ACCOUNTING PRINCIPLES

VOLUME 1

WEYGANDT • KIMMEL • KIESO

9th Edition

STRAYER.
U N I V E R S I T Y

Wiley Custom Learning Solutions

To order books or for customer service, please call 1(800)-CALL-WILEY (225-5945).

Printed in the United States of America.

ISBN 978-1-118-73988-4
Printed and bound by Bind Rite Graphics.

10 9 8 7 6 5 4 3 2 1

Achieve Positive Learning Outcomes

WILEY PLUS

www.wileyplus.com

WileyPLUS combines robust course management tools with interactive teaching and learning resources all in one easy-to-use system.
It has helped over half a million students and instructors achieve positive learning outcomes in their courses.

WileyPLUS contains everything you and your students need—and nothing more, including:

⊕ The entire textbook online—with dynamic links from homework to relevant sections. Students can use the online text and save up to half the cost of buying a new printed book.

⊕ Automated assigning & grading of homework & quizzes.

⊕ An interactive variety of ways to teach and learn the material.

⊕ Instant feedback and help for students… available 24/7.

"WileyPLUS helped me become more prepared. There were more resources available using WileyPLUS than just using a regular [printed] textbook, which helped out significantly. Very helpful...and very easy to use."

– Student Victoria Cazorla,
Dutchess County Community College

See and try WileyPLUS *in action!*
Details and Demo:
www.wileyplus.com

Why WileyPLUS for Accounting?

"It was easier to do my homework problems online and receive quick responses. WileyPLUS helped me understand what I was doing wrong and confirmed what I was doing right."

– Student Brenda Cintron, Accounting Major at UMUC

WileyPLUS helps today's students succeed in the classroom and become globally competitive with step-by-step instruction, instant feedback, and support material to reinforce accounting concepts. Instructors can easily monitor progress by student or by class, and spend more time teaching and less time grading homework.

⊕ **WileyPLUS** *links students directly from homework problems to specific sections of their online text to read about specific topics.*

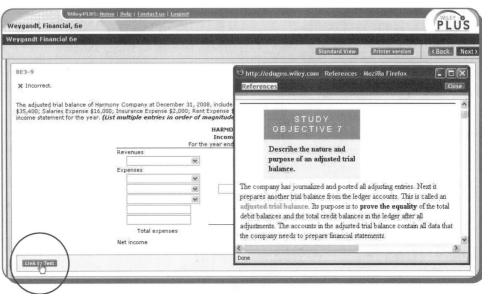

⊕ *Students can also link to contextual help such as interactive tutorials, chapter reviews, and demonstration problems; simulations; and video for visual review or help when they need it most.*

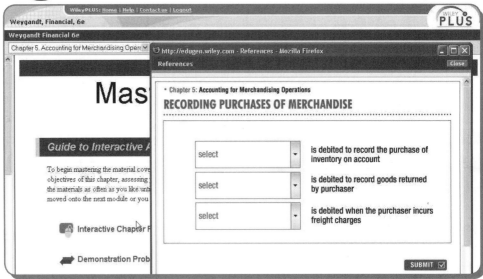

"I really liked the demonstrations and examples with the pictures and interactive quizzes...very helpful. WileyPLUS gave me motivation and confidence... "

– Student Victoria Sniezek, Anne Arundel Community College

www.wileyplus.com

See and try WileyPLUS in action!
Details and Demo: www.wileyplus.com

9th Edition

Accounting Principles

Volume 1: Chapters 1–12

Jerry J. Weygandt PhD, CPA
University of Wisconsin
Madison, Wisconsin

Paul D. Kimmel PhD, CPA
University of Wisconsin—Milwaukee
Milwaukee, Wisconsin

Donald E. Kieso PhD, CPA
Northern Illinois University
DeKalb, Illinois

 John Wiley & Sons, Inc.
WILEY

Dedicated to
Amaya, Christina, Max, Quinn, Venden, Evan, and Nolan, and
their grandmother Enid; Morgan, Cole, and Erin, and their grandmother
Donna; Croix, Marais, and Kale, and their mother Merlynn

Publisher George Hoffman
Associate Publisher Christopher DeJohn
Senior Editor Brian Kamins
Senior Marketing Manager Julia Flohr
Assistant Marketing Manager Carly DeCardia
Executive Marketing Manager Amy Scholz
Senior Production Editor Valerie A. Vargas
Senior Media Editor Allie K. Morris
Development Editor Ann Torbert
Production Management Services Ingrao Associates
Creative Director Harry Nolan
Senior Designer Madelyn Lesure
Project Editor Ed Brislin
Senior Photo Editor Elle Wagner
Editorial Assistant Kathryn Fraser
Marketing Assistant Alana Filipovich
Cover Photo OJO Images/SuperStock

This book was set in Times Ten Roman 10.5/12 by Aptara®, Inc. and printed and bound by RRD-JC. The cover was printed by RRD-JC.

This book is printed on acid free paper. ∞

To order books or for customer service please, call 1-800-CALL WILEY (225-5945).

ISBN-13 978-0470-31755-6

Printed in the United States of America

10 9 8 7 6 5 4 3 2

Dear Student,

Why This Course?
Remember your biology course in high school? Did you have one of those "invisible man" models (or maybe something more high-tech than that) that gave you the opportunity to look "inside" the human body? This accounting course offers something similar: To understand a business, you have to understand the financial insides of a business organization. An accounting course will help you understand the essential financial components of businesses. Whether you are looking at a large multinational company like Microsoft or Starbucks or a single-owner software consulting business or coffee shop, knowing the fundamentals of accounting will help you understand what is happening. As an employee, a manager, an investor, a business owner, or a manager of your own personal finances—any of which roles you will have at some point in your life—you will be much the wiser for having taken this course.

Why This Book?
Hundreds of thousands of students have used this textbook. Your instructor has chosen it for you because of its trusted reputation. The authors have worked hard to keep the book fresh, timely, and accurate.

The book contains features to help you learn best, whatever your learning style. To understand what your learning style is, spend about ten minutes to take the online learning style quiz discussed at the top of page ix and then look at pages ix, x, and xi for how you can apply an understanding of your learning style to this course. Then, when you know more about your own learning style, browse through the Student Owner's Manual online at the book's companion website (www.wiley.com/college/sc/weyprin). It shows you the main features you will find in this textbook and explains their purpose.

How to Succeed?
We've asked many students and many instructors whether there is a secret for success in this course. The nearly unanimous answer turns out to be not much of a secret: "Do the homework." This is one course where doing is learning, and the more time you spend on the homework assignments—using the various tools that this book provides—the more likely you are to learn the essential concepts, techniques, and methods of accounting. Besides the textbook itself, the companion website offers various support resources.

Good luck in this course. We hope you enjoy the experience and that you put to good use throughout a lifetime of success the lessons you learn about accounting and about business! We are sure you will not be disappointed.

Jerry J. Weygandt
Paul D. Kimmel
Donald E. Kieso

ABOUT THE AUTHORS

Jerry J. Weygandt, PhD, CPA, is Arthur Andersen Alumni Professor of Accounting at the University of Wisconsin—Madison. He holds a Ph.D. in accounting from the University of Illinois. Articles by Professor Weygandt have appeared in the *Accounting Review. Journal of Accounting Research, Accounting Horizons, Journal of Accountancy*, and other academic and professional journals. These articles have examined such financial reporting issues as accounting for price-level adjustments, pensions, convertible securities, stock option contracts, and interim reports. Professor Weygandt is author of other accounting and financial reporting books and is a member of the American Accounting Association, the American Institute of Certified Public Accountants, and the Wisconsin Society of Certified Public Accountants. He has seved on numerous committees of the American Accounting Association and as a member of the editorial board of the *Accounting Review;* he also has served as President and Secretary-Treasurer of the American Accounting Association. In addition, he has been actively involved with the American Institute of Certified Public Accountants and has been a member of the Accounting Standards Executive Committee (AcSEC) of that organization. He has served on the FASB task force that examined the reporting issues related to accounting for income taxes and served as a trustee of the Financial Accounting Foundation. Professor Weygandt has received the Chancellor's Award for Excellence in Teaching and the Beta Gamma Sigma Dean's Teaching Award. He is on the board of directors of M & I Bank of Southern Wisconsin. He is the recipient of the Wisconsin Institute of CPA's Outstanding Educator's Award and the Lifetime Achievement Award. In 2001 he received the American Accounting Association's Outstanding Accounting Educator Award.

Paul D. Kimmel, PhD, CPA, received his bachelor's degree from the University of Minnesota and his doctorate in accounting from the University of Wisconsin. He is an Associate Professor at the University of Wisconsin—Milwaukee, and has public accounting experience with Deloitte & Touche (Minneapolis). He was the recipient of the UWM School of Business Advisory Council Teaching Award, the Reggie Taite Excellence in Teaching Award. and a three-time winner of the Outstanding Teaching Assistant Award at the University of Wisconsin. He is also a recipient of the Elijah Watts Sells Award for Honorary Distinction for his results on the CPA exam. He is a member of the American Accounting Association and the Institute of Management Accountants and has published articles in *Accounting Review, Accounting Horizons, Advances in Management Accounting, Managerial Finance, Issues in Accounting Education, Journal of Accounting Education,* as well as other journals. His research interests include accounting for financial instruments and innovation in accounting education. He has published papers and given numerous talks on incorporating critical thinking into accounting education, and helped prepare a catalog of critical thinking resources for the Federated Schools of Accountancy.

Donald E. Kieso, PhD, CPA, received his bachelor's degree from Aurora University and his doctorate in accounting from the University of Illinois. He has served as chairman of the Department of Accountancy and is currently the KPMG Emeritus Professor of Accountancy at Northern Illinois University. He has public accounting experience with Price Waterhouse & Co. (San Francisco and Chicago) and Arthur Andersen & Co. (Chicago) and research experience with the Research Division of the American Institute of Certified Public Accountants (New York). He has done postdoctorate work as a Visiting Scholar at the University of California at Berkeley and is a recipient of NIU's Teaching Excellence Award and four Golden Apple Teaching Awards. Professor Kieso is the author of other accounting and business books and is a member of the American Accounting Association, the American Institute of Certified Public Accountants, and the Illinois CPA Society. He has served as a member of the Board of Directors of the Illinois CPA Society, the AACSB's Accounting Accreditation Committees, the State of Illinois Comptroller's Commission, as Secretary-Treasurer of the Federation of Schools of Accountancy, and as Secretary-Treasurer of the American Accounting Association. Professor Kieso is currently serving on the Board of Trustees and Executive Committee of Aurora University, as a member of the Board of Directors of Kishwaukee Community Hospital, and as Treasurer and Director of Valley West Community Hospital. From 1989 to 1993 he served as a charter member of the national Accounting Education Change Commission. He is the recipient of the Outstanding Accounting Educator Award from the Illinois CPA Society, the FSA's Joseph A. Silvoso Award of Merit, the NIU Foundation's Humanitarian Award for Service to Higher Education, a Distinguished Service Award from the Illinois CPA Society, and in 2003 an honorary doctorate from Aurora University.

WHAT ARE LEARNING STYLES?

Have you ever repeated something to yourself over and over to help remember it? Or does your best friend ask you to draw a map to someplace where the two of you are planning to meet, rather than just *tell* her the directions? If so, then you already have an intuitive sense that people learn in different ways.

Researchers in learning theory have developed various categories of learning styles. Some people, for example, learn best by reading or writing. Others learn best by using various senses—seeing, hearing, feeling, tasting, or even smelling.

When you understand how you learn best, you can make use of learning strategies that will optimize the time you spend studying. To find out what your particular learning style is, go to WileyPLUS and take the learning styles quiz you find there. The quiz will help you determine your primary learning style:

Visual learner	Auditory learner	Haptic learner	Olfactory learner
Print learner	Interactive learner	Kinesthetic learner	

Then, consult the information below and on the following pages for study tips for each learning style. This information will help you better understand your learning style and how to apply it to the study of accounting.

✔ Study Tips for Visual Learners

If you are a **Visual Learner,** you prefer to work with images and diagrams. It is important that you *see* information.

Visual Learning:

- Draw charts/diagrams during lecture.
- Examine textbook figures and graphs.
- Look at images and videos on WileyPLUS and other websites.
- Pay close attention to charts, drawings, and handouts your instructors use.
- Underline; use different colors.
- Use symbols, flow charts, graphs, different arrangements on the page, white spaces.

Visual Reinforcement:

- Make flashcards by drawing tables/charts on one side and definition or description on the other side.
- Use art-based worksheets. Cover labels on images in text and then rewrite the labels.
- Use colored pencils/markers and colored paper to organize information into types.
- Convert your lecture notes into "page pictures." To do this:
  - Use the visual learning strategies outlined above.
  - Reconstruct images in different ways.
  - Redraw pages from memory.
  - Replace words with symbols and initials.
  - Draw diagrams where appropriate.
  - Practice turning your visuals back into words.

If visual learning is your weakness: If you are **not** a Visual Learner but want to improve your visual learning, try re-keying tables/charts from the textbook.

✔ Study Tips for Print Learners

If you are a **Print Learner,** reading will be important but writing will be much more important.

Print Learning:

- Write text lecture notes during lecture.
- Read relevant topics in textbook, especially textbook tables.

- Look at text descriptions in animations and websites.
- Use lists and headings.
- Use dictionaries, glossaries, and definitions.
- Read handouts, textbooks, and supplementary library readings.
- Use lecture notes.

Print Reinforcement:

- Rewrite your notes from class and copy classroom handouts in your own handwriting.
- Make your own flashcards.
- Write out essays summarizing lecture notes or textbook topics.
- Develop mnemonics.
- Identify word relationships.
- Create tables with information extracted from textbook or lecture notes.
- Use text-based worksheets or crossword puzzles.
- Write out words again and again.
- Reread notes silently.
- Rewrite ideas and principles into other words.
- Turn charts, diagrams, and other illustrations into statements.
- Practice writing exam answers.
- Practice with multiple-choice questions.
- Write paragraphs, especially beginnings and endings.
- Write your lists in outline form.
- Arrange your words into hierarchies and points.

If print learning is your weakness: If you are **not** a Print Learner but want to improve your print learning, try covering labels of figures from the textbook and writing in the labels.

✔ Study Tips for Auditory Learners

If you are an **Auditory Learner,** you prefer listening as a way to learn information. Hearing will be very important, and sound helps you focus.

Auditory Learning:

- Make audio recordings during lecture.
- Do not skip class. Hearing the lecture is essential to understanding.

- Play audio files provided by instructor and textbook.
- Listen to narration of animations.
- Attend lectures and tutorials.
- Discuss topics with students and instructors.
- Explain new ideas to other people.
- Leave spaces in your lecture notes for later recall.
- Describe overheads, pictures, and visuals to somebody who was not in class.

Auditory Reinforcement:
- Record yourself reading the notes and listen to the recording.
- Write out transcripts of the audio files.
- Summarize information that you have read, speaking out loud.
- Use a recorder to create self-tests.
- Compose "songs" about information.
- Play music during studying to help focus.
- Expand your notes by talking with others and with information from your textbook.
- Read summarized notes out loud.
- Explain your notes to another auditory learner.
- Talk with the instructor.
- Spend time in quiet places recalling the ideas.
- Say your answers out loud.

If auditory learning is your weakness: If you are **not** an Auditory Learner but want to improve your auditory learning, try writing out the scripts from pre-recorded lectures.

✔ Study Tips for Interactive Learners

If you are an **Interactive Learner,** you will want to share your information. A study group will be important.

Interactive Learning:
- Ask a lot of questions during lecture or laboratory meetings.
- Contact other students, via email or discussion forums, and ask them to explain what they learned.

Interactive Reinforcement:
- "Teach" the content to a group of other students.
- Talking to an empty room may seem odd, but it will be effective for you.
- Discuss information with others, making sure that you both ask and answer questions.
- Work in small group discussions, making a verbal and written summary of what others say.

If interactive learning is your weakness: If you are **not** an Interactive Learner but want to improve your interactive learning, try asking your study partner questions and then repeating them to the instructor.

✔ Study Tips for Haptic Learners

If you are a **Haptic Learner,** you prefer to work with your hands. It is important to physically manipulate material.

Haptic Learning:
- Take blank paper to lecture to draw charts/tables/diagrams.
- Using the textbook, run your fingers along the figures and graphs to get a "feel" for shapes and relationships.

Haptic Reinforcement:
- Trace words and pictures on flash cards.
- Perform electronic exercises that involve drag-and-drop activities.
- Alternate between speaking and writing information.
- Observe someone performing a task that you would like to learn.
- Make sure you have freedom of movement while studying.

If haptic learning is your weakness: If you are **not** a Haptic Learner but want to improve your haptic learning, try spending more time in class working with formulas, financial statements, and tables while speaking or writing down information.

✔ Study Tips for Kinesthetic Learners

If you are a **Kinesthetic Learner,** it will be important that you involve your body during studying.

Kinesthetic Learning:
- Ask permission to get up and move during lecture.
- Participate in role playing activities, in the classroom.
- Use all your senses.
- Use hands-on approaches.
- Go to labs, take field trips.
- Use trial-and-error methods.
- Listen to real-life examples.
- Pay attention to applications.

Kinesthetic Reinforcement:
- Make flash cards, place them on the floor and move around them as you study.
- Move while you are "teaching" the material to others.
- Put examples in your summaries.
- Use case studies and applications to help with principles and abstract concepts.
- Talk about your notes with another Kinesthetic person.
- Use pictures and photographs that illustrate an idea.
- Write practice answers.
- Role-play the exam situation.

If kinesthetic learning is your weakness: If you are **not** a Kinesthetic Learner but want to improve your kinesthetic learning, try moving flash cards to reconstruct balance sheets, income statements, cash flow statements, etc.

✔ Study Tips for Olfactory Learners

If you are an **Olfactory Learner,** you will prefer to use the sense of smell (sometimes taste) and to reinforce learning. This is a rare learning modality.

Olfactory Learning:
- During lecture, use different scented markers to identify different types of information.

Olfactory Reinforcement:
- Rewrite notes with scented markers.
- If possible, go back to the computer lab to do your studying.
- Burn aromatic candles while studying.
- Try to associate the material that you're studying with a pleasant smell or taste.

If olfactory learning is your weakness: If you are **not** an Olfactory Learner, but want to improve your olfactory learning, try surrounding yourself with pleasant scents during study sessions.

WileyPLUS and Textbook Resources for Various Learning Styles

RESOURCES	Visual	Print	Auditory	Interactive	Haptic	Kinesthetic	Olfactory*
Content of textbook		✓					
The Navigator/Feature Story/Preview	✓	✓					
Study Objectives		✓					
Infographics/Illustrations	✓	✓					
Accounting Equation Analyses	✓	✓	✓	✓	✓	✓	
Do It! Exercises/ Comprehensive Do It! Problem/Action Plan	✓	✓		✓	✓	✓	
Graph in *All About You*	✓	✓					
Summary of Study Objectives		✓					
Glossary/Self-study questions		✓		✓	✓	✓	
Questions/Exercises/Problems	✓	✓		✓			
Alternate versions of exercises & Problems (B exercises; Problem sets B&C)	✓	✓		✓			
Financial Reporting/ Comparative Analysis Problems	✓	✓		✓	✓	✓	
Writing activities—Exercises and Problems marked with a pencil icon	✓	✓		✓	✓	✓	
Exploring the Web activity	✓	✓	✓	✓	✓	✓	
Communication Activity		✓		✓	✓	✓	
AAY Activity		✓		✓	✓	✓	
Practice quizzes		✓		✓	✓	✓	
Flash cards	✓	✓		✓	✓	✓	
Audio Reviews/Video Clips/Clicker Content			✓	✓	✓	✓	
Flash Tutorial Reviews (Comprehensive Do It/ Accounting Cycle/Annual Report)	✓	✓	✓	✓	✓	✓	
Crossword Puzzles	✓	✓	✓	✓	✓	✓	
Excel Templates/Excel Working Papers	✓	✓		✓	✓	✓	
Checklist of Key Figures	✓	✓					
Peachtree/Quickbooks/GLS	✓	✓		✓	✓	✓	
Self-study/Self-test web quizzes	✓	✓		✓	✓	✓	

* To improve your learning using your olfactory modality, look at the resources recommended for your other most preferred learning styles. Then, pair olfactory study techniques with other resources, to enhance your learning. For example, you can burn aromatic candles while working on Flash tutorial reviews or Excel templates in WileyPLUS, or you can use scented markers to create flashcards.

ACKNOWLEDGMENTS

From the first edition of this textbook and through the years since, we have benefited greatly from feedback provided by numerous instructors and students of accounting principles courses throughout the country. We offer our thanks to those many people for their criticism, constructive suggestions, and innovative ideas. We are indebted to the following people for their contributions to the most recent editions of the book.

Reviewers and Focus Group Participants for the Ninth Edition

John Ahmad, *Northern Virginia Community College—Annandale;* Colin Battle, *Broward Community College;* Beverly Beatty, *Anne Arundel Community College;* Jaswinder Bhangal, *Chabot College;* Leroy Bugger, *Edison Community College;* Ann Cardozo, *Broward Community College;* Kimberly Charland, *Kansas State University;* Lisa Cole, *Johnson County Community College.*

Tony Dellarte, *Luzerne Community College;* Pam Donahue, *Northern Essex Community College;* Dora Estes, *Volunteer State Community College;* Mary Falkey, *Prince Georges Community College;* Lori Grady, *Bucks County Community College;* Joyce Griffin, *Kansas City Community College;* Lester Hall, *Danville Community College;* Becky Hancock, *El Paso Community College;* Audrey Hunter, *Broward Community College.*

Naomi Karolinski, *Monroe Community College;* Kenneth Koerber, *Bucks County Community College;* Sandra Lang, *McKendree College;* Cathy Xanthaky Larsen, *Middlesex Community College;* David Laurel, *South Texas Community College;* Suneel Maheshwari, *Marshall University;* Lori Major, *Luzerne County Community College;* Jim Martin, *University of Montevallo.*

Yvonne Phang, *Borough of Manhattan Community College;* Mike Prockton, *Finger Lakes Community College;* Richard Sarkisian, *Camden Community College;* Beth Secrest, *Walsh University;* Lois Slutsky, *Broward Community College;* Shafi Ullah, *Broward Community College;* Patricia Walczack, *Lansing Community College;* Kenton Walker, *University of Wyoming;* Patricia Wall, *Middle Tennessee State University.*

Reviewers and Focus Group Participants for Recent Editions

Sylvia Allen, *Los Angeles Valley College;* Matt Anderson, *Michigan State University;* Alan Applebaum, *Broward Community College;* Juanita Ardovany, *Los Angeles Valley College;* Yvonne Baker, *Cincinnati State Tech Community College;* Peter Battelle, *University of Vermont;* Jim Benedum, *Milwaukee Area Technical College;* Bernard Bieg, *Bucks County College;* Michael Blackett, *National American University;* Barry Bomboy, *J. Sargeant Reynolds Community College;* Kent D. Bowen, *Butler County Community College;* David Boyd, *Arkansas State University;* Greg Brookins, *Santa Monica College;* Kurt H. Buerger, *Angelo State University;* Leon Button, *Scottsdale Community College.*

Steve Carlson, *University of North Dakota;* Fatma Cebenoyan, *Hunter College;* Trudy Chiaravelli, *Lansing Community College;* Shifei Chung, *Rowan University;* Siu Chung, *Los Angeles Valley College;* Kenneth Couvillion, *San Joaquin Delta College;* Alan B. Czyzewski, *Indiana State University;* Thomas Davies, *University of South Dakota;* Peggy DeJong, *Kirkwood Community College;* John Delaney, *Augustana College;* Kevin Dooley, *Kapi'olani Community College;* Edmond Douville, *Indiana University Northwest;* Pamela Druger, *Augustana College;* Russell Dunn, *Broward Community College;* John Eagan, *Erie Community College;* Richard Ellison, *Middlesex Community College.*

Raymond Gardner, *Ocean County College;* Richard Ghio, *San Joaquin Delta College;* Amy Haas, *Kingsborough Community College, CUNY;* Jeannie Harrington, *Middle Tennessee State University;* Bonnie Harrison, *College of Southern Maryland;* William Harvey, *Henry Ford Community College;* Michelle Heard, *Metropolitan Community College;* Ruth Henderson, *Union Community College;* Ed Hess, *Butler County Community College;* Kathy Hill, *Leeward Community College;* Patty Holmes, *Des Moines Area Community College;* Zach Holmes, *Oakland Community College;* Paul Holt, *Texas A&M-Kingsville;* Audrey Hunter, *Broward Community College;* Verne Ingram, *Red Rocks Community College.*

Joanne Johnson, *Caldwell Community College;* Anil Khatri, *Bowie State University;* Shirley Kleiner, *Johnson County Community College;* Jo Koehn, *Central Missouri State University;* Ken Koerber, *Bucks County Community College;* Adriana Kulakowski, *Mynderse Academy;* Robert Laycock, *Montgomery College;* Natasha Librizzi, *Madison Area Technical College;* William P. Lovell, *Cayuga Community College;.* Melanie Mackey, *Ocean County College;* Jerry Martens, *Community College of Aurora;* Maureen McBeth, *College of DuPage;* Francis McCloskey, *Community College of Philadelphia;* Chris McNamara, *Finger Lakes Community College;* Edwin Mah, *University of Maryland, University College;* Thomas Marsh, *Northern Virginia Community College—Annandale;* Shea Mears, *Des Moines Area Community College;* Pam Meyer, *University of Louisiana—Lafayette;* Cathy Montesarchio, *Broward Community College.*

Robin Nelson, *Community College of Southern Nevada;* Joseph M. Nicassio, *Westmoreland County Community College;* Michael O'Neill, *Seattle Central Community College;* Mike Palma, *Gwinnett Tech;* George Palz, *Erie Community College;* Michael Papke, *Kellogg Community College;* Ruth Parks, *Kellogg Community College;* Al Partington, *Los Angeles Pierce College;* Jennifer Patty, *Des Moines Area Community College;* Jan Pitera, *Broome Community College;* Laura M. Prosser, *Black Hills State University;* Bill Rencher, *Seminole Community College;* Jenny Resnick, Santa Monica College; Renee Rigoni, *Monroe Community College;* Kathie Rogers, *SUNY Suffolk;* Al Ruggiero, *SUNY Suffolk;* Jill Russell, *Camden County College.*

Roger Sands, *Milwaukee Area Technical College;* Marcia Sandvold, *Des Moines Area Community College;* Kent Schneider, *East Tennessee State University;* Karen Searle, Paul J. Shinal, *Cayuga Community College;* Kevin Sinclair,

Lehigh University; Alice Sineath, *Forsyth Tech Community College;* Leon Singleton, *Santa Monica College;* Michael S. Skaff, *College of the Sequoias;* Jeff Slater, *North Shore Community College;* Lois Slutsky, *Broward Community College;* Dan Small, *J. Sargeant Reynolds Community College;* Lee Smart, *Southwest Tennessee Community College;* James Smith, *Ivy Tech State College;* Carol Springer, *Georgia State University;* Jeff Spoelman, *Grand Rapids Community College;* Norman Sunderman, *Angelo State University.*

Donald Terpstra, *Jefferson; Community College;* Lynda Thompson, *Massasoit Community College;* Sue Van Boven, *Paradise Valley Community College;* Christian Widmer, *Tidewater Community College;* Wanda Wong, *Chabot College;* Pat Walczak, *Lansing Community College;* Carol N. Welsh, *Rowan University;* Idalene Williams, *Metropolitan Community College;* Gloria Worthy, *Southwest Tennessee Community College.*

Thanks also to "perpetual reviewers" Robert Benjamin, *Taylor University;* Charles Malone, Tammy Wend, and Carol Wysocki, all of *Columbia Basin College;* and William Gregg of *Montgomery College.* We appreciate their continuing interest in the book and their regular contributions of ideas to improve it.

Special Thanks

Our thanks also go to the following for their work on the Ninth Edition: Melanie Yon, for preparing end-of-chapter content for WileyPLUS; Sheila Viel, *University of Wisconsin-Milwaukee,* for production of interactive chapter reviews and demonstration problems; Richard Campbell, *Rio Grande College,* for WileyPLUS Accounting Tutors and video material; Naomi Karolinski, *Monroe Community College,* for General Ledger Software review; Sally Nelson, for General Ledger Software review; Chris Tomas, for General Ledger Software review.

Thanks, too, to the following for their authorship of supplements: Linda Batiste, *Baton Rouge Community College,* Test Bank; Mel Coe, *DeVry Institute of Technology, Atlanta,* Peachtree Workbook; Joan Cook, *Milwaukee Area Technical College,* Heritage Home Furniture Practice Set; Larry Falcetto, *Emporia State University,* Test Bank, Instructor's Manual, Campus Cycle Practice Set; Mark Gleason, *Metropolitan State University,* Algorithmic Computerized Test Bank; Larry Falcetto, *Emporia State University,* Test Bank, Lori Grady, *Bucks County Community College,* Web Quizzes; Coby Harmon, *University of California, Santa Barbara,* PowerPoint presentations; Marilyn Hunt, M.A., C.P.A., Problem-Solving Survival Guide; Douglas W. Kieso, *Aurora University,* Study Guide; Jill Misuraca, *Central Connecticut State University,* Web Quizzes; Yvonne Phang, *Borough of Manhattan Community College,* WileyPLUS Web Quizzes. Rex A. Schildhouse, *San Diego Community College—Miramar,* Peachtree Workbook, Excel Workbook and Templates, and QuickBooks Tutorials; Dick Wasson, *Southwestern College,* Excel Working Papers, Working Papers, and Test Bank.

We also thank those who have ensured the accuracy of our supplements: LuAnn Bean, *Florida Institute of Technology;* Jack Borke, *University of Wisconsin—Platteville;*

Robert Derstine, *Villanova University;* Terry Elliott, *Morehead State University;* James Emig, *Villanova University;* Larry Falcetto, *Emporia State University;* Anthony Falgiani, *Western Illinois University;* Jennifer Laudermilch, *PricewaterhouseCoopers;* Kevin McNelis, *New Mexico State University;* Richard Merryman, *Jefferson Community College, State University of New York;* Barbara Muller, *Arizona State University;* Yvonne Phang, *Borough of Manhattan Community College;* John Plouffe, *California State University—Los Angeles;* Renee Rigoni, *Monroe Community College;* Rex Schildhouse, *San Diego Community College–Miramar;* Alice Sineath, *Forsyth Tech Community College;* Teresa Speck, *St. Mary's University;* Lynn Stallworth, *Appalachian State University;* Sheila Viel, *University of Wisconsin—Milwaukee;* Dick Wasson, *Southwestern College;* Bernie Weinrich, *Lindenwood University.*

In addition, special recognition goes to Karen Huffman, *Palomar College,* for her assessment of the text's pedagogy and her suggestions on how to increase its helpfulness to students; to Gary R., Morrison, *Wayne State University,* for his review of the instructional design; and to Nancy Galli, *Palomar College,* for her work on learning styles. Finally, special thanks to Wayne Higley, *Buena Vista University,* for his technical proofing.

Our thanks to the publishing "pros" who contribute to our efforts to publish high-quality products that benefit both teachers and students: Ann Torbert, development editor; Ed Brislin, project editor; Brian Kamins, associate editor; Allie Morris, media editor; Katie Fraser, editorial assistant; Valerie Vargas, senior production editor; Maddy Lesure, textbook designer; Dorothy Sinclair, managing editor; Pam Kennedy, director of production and manufacturing; Ann Berlin, VP of higher education production and manufacturing; Elle Wagner, photo editor; Sandra Rigby, illustration editor; Suzanne Ingrao of Ingrao Associates, project manager; Karyn Morrison, permissions editor; Jane Shifflet of Aptara Inc., product manager at Aptara Inc.; and Amanda Grant, project manager at Elm Street Publishing Services. They provided innumerable services that helped this project take shape.

We also appreciate the exemplary support and professional commitment given us by Chris DeJohn, associate publisher, and the enthusiasm and ideas that Julia Flohr, senior marketing manager, brings to the project.

Finally, our thanks for the support provided by the management of John Wiley & Sons, Inc.—Joe Heider, Vice President of Product and e-Business Development; Bonnie Lieberman, Senior Vice President of the College Division; and Will Pesce, President and Chief Executive Officer of John Wiley & Sons, Inc..

We thank PepsiCo, Inc. for permitting us the use of their 2007 annual reports for our specimen financial statements and accompanying notes.

We will appreciate suggestions and comments from users—instructors and students alike. You can send your thought to us via email at

AccountingAuthors@yahoo.com

Jerry J. Weygandt, *Madison, Wisconsin*
Paul D. Kimmel, *Milwaukee, Wisconsin*
Donald E. Kieso, *DeKalb, Illinois*

BRIEF CONTENTS

APPENDICES

CONTENTS

14   Corporations: Dividends, Retained Earnings, and Income Reporting   606

15   Long-Term Liabilities   642

16   Investments   694

17   Statement of Cash Flows   730

all about YOU

quick guide

The *"All About You"* feature promotes financial literacy. These full-page boxes will get students thinking and talking about how accounting impacts their personal lives. Students are more likely to understand the accounting concept being made within the textbook when accounting material is linked to a familiar topic. Each *All About You* box presents a high-interest issue related to the chapter topic, offers facts about it, poses a situation for students to think about, and offers brief opposing answers as a starting place for further discussion. As a feedback mechanism, the authors' comments and opinions about the situation appear at the end of the chapter.

In addition, an *"All About You" Activity*, located in the *Broadening Your Perspective* section near the end of the assignment material, offers further opportunity to explore aspects of the topic in a homework assignment.

CHAPTER 1   Accounting in Action
Ethics: Managing Personal Financial Reporting (p. 25)
Compares filing for financial aid to corporate financial reporting. Presents facts about student debt loads. Asks whether students should present a negative financial picture to increase the chance of receiving financial aid.

CHAPTER 2   The Recording Process
Your Personal Annual Report (p. 72)
Likens a student's résumé to a company's annual report. Asks students to consider whether firing Radio Shack's CEO for résumé falsehoods was warranted.

CHAPTER 4   Completing the Accounting Cycle
Your Personal Balance Sheet (p. 169)
Walks students through identification of personal assets and personal liabilities. Presents facts about Americans' wealth and attitudes toward saving versus spending. Asks if college is a good time to prepare a personal balance sheet.

CHAPTER 6   Inventories
Employee Theft—An Inside Job (p. 268)
Discusses the problem of inventory theft and how companies keep it in check. Asks students' opinions on the use of video cameras to reduce theft.

CHAPTER 8   Internal Control and Cash
Protecting Yourself from Identity Theft (p. 373)
Likens corporate internal controls to individuals' efforts to protect themselves from identity thieves. Presents facts about how thieves use stolen data. Asks students about the safety of storing personal financial data on computers.

CHAPTER 9   Accounting for Receivables
Should You Be Carrying Plastic? (p. 416)
Discusses the need for individuals to evaluate their credit positions as thoughtfully as companies do. Presents facts about college-student debt and Americans' use of credit cards. Asks whether students should cut up their credit cards.

CHAPTER 10   Plant Assets, Natural Resources, and Intangible Assets
Buying a Wreck of Your Own (p. 460)
Presents information about costs of new versus used cars. Asks whether students could improve their economic well-being by buying a used car.

CHAPTER 11   Current Liabilities and Payroll Accounting
Your Boss Wants to Know If You Jogged Today (p. 506)
Discusses ways to contain costs of health-care spending. Asks students to consider whose responsibility it is to maintain healthy lifestyles to control health-care costs.

CHAPTER 14   Corporations: Dividends, Retained Earnings, and Income Reporting
Corporations Have Governance Structures— Do You? (p. 624)
Discusses codes of ethics in business and at college. Presents facts about abuse of workplace codes of ethics and responses of stockholders. Asks students for opinions on whether schools' codes of ethics serve a useful purpose.

CHAPTER 20   Job Order Cost Accounting
Minding Your Own Business (p. 906)
Focuses on how small business owners calculate product costs. Presents facts about sole proprietorships and franchises. Poses a start-up business idea and asks students to evaluate the cost of labor input.

CHAPTER 22   Cost-Volume-Profit
A Hybrid Dilemma (p. 995)
Explores the cost tradeoffs of hybrid vehicles. Asks students to evaluate the pros and cons of buying a hybrid vehicle.

CHAPTER 23   Budgetary Planning
Avoiding Personal Financial Disaster (p. 1038)
Explores personal budgets for college students. Asks students to look at a budgeting calculator and consider whether student loans should be considered a source of income.

CHAPTER 26   Incremental Analysis and Capital Budgeting
What Is a Degree Worth? (p. 1176)
Presents facts about cost of college, and benefits of college education. Asks students to consider the value of a college education.

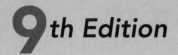
9th Edition

Accounting Principles

Volume 1: Chapters 1–12

Chapter 1

Accounting in Action

STUDY OBJECTIVES

After studying this chapter, you should be able to:

1 Explain what accounting is.
2 Identify the users and uses of accounting.
3 Understand why ethics is a fundamental business concept.
4 Explain generally accepted accounting principles and the cost principle.
5 Explain the monetary unit assumption and the economic entity assumption.
6 State the accounting equation, and define its components.
7 Analyze the effects of business transactions on the accounting equation.
8 Understand the four financial statements and how they are prepared.

✔ The Navigator

✔ The Navigator

Scan **Study Objectives**	■
Read **Feature Story**	■
Read **Preview**	■
Read text and answer **DO IT!** p. 10 ■ p. 13 ■ p. 19 ■ p. 24 ■	
Work **Comprehensive** **DO IT!**	■
Review **Summary of Study Objectives**	■
Answer **Self-Study Questions**	■
Complete **Assignments**	■

The Navigator is a learning system designed to prompt you to use the learning aids in the chapter and set priorities as you study.

Study Objectives give you a framework for learning the specific concepts covered in the chapter.

Feature Story

KNOWING THE NUMBERS

Consider this quote from Harold Geneen, the former chairman of IT&T: "To be good at your business, you have to know the numbers—cold." Success in any business comes back to the numbers. You will rely on them to make decisions, and managers will use them to evaluate your performance. That is true whether your job involves marketing, production, management, or information systems.

In business, accounting and financial statements are the means for communicating the numbers. If you don't know how to read financial statements, you can't really know your business.

When Jack Stack and 11 other managers purchased Springfield ReManufacturing Corporation (SRC) (*www.srcreman.com*) for 10 cents a share, it was a failing

division of International Harvester. Stack had 119 employees who were counting on him for their livelihood, and he knew that the company was on the verge of financial failure.

Stack decided that the company's only chance of survival was to encourage every employee to think like a businessperson and to act like an owner. To accomplish this, all employees at SRC took basic accounting courses and participated in weekly reviews of the company's financial statements. SRC survived, and eventually thrived. To this day, every employee (now numbering more than 1,000) undergoes this same training.

Many other companies have adopted this approach, which is called "open-book management." Even in companies that do not practice open-book management, employers generally assume that managers in all areas of the company are "financially literate."

Taking this course will go a long way to making you financially literate. In this book you will learn how to read and prepare financial statements, and how to use basic tools to evaluate financial results. Appendixes A and B provide real financial statements of two well-known companies, PepsiCo, Inc. and The Coca-Cola Company. Throughout this textbook we attempt to increase your familiarity with financial reporting by providing numerous references, questions, and exercises that encourage you to explore these financial statements.

The Feature Story helps you picture how the chapter topic relates to the real world of accounting and business. You will find references to the story throughout the chapter.

The Navigator

Inside Chapter 1...

- **How Will Accounting Help Me?** (p. 11)

- **What Do General Mills, Walt Disney, and Dunkin' Donuts Have in Common?** (p. 23)

- *All About You:* **Ethics: Managing Personal Financial Reporting** (p. 25)

"Inside Chapter x" lists boxes in the chapter that should be of special interest to you.

Preview of Chapter 1

The opening story about Springfield ReManufacturing Corporation highlights the importance of having good financial information to make effective business decisions. Whatever one's pursuits or occupation, the need for financial information is inescapable. You cannot earn a living, spend money, buy on credit, make an investment, or pay taxes without receiving, using, or dispensing financial information. Good decision making depends on good information.

The purpose of this chapter is to show you that accounting is the system used to provide useful financial information. The content and organization of Chapter 1 are as follows.

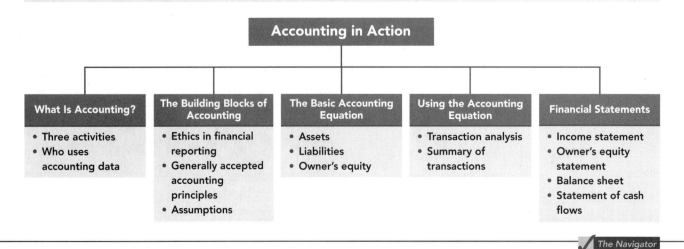

The Navigator

*The **Preview** describes and outlines the major topics and subtopics you will see in the chapter.*

WHAT IS ACCOUNTING?

STUDY OBJECTIVE 1
Explain what accounting is.

Why is accounting so popular? What consistently ranks as one of the top career opportunities in business? What frequently rates among the most popular majors on campus? What was the undergraduate degree chosen by Nike founder Phil Knight, Home Depot co-founder Arthur Blank, former acting director of the Federal Bureau of Investigation (FBI) Thomas Pickard, and numerous members of Congress? Accounting.[1] Why did these people choose accounting? They wanted to understand what was happening financially to their organizations. Accounting is the financial information system that provides these insights. In short, to understand your organization, you have to know the numbers.

Accounting consists of three basic activities—it **identifies**, **records**, and **communicates** the economic events of an organization to interested users. Let's take a closer look at these three activities.

Three Activities

To **identify** economic events, a company selects the **economic events relevant to its business**. Examples of economic events are the sale of snack chips by PepsiCo, providing of telephone services by AT&T, and payment of wages by Ford Motor Company.

---

[1]The appendix to this chapter describes job opportunities for accounting majors and explains why accounting is such a popular major.

Once a company like PepsiCo identifies economic events, it **records** those events in order to provide a history of its financial activities. Recording consists of keeping a **systematic**, **chronological diary of events**, measured in dollars and cents. In recording, PepsiCo also classifies and summarizes economic events.

Finally, PepsiCo **communicates** the collected information to interested users by means of **accounting reports**. The most common of these reports are called **financial statements**. To make the reported financial information meaningful, Kellogg reports the recorded data in a standardized way. It accumulates information resulting from similar transactions. For example, PepsiCo accumulates all sales transactions over a certain period of time and reports the data as one amount in the company's financial statements. Such data are said to be reported **in the aggregate**. By presenting the recorded data in the aggregate, the accounting process simplifies a multitude of transactions and makes a series of activities understandable and meaningful.

A vital element in communicating economic events is the accountant's ability to **analyze and interpret** the reported information. Analysis involves use of ratios, percentages, graphs, and charts to highlight significant financial trends and relationships. Interpretation involves **explaining the uses**, **meaning**, **and limitations of reported data**. Appendix A of this textbook shows the financial statements of PepsiCo, Inc.; Appendix B illustrates the financial statements of The Coca-Cola Company. We refer to these statements at various places throughout the text. At this point, they probably strike you as complex and confusing. By the end of this course, you'll be surprised at your ability to understand, analyze, and interpret them.

Illustration 1-1 summarizes the activities of the accounting process.

Illustration 1-1
The activities of the accounting process

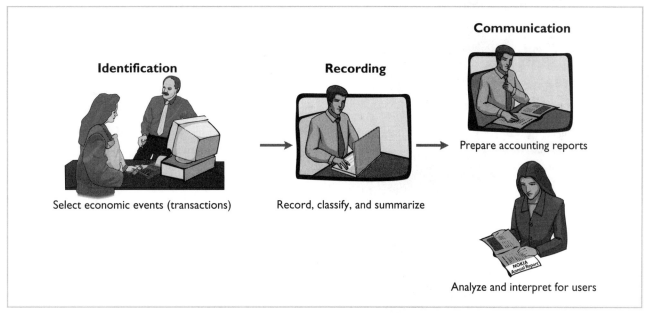

Communication

Identification

Recording

Select economic events (transactions)

Record, classify, and summarize

Prepare accounting reports

Analyze and interpret for users

You should understand that the accounting process **includes** the bookkeeping function. **Bookkeeping** usually involves **only** the recording of economic events. It is therefore just one part of the accounting process. In total, accounting involves **the entire process of identifying**, **recording**, **and communicating economic events.**[2]

Essential terms are printed in blue when they first appear, and are defined in the end-of-chapter glossary.

---

[2]The origins of accounting are generally attributed to the work of Luca Pacioli, an Italian Renaissance mathematician. Pacioli was a close friend and tutor to Leonardo da Vinci and a contemporary of Christopher Columbus. In his 1494 text *Summa de Arithmetica, Geometria, Proportione et Proportionalite,* Pacioli described a system to ensure that financial information was recorded efficiently and accurately.

Who Uses Accounting Data

STUDY OBJECTIVE 2

Identify the users and uses of accounting.

The information that a user of financial information needs depends upon the kinds of decisions the user makes. There are two broad groups of users of financial information: internal users and external users.

INTERNAL USERS

Internal users of accounting information are those individuals inside a company who plan, organize, and run the business. These include marketing managers, production supervisors, finance directors, and company officers. In running a business, internal users must answer many important questions, as shown in Illustration 1-2.

Illustration 1-2
Questions asked by
internal users

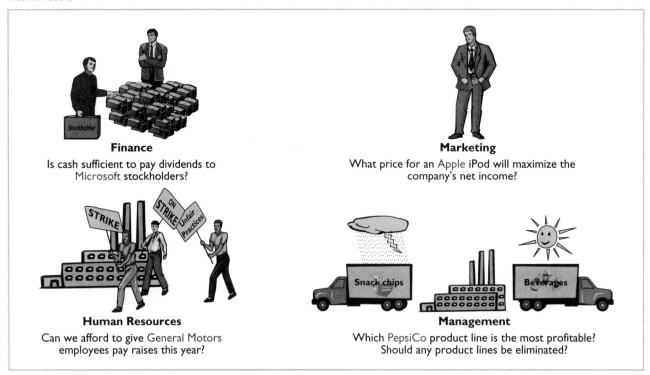

Finance
Is cash sufficient to pay dividends to Microsoft stockholders?

Marketing
What price for an Apple iPod will maximize the company's net income?

Human Resources
Can we afford to give General Motors employees pay raises this year?

Management
Which PepsiCo product line is the most profitable? Should any product lines be eliminated?

To answer these and other questions, internal users need detailed information on a timely basis. **Managerial accounting** provides internal reports to help users make decisions about their companies. Examples are financial comparisons of operating alternatives, projections of income from new sales campaigns, and forecasts of cash needs for the next year.

EXTERNAL USERS

External users are individuals and organizations outside a company who want financial information about the company. The two most common types of external users are investors and creditors. **Investors** (owners) use accounting information to make decisions to buy, hold, or sell ownership shares of a company. **Creditors** (such as suppliers and bankers) use accounting information to evaluate the risks of granting credit or lending money. Illustration 1-3 shows some questions that investors and creditors may ask.

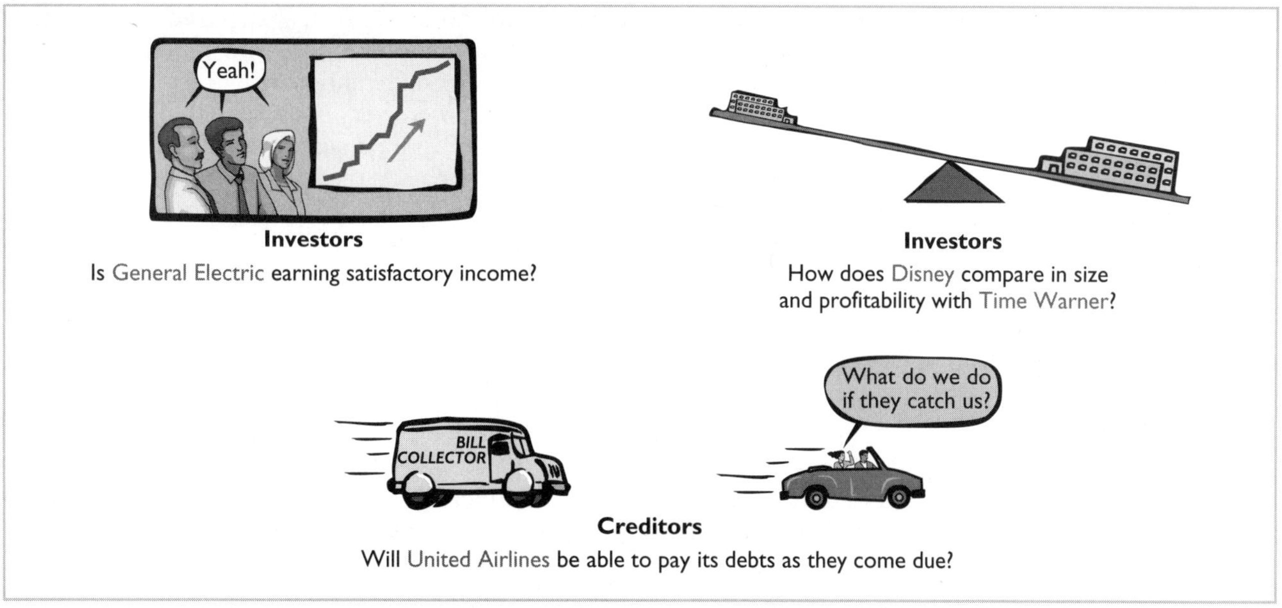
Yeah!
Investors
Is General Electric earning satisfactory income?
Investors
How does Disney compare in size and profitability with Time Warner?
What do we do if they catch us?
BILL COLLECTOR
Creditors
Will United Airlines be able to pay its debts as they come due?

Illustration 1-3
Questions asked by external users

Financial accounting answers these questions. It provides economic and financial information for investors, creditors, and other external users. The information needs of external users vary considerably. **Taxing authorities** (such as the Internal Revenue Service) want to know whether the company complies with tax laws. **Regulatory agencies**, such as the Securities and Exchange Commission and the Federal Trade Commission, want to know whether the company is operating within prescribed rules. **Customers** are interested in whether a company like General Motors will continue to honor product warranties and support its product lines. **Labor unions** such as the Major League Baseball Players Association want to know whether the owners can pay increased wages and benefits.

THE BUILDING BLOCKS OF ACCOUNTING

A doctor follows certain standards in treating a patient's illness. An architect follows certain standards in designing a building. An accountant follows certain standards in reporting financial information. For these standards to work, a fundamental business concept must be at work—ethical behavior.

Ethics in Financial Reporting

STUDY OBJECTIVE 3
Understand why ethics is a fundamental business concept.

People won't gamble in a casino if they think it is rigged. Similarly, people won't play the stock market if they think stock prices are rigged. In recent years the financial press has been full of articles about financial scandals at Enron, WorldCom, HealthSouth, AIG, and others. As the scandals came to light, mistrust of financial reporting in general grew. One article in the *Wall Street Journal* noted that "repeated disclosures about questionable accounting practices have bruised investors' faith in the reliability of earnings reports, which in turn has sent stock prices tumbling."[3] Imagine trying to carry on a business or invest money if you could

[3] "U.S. Share Prices Slump," *Wall Street Journal*, February 21, 2002.

not depend on the financial statements to be honestly prepared. Information would have no credibility. There is no doubt that a sound, well-functioning economy depends on accurate and dependable financial reporting.

United States regulators and lawmakers were very concerned that the economy would suffer if investors lost confidence in corporate accounting because of unethical financial reporting. In response, Congress passed the **Sarbanes-Oxley Act of 2002** (SOX, or Sarbox). Its intent is to reduce unethical corporate behavior and decrease the likelihood of future corporate scandals. As a result of SOX, top management must now certify the accuracy of financial information. In addition, top management now faces much more severe penalties for fraudulent financial activity. Also, SOX calls for increased independence of the outside auditors who review the accuracy of corporate financial statements and increased responsibility of boards of directors in their oversight role.

The standards of conduct by which one's actions are judged as right or wrong, honest or dishonest, fair or not fair, are **ethics**. Effective financial reporting depends on sound ethical behavior. To sensitize you to ethical situations in business and to give you practice at solving ethical dilemmas, we address ethics in a number of ways in this book:

1. A number of the *Feature Stories* and other parts of the text discuss the central importance of ethical behavior to financial reporting.

2. *Ethics Insight* boxes and marginal *Ethics Notes* highlight ethics situations and issues in actual business settings.

3. Many of the *All About You* boxes (near the chapter Summary; see page 25, for example) focus on ethical issues you may face in your college and early-career years.

4. At the end of the chapter, an *Ethics Case* simulates a business situation and asks you to put yourself in the position of a decision maker in that case.

When analyzing these various ethics cases, as well as experiences in your own life, it is useful to apply the three steps outlined in Illustration 1-4.

Ethics Notes help sensitize you to some of the ethical issues in accounting.

> **ETHICS NOTE**
> Circus-founder P.T. Barnum is alleged to have said, "Trust everyone, but cut the deck." What Sarbanes-Oxley does is to provide measures that (like cutting the deck of playing cards) help ensure that fraud will not occur.

Illustration 1-4
Steps in analyzing ethics cases and situations

1. Recognize an ethical situation and the ethical issues involved.
Use your personal ethics to identify ethical situations and issues. Some businesses and professional organizations provide written codes of ethics for guidance in some business situations.

2. Identify and analyze the principal elements in the situation.
Identify the *stakeholders*—persons or groups who may be harmed or benefited. Ask the question: What are the responsibilities and obligations of the parties involved?

3. Identify the alternatives, and weigh the impact of each alternative on various stakeholders.
Select the most ethical alternative, considering all the consequences. Sometimes there will be one right answer. Other situations involve more than one right solution; these situations require an evaluation of each and a selection of the best alternative.

Generally Accepted Accounting Principles

STUDY OBJECTIVE 4
Explain generally accepted accounting principles and the cost principle.

The accounting profession has developed standards that are generally accepted and universally practiced. This common set of standards is called **generally accepted accounting principles (GAAP)**. These standards indicate how to report economic events.

The primary accounting standard-setting body in the United States is the **Financial Accounting Standards Board (FASB)**. The **Securities and Exchange**

Commission (SEC) is the agency of the U.S. government that oversees U.S. financial markets and accounting standard-setting bodies. The SEC relies on the FASB to develop accounting standards, which public companies must follow. Many countries outside of the United States have adopted the accounting standards issued by the **International Accounting Standards Board (IASB)**. In recent years the FASB and IASB have worked closely to try to minimize the differences in their standards and principles.

One important accounting principle is the cost principle. The **cost principle** (or historical cost principle) dictates that companies record assets at their cost. This is true not only at the time the asset is purchased, but also over the time the asset is held. For example, if Best Buy purchases land for $30,000, the company initially reports it in its accounting records at $30,000. But what does Best Buy do if, by the end of the next year, the land has increased in value to $40,000? Under the cost principle it continues to report the land at $30,000.

Critics contend the cost principle is misleading. They argue that market value (the value determined by the market at any particular time) is more useful to financial decision makers than is cost. Those who favor the cost principle counter that cost is the best measure. The reason: Cost can be easily verified, whereas market value is often subjective (it depends on who you ask). Recently, the FASB has changed some accounting rules and now requires that certain investment securities be recorded at their market value. In choosing between cost and market value, the FASB used two qualities that make accounting information useful for decision making—reliability and relevance: In this case, it weighed the **reliability** of cost figures versus the **relevance** of market value.

> **INTERNATIONAL NOTE**
> Over 100 countries use international standards (sometimes called iGAAP). For example, all companies in the European Union follow international standards. The differences between U.S. and international standards are not generally significant. In this book, we highlight any major differences using International Notes like this one.

International Notes highlight differences between U.S. and international accounting standards.

Assumptions

Assumptions provide a foundation for the accounting process. Two main assumptions are the **monetary unit assumption** and the **economic entity assumption**.

> **STUDY OBJECTIVE 5**
> Explain the monetary unit assumption and the economic entity assumption.

MONETARY UNIT ASSUMPTION

The **monetary unit assumption** requires that companies include in the accounting records only transaction data that can be expressed in money terms. This assumption enables accounting to quantify (measure) economic events. The monetary unit assumption is vital to applying the cost principle.

This assumption prevents the inclusion of some relevant information in the accounting records. For example, the health of a company's owner, the quality of service, and the morale of employees are not included. The reason: Companies cannot quantify this information in money terms. Though this information is important, companies record only events that can be measured in money.

ECONOMIC ENTITY ASSUMPTION

An economic entity can be any organization or unit in society. It may be a company (such as Crocs, Inc.), a governmental unit (the state of Ohio), a municipality (Seattle), a school district (St. Louis District 48), or a church (Southern Baptist). The **economic entity assumption** requires that the activities of the entity be kept separate and distinct from the activities of its owner and all other economic entities. To illustrate, Sally Rider, owner of Sally's Boutique, must keep her personal living costs separate from the expenses of the Boutique. Similarly, McDonald's, Coca-Cola, and Cadbury-Schweppes are segregated into separate economic entities for accounting purposes.

> **ETHICS NOTE**
> The importance of the economic entity assumption is illustrated by scandals involving Adelphia. In this case, senior company employees entered into transactions that blurred the line between the employees' financial interests and those of the company. For example, Aldephia guaranteed over $2 billion of loans to the founding family.

Proprietorship. A business owned by one person is generally a *proprietorship*. The owner is often the manager/operator of the business. Small service-type businesses (plumbing companies, beauty salons, and auto repair shops), farms, and small retail stores (antique shops, clothing stores, and used-book stores) are often proprietorships. **Usually only a relatively small amount of money (capital) is necessary to start in business as a proprietorship. The owner (proprietor) receives any profits, suffers any losses, and is personally liable for all debts of the business.** There is no legal distinction between the business as an economic unit and the owner, but the accounting records of the business activities are kept separate from the personal records and activities of the owner.

Partnership. A business owned by two or more persons associated as partners is a *partnership*. In most respects a partnership is like a proprietorship except that more than one owner is involved. Typically a partnership agreement (written or oral) sets forth such terms as initial investment, duties of each partner, division of net income (or net loss), and settlement to be made upon death or withdrawal of a partner. Each partner generally has unlimited personal liability for the debts of the partnership. **Like a proprietorship, for accounting purposes the partnership transactions must be kept separate from the personal activities of the partners.** Partnerships are often used to organize retail and service-type businesses, including professional practices (lawyers, doctors, architects, and certified public accountants).

Corporation. A business organized as a separate legal entity under state corporation law and having ownership divided into transferable shares of stock is a *corporation*. The holders of the shares (stockholders) **enjoy limited liability**; that is, they are not personally liable for the debts of the corporate entity. Stockholders **may transfer all or part of their ownership shares to other investors at any time** (i.e., sell their shares). The ease with which ownership can change adds to the attractiveness of investing in a corporation. Because ownership can be transferred without dissolving the corporation, the corporation **enjoys an unlimited life**.

Although the combined number of proprietorships and partnerships in the United States is more than five times the number of corporations, the revenue produced by corporations is eight times greater. Most of the largest enterprises in the United States—for example, ExxonMobil, General Motors, Wal-Mart, Citigroup, and Microsoft—are corporations.

*The **Do It** exercises ask you to put newly acquired knowledge to work. They outline the Action Plan necessary to complete the exercise, and they show a Solution.*

DO IT!

BASIC CONCEPTS

Indicate whether each of the five statements presented below is true or false.

1. The three steps in the accounting process are identification, recording, and communication.
2. The two most common types of external users are investors and company officers.
3. Congress passed the Sarbanes-Oxley Act of 2002 to reduce unethical behavior and decrease the likelihood of future corporate scandals.
4. The primary accounting standard-setting body in the United States is the Financial Accounting Standards Board (FASB).
5. The cost principle dictates that companies record assets at their cost. In later periods, however, the market value of the asset must be used if market value is higher than its cost.

Solution

1. True   2. False. The two most common types of external users are investors and creditors.   3. True.   4. True.   5. False. The cost principle dictates that companies record assets at their cost. Under the cost principle, the company must also use cost in later periods as well.

Related exercise material: **E1-1, E1-2, E1-3, E1-4,** and DO IT! **1-1.**

action plan

✔ Review the basic concepts learned to date.

✔ Develop an understanding of the key terms used.

ACCOUNTING ACROSS THE ORGANIZATION

How Will Accounting Help Me?

One question that students frequently ask is, "How will the study of accounting help me?" It should help you a great deal, because a working knowledge of accounting is desirable for virtually *every field* of endeavor. Some examples of how accounting is used in other careers include:

General management: Imagine running Ford Motors, Massachusetts General Hospital, Northern Virginia Community College, a Subway franchise, a Trek bike shop. All general managers need to understand where the enterprise's cash comes from and where it goes in order to make wise business decisions.

Marketing: A marketing specialist at a company like Procter & Gamble develops strategies to help the sales force be successful. But making a sale is meaningless unless it is a profitable sale. Marketing people must be sensitive to costs and benefits, which accounting helps them quantify and understand.

Finance: Do you want to be a banker for Bank of America, an investment analyst for Goldman Sachs, a stock broker for Merrill Lynch? These fields rely heavily on accounting. In all of them you will regularly examine and analyze financial statements. In fact, it is difficult to get a good finance job without two or three courses in accounting.

Real estate: Are you interested in being a real estate broker for Prudential Real Estate? Because a third party—the bank—is almost always involved in financing a real estate transaction, brokers must understand the numbers involved: Can the buyer afford to make the payments to the bank? Does the cash flow from an industrial property justify the purchase price? What are the tax benefits of the purchase?

? How might accounting help you?

Accounting Across the Organization boxes demonstrate applications of accounting information in various business functions.

THE BASIC ACCOUNTING EQUATION

The two basic elements of a business are what it owns and what it owes. **Assets** are the resources a business owns. For example, Google has total assets of approximately $18.4 billion. Liabilities and owner's equity are the rights or claims against these resources. Thus, Google has $18.4 billion of claims against its $18.4 billion of assets. Claims of those to whom the company owes money (creditors) are called **liabilities**. Claims of owners are called **owner's equity**. Google has liabilities of $1.4 billion and owners' equity of $17 billion.

We can express the relationship of assets, liabilities, and owner's equity as an equation, as shown in Illustration 1-5 (page 12).

STUDY OBJECTIVE 6

State the accounting equation, and define its components.

Illustration 1-5
The basic accounting
equation

Assets	=	Liabilities	+	Owner's Equity

This relationship is the **basic accounting equation**. Assets must equal the sum of liabilities and owner's equity. Liabilities appear before owner's equity in the basic accounting equation because they are paid first if a business is liquidated.

The accounting equation applies to all **economic entities** regardless of size, nature of business, or form of business organization. It applies to a small proprietorship such as a corner grocery store as well as to a giant corporation such as PepsiCo. The equation provides the **underlying framework** for recording and summarizing economic events.

Let's look in more detail at the categories in the basic accounting equation.

Assets

As noted above, **assets** are resources a business owns. The business uses its assets in carrying out such activities as production and sales. The common characteristic possessed by all assets is **the capacity to provide future services or benefits**. In a business, that service potential or future economic benefit eventually results in cash inflows (receipts). For example, Campus Pizza owns a delivery truck that provides economic benefits from delivering pizzas. Other assets of Campus Pizza are tables, chairs, jukebox, cash register, oven, tableware, and, of course, cash.

Liabilities

Liabilities are claims against assets—that is, existing debts and obligations. Businesses of all sizes usually borrow money and purchase merchandise on credit. These economic activities result in payables of various sorts:

- Campus Pizza, for instance, purchases cheese, sausage, flour, and beverages on credit from suppliers. These obligations are called **accounts payable**.
- Campus Pizza also has a **note payable** to First National Bank for the money borrowed to purchase the delivery truck.
- Campus Pizza may also have **wages payable** to employees and **sales and real estate taxes payable** to the local government.

All of these persons or entities to whom Campus Pizza owes money are its **creditors**.

Creditors may legally force the liquidation of a business that does not pay its debts. In that case, the law requires that creditor claims be paid **before** ownership claims.

Owner's Equity

The ownership claim on total assets is **owner's equity**. It is equal to total assets minus total liabilities. Here is why: The assets of a business are claimed by either creditors or owners. To find out what belongs to owners, we subtract the creditors' claims (the liabilities) from assets. The remainder is the owner's claim on the assets—the owner's equity. Since the claims of creditors must be paid **before** ownership claims, owner's equity is often referred to as **residual equity**.

INCREASES IN OWNER'S EQUITY

In a proprietorship, owner's investments and revenues increase owner's equity.

Investments by Owner. Investments by owner are the assets the owner puts into the business. These investments increase owner's equity. They are recorded in a category called **owner's capital**.

Revenues. Revenues are the **gross increase in owner's equity resulting from business activities entered into for the purpose of earning income**. Generally, revenues result from selling merchandise, performing services, renting property, and lending money. Common sources of revenue are sales, fees, services, commissions, interest, dividends, royalties, and rent.

Revenues usually result in an increase in an asset. They may arise from different sources and are called various names depending on the nature of the business. Campus Pizza, for instance, has two categories of sales revenues—pizza sales and beverage sales.

DECREASES IN OWNER'S EQUITY

In a proprietorship, owner's drawings and expenses decrease owner's equity.

Drawings. An owner may withdraw cash or other assets for personal use. We use a separate classification called drawings to determine the total withdrawals for each accounting period. **Drawings decrease owner's equity.**

Expenses. Expenses are the cost of assets consumed or services used in the process of earning revenue. They are **decreases in owner's equity that result from operating the business**. For example, Campus Pizza recognizes the following expenses: cost of ingredients (meat, flour, cheese, tomato paste, mushrooms, etc.); cost of beverages; wages expense; utility expense (electric, gas, and water expense); telephone expense; delivery expense (gasoline, repairs, licenses, etc.); supplies expense (napkins, detergents, aprons, etc.); rent expense; interest expense; and property tax expense.

In summary, owner's equity is increased by an owner's investments and by revenues from business operations. Owner's equity is decreased by an owner's withdrawals of assets and by expenses. Illustration 1-6 expands the basic accounting equation by showing the accounts that comprise owner's equity. This format is referred to as the **expanded accounting equation**.

HELPFUL HINT

In some places we use the term "owner's equity" and in others we use "owners' equity." *Owner's* (singular, possessive) refers to one owner (the case with a sole proprietorship). *Owners'* (plural, possessive) refers to multiple owners (the case with partnerships or corporations).

| Basic Equation: | Assets = Liabilities | + | Owner's Equity |
| Expanded Equation: | Assets = Liabilities | + | Owner's Capital − Owner's Drawings + Revenues − Expenses |

Illustration 1-6
Expanded accounting equation

DO IT!

Classify the following items as investment by owner (I), owner's drawings (D), revenues (R), or expenses (E). Then indicate whether each item increases or decreases owner's equity.
(1) Rent Expense
(2) Service Revenue
(3) Drawings
(4) Salaries Expense

OWNER'S EQUITY EFFECTS

action plan

✔ Understand the sources of revenue.
✔ Understand what causes expenses.

action plan (cont'd)

✔ Review the rules for changes in owner's equity: Investments and revenues increase owner's equity. Expenses and drawings decrease owner's equity.

✔ Recognize that drawings are withdrawals of cash or other assets from the business for personal use.

Solution

1. Rent Expense is an expense (E); it decreases owner's equity.   2. Service Revenue is revenue (R); it increases owner's equity.   3. Drawings is owner's drawings (D); it decreases owner's equity.   4. Salaries Expense is an expense (E); it decreases owner's equity.

Related exercise material: **BE1-1, BE1-2, BE1-3, BE1-4, BE1-5, E1-5, E1-6, E1-7,** and **DO IT!** **1-2.**

 ✔ The Navigator

USING THE ACCOUNTING EQUATION

STUDY OBJECTIVE 7

Analyze the effects of business transactions on the accounting equation.

Transactions (**business transactions**) are a business's economic events recorded by accountants. Transactions may be external or internal. **External transactions** involve economic events between the company and some outside enterprise. For example, Campus Pizza's purchase of cooking equipment from a supplier, payment of monthly rent to the landlord, and sale of pizzas to customers are external transactions. **Internal transactions** are economic events that occur entirely within one company. The use of cooking and cleaning supplies are internal transactions for Campus Pizza.

Companies carry on many activities that do not represent business transactions. Examples are hiring employees, answering the telephone, talking with customers, and placing merchandise orders. Some of these activities may lead to business transactions: Employees will earn wages, and suppliers will deliver ordered merchandise. The company must analyze each event to find out if it affects the components of the accounting equation. If it does, the company will record the transaction. Illustration 1-7 (page 15) demonstrates the transaction-identification process.

Each transaction must have a dual effect on the accounting equation. For example, if an asset is increased, there must be a corresponding: (1) decrease in another asset, or (2) increase in a specific liability, or (3) increase in owner's equity.

Two or more items could be affected. For example, as one asset is increased $10,000, another asset could decrease $6,000 and a liability could increase $4,000. Any change in a liability or ownership claim is subject to similar analysis.

Transaction Analysis

HELPFUL HINT

You will want to study these transactions until you are sure you understand them. They are not difficult, but understanding them is important to your success in this course. The ability to analyze transactions in terms of the basic accounting equation is essential in accounting.

The following examples are business transactions for a computer programming business during its first month of operations.

Transaction (1). Investment By Owner.   Ray Neal decides to open a computer programming service which he names Softbyte. On September 1, 2010, he invests $15,000 cash in the business. This transaction results in an equal increase in assets and owner's equity. The asset Cash increases $15,000, as does the owner's equity, identified as R. Neal, Capital. The effect of this transaction on the basic equation is:

	Assets	=	**Liabilities**	+	**Owner's Equity**
					R. Neal,
	Cash	=			Capital
(1)	+$15,000	=			+$15,000

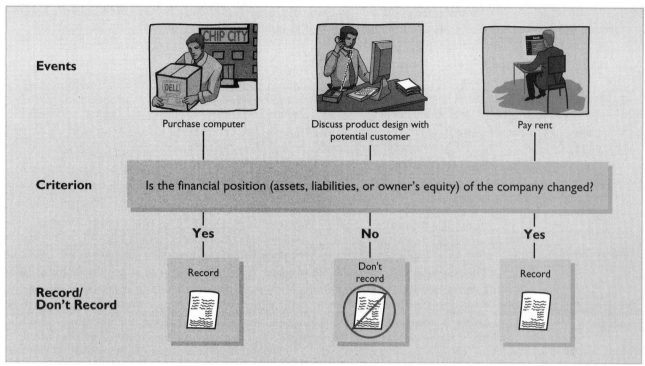

Events | Purchase computer | Discuss product design with potential customer | Pay rent

Criterion | Is the financial position (assets, liabilities, or owner's equity) of the company changed?

Yes | No | Yes

Record/Don't Record | Record | Don't record | Record

Illustration 1-7
Transaction-identification process

Observe that the equality of the accounting equation has been maintained. Note that the investments by the owner do not represent revenues, and they are excluded in determining net income. Therefore it is necessary to make clear that the increase is an investment (increasing R. Neal, Capital) rather than revenue.

Transaction (2). Purchase of Equipment for Cash.   Softbyte purchases computer equipment for $7,000 cash. This transaction results in an equal increase and decrease in total assets, though the composition of assets changes: Cash decreases $7,000, and the asset Equipment increases $7,000. The specific effect of this transaction and the cumulative effect of the first two transactions are:

		Assets			=	**Liabilities**	+	**Owner's Equity**
		Cash	+	Equipment	=			R. Neal, Capital
	Old Bal.	$15,000						$15,000
(2)		−7,000		+$7,000				
	New Bal.	$ 8,000	+	$7,000	=			$15,000
		$15,000						

Observe that total assets are still $15,000. Neal's equity also remains at $15,000, the amount of his original investment.

Transaction (3). Purchase of Supplies on Credit.   Softbyte purchases for $1,600 from Acme Supply Company computer paper and other supplies expected to last several months. Acme agrees to allow Softbyte to pay this bill in October. This transaction is a purchase on account (a credit purchase). Assets increase because of the expected future benefits of using the paper and supplies, and liabilities increase by the amount due Acme Company. The asset Supplies increases $1,600, and the liability Accounts Payable increases by the same amount. The effect on the equation is:

		Assets				=	Liabilities	+	Owner's Equity
		Cash	+ Supplies	+ Equipment	=		Accounts Payable	+	R. Neal, Capital
	Old Bal.	$8,000		$7,000					$15,000
(3)			+$1,600				+$1,600		
	New Bal.	$8,000 +	$1,600 +	$7,000	=		$1,600	+	$15,000
			$16,600					$16,600	

Total assets are now $16,600. This total is matched by a $1,600 creditor's claim and a $15,000 ownership claim.

Transaction (4). Services Provided for Cash. Softbyte receives $1,200 cash from customers for programming services it has provided. This transaction represents Softbyte's principal revenue-producing activity. Recall that **revenue increases owner's equity**. In this transaction, Cash increases $1,200, and revenues (specifically, Service Revenue) increase $1,200. The new balances in the equation are:

		Assets			=	Liabilities	+	Owner's Equity	
		Cash	+ Supplies	+ Equipment	=	Accounts Payable	+	R. Neal, Capital	+ Revenues
	Old Bal.	$8,000	$1,600	$7,000		$1,600		$15,000	
(4)		+$1,200							+$1,200
	New Bal.	$9,200 +	$1,600 +	$7,000	=	$1,600	+	$15,000 +	$1,200
			$17,800					$17,800	

The two sides of the equation balance at $17,800. Service Revenue is included in determining Softbyte's net income.

Note that we do not have room to give details for each individual revenue and expense account in this illustration. Thus, revenues (and expenses when we get to them) are summarized under one column heading for Revenues and one for Expenses. However, it is important to keep track of the category (account) titles affected (e.g., Service Revenue) as they will be needed when we prepare financial statements later in the chapter.

Transaction (5). Purchase of Advertising on Credit. Softbyte receives a bill for $250 from the *Daily News* for advertising but postpones payment until a later date. This transaction results in an increase in liabilities and a decrease in owner's equity. The specific categories involved are Accounts Payable and expenses (specifically, Advertising Expense). The effect on the equation is:

		Assets			=	Liabilities	+	Owner's Equity		
		Cash	+ Supplies	+ Equipment	=	Accounts Payable	+	R. Neal, Capital	+ Revenues	− Expenses
	Old Bal.	$9,200	$1,600	$7,000		$1,600		$15,000	$1,200	
(5)						+250				−$250
	New Bal.	$9,200 +	$1,600 +	$7,000	=	$1,850	+	$15,000 +	$1,200 −	$250
			$17,800					$17,800		

The two sides of the equation still balance at $17,800. Owner's equity decreases when Softbyte incurs the expense. Expenses are not always paid in cash at the time they are incurred. When Softbyte pays at a later date, the liability Accounts Payable will decrease, and the asset Cash will decrease [see Transaction (8)]. The cost of advertising is an expense (rather than an asset) because the company has *used* the benefits. Advertising Expense is included in determining net income.

Transaction (6). Services Provided for Cash and Credit.   Softbyte provides $3,500 of programming services for customers. The company receives cash of $1,500 from customers, and it bills the balance of $2,000 on account. This transaction results in an equal increase in assets and owner's equity. Three specific items are affected: Cash increases $1,500; Accounts Receivable increases $2,000; and Service Revenue increases $3,500. The new balances are as follows.

			Assets				= Liabilities +			Owner's Equity		
	Cash	+	Accounts Receivable +	Supplies +	Equipment =		Accounts Payable	+	R. Neal, Capital +	Revenues	−	Expenses
Old Bal.	$9,200			$1,600	$7,000		$1,850		$15,000	$1,200		$250
(6)	+1,500		+$2,000							+3,500		
New Bal.	$10,700	+	$2,000 +	$1,600 +	$7,000 =		$1,850	+	$15,000 +	$4,700	−	$250
			$21,300							$21,300		

Softbyte earns revenues when it provides the service, and therefore it recognizes $3,500 in revenue. In exchange for this service, it received $1,500 in Cash and Accounts Receivable of $2,000. This Accounts Receivable represents customers' promise to pay $2,000 to Softbyte in the future. When it later receives collections on account, Softbyte will increase Cash and will decrease Accounts Receivable [see Transaction (9)].

Transaction (7). Payment of Expenses.   Softbyte pays the following Expenses in cash for September: store rent $600, salaries of employees $900, and utilities $200. These payments result in an equal decrease in assets and expenses. Cash decreases $1,700, and the specific expense categories (Rent Expense, Salaries Expense, and Utility Expense) decrease owner's equity by the same amount. The effect of these payments on the equation is:

			Assets				= Liabilities +			Owner's Equity		
	Cash	+	Accounts Receivable +	Supplies +	Equipment =		Accounts Payable	+	R. Neal, Capital +	Revenues	−	Expenses
Old Bal.	$10,700		$2,000	$1,600	$7,000		$1,850		$15,000	$4,700		$ 250
(7)	−1,700											−600
												−900
												−200
New Bal.	$9,000	+	$2,000 +	$1,600 +	$7,000 =		$1,850	+	$15,000 +	$4,700	−	$1,950
			$19,600							$19,600		

The two sides of the equation now balance at $19,600. Three lines in the analysis indicate the different types of expenses that have been incurred.

Transaction (8). Payment of Accounts Payable. Softbyte pays its $250 *Daily News* bill in cash. The company previously [in Transaction (5)] recorded the bill as an increase in Accounts Payable and a decrease in owner's equity. This payment "on account" decreases the asset Cash by $250 and also decreases the liability Accounts Payable by $250. The effect of this transaction on the equation is:

	Assets				= Liabilities +		Owner's Equity		
	Cash +	Accounts Receivable +	Supplies +	Equipment =	Accounts Payable +	R. Neal, Capital +	Revenues −	Expenses
Old Bal.	$9,000	$2,000	$1,600	$7,000	$1,850	$15,000	$4,700	$1,950
(8)	−250				−250			
New Bal.	$8,750 +	$2,000 +	$1,600 +	$7,000 =	$1,600 +	$15,000 +	$4,700 −	$1,950
		$19,350				$19,350		

Observe that the payment of a liability related to an expense that has previously been recorded does not affect owner's equity. The company recorded this expense in Transaction (5) and should not record it again.

Transaction (9). Receipt of Cash on Account. Softbyte receives $600 in cash from customers who had been billed for services [in Transaction (6)]. This does not change total assets, but it changes the composition of those assets. Cash increases $600 and Accounts Receivable decreases $600. The new balances are:

	Assets				= Liabilities +		Owner's Equity		
	Cash +	Accounts Receivable +	Supplies +	Equipment =	Accounts Payable +	R. Neal, Capital +	Revenues −	Expenses
Old Bal.	$8,750	$2,000	$1,600	$7,000	$1,600	$15,000	$4,700	$1,950
(9)	+600	−600						
New Bal.	$9,350 +	$1,400 +	$1,600 +	$7,000 =	$1,600 +	$15,000 +	$4,700 −	$1,950
		$19,350				$19,350		

Note that the collection of an account receivable for services previously billed and recorded does not affect owner's equity. Softbyte already recorded this revenue in Transaction (6) and should not record it again.

Transaction (10). Withdrawal of Cash by Owner. Ray Neal withdraws $1,300 in cash from the business for his personal use. This transaction results in an equal decrease in assets and owner's equity. Both Cash and R. Neal, Capital decrease $1,300, as shown below.

	Assets				= Liabilities +		Owner's Equity		
	Cash +	Accounts Receivable +	Supplies +	Equipment =	Accounts Payable +	R. Neal, Capital −	R. Neal, Drawings +	Revenues −	Expenses
Old Bal.	$9,350	$1,400	$1,600	$7,000	$1,600	$15,000		$4,700	$1,950
(10)	−1,300						−$1,300		
New Bal.	$8,050 +	$1,400 +	$1,600 +	$7,000 =	$1,600 +	$15,000 −	$1,300 +	$4,700 −	$1,950
		$18,050				$18,050			

Observe that the effect of a cash withdrawal by the owner is the opposite of the effect of an investment by the owner. **Owner's drawings are not expenses.** Expenses are incurred for the purpose of earning revenue. Drawings do not generate revenue. They are a **disinvestment**. Like owner's investment, the company excludes owner's drawings in determining net income.

Summary of Transactions

Illustration 1-8 summarizes the September transactions of Softbyte to show their cumulative effect on the basic accounting equation. It also indicates the transaction number and the specific effects of each transaction.

	Cash	+ Receivable	+ Supplies	+ Equipment =	Payable	+ R. Neal, Capital	− R. Neal, Drawings	+ Revenues	− Expenses
(1)	+$15,000					+$15,000			
(2)	−7,000			+$7,000					
(3)			+$1,600		+$1,600				
(4)	+1,200							+$1,200	
(5)					+250				−$250
(6)	+1,500	+$2,000						+3,500	
(7)	−600								−600
	−900								−900
	−200								−200
(8)	−250				−250				
(9)	+600	−600							
(10)	−1,300						−$1,300		
	$8,050 +	$1,400 +	$1,600 +	$7,000 =	$1,600 +	$15,000 −	$1,300 +	$4,700 −	$1,950

Assets $18,050

Liabilities + Owner's Equity $18,050

Illustration 1-8
Tabular summary of Softbyte transactions

Illustration 1-8 demonstrates some significant facts:

1. Each transaction is analyzed in terms of its effect on:
   (a) the three components of the basic accounting equation.
   (b) specific items within each component.
2. The two sides of the equation must always be equal.

There! You made it through your first transaction analysis. If you feel a bit shaky on any of the transactions, it might be a good idea at this point to get up, take a short break, and come back again for a 10- to 15-minute review of the transactions, to make sure you understand them before you go on to the next section.

DO IT!

Transactions made by Virmari & Co., a public accounting firm, for the month of August are shown below. Prepare a tabular analysis which shows the effects of these transactions on the expanded accounting equation, similar to that shown in Illustration 1-8.

TABULAR ANALYSIS

action plan

✔ Analyze the effects of each transaction on the accounting equation.

✔ Use appropriate category names (not descriptions).

✔ Keep the accounting equation in balance.

1. The owner invested $25,000 cash in the business.
2. The company purchased $7,000 of office equipment on credit.
3. The company received $8,000 cash in exchange for services performed.
4. The company paid $850 for this month's rent.
5. The owner withdrew $1,000 cash for personal use.

Solution

	Assets		=	Liabilities	+			Owner's Equity			
	Cash	+	Office Equipment	=	Accounts Payable	+	A.Virmari, Capital	–	A.Virmari, Drawings	+	Revenues	–	Expenses
1.	+$25,000						+$25,000					
2.			+$7,000		+$7,000							
3.	+8,000										+$8,000	
4.	–850											–$850
5.	–1,000								–$1,000			
	$31,150	+	$7,000	=	$7,000	+	$25,000	–	$1,000	+	$8,000	–	$850
		$38,150							$38,150			

Related exercise material: **BE1-6, BE1-7, BE1-8, BE1-9, E1-6, E1-7, E1-8, E1-10, E1-11,** and **DO IT!** 1-3.

✔ The Navigator

FINANCIAL STATEMENTS

STUDY OBJECTIVE 8
Understand the four financial statements and how they are prepared.

Companies prepare four financial statements from the summarized accounting data:

1. An **income statement** presents the revenues and expenses and resulting net income or net loss for a specific period of time.
2. An **owner's equity statement** summarizes the changes in owner's equity for a specific period of time.
3. A **balance sheet** reports the assets, liabilities, and owner's equity at a specific date.
4. A **statement of cash flows** summarizes information about the cash inflows (receipts) and outflows (payments) for a specific period of time.

HELPFUL HINT
The income statement, owner's equity statement, and statement of cash flows are all for a *period* of time, whereas the balance sheet is for a *point* in time.

These statements provide relevant financial data for internal and external users.

Illustration 1-9 (page 21) shows the financial statements of Softbyte. Note that the statements are interrelated:

1. Net income of $2,750 on the **income statement** is added to the beginning balance of owner's capital in the **owner's equity statement**.
2. Owner's capital of $16,450 at the end of the reporting period shown in the **owner's equity statement** is reported on the **balance sheet**.
3. Cash of $8,050 on the **balance sheet** is reported on the **statement of cash flows**.

Also, explanatory notes and supporting schedules are an integral part of every set of financial statements. We illustrate these notes and schedules in later chapters of this textbook.

Be sure to carefully examine the format and content of each statement in Illustration 1-9. We describe the essential features of each in the following sections.

SOFTBYTE
Income Statement
For the Month Ended September 30, 2010

Revenues		
Service revenue		$ 4,700
Expenses		
Salaries expense	$900	
Rent expense	600	
Advertising expense	250	
Utilities expense	200	
Total expenses		1,950
Net income		$ 2,750

1

SOFTBYTE
Owner's Equity Statement
For the Month Ended September 30, 2010

R. Neal, Capital September 1		$ –0–
Add: Investments	$15,000	
Net income	2,750	17,750
		17,750
Less: Drawings		1,300
R. Neal, Capital, September 30		$16,450

SOFTBYTE
Balance Sheet
September 30, 2010

Assets

Cash	$ 8,050
Accounts receivable	1,400
Supplies	1,600
Equipment	7,000
Total assets	$18,050

Liabilities and Owner's Equity

Liabilities		
Accounts payable		$ 1,600
Owner's equity		
R. Neal, Capital		16,450
Total liabilities and owner's equity		$18,050

2
3

SOFTBYTE
Statement of Cash Flows
For the Month Ended September 30, 2010

Cash flows from operating activities		
Cash receipts from revenues		$ 3,300
Cash payments for expenses		(1,950)
Net cash provided by operating activities		1,350
Cash flows from investing activities		
Purchase of equipment		(7,000)
Cash flows from financing activities		
Investments by owner	$15,000	
Drawings by owner	(1,300)	13,700
Net increase in cash		8,050
Cash at the beginning of the period		0
Cash at the end of the period		$ 8,050

Illustration 1-9
Financial statements and their interrelationships

HELPFUL HINT
The heading of each statement identifies the company, the type of statement, and the specific date or time period covered by the statement.

HELPFUL HINT
Note that final sums are double-underlined.

HELPFUL HINT
1. Net income is computed first and is needed to determine the ending balance in owner's equity.
2. The ending balance in owner's equity is needed in preparing the balance sheet.
3. The cash shown on the balance sheet is needed in preparing the statement of cash flows.

Income Statement

The income statement reports the revenues and expenses for a specific period of
time. (In Softbyte's case, this is "For the Month Ended September 30, 2010.")
Softbyte's income statement is prepared from the data appearing in the owner's
equity columns of Illustration 1-8.

The income statement lists revenues first, followed by expenses. Finally the
statement shows net income (or net loss). **Net income** results when revenues exceed expenses. A **net loss** occurs when expenses exceed revenues.

Although practice varies, we have chosen in our illustrations and homework
solutions to list expenses in order of magnitude. (We will consider alternative for-
mats for the income statement in later chapters.)

Note that the income statement does **not** include investment and withdrawal
transactions between the owner and the business in measuring net income. For
example, as explained earlier, Ray Neal's withdrawal of cash from Softbyte was not
regarded as a business expense.

Owner's Equity Statement

The owner's equity statement reports the changes in owner's equity for a specific
period of time. The time period is the same as that covered by the income statement. Data for the preparation of the owner's equity statement come from the
owner's equity columns of the tabular summary (Illustration 1-8) and from the income statement. The first line of the statement shows the beginning owner's
equity amount (which was zero at the start of the business). Then come the
owner's investments, net income (or loss), and the owner's drawings. This statement indicates *why* owner's equity has increased or decreased during the period.

What if Softbyte had reported a net loss in its first month? Let's assume that
during the month of September 2010, Softbyte lost $10,000. Illustration 1-10 shows
the presentation of a net loss in the owner's equity statement.

Illustration 1-10
Presentation of net loss

SOFTBYTE Owner's Equity Statement For the Month Ended September 30, 2010		
R. Neal, Capital, September 1		$ –0–
Add: Investments		15,000
		15,000
Less: Drawings	$ 1,300	
Net loss	**10,000**	11,300
R. Neal, Capital, September 30		$ 3,700

If the owner makes any additional investments, the company reports them in the
owner's equity statement as investments.

Balance Sheet

Softbyte's balance sheet reports the assets, liabilities, and owner's equity at a specific date (in Softbyte's case, September 30, 2010). The company prepares the

balance sheet from the column headings of the tabular summary (Illustration 1-8) and the month-end data shown in its last line.

Observe that the balance sheet lists assets at the top, followed by liabilities and owner's equity. Total assets must equal total liabilities and owner's equity. Softbyte reports only one liability—accounts payable—in its balance sheet. In most cases, there will be more than one liability. When two or more liabilities are involved, a customary way of listing is as follows.

Illustration 1-11
Presentation of liabilities

Liabilities	
Notes payable	$10,000
Accounts payable	63,000
Salaries payable	18,000
Total liabilities	$91,000

The balance sheet is a snapshot of the company's financial condition at a specific moment in time (usually the month-end or year-end).

ACCOUNTING ACROSS THE ORGANIZATION

What Do General Mills, Walt Disney, and Dunkin' Donuts Have in Common?

Not every company uses December 31 as the accounting year-end. Some companies whose year-ends differ from December 31 are General Mills, May 27; Walt Disney Productions, September 30; and Dunkin' Donuts Inc., October 31. Why do companies choose the particular year-ends that they do? Many choose to end the accounting year when inventory or operations are at a low. Compiling accounting information requires much time and effort by managers, so companies would rather do it when they aren't as busy operating the business. Also, inventory is easier and less costly to count when it is low.

? What year-end would you likely use if you owned a ski resort and ski rental business? What if you owned a college bookstore? Why choose those year-ends?

Statement of Cash Flows

The statement of cash flows provides information on the cash receipts and payments for a specific period of time. The statement of cash flows reports (1) the cash effects of a company's operations during a period, (2) its investing transactions, (3) its financing transactions, (4) the net increase or decrease in cash during the period, and (5) the cash amount at the end of the period.

Reporting the sources, uses, and change in cash is useful because investors, creditors, and others want to know what is happening to a company's most liquid resource. The statement of cash flows provides answers to the following simple but important questions.

HELPFUL HINT
Investing activities pertain to investments made by the company, not investments made by the owner.

1. Where did cash come from during the period?
2. What was cash used for during the period?
3. What was the change in the cash balance during the period?

As shown in Softbyte's statement of cash flows, cash increased $8,050 during the period. Net cash flow provided from operating activities increased cash $1,350. Cash flow from investing transactions decreased cash $7,000. And cash flow from financing transactions increased cash $13,700. At this time, you need not be concerned with how these amounts are determined. Chapter 17 will examine the statement of cash flows in detail.

DO IT!

FINANCIAL STATEMENT ITEMS

Presented below is selected information related to Flanagan Company at December 31, 2010. Flanagan reports financial information monthly.

Office Equipment	$10,000	Utilities Expense	$ 4,000
Cash	8,000	Accounts Receivable	9,000
Service Revenue	36,000	Wages Expense	7,000
Rent Expense	11,000	Notes Payable	16,500
Accounts Payable	2,000	Drawings	5,000

(a) Determine the total assets of Flanagan Company at December 31, 2010.

(b) Determine the net income that Flanagan Company reported for December 2010.

(c) Determine the owner's equity of Flanagan Company at December 31, 2010.

action plan

✔ Remember the basic accounting equation: assets must equal liabilities plus owner's equity.

✔ Review previous financial statements to determine how total assets, net income, and owner's equity are computed.

Solution

(a) The total assets are $27,000, comprised of Cash $8,000, Accounts Receivable $9,000, and Office Equipment $10,000.

(b) Net income is $14,000, computed as follows:

Revenues		
Service revenue		$36,000
Expenses		
Rent expense	$11,000	
Wages expense	7,000	
Utilities expense	4,000	
Total expenses		22,000
Net income		$14,000

(c) The ending owner's equity of Flanagan Company is $8,500. By rewriting the accounting equation, we can compute owner's equity as assets minus liabilities, as follows:

Total assets [as computed in (a)]		$27,000
Less: Liabilities		
Notes payable	$16,500	
Accounts payable	2,000	18,500
Owner's equity		$ 8,500

Note that it is not possible to determine the company's owner's equity in any other way, because the beginning total for owner's equity is not provided.

The Navigator

Be sure to read **ALL ABOUT YOU:** *Ethics: Managing Personal Financial Reporting* on page 25 for information on how topics in this chapter apply to your personal life.

Ethics: Managing Personal Financial Reporting

When companies need money, they go to investors or creditors. Before investors or creditors will give a company cash, they want to know the company's financial position and performance. They want to see the company's financial statements—the balance sheet and the income statement. When students need money for school, they often apply for financial aid. When you apply for financial aid, you must submit your own version of a financial statement—the Free Application for Federal Student Aid (FAFSA) form.

The FAFSA form asks how much you make (based on your federal income tax return) and how much your parents make. The purpose is to find out how much you own and how much you owe. Why do the Department of Education and your school want this information? Simple: They want to know whether you really need the money. Schools and government-loan funds have limited resources, and they want to make sure that the money goes to those who need it the most. The bottom line is: The worse off you look financially, the more likely you are to get money.

The question is: Should you intentionally make yourself look worse off than you are?

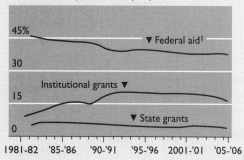

The federal share of assistance is declining
Sources of financial aid as a percentage of total aid used to finance postsecondary expenses

Source for graph: College Board, *Princeton Review*, as reported in "College Admissions: Is Gate Open or Closed?," *Wall Street Journal*, March 25, 2006, p. A7.

✷ Some Facts

* After adjusting for inflation, private-college tuition and fees have increased 37% over the past decade; public-college tuition has risen 54%.

* Two-thirds (65.6%) of undergraduate students graduate with some debt.

* Among graduating seniors, the average debt load is $19,202, according to an analysis of data from the Department of Education's National Postsecondary Student Aid Study. That does not include any debt that their parents might incur.

* Colleges are required to audit the FAFSA forms of at least one-third of their students; some audit 100%. (Compare that to the IRS, which audits a very small percentage of tax returns.) Thus, if you lie on your financial aid forms, there's a very good chance you'll get caught.

Additional information regarding scholarships and loans is available at *www.finaid.org/.* You might find especially interesting the section that discusses how to maximize your chances of obtaining financial aid at *www.finaid.org/fafsa/maximize.phtml.*

✷ What Do You Think?

Consider the following and decide what action you would take:

Suppose you have $4,000 in cash and $4,000 in credit card bills. The more cash and other assets that you have, the less likely you are to get financial aid. Also, if you have a lot of consumer debt (credit card bills), schools are not more likely to loan you money. To increase your chances of receiving aid, should you use the cash to pay off your credit card bills, and therefore make yourself look "worse off" to the financial aid decision makers?

YES: You are playing within the rules. You are not hiding assets. You are simply restructuring your assets and liabilities to best conform with the preferences that are built into the federal aid formulas.

NO: You are engaging in a transaction solely to take advantage of a loophole in the federal aid rules. In doing so, you are potentially depriving someone who is actually worse off than you from receiving aid.

Sources: "College Admissions: Is Gate Open or Closed?," *Wall Street Journal*, March 25, 2006, P. A7; *www.finaid.org.*

Comprehensive DO IT!

*The **Comprehensive Do It!** is a final review of the chapter. The **Action Plan** gives tips about how to approach the problem, and the **Solution** demonstrates both the form and content of complete answers.*

Joan Robinson opens her own law office on July 1, 2010. During the first month of operations, the following transactions occurred.

1. Joan invested $11,000 in cash in the law practice.
2. Paid $800 for July rent on office space.
3. Purchased office equipment on account $3,000.
4. Provided legal services to clients for cash $1,500.
5. Borrowed $700 cash from a bank on a note payable.
6. Performed legal services for client on account $2,000.
7. Paid monthly expenses: salaries $500, utilities $300, and telephone $100.
8. Joan withdraws $1,000 cash for personal use.

Instructions

(a) Prepare a tabular summary of the transactions.
(b) Prepare the income statement, owner's equity statement, and balance sheet at July 31 for Joan Robinson, Attorney.

Solution to Comprehensive DO IT!

(a)

Trans-action	Cash	+	Accounts Receivable	+	Equipment	=	Note Payable	+	Accounts Payable	+	J. Robinson, Capital	−	J. Robinson, Drawings	+	Revenues	−	Expenses
							Liabilities				**Owner's Equity**						
(1)	+$11,000					=					+$11,000						
(2)	−800																−$800
(3)					+$3,000	=			+$3,000								
(4)	+1,500														+$1,500		
(5)	+700						+$700										
(6)			+$2,000												+2,000		
(7)	−500																−500
	−300																−300
	−100																−100
(8)	−1,000												−$1,000				
	$10,500	+	$2,000	+	$3,000	=	$700	+	$3,000	+	$11,000	−	$1,000	+	$3,500	−	$1,700

$15,500

$15,500

action plan

✔ Make sure that assets equal liabilities plus owner's equity after each transaction.

✔ Investments and revenues increase owner's equity. Withdrawals and expenses decrease owner's equity.

✔ Prepare the financial statements in the order listed.

✔ The income statement shows revenues and expenses for a period of time.

✔ The statement of owner's equity shows the changes in owner's equity for the same period of time as the income statement.

✔ The balance sheet reports assets, liabilities, and owner's equity at a specific date.

(b)

JOAN ROBINSON, ATTORNEY
INCOME STATEMENT
Month Ended July 31, 2010

Revenues		
Service revenue		$3,500
Expenses		
Rent expense	$800	
Salaries expense	500	
Utilities expense	300	
Telephone expense	100	
Total expenses		1,700
Net income		$1,800

JOAN ROBINSON, ATTORNEY
STATEMENT OF OWNER'S EQUITY
Month Ended July 31, 2010

J. Robinson, Capital, July 1		$ 0
Add: Investments	$11,000	
Net income	1,800	12,800
		12,800
Less: Drawings		1,000
J. Robinson, Capital, July 31		$11,800

JOAN ROBINSON, ATTORNEY
BALANCE SHEET
July 31, 2010

Assets

Cash	$10,500
Accounts receivable	2,000
Equipment	3,000
Total assets	$15,500

Liabilities and Owner's Equity

Liabilities		
Notes payable		$ 700
Accounts payable		3,000
Total liabilities		3,700
Owner's equity		
J. Robinson, Capital		11,800
Total liabilities and owner's equity		$15,500

 The Navigator

*This would be a good time to return to the **Student Owner's Manual** at the beginning of the book (or look at it for the first time if you skipped it before) to read about the various types of assignment materials that appear at the end of each chapter. Knowing the purpose of the different assignments will help you appreciate what each contributes to your accounting skills and competencies.*

SUMMARY OF STUDY OBJECTIVES

WILEY PLUS

1 **Explain what accounting is.** Accounting is an information system that identifies, records, and communicates the economic events of an organization to interested users.

2 **Identify the users and uses of accounting.** The major users and uses of accounting are as follows: (a) Management uses accounting information in planning, controlling, and evaluating business operations. (b) Investors (owners) decide whether to buy, hold, or sell their financial interests on the basis of accounting data. (c) Creditors (suppliers and bankers) evaluate the risks of granting credit or lending money on the basis of accounting information. Other groups that use accounting information are taxing authorities, regulatory agencies, customers, labor unions, and economic planners.

3 **Understand why ethics is a fundamental business concept.** Ethics are the standards of conduct by which

actions are judged as right or wrong. If you cannot depend on the honesty of the individuals you deal with, effective communication and economic activity would be impossible, and information would have no credibility.

4 **Explain generally accepted accounting principles and the cost principle.** Generally accepted accounting principles are a common set of standards used by accountants. The cost principle states that companies should record assets at their cost.

5 **Explain the monetary unit assumption and the economic entity assumption.** The monetary unit assumption requires that companies include in the accounting records only transaction data that can be expressed in terms of money. The economic entity assumption requires that the activities of each economic entity be kept

separate from the activities of its owner and other economic entities.

6 **State the accounting equation, and define its components.** The basic accounting equation is:

$$\text{Assets} = \text{Liabilities} + \text{Owner's Equity}$$

Assets are resources owned by a business. Liabilities are creditorship claims on total assets. Owner's equity is the ownership claim on total assets.

The expanded accounting equation is:

$$\text{Assets} = \text{Liabilities} + \text{Owner's Capital} - \text{Owner's Drawings} + \text{Revenues} - \text{Expenses}$$

Owner's capital is assets the owner puts into the business. Owner's drawings are the assets the owner withdraws for personal use. Revenues are increases in assets resulting from income-earning activities. Expenses are the costs of assets consumed in the process of earning revenue.

7 **Analyze the effects of business transactions on the accounting equation.** Each business transaction must have a dual effect on the accounting equation. For example, if an individual asset increases, there must be a corresponding (1) decrease in another asset, or (2) increase in a specific liability, or (3) increase in owner's equity.

8 **Understand the four financial statements and how they are prepared.** An income statement presents the revenues and expenses of a company for a specified period of time. An owner's equity statement summarizes the changes in owner's equity that have occurred for a specific period of time. A balance sheet reports the assets, liabilities, and owner's equity of a business at a specific date. A statement of cash flows summarizes information about the cash inflows (receipts) and outflows (payments) for a specific period of time.

GLOSSARY

Accounting The information system that identifies, records, and communicates the economic events of an organization to interested users. (p. 4).

Assets Resources a business owns. (p. 12).

Balance sheet A financial statement that reports the assets, liabilities, and owner's equity at a specific date. (p. 20).

Basic accounting equation Assets = Liabilities + Owner's Equity. (p. 12).

Bookkeeping A part of accounting that involves only the recording of economic events. (p. 5).

Corporation A business organized as a separate legal entity under state corporation law, having ownership divided into transferable shares of stock. (p. 10).

Cost principle An accounting principle that states that companies should record assets at their cost. (p. 9).

Drawings Withdrawal of cash or other assets from an unincorporated business for the personal use of the owner(s). (p. 13).

Economic entity assumption An assumption that requires that the activities of the entity be kept separate and distinct from the activities of its owner and all other economic entities. (p. 9).

Ethics The standards of conduct by which one's actions are judged as right or wrong, honest or dishonest, fair or not fair. (p. 8).

Expanded accounting equation Assets = Liabilities + Owner's Capital − Owner's Drawings + Revenues − Expenses. (p. 13).

Expenses The cost of assets consumed or services used in the process of earning revenue. (p. 13).

Financial accounting The field of accounting that provides economic and financial information for investors, creditors, and other external users. (p. 7).

Financial Accounting Standards Board (FASB) A private organization that establishes generally accepted accounting principles (GAAP). (p. 8).

Generally accepted accounting principles (GAAP) Common standards that indicate how to report economic events. (p. 8).

Income statement A financial statement that presents the revenues and expenses and resulting net income or net loss of a company for a specific period of time. (p. 20).

International Accounting Standards Board (IASB) An accounting standard-setting body that issues standards adopted by many countries outside of the United States. (p. 9).

Investments by owner The assets an owner puts into the business. (p. 13).

Liabilities Creditor claims on total assets. (p. 12).

Managerial accounting The field of accounting that provides internal reports to help users make decisions about their companies. (p. 6).

Monetary unit assumption An assumption stating that companies include in the accounting records only transaction data that can be expressed in terms of money. (p. 9).

Net income The amount by which revenues exceed expenses. (p. 22).

Net loss The amount by which expenses exceed revenues. (p. 22).

Owner's equity The ownership claim on total assets. (p. 12).

Owner's equity statement A financial statement that summarizes the changes in owner's equity for a specific period of time. (p. 20).

Partnership A business owned by two or more persons associated as partners. (p. 10).

Proprietorship A business owned by one person. (p. 10).

Revenues The gross increase in owner's equity resulting from business activities entered into for the purpose of earning income. (p. 13).

Sarbanes-Oxley Act of 2002 (SOX) Law passed by Congress in 2002 intended to reduce unethical corporate behavior. (p. 8).

Securities and Exchange Commission (SEC) A governmental agency that requires companies to file financial reports in accordance with generally accepted accounting principles. (p. 8).

Statement of cash flows A financial statement that summarizes information about the cash inflows (receipts)

and cash outflows (payments) for a specific period of time. (p. 20).

Transactions The economic events of a business that are recorded by accountants. (p. 14).

APPENDIX **Accounting Career Opportunities**

Why is accounting such a popular major and career choice? First, there are a lot of jobs. In many cities in recent years, the demand for accountants exceeded the supply. Not only are there a lot of jobs, but there are a wide array of opportunities. As one accounting organization observed, "accounting is one degree with 360 degrees of opportunity."

> **STUDY OBJECTIVE 9**
> Explain the career opportunities in accounting.

Accounting is also hot because it is obvious that accounting matters. Interest in accounting has increased, ironically, because of the attention caused by the accounting failures of companies such as Enron and WorldCom. These widely publicized scandals revealed the important role that accounting plays in society. Most people want to make a difference, and an accounting career provides many opportunities to contribute to society. Finally, the Sarbanes-Oxley Act of 2002 (SOX) (see page 8) significantly increased the accounting and internal control requirements for corporations. This dramatically increased demand for professionals with accounting training.

Accountants are in such demand that it is not uncommon for accounting students to have accepted a job offer a year before graduation. As the following discussion reveals, the job options of people with accounting degrees are virtually unlimited.

Public Accounting

Individuals in **public accounting** offer expert service to the general public, in much the same way that doctors serve patients and lawyers serve clients. A major portion of public accounting involves **auditing**. In auditing, a certified public accountant (CPA) examines company financial statements and provides an opinion as to how accurately the financial statements present the company's results and financial position. Analysts, investors, and creditors rely heavily on these "audit opinions," which CPAs have the exclusive authority to issue.

Taxation is another major area of public accounting. The work that tax specialists perform includes tax advice and planning, preparing tax returns, and representing clients before governmental agencies such as the Internal Revenue Service.

A third area in public accounting is **management consulting**. It ranges from installing basic accounting software or highly complex enterprise resource planning systems, to providing support services for major marketing projects or merger and acquisition activities.

Many CPAs are entrepreneurs. They form small- or medium-sized practices that frequently specialize in tax or consulting services.

Private Accounting

Instead of working in public accounting, you might choose to be an employee of a for-profit company such as Starbucks, Google, or PepsiCo. In **private** (or **managerial**) **accounting**, you would be involved in activities such as cost accounting (finding the cost of producing specific products), budgeting, accounting information system design and support, or tax planning and preparation. You might also be a member of your company's internal audit team. In response to SOX, the internal auditors' job of reviewing the company's operations to ensure compliance with company policies and to increase efficiency has taken on increased importance.

Alternatively, many accountants work for not-for-profit organizations such as the Red Cross or the Bill and Melinda Gates Foundation, or for museums, libraries, or performing arts organizations.

Opportunities in Government

Another option is to pursue one of the many accounting opportunities in governmental agencies. For example, the Internal Revenue Service (IRS), Federal Bureau of Investigation (FBI), and the Securities and Exchange Commission (SEC) all employ accountants. The FBI has a stated goal that at least 15 percent of its new agents should be CPAs. There is also a very high demand for accounting educators at public colleges and universities and in state and local governments.

Forensic Accounting

Forensic accounting uses accounting, auditing, and investigative skills to conduct investigations into theft and fraud. It is listed among the top 20 career paths of the future. The job of forensic accountants is to catch the perpetrators of the estimated $600 billion per year of theft and fraud occurring at U.S. companies. This includes tracing money-laundering and identity-theft activities as well as tax evasion. Insurance companies hire forensic accountants to detect insurance frauds such as arson, and law offices employ forensic accountants to identify marital assets in divorces. Forensic accountants often have FBI, IRS, or similar government experience.

"Show Me the Money"

How much can a new accountant make? Salary estimates are constantly changing, and salaries vary considerably across the country. At the time this text was written, the following general information was available from Robert Half International.

Illustration 1A-1
Salary estimates for jobs in public and corporate accounting

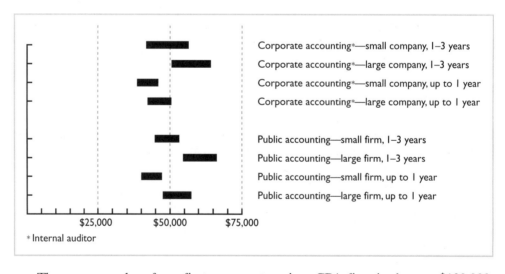

The average salary for a first-year partner in a CPA firm is close to $130,000, with experienced partners often making substantially more. On the corporate side, controllers (the head accountant) can earn $150,000, while chief financial officers can earn as much as $350,000.

For up-to-date salary estimates, as well as a wealth of additional information regarding accounting as a career, check out *www.startheregoplaces.com*.

SUMMARY OF STUDY OBJECTIVE FOR APPENDIX

9 Explain the career opportunities in accounting. Accounting offers many different jobs in fields such as public and private accounting, government, and forensic accounting. Accounting is a popular major because there are many different types of jobs, with unlimited potential for career advancement.

GLOSSARY FOR APPENDIX

Auditing   The examination of financial statements by a certified public accountant in order to express an opinion as to the fairness of presentation. (p. 29).

Forensic accounting   An area of accounting that uses accounting, auditing, and investigative skills to conduct investigations into theft and fraud. (p. 30).

Management consulting   An area of public accounting ranging from development of accounting and computer systems to support services for marketing projects and merger and acquisition activities. (p. 29).

Private (or managerial) accounting   An area of accounting within a company that involves such activities as cost accounting, budgeting, design and support of accounting information systems, and tax planning and preparation. (p. 29).

Public accounting   An area of accounting in which the accountant offers expert service to the general public. (p. 29).

Taxation   An area of public accounting involving tax advice, tax planning, preparing tax returns, and representing clients before governmental agencies. (p. 29).

SELF-STUDY QUESTIONS

Answers are at the end of the chapter.

(SO 1) **1.** Which of the following is *not* a step in the accounting process?
  a. identification.   **c.** recording.
  b. verification.   **d.** communication.

(SO 2) **2.** Which of the following statements about users of accounting information is *incorrect*?
  a. Management is an internal user.
  b. Taxing authorities are external users.
  c. Present creditors are external users.
  d. Regulatory authorities are internal users.

(SO 4) **3.** The cost principle states that:
  a. assets should be initially recorded at cost and adjusted when the market value changes.
  b. activities of an entity are to be kept separate and distinct from its owner.
  c. assets should be recorded at their cost.
  d. only transaction data capable of being expressed in terms of money be included in the accounting records.

(SO 5) **4.** Which of the following statements about basic assumptions is *correct*?
  a. Basic assumptions are the same as accounting principles.
  b. The economic entity assumption states that there should be a particular unit of accountability.
  c. The monetary unit assumption enables accounting to measure employee morale.
  d. Partnerships are not economic entities.

(SO 5) **5.** The three types of business entities are:
  a. proprietorships, small businesses, and partnerships.
  b. proprietorships, partnerships, and corporations.
  c. proprietorships, partnerships, and large businesses.
  d. financial, manufacturing, and service companies.

(SO 6) **6.** Net income will result during a time period when:
  a. assets exceed liabilities.
  b. assets exceed revenues.
  c. expenses exceed revenues.
  d. revenues exceed expenses.

(SO 7) **7.** Performing services on account will have the following effects on the components of the basic accounting equation:
  a. increase assets and decrease owner's equity.
  b. increase assets and increase owner's equity.
  c. increase assets and increase liabilities.
  d. increase liabilities and increase owner's equity.

(SO 7) **8.** As of December 31, 2010, Stoneland Company has assets of $3,500 and owner's equity of $2,000. What are the liabilities for Stoneland Company as of December 31, 2010?
  a. $1,500.   **b.** $1,000.   **c.** $2,500.   **d.** $2,000.

(SO 7) **9.** Which of the following events is *not* recorded in the accounting records?
  a. Equipment is purchased on account.
  b. An employee is terminated.
  c. A cash investment is made into the business.
  d. The owner withdraws cash for personal use.

(SO 7) **10.** During 2010, Gibson Company's assets decreased $50,000 and its liabilities decreased $90,000. Its owner's equity therefore:
  a. increased $40,000.
  b. decreased $140,000.
  c. decreased $40,000.
  d. increased $140,000.

(SO 7) **11.** Payment of an account payable affects the components of the accounting equation in the following way.
  a. Decreases owner's equity and decreases liabilities.
  b. Increases assets and decreases liabilities.

c. Decreases assets and increases owner's equity.

d. Decreases assets and decreases liabilities.

(SO 8) **12.** Which of the following statements is *false*?

    a. A statement of cash flows summarizes information about the cash inflows (receipts) and outflows (payments) for a specific period of time.

    b. A balance sheet reports the assets, liabilities, and owner's equity at a specific date.

    c. An income statement presents the revenues, expenses, changes in owner's equity, and resulting net income or net loss for a specific period of time.

    d. An owner's equity statement summarizes the changes in owner's equity for a specific period of time.

(SO 8) **13.** On the last day of the period, Jim Otto Company buys a $900 machine on credit. This transaction will affect the:

    a. income statement only.

    b. balance sheet only.

c. income statement and owner's equity statement only.

d. income statement, owner's equity statement, and balance sheet.

14. The financial statement that reports assets, liabilities, and (SO 8) owner's equity is the:

    a. income statement.

    b. owner's equity statement.

    c. balance sheet.

    d. statement of cash flow.

*15. Services provided by a public accountant include: (SO 9)

    a. auditing, taxation, and management consulting.

    b. auditing, budgeting, and management consulting.

    c. auditing, budgeting, and cost accounting.

    d. internal auditing, budgeting, and management consulting.

Go to the book's companion website,
www.wiley.com/college/weygandt,
for Additional Self-Study questions.

 The Navigator

QUESTIONS

1. "Accounting is ingrained in our society and it is vital to our economic system." Do you agree? Explain.

2. Identify and describe the steps in the accounting process.

3. (a) Who are internal users of accounting data? (b) How does accounting provide relevant data to these users?

4. What uses of financial accounting information are made by (a) investors and (b) creditors?

5. "Bookkeeping and accounting are the same." Do you agree? Explain.

6. Karen Sommers Travel Agency purchased land for $90,000 cash on December 10, 2010. At December 31, 2010, the land's value has increased to $93,000. What amount should be reported for land on Karen Sommers's balance sheet at December 31, 2010? Explain.

7. What is the monetary unit assumption?

8. What is the economic entity assumption?

9. What are the three basic forms of business organizations for profit-oriented enterprises?

10. Maria Gonzalez is the owner of a successful printing shop. Recently her business has been increasing, and Maria has been thinking about changing the organization of her business from a proprietorship to a corporation. Discuss some of the advantages Maria would enjoy if she were to incorporate her business.

11. What is the basic accounting equation?

12. (a) Define the terms assets, liabilities, and owner's equity.
    (b) What items affect owner's equity?

13. Which of the following items are liabilities of Stanley Jewelry Stores?

    (a) Cash.   **(d)** Accounts receivable.

    (b) Accounts payable.   **(e)** Supplies.

    (c) Drawings.   **(f)** Equipment.

    (g) Salaries payable.   **(i)** Rent expense.

    (h) Service revenue.

14. Can a business enter into a transaction in which only the left side of the basic accounting equation is affected? If so, give an example.

15. Are the following events recorded in the accounting records? Explain your answer in each case.

    (a) The owner of the company dies.

    (b) Supplies are purchased on account.

    (c) An employee is fired.

    (d) The owner of the business withdraws cash from the business for personal use.

16. Indicate how the following business transactions affect the basic accounting equation.

    (a) Paid cash for janitorial services.

    (b) Purchased equipment for cash.

    (c) Invested cash in the business.

    (d) Paid accounts payable in full.

17. Listed below are some items found in the financial statements of Alex Greenspan Co. Indicate in which financial statement(s) the following items would appear.

    (a) Service revenue.   **(d)** Accounts receivable.

    (b) Equipment.   **(e)** Alex Greenspan, Capital.

    (c) Advertising expense.   **(f)** Wages payable.

18. In February 2010, Paula King invested an additional $10,000 in her business, King's Pharmacy, which is organized as a proprietorship. King's accountant, Lance Jones, recorded this receipt as an increase in cash and revenues. Is this treatment appropriate? Why or why not?

19. "A company's net income appears directly on the income statement and the owner's equity statement, and it is included indirectly in the company's balance sheet." Do you agree? Explain.

20. Garcia Enterprises had a capital balance of $168,000 at the beginning of the period. At the end of the accounting period, the capital balance was $198,000.

  (a) Assuming no additional investment or withdrawals during the period, what is the net income for the period?

  (b) Assuming an additional investment of $13,000 but no withdrawals during the period, what is the net income for the period?

21. Summarized operations for J. R. Ross Co. for the month of July are as follows.

Revenues earned: for cash $20,000; on account $70,000.

Expenses incurred: for cash $26,000; on account $40,000.

Indicate for J. R. Ross Co. (a) the total revenues, (b) the total expenses, and (c) net income for the month of July.

22. The basic accounting equation is: Assets = Liabilities + Owner's Equity. Replacing the words in that equation with dollar amounts, what is Coca-Cola's accounting equation at December 31, 2007? (*Hint*: Owner's equity is equivalent to shareowners' equity.)

BRIEF EXERCISES

BE1-1 Presented below is the basic accounting equation. Determine the missing amounts.

Use basic accounting equation.
(SO 6)

	Assets	=	Liabilities	+	Owner's Equity
(a)	$90,000		$50,000		?
(b)	?		$40,000		$70,000
(c)	$94,000		?		$60,000

BE1-2 Given the accounting equation, answer each of the following questions.

Use basic accounting equation.
(SO 6)

(a) The liabilities of McGlone Company are $120,000 and the owner's equity is $232,000. What is the amount of McGlone Company's total assets?

(b) The total assets of Company are $190,000 and its owner's equity is $80,000. What is the amount of its total liabilities?

(c) The total assets of McGlone Co. are $800,000 and its liabilities are equal to one half of its total assets. What is the amount of McGlone Co.'s owner's equity?

BE1-3 At the beginning of the year, Hernandez Company had total assets of $800,000 and total liabilities of $500,000. Answer the following questions.

Use basic accounting equation.
(SO 6)

(a) If total assets increased $150,000 during the year and total liabilities decreased $80,000, what is the amount of owner's equity at the end of the year?

(b) During the year, total liabilities increased $100,000 and owner's equity decreased $70,000. What is the amount of total assets at the end of the year?

(c) If total assets decreased $80,000 and owner's equity increased $120,000 during the year, what is the amount of total liabilities at the end of the year?

BE1-4 Use the expanded accounting equation to answer each of the following questions:

Solve expanded accounting equation.
(SO 6)

(a) The liabilities of Cai Company are $90,000. Meiyu Cai's capital account is $150,000; drawings are $40,000; revenues, $450,000; and expenses, $320,000. What is the amount of Cai Company's total assets?

(b) The total assets of Pereira Company are $57,000. Karen Perry's capital account is $25,000; drawings are $7,000; revenues, $50,000; and expenses, $35,000. What is the amount of the company's total liabilities?

(c) The total assets of Yap Co. are $600,000 and its liabilities are equal to two-thirds of its total assets. What is the amount of Yap Co.'s owner's equity?

BE1-5 Indicate whether each of the following items is an asset (A), liability (L), or part of owner's equity (OE).

Identify assets, liabilities, and owner's equity.
(SO 6)

_____**(a)** Accounts receivable _____**(d)** Office supplies
_____**(b)** Salaries payable _____**(e)** Owner's investment
_____**(c)** Equipment _____**(f)** Notes payable

BE1-6 Presented below are three business transactions. On a sheet of paper, list the letters (a), (b), (c) with columns for assets, liabilities, and owner's equity. For each column, indicate whether the transactions increased (+), decreased (−), or had no effect (NE) on assets, liabilities, and owner's equity.

Determine effect of transactions on basic accounting equation.
(SO 7)

(a) Purchased supplies on account.
(b) Received cash for providing a service.
(c) Paid expenses in cash.

Determine effect of transactions on basic accounting equation.
(SO 7)

BE1-7 Follow the same format as BE1-6 on the previous page. Determine the effect on assets, liabilities, and owner's equity of the following three transactions.

(a) Invested cash in the business.
(b) Withdrawal of cash by owner.
(c) Received cash from a customer who had previously been billed for services provided.

Classify items affecting owner's equity.
(SO 7)

BE1-8 Classify each of the following items as owner's drawing (D), revenue (R), or expense (E).

_____**(a)** Advertising expense   _____**(e)** Bergman, Drawing
_____**(b)** Commission revenue   _____**(f)** Rent revenue
_____**(c)** Insurance expense   _____**(g)** Utilities expense
_____**(d)** Salaries expense

Determine effect of transactions on basic owner's equity.
(SO 7)

BE1-9 Presented below are three transactions. Mark each transaction as affecting owner's investment (I), owner's drawings (D), revenue (R), expense (E), or not affecting owner's equity (NOE).

_____**(a)** Received cash for services performed
_____**(b)** Paid cash to purchase equipment
_____**(c)** Paid employee salaries

Prepare a balance sheet.
(SO 8)

BE1-10 In alphabetical order below are balance sheet items for Lopez Company at December 31, 2010. Kim Lopez is the owner of Lopez Company. Prepare a balance sheet, following the format of Illustration 1-9.

Accounts payable	$90,000
Accounts receivable	$72,500
Cash	$49,000
Kim Lopez, Capital	$31,500

Determine where items appear on financial statements.
(SO 8)

BE1-11 Indicate whether the following items would appear on the income statement (IS), balance sheet (BS), or owner's equity statement (OE).

_____**(a)** Notes payable   _____**(d)** Cash
_____**(b)** Advertising expense   _____**(e)** Service revenue
_____**(c)** Trent Buchanan, Capital

DO IT! REVIEW

WILEY PLUS

Review basic concepts.
(SO 1, 2, 4)

DO IT! 1-1 Indicate whether each of the five statements presented below is true or false.

1. The three steps in the accounting process are identification, recording, and examination.
2. The two most common types of external users are investors and creditors.
3. Congress passed the Sarbanes-Oxley Act of 2002 to ensure that investors invest only in companies that will be profitable.
4. The primary accounting standard-setting body in the United States is the Securities and Exchange Commission (SEC).
5. The cost principle dictates that companies record assets at their cost and continue to report them at their cost over the time the asset is held.

Evaluate effects of transactions on owner's equity.
(SO 6)

DO IT! 1-2 Classify the following items as investment by owner (I), owner's drawings (D), revenues (R), or expenses (E). Then indicate whether each item increases or decreases owner's equity.

(1) Drawings   (3) Advertising Expense
(2) Rent Revenue   (4) Owner puts personal assets into the business

Prepare tabular analysis.
(SO 7)

DO IT! 1-3 Transactions made by Orlando Carbrera and Co., a law firm, for the month of March are shown below. Prepare a tabular analysis which shows the effects of these transactions on the expanded accounting equation, similar to that shown in Illustration 1-8.

1. The company provided $20,000 of services for customers, on credit.
2. The company received $20,000 in cash from customers who had been billed for services [in transaction (1)].
3. The company received a bill for $2,000 of advertising, but will not pay it until a later date.
4. Orlando Carbrera withdrew $5,000 cash from the business for personal use.

DO IT! 1-4   Presented below is selected information related to Broadway Company at December 31, 2010. Broadway reports financial information monthly.

Calculate effects of transactions on financial statement items.

(SO 8)

Accounts Payable	$ 3,000	Salaries Expense	$16,500
Cash	7,000	Note Payable	25,000
Advertising Expense	6,000	Rent Expense	10,500
Service Revenue	54,000	Accounts Receivable	13,500
Equipment	29,000	Drawings	7,500

(a) Determine the total assets of Broadway Company at December 31, 2010.
(b) Determine the net income that Broadway Company reported for December 2010.
(c) Determine the owner's equity of Broadway Company at December 31, 2010.

EXERCISES

E1-1   Urlacher Company performs the following accounting tasks during the year.

_____Analyzing and interpreting information.
_____Classifying economic events.
_____Explaining uses, meaning, and limitations of data.
_____Keeping a systematic chronological diary of events.
_____Measuring events in dollars and cents.
_____Preparing accounting reports.
_____Reporting information in a standard format.
_____Selecting economic activities relevant to the company.
_____Summarizing economic events.

Classify the three activities of accounting.

(SO 1)

Accounting is "an information system that **identifies**, **records**, and **communicates** the economic events of an organization to interested users."

Instructions
Categorize the accounting tasks performed by Urlacher as relating to either the identification (I), recording (R), or communication (C) aspects of accounting.

E1-2   **(a)** The following are users of financial statements.

_____Customers	_____Securities and Exchange Commission
_____Internal Revenue Service	_____Store manager
_____Labor unions	_____Suppliers
_____Marketing manager	_____Vice-president of finance
_____Production supervisor	

Identify users of accounting information.

(SO 2)

Instructions
Identify the users as being either **external users** or **internal users**.

(b) The following questions could be asked by an internal user or an external user.

_____Can we afford to give our employees a pay raise?
_____Did the company earn a satisfactory income?
_____Do we need to borrow in the near future?
_____How does the company's profitability compare to other companies?
_____What does it cost us to manufacture each unit produced?
_____Which product should we emphasize?
_____Will the company be able to pay its short-term debts?

Instructions
Identify each of the questions as being more likely asked by an **internal user** or an **external user**.

E1-3   Larry Smith, president of Smith Company, has instructed Ron Rivera, the head of the accounting department for Smith Company, to report the company's land in the company's accounting reports at its market value of $170,000 instead of its cost of $100,000. Smith says, "Showing the land at $170,000 will make our company look like a better investment when we try to attract new investors next month."

Discuss ethics and the cost principle.

(SO 3)

Instructions
Explain the ethical situation involved for Ron Rivera, identifying the stakeholders and the alternatives.

Use accounting concepts.
(SO 4, 5)

E1-4 The following situations involve accounting principles and assumptions.

1. Grossman Company owns buildings that are worth substantially more than they originally cost. In an effort to provide more relevant information, Grossman reports the buildings at market value in its accounting reports.
2. Jones Company includes in its accounting records only transaction data that can be expressed in terms of money.
3. Caleb Borke, owner of Caleb's Cantina, records his personal living costs as expenses of the Cantina.

Instructions
For each of the three situations, say if the accounting method used is correct or incorrect. If correct, identify which principle or assumption supports the method used. If incorrect, identify which principle or assumption has been violated.

Classify accounts as assets, liabilities, and owner's equity.
(SO 6)

E1-5 Meredith Cleaners has the following balance sheet items.

Accounts payable	Accounts receivable
Cash	Notes payable
Cleaning equipment	Salaries payable
Cleaning supplies	Karin Meredith, Capital

Instructions
Classify each item as an asset, liability, or owner's equity.

Analyze the effect of transactions.
(SO 6, 7)

E1-6 Selected transactions for Evergreen Lawn Care Company are listed below.

1. Made cash investment to start business.
2. Paid monthly rent.
3. Purchased equipment on account.
4. Billed customers for services performed.
5. Withdrew cash for owner's personal use.
6. Received cash from customers billed in (4).
7. Incurred advertising expense on account.
8. Purchased additional equipment for cash.
9. Received cash from customers when service was performed.

Instructions
List the numbers of the above transactions and describe the effect of each transaction on assets, liabilities, and owner's equity. For example, the first answer is: (1) Increase in assets and increase in owner's equity.

Analyze the effect of transactions on assets, liabilities, and owner's equity.
(SO 6, 7)

E1-7 Brandon Computer Timeshare Company entered into the following transactions during May 2010.

1. Purchased computer terminals for $20,000 from Digital Equipment on account.
2. Paid $4,000 cash for May rent on storage space.
3. Received $15,000 cash from customers for contracts billed in April.
4. Provided computer services to Fisher Construction Company for $3,000 cash.
5. Paid Northern States Power Co. $11,000 cash for energy usage in May.
6. Brandon invested an additional $32,000 in the business.
7. Paid Digital Equipment for the terminals purchased in (1) above.
8. Incurred advertising expense for May of $1,200 on account.

Instructions
Indicate with the appropriate letter whether each of the transactions above results in:

(a) an increase in assets and a decrease in assets.
(b) an increase in assets and an increase in owner's equity.
(c) an increase in assets and an increase in liabilities.
(d) a decrease in assets and a decrease in owner's equity.
(e) a decrease in assets and a decrease in liabilities.
(f) an increase in liabilities and a decrease in owner's equity.
(g) an increase in owner's equity and a decrease in liabilities.

E1-8 An analysis of the transactions made by S. Moses & Co., a certified public accounting firm, for the month of August is shown below. The expenses were $650 for rent, $4,900 for salaries, and $500 for utilities.

Analyze transactions and compute net income.
(SO 7)

	Cash	+	Accounts Receivable	+	Supplies	+	Office Equipment	=	Accounts Payable	+	S. Moses, Capital	−	S. Moses, Drawings	+	Revenues	−	Expenses
1.	+$15,000										+$15,000						
2.	−2,000						+$5,000		+$3,000								
3.	−750				+$750												
4.	+4,600		+$3,700												+$8,300		
5.	−1,500								−1,500								
6.	−2,000												−$2,000				
7.	−650																−$650
8.	+450		−450														
9.	−4,900																−4,900
10.									+500								−500

Instructions
(a) ━━━━━▶ Describe each transaction that occurred for the month.
(b) Determine how much owner's equity increased for the month.
(c) Compute the amount of net income for the month.

E1-9 An analysis of transactions for S. Moses & Co. was presented in E1–8.

Prepare financial statements.
(SO 8)

Instructions
Prepare an income statement and an owner's equity statement for August and a balance sheet at August 31, 2010.

E1-10 Lily Company had the following assets and liabilities on the dates indicated.

Determine net income (or loss).
(SO 7)

December 31	Total Assets	Total Liabilities
2009	$400,000	$250,000
2010	$460,000	$300,000
2011	$590,000	$400,000

Lily began business on January 1, 2009, with an investment of $100,000.

Instructions
From an analysis of the change in owner's equity during the year, compute the net income (or loss) for:

(a) 2009, assuming Lily's drawings were $15,000 for the year.
(b) 2010, assuming Lily made an additional investment of $50,000 and had no drawings in 2010.
(c) 2011, assuming Lily made an additional investment of $15,000 and had drawings of $30,000 in 2011.

E1-11 Two items are omitted from each of the following summaries of balance sheet and income statement data for two proprietorships for the year 2010, Craig Cantrel and Mills Enterprises.

Analyze financial statements items.
(SO 6, 7)

	Craig Cantrel	Mills Enterprises
Beginning of year:		
Total assets	$ 95,000	$129,000
Total liabilities	85,000	(c)
Total owner's equity	(a)	80,000
End of year:		
Total assets	160,000	180,000
Total liabilities	120,000	50,000
Total owner's equity	40,000	130,000
Changes during year in owner's equity:		
Additional investment	(b)	25,000
Drawings	24,000	(d)
Total revenues	215,000	100,000
Total expenses	175,000	55,000

Instructions
Determine the missing amounts.

Prepare income statement and owner's equity statement.
(SO 8)

E1-12 The following information relates to Linda Stanley Co. for the year 2010.

Linda Stanley, Capital, January 1, 2010	$ 48,000	Advertising expense	$ 1,800
Linda Stanley, Drawing during 2010	6,000	Rent expense	10,400
Service revenue	62,500	Utilities expense	3,100
Salaries expense	30,000		

Instructions

After analyzing the data, prepare an income statement and an owner's equity statement for the year ending December 31, 2010.

Correct an incorrectly prepared balance sheet.
(SO 8)

E1-13 Mary Close is the bookkeeper for Mendez Company. Mary has been trying to get the balance sheet of Mendez Company to balance. Mendez's balance sheet is shown below.

MENDEZ COMPANY
Balance Sheet
December 31, 2010

Assets		Liabilities	
Cash	$15,000	Accounts payable	$20,000
Supplies	8,000	Accounts receivable	(8,500)
Equipment	46,000	Mendez, Capital	67,500
Mendez, Drawing	10,000	Total liabilities and	
Total assets	$79,000	owner's equity	$79,000

Instructions

Prepare a correct balance sheet.

Compute net income and prepare a balance sheet.
(SO 8)

E1-14 Jan Nab is the sole owner of Deer Park, a public camping ground near the Lake Mead National Recreation Area. Jan has compiled the following financial information as of December 31, 2010.

Revenues during 2010—camping fees	$140,000	Market value of equipment	$140,000
Revenues during 2010—general store	50,000	Notes payable	60,000
Accounts payable	11,000	Expenses during 2010	150,000
Cash on hand	23,000	Supplies on hand	2,500
Original cost of equipment	105,500		

Instructions

(a) Determine Jan Nab's net income from Deer Park for 2010.

(b) Prepare a balance sheet for Deer Park as of December 31, 2010.

Prepare an income statement.
(SO 8)

E1-15 Presented below is financial information related to the 2010 operations of Summers Cruise Company.

Maintenance expense	$ 95,000
Property tax expense (on dock facilities)	10,000
Salaries expense	142,000
Advertising expense	3,500
Ticket revenue	325,000

Instructions

Prepare the 2010 income statement for Summers Cruise Company.

Prepare an owner's equity statement.
(SO 8)

E1-16 Presented below is information related to the sole proprietorship of Kevin Johnson, attorney.

Legal service revenue—2010	$350,000
Total expenses—2010	211,000
Assets, January 1, 2010	85,000
Liabilities, January 1, 2010	62,000
Assets, December 31, 2010	168,000
Liabilities, December 31, 2010	85,000
Drawings—2010	?

Instructions

Prepare the 2010 owner's equity statement for Kevin Johnson's legal practice.

EXERCISES: SET B

Visit the book's companion website at **www.wiley.com/college/weygandt,** and choose the Student Companion site, to access Exercise Set B.

PROBLEMS: SET A

P1-1A   Barone's Repair Shop was started on May 1 by Nancy Barone. A summary of May transactions is presented below.

1. Invested $10,000 cash to start the repair shop.
2. Purchased equipment for $5,000 cash.
3. Paid $400 cash for May office rent.
4. Paid $500 cash for supplies.
5. Incurred $250 of advertising costs in the *Beacon News* on account.
6. Received $5,100 in cash from customers for repair service.
7. Withdrew $1,000 cash for personal use.
8. Paid part-time employee salaries $2,000.
9. Paid utility bills $140.
10. Provided repair service on account to customers $750.
11. Collected cash of $120 for services billed in transaction (10).

Instructions

(a) Prepare a tabular analysis of the transactions, using the following column headings: Cash, Accounts Receivable, Supplies, Equipment, Accounts Payable, N. Barone, Capital; N. Barone, Drawings; Revenues, and Expenses.

(b) From an analysis of the owner's equity columns, compute the net income or net loss for May.

Analyze transactions and compute net income.

(SO 6, 7)

(a) Total assets $12,310

(b) Net income $3,060

P1-2A   Maria Gonzalez opened a veterinary business in Nashville, Tennessee, on August 1. On August 31, the balance sheet showed Cash $9,000, Accounts Receivable $1,700, Supplies $600, Office Equipment $6,000, Accounts Payable $3,600, and M. Gonzalez, Capital $13,700. During September the following transactions occurred.

1. Paid $2,900 cash on accounts payable.
2. Collected $1,300 of accounts receivable.
3. Purchased additional office equipment for $2,100, paying $800 in cash and the balance on account.
4. Earned revenue of $8,000, of which $2,500 is paid in cash and the balance is due in October.
5. Withdrew $1,000 cash for personal use.
6. Paid salaries $1,700, rent for September $900, and advertising expense $300.
7. Incurred utilities expense for month on account $170.
8. Received $10,000 from Capital Bank–money borrowed on a note payable.

Instructions

(a) Prepare a tabular analysis of the September transactions beginning with August 31 balances. The column headings should be as follows: Cash + Accounts Receivable + Supplies + Office Equipment = Notes Payable + Accounts Payable + M. Gonzalez, Capital − M. Gonzalez, Drawings + Revenues − Expenses.

(b) Prepare an income statement for September, an owner's equity statement for September, and a balance sheet at September 30.

Analyze transactions and prepare income statement, owner's equity statement, and balance sheet.

(SO 6, 7, 8)

(a) Total assets $29,800

(b) Net income $4,930
Ending capital $17,630

P1-3A   On May 1, Jeff Wilkins started Skyline Flying School, a company that provides flying lessons, by investing $45,000 cash in the business. Following are the assets and liabilities of the company on May 31, 2010, and the revenues and expenses for the month of May.

Prepare income statement, owner's equity statement, and balance sheet.

(SO 8)

Cash	$ 5,600	Notes Payable	$30,000
Accounts Receivable	7,200	Rent Expense	1,200
Equipment	64,000	Repair Expense	400
Lesson Revenue	7,500	Fuel Expense	2,500
Advertising Expense	500	Insurance Expense	400
		Accounts Payable	800

Jeff Wilkins made no additional investment in May, but he withdrew $1,500 in cash for personal use.

Instructions

(a) Net income $2,500
   Owner's equity $46,000
   Total assets $76,800
(b) Net income $1,900
   Owner's equity $45,400

(a) Prepare an income statement and owner's equity statement for the month of May and a balance sheet at May 31.

(b) Prepare an income statement and owner's equity statement for May assuming the following data are not included above: (1) $900 of revenue was earned and billed but not collected at May 31, and (2) $1,500 of fuel expense was incurred but not paid.

Analyze transactions and prepare financial statements.

(SO 6, 7, 8)

P1-4A   Mark Miller started his own delivery service, Miller Deliveries, on June 1, 2010. The following transactions occurred during the month of June.

June 1 Mark invested $10,000 cash in the business.
      2 Purchased a used van for deliveries for $12,000. Mark paid $2,000 cash and signed a note payable for the remaining balance.
      3 Paid $500 for office rent for the month.
      5 Performed $4,400 of services on account.
      9 Withdrew $200 cash for personal use.
     12 Purchased supplies for $150 on account.
     15 Received a cash payment of $1,250 for services provided on June 5.
     17 Purchased gasoline for $100 on account.
     20 Received a cash payment of $1,500 for services provided.
     23 Made a cash payment of $500 on the note payable.
     26 Paid $250 for utilities.
     29 Paid for the gasoline purchased on account on June 17.
     30 Paid $1,000 for employee salaries.

Instructions

(a) Total assets $23,500

(a) Show the effects of the previous transactions on the accounting equation using the following format.

		Assets				Liabilities		Owner's Equity			
Date	Cash	+ Accounts Receivable	+ Supplies	+ Delivery Van	=	Notes Payable	+ Accounts Payable	+ M. Miller, Capital	− M. Miller, Drawings	+ Revenues	− Expenses

(b) Net income $4,050
(c) Cash $8,200

(b) Prepare an income statement for the month of June.
(c) Prepare a balance sheet at June 30, 2010.

Determine financial statement amounts and prepare owner's equity statement.

(SO 7, 8)

P1-5A   Financial statement information about four different companies is as follows.

	Karma Company	Yates Company	McCain Company	Dench Company
January 1, 2010				
Assets	$ 95,000	$110,000	(g)	$170,000
Liabilities	50,000	(d)	75,000	(j)
Owner's equity	(a)	60,000	45,000	90,000
December 31, 2010				
Assets	(b)	137,000	200,000	(k)
Liabilities	55,000	75,000	(h)	80,000
Owner's equity	60,000	(e)	130,000	170,000
Owner's equity changes in year				
Additional investment	(c)	15,000	10,000	15,000
Drawings	25,000	(f)	14,000	20,000
Total revenues	350,000	420,000	(i)	520,000
Total expenses	320,000	385,000	342,000	(l)

Instructions

(a) Determine the missing amounts. (*Hint:* For example, to solve for (a), Assets − Liabilities = Owner's equity = $45,000.)

(b) Prepare the owner's equity statement for Yates Company.

(c) ━━━━━● Write a memorandum explaining the sequence for preparing financial statements and the interrelationship of the owner's equity statement to the income statement and balance sheet.

PROBLEMS: SET B

P1-1B   On April 1, Vinnie Venuchi established Vinnie's Travel Agency. The following transactions were completed during the month.

Analyze transactions and compute net income.

(SO 6, 7)

1. Invested $15,000 cash to start the agency.
2. Paid $600 cash for April office rent.
3. Purchased office equipment for $3,000 cash.
4. Incurred $700 of advertising costs in the *Chicago Tribune,* on account.
5. Paid $800 cash for office supplies.
6. Earned $11,000 for services rendered: $3,000 cash is received from customers, and the balance of $8,000 is billed to customers on account.
7. Withdrew $500 cash for personal use.
8. Paid *Chicago Tribune* amount due in transaction (4).
9. Paid employees' salaries $2,200.
10. Received $4,000 in cash from customers who have previously been billed in transaction (6).

Instructions

(a) Prepare a tabular analysis of the transactions using the following column headings: Cash, Accounts Receivable, Supplies, Office Equipment, Accounts Payable, V. Venuchi, Capital; V. Venuchi, Drawings; Revenues, and Expenses.

(a) Total assets $22,000

(b) From an analysis of the owner's equity columns, compute the net income or net loss for April.

(b) Net income $7,500

P1-2B   Jenny Brown opened a law office, on July 1, 2010. On July 31, the balance sheet showed Cash $5,000, Accounts Receivable $1,500, Supplies $500, Office Equipment $6,000, Accounts Payable $4,200, and Jenny Brown, Capital $8,800. During August the following transactions occurred.

Analyze transactions and prepare income statement, owner's equity statement, and balance sheet.

(SO 6, 7, 8)

1. Collected $1,200 of accounts receivable.
2. Paid $2,800 cash on accounts payable.
3. Earned revenue of $8,000 of which $3,000 is collected in cash and the balance is due in September.
4. Purchased additional office equipment for $2,000, paying $400 in cash and the balance on account.
5. Paid salaries $2,500, rent for August $900, and advertising expenses $400.
6. Withdrew $700 in cash for personal use.
7. Received $1,500 from Standard Federal Bank—money borrowed on a note payable.
8. Incurred utility expenses for month on account $220.

Instructions

(a) Prepare a tabular analysis of the August transactions beginning with July 31 balances. The column headings should be as follows: Cash + Accounts Receivable + Supplies + Office Equipment = Notes Payable + Accounts Payable + J. Brown, Capital − J. Brown, Drawings + Revenues − Expenses.

(a) Total assets $16,800

(b) Prepare an income statement for August, an owner's equity statement for August, and a balance sheet at August 31.

(b) Net income $3,980
   Ending capital $12,080

P1-3B   On June 1, Michelle Sasse started Divine Creations Co., a company that provides craft opportunities, by investing $15,200 cash in the business. Following are the assets and liabilities of the company at June 30 and the revenues and expenses for the month of June.

Prepare income statement, owner's equity statement, and balance sheet.

(SO 8)

Cash	$13,750	Notes Payable	$9,000
Accounts Receivable	3,000	Accounts Payable	1,200
Service Revenue	7,000	Supplies Expense	1,600
Craft Supplies	2,000	Gas and Oil Expense	200
Advertising Expense	400	Utilities Expense	150
Equipment	10,000		

Michelle made no additional investment in June, but withdrew $1,300 in cash for personal use during the month.

Instructions

(a) Prepare an income statement and owner's equity statement for the month of June and a balance sheet at June 30, 2010.

(a) Net income $4,650
   Owner's equity $18,550
   Total assets $28,750

(b) Prepare an income statement and owner's equity statement for June assuming the following data are not included above: (1) $900 of revenue was earned and billed but not collected at June 30, and (2) $150 of gas and oil expense was incurred but not paid.

(b) Net income $5,400
   Owner's equity $19,300

Analyze transactions and prepare financial statements.

(SO 6, 7, 8)

P1-4B Michelle Rodriguez started her own consulting firm, Rodriguez Consulting, on May 1, 2010. The following transactions occurred during the month of May.

May 1 Michelle invested $7,000 cash in the business.
2 Paid $900 for office rent for the month.
3 Purchased $600 of supplies on account.
5 Paid $125 to advertise in the *County News*.
9 Received $4,000 cash for services provided.
12 Withdrew $1,000 cash for personal use.
15 Performed $6,400 of services on account.
17 Paid $2,500 for employee salaries.
20 Paid for the supplies purchased on account on May 3.
23 Received a cash payment of $4,000 for services provided on account on May 15.
26 Borrowed $5,000 from the bank on a note payable.
29 Purchased office equipment for $3,100 on account.
30 Paid $175 for utilities.

Instructions

(a) Total assets $20,800

(a) Show the effects of the previous transactions on the accounting equation using the following format.

	Assets				Liabilities		Owner's Equity				
Date	Cash +	Accounts Receivable +	Supplies +	Office Equipment =	Notes Payable +	Accounts Payable +	M. Rodriguez, Capital –	M. Rodriguez, Drawing +	Revenues –	Expenses

(b) Net income $6,700
(c) Cash $14,700

(b) Prepare an income statement for the month of May.
(c) Prepare a balance sheet at May 31, 2010.

Determine financial statement amounts and prepare owner's equity statement.

(SO 7, 8)

P1-5B Financial statement information about four different companies is as follows.

	Donatello Company	Raphael Company	Michelangelo Company	Leonardo Company
January 1, 2010				
Assets	$ 80,000	$90,000	(g)	$150,000
Liabilities	48,000	(d)	80,000	(j)
Owner's equity	(a)	40,000	49,000	90,000
December 31, 2010				
Assets	(b)	112,000	180,000	(k)
Liabilities	60,000	72,000	(h)	100,000
Owner's equity	40,000	(e)	70,000	145,000
Owner's equity changes in year				
Additional investment	(c)	8,000	10,000	15,000
Drawings	15,000	(f)	12,000	10,000
Total revenues	350,000	410,000	(i)	500,000
Total expenses	333,000	385,000	350,000	(l)

Instructions

(a) Determine the missing amounts. (*Hint:* For example, to solve for (a), Assets – Liabilities = Owner's equity = $32,000.)

(b) Prepare the owner's equity statement for Donatello Company.

(c) ⬤▬▬▶ Write a memorandum explaining the sequence for preparing financial statements and the interrelationship of the owner's equity statement to the income statement and balance sheet.

PROBLEMS: SET C

Visit the book's companion website at **www.wiley.com/college/weygandt,** and choose the Student Companion site, to access Problem Set C.

CONTINUING COOKIE CHRONICLE

CCC1 Natalie Koebel spent much of her childhood learning the art of cookie-making from her grandmother. They passed many happy hours mastering every type of cookie imaginable and later creating new recipes that were both healthy and delicious. Now at the start of her second year in college, Natalie is investigating various possibilities for starting her own business as part of the requirements of the entrepreneurship program in which she is enrolled.

*The **Continuing Cookie Chronicle** starts in this chapter and continues in every chapter. You also can find this problem at the book's Student Companion site.*

A long-time friend insists that Natalie has to somehow include cookies in her business plan. After a series of brainstorming sessions, Natalie settles on the idea of operating a cookie-making school. She will start on a part-time basis and offer her services in people's homes. Now that she has started thinking about it, the possibilities seem endless. During the fall, she will concentrate on holiday cookies. She will offer individual lessons and group sessions (which will probably be more entertainment than education for the participants). Natalie also decides to include children in her target market.

The first difficult decision is coming up with the perfect name for her business. In the end, she settles on "Cookie Creations" and then moves on to more important issues.

Instructions

(a) What form of business organization—proprietorship, partnership, or corporation—do you recommend that Natalie use for her business? Discuss the benefits and weaknesses of each form and give the reasons for your choice.

(b) Will Natalie need accounting information? If yes, what information will she need and why? How often will she need this information?

(c) Identify specific asset, liability, and equity accounts that Cookie Creations will likely use to record its business transactions.

(d) Should Natalie open a separate bank account for the business? Why or why not?

BROADENING YOUR PERSPECTIVE

FINANCIAL REPORTING AND ANALYSIS

Financial Reporting Problem: PepsiCo, Inc.

BYP1-1 The actual financial statements of PepsiCo, Inc., as presented in the company's 2007 annual report, are contained in Appendix A (at the back of the textbook).

Instructions

Refer to Pepsi's financial statements and answer the following questions.

(a) What were Pepsi's total assets at December 29, 2007? At December 30, 2006?

(b) How much cash (and cash equivalents) did Pepsi have on December 29, 2007?

(c) What amount of accounts payable did Pepsi report on December 29, 2007? On December 30, 2006?

(d) What were Pepsi's net sales in 2005? In 2006? In 2007?

(e) What is the amount of the change in Pepsi's net income from 2006 to 2007?

Comparative Analysis Problem: PepsiCo, Inc. vs. The Coca-Cola Company

BYP1-2 PepsiCo's financial statements are presented in Appendix A. Financial statements of The Coca-Cola Company are presented in Appendix B.

Instructions

(a) Based on the information contained in these financial statements, determine the following for each company.

(1) Total assets at December 29, 2007, for Pepsi and for Coca-Cola at December 31, 2007.

(2) Accounts (notes) receivable, net at December 29, 2007, for Pepsi and at December 31, 2007, for Coca-Cola.

(3) Net sales for year ended in 2007.

(4) Net income for year ended in 2007.

(b) What conclusions concerning the two companies can be drawn from these data?

Exploring the Web

BYP1-3   This exercise will familiarize you with skill requirements, job descriptions, and salaries for accounting careers.

Address: www.careers-in-accounting.com, or go to **www.wiley.com/college/weygandt**

Instructions
Go to the site shown above. Answer the following questions.

(a) What are the three broad areas of accounting (from "Skills and Talents Required")?
(b) List eight skills required in accounting.
(c) How do the three accounting areas differ in terms of these eight required skills?
(d) Explain one of the key job functions in accounting.
(e) Based on the *Smart Money* survey, what is the salary range for a junior staff accountant with Deloitte & Touche?

CRITICAL THINKING

Decision Making Across the Organization

BYP1-4   Mary and Jack Gray, local golf stars, opened the Chip-Shot Driving Range on March 1, 2010, by investing $25,000 of their cash savings in the business. A caddy shack was constructed for cash at a cost of $8,000, and $800 was spent on golf balls and golf clubs. The Grays leased five acres of land at a cost of $1,000 per month and paid the first month's rent. During the first month, advertising costs totaled $750, of which $150 was unpaid at March 31, and $400 was paid to members of the high-school golf team for retrieving golf balls. All revenues from customers were deposited in the company's bank account. On March 15, Mary and Jack withdrew a total of $1,000 in cash for personal living expenses. A $100 utility bill was received on March 31 but was not paid. On March 31, the balance in the company's bank account was $18,900.

Mary and Jack thought they had a pretty good first month of operations. But, their estimates of profitability ranged from a loss of $6,100 to net income of $2,450.

Instructions
With the class divided into groups, answer the following.

(a) How could the Grays have concluded that the business operated at a loss of $6,100? Was this a valid basis on which to determine net income?
(b) How could the Grays have concluded that the business operated at a net income of $2,450? (*Hint:* Prepare a balance sheet at March 31.) Was this a valid basis on which to determine net income?
(c) Without preparing an income statement, determine the actual net income for March.
(d) What was the revenue earned in March?

Communication Activity

BYP1-5   Lynn Benedict, the bookkeeper for New York Company, has been trying to get the balance sheet to balance. The company's balance sheet is shown on the next page.

NEW YORK COMPANY
Balance Sheet
For the Month Ended December 31, 2010

Assets		Liabilities	
Equipment	$25,500	Don Wenger, Capital	$26,000
Cash	9,000	Accounts receivable	(6,000)
Supplies	2,000	Don Wenger, Drawing	(2,000)
Accounts payable	(8,000)	Notes payable	10,500
	$28,500		$28,500

Instructions
Explain to Lynn Benedict in a memo why the original balance sheet is incorrect, and what should be done to correct it.

Ethics Case

BYP1-6   After numerous campus interviews, Steve Baden, a senior at Great Northern College, received two office interview invitations from the Baltimore offices of two large firms. Both firms offered to cover his out-of-pocket expenses (travel, hotel, and meals). He scheduled the interviews for both firms on the same day, one in the morning and one in the afternoon. At the conclusion of each interview, he submitted to both firms his total out-of-pocket expenses for the trip to Baltimore: mileage $112 (280 miles at $0.40), hotel $130, meals $36, parking and tolls $18, for a total of $296. He believes this approach is appropriate. If he had made two trips, his cost would have been two times $296. He is also certain that neither firm knew he had visited the other on that same trip. Within ten days Steve received two checks in the mail, each in the amount of $296.

Instructions
(a) Who are the stakeholders (affected parties) in this situation?
(b) What are the ethical issues in this case?
(c) What would you do in this situation?

"All About You" Activity

BYP1-7   As discussed in the **All About You** feature in this chapter (p. 25), some people are tempted to make their finances look worse to get financial aid. Companies sometimes also manage their financial numbers in order to accomplish certain goals. Earnings management is the planned timing of revenues, expenses, gains, and losses to smooth out bumps in net income. In managing earnings, companies' actions vary from being within the range of ethical activity, to being both unethical and illegal attempts to mislead investors and creditors.

Instructions
Provide responses for each of the following questions.
(a) Discuss whether you think each of the following actions (adapted from *www.finaid.org/ fafsa/maximize.phtml*) to increase the chances of receiving financial aid is ethical.
   (i) Spend down the student's assets and income first, before spending parents' assets and income.
   (ii) Accelerate necessary expenses to reduce available cash. For example, if you need a new car, buy it before applying for financial aid.
   (iii) State that a truly financially dependent child is independent.
   (iv) Have a parent take an unpaid leave of absence for long enough to get below the "threshold" level of income.
(b) What are some reasons why a *company* might want to overstate its earnings?
(c) What are some reasons why a *company* might want to understate its earnings?
(d) Under what circumstances might an otherwise ethical person decide to illegally overstate or understate earnings?

Answers to Insight and Accounting Across the Organization Questions

p. 11 How Will Accounting Help Me?

Q: How might accounting help you?

A: *You will need to understand financial reports in any enterprise with which you are associated. Whether you become a business manager, doctor, lawyer, social worker, teacher, engineer, architect, or entrepreneur, a working knowledge of accounting is relevant.*

p. 23 What Do General Mills, Walt Disney, and Dunkin' Donuts Have in Common?

Q: What year-end would you likely use if you owned a ski resort and ski rental business?

A: *Probable choices for a ski resort would be between May 31 and August 31.*

Q: What if you owned a college bookstore?

A: *For a college bookstore, a likely year-end would be June 30.*

Q: Why choose those year-ends?

A: *The optimum accounting year-end, especially for seasonal businesses, is a point when inventory and activities are lowest.*

Authors' Comments on *All About You: Ethics: Managing Personal Financial Reporting* (p. 25)

In this chapter you saw that there are very specific rules governing the recording of assets, liabilities, revenues, and expenses. However, within these rules there is a lot of room for judgment. It would not be at all unusual for two experienced accountants, when faced with identical situations, to arrive at different results.

Similarly, in reporting your financial situation for financial aid there is a lot of room for judgment. The question is, what kinds of actions are both permissible and ethical, and what kinds of actions are illegal and unethical? It might be argued that paying off your credit card debt to reduce your assets is legal and ethical. It is true that you have intentionally changed the nature of your assets in order to improve your chances of getting aid. You did so, however, through a legitimate transaction. In fact, given the high interest rates charged on credit card bills, it would probably be a good idea to use the cash to pay off your bills even if you aren't applying for aid.

Now, consider an alternative situation. Suppose that you have $10,000 in cash, and you have a sibling who is five years younger than you. Should you "give" the cash to your sibling while you are being considered for financial aid? This would give the appearance of substantially reducing your assets, and thus increase the likelihood that you will receive aid. Most people would argue that this is unethical, and it is probably illegal.

When completing your FAFSA form, don't ignore the following warning on the front of the form: "If you get Federal student aid based on incorrect information, you will have to pay it back; you may also have to pay fines and fees. If you purposely give false or misleading information on your application, you may be fined $20,000, sent to prison, or both."

Answers to Self-Study Questions

1. b   **2.** d   **3.** c   **4.** b   **5.** b   **6.** d   **7.** b   **8.** a   **9.** b   **10.** a   **11.** d   **12.** c   **13.** b   **14.** c   ***15.** a

Chapter 2

The Recording Process

STUDY OBJECTIVES

After studying this chapter, you should be able to:

1 Explain what an account is and how it helps in the recording process.

2 Define debits and credits and explain their use in recording business transactions.

3 Identify the basic steps in the recording process.

4 Explain what a journal is and how it helps in the recording process.

5 Explain what a ledger is and how it helps in the recording process.

6 Explain what posting is and how it helps in the recording process.

7 Prepare a trial balance and explain its purposes.

 The Navigator

✓ The Navigator

Scan **Study Objectives**	■
Read **Feature Story**	■
Read **Preview**	■
Read text and answer **DO IT!** p. 54 ■ p. 57 ■ p. 66 ■ p. 71 ■	
Work **Comprehensive DO IT!** p. 73	■
Review **Summary of Study Objectives**	■
Answer **Self-Study Questions**	■
Complete **Assignments**	■

Feature Story

ACCIDENTS HAPPEN

How organized are you financially? Take a short quiz. Answer *yes* or *no* to each question:

• Does your wallet contain so many cash machine receipts that you've been declared a walking fire hazard?

• Is your wallet such a mess that it is often faster to fish for money in the crack of your car seat than to dig around in your wallet?

• Was LeBron James playing high school basketball the last time you balanced your checkbook?

If you think it is hard to keep track of the many transactions that make up *your* life, imagine what it is like for a major corporation like Fidelity Investments (*www.fidelity.com*). Fidelity is one of the largest mutual fund management firms in the world. If you had your life savings invested at Fidelity Investments, you might be just slightly displeased if, when you called to find out your balance, the representative said, "You know, I kind of remember someone with a name like yours sending us some money—now what did we do with that?"

To ensure the accuracy of your balance and the security of your funds, Fidelity Investments, like all other companies large and small, relies on a sophisticated accounting information system. That's not to say that Fidelity or any other company is error-free. In fact, if you've ever really messed up your checkbook register, you may take some comfort from one accountant's mistake at Fidelity Investments. The accountant failed to include a minus sign while doing a calculation, making what was actually a $1.3 billion loss look like a $1.3 billion gain! Fortunately, like most accounting errors, it was detected before any real harm was done.

No one expects that kind of mistake at a company like Fidelity, which has sophisticated computer systems and top investment managers. In explaining the mistake to shareholders, a spokesperson wrote, "Some people have asked how, in this age of technology, such a mistake could be made. While many of our processes are computerized, accounting systems are complex and dictate that some steps must be handled manually by our managers and accountants, and people can make mistakes."

✓ The Navigator

Inside Chapter 2...

- **What Would Sam Do?** (p. 58)
- **Sarbanes-Oxley Comes to the Rescue** (p. 70)
- ***All About You*: Your Personal Annual Report** (p. 72)

In Chapter 1, we analyzed business transactions in terms of the accounting equation, and we presented the cumulative effects of these transactions in tabular form. Imagine a company like Fidelity Investments (as in the Feature Story) using the same tabular format as Softbyte to keep track of its transactions. In a single day, Fidelity engages in thousands of business transactions. To record each transaction this way would be impractical, expensive, and unnecessary. Instead, companies use a set of procedures and records to keep track of transaction data more easily. This chapter introduces and illustrates these basic procedures and records.

The content and organization of Chapter 2 are as follows.

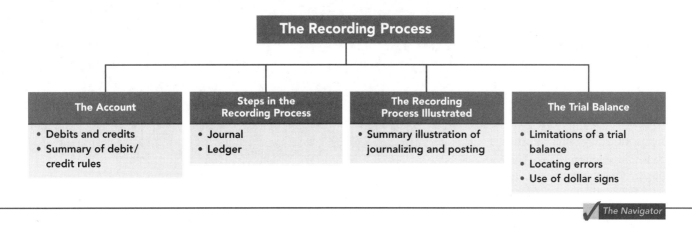

The Recording Process			
The Account	**Steps in the Recording Process**	**The Recording Process Illustrated**	**The Trial Balance**
• Debits and credits • Summary of debit/credit rules	• Journal • Ledger	• Summary illustration of journalizing and posting	• Limitations of a trial balance • Locating errors • Use of dollar signs

✓ *The Navigator*

THE ACCOUNT

STUDY OBJECTIVE 1

Explain what an account is and how it helps in the recording process.

An **account** is an accounting record of increases and decreases in a specific asset, liability, or owner's equity item. For example, Softbyte (the company discussed in Chapter 1) would have separate accounts for Cash, Accounts Receivable, Accounts Payable, Service Revenue, and Salaries Expense. In its simplest form, an account consists of three parts: (1) a title, (2) a left or debit side, and (3) a right or credit side. Because the format of an account resembles the letter T, we refer to it as a **T account**. Illustration 2-1 shows the basic form of an account.

Illustration 2-1
Basic form of account

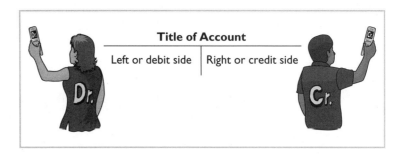

Title of Account

Left or debit side | Right or credit side

The T account is a standard shorthand in accounting, which helps make clear the effects of transactions on individual accounts. We will use it often throughout this book to explain basic accounting relationships.

Debits and Credits

The terms debit and credit are directional signals: Debit indicates left, and credit indicates right. They indicate which side of a T account a number will be recorded on. Entering an amount on the left side of an account is called **debiting** the account. Making an entry on the right side is **crediting** the account. We commonly abbreviate debit as Dr. and credit as Cr.

STUDY OBJECTIVE 2

Define debits and credits and explain their use in recording business transactions.

Having debits on the left and credits on the right is an accounting custom, or rule, like the custom of driving on the right-hand side of the road in the United States. **This rule applies to all accounts.**

Illustration 2-2 shows the recording of debits and credits in an account for the cash transactions of Softbyte. The data are taken from the cash column of the tabular summary in Illustration 1-8 (from page 19), which is reproduced here.

Tabular Summary	Account Form			
Cash	**Cash**			
$15,000	(Debits) 15,000	(Credits)	7,000	
–7,000	1,200		1,700	
1,200	1,500		250	
1,500	600		1,300	
–1,700	Balance 8,050			
–250	(Debit)			
600				
–1,300				
$ 8,050				

Illustration 2-2
Tabular summary compared to account form

In the tabular summary, every positive item represents Softbyte's receipt of cash; every negative amount represents a payment of cash. In the account form we record the increases in cash as debits, and the decreases in cash as credits. Having increases on one side and decreases on the other helps determine the total of each side as well as the overall account balance. The balance, a debit of $8,050, indicates that Softbyte has had $8,050 more increases than decreases in cash.

When the totals of the two sides of an account are compared, an account will have a **debit balance** if the total of the debit amounts exceeds the credits. An account will have a **credit balance** if the credit amounts exceed the debits. The account in Illustration 2-2 has a debit balance.

DEBIT AND CREDIT PROCEDURE

In Chapter 1 you learned the effect of a transaction on the basic accounting equation. Remember that each transaction must affect two or more accounts to keep the basic accounting equation in balance. In other words, for each transaction, debits must equal credits in the accounts. The equality of debits and credits provides the basis for the double-entry system of recording transactions.

In the double-entry system the dual (two-sided) effect of each transaction is recorded in appropriate accounts. This system provides a logical method for recording transactions. It also helps ensure the accuracy of the recorded amounts. The sum of all the debits to the accounts must equal the sum of all the credits.

The double-entry system for determining the equality of the accounting equation is much more efficient than the plus/minus procedure used in Chapter 1. On the following pages, we will illustrate debit and credit procedures in the double-entry system.

INTERNATIONAL NOTE

Rules for accounting for specific events sometimes differ across countries. For example, European companies rely less on historical cost and more on fair value than U.S. companies. Despite the differences, the double-entry accounting system is the basis of accounting systems worldwide.

Assets and Liabilities. Both sides of the accounting equation (Assets = Liabilities + Owner's equity) must be equal. It follows, then, that we must record increases and decreases in assets opposite from each other. In Illustration 2-2, Softbyte entered increases in cash—an asset—on the left side, and decreases in cash on the right side. Therefore, we must enter increases in liabilities on the right or credit side, and decreases in liabilities on the left or debit side. Illustration 2-3 summarizes the effects that debits and credits have on assets and liabilities.

Illustration 2-3
Debit and credit effects—
assets and liabilities

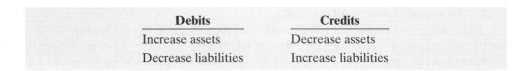

Debits	Credits
Increase assets	Decrease assets
Decrease liabilities	Increase liabilities

Debits to a specific asset account should exceed the credits to that account. Credits to a liability account should exceed debits to that account. **The normal balance of an account is on the side where an increase in the account is recorded.** Thus, asset accounts normally show debit balances, and liability accounts normally show credit balances. Illustration 2-4 shows the normal balances for assets and liabilities.

Illustration 2-4
Normal balances—assets
and liabilities

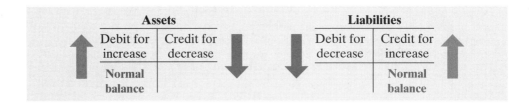

Knowing the normal balance in an account may help you trace errors. For example, a credit balance in an asset account such as Land would indicate a recording error. Similarly, a debit balance in a liability account such as Wages Payable would indicate an error. Occasionally, though, an abnormal balance may be correct. The Cash account, for example, will have a credit balance when a company has overdrawn its bank balance (i.e., written a "bad" check). (Notice that when we are referring to a specific account, we capitalize its name.)

Owner's Equity. As Chapter 1 indicated, owner's investments and revenues increase owner's equity. Owner's drawings and expenses decrease owner's equity. Companies keep accounts for each of these types of transactions.

Owner's Capital. Investments by owners are credited to the Owner's Capital account. Credits increase this account, and debits decrease it. When an owner invests cash in the business, the company debits (increases) Cash and credits (increases) Owner's Capital. When the owner's investment in the business is reduced, Owner's Capital is debited (decreased).

Illustration 2-5 shows the rules of debit and credit for the Owner's Capital account.

Illustration 2-5
Debit and credit effects—
Owner's Capital

Debits	Credits
Decrease Owner's Capital	Increase Owner's Capital

We can diagram the normal balance in Owner's Capital as follows.

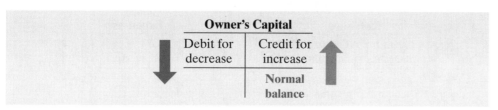

Illustration 2-6
Normal balance—Owner's
Capital

Owner's Drawing.   An owner may withdraw cash or other assets for personal use. Withdrawals could be debited directly to Owner's Capital to indicate a decrease in owner's equity. However, it is preferable to use a separate account, called Owner's Drawing. This separate account makes it easier to determine total withdrawals for each accounting period. Owner's Drawing is increased by debits and decreased by credits. Normally, the drawing account will have a debit balance.

Illustration 2-7 shows the rules of debit and credit for the drawing account.

Debits	Credits
Increase Owner's Drawing	Decrease Owner's Drawing

Illustration 2-7
Debit and credit effects—
Owner's Drawing

We can diagram the normal balance as follows.

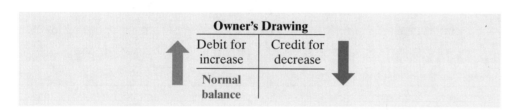

Illustration 2-8
Normal balance—Owner's
Drawing

The Drawing account decreases owner's equity. It is not an income statement account like revenues and expenses.

Revenues and Expenses.   The purpose of earning revenues is to benefit the owner(s) of the business. When a company earns revenues, owner's equity increases. Therefore, **the effect of debits and credits on revenue accounts is the same as their effect on Owner's Capital.** That is, revenue accounts are increased by credits and decreased by debits.

Expenses have the opposite effect: Expenses decrease owner's equity. Since expenses decrease net income, and revenues increase it, it is logical that the increase and decrease sides of expense accounts should be the reverse of revenue accounts. Thus, expense accounts are increased by debits and decreased by credits. Illustration 2-9 shows the rules of debits and credits for revenues and expenses.

HELPFUL HINT

Because revenues increase owner's equity, a revenue account has the same debit/credit rules as the Owner's Capital account. Expenses have the opposite effect.

Debits	Credits
Decrease revenues	Increase revenues
Increase expenses	Decrease expenses

Illustration 2-9
Debit and credit effects—
revenues and expenses

Credits to revenue accounts should exceed debits. Debits to expense accounts should exceed credits. Thus, revenue accounts normally show credit balances, and expense accounts normally show debit balances. We can diagram the normal balances as follows.

Illustration 2-10
Normal balances—revenues
and expenses

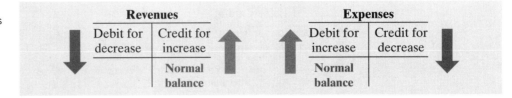

Summary of Debit/Credit Rules

Illustration 2-11 shows a summary of the debit/credit rules and effects on each type
of account. Study this diagram carefully. It will help you understand the fundamentals of the double-entry system.

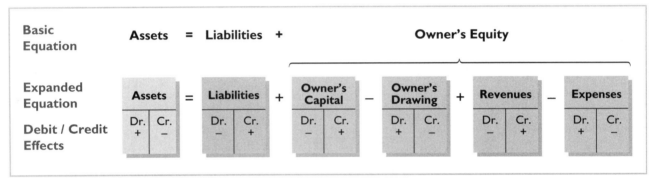

Illustration 2-11
Summary of debit/credit
rules

DO IT!

NORMAL BALANCES

Kate Browne has just rented space in a shopping mall. In this space, she will open
a hair salon, to be called "Hair It Is." A friend has advised Kate to set up a
double-entry set of accounting records in which to record all of her business
transactions.

Identify the balance sheet accounts that Kate will likely need to record the
transactions needed to open her business. Indicate whether the normal balance of
each account is a debit or a credit.

action plan

✔ Determine the types of
accounts needed: Kate will
need asset accounts for
each different type of asset
she invests in the business,
and liability accounts for
any debts she incurs.

✔ Understand the types of
owner's equity accounts:
Only Owner's Capital will
be needed when Kate be-
gins the business. Other
owner's equity accounts
will be needed later.

Solution

Kate would likely need the following accounts in which to record the
transactions necessary to ready her hair salon for opening day:

Cash (debit balance)

Equipment (debit balance)

Supplies (debit balance)

Accounts Payable (credit balance)

If she borrows money: Notes payable
(credit balance)

K. Browne, Capital (credit balance)

Related exercise material: **BE2-1, BE2-2, BE2-5, E2-1, E2-2, E2-4,** and **DO IT!** 2-1.

STEPS IN THE RECORDING PROCESS

In practically every business, there are three basic steps in the recording process:

1. Analyze each transaction for its effects on the accounts.
2. Enter the transaction information in a *journal*.
3. Transfer the journal information to the appropriate accounts in the *ledger*.

Although it is possible to enter transaction information directly into the accounts without using a journal, few businesses do so.

The recording process begins with the transaction. **Business documents**, such as a sales slip, a check, a bill, or a cash register tape, provide evidence of the transaction. The company analyzes this evidence to determine the transaction's effects on specific accounts. The company then enters the transaction in the journal. Finally, it transfers the journal entry to the designated accounts in the ledger. Illustration 2-12 shows the recording process.

STUDY OBJECTIVE 3

Identify the basic steps in the recording process.

ETHICS NOTE

Business documents provide evidence that transactions actually occurred. International Outsourcing Services, LLC, was accused of submitting fraudulent documents (store coupons) to companies such as Kraft Foods and PepsiCo for reimbursement of as much as $250 million. Ensuring that all recorded transactions are backed up by proper business documents reduces the likelihood of fraudulent activity.

Analyze each transaction   Enter transaction in a journal   Transfer journal information to ledger accounts

Illustration 2-12
The recording process

The steps in the recording process occur repeatedly. In Chapter 1, we illustrated the first step, the analysis of transactions, and will give further examples in this and later chapters. The other two steps in the recording process are explained in the next sections.

The Journal

Companies initially record transactions in chronological order (the order in which they occur). Thus, the journal is referred to as the book of original entry. For each transaction the journal shows the debit and credit effects on specific accounts.

STUDY OBJECTIVE 4

Explain what a journal is and how it helps in the recording process.

Companies may use various kinds of journals, but every company has the most basic form of journal, a general journal. Typically, a general journal has spaces for dates, account titles and explanations, references, and two amount columns. See the format of the journal in Illustration 2-13 (on page 56). *Whenever we use the term "journal" in this textbook without a modifying adjective, we mean the general journal.*

The journal makes several significant contributions to the recording process:

1. It discloses in one place the complete effects of a transaction.
2. It provides a chronological record of transactions.
3. It helps to prevent or locate errors because the debit and credit amounts for each entry can be easily compared.

JOURNALIZING

Entering transaction data in the journal is known as journalizing. Companies make separate journal entries for each transaction. A complete entry consists of: (1) the date of the transaction, (2) the accounts and amounts to be debited and credited, and (3) a brief explanation of the transaction.

Illustration 2-13 shows the technique of journalizing, using the first two transactions of Softbyte. On September 1, Ray Neal invested $15,000 cash in the business, and Softbyte purchased computer equipment for $7,000 cash. The number J1 indicates that these two entries are recorded on the first page of the journal. Illustration 2-13 shows the standard form of journal entries for these two transactions. (The boxed numbers correspond to explanations in the list below the illustration.)

Illustration 2-13
Technique of journalizing

GENERAL JOURNAL				J1
Date	**Account Titles and Explanation**	**Ref.**	**Debit**	**Credit**
2010		[5]		
Sept. 1 [2] [1]	Cash		15,000	
[3]	R. Neal, Capital			15,000
[4]	(Owner's investment of cash in business)			
1	Computer Equipment		7,000	
	Cash			7,000
	(Purchase of equipment for cash)			

[1] The date of the transaction is entered in the Date column.

[2] The debit account title (that is, the account to be debited) is entered first at the extreme left margin of the column headed "Account Titles and Explanation," and the amount of the debit is recorded in the Debit column.

[3] The credit account title (that is, the account to be credited) is indented and entered on the next line in the column headed "Account Titles and Explanation," and the amount of the credit is recorded in the Credit column.

[4] A brief explanation of the transaction appears on the line below the credit account title. A space is left between journal entries. The blank space separates individual journal entries and makes the entire journal easier to read.

[5] The column titled Ref. (which stands for Reference) is left blank when the journal entry is made. This column is used later when the journal entries are transferred to the ledger accounts.

It is important to use correct and specific account titles in journalizing. The main criterion is that each title must appropriately describe the content of the account. For example, a company might use Delivery Equipment, Delivery Trucks, or Trucks as the account title used for the cost of delivery trucks. Once a company chooses the specific title to use, it should record under that account title all later transactions involving the account.[1]

---

[1] *In homework problems, you should use specific account titles when they are given.* When account titles are not given, you may select account titles that identify the nature and content of each account. The account titles used in journalizing should not contain explanations such as Cash Paid or Cash Received.

SIMPLE AND COMPOUND ENTRIES

Some entries involve only two accounts, one debit and one credit. (See, for example, the entries in Illustration 2-13.) An entry like these is considered a **simple entry**. Some transactions, however, require more than two accounts in journalizing. An entry that requires three or more accounts is a **compound entry**. To illustrate, assume that on July 1, Butler Company purchases a delivery truck costing $14,000. It pays $8,000 cash now and agrees to pay the remaining $6,000 on account (to be paid later). The compound entry is as follows.

GENERAL JOURNAL					J1
Date	Account Titles and Explanation	Ref.	Debit	Credit	
2010 July 1	Delivery Equipment		14,000		
	Cash			8,000	
	Accounts Payable			6,000	
	(Purchased truck for cash with balance on account)				

Illustration 2-14
Compound journal entry

In a compound entry, the standard format requires that all debits be listed before the credits.

DO IT!

Kate Browne engaged in the following activities in establishing her salon, Hair It Is:

1. Opened a bank account in the name of Hair It Is and deposited $20,000 of her own money in this account as her initial investment.
2. Purchased equipment on account (to be paid in 30 days) for a total cost of $4,800.
3. Interviewed three persons for the position of hair stylist.

In what form (type of record) should Kate record these three activities? Prepare the entries to record the transactions.

RECORDING BUSINESS ACTIVITIES

Solution

Each transaction that is recorded is entered in the general journal. The three activities would be recorded as follows.

1. Cash		20,000	
K. Browne, Capital			20,000
(Owner's investment of cash in business)			
2. Equipment		4,800	
Accounts Payable			4,800
(Purchase of equipment on account)			
3. No entry because no transaction has occurred.			

action plan

✔ Understand which activities need to be recorded and which do not. Any that affect assets, liabilities, or owner's capital should be recorded in a journal.

✔ Analyze the effects of transactions on asset, liability, and owner's equity accounts.

Related exercise material: **BE2-3, BE2-6, E2-3, E2-5, E2-6, E2-7,** and **DO IT!** **2-2**.

✓ *The Navigator*

The Ledger

STUDY OBJECTIVE 5

Explain what a ledger is and how it helps in the recording process.

The entire group of accounts maintained by a company is the **ledger**. The ledger keeps in one place all the information about changes in specific account balances.

Companies may use various kinds of ledgers, but every company has a general ledger. A **general ledger** contains all the asset, liability, and owner's equity accounts, as shown in Illustration 2-15 for J. Lind Company. *Whenever we use the term "ledger" in this textbook, we are referring to the general ledger, unless we specify otherwise.*

Illustration 2-15
The general ledger, which contains all of a company's accounts

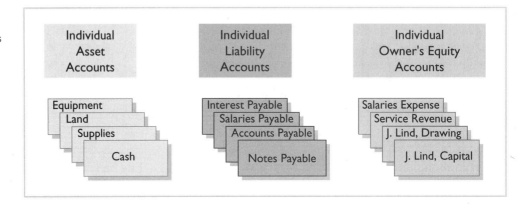

Companies arrange the ledger in the sequence in which they present the accounts in the financial statements, beginning with the balance sheet accounts. First in order are the asset accounts, followed by liability accounts, owner's capital, owner's drawing, revenues, and expenses. Each account is numbered for easier identification.

The ledger provides the balance in each of the accounts. For example, the Cash account shows the amount of cash available to meet current obligations. The Accounts Receivable account shows amounts due from customers. Accounts Payable shows amounts owed to creditors.

ACCOUNTING ACROSS THE ORGANIZATION

What Would Sam Do?

In his autobiography Sam Walton described the double-entry accounting system he used when Wal-Mart was just getting started: "We kept a little pigeonhole on the wall for the cash receipts and paperwork of each [Wal-Mart] store. I had a blue binder ledger book for each store. When we added a store, we added a pigeonhole. We did this at least up to twenty stores. Then once a month, the bookkeeper and I would enter the merchandise, enter the sales, enter the cash, and balance it."

Source: Sam Walton, *Made in America* (New York: Doubleday, 1992), p. 53.

? Why did Sam Walton keep separate pigeonholes and blue binders? Why bother to keep separate records for each store?

STANDARD FORM OF ACCOUNT

The simple T-account form used in accounting textbooks is often very useful for illustration purposes. However, in practice, the account forms used in ledgers are much more structured. Illustration 2-16 shows a typical form, using assumed data from a cash account.

	CASH			NO. 101	
Date	Explanation	Ref.	Debit	Credit	Balance
2010					
June 1			25,000		25,000
2				8,000	17,000
3			4,200		21,200
9			7,500		28,700
17				11,700	17,000
20				250	16,750
30				7,300	9,450

Illustration 2-16
Three-column form
of account

This format is called the **three-column form of account**. It has three money columns—debit, credit, and balance. The balance in the account is determined after each transaction. Companies use the explanation space and reference columns to provide special information about the transaction.

POSTING

Transferring journal entries to the ledger accounts is called posting. This phase of the recording process accumulates the effects of journalized transactions into the individual accounts. Posting involves the following steps.

> **STUDY OBJECTIVE 6**
> Explain what posting is and how it helps in the recording process.

1. In the **ledger**, in the appropriate columns of the account(s) debited, enter the date, journal page, and debit amount shown in the journal.
2. In the reference column of the **journal**, write the account number to which the debit amount was posted.
3. In the **ledger**, in the appropriate columns of the account(s) credited, enter the date, journal page, and credit amount shown in the journal.
4. In the reference column of the **journal**, write the account number to which the credit amount was posted.

Illustration 2-17 (page 60) shows these four steps using Softbyte's first journal entry. The boxed numbers indicate the sequence of the steps.

Posting should be performed in chronological order. That is, the company should post all the debits and credits of one journal entry before proceeding to the next journal entry. Postings should be made on a timely basis to ensure that the ledger is up to date.[2]

The reference column of a ledger account indicates the journal page from which the transaction was posted.[3] The explanation space of the ledger account is used infrequently because an explanation already appears in the journal.

---

[2] *In homework problems, you can journalize all transactions before posting any of the journal entries.*

[3] After the last entry has been posted, the accountant should scan the reference column **in the journal**, to confirm that all postings have been made.

Illustration 2-17
Posting a journal entry

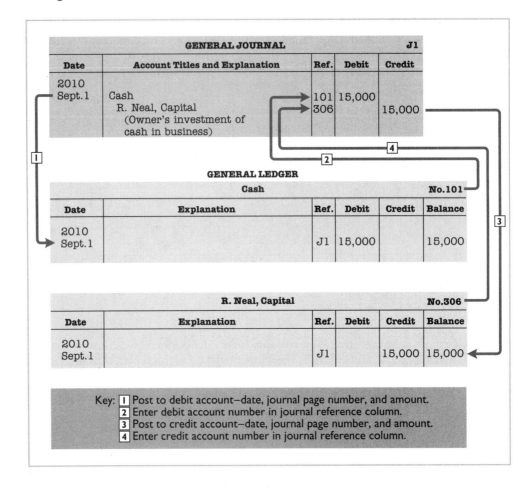

CHART OF ACCOUNTS

The number and type of accounts differ for each company. The number of accounts depends on the amount of detail management desires. For example, the management of one company may want a single account for all types of utility expense. Another may keep separate expense accounts for each type of utility, such as gas, electricity, and water. Similarly, a small company like Softbyte will have fewer accounts than a corporate giant like Dell. Softbyte may be able to manage and report its activities in 20 to 30 accounts, while Dell may require thousands of accounts to keep track of its worldwide activities.

Most companies have a **chart of accounts**. This chart lists the accounts and the account numbers that identify their location in the ledger. The numbering system that identifies the accounts usually starts with the balance sheet accounts and follows with the income statement accounts.

In this and the next two chapters, we will be explaining the accounting for Pioneer Advertising Agency (a service company). Accounts 101–199 indicate asset accounts; 200–299 indicate liabilities; 301–350 indicate owner's equity accounts; 400–499, revenues; 601–799, expenses; 800–899, other revenues; and 900–999, other expenses. Illustration 2-18 (page 61) shows Pioneer's chart of accounts. (C. R. Byrd is Pioneer's owner.) Accounts listed in red are used in this chapter; accounts shown in black are explained in later chapters.

You will notice that there are gaps in the numbering system of the chart of accounts for Pioneer Advertising. Companies leave gaps to permit the insertion of new accounts as needed during the life of the business.

HELPFUL HINT

On the book's endpapers, you also will find an expanded chart of accounts.

PIONEER ADVERTISING AGENCY
Chart of Accounts

Illustration 2-18
Chart of accounts

Assets

101 Cash
112 Accounts Receivable
126 Advertising Supplies
130 Prepaid Insurance
157 Office Equipment
158 Accumulated Depreciation—Office Equipment

Liabilities

200 Notes Payable
201 Accounts Payable
209 Unearned Revenue
212 Salaries Payable
230 Interest Payable

Owner's Equity

301 C. R. Byrd, Capital
306 C. R. Byrd, Drawing
350 Income Summary

Revenues

400 Service Revenue

Expenses

631 Advertising Supplies Expense
711 Depreciation Expense
722 Insurance Expense
726 Salaries Expense
729 Rent Expense
905 Interest Expense

THE RECORDING PROCESS ILLUSTRATED

Illustrations 2-19 through 2-28 show the basic steps in the recording process, using the October transactions of Pioneer Advertising Agency. Pioneer's accounting period is a month. In these illustrations, a basic analysis, an equation analysis, and a debit-credit analysis precede the journal entry and posting of each transaction. For simplicity, we use the T-account form to show the posting instead of the standard account form.

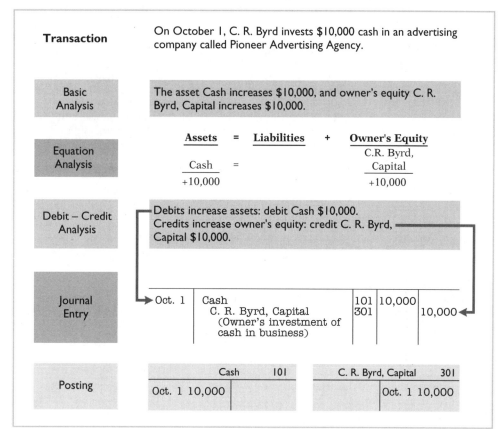

Illustration 2-19
Investment of cash
by owner

Transaction

On October 1, C. R. Byrd invests $10,000 cash in an advertising company called Pioneer Advertising Agency.

Basic Analysis

The asset Cash increases $10,000, and owner's equity C. R. Byrd, Capital increases $10,000.

Equation Analysis

Assets	=	Liabilities	+	Owner's Equity
				C.R. Byrd, Capital
Cash	=			
+10,000				+10,000

Debit – Credit Analysis

Debits increase assets: debit Cash $10,000.
Credits increase owner's equity: credit C. R. Byrd, Capital $10,000.

Journal Entry

Oct. 1	Cash	101	10,000	
	C. R. Byrd, Capital	301		10,000
	(Owner's investment of cash in business)			

Posting

Cash	101
Oct. 1 10,000	

C. R. Byrd, Capital	301
	Oct. 1 10,000

HELPFUL HINT

Follow these steps:
1. Determine what type of account is involved.
2. Determine what items increased or decreased and by how much.
3. Translate the increases and decreases into debits and credits.

Illustration 2-20
Purchase of office
equipment

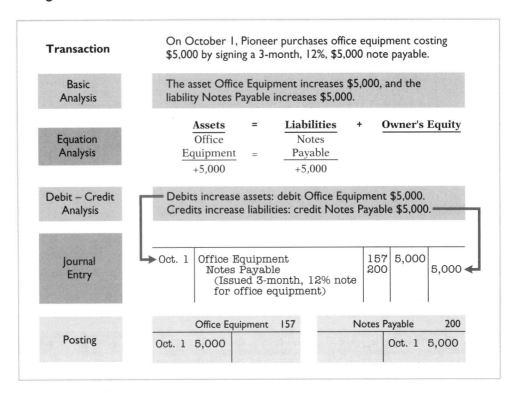

Transaction	On October 1, Pioneer purchases office equipment costing $5,000 by signing a 3-month, 12%, $5,000 note payable.
Basic Analysis	The asset Office Equipment increases $5,000, and the liability Notes Payable increases $5,000.

Equation Analysis

Assets	=	Liabilities	+	Owner's Equity
Office Equipment	=	Notes Payable		
+5,000		+5,000		

Debit – Credit Analysis

Debits increase assets: debit Office Equipment $5,000.
Credits increase liabilities: credit Notes Payable $5,000.

Journal Entry

Oct. 1	Office Equipment	157	5,000	
	Notes Payable	200		5,000
	(Issued 3-month, 12% note for office equipment)			

Posting

Office Equipment	157			Notes Payable	200
Oct. 1 5,000					Oct. 1 5,000

Illustration 2-21
Receipt of cash for future
service

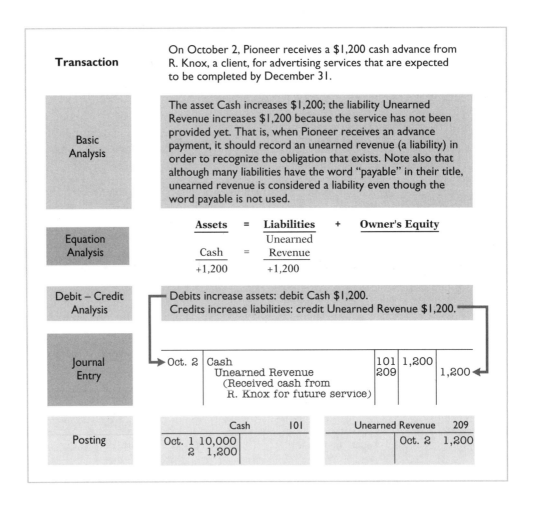

Transaction	On October 2, Pioneer receives a $1,200 cash advance from R. Knox, a client, for advertising services that are expected to be completed by December 31.
Basic Analysis	The asset Cash increases $1,200; the liability Unearned Revenue increases $1,200 because the service has not been provided yet. That is, when Pioneer receives an advance payment, it should record an unearned revenue (a liability) in order to recognize the obligation that exists. Note also that although many liabilities have the word "payable" in their title, unearned revenue is considered a liability even though the word payable is not used.

Equation Analysis

Assets	=	Liabilities	+	Owner's Equity
		Unearned		
Cash	=	Revenue		
+1,200		+1,200		

Debit – Credit Analysis

Debits increase assets: debit Cash $1,200.
Credits increase liabilities: credit Unearned Revenue $1,200.

Journal Entry

Oct. 2	Cash	101	1,200	
	Unearned Revenue	209		1,200
	(Received cash from R. Knox for future service)			

Posting

Cash	101			Unearned Revenue	209
Oct. 1 10,000					Oct. 2 1,200
2 1,200					

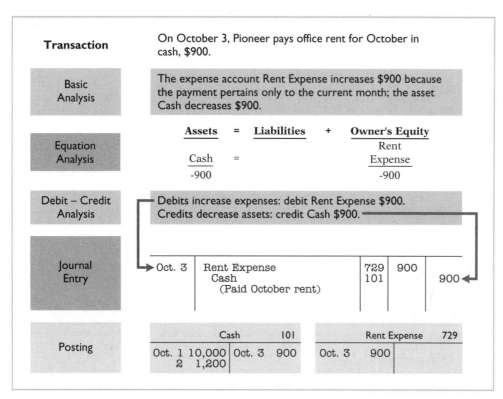

Illustration 2-22
Payment of monthly rent

| Transaction | On October 3, Pioneer pays office rent for October in cash, $900. |

Basic Analysis — The expense account Rent Expense increases $900 because the payment pertains only to the current month; the asset Cash decreases $900.

Equation Analysis

Assets	=	Liabilities	+	Owner's Equity
				Rent
Cash	=			Expense
-900				-900

Debit – Credit Analysis — Debits increase expenses: debit Rent Expense $900. Credits decrease assets: credit Cash $900.

Journal Entry

Oct. 3	Rent Expense	729	900	
	Cash	101		900
	(Paid October rent)			

Posting

Cash			101
Oct. 1	10,000	Oct. 3	900
2	1,200		

Rent Expense		729
Oct. 3	900	

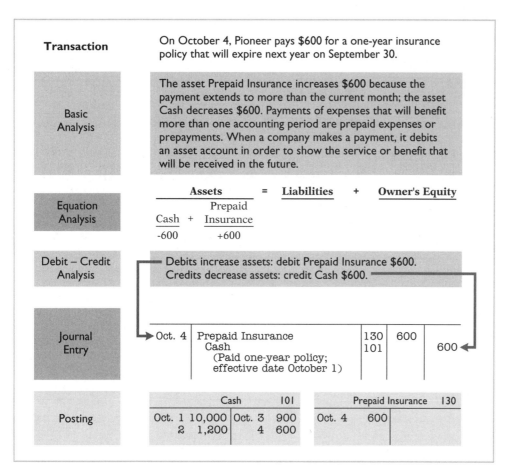

Illustration 2-23
Payment for insurance

| Transaction | On October 4, Pioneer pays $600 for a one-year insurance policy that will expire next year on September 30. |

Basic Analysis — The asset Prepaid Insurance increases $600 because the payment extends to more than the current month; the asset Cash decreases $600. Payments of expenses that will benefit more than one accounting period are prepaid expenses or prepayments. When a company makes a payment, it debits an asset account in order to show the service or benefit that will be received in the future.

Equation Analysis

Assets		=	Liabilities	+	Owner's Equity
	Prepaid				
Cash	+ Insurance	=			
-600	+600				

Debit – Credit Analysis — Debits increase assets: debit Prepaid Insurance $600. Credits decrease assets: credit Cash $600.

Journal Entry

Oct. 4	Prepaid Insurance	130	600	
	Cash	101		600
	(Paid one-year policy; effective date October 1)			

Posting

Cash			101
Oct. 1	10,000	Oct. 3	900
2	1,200	4	600

Prepaid Insurance		130
Oct. 4	600	

Illustration 2-24
Purchase of supplies on
credit

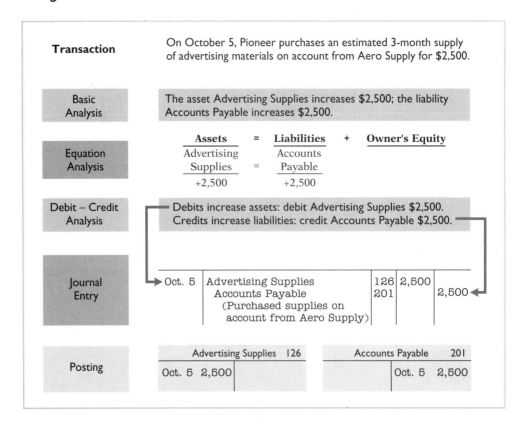

Transaction	On October 5, Pioneer purchases an estimated 3-month supply of advertising materials on account from Aero Supply for $2,500.
Basic Analysis	The asset Advertising Supplies increases $2,500; the liability Accounts Payable increases $2,500.

	Assets	=	Liabilities	+	Owner's Equity
Equation Analysis	Advertising Supplies	=	Accounts Payable		
	+2,500		+2,500		

Debit – Credit Analysis

Debits increase assets: debit Advertising Supplies $2,500.
Credits increase liabilities: credit Accounts Payable $2,500.

Journal Entry

Oct. 5	Advertising Supplies	126	2,500	
	Accounts Payable	201		2,500
	(Purchased supplies on account from Aero Supply)			

Posting

Advertising Supplies	126		Accounts Payable	201
Oct. 5 2,500			Oct. 5 2,500	

Illustration 2-25
Hiring of employees

Event	On October 9, Pioneer hires four employees to begin work on October 15. Each employee is to receive a weekly salary of $500 for a 5-day work week, payable every 2 weeks—first payment made on October 26.
Basic Analysis	A business transaction has not occurred. There is only an agreement between the employer and the employees to enter into a business transaction beginning on October 15. Thus, a debit–credit analysis is not needed because there is no accounting entry. (See transaction of October 26 for first entry.)

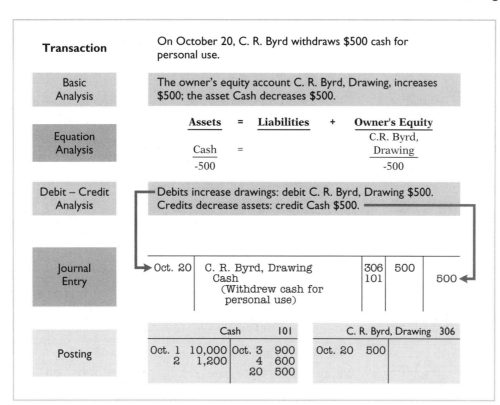

Illustration 2-26
Withdrawal of cash
by owner

Transaction	On October 20, C. R. Byrd withdraws $500 cash for personal use.
Basic Analysis	The owner's equity account C. R. Byrd, Drawing, increases $500; the asset Cash decreases $500.

Equation Analysis

Assets	=	Liabilities	+	Owner's Equity
				C.R. Byrd,
Cash	=			Drawing
-500				-500

Debit – Credit Analysis: Debits increase drawings: debit C. R. Byrd, Drawing $500. Credits decrease assets: credit Cash $500.

Journal Entry:

Oct. 20	C. R. Byrd, Drawing	306	500	
	Cash	101		500
	(Withdrew cash for personal use)			

Posting:

Cash			101		C. R. Byrd, Drawing	306
Oct. 1	10,000	Oct. 3	900	Oct. 20	500	
2	1,200	4	600			
		20	500			

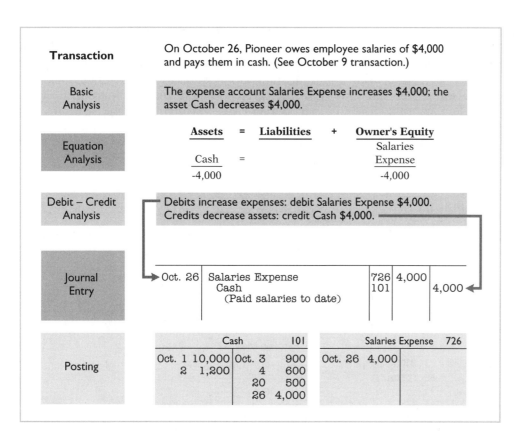

Illustration 2-27
Payment of salaries

Transaction	On October 26, Pioneer owes employee salaries of $4,000 and pays them in cash. (See October 9 transaction.)
Basic Analysis	The expense account Salaries Expense increases $4,000; the asset Cash decreases $4,000.

Equation Analysis

Assets	=	Liabilities	+	Owner's Equity
				Salaries
Cash	=			Expense
-4,000				-4,000

Debit – Credit Analysis: Debits increase expenses: debit Salaries Expense $4,000. Credits decrease assets: credit Cash $4,000.

Journal Entry:

Oct. 26	Salaries Expense	726	4,000	
	Cash	101		4,000
	(Paid salaries to date)			

Posting:

Cash			101		Salaries Expense	726
Oct. 1	10,000	Oct. 3	900	Oct. 26	4,000	
2	1,200	4	600			
		20	500			
		26	4,000			

Illustration 2-28
Receipt of cash for services
provided

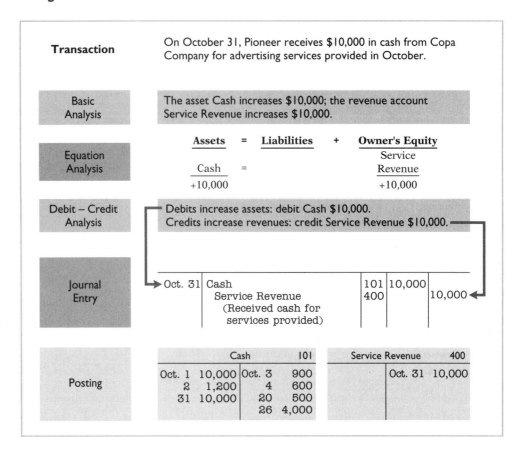

| Transaction | On October 31, Pioneer receives $10,000 in cash from Copa Company for advertising services provided in October. |

Study these transaction analyses carefully. **The purpose of transaction analysis is first to identify the type of account involved, and then to determine whether to make a debit or a credit to the account.** You should always perform this type of analysis before preparing a journal entry. Doing so will help you understand the journal entries discussed in this chapter as well as more complex journal entries in later chapters. In addition, an Accounting Cycle Tutorial in WileyPLUS provides an interactive presentation of the steps in the accounting cycle, using the examples in the illustrations on the preceding pages.

DO IT!

POSTING

Kate Brown recorded the following transactions in a general journal during the month of March.

Mar. 4	Cash		2,280	
	Service Revenue			2,280
15	Wages Expense		400	
	Cash			400
19	Utilities Expense		92	
	Cash			92

Post these entries to the Cash account of the general ledger to determine the ending balance in cash. The beginning balance of cash on March 1 was $600.

Solution

		Cash		
3/1	600		3/15	400
3/4	2,280		3/19	92
3/31 Bal.	2,388			

Related exercise material: **BE2-7, BE2-8, E2-8, E2-12** and **DO IT!** **2-3**.

action plan

✔ Recall that posting involves transferring the journalized debits and credits to specific accounts in the ledger.

✔ Determine the ending balance by netting the total debits and credits.

Summary Illustration of Journalizing and Posting

Illustration 2-29 shows the journal for Pioneer Advertising Agency for October. Illustration 2-30 (on page 68) shows the ledger, with all balances in color.

Date	Account Titles and Explanation	Ref.	Debit	Credit
GENERAL JOURNAL				**PAGE J1**
2010 Oct. 1	Cash	101	10,000	
	C. R. Byrd, Capital	301		10,000
	(Owner's investment of cash in business)			
1	Office Equipment	157	5,000	
	Notes Payable	200		5,000
	(Issued 3-month, 12% note for office equipment)			
2	Cash	101	1,200	
	Unearned Revenue	209		1,200
	(Received cash from R. Knox for future service)			
3	Rent Expense	729	900	
	Cash	101		900
	(Paid October rent)			
4	Prepaid Insurance	130	600	
	Cash	101		600
	(Paid one-year policy; effective date October 1)			
5	Advertising Supplies	126	2,500	
	Accounts Payable	201		2,500
	(Purchased supplies on account from Aero Supply)			
20	C. R. Byrd, Drawing	306	500	
	Cash	101		500
	(Withdrew cash for personal use)			
26	Salaries Expense	726	4,000	
	Cash	101		4,000
	(Paid salaries to date)			
31	Cash	101	10,000	
	Service Revenue	400		10,000
	(Received cash for services provided)			

Illustration 2-29
General journal entries

GENERAL LEDGER

Cash					No. 101
Date	Explanation	Ref.	Debit	Credit	Balance
2010					
Oct. 1		J1	10,000		10,000
2		J1	1,200		11,200
3		J1		900	10,300
4		J1		600	9,700
20		J1		500	9,200
26		J1		4,000	5,200
31		J1	10,000		15,200

Advertising Supplies					No. 126
Date	Explanation	Ref.	Debit	Credit	Balance
2010					
Oct. 5		J1	2,500		2,500

Prepaid Insurance					No. 130
Date	Explanation	Ref.	Debit	Credit	Balance
2010					
Oct. 4		J1	600		600

Office Equipment					No. 157
Date	Explanation	Ref.	Debit	Credit	Balance
2010					
Oct. 1		J1	5,000		5,000

Notes Payable					No. 200
Date	Explanation	Ref.	Debit	Credit	Balance
2010					
Oct. 1		J1		5,000	5,000

Accounts Payable					No. 201
Date	Explanation	Ref.	Debit	Credit	Balance
2010					
Oct. 5		J1		2,500	2,500

Unearned Revenue					No. 209
Date	Explanation	Ref.	Debit	Credit	Balance
2010					
Oct. 2		J1		1,200	1,200

C.R. Byrd, Capital					No. 301
Date	Explanation	Ref.	Debit	Credit	Balance
2010					
Oct. 1		J1		10,000	10,000

C.R. Byrd, Drawing					No. 306
Date	Explanation	Ref.	Debit	Credit	Balance
2010					
Oct. 20		J1	500		500

Service Revenue					No. 400
Date	Explanation	Ref.	Debit	Credit	Balance
2010					
Oct. 31		J1		10,000	10,000

Salaries Expense					No. 726
Date	Explanation	Ref.	Debit	Credit	Balance
2010					
Oct. 26		J1	4,000		4,000

Rent Expense					No. 729
Date	Explanation	Ref.	Debit	Credit	Balance
2010					
Oct. 3		J1	900		900

Illustration 2-30
General ledger

THE TRIAL BALANCE

STUDY OBJECTIVE 7

Prepare a trial balance and explain its purposes.

A trial balance is a list of accounts and their balances at a given time. Customarily, companies prepare a trial balance at the end of an accounting period. They list accounts in the order in which they appear in the ledger. Debit balances appear in the left column and credit balances in the right column.

The primary purpose of a trial balance is to prove (check) that the debits equal the credits after posting. The sum of the debit balances in the trial balance should equal the sum of the credit balances. If the debits and credits do not agree, the company can use the trial balance to uncover errors in journalizing and posting. In addition, the trial balance is useful in preparing financial statements, as we will explain in the next two chapters.

The steps for preparing a trial balance are:

1. List the account titles and their balances in the appropriate debit or credit column.
2. Total the debit and credit columns.
3. Prove the equality of the two columns.

Illustration 2-31 shows the trial balance prepared from Pioneer Advertising's ledger. Note that the total debits equal the total credits.

Illustration 2-31
A trial balance

PIONEER ADVERTISING AGENCY
Trial Balance
October 31, 2010

	Debit	Credit
Cash	$15,200	
Advertising Supplies	2,500	
Prepaid Insurance	600	
Office Equipment	5,000	
Notes Payable		$ 5,000
Accounts Payable		2,500
Unearned Revenue		1,200
C. R. Byrd, Capital		10,000
C. R. Byrd, Drawing	500	
Service Revenue		10,000
Salaries Expense	4,000	
Rent Expense	900	
	$28,700	$28,700

A trial balance is a necessary checkpoint for uncovering certain types of errors. For example, if only the debit portion of a journal entry has been posted, the trial balance would bring this error to light.

Limitations of a Trial Balance

A trial balance does not guarantee freedom from recording errors, however. Numerous errors may exist even though the trial balance columns agree. For example, the trial balance may balance even when:

1. a transaction is not journalized,
2. a correct journal entry is not posted,
3. a journal entry is posted twice,
4. incorrect accounts are used in journalizing or posting, or
5. offsetting errors are made in recording the amount of a transaction.

ETHICS NOTE

An *error* is the result of an unintentional mistake; it is neither ethical nor unethical. An *irregularity* is an intentional misstatement, which *is* viewed as unethical.

As long as equal debits and credits are posted, even to the wrong account or in the wrong amount, the total debits will equal the total credits. **The trial balance does not prove that the company has recorded all transactions or that the ledger is correct.**

Locating Errors

Errors in a trial balance generally result from mathematical mistakes, incorrect postings, or simply transcribing data incorrectly. What do you do if you are faced with a trial balance that does not balance? First determine the amount of the difference between the two columns of the trial balance. After this amount is known, the following steps are often helpful:

1. If the error is $1, $10, $100, or $1,000, re-add the trial balance columns and re-compute the account balances.
2. If the error is divisible by 2, scan the trial balance to see whether a balance equal to half the error has been entered in the wrong column.
3. If the error is divisible by 9, retrace the account balances on the trial balance to see whether they are incorrectly copied from the ledger. For example, if a balance was $12 and it was listed as $21, a $9 error has been made. Reversing the order of numbers is called a **transposition error**.
4. If the error is not divisible by 2 or 9, scan the ledger to see whether an account balance in the amount of the error has been omitted from the trial balance, and scan the journal to see whether a posting of that amount has been omitted.

Use of Dollar Signs

Note that dollar signs do not appear in journals or ledgers. Dollar signs are typically used only in the trial balance and the financial statements. Generally, a dollar sign is shown only for the first item in the column and for the total of that column. A single line (a totaling rule) is placed under the column of figures to be added or subtracted. Total amounts are double-underlined to indicate they are final sums.

Insight boxes provide examples of business situations from various perspectives—ethics, investor, and international. Guideline answers are provided on the last page of the chapter.

ETHICS INSIGHT

Sarbanes-Oxley Comes to the Rescue

While most companies record transactions very carefully, the reality is that mistakes still happen: Bank regulators fined Bank One Corporation (now Chase) $1.8 million; they felt that the unreliability of the bank's accounting system caused it to violate regulatory requirements. Also, in recent years Fannie Mae, the government-chartered mortgage association, announced large accounting errors. These announcements caused investors, regulators, and politicians to fear larger, undetected problems. Finally, before a major overhaul of its accounting system, the financial records of Waste Management Company were in such disarray that of the company's 57,000 employees, 10,000 were receiving pay slips that were in error.

The Sarbanes-Oxley Act was created to minimize the occurrence of errors like these by increasing every employee's responsibility for accurate financial reporting.

? In order for these companies to prepare and issue financial statements, their accounting equations (debits and credits) must have been in balance at year-end. How could these errors or misstatements have occurred?

DO IT!

The following accounts come from the ledger of SnowGo Company at December 31, 2010.

TRIAL BALANCE

157	Equipment	$88,000	301	Roberts, Capital	$20,000
306	Roberts, Drawing	8,000	212	Salaries Payable	2,000
201	Accounts Payable	22,000	200	Notes Payable	19,000
726	Salaries Expense	42,000	722	Insurance Expense	3,000
112	Accounts Receivable	4,000	130	Prepaid Insurance	6,000
400	Service Revenue	95,000	101	Cash	7,000

Prepare a trial balance in good form.

action plan

✔ Determine normal balances and list accounts in the order they appear in the ledger.

✔ Accounts with debit balances appear in the left column, and those with credit balances in the right column.

✔ Total the debit and credit columns to prove equality.

Solution

SnowGo Company
Trial Balance
December 31, 2010

	Debit	Credit
Cash	$ 7,000	
Accounts Receivable	4,000	
Prepaid Insurance	6,000	
Equipment	88,000	
Notes Payable		$ 19,000
Accounts Payable		22,000
Salaries Payable		2,000
Roberts, Capital		20,000
Roberts, Drawing	8,000	
Service Revenue		95,000
Insurance Expense	3,000	
Salaries Expense	42,000	
	$ 158,000	$158,000

Related exercise material: **BE2-9, BE2-10, E2-9, E2-10, E2-11, E2-13, E2-14,** and DO IT! **2-4**.

✔ *The Navigator*

Be sure to read **ALL ABOUT YOU:** *Your Personal Annual Report* on page 72 for information on how topics in this chapter apply to your personal life.

Your Personal Annual Report

If you haven't already done so, in the not-too-distant future you will prepare a résumé. In some ways your résumé is like a company's annual report. Its purpose is to enable others to evaluate your past, in an effort to predict your future.

A résumé is your opportunity to create a positive first impression. It is important that it be impressive—but it should also be accurate. In order to increase their job prospects, some people are tempted to "inflate" their résumés by overstating the importance of some past accomplishments or positions. In fact, you might even think that "everybody does it" and that if you don't do it, you will be at a disadvantage.

✳ Some Facts

Before you turn your résumé into a world-class work of fiction, consider the following:

* David Edmondson, the president and CEO of well-known electronics retailer Radio Shack, overstated his accomplishments by claiming that he had earned a bachelor's of science degree, when in fact he had not. Apparently his employer had not done a background check to ensure the accuracy of his résumé.

* A chief financial officer of Veritas Software lied about having an M.B.A. from Stanford University.

* A former president of the U.S. Olympic Committee lied about having a Ph.D. from Arizona State University. When the truth was discovered, she resigned.

* The University of Notre Dame discovered that its football coach, George O'Leary, lied about his education and football history. He was forced to resign after only five days.

✳ About the Numbers

• A survey by Automatic Data Processing reported that 40% of applicants misrepresented their education or employment history.

• A survey by the Society for Human Resource Management of human resource professionals reported the following responses to the question, "*When investigating the backgrounds of job candidates, how important or unimportant is the discovery of inaccuracies in the job candidate's résumé on your decision to extend a job offer?*"

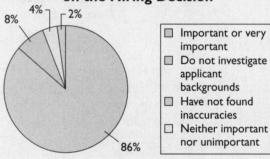

Importance of Résumé Inaccuracies on the Hiring Decision

- 8%
- 4%
- 2%
- 86%

Legend:
- ☐ Important or very important
- ☐ Do not investigate applicant backgrounds
- ☐ Have not found inaccuracies
- ☐ Neither important nor unimportant

Source: Society for Human Resource Management, press release, August 31, 2004, *http://www.shrm.org/press/ntu_published/cms_009624.asp.*

✳ What Do You Think?

Using Radio Shack as an example, what should the company have done when it learned of the falsehoods on Mr. Edmondson's résumé? Should Radio Shack have fired him?

NO: Mr. Edmondson had been a Radio Shack employee for 11 years. He had served the company in a wide variety of positions, and had earned the position of CEO through exceptional performance. While the fact that he lied 11 years earlier on his résumé was unfortunate, his service since then made this past transgression irrelevant. In addition, the company was in the midst of a massive restructuring, which included closing 700 of its 7,000 stores. It could not afford additional upheaval at this time.

YES: Radio Shack is a publicly traded company. Investors, creditors, employees, and others doing business with the company will not trust it if its leader is known to have poor integrity. The "tone at the top" is vital to creating an ethical organization.

Sources: E. White and T. Herrick, "Ethical Breaches Pose Dilemma for Boards: When to Fire a CEO?" *Wall Street Journal*, February 15, 2006; and T. Hanrahan, "Résumé Trouble," *Wall Street Journal*, March 3, 2006.

Tips on resume writing can be found at many websites, such as *http://resume.monster.com/.*

Comprehensive DO IT!

Bob Sample opened the Campus Laundromat on September 1, 2010. During the first month of operations the following transactions occurred.

Sept. 1 Bob invested $20,000 cash in the business.
2 The company paid $1,000 cash for store rent for September.
3 Purchased washers and dryers for $25,000, paying $10,000 in cash and signing a $15,000, 6-month, 12% note payable.
4 Paid $1,200 for a one-year accident insurance policy.
10 Received a bill from the *Daily News* for advertising the opening of the laundromat $200.
20 Bob withdrew $700 cash for personal use.
30 The company determined that cash receipts for laundry services for the month were $6,200.

The chart of accounts for the company is the same as that for Pioneer Advertising Agency plus the following: No. 154 Laundry Equipment, No. 610 Advertising Expense, No. 301 Bob Sample, Capital; and No. 306 Bob Sample, Drawing.

Instructions

(a) Journalize the September transactions. (Use J1 for the journal page number.)
(b) Open ledger accounts and post the September transactions.
(c) Prepare a trial balance at September 30, 2010.

action plan

✔ Make separate journal entries for each transaction.
✔ In journalizing, make sure debits equal credits.
✔ In journalizing, use specific account titles taken from the chart of accounts.
✔ Provide appropriate description of each journal entry.
✔ Arrange ledger in statement order, beginning with the balance sheet accounts.
✔ Post in chronological order.
✔ Use numbers in the reference column to indicate the amount has been posted.
✔ In the trial balance, list accounts in the order in which they appear in the ledger.
✔ List debit balances in the left column, and credit balances in the right column.

Solution to Comprehensive DO IT!

(a) GENERAL JOURNAL **J1**

Date	Account Titles and Explanation	Ref.	Debit	Credit
2010				
Sept. 1	Cash	101	20,000	
	Bob Sample, Capital	301		20,000
	(Owner's investment of cash in business)			
2	Rent Expense	729	1,000	
	Cash	101		1,000
	(Paid September rent)			
3	Laundry Equipment	154	25,000	
	Cash	101		10,000
	Notes Payable	200		15,000
	(Purchased laundry equipment for cash and 6-month, 12% note payable)			
4	Prepaid Insurance	130	1,200	
	Cash	101		1,200
	(Paid one-year insurance policy)			
10	Advertising Expense	610	200	
	Accounts Payable	201		200
	(Received bill from *Daily News* for advertising)			
20	Bob Sample, Drawing	306	700	
	Cash	101		700
	(Withdrew cash for personal use)			
30	Cash	101	6,200	
	Service Revenue	400		6,200
	(Received cash for services provided)			

(b)

GENERAL LEDGER

Cash					No. 101
Date	Explanation	Ref.	Debit	Credit	Balance
2010					
Sept. 1		J1	20,000		20,000
2		J1		1,000	19,000
3		J1		10,000	9,000
4		J1		1,200	7,800
20		J1		700	7,100
30		J1	6,200		13,300

Prepaid Insurance					No. 130
Date	Explanation	Ref.	Debit	Credit	Balance
2010					
Sept. 4		J1	1,200		1,200

Laundry Equipment					No. 154
Date	Explanation	Ref.	Debit	Credit	Balance
2010					
Sept. 3		J1	25,000		25,000

Notes Payable					No. 200
Date	Explanation	Ref.	Debit	Credit	Balance
2010					
Sept. 3		J1		15,000	15,000

Accounts Payable					No. 201
Date	Explanation	Ref.	Debit	Credit	Balance
2010					
Sept. 10		J1		200	200

Bob Sample, Capital					No. 301
Date	Explanation	Ref.	Debit	Credit	Balance
2010					
Sept. 1		J1		20,000	20,000

Bob Sample, Drawing					No. 306
Date	Explanation	Ref.	Debit	Credit	Balance
2010					
Sept. 20		J1	700		700

Service Revenue					No. 400
Date	Explanation	Ref.	Debit	Credit	Balance
2010					
Sept. 30		J1		6,200	6,200

Advertising Expense					No. 610
Date	Explanation	Ref.	Debit	Credit	Balance
2010					
Sept. 10		J1	200		200

Rent Expense					No. 729
Date	Explanation	Ref.	Debit	Credit	Balance
2010					
Sept. 2		J1	1,000		1,000

(c)

CAMPUS LAUNDROMAT
Trial Balance
September 30, 2010

	Debit	Credit
Cash	$13,300	
Prepaid Insurance	1,200	
Laundry Equipment	25,000	
Notes Payable		$15,000
Accounts Payable		200
Bob Sample, Capital		20,000
Bob Sample, Drawing	700	
Service Revenue		6,200
Advertising Expense	200	
Rent Expense	1,000	
	$41,400	$41,400

SUMMARY OF STUDY OBJECTIVES

1 Explain what an account is and how it helps in the recording process. An account is a record of increases and decreases in specific asset, liability, and owner's equity items.

2 Define debits and credits and explain their use in recording business transactions. The terms debit and credit are synonymous with left and right. Assets, drawings, and expenses are increased by debits and decreased by credits. Liabilities, owner's capital, and revenues are increased by credits and decreased by debits.

3 Identify the basic steps in the recording process. The basic steps in the recording process are: (a) analyze each transaction for its effects on the accounts, (b) enter the transaction information in a journal, (c) transfer the journal information to the appropriate accounts in the ledger.

4 Explain what a journal is and how it helps in the recording process. The initial accounting record of a transaction is entered in a journal before the data are entered in the accounts. A journal (a) discloses in one place the complete effects of a transaction, (b) provides a chronological record of transactions, and (c) prevents or locates errors because the debit and credit amounts for each entry can be easily compared.

5 Explain what a ledger is and how it helps in the recording process. The ledger is the entire group of accounts maintained by a company. The ledger keeps in one place all the information about changes in specific account balances.

6 Explain what posting is and how it helps in the recording process. Posting is the transfer of journal entries to the ledger accounts. This phase of the recording process accumulates the effects of journalized transactions in the individual accounts.

7 Prepare a trial balance and explain its purposes. A trial balance is a list of accounts and their balances at a given time. Its primary purpose is to prove the equality of debits and credits after posting. A trial balance also uncovers errors in journalizing and posting and is useful in preparing financial statements.

GLOSSARY

Account A record of increases and decreases in specific asset, liability, or owner's equity items. (p. 50).

Chart of accounts A list of accounts and the account numbers that identify their location in the ledger. (p. 60).

Compound entry A journal entry that involves three or more accounts. (p. 57).

Credit The right side of an account. (p. 51).

Debit The left side of an account. (p. 51).

Double-entry system A system that records in appropriate accounts the dual effect of each transaction. (p. 51).

General journal The most basic form of journal. (p. 55).

General ledger A ledger that contains all asset, liability, and owner's equity accounts. (p. 58).

Journal An accounting record in which transactions are initially recorded in chronological order. (p. 55).

Journalizing The entering of transaction data in the journal. (p. 56).

Ledger The entire group of accounts maintained by a company. (p. 58).

Normal balance An account balance on the side where an increase in the account is recorded. (p. 52).

Posting The procedure of transferring journal entries to the ledger accounts. (p. 59).

Simple entry A journal entry that involves only two accounts. (p. 57).

T account The basic form of an account. (p. 50).

Three-column form of account A form with columns for debit, credit, and balance amounts in an account. (p. 59).

Trial balance A list of accounts and their balances at a given time. (p. 68).

SELF-STUDY QUESTIONS

Answers are at the end of the chapter.

(SO 1) **1.** Which of the following statements about an account is true?
  a. In its simplest form, an account consists of two parts.
  b. An account is an individual accounting record of increases and decreases in specific asset, liability, and owner's equity items.
  c. There are separate accounts for specific assets and liabilities but only one account for owner's equity items.
  d. The left side of an account is the credit or decrease side.

(SO 2) **2.** Debits:
  a. increase both assets and liabilities.
  b. decrease both assets and liabilities.
  c. increase assets and decrease liabilities.
  d. decrease assets and increase liabilities.

3. A revenue account: (SO 2)
  a. is increased by debits.
  b. is decreased by credits.
  c. has a normal balance of a debit.
  d. is increased by credits.

4. Accounts that normally have debit balances are: (SO 2)
  a. assets, expenses, and revenues.
  b. assets, expenses, and owner's capital.
  c. assets, liabilities, and owner's drawings.
  d. assets, owner's drawings, and expenses.

5. The expanded accounting equation is: (SO 2)
  a. Assets + Liabilities = Owner's Capital + Owner's Drawing + Revenues + Expenses
  b. Assets = Liabilities + Owner's Capital + Owner's Drawing + Revenues − Expenses

c. Assets = Liabilities − Owner's Capital − Owner's Drawing − Revenues − Expenses
d. Assets = Liabilities + Owner's Capital − Owner's Drawing + Revenues − Expenses

(SO 3) **6.** Which of the following is *not* part of the recording process?
a. Analyzing transactions.
b. Preparing a trial balance.
c. Entering transactions in a journal.
d. Posting transactions.

(SO 4) **7.** Which of the following statements about a journal is *false*?
a. It is not a book of original entry.
b. It provides a chronological record of transactions.
c. It helps to locate errors because the debit and credit amounts for each entry can be readily compared.
d. It discloses in one place the complete effect of a transaction.

(SO 4) **8.** The purchase of supplies on account should result in:
a. a debit to Supplies Expense and a credit to Cash.
b. a debit to Supplies Expense and a credit to Accounts Payable.
c. a debit to Supplies and a credit to Accounts Payable.
d. a debit to Supplies and a credit to Accounts Receivable.

(SO 5) **9.** The order of the accounts in the ledger is:
a. assets, revenues, expenses, liabilities, owner's capital, owner's drawing.
b. assets, liabilities, owner's capital, owner's drawing, revenues, expenses.
c. owner's capital, assets, revenues, expenses, liabilities, owner's drawing.
d. revenues, assets, expenses, liabilities, owner's capital, owner's drawing.

(SO 5) **10.** A ledger:
a. contains only asset and liability accounts.
b. should show accounts in alphabetical order.
c. is a collection of the entire group of accounts maintained by a company.
d. is a book of original entry.

(SO 6) **11.** Posting:
a. normally occurs before journalizing.
b. transfers ledger transaction data to the journal.
c. is an optional step in the recording process.
d. transfers journal entries to ledger accounts.

(SO 6) **12.** Before posting a payment of $5,000, the Accounts Payable of Senator Company had a normal balance of $16,000. The balance after posting this transaction was:
a. $21,000.
b. $5,000.
c. $11,000.
d. Cannot be determined.

(SO 7) **13.** A trial balance:
a. is a list of accounts with their balances at a given time.
b. proves the mathematical accuracy of journalized transactions.
c. will not balance if a correct journal entry is posted twice.
d. proves that all transactions have been recorded.

(SO 7) **14.** A trial balance will not balance if:
a. a correct journal entry is posted twice.
b. the purchase of supplies on account is debited to Supplies and credited to Cash.
c. a $100 cash drawing by the owner is debited to Owner's Drawing for $1,000 and credited to Cash for $100.
d. a $450 payment on account is debited to Accounts Payable for $45 and credited to Cash for $45.

(SO 7) **15.** The trial balance of Clooney Company had accounts with the following normal balances: Cash $5,000, Revenue $85,000, Salaries Payable $4,000, Salaries Expense $40,000, Rent Expense $10,000, Clooney, Capital $42,000; Clooney, Drawing $15,000; Equipment $61,000. In preparing a trial balance, the total in the debit column is:
a. $131,000.
c. $91,000.
b. $216,000.
d. $116,000.

Go to the book's companion website, **www.wiley.com/college/ weygandt**, for Additional Self-Study questions.

QUESTIONS

1. Describe the parts of a T account.
2. "The terms *debit* and *credit* mean increase and decrease, respectively." Do you agree? Explain.
3. Jeff Hiller, a fellow student, contends that the double-entry system means each transaction must be recorded twice. Is Jeff correct? Explain.
4. Maria Alvarez, a beginning accounting student, believes debit balances are favorable and credit balances are unfavorable. Is Maria correct? Discuss.
5. State the rules of debit and credit as applied to (a) asset accounts, (b) liability accounts, and (c) the owner's equity accounts (revenue, expenses, owner's drawing, and owner's capital).
6. What is the normal balance for each of the following accounts? (a) Accounts Receivable. (b) Cash. (c) Owner's Drawing. (d) Accounts Payable. (e) Service Revenue. (f) Salaries Expense. (g) Owner's Capital.

7. Indicate whether each of the following accounts is an asset, a liability, or an owner's equity account and whether it has a normal debit or credit balance: (a) Accounts Receivable, (b) Accounts Payable, (c) Equipment, (d) Owner's Drawing, (e) Supplies.
8. For the following transactions, indicate the account debited and the account credited.
(a) Supplies are purchased on account.
(b) Cash is received on signing a note payable.
(c) Employees are paid salaries in cash.
9. Indicate whether the following accounts generally will have (a) debit entries only, (b) credit entries only, or (c) both debit and credit entries.
(1) Cash. **(4)** Accounts Payable.
(2) Accounts Receivable. **(5)** Salaries Expense.
(3) Owner's Drawing. **(6)** Service Revenue.
10. What are the basic steps in the recording process?

11. What are the advantages of using a journal in the recording process?

12. (a) When entering a transaction in the journal, should the debit or credit be written first?
    (b) Which should be indented, the debit or credit?

13. Describe a compound entry, and provide an example.

14. (a) Should business transaction debits and credits be recorded directly in the ledger accounts?
    (b) What are the advantages of first recording transactions in the journal and then posting to the ledger?

15. The account number is entered as the last step in posting the amounts from the journal to the ledger. What is the advantage of this step?

16. Journalize the following business transactions.
    (a) Hector Molina invests $9,000 cash in the business.
    (b) Insurance of $800 is paid for the year.
    (c) Supplies of $2,000 are purchased on account.
    (d) Cash of $7,500 is received for services rendered.

17. (a) What is a ledger?
    (b) What is a chart of accounts and why is it important?

18. What is a trial balance and what are its purposes?

19. Jim Benes is confused about how accounting information flows through the accounting system. He believes the flow of information is as follows.
    (a) Debits and credits posted to the ledger.
    (b) Business transaction occurs.
    (c) Information entered in the journal.
    (d) Financial statements are prepared.
    (e) Trial balance is prepared.

    Is Jim correct? If not, indicate to Jim the proper flow of the information.

20. Two students are discussing the use of a trial balance. They wonder whether the following errors, each considered separately, would prevent the trial balance from balancing.
    (a) The bookkeeper debited Cash for $600 and credited Wages Expense for $600 for payment of wages.
    (b) Cash collected on account was debited to Cash for $900 and Service Revenue was credited for $90.

    What would you tell them?

21. **PEPSICO** What are the normal balances for PepsiCo's Cash, Accounts Payable, and Interest Expense accounts?

BRIEF EXERCISES

BE2-1 For each of the following accounts indicate the effects of (a) a debit and (b) a credit on the accounts and (c) the normal balance of the account.

1. Accounts Payable.
2. Advertising Expense.
3. Service Revenue.
4. Accounts Receivable.
5. A. J. Ritter, Capital.
6. A. J. Ritter, Drawing.

Indicate debit and credit effects and normal balance.

(SO 2)

BE2-2 Transactions for the Hank Norris Company for the month of June are presented below. Identify the accounts to be debited and credited for each transaction.

June 1 Hank Norris invests $5,000 cash in a small welding business of which he is the sole proprietor.
      2 Purchases equipment on account for $900.
      3 $800 cash is paid to landlord for June rent.
     12 Bills J. Kronsnoble $300 for welding work done on account.

Identify accounts to be debited and credited.

(SO 2)

BE2-3 Using the data in BE2-2, journalize the transactions. (You may omit explanations.)

Journalize transactions.

(SO 4)

BE2-4 ━━━━▶ Tom Oslow, a fellow student, is unclear about the basic steps in the recording process. Identify and briefly explain the steps in the order in which they occur.

Identify and explain steps in recording process.

(SO 3)

BE2-5 T. J. Carlin has the following transactions during August of the current year. Indicate (a) the effect on the accounting equation and (b) the debit-credit analysis illustrated on pages 61–66 of the text.

Aug. 1 Opens an office as a financial advisor, investing $8,000 in cash.
      4 Pays insurance in advance for 6 months, $1,800 cash.
     16 Receives $800 from clients for services provided.
     27 Pays secretary $1,000 salary.

Indicate basic and debit-credit analysis.

(SO 2)

BE2-6 Using the data in BE2-5, journalize the transactions. (You may omit explanations.)

Journalize transactions.

(SO 4)

Post journal entries to T accounts.

(SO 6)

BE2-7   Selected transactions for the Finney Company are presented in journal form below. Post the transactions to T accounts. Make one T account for each item and determine each account's ending balance.

J1

Date	Account Titles and Explanation	Ref.	Debit	Credit
May 5	Accounts Receivable		5,000	
	Service Revenue			5,000
	(Billed for services provided)			
12	Cash		2,400	
	Accounts Receivable			2,400
	(Received cash in payment of account)			
15	Cash		3,000	
	Service Revenue			3,000
	(Received cash for services provided)			

Post journal entries to standard form of account.

(SO 6)

BE2-8   Selected journal entries for the Finney Company are presented in BE2-7. Post the transactions using the standard form of account.

Prepare a trial balance.

(SO 7)

BE2-9   From the ledger balances given below, prepare a trial balance for the Cleland Company at June 30, 2010. List the accounts in the order shown on page 61 of the text. All account balances are normal.

    Accounts Payable $9,000, Cash $8,800, Cleland, Capital $20,000; Cleland, Drawing $1,200; Equipment $17,000, Service Revenue $8,000, Accounts Receivable $3,000, Salaries Expense $6,000, and Rent Expense $1,000.

Prepare a correct trial balance.

(SO 7)

BE2-10   An inexperienced bookkeeper prepared the following trial balance. Prepare a correct trial balance, assuming all account balances are normal.

KWUN COMPANY
Trial Balance
December 31, 2010

	Debit	Credit
Cash	$14,800	
Prepaid Insurance		$3,500
Accounts Payable		3,000
Unearned Revenue	2,200	
P. Kwun, Capital		13,000
P. Kwun, Drawing		4,500
Service Revenue		25,600
Salaries Expense	18,600	
Rent Expense		2,400
	$35,600	$52,000

DO IT! REVIEW

Identify normal balances.

(SO 2)

DO IT! 2-1   Josh Borke has just rented space in a strip mall. In this space, he will open a photography studio, to be called "Picture This!" A friend has advised Josh to set up a double-entry set of accounting records in which to record all of his business transactions.

    Identify the balance sheet accounts that Josh will likely need to record the transactions needed to open his business. Indicate whether the normal balance of each account is a debit or credit.

Record business activities.

(SO 4)

DO IT! 2-2   Josh Borke engaged in the following activities in establishing his photography studio, Picture This!:

1. Opened a bank account in the name of Picture This! and deposited $8,000 of his own money into this account as his initial investment.
2. Purchased photography supplies at a total cost of $1,100. The business paid $400 in cash and the balance is on account.
3. Obtained estimates on the cost of photography equipment from three different manufacturers.

In what form (type of record) should Josh record these three activities? Prepare the entries to record the transactions.

DO IT! 2-3 Josh Borke recorded the following transactions during the month of April.

Post transactions.

(SO 6)

April 3	Cash	3,400	
	Photography Revenue		3,400
April 16	Rent Expense	600	
	Cash		600
April 20	Salaries Expense	300	
	Cash		300

Post these entries to the Cash T-account of the general ledger to determine the ending balance in cash. The beginning balance in cash on April 1 was $1,600.

DO IT! 2-4 The following accounts are taken from the ledger of Boardin' Company at December 31, 2010.

Prepare a trial balance.

(SO 7)

200	Notes Payable	$20,000		100	Cash	$ 6,000
300	Hawk, Capital	25,000		120	Supplies	5,000
150	Equipment	80,000		522	Supplies Expense	2,000
310	Hawk, Drawing	8,000		220	Salaries Payable	3,000
726	Salaries Expense	38,000		201	Accounts Payable	11,000
400	Service Revenue	88,000		110	Accounts Receivable	8,000

Prepare a trial balance in good form.

EXERCISES

E2-1 Josh Cephus has prepared the following list of statements about accounts.

Analyze statements about accounting and the recording process.

(SO 1)

1. An account is an accounting record of either a specific asset or a specific liability.
2. An account shows only increases, not decreases, in the item it relates to.
3. Some items, such as Cash and Accounts Receivable, are combined into one account.
4. An account has a left, or credit side, and a right, or debit side.
5. A simple form of an account consisting of just the account title, the left side, and the right side, is called a T-account.

Instructions
Identify each statement as true or false. If false, indicate how to correct the statement.

E2-2 Selected transactions for D. Reyes, an interior decorator, in her first month of business, are as follows.

Identify debits, credits, and normal balances.

(SO 2)

Jan. 2 Invested $10,000 cash in business.
3 Purchased used car for $4,000 cash for use in business.
9 Purchased supplies on account for $500.
11 Billed customers $1,800 for services performed.
16 Paid $200 cash for advertising.
20 Received $700 cash from customers billed on January 11.
23 Paid creditor $300 cash on balance owed.
28 Withdrew $1,000 cash for personal use by owner.

Instructions
For each transaction indicate the following.

(a) The basic type of account debited and credited (asset, liability, owner's equity).
(b) The specific account debited and credited (cash, rent expense, service revenue, etc.).
(c) Whether the specific account is increased or decreased.
(d) The normal balance of the specific account.

Use the following format, in which the January 2 transaction is given as an example.

	Account Debited				Account Credited			
	(a)	**(b)**	**(c)**	**(d)**	**(a)**	**(b)**	**(c)**	**(d)**
	Basic	**Specific**		**Normal**	**Basic**	**Specific**		**Normal**
Date	**Type**	**Account**	**Effect**	**Balance**	**Type**	**Account**	**Effect**	**Balance**
Jan. 2	Asset	Cash	Increase	Debit	Owner's Equity	D. Reyes, Capital	Increase	Credit

Journalize transactions.
(SO 4)

E2-3 Data for D. Reyes, interior decorator, are presented in E2-2.

Instructions
Journalize the transactions using journal page J1. (You may omit explanations.)

Analyze transactions and determine their effect on accounts.
(SO 2)

E2-4 Presented below is information related to Hanshew Real Estate Agency.

Oct. 1 Pete Hanshew begins business as a real estate agent with a cash investment of $15,000.
  2 Hires an administrative assistant.
  3 Purchases office furniture for $1,900, on account.
  6 Sells a house and lot for B. Kidman; bills B. Kidman $3,200 for realty services provided.
  27 Pays $700 on the balance related to the transaction of October 3.
  30 Pays the administrative assistant $2,500 in salary for October.

Instructions
Prepare the debit-credit analysis for each transaction as illustrated on pages 61–66.

Journalize transactions.
(SO 4)

E2-5 Transaction data for Hanshew Real Estate Agency are presented in E2-4.

Instructions
Journalize the transactions. (You may omit explanations.)

Analyze transactions and journalize.
(SO 2, 3, 4)

E2-6 Konerko Industries had the following transactions.

1. Borrowed $5,000 from the bank by signing a note.
2. Paid $2,500 cash for a computer.
3. Purchased $700 of supplies on account.

Instructions
(a) Indicate what accounts are increased and decreased by each transaction.
(b) Journalize each transaction. (Omit explanations.)

Analyze transactions and journalize.
(SO 2, 3, 4)

E2-7 Rowand Enterprises had the following selected transactions.

1. Aaron Rowand invested $4,000 cash in the business.
2. Paid office rent of $1,100.
3. Performed consulting services and billed a client $5,200.
4. Aaron Rowand withdrew $700 cash for personal use.

Instructions
(a) Indicate the effect each transaction has on the accounting equation (Assets = Liabilities + Owner's Equity), using plus and minus signs.
(b) Journalize each transaction. (Omit explanations.)

Analyze statements about the ledger.
(SO 5)

E2-8 Josie Feeney has prepared the following list of statements about the general ledger.

1. The general ledger contains all the asset and liability accounts, but no owner's equity accounts.
2. The general ledger is sometimes referred to as simply the ledger.
3. The accounts in the general ledger are arranged in alphabetical order.
4. Each account in the general ledger is numbered for easier identification.
5. The general ledger is a book of original entry.

Instructions
Identify each statement as true or false. If false, indicate how to correct the statement.

Post journal entries and prepare a trial balance.

(SO 6, 7)

E2-9 Selected transactions from the journal of Teresa Gonzalez, investment broker, are presented below.

Date	Account Titles and Explanation	Ref.	Debit	Credit
Aug. 1	Cash		5,000	
	Teresa Gonzalez, Capital			5,000
	(Owner's investment of cash in business)			
10	Cash		2,400	
	Service Revenue			2,400
	(Received cash for services provided)			
12	Office Equipment		5,000	
	Cash			1,000
	Notes Payable			4,000
	(Purchased office equipment for cash and notes payable)			
25	Accounts Receivable		1,600	
	Service Revenue			1,600
	(Billed clients for services provided)			
31	Cash		900	
	Accounts Receivable			900
	(Receipt of cash on account)			

Instructions
(a) Post the transactions to T accounts.
(b) Prepare a trial balance at August 31, 2010.

Journalize transactions from account data and prepare a trial balance.

(SO 4, 7)

E2-10 The T accounts below summarize the ledger of Simon Landscaping Company at the end of the first month of operations.

Cash No. 101
4/1	15,000	4/15	600
4/12	900	4/25	1,500
4/29	400		
4/30	1,000		

Unearned Revenue No. 205
		4/30	1,000

Accounts Receivable No. 112
4/7	3,200	4/29	400

J. Simon, Capital No. 301
		4/1	15,000

Supplies No. 126
4/4	1,800		

Service Revenue No. 400
		4/7	3,200
		4/12	900

Accounts Payable No. 201
4/25	1,500	4/4	1,800

Salaries Expense No. 726
4/15	600		

Instructions
(a) Prepare the complete general journal (including explanations) from which the postings to Cash were made.
(b) Prepare a trial balance at April 30, 2010.

Journalize transactions from account data and prepare a trial balance.

(SO 4, 7)

E2-11 Presented below and on the next page is the ledger for Heerey Co.

Cash No. 101
10/1	5,000	10/4	400
10/10	650	10/12	1,500
10/10	4,000	10/15	250
10/20	500	10/30	300
10/25	2,000	10/31	500

Heerey, Capital No. 301
		10/1	5,000
		10/25	2,000

Heerey, Drawing No. 306
10/30	300		

	Accounts Receivable	**No. 112**		**Service Revenue**	**No. 407**
10/6	800	10/20	500		10/6	800
10/20	940				10/10	650
					10/20	940

	Supplies	**No. 126**		**Store Wages Expense**	**No. 628**
10/4	400			10/31	500

	Furniture	**No. 149**		**Rent Expense**	**No. 729**
10/3	2,000			10/15	250

	Notes Payable	**No. 200**
	10/10	4,000

	Accounts Payable	**No. 201**
10/12	1,500	10/3	2,000

Instructions

(a) Reproduce the journal entries for the transactions that occurred on October 1, 10, and 20, and provide explanations for each.

(b) Determine the October 31 balance for each of the accounts above, and prepare a trial balance at October 31, 2010.

Prepare journal entries and post using standard account form.

(SO 4, 6)

E2-12 Selected transactions for Tina Cordero Company during its first month in business are presented below.

Sept.	1	Invested $10,000 cash in the business.
	5	Purchased equipment for $12,000 paying $5,000 in cash and the balance on account.
	25	Paid $3,000 cash on balance owed for equipment.
	30	Withdrew $500 cash for personal use.

Cordero's chart of accounts shows: No. 101 Cash, No. 157 Equipment, No. 201 Accounts Payable, No. 301 Tina Cordero, Capital; No. 306 Tina Cordero, Drawing.

Instructions

(a) Journalize the transactions on page J1 of the journal. (Omit explanations.)
(b) Post the transactions using the standard account form.

Analyze errors and their effects on trial balance.

(SO 7)

E2-13 The bookkeeper for Sam Kaplin Equipment Repair made a number of errors in journalizing and posting, as described below.

1. A credit posting of $400 to Accounts Receivable was omitted.
2. A debit posting of $750 for Prepaid Insurance was debited to Insurance Expense.
3. A collection from a customer of $100 in payment of its account owed was journalized and posted as a debit to Cash $100 and a credit to Service Revenue $100.
4. A credit posting of $300 to Property Taxes Payable was made twice.
5. A cash purchase of supplies for $250 was journalized and posted as a debit to Supplies $25 and a credit to Cash $25.
6. A debit of $475 to Advertising Expense was posted as $457.

Instructions

For each error:

(a) Indicate whether the trial balance will balance.
(b) If the trial balance will not balance, indicate the amount of the difference.
(c) Indicate the trial balance column that will have the larger total.

Consider each error separately. Use the following form, in which error (1) is given as an example.

Error	(a) In Balance	(b) Difference	(c) Larger Column
(1)	No	$400	debit

E2-14 The accounts in the ledger of Sanford Delivery Service contain the following balances on July 31, 2010.

Prepare a trial balance.
(SO 2, 7)

Accounts Receivable	$ 7,642	Prepaid Insurance	$1,968
Accounts Payable	8,396	Repair Expense	961
Cash	?	Service Revenue	10,610
Delivery Equipment	49,360	Sanford, Drawing	700
Gas and Oil Expense	758	Sanford, Capital	44,636
Insurance Expense	523	Salaries Expense	4,428
Notes Payable	18,450	Salaries Payable	815

Instructions
Prepare a trial balance with the accounts arranged as illustrated in the chapter and fill in the missing amount for Cash.

EXERCISES: SET B

Visit the book's companion website at **www.wiley.com/college/weygandt**, and choose the Student Companion site, to access Exercise Set B.

PROBLEMS: SET A

P2-1A Frontier Park was started on April 1 by C. J. Mendez. The following selected events and transactions occurred during April.

Journalize a series of transactions.
(SO 2, 4)

Apr. 1 Mendez invested $40,000 cash in the business.
  4 Purchased land costing $30,000 for cash.
  8 Incurred advertising expense of $1,800 on account.
  11 Paid salaries to employees $1,500.
  12 Hired park manager at a salary of $4,000 per month, effective May 1.
  13 Paid $1,500 cash for a one-year insurance policy.
  17 Withdrew $1,000 cash for personal use.
  20 Received $5,700 in cash for admission fees.
  25 Sold 100 coupon books for $25 each. Each book contains 10 coupons that entitle the holder to one admission to the park.
  30 Received $8,900 in cash admission fees.
  30 Paid $900 on balance owed for advertising incurred on April 8.

Mendez uses the following accounts: Cash, Prepaid Insurance, Land, Accounts Payable, Unearned Admission Revenue, C. J. Mendez, Capital; C. J. Mendez, Drawing; Admission Revenue, Advertising Expense, and Salaries Expense.

Instructions
Journalize the April transactions.

P2-2A Jane Kent is a licensed CPA. During the first month of operations of her business, the following events and transactions occurred.

Journalize transactions, post, and prepare a trial balance.
(SO 2, 4, 6, 7)

May 1 Kent invested $25,000 cash.
  2 Hired a secretary-receptionist at a salary of $2,000 per month.
  3 Purchased $2,500 of supplies on account from Read Supply Company.
  7 Paid office rent of $900 cash for the month.
  11 Completed a tax assignment and billed client $2,100 for services provided.
  12 Received $3,500 advance on a management consulting engagement.
  17 Received cash of $1,200 for services completed for H. Arnold Co.
  31 Paid secretary-receptionist $2,000 salary for the month.
  31 Paid 40% of balance due Read Supply Company.

Jane uses the following chart of accounts: No. 101 Cash, No. 112 Accounts Receivable, No. 126 Supplies, No. 201 Accounts Payable, No. 205 Unearned Revenue, No. 301 Jane Kent, Capital; No. 400 Service Revenue, No. 726 Salaries Expense, and No. 729 Rent Expense.

Trial balance totals $33,300

Instructions
(a) Journalize the transactions.
(b) Post to the ledger accounts.
(c) Prepare a trial balance on May 31, 2010.

*Journalize and post transactions
and prepare a trial balance.*

(SO 2, 4, 6, 7)

P2-3A   Jack Shellenkamp owns and manages a computer repair service, which had the following trial balance on December 31, 2009 (the end of its fiscal year).

BYTE REPAIR SERVICE
Trial Balance
December 31, 2009

Cash	$ 8,000	
Accounts Receivable	15,000	
Parts Inventory	13,000	
Prepaid Rent	3,000	
Shop Equipment	21,000	
Accounts Payable		$19,000
Jack Shellenkamp, Capital		41,000
	$60,000	$60,000

Summarized transactions for January 2010 were as follows:

1. Advertising costs, paid in cash, $1,000.
2. Additional repair parts inventory acquired on account $4,000.
3. Miscellaneous expenses, paid in cash, $2,000.
4. Cash collected from customers in payment of accounts receivable $14,000.
5. Cash paid to creditors for accounts payable due $15,000.
6. Repair parts used during January $4,000. (*Hint:* Debit this to Repair Parts Expense.)
7. Repair services performed during January: for cash $6,000; on account $9,000.
8. Wages for January, paid in cash, $3,000.
9. Jack's drawings during January were $3,000.

Instructions
(a) Open T accounts for each of the accounts listed in the trial balance, and enter the opening balances for 2010.
(b) Prepare journal entries to record each of the January transactions. (Omit explanations.)
(c) Post the journal entries to the accounts in the ledger. (Add accounts as needed.)
(d) Prepare a trial balance as of January 31, 2010.

Trial balance totals $64,000

Prepare a correct trial balance.

(SO 7)

P2-4A   The trial balance of the Sterling Company shown below does not balance.

STERLING COMPANY
Trial Balance
May 31, 2010

	Debit	Credit
Cash	$5,850	
Accounts Receivable		$2,750
Prepaid Insurance	700	
Equipment	8,000	
Accounts Payable		4,500
Property Taxes Payable	560	
M. Sterling, Capital		11,700
Service Revenue	6,690	
Salaries Expense	4,200	
Advertising Expense		1,100
Property Tax Expense	800	
	$26,800	$20,050

Your review of the ledger reveals that each account has a normal balance. You also discover the following errors (shown on page 85).

1. The totals of the debit sides of Prepaid Insurance, Accounts Payable, and Property Tax Expense were each understated $100.
2. Transposition errors were made in Accounts Receivable and Service Revenue. Based on postings made, the correct balances were $2,570 and $6,960, respectively.
3. A debit posting to Salaries Expense of $200 was omitted.
4. A $1,000 cash drawing by the owner was debited to M. Sterling, Capital for $1,000 and credited to Cash for $1,000.
5. A $520 purchase of supplies on account was debited to Equipment for $520 and credited to Cash for $520.
6. A cash payment of $450 for advertising was debited to Advertising Expense for $45 and credited to Cash for $45.
7. A collection from a customer for $210 was debited to Cash for $210 and credited to Accounts Payable for $210.

Instructions

Prepare a correct trial balance. Note that the chart of accounts includes the following: M. Sterling, Drawing; and Supplies. (*Hint:* It helps to prepare the correct journal entry for the transaction described and compare it to the mistake made.)

Trial balance totals $24,930

P2-5A The Lake Theater is owned by Tony Carpino. All facilities were completed on March 31. At this time, the ledger showed: No. 101 Cash $6,000, No. 140 Land $10,000, No. 145 Buildings (concession stand, projection room, ticket booth, and screen) $8,000, No. 157 Equipment $6,000, No. 201 Accounts Payable $2,000, No. 275 Mortgage Payable $8,000, and No. 301 Tony Carpino, Capital $20,000. During April, the following events and transactions occurred.

Journalize transactions, post, and prepare a trial balance.

(SO 2, 4, 6, 7)

Peachtree

Apr. 2 Paid film rental of $800 on first movie.
    3 Ordered two additional films at $1,000 each.
    9 Received $2,800 cash from admissions.
   10 Made $2,000 payment on mortgage and $1,000 for accounts payable due.
   11 Lake Theater contracted with R. Wynns Company to operate the concession stand. Wynns is to pay 17% of gross concession receipts (payable monthly) for the right to operate the concession stand.
   12 Paid advertising expenses $500.
   20 Received one of the films ordered on April 3 and was billed $1,000. The film will be shown in April.
   25 Received $5,200 cash from admissions.
   29 Paid salaries $2,000.
   30 Received statement from R. Wynns showing gross concession receipts of $1,000 and the balance due to The Lake Theater of $170 ($1,000 × 17%) for April. Wynns paid one-half of the balance due and will remit the remainder on May 5.
   30 Prepaid $900 rental on special film to be run in May.

In addition to the accounts identified above, the chart of accounts shows: No. 112 Accounts Receivable, No. 136 Prepaid Rentals, No. 405 Admission Revenue, No. 406 Concession Revenue, No. 610 Advertising Expense, No. 632 Film Rental Expense, and No. 726 Salaries Expense.

Instructions

(a) Enter the beginning balances in the ledger as of April 1. Insert a check mark (✓) in the reference column of the ledger for the beginning balance.
(b) Journalize the April transactions.
(c) Post the April journal entries to the ledger. Assume that all entries are posted from page 1 of the journal.
(d) Prepare a trial balance on April 30, 2010.

Trial balance totals $36,170

PROBLEMS: SET B

P2-1B Hyzer Disc Golf Course was opened on March 1 by Barry Schultz. The following selected events and transactions occurred during March:

Journalize a series of transactions.

(SO 2, 4)

Mar. 1 Invested $20,000 cash in the business.
    3 Purchased Heeren's Golf Land for $15,000 cash. The price consists of land $12,000, shed $2,000, and equipment $1,000. (Make one compound entry.)

5   Advertised the opening of the driving range and miniature golf course, paying advertising expenses of $700.
6   Paid cash $600 for a one-year insurance policy.
10   Purchased golf discs and other equipment for $1,050 from Innova Company payable in 30 days.
18   Received $340 in cash for golf fees earned.
19   Sold 100 coupon books for $10 each. Each book contains 4 coupons that enable the holder to play one round of disc golf.
25   Withdrew $800 cash for personal use.
30   Paid salaries of $250.
30   Paid Innova Company in full.
31   Received $200 cash for fees earned.

Barry Schultz uses the following accounts: Cash, Prepaid Insurance, Land, Buildings, Equipment, Accounts Payable, Unearned Revenue, B. Schultz, Capital; B. Schultz, Drawing; Golf Revenue, Advertising Expense, and Salaries Expense.

Instructions
Journalize the March transactions.

Journalize transactions, post, and prepare a trial balance.

(SO 2, 4, 6, 7)

P2-2B   Maria Juarez is a licensed dentist. During the first month of the operation of her business, the following events and transactions occurred.

April   1   Invested $40,000 cash.
1   Hired a secretary-receptionist at a salary of $600 per week payable monthly.
2   Paid office rent for the month $1,000.
3   Purchased dental supplies on account from Smile Company $4,000.
10   Provided dental services and billed insurance companies $5,100.
11   Received $1,000 cash advance from Trudy Borke for an implant.
20   Received $2,100 cash for services completed and delivered to John Stanley.
30   Paid secretary-receptionist for the month $2,400.
30   Paid $1,600 to Smile Company for accounts payable due.

Maria uses the following chart of accounts: No. 101 Cash, No. 112 Accounts Receivable, No. 126 Supplies, No. 201 Accounts Payable, No. 205 Unearned Revenue, No. 301 Maria Juarez, Capital; No. 400 Service Revenue, No. 726 Salaries Expense, and No. 729 Rent Expense.

Instructions

Trial balance totals $50,600

(a) Journalize the transactions.
(b) Post to the ledger accounts.
(c) Prepare a trial balance on April 30, 2010.

Journalize transactions, post, and prepare a trial balance.

(SO 2, 4, 6, 7)

P2-3B   Slowhand Services was formed on May 1, 2010. The following transactions took place during the first month.

Transactions on May 1:

1. Eric Clapton invested $50,000 cash in the company, as its sole owner.
2. Hired two employees to work in the warehouse. They will each be paid a salary of $2,800 per month.
3. Signed a 2-year rental agreement on a warehouse; paid $24,000 cash in advance for the first year.
4. Purchased furniture and equipment costing $30,000. A cash payment of $10,000 was made immediately; the remainder will be paid in 6 months.
5. Paid $1,800 cash for a one-year insurance policy on the furniture and equipment.

Transactions during the remainder of the month:

6. Purchased basic office supplies for $500 cash.
7. Purchased more office supplies for $1,500 on account.
8. Total revenues earned were $20,000—$8,000 cash and $12,000 on account.
9. Paid $400 to suppliers for accounts payable due.
10. Received $3,000 from customers in payment of accounts receivable.
11. Received utility bills in the amount of $200, to be paid next month.
12. Paid the monthly salaries of the two employees, totalling $5,600.

Instructions

Trial balance totals $91,300

(a) Prepare journal entries to record each of the events listed. (Omit explanations.)

(b) Post the journal entries to T accounts.
(c) Prepare a trial balance as of May 31, 2010.

P2-4B   The trial balance of Syed Moiz Co. shown below does not balance.

Prepare a correct trial balance.
(SO 7)

SYED MOIZ CO.
Trial Balance
June 30, 2010

	Debit	Credit
Cash		$ 3,340
Accounts Receivable	$ 2,731	
Supplies	1,200	
Equipment	2,600	
Accounts Payable		3,666
Unearned Revenue	1,100	
S. Moiz, Capital		8,000
S. Moiz, Drawing	800	
Service Revenue		2,480
Salaries Expense	3,200	
Office Expense	810	
	$12,441	$17,486

Each of the listed accounts has a normal balance per the general ledger. An examination of the ledger and journal reveals the following errors.

1. Cash received from a customer in payment of its account was debited for $480, and Accounts Receivable was credited for the same amount. The actual collection was for $840.
2. The purchase of a computer on account for $620 was recorded as a debit to Supplies for $620 and a credit to Accounts Payable for $620.
3. Services were performed on account for a client for $890. Accounts Receivable was debited for $890, and Service Revenue was credited for $89.
4. A debit posting to Salaries Expense of $700 was omitted.
5. A payment of a balance due for $306 was credited to Cash for $306 and credited to Accounts Payable for $360.
6. The withdrawal of $600 cash for Moiz's personal use was debited to Salaries Expense for $600 and credited to Cash for $600.

Instructions
Prepare a correct trial balance. (*Hint:* It helps to prepare the correct journal entry for the transaction described and compare it to the mistake made).

Trial balance totals $15,381

P2-5B   The Josie Theater, owned by Josie Micheals, will begin operations in March. The Josie will be unique in that it will show only triple features of sequential theme movies. As of March 1, the ledger of Josie showed: No. 101 Cash $9,000, No. 140 Land $24,000, No. 145 Buildings (concession stand, projection room, ticket booth, and screen) $10,000, No. 157 Equipment $10,000, No. 201 Accounts Payable $7,000, and No. 301 J. Micheals, Capital $46,000. During the month of March the following events and transactions occurred.

Journalize transactions, post, and prepare a trial balance.
(SO 2, 4, 6, 7)
 GLS

Mar. 2   Rented the three Indiana Jones movies to be shown for the first 3 weeks of March. The film rental was $3,500; $1,500 was paid in cash and $2,000 will be paid on March 10.
  3   Ordered the *Lord of the Rings* movies to be shown the last 10 days of March. It will cost $200 per night.
  9   Received $4,000 cash from admissions.
  10   Paid balance due on Indiana Jones movies rental and $2,100 on March 1 accounts payable.
  11   Josie Theater contracted with Stephanie Becker to operate the concession stand. Becker is to pay 15% of gross concession receipts (payable monthly) for the right to operate the concession stand.
  12   Paid advertising expenses $450.
  20   Received $5,000 cash from customers for admissions.

20 Received the *Lord of Rings* movies and paid the rental fee of $2,000.

31 Paid salaries of $2,500.

31 Received statement from Stephanie Becker showing gross receipts from concessions of $6,000 and the balance due to Josie Theater of $900 ($6,000 × 15%) for March. Becker paid one-half the balance due and will remit the remainder on April 5.

31 Received $9,000 cash from customers for admissions.

In addition to the accounts identified above, the chart of accounts includes: No. 112 Accounts Receivable, No. 405 Admission Revenue, No. 406 Concession Revenue, No. 610 Advertising Expense, No. 632 Film Rental Expense, and No. 726 Salaries Expense.

Instructions

(a) Enter the beginning balances in the ledger. Insert a check mark (✓) in the reference column of the ledger for the beginning balance.

(b) Journalize the March transactions.

(c) Post the March journal entries to the ledger. Assume that all entries are posted from page 1 of the journal.

Trial balance totals $69,800

(d) Prepare a trial balance on March 31, 2010.

PROBLEMS: SET C

Visit the book's companion website at **www.wiley.com/college/weygandt**, and choose the Student Companion site, to access Problem Set C.

CONTINUING COOKIE CHRONICLE

(*Note*: This is a continuation of the Cookie Chronicle from Chapter 1.)

CCC2 After researching the different forms of business organization, Natalie Koebel decides to operate "Cookie Creations" as a proprietorship. She then starts the process of getting the business running.

Go to the book's companion website,
www.wiley.com/college/weygandt,
to see the completion of this problem.

BROADENING YOUR PERSPECTIVE

FINANCIAL REPORTING AND ANALYSIS

Financial Reporting Problem: PepsiCo, Inc.

BYP2-1 The financial statements of PepsiCo, Inc. are presented in Appendix A. The notes accompanying the statements contain the following selected accounts, stated in millions of dollars.

Accounts Payable   Income Taxes Payable
Accounts Receivable   Interest Expense
Property, Plant, and Equipment   Inventory

Instructions

(a) Answer the following questions.

(1) What is the increase and decrease side for each account?

(2) What is the normal balance for each account?

(b) Identify the probable other account in the transaction and the effect on that account when:

(1) Accounts Receivable is decreased.

(2) Accounts Payable is decreased.

(3) Inventory is increased.

(c) Identify the other account(s) that ordinarily would be involved when:
   (1) Interest Expense is increased.
   (2) Property, Plant, and Equipment is increased.

Comparative Analysis Problem: PepsiCo, Inc. vs. The Coca-Cola Company

BYP2-2   PepsiCo's financial statements are presented in Appendix A. Financial statements of The Coca-Cola Company are presented in Appendix B.

Instructions

(a) Based on the information contained in the financial statements, determine the normal balance of the listed accounts for each company.

Pepsi	Coca-Cola
1. Inventory	**1.** Accounts Receivable
2. Property, Plant, and Equipment	**2.** Cash and Cash Equivalents
3. Accounts Payable	**3.** Cost of Goods Sold
4. Interest Expense	**4.** Sales (revenue)

(b) Identify the other account ordinarily involved when:
   (1) Accounts Receivable is increased.
   (2) Wages Payable is decreased.
   (3) Property, Plant, and Equipment is increased.
   (4) Interest Expense is increased.

Exploring the Web

BYP2-3   Much information about specific companies is available on the World Wide Web. Such information includes basic descriptions of the company's location, activities, industry, financial health, and financial performance.

Address: biz.yahoo.com/i, or go to **www.wiley.com/college/weygandt**

Steps

1. Type in a company name, or use index to find company name.
2. Choose **Profile**. Perform instructions (a)–(c) below.
3. Click on the company's specific industry to identify competitors. Perform instructions (d)–(g) below.

Instructions

Answer the following questions.

(a) What is the company's industry?
(b) What was the company's total sales?
(c) What was the company's net income?
(d) What are the names of four of the company's competitors?
(e) Choose one of these competitors.
(f) What is this competitor's name? What were its sales? What was its net income?
(g) Which of these two companies is larger by size of sales? Which one reported higher net income?

CRITICAL THINKING

Decision Making Across the Organization

BYP2-4   Lisa Ortega operates Ortega Riding Academy. The academy's primary sources of revenue are riding fees and lesson fees, which are paid on a cash basis. Lisa also boards horses for owners, who are billed monthly for boarding fees. In a few cases, boarders pay in advance of expected use. For its revenue transactions, the academy maintains the following accounts: No. 1 Cash, No. 5 Boarding Accounts Receivable, No. 27 Unearned Boarding Revenue, No. 51 Riding Revenue, No. 52 Lesson Revenue, and No. 53 Boarding Revenue.

The academy owns 10 horses, a stable, a riding corral, riding equipment, and office equipment. These assets are accounted for in accounts No. 11 Horses, No. 12 Building, No. 13 Riding Corral, No. 14 Riding Equipment, and No. 15 Office Equipment.

For its expenses, the academy maintains the following accounts: No. 6 Hay and Feed Supplies, No. 7 Prepaid Insurance, No. 21 Accounts Payable, No. 60 Salaries Expense, No. 61 Advertising Expense, No. 62 Utilities Expense, No. 63 Veterinary Expense, No. 64 Hay and Feed Expense, and No. 65 Insurance Expense.

Lisa makes periodic withdrawals of cash for personal living expenses. To record Lisa's equity in the business and her drawings, two accounts are maintained: No. 50 Lisa Ortega, Capital, and No. 51 Lisa Ortega, Drawing.

During the first month of operations an inexperienced bookkeeper was employed. Lisa Ortega asks you to review the following eight entries of the 50 entries made during the month. In each case, the explanation for the entry is correct.

May	1	Cash	18,000	
		Lisa Ortega, Capital		18,000
		(Invested $18,000 cash in business)		
	5	Cash	250	
		Riding Revenue		250
		(Received $250 cash for lessons provided)		
	7	Cash	300	
		Boarding Revenue		300
		(Received $300 for boarding of horses beginning June 1)		
	14	Riding Equipment	80	
		Cash		800
		(Purchased desk and other office equipment for $800 cash)		
	15	Salaries Expense	400	
		Cash		400
		(Issued check to Lisa Ortega for personal use)		
	20	Cash	148	
		Riding Revenue		184
		(Received $184 cash for riding fees)		
	30	Veterinary Expense	75	
		Accounts Payable		75
		(Received bill of $75 from veterinarian for services rendered)		
	31	Hay and Feed Expense	1,700	
		Cash		1,700
		(Purchased an estimated 2 months' supply of feed and hay for $1,700 on account)		

Instructions

With the class divided into groups, answer the following.

(a) Identify each journal entry that is correct. For each journal entry that is incorrect, prepare the entry that should have been made by the bookkeeper.

(b) Which of the incorrect entries would prevent the trial balance from balancing?

(c) What was the correct net income for May, assuming the bookkeeper reported net income of $4,500 after posting all 50 entries?

(d) What was the correct cash balance at May 31, assuming the bookkeeper reported a balance of $12,475 after posting all 50 entries (and the only errors occurred in the items listed above)?

Communication Activity

BYP2-5 Woderson's Maid Company offers home cleaning service. Two recurring transactions for the company are billing customers for services rendered and paying employee salaries. For example, on March 15, bills totaling $6,000 were sent to customers and $2,000 was paid in salaries to employees.

Instructions

Write a memo to your instructor that explains and illustrates the steps in the recording process for each of the March 15 transactions. Use the format illustrated in the text under the heading, "The Recording Process Illustrated" (p. 61).

Ethics Case

BYP2-6   Mary Jansen is the assistant chief accountant at Casey Company, a manufacturer of computer chips and cellular phones. The company presently has total sales of $20 million. It is the end of the first quarter. Mary is hurriedly trying to prepare a general ledger trial balance so that quarterly financial statements can be prepared and released to management and the regulatory agencies. The total credits on the trial balance exceed the debits by $1,000. In order to meet the 4 p.m. deadline, Mary decides to force the debits and credits into balance by adding the amount of the difference to the Equipment account. She chose Equipment because it is one of the larger account balances; percentage-wise, it will be the least misstated. Mary "plugs" the difference! She believes that the difference will not affect anyone's decisions. She wishes that she had another few days to find the error but realizes that the financial statements are already late.

Instructions

(a) Who are the stakeholders in this situation?

(b) What are the ethical issues involved in this case?

(c) What are Mary's alternatives?

"All About You" Activity

BYP2-7   Every company needs to plan in order to move forward. Its top management must consider where it wants the company to be in three to five years. Like a company, you need to think about where you want to be three to five years from now, and you need to start taking steps now in order to get there. With some forethought, you can help yourself avoid a situation, like those described in the **All About You** feature in this chapter (p. 72), in which your résumé seems to need creative writing.

Instructions

Provide responses to each of the following items.

(a) Where would you like to be working in three to five years? Describe your plan for getting there by identifying between five and 10 specific steps that you need to take in order to get there.

(b) In order to get the job you want, you will need a résumé. Your résumé is the equivalent of a company's annual report. It needs to provide relevant and reliable information about your past accomplishments so that employers can decide whether to "invest" in you. Do a search on the Internet to find a good résumé format. What are the basic elements of a résumé?

(c) A company's annual report provides information about a company's accomplishments. In order for investors to use the annual report, the information must be reliable; that is, users must have faith that the information is accurate and believable. How can you provide assurance that the information on your résumé is reliable?

(d) Prepare a résumé assuming that you have accomplished the five to 10 specific steps you identified in part (a). Also, provide evidence that would give assurance that the information is reliable.

Answers to Insight and Accounting Across the Organization Questions

p. 58   What Would Sam Do?

Q: Why did Sam Walton keep separate pigeonholes and blue binders?

A: *Using separate pigeonholes and blue binders for each store enabled Walton to accumulate and track the performance of each individual store easily.*

Q: Why bother to keep separate records for each store?

A: *Keeping separate records for each store provided Walton with more information about performance of individual stores and managers, and greater control. Walton would want and need the same advantages if he were starting his business today. The difference is that he might now use a computerized system for small businesses.*

p. 70 Sarbanes-Oxley Comes to the Rescue

Q: In order for these companies to prepare and issue financial statements, their accounting equations (debits and credits) must have been in balance at year-end. How could these errors or mis-statements have occurred?

A: *A company's accounting equation (as expressed in its books) can be in balance yet its financial statements have errors or misstatements because of the following: entire transactions were not recorded, transactions were recorded at wrong amounts; transactions were recorded in the wrong accounts; transactions were recorded in the wrong accounting period. Audits of financial statements uncover some, but not all, errors or mis-statements.*

Authors' Comments on *All About You: Your Personal Annual Report* (p. 72)

The decision whether to fire Mr. Edmondson was the responsibility of Radio Shack's board of directors, which is elected by the company's shareholders to oversee management. The board initially announced its support for the CEO. After further investigation, the board encouraged Mr. Edmondson to resign, which he did. In contrast, when Bausch & Lomb's CEO offered to resign in a similar situation, the company's board refused to accept his resignation. Board members stated that they felt he was still the best person for the position.

Radio Shack says that although it did a reference check at the time of Mr. Edmondson's hiring, it did not check his educational credentials. Under the Sarbanes-Oxley Act of 2002, companies must now perform thorough background checks as part of a check of internal controls. The bottom line: Your résumé must be a fair and accurate depiction of your past.

Answers to Self-Study Questions

1. b   **2.** c   **3.** d   **4.** d   **5.** d   **6.** b   **7.** a   **8.** c   **9.** b   **10.** c   **11.** d   **12.** c   **13.** a
14. c   **15.** a

Chapter **3**

Adjusting the Accounts

Feature Story

WHAT WAS YOUR PROFIT?

The accuracy of the financial reporting system depends on answers to a few fundamental questions: At what point has revenue been earned? At what point is the earnings process complete? When have expenses really been incurred?

During the 1990s' boom in the stock prices of dot-com companies, many dot-coms earned most of their revenue from selling advertising space on their websites. To boost reported revenue, some dot-coms began swapping website ad space. Company A would put an ad for its website on company B's website, and company B would put an ad for its website on company A's website. No money changed hands, but each company recorded revenue (for the value of the space that it gave the other company on its site). This practice did little to boost net income, and it resulted in no additional cash flow—but it did boost *reported revenue*. Regulators eventually put an end to this misleading practice.

Another type of transgression results from companies recording revenues or expenses in the wrong year. In fact, shifting revenues and expenses is one of the most common abuses of financial accounting. Xerox, for example, admitted reporting billions of dollars of lease revenue in periods earlier than it should have been reported. And WorldCom stunned the financial markets with its admission that it had boosted net income by billions of dollars by delaying the recognition of expenses until later years.

Unfortunately, revelations such as these have become all too common in the corporate world. It is no wonder that a U.S. Trust survey of affluent Americans reported that 85% of respondents believed that there should be tighter regulation of financial disclosures; 66% said they did not trust the management of publicly traded companies.

Why did so many companies violate basic financial reporting rules and sound ethics? Many speculate that as stock prices climbed, executives were under increasing pressure to meet higher and higher earnings expectations. If actual results weren't as good as hoped for, some gave in to temptation and "adjusted" their numbers to meet market expectations.

✓ *The Navigator*

Inside Chapter 3...

In Chapter 1 you learned a neat little formula: Net income = Revenues − Expenses. In Chapter 2 you learned some rules for recording revenue and expense transactions. Guess what? Things are not really that nice and neat. In fact, it is often difficult for companies to determine in what time period they should report some revenues and expenses. In other words, in measuring net income, timing is everything.

The content and organization of Chapter 3 are as follows.

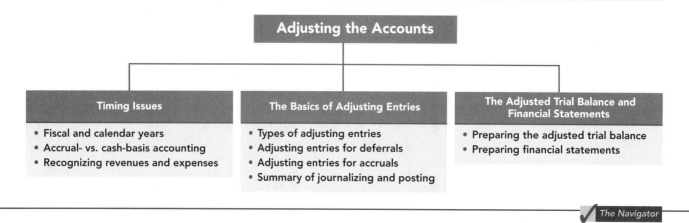

The Navigator

TIMING ISSUES

STUDY OBJECTIVE 1

Explain the time period assumption.

We would need no adjustments if we could wait to prepare financial statements until a company ended its operations. At that point, we could easily determine its final balance sheet and the amount of lifetime income it earned.

However, all companies find it desirable to report the results of their activities on a frequent basis. For example, management usually wants monthly financial statements, and the Internal Revenue Service requires all businesses to file annual tax returns. Therefore, **accountants divide the economic life of a business into artificial time periods**. This convenient assumption is referred to as the time period assumption.

Many business transactions affect more than one of these arbitrary time periods. For example, the airplanes purchased by Southwest Airlines five years ago are still in use today. We must determine the relevance of each business transaction to specific accounting periods. (How much of the cost of an airplane contributed to operations this year?)

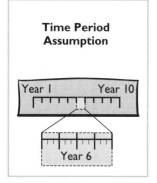

Time Period Assumption

ALTERNATIVE TERMINOLOGY

The time period assumption is also called the *periodicity assumption.*

Fiscal and Calendar Years

Both small and large companies prepare financial statements periodically in order to assess their financial condition and results of operations. **Accounting time periods are generally a month, a quarter, or a year.** Monthly and quarterly time periods are called interim periods. Most large companies must prepare both quarterly and annual financial statements.

An accounting time period that is one year in length is a fiscal year. A fiscal year usually begins with the first day of a month and ends twelve months later on the last day of a month. Most businesses use the calendar year (January 1 to December 31) as their accounting period. Some do not. Companies whose fiscal year differs from the calendar year include Delta Air Lines, June 30, and Walt Disney Productions, September 30. Sometimes a company's year-end will vary from year to year. For example, PepsiCo's fiscal year ends on the Friday closest to December 31, which was December 30 in 2006 and December 29 in 2007.

Accrual- vs. Cash-Basis Accounting

What you will learn in this chapter is accrual-basis accounting. Under the accrual basis, companies record transactions that change a company's financial statements **in the periods in which the events occur**. For example, using the accrual basis to determine net income means companies recognize revenues when earned (rather than when they receive cash). It also means recognizing expenses when incurred (rather than when paid).

An alternative to the accrual basis is the cash basis. Under cash-basis accounting, companies record revenue when they receive cash. They record an expense when they pay out cash. The cash basis seems appealing due to its simplicity, but it often produces misleading financial statements. It fails to record revenue that a company has earned but for which it has not received the cash. Also, it does not match expenses with earned revenues. **Cash-basis accounting is not in accordance with generally accepted accounting principles (GAAP).**

Individuals and some small companies do use cash-basis accounting. The cash basis is justified for small businesses because they often have few receivables and payables. Medium and large companies use accrual-basis accounting.

Recognizing Revenues and Expenses

It can be difficult to determine the amount of revenues and expenses to report in a given accounting period. Two principles help in this task: the revenue recognition principle and the matching principle.

REVENUE RECOGNITION PRINCIPLE

The revenue recognition principle dictates that companies recognize revenue in the accounting period in which it is earned. In a service enterprise, revenue is considered to be earned at the time the service is performed. To illustrate, assume that Dave's Dry Cleaning cleans clothing on June 30 but customers do not claim and pay for their clothes until the first week of July. Under the revenue recognition principle, Dave's earns revenue in June when it performed the service, rather than in July when it received the cash. At June 30, Dave's would report a receivable on its balance sheet and revenue in its income statement for the service performed.

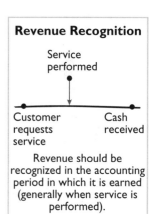

Revenue Recognition

Service performed

Customer requests service — Cash received

Revenue should be recognized in the accounting period in which it is earned (generally when service is performed).

MATCHING PRINCIPLE

Accountants follow a simple rule in recognizing expenses: "Let the expenses follow the revenues." That is, expense recognition is tied to revenue recognition. In the dry cleaning example, this principle means that Dave's should report the salary expense incurred in performing the June 30 cleaning service in the income statement for the same period in which it recognizes the service revenue. The critical issue in expense recognition is when the expense makes its contribution to revenue. This may or may not be the same period in which the expense is paid. If Dave's does not pay the salary incurred on June 30 until July, it would report salaries payable on its June 30 balance sheet.

This practice of expense recognition is referred to as the matching principle. It dictates that efforts (expenses) be matched with accomplishments (revenues). Illustration 3-1 (page 98) summarizes the revenue and expense recognition principles.

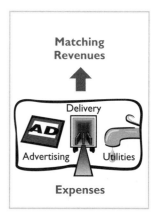

Matching Revenues

Delivery

Advertising   Utilities

Expenses

Illustration 3-1
GAAP relationships in revenue and expense recognition

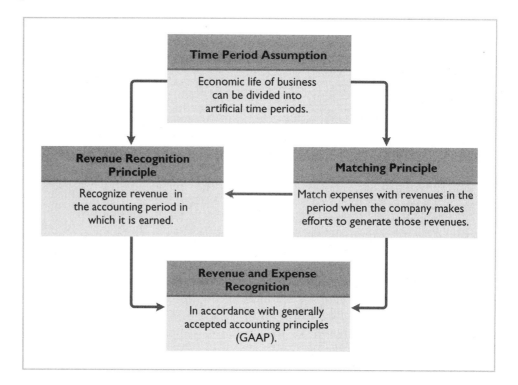

ACCOUNTING ACROSS THE ORGANIZATION

How Long Will "The Force" Be with Us?

Suppose you are filmmaker George Lucas and you spent $11 million to produce Twentieth Century Fox's film *Star Wars*. Over what period should the studio expense the cost?

Yes, it should expense the cost over the economic life of the film. But what *is* its economic life? You must estimate how much revenue you will earn from box office sales, video sales, television, and games and toys—a period that could be less than a year or more than 20 years, as is the case for *Star Wars*. Originally released in 1977, and rereleased in 1997, domestic revenues total over $500 million for *Star Wars* and continue to grow.

? What accounting principle does this example illustrate? How will financial results be affected if the expenses are recognized over a period that is *less than* that used for revenues? How will financial results be affected if the expenses are recognized over a period that is *longer than* that used for revenues?

DO IT!

TIMING CONCEPTS

Numerous timing concepts are discussed on pages 96 to 97. A list of concepts is provided on page 99, on the left, with a description of the concept on the right. There are more descriptions provided than concepts. Match the description of the concept to the concept.

1. _____ Accrual basis accounting.
2. _____ Calendar year.
3. _____ Time period assumption.
4. _____ Matching principle.

(a) Monthly and quarterly time periods.
(b) Efforts (expenses) should be matched with accomplishments (revenues).
(c) Accountants divide the economic life of a business into artificial time periods.
(d) Companies record revenues when they receive cash and record expenses when they pay out cash.
(e) An accounting time period that is one year in length.
(f) An accounting time period that starts on January 1 and ends on December 31.
(g) Companies record transactions in the period in which the events occur.

action plan

✔ Review the glossary terms identified on pages 96–97.

✔ Study carefully the revenue recognition principle, the matching principle, and the time period assumption.

Solution

1. g   2. f   3. c   4. b

Related exercise material: **E3-1, E3-2, E3-3,** and DO IT! **3-1.**

 The Navigator

THE BASICS OF ADJUSTING ENTRIES

In order for revenues and expenses to be reported in the correct period, companies make adjusting entries at the end of the accounting period. **Adjusting entries ensure that the revenue recognition and matching principles are followed.** Adjusting entries make it possible to report correct amounts on the balance sheet and on the income statement.

The trial balance—the first summarization of the transaction data—may not contain up-to-date and complete data. This is true for several reasons:

1. Some events are not recorded daily because it is not efficient to do so. For example, companies do not record the daily use of supplies or the earning of wages by employees.

2. Some costs are not recorded during the accounting period because they expire with the passage of time rather than as a result of daily transactions. Examples are rent, insurance, and charges related to the use of equipment.

3. Some items may be unrecorded. An example is a utility bill that the company will not receive until the next accounting period.

A company must make adjusting entries every time it prepares financial statements. It analyzes each account in the trial balance to determine whether it is complete and up-to-date. For example, the company may need to make inventory counts of supplies. It may also need to prepare supporting schedules of insurance policies, rental agreements, and other contractual commitments. Because the adjusting and closing process can be time-consuming, companies often prepare adjusting entries after the balance sheet date, but date them as of the balance sheet date.

STUDY OBJECTIVE 3

Explain the reasons for adjusting entries.

 WILEY PLUS

Accounting Cycle Tutorial— Making Adjusting Entries

HELPFUL HINT

Adjusting entries are needed to enable financial statements to conform to GAAP.

Types of Adjusting Entries

Adjusting entries are classified as either **deferrals** or **accruals**. As Illustration 3-2 shows, each of these classes has two subcategories.

STUDY OBJECTIVE 4

Identify the major types of adjusting entries.

Illustration 3-2
Categories of adjusting
entries

Deferrals

1. **Prepaid Expenses.** Expenses paid in cash and recorded as assets before they are used or consumed.

2. **Unearned Revenues.** Cash received and recorded as liabilities before revenue is earned.

Accruals

1. **Accrued Revenues.** Revenues earned but not yet received in cash or recorded.

2. **Accrued Expenses.** Expenses incurred but not yet paid in cash or recorded.

The following pages explain each type of adjustment and show examples. Each example is based on the October 31 trial balance of Pioneer Advertising Agency, from Chapter 2 and reproduced in Illustration 3-3.

Illustration 3-3
Trial balance

PIONEER ADVERTISING AGENCY
Trial Balance
October 31, 2010

	Debit	Credit
Cash	$15,200	
Advertising Supplies	2,500	
Prepaid Insurance	600	
Office Equipment	5,000	
Notes Payable		$ 5,000
Accounts Payable		2,500
Unearned Revenue		1,200
C. R. Byrd, Capital		10,000
C. R. Byrd, Drawing	500	
Service Revenue		10,000
Salaries Expense	4,000	
Rent Expense	900	
	$28,700	$28,700

We assume that Pioneer Advertising uses an accounting period of one month, and thus it makes monthly adjusting entries. The entries are dated October 31.

Adjusting Entries for Deferrals

STUDY OBJECTIVE 5

Prepare adjusting entries for deferrals.

Deferrals are either prepaid expenses or unearned revenues. Companies make adjustments for deferrals to record the portion of the deferral that represents the **expense incurred or the revenue earned** in the current period.

PREPAID EXPENSES

Just as you might pay for your car insurance six months in advance, companies will pay in advance for some items that cover more than one period. Because accrual accounting requires that expenses are recognized only in the period in which they are incurred, these prepayments are recorded as assets called **prepaid expenses** or **prepayments**. When expenses are prepaid, an asset account is increased (debited) to show the service or benefit that the company will receive in the future. Examples of common prepayments are insurance, supplies, advertising, and rent. In addition, companies make prepayments when they purchase buildings and equipment.

Prepaid expenses are costs that expire either with the passage of time (e.g., rent and insurance) **or through use** (e.g., supplies). The expiration of these costs does not require daily journal entries. Companies postpone recognizing these costs until they prepare financial statements. At each statement date, they make adjusting entries: (1) to record the expenses that apply to the current accounting period, and (2) to show the unexpired costs in the asset accounts.

Prior to adjustment for prepaid expenses, assets are overstated and expenses are understated. As shown in Illustration 3-4, **an adjusting entry for prepaid expense increases (debits) an expense account and a decreases (credits) an asset account**.

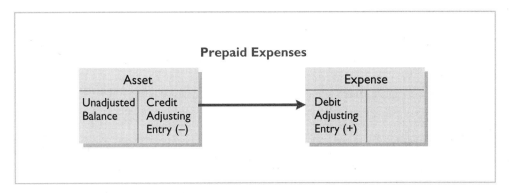

Illustration 3-4
Adjusting entries for prepaid expenses

On the next few pages, we will look in more detail at some specific types of prepaid expenses, beginning with supplies.

Supplies. Businesses use various types of supplies such as paper, envelopes, and printer cartridges. Companies generally debit supplies to an asset account when they acquire them. In the course of operations, supplies are used, but companies postpone recognizing their use until the adjustment process. At the end of the accounting period, a company counts the remaining supplies. The difference between the balance in the Supplies (asset) account and the supplies on hand represents the supplies used (an expense) for the period.

Pioneer Advertising Agency purchased advertising supplies costing $2,500 on October 5. Pioneer recorded that transaction by increasing (debiting) the asset Advertising Supplies. This account shows a balance of $2,500 in the October 31 trial balance. An inventory count at the close of business on October 31 reveals that $1,000 of supplies are still on hand. Thus, the cost of supplies used is $1,500 ($2,500 − $1,000). Pioneer makes the following adjusting entry.

Supplies

Oct.5

Supplies purchased; record asset

Oct.31
Supplies used; record supplies expense

Equation analyses summarize the effects of the transaction on the elements of the accounting equation.

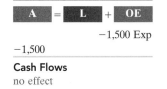

A	=	L	+	OE
				−1,500 Exp
−1,500				

Cash Flows
no effect

Oct. 31	Advertising Supplies Expense	1,500	
	Advertising Supplies		1,500
	(To record supplies used)		

After the adjusting entry is posted, the two supplies accounts show:

Illustration 3-5
Supplies accounts after
adjustment

Advertising Supplies				Advertising Supplies Expense	
10/5	2,500	10/31 **Adj.**	1,500	10/31 **Adj.** 1,500	
10/31 Bal.	1,000				

The asset account Advertising Supplies now shows a balance of $1,000, which is equal to the cost of supplies on hand at the statement date. In addition, Advertising Supplies Expense shows a balance of $1,500, which equals the cost of supplies used in October. **If Pioneer does not make the adjusting entry, October expenses will be understated and net income overstated by $1,500. Also, both assets and owner's equity will be overstated by $1,500 on the October 31 balance sheet.**

Insurance. Companies purchase insurance to protect themselves from losses due to fire, theft, and other unforeseen events. Insurance must be paid in advance. Insurance premiums (payments) normally are recorded as an increase (a debit) to the asset account Prepaid Insurance. At the financial statement date companies increase (debit) Insurance Expense and decrease (credit) Prepaid Insurance for the cost that has expired during the period.

On October 4, Pioneer Advertising Agency paid $600 for a one-year fire insurance policy. Coverage began on October 1. Pioneer recorded the payment by increasing (debiting) Prepaid Insurance. This account shows a balance of $600 in the October 31 trial balance. Insurance of $50 ($600 ÷ 12) expires each month. Thus, Pioneer makes the following adjusting entry.

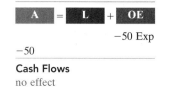

Insurance

Oct.4
Insurance purchased;
record asset

Insurance Policy			
Oct $50	Nov $50	Dec $50	Jan $50
Feb $50	March $50	April $50	May $50
June $50	July $50	Aug $50	Sept $50
1 YEAR $600			

Oct.31
Insurance expired;
record insurance expense

A	=	L	+	OE

-50 Exp
-50

Cash Flows
no effect

Oct. 31	Insurance Expense	50	
	Prepaid Insurance		50
	(To record insurance expired)		

After Pioneer posts the adjusting entry, the accounts show:

Illustration 3-6
Insurance accounts after
adjustment

Prepaid Insurance				Insurance Expense	
10/4	600	10/31 **Adj.**	50	10/31 **Adj.** 50	
10/31 Bal.	550				

The asset Prepaid Insurance shows a balance of $550. This amount represents the unexpired cost for the remaining 11 months of coverage. The $50 balance in Insurance Expense equals the insurance cost that has expired in October. If Pioneer does not make this adjustment, October expenses will be understated and net income overstated by $50. Also, both assets and owner's equity will be overstated by $50 on the October 31 balance sheet.

Depreciation. Companies typically own buildings, equipment, and vehicles. These long-lived assets provide service for a number of years. Thus, each is recorded as an asset, rather than an expense, in the year it is acquired. As explained in Chapter 1, companies record such assets **at cost**, as required by the cost principle. The term of service is referred to as the useful life.

According to the matching principle, companies then report a portion of the cost of a long-lived asset as an expense during each period of the asset's useful life. Depreciation is the process of allocating the cost of an asset to expense over its useful life in a rational and systematic manner.

Need for Depreciation Adjustment. From an accounting standpoint, acquiring long-lived assets is essentially a long-term prepayment for services. Companies need to make periodic adjusting entries for depreciation, just as they do for other prepaid expenses. These entries recognize the cost that has been used (an expense) during the period and report the unexpired cost (an asset) at the end of the period.

When a company acquires a long-lived asset, it does not know its exact useful life. The asset may be useful for a longer or shorter time than expected, depending on various factors. Thus, **depreciation is an estimate** rather than a factual measurement of expired cost. A common procedure in computing depreciation expense is to divide the cost of the asset by its useful life. For example, if cost is $10,000 and useful life is expected to be 10 years, annual depreciation is $1,000.[1]

Pioneer Advertising estimates depreciation on the office equipment to be $480 a year, or $40 per month. Thus, Pioneer makes the following adjusting entry to record depreciation for October.

Oct. 31	Depreciation Expense	40	
	Accumulated Depreciation—Office Equipment		40
	(To record monthly depreciation)		

After the adjusting entry is posted, the accounts show:

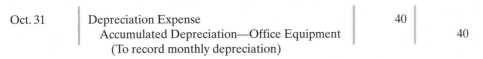

Illustration 3-7
Accounts after adjustment for depreciation

The balance in the accumulated depreciation account will increase $40 each month. After journalizing and posting the adjusting entry at November 30, the balance will be $80; at December 31, $120; and so on.

Statement Presentation. Accumulated Depreciation—Office Equipment is a contra asset account. That means that it is offset against an asset account on the balance sheet. This accumulated depreciation account appears just after the account it offsets (in this case, Office Equipment) on the balance sheet. Its normal balance is a credit.

HELPFUL HINT
All contra accounts have increases, decreases, and normal balances *opposite to* the account to which they relate.

---
[1] Chapter 10 addresses the computation of depreciation expense in detail.

An alternative to using a contra asset account would be to decrease (credit) the asset account (e.g., Office Equipment) directly for the depreciation each month. But use of the contra account is preferable for a simple reason: it discloses *both* the original cost of the equipment *and* the total cost that has expired to date.

In the balance sheet, Pioneer deducts Accumulated Depreciation—Office Equipment from the related asset account, as follows.

Illustration 3-8
Balance sheet presentation of accumulated depreciation

Office equipment	$5,000	
Less: Accumulated depreciation—office equipment	40	**$4,960**

ALTERNATIVE TERMINOLOGY

Book value is sometimes referred to as *carrying value* or *unexpired cost.*

The difference between the cost of any depreciable asset and its related accumulated depreciation is its **book value**. In Illustration 3-8, the book value of the equipment at the balance sheet date is $4,960. The book value of an asset generally differs from its **market value**—the price at which the asset could be sold in the marketplace. Remember that depreciation is a means of cost allocation, not a matter of market valuation.

Depreciation expense identifies that portion of the asset's cost that has expired during the period (in this case, in October). As for other prepaid adjustments, the omission of this adjusting entry would cause total assets, total owner's equity, and net income to be overstated and depreciation expense to be understated.

If the company owns additional long-lived assets, such as store equipment or buildings, it records depreciation expense on each of those items. It also establishes related accumulated depreciation accounts, such as: Accumulated Depreciation—Store Equipment; and Accumulated Depreciation—Buildings.

Illustration 3-9 summarizes the accounting for prepaid expenses.

Illustration 3-9
Accounting for prepaid expenses

ACCOUNTING FOR PREPAID EXPENSES			
Examples	**Reason for Adjustment**	**Accounts Before Adjustment**	**Adjusting Entry**
Insurance, supplies, advertising, rent, depreciation	Prepaid expenses recorded in asset accounts have been used.	Assets over-stated. Expenses understated.	Dr. Expenses Cr. Assets

Unearned Revenues

Oct.2 — Thank you in advance for your work

I will finish by Dec. 31

~$1,200

Cash is received in advance; liability is recorded

Oct.31
Some service has been provided; some revenue is recorded

UNEARNED REVENUES

Companies record cash received before revenue is earned by increasing a liability account called **unearned revenues**. Examples are rent, magazine subscriptions, and customer deposits for future service. Airlines such as United, American, and Southwest, for instance, treat receipts from the sale of tickets as unearned revenue until they provide the flight service. Similarly, colleges consider tuition received prior to the start of a semester as unearned revenue.

Unearned revenues are the opposite of prepaid expenses. Indeed, unearned revenue on the books of one company is likely to be a prepayment on the books of the company that made the advance payment. For example, a landlord will have unearned rent revenue when a tenant has prepaid rent.

When a company receives cash for future services, it increases (credits) an unearned revenue account (a liability) to recognize the liability. Later, the company earns revenues by providing service. It may not be practical to make daily journal entries as the revenue is earned. Instead, we delay recognizing earned revenue until the end of the period. Then the company makes an adjusting entry to record the revenue that has been earned and to show the liability that remains. Typically, prior to adjustment, liabilities are overstated and revenues are understated. Therefore, as shown in Illustration 3-10, the adjusting entry for unearned revenues results in a decrease (a debit) to a liability account and an increase (a credit) to a revenue account.

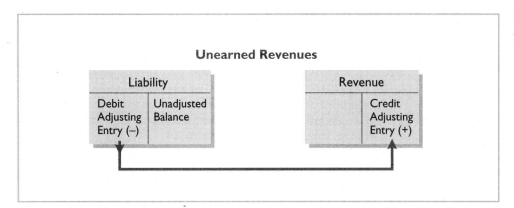

Illustration 3-10
Adjusting entries for
unearned revenues

Pioneer Advertising Agency received $1,200 on October 2 from R. Knox for advertising services expected to be completed by December 31. Pioneer credited the payment to Unearned Service Revenue; this account shows a balance of $1,200 in the October 31 trial balance. Analysis reveals that the company earned $400 of those fees in October. Thus, it makes the following adjusting entry.

ALTERNATIVE
TERMINOLOGY

Unearned revenue is
sometimes referred to
as *deferred revenue*.

Oct. 31	Unearned Revenue	400	
	Service Revenue		400
	(To record revenue for services provided)		

After the company posts the adjusting entry, the accounts show:

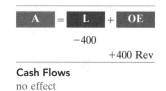

Cash Flows
no effect

Unearned Revenue				Service Revenue		
10/31 **Adj.**	**400**	10/2	1,200		10/31 Bal.	10,000
		10/31 Bal.	800		31 **Adj.**	**400**

Illustration 3-11
Revenue accounts after
prepayments adjustment

The liability Unearned Revenue now shows a balance of $800. That amount represents the remaining prepaid advertising services to be performed in the future. At the same time, Service Revenue shows total revenue of $10,400 earned in October. Without this adjustment, revenues and net income are understated by $400 in the income statement. Also, liabilities are overstated and owner's equity understated by $400 on the October 31 balance sheet.

Illustration 3-12 summarizes the accounting for unearned revenues.

Illustration 3-12
Accounting for unearned
revenues

	ACCOUNTING FOR UNEARNED REVENUES		
Examples	Reason for Adjustment	Accounts Before Adjustment	Adjusting Entry
Rent, magazine subscriptions, customer deposits for future service	Unearned revenues recorded in liability accounts have been earned.	Liabilities overstated. Revenues understated.	Dr. Liabilities Cr. Revenues

ACCOUNTING ACROSS THE ORGANIZATION

Turning Gift Cards into Revenue

Those of you interested in marketing know that gift cards are among the hottest tools in merchandising today. Customers purchase gift cards and give them to someone for later use. In a recent year gift-card sales topped $95 billion.

Although these programs are popular with marketing executives, they create accounting questions. Should revenue be recorded at the time the gift card is sold, or when it is used by the customer? How should expired gift cards be accounted for? In its 2007 balance sheet Best Buy reported unearned revenue related to gift cards of $300 million.

Source: Robert Berner, "Gift Cards: No Gift to Investors," *Business Week* (March 14, 2005), p. 86.

? Suppose that Robert Jones purchases a $100 gift card at Best Buy on December 24, 2010, and gives it to his wife, Devon, on December 25, 2010. On January 3, 2011, Devon uses the card to purchase $100 worth of CDs. When do you think Best Buy should recognize revenue, and why?

DO IT!

ADJUSTING ENTRIES—DEFERRALS

action plan

✔ Make adjusting entries at the end of the period for revenues earned and expenses incurred in the period.

✔ Don't forget to make adjusting entries for prepayments. Failure to adjust for prepayments leads to overstatement of the asset or liability and related understatement of the expense or revenue.

The ledger of Hammond, Inc. on March 31, 2010, includes the following selected accounts before adjusting entries.

	Debit	Credit
Prepaid Insurance	3,600	
Office Supplies	2,800	
Office Equipment	25,000	
Accumulated Depreciation—Office Equipment		5,000
Unearned Revenue		9,200

An analysis of the accounts shows the following.

1. Insurance expires at the rate of $100 per month.
2. Supplies on hand total $800.
3. The office equipment depreciates $200 a month.
4. One-half of the unearned revenue was earned in March.

Prepare the adjusting entries for the month of March.

Solution

1. Insurance Expense	100	
Prepaid Insurance		100
(To record insurance expired)		
2. Office Supplies Expense	2,000	
Office Supplies		2,000
(To record supplies used)		
3. Depreciation Expense	200	
Accumulated Depreciation—Office Equipment		200
(To record monthly depreciation)		
4. Unearned Revenue	4,600	
Service Revenue		4,600
(To record revenue for services provided)		

Related exercise material: **BE3-3, BE3-4, BE3-5, BE3-6**, and **DO IT!** 3-2.

The Navigator

Adjusting Entries for Accruals

The second category of adjusting entries is **accruals**. Companies make adjusting entries for accruals to record revenues earned and expenses incurred in the current accounting period that have not been recognized through daily entries.

ACCRUED REVENUES

Revenues earned but not yet recorded at the statement date are **accrued revenues**. Accrued revenues may accumulate (accrue) with the passing of time, as in the case of interest revenue and rent revenue. Or they may result from services that have been performed but are neither billed nor collected. The former are unrecorded because the earning process (e.g., of interest and rent) does not involve daily transactions. The latter may be unrecorded because the company has provided only a portion of the total service.

An adjusting entry for accrued revenues serves two purposes: (1) It shows the receivable that exists at the balance sheet date, and (2) it records the revenues earned during the period. Prior to adjustment, both assets and revenues are understated. Therefore, as Illustration 3-13 shows, **an adjusting entry for accrued revenues increases (debits) an asset account and increases (credits) a revenue account**.

Accrued Revenues

Oct.31

Revenue and receivable are recorded for unbilled services

Nov.10

Cash is received; receivable is reduced

Illustration 3-13
Adjusting entries for accrued revenues

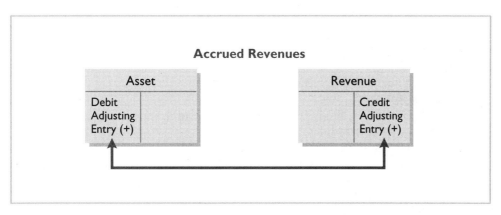

Accrued Revenues

In October Pioneer Advertising Agency earned $200 for advertising services that have not been recorded. Pioneer makes the following adjusting entry on October 31.

A	=	L	+	OE
+200				
				+200 Rev

Cash Flows
no effect

Oct. 31	Accounts Receivable	200	
	Service Revenue		200
	(To record revenue for services provided)		

After Pioneer posts the adjusting entry, the accounts show:

Illustration 3-14
Receivable and revenue accounts after accrual adjustment

Accounts Receivable		Service Revenue	
10/31 **Adj.** 200		10/31	10,000
		31	400
		31 **Adj.**	200
		10/31 Bal.	10,600

A	=	L	+	OE
+200				
−200				

Cash Flows
+200

The asset Accounts Receivable indicates that clients owe $200 at the balance sheet date. The balance of $10,600 in Service Revenue represents the total revenue Pioneer earned during the month ($10,000 + $400 + $200). Without the adjusting entry, assets and owner's equity on the balance sheet, and revenues and net income on the income statement, are understated.

On November 10, Pioneer receives cash of $200 for the services performed in October and makes the following entry.

Nov. 10	Cash	200	
	Accounts Receivable		200
	(To record cash collected on account)		

The company records collection of cash on account with a debit (increase) to Cash and a credit (decrease) to Accounts Receivable.

Illustration 3-15 summarizes the accounting for accrued revenues.

Illustration 3-15
Accounting for accrued revenues

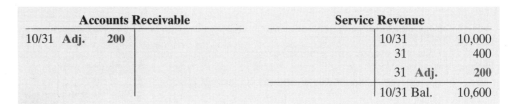

ACCOUNTING FOR ACCRUED REVENUES			
Examples	Reason for Adjustment	Accounts Before Adjustment	Adjusting Entry
Interest, rent, services performed but not collected	Revenues have been earned but not yet received in cash or recorded.	Assets understated. Revenues understated.	Dr. Assets Cr. Revenues

ACCRUED EXPENSES

Expenses incurred but not yet paid or recorded at the statement date are **accrued expenses.** Interest, rent, taxes, and salaries are typical accrued expenses. Accrued expenses result from the same causes as accrued revenues. In fact, an accrued expense on the books of one company is an accrued revenue to another company. For example, Pioneer's $200 accrual of revenue is an accrued expense to the client that received the service.

An adjusting entry for accrued expenses serves two purposes: (1) It records the obligations that exist at the balance sheet date, and (2) it recognizes the expenses of the current accounting period. Prior to adjustment, both liabilities and expenses are understated. Therefore, as Illustration 3-16 shows, **an adjusting entry for accrued expenses increases (debits) an expense account and increases (credits) a liability account**.

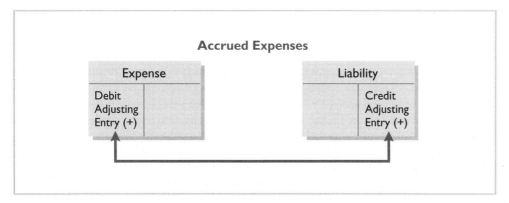

Illustration 3-16
Adjusting entries for accrued expenses

On the next few pages, we will look in more detail at some specific types of accrued expenses, beginning with accrued interest.

Accrued Interest.   Pioneer Advertising Agency signed a $5,000, 3-month note payable on October 1. The note requires Pioneer to pay interest at an annual rate of 12%.

Three factors determine the amount of interest accumulation: (1) the face value of the note, (2) the interest rate, which is always expressed as an annual rate, and (3) the length of time the note is outstanding. For Pioneer, the total interest due on the note at its due date is $150 ($5,000 face value × 12% interest rate × 3/12 time period). The interest is thus $50 per month. Illustration 3-17 shows the formula for computing interest and its application to Pioneer Advertising Agency for the month of October.[2] Note that the time period is expressed as a fraction of a year.

> **HELPFUL HINT**
>
> **Interest is a cost of borrowing money that accumulates with the passage of time.**

Face Value of Note	×	Annual Interest Rate	×	Time in Terms of One Year	=	Interest
$5,000	×	12%	×	1/12	=	**$50**

Illustration 3-17
Formula for computing interest

Pioneer makes the following accrued expense adjusting entry on October 31.

Oct. 31	Interest Expense		50	
	Interest Payable			50
	(To record interest on notes payable)			

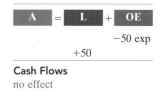

Cash Flows
no effect

---

[2]We will consider the computation of interest in more depth in later chapters.

After the company posts this adjusting entry, the accounts show:

Illustration 3-18
Interest accounts after
adjustment

Interest Expense	Interest Payable
10/31 **Adj.** 50	10/31 **Adj.** 50

Interest Expense shows the interest charges for the month of October. Interest Payable shows the amount of interest owed at the statement date. (As of October 31, they are the same because October is the first month of the note payable.) Pioneer will not pay the interest until the note comes due at the end of three months. Companies use the Interest Payable account, instead of crediting (increasing) Notes Payable, in order to disclose the two types of obligations—interest and principal—in the accounts and statements. Without this adjusting entry, liabilities and interest expense are understated, and net income and owner's equity are overstated.

Accrued Salaries.   Companies pay for some types of expenses after the services have been performed. Examples are employee salaries and commissions. Pioneer last paid salaries on October 26; the next payday is November 9. As the calendar in Illustration 3-19 shows, three working days remain in October (October 29–31).

Illustration 3-19
Calendar showing Pioneer's
pay periods

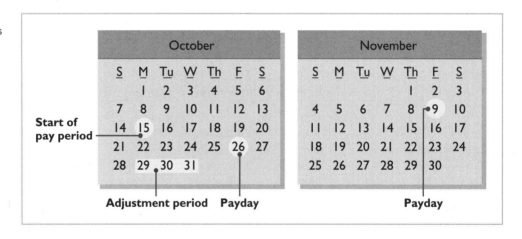

At October 31, the salaries for the last three days of the month represent an accrued expense and a related liability. The employees receive total salaries of $2,000 for a five-day work week, or $400 per day. Thus, accrued salaries at October 31 are $1,200 ($400 × 3). Pioneer makes the following adjusting entry:

A	=	L	+	OE
				−1,200 exp
		+1,200		

Cash Flows
no effect

Oct. 31	Salaries Expense	1,200	
	Salaries Payable		1,200
	(To record accrued salaries)		

After the company posts this adjusting entry, the accounts show:

Salaries Expense				Salaries Payable			
10/26		4,000				10/31 Adj.	1,200
31 Adj.		1,200					
10/31 Bal.		5,200					

Illustration 3-20
Salary accounts after adjustment

After this adjustment, the balance in Salaries Expense of $5,200 (13 days × $400) is the actual salary expense for October. The balance in Salaries Payable of $1,200 is the amount of the liability for salaries Pioneer owes as of October 31. Without the $1,200 adjustment for salaries, Pioneer's expenses are understated $1,200, and its liabilities are understated $1,200.

Pioneer Advertising pays salaries every two weeks. The next payday is November 9, when the company will again pay total salaries of $4,000. The payment will consist of $1,200 of salaries payable at October 31 plus $2,800 of salaries expense for November (7 working days as shown in the November calendar × $400). Therefore, Pioneer makes the following entry on November 9.

Nov. 9	Salaries Payable	1,200	
	Salaries Expense	2,800	
	Cash		4,000
	(To record November 9 payroll)		

A = L + OE
−1,200
−2,800 Exp
−4,000
Cash Flows
−4,000

This entry eliminates the liability for Salaries Payable that Pioneer recorded in the October 31 adjusting entry. It also records the proper amount of Salaries Expense for the period between November 1 and November 9.

Illustration 3-21 summarizes the accounting for accrued expenses.

Illustration 3-21
Accounting for accrued expenses

	ACCOUNTING FOR ACCRUED EXPENSES		
Examples	Reason for Adjustment	Accounts Before Adjustment	Adjusting Entry
Interest, rent, salaries	Expenses have been incurred but not yet paid in cash or recorded.	Expenses understated. Liabilities understated.	Dr. Expenses Cr. Liabilities

DO IT!

Calvin and Hobbes are the new owners of Micro Computer Services. At the end of August 2010, their first month of ownership, Calvin and Hobbes are trying to prepare monthly financial statements. They have the following information for the month.

1. At August 31, Calvin and Hobbes owed employees $800 in salaries that the company will pay on September 1.
2. On August 1, Calvin and Hobbes borrowed $30,000 from a local bank on a 15-year note. The annual interest rate is 10%.
3. Service revenue unrecorded in August totaled $1,100.

Prepare the adjusting entries needed at August 31, 2010.

ADJUSTING ENTRIES— ACCRUALS

action plan

✔ Make adjusting entries at the end of the period for revenues earned and expenses incurred in the period.

✔ Don't forget to make adjusting entries for accruals. Adjusting entries for accruals will increase both a balance sheet and an income statement account.

Solution

	Debit	Credit
1. Salaries Expense	800	
Salaries Payable		800
(To record accrued salaries)		
2. Interest Expense	250	
Interest Payable		250
(To record interest)		
($30,000 × 10% × 1/12 = $250)		
3. Accounts Receivable	1,100	
Service Revenue		1,100
(To record revenue for services provided)		

Related exercise material: **BE3-7, E3-5, E3-6, E3-7, E3-8, E3-9, E3-10, E3-11, E3-12,** and **DO IT!** **E3-3.**

 The Navigator

Summary of Journalizing and Posting

Illustrations 3-22 and 3-23 show the journalizing and posting of adjusting entries for Pioneer Advertising Agency on October 31. The ledger identifies all adjustments by the reference J2 because they have been recorded on page 2 of the general journal. The company may insert a center caption "Adjusting Entries" between the last transaction entry and the first adjusting entry in the journal. When you review the general ledger in Illustration 3-23, note that the entries highlighted in color are the adjustments.

Illustration 3-22
General journal showing adjusting entries

HELPFUL HINT

(1) Adjusting entries should not involve debits or credits to cash.
(2) Evaluate whether the adjustment makes sense. For example, an adjustment to recognize supplies used should increase supplies expense.
(3) Double-check all computations.
(4) Each adjusting entry affects one balance sheet account and one income statement account.

GENERAL JOURNAL					J2
Date	**Account Titles and Explanation**	**Ref.**	**Debit**	**Credit**	
2010	Adjusting Entries				
Oct. 31	Advertising Supplies Expense	631	1,500		
	Advertising Supplies	126		1,500	
	(To record supplies used)				
31	Insurance Expense	722	50		
	Prepaid Insurance	130		50	
	(To record insurance expired)				
31	Depreciation Expense	711	40		
	Accumulated Depreciation—Office Equipment	158		40	
	(To record monthly depreciation)				
31	Unearned Revenue	209	400		
	Service Revenue	400		400	
	(To record revenue for services provided)				
31	Accounts Receivable	112	200		
	Service Revenue	400		200	
	(To record revenue for services provided)				
31	Interest Expense	905	50		
	Interest Payable	230		50	
	(To record interest on notes payable)				
31	Salaries Expense	726	1,200		
	Salaries Payable	212		1,200	
	(To record accrued salaries)				

Illustration 3-23
General ledger after adjustment

GENERAL LEDGER

Cash   No. 101

Date	Explanation	Ref.	Debit	Credit	Balance
2010					
Oct. 1		J1	10,000		10,000
2		J1	1,200		11,200
3		J1		900	10,300
4		J1		600	9,700
20		J1		500	9,200
26		J1		4,000	5,200
31		J1	10,000		15,200

Accounts Receivable   No. 112

Date	Explanation	Ref.	Debit	Credit	Balance
2010					
Oct. 31	Adj. entry	J2	200		200

Advertising Supplies   No. 126

Date	Explanation	Ref.	Debit	Credit	Balance
2010					
Oct. 5		J1	2,500		2,500
31	Adj. entry	J2		1,500	1,000

Prepaid Insurance   No. 130

Date	Explanation	Ref.	Debit	Credit	Balance
2010					
Oct. 4		J1	600		600
31	Adj. entry	J2		50	550

Office Equipment   No. 157

Date	Explanation	Ref.	Debit	Credit	Balance
2010					
Oct. 1		J1	5,000		5,000

Accumulated Depreciation—Office Equipment   No. 158

Date	Explanation	Ref.	Debit	Credit	Balance
2010					
Oct. 31	Adj. entry	J2		40	40

Notes Payable   No. 200

Date	Explanation	Ref.	Debit	Credit	Balance
2010					
Oct. 1		J1		5,000	5,000

Accounts Payable   No. 201

Date	Explanation	Ref.	Debit	Credit	Balance
2010					
Oct. 5		J1		2,500	2,500

Unearned Revenue   No. 209

Date	Explanation	Ref.	Debit	Credit	Balance
2010					
Oct. 2		J1		1,200	1,200
31	Adj. entry	J2	400		800

Salaries Payable   No. 212

Date	Explanation	Ref.	Debit	Credit	Balance
2010					
Oct. 31	Adj. entry	J2		1,200	1,200

Interest Payable   No. 230

Date	Explanation	Ref.	Debit	Credit	Balance
2010					
Oct. 31	Adj. entry	J2		50	50

C. R. Byrd, Capital   No. 301

Date	Explanation	Ref.	Debit	Credit	Balance
2010					
Oct. 1		J1		10,000	10,000

C. R. Byrd, Drawing   No. 306

Date	Explanation	Ref.	Debit	Credit	Balance
2010					
Oct. 20		J1	500		500

Service Revenue   No. 400

Date	Explanation	Ref.	Debit	Credit	Balance
2010					
Oct. 31		J1		10,000	10,000
31	Adj. entry	J2		400	10,400
31	Adj. entry	J2		200	10,600

Advertising Supplies Expense   No. 631

Date	Explanation	Ref.	Debit	Credit	Balance
2010					
Oct. 31	Adj. entry	J2	1,500		1,500

Depreciation Expense   No. 711

Date	Explanation	Ref.	Debit	Credit	Balance
2010					
Oct. 31	Adj. entry	J2	40		40

Insurance Expense   No. 722

Date	Explanation	Ref.	Debit	Credit	Balance
2010					
Oct. 31	Adj. entry	J2	50		50

Salaries Expense   No. 726

Date	Explanation	Ref.	Debit	Credit	Balance
2010					
Oct. 26		J1	4,000		4,000
31	Adj. entry	J2	1,200		5,200

Rent Expense   No. 729

Date	Explanation	Ref.	Debit	Credit	Balance
2010					
Oct. 3		J1	900		900

Interest Expense   No. 905

Date	Explanation	Ref.	Debit	Credit	Balance
2010					
Oct. 31	Adj. entry	J2	50		50

THE ADJUSTED TRIAL BALANCE
AND FINANCIAL STATEMENTS

STUDY OBJECTIVE 7
Describe the nature and purpose of an adjusted trial balance.

The company has journalized and posted all adjusting entries. Next it prepares another trial balance from the ledger accounts. This is called an **adjusted trial balance**. Its purpose is to **prove the equality** of the total debit balances and the total credit balances in the ledger after all adjustments. The accounts in the adjusted trial balance contain all data that the company needs to prepare financial statements.

Preparing the Adjusted Trial Balance

Illustration 3-24 presents the adjusted trial balance for Pioneer Advertising Agency, prepared from the ledger accounts in Illustration 3-23. The amounts highlighted in color are those affected by the adjusting entries. Compare these amounts to those in the unadjusted trial balance in Illustration 3-3 on page 100. In this comparison, you will see that there are more accounts in the adjusted trial balance as a result of the adjusting entries made at the end of the month.

Illustration 3-24
Adjusted trial balance

PIONEER ADVERTISING AGENCY
Adjusted Trial Balance
October 31, 2010

	Dr.	Cr.
Cash	$15,200	
Accounts Receivable	200	
Advertising Supplies	1,000	
Prepaid Insurance	550	
Office Equipment	5,000	
Accumulated Depreciation—Office Equipment		$ 40
Notes Payable		5,000
Accounts Payable		2,500
Unearned Revenue		800
Salaries Payable		1,200
Interest Payable		50
C. R. Byrd, Capital		10,000
C. R. Byrd, Drawing	500	
Service Revenue		10,600
Salaries Expense	5,200	
Advertising Supplies Expense	1,500	
Rent Expense	900	
Insurance Expense	50	
Interest Expense	50	
Depreciation Expense	40	
	$30,190	$30,190

Preparing Financial Statements

Companies can prepare financial statements directly from the adjusted trial balance. Illustrations 3-25 (below) and 3-26 (on page 116) show the interrelationships of data in the adjusted trial balance and the financial statements.

As Illustration 3-25 shows, companies first prepare the income statement from the revenue and expense accounts. Next, they use the owner's capital and drawing accounts and the net income (or net loss) from the income statement to prepare the owner's equity statement. As Illustration 3-26 (page 116) shows, companies then prepare the balance sheet from the asset and liability accounts and the ending owner's capital balance as reported in the owner's equity statement.

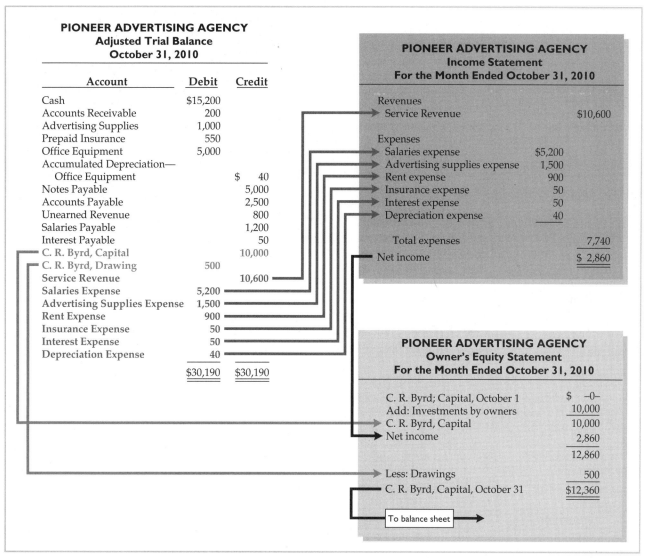

Illustration 3-25
Preparation of the income statement and owner's equity statement from the adjusted trial balance

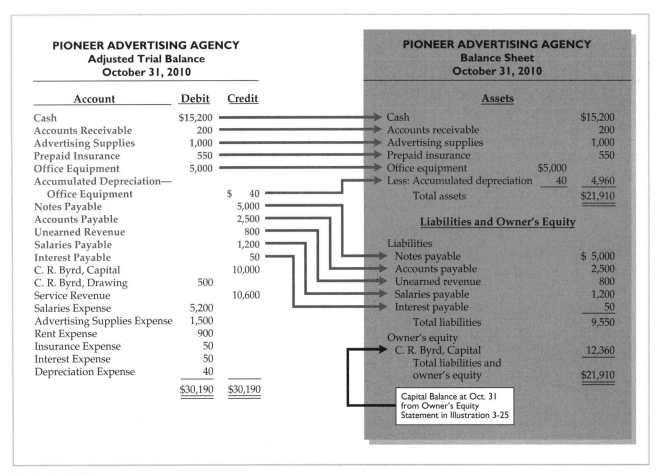

Illustration 3-26
Preparation of the balance
sheet from the adjusted trial
balance

DO IT!

TRIAL BALANCE

Skolnick Co. was organized on April 1, 2010. The company prepares quarterly financial statements. The adjusted trial balance amounts at June 30 are shown below.

Debits		Credits	
Cash	$ 6,700	Accumulated Depreciation—	$ 850
Accounts Receivable	600	Equipment	
Prepaid Rent	900	Notes Payable	5,000
Supplies	1,000	Accounts Payable	1,510
Equipment	15,000	Salaries Payable	400
Bob Skolnick, Drawing	600	Interest Payable	50
Salaries Expense	9,400	Unearned Rent	500
Rent Expense	1,500	Bob Skolnick, Capital	14,000
Depreciation Expense	850	Commission Revenue	14,200
Supplies Expense	200	Rent Revenue	800
Utilities Expense	510		
Interest Expense	50		
Total debits	$37,310	Total credits	$37,310

(a) Determine the net income for the quarter April 1 to June 30.
(b) Determine the total assets and total liabilities at June 30, 2010.
(c) Determine the amount for Bob Skolnick, Capital at June 30, 2010.

action plan

✔ In an adjusted trial balance, all assets, liability, revenue and expense accounts are properly stated.

✔ To determine the ending balance in Bob Skolnick, Capital at June 30, 2010, it is necessary to adjust this amount by net income and drawings.

Solution

(a) The net income is determined by adding revenue and subtracting expenses. The net income is computed as follows:

Revenues		
Commission revenue	$14,200	
Rent revenue	800	
Total revenues		$15,000
Expenses		
Salaries expense	$ 9,400	
Rent expense	1,500	
Depreciation expense	850	
Supplies expense	200	
Utilities expense	510	
Interest expense	50	
Total expenses		12,510
Net income		$ 2,490

(b) Total assets and liabilities are computed as follows:

Assets			Liabilities	
Cash		$ 6,700	Notes payable	$5,000
Accounts receivable		600	Accounts payable	1,510
Prepaid rent		900	Salaries payable	400
Supplies		1,000	Interest payable	50
Equipment	$15,000		Unearned rent	500
Less: Accumulated				
depreciation	850	14,150		
Total assets		$23,350	Total liabilities	$7,460

(c) Bob Skolnick, Capital at June 30, 2010, can be computed in two ways. Using the basic accounting equation (Assets = Liabilities + Owner's equity), we find that total assets are $23,350 and total liabilities are $7,460; therefore owner's equity (Bob Skolnick, Capital) is $15,890 ($23,350 − $7,460).

Another way to compute Skolnick, Capital at June 30, 2010, is as follows:

Bob Skolnick, Capital, April 1		$ −0−
Add: Investments	$14,000	
Net income	2,490	16,490
Less: Drawings		600
Bob Skolnick, Capital, June 30		$15,890

Related exercise material: **BE3-9, BE3-10, E3-11, E3-13, E3-14,** and **DO IT!** **3-4.**

✔ The Navigator

Comprehensive **DO IT!**

Terry Thomas opens the Green Thumb Lawn Care Company on April 1. At April 30, the trial balance shows the following balances for selected accounts.

Prepaid Insurance	$ 3,600
Equipment	28,000
Notes Payable	20,000
Unearned Revenue	4,200
Service Revenue	1,800

Analysis reveals the following additional data.

1. Prepaid insurance is the cost of a 2-year insurance policy, effective April 1.
2. Depreciation on the equipment is $500 per month.
3. The note payable is dated April 1. It is a 6-month, 12% note.
4. Seven customers paid for the company's 6 months' lawn service package of $600 beginning in April. The company performed services for these customers in April.
5. Lawn services provided other customers but not recorded at April 30 totaled $1,500.

Instructions

Prepare the adjusting entries for the month of April. Show computations.

action plan

✔ Note that adjustments are being made for one month.

✔ Make computations carefully.

✔ Select account titles carefully.

✔ Make sure debits are made first and credits are indented.

✔ Check that debits equal credits for each entry.

Solution to Comprehensive **DO IT!**

GENERAL JOURNAL   J1

Date	Account Titles and Explanation	Ref.	Debit	Credit
	Adjusting Entries			
Apr. 30	Insurance Expense		150	
	Prepaid Insurance			150
	(To record insurance expired:			
	$3,600 ÷ 24 = $150 per month)			
30	Depreciation Expense		500	
	Accumulated Depreciation—Equipment			500
	(To record monthly depreciation)			
30	Interest Expense		200	
	Interest Payable			200
	(To record interest on notes payable:			
	$20,000 × 12% × 1/12 = $200)			
30	Unearned Revenue		700	
	Service Revenue			700
	(To record service revenue: $600 ÷ 6 = $100;			
	$100 per month × 7 = $700)			
30	Accounts Receivable		1,500	
	Service Revenue			1,500
	(To record revenue for services provided)			

✔ *The Navigator*

SUMMARY OF STUDY OBJECTIVES

1 Explain the time period assumption. The time period assumption assumes that the economic life of a business is divided into artificial time periods.

2 Explain the accrual basis of accounting. Accrual-basis accounting means that companies record events that

change a company's financial statements in the periods in which those events occur, rather than in the periods in which the company receives or pays cash.

3 Explain the reasons for adjusting entries. Companies make adjusting entries at the end of an accounting period.

Such entries ensure that companies record revenues in the period in which they are earned and that they recognize expenses in the period in which they are incurred.

4 **Identify the major types of adjusting entries.** The major types of adjusting entries are deferrals (prepaid expenses and unearned revenues), and accruals (accrued revenues and accrued expenses).

5 **Prepare adjusting entries for deferrals.** Deferrals are either prepaid expenses or unearned revenues. Companies make adjusting entries for deferrals to record the portion of the prepayment that represents the expense incurred or the revenue earned in the current accounting period.

6 **Prepare adjusting entries for accruals.** Accruals are either accrued revenues or accrued expenses. Companies make adjusting entries for accruals to record revenues earned and expenses incurred in the current accounting period that have not been recognized through daily entries.

7 **Describe the nature and purpose of an adjusted trial balance.** An adjusted trial balance shows the balances of all accounts, including those that have been adjusted, at the end of an accounting period. Its purpose is to prove the equality of the total debit balances and total credit balances in the ledger after all adjustments.

The Navigator

GLOSSARY

Accrual-basis accounting Accounting basis in which companies record transactions that change a company's financial statements in the periods in which the events occur. (p. 97).

Accruals Adjusting entries for either accrued revenues or accrued expenses. (p. 99).

Accrued expenses Expenses incurred but not yet paid in cash or recorded. (p. 108).

Accrued revenues Revenues earned but not yet received in cash or recorded. (p. 107).

Adjusted trial balance A list of accounts and their balances after the company has made all adjustments. (p. 114).

Adjusting entries Entries made at the end of an accounting period to ensure that companies follow the revenue recognition and matching principles. (p. 99).

Book value The difference between the cost of a depreciable asset and its related accumulated depreciation. (p. 104).

Calendar year An accounting period that extends from January 1 to December 31. (p. 96).

Cash-basis accounting Accounting basis in which companies record revenue when they receive cash and an expense when they pay cash. (p. 97).

Contra asset account An account offset against an asset account on the balance sheet. (p. 103).

Deferrals Adjusting entries for either prepaid expenses or unearned revenues. (p. 99).

Depreciation The allocation of the cost of an asset to expense over its useful life in a rational and systematic manner. (p. 103).

Fiscal year An accounting period that is one year in length. (p. 96).

Interim periods Monthly or quarterly accounting time periods. (p. 96).

Matching principle The principle that companies match efforts (expenses) with accomplishments (revenues). (p. 97).

Prepaid expenses Expenses paid in cash that benefit more than one accounting period and that are recorded as assets. (p. 100).

Revenue recognition principle The principle that companies recognize revenue in the accounting period in which it is earned. (p. 97).

Time period assumption An assumption that accountants can divide the economic life of a business into artificial time periods. (p. 96).

Unearned revenues Cash received and recorded as liabilities before revenue is earned. (p. 104).

Useful life The length of service of a long-lived asset. (p. 103).

APPENDIX Alternative Treatment of Prepaid Expenses and Unearned Revenues

In discussing adjusting entries for prepaid expenses and unearned revenues, we illustrated transactions for which companies made the initial entries to balance sheet accounts. In the case of prepaid expenses, the company debited the prepayment to an asset account. In the case of unearned revenue, the company credited a liability account to record the cash received.

STUDY OBJECTIVE 8
Prepare adjusting entries for the alternative treatment of deferrals.

Some companies use an alternative treatment: (1) When a company prepays an expense, it debits that amount to an expense account. (2) When it receives payment for future services, it credits the amount to a revenue account. In this appendix, we describe the circumstances that justify such entries and the different adjusting entries that may be required. This alternative treatment of prepaid expenses and unearned revenues has the same effect on the financial statements as the procedures described in the chapter.

Prepaid Expenses

Prepaid expenses become expired costs either through the passage of time (e.g., insurance) or through consumption (e.g., advertising supplies). If, at the time of purchase, the company expects to consume the supplies before the next financial statement date, **it may choose to debit (increase) an expense account rather than an asset account.** This alternative treatment is simply more convenient.

Assume that Pioneer Advertising expects that it will use before the end of the month all of the supplies purchased on October 5. A debit of $2,500 to Advertising Supplies Expense (rather than to the asset account Advertising Supplies) on October 5 will eliminate the need for an adjusting entry on October 31. At October 31, the Advertising Supplies Expense account will show a balance of $2,500, which is the cost of supplies used between October 5 and October 31.

But what if the company does not use all the supplies? For example, what if an inventory of $1,000 of advertising supplies remains on October 31? Obviously, the company would need to make an adjusting entry. Prior to adjustment, the expense account Advertising Supplies Expense is overstated $1,000, and the asset account Advertising Supplies is understated $1,000. Thus Pioneer makes the following adjusting entry.

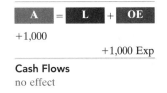

Oct. 31	Advertising Supplies	1,000	
	Advertising Supplies Expense		1,000
	(To record supplies inventory)		

After the company posts the adjusting entry, the accounts show:

Illustration 3A-1
Prepaid expenses accounts after adjustment

Advertising Supplies		Advertising Supplies Expense	
10/31 **Adj.** 1,000		10/5 2,500	10/31 **Adj.** 1,000
		10/31 **Bal.** 1,500	

After adjustment, the asset account Advertising Supplies shows a balance of $1,000, which is equal to the cost of supplies on hand at October 31. In addition, Advertising Supplies Expense shows a balance of $1,500. This is equal to the cost of supplies used between October 5 and October 31. Without the adjusting entry expenses are overstated and net income is understated by $1,000 in the October income statement. Also, both assets and owner's equity are understated by $1,000 on the October 31 balance sheet.

Illustration 3A-2 compares the entries and accounts for advertising supplies in the two adjustment approaches.

Illustration 3A-2
Adjustment approaches—a comparison

Prepayment Initially Debited to Asset Account (per chapter)			Prepayment Initially Debited to Expense Account (per appendix)		
Oct. 5	Advertising Supplies	2,500	Oct. 5	Advertising Supplies	
	Accounts Payable	2,500		Expense	2,500
				Accounts Payable	2,500
Oct. 31	Advertising Supplies		Oct. 31	Advertising Supplies	1,000
	Expense	1,500		Advertising Supplies	
	Advertising Supplies	1,500		Expense	1,000

After Pioneer posts the entries, the accounts appear as follows.

(per chapter) Advertising Supplies		(per appendix) Advertising Supplies	
10/5 2,500	10/31 Adj. 1,500	10/31 Adj. 1,000	
10/31 Bal. 1,000			

Advertising Supplies Expense		Advertising Supplies Expense	
10/31 Adj. 1,500		10/5 2,500	10/31 Adj. 1,000
		10/31 Bal. 1,500	

Note that the account balances under each alternative are the same at October 31: Advertising Supplies $1,000, and Advertising Supplies Expense $1,500.

Unearned Revenues

Unearned revenues become earned either through the passage of time (e.g., unearned rent) or through providing the service (e.g., unearned fees). Similar to the case for prepaid expenses, companies may credit (increase) a revenue account when they receive cash for future services.

To illustrate, assume that Pioneer Advertising received $1,200 for future services on October 2. Pioneer expects to perform the services before October 31.[3] In such a case, the company credits Service Revenue. If it in fact earns the revenue before October 31, no adjustment is needed.

However, if at the statement date Pioneer has not performed $800 of the services, it would make an adjusting entry. Without the entry, the revenue account Service Revenue is overstated $800, and the liability account Unearned Revenue is understated $800. Thus, Pioneer makes the following adjusting entry.

Oct. 31	Service Revenue	800	
	Unearned Revenue		800
	(To record unearned revenue)		

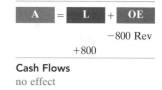

A	=	L	+	OE
				−800 Rev
		+800		

Cash Flows
no effect

After Pioneer posts the adjusting entry, the accounts show:

Unearned Revenue		Service Revenue			
	10/31 Adj. 800	10/31 Adj. 800	10/2 1,200		
			10/31 Bal. 400		

The liability account Unearned Revenue shows a balance of $800. This equals the services that will be provided in the future. In addition, the balance in Service Revenue equals the services provided in October. Without the adjusting entry, both revenues and net income are overstated by $800 in the October income statement. Also, liabilities are understated by $800, and owner's equity is overstated by $800 on the October 31 balance sheet.

Illustration 3A-5, (page 122) compares the entries and accounts for service revenue earned and unearned in the two adjustment approaches.

---

[3]This example focuses only on the alternative treatment of unearned revenues. In the interest of simplicity, we have ignored the entries to Service Revenue pertaining to the immediate earning of revenue ($10,000) and the adjusting entry for accrued revenue ($200).

Illustration 3A-5
Adjustment approaches—a comparison

Unearned Revenue Initially Credited to Liability Account (per chapter)			Unearned Revenue Initially Credited to Revenue Account (per appendix)		
Oct. 2	Cash	1,200	Oct. 2	Cash	1,200
	Unearned Revenue	1,200		Service Revenue	1,200
Oct. 31	Unearned Revenue	400	Oct. 31	Service Revenue	800
	Service Revenue	400		Unearned Revenue	800

After Pioneer posts the entries, the accounts appear as follows.

Illustration 3A-6
Comparison of accounts

(per chapter) Unearned Revenue				(per appendix) Unearned Revenue			
10/31 Adj.	400	10/2	1,200			10/31 Adj.	800
		10/31 Bal.	800				

Service Revenue				Service Revenue			
		10/31 Adj.	400	10/31 Adj.	800	10/2	1,200
						10/31 Bal.	400

Note that the balances in the accounts are the same under the two alternatives: Unearned Revenue $800, and Service Revenue $400.

Summary of Additional Adjustment Relationships

Illustration 3A-7
Summary of basic relationships for deferrals

Illustration 3A-7 provides a summary of basic relationships for deferrals.

Type of Adjustment	Reason for Adjustment	Account Balances before Adjustment	Adjusting Entry
1. Prepaid expenses	(a) Prepaid expenses initially recorded in asset accounts have been used.	Assets overstated Expenses understated	Dr. Expenses Cr. Assets
	(b) Prepaid expenses initially recorded in expense accounts have not been used.	Assets understated Expenses overstated	Dr. Assets Cr. Expenses
2. Unearned revenues	(a) Unearned revenues initially recorded in liability accounts have been earned.	Liabilities overstated Revenues understated	Dr. Liabilities Cr. Revenues
	(b) Unearned revenues initially recorded in revenue accounts have not been earned.	Liabilities understated Revenues overstated	Dr. Revenues Cr. Liabilities

Alternative adjusting entries **do not apply** to accrued revenues and accrued expenses because **no entries occur before companies make these types of adjusting entries**.

SUMMARY OF STUDY OBJECTIVE FOR APPENDIX

8 Prepare adjusting entries for the alternative treatment of deferrals. Companies may initially debit prepayments to an expense account. Likewise, they may credit unearned revenues to a revenue account. At the end of the period, these accounts may be overstated. The adjusting entries for prepaid expenses are a debit to an asset account and a credit to an expense account. Adjusting entries for unearned revenues are a debit to a revenue account and a credit to a liability account.

Note: All asterisked Questions, Exercises, and Problems relate to material in the appendix to the chapter.

SELF-STUDY QUESTIONS

Answers are at the end of the chapter.

(SO 1) **1.** The time period assumption states that:
   a. revenue should be recognized in the accounting period in which it is earned.
   b. expenses should be matched with revenues.
   c. the economic life of a business can be divided into artificial time periods.
   d. the fiscal year should correspond with the calendar year.

(SO 1) **2.** The time period assumption states that:
   a. companies must wait until the calendar year is completed to prepare financial statements.
   b. companies use the fiscal year to report financial information.
   c. the economic life of a business can be divided into artificial time periods.
   d. companies record information in the time period in which the events occur.

(SO 2) **3.** One of the following statements about the accrual basis of accounting is *false*. That statement is:
   a. Events that change a company's financial statements are recorded in the periods in which the events occur.
   b. Revenue is recognized in the period in which it is earned.
   c. This basis is in accord with generally accepted accounting principles.
   d. Revenue is recorded only when cash is received, and expense is recorded only when cash is paid.

(SO 2) **4.** The principle or assumption dictating that efforts (expenses) be matched with accomplishments (revenues) is the:
   a. matching principle.
   b. cost assumption.
   c. periodicity principle.
   d. revenue recognition principle.

(SO 3) **5.** Adjusting entries are made to ensure that:
   a. expenses are recognized in the period in which they are incurred.
   b. revenues are recorded in the period in which they are earned.
   c. balance sheet and income statement accounts have correct balances at the end of an accounting period.
   d. all of the above.

(SO 4) **6.** Each of the following is a major type (or category) of adjusting entries *except:*
   a. prepaid expenses.
   b. accrued revenues.
   c. accrued expenses.
   d. earned revenues.

(SO 5) **7.** The trial balance shows Supplies $1,350 and Supplies Expense $0. If $600 of supplies are on hand at the end of the period, the adjusting entry is:

a. Supplies	600	
Supplies Expense		600
b. Supplies	750	
Supplies Expense		750

c. Supplies Expense	750	
Supplies		750
d. Supplies Expense	600	
Supplies		600

8. Adjustments for prepaid expenses: (SO 5)
   a. decrease assets and increase revenues.
   b. decrease expenses and increase assets.
   c. decrease assets and increase expenses.
   d. decrease revenues and increase assets.

9. Accumulated Depreciation is: (SO 5)
   a. a contra asset account.
   b. an expense account.
   c. an owner's equity account.
   d. a liability account.

10. Queenan Company computes depreciation on delivery (SO 5) equipment at $1,000 for the month of June. The adjusting entry to record this depreciation is as follows:

a. Depreciation Expense	1,000	
Accumulated Depreciation—		
Queenan Company		1,000
b. Depreciation Expense	1,000	
Delivery Equipment		1,000
c. Depreciation Expense	1,000	
Accumulated Depreciation—		
Delivery Equipment		1,000
d. Delivery Equipment Expense	1,000	
Accumulated Depreciation—		
Delivery Equipment		1,000

11. Adjustments for unearned revenues: (SO 5)
   a. decrease liabilities and increase revenues.
   b. have an assets and revenues account relationship.
   c. increase assets and increase revenues.
   d. decrease revenues and decrease assets.

12. Adjustments for accrued revenues: (SO 6)
   a. have a liabilities and revenues account relationship.
   b. have an assets and revenues account relationship.
   c. decrease assets and revenues.
   d. decrease liabilities and increase revenues.

13. Kathy Siska earned a salary of $400 for the last week of (SO 6) September. She will be paid on October 1. The adjusting entry for Kathy's employer at September 30 is:
   a. No entry is required.

b. Salaries Expense	400	
Salaries Payable		400
c. Salaries Expense	400	
Cash		400
d. Salaries Payable	400	
Cash		400

14. Which of the following statements is *incorrect* concerning (SO 7) the adjusted trial balance?
   a. An adjusted trial balance proves the equality of the total debit balances and the total credit balances in the ledger after all adjustments are made.
   b. The adjusted trial balance provides the primary basis for the preparation of financial statements.

c. The adjusted trial balance lists the account balances segregated by assets and liabilities.

d. The adjusted trial balance is prepared after the adjusting entries have been journalized and posted.

(SO 8) *15. The trial balance shows Supplies $0 and Supplies Expense $1,500. If $800 of supplies are on hand at the end of the period, the adjusting entry is:

a. Debit Supplies $800 and credit Supplies Expense $800.

b. Debit Supplies Expense $800 and credit Supplies $800.

c. Debit Supplies $700 and credit Supplies Expense $700.

d. Debit Supplies Expense $700 and credit Supplies $700.

Go to the book's companion website, **www.wiley.com/college/weygandt**, for Additional Self-Study questions.

 The Navigator

QUESTIONS

1. (a) How does the time period assumption affect an accountant's analysis of business transactions?

(b) Explain the terms *fiscal year, calendar year*, and *interim periods*.

2. State two generally accepted accounting principles that relate to adjusting the accounts.

3. Rick Marsh, a lawyer, accepts a legal engagement in March, performs the work in April, and is paid in May. If Marsh's law firm prepares monthly financial statements, when should it recognize revenue from this engagement? Why?

4. Why do accrual-basis financial statements provide more useful information than cash-basis statements?

5. In completing the engagement in question 3, Marsh pays no costs in March, $2,000 in April, and $2,500 in May (incurred in April). How much expense should the firm deduct from revenues in the month when it recognizes the revenue? Why?

6. "Adjusting entries are required by the cost principle of accounting." Do you agree? Explain.

7. Why may a trial balance not contain up-to-date and complete financial information?

8. Distinguish between the two categories of adjusting entries, and identify the types of adjustments applicable to each category.

9. What is the debit/credit effect of a prepaid expense adjusting entry?

10. "Depreciation is a valuation process that results in the reporting of the fair market value of the asset." Do you agree? Explain.

11. Explain the differences between depreciation expense and accumulated depreciation.

12. Shinn Company purchased equipment for $18,000. By the current balance sheet date, $6,000 had been depreciated. Indicate the balance sheet presentation of the data.

13. What is the debit/credit effect of an unearned revenue adjusting entry?

14. A company fails to recognize revenue earned but not yet received. Which of the following accounts are involved in the adjusting entry: (a) asset, (b) liability, (c) revenue, or (d) expense? For the accounts selected, indicate whether they would be debited or credited in the entry.

15. A company fails to recognize an expense incurred but not paid. Indicate which of the following accounts is debited and which is credited in the adjusting entry: (a) asset, (b) liability, (c) revenue, or (d) expense.

16. A company makes an accrued revenue adjusting entry for $900 and an accrued expense adjusting entry for $700. How much was net income understated prior to these entries? Explain.

17. On January 9, a company pays $5,000 for salaries, of which $2,000 was reported as Salaries Payable on December 31. Give the entry to record the payment.

18. For each of the following items before adjustment, indicate the type of adjusting entry (prepaid expense, unearned revenue, accrued revenue, and accrued expense) that is needed to correct the misstatement. If an item could result in more than one type of adjusting entry, indicate each of the types.

(a) Assets are understated.

(b) Liabilities are overstated.

(c) Liabilities are understated.

(d) Expenses are understated.

(e) Assets are overstated.

(f) Revenue is understated.

19. One-half of the adjusting entry is given below. Indicate the account title for the other half of the entry.

(a) Salaries Expense is debited.

(b) Depreciation Expense is debited.

(c) Interest Payable is credited.

(d) Supplies is credited.

(e) Accounts Receivable is debited.

(f) Unearned Service Revenue is debited.

20. "An adjusting entry may affect more than one balance sheet or income statement account." Do you agree? Why or why not?

21. Why is it possible to prepare financial statements directly from an adjusted trial balance?

***22.** Adel Company debits Supplies Expense for all purchases of supplies and credits Rent Revenue for all advanced rentals. For each type of adjustment, give the adjusting entry.

23. PEPSICO What was PepsiCo's depreciation expense for 2007 and 2006?

BRIEF EXERCISES

BE3-1 The ledger of Dey Company includes the following accounts. Explain why each account may require adjustment.

(a) Prepaid Insurance   **(c)** Unearned Revenue
(b) Depreciation Expense   **(d)** Interest Payable

Indicate why adjusting entries are needed.
(SO 3)

BE3-2 Nunez Company accumulates the following adjustment data at December 31. Indicate **(a)** the type of adjustment (prepaid expense, accrued revenues and so on), and **(b)** the status of accounts before adjustment (overstated or understated).

1. Supplies of $100 are on hand.
2. Services provided but not recorded total $900.
3. Interest of $200 has accumulated on a note payable.
4. Rent collected in advance totaling $800 has been earned.

Identify the major types of adjusting entries.
(SO 4)

BE3-3 Windsor Advertising Company's trial balance at December 31 shows Advertising Supplies $6,700 and Advertising Supplies Expense $0. On December 31, there are $2,700 of supplies on hand. Prepare the adjusting entry at December 31, and using T accounts, enter the balances in the accounts, post the adjusting entry, and indicate the adjusted balance in each account.

Prepare adjusting entry for supplies.
(SO 5)

BE3-4 At the end of its first year, the trial balance of Denton Company shows Equipment $30,000 and zero balances in Accumulated Depreciation—Equipment and Depreciation Expense. Depreciation for the year is estimated to be $5,000. Prepare the adjusting entry for depreciation at December 31, post the adjustments to T accounts, and indicate the balance sheet presentation of the equipment at December 31.

Prepare adjusting entry for depreciation.
(SO 5)

BE3-5 On July 1, 2010, Spahn Co. pays $18,000 to Randle Insurance Co. for a 3-year insurance contract. Both companies have fiscal years ending December 31. For Spahn Co., journalize and post the entry on July 1 and the adjusting entry on December 31.

Prepare adjusting entry for prepaid expense.
(SO 5)

BE3-6 Using the data in BE3-5, journalize and post the entry on July 1 and the adjusting entry on December 31 for Randle Insurance Co. Randle uses the accounts Unearned Insurance Revenue and Insurance Revenue.

Prepare adjusting entry for unearned revenue.
(SO 5)

BE3-7 The bookkeeper for Oglesby Company asks you to prepare the following accrued adjusting entries at December 31.

1. Interest on notes payable of $400 is accrued.
2. Services provided but not recorded total $1,500.
3. Salaries earned by employees of $900 have not been recorded.

Use the following account titles: Service Revenue, Accounts Receivable, Interest Expense, Interest Payable, Salaries Expense, and Salaries Payable.

Prepare adjusting entries for accruals.
(SO 6)

BE3-8 The trial balance of Bair Company includes the following balance sheet accounts. Identify the accounts that may require adjustment. For each account that requires adjustment, indicate **(a)** the type of adjusting entry (prepaid expenses, unearned revenues, accrued revenues, and accrued expenses) and **(b)** the related account in the adjusting entry.

Accounts Receivable   Interest Payable
Prepaid Insurance   Unearned Service Revenue
Accumulated Depreciation—Equipment

Analyze accounts in an unadjusted trial balance.
(SO 4)

BE3-9 The adjusted trial balance of Harmony Company at December 31, 2010, includes the following accounts: S. Harmony, Capital $15,600; S. Harmony, Drawing $6,000; Service Revenue $35,400; Salaries Expense $16,000; Insurance Expense $2,000; Rent Expense $4,000; Supplies Expense $1,500; and Depreciation Expense $1,300. Prepare an income statement for the year.

Prepare an income statement from an adjusted trial balance.
(SO 7)

BE3-10 Partial adjusted trial balance data for Harmony Company is presented in BE3-9. The balance in S. Harmony, Capital is the balance as of January 1. Prepare an owner's equity statement for the year assuming net income is $10,600 for the year.

Prepare an owner's equity statement from an adjusted trial balance.
(SO 7)

*BE3-11 Duncan Company records all prepayments in income statement accounts. At April 30, the trial balance shows Supplies Expense $2,800, Service Revenue $9,200, and zero balances in related balance sheet accounts. Prepare the adjusting entries at April 30 assuming **(a)** $1,000 of supplies on hand and **(b)** $3,000 of service revenue should be reported as unearned.

Prepare adjusting entries under alternative treatment of deferrals.
(SO 8)

DO IT! REVIEW

Identify timing concepts.
(SO 1, 2)

DO IT! 3-1 Numerous timing concepts are discussed on pages 96 and 97. A list of concepts is provided below, on the left, with a description of the concept on the right. There are more descriptions provided than concepts. Match the description of the concept to the concept.

1. ____ Cash basis accounting.
2. ____ Fiscal year.
3. ____ Revenue recognition principle.
4. ____ Matching principle.

(a) Monthly and quarterly time periods.
(b) Accountants divide the economic life of a business into artificial time periods.
(c) Efforts (expenses) should be matched with accomplishments (revenues).
(d) Companies record revenues when they receive cash and record expenses when they pay out cash.
(e) An accounting time period that is one year in length.
(f) An accounting time period that starts on January 1 and ends on December 31.
(g) Companies record transactions in the period in which the events occur.
(h) Recognize revenue in the accounting period in which it is earned.

Prepare adjusting entries for deferrals.
(SO 5)

DO IT! 3-2 The ledger of Buerhle, Inc. on March 31, 2010, includes the following selected accounts before adjusting entries.

	Debit	Credit
Prepaid Insurance	2,400	
Office Supplies	2,500	
Office Equipment	30,000	
Unearned Revenue		10,000

An analysis of the accounts shows the following:

1. Insurance expires at the rate of $300 per month.
2. Supplies on hand total $900.
3. The office equipment depreciates $500 per month.
4. 2/5 of the unearned revenue was earned in March.

Prepare the adjusting entries for the month of March.

Prepare adjusting entries for accruals.
(SO 6)

DO IT! 3-3 Jose Contreras is the new owner of Curveball Computer Services. At the end of July 2010, his first month of ownership, Jose is trying to prepare monthly financial statements. He has the following information for the month.

1. At July 31, Contreras owed employees $1,100 in salaries that the company will pay in August.
2. On July 1, Contreras borrowed $20,000 from a local bank on a 10-year note. The annual interest rate is 12%.
3. Service revenue unrecorded in July totaled $1,600.

Prepare the adjusting entries needed at July 31, 2010.

Calculate amounts for trial balance.
(SO 7)

DO IT! 3-4 Danks Co. was organized on April 1, 2010. The company prepares quarterly financial statements. The adjusted trial balance amounts at June 30 are shown below.

Debits		Credits	
Cash	$ 5,360	Accumulated Depreciation—	$ 700
Accounts Receivable	480	Equipment	
Prepaid Rent	720	Notes Payable	4,000
Supplies	800	Accounts Payable	1,200
Equipment	12,000	Salaries Payable	300
John Danks, Drawing	500	Interest Payable	40
Salaries Expense	7,520	Unearned Rent	400
Rent Expense	1,200	John Danks, Capital	11,200
Depreciation Expense	700	Commission revenue	11,360
Supplies Expense	160	Rent revenue	690
Utilities Expense	410	Total credits	$29,890
Interest Expense	40		
Total debits	$29,890		

(a) Determine the net income for the quarter April 1 to June 30.
(b) Determine the total assets and total liabilities at June 30, 2010 for Danks Company.
(c) Determine the amount that appears for John Danks, Capital at June 30, 2010.

EXERCISES

E3-1   Jo Seacat has prepared the following list of statements about the time period assumption.

1. Adjusting entries would not be necessary if a company's life were not divided into artificial time periods.
2. The IRS requires companies to file annual tax returns.
3. Accountants divide the economic life of a business into artificial time periods, but each transaction affects only one of these periods.
4. Accounting time periods are generally a month, a quarter, or a year.
5. A time period lasting one year is called an interim period.
6. All fiscal years are calendar years, but not all calendar years are fiscal years.

Explain the time period assumption.

(SO 1)

Instructions
Identify each statement as true or false. If false, indicate how to correct the statement.

E3-2   On numerous occasions, proposals have surfaced to put the federal government on the accrual basis of accounting. This is no small issue. If this basis were used, it would mean that billions in unrecorded liabilities would have to be booked, and the federal deficit would increase substantially.

Distinguish between cash and accrual basis of accounting.

(SO 2)

Instructions
(a) What is the difference between accrual-basis accounting and cash-basis accounting?
(b) Why would politicians prefer the cash basis over the accrual basis?
(c) Write a letter to your senator explaining why the federal government should adopt the accrual basis of accounting.

E3-3   Conan Industries collected $100,000 from customers in 2010. Of the amount collected, $25,000 was from revenue earned on account in 2009. In addition, Conan earned $40,000 of revenue in 2010, which will not be collected until 2011.

    Conan Industries also paid $70,000 for expenses in 2010. Of the amount paid, $30,000 was for expenses incurred on account in 2009. In addition, Conan incurred $42,000 of expenses in 2010, which will not be paid until 2011.

Compute cash and accrual accounting income.

(SO 2)

Instructions
(a) Compute 2010 cash-basis net income.
(b) Compute 2010 accrual-basis net income.

E3-4   Emeril Corporation encounters the following situations:

1. Emeril collects $1,000 from a customer in 2010 for services to be performed in 2011.
2. Emeril incurs utility expense which is not yet paid in cash or recorded.
3. Emeril's employees worked 3 days in 2010, but will not be paid until 2011.
4. Emeril earned service revenue but has not yet received cash or recorded the transaction.
5. Emeril paid $2,000 rent on December 1 for the 4 months starting December 1.
6. Emeril received cash for future services and recorded a liability until the revenue was earned.
7. Emeril performed consulting services for a client in December 2010. On December 31, it billed the client $1,200.
8. Emeril paid cash for an expense and recorded an asset until the item was used up.
9. Emeril purchased $900 of supplies in 2010; at year-end, $400 of supplies remain unused.
10. Emeril purchased equipment on January 1, 2010; the equipment will be used for 5 years.
11. Emeril borrowed $10,000 on October 1, 2010, signing an 8% one-year note payable.

Identify the type of adjusting entry needed.

(SO 4)

Instructions
Identify what type of adjusting entry (prepaid expense, unearned revenue, accrued expense, accrued revenue) is needed in each situation, at December 31, 2010.

Prepare adjusting entries from selected data.

(SO 5, 6)

E3-5 Drew Carey Company has the following balances in selected accounts on December 31, 2010.

Accounts Receivable	$ -0-
Accumulated Depreciation—Equipment	-0-
Equipment	7,000
Interest Payable	-0-
Notes Payable	10,000
Prepaid Insurance	2,100
Salaries Payable	-0-
Supplies	2,450
Unearned Consulting Revenue	40,000

All the accounts have normal balances. The information below has been gathered at December 31, 2010.

1. Drew Carey Company borrowed $10,000 by signing a 12%, one-year note on September 1, 2010.
2. A count of supplies on December 31, 2010, indicates that supplies of $800 are on hand.
3. Depreciation on the equipment for 2010 is $1,000.
4. Drew Carey Company paid $2,100 for 12 months of insurance coverage on June 1, 2010.
5. On December 1, 2010, Drew Carey collected $40,000 for consulting services to be performed from December 1, 2010, through March 31, 2011.
6. Drew Carey performed consulting services for a client in December 2010. The client will be billed $4,200.
7. Drew Carey Company pays its employees total salaries of $9,000 every Monday for the preceding 5-day week (Monday through Friday). On Monday, December 29, employees were paid for the week ending December 26. All employees worked the last 3 days of 2010.

Instructions

Prepare adjusting entries for the seven items described above.

Identify types of adjustments and account relationships.

(SO 4, 5, 6)

E3-6 Affleck Company accumulates the following adjustment data at December 31.

1. Services provided but not recorded total $750.
2. Store supplies of $300 have been used.
3. Utility expenses of $225 are unpaid.
4. Unearned revenue of $260 has been earned.
5. Salaries of $900 are unpaid.
6. Prepaid insurance totaling $350 has expired.

Instructions

For each of the above items indicate the following.

(a) The type of adjustment (prepaid expense, unearned revenue, accrued revenue, or accrued expense).
(b) The status of accounts before adjustment (overstatement or understatement).

Prepare adjusting entries from selected account data.

(SO 5, 6)

E3-7 The ledger of Piper Rental Agency on March 31 of the current year includes the following selected accounts before adjusting entries have been prepared.

	Debit	Credit
Prepaid Insurance	$ 3,600	
Supplies	2,800	
Equipment	25,000	
Accumulated Depreciation—Equipment		$ 8,400
Notes Payable		20,000
Unearned Rent Revenue		9,900
Rent Revenue		60,000
Interest Expense	–0–	
Wages Expense	14,000	

An analysis of the accounts shows the following.

1. The equipment depreciates $400 per month.
2. One-third of the unearned rent revenue was earned during the quarter.
3. Interest of $500 is accrued on the notes payable.
4. Supplies on hand total $700.
5. Insurance expires at the rate of $200 per month.

Instructions

Prepare the adjusting entries at March 31, assuming that adjusting entries are made **quarterly**. Additional accounts are: Depreciation Expense, Insurance Expense, Interest Payable, and Supplies Expense.

E3-8   Andy Wright, D.D.S., opened a dental practice on January 1, 2010. During the first month of operations the following transactions occurred.

Prepare adjusting entries.

(SO 5, 6)

1. Performed services for patients who had dental plan insurance. At January 31, $875 of such services was earned but not yet recorded.
2. Utility expenses incurred but not paid prior to January 31 totaled $520.
3. Purchased dental equipment on January 1 for $80,000, paying $20,000 in cash and signing a $60,000, 3-year note payable. The equipment depreciates $400 per month. Interest is $500 per month.
4. Purchased a one-year malpractice insurance policy on January 1 for $12,000.
5. Purchased $1,600 of dental supplies. On January 31, determined that $400 of supplies were on hand.

Instructions

Prepare the adjusting entries on January 31. Account titles are: Accumulated Depreciation— Dental Equipment, Depreciation Expense, Service Revenue, Accounts Receivable, Insurance Expense, Interest Expense, Interest Payable, Prepaid Insurance, Supplies, Supplies Expense, Utilities Expense, and Utilities Payable.

E3-9   The trial balance for Pioneer Advertising Agency is shown in Illustration 3-3, p. 100. In lieu of the adjusting entries shown in the text at October 31, assume the following adjustment data.

Prepare adjusting entries.

(SO 5, 6)

1. Advertising supplies on hand at October 31 total $500.
2. Expired insurance for the month is $100.
3. Depreciation for the month is $50.
4. Unearned revenue earned in October totals $600.
5. Services provided but not recorded at October 31 are $300.
6. Interest accrued at October 31 is $70.
7. Accrued salaries at October 31 are $1,500.

Instructions

Prepare the adjusting entries for the items above.

E3-10   The income statement of Benning Co. for the month of July shows net income of $1,400 based on Service Revenue $5,500, Wages Expense $2,300, Supplies Expense $1,200, and Utilities Expense $600. In reviewing the statement, you discover the following.

Prepare correct income statement.

(SO 2, 5, 6, 7)

1. Insurance expired during July of $400 was omitted.
2. Supplies expense includes $200 of supplies that are still on hand at July 31.
3. Depreciation on equipment of $150 was omitted.
4. Accrued but unpaid wages at July 31 of $300 were not included.
5. Services provided but unrecorded totaled $500.

Instructions

Prepare a correct income statement for July 2010.

E3-11   A partial adjusted trial balance of Sila Company at January 31, 2010, shows the following.

Analyze adjusted data.

(SO 4, 5, 6, 7)

SILA COMPANY
Adjusted Trial Balance
January 31, 2010

	Debit	**Credit**
Supplies	$ 850	
Prepaid Insurance	2,400	
Salaries Payable		$ 800
Unearned Revenue		750
Supplies Expense	950	
Insurance Expense	400	
Salaries Expense	1,800	
Service Revenue		2,000

Instructions

Answer the following questions, assuming the year begins January 1.

(a) If the amount in Supplies Expense is the January 31 adjusting entry, and $500 of supplies was purchased in January, what was the balance in Supplies on January 1?

(b) If the amount in Insurance Expense is the January 31 adjusting entry, and the original insurance premium was for one year, what was the total premium and when was the policy purchased?

(c) If $3,500 of salaries was paid in January, what was the balance in Salaries Payable at December 31, 2009?

(d) If $1,600 was received in January for services performed in January, what was the balance in Unearned Revenue at December 31, 2009?

Journalize basic transactions and adjusting entries.
(SO 5, 6, 7)

E3-12 Selected accounts of Tabor Company are shown below.

Supplies Expense

7/31	800

Supplies

7/1 Bal.	1,100	7/31	800
7/10	400		

Salaries Payable

		7/31	1,200

Accounts Receivable

7/31	500		

Unearned Revenue

7/31	900	7/1 Bal.	1,500
		7/20	1,000

Salaries Expense

7/15	1,200		
7/31	1,200		

Service Revenue

		7/14	2,000
		7/31	900
		7/31	500

Instructions

After analyzing the accounts, journalize **(a)** the July transactions and **(b)** the adjusting entries that were made on July 31. (*Hint:* July transactions were for cash.)

Prepare adjusting entries from analysis of trial balances.
(SO 5, 6, 7)

E3-13 The trial balances before and after adjustment for Garcia Company at the end of its fiscal year are presented below.

GARCIA COMPANY
Trial Balance
August 31, 2010

	Before Adjustment Dr.	Before Adjustment Cr.	After Adjustment Dr.	After Adjustment Cr.
Cash	$10,400		$10,400	
Accounts Receivable	8,800		9,800	
Office Supplies	2,300		700	
Prepaid Insurance	4,000		2,500	
Office Equipment	14,000		14,000	
Accumulated Depreciation—Office Equipment		$ 3,600		$ 4,500
Accounts Payable		5,800		5,800
Salaries Payable		–0–		1,100
Unearned Rent Revenue		1,500		600
T. Garcia, Capital		15,600		15,600
Service Revenue		34,000		35,000
Rent Revenue		11,000		11,900
Salaries Expense	17,000		18,100	
Office Supplies Expense	–0–		1,600	
Rent Expense	15,000		15,000	
Insurance Expense	–0–		1,500	
Depreciation Expense	–0–		900	
	$71,500	$71,500	$74,500	$74,500

Instructions

Prepare the adjusting entries that were made.

E3-14 The adjusted trial balance for Garcia Company is given in E3-13.

Prepare financial statements from adjusted trial balance.

(SO 7)

Instructions

Prepare the income and owner's equity statements for the year and the balance sheet at August 31.

E3-15 The following data are taken from the comparative balance sheets of Girard Billiards Club, which prepares its financial statements using the accrual basis of accounting.

Record transactions on accrual basis; convert revenue to cash receipts.

(SO 5, 6)

December 31	2010	2009
Fees receivable from members	$14,000	$ 9,000
Unearned fees revenue	17,000	25,000

Fees are billed to members based upon their use of the club's facilities. Unearned fees arise from the sale of gift certificates, which members can apply to their future use of club facilities. The 2010 income statement for the club showed that fees revenue of $153,000 was earned during the year.

Instructions

(*Hint:* You will probably find it helpful to use T accounts to analyze these data.)

(a) Prepare journal entries for each of the following events that took place during 2010.
  (1) Fees receivable from 2009 were all collected.
  (2) Gift certificates outstanding at the end of 2009 were all redeemed.
  (3) An additional $35,000 worth of gift certificates were sold during 2010. A portion of these was used by the recipients during the year; the remainder was still outstanding at the end of 2010.
  (4) Fees for 2010 for services provided to members were billed to members.
  (5) Fees receivable for 2010 (i.e., those billed in item [4] above) were partially collected.

(b) Determine the amount of cash received by the club, with respect to fees, during 2010.

*E3-16 Colin Mochrie Company has the following balances in selected accounts on December 31, 2010.

Journalize adjusting entries.

(SO 8)

Consulting Revenue	$40,000
Insurance Expense	2,100
Supplies Expense	2,450

All the accounts have normal balances. Colin Mochrie Company debits prepayments to expense accounts when paid, and credits unearned revenues to revenue accounts when received. The following information below has been gathered at December 31, 2010.

1. Colin Mochrie Company paid $2,100 for 12 months of insurance coverage on June 1, 2010.
2. On December 1, 2010, Colin Mochrie Company collected $40,000 for consulting services to be performed from December 1, 2010, through March 31, 2011.
3. A count of supplies on December 31, 2010, indicates that supplies of $800 are on hand.

Instructions

Prepare the adjusting entries needed at December 31, 2010.

*E3-17 At Natasha Company, prepayments are debited to expense when paid, and unearned revenues are credited to revenue when received. During January of the current year, the following transactions occurred.

Journalize transactions and adjusting entries.

(SO 8)

Jan. 2 Paid $1,800 for fire insurance protection for the year.
    10 Paid $1,700 for supplies.
    15 Received $6,100 for services to be performed in the future.

On January 31, it is determined that $2,500 of the services fees have been earned and that there are $800 of supplies on hand.

Instructions

(a) Journalize and post the January transactions. (Use T accounts.)
(b) Journalize and post the adjusting entries at January 31.
(c) Determine the ending balance in each of the accounts.

EXERCISES: SET B

Visit the book's companion website at **www.wiley.com/college/weygandt**, and choose the Student Companion site, to access Exercise Set B.

PROBLEMS: SET A

Prepare adjusting entries, post to ledger accounts, and prepare adjusted trial balance.

(SO 5, 6, 7)

P3-1A Tony Masasi started his own consulting firm, Masasi Company, on June 1, 2010. The trial balance at June 30 is shown below.

MASASI COMPANY
Trial Balance
June 30, 2010

Account Number		Debit	Credit
101	Cash	$ 7,150	
112	Accounts Receivable	6,000	
126	Supplies	2,000	
130	Prepaid Insurance	3,000	
157	Office Equipment	15,000	
201	Accounts Payable		$ 4,500
209	Unearned Service Revenue		4,000
301	T. Masasi, Capital		21,750
400	Service Revenue		7,900
726	Salaries Expense	4,000	
729	Rent Expense	1,000	
		$38,150	$38,150

In addition to those accounts listed on the trial balance, the chart of accounts for Masasi Company also contains the following accounts and account numbers: No. 158 Accumulated Depreciation—Office Equipment, No. 212 Salaries Payable, No. 244 Utilities Payable, No. 631 Supplies Expense, No. 711 Depreciation Expense, No. 722 Insurance Expense, and No. 732 Utilities Expense.

Other data:

1. Supplies on hand at June 30 are $600.
2. A utility bill for $150 has not been recorded and will not be paid until next month.
3. The insurance policy is for a year.
4. $2,500 of unearned service revenue has been earned at the end of the month.
5. Salaries of $2,000 are accrued at June 30.
6. The office equipment has a 5-year life with no salvage value. It is being depreciated at $250 per month for 60 months.
7. Invoices representing $1,000 of services performed during the month have not been recorded as of June 30.

Instructions

(a) Prepare the adjusting entries for the month of June. Use J3 as the page number for your journal.

(b) Post the adjusting entries to the ledger accounts. Enter the totals from the trial balance as beginning account balances and place a check mark in the posting reference column.

(c) Prepare an adjusted trial balance at June 30, 2010.

(c) Adj. trial balance $41,550

P3-2A   Neosho River Resort opened for business on June 1 with eight air-conditioned units. Its trial balance before adjustment on August 31 is as follows.

Prepare adjusting entries, post, and prepare adjusted trial balance, and financial statements.

(SO 5, 6, 7)

NEOSHO RIVER RESORT
Trial Balance
August 31, 2010

Account Number		Debit	Credit
101	Cash	$ 19,600	
126	Supplies	3,300	
130	Prepaid Insurance	6,000	
140	Land	25,000	
143	Cottages	125,000	
149	Furniture	26,000	
201	Accounts Payable		$ 6,500
209	Unearned Rent Revenue		7,400
275	Mortgage Payable		80,000
301	P. Harder, Capital		100,000
306	P. Harder, Drawing	5,000	
429	Rent Revenue		80,000
622	Repair Expense	3,600	
726	Salaries Expense	51,000	
732	Utilities Expense	9,400	
		$273,900	$273,900

In addition to those accounts listed on the trial balance, the chart of accounts for Neosho River Resort also contains the following accounts and account numbers: No. 112 Accounts Receivable, No. 144 Accumulated Depreciation—Cottages, No. 150 Accumulated Depreciation—Furniture, No. 212 Salaries Payable, No. 230 Interest Payable, No. 620 Depreciation Expense—Cottages, No. 621 Depreciation Expense—Furniture, No. 631 Supplies Expense, No. 718 Interest Expense, and No. 722 Insurance Expense.

Other data:

1. Insurance expires at the rate of $400 per month.
2. A count on August 31 shows $600 of supplies on hand.
3. Annual depreciation is $6,000 on cottages and $2,400 on furniture.
4. Unearned rent revenue of $4,100 was earned prior to August 31.
5. Salaries of $400 were unpaid at August 31.
6. Rentals of $1,000 were due from tenants at August 31. (Use Accounts Receivable.)
7. The mortgage interest rate is 9% per year. (The mortgage was taken out on August 1.)

Instructions

(a) Journalize the adjusting entries on August 31 for the 3-month period June 1–August 31.

(b) Prepare a ledger using the three-column form of account. Enter the trial balance amounts and post the adjusting entries. (Use J1 as the posting reference.)

(c) Prepare an adjusted trial balance on August 31.

(d) Prepare an income statement and an owner's equity statement for the 3 months ending August 31 and a balance sheet as of August 31.

(c) Adj. trial balance $278,000
(d) Net income $14,100
Ending capital balance $109,100
Total assets $199,900

P3-3A   Fernetti Advertising Agency was founded by John Fernetti in January of 2009. Presented on page 134 are both the adjusted and unadjusted trial balances as of December 31, 2010.

Prepare adjusting entries and financial statements.

(SO 5, 6, 7)

FERNETTI ADVERTISING AGENCY
Trial Balance
December 31, 2010

	Unadjusted		Adjusted	
	Dr.	**Cr.**	**Dr.**	**Cr.**
Cash	$ 11,000		$ 11,000	
Accounts Receivable	20,000		22,500	
Art Supplies	8,600		5,000	
Prepaid Insurance	3,350		2,500	
Printing Equipment	60,000		60,000	
Accumulated Depreciation		$ 28,000		$ 34,000
Accounts Payable		5,000		5,000
Interest Payable		–0–		150
Notes Payable		5,000		5,000
Unearned Advertising Fees		7,200		5,600
Salaries Payable		–0–		1,300
J. Fernetti, Capital		25,500		25,500
J. Fernetti, Drawing	12,000		12,000	
Advertising Revenue		58,600		62,700
Salaries Expense	10,000		11,300	
Insurance Expense			850	
Interest Expense	350		500	
Depreciation Expense			6,000	
Art Supplies Expense			3,600	
Rent Expense	4,000		4,000	
	$129,300	$129,300	$139,250	$139,250

Instructions
(a) Journalize the annual adjusting entries that were made.
(b) Prepare an income statement and a statement of owner's equity for the year ending December 31, 2010, and a balance sheet at December 31.
(c) Answer the following questions.
  (1) If the note has been outstanding 6 months, what is the annual interest rate on that note?
  (2) If the company paid $12,500 in salaries in 2010, what was the balance in Salaries Payable on December 31, 2009?

(b) Net income $36,450
Ending capital $49,950
Total assets $67,000
(c) (1) 6%
(2) $2,500

Preparing adjusting entries.
(SO 5, 6)
1. Salaries expense $2,320

P3-4A A review of the ledger of Remington Company at December 31, 2010, produces the following data pertaining to the preparation of annual adjusting entries.

1. Salaries Payable $0. There are eight salaried employees. Salaries are paid every Friday for the current week. Five employees receive a salary of $800 each per week, and three employees earn $600 each per week. Assume December 31 is a Tuesday. Employees do not work weekends. All employees worked the last 2 days of December.

2. Rent revenue $74,000

2. Unearned Rent $324,000. The company began subleasing office space in its new building on November 1. At December 31, the company had the following rental contracts that are paid in full for the entire term of the lease.

Date	Term (in months)	Monthly Rent	Number of Leases
Nov. 1	6	$4,000	5
Dec. 1	6	$8,500	4

3. Advertising expense $4,800

3. Prepaid Advertising $15,000. This balance consists of payments on two advertising contracts. The contracts provide for monthly advertising in two trade magazines. The terms of the contracts are as follows.

Contract	Date	Amount	Number of Magazine Issues
A650	May 1	$5,400	12
B974	Oct. 1	9,600	24

The first advertisement runs in the month in which the contract is signed.

4. Notes Payable $120,000. This balance consists of a note for one year at an annual interest rate of 9%, dated June 1.

4. Interest expense $6,300

Instructions

Prepare the adjusting entries at December 31, 2010. (Show all computations.)

P3-5A On September 1, 2010, the account balances of Rand Equipment Repair were as follows.

Journalize transactions and follow through accounting cycle to preparation of financial statements.

(SO 5, 6, 7)

No.	Debits		No.	Credits	
101	Cash	$ 4,880	154	Accumulated Depreciation	$ 1,500
112	Accounts Receivable	3,520	201	Accounts Payable	3,400
126	Supplies	2,000	209	Unearned Service Revenue	1,400
153	Store Equipment	15,000	212	Salaries Payable	500
			301	J. Rand, Capital	18,600
		$25,400			$25,400

During September the following summary transactions were completed.

Sept. 8 Paid $1,400 for salaries due employees, of which $900 is for September.
10 Received $1,200 cash from customers on account.
12 Received $3,400 cash for services performed in September.
15 Purchased store equipment on account $3,000.
17 Purchased supplies on account $1,200.
20 Paid creditors $4,500 on account.
22 Paid September rent $500.
25 Paid salaries $1,250.
27 Performed services on account and billed customers for services provided $1,500.
29 Received $650 from customers for future service.

Adjustment data consist of:

1. Supplies on hand $1,200.
2. Accrued salaries payable $400.
3. Depreciation is $100 per month.
4. Unearned service revenue of $1,450 is earned.

Instructions

(a) Enter the September 1 balances in the ledger accounts.
(b) Journalize the September transactions.
(c) Post to the ledger accounts. Use J1 for the posting reference. Use the following additional accounts: No. 407 Service Revenue, No. 615 Depreciation Expense, No. 631 Supplies Expense, No. 726 Salaries Expense, and No. 729 Rent Expense.
(d) Prepare a trial balance at September 30.
(e) Journalize and post adjusting entries.
(f) Prepare an adjusted trial balance.
(g) Prepare an income statement and an owner's equity statement for September and a balance sheet at September 30 on the next page.

(d) Trial balance $30,150
(f) Adj. trial balance $30,650
(g) Net income $1,200
Ending capital $19,800
Total assets $23,900

*P3-6A Givens Graphics Company was organized on January 1, 2010, by Sue Givens. At the end of the first 6 months of operations, the trial balance contained the accounts on the next page.

Prepare adjusting entries, adjusted trial balance, and financial statements using appendix.

(SO 5, 6, 7, 8)

Debits		Credits	
Cash	$ 9,500	Notes Payable	$ 20,000
Accounts Receivable	14,000	Accounts Payable	9,000
Equipment	45,000	Sue Givens, Capital	22,000
Insurance Expense	1,800	Graphic Revenue	52,100
Salaries Expense	30,000	Consulting Revenue	6,000
Supplies Expense	3,700		
Advertising Expense	1,900		
Rent Expense	1,500		
Utilities Expense	1,700		
	$109,100		$109,100

Analysis reveals the following additional data.

1. The $3,700 balance in Supplies Expense represents supplies purchased in January. At June 30, $1,300 of supplies was on hand.
2. The note payable was issued on February 1. It is a 9%, 6-month note.
3. The balance in Insurance Expense is the premium on a one-year policy, dated March 1, 2010.
4. Consulting fees are credited to revenue when received. At June 30, consulting fees of $1,500 are unearned.
5. Graphic revenue earned but unrecorded at June 30 totals $2,000.
6. Depreciation is $2,000 per year.

Instructions
(a) Journalize the adjusting entries at June 30. (Assume adjustments are recorded every 6 months.)
(b) Prepare an adjusted trial balance.
(c) Prepare an income statement and owner's equity statement for the 6 months ended June 30 and a balance sheet at June 30.

(b) Adj. trial balance $112,850
(c) Net income $18,750
   Ending capital $40,750
   Total assets $72,000

PROBLEMS: SET B

Prepare adjusting entries, post to ledger accounts, and prepare an adjusted trial balance.

(SO 5, 6, 7)

P3-1B Ken Ham started his own consulting firm, Hambone Consulting, on May 1, 2010. The trial balance at May 31 is as follows.

HAMBONE CONSULTING
Trial Balance
May 31, 2010

Account Number		Debit	Credit
101	Cash	$ 5,700	
112	Accounts Receivable	6,000	
126	Supplies	1,900	
130	Prepaid Insurance	3,600	
149	Office Furniture	10,200	
201	Accounts Payable		$ 4,500
209	Unearned Service Revenue		2,000
301	K. Ham, Capital		17,700
400	Service Revenue		7,500
726	Salaries Expense	3,400	
729	Rent Expense	900	
		$31,700	$31,700

In addition to those accounts listed on the trial balance, the chart of accounts for Hambone Consulting also contains the following accounts and account numbers: No. 150 Accumulated Depreciation—Office Furniture, No. 212 Salaries Payable, No. 229 Travel Payable, No. 631

Supplies Expense, No. 717 Depreciation Expense, No. 722 Insurance Expense, and No. 736 Travel Expense.

Other data:

1. $900 of supplies have been used during the month.
2. Travel expense incurred but not paid on May 31, 2010, $250.
3. The insurance policy is for 2 years.
4. $400 of the balance in the unearned service revenue account remains unearned at the end of the month.
5. May 31 is a Wednesday, and employees are paid on Fridays. Hambone Consulting has two employees, who are paid $800 each for a 5-day work week.
6. The office furniture has a 5-year life with no salvage value. It is being depreciated at $170 per month for 60 months.
7. Invoices representing $1,200 of services performed during the month have not been recorded as of May 31.

Instructions

(a) Prepare the adjusting entries for the month of May. Use J4 as the page number for your journal.
(b) Post the adjusting entries to the ledger accounts. Enter the totals from the trial balance as beginning account balances and place a check mark in the posting reference column.
(c) Prepare an adjusted trial balance at May 31, 2010.

(c) Adj. trial balance $34,280

P3-2B   The Mound View Motel opened for business on May 1, 2010. Its trial balance before adjustment on May 31 is as follows.

Prepare adjusting entries, post, and prepare adjusted trial balance, and financial statements.

(SO 5, 6, 7)

MOUND VIEW MOTEL
Trial Balance
May 31, 2010

Account Number		Debit	Credit
101	Cash	$ 3,500	
126	Supplies	2,200	
130	Prepaid Insurance	2,280	
140	Land	12,000	
141	Lodge	60,000	
149	Furniture	15,000	
201	Accounts Payable		$ 4,800
209	Unearned Rent Revenue		3,300
275	Mortgage Payable		35,000
301	Kevin Henry, Capital		46,380
429	Rent Revenue		10,300
610	Advertising Expense	600	
726	Salaries Expense	3,300	
732	Utilities Expense	900	
		$99,780	$99,780

In addition to those accounts listed on the trial balance, the chart of accounts for Mound View Motel also contains the following accounts and account numbers: No. 142 Accumulated Depreciation—Lodge, No. 150 Accumulated Depreciation—Furniture, No. 212 Salaries Payable, No. 230 Interest Payable, No. 619 Depreciation Expense—Lodge, No. 621 Depreciation Expense—Furniture, No. 631 Supplies Expense, No. 718 Interest Expense, and No. 722 Insurance Expense.

Other data:

1. Prepaid insurance is a 1-year policy starting May 1, 2010.
2. A count of supplies shows $750 of unused supplies on May 31.
3. Annual depreciation is $3,000 on the lodge and $2,700 on furniture.
4. The mortgage interest rate is 12%. (The mortgage was taken out on May 1.)
5. Two-thirds of the unearned rent revenue has been earned.
6. Salaries of $750 are accrued and unpaid at May 31.

Instructions

(a) Journalize the adjusting entries on May 31.

(b) Prepare a ledger using the three-column form of account. Enter the trial balance amounts and post the adjusting entries. (Use J1 as the posting reference.)

(c) Adj. trial balance $101,355

(d) Net income $4,485
Ending capital balance $50,865
Total assets $92,865

(c) Prepare an adjusted trial balance on May 31.

(d) Prepare an income statement and an owner's equity statement for the month of May and a balance sheet at May 31.

Prepare adjusting entries and financial statements.

(SO 5, 6, 7)

P3-3B Poblano Co. was organized on July 1, 2010. Quarterly financial statements are prepared. The unadjusted and adjusted trial balances as of September 30 are shown below.

POBLANO CO.
Trial Balance
September 30, 2010

	Unadjusted Dr.	Unadjusted Cr.	Adjusted Dr.	Adjusted Cr.
Cash	$ 8,700		$ 8,700	
Accounts Receivable	10,400		11,200	
Supplies	1,500		900	
Prepaid Rent	2,200		1,300	
Equipment	18,000		18,000	
Accumulated Depreciation—Equipment				$ 500
Notes Payable		$ 10,000		10,000
Accounts Payable		2,500		2,500
Salaries Payable				725
Interest Payable				100
Unearned Rent Revenue		1,900		1,050
Rikki Poblano, Capital		22,000		22,000
Rikki Poblano, Drawing	1,600		1,600	
Commission Revenue		16,000		16,800
Rent Revenue		1,410		2,260
Salaries Expense	8,000		8,725	
Rent Expense	1,900		2,800	
Depreciation Expense			500	
Supplies Expense			600	
Utilities Expense	1,510		1,510	
Interest Expense			100	
	$53,810	$53,810	$55,935	$55,935

Instructions

(a) Journalize the adjusting entries that were made.

(b) Net income $4,825
Ending capital $25,225
Total assets $39,600

(b) Prepare an income statement and an owner's equity statement for the 3 months ending September 30 and a balance sheet at September 30.

(c) If the note bears interest at 12%, how many months has it been outstanding?

Prepare adjusting entries

(SO 5, 6)

P3-4B A review of the ledger of Obi Company at December 31, 2010, produces the following data pertaining to the preparation of annual adjusting entries.

1. Insurance expense $4,650

1. Prepaid Insurance $9,900. The company has separate insurance policies on its buildings and its motor vehicles. Policy B4564 on the building was purchased on April 1, 2009, for $7,200. The policy has a term of 3 years. Policy A2958 on the vehicles was purchased on January 1, 2010, for $4,500. This policy has a term of 2 years.

2. Subscription revenue $6,375

2. Unearned Subscriptions $45,000. The company began selling magazine subscriptions in 2010 on an annual basis. The magazine is published monthly. The selling price of a subscription is $45. A review of subscription contracts reveals the following.

Subscription Date	Number of Subscriptions
October 1	200
November 1	300
December 1	500
	1,000

3. Notes Payable $100,000. This balance consists of a note for 9 months at an annual interest rate of 9%, dated November 1.

4. Salaries Payable $0. There are eight salaried employees. Salaries are paid every Friday for the current week. Five employees receive a salary of $700 each per week, and three employees earn $500 each per week. Assume December 31 is a Tuesday. Employees do not work weekends. All employees worked the last 2 days of December.

3. Interest expense $1,500

4. Salaries expense $2,000

Instructions
Prepare the adjusting entries at December 31, 2010.

P3-5B On November 1, 2010, the account balances of Morelli Equipment Repair were as follows.

Journalize transactions and follow through accounting cycle to preparation of financial statements.

(SO 5, 6, 7)

No.	Debits		No.	Credits	
101	Cash	$ 2,400	154	Accumulated Depreciation	$ 2,000
112	Accounts Receivable	4,250	201	Accounts Payable	2,600
126	Supplies	1,800	209	Unearned Service Revenue	1,200
153	Store Equipment	12,000	212	Salaries Payable	700
			301	V. Morelli, Capital	13,950
		$20,450			$20,450

During November the following summary transactions were completed.

Nov. 8 Paid $1,700 for salaries due employees, of which $700 is for October salaries.
  10 Received $3,420 cash from customers on account.
  12 Received $3,100 cash for services performed in November.
  15 Purchased store equipment on account $2,000.
  17 Purchased supplies on account $700.
  20 Paid creditors on account $2,700.
  22 Paid November rent $400.
  25 Paid salaries $1,700.
  27 Performed services on account and billed customers for services provided $900.
  29 Received $600 from customers for future service.

Adjustment data consist of:

1. Supplies on hand $1,200.
2. Accrued salaries payable $400.
3. Depreciation for the month is $200.
4. Unearned service revenue of $1,250 is earned.

Instructions
(a) Enter the November 1 balances in the ledger accounts.
(b) Journalize the November transactions.
(c) Post to the ledger accounts. Use J1 for the posting reference. Use the following additional accounts: No. 407 Service Revenue, No. 615 Depreciation Expense, No. 631 Supplies Expense, No. 726 Salaries Expense, and No. 729 Rent Expense.
(d) Prepare a trial balance at November 30.
(e) Journalize and post adjusting entries.
(f) Prepare an adjusted trial balance.
(g) Prepare an income statement and an owner's equity statement for November and a balance sheet at November 30.

(d) Trial balance $24,350

(f) Adj. trial balance $24,950
(g) Net income $250; Ending capital $14,200
    Total assets $17,750

PROBLEMS: SET C

Visit the book's companion website at **www.wiley.com/college/weygandt**, and choose the Student Companion site, to access Problem Set C.

CONTINUING COOKIE CHRONICLE

(*Note*: This is a continuation of the Cookie Chronicle from Chapters 1 and 2.)

CCC3 It is the end of November and Natalie has been in touch with her grandmother. Her grandmother asked Natalie how well things went in her first month of business. Natalie, too, would like to know if she has been profitable or not during November. Natalie realizes that in order to determine Cookie Creations' income, she must first make adjustments.

Go to the book's companion website,
www.wiley.com/college/weygandt,
to see the completion of this problem.

BROADENING YOUR PERSPECTIVE

FINANCIAL REPORTING AND ANALYSIS

Financial Reporting Problem: PepsiCo, Inc.

BYP3-1 The financial statements of PepsiCo, Inc. are presented in Appendix A at the end of this textbook.

Instructions
(a) Using the consolidated financial statements and related information, identify items that may result in adjusting entries for prepayments.
(b) Using the consolidated financial statements and related information, identify items that may result in adjusting entries for accruals.
(c) Using the Selected Financial Data and 5-Year Summary, what has been the trend since 2003 for net income?

Comparative Analysis Problem: PepsiCo, Inc. vs. The Coca-Cola Company

BYP3-2 PepsiCo's financial statements are presented in Appendix A. Financial statements for The Coca-Cola Company are presented in Appendix B.

Instructions
Based on information contained in these financial statements, determine the following for each company.

(a) Net increase (decrease) in property, plant, and equipment (net) from 2006 to 2007.
(b) Increase (decrease) in selling, general, and administrative expenses from 2006 to 2007.
(c) Increase (decrease) in long-term debt (obligations) from 2006 to 2007.
(d) Increase (decrease) in net income from 2006 to 2007.
(e) Increase (decrease) in cash and cash equivalents from 2006 to 2007.

Exploring the Web

BYP3-3 A wealth of accounting-related information is available via the Internet. For example the Rutgers Accounting Web offers access to a great variety of sources.

Address: www.accounting.rutgers.edu/ or go to **www.wiley.com/college/weygandt**

Steps: Click on **Accounting Resources**. (*Note*: Once on this page, you may have to click on the **text only** box to access the available information.)

Instructions
(a) List the categories of information available through the **Accounting Resources** page.
(b) Select any one of these categories and briefly describe the types of information available.

CRITICAL THINKING

Decision Making Across the Organization

BYP3-4 Happy Camper Park was organized on April 1, 2009, by Amaya Berge. Amaya is a good manager but a poor accountant. From the trial balance prepared by a part-time bookkeeper, Amaya prepared the following income statement for the quarter that ended March 31, 2010.

HAPPY CAMPER PARK
Income Statement
For the Quarter Ended March 31, 2010

Revenues		
Rental revenue		$90,000
Operating expenses		
Advertising	$ 5,200	
Wages	29,800	
Utilities	900	
Depreciation	800	
Repairs	4,000	
Total operating expenses		40,700
Net income		$49,300

Amaya thought that something was wrong with the statement because net income had never exceeded $20,000 in any one quarter. Knowing that you are an experienced accountant, she asks you to review the income statement and other data.

You first look at the trial balance. In addition to the account balances reported above in the income statement, the ledger contains the following additional selected balances at March 31, 2010.

Supplies	$ 6,200
Prepaid Insurance	7,200
Notes Payable	12,000

You then make inquiries and discover the following.

1. Rental revenues include advanced rentals for summer occupancy $15,000.
2. There were $1,700 of supplies on hand at March 31.
3. Prepaid insurance resulted from the payment of a one-year policy on January 1, 2010.
4. The mail on April 1, 2010, brought the following bills: advertising for week of March 24, $110; repairs made March 10, $260; and utilities, $180.
5. There are four employees, who receive wages totaling $300 per day. At March 31, 2 days' wages have been incurred but not paid.
6. The note payable is a 3-month, 10% note dated January 1, 2010.

Instructions
With the class divided into groups, answer the following.

(a) Prepare a correct income statement for the quarter ended March 31, 2010.
(b) Explain to Amaya the generally accepted accounting principles that she did not recognize in preparing her income statement and their effect on her results.

Communication Activity

BYP3-5 In reviewing the accounts of Keri Ann Co. at the end of the year, you discover that adjusting entries have not been made.

Instructions

Write a memo to Keri Ann Nickels, the owner of Keri Ann Co., that explains the following: the nature and purpose of adjusting entries, why adjusting entries are needed, and the types of adjusting entries that may be made.

Ethics Case

BYP3-6   Bluestem Company is a pesticide manufacturer. Its sales declined greatly this year due to the passage of legislation outlawing the sale of several of Bluestem's chemical pesticides. In the coming year, Bluestem will have environmentally safe and competitive chemicals to replace these discontinued products. Sales in the next year are expected to greatly exceed any prior year's. The decline in sales and profits appears to be a one-year aberration. But even so, the company president fears a large dip in the current year's profits. He believes that such a dip could cause a significant drop in the market price of Bluestem's stock and make the company a takeover target.

   To avoid this possibility, the company president calls in Cathi Bell, controller, to discuss this period's year-end adjusting entries. He urges her to accrue every possible revenue and to defer as many expenses as possible. He says to Cathi, "We need the revenues this year, and next year can easily absorb expenses deferred from this year. We can't let our stock price be hammered down!" Cathi didn't get around to recording the adjusting entries until January 17, but she dated the entries December 31 as if they were recorded then. Cathi also made every effort to comply with the president's request.

Instructions

(a) Who are the stakeholders in this situation?

(b) What are the ethical considerations of (1) the president's request and (2) Cathi's dating the adjusting entries December 31?

(c) Can Cathi accrue revenues and defer expenses and still be ethical?

 ## "All About You" Activity

BYP3-7   Companies must report or disclose in their financial statements information about all liabilities, including potential liabilities related to environmental clean-up. There are many situations in which you will be asked to provide personal financial information about your assets, liabilities, revenue, and expenses. Sometimes you will face difficult decisions regarding what to disclose and how to disclose it.

Instructions

Suppose that you are putting together a loan application to purchase a home. Based on your income and assets, you qualify for the mortgage loan, but just barely. How would you address each of the following situations in reporting your financial position for the loan application? Provide responses for each of the following questions.

(a) You signed a guarantee for a bank loan that a friend took out for $20,000. If your friend doesn't pay, you will have to pay. Your friend has made all of the payments so far, and it appears he will be able to pay in the future.

(b) You were involved in an auto accident in which you were at fault. There is the possibility that you may have to pay as much as $50,000 as part of a settlement. The issue will not be resolved before the bank processes your mortgage request.

(c) The company at which you work isn't doing very well, and it has recently laid off employees. You are still employed, but it is quite possible that you will lose your job in the next few months.

 ## Answers to Insight and Accounting Across the Organization Questions

p. 98   How Long Will "The Force" Be with Us?

Q: What accounting principle does this example illustrate?

A: *This situation demonstrates the difficulty of matching expenses to revenues.*

Q: How will financial results be affected if the expenses are recognized over a period that is *less than* that used for revenues?

A: *If expenses are recognized over a period that is* less than *that used for revenues, earnings will be understated during the early years and overstated during the later years.*

Q: What if the expenses are recognized over a period that is *longer than* that used for revenues?

A: *If the expenses are recognized over a period that is longer than that used for revenues, earnings will be overstated during the early years and understated in later years. In either case, management and stockholders could be misled.*

p. 106 Turning Gift Cards into Revenue

Q: Suppose that Robert Jones purchases a $100 gift card at Best Buy on December 24, 2010, and gives it to his wife, Devon, on December 25, 2010. On January 3, 2011, Devon uses the card to purchase $100 worth of CDs. When do you think Best Buy should recognize revenue, and why?

A: *According to the revenue recognition principle, companies should recognize revenue when earned. In this case revenue is not earned until Best Buy provides the goods. Thus, when Best Buy receives cash in exchange for the gift card on December 24, 2010, it should recognize a liability, Unearned Revenue, for $100. On January 3, 2011, when Devon Jones exchanges the card for merchandise, Best Buy should recognize revenue and eliminate $100 from the balance in the Unearned Revenue account.*

Answers to Self-Study Questions

1. c   2. c   3. d   4. a   5. d   6. d   7. c   8. c   9. a   10. c   11. a   12. b   13. b
14. c   *15. a

Remember to go back to the Navigator box on the chapter-opening page and check off your completed work.

Completing the Accounting Cycle

Feature Story

EVERYONE LIKES TO WIN

When Ted Castle was a hockey coach at the University of Vermont, his players were self-motivated by their desire to win. Hockey was a game you either won or lost. But at Rhino Foods, Inc., a bakery-foods company he founded in Burlington, Vermont, he discovered that manufacturing-line workers were not so self-motivated. Ted thought, what if he turned the food-making business into a game, with rules, strategies, and trophies?

Ted knew that in a game knowing the score is all-important. He felt that only if the employees know the score—know exactly how the business is doing daily, weekly, monthly—could he turn food-making into a game. But Rhino is a closely held, family-owned business, and its financial statements

and profits were confidential. Ted wondered, should he open Rhino's books to the employees?

A consultant put Ted's concerns in perspective when he said, "Imagine you're playing touch football. You play for an hour or two, and the whole time I'm sitting there with a book, keeping score. All of a sudden I blow the whistle, and I say, 'OK, that's it. Everybody go home.' I close my book and walk away. How would you feel?" Ted opened his books and revealed the financial statements to his employees.

The next step was to teach employees the rules and strategies of how to "win" at making food. The first lesson: "Your opponent at Rhino is expenses. You must cut and control expenses." Ted and his staff distilled those lessons into daily scorecards—production reports and income statements—that keep Rhino's employees up-to-date on the game. At noon each day, Ted posts the previous day's results at the entrance to the production room. Everyone checks whether they made or lost money on what they produced the day before. And it's not just an academic exercise: There's a bonus check for each employee at the end of every four-week "game" that meets profitability guidelines.

Rhino has flourished since the first game. Employment has increased from 20 to 130 people, while both revenues and profits have grown dramatically.

The Navigator

Inside Chapter 4...

At Rhino Foods, Inc., financial statements help employees understand what is happening in the business. In Chapter 3, we prepared financial statements directly from the adjusted trial balance. However, with so many details involved in the end-of-period accounting procedures, it is easy to make errors. One way to minimize errors in the records and to simplify the end-of-period procedures is to use a worksheet.

In this chapter we will explain the role of the worksheet in accounting. We also will study the remaining steps in the accounting cycle, especially the closing process, again using Pioneer Advertising Agency as an example. Then we will consider correcting entries and classified balance sheets. The content and organization of Chapter 4 are as follows.

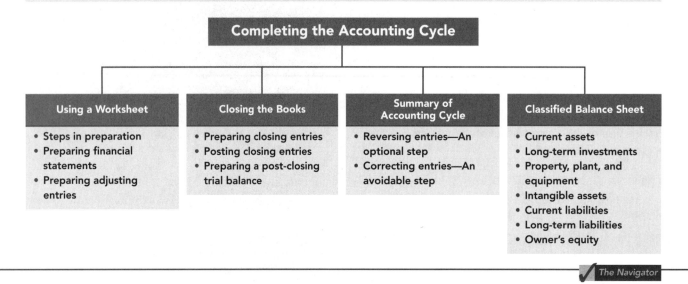

Completing the Accounting Cycle

Using a Worksheet	Closing the Books	Summary of Accounting Cycle	Classified Balance Sheet
• Steps in preparation • Preparing financial statements • Preparing adjusting entries	• Preparing closing entries • Posting closing entries • Preparing a post-closing trial balance	• Reversing entries—An optional step • Correcting entries—An avoidable step	• Current assets • Long-term investments • Property, plant, and equipment • Intangible assets • Current liabilities • Long-term liabilities • Owner's equity

The Navigator

USING A WORKSHEET

STUDY OBJECTIVE 1
Prepare a worksheet.

A **worksheet** is a multiple-column form used in the adjustment process and in preparing financial statements. As its name suggests, the worksheet is a working tool. **It is not a permanent accounting record**; it is neither a journal nor a part of the general ledger. The worksheet is merely a device used in preparing adjusting entries and the financial statements. Companies generally computerize worksheets using an electronic spreadsheet program such as Excel.

Illustration 4-1 shows the basic form of a worksheet and the five steps for preparing it. Each step is performed in sequence. **The use of a worksheet is optional.** When a company chooses to use one, it prepares financial statements from the worksheet. It enters the adjustments in the worksheet columns and then journalizes and posts the adjustments after it has prepared the financial statements. Thus, worksheets make it possible to provide the financial statements to management and other interested parties at an earlier date.

Steps in Preparing a Worksheet

We will use the October 31 trial balance and adjustment data of Pioneer Advertising, from Chapter 3, to illustrate how to prepare a worksheet. We describe each step of the process and demonstrate these steps in Illustrations 4-2 (page 148) and transparencies 4-3A, B, C, and D.

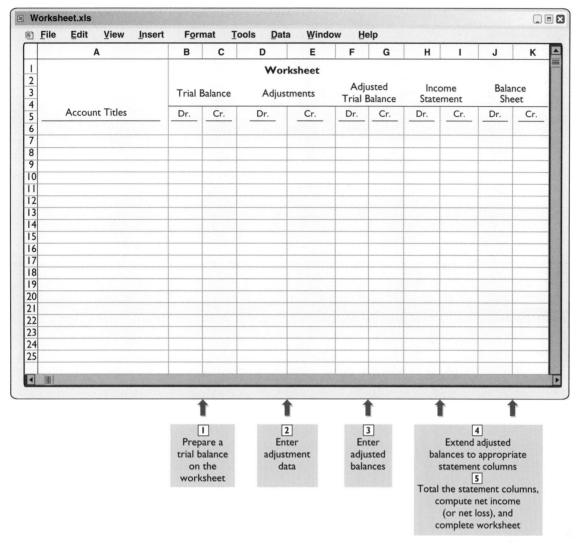

Illustration 4-1
Form and procedure for a worksheet

STEP 1. PREPARE A TRIAL BALANCE ON THE WORKSHEET

Enter all ledger accounts with balances in the account titles space. Enter debit and credit amounts from the ledger in the trial balance columns. Illustration 4-2 shows the worksheet trial balance for Pioneer Advertising Agency. This trial balance is the same one that appears in Illustration 2-31 (page 69) and Illustration 3-3 (page 100).

STEP 2. ENTER THE ADJUSTMENTS IN THE ADJUSTMENTS COLUMNS

Turn over the first transparency, Illustration 4-3A. When using a worksheet, enter all adjustments in the adjustments columns. In entering the adjustments, use applicable trial balance accounts. If additional accounts are needed, insert them on the lines immediately below the trial balance totals. A different letter identifies the debit and credit for each adjusting entry. The term used to describe this process is **keying. Companies do not journalize the adjustments until after they complete the worksheet and prepare the financial statements.**

(**Note:** Text continues on page 149, following acetate overlays.)

Illustration 4-2
Preparing a trial balance

Pioneer Advertising.xls

File   Edit   View   Insert   Format   Tools   Data   Window   Help

	A	B	C	D	E	F	G	H	I	J	K
		PIONEER ADVERTISING AGENCY									
		Worksheet									
		For the Month Ended October 31, 2010									
	Account Titles	Trial Balance		Adjustments		Adjusted Trial Balance		Income Statement		Balance Sheet	
		Dr.	Cr.	Dr.	Cr.	Dr.	Cr.	Dr.	Cr.	Dr.	Cr.
8	Cash	15,200									
9	Advertising Supplies	2,500									
10	Prepaid Insurance	600									
11	Office Equipment	5,000									
12	Notes Payable		5,000								
13	Accounts Payable		2,500								
14	Unearned Revenue		1,200								
15	C. R. Byrd, Capital		10,000								
16	C. R. Byrd, Drawing	500									
17	Service Revenue		10,000								
18											
19	Salaries Expense	4,000									
20	Rent Expense	900									
21	Totals	28,700	28,700								

Include all accounts with balances from ledger.

Trial balance amounts come directly from ledger accounts.

Illustratio

Enterin g t

Add ac
as nee
the adj

(a) Sup
(b) Insu
(c) Dep
(d) Ser
(e) Ser
(f) Inte
(g) Sala

The adjustments for Pioneer Advertising Agency are the same as the adjustments illustrated on page 112. They are keyed in the adjustments columns of the worksheet as follows.

(a) Pioneer debits an additional account, Advertising Supplies Expense, $1,500 for the cost of supplies used, and credits Advertising Supplies $1,500.

(b) Pioneer debits an additional account, Insurance Expense, $50 for the insurance that has expired, and credits Prepaid Insurance $50.

(c) The company needs two additional depreciation accounts. It debits Depreciation Expense $40 for the month's depreciation, and credits Accumulated Depreciation—Office Equipment $40.

(d) Pioneer debits Unearned Revenue $400 for services provided, and credits Service Revenue $400.

(e) Pioneer debits an additional account, Accounts Receivable, $200 for services provided but not billed, and credits Service Revenue $200.

(f) The company needs two additional accounts relating to interest. It debits Interest Expense $50 for accrued interest, and credits Interest Payable $50.

(g) Pioneer debits Salaries Expense $1,200 for accrued salaries, and credits an additional account, Salaries Payable, $1,200.

After Pioneer has entered all the adjustments, the adjustments columns are totaled to prove their equality.

STEP 3. ENTER ADJUSTED BALANCES IN THE ADJUSTED TRIAL BALANCE COLUMNS

Turn over the second transparency, Illustration 4-3B. Pioneer determines the adjusted balance of an account by combining the amounts entered in the first four columns of the worksheet for each account. For example, the Prepaid Insurance account in the trial balance columns has a $600 debit balance and a $50 credit in the adjustments columns. The result is a $550 debit balance recorded in the adjusted trial balance columns. **For each account, the amount in the adjusted trial balance columns is the balance that will appear in the ledger after journalizing and posting the adjusting entries.** The balances in these columns are the same as those in the adjusted trial balance in Illustration 3-24 (page 114).

After Pioneer has entered all account balances in the adjusted trial balance columns, the columns are totaled to prove their equality. If the column totals do not agree, the financial statement columns will not balance and the financial statements will be incorrect.

STEP 4. EXTEND ADJUSTED TRIAL BALANCE AMOUNTS TO APPROPRIATE FINANCIAL STATEMENT COLUMNS

Turn over the third transparency, Illustration 4-3C. The fourth step is to extend adjusted trial balance amounts to the income statement and balance sheet columns of the worksheet. Pioneer enters balance sheet accounts in the appropriate balance sheet debit and credit columns. For instance, it enters Cash in the balance sheet debit column, and Notes Payable in the credit column. Pioneer extends Accumulated Depreciation to the balance sheet credit column; the reason is that accumulated depreciation is a contra-asset account with a credit balance.

Because the worksheet does not have columns for the owner's equity statement, Pioneer extends the balance in owner's capital to the balance sheet credit column. In addition, it extends the balance in owner's drawing to the balance sheet debit column because it is an owner's equity account with a debit balance.

HELPFUL HINT

Every adjusted trial balance amount must be extended to one of the four statement columns.

The company enters the expense and revenue accounts such as Salaries Expense and Service Revenue in the appropriate income statement columns. Illustration 4-3C shows all of these extensions.

STEP 5. TOTAL THE STATEMENT COLUMNS, COMPUTE THE NET INCOME (OR NET LOSS), AND COMPLETE THE WORKSHEET

Turn over the fourth transparency, Illustration 4-3D. The company now must total each of the financial statement columns. The net income or loss for the period is the difference between the totals of the two income statement columns. If total credits exceed total debits, the result is net income. In such a case, as shown in Illustration 4-3D, the company inserts the words "Net Income" in the account titles space. It then enters the amount in the income statement debit column and the balance sheet credit column. **The debit amount balances the income statement columns; the credit amount balances the balance sheet columns.** In addition, the credit in the balance sheet column indicates the increase in owner's equity resulting from net income.

What if total debits in the income statement columns exceed total credits? In that case, the company has a net loss. It enters the amount of the net loss in the income statement credit column and the balance sheet debit column.

After entering the net income or net loss, the company determines new column totals. The totals shown in the debit and credit income statement columns will match. So will the totals shown in the debit and credit balance sheet columns. If either the income statement columns or the balance sheet columns are not equal after the net income or net loss has been entered, there is an error in the worksheet. Illustration 4-3D shows the completed work sheet for Pioneer Advertising Agency.

Preparing Financial Statements from a Worksheet

After a company has completed a worksheet, it has at hand all the data required for preparation of financial statements. The income statement is prepared from the income statement columns. The balance sheet and owner's equity statement are prepared from the balance sheet columns. Illustration 4-4 (page 151) shows the financial statements prepared from Pioneer's worksheet. At this point, the company has not journalized or posted adjusting entries. Therefore, ledger balances for some accounts are not the same as the financial statement amounts.

The amount shown for owner's capital on the worksheet is the account balance **before considering drawings and net income (or loss).** When the owner has made no additional investments of capital during the period, this worksheet amount for owner's capital is the balance at the beginning of the period.

Using a worksheet, companies can prepare financial statements before they journalize and post adjusting entries. **However, the completed worksheet is not a substitute for formal financial statements.** The format of the data in the financial statement columns of the worksheet is not the same as the format of the financial statements. **A worksheet is essentially a working tool of the accountant;** companies do not distribute it to management and other parties.

Accounting Cycle Tutorial—
Preparing Financial
Statements and Closing the
Books

Preparing Adjusting Entries from a Worksheet

A worksheet is not a journal, and it cannot be used as a basis for posting to ledger accounts. To adjust the accounts, the company must journalize the adjustments and

Illustration 4-4
Financial statements from a
worksheet

PIONEER ADVERTISING AGENCY
Income Statement
For the Month Ended October 31, 2010

Revenues		
Service revenue		$10,600
Expenses		
Salaries expense	$5,200	
Advertising supplies expense	1,500	
Rent expense	900	
Insurance expense	50	
Interest expense	50	
Depreciation expense	40	
Total expenses		7,740
Net income		$ 2,860

PIONEER ADVERTISING AGENCY
Owner's Equity Statement
For the Month Ended October 31, 2010

C. R. Byrd, Capital, October 1		$ –0–
Add: Investments	$10,000	
Net income	2,860	12,860
		12,860
Less: Drawings		500
C. R. Byrd, Capital, October 31		$12,360

PIONEER ADVERTISING AGENCY
Balance Sheet
October 31, 2010

Assets

Cash		$15,200
Accounts receivable		200
Advertising supplies		1,000
Prepaid insurance		550
Office equipment	$5,000	
Less: Accumulated depreciation	40	4,960
Total assets		$21,910

Liabilities and Owner's Equity

Liabilities		
Notes payable	$5,000	
Accounts payable	2,500	
Interest payable	50	
Unearned revenue	800	
Salaries payable	1,200	
Total liabilities		$ 9,550
Owner's equity		
C. R. Byrd, Capital		12,360
Total liabilities and owner's equity		$21,910

post them to the ledger. **The adjusting entries are prepared from the adjustments columns of the worksheet.** The reference letters in the adjustments columns and the explanations of the adjustments at the bottom of the worksheet help identify the adjusting entries. The journalizing and posting of adjusting entries **follows** the preparation of financial statements when a worksheet is used. The adjusting entries on October 31 for Pioneer Advertising Agency are the same as those shown in Illustration 3-22 (page 112).

DO IT!

WORKSHEET

Susan Elbe is preparing a worksheet. Explain to Susan how she should extend the following adjusted trial balance accounts to the financial statement columns of the worksheet.

> Cash
> Accumulated Depreciation
> Accounts Payable
> Julie Kerr, Drawing
> Service Revenue
> Salaries Expense

action plan

✔ Balance sheet: Extend assets to debit column. Extend liabilities to credit column. Extend contra assets to credit column. Extend drawing account to debit column.

✔ Income statement: Extend expenses to debit column. Extend revenues to credit column.

Solution

Income statement debit column—Salaries Expense
Income statement credit column—Service Revenue
Balance sheet debit column—Cash; Julie Kerr, Drawing
Balance sheet credit column—Accumulated Depreciation; Accounts Payable

Related exercise material: **BE4-1, BE4-2, BE4-3, E4-1, E4-2, E4-5, E4-6,** and **DO IT! 4-1.**

✔ *The Navigator*

CLOSING THE BOOKS

STUDY OBJECTIVE 2

Explain the process of closing the books.

ALTERNATIVE TERMINOLOGY

Temporary accounts are sometimes called *nominal accounts*, and permanent accounts are sometimes called *real accounts*.

At the end of the accounting period, the company makes the accounts ready for the next period. This is called **closing the books**. In closing the books, the company distinguishes between temporary and permanent accounts.

Temporary accounts relate only to a given accounting period. They include all income statement accounts and the owner's drawing account. The company closes all temporary accounts at the end of the period.

In contrast, **permanent accounts** relate to one or more future accounting periods. They consist of all balance sheet accounts, including the owner's capital account. Permanent accounts are not closed from period to period. Instead, the company carries forward the balances of permanent accounts into the next accounting period. Illustration 4-5 identifies the accounts in each category.

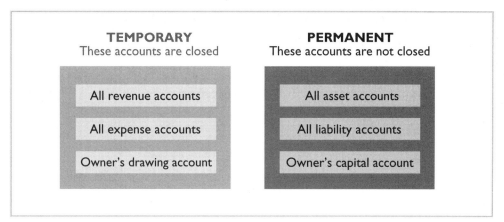

Illustration 4-5
Temporary versus permanent accounts

HELPFUL HINT

A contra-asset account, such as accumulated depreciation, is a permanent account also.

Preparing Closing Entries

At the end of the accounting period, the company transfers temporary account balances to the permanent owner's equity account, Owner's Capital, by means of closing entries.[1]

Closing entries formally recognize in the ledger the transfer of net income (or net loss) and owner's drawing to owner's capital. The owner's equity statement shows the results of these entries. **Closing entries also produce a zero balance in each temporary account.** The temporary accounts are then ready to accumulate data in the next accounting period separate from the data of prior periods. Permanent accounts are not closed.

Journalizing and posting closing entries is a required step in the accounting cycle. (See Illustration 4-12 on page 160.) The company performs this step after it has prepared financial statements. In contrast to the steps in the cycle that you have already studied, companies generally journalize and post closing entries **only at the end of the annual accounting period**. Thus, all temporary accounts will contain data for the entire year.

In preparing closing entries, companies could close each income statement account directly to owner's capital. However, to do so would result in excessive detail in the permanent Owner's Capital account. Instead, companies close the revenue and expense accounts to another temporary account, Income Summary, and they transfer the resulting net income or net loss from this account to owner's capital.

Companies **record closing entries in the general journal**. A center caption, Closing Entries, inserted in the journal between the last adjusting entry and the first closing entry, identifies these entries. Then the company posts the closing entries to the ledger accounts.

Companies generally prepare closing entries directly from the adjusted balances in the ledger. They could prepare separate closing entries for each nominal account, but the following four entries accomplish the desired result more efficiently:

1. Debit each revenue account for its balance, and credit Income Summary for total revenues.

2. Debit Income Summary for total expenses, and credit each expense account for its balance.

---

[1] We explain closing entries for a partnership and for a corporation in Chapters 12 and 13, respectively.

3. Debit Income Summary and credit Owner's Capital for the amount of net income.

4. Debit Owner's Capital for the balance in the Owner's Drawing account, and credit Owner's Drawing for the same amount.

Illustration 4-6 presents a diagram of the closing process. In it, the boxed numbers refer to the four entries required in the closing process.

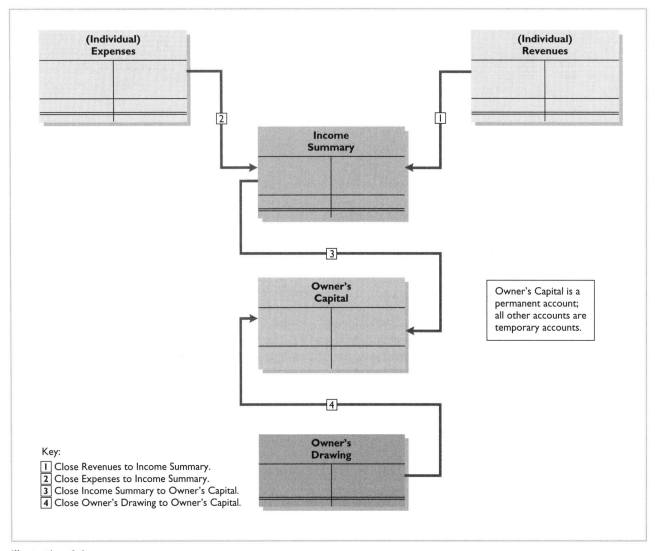

Key:
1 Close Revenues to Income Summary.
2 Close Expenses to Income Summary.
3 Close Income Summary to Owner's Capital.
4 Close Owner's Drawing to Owner's Capital.

Owner's Capital is a permanent account; all other accounts are temporary accounts.

Illustration 4-6
Diagram of closing process—proprietorship

If there were a net loss (because expenses exceeded revenues), entry 3 in Illustration 4-6 would be reversed: there would be a credit to Income Summary and a debit to Owner's Capital.

CLOSING ENTRIES ILLUSTRATED

In practice, companies generally prepare closing entries only at the end of the annual accounting period. However, to illustrate the journalizing and posting of closing entries, we will assume that Pioneer Advertising Agency closes its books monthly. Illustration 4-7 shows the closing entries at October 31. (The numbers in parentheses before each entry correspond to the four entries diagrammed in Illustration 4-6.)

Illustration 4-7
Closing entries journalized

Date	Account Titles and Explanation	Ref.	Debit	Credit
	GENERAL JOURNAL			**J3**
	<u>Closing Entries</u>			
	(1)			
2010				
Oct. 31	Service Revenue	400	10,600	
	Income Summary	350		10,600
	(To close revenue account)			
	(2)			
31	Income Summary	350	7,740	
	Advertising Supplies Expense	631		1,500
	Depreciation Expense	711		40
	Insurance Expense	722		50
	Salaries Expense	726		5,200
	Rent Expense	729		900
	Interest Expense	905		50
	(To close expense accounts)			
	(3)			
31	Income Summary	350	2,860	
	C. R. Byrd, Capital	301		2,860
	(To close net income to capital)			
	(4)			
31	C. R. Byrd, Capital	301	500	
	C. R. Byrd, Drawing	306		500
	(To close drawings to capital)			

Note that the amounts for Income Summary in entries (1) and (2) are the totals of the income statement credit and debit columns, respectively, in the worksheet.

A couple of cautions in preparing closing entries: (1) Avoid unintentionally doubling the revenue and expense balances rather than zeroing them. (2) Do not close Owner's Drawing through the Income Summary account. **Owner's Drawing is not an expense, and it is not a factor in determining net income.**

Posting Closing Entries

Illustration 4-8 (page 156) shows the posting of the closing entries and the ruling of the accounts. Note that all temporary accounts have zero balances after posting the closing entries. In addition, notice that the balance in owner's capital (C. R. Byrd, Capital) represents the total equity of the owner at the end of the accounting period. This balance is shown on the balance sheet and is the ending capital reported on the owner's equity statement, as shown in Illustration 4-4 on page 151. Pioneer uses the Income Summary account only in closing. It does not journalize and post entries to this account during the year.

As part of the closing process, Pioneer totals, balances, and double-rules its temporary accounts—revenues, expenses, and owner's drawing, as shown in T account form in Illustration 4-8. It does not close its permanent accounts—assets, liabilities, and owner's capital. Instead, Pioneer draws a single rule beneath the current-period entries for the permanent accounts. The account balance is then entered below the single rule and is carried forward to the next period. (For example, see C. R. Byrd, Capital.)

HELPFUL HINT

The balance in Income Summary before it is closed must equal the net income or net loss for the period.

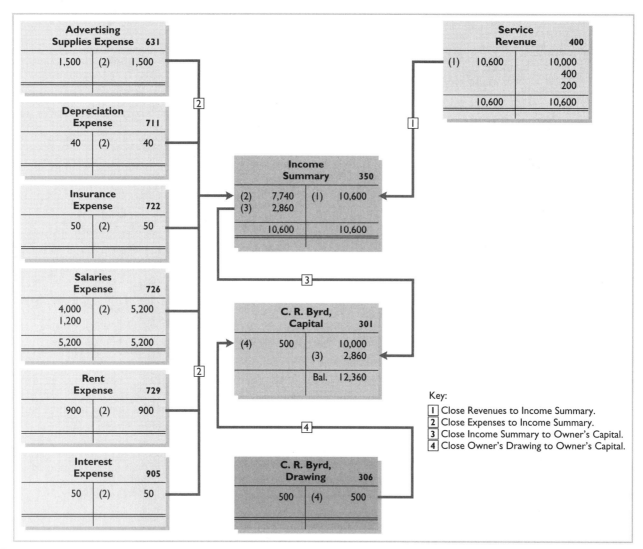

Illustration 4-8
Posting of closing entries

DO IT!

CLOSING ENTRIES

The worksheet for Hancock Company shows the following in the financial statement columns:

R. Hancock, Drawing $15,000
R. Hancock, Capital $42,000
Net income $18,000

action plan

✔ Close Income Summary to Owner's Capital.
✔ Close Owner's Drawing to Owner's Capital.

Prepare the closing entries at December 31 that affect owner's capital.

Solution

Dec. 31	Income Summary	18,000	
	R. Hancock, Capital		18,000
	(To close net income to capital)		
31	R. Hancock, Capital	15,000	
	R. Hancock, Drawing		15,000
	(To close drawings to capital)		

Related exercise material: **BE4-4, BE4-5, BE4-6, BE4-7, BE4-8, E4-4, E4-7, E4-8, E4-10, E4-11,** and **DO IT!** 4-2.

✔ *The Navigator*

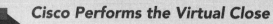

ACCOUNTING ACROSS THE ORGANIZATION

Cisco Performs the Virtual Close

Technology has dramatically shortened the closing process. Recent surveys have reported that the average company now takes only six to seven days to close, rather than 20 days. But a few companies do much better. Cisco Systems can perform a "virtual close"—closing within 24 hours on any day in the quarter. The same is true at Lockheed Martin Corp., which improved its closing time by 85% in just the last few years. Not very long ago it took 14 to 16 days. Managers at these companies emphasize that this increased speed has not reduced the accuracy and completeness of the data.

This is not just showing off. Knowing exactly where you are financially all of the time allows the company to respond faster than competitors. It also means that the hundreds of people who used to spend 10 to 20 days a quarter tracking transactions can now be more usefully employed on things such as mining data for business intelligence to find new business opportunities.

Source: "Reporting Practices: Few Do It All," *Financial Executive*, November 2003, p. 11.

 Who else benefits from a shorter closing process?

Preparing a Post-Closing Trial Balance

After Pioneer has journalized and posted all closing entries, it prepares another trial balance, called a **post-closing trial balance**, from the ledger. The post-closing trial balance lists permanent accounts and their balances after journalizing and posting of closing entries. The purpose of the post-closing trial balance is **to prove the equality of the permanent account balances carried forward into the next accounting period**. Since all temporary accounts will have zero balances, **the post-closing trial balance will contain only permanent—balance sheet—accounts**.

Illustration 4-9 shows the post-closing trial balance for Pioneer Advertising Agency.

> **STUDY OBJECTIVE 3**
>
> Describe the content and purpose of a post-closing trial balance.

Illustration 4-9
Post-closing trial balance

PIONEER ADVERTISING AGENCY Post-Closing Trial Balance October 31, 2010		
	Debit	**Credit**
Cash	$15,200	
Accounts Receivable	200	
Advertising Supplies	1,000	
Prepaid Insurance	550	
Office Equipment	5,000	
Accumulated Depreciation—Office Equipment		$ 40
Notes Payable		5,000
Accounts Payable		2,500
Unearned Revenue		800
Salaries Payable		1,200
Interest Payable		50
C. R. Byrd, Capital		12,360
	$21,950	$21,950

Pioneer prepares the post-closing trial balance from the permanent accounts in the ledger. Illustration 4-10 shows the permanent accounts in Pioneer's general ledger.

Illustration 4-10
General ledger, permanent accounts

(Permanent Accounts Only)

GENERAL LEDGER

Cash — No. 101

Date	Explanation	Ref.	Debit	Credit	Balance
2010					
Oct. 1		J1	10,000		10,000
2		J1	1,200		11,200
3		J1		900	10,300
4		J1		600	9,700
20		J1		500	9,200
26		J1		4,000	5,200
31		J1	10,000		**15,200**

Accounts Receivable — No. 112

Date	Explanation	Ref.	Debit	Credit	Balance
2010					
Oct. 31	Adj. entry	J2	**200**		200

Advertising Supplies — No. 126

Date	Explanation	Ref.	Debit	Credit	Balance
2010					
Oct. 5		J1	2,500		2,500
31	Adj. entry	J2		**1,500**	1,000

Prepaid Insurance — No. 130

Date	Explanation	Ref.	Debit	Credit	Balance
2010					
Oct. 4		J1	600		600
31	Adj. entry	J2		**50**	550

Office Equipment — No. 157

Date	Explanation	Ref.	Debit	Credit	Balance
2010					
Oct. 1		J1	5,000		**5,000**

Accumulated Depreciation—Office Equipment — No. 158

Date	Explanation	Ref.	Debit	Credit	Balance
2010					
Oct. 31	Adj. entry	J2		**40**	40

Notes Payable — No. 200

Date	Explanation	Ref.	Debit	Credit	Balance
2010					
Oct. 1		J1		5,000	**5,000**

Accounts Payable — No. 201

Date	Explanation	Ref.	Debit	Credit	Balance
2010					
Oct. 5		J1		2,500	**2,500**

Unearned Revenue — No. 209

Date	Explanation	Ref.	Debit	Credit	Balance
2010					
Oct. 2		J1		1,200	1,200
31	Adj. entry	J2	400		800

Salaries Payable — No. 212

Date	Explanation	Ref.	Debit	Credit	Balance
2010					
Oct. 31	Adj. entry	J2		**1,200**	1,200

Interest Payable — No. 230

Date	Explanation	Ref.	Debit	Credit	Balance
2010					
Oct. 31	Adj. entry	J2		**50**	50

C. R. Byrd, Capital — No. 301

Date	Explanation	Ref.	Debit	Credit	Balance
2010					
Oct. 1		J1		10,000	10,000
31	Closing entry	J3		2,860	12,860
31	Closing entry	J3	500		12,360

Note: The permanent accounts for Pioneer Advertising Agency are shown here; Illustration 4-11 shows the temporary accounts. Both permanent and temporary accounts are part of the general ledger; they are segregated here to aid in learning.

A post-closing trial balance provides evidence that the company has properly journalized and posted the closing entries. It also shows that the accounting equation is in balance at the end of the accounting period. However, like the trial balance, it does not prove that Pioneer has recorded all transactions or that the ledger is correct. For example, the post-closing trial balance still will balance even if a transaction is not journalized and posted or if a transaction is journalized and posted twice.

The remaining accounts in the general ledger are temporary accounts, shown in Illustration 4-11. After Pioneer correctly posts the closing entries, each temporary account has a zero balance. These accounts are double-ruled to finalize the closing process.

Illustration 4-11
General ledger, temporary accounts

(Temporary Accounts Only)

GENERAL LEDGER

C. R. Byrd, Drawing No. 306

Date	Explanation	Ref.	Debit	Credit	Balance
2010					
Oct. 20		J1	500		500
31	Closing entry	J3		500	–0–

Income Summary No. 350

Date	Explanation	Ref.	Debit	Credit	Balance
2010					
Oct. 31	Closing entry	J3		10,600	10,600
31	Closing entry	J3	7,740		2,860
31	Closing entry	J3	2,860		–0–

Service Revenue No. 400

Date	Explanation	Ref.	Debit	Credit	Balance
2010					
Oct. 31		J1		10,000	10,000
31	Adj. entry	J2		400	10,400
31	Adj. entry	J2		200	10,600
31	Closing entry	J3	10,600		–0–

Advertising Supplies Expense No. 631

Date	Explanation	Ref.	Debit	Credit	Balance
2010					
Oct. 31	Adj. entry	J2	1,500		1,500
31	Closing entry	J3		1,500	–0–

Depreciation Expense No. 711

Date	Explanation	Ref.	Debit	Credit	Balance
2010					
Oct. 31	Adj. entry	J2	40		40
31	Closing entry	J3		40	–0–

Insurance Expense No. 722

Date	Explanation	Ref.	Debit	Credit	Balance
2010					
Oct. 31	Adj. entry	J2	50		50
31	Closing entry	J3		50	–0–

Salaries Expense No. 726

Date	Explanation	Ref.	Debit	Credit	Balance
2010					
Oct. 26		J1	4,000		4,000
31	Adj. entry	J2	1,200		5,200
31	Closing entry	J3		5,200	–0–

Rent Expense No. 729

Date	Explanation	Ref.	Debit	Credit	Balance
2010					
Oct. 3		J1	900		900
31	Closing entry	J3		900	–0–

Interest Expense No. 905

Date	Explanation	Ref.	Debit	Credit	Balance
2010					
Oct. 31	Adj. entry	J2	50		50
31	Closing entry	J3		50	–0–

Note: The temporary accounts for Pioneer Advertising Agency are shown here; Illustration 4-10 shows the permanent accounts. Both permanent and temporary accounts are part of the general ledger; they are segregated here to aid in learning.

SUMMARY OF THE ACCOUNTING CYCLE

Illustration 4-12 (page 160) summarizes the steps in the accounting cycle. You can see that the cycle begins with the analysis of business transactions and ends with the preparation of a post-closing trial balance.

STUDY OBJECTIVE 4
State the required steps in the accounting cycle.

Steps 1–3 may occur daily during the accounting period, as explained in Chapter 2. Companies perform Steps 4–7 on a periodic basis, such as monthly, quarterly, or annually. Steps 8 and 9—closing entries, and a post-closing trial balance—usually take place only at the end of a company's **annual** accounting period.

Illustration 4-12
Steps in the accounting
cycle

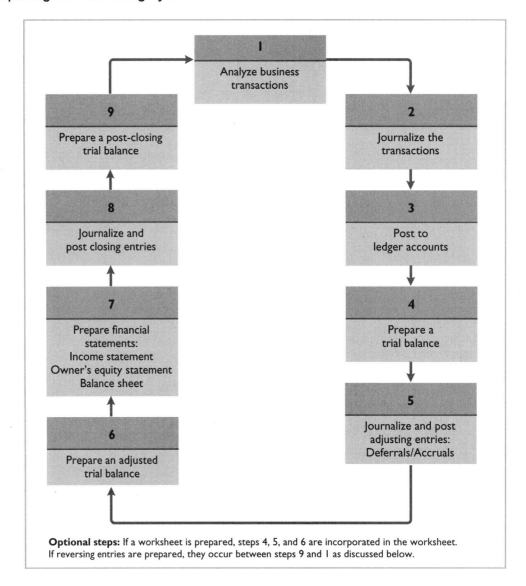

Optional steps: If a worksheet is prepared, steps 4, 5, and 6 are incorporated in the worksheet. If reversing entries are prepared, they occur between steps 9 and 1 as discussed below.

There are also two **optional steps** in the accounting cycle. As you have seen, companies may use a worksheet in preparing adjusting entries and financial statements. In addition, they may use reversing entries, as explained below.

Reversing Entries—An Optional Step

Some accountants prefer to reverse certain adjusting entries by making a **reversing entry** at the beginning of the next accounting period. A reversing entry is the exact opposite of the adjusting entry made in the previous period. **Use of reversing entries is an optional bookkeeping procedure; it is not a required step in the accounting cycle.** Accordingly, we have chosen to cover this topic in an appendix at the end of the chapter.

Correcting Entries—An Avoidable Step

STUDY OBJECTIVE 5

Explain the approaches to preparing correcting entries.

Unfortunately, errors may occur in the recording process. Companies should correct errors, **as soon as they discover them,** by journalizing and posting **correcting entries.** If the accounting records are free of errors, no correcting entries are needed.

You should recognize several differences between correcting entries and adjusting entries. First, adjusting entries are an integral part of the accounting cycle. Correcting entries, on the other hand, are unnecessary if the records are error-free. Second, companies journalize and post adjustments **only at the end of an accounting period**. In contrast, companies make correcting entries **whenever they discover an error**. Finally, adjusting entries always affect at least one balance sheet account and one income statement account. In contrast, correcting entries may involve any combination of accounts in need of correction. **Correcting entries must be posted before closing entries.**

To determine the correcting entry, it is useful to compare the incorrect entry with the correct entry. Doing so helps identify the accounts and amounts that should—and should not—be corrected. After comparison, the accountant makes an entry to correct the accounts. The following two cases for Mercato Co. illustrate this approach.

CASE 1

On May 10, Mercato Co. journalized and posted a $50 cash collection on account from a customer as a debit to Cash $50 and a credit to Service Revenue $50. The company discovered the error on May 20, when the customer paid the remaining balance in full.

Incorrect Entry (May 10)			Correct Entry (May 10)		
Cash	50		Cash	50	
Service Revenue		50	Accounts Receivable		50

Illustration 4-13
Comparison of entries

Comparison of the incorrect entry with the correct entry reveals that the debit to Cash $50 is correct. However, the $50 credit to Service Revenue should have been credited to Accounts Receivable. As a result, both Service Revenue and Accounts Receivable are overstated in the ledger. Mercato makes the following correcting entry.

	Correcting Entry		
May 20	Service Revenue	50	
	Accounts Receivable		50
	(To correct entry of May 10)		

Illustration 4-14
Correcting entry

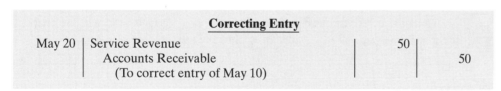

A = L + OE

−50   −50 Rev

Cash Flows
no effect

CASE 2

On May 18, Mercato purchased on account office equipment costing $450. The transaction was journalized and posted as a debit to Delivery Equipment $45 and a credit to Accounts Payable $45. The error was discovered on June 3, when Mercato received the monthly statement for May from the creditor.

Incorrect Entry (May 18)			Correct Entry (May 18)		
Delivery Equipment	45		Office Equipment	450	
Accounts Payable		45	Accounts Payable		450

Illustration 4-15
Comparison of entries

Comparison of the two entries shows that three accounts are incorrect. Delivery Equipment is overstated $45; Office Equipment is understated $450; and Accounts Payable is understated $405. Mercato makes the following correcting entry.

Illustration 4-16
Correcting entry

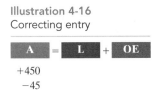

+450
−45
+405

Cash Flows
no effect

Correcting Entry			
June 3	Office Equipment	450	
	Delivery Equipment		45
	Accounts Payable		405
	(To correct entry of May 18)		

Instead of preparing a correcting entry, **it is possible to reverse the incorrect entry and then prepare the correct entry**. This approach will result in more entries and postings than a correcting entry, but it will accomplish the desired result.

ACCOUNTING ACROSS THE ORGANIZATION

Yale Express Loses Some Transportation Bills

Yale Express, a short-haul trucking firm, turned over much of its cargo to local truckers to complete deliveries. Yale collected the entire delivery charge; when billed by the local trucker, Yale sent payment for the final phase to the local trucker. Yale used a cutoff period of 20 days into the next accounting period in making its adjusting entries for accrued liabilities. That is, it waited 20 days to receive the local truckers' bills to determine the amount of the unpaid but incurred delivery charges as of the balance sheet date.

On the other hand, Republic Carloading, a nationwide, long-distance freight forwarder, frequently did not receive transportation bills from truckers to whom it passed on cargo until months after the year-end. In making its year-end adjusting entries, Republic waited for months in order to include all of these outstanding transportation bills.

When Yale Express merged with Republic Carloading, Yale's vice president employed the 20-day cutoff procedure for both firms. As a result, millions of dollars of Republic's accrued transportation bills went unrecorded. When the company detected the error and made correcting entries, these and other errors changed a reported profit of $1.14 million into a loss of $1.88 million!

? What might Yale Express's vice president have done to produce more accurate financial statements without waiting months for Republic's outstanding transportation bills?

THE CLASSIFIED BALANCE SHEET

STUDY OBJECTIVE 6

Identify the sections of a classified balance sheet.

The balance sheet presents a snapshot of a company's financial position at a point in time. To improve users' understanding of a company's financial position, companies often group similar assets and similar liabilities together. This is useful because it tells you that items within a group have similar economic characteristics. A **classified balance sheet** generally contains the standard classifications listed in Illustration 4-17.

Illustration 4-17
Standard balance sheet
classifications

Assets	Liabilities and Owner's Equity
Current assets	Current liabilities
Long-term investments	Long-term liabilities
Property, plant, and equipment	Owner's (Stockholders') equity
Intangible assets	

These groupings help readers determine such things as (1) whether the company has enough assets to pay its debts as they come due, and (2) the claims of short- and long-term creditors on the company's total assets. Many of these groupings can be seen in the balance sheet of Franklin Company shown in Illustration 4-18 below. In the sections that follow, we explain each of these groupings.

Illustration 4-18
Classified balance sheet

FRANKLIN COMPANY
Balance Sheet
October 31, 2010

Assets

Current assets			
Cash		$ 6,600	
Short-term investments		2,000	
Accounts receivable		7,000	
Notes receivable		1,000	
Inventories		3,000	
Supplies		2,100	
Prepaid insurance		400	
Total current assets			$22,100
Long-term investments			
Investment in stock of Walters Corp.		5,200	
Investment in real estate		2,000	7,200
Property, plant, and equipment			
Land		10,000	
Office equipment	$24,000		
Less: Accumulated depreciation	5,000	19,000	29,000
Intangible assets			
Patents			3,100
Total assets			$61,400

Liabilities and Owner's Equity

Current liabilities		
Notes payable	$11,000	
Accounts payable	2,100	
Salaries payable	1,600	
Unearned revenue	900	
Interest payable	450	
Total current liabilities		$16,050
Long-term liabilities		
Mortgage note payable	10,000	
Notes payable	1,300	
Total long-term liabilities		11,300
Total liabilities		27,350
Owner's equity		
B. Franklin, Capital		34,050
Total liabilities and owner's equity		$61,400

HELPFUL HINT

Recall that the basic accounting equation is Assets = Liabilities + Owner's Equity.

Current Assets

Current assets are assets that a company expects to convert to cash or use up within one year. In Illustration 4-18, Franklin Company had current assets of $22,100. For most businesses the cutoff for classification as current assets is one year from the balance sheet date. For example, accounts receivable are current assets because the company will collect them and convert them to cash within one year. Supplies is a current asset because the company expects to use it up in operations within one year.

Some companies use a period longer than one year to classify assets and liabilities as current because they have an operating cycle longer than one year. The operating cycle of a company is the average time that it takes to purchase inventory, sell it on account, and then collect cash from customers. For most businesses this cycle takes less than a year, so they use a one-year cutoff. But, for some businesses, such as vineyards or airplane manufacturers, this period may be longer than a year. **Except where noted, we will assume that companies use one year to determine whether an asset or liability is current or long-term.**

Common types of current assets are (1) cash, (2) short-term investments (such as short-term U.S. government securities), (3) receivables (notes receivable, accounts receivable, and interest receivable), (4) inventories, and (5) prepaid expenses (insurance and supplies). **On the balance sheet, companies usually list these items in the order in which they expect to convert them into cash.**

Illustration 4-19 presents the current assets of Southwest Airlines Co.

Illustration 4-19
Current assets section

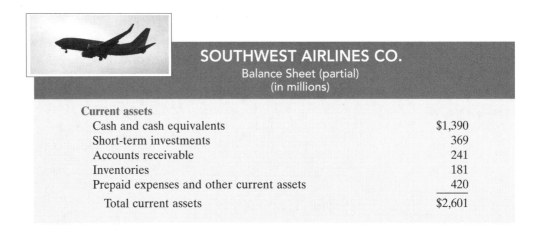

SOUTHWEST AIRLINES CO.
Balance Sheet (partial)
(in millions)

Current assets	
Cash and cash equivalents	$1,390
Short-term investments	369
Accounts receivable	241
Inventories	181
Prepaid expenses and other current assets	420
Total current assets	$2,601

As explained later in the chapter, a company's current assets are important in assessing its short-term debt-paying ability.

Long-Term Investments

Long-term investments are generally, (1) investments in stocks and bonds of other companies that are normally held for many years, and (2) long-term assets such as land or buildings that a company is not currently using in its operating activities. In Illustration 4-18 Franklin Company reported total long-term investments of $7,200 on its balance sheet.

Yahoo! Inc. reported long-term investments in its balance sheet as shown in Illustration 4-20.

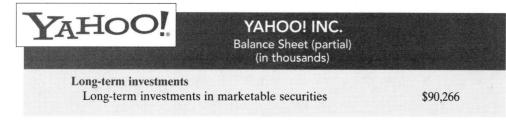

YAHOO! INC.
Balance Sheet (partial)
(in thousands)

Long-term investments	
Long-term investments in marketable securities	$90,266

Illustration 4-20
Long-term investments
section

Property, Plant, and Equipment

Property, plant, and equipment are assets with relatively long useful lives that a company is currently using in operating the business. This category (sometimes called *fixed assets*) includes land, buildings, machinery and equipment, delivery equipment, and furniture. In Illustration 4-18 Franklin Company reported property, plant, and equipment of $29,000.

Depreciation is the practice of allocating the cost of assets to a number of years. Companies do this by systematically assigning a portion of an asset's cost as an expense each year (rather than expensing the full purchase price in the year of purchase). The assets that the company depreciates are reported on the balance sheet at cost less accumulated depreciation. The **accumulated depreciation** account shows the total amount of depreciation that the company has expensed thus far in the asset's life. In Illustration 4-18 Franklin Company reported accumulated depreciation of $5,000.

Illustration 4-21 presents the property, plant, and equipment of Cooper Tire & Rubber Company.

> **INTERNATIONAL NOTE**
> In 2007 China adopted international financial reporting standards. This was done in an effort to reduce fraud and increase investor confidence in financial reports. Under these standards, many items, such as property, plant, and equipment, may be reported at current market values, rather than historical cost.

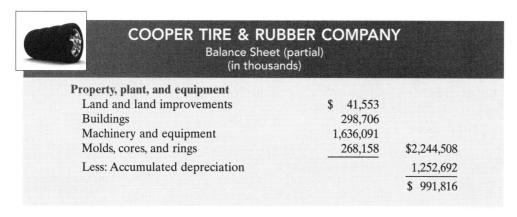

COOPER TIRE & RUBBER COMPANY
Balance Sheet (partial)
(in thousands)

Property, plant, and equipment		
Land and land improvements	$ 41,553	
Buildings	298,706	
Machinery and equipment	1,636,091	
Molds, cores, and rings	268,158	$2,244,508
Less: Accumulated depreciation		1,252,692
		$ 991,816

Illustration 4-21
Property, plant, and
equipment section

Intangible Assets

Many companies have long-lived assets that do not have physical substance yet often are very valuable. We call these assets **intangible assets**. One common intangible asset is goodwill. Others include patents, copyrights, and trademarks or trade names that give the company **exclusive right** of use for a specified period of time. In Illustration 4-18 Franklin Company reported intangible assets of $3,100.

> **HELPFUL HINT**
> Sometimes intangible assets are reported under a broader heading called *"Other assets."*

Illustration 4-22 shows the intangible assets of media giant Time Warner, Inc.

Illustration 4-22
Intangible assets section

TIME WARNER, INC.
Balance Sheet (partial)
(in millions)

Intangible assets	
Goodwill	$40,953
Film library	2,690
Customer lists	2,540
Cable television franchises	38,048
Sports franchises	262
Brands, trademarks, and other intangible assets	8,313
	$92,806

DO IT!

ASSETS SECTION OF BALANCE SHEET

Baxter Hoffman recently received the following information related to Hoffman Company's December 31, 2010, balance sheet.

Prepaid expenses	$ 2,300	Inventory	$3,400
Cash	800	Accumulated depreciation	2,700
Property, plant, and equipment	10,700	Accounts receivable	1,100

Prepare the assets section of Hoffman Company's balance sheet.

action plan

✔ Present current assets first. Current assets are cash and other resources that the company expects to convert to cash or use up within one year.

✔ Present current assets in the order in which the company expects to convert them into cash.

✔ Subtract accumulated depreciation from property, plant, and equipment to determine net property, plant, and equipment.

Solution

Assets

Current assets		
Cash	$ 800	
Accounts receivable	1,100	
Inventory	3,400	
Prepaid expenses	2,300	
Total current assets		$ 7,600
Property, plant, and equipment	10,700	
Less: Accumulated depreciation	2,700	8,000
Total assets		$15,600

Related exercise material: **BE4-10** and **DO IT!** 4-3.

 The Navigator

Current Liabilities

ETHICS NOTE

A company that has more current assets than current liabilities can increase the ratio of current assets to current liabilities by using cash to pay off some current liabilities. This gives the appearance of being more liquid. Do you think this move is ethical?

In the liabilities and owners' equity section of the balance sheet, the first grouping is current liabilities. **Current liabilities** are obligations that the company is to pay within the coming year. Common examples are accounts payable, wages payable, bank loans payable, interest payable, and taxes payable. Also included as current liabilities are current maturities of long-term obligations—payments to be made within the next year on long-term obligations. In Illustration 4-18 Franklin Company reported five different types of current liabilities, for a total of $16,050.

Within the current liabilities section, companies usually list notes payable first, followed by accounts payable. Other items then follow in the order of their magnitude. *In your homework, you should present notes payable first, followed by accounts payable, and then other liabilities in order of magnitude.*

Illustration 4-23 shows the current liabilities section adapted from the balance sheet of Marcus Corporation.

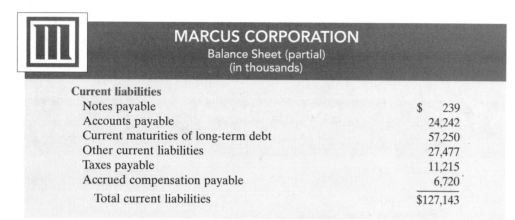

MARCUS CORPORATION
Balance Sheet (partial)
(in thousands)

Current liabilities	
Notes payable	$ 239
Accounts payable	24,242
Current maturities of long-term debt	57,250
Other current liabilities	27,477
Taxes payable	11,215
Accrued compensation payable	6,720
Total current liabilities	$127,143

Illustration 4-23
Current liabilities section

Users of financial statements look closely at the relationship between current assets and current liabilities. This relationship is important in evaluating a company's **liquidity**—its ability to pay obligations expected to be due within the next year. When current assets exceed current liabilities at the balance sheet date, the likelihood for paying the liabilities is favorable. When the reverse is true, short-term creditors may not be paid, and the company may ultimately be forced into bankruptcy.

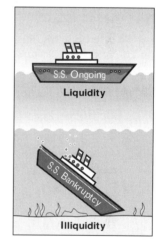

Long-Term Liabilities

Long-term liabilities are obligations that a company expects to pay **after** one year. Liabilities in this category include bonds payable, mortgages payable, long-term notes payable, lease liabilities, and pension liabilities. Many companies report long-term debt maturing after one year as a single amount in the balance sheet and show the details of the debt in notes that accompany the financial statements. Others list the various types of long-term liabilities. In Illustration 4-18 Franklin Company reported long-term liabilities of $11,300. *In your homework, list long-term liabilities in the order of their magnitude.*

Illustration 4-24 shows the long-term liabilities that The Procter & Gamble Company reported in its balance sheet.

THE PROCTER & GAMBLE COMPANY
Balance Sheet (partial)
(in millions)

Long-term liabilities	
Long-term debt	$23,375
Deferred income taxes	12,015
Other noncurrent liabilities	5,147
Total long-term liabilities	$40,537

Illustration 4-24
Long-term liabilities section

Owner's Equity

The content of the owner's equity section varies with the form of business organization. In a proprietorship, there is one capital account. In a partnership, there is a capital account for each partner. Corporations divide owners' equity into two accounts—Capital Stock and Retained Earnings. Corporations record stockholders' investments in the company by debiting an asset account and crediting the Capital Stock account. They record in the Retained Earnings account income retained for use in the business. Corporations combine the Capital Stock and Retained Earnings accounts and report them on the balance sheet as **stockholders' equity**. (We'll learn more about these corporation accounts in later chapters.) Nordstrom, Inc. recently reported its stockholders' equity section as follows.

Illustration 4-25
Stockholders' equity section

NORDSTROM, INC.
Balance Sheet (partial)
($ in thousands)

Stockholders' equity	
Common stock, 271,331 shares	$ 685,934
Retained earnings	1,406,747
Total stockholders' equity	$2,092,681

DO IT!

BALANCE SHEET CLASSIFICATIONS

The following accounts were taken from the financial statements of Callahan Company.

_____ Salaries payable
_____ Service revenue
_____ Interest payable
_____ Goodwill
_____ Short-term investments
_____ Mortgage note payable due in 3 years
_____ Investment in real estate
_____ Delivery truck
_____ Accumulated depreciation
_____ Depreciation expense
_____ R. Callahan, Capital
_____ Unearned revenue

Match each of the following accounts to its proper balance sheet classification, shown below. If the item would not appear on a balance sheet, use "NA."

Current assets (CA)
Long-term investments (LTI)
Property, plant, and equipment (PPE)
Intangible assets (IA)

Current liabilities (CL)
Long-term liabilities (LTL)
Owner's equity (OE)

action plan

✔ Analyze whether each account is an asset, liability, or owner's equity item.

✔ Determine if asset and liability items are short-term or long-term.

Solution

__CL__	Salaries payable		__LTI__	Investment in real estate
__NA__	Service revenue		__PPE__	Delivery truck
__CL__	Interest payable		__PPE__	Accumulated depreciation
__IA__	Goodwill		__NA__	Depreciation expense
__CA__	Short-term investments		__OE__	R. Callahan, Capital
__LTL__	Mortgage note payable due in 3 years		__CL__	Unearned revenue

---

Related exercise material: **BE4-11, E4-14, E4-15, E4-16, E4-17,** and DO IT! **4-4.**

 Be sure to read **ALL ABOUT YOU:** *Your Personal Balance Sheet* on page 169 for information on how topics in this chapter apply to your personal life.

all about Y✸U

Your Personal Balance Sheet

By now you should be pretty comfortable with how to prepare a company's balance sheet. Maybe it is time for us to look at *your* personal financial position.

What are your personal assets? These are the items of value that you own. Some of your assets are *liquid*—cash or items that are easily converted to cash. Others, like cars, real estate, and some types of investments, are less liquid. Some assets, like houses and investments, tend to rise in value over time, which increases your net worth. Other assets, such as cars, tend to fall in value over time, decreasing your net worth.

What are your personal liabilities—the amounts that you owe to others? Student loans, car loans, credit card bills, and amounts owed to relatives are all personal liabilities. These liabilities are either current (to be repaid within 12 months) or long-term.

The difference between your assets and liabilities is, to use the terminology of the accounting equation, your "owner's equity." In personal finance terminology, this is your *net worth*. Having a high net worth does not guarantee happiness—but most believe that it is better than being broke. By monitoring your personal balance sheet, you can begin to take control of your financial future.

✸ Some Facts

* 48% of Americans think they know how much wealth they have.

* 2005 was the first year since the Depression when Americans spent more money than they made.

* The total net worth of U.S. households hit a record of $51.09 trillion during 2005.

* Economists note that a rise in house prices actually results in a fall in individual savings. It has been documented that a $1,000 rise in the value of a home results in a $50 fall in savings per year, presumably because homeowners feel more wealthy and therefore spend more (save less).

* When asked about very important wealth-building strategies for all Americans, 16% said "win the lottery."

✸ About the Numbers

Your ability to make good financial decisions is often influenced by your attitudes toward saving versus spending. The authors of a recent study conclude that "people commonly fall prey to psychologically driven impulses that affect their financial decisions." For example, when individuals were asked whether could they save 20% of their household income, nearly half said they couldn't. But, when asked if they could spend less, well more than half (71%) said they could live comfortably on 80% of their income. This clearly is inconsistent thinking: If you can live on 80% of your current income, you can save 20% of your current income.

"How much could you save?"

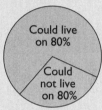

Nearly half could not comfortably **save 20%** of household's **annual income** at this point in life.

BUT

71% said they could comfortably **live on 80%** of household's **annual income** at this point in life.

Source: Northwestern Mutual Life, *www.nmfn.com/contentassets/pdfs/fin_misbehav.pdf*, p. 6.

✸ What Do You Think?

Should you prepare a personal balance sheet?

YES: In order to attain your desired financial objectives, you need to set goals early. The personal balance sheet provides a benchmark by which you can measure progress toward your financial goals. You need to do it now so that you begin to develop good financial habits. It provides a mechanism so that you don't allow your finances to get too "out-of-whack" while you are in school. That is, you don't want to dig too deep a hole.

NO: Your financial situation right now bears very little resemblance to what it will look like after you graduate. At that point, you will have a better job, and you won't have to pay tuition. Right now, you're just "bleeding cash."

Sources: Andrew Blackman, "How to Calculate Your Savings Rate; For Americans in 2005, Earnings Didn't Keep Pace with Boom in Spending," *Wall Street Journal*, January 3, 2006, p. D2; "Financial Planners Share Views on Saving," Consumer Federation of America and Financial Planning Association, January 2006.

Comprehensive DO IT!

At the end of its first month of operations, Watson Answering Service has the following unadjusted trial balance.

WATSON ANSWERING SERVICE
August 31, 2010
Trial Balance

	Debit	Credit
Cash	$ 5,400	
Accounts Receivable	2,400	
Supplies	2,800	
Prepaid Insurance	1,300	
Equipment	60,000	
Notes Payable		$40,000
Accounts Payable		2,400
Ray Watson, Capital		30,000
Ray Watson, Drawing	1,000	
Service Revenue		4,900
Salaries Expense	3,200	
Utilities Expense	800	
Advertising Expense	400	
	$77,300	$77,300

action plan

✔ In completing the worksheet, be sure to (a) key the adjustments; (b) start at the top of the adjusted trial balance columns and extend adjusted balances to the correct statement columns; and (c) enter net income (or net loss) in the proper columns.

✔ In preparing a classified balance sheet, know the contents of each of the sections.

✔ In journalizing closing entries, remember that there are only four entries and that owner's drawing is closed to owner's capital.

Other data:

1. Insurance expires at the rate of $200 per month.
2. $1,000 of supplies are on hand at August 31.
3. Monthly depreciation on the equipment is $900.
4. Interest of $500 on the notes payable has accrued during August.

Instructions

(a) Prepare a worksheet.
(b) Prepare a classified balance sheet assuming $35,000 of the notes payable are long-term.
(c) Journalize the closing entries.

Solution to Comprehensive DO IT!

(a)
WATSON ANSWERING SERVICE
Worksheet For the Month Ended August 31, 2010

Account Titles	Trial Balance Dr.	Trial Balance Cr.	Adjustments Dr.	Adjustments Cr.	Adjusted Trial Balance Dr.	Adjusted Trial Balance Cr.	Income Statement Dr.	Income Statement Cr.	Balance Sheet Dr.	Balance Sheet Cr.
Cash	5,400				5,400				5,400	
Accounts Receivable	2,800				2,800				2,800	
Supplies	1,300			(b) 300	1,000				1,000	
Prepaid Insurance	2,400			(a) 200	2,200				2,200	
Equipment	60,000				60,000				60,000	
Notes Payable		40,000				40,000				40,000
Accounts Payable		2,400				2,400				2,400
Ray Watson, Capital		30,000				30,000				30,000
Ray Watson, Drawing	1,000				1,000				1,000	
Service Revenue		4,900				4,900		4,900		
Salaries Expense	3,200				3,200		3,200			
Utilities Expense	800				800		800			
Advertising Expense	400				400		400			
Totals	77,300	77,300								

Account Titles	Trial Balance		Adjustments		Adjusted Trial Balance		Income Statement		Balance Sheet	
	Dr.	Cr.	Dr.	Cr.	Dr.	Cr.	Dr.	Cr.	Dr.	Cr.
Insurance Expense			(a) 200		200		200			
Supplies Expense			(b) 300		300		300			
Depreciation Expense			(c) 900		900		900			
Accumulated Depreciation—Equipment				(c) 900		900				900
Interest Expense			(d) 500		500		500			
Interest Payable				(d) 500		500				500
Totals			1,900	1,900	78,700	78,700	6,300	4,900	72,400	73,800
Net Loss								1,400	1,400	
Totals							6,300	6,300	73,800	73,800

Explanation: (a) Insurance expired, (b) Supplies used, (c) Depreciation expensed, (d) Interest accrued.

(b)

WATSON ANSWERING SERVICE
Balance Sheet
August 31, 2010

Assets

Current assets

Cash	$ 5,400	
Accounts receivable	2,800	
Supplies	1,000	
Prepaid insurance	2,200	
Total current assets		$11,400

Property, plant, and equipment

Equipment	$60,000	
Less: Accumulated depreciation—equipment	900	59,100
Total assets		$70,500

Liabilities and Owner's Equity

Current liabilities

Notes payable	$5,000	
Accounts payable	2,400	
Interest payable	500	
Total current liabilities		$ 7,900

Long-term liabilities

Notes payable		35,000
Total liabilities		42,900

Owner's equity

Ray Watson, Capital		27,600*
Total liabilities and owner's equity		$70,500

*Ray Watson, Capital, $30,000 less drawings $1,000 and net loss $1,400.

(c)

Aug. 31	Service Revenue	4,900	
	Income Summary		4,900
	(To close revenue account)		

31	Income Summary	6,300		
	Salaries Expense		3,200	
	Depreciation Expense		900	
	Utilities Expense		800	
	Interest Expense		500	
	Advertising Expense		400	
	Supplies Expense		300	
	Insurance Expense		200	
	(To close expense accounts)			
31	Ray Watson, Capital	1,400		
	Income Summary		1,400	
	(To close net loss to capital)			
31	Ray Watson, Capital	1,000		
	Ray Watson, Drawing		1,000	
	(To close drawings to capital)			

SUMMARY OF STUDY OBJECTIVES

1 Prepare a worksheet. The steps in preparing a worksheet are: (a) Prepare a trial balance on the worksheet. (b) Enter the adjustments in the adjustments columns. (c) Enter adjusted balances in the adjusted trial balance columns. (d) Extend adjusted trial balance amounts to appropriate financial statement columns. (e) Total the statement columns, compute net income (or net loss), and complete the worksheet.

2 Explain the process of closing the books. Closing the books occurs at the end of an accounting period. The process is to journalize and post closing entries and then rule and balance all accounts. In closing the books, companies make separate entries to close revenues and expenses to Income Summary, Income Summary to Owner's Capital, and Owner's Drawings to Owner's Capital. Only temporary accounts are closed.

3 Describe the content and purpose of a post-closing trial balance. A post-closing trial balance contains the balances in permanent accounts that are carried forward to the next accounting period. The purpose of this trial balance is to prove the equality of these balances.

4 State the required steps in the accounting cycle. The required steps in the accounting cycle are: (1) analyze business transactions, (2) journalize the transactions, (3) post to ledger accounts, (4) prepare a trial balance, (5) journalize and post adjusting entries, (6) prepare an adjusted trial balance, (7) prepare financial statements, (8) journalize and post closing entries, and (9) prepare a post-closing trial balance.

5 Explain the approaches to preparing correcting entries. One way to determine the correcting entry is to compare the incorrect entry with the correct entry. After comparison, the company makes a correcting entry to correct the accounts. An alternative to a correcting entry is to reverse the incorrect entry and then prepare the correct entry.

6 Identify the sections of a classified balance sheet. A classified balance sheet categorizes assets as current assets; long-term investments; property, plant, and equipment; and intangibles. Liabilities are classified as either current or long-term. There is also an owner's (owners') equity section, which varies with the form of business organization.

GLOSSARY

Classified balance sheet   A balance sheet that contains standard classifications or sections. (p. 162).

Closing entries   Entries made at the end of an accounting period to transfer the balances of temporary accounts to a permanent owner's equity account, Owner's Capital. (p. 153).

Correcting entries   Entries to correct errors made in recording transactions. (p. 160).

Current assets   Assets that a company expects to convert to cash or use up within one year. (p. 164).

Current liabilities   Obligations that a company expects to pay from existing current assets within the coming year. (p. 166).

Income Summary   A temporary account used in closing revenue and expense accounts. (p. 153).

Intangible assets   Noncurrent assets that do not have physical substance. (p. 165).

Liquidity The ability of a company to pay obligations expected to be due within the next year. (p. 167).

Long-term investments Generally, (1) investments in stocks and bonds of other companies that companies normally hold for many years, and (2) long-term assets, such as land and buildings, not currently being used in operations. (p. 164).

Long-term liabilities Obligations that a company expects to pay after one year. (p. 167).

Operating cycle The average time that it takes to go from cash to cash in producing revenues. (p. 164).

Permanent (real) accounts Accounts that relate to one or more accounting periods. Consist of all balance sheet accounts. Balances are carried forward to next accounting period. (p. 152).

Post-closing trial balance A list of permanent accounts and their balances after a company has journalized and posted closing entries. (p. 157).

Property, plant, and equipment Assets with relatively long useful lives and currently being used in operations. (p. 165).

Reversing entry An entry, made at the beginning of the next accounting period, that is the exact opposite of the adjusting entry made in the previous period. (p. 160).

Stockholders' equity The ownership claim of shareholders on total assets. It is to a corporation what owner's equity is to a proprietorship. (p. 168).

Temporary (nominal) accounts Accounts that relate only to a given accounting period. Consist of all income statement accounts and owner's drawing account. All temporary accounts are closed at end of the accounting period. (p. 152).

Worksheet A multiple-column form that may be used in making adjusting entries and in preparing financial statements. (p. 146).

APPENDIX **Reversing Entries**

After preparing the financial statements and closing the books, it is often helpful to reverse some of the adjusting entries before recording the regular transactions of the next period. Such entries are **reversing entries**. Companies make **a reversing entry at the beginning of the next accounting period**. Each reversing entry **is the exact opposite of the adjusting entry made in the previous period**. The recording of reversing entries is an **optional step** in the accounting cycle.

STUDY OBJECTIVE 7
Prepare reversing entries.

The purpose of reversing entries is to simplify the recording of a subsequent transaction related to an adjusting entry. For example, in Chapter 3 (page 111), the payment of salaries after an adjusting entry resulted in two debits: one to Salaries Payable and the other to Salaries Expense. With reversing entries, the company can debit the entire subsequent payment to Salaries Expense. **The use of reversing entries does not change the amounts reported in the financial statements.** What it does is simplify the recording of subsequent transactions.

Reversing Entries Example

Companies most often use reversing entries to reverse two types of adjusting entries: accrued revenues and accrued expenses. To illustrate the optional use of reversing entries for accrued expenses, we will use the salaries expense transactions for Pioneer Advertising Agency as illustrated in Chapters 2, 3, and 4. The transaction and adjustment data are as follows.

1. October 26 (initial salary entry): Pioneer pays $4,000 of salaries earned between October 15 and October 26.

2. October 31 (adjusting entry): Salaries earned between October 29 and October 31 are $1,200. The company will pay these in the November 9 payroll.

3. November 9 (subsequent salary entry): Salaries paid are $4,000. Of this amount, $1,200 applied to accrued wages payable and $2,800 was earned between November 1 and November 9.

Illustration 4A-1 shows the entries with and without reversing entries.

Without Reversing Entries (per chapter)			With Reversing Entries (per appendix)	
Initial Salary Entry			**Initial Salary Entry**	
Oct. 26 Salaries Expense	4,000		Oct. 26 (Same entry)	
Cash		4,000		
Adjusting Entry			**Adjusting Entry**	
Oct. 31 Salaries Expense	1,200		Oct. 31 (Same entry)	
Salaries Payable		1,200		
Closing Entry			**Closing Entry**	
Oct. 31 Income Summary	5,200		Oct. 31 (Same entry)	
Salaries Expense		5,200		
Reversing Entry			**Reversing Entry**	
Nov. 1 No reversing entry is made.			Nov. 1 **Salaries Payable**	1,200
			Salaries Expense	1,200
Subsequent Salary Entry			**Subsequent Salary Entry**	
Nov. 9 Salaries Payable	1,200		Nov. 9 **Salaries Expense**	4,000
Salaries Expense	2,800		**Cash**	4,000
Cash		4,000		

Illustration 4A-1
Comparative entries—not reversing vs. reversing

The first three entries are the same whether or not Pioneer uses reversing entries. The last two entries are different. The November 1 **reversing entry** eliminates the $1,200 balance in Salaries Payable created by the October 31 adjusting entry. The reversing entry also creates a $1,200 credit balance in the Salaries Expense account. As you know, it is unusual for an expense account to have a credit balance. The balance is correct in this instance, though, because it anticipates that the entire amount of the first salary payment in the new accounting period will be debited to Salaries Expense. This debit will eliminate the credit balance. The resulting debit balance in the expense account will equal the salaries expense incurred in the new accounting period ($2,800 in this example).

If Pioneer makes reversing entries, it can debit all cash payments of expenses to the expense account. This means that on November 9 (and every payday) Pioneer can debit Salaries Expense for the amount paid, without regard to any accrued salaries payable. Being able to make the **same entry each time** simplifies the recording process: The company can record subsequent transactions as if the related adjusting entry had never been made.

Illustration 4A-2 shows the posting of the entries with reversing entries.

Illustration 4A-2
Postings with reversing entries

Salaries Expense				Salaries Payable			
10/26 Paid	4,000	10/31 Closing	5,200	11/1 Reversing	1,200	10/31 Adjusting	1,200
31 Adjusting	1,200						
	5,200		5,200				
11/9 Paid	4,000	11/1 Reversing	1,200				

A company can also use reversing entries for accrued revenue adjusting entries. For Pioneer Advertising, the adjusting entry was: Accounts Receivable (Dr.) $200 and Service Revenue (Cr.) $200. Thus, the reversing entry on November 1 is:

Nov. 1	Service Revenue	200	
	Accounts Receivable		200
	(To reverse October 31 adjusting entry)		

−200

Cash Flows
no effect

When Pioneer collects the accrued service revenue, it debits Cash and credits Service Revenue.

SUMMARY OF STUDY OBJECTIVE FOR APPENDIX

7 Prepare reversing entries. Reversing entries are the opposite of the adjusting entries made in the preceding period. Some companies choose to make reversing entries at the beginning of a new accounting period to simplify the recording of later transactions related to the adjusting entries. In most cases, only accrued adjusting entries are reversed.

Note: All asterisked Questions, Exercises, and Problems relate to material in the appendix to the chapter.

SELF-STUDY QUESTIONS

Answers are at the end of the chapter.

(SO 1) **1.** Which of the following statements is *incorrect* concerning the worksheet?
   a. The worksheet is essentially a working tool of the accountant.
   b. The worksheet is distributed to management and other interested parties.
   c. The worksheet cannot be used as a basis for posting to ledger accounts.
   d. Financial statements can be prepared directly from the worksheet before journalizing and posting the adjusting entries.

(SO 1) **2.** In a worksheet, net income is entered in the following columns:
   a. income statement (Dr) and balance sheet (Dr).
   b. income statement (Cr) and balance sheet (Dr).
   c. income statement (Dr) and balance sheet (Cr).
   d. income statement (Cr) and balance sheet (Cr).

(SO 1) **3.** In the unadjusted trial balance of its worksheet for the year ended December 31, 2010, Taitum Company reported Office Equipment of $120,000. The year-end adjusting entries require an adjustment of $15,000 for depreciation expense for the office equipment. After adjustment, the following adjusted amount should be reported:
   a. A debit of $105,000 for Office Equipment in the balance sheet column.
   b. A credit of $15,000 for Depreciation Expense—Office Equipment in the income statement column.
   c. A debit of $120,000 for Office Equipment in the balance sheet column.
   d. A debit of $15,000 for Accumulated Deprecation—Office Equipment in the balance sheet column.

(SO 2) **4.** An account that will have a zero balance after closing entries have been journalized and posted is:
   a. Service Revenue.
   b. Advertising Supplies.

   c. Prepaid Insurance.
   d. Accumulated Depreciation.

(SO 2) **5.** When a net loss has occurred, Income Summary is:
   a. debited and Owner's Capital is credited.
   b. credited and Owner's Capital is debited.
   c. debited and Owner's Drawing is credited.
   d. credited and Owner's Drawing is debited.

(SO 2) **6.** The closing process involves separate entries to close (1) expenses, (2) drawings, (3) revenues, and (4) income summary. The correct sequencing of the entries is:
   a. (4), (3), (2), (1)
   b. (1), (2), (3), (4)
   c. (3), (1), (4), (2)
   d. (3), (2), (1), (4)

(SO 3) **7.** Which types of accounts will appear in the post-closing trial balance?
   a. Permanent (real) accounts.
   b. Temporary (nominal) accounts.
   c. Accounts shown in the income statement columns of a work sheet.
   d. None of the above.

(SO 4) **8.** All of the following are required steps in the accounting cycle *except*:
   a. journalizing and posting closing entries.
   b. preparing financial statements.
   c. journalizing the transactions.
   d. preparing a work sheet.

(SO 4) **9.** The proper order of the following steps in the accounting cycle is:
   a. prepare unadjusted trial balance, journalize transactions, post to ledger accounts, journalize and post adjusting entries.
   b. journalize transactions, prepare unadjusted trial balance, post to ledger accounts, journalize and post adjusting entries.

c. journalize transactions, post to ledger accounts, prepare unadjusted trial balance, journalize and post adjusting entries.

d. prepare unadjusted trial balance, journalize and post adjusting entries, journalize transactions, post to ledger accounts.

(SO 5) **10.** When Alexander Company purchased supplies worth $500, it incorrectly recorded a credit to Supplies for $5,000 and a debit to Cash for $5,000. Before correcting this error:

a. Cash is overstated and Supplies is overstated.

b. Cash is understated and Supplies is understated.

c. Cash is understated and Supplies is overstated.

d. Cash is overstated and Supplies is understated.

(SO 5) **11.** Cash of $100 received at the time the service was provided was journalized and posted as a debit to Cash $100 and a credit to Accounts Receivable $100. Assuming the incorrect entry is not reversed, the correcting entry is:

a. debit Service Revenue $100 and credit Accounts Receivable $100.

b. debit Accounts Receivable $100 and credit Service Revenue $100.

c. debit Cash $100 and credit Service Revenue $100.

d. debit Accounts Receivable $100 and credit Cash $100.

(SO 6) **12.** The correct order of presentation in a classified balance sheet for the following current assets is:

a. accounts receivable, cash, prepaid insurance, inventories.

b. cash, inventories, accounts receivable, prepaid insurance.

c. cash, accounts receivable, inventories, prepaid insurance.

d. inventories, cash, accounts receivable, prepaid insurance.

(SO 6) **13.** A company has purchased a tract of land. It expects to build a production plant on the land in approximately 5 years. During the 5 years before construction, the land will be idle. The land should be reported as:

a. property, plant, and equipment.

b. land expense.

c. a long-term investment.

d. an intangible asset.

(SO 6) **14.** In a classified balance sheet, assets are usually classified using the following categories:

a. current assets; long-term assets; property, plant, and equipment; and intangible assets.

b. current assets; long-term investments; property, plant, and equipment; and tangible assets.

c. current assets; long-term investments; tangible assets; and intangible assets.

d. current assets; long-term investments; property, plant, and equipment; and intangible assets.

(SO 6) **15.** Current assets are listed:

a. by expected conversion to cash.

b. by importance.

c. by longevity.

d. alphabetically.

*(SO 7) **16.** On December 31, Frank Voris Company correctly made an adjusting entry to recognize $2,000 of accrued salaries payable. On January 8 of the next year, total salaries of $3,400 were paid. Assuming the correct reversing entry was made on January 1, the entry on January 8 will result in a credit to Cash $3,400 and the following debit(s):

a. Salaries Payable $1,400, and Salaries Expense $2,000.

b. Salaries Payable $2,000 and Salaries Expense $1,400.

c. Salaries Expense $3,400.

d. Salaries Payable $3,400.

Go to the book's companion website, **www.wiley.com/college/weygandt**, for additional Self-Study Questions.

 The Navigator

QUESTIONS

1. "A worksheet is a permanent accounting record and its use is required in the accounting cycle." Do you agree? Explain.

2. Explain the purpose of the worksheet.

3. What is the relationship, if any, between the amount shown in the adjusted trial balance column for an account and that account's ledger balance?

4. If a company's revenues are $125,000 and its expenses are $113,000, in which financial statement columns of the worksheet will the net income of $12,000 appear? When expenses exceed revenues, in which columns will the difference appear?

5. Why is it necessary to prepare formal financial statements if all of the data are in the statement columns of the worksheet?

6. Identify the account(s) debited and credited in each of the four closing entries, assuming the company has net income for the year.

7. Describe the nature of the Income Summary account and identify the types of summary data that may be posted to this account.

8. What are the content and purpose of a post-closing trial balance?

9. Which of the following accounts would not appear in the post-closing trial balance? Interest Payable; Equipment; Depreciation Expense; Jennifer Shaeffer, Drawing; Unearned Revenue; Accumulated Depreciation—Equipment; and Service Revenue.

10. Distinguish between a reversing entry and an adjusting entry. Are reversing entries required?

11. Indicate, in the sequence in which they are made, the three required steps in the accounting cycle that involve journalizing.

12. Identify, in the sequence in which they are prepared, the three trial balances that are often used to report financial information about a company.

13. How do correcting entries differ from adjusting entries?

14. What standard classifications are used in preparing a classified balance sheet?

15. What is meant by the term "operating cycle?"

16. Define current assets. What basis is used for arranging individual items within the current assets section?

17. Distinguish between long-term investments and property, plant, and equipment.

18. (a) What is the term used to describe the owner's equity section of a corporation? (b) Identify the two owners' equity accounts in a corporation and indicate the purpose of each.

19. ®PEPSICO Using PepsiCo's annual report, determine its current liabilities at December 29, 2007, and December 30,

2006. Were current liabilities higher or lower than current assets in these two years?

*20. Sanchez Company prepares reversing entries. If the adjusting entry for interest payable is reversed, what type of an account balance, if any, will there be in Interest Payable and Interest Expense after the reversing entry is posted?

*21. At December 31, accrued salaries payable totaled $3,500. On January 10, total salaries of $8,000 are paid. (a) Assume that reversing entries are made at January 1. Give the January 10 entry, and indicate the Salaries Expense account balance after the entry is posted. (b) Repeat part (a) assuming reversing entries are not made.

BRIEF EXERCISES

BE4-1 The steps in using a worksheet are presented in random order below. List the steps in the proper order by placing numbers 1–5 in the blank spaces.

(a) _____ Prepare a trial balance on the worksheet.
(b) _____ Enter adjusted balances.
(c) _____ Extend adjusted balances to appropriate statement columns.
(d) _____ Total the statement columns, compute net income (loss), and complete the worksheet.
(e) _____ Enter adjustment data.

List the steps in preparing a worksheet.
(SO 1)

BE4-2 The ledger of Ley Company includes the following unadjusted balances: Prepaid Insurance $3,000, Service Revenue $58,000, and Salaries Expense $25,000. Adjusting entries are required for (a) expired insurance $1,200; (b) services provided $1,100, but unbilled and uncollected; and (c) accrued salaries payable $800. Enter the unadjusted balances and adjustments into a worksheet and complete the worksheet for all accounts. *Note:* You will need to add the following accounts: Accounts Receivable, Salaries Payable, and Insurance Expense.

Prepare partial worksheet.
(SO 1)

BE4-3 The following selected accounts appear in the adjusted trial balance columns of the worksheet for Batan Company: Accumulated Depreciation; Depreciation Expense; N. Batan, Capital; N. Batan, Drawing; Service Revenue; Supplies; and Accounts Payable. Indicate the financial statement column (income statement Dr., balance sheet Cr., etc.) to which each balance should be extended.

Identify worksheet columns for selected accounts.
(SO 1)

BE4-4 The ledger of Swann Company contains the following balances: D. Swann, Capital $30,000; D. Swann, Drawing $2,000; Service Revenue $50,000; Salaries Expense $27,000; and Supplies Expense $4,000. Prepare the closing entries at December 31.

Prepare closing entries from ledger balances.
(SO 2)

BE4-5 Using the data in BE4-4, enter the balances in T accounts, post the closing entries, and rule and balance the accounts.

Post closing entries; rule and balance T accounts.
(SO 2)

BE4-6 The income statement for Crestwood Golf Club for the month ending July 31 shows Green Fee Revenue $13,600, Salaries Expense $8,200, Maintenance Expense $2,500, and Net Income $2,900. Prepare the entries to close the revenue and expense accounts. Post the entries to the revenue and expense accounts, and complete the closing process for these accounts using the three-column form of account.

Journalize and post closing entries using the three-column form of account.
(SO 2)

BE4-7 Using the data in BE4-3, identify the accounts that would be included in a post-closing trial balance.

Identify post-closing trial balance accounts.
(SO 3)

List the required steps in the accounting cycle in sequence.
(SO 4)

BE4-8 The steps in the accounting cycle are listed in random order below. List the steps in proper sequence, assuming no worksheet is prepared, by placing numbers 1–9 in the blank spaces.

(a) _____ Prepare a trial balance.
(b) _____ Journalize the transactions.
(c) _____ Journalize and post closing entries.
(d) _____ Prepare financial statements.
(e) _____ Journalize and post adjusting entries.
(f) _____ Post to ledger accounts.
(g) _____ Prepare a post-closing trial balance.
(h) _____ Prepare an adjusted trial balance.
(i) _____ Analyze business transactions.

Prepare correcting entries.
(SO 5)

BE4-9 At Batavia Company, the following errors were discovered after the transactions had been journalized and posted. Prepare the correcting entries.

1. A collection on account from a customer for $780 was recorded as a debit to Cash $780 and a credit to Service Revenue $780.
2. The purchase of store supplies on account for $1,570 was recorded as a debit to Store Supplies $1,750 and a credit to Accounts Payable $1,750.

Prepare the current assets section of a balance sheet.
(SO 6)

BE4-10 The balance sheet debit column of the worksheet for Diaz Company includes the following accounts: Accounts Receivable $12,500; Prepaid Insurance $3,600; Cash $15,400; Supplies $5,200, and Short-term Investments $6,700. Prepare the current assets section of the balance sheet, listing the accounts in proper sequence.

Classify accounts on balance sheet.
(SO 6)

BE4-11 The following are the major balance sheet classifications:

Current assets (CA)
Long-term investments (LTI)
Property, plant, and equipment (PPE)
Intangible assets (IA)

Current liabilities (CL)
Long-term liabilities (LTL)
Owner's equity (OE)

Match each of the following accounts to its proper balance sheet classification.

_____ Accounts payable
_____ Accounts receivable
_____ Accumulated depreciation
_____ Building
_____ Cash
_____ Copyrights

_____ Income tax payable
_____ Investment in long-term bonds
_____ Land
_____ Merchandise inventory
_____ Patent
_____ Supplies

Prepare reversing entries.
(SO 7)

*BE4-12 At October 31, Nathan Company made an accrued expense adjusting entry of $1,400 for salaries. Prepare the reversing entry on November 1, and indicate the balances in Salaries Payable and Salaries Expense after posting the reversing entry.

DO IT! REVIEW

Prepare a worksheet.
(SO 1)

DO IT! 4-1 Vladimir Klitschko is preparing a worksheet. Explain to Vladimir how he should extend the following adjusted trial balance accounts to the financial statement columns of the worksheet.

Service Revenue
Notes Payable
V. Klitschko, Capital

Accounts Receivable
Accumulated Depreciation
Utilities Expense

Prepare closing entries.
(SO 5)

DO IT! 4-2 The worksheet for Adams Company shows the following in the financial statement columns.

J. Q. Adams, Drawing $22,000
J. Q. Adams, Capital   70,000
Net income   29,000

Prepare the closing entries at December 31 that affect owner's capital.

DO IT! 4-3 Javier Vasquez recently received the following information related to Vasquez Company's December 31, 2010, balance sheet.

Prepare assets section of the balance sheet.

(SO 6)

Inventories	$ 2,900	Short-term investments	$ 120
Cash	13,400	Accumulated depreciation	5,700
Equipment	21,700	Accounts receivable	4,300
Investments in stock (long-term)	6,500		

Prepare the assets section of Vasquez Company's classified balance sheet.

DO IT! 4-4 The following accounts were taken from the financial statements of Crofoot Company.

Match accounts to balance sheet classifications.

(SO 6)

_____ Interest revenue
_____ Utilities payable
_____ Accounts payable
_____ Supplies
_____ Bonds payable
_____ Trademarks

_____ J. Crofoot, Capital
_____ Accumulated depreciation
_____ Machinery
_____ Salaries expense
_____ Investment in real estate
_____ Unearned rent

Match each of the accounts to its proper balance sheet classification, as shown below. If the item would not appear on a balance sheet, use "NA."

Current assets (CA)
Long-term investments (LTI)
Property, plant, and equipment (PPE)
Intangible assets (IA)

Current liabilities (CL)
Long-term liabilities (LTL)
Owner's equity (OE)

EXERCISES

E4-1 The trial balance columns of the worksheet for Briscoe Company at June 30, 2010, are as follows.

Complete the worksheet.

(SO 1)

BRISCOE COMPANY
Worksheet
for the Month Ended June 30, 2010

Account Titles	Trial Balance	
	Dr.	Cr.
Cash	$2,320	
Accounts Receivable	2,440	
Supplies	1,880	
Accounts Payable		$1,120
Unearned Revenue		240
Lenny Briscoe, Capital		3,600
Service Revenue		2,400
Salaries Expense	560	
Miscellaneous Expense	160	
	$7,360	$7,360

Other data:

1. A physical count reveals $300 of supplies on hand.
2. $100 of the unearned revenue is still unearned at month-end.
3. Accrued salaries are $280.

Instructions
Enter the trial balance on a worksheet and complete the worksheet.

Complete the worksheet.

(SO 1)

E4-2 The adjusted trial balance columns of the worksheet for Goode Company are as follows.

GOODE COMPANY
Worksheet (partial)
for the Month Ended April 30, 2010

	Adjusted Trial Balance		Income Statement		Balance Sheet	
Account Titles	**Dr.**	**Cr.**	**Dr.**	**Cr.**	**Dr.**	**Cr.**
Cash	13,752					
Accounts Receivable	7,840					
Prepaid Rent	2,280					
Equipment	23,050					
Accumulated Depreciation		4,921				
Notes Payable		5,700				
Accounts Payable		5,672				
T. Goode, Capital		30,960				
T. Goode, Drawing	3,650					
Service Revenue		15,590				
Salaries Expense	10,840					
Rent Expense	760					
Depreciation Expense	671					
Interest Expense	57					
Interest Payable		57				
Totals	62,900	62,900				

Instructions

Complete the worksheet.

Prepare financial statements from worksheet.

(SO 1, 6)

E4-3 Worksheet data for Goode Company are presented in E4-2. The owner did not make any additional investments in the business in April.

Instructions

Prepare an income statement, an owner's equity statement, and a classified balance sheet.

Journalize and post closing entries and prepare a post-closing trial balance.

(SO 2, 3)

E4-4 Worksheet data for Goode Company are presented in E4-2.

Instructions

(a) Journalize the closing entries at April 30.
(b) Post the closing entries to Income Summary and T. Goode, Capital. Use T accounts.
(c) Prepare a post-closing trial balance at April 30.

Prepare adjusting entries from a worksheet, and extend balances to worksheet columns.

(SO 1)

E4-5 The adjustments columns of the worksheet for Mears Company are shown below.

	Adjustments	
Account Titles	**Debit**	**Credit**
Accounts Receivable	600	
Prepaid Insurance		400
Accumulated Depreciation		900
Salaries Payable		500
Service Revenue		600
Salaries Expense	500	
Insurance Expense	400	
Depreciation Expense	900	
	2,400	2,400

Instructions
(a) Prepare the adjusting entries.
(b) Assuming the adjusted trial balance amount for each account is normal, indicate the financial statement column to which each balance should be extended.

E4-6   Selected worksheet data for Nicholson Company are presented below.

Derive adjusting entries from worksheet data.

(SO 1)

Account Titles	Trial Balance		Adjusted Trial Balance	
	Dr.	**Cr.**	**Dr.**	**Cr.**
Accounts Receivable	?		34,000	
Prepaid Insurance	26,000		20,000	
Supplies	7,000		?	
Accumulated Depreciation		12,000		?
Salaries Payable		?		5,000
Service Revenue		88,000		97,000
Insurance Expense			?	
Depreciation Expense			10,000	
Supplies Expense			5,000	
Salaries Expense	?		49,000	

Instructions
(a) Fill in the missing amounts.
(b) Prepare the adjusting entries that were made.

E4-7   Emil Skoda Company had the following adjusted trial balance.

Prepare closing entries, and prepare a post-closing trial balance.

(SO 2, 3)

EMIL SKODA COMPANY
Adjusted Trial Balance
for the Month Ended June 30, 2010

Account Titles	Adjusted Trial Balance	
	Debits	**Credits**
Cash	$3,712	
Accounts Receivable	3,904	
Supplies	480	
Accounts Payable		$1,792
Unearned Revenue		160
Emil Skoda, Capital		5,760
Emil Skoda, Drawing	300	
Service Revenue		4,064
Salaries Expense	1,344	
Miscellaneous Expense	256	
Supplies Expense	2,228	
Salaries Payable		448
	$12,224	$12,224

Instructions
(a) Prepare closing entries at June 30, 2010.
(b) Prepare a post-closing trial balance.

E4-8   Apachi Company ended its fiscal year on July 31, 2010. The company's adjusted trial balance as of the end of its fiscal year is as shown at the top of page 182.

Journalize and post closing entries, and prepare a post-closing trial balance.

(SO 2, 3)

APACHI COMPANY
Adjusted Trial Balance
July 31, 2010

No.	Account Titles	Debits	Credits
101	Cash	$ 14,840	
112	Accounts Receivable	8,780	
157	Equipment	15,900	
167	Accumulated Depreciation		$ 7,400
201	Accounts Payable		4,220
208	Unearned Rent Revenue		1,800
301	B. J. Apachi, Capital		45,200
306	B. J. Apachi, Drawing	16,000	
404	Commission Revenue		65,000
429	Rent Revenue		6,500
711	Depreciation Expense	4,000	
720	Salaries Expense	55,700	
732	Utilities Expense	14,900	
		$130,120	$130,120

Instructions

(a) Prepare the closing entries using page J15.

(b) Post to B. J. Apachi, Capital and No. 350 Income Summary accounts. (Use the three-column form.)

(c) Prepare a post-closing trial balance at July 31.

Prepare financial statements.
(SO 6)

E4-9 The adjusted trial balance for Apachi Company is presented in E4-8.

Instructions

(a) Prepare an income statement and an owner's equity statement for the year. Apachi did not make any capital investments during the year.

(b) Prepare a classified balance sheet at July 31.

Answer questions related to the accounting cycle.
(SO 4)

E4-10 Josh Borke has prepared the following list of statements about the accounting cycle.

1. "Journalize the transactions" is the first step in the accounting cycle.
2. Reversing entries are a required step in the accounting cycle.
3. Correcting entries do not have to be part of the accounting cycle.
4. If a worksheet is prepared, some steps of the accounting cycle are incorporated into the worksheet.
5. The accounting cycle begins with the analysis of business transactions and ends with the preparation of a post-closing trial balance.
6. All steps of the accounting cycle occur daily during the accounting period.
7. The step of "post to the ledger accounts" occurs before the step of "journalize the transactions."
8. Closing entries must be prepared before financial statements can be prepared.

Instructions

Identify each statement as true or false. If false, indicate how to correct the statement.

Prepare closing entries.
(SO 2)

E4-11 Selected accounts for Nina's Salon are presented below. All June 30 postings are from closing entries.

Salaries Expense			
6/10	3,200	6/30	8,800
6/28	5,600		

Service Revenue			
6/30	15,100	6/15	6,700
		6/24	8,400

Nina Cole, Capital			
6/30	2,500	6/1	12,000
		6/30	2,000
		Bal.	11,500

Supplies Expense			
6/12	600	6/30	1,300
6/24	700		

Rent Expense			
6/1	3,000	6/30	3,000

Nina Cole, Drawing			
6/13	1,000	6/30	2,500
6/25	1,500		

Instructions

(a) Prepare the closing entries that were made.

(b) Post the closing entries to Income Summary.

E4-12 Max Weinberg Company discovered the following errors made in January 2010.

Prepare correcting entries.

(SO 5)

1. A payment of Salaries Expense of $600 was debited to Equipment and credited to Cash, both for $600.
2. A collection of $1,000 from a client on account was debited to Cash $100 and credited to Service Revenue $100.
3. The purchase of equipment on account for $980 was debited to Equipment $890 and credited to Accounts Payable $890.

Instructions

(a) Correct the errors by reversing the incorrect entry and preparing the correct entry.

(b) Correct the errors without reversing the incorrect entry.

E4-13 Mason Company has an inexperienced accountant. During the first 2 weeks on the job, the accountant made the following errors in journalizing transactions. All entries were posted as made.

Prepare correcting entries.

(SO 5)

1. A payment on account of $630 to a creditor was debited to Accounts Payable $360 and credited to Cash $360.
2. The purchase of supplies on account for $560 was debited to Equipment $56 and credited to Accounts Payable $56.
3. A $400 withdrawal of cash for M. Mason's personal use was debited to Salaries Expense $400 and credited to Cash $400.

Instructions

Prepare the correcting entries.

E4-14 The adjusted trial balance for Karr Bowling Alley at December 31, 2010, contains the following accounts.

Prepare a classified balance sheet.

(SO 6)

Debits		Credits	
Building	$128,800	Sue Karr, Capital	$115,000
Accounts Receivable	14,520	Accumulated Depreciation—Building	42,600
Prepaid Insurance	4,680	Accounts Payable	12,300
Cash	18,040	Note Payable	97,780
Equipment	62,400	Accumulated Depreciation—Equipment	18,720
Land	64,000	Interest Payable	2,600
Insurance Expense	780	Bowling Revenues	14,180
Depreciation Expense	7,360		$303,180
Interest Expense	2,600		
	$303,180		

Instructions

(a) Prepare a classified balance sheet; assume that $13,900 of the note payable will be paid in 2011.

(b) Comment on the liquidity of the company.

E4-15 The following are the major balance sheet classifications.

Classify accounts on balance sheet.

(SO 6)

Current assets (CA)

Long-term investments (LTI)

Property, plant, and equipment (PPE)

Intangible assets (IA)

Current liabilities (CL)

Long-term liabilities (LTL)

Owner's equity (OE)

Instructions

Classify each of the following accounts taken from Roberts Company's balance sheet.

_____ Accounts payable

_____ Accounts receivable

_____ Accumulated depreciation

_____ Buildings

_____ Cash	_____ Land
_____ Roberts, Capital	_____ Long-term debt
_____ Patents	_____ Supplies
_____ Salaries payable	_____ Office equipment
_____ Inventories	_____ Prepaid expenses
_____ Investments	

Prepare a classified balance sheet.

(SO 6)

E4-16 The following items were taken from the financial statements of R. Stevens Company. (All dollars are in thousands.)

Long-term debt	$ 943	Accumulated depreciation	5,655
Prepaid expenses	880	Accounts payable	1,444
Property, plant, and equipment	11,500	Notes payable after 2011	368
Long-term investments	264	R. Stevens, Capital	13,063
Short-term investments	3,690	Accounts receivable	1,696
Notes payable in 2011	481	Inventories	1,256
Cash	$ 2,668		

Instructions
Prepare a classified balance sheet in good form as of December 31, 2010.

Prepare financial statements.

(SO 1, 6)

E4-17 These financial statement items are for B. Snyder Company at year-end, July 31, 2010.

Salaries payable	$ 2,080	Note payable (long-term)	$ 1,800
Salaries expense	51,700	Cash	24,200
Utilities expense	22,600	Accounts receivable	9,780
Equipment	18,500	Accumulated depreciation	6,000
Accounts payable	4,100	B. Snyder, Drawing	4,000
Commission revenue	61,100	Depreciation expense	4,000
Rent revenue	8,500	B. Snyder, Capital (beginning of the year)	51,200

Instructions
(a) Prepare an income statement and an owner's equity statement for the year. The owner did not make any new investments during the year.
(b) Prepare a classified balance sheet at July 31.

Use reversing entries.

(SO 7)

*E4-18 LaBamba Company pays salaries of $10,000 every Monday for the preceding 5-day week (Monday through Friday). Assume December 31 falls on a Tuesday, so LaBamba's employes have worked 2 days without being paid.

Instructions
(a) Assume the company does not use reversing entries. Prepare the December 31 adjusting entry and the entry on Monday, January 6, when LaBamba pays the payroll.
(b) Assume the company does use reversing entries. Prepare the December 31 adjusting entry, the January 1 reversing entry, and the entry on Monday, January 6, when LaBamba pays the payroll.

Prepare closing and reversing entries.

(SO 2, 4, 7)

*E4-19 On December 31, the adjusted trial balance of Oslo Employment Agency shows the following selected data.

Accounts Receivable	$24,000	Commission Revenue	$92,000
Interest Expense	7,800	Interest Payable	1,500

Analysis shows that adjusting entries were made to (1) accrue $4,500 of commission revenue and (2) accrue $1,500 interest expense.

Instructions
(a) Prepare the closing entries for the temporary accounts shown above at December 31.
(b) Prepare the reversing entries on January 1.
(c) Post the entries in (a) and (b). Rule and balance the accounts. (Use T accounts.)
(d) Prepare the entries to record (1) the collection of the accrued commissions on January 10 and (2) the payment of all interest due ($2,500) on January 15.
(e) Post the entries in (d) to the temporary accounts.

EXERCISES: SET B

Visit the book's companion website at **www.wiley.com/college/weygandt**, and choose the Student Companion site, to access Exercise Set B.

PROBLEMS: SET A

P4-1A Thomas Magnum began operations as a private investigator on January 1, 2010. The trial balance columns of the worksheet for Thomas Magnum, P.I. at March 31 are as follows.

Prepare worksheet, financial statements, and adjusting and closing entries.

(SO 1, 2, 3, 6)

THOMAS MAGNUM, P.I.
Worksheet
For the Quarter Ended March 31, 2010

Account Titles	Trial Balance Dr.	Cr.
Cash	11,400	
Accounts Receivable	5,620	
Supplies	1,050	
Prepaid Insurance	2,400	
Equipment	30,000	
Notes Payable		10,000
Accounts Payable		12,350
T. Magnum, Capital		20,000
T. Magnum, Drawing	600	
Service Revenue		13,620
Salaries Expense	2,200	
Travel Expense	1,300	
Rent Expense	1,200	
Miscellaneous Expense	200	
	55,970	55,970

Other data:

1. Supplies on hand total $380.
2. Depreciation is $1,000 per quarter.
3. Interest accrued on 6-month note payable, issued January 1, $300.
4. Insurance expires at the rate of $200 per month.
5. Services provided but unbilled at March 31 total $530.

Instructions
(a) Enter the trial balance on a worksheet and complete the worksheet.
(b) Prepare an income statement and owner's equity statement for the quarter and a classified balance sheet at March 31. T. Magnum did not make any additional investments in the business during the quarter ended March 31, 2010.
(c) Journalize the adjusting entries from the adjustments columns of the worksheet.
(d) Journalize the closing entries from the financial statement columns of the worksheet.

(a) Adjusted trial balance $57,800

(b) Net income $6,680
Total assets $48,730

P4-2A The adjusted trial balance columns of the worksheet for Porter Company are as follows.

Complete worksheet; prepare financial statements, closing entries, and post-closing trial balance.

(SO 1, 2, 3, 6)

PORTER COMPANY
Worksheet
For the Year Ended December 31, 2010

Account No.	Account Titles	Adjusted Trial Balance Dr.	Cr.
101	Cash	18,800	
112	Accounts Receivable	16,200	
126	Supplies	2,300	

Account No.	Account Titles	Adjusted Trial Balance Dr.	Cr.
130	Prepaid Insurance	4,400	
151	Office Equipment	44,000	
152	Accumulated Depreciation—Office Equipment		20,000
200	Notes Payable		20,000
201	Accounts Payable		8,000
212	Salaries Payable		2,600
230	Interest Payable		1,000
301	B. Porter, Capital		36,000
306	B. Porter, Drawing	12,000	
400	Service Revenue		77,800
610	Advertising Expense	12,000	
631	Supplies Expense	3,700	
711	Depreciation Expense	8,000	
722	Insurance Expense	4,000	
726	Salaries Expense	39,000	
905	Interest Expense	1,000	
	Totals	165,400	165,400

(a) Net income $10,100
(b) Current assets $41,700
Current liabilities $21,600

(e) Post-closing trial balance $85,700

Prepare financial statements, closing entries, and post-closing trial balance.

(SO 1, 2, 3, 6)

Instructions
(a) Complete the worksheet by extending the balances to the financial statement columns.
(b) Prepare an income statement, owner's equity statement, and a classified balance sheet. $10,000 of the notes payable become due in 2011. B. Porter did not make any additional investments in the business during 2010.
(c) Prepare the closing entries. Use J14 for the journal page.
(d) Post the closing entries. Use the three-column form of account. Income Summary is account No. 350.
(e) Prepare a post-closing trial balance.

P4-3A The completed financial statement columns of the worksheet for Woods Company are shown below.

WOODS COMPANY
Worksheet
For the Year Ended December 31, 2010

Account No.	Account Titles	Income Statement Dr.	Cr.	Balance Sheet Dr.	Cr.
101	Cash			8,200	
112	Accounts Receivable			7,500	
130	Prepaid Insurance			1,800	
157	Equipment			28,000	
167	Accumulated Depreciation				8,600
201	Accounts Payable				11,700
212	Salaries Payable				3,000
301	S. Woods, Capital				34,000
306	S. Woods, Drawing			7,200	
400	Service Revenue		44,000		
622	Repair Expense	5,400			
711	Depreciation Expense	2,800			
722	Insurance Expense	1,200			
726	Salaries Expense	35,200			
732	Utilities Expense	4,000			
	Totals	48,600	44,000	52,700	57,300
	Net Loss		4,600	4,600	
		48,600	48,600	57,300	57,300

Instructions

(a) Prepare an income statement, owner's equity statement, and a classified balance sheet. S. Woods made an additional investment in the business of $4,000 during 2010.

(b) Prepare the closing entries.

(c) Post the closing entries and rule and balance the accounts. Use T accounts. Income Summary is account No. 350.

(d) Prepare a post-closing trial balance.

(a) Net loss $4,600
Ending capital $22,200
Total assets $36,900

(d) Post-closing trial balance
$45,500

P4-4A Disney Amusement Park has a fiscal year ending on September 30. Selected data from the September 30 worksheet are presented below.

Complete worksheet; prepare classified balance sheet, entries, and post-closing trial balance.

(SO 1, 2, 3, 6)

DISNEY AMUSEMENT PARK
Worksheet
For the Year Ended September 30, 2010

	Trial Balance Dr.	Trial Balance Cr.	Adjusted Trial Balance Dr.	Adjusted Trial Balance Cr.
Cash	41,400		41,400	
Supplies	18,600		1,200	
Prepaid Insurance	31,900		8,900	
Land	80,000		80,000	
Equipment	120,000		120,000	
Accumulated Depreciation		36,200		42,200
Accounts Payable		14,600		14,600
Unearned Admissions Revenue		3,700		2,000
Mortgage Note Payable		50,000		50,000
L. Disney, Capital		109,700		109,700
L. Disney, Drawing	14,000		14,000	
Admissions Revenue		277,500		279,200
Salaries Expense	105,000		105,000	
Repair Expense	30,500		30,500	
Advertising Expense	9,400		9,400	
Utilities Expense	16,900		16,900	
Property Taxes Expense	18,000		21,000	
Interest Expense	6,000		10,000	
Totals	491,700	491,700		
Insurance Expense			23,000	
Supplies Expense			17,400	
Interest Payable				4,000
Depreciation Expense			6,000	
Property Taxes Payable				3,000
Totals			504,700	504,700

Instructions

(a) Prepare a complete worksheet.

(b) Prepare a classified balance sheet. (*Note*: $10,000 of the mortgage note payable is due for payment in the next fiscal year.)

(c) Journalize the adjusting entries using the worksheet as a basis.

(d) Journalize the closing entries using the worksheet as a basis.

(e) Prepare a post-closing trial balance.

(a) Net income $40,000

(b) Total current assets
$51,500

(e) Post-closing trial balance
$251,500

P4-5A Laura Eddy opened Eddy's Carpet Cleaners on March 1. During March, the following transactions were completed.

Complete all steps in accounting cycle.

(SO 1, 2, 3, 4, 6)

Mar. 1 Invested $10,000 cash in the business.
1 Purchased used truck for $6,000, paying $3,000 cash and the balance on account.
3 Purchased cleaning supplies for $1,200 on account.
5 Paid $1,200 cash on one-year insurance policy effective March 1.

14 Billed customers $4,800 for cleaning services.
18 Paid $1,500 cash on amount owed on truck and $500 on amount owed on cleaning supplies.
20 Paid $1,800 cash for employee salaries.
21 Collected $1,400 cash from customers billed on March 14.
28 Billed customers $2,500 for cleaning services.
31 Paid gas and oil for month on truck $200.
31 Withdrew $700 cash for personal use.

The chart of accounts for Eddy's Carpet Cleaners contains the following accounts: No. 101 Cash, No. 112 Accounts Receivable, No. 128 Cleaning Supplies, No. 130 Prepaid Insurance, No. 157 Equipment, No. 158 Accumulated Depreciation—Equipment, No. 201 Accounts Payable, No. 212 Salaries Payable, No. 301 L. Eddy, Capital; No. 306, L. Eddy, Drawing; No. 350 Income Summary, No. 400 Service Revenue, No. 633 Gas & Oil Expense, No. 634 Cleaning Supplies Expense, No. 711 Depreciation Expense, No. 722 Insurance Expense, and No. 726 Salaries Expense.

Instructions
(a) Journalize and post the March transactions. Use page J1 for the journal and the three-column form of account.

(b) Trial balance $19,500

(b) Prepare a trial balance at March 31 on a worksheet.

(c) Adjusted trial balance $20,950

(c) Enter the following adjustments on the worksheet and complete the worksheet.
  (1) Earned but unbilled revenue at March 31 was $700.
  (2) Depreciation on equipment for the month was $250.
  (3) One-twelfth of the insurance expired.
  (4) An inventory count shows $400 of cleaning supplies on hand at March 31.
  (5) Accrued but unpaid employee salaries were $500.

(d) Net income $4,350
Total assets $16,350

(d) Prepare the income statement and owner's equity statement for March and a classified balance sheet at March 31.

(e) Journalize and post adjusting entries. Use page J2 for the journal.

(f) Journalize and post closing entries and complete the closing process. Use page J3 for the journal.

(g) Post-closing trial balance $16,600

(g) Prepare a post-closing trial balance at March 31.

Analyze errors and prepare correcting entries and trial balance.

(SO 5)

P4-6A Joe Edmonds, CPA, was retained by Fox Cable to prepare financial statements for April 2010. Edmonds accumulated all the ledger balances per Fox's records and found the following.

FOX CABLE
Trial Balance
April 30, 2010

	Debit	Credit
Cash	$ 4,100	
Accounts Receivable	3,200	
Supplies	800	
Equipment	10,600	
Accumulated Depreciation		$ 1,350
Accounts Payable		2,100
Salaries Payable		700
Unearned Revenue		890
A. Manion, Capital		12,900
Service Revenue		5,450
Salaries Expense	3,300	
Advertising Expense	600	
Miscellaneous Expense	290	
Depreciation Expense	500	
	$23,390	$23,390

Joe Edmonds reviewed the records and found the following errors.

1. Cash received from a customer on account was recorded as $960 instead of $690.
2. A payment of $65 for advertising expense was entered as a debit to Miscellaneous Expense $65 and a credit to Cash $65.
3. The first salary payment this month was for $1,900, which included $700 of salaries payable on March 31. The payment was recorded as a debit to Salaries Expense $1,900 and a credit to Cash $1,900. (No reversing entries were made on April 1.)
4. The purchase on account of a printer costing $290 was recorded as a debit to Supplies and a credit to Accounts Payable for $290.
5. A cash payment of repair expense on equipment for $95 was recorded as a debit to Equipment $59 and a credit to Cash $59.

Instructions
(a) Prepare an analysis of each error showing (1) the incorrect entry, (2) the correct entry, and (3) the correcting entry. Items 4 and 5 occurred on April 30, 2010.
(b) Prepare a correct trial balance.

Trial balance $22,690

PROBLEMS: SET B

P4-1B   The trial balance columns of the worksheet for Sasse Roofing at March 31, 2010, are as follows.

Prepare a worksheet, financial statements, and adjusting and closing entries.

(SO 1, 2, 3, 6)

SASSE ROOFING
Worksheet
For the Month Ended March 31, 2010

	Trial Balance	
Account Titles	**Dr.**	**Cr.**
Cash	4,500	
Accounts Receivable	3,200	
Roofing Supplies	2,000	
Equipment	11,000	
Accumulated Depreciation—Equipment		1,250
Accounts Payable		2,500
Unearned Revenue		550
J. Sasse, Capital		12,900
J. Sasse, Drawing	1,100	
Service Revenue		6,300
Salaries Expense	1,300	
Miscellaneous Expense	400	
	23,500	23,500

Other data:

1. A physical count reveals only $650 of roofing supplies on hand.
2. Depreciation for March is $250.
3. Unearned revenue amounted to $170 at March 31.
4. Accrued salaries are $600.

Instructions
(a) Enter the trial balance on a worksheet and complete the worksheet.
(b) Prepare an income statement and owner's equity statement for the month of March and a classified balance sheet at March 31. J. Sasse did not make any additional investments in the business in March.
(c) Journalize the adjusting entries from the adjustments columns of the worksheet.
(d) Journalize the closing entries from the financial statement columns of the worksheet.

(a) Adjusted trial balance $24,350

*(b) Net income $2,780
Total assets $17,850*

Complete worksheet; prepare financial statements, closing entries, and post-closing trial balance.

(SO 1, 2, 3, 6)

P4-2B The adjusted trial balance columns of the worksheet for Rachel Company, owned by Toni Rachel, are as follows.

RACHEL COMPANY
Worksheet
For the Year Ended December 31, 2010

Account No.	Account Titles	Adjusted Trial Balance Dr.	Cr.
101	Cash	8,100	
112	Accounts Receivable	10,800	
126	Supplies	1,500	
130	Prepaid Insurance	2,000	
151	Office Equipment	24,000	
152	Accumulated Depreciation—Office Equipment		5,600
200	Notes Payable		15,000
201	Accounts Payable		6,100
212	Salaries Payable		2,400
230	Interest Payable		600
301	T. Rachel, Capital		15,800
306	T. Rachel, Drawing	7,000	
400	Service Revenue		61,000
610	Advertising Expense	8,400	
631	Supplies Expense	4,000	
711	Depreciation Expense	5,600	
722	Insurance Expense	3,500	
726	Salaries Expense	31,000	
905	Interest Expense	600	
	Totals	106,500	106,500

Instructions

(a) Net income $7,900

(b) Current assets $22,400; Current liabilities $18,100

(e) Post-closing trial balance $46,400

(a) Complete the worksheet by extending the balances to the financial statement columns.

(b) Prepare an income statement, owner's equity statement, and a classified balance sheet. (*Note:* $9,000 of the notes payable become due in 2011.) Toni Rachel did not make any additional investments in the business during the year.

(c) Prepare the closing entries. Use J14 for the journal page.

(d) Post the closing entries. Use the three-column form of account. Income Summary is No. 350.

(e) Prepare a post-closing trial balance.

Prepare financial statements, closing entries, and post-closing trial balance.

(SO 1, 2, 3, 6)

P4-3B The completed financial statement columns of the worksheet for Muddy Company are shown below and on the next page.

MUDDY COMPANY
Worksheet
For the Year Ended December 31, 2010

Account No.	Account Titles	Income Statement Dr.	Cr.	Balance Sheet Dr.	Cr.
101	Cash			17,900	
112	Accounts Receivable			10,800	
130	Prepaid Insurance			2,800	
157	Equipment			21,000	
167	Accumulated Depreciation				4,500
201	Accounts Payable				9,000
212	Salaries Payable				2,400
301	Melissa Muddy, Capital				28,500
306	Melissa Muddy, Drawing			11,000	

Account		Income Statement		Balance Sheet	
No.	Account Titles	Dr.	Cr.	Dr.	Cr.
400	Service Revenue		56,000		
622	Repair Expense	1,600			
711	Depreciation Expense	2,100			
722	Insurance Expense	1,800			
726	Salaries Expense	30,000			
732	Utilities Expense	1,400			
	Totals	36,900	56,000	63,500	44,400
	Net Income	19,100			19,100
		56,000	56,000	63,500	63,500

Instructions

(a) Prepare an income statement, an owner's equity statement, and a classified balance sheet.

(b) Prepare the closing entries. Melissa did not make any additional investments during the year.

(c) Post the closing entries and rule and balance the accounts. Use T accounts. Income Summary is account No. 350.

(d) Prepare a post-closing trial balance.

(a) Ending capital $36,600; Total current assets $31,500

(d) Post-closing trial balance $52,500

P4-4B   Rockford Management Services began business on January 1, 2010, with a capital investment of $120,000. The company manages condominiums for owners (Service Revenue) and rents space in its own office building (Rent Revenue). The trial balance and adjusted trial balance columns of the worksheet at the end of the first year are as follows.

Complete worksheet; prepare classified balance sheet, entries, and post-closing trial balance.

(SO 1, 2, 3, 6)

ROCKFORD MANAGEMENT SERVICES
Worksheet
For the Year Ended December 31, 2010

Account Titles	Trial Balance		Adjusted Trial Balance	
	Dr.	Cr.	Dr.	Cr.
Cash	13,800		13,800	
Accounts Receivable	28,300		28,300	
Prepaid Insurance	3,600		2,400	
Land	67,000		67,000	
Building	127,000		127,000	
Equipment	59,000		59,000	
Accounts Payable		12,500		12,500
Unearned Rent Revenue		6,000		2,000
Mortgage Note Payable		120,000		120,000
R. Neillsen, Capital		144,000		144,000
R. Neillsen, Drawing	22,000		22,000	
Service Revenue		90,700		90,700
Rent Revenue		29,000		33,000
Salaries Expense	42,000		42,000	
Advertising Expense	20,500		20,500	
Utilities Expense	19,000		19,000	
Totals	402,200	402,200		
Insurance Expense			1,200	
Depreciation Expense—Building			3,000	
Accumulated Depreciation—Building				3,000
Depreciation Expense—Equipment			4,700	
Accumulated Depreciation—Equipment				4,700
Interest Expense			11,000	
Interest Payable				11,000
Totals			420,900	420,900

Instructions

(a) Net income $22,300

(b) Total current assets $44,500

(e) Post-closing trial balance $297,500

(a) Prepare a complete worksheet.

(b) Prepare a classified balance sheet. (*Note:* $20,000 of the mortgage note payable is due for payment next year.)

(c) Journalize the adjusting entries.

(d) Journalize the closing entries.

(e) Prepare a post-closing trial balance.

Complete all steps in accounting cycle.

(SO 1, 2, 3, 4, 6)

P4-5B   Lee Chang opened Chang's Cleaning Service on July 1, 2010. During July the following transactions were completed.

July 1   Chang invested $20,000 cash in the business.
     1   Purchased used truck for $9,000, paying $4,000 cash and the balance on account.
     3   Purchased cleaning supplies for $2,100 on account.
     5   Paid $1,800 cash on one-year insurance policy effective July 1.
    12   Billed customers $4,500 for cleaning services.
    18   Paid $1,500 cash on amount owed on truck and $1,400 on amount owed on cleaning supplies.
    20   Paid $2,000 cash for employee salaries.
    21   Collected $3,400 cash from customers billed on July 12.
    25   Billed customers $9,000 for cleaning services.
    31   Paid gas and oil for month on truck $350.
    31   Withdraw $1,600 cash for personal use.

The chart of accounts for Chang's Cleaning Service contains the following accounts: No. 101 Cash, No. 112 Accounts Receivable, No. 128 Cleaning Supplies, No. 130 Prepaid Insurance, No. 157 Equipment, No. 158 Accumulated Depreciation—Equipment, No. 201 Accounts Payable, No. 212 Salaries Payable, No. 301 Lee Chang, Capital; No. 306 Lee Chang, Drawing; No. 350 Income Summary, No. 400 Service Revenue, No. 633 Gas & Oil Expense, No. 634 Cleaning Supplies Expense, No. 711 Depreciation Expense, No. 722 Insurance Expense, and No. 726 Salaries Expense.

Instructions

(b) Trial balance $37,700

(c) Adjusted trial balance $41,900

(d) Net income $10,800; Total assets $34,400

(g) Post-closing trial balance $34,900

(a) Journalize and post the July transactions. Use page J1 for the journal and the three-column form of account.

(b) Prepare a trial balance at July 31 on a worksheet.

(c) Enter the following adjustments on the worksheet and complete the worksheet.

   (1) Services provided but unbilled and uncollected at July 31 were $2,700.

   (2) Depreciation on equipment for the month was $500.

   (3) One-twelfth of the insurance expired.

   (4) An inventory count shows $700 of cleaning supplies on hand at July 31.

   (5) Accrued but unpaid employee salaries were $1,000.

(d) Prepare the income statement and owner's equity statement for July and a classified balance sheet at July 31.

(e) Journalize and post adjusting entries. Use page J2 for the journal.

(f) Journalize and post closing entries and complete the closing process. Use page J3 for the journal.

(g) Prepare a post-closing trial balance at July 31.

PROBLEMS: SET C

Visit the book's companion website at **www.wiley.com/college/weygandt**, and choose the Student Companion site, to access Problem Set C.

COMPREHENSIVE PROBLEM: CHAPTERS 2 TO 4

Julie Molony opened Julie's Maids Cleaning Service on July 1, 2010. During July, the company completed the following transactions.

July 1   Invested $14,000 cash in the business.
     1   Purchased a used truck for $10,000, paying $3,000 cash and the balance on account.
     3   Purchased cleaning supplies for $800 on account.

   5 Paid $1,800 on a one-year insurance policy, effective July 1.
  12 Billed customers $3,800 for cleaning services.
  18 Paid $1,000 of amount owed on truck, and $400 of amount owed on cleaning supplies.
  20 Paid $1,600 for employee salaries.
  21 Collected $1,400 from customers billed on July 12.
  25 Billed customers $1,500 for cleaning services.
  31 Paid gas and oil for the month on the truck, $400.
  31 Withdrew $600 cash for personal use.

The chart of accounts for Julie's Maids Cleaning Service contains the following accounts: No. 101 Cash, No. 112 Accounts Receivable, No. 128 Cleaning Supplies, No. 130 Prepaid Insurance, No. 157 Equipment, No. 158 Accumulated Depreciation—Equipment, No. 201 Accounts Payable, No. 212 Salaries Payable, No. 301, Julie Molony, Capital; No. 306 Julie Molony, Drawing; No. 350 Income Summary, No. 400 Service Revenue, No. 633 Gas & Oil Expense, No. 634 Cleaning Supplies Expense, No. 711 Depreciation Expense, No. 722 Insurance Expense, and No. 726 Salaries Expense.

Instructions

(a) Journalize and post the July transactions. Use page J1 for the journal.

(b) Prepare a trial balance at July 31 on a worksheet.

(b) Trial balance totals $25,700

(c) Enter the following adjustments on the worksheet, and complete the worksheet.
   (1) Earned but unbilled fees at July 31 were $1,300.
   (2) Depreciation on equipment for the month was $200.
   (3) One-twelfth of the insurance expired.
   (4) An inventory count shows $100 of cleaning supplies on hand at July 31.
   (5) Accrued but unpaid employee salaries were $500.

(d) Prepare the income statement and statement of owner's equity for July, and a classified balance sheet at July 31, 2010.

*(d) Net income $3,050
Total assets $23,350*

(e) Journalize and post the adjusting entries. Use page J2 for the journal.

(f) Journalize and post the closing entries, and complete the closing process. Use page J3 for the journal.

(g) Prepare a post-closing trial balance at July 31.

(g) Trial balance totals $23,550

CONTINUING COOKIE CHRONICLE

(*Note*: This is a continuation of the Cookie Chronicle from Chapters 1 through 3.)

CCC4 Natalie had a very busy December. At the end of the month after journalizing and posting the December transactions and adjusting entries, Natalie prepared an adjusted trial balance. Using that information, she wants to prepare financial statements for the year-end, closing entries, and a post-closing trial balance.

Go to the book's companion website,
www.wiley.com/college/weygandt,
to see the completion of this problem.

BROADENING YOUR PERSPECTIVE

FINANCIAL REPORTING AND ANALYSIS

Financial Reporting Problem: PepsiCo, Inc.

BYP4-1 The financial statements of PepsiCo, Inc. are presented in Appendix A at the end of this textbook.

Instructions

Answer the questions on the following page using the Consolidated Balance Sheet and the Notes to Consolidated Financial Statements section.

(a) What were PepsiCo's total current assets at December 29, 2007 and December 30, 2006?
(b) Are assets that PepsiCo included under current assets listed in proper order? Explain.
(c) How are PepsiCo's assets classified?
(d) What are "cash equivalents"?
(e) What were PepsiCo's total current liabilities at December 29, 2007 and December 30, 2006?

Comparative Analysis Problem: PepsiCo, Inc. vs. The Coca-Cola Company

BYP4-2 PepsiCo's financial statements are presented in Appendix A. Financial statements for The Coca-Cola Company are presented in Appendix B.

Instructions
(a) Based on the information contained in these financial statements, determine each of the following for PepsiCo at December 29, 2007, and for Coca-Cola at December 31, 2007.
  (1) Total current assets.
  (2) Net amount of property, plant, and equipment (land, buildings, and equipment).
  (3) Total current liabilities.
  (4) Total stockholders' (shareholders') equity.
(b) What conclusions concerning the companies' respective financial positions can be drawn?

Exploring the Web

BYP4-3 Numerous companies have established home pages on the Internet, e.g., Capt'n Eli Root Beer Company *(www.captneli.com/rootbeer.php)* and Kodak *(www.kodak.com)*.

Instructions
Examine the home pages of any two companies and answer the following questions.

(a) What type of information is available?
(b) Is any accounting-related information presented?
(c) Would you describe the home page as informative, promotional, or both? Why?

CRITICAL THINKING

Decision Making Across the Organization

BYP4-4 Whitegloves Janitorial Service was started 2 years ago by Nancy Kohl. Because business has been exceptionally good, Nancy decided on July 1, 2010, to expand operations by acquiring an additional truck and hiring two more assistants. To finance the expansion, Nancy obtained on July 1, 2010, a $25,000, 10% bank loan, payable $10,000 on July 1, 2011, and the balance on July 1, 2012. The terms of the loan require the borrower to have $10,000 more current assets than current liabilities at December 31, 2010. If these terms are not met, the bank loan will be refinanced at 15% interest. At December 31, 2010, the accountant for Whitegloves Janitorial Service Inc. prepared the balance sheet shown on page 195.

Nancy presented the balance sheet to the bank's loan officer on January 2, 2011, confident that the company had met the terms of the loan. The loan officer was not impressed. She said, "We need financial statements audited by a CPA." A CPA was hired and immediately realized that the balance sheet had been prepared from a trial balance and not from an adjusted trial balance. The adjustment data at the balance sheet date consisted of the following.

(1) Earned but unbilled janitorial services were $3,700.
(2) Janitorial supplies on hand were $2,500.
(3) Prepaid insurance was a 3-year policy dated January 1, 2010.
(4) December expenses incurred but unpaid at December 31, $500.
(5) Interest on the bank loan was not recorded.

(6) The amounts for property, plant, and equipment presented in the balance sheet were reported net of accumulated depreciation (cost less accumulated depreciation). These amounts were $4,000 for cleaning equipment and $5,000 for delivery trucks as of January 1, 2010. Depreciation for 2010 was $2,000 for cleaning equipment and $5,000 for delivery trucks.

WHITEGLOVES JANITORIAL SERVICE
Balance Sheet
December 31, 2010

Assets		Liabilities and Owner's Equity	
Current assets		**Current liabilities**	
Cash	$ 6,500	Notes payable	$10,000
Accounts receivable	9,000	Accounts payable	2,500
Janitorial supplies	5,200	Total current liabilities	12,500
Prepaid insurance	4,800	**Long-term liability**	
Total current assets	25,500	Notes payable	15,000
Property, plant, and equipment		Total liabilities	27,500
Cleaning equipment (net)	22,000	**Owner's equity**	
Delivery trucks (net)	34,000	Nancy Kohl, Capital	54,000
Total property, plant, and equipment	56,000		
Total assets	$81,500	Total liabilities and owner's equity	$81,500

Instructions
With the class divided into groups, answer the following.

(a) Prepare a correct balance sheet.
(b) Were the terms of the bank loan met? Explain.

Communication Activity

BYP4-5   The accounting cycle is important in understanding the accounting process.

Instructions
Write a memo to your instructor that lists the steps of the accounting cycle in the order they should be completed. End with a paragraph that explains the optional steps in the cycle.

Ethics Case

BYP4-6   As the controller of Breathless Perfume Company, you discover a misstatement that overstated net income in the prior year's financial statements. The misleading financial statements appear in the company's annual report which was issued to banks and other creditors less than a month ago. After much thought about the consequences of telling the president, Jerry McNabb, about this misstatement, you gather your courage to inform him. Jerry says, "Hey! What they don't know won't hurt them. But, just so we set the record straight, we'll adjust this year's financial statements for last year's misstatement. We can absorb that misstatement better in this year than in last year anyway! Just don't make such a mistake again."

Instructions
(a) Who are the stakeholders in this situation?
(b) What are the ethical issues in this situation?
(c) What would you do as a controller in this situation?

"All About You" Activity

BYP4-7   Companies prepare balance sheets in order to know their financial position at a specific point in time. This enables them to make a comparison to their position at previous points in time, and gives them a basis for planning for the future. As discussed in the **All About You**

feature in this chapter, in order to evaluate your financial position you need to prepare a personal balance sheet. Assume that you have compiled the following information regarding your finances. (*Hint:* Some of the items might not be used in your personal balance sheet.)

Amount owed on student loan balance (long-term)	$5,000
Balance in checking account	1,200
Certificate of deposit (6-month)	3,000
Annual earnings from part-time job	11,300
Automobile	7,000
Balance on automobile loan (current portion)	1,500
Balance on automobile loan (long-term portion)	4,000
Home computer	800
Amount owed to you by younger brother	300
Balance in money market account	1,800
Annual tuition	6,400
Video and stereo equipment	1,250
Balance owed on credit card (current portion)	150
Balance owed on credit card (long-term portion)	1,650

Instructions
Prepare a personal balance sheet using the format you have learned for a classified balance sheet for a company. For the capital account, use M. Y. Own, Capital.

Answers to Insight and Accounting Across the Organization Questions

p. 157 Cisco Performs the Virtual Close
Q: Who else benefits from a shorter closing process?
A: *Investors benefit from a shorter closing process. The shorter the closing, the sooner the company can report its financial results. This means that the financial information is more timely, and therefore more relevant to investors.*

p. 162 Yale Express Loses Some Transportation Bills
Q: What might Yale Express's vice president have done to produce more accurate financial statements without waiting months for Republic's outstanding transportation bills?
A: *Yale's vice president could have engaged his accountants and auditors to prepare an adjusting entry based on an estimate of the outstanding transportation bills. (The estimate could have been made using past experience and the current volume of business.)*

Authors' Comments on *All About You:* Your Personal Balance Sheet (p. 169)

By deciding to go to school after high school, you have taken a big step toward improving your long-term personal finances. Post-high-school education increases your job opportunities, which increases your earning potential.

Although it is true that your earnings will probably increase considerably when you graduate, you should not wait until graduation to lay the groundwork for a sound financial plan. If you do not monitor your finances closely while you are in school, you could easily dig a deep hole that would be difficult to get out of. Controlling your spending now will give you better control of your personal finances by the time you graduate. A first step toward taking control of your finances is preparing a personal balance sheet. In later chapters we discuss topics that will give you the tools that you need to improve your financial position.

Software is available to help you identify your assets and liabilities and determine your net worth. See for example the net worth calculator at *http://www.bygpub.com/finance/NetWorthCalc.htm.*

Answers to Self-Study Questions
1. b **2.** c **3.** c **4.** a **5.** b **6.** c **7.** a **8.** d **9.** c **10.** d **11.** b **12.** c **13.** c **14.** d **15.** a ***16.** c

Chapter 5

Accounting for Merchandising Operations

STUDY OBJECTIVES

After studying this chapter, you should be able to:

1 Identify the differences between service and merchandising companies.
2 Explain the recording of purchases under a perpetual inventory system.
3 Explain the recording of sales revenues under a perpetual inventory system.
4 Explain the steps in the accounting cycle for a merchandising company.
5 Distinguish between a multiple-step and a single-step income statement.
6 Explain the computation and importance of gross profit.

✓ The Navigator

✓ The Navigator

Scan **Study Objectives** ▪

Read **Feature Story** ▪

Read **Preview** ▪

Read text and answer **DO IT!**
p. 207 ▪   p. 210 ▪   p. 213 ▪   p. 218

Work **Comprehensive DO IT!** p. 219 ▪

Review **Summary of Study Objectives** ▪

Answer **Self-Study Questions** ▪

Complete **Assignments** ▪

Feature Story

WHO DOESN'T SHOP AT WAL-MART?

In his book *The End of Work*, Jeremy Rifkin notes that until the 20th century the word *consumption* evoked negative images. To be labeled a "consumer" was an insult. In fact, one of the deadliest diseases in history, tuberculosis, was often referred to as "consumption." Twentieth-century merchants realized, however, that in order to prosper, they had to convince people of the need for things not previously needed. For example, General Motors made annual changes in its cars so that people would be discontented with the cars they already owned. Thus began consumerism.

Today consumption describes the U.S. lifestyle in a nutshell. We consume twice as much today per person as we did at the end of World War II. The amount of U.S. retail space per person is vastly greater than that of any other country. It appears that we live to shop.

The first great retail giant was Sears, Roebuck and Company. It started as a catalog company enabling people in rural areas to buy things by mail. For decades it was the uncontested merchandising leader.

Today Wal-Mart (*www.walmart.com*) is the undisputed champion provider of basic (and perhaps not-so-basic) human needs. Wal-Mart opened its first store in 1962, and it now has more than 6,000 stores, serving more than 100 million customers every week. A key cause of Wal-Mart's incredible growth is its amazing system of inventory control and distribution. Wal-Mart has a management information system that employs six satellite channels, from which company computers receive 8.4 million updates every minute on what items customers buy and the relationship among items sold to each person.

Measured by sales revenues, Wal-Mart is the largest company in the world. In six years it went from selling almost no groceries to being America's largest grocery retailer.

It would appear that things have never looked better at Wal-Mart. On the other hand, a *Wall Street Journal* article entitled "How to Sell More to Those Who Think It's Cool to Be Frugal" suggests that consumerism as a way of life might be dying. Don't bet your wide-screen TV on it, though.

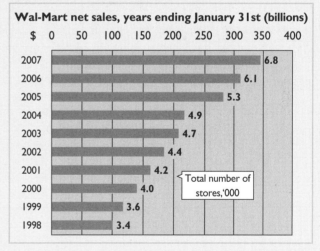

Wal-Mart net sales, years ending January 31st (billions)

Year	Net sales	Total number of stores, '000
2007		6.8
2006		6.1
2005		5.3
2004		4.9
2003		4.7
2002		4.4
2001		4.2
2000		4.0
1999		3.6
1998		3.4

Sources: "How Big Can It Grow?" *The Economist*, April 17, 2004, pp. 67–69; and *www.walmart.com* (accessed March 17, 2008).

✓ The Navigator

Inside Chapter 5...

Merchandising is one of the largest and most influential industries in the United States. It is likely that a number of you will work for a merchandiser. Therefore, understanding the financial statements of merchandising companies is important. In this chapter you will learn the basics about reporting merchandising transactions. In addition, you will learn how to prepare and analyze a commonly used form of the income statement—the multiple-step income statement. The content and organization of the chapter are as follows.

Accounting for Merchandising Operations

Merchandising Operations	Recording Purchases of Merchandise	Recording Sales of Merchandise	Completing the Accounting Cycle	Forms of Financial Statements
• Operating cycles • Flow of costs—perpetual and periodic inventory systems	• Freight costs • Purchase returns and allowances • Purchase discounts • Summary of purchasing transactions	• Sales returns and allowances • Sales discounts	• Adjusting entries • Closing entries • Summary of merchandising entries	• Multiple-step income statement • Single-step income statement • Classified balance sheet

✓ *The Navigator*

MERCHANDISING OPERATIONS

Wal-Mart, Kmart, and Target are called merchandising companies because they buy and sell merchandise rather than perform services as their primary source of revenue. Merchandising companies that purchase and sell directly to consumers are called **retailers**. Merchandising companies that sell to retailers are known as **wholesalers**. For example, retailer Walgreens might buy goods from wholesaler McKesson; retailer Office Depot might buy office supplies from wholesaler United Stationers. The primary source of revenues for merchandising companies is the sale of merchandise, often referred to simply as **sales revenue** or **sales**. A merchandising company has two categories of expenses: cost of goods sold and operating expenses.

Cost of goods sold is the total cost of merchandise sold during the period. This expense is directly related to the revenue recognized from the sale of goods. Illustration 5-1 shows the income measurement process for a merchandising

Illustration 5-1
Income measurement process for a merchandising company

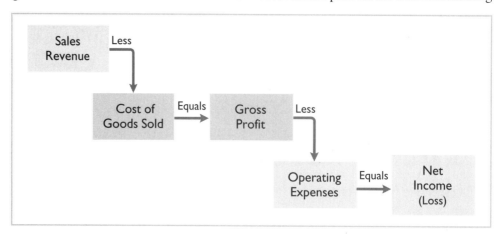

company. The items in the two blue boxes are unique to a merchandising company; they are not used by a service company.

Operating Cycles

The operating cycle of a merchandising company ordinarily is longer than that of a service company. The purchase of merchandise inventory and its eventual sale lengthen the cycle. Illustration 5-2 contrasts the operating cycles of service and merchandising companies. Note that the added asset account for a merchandising company is the Merchandise Inventory account. Companies report merchandise inventory as a current asset on the balance sheet.

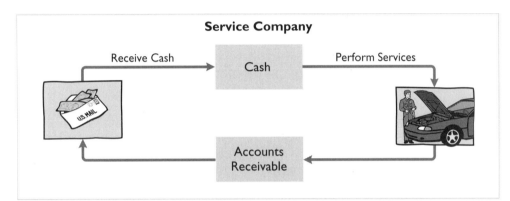

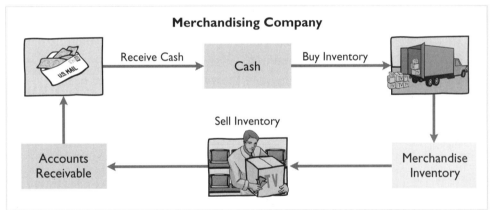

Illustration 5-2
Operating cycles for a
service company and a
merchandising company

Flow of Costs

The flow of costs for a merchandising company is as follows: Beginning inventory is added to the cost of goods purchased to arrive at cost of goods available for sale. Cost of goods available for sale is assigned to the cost of goods sold (goods sold this period) and ending inventory (goods to be sold in the future). Illustration 5-3 (page 202) describes these relationships. Companies use one of two systems to account for inventory: a **perpetual inventory system** or a **periodic inventory system**.

PERPETUAL SYSTEM

In a **perpetual inventory system**, companies keep detailed records of the cost of each inventory purchase and sale. These records continuously—perpetually—show the inventory that should be on hand for every item. For example, a Ford dealership has separate inventory records for each automobile, truck, and van on its lot and showroom floor. Similarly, a Kroger grocery store uses bar codes and optical

HELPFUL HINT

For control purposes companies take a physical inventory count under the perpetual system, even though it is not needed to determine cost of goods sold.

Illustration 5-3
Flow of costs

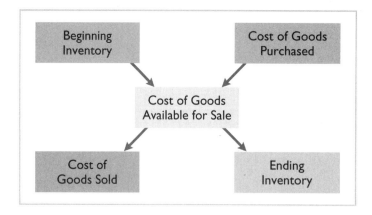

scanners to keep a daily running record of every box of cereal and every jar of jelly that it buys and sells. Under a perpetual inventory system, a company determines the cost of goods sold **each time a sale occurs**.

PERIODIC SYSTEM

In a **periodic inventory system**, companies do not keep detailed inventory records of the goods on hand throughout the period. Instead, they determine the cost of goods sold **only at the end of the accounting period**—that is, periodically. At that point, the company takes a physical inventory count to determine the cost of goods on hand.

To determine the cost of goods sold under a periodic inventory system, the following steps are necessary:

1. Determine the cost of goods on hand at the beginning of the accounting period.
2. Add to it the cost of goods purchased.
3. Subtract the cost of goods on hand at the end of the accounting period.

Illustration 5-4 graphically compares the sequence of activities and the timing of the cost of goods sold computation under the two inventory systems.

Illustration 5-4
Comparing perpetual and
periodic inventory systems

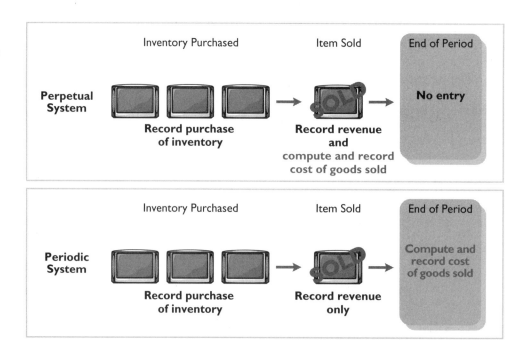

ADDITIONAL CONSIDERATIONS

Companies that sell merchandise with high unit values, such as automobiles, furniture, and major home appliances, have traditionally used perpetual systems. The growing use of computers and electronic scanners has enabled many more companies to install perpetual inventory systems. The perpetual inventory system is so named because the accounting records continuously—perpetually—show the quantity and cost of the inventory that should be on hand at any time.

A perpetual inventory system provides better control over inventories than a periodic system. Since the inventory records show the quantities that should be on hand, the company can count the goods at any time to see whether the amount of goods actually on hand agrees with the inventory records. If shortages are uncovered, the company can investigate immediately. Although a perpetual inventory system requires additional clerical work and additional cost to maintain the subsidiary records, a computerized system can minimize this cost. As noted in the Feature Story, much of Wal-Mart's success is attributed to its sophisticated inventory system.

Some businesses find it either unnecessary or uneconomical to invest in a computerized perpetual inventory system. Many small merchandising businesses, in particular, find that a perpetual inventory system costs more than it is worth. Managers of these businesses can control their merchandise and manage day-to-day operations using a periodic inventory system.

Because the perpetual inventory system is growing in popularity and use, we illustrate it in this chapter. Appendix 5A describes the journal entries for the periodic system.

INVESTOR INSIGHT

Morrow Snowboards Improves Its Stock Appeal

Investors are often eager to invest in a company that has a hot new product. However, when snowboard maker Morrow Snowboards, Inc., issued shares of stock to the public for the first time, some investors expressed reluctance to invest in Morrow because of a number of accounting control problems. To reduce investor concerns, Morrow implemented a perpetual inventory system to improve its control over inventory. In addition, it stated that it would perform a physical inventory count every quarter until it felt that the perpetual inventory system was reliable.

? If a perpetual system keeps track of inventory on a daily basis, why do companies ever need to do a physical count?

RECORDING PURCHASES OF MERCHANDISE

Companies purchase inventory using cash or credit (on account). They normally record purchases when they receive the goods from the seller. Business documents provide written evidence of the transaction. A canceled check or a cash register receipt, for example, indicates the items purchased and amounts paid for each cash purchase. Companies record cash purchases by an increase in Merchandise Inventory and a decrease in Cash.

A **purchase invoice** should support each credit purchase. This invoice indicates the total purchase price and other relevant information. The purchaser uses the

STUDY OBJECTIVE 2

Explain the recording of purchases under a perpetual inventory system.

copy of the sales invoice sent by the seller as a purchase invoice. In Illustration 5-5, for example, Sauk Stereo (the buyer) uses as a purchase invoice the sales invoice prepared by PW Audio Supply, Inc. (the seller).

Illustration 5-5
Sales invoice used as purchase invoice by Sauk Stereo

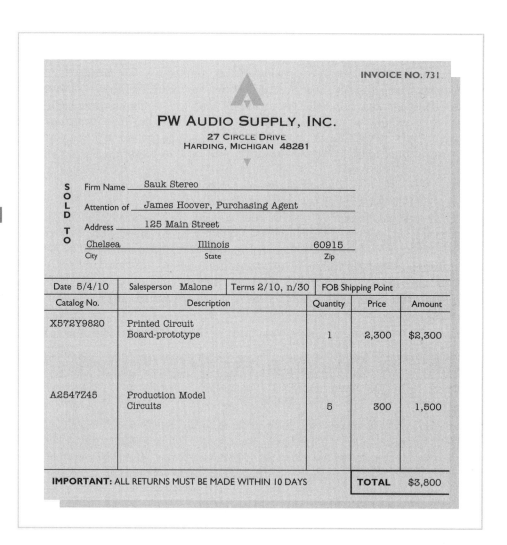

To better understand the contents of this invoice, identify these items:
1. Seller
2. Invoice date
3. Purchaser
4. Salesperson
5. Credit terms
6. Freight terms
7. Goods sold: catalog number, description, quantity, price per unit
8. Total invoice amount

Sauk Stereo makes the following journal entry to record its purchase from PW Audio Supply. The entry increases (debits) Merchandise Inventory and increases (credits) Accounts Payable.

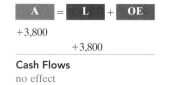

+3,800

     +3,800

Cash Flows
no effect

May	4	Merchandise Inventory	3,800	
		Accounts Payable		3,800
		(To record goods purchased on account from PW Audio Supply)		

Under the perpetual inventory system, companies record in the Merchandise Inventory account the purchase of goods they intend to sell. Thus, Wal-Mart would increase (debit) Merchandise Inventory for clothing, sporting goods, and anything else purchased for resale to customers.

Not all purchases are debited to Merchandise Inventory, however. Companies record purchases of assets acquired for use and not for resale, such as supplies, equipment, and similar items, as increases to specific asset accounts rather than to Merchandise Inventory. For example, to record the purchase of materials used to make shelf signs or for cash register receipt paper, Wal-Mart would increase Supplies.

Freight Costs

The sales agreement should indicate who—the seller or the buyer—is to pay for transporting the goods to the buyer's place of business. When a common carrier such as a railroad, trucking company, or airline transports the goods, the carrier prepares a freight bill in accord with the sales agreement.

Freight terms are expressed as either FOB shipping point or FOB destination. The letters FOB mean **free on board**. Thus, FOB shipping point means that the seller places the goods free on board the carrier, and the buyer pays the freight costs. Conversely, FOB destination means that the seller places the goods free on board to the buyer's place of business, and the seller pays the freight. For example, the sales invoice in Illustration 5-5 indicates FOB shipping point. Thus, the buyer (Sauk Stereo) pays the freight charges. Illustration 5-6 illustrates these shipping terms.

Illustration 5-6
Shipping terms

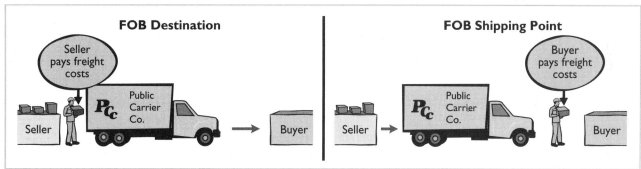

When the purchaser incurs the freight costs, it debits (increases) the account Merchandise Inventory for those costs. For example, if upon delivery of the goods on May 6, Sauk Stereo pays Acme Freight Company $150 for freight charges, the entry on Sauk Stereo's books is:

May 6	Merchandise Inventory	150	
	Cash		150
	(To record payment of freight on goods purchased)		

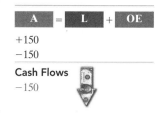

Thus, any freight costs incurred by the buyer are part of the cost of merchandise purchased. The reason: Inventory cost should include any freight charges necessary to deliver the goods to the buyer.

In contrast, **freight costs incurred by the seller on outgoing merchandise are an operating expense to the seller.** These costs increase an expense account titled Freight-out or Delivery Expense. If the freight terms on the invoice in Illustration 5-5 had required PW Audio Supply to pay the freight charges, the entry by PW Audio Supply would have been:

May 4	Freight-out (or Delivery Expense)	150	
	Cash		150
	(To record payment of freight on goods sold)		

When the seller pays the freight charges, it will usually establish a higher invoice price for the goods to cover the shipping expense.

Purchase Returns and Allowances

A purchaser may be dissatisfied with the merchandise received because the goods are damaged or defective, of inferior quality, or do not meet the purchaser's specifications. In such cases, the purchaser may return the goods to the seller for credit if the sale was made on credit, or for a cash refund if the purchase was for cash. This transaction is known as a **purchase return**. Alternatively, the purchaser may choose to keep the merchandise if the seller is willing to grant an allowance (deduction) from the purchase price. This transaction is known as a **purchase allowance**.

Assume that on May 8 Sauk Stereo returned to PW Audio Supply goods costing $300. The following entry by Sauk Stereo for the returned merchandise decreases (debits) Accounts Payable and decreases (credits) Merchandise Inventory.

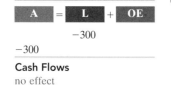

Cash Flows
no effect

May 8	Accounts Payable	300	
	Merchandise Inventory		300
	(To record return of goods purchased		
	from PW Audio Supply)		

Because Sauk Stereo increased Merchandise Inventory when the goods were received, Merchandise Inventory is decreased when Sauk returns the goods (or when it is granted an allowance).

Purchase Discounts

The credit terms of a purchase on account may permit the buyer to claim a cash discount for prompt payment. The buyer calls this cash discount a **purchase discount**. This incentive offers advantages to both parties: The purchaser saves money, and the seller shortens the operating cycle by more quickly converting the accounts receivable into cash.

Credit terms specify the amount of the cash discount and time period in which it is offered. They also indicate the time period in which the purchaser is expected to pay the full invoice price. In the sales invoice in Illustration 5-5 (page 204) credit terms are 2/10, n/30, which is read "two-ten, net thirty." This means that the buyer may take a 2% cash discount on the invoice price less ("net of") any returns or allowances, if payment is made within 10 days of the invoice date (the **discount period**). If the buyer does not pay in that time, the invoice price, less any returns or allowances, is due 30 days from the invoice date.

HELPFUL HINT

The term *net* in "net 30" means the remaining amount due after subtracting any sales returns and allowances and partial payments.

Alternatively, the discount period may extend to a specified number of days following the month in which the sale occurs. For example, 1/10 EOM (end of month) means that a 1% discount is available if the invoice is paid within the first 10 days of the next month.

When the seller elects not to offer a cash discount for prompt payment, credit terms will specify only the maximum time period for paying the balance due. For example, the invoice may state the time period as n/30, n/60, or n/10 EOM. This means, respectively, that the buyer must pay the net amount in 30 days, 60 days, or within the first 10 days of the next month.

When the buyer pays an invoice within the discount period, the amount of the discount decreases Merchandise Inventory. Why? Because companies record inventory at cost and, by paying within the discount period, the merchandiser has reduced that cost. To illustrate, assume Sauk Stereo pays the balance due of $3,500 (gross invoice price of $3,800 less purchase returns and allowances of $300) on May 14, the last day of the discount period. The cash discount is $70 ($3,500 × 2%), and Sauk Stereo pays $3,430 ($3,500 − $70). The entry Sauk makes to record its May 14 payment decreases (debits) Accounts Payable by the amount of the gross invoice price, reduces (credits) Merchandise Inventory by the $70 discount, and reduces (credits) Cash by the net amount owed.

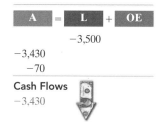

May 14	Accounts Payable	3,500	
	Cash		3,430
	Merchandise Inventory		70
	(To record payment within discount period)		

$A = L + OE$
−3,500
−3,430
−70
Cash Flows
−3,430

If Sauk Stereo failed to take the discount, and instead made full payment of $3,500 on June 3, it would debit Accounts Payable and credit Cash for $3,500 each.

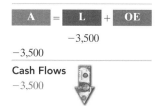

June 3	Accounts Payable	3,500	
	Cash		3,500
	(To record payment with no discount taken)		

$A = L + OE$
−3,500
−3,500
Cash Flows
−3,500

As a rule, a company usually should take all available discounts. Passing up the discount may be viewed as **paying interest** for use of the money. For example, passing up the discount offered by PW Audio would be comparable to Sauk Stereo paying an interest rate of 2% for the use of $3,500 for 20 days. This is the equivalent of an annual interest rate of approximately 36.5% (2% × 365/20). Obviously, it would be better for Sauk Stereo to borrow at prevailing bank interest rates of 6% to 10% than to lose the discount.

Summary of Purchasing Transactions

The following T account (with transaction descriptions in blue) provides a summary of the effect of the previous transactions on Merchandise Inventory. Sauk originally purchased $3,800 worth of inventory for resale. It then returned $300 of goods. It paid $150 in freight charges, and finally, it received a $70 discount off the balance owed because it paid within the discount period. This results in a balance in Merchandise Inventory of $3,580.

Merchandise Inventory

Purchase	May 4	3,800	May 8	300	Purchase return
Freight-in	6	150	14	70	Purchase discount
Balance		3,580			

DO IT!

On September 5, De La Hoya Company buys merchandise on account from Junot Diaz Company. The selling price of the goods is $1,500, and the cost to Diaz Company was $800. On September 8, De La Hoya returns defective goods with a selling price of $200 and a scrap value of $80. Record the transactions on the books of De La Hoya Company.

PURCHASE TRANSACTIONS

action plan

✔ Purchaser records goods at cost.

✔ When goods are returned, purchaser reduces Merchandise Inventory.

Solution

Sept.	5	Merchandise Inventory	1,500	
		Accounts Payable		1,500
		(To record goods purchased on account)		
	8	Accounts Payable	200	
		Merchandise Inventory		200
		(To record return of defective goods)		

Related exercise material: **BE5-2, BE5-4, E5-2, E5-3, E5-4,** and **DO IT!** 5-1.

 The Navigator

RECORDING SALES OF MERCHANDISE

STUDY OBJECTIVE 3

Explain the recording of sales revenues under a perpetual inventory system.

Companies record sales revenues, like service revenues, when earned, in compliance with the revenue recognition principle. Typically, companies earn sales revenues when the goods transfer from the seller to the buyer. At this point the sales transaction is complete and the sales price established.

Sales may be made on credit or for cash. A **business document** should support every sales transaction, to provide written evidence of the sale. **Cash register tapes** provide evidence of cash sales. A sales invoice, like the one shown in Illustration 5-5 (page 204), provides support for a credit sale. The original copy of the invoice goes to the customer, and the seller keeps a copy for use in recording the sale. The invoice shows the date of sale, customer name, total sales price, and other relevant information.

The seller makes two entries for each sale. The first entry records the sale: The seller increases (debits) Cash (or Accounts Receivable, if a credit sale), and also increases (credits) Sales for the invoice price of the goods. The second entry records the cost of the merchandise sold: The seller increases (debits) Cost of Goods Sold, and also decreases (credits) Merchandise Inventory for the cost of those goods. As a result, the Merchandise Inventory account will show at all times the amount of inventory that should be on hand.

To illustrate a credit sales transaction, PW Audio Supply records its May 4 sale of $3,800 to Sauk Stereo (see Illustration 5-5) as follows. (Here, we assume the merchandise cost PW Audio Supply $2,400.)

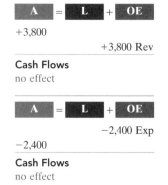

A = L + OE

+3,800

     +3,800 Rev

Cash Flows
no effect

A = L + OE

     −2,400 Exp

−2,400

Cash Flows
no effect

May	4	Accounts Receivable	3,800	
		Sales		3,800
		(To record credit sale to Sauk Stereo		
		per invoice #731)		
	4	Cost of Goods Sold	2,400	
		Merchandise Inventory		2,400
		(To record cost of merchandise sold on		
		invoice #731 to Sauk Stereo)		

For internal decision-making purposes, merchandising companies may use more than one sales account. For example, PW Audio Supply may decide to keep separate sales accounts for its sales of TV sets, DVD recorders, and satellite radio receivers. Wal-Mart might use separate accounts for sporting goods, children's clothing, and hardware—or it might have even more narrowly defined accounts. By using separate sales accounts for major product lines, rather than a single combined sales account, company management can more closely monitor sales trends and respond more strategically to changes in sales patterns. For example, if HDTV sales are increasing while DVD-player sales are decreasing, PW Audio Supply might reevaluate both its advertising and pricing policies on these items to ensure they are optimal.

On its income statement presented to outside investors, a merchandising company normally would provide only a single sales figure—the sum of all of its individual sales accounts. This is done for two reasons. First, providing detail on all of its individual sales accounts would add considerable length to its income statement. Second, companies do not want their competitors to know the details of their operating results. However, Microsoft recently expanded its disclosure of revenue from three to five types. The reason: The additional categories will better enable financial statement users to evaluate the growth of the company's consumer and Internet businesses.

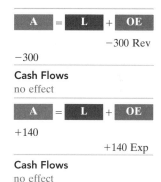

ETHICS NOTE
Many companies are trying to improve the quality of their financial reporting. For example, General Electric now provides more detail on its revenues and operating profits.

Sales Returns and Allowances

We now look at the "flipside" of purchase returns and allowances, which the seller records as **sales returns and allowances**. PW Audio Supply's entries to record credit for returned goods involve (1) an increase in Sales Returns and Allowances and a decrease in Accounts Receivable at the $300 selling price, and (2) an increase in Merchandise Inventory (assume a $140 cost) and a decrease in Cost of Goods Sold as shown below (assuming that the goods were not defective).

May	8	Sales Returns and Allowances	300	
		Accounts Receivable		300
		(To record credit granted to Sauk Stereo for returned goods)		
	8	Merchandise Inventory	140	
		Cost of Goods Sold		140
		(To record cost of goods returned)		

A	=	L	+	OE
				−300 Rev
−300				

Cash Flows
no effect

A	=	L	+	OE
+140				
				+140 Exp

Cash Flows
no effect

If Sauk returns goods because they are damaged or defective, then PW Audio Supply's entry to Merchandise Inventory and Cost of Goods Sold should be for the estimated value of the returned goods, rather than their cost. For example, if the returned goods were defective and had a scrap value of $50, PW Audio would debit Merchandise Inventory for $50, and would credit Cost of Goods Sold for $50.

Sales Returns and Allowances is a **contra-revenue account** to Sales. The normal balance of Sales Returns and Allowances is a debit. Companies use a contra account, instead of debiting Sales, to disclose in the accounts and in the income statement the amount of sales returns and allowances. Disclosure of this information is important to management: Excessive returns and allowances may suggest problems—inferior merchandise, inefficiencies in filling orders, errors in billing customers, or delivery or shipment mistakes. Moreover, a decrease (debit) recorded directly to Sales would obscure the relative importance of sales returns and allowances as a percentage of sales. It also could distort comparisons between total sales in different accounting periods.

ACCOUNTING ACROSS THE ORGANIZATION

Should Publishers Have Liberal Return Policies?

In most industries sales returns are relatively minor. In the publishing industry, however, bookstores are allowed to return unsold hardcover books to the publisher. Marketing managers at the publishing companies argue that these generous return policies are necessary to encourage bookstores to buy a broader range of books, instead of focusing just on "sure things."

But with returns of hardcover books now exceeding 34% of sales, this generous return policy is taking its toll on net income. Production and inventory managers are quick to point out the many costs of excess returns. Publishers must pay to have the books shipped back to their warehouse, sorted, and then shipped to discounters. If the discounters don't sell them, the books are repackaged again, shipped back to the publisher, and destroyed. Some bookstores and publishers have proposed adopting a "no returns" policy, but no company wants to be the first to implement it.

Source: Jeffrey A Trachtenberg, "Quest for Best Seller Creates a Pileup of Returned Books," *Wall Street Journal* (June 3, 2005), p. A1.

 If a company expects significant returns, what are the implications for revenue recognition?

Sales Discounts

As mentioned earlier, the seller may offer the customer a cash discount—called by the seller a sales discount—for the prompt payment of the balance due. It is based on the invoice price less returns and allowances, if any. The seller increases (debits) the Sales Discounts account for discounts that are taken. For example, PW Audio Supply makes the following entry to record the cash receipt on May 14 from Sauk Stereo within the discount period.

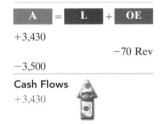

A	=	L	+	OE
+3,430				
				−70 Rev
−3,500				

Cash Flows
+3,430

May 14	Cash	3,430	
	Sales Discounts	70	
	Accounts Receivable		3,500
	(To record collection within 2/10, n/30		
	discount period from Sauk Stereo)		

Like Sales Returns and Allowances, Sales Discounts is a **contra-revenue account** to Sales. Its normal balance is a debit. PW Audio uses this account, instead of debiting sales, to disclose the amount of cash discounts taken by customers. If Sauk Stereo does not take the discount, PW Audio Supply increases Cash for $3,500 and decreases Accounts Receivable for the same amount at the date of collection.

DO IT!

SALES TRANSACTIONS

Assume information similar to that in the Do It! on page 207. That is: On September 5, De La Hoya Company buys merchandise on account from Junot Diaz Company. The selling price of the goods is $1,500, and the cost to Diaz

Company was $800. On September 8, De La Hoya returns defective goods with a selling price of $200 and a scrap value of $80. Record the transactions on the books of Junot Diaz Company.

action plan

✔ Seller records both the sale and the cost of goods sold at the time of the sale.

✔ When goods are returned, the seller records the return in a contra account, Sales Returns and Allowances, and reduces Accounts Receivable. Any goods returned increase Merchandise Inventory and reduce Cost of Goods Sold.

✔ Record merchandise inventory at its market value (scrap value).

Solution

Sept.	5	Accounts Receivable	1,500	
		Sales		1,500
		(To record credit sale)		
	5	Cost of Goods Sold	800	
		Merchandise Inventory		800
		(To record cost of goods sold on account)		
Sept.	8	Sales Returns and Allowances	200	
		Accounts Receivable		200
		(To record credit granted for receipt of returned goods)		
	8	Merchandise Inventory	80	
		Cost of Goods Sold		80
		(To record scrap value of goods returned)		

Related exercise material: **BE5-2, BE5-3, E5-3, E5-4, E5-5**, and **DO IT!** 5-2.

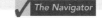 ✔ *The Navigator*

COMPLETING THE ACCOUNTING CYCLE

Up to this point, we have illustrated the basic entries for transactions relating to purchases and sales in a perpetual inventory system. Now we consider the remaining steps in the accounting cycle for a merchandising company. Each of the required steps described in Chapter 4 for service companies apply to merchandising companies. Appendix 5B to this chapter shows use of a worksheet by a merchandiser (an optional step).

Adjusting Entries

A merchandising company generally has the same types of adjusting entries as a service company. However, a merchandiser using a perpetual system will require one additional adjustment to make the records agree with the actual inventory on hand. Here's why: At the end of each period, for control purposes, a merchandising company that uses a perpetual system will take a physical count of its goods on hand. The company's unadjusted balance in Merchandise Inventory usually does not agree with the actual amount of inventory on hand. The perpetual inventory records may be incorrect due to recording errors, theft, or waste. Thus, the company needs to adjust the perpetual records to make the recorded inventory amount agree with the inventory on hand. **This involves adjusting Merchandise Inventory and Cost of Goods Sold.**

For example, suppose that PW Audio Supply has an unadjusted balance of $40,500 in Merchandise Inventory. Through a physical count, PW Audio determines that its actual merchandise inventory at year-end is $40,000. The company would make an adjusting entry as follows.

Cost of Goods Sold	500	
Merchandise Inventory		500
(To adjust inventory to physical count)		

Closing Entries

A merchandising company, like a service company, closes to Income Summary all accounts that affect net income. In journalizing, the company credits all temporary accounts with debit balances, and debits all temporary accounts with credit balances, as shown below for PW Audio Supply. Note that PW Audio closes Cost of Goods Sold to Income Summary.

HELPFUL HINT

The easiest way to prepare the first two closing entries is to identify the temporary accounts by their balances and then prepare one entry for the credits and one for the debits.

Dec. 31	Sales	480,000	
	Income Summary		480,000
	(To close income statement accounts with		
	credit balances)		
31	Income Summary	450,000	
	Sales Returns and Allowances		12,000
	Sales Discounts		8,000
	Cost of Goods Sold		316,000
	Store Salaries Expense		45,000
	Administrative Salaries Expense		19,000
	Freight-out		7,000
	Advertising Expense		16,000
	Utilities Expense		17,000
	Depreciation Expense		8,000
	Insurance Expense		2,000
	(To close income statement accounts with		
	debit balances)		
31	Income Summary	30,000	
	R.A. Lamb, Capital		30,000
	(To close net income to capital)		
31	R.A. Lamb, Capital	15,000	
	R.A. Lamb, Drawing		15,000
	(To close drawings to capital)		

After PW Audio has posted the closing entries, all temporary accounts have zero balances. Also, R.A. Lamb, Capital has a balance that is carried over to the next period.

Summary of Merchandising Entries

Illustration 5-7 summarizes the entries for the merchandising accounts using a perpetual inventory system.

Transactions	Daily Recurring Entries	Dr.	Cr.
Sales Transactions			
Selling merchandise to customers.	Cash or Accounts Receivable	XX	
	Sales		XX
	Cost of Goods Sold	XX	
	Merchandise Inventory		XX
Granting sales returns or allowances to customers.	Sales Returns and Allowances	XX	
	Cash or Accounts Receivable		XX
	Merchandise Inventory	XX	
	Cost of Goods Sold		XX
Paying freight costs on sales; FOB destination.	Freight-out	XX	
	Cash		XX
Receiving payment from customers within discount period.	Cash	XX	
	Sales Discounts	XX	
	Accounts Receivable		XX
Purchase Transactions			
Purchasing merchandise for resale.	Merchandise Inventory	XX	
	Cash or Accounts Payable		XX
Paying freight costs on merchandise purchased; FOB shipping point.	Merchandise Inventory	XX	
	Cash		XX
Receiving purchase returns or allowances from suppliers.	Cash or Accounts Payable	XX	
	Merchandise Inventory		XX
Paying suppliers within discount period.	Accounts Payable	XX	
	Merchandise Inventory		XX
	Cash		XX

Events	Adjusting and Closing Entries	Dr.	Cr.
Adjust because book amount is higher than the inventory amount determined to be on hand.	Cost of Goods Sold	XX	
	Merchandise Inventory		XX
Closing temporary accounts with credit balances.	Sales	XX	
	Income Summary		XX
Closing temporary accounts with debit balances.	Income Summary	XX	
	Sales Returns and Allowances		XX
	Sales Discounts		XX
	Cost of Goods Sold		XX
	Freight-out		XX
	Expenses		XX

Illustration 5-7
Daily recurring and adjusting and closing entries

DO IT!

The trial balance of Celine's Sports Wear Shop at December 31 shows Merchandise Inventory $25,000, Sales $162,400, Sales Returns and Allowances $4,800, Sales Discounts $3,600, Cost of Goods Sold $110,000, Rental Revenue $6,000, Freight-out $1,800, Rent Expense $8,800, and Salaries and Wages Expense $22,000. Prepare the closing entries for the above accounts.

CLOSING ENTRIES

action plan

✔ Close all temporary accounts with credit balances to Income Summary by debiting these accounts.

✔ Close all temporary accounts with debit balances, except drawings, to Income Summary by crediting these accounts.

Solution The two closing entries are:

Dec. 31	Sales	162,400	
	Rental Revenue	6,000	
	Income Summary		168,400
	(To close accounts with credit balances)		
31	Income Summary	151,000	
	Cost of Goods Sold		110,000
	Sales Returns and Allowances		4,800
	Sales Discounts		3,600
	Freight-out		1,800
	Rent Expense		8,800
	Salaries and Wages Expense		22,000
	(To close accounts with debit balances)		

Related exercise material: **BE5-5, BE5-6, E5-6, E5-7, E5-8,** and **DO IT!** **5-3.**

FORMS OF FINANCIAL STATEMENTS

STUDY OBJECTIVE 5

Distinguish between a multiple-step and a single-step income statement.

Merchandising companies widely use the classified balance sheet introduced in Chapter 4 and one of two forms for the income statement. This section explains the use of these financial statements by merchandisers.

Multiple-Step Income Statement

The **multiple-step income statement** is so named because it shows several steps in determining net income. Two of these steps relate to the company's principal operating activities. A multiple-step statement also distinguishes between **operating** and **non-operating activities**. Finally, the statement also highlights intermediate components of income and shows subgroupings of expenses.

INCOME STATEMENT PRESENTATION OF SALES

The multiple-step income statement begins by presenting **sales revenue**. It then deducts contra-revenue accounts—sales returns and allowances, and sales discounts—to arrive at **net sales**. Illustration 5-8 presents the sales revenues section for PW Audio Supply, using assumed data.

Illustration 5-8
Computation of net sales

PW AUDIO SUPPLY
Income Statement (partial)

Sales revenues		
Sales		$480,000
Less: Sales returns and allowances	$12,000	
Sales discounts	8,000	20,000
Net sales		**$460,000**

This presentation discloses the key data about the company's principal revenue-producing activities.

GROSS PROFIT

From Illustration 5-1, you learned that companies deduct from sales revenue the cost of goods sold in order to determine **gross profit**. For this computation, companies use

net sales as the amount of sales revenue. On the basis of the sales data in Illustration 5-8 (net sales of $460,000) and cost of goods sold under the perpetual inventory system (assume $316,000), PW Audio's gross profit is $144,000, computed as follows.

STUDY OBJECTIVE 6
Explain the computation and importance of gross profit.

Net sales	$460,000
Cost of goods sold	316,000
Gross profit	**$144,000**

Illustration 5-9
Computation of gross profit

We also can express a company's gross profit as a percentage, called the gross profit rate. To do so, we divide the amount of gross profit by net sales. For PW Audio, the **gross profit rate** is 31.3%, computed as follows.

Gross Profit	÷	Net Sales	=	Gross Profit Rate
$144,000	÷	$460,000	=	**31.3%**

Illustration 5-10
Gross profit rate formula and computation

Analysts generally consider the gross profit **rate** to be more useful than the gross profit **amount**. The rate expresses a more meaningful (qualitative) relationship between net sales and gross profit. For example, a gross profit of $1,000,000 may sound impressive. But if it is the result of a gross profit rate of only 7%, it is not so impressive. The gross profit rate tells how many cents of each sales dollar go to gross profit.

Gross profit represents the **merchandising profit** of a company. It is not a measure of the overall profitability, because operating expenses are not yet deducted. But managers and other interested parties closely watch the amount and trend of gross profit. They compare current gross profit with amounts reported in past periods. They also compare the company's gross profit rate with rates of competitors and with industry averages. Such comparisons provide information about the effectiveness of a company's purchasing function and the soundness of its pricing policies.

OPERATING EXPENSES AND NET INCOME

Operating expenses are the next component in measuring net income for a merchandising company. They are the expenses incurred in the process of earning sales revenue. These expenses are similar in merchandising and service enterprises. At PW Audio, operating expenses were $114,000. The company determines its net income by subtracting operating expenses from gross profit. Thus, net income is $30,000, as shown below.

Gross profit	$144,000
Operating expenses	**114,000**
Net income	$ 30,000

Illustration 5-11
Operating expenses in computing net income

The net income amount is the so-called "bottom line" of a company's income statement.

NONOPERATING ACTIVITIES

Nonoperating activities consist of various revenues and expenses and gains and losses that are unrelated to the company's main line of operations. When nonoperating items are included, the label "Income from operations" (or "Operating income") precedes them. This label clearly identifies the results of the company's normal operations, an amount determined by

ETHICS NOTE
Companies manage earnings in various ways. ConAgra Foods recorded a nonrecurring gain for $186 million from the sale of Pilgrim's Pride stock to help meet an earnings projection for the quarter.

subtracting cost of goods sold and operating expenses from net sales. The results of nonoperating activities are shown in the categories "Other revenues and gains" and "Other expenses and losses." Illustration 5-12 lists examples of each.

Illustration 5-12
Other items of nonoperating activities

Other Revenues and Gains
Interest revenue from notes receivable and marketable securities.
Dividend revenue from investments in capital stock.
Rent revenue from subleasing a portion of the store.
Gain from the sale of property, plant, and equipment.
Other Expenses and Losses
Interest expense on notes and loans payable.
Casualty losses from recurring causes, such as vandalism and accidents.
Loss from the sale or abandonment of property, plant, and equipment.
Loss from strikes by employees and suppliers.

Merchandising companies report the nonoperating activities in the income statement immediately after the company's primary operating activities. Illustration 5-13 shows these sections for PW Audio Supply, Inc., using assumed data.

Illustration 5-13
Multiple-step income statement

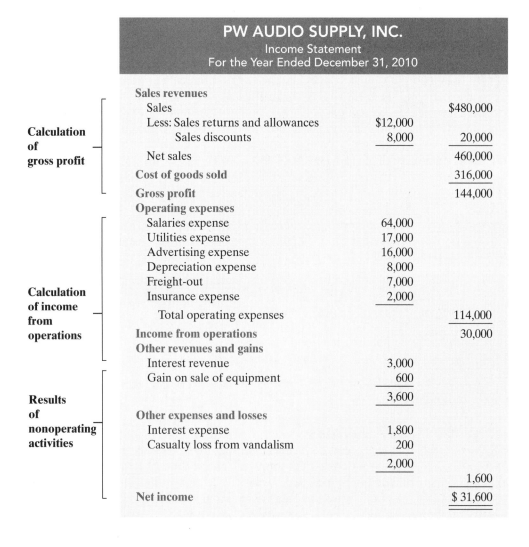

PW AUDIO SUPPLY, INC.
Income Statement
For the Year Ended December 31, 2010

Sales revenues			
Sales			$480,000
Less: Sales returns and allowances		$12,000	
Sales discounts		8,000	20,000
Net sales			460,000
Cost of goods sold			316,000
Gross profit			144,000
Operating expenses			
Salaries expense		64,000	
Utilities expense		17,000	
Advertising expense		16,000	
Depreciation expense		8,000	
Freight-out		7,000	
Insurance expense		2,000	
Total operating expenses			114,000
Income from operations			30,000
Other revenues and gains			
Interest revenue		3,000	
Gain on sale of equipment		600	
		3,600	
Other expenses and losses			
Interest expense		1,800	
Casualty loss from vandalism		200	
		2,000	
			1,600
Net income			$ 31,600

Calculation of gross profit

Calculation of income from operations

Results of nonoperating activities

The distinction between operating and nonoperating activities is crucial to many external users of financial data. These users view operating income as sustainable and many nonoperating activities as nonrecurring. Therefore, when forecasting next year's income, analysts put the most weight on this year's operating income, and less weight on this year's nonoperating activities.

Single-Step Income Statement

Another income statement format is the single-step income statement. The statement is so named because only one step—subtracting total expenses from total revenues—is required in determining net income.

In a single-step statement, all data are classified into two categories: (1) **revenues**, which include both operating revenues and other revenues and gains; and (2) **expenses**, which include cost of goods sold, operating expenses, and other expenses and losses. Illustration 5-14 shows a single-step statement for PW Audio Supply.

PW AUDIO SUPPLY
Income Statement
For the Year Ended December 31, 2010

Revenues		
Net sales		$460,000
Interest revenue		3,000
Gain on sale of equipment		600
Total revenues		463,600
Expenses		
Cost of goods sold	$316,000	
Operating expenses	114,000	
Interest expense	1,800	
Casualty loss from vandalism	200	
Total expenses		432,000
Net income		$ 31,600

Illustration 5-14
Single-step income statement

There are two primary reasons for using the single-step format: (1) A company does not realize any type of profit or income until total revenues exceed total expenses, so it makes sense to divide the statement into these two categories. (2) The format is simpler and easier to read. *For homework problems, however, you should use the single-step format only when specifically instructed to do so.*

Classified Balance Sheet

In the balance sheet, merchandising companies report merchandise inventory as a current asset immediately below accounts receivable. Recall from Chapter 4 that companies generally list current asset items in the order of their closeness to cash (liquidity). Merchandise inventory is less close to cash than accounts receivable, because the goods must first be sold and then collection made from the customer. Illustration 5-15 (page 218) presents the assets section of a classified balance sheet for PW Audio Supply.

Illustration 5-15
Assets section of a classified
balance sheet

PW AUDIO SUPPLY
Balance Sheet (Partial)
December 31, 2010

Assets

Current assets		
Cash		$ 9,500
Accounts receivable		16,100
Merchandise inventory		40,000
Prepaid insurance		1,800
Total current assets		67,400
Property, plant, and equipment		
Store equipment	$80,000	
Less: Accumulated depreciation—store equipment	24,000	56,000
Total assets		$123,400

HELPFUL HINT

The $40,000 is the *cost* of the inventory on hand, not its expected selling price.

DO IT!

FINANCIAL STATEMENT CLASSIFICATIONS

You are presented with the following list of accounts from the adjusted trial balance for merchandiser Gorman Company. Indicate in which financial statement and under what classification each of the following would be reported.

Accounts Payable	Interest Payable
Accounts Receivable	Land
Accumulated Depreciation—Office Building	Merchandise Inventory
Accumulated Depreciation—Store Equipment	Notes Payable (due in 3 years)
Advertising Expense	Office Building
Depreciation Expense	Property Tax Payable
B. Gorman, Capital	Salaries Expense
B. Gorman, Drawing	Salaries Payable
Cash	Sales Returns and Allowances
Freight-out	Store Equipment
Gain on Sale of Equipment	Sales Revenue
Insurance Expense	Utilities Expense
Interest Expense	

action plan

✔ Review the major sections of the income statement, sales revenues, cost of goods sold, operating expenses, other revenues and gains, and other expenses and losses.

✔ Add net income and investments to beginning capital and deduct drawings to arrive at ending capital in the statement of owner's equity.

✔ Review the major sections of the balance sheet, income statement, and statement of owner's equity.

Solution

Account	Financial Statement	Classification
Accounts Payable	Balance sheet	Current liabilities
Accounts Receivable	Balance sheet	Current assets
Accumulated Depreciation— Office Building	Balance sheet	Property, plant, and equipment
Accumulated Depreciation— Store Equipment	Balance sheet	Property, plant, and equipment
Advertising Expense	Income statement	Operating expenses
Depreciation Expense	Income statement	Operating expenses

B. Gorman, Capital	Statement of owner's equity	Beginning balance
B. Gorman, Drawing	Statement of owner's equity	Deduction section
Cash	Balance sheet	Current assets
Freight-out	Income statement	Operating expenses
Gain on Sale of Equipment	Income statement	Other revenues and gains
Insurance Expense	Income statement	Operating expenses
Interest Expense	Income statement	Other expenses and losses
Interest Payable	Balance sheet	Current liabilities
Land	Balance sheet	Property, plant, and equipment
Merchandise Inventory	Balance sheet	Current assets
Notes Payable	Balance sheet	Long-term liabilities
Office Building	Balance sheet	Property, plant, and equipment
Property Tax Payable	Balance sheet	Current liabilities
Salaries Expense	Income statement	Operating expenses
Salaries Payable	Balance sheet	Current liabilities
Sales Returns and Allowances	Income statement	Sales revenues
Store Equipment	Balance sheet	Property, plant, and equipment
Sales Revenue	Income statement	Sales revenues
Utilities Expense	Income statement	Operating expenses

Related exercise material: **BE5-7, BE5-8, BE5-9, E5-9, E5-10, E5-12, E5-13, E5-14,** and **DO IT! 5-4.**

Comprehensive **DO IT!**

The adjusted trial balance columns of Falcetto Company's worksheet for the year ended December 31, 2010, are as follows.

Debit		Credit	
Cash	14,500	Accumulated Depreciation	18,000
Accounts Receivable	11,100	Notes Payable	25,000
Merchandise Inventory	29,000	Accounts Payable	10,600
Prepaid Insurance	2,500	Larry Falcetto, Capital	81,000
Store Equipment	95,000	Sales	536,800
Larry Falcetto, Drawing	12,000	Interest Revenue	2,500
Sales Returns and Allowances	6,700		673,900
Sales Discounts	5,000		
Cost of Goods Sold	363,400		
Freight-out	7,600		
Advertising Expense	12,000		
Salaries Expense	56,000		
Utilities Expense	18,000		
Rent Expense	24,000		
Depreciation Expense	9,000		
Insurance Expense	4,500		
Interest Expense	3,600		
	673,900		

action plan

✔ Remember that the key components of the income statement are net sales, cost of goods sold, gross profit, total operating expenses, and net income (loss). Report these components in the right-hand column of the income statement.

✔ Put nonoperating items after income from operations.

Instructions

Prepare a multiple-step income statement for Falcetto Company.

Solution to Comprehensive **DO IT!**

FALCETTO COMPANY
Income Statement
For the Year Ended December 31, 2010

Sales revenues		
Sales		$536,800
Less: Sales returns and allowances	$6,700	
Sales discounts	5,000	11,700
Net sales		525,100
Cost of goods sold		363,400
Gross profit		161,700
Operating expenses		
Salaries expense	56,000	
Rent expense	24,000	
Utilities expense	18,000	
Advertising expense	12,000	
Depreciation expense	9,000	
Freight-out	7,600	
Insurance expense	4,500	
Total operating expenses		131,100
Income from operations		30,600
Other revenues and gains		
Interest revenue	2,500	
Other expenses and losses		
Interest expense	3,600	1,100
Net income		$ 29,500

✓ *The Navigator*

SUMMARY OF STUDY OBJECTIVES

1 **Identify the differences between service and merchandising companies.** Because of inventory, a merchandising company has sales revenue, cost of goods sold, and gross profit. To account for inventory, a merchandising company must choose between a perpetual and a periodic inventory system.

2 **Explain the recording of purchases under a perpetual inventory system.** The company debits the Merchandise Inventory account for all purchases of merchandise and freight-in, and credits it for purchase discounts and purchase returns and allowances.

3 **Explain the recording of sales revenues under a perpetual inventory system.** When a merchandising company sells inventory, it debits Accounts Receivable (or Cash), and credits Sales for the **selling price** of the merchandise. At the same time, it debits Cost of Goods Sold, and credits Merchandise Inventory for the **cost** of the inventory items sold.

4 **Explain the steps in the accounting cycle for a merchandising company.** Each of the required steps in the

accounting cycle for a service company applies to a merchandising company. A worksheet is again an optional step. Under a perpetual inventory system, the company must adjust the Merchandise Inventory account to agree with the physical count.

5 **Distinguish between a multiple-step and a single-step income statement.** A multiple-step income statement shows numerous steps in determining net income, including nonoperating activities sections. A single-step income statement classifies all data under two categories, revenues or expenses, and determines net income in one step.

6 **Explain the computation and importance of gross profit.** Merchandising companies compute gross profit by subtracting cost of goods sold from net sales. Gross profit represents the merchandising profit of a company. Managers and other interested parties closely watch the amount and trend of gross profit and of the gross profit rate.

✓ *The Navigator*

GLOSSARY

Contra-revenue account   An account that is offset against a revenue account on the income statement. (p. 209).

Cost of goods sold   The total cost of merchandise sold during the period. (p. 200).

FOB destination   Freight terms indicating that the seller places the goods free on board to the buyer's place of business, and the seller pays the freight. (p. 205).

FOB shipping point   Freight terms indicating that the seller places goods free on board the carrier, and the buyer pays the freight costs. (p. 205).

Gross profit   The excess of net sales over the cost of goods sold. (p. 214).

Gross profit rate   Gross profit expressed as a percentage, by dividing the amount of gross profit by net sales. (p. 215).

Income from operations   Income from a company's principal operating activity; determined by subtracting cost of goods sold and operating expenses from net sales. (p. 215).

Multiple-step income statement   An income statement that shows several steps in determining net income. (p. 214).

Net sales   Sales less sales returns and allowances and less sales discounts. (p. 214).

Nonoperating activities   Various revenues, expenses, gains, and losses that are unrelated to a company's main line of operations. (p. 215).

Operating expenses   Expenses incurred in the process of earning sales revenues. (p. 215).

Other expenses and losses   A nonoperating-activities section of the income statement that shows expenses and losses unrelated to the company's main line of operations. (p. 216).

Other revenues and gains   A nonoperating-activities section of the income statement that shows revenues and gains unrelated to the company's main line of operations. (p. 216).

Periodic inventory system   An inventory system under which the company does not keep detailed inventory records throughout the accounting period but determines the cost of goods sold only at the end of an accounting period. (p. 202).

Perpetual inventory system   An inventory system under which the company keeps detailed records of the cost of each inventory purchase and sale and the records continuously show the inventory that should be on hand. (p. 201).

Purchase allowance   A deduction made to the selling price of merchandise, granted by the seller so that the buyer will keep the merchandise. (p. 206).

Purchase discount   A cash discount claimed by a buyer for prompt payment of a balance due. (p. 206).

Purchase invoice   A document that supports each credit purchase. (p. 203).

Purchase return   A return of goods from the buyer to the seller for a cash or credit refund. (p. 206).

Sales discount   A reduction given by a seller for prompt payment of a credit sale. (p. 210).

Sales invoice   A document that supports each credit sale. (p. 208).

Sales returns and allowances   Purchase returns and allowances from the seller's perspective. See *Purchase return* and *Purchase allowance,* above. (p. 209).

Sales revenue (Sales)   The primary source of revenue in a merchandising company. (p. 200).

Single-step income statement   An income statement that shows only one step in determining net income. (p. 217).

APPENDIX 5A Periodic Inventory System

As described in this chapter, companies may use one of two basic systems of accounting for inventories: (1) the perpetual inventory system or (2) the periodic inventory system. In the chapter we focused on the characteristics of the perpetual inventory system. In this appendix we discuss and illustrate the **periodic inventory system.** One key difference between the two systems is the point at which the company computes cost of goods sold. For a visual reminder of this difference, refer back to Illustration 5-4 on page 202.

> **STUDY OBJECTIVE 7**
> Explain the recording of purchases and sales of inventory under a periodic inventory system.

Determining Cost of Goods Sold Under a Periodic System

When a company uses a perpetual inventory system, it records all transactions affecting inventory (such as purchases, freight costs, returns, and discounts) directly to the Merchandise Inventory account. In addition, at the time of each sale the perpetual system requires a reduction in Merchandise Inventory and an increase in Cost of Goods Sold.

Under a periodic system, however, the company uses **separate accounts** to record purchases, freight costs, returns, and discounts. Also, the company does not maintain a running account of changes in inventory. Instead, at the end of the period, it calculates the balance in ending inventory, as well as the cost of goods sold for the period. Illustration 5A-1 shows the calculation of cost of goods sold for PW Audio Supply, using a periodic inventory system. Note that it includes (here, in blue type) separate amounts for beginning inventory, cost of goods purchased, and ending inventory. These are the inputs to the cost of goods sold computation under a periodic system.

Illustration 5A-1
Cost of goods sold for a merchandising company using a periodic inventory system

Cost of goods sold			
Inventory, January 1			$36,000
Purchases		$325,000	
Less: Purchase returns and allowances	$10,400		
Purchase discounts	6,800	17,200	
Net purchases		307,800	
Add: Freight-in		12,200	
Cost of goods purchased			320,000
Cost of goods available for sale			356,000
Inventory, December 31			40,000
Cost of goods sold			316,000

HELPFUL HINT
Reading from right to left, the second column identifies the primary items that make up cost of goods sold of $316,000. The third column explains cost of goods purchased of $320,000. The fourth column reports contra-purchase items of $17,200.

A company reports merchandise inventory in the current assets section whether it uses a periodic or a perpetual system.

Recording Merchandise Transactions

In a **periodic inventory system**, companies record revenues from the sale of merchandise when sales are made, just as in a perpetual system. Unlike the perpetual system, however, companies **do not attempt on the date of sale to record the cost of the merchandise sold**. Instead, they take a physical inventory count at the **end of the period** to determine (1) the cost of the merchandise then on hand and (2) the cost of the goods sold during the period. And, **under a periodic system**, **companies record purchases of merchandise in the Purchases account rather than the Merchandise Inventory account**. Also, in a periodic system, purchase returns and allowances, purchase discounts, and freight costs on purchases are recorded in separate accounts.

To illustrate the recording of merchandise transactions under a periodic inventory system, we will use purchase/sale transactions between PW Audio Supply, Inc. and Sauk Stereo, as illustrated for the perpetual inventory system in this chapter.

Recording Purchases of Merchandise

HELPFUL HINT
Be careful not to debit purchases of equipment or supplies to a Purchases account.

On the basis of the sales invoice (Illustration 5-5, shown on page 204) and receipt of the merchandise ordered from PW Audio Supply, Sauk Stereo records the $3,800 purchase as follows.

May 4	Purchases	3,800	
	Accounts Payable		3,800
	(To record goods purchased on account from PW Audio Supply)		

Purchases is a temporary account whose normal balance is a debit.

FREIGHT COSTS

When the purchaser directly incurs the freight costs, it debits the account Freight-in (or Transportation-in). For example, if Sauk pays Acme Freight Company $150 for freight charges on its purchase from PW Audio Supply on May 6, the entry on Sauk's books is:

May 6	Freight-in (Transportation-in)	150	
	Cash		150
	(To record payment of freight on goods		
	purchased)		

Like Purchases, Freight-in is a temporary account whose normal balance is a debit. **Freight-in is part of cost of goods purchased.** The reason is that cost of goods purchased should include any freight charges necessary to bring the goods to the purchaser. Freight costs are not subject to a purchase discount. Purchase discounts apply only to the invoice cost of the merchandise.

PURCHASE RETURNS AND ALLOWANCES

Sauk Stereo returns $300 of goods to PW Audio Supply and prepares the following entry to recognize the return.

May 8	Accounts Payable	300	
	Purchase Returns and Allowances		300
	(To record return of goods		
	purchased from PW Audio Supply)		

Purchase Returns and Allowances is a temporary account whose normal balance is a credit.

PURCHASE DISCOUNTS

On May 14 Sauk Stereo pays the balance due on account to PW Audio Supply, taking the 2% cash discount allowed by PW Audio for payment within 10 days. Sauk Stereo records the payment and discount as follows.

May 14	Accounts Payable ($3,800 − $300)	3,500	
	Purchase Discounts ($3,500 × .02)		70
	Cash		3,430
	(To record payment within the		
	discount period)		

Purchase Discounts is a temporary account whose normal balance is a credit.

Recording Sales of Merchandise

The seller, PW Audio Supply, records the sale of $3,800 of merchandise to Sauk Stereo on May 4 (sales invoice No. 731, Illustration 5-5, page 204) as follows.

May 4	Accounts Receivable	3,800	
	Sales		3,800
	(To record credit sales per invoice #731		
	to Sauk Stereo)		

SALES RETURNS AND ALLOWANCES

To record the returned goods received from Sauk Stereo on May 8, PW Audio Supply records the $300 sales return as follows.

May 8	Sales Returns and Allowances	300	
	Accounts Receivable		300
	(To record credit granted to Sauk		
	Stereo for returned goods)		

SALES DISCOUNTS

On May 14, PW Audio Supply receives payment of $3,430 on account from Sauk Stereo. PW Audio honors the 2% cash discount and records the payment of Sauk's account receivable in full as follows.

May 14	Cash	3,430	
	Sales Discounts ($3,500 × .02)	70	
	Accounts Receivable ($3,800 − $300)		3,500
	(To record collection within 2/10, n/30		
	discount period from Sauk Stereo)		

COMPARISON OF ENTRIES—PERPETUAL VS. PERIODIC

Illustration 5A-2 summarizes the periodic inventory entries shown in this appendix and compares them to the perpetual-system entries from the chapter. Entries that differ in the two systems are shown in color.

Illustration 5A-2
Comparison of entries for perpetual and periodic inventory systems

ENTRIES ON SAUK STEREO'S BOOKS

	Transaction	Perpetual Inventory System			Periodic Inventory System		

May 4	Purchase of merchandise on credit.	Merchandise Inventory
		  Accounts Payable
			3,800	3,800	Purchases
					  Accounts Payable
						3,800	3,800

May 6	Freight costs on purchases.	Merchandise Inventory
		  Cash
			150	150	Freight-in
					  Cash
						150	150

May 8	Purchase returns and allowances.	Accounts Payable
		  Merchandise Inventory
			300	300	Accounts Payable
					  Purchase Returns
					  and Allowances
						300	300

May 14	Payment on account with a discount.	Accounts Payable
		  Cash
		  Merchandise Inventory
			3,500	3,430
				70
					Accounts Payable
					  Cash
					  Purchase Discounts
						3,500	3,430
							70

ENTRIES ON PW AUDIO SUPPLY'S BOOKS

	Transaction	Perpetual Inventory System			Periodic Inventory System		

May 4	Sale of merchandise on credit.	Accounts Receivable
		  Sales Revenue
			3,800	3,800	Accounts Receivable
					  Sales Revenue
						3,800	3,800

		Cost of Goods Sold
		  Merchandise Inventory
			2,400	2,400	No entry for cost of
					  goods sold		

May 8	Return of merchandise sold.	Sales Returns and
		Allowances
		  Accounts Receivable
			300	300	Sales Returns and
					Allowances
					  Accounts Receivable
						300	300

		Merchandise Inventory Cost of Goods Sold	140	140	No entry		

May 14	Cash received on account with a discount.	Cash
		Sales Discounts
		  Accounts Receivable
			3,430
			70
				3,500	Cash
					Sales Discounts
					  Accounts Receivable
						3,430
						70
							3,500

SUMMARY OF STUDY OBJECTIVE FOR APPENDIX 5A

7 Explain the recording of purchases and sales of inventory under a periodic inventory system. In recording purchases under a periodic system, companies must make entries for (a) cash and credit purchases, (b) purchase returns and allowances, (c) purchase discounts, and (d) freight costs. In recording sales, companies must make entries for (a) cash and credit sales, (b) sales returns and allowances, and (c) sales discounts.

APPENDIX 5B **Worksheet for a Merchandising Company**

Using a Worksheet

As indicated in Chapter 4, a worksheet enables companies to prepare financial statements before they journalize and post adjusting entries. The steps in preparing a worksheet for a merchandising company are the same as for a service enterprise (see pages 147–150). Illustration 5B-1 shows the worksheet for PW Audio Supply (excluding nonoperating items). The unique accounts for a merchandiser using a perpetual inventory system are in boldface letters and in red.

> **STUDY OBJECTIVE 8**
> Prepare a worksheet for a merchandising company.

PW Audio Supply.xls

File   Edit   View   Insert   Format   Tools   Data   Window   Help

PW AUDIO SUPPLY
Worksheet
For the Year Ended December 31, 2010

Accounts	Trial Balance Dr.	Trial Balance Cr.	Adjustments Dr.	Adjustments Cr.	Adjusted Trial Balance Dr.	Adjusted Trial Balance Cr.	Income Statement Dr.	Income Statement Cr.	Balance Sheet Dr.	Balance Sheet Cr.
Cash	9,500				9,500				9,500	
Accounts Receivable	16,100				16,100				16,100	
Merchandise Inventory	40,500			(a) 500	40,000				40,000	
Prepaid Insurance	3,800			(b) 2,000	1,800				1,800	
Store Equipment	80,000				80,000				80,000	
Accumulated Depreciation		16,000		(c) 8,000		24,000				24,000
Accounts Payable		20,400				20,400				20,400
R. A. Lamb, Capital		83,000				83,000				83,000
R. A. Lamb, Drawing	15,000				15,000				15,000	
Sales		480,000				480,000		480,000		
Sales Returns and Allowances	12,000				12,000		12,000			
Sales Discounts	8,000				8,000		8,000			
Cost of Goods Sold	315,500		(a) 500		316,000		316,000			
Freight-out	7,000				7,000		7,000			
Advertising Expense	16,000				16,000		16,000			
Admin. Sal. Exp.	19,000				19,000		19,000			
Salaries Expense	59,000		(d) 5,000		64,000		64,000			
Utilities Expense	17,000				17,000		17,000			
Totals	599,400	599,400								
Insurance Expense			(b) 2,000		2,000		2,000			
Depreciation Expense			(c) 8,000		8,000		8,000			
Salaries Payable				(d) 5,000		5,000				5,000
Totals			15,500	15,500	612,400	612,400	450,000	480,000	162,400	132,400
Net Income							30,000			30,000
Totals							480,000	480,000	162,400	162,400

Key: (a) Adjustment to inventory on hand. (b) Insurance expired. (c) Depreciation expense. (d) Salaries accrued.

Illustration 5B-1 Worksheet for merchandising company

TRIAL BALANCE COLUMNS

Data for the trial balance come from the ledger balances of PW Audio Supply at December 31. The amount shown for Merchandise Inventory, $40,500, is the year-end inventory amount from the perpetual inventory system.

ADJUSTMENTS COLUMNS

A merchandising company generally has the same types of adjustments as a service company. As you see in the worksheet, adjustments (b), (c), and (d) are for insurance, depreciation, and salaries. Pioneer Advertising Agency, as illustrated in Chapters 3 and 4, also had these adjustments. Adjustment (a) was required to adjust the perpetual inventory carrying amount to the actual count.

After PW Audio enters all adjustments data on the worksheet, it establishes the equality of the adjustments column totals. It then extends the balances in all accounts to the adjusted trial balance columns.

ADJUSTED TRIAL BALANCE

The adjusted trial balance shows the balance of all accounts after adjustment at the end of the accounting period.

INCOME STATEMENT COLUMNS

Next, the merchandising company transfers the accounts and balances that affect the income statement from the adjusted trial balance columns to the income statement columns. PW Audio Supply shows sales of $480,000 in the credit column. It shows the contra-revenue accounts Sales Returns and Allowances $12,000 and Sales Discounts $8,000 in the debit column. The difference of $460,000 is the net sales shown on the income statement (Illustration 5-13, page 216).

Finally, the company totals all the credits in the income statement column and compares those totals to the total of the debits in the income statement column. If the credits exceed the debits, the company has net income. PW Audio Supply has net income of $30,000. If the debits exceed the credits, the company would report a net loss.

BALANCE SHEET COLUMNS

The major difference between the balance sheets of a service company and a merchandiser is inventory. PW Audio Supply shows the ending inventory amount of $40,000 in the balance sheet debit column. The information to prepare the owner's equity statement is also found in these columns. That is, the capital account of R. A. Lamb is $83,000. The drawings for R. A. Lamb are $15,000. Net income results when the total of the debit column exceeds the total of the credit column in the balance sheet columns. A net loss results when the total of the credits exceeds the total of the debit balances.

SUMMARY OF STUDY OBJECTIVE

8 Prepare a worksheet for a merchandising company. The steps in preparing a worksheet for a merchandising company are the same as for a service company. The unique accounts for a merchandiser are Merchandise Inventory, Sales, Sales Returns and Allowances, Sales Discounts, and Cost of Goods Sold.

*Note: All **asterisked** Questions, Exercises, and Problems relate to material in the appendices to the chapter.

SELF-STUDY QUESTIONS

Answers are at the end of the chapter.

(SO 1) **1.** Gross profit will result if:
a. operating expenses are less than net income.
b. sales revenues are greater than operating expenses.
c. sales revenues are greater than cost of goods sold.
d. operating expenses are greater than cost of goods sold.

2. Under a perpetual inventory system, when goods are (SO 2) purchased for resale by a company:
a. purchases on account are debited to Merchandise Inventory.
b. purchases on account are debited to Purchases.
c. purchase returns are debited to Purchase Returns and Allowances.
d. freight costs are debited to Freight-out.

(SO 3) **3.** The sales accounts that normally have a debit balance are:
   a. Sales Discounts.
   b. Sales Returns and Allowances.
   c. both (a) and (b).
   d. neither (a) nor (b).

(SO 3) **4.** A credit sale of $750 is made on June 13, terms 2/10, net/30. A return of $50 is granted on June 16. The amount received as payment in full on June 23 is:
   a. $700.
   b. $686.
   c. $685.
   d. $650.

(SO 2) **5.** Which of the following accounts will normally appear in the ledger of a merchandising company that uses a perpetual inventory system?
   a. Purchases.
   b. Freight-in.
   c. Cost of Goods Sold.
   d. Purchase Discounts.

(SO 3) **6.** To record the sale of goods for cash in a perpetual inventory system:
   a. only one journal entry is necessary to record cost of goods sold and reduction of inventory.
   b. only one journal entry is necessary to record the receipt of cash and the sales revenue.
   c. two journal entries are necessary: one to record the receipt of cash and sales revenue, and one to record the cost of goods sold and reduction of inventory.
   d. two journal entries are necessary: one to record the receipt of cash and reduction of inventory, and one to record the cost of goods sold and sales revenue.

(SO 4) **7.** The steps in the accounting cycle for a merchandising company are the same as those in a service company *except*:
   a. an additional adjusting journal entry for inventory may be needed in a merchandising company.
   b. closing journal entries are not required for a merchandising company.
   c. a post-closing trial balance is not required for a merchandising company.
   d. a multiple-step income statement is required for a merchandising company.

(SO 5) **8.** The multiple-step income statement for a merchandising company shows each of the following features *except*:
   a. gross profit.
   b. cost of goods sold.
   c. a sales revenue section.
   d. investing activities section.

(SO 6) **9.** If sales revenues are $400,000, cost of goods sold is $310,000, and operating expenses are $60,000, the gross profit is:

   a. $30,000.
   b. $90,000.
   c. $340,000.
   d. $400,000.

(SO 5) **10.** A single-step income statement:
   a. reports gross profit.
   b. does not report cost of goods sold.
   c. reports sales revenues and "Other revenues and gains" in the revenues section of the income statement.
   d. reports operating income separately.

(SO 5) **11.** Which of the following appears on both a single-step and a multiple-step income statement?
   a. merchandise inventory.
   b. gross profit.
   c. income from operations.
   d. cost of goods sold.

(SO 7) *****12.** In determining cost of goods sold:
   a. purchase discounts are deducted from net purchases.
   b. freight-out is added to net purchases.
   c. purchase returns and allowances are deducted from net purchases.
   d. freight-in is added to net purchases.

(SO 7) *****13.** If beginning inventory is $60,000, cost of goods purchased is $380,000, and ending inventory is $50,000, cost of goods sold is:
   a. $390,000.
   b. $370,000.
   c. $330,000.
   d. $420,000.

(SO 7) *****14.** When goods are purchased for resale by a company using a periodic inventory system:
   a. purchases on account are debited to Merchandise Inventory.
   b. purchases on account are debited to Purchases.
   c. purchase returns are debited to Purchase Returns and Allowances.
   d. freight costs are debited to Purchases.

(SO 8) *****15.** In a worksheet, Merchandise Inventory is shown in the following columns:
   a. Adjusted trial balance debit and balance sheet debit.
   b. Income statement debit and balance sheet debit.
   c. Income statement credit and balance sheet debit.
   d. Income statement credit and adjusted trial balance debit.

   Go to the book's companion website, **www.wiley.com/college/weygandt**, for Additional Self-Study questions.

 The Navigator

QUESTIONS

1. (a) "The steps in the accounting cycle for a merchandising company are different from the accounting cycle for a service company." Do you agree or disagree? (b) Is the measurement of net income for a merchandising company conceptually the same as for a service company? Explain.

2. Why is the normal operating cycle for a merchandising company likely to be longer than for a service company?

3. (a) How do the components of revenues and expenses differ between merchandising and service companies? (b) Explain the income measurement process in a merchandising company.

4. How does income measurement differ between a merchandising and a service company?

5. When is cost of goods sold determined in a perpetual inventory system?

6. Distinguish between FOB shipping point and FOB destination. Identify the freight terms that will result in a debit to Merchandise Inventory by the purchaser and a debit to Freight-out by the seller.

7. Explain the meaning of the credit terms 2/10, n/30.

8. Goods costing $2,000 are purchased on account on July 15 with credit terms of 2/10, n/30. On July 18 a $200 credit memo is received from the supplier for damaged goods. Give the journal entry on July 24 to record payment of the balance due within the discount period using a perpetual inventory system.

9. Joan Roland believes revenues from credit sales may be earned before they are collected in cash. Do you agree? Explain.

10. (a) What is the primary source document for recording (1) cash sales, (2) credit sales. (b) Using XXs for amounts, give the journal entry for each of the transactions in part (a).

11. A credit sale is made on July 10 for $900, terms 2/10, n/30. On July 12, $100 of goods are returned for credit. Give the journal entry on July 19 to record the receipt of the balance due within the discount period.

12. Explain why the Merchandise Inventory account will usually require adjustment at year-end.

13. Prepare the closing entries for the Sales account, assuming a balance of $200,000 and the Cost of Goods Sold account with a $145,000 balance.

14. What merchandising account(s) will appear in the post-closing trial balance?

15. Reese Co. has sales revenue of $105,000, cost of goods sold of $70,000, and operating expenses of $20,000. What is its gross profit and its gross profit rate?

16. Ann Fort Company reports net sales of $800,000, gross profit of $370,000, and net income of $240,000. What are its operating expenses?

17. Identify the distinguishing features of an income statement for a merchandising company.

18. Identify the sections of a multiple-step income statement that relate to (a) operating activities, and (b) nonoperating activities.

19. How does the single-step form of income statement differ from the multiple-step form?

20. **PEPSICO** Determine PepsiCo's gross profit rate for 2007 and 2006. Indicate whether it increased or decreased from 2006 to 2007.

*21. Identify the accounts that are added to or deducted from Purchases to determine the cost of goods purchased. For each account, indicate whether it is added or deducted.

*22. Goods costing $3,000 are purchased on account on July 15 with credit terms of 2/10, n/30. On July 18 a $200 credit was received from the supplier for damaged goods. Give the journal entry on July 24 to record payment of the balance due within the discount period, assuming a periodic inventory system.

*23. Indicate the columns of the work sheet in which (a) merchandise inventory and (b) cost of goods sold will be shown.

BRIEF EXERCISES

Compute missing amounts in determining net income.
(SO 1)

BE5-1 Presented below are the components in Waegelain Company's income statement. Determine the missing amounts.

	Sales	Cost of Goods Sold	Gross Profit	Operating Expenses	Net Income
(a)	$75,000	?	$30,000	?	$10,800
(b)	$108,000	$70,000	?	?	$29,500
(c)	?	$71,900	$79,600	$39,500	?

Journalize perpetual inventory entries.
(SO 2, 3)

BE5-2 Hollins Company buys merchandise on account from Gordon Company. The selling price of the goods is $780, and the cost of the goods is $520. Both companies use perpetual inventory systems. Journalize the transaction on the books of both companies.

Journalize sales transactions.
(SO 3)

BE5-3 Prepare the journal entries to record the following transactions on Monroe Company's books using a perpetual inventory system.

(a) On March 2, Monroe Company sold $900,000 of merchandise to Churchill Company, terms 2/10, n/30. The cost of the merchandise sold was $620,000.

(b) On March 6, Churchill Company returned $120,000 of the merchandise purchased on March 2. The cost of the returned merchandise was $90,000.

(c) On March 12, Monroe Company received the balance due from Churchill Company.

BE5-4   From the information in BE5-3, prepare the journal entries to record these transactions on Churchill Company's books under a perpetual inventory system.

Journalize purchase transactions.
(SO 2)

BE5-5   At year-end the perpetual inventory records of Garbo Company showed merchandise inventory of $98,000. The company determined, however, that its actual inventory on hand was $96,500. Record the necessary adjusting entry.

Prepare adjusting entry for merchandise inventory.
(SO 4)

BE5-6   Bleeker Company has the following merchandise account balances: Sales $195,000, Sales Discounts $2,000, Cost of Goods Sold $105,000, and Merchandise Inventory $40,000. Prepare the entries to record the closing of these items to Income Summary.

Prepare closing entries for merchandise accounts.
(SO 4)

BE5-7   Maulder Company provides the following information for the month ended October 31, 2010: Sales on credit $280,000, cash sales $100,000, sales discounts $13,000, sales returns and allowances $11,000. Prepare the sales revenues section of the income statement based on this information.

Prepare sales revenues section of income statement.
(SO 5)

BE5-8   ⬤▬▬▶ Explain where each of the following items would appear on (1) a multiple-step income statement, and on (2) a single-step income statement: **(a)** gain on sale of equipment, **(b)** interest expense, **(c)** casualty loss from vandalism, and **(d)** cost of goods sold.

Contrast presentation in multiple-step and single-step income statements.
(SO 5)

BE5-9   Assume Baja Company has the following reported amounts: Sales $510,000, Sales returns and allowances $15,000, Cost of goods sold $350,000, Operating expenses $110,000. Compute the following: **(a)** net sales, **(b)** gross profit, **(c)** income from operations, and **(d)** gross profit rate. (Round to one decimal place.)

Compute net sales, gross profit, income from operations, and gross profit rate.
(SO 5, 6)

*BE5-10   Assume that Alshare Company uses a periodic inventory system and has these account balances: Purchases $450,000; Purchase Returns and Allowances $11,000; Purchase Discounts $8,000; and Freight-in $16,000. Determine net purchases and cost of goods purchased.

Compute net purchases and cost of goods purchased.
(SO 7)

*BE5-11   Assume the same information as in BE5-10 and also that Alshare Company has beginning inventory of $60,000, ending inventory of $90,000, and net sales of $630,000. Determine the amounts to be reported for cost of goods sold and gross profit.

Compute cost of goods sold and gross profit.
(SO 6, 7)

*BE5-12   Prepare the journal entries to record these transactions on Allied Company's books using a periodic inventory system.

Journalize purchase transactions.
(SO 7)

(a) On March 2, Allied Company purchased $1,000,000 of merchandise from B. Streisand Company, terms 2/10, n/30.

(b) On March 6 Allied Company returned $130,000 of the merchandise purchased on March 2.

(c) On March 12 Allied Company paid the balance due to B. Streisand Company.

*BE5-13   Presented below is the format of the worksheet presented in the chapter.

Identify worksheet columns for selected accounts.
(SO 8)

Trial Balance		Adjustments		Adjusted Trial Balance		Income Statement		Balance Sheet	
Dr.	Cr.	Dr.	Cr.	Dr.	Cr.	Dr.	Cr.	Dr.	Cr.

Indicate where the following items will appear on the worksheet: **(a)** Cash, **(b)** Merchandise Inventory, **(c)** Sales, **(d)** Cost of goods sold.

Example:
Cash: Trial balance debit column; Adjusted trial balance debit column; and Balance sheet debit column.

DO IT! REVIEW

Record transactions of purchasing company.
(SO 2)

DO IT! 5-1 On October 5, Lane Company buys merchandise on account from O'Brien Company. The selling price of the goods is $5,000, and the cost to O'Brien Company is $3,000. On October 8, Lane returns defective goods with a selling price of $700 and a scrap value of $250. Record the transactions on the books of Lane Company.

Record transactions of selling company.
(SO 3)

DO IT! 5-2 Assume information similar to that in Do It! 5-1. That is: On October 5, Lane Company buys merchandise on account from O'Brien Company. The selling price of the goods is $5,000, and the cost to O'Brien Company is $3,000. On October 8, Lane returns defective goods with a selling price of $700 and a scrap value of $250. Record the transactions on the books of O'Brien Company.

Prepare closing entries for a merchandising company.
(SO 4)

DO IT! 5-3 The trial balance of Dionne's Boutique at December 31 shows Merchandise Inventory $21,000, Sales $136,000, Sales Returns and Allowances $4,000, Sales Discounts $3,000, Cost of Goods Sold $92,400, Interest Revenue $5,000, Freight-out $1,500, Utilities Expense $7,400, Salaries Expense $18,500. Prepare the closing entries for the Dionne's accounts.

Classify financial statement accounts.
(SO 5)

DO IT! 5-4 Smith Company is preparing its multiple-step income statement, statement of owner's equity, and classified balance sheet. Using the column heads *Account, Financial Statement*, and *Classification*, indicate in which financial statement and under what classification each of the following would be reported.

Account	**Financial Statement**	**Classification**
Accounts Payable		
Accounts Receivable		
Accumulated Depreciation— Office Building		
Cash		
Casualty Loss from Vandalism		
Cost of Goods Sold		
Delivery Equipment		
Depreciation Expense		
E. Smith, Capital		
E. Smith, Drawing		
Freight-out		
Insurance Expense		
Interest Payable		
Land		
Merchandise Inventory		
Notes Payable (due in 5 years)		
Property Tax Payable		
Salaries Expense		
Salaries Payable		
Sales Returns and Allowances		
Sales Revenues		
Unearned Rent		
Utilities Expense		
Warehouse		

EXERCISES

Answer general questions about merchandisers.
(SO 1)

E5-1 Mr. Wellington has prepared the following list of statements about service companies and merchandisers.

1. Measuring net income for a merchandiser is conceptually the same as for a service company.
2. For a merchandiser, sales less operating expenses is called gross profit.
3. For a merchandiser, the primary source of revenues is the sale of inventory.
4. Sales salaries is an example of an operating expense.
5. The operating cycle of a merchandiser is the same as that of a service company.
6. In a perpetual inventory system, no detailed inventory records of goods on hand are maintained.

7. In a periodic inventory system, the cost of goods sold is determined only at the end of the accounting period.
8. A periodic inventory system provides better control over inventories than a perpetual system.

Instructions
Identify each statement as true or false. If false, indicate how to correct the statement.

E5-2 Information related to Steffens Co. is presented below.

Journalize purchases transactions.
(SO 2)

1. On April 5, purchased merchandise from Bryant Company for $25,000 terms 2/10, net/30, FOB shipping point.
2. On April 6 paid freight costs of $900 on merchandise purchased from Bryant.
3. On April 7, purchased equipment on account for $26,000.
4. On April 8, returned damaged merchandise to Bryant Company and was granted a $4,000 credit for returned merchandise.
5. On April 15 paid the amount due to Bryant Company in full.

Instructions
(a) Prepare the journal entries to record these transactions on the books of Steffens Co. under a perpetual inventory system.
(b) Assume that Steffens Co. paid the balance due to Bryant Company on May 4 instead of April 15. Prepare the journal entry to record this payment.

E5-3 On September 1, Howe Office Supply had an inventory of 30 calculators at a cost of $18 each. The company uses a perpetual inventory system. During September, the following transactions occurred.

Journalize perpetual inventory entries.
(SO 2, 3)

Sept. 6   Purchased 80 calculators at $20 each from DeVito Co. for cash.
      9   Paid freight of $80 on calculators purchased from DeVito Co.
     10   Returned 2 calculators to DeVito Co. for $42 credit (including freight) because they did not meet specifications.
     12   Sold 26 calculators costing $21 (including freight) for $31 each to Mega Book Store, terms n/30.
     14   Granted credit of $31 to Mega Book Store for the return of one calculator that was not ordered.
     20   Sold 30 calculators costing $21 for $31 each to Barbara's Card Shop, terms n/30.

Instructions
Journalize the September transactions.

E5-4 On June 10, Meredith Company purchased $8,000 of merchandise from Leinert Company, FOB shipping point, terms 2/10, n/30. Meredith pays the freight costs of $400 on June 11. Damaged goods totaling $300 are returned to Leinert for credit on June 12. The scrap value of these goods is $150. On June 19, Meredith pays Leinert Company in full, less the purchase discount. Both companies use a perpetual inventory system.

Prepare purchase and sale entries.
(SO 2, 3)

Instructions
(a) Prepare separate entries for each transaction on the books of Meredith Company.
(b) Prepare separate entries for each transaction for Leinert Company. The merchandise purchased by Meredith on June 10 had cost Leinert $5,000.

E5-5 Presented below are transactions related to Wheeler Company.

Journalize sales transactions.
(SO 3)

1. On December 3, Wheeler Company sold $500,000 of merchandise to Hashmi Co., terms 2/10, n/30, FOB shipping point. The cost of the merchandise sold was $350,000.
2. On December 8, Hashmi Co. was granted an allowance of $27,000 for merchandise purchased on December 3.
3. On December 13, Wheeler Company received the balance due from Hashmi Co.

Instructions
(a) Prepare the journal entries to record these transactions on the books of Wheeler Company using a perpetual inventory system.
(b) Assume that Wheeler Company received the balance due from Hashmi Co. on January 2 of the following year instead of December 13. Prepare the journal entry to record the receipt of payment on January 2.

Prepare sales revenues section and closing entries.

(SO 4, 5)

E5-6 The adjusted trial balance of Zambrana Company shows the following data pertaining to sales at the end of its fiscal year October 31, 2010: Sales $800,000, Freight-out $16,000, Sales Returns and Allowances $25,000, and Sales Discounts $15,000.

Instructions

(a) Prepare the sales revenues section of the income statement.

(b) Prepare separate closing entries for (1) sales, and (2) the contra accounts to sales.

Prepare adjusting and closing entries.

(SO 4)

E5-7 Peter Kalle Company had the following account balances at year-end: cost of goods sold $60,000; merchandise inventory $15,000; operating expenses $29,000; sales $108,000; sales discounts $1,200; and sales returns and allowances $1,700. A physical count of inventory determines that merchandise inventory on hand is $14,100.

Instructions

(a) Prepare the adjusting entry necessary as a result of the physical count.

(b) Prepare closing entries.

Prepare adjusting and closing entries.

(SO 4)

E5-8 Presented is information related to Rogers Co. for the month of January 2010.

Ending inventory per perpetual records	$ 21,600	Insurance expense	$ 12,000
		Rent expense	20,000
Ending inventory actually on hand	21,000	Salary expense	61,000
		Sales discounts	10,000
Cost of goods sold	218,000	Sales returns and allowances	13,000
Freight-out	7,000	Sales	350,000

Instructions

(a) Prepare the necessary adjusting entry for inventory.

(b) Prepare the necessary closing entries.

Prepare multiple-step income statement.

(SO 5, 6)

E5-9 Presented below is information for Obley Company for the month of March 2010.

Cost of goods sold	$212,000	Rent expense	$ 32,000
Freight-out	7,000	Sales discounts	8,000
Insurance expense	12,000	Sales returns and allowances	13,000
Salary expense	58,000	Sales	370,000

Instructions

(a) Prepare a multiple-step income statement.

(b) Compute the gross profit rate.

Prepare multiple-step and single-step income statements.

(SO 5)

E5-10 In its income statement for the year ended December 31, 2010, Pele Company reported the following condensed data.

Operating expenses	$ 925,000	Interest revenue	$ 28,000
Cost of goods sold	1,289,000	Loss on sale of equipment	10,000
Interest expense	$ 70,000	Net sales	2,312,000

Instructions

(a) Prepare a multiple-step income statement.

(b) Prepare a single-step income statement.

Prepare correcting entries for sales and purchases.

(SO 2, 3)

E5-11 An inexperienced accountant for Blaufuss Company made the following errors in recording merchandising transactions.

1. A $175 refund to a customer for faulty merchandise was debited to Sales $175 and credited to Cash $175.

2. A $180 credit purchase of supplies was debited to Merchandise Inventory $180 and credited to Cash $180.

3. A $110 sales discount was debited to Sales.
4. A cash payment of $20 for freight on merchandise purchases was debited to Freight-out $200 and credited to Cash $200.

Instructions
Prepare separate correcting entries for each error, assuming that the incorrect entry is not reversed. (Omit explanations.)

E5-12   In 2010, Walter Payton Company had net sales of $900,000 and cost of goods sold of $540,000. Operating expenses were $230,000, and interest expense was $11,000. Payton prepares a multiple-step income statement.

Compute various income measures.
(SO 5, 6)

Instructions
(a) Compute Payton's gross profit.
(b) Compute the gross profit rate. Why is this rate computed by financial statement users?
(c) What is Payton's income from operations and net income?
(d) If Payton prepared a single-step income statement, what amount would it report for net income?
(e) In what section of its classified balance sheet should Payton report merchandise inventory?

E5-13   Presented below is financial information for two different companies.

Compute missing amounts and compute gross profit rate.
(SO 5, 6)

	Nam Company	Mayo Company
Sales	$90,000	(d)
Sales returns	(a)	$ 5,000
Net sales	84,000	100,000
Cost of goods sold	56,000	(e)
Gross profit	(b)	41,500
Operating expenses	15,000	(f)
Net income	(c)	15,000

Instructions
(a) Determine the missing amounts.
(b) Determine the gross profit rates. (Round to one decimal place.)

E5-14   Financial information is presented below for three different companies.

Compute missing amounts.
(SO 5)

	Natural Cosmetics	Mattar Grocery	Allied Wholesalers
Sales	$90,000	$ (e)	$144,000
Sales returns and allowances	(a)	5,000	12,000
Net sales	81,000	95,000	(i)
Cost of goods sold	56,000	(f)	(j)
Gross profit	(b)	38,000	24,000
Operating expenses	15,000	(g)	18,000
Income from operations	(c)	(h)	(k)
Other expenses and losses	4,000	7,000	(l)
Net income	(d)	11,000	5,000

Instructions
Determine the missing amounts.

*E5-15   The trial balance of G. Durler Company at the end of its fiscal year, August 31, 2010, includes these accounts: Merchandise Inventory $17,200; Purchases $149,000; Sales $190,000; Freight-in $4,000; Sales Returns and Allowances $3,000; Freight-out $1,000; and Purchase Returns and Allowances $2,000. The ending merchandise inventory is $25,000.

Prepare cost of goods sold section.
(SO 7)

Instructions
Prepare a cost of goods sold section for the year ending August 31 (periodic inventory).

*Compute various income
statement items.*

(SO 7)

*E5-16   On January 1, 2010, Rachael Ray Corporation had merchandise inventory of $50,000. At December 31, 2010, Rachael Ray had the following account balances.

Freight-in	$ 4,000
Purchases	500,000
Purchase discounts	6,000
Purchase returns and allowances	2,000
Sales	800,000
Sales discounts	5,000
Sales returns and allowances	10,000

At December 31, 2010, Rachael Ray determines that its ending inventory is $60,000.

Instructions
(a) Compute Rachael Ray's 2010 gross profit.
(b) Compute Rachael Ray's 2010 operating expenses if net income is $130,000 and there are no nonoperating activities.

*Prepare cost of goods sold
section.*

(SO 7)

*E5-17   Below is a series of cost of goods sold sections for companies B, F, L, and R.

	B	F	L	R
Beginning inventory	$ 150	$ 70	$1,000	$ (j)
Purchases	1,600	1,080	(g)	43,590
Purchase returns and allowances	40	(d)	290	(k)
Net purchases	(a)	1,030	6,210	41,090
Freight-in	110	(e)	(h)	2,240
Cost of goods purchased	(b)	1,280	7,940	(l)
Cost of goods available for sale	1,820	1,350	(i)	49,530
Ending inventory	310	(f)	1,450	6,230
Cost of goods sold	(c)	1,230	7,490	43,300

Instructions
Fill in the lettered blanks to complete the cost of goods sold sections.

*Journalize purchase
transactions.*

(SO 7)

*E5-18   This information relates to Martinez Co.

1. On April 5 purchased merchandise from D. Norlan Company for $20,000, terms 2/10, net/30, FOB shipping point.
2. On April 6 paid freight costs of $900 on merchandise purchased from D. Norlan Company.
3. On April 7 purchased equipment on account for $26,000.
4. On April 8 returned some of April 5 merchandise, which cost $2,800, to D. Norlan Company.
5. On April 15 paid the amount due to D. Norlan Company in full.

Instructions
(a) Prepare the journal entries to record these transactions on the books of Martinez Co. using a periodic inventory system.
(b) Assume that Martinez Co. paid the balance due to D. Norlan Company on May 4 instead of April 15. Prepare the journal entry to record this payment.

*Journalize purchase
transactions.*

(SO 7)

*E5-19   Presented below is information related to Chevalier Co.

1. On April 5, purchased merchandise from Paris Company for $22,000, terms 2/10, net/30, FOB shipping point.
2. On April 6, paid freight costs of $800 on merchandise purchased from Paris.
3. On April 7, purchased equipment on account from Wayne Higley Mfg. Co. for $26,000.
4. On April 8, returned merchandise, which cost $4,000, to Paris Company.
5. On April 15, paid the amount due to Paris Company in full.

Instructions
(a) Prepare the journal entries to record these transactions on the books of Chevalier Co. using a periodic inventory system.
(b) Assume that Chevalier Co. paid the balance due to Paris Company on May 4 instead of April 15. Prepare the journal entry to record this payment.

*E5-20   Presented below are selected accounts for Carpenter Company as reported in the worksheet at the end of May 2010.

Complete worksheet.
(SO 8)

Accounts	Adjusted Trial Balance		Income Statement		Balance Sheet	
	Dr.	Cr.	Dr.	Cr.	Dr.	Cr.
Cash	9,000					
Merchandise Inventory	76,000					
Sales		450,000				
Sales Returns and Allowances	10,000					
Sales Discounts	9,000					
Cost of Goods Sold	300,000					

Instructions

Complete the worksheet by extending amounts reported in the adjusted trial balance to the appropriate columns in the work sheet. Do not total individual columns.

*E5-21   The trial balance columns of the worksheet for Green Company at June 30, 2010, are as follows.

Prepare a worksheet.
(SO 8)

GREEN COMPANY
Worksheet
For the Month Ended June 30, 2010

Account Titles	Trial Balance	
	Debit	Credit
Cash	$ 2,320	
Accounts Receivable	2,440	
Merchandise Inventory	11,640	
Accounts Payable		$ 1,120
Ed Green, Capital		3,600
Sales		42,400
Cost of Goods Sold	20,560	
Operating Expenses	10,160	
	$47,120	$47,120

Other data:
Operating expenses incurred on account, but not yet recorded, total $1,500.

Instructions

Enter the trial balance on a worksheet and complete the worksheet.

EXERCISES: SET B

Visit the book's companion website at **www.wiley.com/college/weygandt**, and choose the Student Companion site, to access Exercise Set B.

PROBLEMS: SET A

P5-1A   Sansomite Co. distributes suitcases to retail stores and extends credit terms of 1/10, n/30 to all of its customers. At the end of June, Sansomite's inventory consisted of suitcases costing $1,200. During the month of July the following merchandising transactions occurred.

Journalize purchase and sales transactions under a perpetual inventory system.
(SO 2, 3)

July 1   Purchased suitcases on account for $1,800 from Trunk Manufacturers, FOB destination, terms 2/10, n/30. The appropriate party also made a cash payment of $100 for freight on this date.

3 Sold suitcases on account to Satchel World for $2,000. The cost of suitcases sold is $1,200.

9 Paid Trunk Manufacturers in full.

12 Received payment in full from Satchel World.

17 Sold suitcases on account to The Going Concern for $1,500. The cost of the suitcases sold was $900.

18 Purchased suitcases on account for $1,700 from Kingman Manufacturers, FOB shipping point, terms 1/10, n/30. The appropriate party also made a cash payment of $100 for freight on this date.

20 Received $300 credit (including freight) for suitcases returned to Kingman Manufacturers.

21 Received payment in full from The Going Concern.

22 Sold suitcases on account to Fly-By-Night for $2,250. The cost of suitcases sold was $1,350.

30 Paid Kingman Manufacturers in full.

31 Granted Fly-By-Night $200 credit for suitcases returned costing $120.

Sansomite's chart of accounts includes the following: No. 101 Cash, No. 112 Accounts Receivable, No. 120 Merchandise Inventory, No. 201 Accounts Payable, No. 401 Sales, No. 412 Sales Returns and Allowances, No. 414 Sales Discounts, No. 505 Cost of Goods Sold.

Instructions

Journalize the transactions for the month of July for Sansomite using a perpetual inventory system.

Journalize, post, and prepare a partial income statement.

(SO 2, 3, 5, 6)

P5-2A Olaf Distributing Company completed the following merchandising transactions in the month of April. At the beginning of April, the ledger of Olaf showed Cash of $9,000 and M. Olaf, Capital of $9,000.

Apr. 2 Purchased merchandise on account from Dakota Supply Co. $6,900, terms 1/10, n/30.

4 Sold merchandise on account $5,500, FOB destination, terms 1/10, n/30. The cost of the merchandise sold was $4,100.

5 Paid $240 freight on April 4 sale.

6 Received credit from Dakota Supply Co. for merchandise returned $500.

11 Paid Dakota Supply Co. in full, less discount.

13 Received collections in full, less discounts, from customers billed on April 4.

14 Purchased merchandise for cash $3,800.

16 Received refund from supplier for returned goods on cash purchase of April 14, $500.

18 Purchased merchandise from Skywalker Distributors $4,500, FOB shipping point, terms 2/10, n/30.

20 Paid freight on April 18 purchase $100.

23 Sold merchandise for cash $6,400. The merchandise sold had a cost of $5,120.

26 Purchased merchandise for cash $2,300.

27 Paid Skywalker Distributors in full, less discount.

29 Made refunds to cash customers for defective merchandise $90. The returned merchandise had a scrap value of $30.

30 Sold merchandise on account $3,700, terms n/30. The cost of the merchandise sold was $2,800.

Olaf Company's chart of accounts includes the following: No. 101 Cash, No. 112 Accounts Receivable, No. 120 Merchandise Inventory, No. 201 Accounts Payable, No. 301 M. Olaf, Capital, No. 401 Sales, No. 412 Sales Returns and Allowances, No. 414 Sales Discounts, No. 505 Cost of Goods Sold, and No. 644 Freight-out.

Instructions

(a) Journalize the transactions using a perpetual inventory system.

(b) Enter the beginning cash and capital balances, and post the transactions. (Use J1 for the journal reference.)

(c) Gross profit $3,465

(c) Prepare the income statement through gross profit for the month of April 2010.

Prepare financial statements and adjusting and closing entries.

(SO 4, 5)

P5-3A Maine Department Store is located near the Village Shopping Mall. At the end of the company's calendar year on December 31, 2010, the following accounts appeared in two of its trial balances.

	Unadjusted	Adjusted		Unadjusted	Adjusted
Accounts Payable	$ 79,300	$ 79,300	Interest Payable		$ 8,000
Accounts Receivable	50,300	50,300	Interest Revenue	$ 4,000	4,000
Accumulated Depr.—Building	42,100	52,500	Merchandise Inventory	75,000	75,000
Accumulated Depr.—Equipment	29,600	42,900	Mortgage Payable	80,000	80,000
Building	190,000	190,000	Office Salaries Expense	32,000	32,000
Cash	23,800	23,800	Prepaid Insurance	9,600	2,400
B. Maine, Capital	176,600	176,600	Property Tax Expense		4,800
Cost of Goods Sold	412,700	412,700	Property Taxes Payable		4,800
Depr. Expense—Building		10,400	Sales Salaries Expense	76,000	76,000
Depr. Expense—Equipment		13,300	Sales	628,000	628,000
B. Maine, Drawing	28,000	28,000	Sales Commissions Expense	10,200	14,500
Equipment	110,000	110,000	Sales Commissions Payable		4,300
Insurance Expense		7,200	Sales Returns and Allowances	8,000	8,000
Interest Expense	3,000	11,000	Utilities Expense	11,000	12,000
			Utilities Expense Payable		1,000

Instructions

(a) Prepare a multiple-step income statement, an owner's equity statement, and a classified balance sheet. $20,000 of the mortgage payable is due for payment next year.

(b) Journalize the adjusting entries that were made.

(c) Journalize the closing entries that are necessary.

(a) Net income $30,100
 Capital $178,700
 Total assets $356,100

P5-4A   J. Hafner, a former professional tennis star, operates Hafner's Tennis Shop at the Miller Lake Resort. At the beginning of the current season, the ledger of Hafner's Tennis Shop showed Cash $2,500, Merchandise Inventory $1,700, and J. Hafner, Capital $4,200. The following transactions were completed during April.

Journalize, post, and prepare a trial balance.

(SO 2, 3, 4)

GLS
  Peachtree

Apr. 4   Purchased racquets and balls from Wellman Co. $840, FOB shipping point, terms 2/10, n/30.

   6   Paid freight on purchase from Wellman Co. $40.

   8   Sold merchandise to members $1,150, terms n/30. The merchandise sold had a cost of $790.

  10   Received credit of $40 from Wellman Co. for a racquet that was returned.

  11   Purchased tennis shoes from Venus Sports for cash, $420.

  13   Paid Wellman Co. in full.

  14   Purchased tennis shirts and shorts from Serena's Sportswear $900, FOB shipping point, terms 3/10, n/60.

  15   Received cash refund of $50 from Venus Sports for damaged merchandise that was returned.

  17   Paid freight on Serena's Sportswear purchase $30.

  18   Sold merchandise to members $810, terms n/30. The cost of the merchandise sold was $530.

  20   Received $500 in cash from members in settlement of their accounts.

  21   Paid Serena's Sportswear in full.

  27   Granted an allowance of $30 to members for tennis clothing that did not fit properly.

  30   Received cash payments on account from members, $660.

The chart of accounts for the tennis shop includes the following: No. 101 Cash, No. 112 Accounts Receivable, No. 120 Merchandise Inventory, No. 201 Accounts Payable, No. 301 J. Hafner, Capital, No. 401 Sales, No. 412 Sales Returns and Allowances, No. 505 Cost of Goods Sold.

Instructions

(a) Journalize the April transactions using a perpetual inventory system.

(b) Enter the beginning balances in the ledger accounts and post the April transactions. (Use J1 for the journal reference.)

(c) Prepare a trial balance on April 30, 2010.

(c) Total debits $6,160

Determine cost of goods sold and gross profit under periodic approach.

(SO 6, 7)

*P5-5A   At the end of Gordman Department Store's fiscal year on December 31, 2010, these accounts appeared in its adjusted trial balance.

Freight-in	$ 5,600
Merchandise Inventory	40,500
Purchases	447,000
Purchase Discounts	12,000
Purchase Returns and Allowances	6,400
Sales	718,000
Sales Returns and Allowances	8,000

Additional facts:

1. Merchandise inventory on December 31, 2010, is $75,000.
2. Note that Gordman Department Store uses a periodic system.

Instructions

Gross profit $310,300

Prepare an income statement through gross profit for the year ended December 31, 2010.

Calculate missing amounts and assess profitability.

(SO 6, 7)

*P5-6A   Kristen Montana operates a retail clothing operation. She purchases all merchandise inventory on credit and uses a periodic inventory system. The accounts payable account is used for recording inventory purchases only; all other current liabilities are accrued in separate accounts. You are provided with the following selected information for the fiscal years 2007, 2008, 2009, and 2010.

	2007	**2008**	**2009**	**2010**
Inventory (ending)	$ 13,000	$ 11,300	$ 14,700	$ 12,200
Accounts payable (ending)	20,000			
Sales		225,700	227,600	219,500
Purchases of merchandise inventory on account		146,000	145,000	129,000
Cash payments to suppliers		135,000	161,000	127,000

Instructions

(a) 2009 $141,600

(c) 2009 Ending accts payable $15,000

(a) Calculate cost of goods sold for each of the 2008, 2009, and 2010 fiscal years.
(b) Calculate the gross profit for each of the 2008, 2009, and 2010 fiscal years.
(c) Calculate the ending balance of accounts payable for each of the 2008, 2009, and 2010 fiscal years.
(d) Sales declined in fiscal 2010. Does that mean that profitability, as measured by the gross profit rate, necessarily also declined? Explain, calculating the gross profit rate for each fiscal year to help support your answer. (Round to one decimal place.)

Journalize, post, and prepare trial balance and partial income statement using periodic approach.

(SO 7)

*P5-7A   At the beginning of the current season, the ledger of Village Tennis Shop showed Cash $2,500; Merchandise Inventory $1,700; and Angie Wilbert, Capital $4,200. The following transactions were completed during April.

Apr. 4   Purchased racquets and balls from Denton Co. $740, terms 3/10, n/30.
       6   Paid freight on Denton Co. purchase $60.
       8   Sold merchandise to members $900, terms n/30.
      10   Received credit of $40 from Denton Co. for a racquet that was returned.
      11   Purchased tennis shoes from Newbee Sports for cash $300.
      13   Paid Denton Co. in full.
      14   Purchased tennis shirts and shorts from Venus's Sportswear $600, terms 2/10, n/60.
      15   Received cash refund of $50 from Newbee Sports for damaged merchandise that was returned.
      17   Paid freight on Venus's Sportswear purchase $30.
      18   Sold merchandise to members $1,000, terms n/30.
      20   Received $500 in cash from members in settlement of their accounts.
      21   Paid Venus's Sportswear in full.
      27   Granted an allowance of $30 to members for tennis clothing that did not fit properly.
      30   Received cash payments on account from members $500.

The chart of accounts for the tennis shop includes Cash; Accounts Receivable; Merchandise Inventory; Accounts Payable; Angie Wilbert, Capital; Sales; Sales Returns and Allowances; Purchases; Purchase Returns and Allowances; Purchase Discounts; and Freight-in.

Instructions
(a) Journalize the April transactions using a periodic inventory system.
(b) Using T accounts, enter the beginning balances in the ledger accounts and post the April transactions.
(c) Prepare a trial balance on April 30, 2010.
(d) Prepare an income statement through gross profit, assuming merchandise inventory on hand at April 30 is $2,296.

(c) Tot. trial balance $6,223
(d) Gross profit $ 859

*P5-8A   The trial balance of Terry Manning Fashion Center contained the following accounts at November 30, the end of the company's fiscal year.

Complete accounting cycle beginning with a worksheet.
(SO 4, 5, 6, 8)

TERRY MANNING FASHION CENTER
Trial Balance
November 30, 2010

	Debit	Credit
Cash	$ 28,700	
Accounts Receivable	30,700	
Merchandise Inventory	44,700	
Store Supplies	6,200	
Store Equipment	85,000	
Accumulated Depreciation—Store Equipment		$ 22,000
Delivery Equipment	48,000	
Accumulated Depreciation—Delivery Equipment		6,000
Notes Payable		51,000
Accounts Payable		48,500
Terry Manning, Capital		110,000
Terry Manning, Drawing	12,000	
Sales		755,200
Sales Returns and Allowances	8,800	
Cost of Goods Sold	497,400	
Salaries Expense	140,000	
Advertising Expense	24,400	
Utilities Expense	14,000	
Repair Expense	12,100	
Delivery Expense	16,700	
Rent Expense	24,000	
Totals	$992,700	$992,700

Adjustment data:

1. Store supplies on hand totaled $2,500.
2. Depreciation is $9,000 on the store equipment and $5,000 on the delivery equipment.
3. Interest of $4,080 is accrued on notes payable at November 30.
4. Merchandise inventory actually on hand is $44,400.

Instructions
(a) Enter the trial balance on a worksheet, and complete the worksheet.
(b) Prepare a multiple-step income statement and an owner's equity statement for the year, and a classified balance sheet as of November 30, 2010. Notes payable of $30,000 are due in January 2011.
(c) Journalize the adjusting entries.
(d) Journalize the closing entries.
(e) Prepare a post-closing trial balance.

(a) Adj. trial balance
* $1,010,780*
* Net loss $4,280*

(b) Gross profit $248,700
* Total assets $197,300*

PROBLEMS: SET B

P5-1B   Paul's Book Warehouse distributes hardcover books to retail stores and extends credit terms of 2/10, n/30 to all of its customers. At the end of May, Paul's inventory consisted of books purchased for $1,800. During June the following merchandising transactions occurred.

Journalize purchase and sales transactions under a perpetual inventory system.

(SO 2, 3)

June 1 Purchased books on account for $1,200 from Logan Publishers, FOB destination, terms 2/10, n/30. The appropriate party also made a cash payment of $50 for the freight on this date.
       3 Sold books on account to Reading Rainbow for $2,400.
       6 Received $100 credit for books returned to Logan Publishers.
       9 Paid Logan Publishers in full, less discount.
      15 Received payment in full from Reading Rainbow.
      17 Sold books on account to Cheap Books for $1,800. The cost of the books sold was $1,080.
      20 Purchased books on account for $1,500 from Phantom Publishers, FOB destination, terms 2/15, n/30. The appropriate party also made a cash payment of $50 for the freight on this date.
      24 Received payment in full from Cheap Books.
      26 Paid Phantom Publishers in full, less discount.
      28 Sold books on account to Willow Bookstore for $1,300. The cost of the books sold was $780.
      30 Granted Willow Bookstore $120 credit for books returned costing $72.

Paul's Book Warehouse's chart of accounts includes the following: No. 101 Cash, No. 112 Accounts Receivable, No. 120 Merchandise Inventory, No. 201 Accounts Payable, No. 401 Sales, No. 412 Sales Returns and Allowances, No. 414 Sales Discounts, No. 505 Cost of Goods Sold.

Instructions

Journalize the transactions for the month of June for Paul's Book Warehouse using a perpetual inventory system.

Journalize, post, and prepare a partial income statement.

(SO 2, 3, 5, 6)

GLS

P5-2B Newman Hardware Store completed the following merchandising transactions in the month of May. At the beginning of May, the ledger of Newman showed Cash of $5,000 and Newman, Capital of $5,000.

May 1 Purchased merchandise on account from Jerry's Wholesale Supply $4,200, terms 2/10, n/30.
      2 Sold merchandise on account $2,100, terms 1/10, n/30. The cost of the merchandise sold was $1,300.
      5 Received credit from Jerry's Wholesale Supply for merchandise returned $300.
      9 Received collections in full, less discounts, from customers billed on sales of $2,100 on May 2.
     10 Paid Jerry's Wholesale Supply in full, less discount.
     11 Purchased supplies for cash $400.
     12 Purchased merchandise for cash $1,400.
     15 Received refund for poor quality merchandise from supplier on cash purchase $150.
     17 Purchased merchandise from Cosmo Distributors $1,300, FOB shipping point, terms 2/10, n/30.
     19 Paid freight on May 17 purchase $130.
     24 Sold merchandise for cash $3,200. The merchandise sold had a cost of $2,000.
     25 Purchased merchandise from Costanza, Inc. $550, FOB destination, terms 2/10, n/30.
     27 Paid Cosmo Distributors in full, less discount.
     29 Made refunds to cash customers for defective merchandise $60. The returned merchandise had a scrap value of $10.
     31 Sold merchandise on account $900, terms n/30. The cost of the merchandise sold was $560.

Newman Hardware's chart of accounts includes the following: No. 101 Cash, No. 112 Accounts Receivable, No. 120 Merchandise Inventory, No. 126 Supplies, No. 201 Accounts Payable, No. 301 Newman, Capital, No. 401 Sales, No. 412 Sales Returns and Allowances, No. 414 Sales Discounts, No. 505 Cost of Goods Sold.

Instructions

(a) Journalize the transactions using a perpetual inventory system.
(b) Enter the beginning cash and capital balances and post the transactions. (Use J1 for the journal reference.)

(c) Gross profit $2,269

(c) Prepare an income statement through gross profit for the month of May 2010.

Prepare financial statements and adjusting and closing entries.

(SO 4, 5)

P5-3B Tarp Department Store is located in midtown Platteville. During the past several years, net income has been declining because of suburban shopping centers. At the end of the company's fiscal year on November 30, 2010, the following accounts appeared in two of its trial balances.

	Unadjusted	Adjusted		Unadjusted	Adjusted
Accounts Payable	$ 25,200	$ 25,200	Interest Revenue	$ 8,000	$ 8,000
Accounts Receivable	30,500	30,500	Merchandise Inventory	29,000	29,000
Accumulated Depr.—Delivery Equip.	10,000	15,000	Notes Payable	37,000	37,000
Accumulated Depr.—Store Equip.	24,000	32,000	Prepaid Insurance	10,500	3,500
Cash	6,000	6,000	Property Tax Expense		2,800
J. Tarp, Capital	101,700	101,700	Property Taxes Payable		2,800
Cost of Goods Sold	507,000	507,000	Rent Expense	15,000	15,000
Delivery Expense	6,500	6,500	Salaries Expense	96,000	96,000
Delivery Equipment	46,000	46,000	Sales	680,000	680,000
Depr. Expense—Delivery Equip.		5,000	Sales Commissions Expense	6,500	11,200
Depr. Expense—Store Equip.		8,000	Sales Commissions Payable		4,700
J. Tarp, Drawing	10,000	10,000	Sales Returns and Allowances	8,000	8,000
Insurance Expense		7,000	Store Equip.	100,000	100,000
Interest Expense	6,400	6,400	Utilities Expense	8,500	8,500

Instructions

(a) Prepare a multiple-step income statement, an owner's equity statement, and a classified balance sheet. Notes payable are due in 2013.

(b) Journalize the adjusting entries that were made.

(c) Journalize the closing entries that are necessary.

(a) Net income $6,600
Capital $98,300
Total assets $168,000

P5-4B Caleb Borke, a former disc golf star, operates Caleb's Discorama. At the beginning of the current season on April 1, the ledger of Caleb's Discorama showed Cash $1,800, Merchandise Inventory $2,500, and C. Borke, Capital $4,300. The following transactions were completed during April.

Journalize, post, and prepare a trial balance.
(SO 2, 3, 4)

Apr. 5 Purchased golf discs, bags, and other inventory on account from Innova Co. $1,200, FOB shipping point, terms 2/10, n/60.

  7 Paid freight on Innovas purchase $50.

  9 Received credit from Innova Co. for merchandise returned $100.

 10 Sold merchandise on account for $900, terms n/30. The merchandise sold had a cost of $540.

 12 Purchased disc golf shirts and other accessories on account from Lightning Sportswear $670, terms 1/10, n/30.

 14 Paid Innova Co. in full, less discount.

 17 Received credit from Lightning Sportswear for merchandise returned $70.

 20 Made sales on account for $560, terms n/30. The cost of the merchandise sold was $340.

 21 Paid Lightning Sportswear in full, less discount.

 27 Granted an allowance to members for clothing that was flawed $30.

 30 Received payments on account from customers $800.

The chart of accounts for the store includes the following: No. 101 Cash, No. 112 Accounts Receivable, No. 120 Merchandise Inventory, No. 201 Accounts Payable, No. 301 C. Borke, Capital, No. 401 Sales, No. 412 Sales Returns and Allowances, No. 505 Cost of Goods Sold.

Instructions

(a) Journalize the April transactions using a perpetual inventory system.

(b) Enter the beginning balances in the ledger accounts and post the April transactions. (Use J1 for the journal reference.)

(c) Prepare a trial balance on April 30, 2010.

(c) Total debits $5,760

*P5-5B At the end of Duckworth Department Store's fiscal year on November 30, 2010, these accounts appeared in its adjusted trial balance.

Determine cost of goods sold and gross profit under periodic approach.
(SO 6, 7)

Freight-in	$ 4,500
Merchandise Inventory	40,000
Purchases	585,000
Purchase Discounts	6,300
Purchase Returns and Allowances	2,700
Sales	810,000
Sales Returns and Allowances	18,000

Additional facts:
1. Merchandise inventory on November 30, 2010, is $32,600.
2. Note that Duckworth Department Store uses a periodic system.

Instructions

Gross profit $204,100

Prepare an income statement through gross profit for the year ended November 30, 2010.

Calculate missing amounts and assess profitability.

(SO 6, 7)

*P5-6B Letterman Inc. operates a retail operation that purchases and sells home entertainment products. The company purchases all merchandise inventory on credit and uses a periodic inventory system. The accounts payable account is used for recording inventory purchases only; all other current liabilities are accrued in separate accounts. You are provided with the following selected information for the fiscal years 2007 through 2010, inclusive.

	2007	2008	2009	2010
Income Statement Data				
Sales		$53,300	$ (e)	$45,200
Cost of goods sold		(a)	13,800	14,300
Gross profit		38,300	33,800	(i)
Operating expenses		34,900	(f)	28,600
Net income		$ (b)	$ 2,500	$ (j)
Balance Sheet Data				
Merchandise inventory	$7,200	$ (c)	$8,100	$ (k)
Accounts payable	3,200	3,600	2,500	(l)
Additional Information				
Purchases of merchandise inventory on account		$14,200	$ (g)	$13,200
Cash payments to suppliers		(d)	(h)	13,600

Instructions

(c) $6,400

(g) $15,500

(i) $30,900

(a) Calculate the missing amounts.
(b) Sales declined over the 3-year fiscal period, 2008–2010. Does that mean that profitability necessarily also declined? Explain, computing the gross profit rate and the profit margin ratio for each fiscal year to help support your answer. (Round to one decimal place.)

Journalize, post, and prepare trial balance and partial income statement using periodic approach.

(SO 7)

*P5-7B At the beginning of the current season on April 1, the ledger of Five Pines Pro Shop showed Cash $3,000; Merchandise Inventory $4,000; and Irene Tiger, Capital $7,000. These transactions occurred during April 2010.

Apr. 5 Purchased golf bags, clubs, and balls on account from Mickelson Co. $1,200, FOB shipping point, terms 2/10, n/60.
      7 Paid freight on Mickelson Co. purchases $50.
      9 Received credit from Mickelson Co. for merchandise returned $100.
     10 Sold merchandise on account to members $600, terms n/30.
     12 Purchased golf shoes, sweaters, and other accessories on account from Dagger Sportswear $340, terms 1/10, n/30.
     14 Paid Mickelson Co. in full.
     17 Received credit from Dagger Sportswear for merchandise returned $40.
     20 Made sales on account to members $600, terms n/30.
     21 Paid Dagger Sportswear in full.
     27 Granted credit to members for clothing that had flaws $35.
     30 Received payments on account from members $650.

The chart of accounts for the pro shop includes Cash; Accounts Receivable, Merchandise Inventory; Accounts Payable; Irene Tiger, Capital; Sales; Sales Returns and Allowances; Purchases; Purchase Returns and Allowances; Purchase Discounts, and Freight-in.

Instructions

(a) Journalize the April transactions using a periodic inventory system.
(b) Using T accounts, enter the beginning balances in the ledger accounts and post the April transactions.

(c) Tot. trial balance $8,365

Gross profit $466

(c) Prepare a trial balance on April 30, 2010.
(d) Prepare an income statement through gross profit, assuming merchandise inventory on hand at April 30 is $4,726.

PROBLEMS: SET C

Visit the book's companion website at **www.wiley.com/college/weygandt**, and choose the Student Companion site, to access Problem Set C.

CONTINUING COOKIE CHRONICLE

(*Note:* This is a continuation of the Cookie Chronicle from Chapters 1 through 4.)

CCC5 Because Natalie has had such a successful first few months, she is considering other opportunities to develop her business. One opportunity is the sale of fine European mixers. The owner of Kzinski Supply Company has approached Natalie to become the exclusive U.S. distributor of these fine mixers in her state. The current cost of a mixer is approximately $525 (U.S.), and Natalie would sell each one for $1,050. Natalie comes to you for advice on how to account for these mixers.

Go to the book's companion website,
www.wiley.com/college/weygandt,
to see the completion of this problem.

BROADENING YOUR PERSPECTIVE

FINANCIAL REPORTING AND ANALYSIS

Financial Reporting Problem: PepsiCo, Inc.

BYP5-1 The financial statements of PepsiCo, Inc. are presented in Appendix A at the end of this textbook.

Instructions
Answer the following questions using PepsiCo's Consolidated Statement of Income.

(a) What was the percentage change in (1) sales and in (2) net income from 2005 to 2006 and from 2006 to 2007?
(b) What was the company's gross profit rate in 2005, 2006, and 2007?
(c) What was the company's percentage of net income to net sales in 2005, 2006, and 2007? Comment on any trend in this percentage.

Comparative Analysis Problem: PepsiCo, Inc. vs. The Coca-Cola Company

BYP5-2 PepsiCo's financial statements are presented in Appendix A. Financial statements of The Coca-Cola Company are presented in Appendix B.

Instructions
(a) Based on the information contained in these financial statements, determine each of the following for each company.
  (1) Gross profit for 2007.
  (2) Gross profit rate for 2007.
  (3) Operating income for 2007.
  (4) Percent change in operating income from 2006 to 2007.
(b) What conclusions concerning the relative profitability of the two companies can you draw from these data?

Exploring the Web

BYP5-3   No financial decision maker should ever rely solely on the financial information reported in the annual report to make decisions. It is important to keep abreast of financial news. This activity demonstrates how to search for financial news on the Web.

Address: biz.yahoo.com/i, or go to **www.wiley.com/college/weygandt**

Steps:
1. Type in either PepsiCo or Coca-Cola.
2. Choose **News**.
3. Select an article that sounds interesting to you.

Instructions
(a) What was the source of the article? (For example, Reuters, Businesswire, PR Newswire.)
(b) Pretend that you are a personal financial planner and that one of your clients owns stock in the company. Write a brief memo to your client, summarizing the article and explaining the implications of the article for their investment.

CRITICAL THINKING

Decision Making Across the Organization

BYP5-4   Three years ago, Carrie Dungy and her brother-in-law Luke Barber opened FedCo Department Store. For the first two years, business was good, but the following condensed income results for 2009 were disappointing.

FEDCO DEPARTMENT STORE
Income Statement
For the Year Ended December 31, 2009

Net sales		$700,000
Cost of goods sold		553,000
Gross profit		147,000
Operating expenses		
Selling expenses	$100,000	
Administrative expenses	20,000	120,000
Net income		$ 27,000

Carrie believes the problem lies in the relatively low gross profit rate (gross profit divided by net sales) of 21%. Luke believes the problem is that operating expenses are too high.

Carrie thinks the gross profit rate can be improved by making both of the following changes. She does not anticipate that these changes will have any effect on operating expenses.

1. Increase average selling prices by 17%. This increase is expected to lower sales volume so that total sales will increase only 6%.
2. Buy merchandise in larger quantities and take all purchase discounts. These changes are expected to increase the gross profit rate by 3 percentage points.

Luke thinks expenses can be cut by making both of the following changes. He feels that these changes will not have any effect on net sales.

1. Cut 2009 sales salaries of $60,000 in half and give sales personnel a commission of 2% of net sales.
2. Reduce store deliveries to one day per week rather than twice a week; this change will reduce 2009 delivery expenses of $30,000 by 40%.

Carrie and Luke come to you for help in deciding the best way to improve net income.

Instructions

With the class divided into groups, answer the following.

(a) Prepare a condensed income statement for 2010 assuming (1) Carrie's changes are implemented and (2) Luke's ideas are adopted.

(b) What is your recommendation to Carrie and Luke?

(c) Prepare a condensed income statement for 2010 assuming both sets of proposed changes are made.

Communication Activity

BYP5-5   The following situation is in chronological order.

1. Flutie decides to buy a surfboard.
2. He calls Surfing USA Co. to inquire about their surfboards.
3. Two days later he requests Surfing USA Co. to make him a surfboard.
4. Three days later, Surfing USA Co. sends him a purchase order to fill out.
5. He sends back the purchase order.
6. Surfing USA Co. receives the completed purchase order.
7. Surfing USA Co. completes the surfboard.
8. Flutie picks up the surfboard.
9. Surfing USA Co. bills Flutie.
10. Surfing USA Co. receives payment from Flutie.

Instructions

In a memo to the president of Surfing USA Co., answer the following.

(a) When should Surfing USA Co. record the sale?

(b) Suppose that with his purchase order, Flutie is required to make a down payment. Would that change your answer?

Ethics Case

BYP5-6   Laura McAntee was just hired as the assistant treasurer of Dorchester Stores. The company is a specialty chain store with nine retail stores concentrated in one metropolitan area. Among other things, the payment of all invoices is centralized in one of the departments Laura will manage. Her primary responsibility is to maintain the company's high credit rating by paying all bills when due and to take advantage of all cash discounts.

Danny Feeney, the former assistant treasurer who has been promoted to treasurer, is training Laura in her new duties. He instructs Laura that she is to continue the practice of preparing all checks "net of discount" and dating the checks the last day of the discount period. "But," Danny continues, "we always hold the checks at least 4 days beyond the discount period before mailing them. That way we get another 4 days of interest on our money. Most of our creditors need our business and don't complain. And, if they scream about our missing the discount period, we blame it on the mail room or the post office. We've only lost one discount out of every hundred we take that way. I think everybody does it. By the way, welcome to our team!"

Instructions

(a) What are the ethical considerations in this case?

(b) Who are the stakeholders that are harmed or benefitted in this situation?

(c) Should Laura continue the practice started by Danny? Does she have any choice?

"All About You" Activity

BYP5-7   There are many situations in business where it is difficult to determine the proper period in which to record revenue. Suppose that after graduation with a degree in finance, you take a job as a manager at a consumer electronics store called Atlantis Electronics. The company has expanded rapidly in order to compete with Best Buy and Circuit City. Atlantis has also begun selling gift cards for its electronic products. The cards are available in any dollar amount, and allow the holder of the card to purchase an item for up to 2 years from the time the card is purchased. If the card is not used during that 2 years, it expires.

Instructions

Answer the following questions: At what point should the revenue from the gift cards be recognized? Should the revenue be recognized at the time the card is sold, or should it be recorded when the card is redeemed? Explain the reasoning to support your conclusion.

Answers to Insight and Accounting Across the Organization Questions

p. 203 Morrow Snowboards Improves Its Stock Appeal

Q: If a perpetual system keeps track of inventory on a daily basis, why do companies ever need to do a physical count?

A: *A perpetual system keeps track of all sales and purchases on a continuous basis. This provides a constant record of the number of units in the inventory. However, if employees make errors in recording sales or purchases or shrinkage occurs because of fraud and waste, the inventory value will not be correct. Thus, all companies do a physical count of inventory at least once a year.*

p. 210 Should Publishers Have Liberal Return Policies?

Q: If a company expects significant returns, what are the implications for revenue recognition?

A: *If a company expects significant returns, it should make an adjusting entry at the end of the year reducing sales by the estimated amount of sales returns. This is necessary to avoid overstating the amount of revenue recognized in the period.*

Answers to Self-Study Questions

1. c   **2.** a   **3.** c   **4.** b   **5.** c   **6.** c   **7.** a   **8.** d   **9.** b   **10.** c   **11.** d   *12. d   *13. a
*14. b   *15. a

Chapter 6

Inventories

Feature Story

"WHERE IS THAT SPARE BULLDOZER BLADE?"

Let's talk inventory—big, bulldozer-size inventory. Caterpillar Inc. (*www.cat.com*) is the world's largest manufacturer of construction and mining equipment, diesel and natural gas engines, and industrial gas turbines. It sells its products in over 200 countries, making it one of the most successful U.S. exporters. More than 70% of its productive assets are located domestically, and nearly 50% of its sales are foreign.

During the 1980s Caterpillar's profitability suffered, but today it is very successful. A big part of this turnaround can be attributed to effective management of its inventory. In 2007 one of Caterpillar's biggest trucks was selling for $2.5 million. Now imagine what it costs Caterpillar to have too many bulldozers sitting around in inventory—a situation the company definitely wants to avoid. Conversely, Caterpillar must make sure it has enough inventory to meet demand.

During a recent 7-year period, Caterpillar's sales increased by 100%, while its inventory increased by only 50%. To achieve this dramatic reduction in the amount of resources tied up in inventory, while continuing to meet customers' needs, Caterpillar used a two-pronged approach. First, it completed a factory modernization program, which dramatically increased its production efficiency. The program reduced by 60% the amount of inventory the company processed at any one time. It also reduced by an incredible 75% the time it takes to manufacture a part.

Second, Caterpillar dramatically improved its parts distribution system. It ships more than 100,000 items daily from its 23 distribution centers strategically located around the world (10 *million* square feet of warehouse space—remember, we're talking bulldozers). The company can virtually guarantee that it can get any part to anywhere in the world within 24 hours.

In 2006 Caterpillar had record exports, profits, and revenues. It would seem that things couldn't be better. But industry analysts, as well as the company's managers, thought otherwise. In order to maintain Caterpillar's position as the industry leader, management began another major overhaul of inventory production and inventory management processes. The goal: Within four years the company wants to have cut the number of repairs in half, increased productivity by 20%, and increased inventory turnover by 40%.

In short, Caterpillar's ability to manage its inventory has been a key reason for its past success, and inventory management will very likely play a huge part in its ability to succeed in the future.

✔ The Navigator

Inside Chapter 6...

In the previous chapter, we discussed the accounting for merchandise inventory using a perpetual inventory system. In this chapter, we explain the methods used to calculate the cost of inventory on hand at the balance sheet date and the cost of goods sold.

The content and organization of this chapter are as follows.

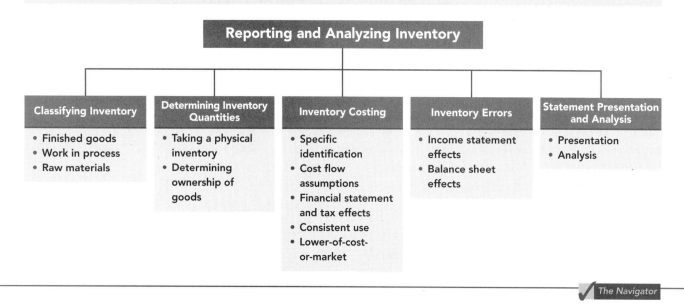

The Navigator

CLASSIFYING INVENTORY

How a company classifies its inventory depends on whether the firm is a merchandiser or a manufacturer. In a *merchandising* company, such as those described in Chapter 5, inventory consists of many different items. For example, in a grocery store, canned goods, dairy products, meats, and produce are just a few of the inventory items on hand. These items have two common characteristics: (1) They are owned by the company, and (2) they are in a form ready for sale to customers in the ordinary course of business. Thus, merchandisers need only one inventory classification, **merchandise inventory**, to describe the many different items that make up the total inventory.

In a *manufacturing* company, some inventory may not yet be ready for sale. As a result, manufacturers usually classify inventory into three categories: finished goods, work in process, and raw materials. **Finished goods inventory** is manufactured items that are completed and ready for sale. **Work in process** is that portion of manufactured inventory that has been placed into the production process but is not yet complete. **Raw materials** are the basic goods that will be used in production but have not yet been placed into production.

For example, Caterpillar classifies earth-moving tractors completed and ready for sale as **finished goods**. It classifies the tractors on the assembly line in various stages of production as **work in process**. The steel, glass, tires, and other components that are on hand waiting to be used in the production of tractors are identified as **raw materials**.

By observing the levels and changes in the levels of these three inventory types, financial statement users can gain insight into management's production plans. For example, low levels of raw materials and high levels of finished goods suggest that management believes it has enough inventory on hand, and production will be slowing down—perhaps in anticipation of a recession. On the other hand, high levels of raw materials and low levels of finished goods probably indicate that management is planning to step up production.

> **HELPFUL HINT**
>
> Regardless of the classification, companies report all inventories under Current Assets on the balance sheet.

Many companies have significantly lowered inventory levels and costs using **just-in-time (JIT) inventory** methods. Under a just-in-time method, companies manufacture or purchase goods just in time for use. Dell is famous for having developed a system for making computers in response to individual customer requests. Even though it makes each computer to meet each customer's particular specifications, Dell is able to assemble the computer and put it on a truck in less than 48 hours. By integrating its information systems with those of its suppliers, Dell reduced its inventories to nearly zero. This is a huge advantage in an industry where products become obsolete nearly overnight.

The accounting concepts discussed in this chapter apply to the inventory classifications of both merchandising and manufacturing companies. Our focus here is on merchandise inventory.

ACCOUNTING ACROSS THE ORGANIZATION

How Wal-Mart Tracks Inventory

Wal-Mart improved its inventory control with the introduction of electronic product codes using radio frequency identification (RFID) technology. Much like bar codes, which tell a retailer the number of boxes of a specific product it has, RFID goes a step farther, helping to distinguish one box of a specific product from another.

Companies currently use RFID to track shipments from supplier to distribution center to store. Other potential uses include help with monitoring product expiration dates and acting quickly on product recalls. Wal-Mart also anticipates faster returns and warranty processing using RFID. This technology will further assist Wal-Mart managers in their efforts to ensure that their stores have just the right type of inventory, in just the right amount, in just the right place. RFID is expensive: Best Buy, for example, has spent millions researching how to integrate RFID.

? Why is inventory control important to managers such as those at Wal-Mart and Best Buy?

DETERMINING INVENTORY QUANTITIES

No matter whether they are using a periodic or perpetual inventory system, all companies need to determine inventory quantities at the end of the accounting period. When using a perpetual system, companies take a physical inventory for two purposes: The first purpose is to check the accuracy of their perpetual inventory records. The second is to determine the amount of inventory lost due to wasted raw materials, shoplifting, or employee theft.

Companies using a periodic inventory system must take a physical inventory for two *different* purposes: to determine the inventory on hand at the balance sheet date, and to determine the cost of goods sold for the period.

Determining inventory quantities involves two steps: (1) taking a physical inventory of goods on hand and (2) determining the ownership of goods.

> **STUDY OBJECTIVE 1**
> Describe the steps in determining inventory quantities.

Taking a Physical Inventory

Taking a physical inventory involves actually counting, weighing, or measuring each kind of inventory on hand. In many companies, taking an inventory is a formidable task. Retailers such as Target, True Value Hardware, or Home Depot have thousands of different inventory items. An inventory count is generally more accurate when goods are not being sold or received during the counting. Consequently, companies often "take inventory" when the business is closed or when business is slow. Many retailers close early on a chosen day in January—after the holiday sales and returns, when inventories are at their lowest level—to count inventory. Recall from Chapter 5 that Wal-Mart had a year-end of January 31. Companies take the physical inventory at the end of the accounting period.[1]

Determining Ownership of Goods

One challenge in computing inventory quantities is determining what inventory a company owns. To determine ownership of goods, two questions must be answered: Do all of the goods included in the count belong to the company? Does the company own any goods that were not included in the count?

GOODS IN TRANSIT

A complication in determining ownership is **goods in transit** (on board a truck, train, ship, or plane) at the end of the period. The company may have purchased goods that have not yet been received, or it may have sold goods that have not yet been delivered. To arrive at an accurate count, the company must determine ownership of these goods.

Goods in transit should be included in the inventory of the company that has legal title to the goods. Legal title is determined by the terms of the sale, as shown in Illustration 6-1 and described below.

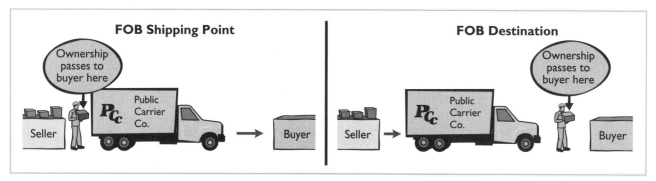

Illustration 6-1
Terms of sale

1. When the terms are **FOB (free on board) shipping point**, ownership of the goods passes to the buyer when the public carrier accepts the goods from the seller.

2. When the terms are **FOB destination**, ownership of the goods remains with the seller until the goods reach the buyer.

If goods in transit at the statement date are ignored, inventory quantities may be seriously miscounted. Assume, for example, that Hargrove Company

---

[1]To estimate the cost of inventory when a physical inventory cannot be taken (e.g., the inventory is destroyed) or when it is inconvenient (e.g., during interim periods), companies can use estimation methods. We discuss these methods—gross profit method and retail inventory method—in Appendix 6B.

has 20,000 units of inventory on hand on December 31. It also has the following goods in transit: (1) sales of 1,500 units shipped December 31 FOB destination, and (2) purchases of 2,500 units shipped FOB shipping point by the seller on December 31. Hargrove has legal title to both the 1,500 units sold and the 2,500 units purchased. If the company ignores the units in transit, it would understate inventory quantities by 4,000 units (1,500 + 2,500).

As we will see later in the chapter, inaccurate inventory counts affect not only the inventory amount shown on the balance sheet but also the cost of goods sold calculation on the income statement.

CONSIGNED GOODS

In some lines of business, it is common to hold the goods of other parties and try to sell the goods for them for a fee, but without taking ownership of the goods. These are called **consigned goods**.

For example, you might have a used car that you would like to sell. If you take the item to a dealer, the dealer might be willing to put the car on its lot and charge you a commission if it is sold. Under this agreement the dealer **would not take ownership** of the car, which would still belong to you. Therefore, if an inventory count were taken, the car would not be included in the dealer's inventory.

Many car, boat, and antique dealers sell goods on consignment to keep their inventory costs down and to avoid the risk of purchasing an item that they won't be able to sell. Today even some manufacturers are making consignment agreements with their suppliers in order to keep their inventory levels low.

> **ETHICS NOTE**
> **Employees of** Craig Consumer Electronics **allegedly overstated the company's inventory figures by improperly classifying defective goods as either new or refurbished. They also were accused of stating that the company owned goods from suppliers when in fact the company did not own the shipments, or the shipments did not even exist.**

DO IT!

Hasbeen Company completed its inventory count. It arrived at a total inventory value of $200,000. As a new member of Hasbeen's accounting department, you have been given the information listed below. Discuss how this information affects the reported cost of inventory.

RULES OF OWNERSHIP

1. Hasbeen included in the inventory goods held on consignment for Falls Co., costing $15,000.

2. The company did not include in the count purchased goods of $10,000 which were in transit (terms: FOB shipping point).

3. The company did not include in the count sold inventory with a cost of $12,000 which was in transit (terms: FOB shipping point).

Solution

The goods of $15,000 held on consignment should be deducted from the inventory count. The goods of $10,000 purchased FOB shipping point should be added to the inventory count. Sold goods of $12,000 which were in transit FOB shipping point should not be included in the ending inventory. Thus, inventory should be carried at $195,000 ($200,000 − $15,000 + $10,000).

action plan

✔ Apply the rules of ownership to goods held on consignment.

✔ Apply the rules of ownership to goods in transit FOB shipping point.

Related exercise material: **BE6-1, E6-1, E6-2,** and **DO IT! 6-1.**

INVENTORY COSTING

After a company has determined the quantity of units of inventory, it applies unit costs to the quantities to compute the total cost of the inventory and the cost of goods sold. This process can be complicated if a company has purchased inventory items at different times and at different prices.

For example, assume that Crivitz TV Company purchases three identical 46-inch TVs on different dates at costs of $700, $750, and $800. During the year Crivitz sold two sets at $1,200 each. These facts are summarized in Illustration 6-2.

Illustration 6-2
Data for inventory costing example

Purchases			
February 3	1 TV	at	$700
March 5	1 TV	at	$750
May 22	1 TV	at	$800
Sales			
June 1	2 TVs	for	$2,400 ($1,200 × 2)

Cost of goods sold will differ depending on which two TVs the company sold. For example, it might be $1,450 ($700 + $750), or $1,500 ($700 + $800), or $1,550 ($750 + $800). In this section we discuss alternative costing methods available to Crivitz.

Specific Identification

If Crivitz sold the TVs it purchased on February 3 and May 22, then its cost of goods sold is $1,500 ($700 + $800), and its ending inventory is $750. If Crivitz can positively identify which particular units it sold and which are still in ending inventory, it can use the **specific identification method** of inventory costing (see Illustration 6-3). Using this method, companies can accurately determine ending inventory and cost of goods sold.

Illustration 6-3
Specific identification method

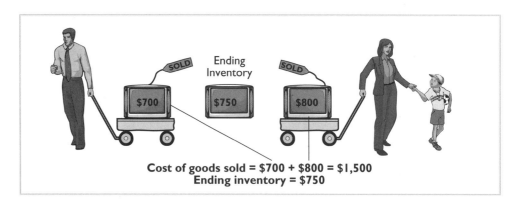

Cost of goods sold = $700 + $800 = $1,500
Ending inventory = $750

Specific identification requires that companies keep records of the original cost of each individual inventory item. Historically, specific identification was possible only when a company sold a limited variety of high-unit-cost items that could be identified clearly from the time of purchase through the time of sale. Examples of such products are cars, pianos, or expensive antiques.

Today, bar coding, electronic product codes, and radio frequency identification make it theoretically possible to do specific identification with nearly any type of product. The reality is, however, that this practice is still relatively rare. Instead, rather than keep track of the cost of each particular item sold, most companies make assumptions, called **cost flow assumptions**, about which units were sold.

Cost Flow Assumptions

Because specific identification is often impractical, other cost flow methods are permitted. These differ from specific identification in that they **assume** flows of costs that may be unrelated to the physical flow of goods. There are three assumed cost flow methods:

1. First-in, first-out (FIFO)
2. Last-in, first-out (LIFO)
3. Average-cost

> **ETHICS NOTE**
> A major disadvantage of the specific identification method is that management may be able to manipulate net income. For example, it can boost net income by selling units purchased at a low cost, or reduce net income by selling units purchased at a high cost.

There is no accounting requirement that the cost flow assumption be consistent with the physical movement of the goods. Company management selects the appropriate cost flow method.

To illustrate these three inventory cost flow methods, we will assume that Houston Electronics uses a periodic inventory system. The information for its Astro condensors is shown in Illustration 6-4.[2] (An appendix to this chapter presents the use of these methods under a perpetual system.)

HOUSTON ELECTRONICS
Astro Condensers

Date	Explanation	Units	Unit Cost	Total Cost
Jan. 1	Beginning inventory	100	$10	$ 1,000
Apr. 15	Purchase	200	11	2,200
Aug. 24	Purchase	300	12	3,600
Nov. 27	Purchase	400	13	5,200
	Total	1,000		$12,000

Illustration 6-4
Cost of goods available for sale

The company had a total of 1,000 units available that it could have sold during the period. The total cost of these units was $12,000. A physical inventory at the end of the year determined that during the year Houston sold 550 units and had 450 units in inventory at December 31. The question then is how to determine what prices to use to value the goods sold and the ending inventory. The sum of the cost allocated to the units sold plus the cost of the units in inventory must be $12,000, the total cost of all goods available for sale.

FIRST-IN, FIRST-OUT (FIFO)

The FIFO (first-in, first-out) method assumes that the **earliest goods** purchased are the first to be sold. FIFO often parallels the actual physical flow of merchandise; it generally is good business practice to sell the oldest units first. Under the FIFO method, therefore, the **costs** of the earliest goods purchased are the first to be recognized

[2]**We have chosen to use the periodic approach for a number of reasons:** First, many companies that use a perpetual inventory system use it to keep track of units on hand, but then determine cost of goods sold at the end of the period using one of the three cost flow approaches applied under essentially a periodic approach. In addition, because of the complexity, few companies use average cost on a perpetual basis. Also, most companies that use perpetual LIFO employ dollar-value LIFO, which is presented in more advanced texts. Furthermore, FIFO gives the same results under either perpetual or periodic. And finally, it is easier to demonstrate the cost flow assumptions under the periodic system, which makes it more pedagogically appropriate.

in determining cost of goods sold. (This does not necessarily mean that the oldest units *are* sold first, but that the costs of the oldest units are *recognized* first. In a bin of picture hangers at the hardware store, for example, no one really knows, nor would it matter, which hangers are sold first.) Illustration 6-5 shows the allocation of the cost of goods available for sale at Houston Electronics under FIFO.

Illustration 6-5
Allocation of costs—FIFO method

HELPFUL HINT

Note the sequencing of the allocation: (1) Compute ending inventory, and (2) determine cost of goods sold.

HELPFUL HINT

Another way of thinking about the calculation of FIFO **ending inventory** is the *LISH assumption*— last in still here.

COST OF GOODS AVAILABLE FOR SALE

Date	Explanation	Units	Unit Cost	Total Cost
Jan. 1	Beginning inventory	100	$10	$ 1,000
Apr. 15	Purchase	200	11	2,200
Aug. 24	Purchase	300	12	3,600
Nov. 27	Purchase	400	13	5,200
	Total	1,000		$12,000

STEP 1: ENDING INVENTORY

Date	Units	Unit Cost	Total Cost
Nov. 27	400	$13	$5,200
Aug. 24	50	12	600
Total	450		$5,800

STEP 2: COST OF GOODS SOLD

Cost of goods available for sale	$12,000
Less: Ending inventory	5,800
Cost of goods sold	$ 6,200

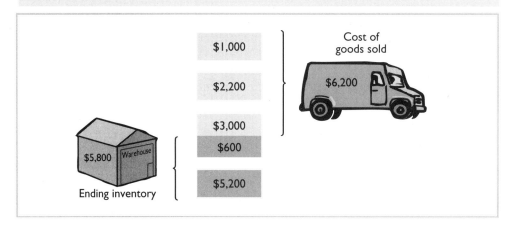

Under FIFO, since it is assumed that the first goods purchased were the first goods sold, ending inventory is based on the prices of the most recent units purchased. That is, **under FIFO, companies obtain the cost of the ending inventory by taking the unit cost of the most recent purchase and working backward until all units of inventory have been costed**. In this example, Houston Electronics prices the 450 units of ending inventory using the *most recent* prices. The last purchase was 400 units at $13 on November 27. The remaining 50 units are priced using the unit cost of the second most recent purchase, $12, on August 24. Next, Houston Electronics calculates cost of goods sold by subtracting the cost of the units **not sold** (ending inventory) from the cost of all goods available for sale.

Illustration 6-6 demonstrates that companies also can calculate cost of goods sold by pricing the 550 units sold using the prices of the first 550 units acquired. Note that of the 300 units purchased on August 24, only 250 units are assumed sold. This agrees with our calculation of the cost of ending inventory, where 50 of these units were assumed unsold and thus included in ending inventory.

Date	Units	Unit Cost	Total Cost
Jan. 1	100	$10	$1,000
Apr. 15	200	11	2,200
Aug. 24	250	12	3,000
Total	550		$6,200

Illustration 6-6
Proof of cost of goods sold

LAST-IN, FIRST-OUT (LIFO)

The **LIFO (last-in, first-out) method** assumes that the **latest goods** purchased are the first to be sold. LIFO seldom coincides with the actual physical flow of inventory. (Exceptions include goods stored in piles, such as coal or hay, where goods are removed from the top of the pile as they are sold.) Under the LIFO method, the **costs** of the latest goods purchased are the first to be recognized in determining cost of goods sold. Illustration 6-7 shows the allocation of the cost of goods available for sale at Houston Electronics under LIFO.

COST OF GOODS AVAILABLE FOR SALE

Date	Explanation	Units	Unit Cost	Total Cost
Jan. 1	Beginning inventory	100	$10	$ 1,000
Apr. 15	Purchase	200	11	2,200
Aug. 24	Purchase	300	12	3,600
Nov. 27	Purchase	400	13	5,200
	Total	1,000		$12,000

Illustration 6-7
Allocation of costs—LIFO method

STEP 1: ENDING INVENTORY   STEP 2: COST OF GOODS SOLD

Date	Units	Unit Cost	Total Cost		
Jan. 1	100	$10	$1,000	Cost of goods available for sale	$12,000
Apr. 15	200	11	2,200	Less: Ending inventory	5,000
Aug. 24	150	12	1,800	Cost of goods sold	$ 7,000
Total	450		$5,000		

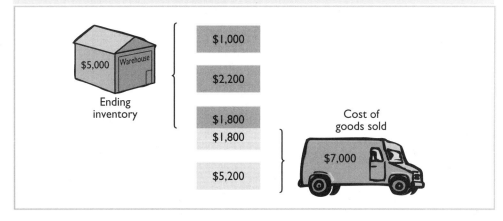

Under LIFO, since it is assumed that the first goods sold were those that were most recently purchased, ending inventory is based on the prices of the oldest units purchased. That is, **under LIFO, companies obtain the cost of the ending inventory**

by taking the unit cost of the earliest goods available for sale and working forward until all units of inventory have been costed. In this example, Houston Electronics prices the 450 units of ending inventory using the *earliest* prices. The first purchase was 100 units at $10 in the January 1 beginning inventory. Then 200 units were purchased at $11. The remaining 150 units needed are priced at $12 per unit (August 24 purchase). Next, Houston Electronics calculates cost of goods sold by subtracting the cost of the units **not sold** (ending inventory) from the cost of all goods available for sale.

Illustration 6-8 demonstrates that companies also can calculate cost of goods sold by pricing the 550 units sold using the prices of the last 550 units acquired. Note that of the 300 units purchased on August 24, only 150 units are assumed sold. This agrees with our calculation of the cost of ending inventory, where 150 of these units were assumed unsold and thus included in ending inventory.

Illustration 6-8
Proof of cost of goods sold

Date	Units	Unit Cost	Total Cost
Nov. 27	400	$13	$5,200
Aug. 24	150	12	1,800
Total	550		$7,000

Under a periodic inventory system, which we are using here, **all goods purchased during the period are assumed to be available for the first sale, regardless of the date of purchase**.

AVERAGE-COST

The average-cost method allocates the cost of goods available for sale on the basis of the weighted average unit cost incurred. The average-cost method assumes that goods are similar in nature. Illustration 6-9 presents the formula and a sample computation of the weighted-average unit cost.

Illustration 6-9
Formula for weighted average unit cost

Cost of Goods Available for Sale	÷	Total Units Available for Sale	=	Weighted Average Unit Cost
$12,000	÷	1,000	=	**$12.00**

The company then applies the weighted average unit cost to the units on hand to determine the cost of the ending inventory. Illustration 6-10 shows the allocation of the cost of goods available for sale at Houston Electronics using average cost.

We can verify the cost of goods sold under this method by multiplying the units sold times the weighted average unit cost ($550 \times \$12 = \$6,600$). Note that this method does not use the average of the unit costs. That average is $11.50 ($10 + $11 + $12 + $13 = $46; $46 ÷ 4). The average cost method instead uses the average **weighted by** the quantities purchased at each unit cost.

COST OF GOODS AVAILABLE FOR SALE

Illustration 6-10
Allocation of costs—
average-cost method

Date	Explanation	Units	Unit Cost	Total Cost
Jan. 1	Beginning inventory	100	$10	$ 1,000
Apr. 15	Purchase	200	11	2,200
Aug. 24	Purchase	300	12	3,600
Nov. 27	Purchase	400	13	5,200
	Total	1,000		$12,000

STEP 1: ENDING INVENTORY   ### STEP 2: COST OF GOODS SOLD

$12,000 ÷ 1,000 = $12.00

Units	Unit Cost	Total Cost
450	$12.00	$5,400

Cost of goods available for sale	$12,000
Less: Ending inventory	5,400
Cost of goods sold	$ 6,600

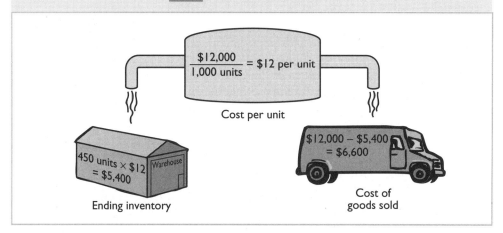

$$\frac{\$12,000}{1,000 \text{ units}} = \$12 \text{ per unit}$$

Cost per unit

450 units × $12 = $5,400   Warehouse

Ending inventory

$12,000 − $5,400 = $6,600

Cost of goods sold

DO IT!

The accounting records of Shumway Ag Implement show the following data.

COST FLOW METHODS

Beginning inventory	4,000 units at $ 3
Purchases	6,000 units at $ 4
Sales	7,000 units at $12

Determine the cost of goods sold during the period under a periodic inventory system using (a) the FIFO method, (b) the LIFO method, and (c) the average-cost method.

action plan

✔ Understand the periodic inventory system.

✔ Compute cost of goods available for sale.

✔ Compute ending inventory.

✔ Determine cost of goods sold.

Solution

Cost of goods available for sale = (4,000 × $3) + (6,000 × $4) = $36,000

Ending inventory = 10,000 − 7,000 = 3,000 units

(a) FIFO: $36,000 − (3,000 × $4) = $24,000

(b) LIFO: $36,000 − (3,000 × $3) = 27,000

(c) Average cost per unit: [(4,000 @ $3) + (6,000 @ $4)] ÷ 10,000 = $3.60
    Average-cost: $36,000 − (3,000 × $3.60) = $25,200

Related exercise material: **BE6-3, BE6-4, BE6-5, E6-3, E6-4, E6-5, E6-6, E6-7, E6-8,** and **DO IT!** **6-2.**

 ✔ *The Navigator*

Financial Statement and Tax Effects of Cost Flow Methods

STUDY OBJECTIVE 3

Explain the financial effects of the inventory cost flow assumptions.

Each of the three assumed cost flow methods is acceptable for use. For example, Reebok International Ltd. and Wendy's International currently use the FIFO method of inventory costing. Campbell Soup Company, Krogers, and Walgreen Drugs use LIFO for part or all of their inventory. Bristol-Myers Squibb, Starbucks, and Motorola use the average-cost method. In fact, a company may also use more than one cost flow method at the same time. Black & Decker Manufacturing Company, for example, uses LIFO for domestic inventories and FIFO for foreign inventories. Illustration 6-11 (in the margin) shows the use of the three cost flow methods in the 600 largest U.S. companies.

The reasons companies adopt different inventory cost flow methods are varied, but they usually involve one of three factors: (1) income statement effects, (2) balance sheet effects, or (3) tax effects.

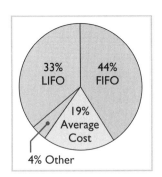

Illustration 6-11
Use of cost flow methods in major U.S. companies

INCOME STATEMENT EFFECTS

To understand why companies might choose a particular cost flow method, let's examine the effects of the different cost flow assumptions on the financial statements of Houston Electronics. The condensed income statements in Illustration 6-12 assume that Houston sold its 550 units for $11,500, had operating expenses of $2,000, and is subject to an income tax rate of 30%.

Illustration 6-12
Comparative effects of cost flow methods

HOUSTON ELECTRONICS Condensed Income Statements			
	FIFO	**LIFO**	**Average Cost**
Sales	$11,500	$11,500	$11,500
Beginning inventory	1,000	1,000	1,000
Purchases	11,000	11,000	11,000
Cost of goods available for sale	12,000	12,000	12,000
Ending inventory	5,800	5,000	5,400
Cost of goods sold	6,200	7,000	6,600
Gross profit	5,300	4,500	4,900
Operating expenses	2,000	2,000	2,000
Income before income taxes[3]	3,300	2,500	2,900
Income tax expense (30%)	990	750	870
Net income	$ 2,310	$ 1,750	$ 2,030

Note the cost of goods available for sale ($12,000) is the same under each of the three inventory cost flow methods. However, the ending inventories and the costs of goods sold are different. This difference is due to the unit costs that the company allocated to cost of goods sold and to ending inventory. Each dollar of difference in ending inventory results in a corresponding dollar difference in income before income taxes. For Houston, an $800 difference exists between FIFO and LIFO cost of goods sold.

---

[3]We are assuming that Houston Electronics is a corporation, and corporations are required to pay income taxes.

In periods of changing prices, the cost flow assumption can have a significant impact on income and on evaluations based on income. In most instances, prices are rising (inflation). In a period of inflation, FIFO produces a higher net income because the lower unit costs of the first units purchased are matched against revenues. In a period of rising prices (as is the case in the Houston example), FIFO reports the highest net income ($2,310) and LIFO the lowest ($1,750); average cost falls in the middle ($2,030). If prices are falling, the results from the use of FIFO and LIFO are reversed: FIFO will report the lowest net income and LIFO the highest.

To management, higher net income is an advantage: It causes external users to view the company more favorably. In addition, management bonuses, if based on net income, will be higher. Therefore, when prices are rising (which is usually the case), companies tend to prefer FIFO because it results in higher net income.

Some argue that the use of LIFO in a period of inflation enables the company to avoid reporting **paper** (or **phantom**) **profit** as economic gain. To illustrate, assume that Kralik Company buys 200 units of a product at $20 per unit on January 10 and 200 more on December 31 at $24 each. During the year, Kralik sells 200 units at $30 each. Illustration 6-13 shows the results under FIFO and LIFO.

	FIFO	**LIFO**
Sales (200 × $30)	$6,000	$6,000
Cost of goods sold	4,000 (200 × $20)	4,800 (200 × $24)
Gross profit	$2,000	$1,200

Illustration 6-13
Income statement effects compared

Under LIFO, Kralik Company has recovered the current replacement cost ($4,800) of the units sold. Thus, the gross profit in economic terms is real. However, under FIFO, the company has recovered only the January 10 cost ($4,000). To replace the units sold, it must reinvest $800 (200 × $4) of the gross profit. Thus, $800 of the gross profit is said to be phantom or illusory. As a result, reported net income is also overstated in real terms.

BALANCE SHEET EFFECTS

A major advantage of the FIFO method is that in a period of inflation, the costs allocated to ending inventory will approximate their current cost. For example, for Houston Electronics, 400 of the 450 units in the ending inventory are costed under FIFO at the higher November 27 unit cost of $13.

Conversely, a major shortcoming of the LIFO method is that in a period of inflation, the costs allocated to ending inventory may be significantly understated in terms of current cost. The understatement becomes greater over prolonged periods of inflation if the inventory includes goods purchased in one or more prior accounting periods. For example, Caterpillar has used LIFO for 50 years. Its balance sheet shows ending inventory of $4,675 million. But the inventory's actual current cost if FIFO had been used is $6,799 million.

TAX EFFECTS

We have seen that both inventory on the balance sheet and net income on the income statement are higher when companies use FIFO in a period of inflation. Yet, many companies have selected LIFO. Why? The reason is that LIFO results in the lowest income taxes (because of lower net income) during times of rising prices. For example, at Houston Electronics, income taxes are $750 under LIFO, compared to $990 under FIFO. The tax savings of $240 makes more cash available for use in the business.

HELPFUL HINT

A tax rule, often referred to as the *LIFO conformity rule*, requires that if companies use LIFO for tax purposes they must also use it for financial reporting purposes. This means that if a company chooses the LIFO method to reduce its tax bills, it will also have to report lower net income in its financial statements.

Using Inventory Cost Flow Methods Consistently

Whatever cost flow method a company chooses, it should use that method consistently from one accounting period to another. This approach is often referred to as the **consistency principle**, which means that a company uses the same accounting principles and methods from year to year. Consistent application enhances the comparability of financial statements over successive time periods. In contrast, using the FIFO method one year and the LIFO method the next year would make it difficult to compare the net incomes of the two years.

Although consistent application is preferred, it does not mean that a company may *never* change its inventory costing method. When a company adopts a different method, it should disclose in the financial statements the change and its effects on net income. Illustration 6-14 shows a typical disclosure, using information from financial statements of Quaker Oats (now a unit of PepsiCo).

Illustration 6-14
Disclosure of change in cost flow method

QUAKER OATS
Notes to the Financial Statements

Note 1: Effective July 1, the Company adopted the LIFO cost flow assumption for valuing the majority of U.S. Grocery Products inventories. The Company believes that the use of the LIFO method better matches current costs with current revenues. The effect of this change on the current year was to decrease net income by $16.0 million.

INTERNATIONAL INSIGHT

Is LIFO Fair?

Exxon Mobil Corporation, like many U.S. companies, uses LIFO to value its inventory for financial reporting and tax purposes. In one recent year, this resulted in a cost of goods sold figure that was $5.6 billion higher than under FIFO. By increasing cost of goods sold, Exxon Mobil reduces net income, which reduces taxes. Critics say that LIFO provides an unfair "tax dodge." As Congress looks for more sources of tax revenue, some lawmakers favor the elimination of LIFO. Supporters of LIFO argue that the method is conceptually sound because it matches current costs with current revenues. In addition, they point out that this matching provides protection against inflation.

International accounting standards do not allow the use of LIFO. Because of this, the net income of foreign oil companies such as BP and Royal Dutch Shell are not directly comparable to U.S. companies, which makes analysis difficult.

Source: David Reilly, "Big Oil's Accounting Methods Fuel Criticism," *Wall Street Journal,* August 8, 2006, p. C1.

? What are the arguments for and against the use of LIFO?

Lower-of-Cost-or-Market

STUDY OBJECTIVE 4

Explain the lower-of-cost-or-market basis of accounting for inventories.

The value of inventory for companies selling high-technology or fashion goods can drop very quickly due to changes in technology or fashions. These circumstances sometimes call for inventory valuation methods other than those presented so far. For example, purchasing managers at Ford decided to make a large purchase of palladium, a precious metal used in vehicle emission devices. They made this purchase because they feared a future shortage. The shortage did not materialize, and by the end of the year the price of palladium had plummeted. Ford's inventory was then worth $1 billion less than its original cost. Do you think Ford's inventory should have been stated at cost, in accordance with the cost principle, or at its lower replacement cost?

As you probably reasoned, this situation requires a departure from the cost basis of accounting. When the value of inventory is lower than its cost, companies can "write down" the inventory to its market value. This is done by valuing the inventory at the **lower-of-cost-or-market (LCM)** in the period in which the price decline occurs. LCM is an example of the accounting concept of **conservatism**, which means that the best choice among accounting alternatives is the method that is least likely to overstate assets and net income.

Companies apply LCM to the items in inventory after they have used one of the cost flow methods (specific identification, FIFO, LIFO, or average cost) to determine cost. Under the LCM basis, market is defined as **current replacement cost**, not selling price. For a merchandising company, market is the cost of purchasing the same goods at the present time from the usual suppliers in the usual quantities. Current replacement cost is used because a decline in the replacement cost of an item usually leads to a decline in the selling price of the item.

To illustrate the application of LCM, assume that Ken Tuckie TV has the following lines of merchandise with costs and market values as indicated. LCM produces the results shown in Illustration 6-15. Note that the amounts shown in the final column are the lower-of-cost-or-market amounts for each item.

	Cost	Market	Lower-of-Cost-or-Market
Flatscreen TVs	$ 60,000	$ 55,000	$ 55,000
Satellite radios	45,000	52,000	45,000
DVD recorders	48,000	45,000	45,000
DVDs	15,000	14,000	14,000
Total inventory			$159,000

Illustration 6-15
Computation of lower-of-cost-or-market

INVENTORY ERRORS

Unfortunately, errors occasionally occur in accounting for inventory. In some cases, errors are caused by failure to count or price the inventory correctly. In other cases, errors occur because companies do not properly recognize the transfer of legal title to goods that are in transit. When errors occur, they affect both the income statement and the balance sheet.

STUDY OBJECTIVE 5
Indicate the effects of inventory errors on the financial statements.

Income Statement Effects

Under a periodic inventory system, both the beginning and ending inventories appear in the income statement. The ending inventory of one period automatically becomes the beginning inventory of the next period. Thus, inventory errors affect the computation of cost of goods sold and net income in two periods.

The effects on cost of goods sold can be computed by entering incorrect data in the formula in Illustration 6-16 and then substituting the correct data.

Beginning Inventory	+	Cost of Goods Purchased	−	Ending Inventory	=	Cost of Goods Sold

Illustration 6-16
Formula for cost of goods sold

If the error understates *beginning* inventory, cost of goods sold will be understated. If the error understates *ending* inventory, cost of goods sold will be overstated. Illustration 6-17 shows the effects of inventory errors on the current year's income statement.

When Inventory Error:	Cost of Goods Sold Is:	Net Income Is:
Understates beginning inventory	Understated	Overstated
Overstates beginning inventory	Overstated	Understated
Understates ending inventory	Overstated	Understated
Overstates ending inventory	Understated	Overstated

ETHICS NOTE

Inventory fraud increases during recessions. Such fraud includes pricing inventory at amounts in excess of its actual value, or claiming to have inventory when no inventory exists. Inventory fraud usually overstates ending inventory, thereby understating cost of goods sold and creating higher income.

So far, the effects of inventory errors are fairly straightforward. Now, though, comes the (at first) surprising part: An error in the ending inventory of the current period will have a **reverse effect on net income of the next accounting period**. Illustration 6-18 shows this effect. As you study the illustration, you will see that the reverse effect comes from the fact that understating ending inventory in 2010 results in understating beginning inventory in 2011 and overstating net income in 2011.

Over the two years, though, total net income is correct because the errors **offset each other**. Notice that total income using incorrect data is $35,000 ($22,000 + $13,000), which is the same as the total income of $35,000 ($25,000 + $10,000) using correct data. Also note in this example that an error in the beginning inventory does not result in a corresponding error in the ending inventory for that period. The correctness of the ending inventory depends entirely on the accuracy of taking and costing the inventory at the balance sheet date under the periodic inventory system.

SAMPLE COMPANY
Condensed Income Statements

	2010 Incorrect		2010 Correct		2011 Incorrect		2011 Correct	
Sales		$80,000		$80,000		$90,000		$90,000
Beginning inventory	$20,000		$20,000		$12,000		$15,000	
Cost of goods purchased	40,000		40,000		68,000		68,000	
Cost of goods available for sale	60,000		60,000		80,000		83,000	
Ending inventory	12,000		15,000		23,000		23,000	
Cost of goods sold		48,000		45,000		57,000		60,000
Gross profit		32,000		35,000		33,000		30,000
Operating expenses		10,000		10,000		20,000		20,000
Net income		$22,000		$25,000		$13,000		$10,000

$(3,000) Net income understated

$3,000 Net income overstated

The errors cancel. Thus the combined total income for the 2-year period is correct.

Balance Sheet Effects

Companies can determine the effect of ending inventory errors on the balance sheet by using the basic accounting equation: Assets = Liabilities + Owner's Equity. Errors in the ending inventory have the effects shown in Illustration 6-19.

Ending Inventory Error	Assets	Liabilities	Owner's Equity
Overstated	Overstated	No effect	Overstated
Understated	Understated	No effect	Understated

Illustration 6-19
Effects of ending inventory errors on balance sheet

DO IT!

(a) Tracy Company sells three different types of home heating stoves (wood, gas, and pellet). The cost and market value of its inventory of stoves are as follows.

	Cost	Market
Gas	$ 84,000	$ 79,000
Wood	250,000	280,000
Pellet	112,000	101,000

Determine the value of the company's inventory under the lower-of-cost-or-market approach.

Solution

The lowest value for each inventory type is: gas $79,000, wood $250,000, and pellet $101,000. The total inventory value is the sum of these amounts, $430,000.

(b) Visual Company overstated its 2010 ending inventory by $22,000. Determine the impact this error has on ending inventory, cost of goods sold, and owner's equity in 2010 and 2011.

Solution

	2010	2011
Ending inventory	$22,000 overstated	No effect
Cost of goods sold	$22,000 understated	$22,000 overstated
Owner's equity	$22,000 overstated	No effect

Related exercise material: **BE6-7, BE6-8, E6-9, E6-10, E6-11, E6-12,** and **DO IT! 6-3.**

✔ *The Navigator*

LCM BASIS; INVENTORY ERRORS

action plan

✔ Determine whether cost or market value is lower for each inventory type.

✔ Sum the lowest value of each inventory type to determine the total value of inventory.

action plan

✔ An ending inventory error in one period will have an equal and opposite effect on cost of goods sold and net income in the next period.

✔ After two years, the errors have offset each other.

STATEMENT PRESENTATION AND ANALYSIS

Presentation

As indicated in Chapter 5, inventory is classified in the balance sheet as a current asset immediately below receivables. In a multiple-step income statement, cost of goods sold is subtracted from sales. There also should be disclosure of (1) the major inventory classifications, (2) the basis of accounting (cost, or lower-of-cost-or-market), and (3) the cost method (FIFO, LIFO, or average).

Wal-Mart, for example, in its January 31, 2008, balance sheet reported inventories of $35,180 million under current assets. The accompanying notes to the financial statements, as shown in Illustration 6-20, disclosed the following information.

Illustration 6-20
Inventory disclosures by
Wal-Mart

WAL-MART STORES, INC.
Notes to the Financial Statements

Note 1. Summary of Significant Accounting Policies

Inventories

The Company values inventories at the lower of cost or market as determined primarily by the retail method of accounting, using the last-in, first-out ("LIFO") method for substantially all of the Wal-Mart Stores segments' merchandise inventories. SAM'S CLUB merchandise and merchandise in our distribution warehouses are valued based on the weighted average cost using the LIFO method. Inventories of foreign operations are primarily valued by the retail method of accounting, using the first-in, first-out ("FIFO") method. At January 31, 2008 and 2007, our inventories valued at LIFO approximate those inventories as if they were valued at FIFO.

As indicated in this note, Wal-Mart values its inventories at the lower-of-cost-or-market using LIFO and FIFO.

Analysis

The amount of inventory carried by a company has significant economic consequences. And inventory management is a double-edged sword that requires constant attention. On the one hand, management wants to have a great variety and quantity on hand so that customers have a wide selection and items are always in stock. But such a policy may incur high carrying costs (e.g., investment, storage, insurance, obsolescence, and damage). On the other hand, low inventory levels lead to stockouts and lost sales. Common ratios used to manage and evaluate inventory levels are inventory turnover and a related measure, days in inventory.

STUDY OBJECTIVE 6
Compute and interpret the inventory turnover ratio.

Inventory turnover measures the number of times on average the inventory is sold during the period. Its purpose is to measure the liquidity of the inventory. The inventory turnover is computed by dividing cost of goods sold by the average inventory during the period. Unless seasonal factors are significant, average inventory can be computed from the beginning and ending inventory balances. For example, Wal-Mart reported in its 2008 annual report a beginning inventory of $33,685 million, an ending inventory of $35,180 million, and cost of goods sold for the year ended January 31, 2008, of $286,515 million. The inventory turnover formula and computation for Wal-Mart are shown below.

Illustration 6-21
Inventory turnover formula
and computation for
Wal-Mart

Cost of Goods Sold	÷	Average Inventory	=	Inventory Turnover
$286,515	÷	$\dfrac{\$33,685 + \$35,180}{2}$	=	8.3 times

A variant of the inventory turnover ratio is **days in inventory**. This measures the average number of days inventory is held. It is calculated as 365 divided by the inventory turnover ratio. For example, Wal-Mart's inventory turnover of 8.3 times divided into 365 is approximately 44 days. This is the approximate time that it takes a company to sell the inventory once it arrives at the store.

There are typical levels of inventory in every industry. Companies that are able to keep their inventory at lower levels and higher turnovers and still satisfy customer needs are the most successful.

DO IT!

Early in 2010 Westmoreland Company switched to a just-in-time inventory system. Its sales, cost of goods sold, and inventory amounts for 2009 and 2010 are shown below.

INVENTORY TURNOVER

	2009	2010
Sales	$2,000,000	$1,800,000
Cost of goods sold	1,000,000	910,000
Beginning inventory	290,000	210,000
Ending inventory	210,000	50,000

Determine the inventory turnover and days in inventory for 2009 and 2010. Discuss the changes in the amount of inventory, the inventory turnover and days in inventory, and the amount of sales across the two years.

action plan

✔ To find the inventory turnover ratio, divide cost of goods sold by average inventory.

✔ To determine days in inventory, divide 365 days by the inventory turnover ratio.

✔ Just-in-time inventory reduces the amount of inventory on hand, which reduces carrying costs. Reducing inventory levels by too much has potential negative implications for sales.

Solution

	2009		2010	
Inventory turnover ratio	$\dfrac{\$1,000,000}{(\$290,000 + \$210,000)/2}$	= 4	$\dfrac{\$910,000}{(\$210,000 + \$50,000)/2}$	= 7
Days in inventory	365 ÷ 4 = 91.3 days		365 ÷ 7 = 52.1 days	

The company experienced a very significant decline in its ending inventory as a result of the just-in-time inventory. This decline improved its inventory turnover ratio and its days in inventory. However, its sales declined by 10%. It is possible that this decline was caused by the dramatic reduction in the amount of inventory that was on hand, which increased the likelihood of "stock-outs." To determine the optimal inventory level, management must weigh the benefits of reduced inventory against the potential lost sales caused by stock-outs.

Related exercise material: **BE6-9, E6-13, E6-14**, and **DO IT!** 6-4.

 The Navigator

 Be sure to read **ALL ABOUT YOU:** *Employee Theft—An Inside Job* on page 268 for information on how topics in this chapter apply to your personal life.

all about YOU

Employee Theft—An Inside Job

Inventory theft is a huge problem for many businesses. Few employees would be as bold as the character in a Johnny Cash song, who while working on an assembly line in Detroit, steals an entire car, one piece at a time, over the course of many years (*www.lyricsdomain.com/10/johnny_cash/one_piece_at_a_time.html*). Nonetheless, at most companies, employees are the primary culprits. While you might think that a free pizza or steak at the end of your shift isn't hurting anybody, the statistics below show that such pilferage really adds up.

Many companies use sophisticated technologies to monitor their customers and employees in order to keep their inventory from walking off. Examples include closed-circuit video cameras and radio frequency identification (RFID). Other companies use techniques that don't rely on technology, such as taking frequent (in some cases, daily) inventory counts, having employees keep all personal belongings and bags in a separate changing room, and making surprise checks of employees' bags as they leave. An increasing number of companies are setting up toll-free phone numbers that employees or customers can call to report suspicious behavior, sometimes for a reward.

✱ Some Facts

✱ The National Food Service Security Council estimates that employee theft costs U.S. restaurants $15 billion to $25 billion annually.

✱ The average supermarket has inventory shrinkage losses of 2.28% of sales, or $224,808 per year. Average net profit is only 1.1% of sales, so inventory shrinkage is twice the level of profits.

✱ Fear of getting caught and being fired ranks among one of the top reasons employees give, in surveys of reasons why they do not steal from their employer.

✱ Tips from customers are the No. 1 way that many stores catch thieving employees.

✱ The average employee caught stealing costs his or her company $1,341, while the average loss from a shoplifting incident is only $207.

✱ About the Numbers

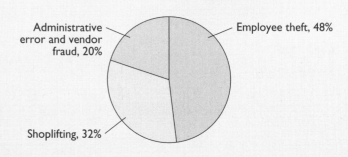

Where Did the Inventory Go?

- Employee theft, 48%
- Shoplifting, 32%
- Administrative error and vendor fraud, 20%

Source: Data from 2003 National Retail Security Survey, University of Florida.

✱ What Do You Think?

Suppose you own a number of wine shops selling mid-level as well as expensive bottled wine. You have been experiencing significant losses from theft at your stores. You suspect that it is a combination of both employee and customer theft. Assuming that it would be cost-effective, would you install video cameras to reduce both employee theft and customer theft?

YES: Most employees and customers are honest. However, some will steal if given the opportunity. Management has a responsibility to employ reasonable, cost-effective approaches to safeguard company assets.

NO: The use of video technology to monitor employees and customers sends a message of distrust. You run the risk of alienating your employees (who may well figure out a way around the cameras anyway). Cameras might also reduce the welcoming atmosphere for your customers, who might find the cameras offensive.

Sources: Bob Ingram, "Shrink Has Shrunk," *Supermarket Business*, September 15, 2000, p. 65; Lisa Bertagnoli, "Wrapping up Shrink," *Restaurants & Institutions*, May 1, 2005, pp. 89–90; Naomi R. Kooker, "Taking Aim at Crime," *Nation's Restaurant News*, May 22, 2000, pp. 114–118.

The authors' comments on this situation appear on page 298.

Comprehensive **DO IT!** *1*

Gerald D. Englehart Company has the following inventory, purchases, and sales data for the month of March.

Inventory: March 1	200 units @ $4.00	$ 800
Purchases:		
March 10	500 units @ $4.50	2,250
March 20	400 units @ $4.75	1,900
March 30	300 units @ $5.00	1,500
Sales:		
March 15	500 units	
March 25	400 units	

The physical inventory count on March 31 shows 500 units on hand.

Instructions

Under a **periodic inventory system**, determine the cost of inventory on hand at March 31 and the cost of goods sold for March under (a) (FIFO), (b) (LIFO), and (c) average-cost.

action plan

✔ Compute the total goods available for sale, in both units and dollars.

✔ Compute the cost of ending inventory under the periodic FIFO method by allocating to the units on hand the **latest costs**.

✔ Compute the cost of ending inventory under the periodic LIFO method by allocating to the units on hand the **earliest costs**.

✔ Compute the cost of ending inventory under the periodic average-cost method by allocating to the units on hand a **weighted-average cost**.

Solution to Comprehensive **DO IT!** *1*

The cost of goods available for sale is $6,450, as follows.

Inventory:	200 units @ $4.00	$ 800
Purchases:		
March 10	500 units @ $4.50	2,250
March 20	400 units @ $4.75	1,900
March 30	300 units @ $5.00	1,500
Total:	1,400	$6,450

Under a **periodic inventory system**, the cost of goods sold under each cost flow method is as follows.

FIFO Method

Ending inventory:

Date	Units	Unit Cost	Total Cost	
March 30	300	$5.00	$1,500	
March 20	200	4.75	950	$2,450

Cost of goods sold: $6,450 − $2,450 = $4,000

LIFO Method

Ending inventory:

Date	Units	Unit Cost	Total Cost	
March 1	200	$4.00	$ 800	
March 10	300	4.50	1,350	$2,150

Cost of goods sold: $6,450 − $2,150 = $4,300

Average-Cost Method

Average unit cost: $6,450 ÷ 1,400 = $4.61
Ending inventory: 500 × $4.61 = $2,305

Cost of goods sold: $6,450 − $2,305 = $4,145

SUMMARY OF STUDY OBJECTIVES

1 **Describe the steps in determining inventory quantities.** The steps are (1) take a physical inventory of goods on hand and (2) determine the ownership of goods in transit or on consignment.

2 **Explain the accounting for inventories and apply the inventory cost flow methods.** The primary basis of accounting for inventories is cost. Cost of goods available for sale includes (a) cost of beginning inventory and (b) cost of goods purchased. The inventory cost flow methods are: specific identification and three assumed cost flow methods—FIFO, LIFO, and average-cost.

3 **Explain the financial effects of the inventory cost flow assumptions.** Companies may allocate the cost of goods available for sale to cost of goods sold and ending inventory by specific identification or by a method based on an assumed cost flow. When prices are rising, the first-in, first-out (FIFO) method results in lower cost of goods sold and higher net income than the other methods. The reverse is true when prices are falling. In the balance sheet, FIFO results in an ending inventory that is closest to current value; inventory under LIFO is the farthest from current value. LIFO results in the lowest income taxes.

4 **Explain the lower-of-cost-or-market basis of accounting for inventories.** Companies may use the lower-of-cost-or-market (LCM) basis when the current replacement cost (market) is less than cost. Under LCM, companies recognize the loss in the period in which the price decline occurs.

5 **Indicate the effects of inventory errors on the financial statements.** *In the income statement of the current year:* (a) An error in beginning inventory will have a reverse effect on net income. (b) An error in ending inventory will have a similar effect on net income. In the following period, its effect on net income for that period is reversed, and total net income for the two years will be correct.

   In the balance sheet: Ending inventory errors will have the same effect on total assets and total stockholders' equity and no effect on liabilities.

6 **Compute and interpret the inventory turnover ratio.** The inventory turnover ratio is cost of goods sold divided by average inventory. To convert it to average days in inventory, divide 365 days by the inventory turnover ratio.

GLOSSARY

Average-cost method Inventory costing method that uses the weighted average unit cost to allocate to ending inventory and cost of goods sold the cost of goods available for sale. (p. 258).

Conservatism Concept that dictates that when in doubt, choose the method that will be least likely to overstate assets and net income. (p. 263).

Consigned goods Goods held for sale by one party although ownership of the goods is retained by another party. (p. 253).

Consistency principle Dictates that a company use the same accounting principles and methods from year to year. (p. 262).

Current replacement cost The current cost to replace an inventory item. (p. 263).

Days in inventory Measure of the average number of days inventory is held; calculated as 365 divided by inventory turnover ratio. (p. 267).

Finished goods inventory Manufactured items that are completed and ready for sale. (p. 250).

First-in, first-out (FIFO) method Inventory costing method that assumes that the costs of the earliest goods purchased are the first to be recognized as cost of goods sold. (p. 255).

FOB (free on board) destination Freight terms indicating that ownership of the goods remains with the seller until the goods reach the buyer. (p. 252).

FOB (free on board) shipping point Freight terms indicating that ownership of the goods passes to the buyer when the public carrier accepts the goods from the seller. (p. 252).

Inventory turnover A ratio that measures the number of times on average the inventory sold during the period; computed by dividing cost of goods sold by the average inventory during the period. (p. 266).

Just-in-time (JIT) inventory method Inventory system in which companies manufacture or purchase goods just in time for use. (p. 251).

Last-in, first-out (LIFO) method Inventory costing method that assumes the costs of the latest units purchased are the first to be allocated to cost of goods sold. (p. 257).

Lower-of-cost-or-market (LCM) basis A basis whereby inventory is stated at the lower of either its cost or its market value as determined by current replacement cost. (p. 263).

Raw materials Basic goods that will be used in production but have not yet been placed into production. (p. 250).

Specific identification method An actual physical flow costing method in which items still in inventory are specifically costed to arrive at the total cost of the ending inventory. (p. 254).

Weighted average unit cost Average cost that is weighted by the number of units purchased at each unit cost. (p. 258).

Work in process That portion of manufactured inventory that has been placed into the production process but is not yet complete. (p. 250).

APPENDIX 6A **Inventory Cost Flow Methods in Perpetual Inventory Systems**

What inventory cost flow methods do companies employ if they use a perpetual inventory system? Simple—they can use any of the inventory cost flow methods described in the chapter. To illustrate the application of the three assumed cost flow methods (FIFO, LIFO, and average-cost), we will use the data shown in Illustration 6A-1 and in this chapter for Houston Electronic's Astro Condenser.

STUDY OBJECTIVE 7
Apply the inventory cost flow methods to perpetual inventory records.

Illustration 6A-1
Inventoriable units and costs

HOUSTON ELECTRONICS
Astro Condensers

Date	Explanation	Units	Unit Cost	Total Cost	Balance in Units
1/1	Beginning inventory	100	$10	$ 1,000	100
4/15	Purchases	200	11	2,200	300
8/24	Purchases	300	12	3,600	600
9/10	Sale	550			50
11/27	Purchases	400	13	5,200	450
				$12,000	

First-In, First-Out (FIFO)

Under FIFO, the company charges to cost of goods sold the cost of the earliest goods on hand **prior to each sale**. Therefore, the cost of goods sold on September 10 consists of the units on hand January 1 and the units purchased April 15 and August 24. Illustration 6A-2 shows the inventory under a FIFO method perpetual system.

Illustration 6A-2
Perpetual system—FIFO

Date	Purchases	Cost of Goods Sold	Balance (in units and cost)
January 1			(100 @ $10) $ 1,000
April 15	(200 @ $11) $2,200		(100 @ $10) (200 @ $11) } $3,200
August 24	(300 @ $12) $3,600		(100 @ $10) (200 @ $11) (300 @ $12) } $6,800
September 10		(100 @ $10) (200 @ $11) (250 @ $12) $6,200	(50 @ $12) $ 600
November 27	(400 @ $13) $5,200		(50 @ $12) (400 @ $13) } $5,800

Cost of goods sold

Ending inventory

The ending inventory in this situation is $5,800, and the cost of goods sold is $6,200 [(100 @ $10) + (200 @ $11) + (250 @ $12)].

Compare Illustrations 6-5 (page 256) and 6A-2. You can see that the results under FIFO in a perpetual system are the **same as in a periodic system**. In both cases, the ending inventory is $5,800 and cost of goods sold is $6,200. Regardless of the system, the first costs in are the costs assigned to cost of goods sold.

Last-In, First-Out (LIFO)

Under the LIFO method using a perpetual system, the company charges to cost of goods sold the cost of the most recent purchase prior to sale. Therefore, the cost of the goods sold on September 10 consists of all the units from the August 24 and April 15 purchases plus 50 of the units in beginning inventory. Illustration 6A-3 shows the computation of the ending inventory under the LIFO method.

Illustration 6A-3
Perpetual system—LIFO

Date	Purchases	Cost of Goods Sold	Balance (in units and cost)	
January 1			(100 @ $10)	$1,000
April 15	(200 @ $11) $2,200		(100 @ $10) (200 @ $11)	} $3,200
August 24	(300 @ $12) $3,600		(100 @ $10) (200 @ $11) (300 @ $12)	} $6,800
September 10		(300 @ $12) (200 @ $11) (50 @ $10) ——— $6,300	(50 @ $10)	$ 500
November 27	(400 @ $13) $5,200		(50 @ $10) (400 @ $13)	} $5,700

Cost of goods sold

Ending inventory

The use of LIFO in a perpetual system will usually produce cost allocations that differ from those using LIFO in a periodic system. In a perpetual system, the company allocates the latest units purchased *prior to each sale* to cost of goods sold. In contrast, in a periodic system, the latest units purchased *during the period* are allocated to cost of goods sold. Thus, when a purchase is made after the last sale, the LIFO periodic system will apply this purchase to the previous sale. Compare Illustrations 6-7 (page 257) and 6A-3. Illustration 6-7 shows that the 400 units at $13 purchased on November 27 applied to the sale of 550 units on September 10. Under the LIFO perpetual system in Illustration 6A-3, the 400 units at $13 purchased on November 27 are all applied to the ending inventory.

The ending inventory in this LIFO perpetual illustration is $5,700, and cost of goods sold is $6,300, as compared to the LIFO periodic illustration (on page 257) where the ending inventory is $5,000 and cost of goods sold is $7,000.

Average-Cost

The average-cost method in a perpetual inventory system is called the **moving-average method**. Under this method the company computes a new average **after each purchase**, by dividing the cost of goods available for sale by the units on hand. They then apply the average cost to: (1) the units sold, to determine the cost of goods sold, and (2) the remaining units on hand, to determine the ending inventory amount. Illustration 6A-4 shows the application of the moving-average cost method by Houston Electronics.

Illustration 6A-4
Perpetual system—average-cost method

Date	Purchases	Cost of Goods Sold	Balance (in units and cost)	
January 1			(100 @ $10)	$1,000
April 15	(200 @ $11) $2,200		(300 @ $10.667)	$3,200
August 24	(300 @ $12) $3,600		(600 @ $11.333)	$6,800
September 10		(550 @ $11.333) ——— $6,233	(50 @ $11.333)	$ 567
November 27	(400 @ $13) $5,200		(450 @ $12.816)	$5,767

Cost of goods sold

Ending inventory

As indicated above, Houston Electronics computes **a new average each time it makes a purchase**. On April 15, after it buys 200 units for $2,200, a total of 300 units costing $3,200 ($1,000 + $2,200) are on hand. The average unit cost is $10.667 ($3,200 ÷ 300). On August 24, after Houston Electronics buys 300 units for $3,600, a total of 600 units costing $6,800 ($1,000 + $2,200 + $3,600) are on hand, at an average cost per unit of $11.333 ($6,800 ÷ 600). Houston Electronics uses this unit cost of $11.333 in costing sales until it makes another purchase, when the company computes a new unit cost. Accordingly, the unit cost of the 550 units sold on September 10 is $11.333, and the total cost of goods sold is $6,233. On November 27, following the purchase of 400 units for $5,200, there are 450 units on hand costing $5,767 ($567 + $5,200) with a new average cost of $12.816 ($5,767 ÷ 450).

Compare this moving-average cost under the perpetual inventory system to Illustration 6-10 (on page 259) showing the average-cost method under a periodic inventory system.

Comprehensive **DO IT!** *2*

Comprehensive Do It! 1 on page 269 showed cost of goods sold computations under a periodic inventory system. Now let's assume that Gerald D. Englehart Company uses a perpetual inventory system. The company has the same inventory, purchases, and sales data for the month of March as shown earlier:

Inventory:	March 1	200 units @ $4.00	$ 800
Purchases:	March 10	500 units @ $4.50	2,250
	March 20	400 units @ $4.75	1,900
	March 30	300 units @ $5.00	1,500
Sales:	March 15	500 units	
	March 25	400 units	

The physical inventory count on March 31 shows 500 units on hand.

Instructions

Under a **perpetual inventory system**, determine the cost of inventory on hand at March 31 and the cost of goods sold for March under (a) FIFO, (b) LIFO, and (c) average-cost.

action plan

✔ Compute the cost of goods sold under the perpetual FIFO method by allocating to the goods sold the **earliest** cost of goods purchased.

✔ Compute the cost of goods sold under the perpetual LIFO method by allocating to the goods sold the **latest** cost of goods purchased.

✔ Compute the cost of goods sold under the perpetual average-cost method by allocating to the goods sold a **moving-average** cost.

Solution to Comprehensive **DO IT!** 2

The cost of goods available for sale is $6,450, as follows.

Inventory:		200 units @ $4.00	$ 800
Purchases:	March 10	500 units @ $4.50	2,250
	March 20	400 units @ $4.75	1,900
	March 30	300 units @ $5.00	1,500
Total:		1,400	$6,450

Under a **perpetual inventory system**, the cost of goods sold under each cost flow method is as follows.

FIFO Method

Date	Purchases	Cost of Goods Sold	Balance
March 1			(200 @ $4.00) $ 800
March 10	(500 @ $4.50) $2,250		(200 @ $4.00) ⎱ $3,050 (500 @ $4.50) ⎰
March 15		(200 @ $4.00) (300 @ $4.50) —————— $2,150	(200 @ $4.50) $ 900

Date	Purchases	Cost of Goods Sold	Balance
March 20	(400 @ $4.75) $1,900		(200 @ $4.50)⎫ (400 @ $4.75)⎬ $2,800
March 25		(200 @ $4.50) (200 @ $4.75)	(200 @ $4.75) $ 950
		$1,850	
March 30	(300 @ $5.00) $1,500		(200 @ $4.75)⎫ (300 @ $5.00)⎬ $2,450
	Ending inventory, $2,450	Cost of goods sold: $2,150 + $1,850 = $4,000	

LIFO Method

Date	Purchases	Cost of Goods Sold	Balance
March 1			(200 @ $4.00) $ 800
March 10	(500 @ $4.50) $2,250		(200 @ $4.00)⎫ (500 @ $4.50)⎬ $3,050
March 15		(500 @ $4.50) $2,250	(200 @ $4.00) $ 800
March 20	(400 @ $4.75) $1,900		(200 @ $4.00)⎫ (400 @ $4.75)⎬ $2,700
March 25		(400 @ $4.75) $1,900	(200 @ $4.00) $ 800
March 30	(300 @ $5.00) $1,500		(200 @ $4.00)⎫ (300 @ $5.00)⎬ $2,300
	Ending inventory, $2,300	Cost of goods sold: $2,250 + $1,900 = $4,150	

Moving-Average Cost Method

Date	Purchases	Cost of Goods Sold	Balance
March 1			(200 @ $ 4.00) $ 800
March 10	(500 @ $4.50) $2,250		(700 @ $4.357) $3,050
March 15		(500 @ $4.357) $2,179	(200 @ $4.357) $ 871
March 20	(400 @ $4.75) $1,900		(600 @ $4.618) $2,771
March 25		(400 @ $4.618) $1,847	(200 @ $4.618) $ 924
March 30	(300 @ $5.00) $1,500		(500 @ $4.848) $2,424
	Ending inventory, $2,424	Cost of goods sold: $2,179 + $1,847 = $4,026	

✓ *The Navigator*

SUMMARY OF STUDY OBJECTIVE FOR APPENDIX 6A

7 Apply the inventory cost flow methods to perpetual inventory records. Under FIFO and a perpetual inventory system, companies charge to cost of goods sold the cost of the earliest goods on hand prior to each sale. Under LIFO and a perpetual system, companies charge to cost of goods sold the cost of the most recent purchase prior to sale. Under the moving-average (average cost) method and a perpetual system, companies compute a new average cost after each purchase.

APPENDIX 6B Estimating Inventories

STUDY OBJECTIVE 8

Describe the two methods of estimating inventories.

In the chapter we assumed that a company would be able to physically count its inventory. What if it cannot? What if the inventory were destroyed by fire or flood, for example? In that case, the company would use an estimate.

Two circumstances explain why companies sometimes estimate inventories. First, a casualty such as fire, flood, or earthquake may make it impossible to take a physical inventory. Second, managers may want monthly or quarterly financial statements, but a physical inventory is taken only annually. The need for estimating inventories occurs primarily with a periodic inventory system because of the absence of perpetual inventory records.

There are two widely used methods of estimating inventories: (1) the gross profit method, and (2) the retail inventory method.

Gross Profit Method

The **gross profit method** estimates the cost of ending inventory by applying a gross profit rate to net sales. This method is relatively simple, but effective. Accountants, auditors, and managers frequently use the gross profit method to test the reasonableness of the ending inventory amount. It will detect large errors.

To use this method, a company needs to know its net sales, cost of goods available for sale, and gross profit rate. The company then can estimate its gross profit for the period. Illustration 6B-1 shows the formulas for using the gross profit method.

Illustration 6B-1
Gross profit method formulas

To illustrate, assume that Kishwaukee Company wishes to prepare an income statement for the month of January. Its records show net sales of $200,000, beginning inventory $40,000, and cost of goods purchased $120,000. In the preceding year, the company realized a 30% gross profit rate. It expects to earn the same rate this year. Given these facts and assumptions, Kishwaukee can compute the estimated cost of the ending inventory at January 31 under the gross profit method as follows.

Step 1:

Net sales	$200,000
Less: Estimated gross profit (30% × $200,000)	60,000
Estimated cost of goods sold	**$140,000**

Step 2:

Beginning inventory	$ 40,000
Cost of goods purchased	120,000
Cost of goods available for sale	160,000
Less: Estimated cost of goods sold	140,000
Estimated cost of ending inventory	**$ 20,000**

Illustration 6B-2
Example of gross profit method

The gross profit method is based on the assumption that the gross profit rate will remain constant. But it may not remain constant, due to a change in merchandising policies or in market conditions. In such cases, the company should adjust the rate to reflect current operating conditions. In some cases, companies can obtain a more accurate estimate by applying this method on a department or product-line basis.

Note that companies should not use the gross profit method to prepare financial statements at the end of the year. These statements should be based on a physical inventory count.

Retail Inventory Method

A retail store such as Home Depot, Ace Hardware, or Wal-Mart has thousands of different types of merchandise at low unit costs. In such cases it is difficult and time-consuming to apply unit costs to inventory quantities. An alternative is to use the **retail inventory method** to estimate the cost of inventory. Most retail companies can establish a relationship between cost and sales price. The company then applies the cost-to-retail percentage to the ending inventory at retail prices to determine inventory at cost.

Under the retail inventory method, a company's records must show both the cost and retail value of the goods available for sale. Illustration 6B-3 presents the formulas for using the retail inventory method.

Illustration 6B-3
Retail inventory method formulas

Step 1:	Goods Available for Sale at Retail	− Net Sales	=	Ending Inventory at Retail
Step 2:	Goods Available for Sale at Cost	÷ Goods Available for Sale at Retail	=	Cost-to-Retail Ratio
Step 3:	Ending Inventory at Retail	× Cost-to-Retail Ratio	=	Estimated Cost of Ending Inventory

We can demonstrate the logic of the retail method by using unit-cost data. Assume that Ortiz Inc. has marked 10 units purchased at $7 to sell for $10 per unit. Thus, the cost-to-retail ratio is 70% ($70 ÷ $100). If four units remain unsold, their retail value is $40 (4 × $10), and their cost is $28 ($40 × 70%). This amount agrees with the total cost of goods on hand on a per unit basis (4 × $7).

Illustration 6B-4 shows application of the retail method for Valley West Co. Note that it is not necessary to take a physical inventory to determine the estimated cost of goods on hand at any given time.

Illustration 6B-4
Application of retail inventory method

	At Cost	At Retail
Beginning inventory	$14,000	$ 21,500
Goods purchased	61,000	78,500
Goods available for sale	$75,000	100,000
Net sales		70,000
Step (1) Ending inventory at retail =		$ 30,000
Step (2) Cost-to-retail ratio $75,000 ÷ $100,000 = 75%		
Step (3) Estimated cost of ending inventory = $30,000 × 75% = $22,500		

The retail inventory method also facilitates taking a physical inventory at the end of the year. Valley West can value the goods on hand at the prices marked on the merchandise, and then apply the cost-to-retail ratio to the goods on hand at retail to determine the ending inventory at cost.

The major disadvantage of the retail method is that it is an averaging technique. Thus, it may produce an incorrect inventory valuation if the mix of the ending inventory is not representative of the mix in the goods available for sale. Assume, for example, that the cost-to-retail ratio of 75% for Valley West Co. consists of equal proportions of inventory items that have cost-to-retail ratios of 70%, 75%, and 80%. If the ending inventory contains only items with a 70% ratio, an incorrect inventory cost will result. Companies can minimize this problem by applying the retail method on a department or product-line basis.

> **HELPFUL HINT**
>
> In determining inventory at retail, companies use selling prices of the units.

SUMMARY OF STUDY OBJECTIVE FOR APPENDIX 6B

8 Describe the two methods of estimating inventories. The two methods of estimating inventories are the gross profit method and the retail inventory method. Under the gross profit method, companies apply a gross profit rate to net sales to determine estimated cost of goods sold. They then subtract estimated cost of goods sold from cost of goods available for sale to determine the estimated cost of the ending inventory.

Under the retail inventory method, companies compute a cost-to-retail ratio by dividing the cost of goods available for sale by the retail value of the goods available for sale. They then apply this ratio to the ending inventory at retail to determine the estimated cost of the ending inventory.

GLOSSARY FOR APPENDIX 6B

Gross profit method A method for estimating the cost of the ending inventory by applying a gross profit rate to net sales and subtracting estimated cost of goods sold from cost of goods available for sale. (p. 275).

Retail inventory method A method for estimating the cost of the ending inventory by applying a cost-to-retail ratio to the ending inventory at retail. (p. 276).

*Note: All **asterisked** Questions, Exercises, and Problems relate to material in the appendices to the chapter.

SELF-STUDY QUESTIONS

Answers are at the end of the chapter.

(SO 1) **1.** Which of the following should *not* be included in the physical inventory of a company?
  a. Goods held on consignment from another company.
  b. Goods shipped on consignment to another company.
  c. Goods in transit from another company shipped FOB shipping point.
  d. None of the above.

(SO 1) **2.** As a result of a thorough physical inventory, Railway Company determined that it had inventory worth $180,000 at December 31, 2010. This count did not take into consideration the following facts: Rogers Consignment store currently has goods worth $35,000 on its sales floor that belong to Railway but are being sold on consignment by Rogers. The selling price of these goods is $50,000. Railway purchased $13,000 of goods that were shipped on December 27, FOB destination, that will be received by Railway on January 3. Determine the correct amount of inventory that Railway should report.
  a. $230,000.
  b. $215,000.
  c. $228,000.
  d. $193,000.

3. Cost of goods available for sale consist of two elements: (SO 2) beginning inventory and
  a. ending inventory.
  b. cost of goods purchased.
  c. cost of goods sold.
  d. all of the above.

4. Tinker Bell Company has the following: (SO 2)

	Units	Unit Cost
Inventory, Jan. 1	8,000	$11
Purchase, June 19	13,000	12
Purchase, Nov. 8	5,000	13

If Tinker Bell has 9,000 units on hand at December 31, the cost of the ending inventory under FIFO is:
a. $99,000.
c. $113,000.
b. $108,000.
d. $117,000.

(SO 2) **5.** Using the data in Question 4 above, the cost of the ending inventory under LIFO is:
a. $113,000.
c. $99,000.
b. $108,000.
d. $100,000.

(SO 2) **6.** Davidson Electronics has the following:

	Units	Unit Cost
Inventory, Jan. 1	5,000	$ 8
Purchase, April 2	15,000	$10
Purchase, Aug. 28	20,000	$12

If Davidson has 7,000 units on hand at December 31, the cost of ending inventory under the average-cost method is:
a. $84,000.
c. $56,000.
b. $70,000.
d. $75,250.

(SO 3) **7.** In periods of rising prices, LIFO will produce:
a. higher net income than FIFO.
b. the same net income as FIFO.
c. lower net income than FIFO.
d. higher net income than average costing.

(SO 3) **8.** Factors that affect the selection of an inventory costing method do *not* include:
a. tax effects.
b. balance sheet effects.
c. income statement effects.
d. perpetual vs. periodic inventory system.

(SO 4) **9.** Rickety Company purchased 1,000 widgets and has 200 widgets in its ending inventory at a cost of $91 each and a current replacement cost of $80 each. The ending inventory under lower of cost or market is:
a. $91,000.
c. $18,200.
b. $80,000.
d. $16,000.

(SO 5) **10.** Atlantis Company's ending inventory is understated $4,000. The effects of this error on the current year's cost of goods sold and net income, respectively, are:
a. understated, overstated.
b. overstated, understated.
c. overstated, overstated.
d. understated, understated.

(SO 4) **11.** Harold Company overstated its inventory by $15,000 at December 31, 2010. It did not correct the error in 2010 or 2011. As a result, Harold's owner's equity was:

a. overstated at December 31, 2010, and understated at December 31, 2011.
b. overstated at December 31, 2010, and properly stated at December 31, 2011.
c. understated at December 31, 2010, and understated at December 31, 2011.
d. overstated at December 31, 2010, and overstated at December 31, 2011.

12. Which of these would cause the inventory turnover ratio (SO 6) to increase the most?
a. Increasing the amount of inventory on hand.
b. Keeping the amount of inventory on hand constant but increasing sales.
c. Keeping the amount of inventory on hand constant but decreasing sales.
d. Decreasing the amount of inventory on hand and increasing sales.

13. Carlos Company had beginning inventory of $80,000, ending inventory of $110,000, cost of goods sold of $285,000, (SO 5) and sales of $475,000. Carlos's days in inventory is:
a. 73 days.
b. 121.7 days.
c. 102.5 days.
d. 84.5 days.

*14. Songbird Company has sales of $150,000 and cost of (SO 8) goods available for sale of $135,000. If the gross profit rate is 30%, the estimated cost of the ending inventory under the gross profit method is:
a. $15,000.
b. $30,000.
c. $45,000.
d. $75,000.

*15. In a perpetual inventory system, (SO 7)
a. LIFO cost of goods sold will be the same as in a periodic inventory system.
b. average costs are based entirely on unit cost averages.
c. a new average is computed under the average-cost method after each sale.
d. FIFO cost of goods sold will be the same as in a periodic inventory system.

Go to the book's companion website,
www.wiley.com/college/weygandt,
for Additional Self-Study questions.

 The Navigator

QUESTIONS

1. "The key to successful business operations is effective inventory management." Do you agree? Explain.

2. An item must possess two characteristics to be classified as inventory by a merchandiser. What are these two characteristics?

3. Your friend Tom Witt has been hired to help take the physical inventory in Hawkeye Hardware Store. Explain to Tom Witt what this job will entail.

4. (a) Reeves Company ships merchandise to Cox Company on December 30. The merchandise reaches the buyer on January 6. Indicate the terms of sale that will result in the goods being included in (1) Reeves's December 31 inventory, and (2) Cox's December 31 inventory.
(b) Under what circumstances should Reeves Company include consigned goods in its inventory?

5. Jim's Hat Shop received a shipment of hats for which it paid the wholesaler $2,970. The price of the hats was $3,000 but Jim's was given a $30 cash discount and required to pay freight charges of $50. In addition, Jim's paid $130 to cover the travel expenses of an employee who negotiated the purchase of the hats. What amount will Jim's record for inventory? Why?

6. Explain the difference between the terms FOB shipping point and FOB destination.

7. David Shannon believes that the allocation of inventoriable costs should be based on the actual physical flow of the goods. Explain to David why this may be both impractical and inappropriate.

8. What is a major advantage and a major disadvantage of the specific identification method of inventory costing?

9. "The selection of an inventory cost flow method is a decision made by accountants." Do you agree? Explain. Once a method has been selected, what accounting requirement applies?

10. Which assumed inventory cost flow method:
    (a) usually parallels the actual physical flow of merchandise?
    (b) assumes that goods available for sale during an accounting period are identical?
    (c) assumes that the latest units purchased are the first to be sold?

11. In a period of rising prices, the inventory reported in Plato Company's balance sheet is close to the current cost of the inventory. Cecil Company's inventory is considerably below its current cost. Identify the inventory cost flow method being used by each company. Which company has probably been reporting the higher gross profit?

12. Casey Company has been using the FIFO cost flow method during a prolonged period of rising prices. During the same time period, Casey has been paying out all of its net income as dividends. What adverse effects may result from this policy?

13. Peter Lunde is studying for the next accounting mid-term examination. What should Peter know about (a) departing from the cost basis of accounting for inventories and (b) the meaning of "market" in the lower-of-cost-or-market method?

14. Garitson Music Center has 5 CD players on hand at the balance sheet date. Each cost $400. The current replace-

ment cost is $380 per unit. Under the lower-of-cost-or-market basis of accounting for inventories, what value should be reported for the CD players on the balance sheet? Why?

15. Ruthie Stores has 20 toasters on hand at the balance sheet data. Each cost $27. The current replacement cost is $30 per unit. Under the lower-of-cost-or-market basis of accounting for inventories, what value should Ruthie report for the toasters on the balance sheet? Why?

16. Mintz Company discovers in 2010 that its ending inventory at December 31, 2009, was $7,000 understated. What effect will this error have on (a) 2009 net income, (b) 2010 net income, and (c) the combined net income for the 2 years?

17. Willingham Company's balance sheet shows Inventories $162,800. What additional disclosures should be made?

18. Under what circumstances might inventory turnover be too high? That is, what possible negative consequences might occur?

19. 🌐 **PEPSICO** What inventory cost flow does PepsiCo use for its inventories? (*Hint:* you will need to examine the notes for PepsiCo's financial statements.)

*20. "When perpetual inventory records are kept, the results under the FIFO and LIFO methods are the same as they would be in a periodic inventory system." Do you agree? Explain.

*21. How does the average-cost method of inventory costing differ between a perpetual inventory system and a periodic inventory system?

*22. When is it necessary to estimate inventories?

*23. Both the gross profit method and the retail inventory method are based on averages. For each method, indicate the average used, how it is determined, and how it is applied.

*24. Maureen Company has net sales of $400,000 and cost of goods available for sale of $300,000. If the gross profit rate is 35%, what is the estimated cost of the ending inventory? Show computations.

*25. Milo Shoe Shop had goods available for sale in 2008 with a retail price of $120,000. The cost of these goods was $84,000. If sales during the period were $80,000, what is the ending inventory at cost using the retail inventory method?

BRIEF EXERCISES

BE6-1 Smart Company identifies the following items for possible inclusion in the taking of a physical inventory. Indicate whether each item should be included or excluded from the inventory taking.

Identify items to be included in taking a physical inventory.

(SO 1)

(a) Goods shipped on consignment by Smart to another company.
(b) Goods in transit from a supplier shipped FOB destination.
(c) Goods sold but being held for customer pickup.
(d) Goods held on consignment from another company.

Identify the components of goods available for sale.

(SO 2)

BE6-2 The ledger of Gomez Company includes the following items: **(a)** Freight-in, **(b)** Purchase Returns and Allowances, **(c)** Purchases, **(d)** Sales Discounts, **(e)** Purchase Discounts. Identify which items are included in goods available for sale.

Compute ending inventory using FIFO and LIFO.

(SO 2)

BE6-3 In its first month of operations, Quirk Company made three purchases of merchandise in the following sequence: (1) 300 units at $6, (2) 400 units at $7, and (3) 200 units at $8. Assuming there are 360 units on hand, compute the cost of the ending inventory under the **(a)** FIFO method and **(b)** LIFO method. Quirk uses a periodic inventory system.

Compute the ending inventory using average-cost.

(SO 2)

BE6-4 Data for Quirk Company are presented in BE6-3. Compute the cost of the ending inventory under the average-cost method, assuming there are 360 units on hand.

Explain the financial statement effect of inventory cost flow assumptions.

(SO 3)

BE6-5 The management of Hoyt Corp. is considering the effects of various inventory-costing methods on its financial statements and its income tax expense. Assuming that the price the company pays for inventory is increasing, which method will:

(a) provide the highest net income?
(b) provide the highest ending inventory?
(c) result in the lowest income tax expense?
(d) result in the most stable earnings over a number of years?

Explain the financial statement effect of inventory cost flow assumptions.

(SO 3)

BE6-6 In its first month of operation, Gulletson Company purchased 100 units of inventory for $6, then 200 units for $7, and finally 150 units for $8. At the end of the month, 180 units remained. Compute the amount of phantom profit that would result if the company used FIFO rather than LIFO. Explain why this amount is referred to as phantom profit. The company uses the periodic method.

Determine the LCM valuation using inventory categories.

(SO 4)

BE6-7 Alou Appliance Center accumulates the following cost and market data at December 31.

Inventory Categories	Cost Data	Market Data
Cameras	$12,000	$12,100
Camcorders	9,500	9,700
DVD players	14,000	12,800

Compute the lower-of-cost-or-market valuation for the company's total inventory.

Determine correct income statement amounts.

(SO 5)

BE6-8 Cody Company reports net income of $90,000 in 2010. However, ending inventory was understated $10,000. What is the correct net income for 2010? What effect, if any, will this error have on total assets as reported in the balance sheet at December 31, 2010?

Compute inventory turnover and days in inventory.

(SO 6)

BE6-9 At December 31, 2010, the following information was available for J. Graff Company: ending inventory $40,000, beginning inventory $60,000, cost of goods sold $270,000, and sales revenue $380,000. Calculate inventory turnover and days in inventory for J. Graff Company.

Apply cost flow methods to perpetual inventory records.

(SO 7)

*BE6-10 Jensen's Department Store uses a perpetual inventory system. Data for product E2-D2 include the following purchases.

Date	Number of Units	Unit Price
May 7	50	$10
July 28	30	13

On June 1 Jensen's sold 30 units, and on August 27, 40 more units. Prepare the perpetual inventory schedule for the above transactions using (1) FIFO, (2) LIFO, and (3) moving-average cost.

Apply the gross profit method.

(SO 8)

*BE6-11 At May 31, Creole Company has net sales of $330,000 and cost of goods available for sale of $230,000. Compute the estimated cost of the ending inventory, assuming the gross profit rate is 35%.

Apply the retail inventory method.

(SO 8)

*BE6-12 On June 30, Fabre Fabrics has the following data pertaining to the retail inventory method: Goods available for sale: at cost $35,000, at retail $50,000; net sales $40,000, and ending inventory at retail $8,000. Compute the estimated cost of the ending inventory using the retail inventory method.

DO IT! REVIEW

DO IT! 6-1   Neverwas Company just took its physical inventory. The count of inventory items on hand at the company's business locations resulted in a total inventory cost of $300,000. In reviewing the details of the count and related inventory transactions, you have discovered the following.

Apply rules of ownership to determine inventory cost.

(SO 1)

1. Neverwas has sent inventory costing $26,000 on consignment to Niagara Company. All of this inventory was at Niagara's showrooms on December 31.
2. The company did not include in the count inventory (cost, $20,000) that was sold on December 28, terms FOB shipping point. The goods were in transit on December 31.
3. The company did not include in the count inventory (cost, $17,000) that was purchased with terms of FOB shipping point. The goods were in transit on December 31.

Compute the correct December 31 inventory.

DO IT! 6-2   The accounting records of Oots Electronics show the following data.

Compute cost of goods sold under different cost flow methods.

(SO 2)

Beginning inventory	3,000 units at $5
Purchases	8,000 units at $7
Sales	9,200 units at $10

Determine cost of goods sold during the period under a periodic inventory system using (a) the FIFO method, (b) the LIFO method, and (c) the average-cost method. (Round unit cost to nearest tenth of a cent.)

DO IT! 6-3   (a) Blank Company sells three different categories of tools (small, medium and large). The cost and market value of its inventory of tools are as follows.

Compute inventory value under LCM.

(SO 5)

	Cost	Market
Small	$ 64,000	$ 73,000
Medium	290,000	260,000
Large	152,000	171,000

Determine the value of the company's inventory under the lower-of-cost-or-market approach.

(b) Audio Company understated its 2010 ending inventory by $31,000. Determine the impact this error has on ending inventory, cost of goods sold, and owner's equity in 2010 and 2011.

DO IT! 6-4   Early in 2010 Aragon Company switched to a just-in-time inventory system. Its sales, cost of goods sold, and inventory amounts for 2009 and 2010 are shown below.

Compute inventory turnover ratio and assess inventory level.

(SO 6)

	2009	2010
Sales	$3,120,000	$3,713,000
Cost of goods sold	1,200,000	1,425,000
Beginning inventory	180,000	220,000
Ending inventory	220,000	80,000

Determine the inventory turnover and days in inventory for 2009 and 2010. Discuss the changes in the amount of inventory, the inventory turnover and days in inventory, and the amount of sales across the two years.

EXERCISES

E6-1   Premier Bank and Trust is considering giving Lima Company a loan. Before doing so, they decide that further discussions with Lima's accountant may be desirable. One area of particular concern is the inventory account, which has a year-end balance of $297,000. Discussions with the accountant reveal the following.

Determine the correct inventory amount.

(SO 1)

1. Lima sold goods costing $38,000 to Comerica Company, FOB shipping point, on December 28. The goods are not expected to arrive at Comerica until January 12. The goods were not included in the physical inventory because they were not in the warehouse.
2. The physical count of the inventory did not include goods costing $95,000 that were shipped to Lima FOB destination on December 27 and were still in transit at year-end.
3. Lima received goods costing $22,000 on January 2. The goods were shipped FOB shipping point on December 26 by Galant Co. The goods were not included in the physical count.

4. Lima sold goods costing $35,000 to Emerick Co., FOB destination, on December 30. The goods were received at Emerick on January 8. They were not included in Lima's physical inventory.

5. Lima received goods costing $44,000 on January 2 that were shipped FOB destination on December 29. The shipment was a rush order that was supposed to arrive December 31. This purchase was included in the ending inventory of $297,000.

Instructions

Determine the correct inventory amount on December 31.

Determine the correct inventory amount.

(SO 1)

E6-2 Kale Thompson, an auditor with Sneed CPAs, is performing a review of Strawser Company's inventory account. Strawser did not have a good year and top management is under pressure to boost reported income. According to its records, the inventory balance at year-end was $740,000. However, the following information was not considered when determining that amount.

1. Included in the company's count were goods with a cost of $250,000 that the company is holding on consignment. The goods belong to Superior Corporation.

2. The physical count did not include goods purchased by Strawser with a cost of $40,000 that were shipped FOB destination on December 28 and did not arrive at Strawser's warehouse until January 3.

3. Included in the inventory account was $17,000 of office supplies that were stored in the warehouse and were to be used by the company's supervisors and managers during the coming year.

4. The company received an order on December 29 that was boxed and was sitting on the loading dock awaiting pick-up on December 31. The shipper picked up the goods on January 1 and delivered them on January 6. The shipping terms were FOB shipping point. The goods had a selling price of $40,000 and a cost of $30,000. The goods were not included in the count because they were sitting on the dock.

5. On December 29 Strawser shipped goods with a selling price of $80,000 and a cost of $60,000 to District Sales Corporation FOB shipping point. The goods arrived on January 3. District Sales had only ordered goods with a selling price of $10,000 and a cost of $8,000. However, a sales manager at Strawser had authorized the shipment and said that if District wanted to ship the goods back next week, it could.

6. Included in the count was $40,000 of goods that were parts for a machine that the company no longer made. Given the high-tech nature of Strawser's products, it was unlikely that these obsolete parts had any other use. However, management would prefer to keep them on the books at cost, "since that is what we paid for them, after all."

Instructions

Prepare a schedule to determine the correct inventory amount. Provide explanations for each item above, saying why you did or did not make an adjustment for each item.

Calculate cost of goods sold using specific identification and FIFO.

(SO 2, 3)

E6-3 On December 1, Bargain Electronics Ltd. has three DVD players left in stock. All are identical, all are priced to sell at $150. One of the three DVD players left in stock, with serial #1012, was purchased on June 1 at a cost of $100. Another, with serial #1045, was purchased on November 1 for $90. The last player, serial #1056, was purchased on November 30 for $80.

Instructions

(a) Calculate the cost of goods sold using the FIFO periodic inventory method assuming that two of the three players were sold by the end of December, Bargain Electronic's year-end.

(b) If Bargain Electronics used the specific identification method instead of the FIFO method, how might it alter its earnings by "selectively choosing" which particular players to sell to the two customers? What would Bargain's cost of goods sold be if the company wished to minimize earnings? Maximize earnings?

(c) Which of the two inventory methods do you recommend that Bargain use? Explain why.

Compute inventory and cost of goods sold using FIFO and LIFO.

(SO 2)

E6-4 Boarders sells a snowboard, Xpert, that is popular with snowboard enthusiasts. Below is information relating to Boarders's purchases of Xpert snowboards during September. During the same month, 121 Xpert snowboards were sold. Boarders uses a periodic inventory system.

Date	Explanation	Units	Unit Cost	Total Cost
Sept. 1	Inventory	26	$ 97	$ 2,522
Sept. 12	Purchases	45	102	4,590
Sept. 19	Purchases	20	104	2,080
Sept. 26	Purchases	50	105	5,250
	Totals	141		$14,442

Instructions
(a) Compute the ending inventory at September 30 and cost of goods sold using the FIFO and LIFO methods. Prove the amount allocated to cost of goods sold under each method.
(b) For both FIFO and LIFO, calculate the sum of ending inventory and cost of goods sold. What do you notice about the answers you found for each method?

E6-5 Catlet Co. uses a periodic inventory system. Its records show the following for the month of May, in which 65 units were sold.

Compute inventory and cost of goods sold using FIFO and LIFO.

(SO 2)

		Units	Unit Cost	Total Cost
May 1	Inventory	30	$ 8	$240
15	Purchases	25	11	275
24	Purchases	35	12	420
	Totals	90		$935

Instructions
Compute the ending inventory at May 31 and cost of goods sold using the FIFO and LIFO methods. Prove the amount allocated to cost of goods sold under each method.

E6-6 Yount Company reports the following for the month of June.

Compute inventory and cost of goods sold using FIFO and LIFO.

(SO 2, 3)

		Units	Unit Cost	Total Cost
June 1	Inventory	200	$5	$1,000
12	Purchase	300	6	1,800
23	Purchase	500	7	3,500
30	Inventory	120		

Instructions
(a) Compute the cost of the ending inventory and the cost of goods sold under (1) FIFO and (2) LIFO.
(b) Which costing method gives the higher ending inventory? Why?
(c) Which method results in the higher cost of goods sold? Why?

E6-7 Jones Company had 100 units in beginning inventory at a total cost of $10,000. The company purchased 200 units at a total cost of $26,000. At the end of the year, Jones had 80 units in ending inventory.

Compute inventory under FIFO, LIFO, and average-cost.

(SO 2, 3)

Instructions
(a) Compute the cost of the ending inventory and the cost of goods sold under (1) FIFO, (2) LIFO, and (3) average-cost.
(b) Which cost flow method would result in the highest net income?
(c) Which cost flow method would result in inventories approximating current cost in the balance sheet?
(d) Which cost flow method would result in Jones paying the least taxes in the first year?

E6-8 Inventory data for Yount Company are presented in E6-6.

Compute inventory and cost of goods sold using average-cost.

(SO 2, 3)

Instructions
(a) Compute the cost of the ending inventory and the cost of goods sold using the average-cost method.

(b) Will the results in (a) be higher or lower than the results under (1) FIFO and (2) LIFO?
(c) Why is the average unit cost not $6?

Determine ending inventory under LCM.
(SO 4)

E6-9 Americus Camera Shop uses the lower-of-cost-or-market basis for its inventory. The following data are available at December 31.

Item	Units	Unit Cost	Market
Cameras:			
Minolta	5	$170	$156
Canon	6	150	152
Light meters:			
Vivitar	12	125	115
Kodak	14	120	135

Instructions
Determine the amount of the ending inventory by applying the lower-of-cost-or-market basis.

Compute lower-of-cost-or-market.
(SO 4)

E6-10 Conan Company applied FIFO to its inventory and got the following results for its ending inventory.

Cameras	100 units at a cost per unit of $65
DVD players	150 units at a cost per unit of $75
iPods	125 units at a cost per unit of $80

The cost of purchasing units at year-end was VCRs $71, DVD players $69, and iPods $78.

Instructions
Determine the amount of ending inventory at lower-of-cost-or-market.

Determine effects of inventory errors.
(SO 5)

E6-11 Lebo Hardware reported cost of goods sold as follows.

	2010	2011
Beginning inventory	$ 20,000	$ 30,000
Cost of goods purchased	150,000	175,000
Cost of goods available for sale	170,000	205,000
Ending inventory	30,000	35,000
Cost of goods sold	$140,000	$170,000

Lebo made two errors: (1) 2010 ending inventory was overstated $3,000, and (2) 2011 ending inventory was understated $6,000.

Instructions
Compute the correct cost of goods sold for each year.

Prepare correct income statements.
(SO 5)

E6-12 Staley Watch Company reported the following income statement data for a 2-year period.

	2010	2011
Sales	$210,000	$250,000
Cost of goods sold		
Beginning inventory	32,000	44,000
Cost of goods purchased	173,000	202,000
Cost of goods available for sale	205,000	246,000
Ending inventory	44,000	52,000
Cost of goods sold	161,000	194,000
Gross profit	$ 49,000	$ 56,000

Staley uses a periodic inventory system. The inventories at January 1, 2010, and December 31, 2011, are correct. However, the ending inventory at December 31, 2010, was overstated $5,000.

Instructions
(a) Prepare correct income statement data for the 2 years.
(b) What is the cumulative effect of the inventory error on total gross profit for the 2 years?
(c) ⬤━━━▶ Explain in a letter to the president of Staley Company what has happened—i.e., the nature of the error and its effect on the financial statements.

E6-13   This information is available for Santo's Photo Corporation for 2009, 2010, and 2011.

Compute inventory turnover, days in inventory, and gross profit rate.
(SO 6)

	2009	2010	2011
Beginning inventory	$ 100,000	$ 300,000	$ 400,000
Ending inventory	300,000	400,000	480,000
Cost of goods sold	900,000	1,120,000	1,300,000
Sales	1,200,000	1,600,000	1,900,000

Instructions
Calculate inventory turnover, days in inventory, and gross profit rate (from Chapter 5) for Santo's Photo Corporation for 2009, 2010, 2011. Comment on any trends.

E6-14   The cost of goods sold computations for O'Brien Company and Weinberg Company are shown below.

Compute inventory turnover and days in inventory.
(SO 6)

	O'Brien Company	Weinberg Company
Beginning inventory	$ 45,000	$ 71,000
Cost of goods purchased	200,000	290,000
Cost of goods available for sale	245,000	361,000
Ending inventory	55,000	69,000
Cost of goods sold	$190,000	$292,000

Instructions
(a) Compute inventory turnover and days in inventory for each company.
(b) Which company moves its inventory more quickly?

*E6-15   Klugman Appliance uses a perpetual inventory system. For its flat-screen television sets, the January 1 inventory was 3 sets at $600 each. On January 10, Klugman purchased 6 units at $660 each. The company sold 2 units on January 8 and 4 units on January 15.

Apply cost flow methods to perpetual records.
(SO 7)

Instructions
Compute the ending inventory under (1) FIFO, (2) LIFO, and (3) moving-average cost.

*E6-16   Yount Company reports the following for the month of June.

Calculate inventory and cost of goods sold using three cost flow methods in a perpetual inventory system.
(SO 7)

Date	Explanation	Units	Unit Cost	Total Cost
June 1	Inventory	200	$5	$1,000
12	Purchase	300	6	1,800
23	Purchase	500	7	3,500
30	Inventory	120		

Instructions
(a) Calculate the cost of the ending inventory and the cost of goods sold for each cost flow assumption, using a perpetual inventory system. Assume a sale of 400 units occurred on June 15 for a selling price of $8 and a sale of 480 units on June 27 for $9.
(b) How do the results differ from E6-6 and E6-8?
(c) Why is the average unit cost not $6 [($5 + $6 + $7) ÷ 3 = $6]?

*E6-17   Information about Boarders is presented in E6-4. Additional data regarding Boarders' sales of Xpert snowboards are provided below. Assume that Boarders uses a perpetual inventory system.

Apply cost flow methods to perpetual records.
(SO 7)

Date		Units	Unit Price	Total Cost
Sept. 5	Sale	12	$199	$ 2,388
Sept. 16	Sale	50	199	9,950
Sept. 29	Sale	59	209	12,331
	Totals	121		$24,669

Instructions

(a) Compute ending inventory at September 30 using FIFO, LIFO, and moving-average cost.

(b) Compare ending inventory using a perpetual inventory system to ending inventory using a periodic inventory system (from E6-4).

(c) Which inventory cost flow method (FIFO, LIFO) gives the same ending inventory value under both periodic and perpetual? Which method gives different ending inventory values?

Use the gross profit method to estimate inventory.

(SO 8)

*E6-18 Doc Gibbs Company reported the following information for November and December 2010.

	November	December
Cost of goods purchased	$500,000	$ 610,000
Inventory, beginning-of-month	100,000	120,000
Inventory, end-of-month	120,000	????
Sales	800,000	1,000,000

Doc Gibbs's ending inventory at December 31 was destroyed in a fire.

Instructions

(a) Compute the gross profit rate for November.

(b) Using the gross profit rate for November, determine the estimated cost of inventory lost in the fire.

Determine merchandise lost using the gross profit method of estimating inventory.

(SO 8)

*E6-19 The inventory of Faber Company was destroyed by fire on March 1. From an examination of the accounting records, the following data for the first 2 months of the year are obtained: Sales $51,000, Sales Returns and Allowances $1,000, Purchases $31,200, Freight-in $1,200, and Purchase Returns and Allowances $1,400.

Instructions

Determine the merchandise lost by fire, assuming:

(a) A beginning inventory of $20,000 and a gross profit rate of 40% on net sales.

(b) A beginning inventory of $30,000 and a gross profit rate of 30% on net sales.

Determine ending inventory at cost using retail method.

(SO 8)

*E6-20 Quayle Shoe Store uses the retail inventory method for its two departments, Women's Shoes and Men's Shoes. The following information for each department is obtained.

Item	Women's Department	Men's Department
Beginning inventory at cost	$ 32,000	$ 45,000
Cost of goods purchased at cost	148,000	136,300
Net sales	178,000	185,000
Beginning inventory at retail	46,000	60,000
Cost of goods purchased at retail	179,000	185,000

Instructions

Compute the estimated cost of the ending inventory for each department under the retail inventory method.

EXERCISES: SET B

Visit the book's companion website at **www.wiley.com/college/weygandt**, and choose the Student Companion site, to access Exercise Set B.

PROBLEMS: SET A

P6-1A Heath Limited is trying to determine the value of its ending inventory at February 28, 2008, the company's year end. The accountant counted everything that was in the warehouse as of February 28, which resulted in an ending inventory valuation of $48,000. However, she didn't know how to treat the following transactions so she didn't record them.

Determine items and amounts to be recorded in inventory.
(SO 1)

(a) On February 26, Heath shipped to a customer goods costing $800. The goods were shipped FOB shipping point, and the receiving report indicates that the customer received the goods on March 2.

(b) On February 26, Seller Inc. shipped goods to Heath FOB destination. The invoice price was $350. The receiving report indicates that the goods were received by Heath on March 2.

(c) Heath had $500 of inventory at a customer's warehouse "on approval." The customer was going to let Heath know whether it wanted the merchandise by the end of the week, March 4.

(d) Heath also had $400 of inventory on consignment at a Jasper craft shop.

(e) On February 26, Heath ordered goods costing $750. The goods were shipped FOB shipping point on February 27. Heath received the goods on March 1.

(f) On February 28, Heath packaged goods and had them ready for shipping to a customer FOB destination. The invoice price was $350; the cost of the items was $250. The receiving report indicates that the goods were received by the customer on March 2.

(g) Heath had damaged goods set aside in the warehouse because they are no longer saleable. These goods originally cost $400 and, originally, Heath expected to sell these items for $600.

Instructions

For each of the above transactions, specify whether the item in question should be included in ending inventory, and if so, at what amount. For each item that is not included in ending inventory, indicate who owns it and what account, if any, it should have been recorded in.

P6-2A Glanville Distribution markets CDs of the performing artist Harrilyn Clooney. At the beginning of March, Glanville had in beginning inventory 1,500 Clooney CDs with a unit cost of $7. During March Glanville made the following purchases of Clooney CDs.

Determine cost of goods sold and ending inventory using FIFO, LIFO, and average-cost with analysis.
(SO 2, 3)

March 5	3,000 @ $8	March 21	4,000 @ $10
March 13	5,500 @ $9	March 26	2,000 @ $11

During March 12,500 units were sold. Glanville uses a periodic inventory system.

Instructions

(a) Determine the cost of goods available for sale.

(b) Determine (1) the ending inventory and (2) the cost of goods sold under each of the assumed cost flow methods (FIFO, LIFO, and average-cost). Prove the accuracy of the cost of goods sold under the FIFO and LIFO methods.

(b)(2) Cost of goods sold:
FIFO $109,000
LIFO $119,500
Average $114,062

(c) Which cost flow method results in (1) the highest inventory amount for the balance sheet and (2) the highest cost of goods sold for the income statement?

P6-3A Eddings Company had a beginning inventory of 400 units of Product XNA at a cost of $8.00 per unit. During the year, purchases were:

Determine cost of goods sold and ending inventory using FIFO, LIFO, and average-cost with analysis.
(SO 2, 3)

Feb. 20	600 units at $9	Aug. 12	300 units at $11
May 5	500 units at $10	Dec. 8	200 units at $12

Eddings Company uses a periodic inventory system. Sales totaled 1,500 units.

Instructions

(a) Determine the cost of goods available for sale.

(b) Determine (1) the ending inventory, and (2) the cost of goods sold under each of the assumed cost flow methods (FIFO, LIFO, and average). Prove the accuracy of the cost of goods sold under the FIFO and LIFO methods.

(b) Cost of goods sold:
FIFO $13,600
LIFO $15,200
Average $14,475

(c) Which cost flow method results in (1) the lowest inventory amount for the balance sheet, and (2) the lowest cost of goods sold for the income statement?

Compute ending inventory, prepare income statements, and answer questions using FIFO and LIFO.

(SO 2, 3)

P6-4A The management of Morales Co. is reevaluating the appropriateness of using its present inventory cost flow method, which is average-cost. They request your help in determining the results of operations for 2010 if either the FIFO method or the LIFO method had been used. For 2010, the accounting records show the following data.

Inventories		Purchases and Sales	
Beginning (15,000 units)	$32,000	Total net sales (215,000 units)	$865,000
Ending (30,000 units)		Total cost of goods purchased (230,000 units)	595,000

Purchases were made quarterly as follows.

Quarter	Units	Unit Cost	Total Cost
1	60,000	$2.40	$144,000
2	50,000	2.50	125,000
3	50,000	2.60	130,000
4	70,000	2.80	196,000
	230,000		$595,000

Operating expenses were $147,000, and the company's income tax rate is 34%.

Instructions

(a) Prepare comparative condensed income statements for 2010 under FIFO and LIFO. (Show computations of ending inventory.)

(b) ◄━━━ Answer the following questions for management.

(1) Which cost flow method (FIFO or LIFO) produces the more meaningful inventory amount for the balance sheet? Why?

(2) Which cost flow method (FIFO or LIFO) produces the more meaningful net income? Why?

(3) Which cost flow method (FIFO or LIFO) is more likely to approximate actual physical flow of the goods? Why?

(4) How much additional cash will be available for management under LIFO than under FIFO? Why?

(5) Will gross profit under the average-cost method be higher or lower than (a) FIFO and (b) LIFO? (*Note:* It is not necessary to quantify your answer.)

(a) Net income
FIFO $115,500
LIFO $104,940
(b)(4) $5,440

Calculate ending inventory, cost of goods sold, gross profit, and gross profit rate under periodic method; compare results.

(SO 2, 3)

Peachtree

P6-5A You are provided with the following information for Pavey Inc. for the month ended October 31, 2010. Pavey uses a periodic method for inventory.

Date	Description	Units	Unit Cost or Selling Price
October 1	Beginning inventory	60	$25
October 9	Purchase	120	26
October 11	Sale	100	35
October 17	Purchase	70	27
October 22	Sale	60	40
October 25	Purchase	80	28
October 29	Sale	110	40

Instructions

(a)(iii) Gross profit:
LIFO $3,050
FIFO $3,230
Average $3,141

(a) Calculate (i) ending inventory, (ii) cost of goods sold, (iii) gross profit, and (iv) gross profit rate under each of the following methods.

(1) LIFO.
(2) FIFO.
(3) Average-cost.

(b) Compare results for the three cost flow assumptions.

P6-6A You have the following information for Bernelli Diamonds. Bernelli Diamonds uses the periodic method of accounting for its inventory transactions. Bernelli only carries one brand and size of diamonds—all are identical. Each batch of diamonds purchased is carefully coded and marked with its purchase cost.

Compare specific identification, FIFO and LIFO under periodic method; use cost flow assumption to influence earnings.

(SO 2, 3)

March 1	Beginning inventory 150 diamonds at a cost of $300 per diamond.
March 3	Purchased 200 diamonds at a cost of $350 each.
March 5	Sold 180 diamonds for $600 each.
March 10	Purchased 350 diamonds at a cost of $375 each.
March 25	Sold 400 diamonds for $650 each.

Instructions

(a) Assume that Bernelli Diamonds uses the specific identification cost flow method.

(1) Demonstrate how Bernelli Diamonds could maximize its gross profit for the month by specifically selecting which diamonds to sell on March 5 and March 25.

(2) Demonstrate how Bernelli Diamonds could minimize its gross profit for the month by selecting which diamonds to sell on March 5 and March 25.

(b) Assume that Bernelli Diamonds uses the FIFO cost flow assumption. Calculate cost of goods sold. How much gross profit would Bernelli Diamonds report under this cost flow assumption?

(c) Assume that Bernelli Diamonds uses the LIFO cost flow assumption. Calculate cost of goods sold. How much gross profit would the company report under this cost flow assumption?

(d) Which cost flow method should Bernelli Diamonds select? Explain.

(a) Gross profit:
  (1) Maximum $166,750

  (2) Minimum $157,750

P6-7A The management of Utley Inc. asks your help in determining the comparative effects of the FIFO and LIFO inventory cost flow methods. For 2010 the accounting records show these data.

Compute ending inventory, prepare income statements, and answer questions using FIFO and LIFO.

(SO 2, 3)

Inventory, January 1 (10,000 units)	$ 35,000
Cost of 120,000 units purchased	504,500
Selling price of 100,000 units sold	665,000
Operating expenses	130,000

Units purchased consisted of 35,000 units at $4.00 on May 10; 60,000 units at $4.20 on August 15; and 25,000 units at $4.50 on November 20. Income taxes are 28%.

Instructions

(a) Prepare comparative condensed income statements for 2010 under FIFO and LIFO. (Show computations of ending inventory.)

(b) ▬▬▬▬ Answer the following questions for management in the form of a business letter.

(1) Which inventory cost flow method produces the most meaningful inventory amount for the balance sheet? Why?

(2) Which inventory cost flow method produces the most meaningful net income? Why?

(3) Which inventory cost flow method is most likely to approximate the actual physical flow of the goods? Why?

(4) How much more cash will be available for management under LIFO than under FIFO? Why?

(5) How much of the gross profit under FIFO is illusionary in comparison with the gross profit under LIFO?

Gross profit:
  FIFO $259,000
  LIFO $240,500

*P6-8A Vasquez Ltd. is a retailer operating in Edmonton, Alberta. Vasquez uses the perpetual inventory method. All sales returns from customers result in the goods being returned to inventory; the inventory is not damaged. Assume that there are no credit transactions; all amounts are settled in cash. You are provided with the following information for Vasquez Ltd. for the month of January 2010.

Calculate cost of goods sold and ending inventory for FIFO, average-cost, and LIFO under the perpetual system; compare gross profit under each assumption.

(SO 7)

Date	Description	Quantity	Unit Cost or Selling Price
December 31	Ending inventory	150	$17
January 2	Purchase	100	21
January 6	Sale	150	40
January 9	Sale return	10	40
January 9	Purchase	75	24
January 10	Purchase return	15	24
January 10	Sale	50	45
January 23	Purchase	100	28
January 30	Sale	110	50

Gross profit:
LIFO $6,330
FIFO $7,500
Average $7,090

Instructions

(a) For each of the following cost flow assumptions, calculate (i) cost of goods sold, (ii) ending inventory, and (iii) gross profit.

(1) LIFO.   **(2)** FIFO.   **(3)** Moving-average-cost.

(b) Compare results for the three cost flow assumptions.

Determine ending inventory under a perpetual inventory system.

(SO 7)

*P6-9A Sandoval Appliance Mart began operations on May 1. It uses a perpetual inventory system. During May the company had the following purchases and sales for its Model 25 Sureshot camera.

	Purchases		
Date	**Units**	**Unit Cost**	**Sales Units**
May 1	7	$150	
4			4
8	8	$170	
12			5
15	6	$185	
20			3
25			4

Instructions

(a) FIFO $925
Average $874
LIFO $790

(a) Determine the ending inventory under a perpetual inventory system using (1) FIFO, (2) moving-average cost, and (3) LIFO.

(b) Which costing method produces (1) the highest ending inventory valuation and (2) the lowest ending inventory valuation?

Estimate inventory loss using gross profit method.

(SO 8)

*P6-10A Saffordville Company lost 70% of its inventory in a fire on March 25, 2010. The accounting records showed the following gross profit data for February and March.

	February	**March (to 3/25)**
Net sales	$300,000	$250,000
Net purchases	197,800	191,000
Freight-in	2,900	4,000
Beginning inventory	4,500	13,200
Ending inventory	13,200	?

Saffordville Company is fully insured for fire losses but must prepare a report for the insurance company.

Instructions

(a) Compute the gross profit rate for the month of February.

(b) Using the gross profit rate for February, determine both the estimated total inventory and inventory lost in the fire in March.

Compute ending inventory using retail method.

(SO 8)

*P6-11A Neer Department Store uses the retail inventory method to estimate its monthly ending inventories. The following information is available for two of its departments at August 31, 2010.

	Sporting Goods		**Jewelry and Cosmetics**	
	Cost	**Retail**	**Cost**	**Retail**
Net sales		$1,000,000		$1,160,000
Purchases	$675,000	1,066,000	$741,000	1,158,000
Purchase returns	(26,000)	(40,000)	(12,000)	(20,000)
Purchase discounts	(12,360)	—	(2,440)	—
Freight-in	9,000	—	14,000	—
Beginning inventory	47,360	74,000	39,440	62,000

At December 31, Neer Department Store takes a physical inventory at retail. The actual retail values of the inventories in each department are Sporting Goods $95,000, and Jewelry and Cosmetics $44,000.

Instructions
(a) Determine the estimated cost of the ending inventory for each department on **August 31**, 2010, using the retail inventory method.
(b) Compute the ending inventory at cost for each department at **December 31**, assuming the cost-to-retail ratios are 60% for Sporting Goods and 64% for Jewelry and Cosmetics.

PROBLEMS: SET B

P6-1B   Elms Country Limited is trying to determine the value of its ending inventory as of February 28, 2010, the company's year-end. The following transactions occurred, and the accountant asked your help in determining whether they should be recorded or not.

Determine items and amounts to be recorded in inventory.

(SO 1)

(a) On February 26, Elms shipped goods costing $800 to a customer and charged the customer $1,000. The goods were shipped with terms FOB shipping point and the receiving report indicates that the customer received the goods on March 2.
(b) On February 26, Brad Inc. shipped goods to Elms under terms FOB shipping point. The invoice price was $450 plus $30 for freight. The receiving report indicates that the goods were received by Elms on March 2.
(c) Elms had $650 of inventory isolated in the warehouse. The inventory is designated for a customer who has requested that the goods be shipped on March 10.
(d) Also included in Elms's warehouse is $700 of inventory that Art Producers shipped to Elms on consignment.
(e) On February 26, Elms issued a purchase order to acquire goods costing $900. The goods were shipped with terms FOB destination on February 27. Elms received the goods on March 2.
(f) On February 26, Elms shipped goods to a customer under terms FOB destination. The invoice price was $350; the cost of the items was $200. The receiving report indicates that the goods were received by the customer on March 2.

Instructions
For each of the above transactions, specify whether the item in question should be included in ending inventory, and if so, at what amount.

P6-2B   Soul Patrol Distribution markets CDs of the performing artist Taylor Hicks. At the beginning of October, Soul Patrol had in beginning inventory 2,000 of Hicks's CDs with a unit cost of $7. During October Soul Patrol made the following purchases of Hicks's CDs.

Determine cost of goods sold and ending inventory using FIFO, LIFO, and average-cost with analysis.

(SO 2, 3)

Oct. 3	3,000 @ $8	Oct. 19	3,000 @ $10
Oct. 9	3,500 @ $9	Oct. 25	3,500 @ $11

During October, 11,400 units were sold. Soul Patrol uses a periodic inventory system.

Instructions
(a) Determine the cost of goods available for sale.
(b) Determine (1) the ending inventory and (2) the cost of goods sold under each of the assumed cost flow methods (FIFO, LIFO, and average-cost). Prove the accuracy of the cost of goods sold under the FIFO and LIFO methods.
(c) Which cost flow method results in (1) the highest inventory amount for the balance sheet and (2) the highest cost of goods sold for the income statement?

(b)(2) Cost of goods sold:
FIFO $98,500
LIFO $111,200
Average $104,880

P6-3B   Lobster Company had a beginning inventory on January 1 of 150 units of Product BU-54 at a cost of $20 per unit. During the year, the following purchases were made.

Determine cost of goods sold and ending inventory, using FIFO, LIFO, and average-cost with analysis.

(SO 2, 3)

Mar. 15	400 units at $23	Sept. 4	350 units at $26
July 20	250 units at $24	Dec. 2	100 units at $29

1,000 units were sold. Lobster Company uses a periodic inventory system.

Instructions

(b)(2) Cost of goods sold:
FIFO $23,400
LIFO $24,900
Average $24,160

(a) Determine the cost of goods available for sale.

(b) Determine (1) the ending inventory, and (2) the cost of goods sold under each of the assumed cost flow methods (FIFO, LIFO, and average-cost). Prove the accuracy of the cost of goods sold under the FIFO and LIFO methods.

(c) Which cost flow method results in (1) the highest inventory amount for the balance sheet, and (2) the highest cost of goods sold for the income statement?

Compute ending inventory, prepare income statements, and answer questions using FIFO and LIFO.

(SO 2, 3)

P6-4B   The management of Moner Inc. is reevaluating the appropriateness of using its present inventory cost flow method, which is average-cost. The company requests your help in determining the results of operations for 2010 if either the FIFO or the LIFO method had been used. For 2010 the accounting records show these data:

Inventories		Purchases and Sales	
Beginning (8,000 units)	$16,000	Total net sales (180,000 units)	$747,000
Ending (18,000 units)		Total cost of goods purchased (190,000 units)	468,000

Purchases were made quarterly as follows.

Quarter	Units	Unit Cost	Total Cost
1	50,000	$2.20	$110,000
2	40,000	2.40	96,000
3	40,000	2.50	100,000
4	60,000	2.70	162,000
	190,000		$468,000

Operating expenses were $130,000, and the company's income tax rate is 40%.

Instructions

(a) Gross profit:
FIFO $311,600
LIFO $301,000

(a) Prepare comparative condensed income statements for 2010 under FIFO and LIFO. (Show computations of ending inventory.)

(b) ~~~~~~~~Answer the following questions for management.

  (1) Which cost flow method (FIFO or LIFO) produces the more meaningful inventory amount for the balance sheet? Why?

  (2) Which cost flow method (FIFO or LIFO) produces the more meaningful net income? Why?

  (3) Which cost flow method (FIFO or LIFO) is more likely to approximate the actual physical flow of goods? Why?

  (4) How much more cash will be available for management under LIFO than under FIFO? Why?

  (5) Will gross profit under the average-cost method be higher or lower than FIFO? Than LIFO? (*Note*: It is not necessary to quantify your answer.)

Calculate ending inventory, cost of goods sold, gross profit, and gross profit rate under periodic method; compare results.

(SO 2, 3)

P6-5B   You are provided with the following information for Web Inc. for the month ended June 30, 2010. Web uses the periodic method for inventory.

Date	Description	Quantity	Unit Cost or Selling Price
June 1	Beginning inventory	40	$40
June 4	Purchase	135	44
June 10	Sale	110	70
June 11	Sale return	15	70
June 18	Purchase	55	46
June 18	Purchase return	10	46
June 25	Sale	65	75
June 28	Purchase	30	50

Instructions

(a) Calculate (i) ending inventory, (ii) cost of goods sold, (iii) gross profit, and (iv) gross profit rate under each of the following methods.

    (1) LIFO.   **(2)** FIFO.   **(3)** Average-cost.

(b) Compare results for the three cost flow assumptions.

(a)(iii) Gross profit:
   LIFO $4,215
   FIFO $4,645
   Average $4,414.60

P6-6B   You are provided with the following information for Mondello Inc. Mondello Inc. uses the periodic method of accounting for its inventory transactions.

Compare specific identification, FIFO, and LIFO under periodic method; use cost flow assumption to justify price increase.

(SO 2, 3)

March 1	Beginning inventory 2,000 liters at a cost of 60¢ per liter.
March 3	Purchased 2,500 liters at a cost of 65¢ per liter.
March 5	Sold 2,200 liters for $1.05 per liter.
March 10	Purchased 4,000 liters at a cost of 72¢ per liter.
March 20	Purchased 2,500 liters at a cost of 80¢ per liter.
March 30	Sold 5,000 liters for $1.25 per liter.

Instructions

(a) Prepare partial income statements through gross profit, and calculate the value of ending inventory that would be reported on the balance sheet, under each of the following cost flow assumptions. Round ending Inventory and cost of goods sold to the nearest dollar.

  (1) Specific identification method assuming:

    (i) the March 5 sale consisted of 1,100 liters from the March 1 beginning inventory and 1,100 liters from the March 3 purchase; and

    (ii) the March 30 sale consisted of the following number of units sold from beginning inventory and each purchase: 450 liters from March 1; 550 liters from March 3; 2,900 liters from March 10; 1,100 liters from March 20.

  (2) FIFO.

  (3) LIFO.

(b) How can companies use a cost flow method to justify price increases? Which cost flow method would best support an argument to increase prices?

(a)(1) Gross profit:
  Specific identification
        $3,590

(2) FIFO $3,791
(3) LIFO $3,225

P6-7B   The management of Clare Co. asks your help in determining the comparative effects of the FIFO and LIFO inventory cost flow methods. For 2010, the accounting records show the following data.

Compute ending inventory, prepare income statements, and answer questions using FIFO and LIFO.

(SO 2, 3)

Inventory, January 1 (10,000 units)	$ 45,000
Cost of 100,000 units purchased	532,000
Selling price of 80,000 units sold	700,000
Operating expenses	140,000

Units purchased consisted of 35,000 units at $5.10 on May 10; 35,000 units at $5.30 on August 15; and 30,000 units at $5.60 on November 20. Income taxes are 30%.

Instructions

(a) Prepare comparative condensed income statements for 2010 under FIFO and LIFO. (Show computations of ending inventory.)

(b) ━━━Answer the following questions for management.

  (1) Which inventory cost flow method produces the most meaningful inventory amount for the balance sheet? Why?

  (2) Which inventory cost flow method produces the most meaningful net income? Why?

  (3) Which inventory cost flow method is most likely to approximate actual physical flow of the goods? Why?

  (4) How much additional cash will be available for management under LIFO than under FIFO? Why?

  (5) How much of the gross profit under FIFO is illusory in comparison with the gross profit under LIFO?

(a) Net income
   FIFO $105,700
   LIFO $91,000

P6-8B   Hector Inc. is a retailer operating in British Columbia. Hector uses the perpetual inventory method. All sales returns from customers result in the goods being returned to inventory; the inventory is not damaged. Assume that there are no credit transactions; all amounts are settled in cash. You are provided with the following information for Hector Inc. for the month of January 2010.

Calculate cost of goods sold and ending inventory under LIFO, FIFO, and average-cost under the perpetual system; compare gross profit under each assumption.

(SO 7)

Date	Description	Quantity	Unit Cost or Selling Price
January 1	Beginning inventory	100	$15
January 5	Purchase	150	18
January 8	Sale	110	28
January 10	Sale return	10	28
January 15	Purchase	55	20
January 16	Purchase return	5	20
January 20	Sale	80	32
January 25	Purchase	30	22

Instructions

Gross profit:
LIFO $2,020
FIFO $2,420
Average $2,272

(a) For each of the following cost flow assumptions, calculate (i) cost of goods sold, (ii) ending inventory, and (iii) gross profit.
    (1) LIFO.   **(2)** FIFO.   **(3)** Moving-average-cost.
(b) Compare results for the three cost flow assumptions.

Determine ending inventory under a perpetual inventory system.

(SO 7)

P6-9B   Fontana Co. began operations on July 1. It uses a perpetual inventory system. During July the company had the following purchases and sales.

	Purchases		
Date	Units	Unit Cost	Sales Units
July 1	5	$120	
July 6			4
July 11	7	$136	
July 14			3
July 21	8	$147	
July 27			6

Instructions

(a) Ending inventory
FIFO $1,029
Avg. $994
LIFO $958

(a) Determine the ending inventory under a perpetual inventory system using (1) FIFO, (2) moving-average cost, and (3) LIFO.
(b) Which costing method produces the highest ending inventory valuation?

Compute gross profit rate and inventory loss using gross profit method.

(SO 8)

P6-10B   O'Reilly Company lost all of its inventory in a fire on December 26, 2010. The accounting records showed the following gross profit data for November and December.

	November	December (to 12/26)
Net sales	$600,000	$700,000
Beginning inventory	32,000	36,000
Purchases	377,000	424,000
Purchase returns and allowances	13,300	14,900
Purchase discounts	8,500	9,500
Freight-in	8,800	9,900
Ending inventory	36,000	?

O'Reilly is fully insured for fire losses but must prepare a report for the insurance company.

Instructions

(a) Compute the gross profit rate for November.
(b) Using the gross profit rate for November, determine the estimated cost of the inventory lost in the fire.

Compute ending inventory using retail method.

(SO 8)

P6-11B   Fond du Lac Books uses the retail inventory method to estimate its monthly ending inventories. The following information is available for two of its departments at October 31, 2010.

	Hardcovers		Paperbacks	
	Cost	Retail	Cost	Retail
Beginning inventory	$ 420,000	$ 700,000	$ 280,000	$ 360,000
Purchases	2,135,000	3,200,000	1,155,000	1,540,000
Freight-in	24,000		12,000	
Purchase discounts	44,000		22,000	
Net sales		3,100,000		1,570,000

At December 31, Fond du Lac Books takes a physical inventory at retail. The actual retail values of the inventories in each department are Hardcovers $790,000 and Paperbacks $335,000.

Instructions

(a) Determine the estimated cost of the ending inventory for each department at **October 31**, 2010, using the retail inventory method.

(b) Compute the ending inventory at cost for each department at **December 31**, assuming the cost-to-retail ratios for the year are 65% for hardcovers and 75% for paperbacks.

PROBLEMS: SET C

Visit the book's companion website at **www.wiley.com/college/weygandt**, and choose the Student Companion site, to access Problem Set C.

CONTINUING COOKIE CHRONICLE

(*Note:* This is a continuation of the Cookie Chronicle from Chapters 1 through 5.)

CCC6 Natalie is busy establishing both divisions of her business (cookie classes and mixer sales) and completing her business degree. Her goals for the next 11 months are to sell one mixer per month and to give two to three classes per week.

The cost of the fine European mixers is expected to increase. Natalie has just negotiated new terms with Kzinski that include shipping costs in the negotiated purchase price (mixers will be shipped FOB destination). Natalie must choose a cost flow assumption for her mixer inventory.

Go to the book's companion website,
www.wiley.com/college/weygandt,
to see the completion of this problem.

BROADENING YOUR PERSPECTIVE

FINANCIAL REPORTING AND ANALYSIS

Financial Reporting Problem: PepsiCo, Inc.

BYP6-1 The notes that accompany a company's financial statements provide informative details that would clutter the amounts and descriptions presented in the statements. Refer to the financial statements of PepsiCo, Inc. and the Notes to Consolidated Financial Statements in Appendix A.

 PEPSICO

Instructions

Answer the following questions. Complete the requirements in millions of dollars, as shown in PepsiCo's annual report.

(a) What did PepsiCo report for the amount of inventories in its consolidated balance sheet at December 29, 2007? At December 30, 2006?

(b) Compute the dollar amount of change and the percentage change in inventories between 2006 and 2007. Compute inventory as a percentage of current assets at December 29, 2007.

(c) How does PepsiCo value its inventories? Which inventory cost flow method does PepsiCo use? (See Notes to the Financial Statements.)

(d) What is the cost of sales (cost of goods sold) reported by PepsiCo for 2007, 2006, and 2005? Compute the percentage of cost of sales to net sales in 2007.

Comparative Analysis Problem: PepsiCo, Inc. vs. The Coca-Cola Company

BYP6-2   PepsiCo's financial statements are presented in Appendix A. Financial statements of The Coca-Cola Company are presented in Appendix B.

Instructions

(a) Based on the information contained in these financial statements, compute the following 2007 ratios for each company.
  (1) Inventory turnover ratio
  (2) Days in inventory

(b) What conclusions concerning the management of the inventory can you draw from these data?

Exploring the Web

BYP6-3   A company's annual report usually will identify the inventory method used. Knowing that, you can analyze the effects of the inventory method on the income statement and balance sheet.

Address: www.cisco.com, or go to **www.wiley.com/college/weygandt**

Instructions

Answer the following questions based on the current year's Annual Report on Cisco's Web site.

(a) At Cisco's fiscal year-end, what was the inventory on the balance sheet?
(b) How has this changed from the previous fiscal year-end?
(c) How much of the inventory was finished goods?
(d) What inventory method does Cisco use?

CRITICAL THINKING

Decision Making Across the Organization

BYP6-4   On April 10, 2010, fire damaged the office and warehouse of Inwood Company. Most of the accounting records were destroyed, but the following account balances were determined as of March 31, 2010: Merchandise Inventory, January 1, 2010, $80,000; Sales (January 1–March 31, 2010), $180,000; Purchases (January 1–March 31, 2010) $94,000.

The company's fiscal year ends on December 31. It uses a periodic inventory system.

From an analysis of the April bank statement, you discover cancelled checks of $4,200 for cash purchases during the period April 1–10. Deposits during the same period totaled $18,500. Of that amount, 60% were collections on accounts receivable, and the balance was cash sales.

Correspondence with the company's principal suppliers revealed $12,400 of purchases on account from April 1 to April 10. Of that amount, $1,600 was for merchandise in transit on April 10 that was shipped FOB destination.

Correspondence with the company's principal customers produced acknowledgments of credit sales totaling $37,000 from April 1 to April 10. It was estimated that $5,600 of credit sales will never be acknowledged or recovered from customers.

Inwood Company reached an agreement with the insurance company that its fire-loss claim should be based on the average of the gross profit rates for the preceding 2 years. The financial statements for 2008 and 2009 showed the following data.

	2009	2008
Net sales	$600,000	$480,000
Cost of goods purchased	404,000	356,000
Beginning inventory	60,000	40,000
Ending inventory	80,000	60,000

Inventory with a cost of $17,000 was salvaged from the fire.

Instructions

With the class divided into groups, answer the following.

(a) Determine the balances in (1) Sales and (2) Purchases at April 10.
*(b) Determine the average profit rate for the years 2008 and 2009. (*Hint:* Find the gross profit rate for each year and divide the sum by 2.)
*(c) Determine the inventory loss as a result of the fire, using the gross profit method.

Communication Activity

BYP6-5   You are the controller of Small Toys Inc. Janice LeMay, the president, recently mentioned to you that she found an error in the 2009 financial statements which she believes has corrected itself. She determined, in discussions with the Purchasing Department, that 2009 ending inventory was overstated by $1 million. Janice says that the 2010 ending inventory is correct. Thus she assumes that 2010 income is correct. Janice says to you, "What happened has happened—there's no point in worrying about it anymore."

Instructions

You conclude that Janice is incorrect. Write a brief, tactful memo to Janice, clarifying the situation.

Ethics Case

BYP6-6   B. J. Ortiz Wholesale Corp. uses the LIFO method of inventory costing. In the current year, profit at B. J. Ortiz is running unusually high. The corporate tax rate is also high this year, but it is scheduled to decline significantly next year. In an effort to lower the current year's net income and to take advantage of the changing income tax rate, the president of B. J. Ortiz Wholesale instructs the plant accountant to recommend to the purchasing department a large purchase of inventory for delivery 3 days before the end of the year. The price of the inventory to be purchased has doubled during the year, and the purchase will represent a major portion of the ending inventory value.

Instructions

(a) What is the effect of this transaction on this year's and next year's income statement and income tax expense? Why?
(b) If B. J. Ortiz Wholesale had been using the FIFO method of inventory costing, would the president give the same directive?
(c) Should the plant accountant order the inventory purchase to lower income? What are the ethical implications of this order?

"All About You" Activity

BYP6-7   Some of the largest business frauds ever perpetrated have involved the misstatement of inventory. Two classics were at Leslie Fay Cos, and McKesson Corporation.

Instructions
There is considerable information regarding inventory frauds available on the Internet. Search for information about one of the two cases mentioned above, or inventory fraud at any other company, and prepare a short explanation of the nature of the inventory fraud.

Answers to Insight and Accounting Across the Organization Questions

p. 251 How Wal-Mart Tracks Inventory
Q: Why is inventory control important to managers such as those at Wal-Mart and Best Buy?
A: *In the very competitive environment of discount retailing, where Wal-Mart is the major player, small differences in price matter to the customer. Wal-Mart sells a high volume of inventory at a low gross profit rate. When operating in a high-volume, low-margin environment, small cost savings can mean the difference between being profitable or going out of business. The same holds true for Best Buy.*

p. 262 Is LIFO Fair?
Q: What are the arguments for and against the use of LIFO?
A: *Proponents of LIFO argue that it is conceptually superior because it matches the most recent cost with the most recent selling price. Critics contend that it artificially understates the company's net income and consequently reduces tax payments. Also, because most foreign companies are not allowed to use LIFO, its use by U.S. companies reduces the ability of investors to compare results across companies.*

Authors' Comments on *All About You*: Employee Theft—An Inside Job (p. 268)

Opinions regarding video technology differ greatly. One chief operating officer of a pub and restaurant chain says his company considers them "Big Brother-ish and demeaning." However, others feel that they are sometimes the only effective option. When properly implemented, theft-reduction procedures don't need to offend employees or customers. Wal-Mart has long employed senior citizens as greeters at its stores. Many people don't realize that these "greeters" are actually part of Wal-Mart's anti-shoplifting efforts.

Also, the need for video cameras depends, in part, on the nature of the product. In business environments where the inventory is of lower value, and/or not easily stolen, other techniques can be effective. However, in the case of expensive inventory items that can be easily concealed (such as expensive bottles of wine), reliance on video surveillance may be necessary.

Answers to Self-Study Questions

1. a **2.** b **3.** b **4.** c **5.** d **6.** d **7.** c **8.** d **9.** d **10.** b **11.** b **12.** d **13.** b
*14. b ***15.** d

Chapter 7

Accounting Information Systems

Feature Story

QUICKBOOKS® HELPS THIS RETAILER SELL GUITARS

Starting a small business requires many decisions. For example, you have to decide where to locate, how much space you need, how much inventory to have, how many employees to hire, and where to advertise. Small business owners are typically so concerned about the product and sales side of their business that they often do not give enough thought to something that is critical to their success—how to keep track of financial results.

Small business owners today can choose either manual or computerized accounting systems. For example, Paul and Laura West are the owners of the first independent dealership of Carvin guitars and professional audio equipment. When they founded their company, in Sacramento, California, they decided to purchase a computerized accounting system that would integrate many aspects of their retail operations. They wanted their accounting software to manage their inventory of guitars and amplifiers, ring up sales, record and report financial data, and process credit card and debit card transactions. They evaluated a number of options and chose QuickBooks® by Intuit Inc.

QuickBooks®, like most other popular software packages, has programs designed for the needs of a specific business, which in this case is retailing. This QuickBooks® retailing package automatically collects sales information from its point-of-sale scanning devices. It also keeps track of inventory levels and automatically generates purchase orders for popular items when re-order points are reached. It even supports sales efforts by compiling a customer database from which the Wests send out targeted direct mailings to potential customers. The computerized system enables data files to be emailed to the company's accountant. This keeps costs down and makes it easier and more efficient to generate financial reports as needed. The Wests believe that the investment in the computerized system has saved them time and money and allowed them to spend more time on other aspects of their business.

Source: Intuit Inc., "QuickBooks® and ProAdvisor® Help Make Guitar Store a Hit," *Journal of Accountancy*, May 2006, p. 101.

 ✓ The Navigator

Inside Chapter 7...

As you see from the Feature Story, a reliable information system is a necessity for any company. Whether companies use pen, pencil, or computers in maintaining accounting records, certain principles and procedures apply. The purpose of this chapter is to explain and illustrate these features.

The content and organization of Chapter 7 are as follows.

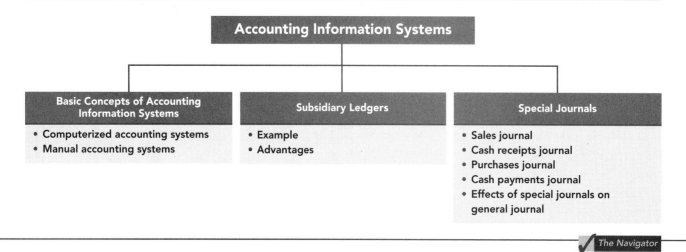

Accounting Information Systems

Basic Concepts of Accounting Information Systems	Subsidiary Ledgers	Special Journals
• Computerized accounting systems • Manual accounting systems	• Example • Advantages	• Sales journal • Cash receipts journal • Purchases journal • Cash payments journal • Effects of special journals on general journal

✓ *The Navigator*

BASIC CONCEPTS OF ACCOUNTING INFORMATION SYSTEMS

STUDY OBJECTIVE 1

Identify the basic concepts of an accounting information system.

The **accounting information system** collects and processes transaction data and communicates financial information to decision makers. It includes each of the steps in the accounting cycle that you studied in earlier chapters. It also includes the documents that provide evidence of the transactions, and the records, trial balances, worksheets, and financial statements that result. An **accounting system** may be either manual or computerized. Most businesses these days use some sort of computerized accounting system, whether it is an off-the-shelf system for small businesses, like QuickBooks or Peachtree, or a more complex custom-made system.

Efficient and effective accounting information systems are based on certain basic principles. These principles, as described in Illustration 7-1 (page 303), are: (1) cost effectiveness, (2) usefulness, and (3) flexibility. If the accounting system is cost effective, provides useful output, and has the flexibility to meet future needs, it can contribute to both individual and organizational goals.

Computerized Accounting Systems

Many small businesses eventually replace their manual accounting system with a computerized general ledger accounting system. **General ledger accounting systems** are software programs that integrate the various accounting functions related to sales, purchases, receivables, payables, cash receipts and disbursements, and payroll. They also generate financial statements. Computerized systems have a number of advantages over manual systems. First, the company typically enters data only once in a computerized system. Second, because the computer does most steps automatically, many errors resulting from human intervention in a manual system,

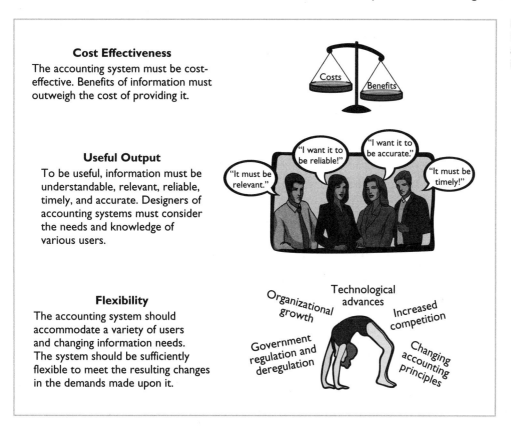

Illustration 7-1
Principles of an efficient
and effective accounting
information system

such as errors in posting or preparation of financial statements, are eliminated. Computerized systems also provide information up-to-the-minute. More timely information results in better business decisions. Many different general ledger software packages are available.

CHOOSING A SOFTWARE PACKAGE

To identify the right software for your business, you must understand your company's operations. For example, consider its needs with regard to inventory, billing, payroll, and cash management. In addition, the company might have specific needs that are not supported by all software systems. For example, you might want to track employees' hours on individual jobs or to extract information for determining sales commissions. Choosing the right system is critical because installation of even a basic system is time-consuming, and learning a new system will require many hours of employee time.

ENTRY-LEVEL SOFTWARE

Software publishers tend to classify businesses into groups based on revenue and the number of employees. Companies with revenues of less than $5 million and up to 20 employees generally use **entry-level programs**. The two leading entry-level programs are Intuit's QuickBooks and Sage Software's Peachtree. These programs control more than 90% of the market. Each of these entry-level programs comes in many different industry-specific versions. For example, some are designed for very specific industry applications such as restaurants, retailing, construction, manufacturing, or nonprofit. *(Both QuickBooks and Peachtree, as well as this textbook's general ledger system, can be used in working many of the problems in this textbook.)*

Quality entry-level packages typically involve more than recording transactions and preparing financial statements. Here are some common features and benefits:

- **Easy data access and report preparation.** Users can easily access information related to specific customers or suppliers. For example, you can view all transactions, invoices, payments, as well as contact information for a specific client.

- **Audit trail.** As a result of the Sarbanes-Oxley Act, companies are now far more concerned that their accounting system minimizes opportunities for fraud. Many programs provide an "audit trail" that enables the tracking of all transactions.

> **ETHICS NOTE**
>
> Entire books and movies have used computer-system tampering as a major theme. Most programmers would agree that tamper-proofing and debugging programs are the most difficult and time-consuming phases of their jobs.

- **Internal controls.** Some systems have an internal accounting review that identifies suspicious transactions or likely mistakes such as wrong account numbers or duplicate transactions.

- **Customization.** This feature enables the company to create data fields specific to the needs of its business.

- **Network-compatibility.** Multiple users in the company can access the system at the same time.

ENTERPRISE RESOURCE PLANNING SYSTEMS

Enterprise resource planning (ERP) systems are typically used by manufacturing companies with more than 500 employees and $500 million in sales. The best-known of these systems are SAP (the most widely used) by SAP AG, J.D. Edwards' ERP, and Oracle's Financials. ERP systems go far beyond the functions of an entry-level general ledger package. They integrate all aspects of the organization, including accounting, sales, human resource management, and manufacturing. Because of the complexity of an ERP system, implementation can take three years and cost five times as much as the purchase price of the system. Purchase and implementation of ERP systems can cost from $250,000 to as much as $50 million for the largest multinational corporations.

ETHICS INSIGHT

Curbing Fraudulent Activity with Software

The Sarbanes-Oxley Act (SOX) requires that companies demonstrate that they have adequate controls in place to detect significant fraudulent behavior by employees. As of November 2005 about 15% of publicly traded companies reported at least one material weakness in their controls that needed to be remedied.

The SOX requirements have created a huge market for software that can monitor and trace every recorded transaction and adjusting entry. This enables companies to pinpoint *who* used the accounting system and *when* they used it. These systems also require "electronic signatures" by employees for all significant transactions. Such signatures verify that employees have followed all required procedures, and that all actions are properly authorized. SOX-related technology spending was estimated to be approximately $2 billion in 2005. One firm that specializes in compliance software had 10 clients prior to SOX and 250 after SOX.

Source: W. M. Bulkeley and C. Forelle, "Anti-Crime Program: How Corporate Scandals Gave Tech Firms a New Business Line," *Wall Street Journal,* December 9, 2005, p. A1.

? Why might this software help reduce fraudulent activity by employees?

Manual Accounting Systems

Manual accounting systems perform each of the steps in the accounting cycle by hand. For example, someone manually enters each accounting transaction in the journal and manually posts each to the ledger. Other manual computations must be made to obtain ledger account balances and to prepare a trial balance and financial statements. In the remainder of this chapter, we illustrate the use of a manual system.

You might be wondering, "Why cover manual accounting systems if the real world uses computerized systems?" First, small businesses still abound. Most of them begin operations with manual accounting systems and convert to computerized systems as the business grows. You may work in a small business, or start your own someday, so it is useful to know how a manual system works. Second, to understand what computerized accounting systems do, you also need to understand manual accounting systems.

The manual accounting system represented in the first six chapters of this textbook is satisfactory in a company with a low volume of transactions. However, in most companies, it is necessary to add additional ledgers and journals to the accounting system to record transaction data efficiently.

SUBSIDIARY LEDGERS

Imagine a business that has several thousand charge (credit) customers and shows the transactions with these customers in only one general ledger account—Accounts Receivable. It would be nearly impossible to determine the balance owed by an individual customer at any specific time. Similarly, the amount payable to one creditor would be difficult to locate quickly from a single Accounts Payable account in the general ledger.

STUDY OBJECTIVE 2

Describe the nature and purpose of a subsidiary ledger.

Instead, companies use subsidiary ledgers to keep track of individual balances. A **subsidiary ledger** is a group of accounts with a common characteristic (for example, all accounts receivable). It is an addition to, and an expansion of, the general ledger. The subsidiary ledger frees the general ledger from the details of individual balances.

Two common subsidiary ledgers are:

1. The **accounts receivable** (or **customers'**) **subsidiary ledger**, which collects transaction data of individual customers.

2. The **accounts payable** (or **creditors'**) **subsidiary ledger**, which collects transaction data of individual creditors.

In each of these subsidiary ledgers, companies usually arrange individual accounts in alphabetical order.

A general ledger account summarizes the detailed data from a subsidiary ledger. For example, the detailed data from the accounts receivable subsidiary ledger are summarized in Accounts Receivable in the general ledger. The general ledger account that summarizes subsidiary ledger data is called a **control account**. Illustration 7-2 (page 306) presents an overview of the relationship of subsidiary ledgers to the general ledger. There, the general ledger control accounts and subsidiary ledger accounts are in green. Note that cash and owner's capital in this illustration are not control accounts because there are no subsidiary ledger accounts related to these accounts.

At the end of an accounting period, each general ledger control account balance must equal the composite balance of the individual accounts in the related subsidiary ledger. For example, the balance in Accounts Payable in Illustration 7-2 must equal the total of the subsidiary balances of Creditors X + Y + Z.

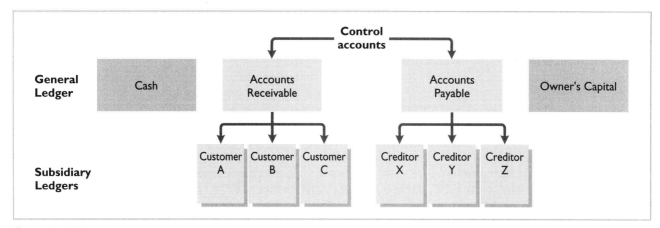

Illustration 7-2
Relationship of general
ledger and subsidiary ledgers

Subsidiary Ledger Example

Illustration 7-3 provides an example of a control account and subsidiary ledger for
Pujols Enterprises. (Due to space considerations, the explanation column in these
accounts is not shown in this and subsequent illustrations.) Illustration 7-3 is based
on the transactions listed in Illustration 7-4.

Illustration 7-3
Relationship between gen-
eral and subsidiary ledgers

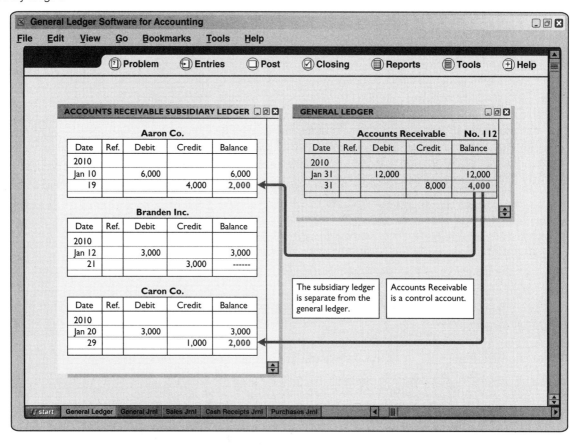

Illustration 7-4
Sales and collection
transactions

Credit Sales			Collections on Account		
Jan. 10	Aaron Co.	$ 6,000	Jan. 19	Aaron Co.	$ 4,000
12	Branden Inc.	3,000	21	Branden Inc.	3,000
20	Caron Co.	3,000	29	Caron Co.	1,000
		$12,000			$ 8,000

Pujols can reconcile the total debits ($12,000) and credits ($8,000) in Accounts Receivable in the general ledger to the detailed debits and credits in the subsidiary accounts. Also, the balance of $4,000 in the control account agrees with the total of the balances in the individual accounts (Aaron Co. $2,000 + Branden Inc. $0 + Caron Co. $2,000) in the subsidiary ledger.

As Illustration 7-3 shows, companies make monthly postings to the control accounts in the general ledger. This practice allows them to prepare monthly financial statements. Companies post to the individual accounts in the subsidiary ledger daily. Daily posting ensures that account information is current. This enables the company to monitor credit limits, bill customers, and answer inquiries from customers about their account balances.

Advantages of Subsidiary Ledgers

Subsidiary ledgers have several advantages:

1. **They show in a single account transactions affecting one customer or one creditor**, thus providing up-to-date information on specific account balances.
2. **They free the general ledger of excessive details.** As a result, a trial balance of the general ledger does not contain vast numbers of individual account balances.
3. **They help locate errors in individual accounts** by reducing the number of accounts in one ledger and by using control accounts.
4. **They make possible a division of labor** in posting. One employee can post to the general ledger while someone else posts to the subsidiary ledgers.

ACCOUNTING ACROSS THE ORGANIZATION

"I'm John Smith, a.k.a. 13695071642"

Rather than relying on customer or creditor names in a subsidiary ledger, a computerized system expands the account number of the control account in a prespecified manner. For example, if Accounts Receivable was numbered 10010, the first account in the accounts receivable subsidiary ledger might be numbered 10010–0001. Most systems allow inquiries about specific accounts in the subsidiary ledger (by account number) or about the control account. With the latter, the system would automatically total all the subsidiary accounts whenever an inquiry to the control account was made.

? Why use numbers to identify names in a computerized system?

DO IT!

Presented below is information related to Sims Company for its first month of operations. Determine the balances that appear in the accounts payable subsidiary ledger. What Accounts Payable balance appears in the general ledger at the end of January?

SUBSIDIARY LEDGERS

Credit Purchases			Cash Paid		
Jan. 5	Devon Co.	$11,000	Jan. 9	Devon Co.	$7,000
11	Shelby Co.	7,000	14	Shelby Co.	2,000
22	Taylor Co.	14,000	27	Taylor Co.	9,000

action plan

✔ Subtract cash paid from credit purchases to determine the balances in the accounts payable subsidiary ledger.

✔ Sum the individual balances to determine the Accounts Payable balance.

Solution

Subsidiary ledger balances:

Devon Co. $4,000 ($11,000 − $7,000)

Shelby Co. $5,000 ($7,000 − $2,000)

Taylor Co. $5,000 ($14,000 − $9,000)

General ledger Accounts Payable balance: $14,000 ($4,000 + $5,000 + $5,000)

Related exercise material: **BE7-4, BE7-5, E7-1, E7-2, E7-4, E7-5,** and **DO IT!** **7-1.**

SPECIAL JOURNALS

STUDY OBJECTIVE 3

Explain how companies use special journals in journalizing.

So far you have learned to journalize transactions in a two-column general journal and post each entry to the general ledger. This procedure is satisfactory in only the very smallest companies. To expedite journalizing and posting, most companies use special journals **in addition to the general journal**.

Companies use **special journals** to record similar types of transactions. Examples are all sales of merchandise on account, or all cash receipts. The types of transactions that occur frequently in a company determine what special journals the company uses. Most merchandising enterprises record daily transactions using the journals shown in Illustration 7-5.

Illustration 7-5
Use of special journals and the general journal

Sales Journal	Cash Receipts Journal	Purchases Journal	Cash Payments Journal	General Journal
Used for:	Used for:	Used for:	Used for:	Used for:
All sales of merchandise on account	All cash received (including cash sales)	All purchases of merchandise on account	All cash paid (including cash purchases)	Transactions that cannot be entered in a special journal, including correcting, adjusting, and closing entries

If a transaction cannot be recorded in a special journal, the company records it in the general journal. For example, if a company had special journals for only the four types of transactions listed above, it would record purchase returns and allowances in the general journal. Similarly, **correcting, adjusting, and closing entries are recorded in the general journal**. In some situations, companies might use special journals other than those listed above. For example, when sales returns and allowances are frequent, a company might use a special journal to record these transactions.

Special journals **permit greater division of labor** because several people can record entries in different journals at the same time. For example, one employee may journalize all cash receipts, and another may journalize all credit sales. Also, the use of special journals **reduces the time needed to complete the posting process.** With special journals, companies may post some accounts monthly, instead of daily, as we will illustrate later in the chapter. On the following pages, we discuss the four special journals shown in Illustration 7-5.

Sales Journal

In the sales journal, companies record **sales of merchandise on account**. Cash sales of merchandise go in the cash receipts journal. Credit sales of assets other than merchandise go in the general journal.

JOURNALIZING CREDIT SALES

To demonstrate use of a sales journal, we will use data for Karns Wholesale Supply, which uses a **perpetual inventory system**. Under this system, each entry in the sales journal results in one entry **at selling price** and another entry **at cost**. The entry at selling price is a debit to Accounts Receivable (a control account) and a credit of equal amount to Sales. The entry at cost is a debit to Cost of Goods Sold and a credit of equal amount to Merchandise Inventory (a control account). Using a sales journal with two amount columns, the company can show on only one line a sales transaction at both selling price and cost. Illustration 7-6 shows this two-column sales journal of Karns Wholesale Supply, using assumed credit sales transactions (for sales invoices 101–107).

HELPFUL HINT

Postings are also made daily to individual ledger accounts in the inventory subsidiary ledger to maintain a perpetual inventory.

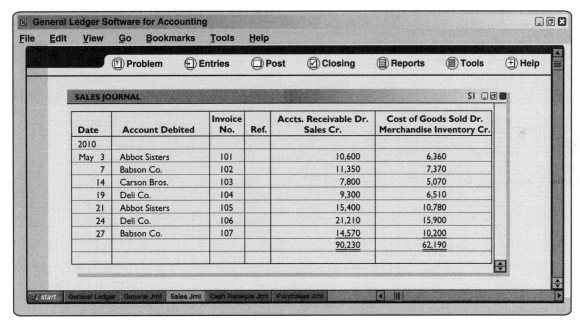

Illustration 7-6
Journalizing the sales journal—perpetual inventory system

Date	Account Debited	Invoice No.	Ref.	Accts. Receivable Dr. Sales Cr.	Cost of Goods Sold Dr. Merchandise Inventory Cr.
2010					
May 3	Abbot Sisters	101		10,600	6,360
7	Babson Co.	102		11,350	7,370
14	Carson Bros.	103		7,800	5,070
19	Deli Co.	104		9,300	6,510
21	Abbot Sisters	105		15,400	10,780
24	Deli Co.	106		21,210	15,900
27	Babson Co.	107		14,570	10,200
				90,230	62,190

Note that, unlike the general journal, an explanation is not required for each entry in a special journal. Also, note that use of prenumbered invoices ensures that all invoices are journalized. Finally, note that the reference (Ref.) column is not used in journalizing. It is used in posting the sales journal, as explained in the next section.

POSTING THE SALES JOURNAL

Companies make daily postings from the sales journal **to the individual accounts receivable** in the subsidiary ledger. Posting **to the general ledger** is done **monthly**. Illustration 7-7 shows both the daily and monthly postings.

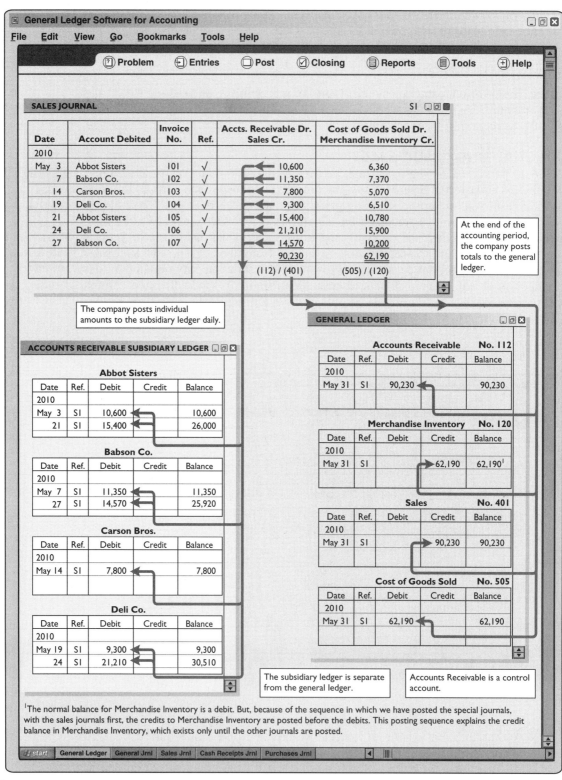

Illustration 7-7
Posting the sales journal

A check mark (✓) is inserted in the reference posting column to indicate that the daily posting to the customer's account has been made. If the subsidiary ledger accounts were numbered, the account number would be entered in place of the check mark. At the end of the month, Karns posts the column totals of the sales journal to the general ledger. Here, the column totals are as follows: From the selling-price column, a debit of $90,230 to Accounts Receivable (account No. 112), and a credit of $90,230 to Sales (account No. 401). From the cost column, a debit of $62,190 to Cost of Goods Sold (account No. 505), and a credit of $62,190 to Merchandise Inventory (account No. 120). Karns inserts the account numbers below the column totals to indicate that the postings have been made. In both the general ledger and subsidiary ledger accounts, the reference **S1** indicates that the posting came from page 1 of the sales journal.

PROVING THE LEDGERS

The next step is to "prove" the ledgers. To do so, Karns must determine two things: (1) The total of the general ledger debit balances must equal the total of the general ledger credit balances. (2) The sum of the subsidiary ledger balances must equal the balance in the control account. Illustration 7-8 shows the proof of the postings from the sales journal to the general and subsidiary ledger.

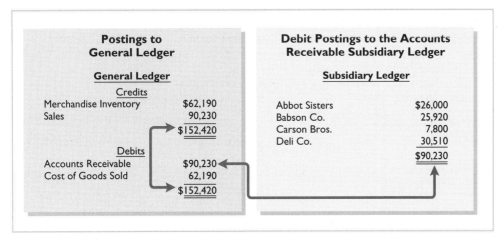

Illustration 7-8
Proving the equality of the postings from the sales journal

ADVANTAGES OF THE SALES JOURNAL

The use of a special journal to record sales on account has a number of advantages. First, the one-line entry for each sales transaction saves time. In the sales journal, it is not necessary to write out the four account titles for each transaction. Second, only totals, rather than individual entries, are posted to the general ledger. This saves posting time and reduces the possibilities of errors in posting. Finally, a division of labor results, because one individual can take responsibility for the sales journal.

Cash Receipts Journal

In the **cash receipts journal**, companies record all receipts of cash. The most common types of cash receipts are cash sales of merchandise and collections of accounts receivable. Many other possibilities exist, such as receipt of money from bank loans and cash proceeds from disposal of equipment. A one- or two-column cash receipts journal would not have space enough for all possible cash receipt transactions. Therefore, companies use a multiple-column cash receipts journal.

Generally, a cash receipts journal includes the following columns: debit columns for Cash and Sales Discounts, and credit columns for Accounts Receivable, Sales, and "Other" accounts. Companies use the "Other Accounts" category when the cash receipt does not involve a cash sale or a collection of accounts receivable. Under a perpetual inventory system, each sales entry also is accompanied by an entry that debits Cost of Goods Sold and credits Merchandise Inventory for the cost of the merchandise sold. Illustration 7-9 (page 313) shows a six-column cash receipts journal.

Companies may use additional credit columns if these columns significantly reduce postings to a specific account. For example, a loan company, such as Household International, receives thousands of cash collections from customers. Using separate credit columns for Loans Receivable and Interest Revenue, rather than the Other Accounts credit column, would reduce postings.

JOURNALIZING CASH RECEIPTS TRANSACTIONS

To illustrate the journalizing of cash receipts transactions, we will continue with the May transactions of Karns Wholesale Supply. Collections from customers relate to the entries recorded in the sales journal in Illustration 7-6. The entries in the cash receipts journal are based on the following cash receipts.

May   1   D. A. Karns makes an investment of $5,000 in the business.
        7   Cash sales of merchandise total $1,900 (cost, $1,240).
      10   Received a check for $10,388 from Abbot Sisters in payment of invoice No. 101 for $10,600 less a 2% discount.
      12   Cash sales of merchandise total $2,600 (cost, $1,690).
      17   Received a check for $11,123 from Babson Co. in payment of invoice No. 102 for $11,350 less a 2% discount.
      22   Received cash by signing a note for $6,000.
      23   Received a check for $7,644 from Carson Bros. in full for invoice No. 103 for $7,800 less a 2% discount.
      28   Received a check for $9,114 from Deli Co. in full for invoice No. 104 for $9,300 less a 2% discount.

Further information about the columns in the cash receipts journal is listed below.

Debit Columns:

1. **Cash.** Karns enters in this column the amount of cash actually received in each transaction. The column total indicates the total cash receipts for the month.

2. **Sales Discounts.** Karns includes a Sales Discounts column in its cash receipts journal. By doing so, it does not need to enter sales discount items in the general journal. As a result, the cash receipts journal shows on one line the collection of an account receivable within the discount period.

Credit Columns:

3. **Accounts Receivable.** Karns uses the Accounts Receivable column to record cash collections on account. The amount entered here is the amount to be credited to the individual customer's account.

4. **Sales.** The Sales column records all cash sales of merchandise. Cash sales of other assets (plant assets, for example) are not reported in this column.

5. **Other Accounts.** Karns uses the Other Accounts column whenever the credit is other than to Accounts Receivable or Sales. For example, in the first entry, Karns enters $5,000 as a credit to D. A. Karns, Capital. This column is often referred to as the sundry accounts column.

Debit and Credit Column:

6. **Cost of Goods Sold and Merchandise Inventory.** This column records debits to Cost of Goods Sold and credits to Merchandise Inventory.

HELPFUL HINT

When is an account title entered in the "Account Credited" column of the cash receipts journal? Answer: A *subsidiary ledger* account is entered when the entry involves a collection of accounts receivable. A *general ledger* account is entered when the account is not shown in a special column (and an amount must be entered in the Other Accounts column). Otherwise, no account is shown in the "Account Credited" column.

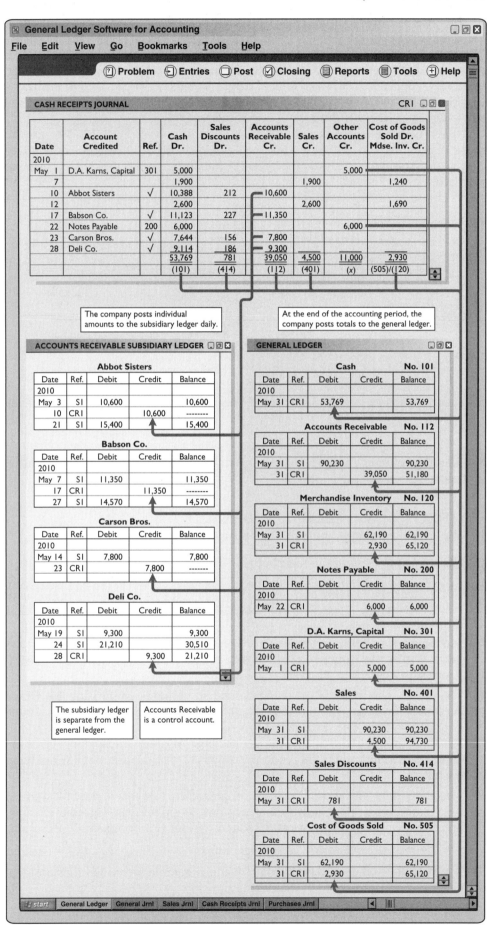

Illustration 7-9
Journalizing and posting the cash receipts journal

In a multi-column journal, generally only one line is needed for each entry. Debit and credit amounts for each line must be equal. When Karns journalizes the collection from Abbot Sisters on May 10, for example, three amounts are indicated. Note also that the Account Credited column identifies both general ledger and subsidiary ledger account titles. General ledger accounts are illustrated in the May 1 and May 22 entries. A subsidiary account is illustrated in the May 10 entry for the collection from Abbot Sisters.

When Karns has finished journalizing a multi-column journal, it totals the amount columns and compares the totals to prove the equality of debits and credits. Illustration 7-10 shows the proof of the equality of Karns's cash receipts journal.

Illustration 7-10
Proving the equality of the cash receipts journal

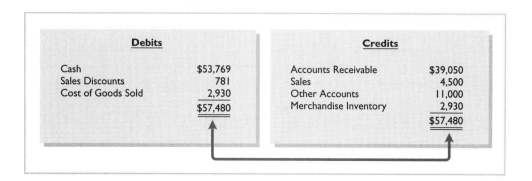

Debits		Credits	
Cash	$53,769	Accounts Receivable	$39,050
Sales Discounts	781	Sales	4,500
Cost of Goods Sold	2,930	Other Accounts	11,000
	$57,480	Merchandise Inventory	2,930
			$57,480

Totaling the columns of a journal and proving the equality of the totals is called **footing** and **cross-footing** a journal.

POSTING THE CASH RECEIPTS JOURNAL

Posting a multi-column journal involves the following steps.

1. **At the end of the month**, the company posts all column totals, except for the Other Accounts total, to the account title(s) specified in the column heading (such as Cash or Accounts Receivable). The company then enters account numbers below the column totals to show that they have been posted. For example, Karns has posted cash to account No. 101, accounts receivable to account No. 112, merchandise inventory to account No. 120, sales to account No. 401, sales discounts to account No. 414, and cost of goods sold to account No. 505.

2. The company **separately posts the individual amounts comprising the Other Accounts total** to the general ledger accounts specified in the Account Credited column. See, for example, the credit posting to D. A. Karns, Capital. The total amount of this column has not been posted. The symbol (X) is inserted below the total to this column to indicate that the amount has not been posted.

3. The individual amounts in a column, posted in total to a control account (Accounts Receivable, in this case), are posted **daily to the subsidiary ledger** account specified in the Account Credited column. See, for example, the credit posting of $10,600 to Abbot Sisters.

The symbol **CR**, used in both the subsidiary and general ledgers, identifies postings from the cash receipts journal.

PROVING THE LEDGERS

After posting of the cash receipts journal is completed, Karns proves the ledgers. As shown in Illustration 7-11, the general ledger totals agree. Also, the sum of the subsidiary ledger balances equals the control account balance.

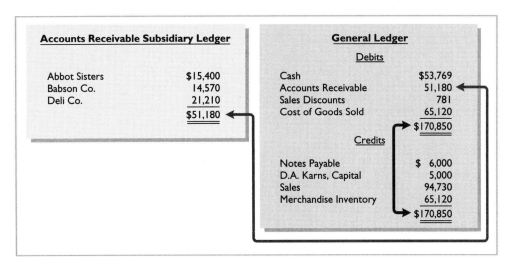

Illustration 7-11
Proving the ledgers after posting the sales and the cash receipts journals

Purchases Journal

In the **purchases journal**, companies record all purchases of merchandise on account. Each entry in this journal results in a debit to Merchandise Inventory and a credit to Accounts Payable. Illustration 7-13 (on page 316) shows the purchases journal for Karns Wholesale Supply.

When using a one-column purchases journal (as in Illustration 7-13), a company cannot journalize other types of purchases on account or cash purchases in it. For example, in the purchases journal in Illustration 7-13, Karns would have to record credit purchases of equipment or supplies in the general journal. Likewise, all cash purchases would be entered in the cash payments journal. As illustrated later, companies that make numerous credit purchases for items other than merchandise often expand the purchases journal to a multi-column format. (See Illustration 7-15 on page 317.)

JOURNALIZING CREDIT PURCHASES OF MERCHANDISE

The journalizing procedure is similar to that for a sales journal. Companies make entries in the purchases journal from purchase invoices. In contrast to the sales journal, the purchases journal may not have an invoice number column, because invoices received from different suppliers will not be in numerical sequence. To ensure that they record all purchase invoices, some companies consecutively number each invoice upon receipt and then use an internal document number column in the purchases journal. The entries for Karns Wholesale Supply are based on the assumed credit purchases listed in Illustration 7-12.

Date	Supplier	Amount
5/6	Jasper Manufacturing Inc.	$11,000
5/10	Eaton and Howe Inc.	7,200
5/14	Fabor and Son	6,900
5/19	Jasper Manufacturing Inc.	17,500
5/26	Fabor and Son	8,700
5/29	Eaton and Howe Inc.	12,600

Illustration 7-12
Credit purchases transactions

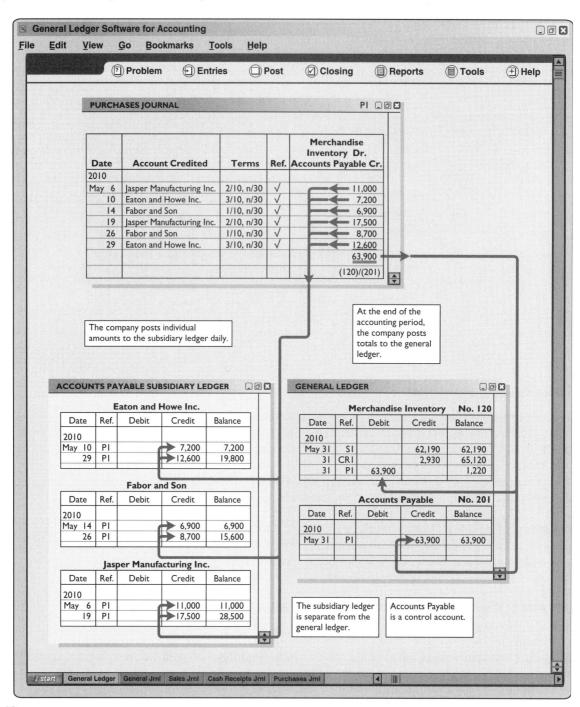

Illustration 7-13
Journalizing and posting the
purchases journal

POSTING THE PURCHASES JOURNAL

The procedures for posting the purchases journal are similar to those for the sales journal. In this case, Karns makes **daily** postings to the **accounts payable ledger**; it makes **monthly** postings to Merchandise Inventory and Accounts Payable in the general ledger. In both ledgers, Karns uses **P1** in the reference column to show that the postings are from page 1 of the purchases journal.

Proof of the equality of the postings from the purchases journal to both ledgers is shown in Illustration 7-14.

HELPFUL HINT

Postings to subsidiary ledger accounts are done daily because it is often necessary to know a current balance for the subsidiary accounts.

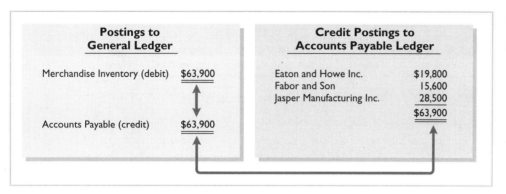

Illustration 7-14
Proving the equality of the
purchases journal

EXPANDING THE PURCHASES JOURNAL

As noted earlier, some companies expand the purchases journal to include all types of purchases on account. Instead of one column for merchandise inventory and accounts payable, they use a multiple-column format. This format usually includes a credit column for Accounts Payable and debit columns for purchases of Merchandise Inventory, Office Supplies, Store Supplies, and Other Accounts. Illustration 7-15 shows a multi-column purchases journal for Hanover Co. The posting procedures are similar to those shown earlier for posting the cash receipts journal.

HELPFUL HINT

A single-column purchases
journal needs only to be
footed to prove the
equality of debits and
credits.

Illustration 7-15
Multi-column purchases
journal

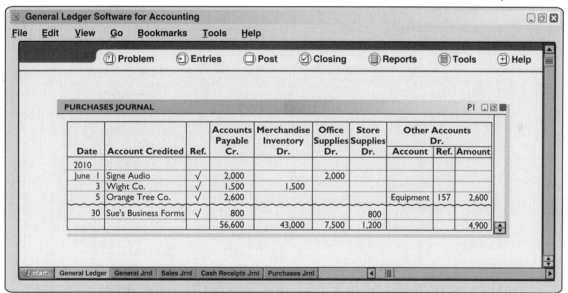

Cash Payments Journal

In a **cash payments (cash disbursements) journal**, companies record all disbursements of cash. Entries are made from prenumbered checks. Because companies make cash payments for various purposes, the cash payments journal has multiple columns. Illustration 7-16 (page 318) shows a four-column journal.

JOURNALIZING CASH PAYMENTS TRANSACTIONS

The procedures for journalizing transactions in this journal are similar to those for the cash receipts journal. Karns records each transaction on one line, and for each line there must be equal debit and credit amounts. The entries in the cash payments

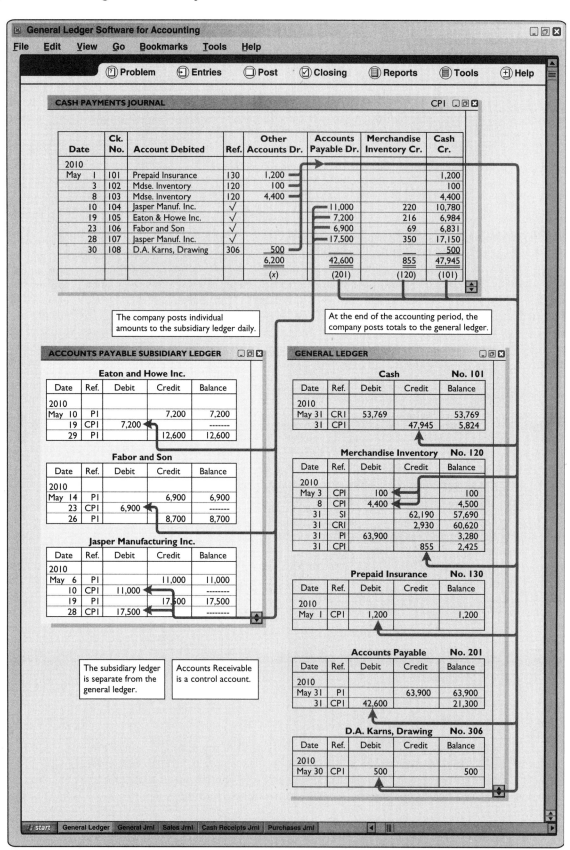

Illustration 7-16
Journalizing and posting the
cash payments journal

journal in Illustration 7-16 are based on the following transactions for Karns Wholesale Supply.

May 1 Issued check No. 101 for $1,200 for the annual premium on a fire insurance policy.
     3 Issued check No. 102 for $100 in payment of freight when terms were FOB shipping point.
     8 Issued check No. 103 for $4,400 for the purchase of merchandise.
    10 Sent check No. 104 for $10,780 to Jasper Manufacturing Inc. in payment of May 6 invoice for $11,000 less a 2% discount.
    19 Mailed check No. 105 for $6,984 to Eaton and Howe Inc. in payment of May 10 invoice for $7,200 less a 3% discount.
    23 Sent check No. 106 for $6,831 to Fabor and Son in payment of May 14 invoice for $6,900 less a 1% discount.
    28 Sent check No. 107 for $17,150 to Jasper Manufacturing Inc. in payment of May 19 invoice for $17,500 less a 2% discount.
    30 Issued check No. 108 for $500 to D. A. Karns as a cash withdrawal for personal use.

Note that whenever Karns enters an amount in the Other Accounts column, it must identify a specific general ledger account in the Account Debited column. The entries for checks No. 101, 102, 103, and 108 illustrate this situation. Similarly, Karns must identify a subsidiary account in the Account Debited column whenever it enters an amount in the Accounts Payable column. See, for example, the entry for check No. 104.

After Karns journalizes the cash payments journal, it totals the columns. The totals are then balanced to prove the equality of debits and credits.

POSTING THE CASH PAYMENTS JOURNAL

The procedures for posting the cash payments journal are similar to those for the cash receipts journal. Karns posts the amounts recorded in the Accounts Payable column individually to the subsidiary ledger and in total to the control account. It posts Merchandise Inventory and Cash only in total at the end of the month. Transactions in the Other Accounts column are posted individually to the appropriate account(s) affected. The company does not post totals for the Other Accounts column.

Illustration 7-16 shows the posting of the cash payments journal. Note that Karns uses the symbol **CP** as the posting reference. After postings are completed, the company proves the equality of the debit and credit balances in the general ledger. In addition, the control account balances should agree with the subsidiary ledger total balance. Illustration 7-17 shows the agreement of these balances.

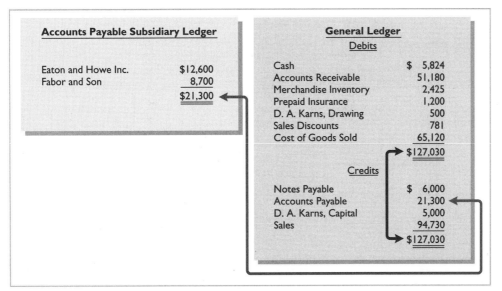

Illustration 7-17
Proving the ledgers after postings from the sales, cash receipts, purchases, and cash payments journals

Effects of Special Journals on the General Journal

Special journals for sales, purchases, and cash substantially reduce the number of entries that companies make in the general journal. **Only transactions that cannot be entered in a special journal are recorded in the general journal.** For example, a company may use the general journal to record such transactions as granting of credit to a customer for a sales return or allowance, granting of credit from a supplier for purchases returned, acceptance of a note receivable from a customer, and purchase of equipment by issuing a note payable. Also, **correcting, adjusting, and closing entries are made in the general journal.**

The general journal has columns for date, account title and explanation, reference, and debit and credit amounts. When control and subsidiary accounts are not involved, the procedures for journalizing and posting of transactions are the same as those described in earlier chapters. When control and subsidiary accounts *are* involved, companies make two changes from the earlier procedures:

1. In **journalizing**, they identify both the control and the subsidiary accounts.

2. In **posting**, there must be a **dual posting**: once to the control account and once to the subsidiary account.

To illustrate, assume that on May 31, Karns Wholesale Supply returns $500 of merchandise for credit to Fabor and Son. Illustration 7-18 shows the entry in the general journal and the posting of the entry. Note that if Karns receives cash instead of credit on this return, then it would record the transaction in the cash receipts journal.

Illustration 7-18
Journalizing and posting the general journal

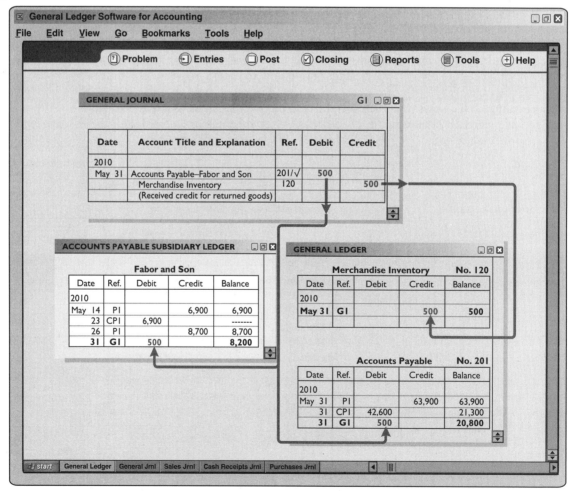

Note that the general journal indicates two accounts (Accounts Payable, and Fabor and Son) for the debit, and two postings ("201/✓") in the reference column. One debit is posted to the control account and another debit to the creditor's account in the subsidiary ledger.

DO IT!

Swisher Company had the following transactions during March.

SPECIAL JOURNALS

1. Collected cash on account from Oakland Company.
2. Purchased equipment by signing a note payable.
3. Sold merchandise on account.
4. Purchased merchandise on account.
5. Paid $2,400 for a 2-year insurance policy.

Identify the journal in which each of the transactions above is recorded.

action plan

✔ Determine if the transaction involves the receipt of cash (cash receipts journal) or the payment of cash (cash payments journal).

Solution

1. Collected cash on account from Oakland Company.	Cash receipts journal
2. Purchased equipment by signing a note payable.	General journal
3. Sold merchandise on account.	Sales journal
4. Purchased merchandise on account.	Purchases journal
5. Paid $2,400 for a 2-year insurance policy.	Cash payments journal

✔ Determine if the transaction is a sale of merchandise on account (sales journal) or a purchase of merchandise on account (purchases journal).

✔ All other transactions are recorded in the general journal.

Related exercise material: **BE7-6, BE7-7, BE7-8, BE7-9, E7-6, E7-7, E7-8, E7-10**, and **DO IT!** 7-2.

Comprehensive DO IT!

Cassandra Wilson Company uses a six-column cash receipts journal with the following columns:

Cash (Dr.)	Other Accounts (Cr.)
Sales Discounts (Dr.)	Cost of Goods Sold (Dr.) and
Accounts Receivable (Cr.)	Merchandise Inventory (Cr.)
Sales (Cr.)	

Cash receipts transactions for the month of July 2010 are as follows.

July	3	Cash sales total $5,800 (cost, $3,480).
	5	Received a check for $6,370 from Jeltz Company in payment of an invoice dated June 26 for $6,500, terms 2/10, n/30.
	9	Cassandra Wilson, the proprietor, made an additional investment of $5,000 in cash in the business.
	10	Cash sales total $12,519 (cost, $7,511).
	12	Received a check for $7,275 from R. Eliot & Co. in payment of a $7,500 invoice dated July 3, terms 3/10, n/30.
	15	Received a customer advance of $700 cash for future sales.
	20	Cash sales total $15,472 (cost, $9,283).
	22	Received a check for $5,880 from Beck Company in payment of $6,000 invoice dated July 13, terms 2/10, n/30.
	29	Cash sales total $17,660 (cost, $10,596).
	31	Received cash of $200 on interest earned for July.

action plan

✔ Record all cash receipts in the cash receipts journal.

✔ The "account credited" indicates items posted individually to the subsidiary ledger or to the general ledger.

✔ Record cash sales in the cash receipts journal—not in the sales journal.

✔ The total debits must equal the total credits.

Instructions

(a) Journalize the transactions in the cash receipts journal.

(b) Contrast the posting of the Accounts Receivable and Other Accounts columns.

Solution to Comprehensive **DO IT!**

(a)

CASSANDRA WILSON COMPANY

Cash Receipts Journal CR1

Date	Account Credited	Ref.	Cash Dr.	Sales Discounts Dr.	Accounts Receivable Cr.	Sales Cr.	Other Accounts Cr.	Cost of Goods Sold Dr. Mdse. Inv. Cr.
2010								
7/3			5,800			5,800		3,480
5	Jeltz Company		6,370	130	6,500			
9	C. Wilson, Capital		5,000				5,000	
10			12,519			12,519		7,511
12	R. Eliot & Co.		7,275	225	7,500			
15	Unearned Revenue		700				700	
20			15,472			15,472		9,283
22	Beck Company		5,880	120	6,000			
29			17,660			17,660		10,596
31	Interest Revenue		200				200	
			76,876	475	20,000	51,451	5,900	30,870

(b) The Accounts Receivable column total is posted as a credit to Accounts Receivable. The individual amounts are credited to the customers' accounts identified in the Account Credited column, which are maintained in the accounts receivable subsidiary ledger.

The amounts in the Other Accounts column are posted individually. They are credited to the account titles identified in the Account Credited column.

SUMMARY OF STUDY OBJECTIVES

1 Identify the basic concepts of an accounting information system. The basic principles in developing an accounting information system are cost effectiveness, useful output, and flexibility. Most companies use a computerized accounting system. Smaller companies use entry-level software such as QuickBooks or Peachtree. Larger companies use custom-made software packages which often integrate all aspects of the organization.

2 Describe the nature and purpose of a subsidiary ledger. A subsidiary ledger is a group of accounts with a common characteristic. It facilitates the recording process by freeing the general ledger from details of individual balances.

3 Explain how companies use special journals in journalizing. Companies use special journals to group similar types of transactions. In a special journal, generally only one line is used to record a complete transaction.

4 Indicate how companies post a multi-column journal. In posting a multi-column journal:
(a) Companies post all column totals except for the Other Accounts column once at the end of the month to the account title specified in the column heading.
(b) Companies do not post the total of the Other Accounts column. Instead, the individual amounts comprising the total are posted separately to the general ledger accounts specified in the Account Credited (Debited) column.
(c) The individual amounts in a column posted in total to a control account are posted daily to the subsidiary ledger accounts specified in the Account Credited (Debited) column.

GLOSSARY

Accounting information system A system that collects and processes transaction data, and communicates financial information to decision makers. (p. 302).

Accounts payable (creditors') subsidiary ledger A subsidiary ledger that collects transaction data of individual creditors. (p. 305).

Accounts receivable (customers') subsidiary ledger A subsidiary ledger that collects transaction data of individual customers. (p. 305).

Cash payments (disbursements) journal A special journal that records all cash paid. (p. 317).

Cash receipts journal A special journal that records all cash received. (p. 311).

Control account An account in the general ledger that summarizes subsidiary ledger. (p. 305).

Manual accounting system A system in which someone performs each of the steps in the accounting cycle by hand. (p. 305).

Purchases journal A special journal that records all purchases of merchandise on account. (p. 315).

Sales journal A special journal that records all sales of merchandise on account. (p. 309).

Special journal A journal that records similar types of transactions, such as all credit sales. (p. 308).

Subsidiary ledger A group of accounts with a common characteristic. (p. 305).

SELF-STUDY QUESTIONS

Answers are at the end of the chapter.

(SO 1) **1.** The basic principles of an accounting information system include all of the following *except*:
    a. cost effectiveness.
    b. flexibility.
    c. useful output.
    d. periodicity.

(SO 1) **2.** Which of the following is *not* an advantage of computerized accounting systems?
    a. Data is entered only once in computerized accounting systems.
    b. Computerized accounting systems provide up-to-date information.
    c. Computerized accounting systems eliminate entering of transaction information.
    d. Computerized accounting systems eliminate many errors resulting from human intervention.

(SO 2) **3.** Which of the following is *incorrect* concerning subsidiary ledgers?
    a. The purchases ledger is a common subsidiary ledger for creditor accounts.
    b. The accounts receivable ledger is a subsidiary ledger.
    c. A subsidiary ledger is a group of accounts with a common characteristic.
    d. An advantage of the subsidiary ledger is that it permits a division of labor in posting.

(SO 2) **4.** Two common subsidiary ledgers are:
    a. accounts receivable and cash receipts.
    b. accounts payable and cash payments.
    c. accounts receivable and accounts payable.
    d. sales and cost of goods sold.

(SO 2) **5.** At the beginning of the month, the accounts receivable subsidiary ledger showed balances for Apple Company $5,000 and Berry Company $7,000. During the month, credit sales were made to Apple $6,000, Berry $4,500, and Cantaloupe $8,500. Cash was collected on account from Berry $11,500 and Cantaloupe $3,000. At the end of the month, the control account Accounts Receivable in the general ledger should have a balance of:
    a. $11,000.
    b. $12,000.
    c. $16,500.
    d. $31,000.

6. A sales journal will be used for: (SO 3)

	Credit Sales	Cash Sales	Sales Discounts
a.	no	yes	yes
b.	yes	no	yes
c.	yes	no	no
d.	yes	yes	no

7. A purchase of equipment on account is recorded in the: (SO 3)
    a. cash receipts journal.
    b. purchases journal.
    c. cash payments journal.
    d. general journal.

8. A purchase of equipment using cash is recorded in the: (SO 3)
    a. cash receipts journal.
    b. purchases journal.
    c. cash payments journal.
    d. general journal.

9. Which of the following statements is *correct*? (SO 3, 4)
    a. The sales discount column is included in the cash receipts journal.
    b. The purchases journal records all purchases of merchandise whether for cash or on account.
    c. The cash receipts journal records sales on account.
    d. Merchandise returned by the buyer is recorded by the seller in the purchases journal.

(SO 4) **10.** Dotel Company's cash receipts journal includes an Accounts Receivable column and an Other Accounts column. At the end of the month, these columns are posted to the general ledger as:

	Accounts Receivable	Other Accounts
a.	a column total	a column total
b.	individual amounts	a column total
c.	individual amounts	individual amounts
d.	a column total	individual amounts

(SO 4) **11.** Which of the following is *incorrect* concerning the posting of the cash receipts journal?
   a. The total of the Other Accounts column is not posted.
   b. All column totals except the total for the Other Accounts column are posted once at the end of the month to the account title(s) specified in the column heading.
   c. The totals of all columns are posted daily to the accounts specified in the column heading.
   d. The individual amounts in a column posted in total to a control account are posted daily to the subsidiary ledger account specified in the Account Credited column.

(SO 4) **12.** Postings from the purchases journal to the subsidiary ledger are generally made:
   a. yearly.
   b. monthly.
   c. weekly.
   d. daily.

13. Which statement is *incorrect* regarding the general journal? (SO 3)
   a. Only transactions that cannot be entered in a special journal are recorded in the general journal.
   b. Dual postings are always required in the general journal.
   c. The general journal may be used to record acceptance of a note receivable in payment of an account receivable.
   d. Correcting, adjusting, and closing entries are made in the general journal.

14. When companies use special journals: (SO 3)
   a. they record all purchase transactions in the purchases journal.
   b. they record all cash received, except from cash sales, in the cash receipts journal.
   c. they record all cash disbursements in the cash payments journal.
   d. a general journal is not necessary.

15. If a customer returns goods for credit, the selling company (SO 3) normally makes an entry in the:
   a. cash payments journal.
   b. sales journal.
   c. general journal.
   d. cash receipts journal.

Go to the book's companion website, **www.wiley.com/college/weygandt**, for Additional Self-Study questions.

The Navigator

QUESTIONS

1. (a) What is an accounting information system? (b) "An accounting information system applies only to a manual system." Do you agree? Explain.

2. Certain principles should be followed in the development of an accounting information system. Identify and explain each of the principles.

3. What are common features of computerized accounting packages beyond recording transactions and preparing financial statements?

4. How does an enterprise resource planning (ERP) system differ from an entry-level computerized accounting system?

5. What are the advantages of using subsidiary ledgers?

6. (a) When do companies normally post to (1) the subsidiary accounts and (2) the general ledger control accounts? (b) Describe the relationship between a control account and a subsidiary ledger.

7. Identify and explain the four special journals discussed in the chapter. List an advantage of using each of these journals rather than using only a general journal.

8. Thogmartin Company uses special journals. It recorded in a sales journal a sale made on account to R. Peters for $435. A few days later, R. Peters returns $70 worth of merchandise for credit. Where should Thogmartin Company record the sales return? Why?

9. A $500 purchase of merchandise on account from Lore Company was properly recorded in the purchases

journal. When posted, however, the amount recorded in the subsidiary ledger was $50. How might this error be discovered?

10. Why would special journals used in different businesses not be identical in format? What type of business would maintain a cash receipts journal but not include a column for accounts receivable?

11. The cash and the accounts receivable columns in the cash receipts journal were mistakenly overadded by $4,000 at the end of the month. (a) Will the customers' ledger agree with the Accounts Receivable control account? (b) Assuming no other errors, will the trial balance totals be equal?

12. One column total of a special journal is posted at month-end to only two general ledger accounts. One of these two accounts is Accounts Receivable. What is the name of this special journal? What is the other general ledger account to which that same month-end total is posted?

13. In what journal would the following transactions be recorded? (Assume that a two-column sales journal and a single-column purchases journal are used.)
   (a) Recording of depreciation expense for the year.
   (b) Credit given to a customer for merchandise purchased on credit and returned.
   (c) Sales of merchandise for cash.
   (d) Sales of merchandise on account.
   (e) Collection of cash on account from a customer.
   (f) Purchase of office supplies on account.

14. In what journal would the following transactions be recorded? (Assume that a two-column sales journal and a single-column purchases journal are used.)
- **(a)** Cash received from signing a note payable.
- **(b)** Investment of cash by the owner of the business.
- **(c)** Closing of the expense accounts at the end of the year.
- **(d)** Purchase of merchandise on account.
- **(e)** Credit received for merchandise purchased and returned to supplier.
- **(f)** Payment of cash on account due a supplier.

15. What transactions might be included in a multiple-column purchases journal that would not be included in a single-column purchases journal?

16. Give an example of a transaction in the general journal that causes an entry to be posted twice (i.e., to two accounts), one in the general ledger, the other in the subsidiary ledger. Does this affect the debit/credit equality of the general ledger?

17. Give some examples of appropriate general journal transactions for an organization using special journals.

BRIEF EXERCISES

BE7-1   Indicate whether each of the following statements is true or false.

1. When designing an accounting system, we need to think about the needs and knowledge of both the top managers and various other users.
2. When the environment changes as a result of technological advances, increased competition, or government regulation, an accounting system does not have to be sufficiently flexible to meet the changes in order to save money.
3. In developing an accounting system, cost is relevant. The benefits obtained from the information disseminated must outweigh the cost of providing it.

Identify basic concepts of an accounting information system.
(SO 1)

BE7-2   Here is a list of words or phrases related to computerized accounting systems.

1. Entry-level software.
2. Enterprise resource planning systems.
3. Network-compatible.
4. Audit trail.
5. Internal control.

Identify basic concepts of an accounting information system.
(SO 1)

Instructions

Match each word or phrase with the best description of it.

_____**(a)** Allows multiple users to access the system at the same time.

_____**(b)** Enables the tracking of all transactions.

_____**(c)** Identifies suspicious transactions or likely mistakes such as wrong account numbers or duplicate transactions.

_____**(d)** Large-scale computer systems that integrate all aspects of the organization including accounting, sales, human resource management, and manufacturing.

_____**(e)** System for companies with revenues of less than $5 million and up to 20 employees.

BE7-3   Beka Borke has prepared the following list of statements about accounting information systems.

1. The accounting information system includes each of the steps of the accounting cycle, the documents that provide evidence of transactions that have occurred, and the accounting records.
2. The benefits obtained from information provided by the accounting information system need not outweigh the cost of providing that information.
3. Designers of accounting systems must consider the needs and knowledge of various users.
4. If an accounting information system is cost-effective and provides useful output, it does not need to be flexible.

Identify basic concepts of an accounting information system.
(SO 1)

Instructions

Identify each statement as true or false. If false, indicate how to correct the statement.

BE7-4   Presented below is information related to Kienholz Company for its first month of operations. Identify the balances that appear in the accounts receivable subsidiary ledger and the accounts receivable balance that appears in the general ledger at the end of January.

Identify subsidiary ledger balances.
(SO 2)

Credit Sales			Cash Collections		
Jan. 7	Agler Co.	$10,000	Jan. 17	Agler Co.	$7,000
15	Barto Co.	6,000	24	Barto Co.	4,000
23	Maris Co.	9,000	29	Maris Co.	9,000

Identify subsidiary ledger accounts.

(SO 2)

BE7-5 Identify in what ledger (general or subsidiary) each of the following accounts is shown.

1. Rent Expense
2. Accounts Receivable—Char
3. Notes Payable
4. Accounts Payable—Thebeau

Identify special journals.

(SO 3)

BE7-6 Identify the journal in which each of the following transactions is recorded.

1. Cash sales
2. Owner withdrawal of cash
3. Cash purchase of land
4. Credit sales
5. Purchase of merchandise on account
6. Receipt of cash for services performed

Identify entries to cash receipts journal.

(SO 3)

BE7-7 Indicate whether each of the following debits and credits is included in the cash receipts journal. (Use "Yes" or "No" to answer this question.)

1. Debit to Sales
2. Credit to Merchandise Inventory
3. Credit to Accounts Receivable
4. Debit to Accounts Payable

Identify transactions for special journals.

(SO 3)

BE7-8 Galindo Co. uses special journals and a general journal. Identify the journal in which each of the following transactions is recorded.

(a) Purchased equipment on account.
(b) Purchased merchandise on account.
(c) Paid utility expense in cash.
(d) Sold merchandise on account.

Identify transactions for special journals.

(SO 3)

BE7-9 Identify the special journal(s) in which the following column headings appear.

1. Sales Discounts Dr.
2. Accounts Receivable Cr.
3. Cash Dr.
4. Sales Cr.
5. Merchandise Inventory Dr.

Indicate postings to cash receipts journal.

(SO 4)

BE7-10 Kidwell Computer Components Inc. uses a multi-column cash receipts journal. Indicate which column(s) is/are posted only in total, only daily, or both in total and daily.

1. Accounts Receivable
2. Sales Discounts
3. Cash
4. Other Accounts

DO IT! REVIEW

Determine subsidiary and general ledger balances.

(SO 2)

DO IT! 7-1 Presented below is information related to City Company for its first month of operations. Determine the balances that appear in the accounts payable subsidiary ledger. What Accounts Payable balance appears in the general ledger at the end of January?

Credit Purchases			Cash Paid		
Jan. 6	Eli Company	$ 9,000	Jan. 11	Eli Company	$ 6,500
Jan. 10	Teddy Company	12,000	Jan. 16	Teddy Company	12,000
Jan. 23	U-2 Company	10,000	Jan. 29	U-2 Company	7,700

Identify special journals.

(SO 3)

DO IT! 7-2 Nick Company had the following transactions during April.

1. Sold merchandise on account.
2. Purchased merchandise on account.
3. Collected cash from a sale to Athletic Company.
4. Recorded accrued interest on a note payable.
5. Paid $2,000 for supplies.

Identify the journal in which each of the transactions above is recorded.

E7-1 Donahue Company uses both special journals and a general journal as described in this chapter. On June 30, after all monthly postings had been completed, the Accounts Receivable control account in the general ledger had a debit balance of $320,000; the Accounts Payable control account had a credit balance of $77,000.

    The July transactions recorded in the special journals are summarized below. No entries affecting accounts receivable and accounts payable were recorded in the general journal for July.

Sales journal	Total sales $161,400
Purchases journal	Total purchases $56,400
Cash receipts journal	Accounts receivable column total $131,000
Cash payments journal	Accounts payable column total $47,500

Instructions
(a) What is the balance of the Accounts Receivable control account after the monthly postings on July 31?
(b) What is the balance of the Accounts Payable control account after the monthly postings on July 31?
(c) To what account(s) is the column total of $161,400 in the sales journal posted?
(d) To what account(s) is the accounts receivable column total of $131,000 in the cash receipts journal posted?

Determine control account balances, and explain posting of special journals.
(SO 2, 4)

E7-2 Presented below is the subsidiary accounts receivable account of Jeremy Dody.

Date	Ref.	Debit	Credit	Balance
2010				
Sept. 2	S31	61,000		61,000
9	G4		14,000	47,000
27	CR8		47,000	—

Instructions
 Write a memo to Andrea Barden, chief financial officer, that explains each transaction.

Explain postings to subsidiary ledger.
(SO 2)

E7-3 On September 1 the balance of the Accounts Receivable control account in the general ledger of Seaver Company was $10,960. The customers' subsidiary ledger contained account balances as follows: Ruiz $1,440, Kingston $2,640, Bannister $2,060, Crampton $4,820. At the end of September the various journals contained the following information.

Sales journal: Sales to Crampton $800; to Ruiz $1,260; to Iman $1,330; to Bannister $1,100.
Cash receipts journal: Cash received from Bannister $1,310; from Crampton $2,300; from Iman $380; from Kingston $1,800; from Ruiz $1,240.
General journal: An allowance is granted to Crampton $220.

Instructions
(a) Set up control and subsidiary accounts and enter the beginning balances. Do not construct the journals.
(b) Post the various journals. Post the items as individual items or as totals, whichever would be the appropriate procedure. (No sales discounts given.)
(c) Prepare a list of customers and prove the agreement of the controlling account with the subsidiary ledger at September 30, 2010.

Post various journals to control and subsidiary accounts.
(SO 2, 4)

E7-4 Yu Suzuki Company has a balance in its Accounts Receivable control account of $11,000 on January 1, 2010. The subsidiary ledger contains three accounts: Smith Company, balance $4,000; Green Company, balance $2,500; and Koyan Company. During January, the following receivable-related transactions occurred.

	Credit Sales	Collections	Returns
Smith Company	$9,000	$8,000	$ -0-
Green Company	7,000	2,500	3,000
Koyan Company	8,500	9,000	-0-

Determine control and subsidiary ledger balances for accounts receivable.
(SO 2)

Instructions

(a) What is the January 1 balance in the Koyan Company subsidiary account?

(b) What is the January 31 balance in the control account?

(c) Compute the balances in the subsidiary accounts at the end of the month.

(d) Which January transaction would not be recorded in a special journal?

Determine control and
subsidiary ledger balances
for accounts payable.

(SO 2)

E7-5   Nobo Uematsu Company has a balance in its Accounts Payable control account of $8,250 on January 1, 2010. The subsidiary ledger contains three accounts: Jones Company, balance $3,000; Brown Company, balance $1,875; and Aatski Company. During January, the following payable-related transactions occurred.

	Purchases	Payments	Returns
Jones Company	$6,750	$6,000	$ -0-
Brown Company	5,250	1,875	2,250
Aatski Company	6,375	6,750	-0-

Instructions

(a) What is the January 1 balance in the Aatski Company subsidiary account?

(b) What is the January 31 balance in the control account?

(c) Compute the balances in the subsidiary accounts at the end of the month.

(d) Which January transaction would not be recorded in a special journal?

Record transactions in sales
and purchases journal.

(SO 2, 3)

E7-6   Montalvo Company uses special journals and a general journal. The following transactions occurred during September 2010.

Sept. 2   Sold merchandise on account to T. Hossfeld, invoice no. 101, $720, terms n/30. The cost of the merchandise sold was $420.

10   Purchased merchandise on account from L. Rincon $600, terms 2/10, n/30.

12   Purchased office equipment on account from R. Press $6,500.

21   Sold merchandise on account to P. Lowther, invoice no. 102 for $800, terms 2/10, n/30. The cost of the merchandise sold was $480.

25   Purchased merchandise on account from W. Barone $860, terms n/30.

27   Sold merchandise to S. Miller for $700 cash. The cost of the merchandise sold was $400.

Instructions

(a) Prepare a sales journal (see Illustration 7-7) and a single-column purchase journal (see Illustration 7-13). (Use page 1 for each journal.)

(b) Record the transaction(s) for September that should be journalized in the sales journal and the purchases journal.

Record transactions in cash
receipts and cash payments
journal.

(SO 2, 3)

E7-7   Pherigo Co. uses special journals and a general journal. The following transactions occurred during May 2010.

May 1   I. Pherigo invested $50,000 cash in the business.

2   Sold merchandise to B. Sherrick for $6,300 cash. The cost of the merchandise sold was $4,200.

3   Purchased merchandise for $7,200 from J. DeLeon using check no. 101.

14   Paid salary to H. Potter $700 by issuing check no. 102.

16   Sold merchandise on account to K. Kimbell for $900, terms n/30. The cost of the merchandise sold was $630.

22   A check of $9,000 is received from M. Moody in full for invoice 101; no discount given.

Instructions

(a) Prepare a multiple-column cash receipts journal (see Illustration 7-9) and a multiple-column cash payments journal (see Illustration 7-16). (Use page 1 for each journal.)

(b) Record the transaction(s) for May that should be journalized in the cash receipts journal and cash payments journal.

Explain journalizing in cash
journals.

(SO 3)

E7-8   Wick Company uses the columnar cash journals illustrated in the textbook. In April, the following selected cash transactions occurred.

1. Made a refund to a customer as an allowance for damaged goods.
2. Received collection from customer within the 3% discount period.
3. Purchased merchandise for cash.
4. Paid a creditor within the 3% discount period.
5. Received collection from customer after the 3% discount period had expired.

6. Paid freight on merchandise purchased.
7. Paid cash for office equipment.
8. Received cash refund from supplier for merchandise returned.
9. Withdrew cash for personal use of owner.
10. Made cash sales.

Instructions
Indicate **(a)** the journal, and **(b)** the columns in the journal that should be used in recording each transaction.

E7-9   Velasquez Company has the following selected transactions during March.

Journalize transactions in general journal and explain postings.
(SO 2, 4)

Mar. 2   Purchased equipment costing $9,400 from Chang Company on account.
       5   Received credit of $410 from Lyden Company for merchandise damaged in shipment to Velasquez.
       7   Issued credit of $400 to Higley Company for merchandise the customer returned. The returned merchandise had a cost of $260.

Velasquez Company uses a one-column purchases journal, a sales journal, the columnar cash journals used in the text, and a general journal.

Instructions
(a) Journalize the transactions in the general journal.
(b) ▬▬▬▬▶ In a brief memo to the president of Velasquez Company, explain the postings to the control and subsidiary accounts from each type of journal.

E7-10   Below are some typical transactions incurred by Kwun Company.

Indicate journalizing in special journals.
(SO 3)

1. Payment of creditors on account.
2. Return of merchandise sold for credit.
3. Collection on account from customers.
4. Sale of land for cash.
5. Sale of merchandise on account.
6. Sale of merchandise for cash.
7. Received credit for merchandise purchased on credit.
8. Sales discount taken on goods sold.
9. Payment of employee wages.
10. Income summary closed to owner's capital.
11. Depreciation on building.
12. Purchase of office supplies for cash.
13. Purchase of merchandise on account.

Instructions
For each transaction, indicate whether it would normally be recorded in a cash receipts journal, cash payments journal, sales journal, single-column purchases journal, or general journal.

E7-11   The general ledger of Sanchez Company contained the following Accounts Payable control account (in T-account form). Also shown is the related subsidiary ledger.

Explain posting to control account and subsidiary ledger.
(SO 2, 4)

GENERAL LEDGER

Accounts Payable

Feb. 15	General journal	1,400	Feb. 1	Balance	26,025
28	?	?	5	General journal	265
			11	General journal	550
			28	Purchases	13,400
			Feb. 28	Balance	9,500

ACCOUNTS PAYABLE LEDGER

Perez			**Tebbetts**		
	Feb. 28	Bal. 4,600		Feb. 28 Bal. ?	

Zerbe		
	Feb. 28	Bal. 2,300

Instructions

(a) Indicate the missing posting reference and amount in the control account, and the missing ending balance in the subsidiary ledger.

(b) Indicate the amounts in the control account that were dual-posted (i.e., posted to the control account and the subsidiary accounts).

Prepare purchases and general journals.
(SO 2, 3)

E7-12 Selected accounts from the ledgers of Lockhart Company at July 31 showed the following.

GENERAL LEDGER

Store Equipment — No. 153

Date	Explanation	Ref.	Debit	Credit	Balance
July 1		G1	3,900		3,900

Accounts Payable — No. 201

Date	Explanation	Ref.	Debit	Credit	Balance
July 1		G1		3,900	3,900
15		G1		400	4,300
18		G1	100		4,200
25		G1	200		4,000
31		P1		8,300	12,300

Merchandise Inventory — No. 120

Date	Explanation	Ref.	Debit	Credit	Balance
July 15		G1	400		400
18		G1		100	300
25		G1		200	100
31		P1	8,300		8,400

ACCOUNTS PAYABLE LEDGER

Albin Equipment Co.

Date	Explanation	Ref.	Debit	Credit	Balance
July 1		G1		3,900	3,900

Drago Co.

Date	Explanation	Ref.	Debit	Credit	Balance
July 14		P1		1,100	1,100
25		G1	200		900

Brian Co.

Date	Explanation	Ref.	Debit	Credit	Balance
July 3		P1		2,400	2,400
20		P1		700	3,100

Erik Co.

Date	Explanation	Ref.	Debit	Credit	Balance
July 12		P1		500	500
21		P1		600	1,100

Chacon Corp

Date	Explanation	Ref.	Debit	Credit	Balance
July 17		P1		1,400	1,400
18		G1	100		1,300
29		P1		1,600	2,900

Heinen Inc.

Date	Explanation	Ref.	Debit	Credit	Balance
July 15		G1		400	400

Instructions

From the data prepare:

(a) the single-column purchases journal for July.

(b) the general journal entries for July.

Determine correct posting amount to control account.
(SO 4)

E7-13 Kansas Products uses both special journals and a general journal as described in this chapter. Kansas also posts customers' accounts in the accounts receivable subsidiary ledger. The postings for the most recent month are included in the subsidiary T accounts below.

Bargo			
Bal.	340		250
	200		

Leary			
Bal.	150		150
	240		

Carol			
Bal.	–0–		145
	145		

Paul			
Bal.	120		120
	190		
	150		

Instructions

Determine the correct amount of the end-of-month posting from the sales journal to the Accounts Receivable control account.

E7-14 Selected account balances for Matisyahu Company at January 1, 2010, are presented below.

Compute balances in various accounts.

(SO 4)

Accounts Payable	$14,000
Accounts Receivable	22,000
Cash	17,000
Inventory	13,500

Matisyahu's sales journal for January shows a total of $100,000 in the selling price column, and its one-column purchases journal for January shows a total of $72,000.

The column totals in Matisyahu's cash receipts journal are: Cash Dr. $61,000; Sales Discounts Dr. $1,100; Accounts Receivable Cr. $45,000; Sales Cr. $6,000; and Other Accounts Cr. $11,100.

The column totals in Matisyahu's cash payments journal for January are: Cash Cr. $55,000; Inventory Cr. $1,000; Accounts Payable Dr. $46,000; and Other Accounts Dr. $10,000. Matisyahu's total cost of goods sold for January is $63,600.

Accounts Payable, Accounts Receivable, Cash, Inventory, and Sales are not involved in the "Other Accounts" column in either the cash receipts or cash payments journal, and are not involved in any general journal entries.

Instructions

Compute the January 31 balance for Matisyahu in the following accounts.
(a) Accounts Payable.
(b) Accounts Receivable.
(c) Cash.
(d) Inventory.
(e) Sales.

EXERCISES: SET B

Visit the book's companion website at **www.wiley.com/college/weygandt**, and choose the Student Companion site, to access Exercise Set B.

PROBLEMS: SET A

P7-1A Grider Company's chart of accounts includes the following selected accounts.

Journalize transactions in cash receipts journal; post to control account and subsidiary ledger.

(SO 2, 3, 4)

101 Cash	401 Sales
112 Accounts Receivable	414 Sales Discounts
120 Merchandise Inventory	505 Cost of Goods Sold
301 O. Grider, Capital	

On April 1 the accounts receivable ledger of Grider Company showed the following balances: Ogden $1,550, Chelsea $1,200, Eggleston Co. $2,900, and Baez $1,800. The April transactions involving the receipt of cash were as follows.

Apr. 1 The owner, O. Grider, invested additional cash in the business $7,200.
4 Received check for payment of account from Baez less 2% cash discount.
5 Received check for $920 in payment of invoice no. 307 from Eggleston Co.
8 Made cash sales of merchandise totaling $7,245. The cost of the merchandise sold was $4,347.
10 Received check for $600 in payment of invoice no. 309 from Ogden.
11 Received cash refund from a supplier for damaged merchandise $740.
23 Received check for $1,500 in payment of invoice no. 310 from Eggleston Co.
29 Received check for payment of account from Chelsea.

Instructions
(a) Journalize the transactions above in a six-column cash receipts journal with columns for Cash Dr., Sales Discounts Dr., Accounts Receivable Cr., Sales Cr., Other Accounts Cr., and Cost of Goods Sold Dr./Merchandise Inventory Cr. Foot and crossfoot the journal.
(b) Insert the beginning balances in the Accounts Receivable control and subsidiary accounts, and post the April transactions to these accounts.
(c) Prove the agreement of the control account and subsidiary account balances.

(a) Balancing totals $21,205

(c) Accounts Receivable $1,430

Journalize transactions in cash payments journal; post to control account and subsidiary ledgers.

(SO 2, 3, 4)

P7-2A Ming Company's chart of accounts includes the following selected accounts.

101	Cash	201	Accounts Payable
120	Merchandise Inventory	306	T. Ming, Drawing
130	Prepaid Insurance	505	Cost of Goods Sold
157	Equipment		

On October 1 the accounts payable ledger of Ming Company showed the following balances: Bovary Company $2,700, Nyman Co. $2,500, Pyron Co. $1,800, and Sims Company $3,700. The October transactions involving the payment of cash were as follows.

Oct. 1 Purchased merchandise, check no. 63, $300.
3 Purchased equipment, check no. 64, $800.
5 Paid Bovary Company balance due of $2,700, less 2% discount, check no. 65, $2,646.
10 Purchased merchandise, check no. 66, $2,250.
15 Paid Pyron Co. balance due of $1,800, check no. 67.
16 T. Ming, the owner, pays his personal insurance premium of $400, check no. 68.
19 Paid Nyman Co. in full for invoice no. 610, $1,600 less 2% cash discount, check no. 69, $1,568.
29 Paid Sims Company in full for invoice no. 264, $2,500, check no. 70.

Instructions

(a) Balancing totals $12,350

(a) Journalize the transactions above in a four-column cash payments journal with columns for Other Accounts Dr., Accounts Payable Dr., Merchandise Inventory Cr., and Cash Cr. Foot and crossfoot the journal.

(b) Insert the beginning balances in the Accounts Payable control and subsidiary accounts, and post the October transactions to these accounts.

(c) Accounts Payable $2,100

(c) Prove the agreement of the control account and the subsidiary account balances.

Journalize transactions in multi-column purchases journal; post to the general and subsidiary ledgers.

(SO 2, 3, 4)

P7-3A The chart of accounts of Lopez Company includes the following selected accounts.

112	Accounts Receivable	401	Sales
120	Merchandise Inventory	412	Sales Returns and Allowances
126	Supplies	505	Cost of Goods Sold
157	Equipment	610	Advertising Expense
201	Accounts Payable		

In July the following selected transactions were completed. All purchases and sales were on account. The cost of all merchandise sold was 70% of the sales price.

July 1 Purchased merchandise from Fritz Company $8,000.
2 Received freight bill from Wayward Shipping on Fritz purchase $400.
3 Made sales to Pinick Company $1,300, and to Wayne Bros. $1,500.
5 Purchased merchandise from Moon Company $3,200.
8 Received credit on merchandise returned to Moon Company $300.
13 Purchased store supplies from Cress Supply $720.
15 Purchased merchandise from Fritz Company $3,600 and from Anton Company $3,300.
16 Made sales to Sager Company $3,450 and to Wayne Bros. $1,570.
18 Received bill for advertising from Lynda Advertisements $600.
21 Sales were made to Pinick Company $310 and to Haddad Company $2,800.
22 Granted allowance to Pinick Company for merchandise damaged in shipment $40.
24 Purchased merchandise from Moon Company $3,000.
26 Purchased equipment from Cress Supply $900.
28 Received freight bill from Wayward Shipping on Moon purchase of July 24, $380.
30 Sales were made to Sager Company $5,600.

Instructions

(a) Purchases journal—
Accounts Payable $24,100
Sales column total $16,530

(a) Journalize the transactions above in a purchases journal, a sales journal, and a general journal. The purchases journal should have the following column headings: Date, Account Credited (Debited), Ref., Accounts Payable Cr., Merchandise Inventory Dr., and Other Accounts Dr.

(c) Accounts Receivable $16,490
Accounts Payable $23,800

(b) Post to both the general and subsidiary ledger accounts. (Assume that all accounts have zero beginning balances.)

(c) Prove the agreement of the control and subsidiary accounts.

Journalize transactions in special journals.

(SO 2, 3, 4)

P7-4A Selected accounts from the chart of accounts of Boyden Company are shown below.

101	Cash	120	Merchandise Inventory
112	Accounts Receivable	126	Supplies

157	Equipment	414	Sales Discounts
201	Accounts Payable	505	Cost of Goods Sold
401	Sales	726	Salaries Expense
412	Sales Returns and Allowances		

The cost of all merchandise sold was 60% of the sales price. During January, Boyden completed the following transactions.

Jan.	3	Purchased merchandise on account from Wortham Co. $10,000.
	4	Purchased supplies for cash $80.
	4	Sold merchandise on account to Milam $5,250, invoice no. 371, terms 1/10, n/30.
	5	Returned $300 worth of damaged goods purchased on account from Wortham Co. on January 3.
	6	Made cash sales for the week totaling $3,150.
	8	Purchased merchandise on account from Noyes Co. $4,500.
	9	Sold merchandise on account to Connor Corp. $6,400, invoice no. 372, terms 1/10, n/30.
	11	Purchased merchandise on account from Betz Co. $3,700.
	13	Paid in full Wortham Co. on account less a 2% discount.
	13	Made cash sales for the week totaling $6,260.
	15	Received payment from Connor Corp. for invoice no. 372.
	15	Paid semi-monthly salaries of $14,300 to employees.
	17	Received payment from Milam for invoice no. 371.
	17	Sold merchandise on account to Bullock Co. $1,200, invoice no. 373, terms 1/10, n/30.
	19	Purchased equipment on account from Murphy Corp. $5,500.
	20	Cash sales for the week totaled $3,200.
	20	Paid in full Noyes Co. on account less a 2% discount.
	23	Purchased merchandise on account from Wortham Co. $7,800.
	24	Purchased merchandise on account from Forgetta Corp. $5,100.
	27	Made cash sales for the week totaling $4,230.
	30	Received payment from Bullock Co. for invoice no. 373.
	31	Paid semi-monthly salaries of $13,200 to employees.
	31	Sold merchandise on account to Milam $9,330, invoice no. 374, terms 1/10, n/30.

Boyden Company uses the following journals.

1. Sales journal.
2. Single-column purchases journal.
3. Cash receipts journal with columns for Cash Dr., Sales Discounts Dr., Accounts Receivable Cr., Sales Cr., Other Accounts Cr., and Cost of Goods Sold Dr./Merchandise Inventory Cr.
4. Cash payments journal with columns for Other Accounts Dr., Accounts Payable Dr., Merchandise Inventory Cr., and Cash Cr.
5. General journal.

Instructions
Using the selected accounts provided:
(a) Record the January transactions in the appropriate journal noted.
(b) Foot and crossfoot all special journals.
(c) Show how postings would be made by placing ledger account numbers and checkmarks as needed in the journals. (Actual posting to ledger accounts is not required.)

(a) Sales journal $22,180
Purchases journal $31,100
Cash receipts journal balancing total $29,690
Cash payments journal balancing total $41,780

P7-5A Presented below are the purchases and cash payments journals for Reyes Co. for its first month of operations.

Journalize in sales and cash receipts journals; post; prepare a trial balance; prove control to subsidiary; prepare adjusting entries; prepare an adjusted trial balance.

(SO 2, 3, 4)

PURCHASES JOURNAL   P1

Date	Account Credited	Ref.	Merchandise Inventory Dr. Accounts Payable Cr.
July 4	G. Clemens		6,800
5	A. Ernst		8,100
11	J. Happy		5,920
13	C. Tabor		15,300
20	M. Sneezy		7,900
			44,020

CASH PAYMENTS JOURNAL   CP1

Date	Account Debited	Ref.	Other Accounts Dr.	Accounts Payable Dr.	Merchandise Inventory Cr.	Cash Cr.
July 4	Store Supplies		600			600
10	A. Ernst			8,100	81	8,019
11	Prepaid Rent		6,000			6,000
15	G. Clemens			6,800		6,800
19	Reyes, Drawing		2,500			2,500
21	C. Tabor			15,300	153	15,147
			9,100	30,200	234	39,066

In addition, the following transactions have not been journalized for July. The cost of all merchandise sold was 65% of the sales price.

July 1   The founder, D. Reyes, invests $80,000 in cash.
6   Sell merchandise on account to Ewing Co. $6,200 terms 1/10, n/30.
7   Make cash sales totaling $6,000.
8   Sell merchandise on account to S. Beauty $3,600, terms 1/10, n/30.
10   Sell merchandise on account to W. Pitts $4,900, terms 1/10, n/30.
13   Receive payment in full from S. Beauty.
16   Receive payment in full from W. Pitts.
20   Receive payment in full from Ewing Co.
21   Sell merchandise on account to H. Prince $5,000, terms 1/10, n/30.
29   Returned damaged goods to G. Clemens and received cash refund of $420.

Instructions
(a) Open the following accounts in the general ledger.

101 Cash
112 Accounts Receivable
120 Merchandise Inventory
127 Store Supplies
131 Prepaid Rent
201 Accounts Payable
301 Reyes, Capital
306 Reyes, Drawing
401 Sales
414 Sales Discounts
505 Cost of Goods Sold
631 Supplies Expense
729 Rent Expense

(b) Sales journal total
    $19,700
    Cash receipts journal
    balancing totals $101,120

(e) Totals $119,520
(f) Accounts Receivable
    $5,000
    Accounts Payable $13,820
(h) Totals $119,520

(b) Journalize the transactions that have not been journalized in the sales journal, the cash receipts journal (see Illustration 7-9), and the general journal.
(c) Post to the accounts receivable and accounts payable subsidiary ledgers. Follow the sequence of transactions as shown in the problem.
(d) Post the individual entries and totals to the general ledger.
(e) Prepare a trial balance at July 31, 2010.
(f) Determine whether the subsidiary ledgers agree with the control accounts in the general ledger.
(g) The following adjustments at the end of July are necessary.
   (1) A count of supplies indicates that $140 is still on hand.
   (2) Recognize rent expense for July, $500.
   Prepare the necessary entries in the general journal. Post the entries to the general ledger.
(h) Prepare an adjusted trial balance at July 31, 2010.

Journalize in special journals; post; prepare a trial balance.

(SO 2, 3, 4)   GLS

P7-6A   The post-closing trial balance for Cortez Co. is as follows.

CORTEZ CO.
Post-Closing Trial Balance
December 31, 2010

	Debit	Credit
Cash	$ 41,500	
Accounts Receivable	15,000	
Notes Receivable	45,000	
Merchandise Inventory	23,000	
Equipment	6,450	
Accumulated Depreciation—Equipment		$ 1,500
Accounts Payable		43,000
B. Cortez, Capital		86,450
	$130,950	$130,950

The subsidiary ledgers contain the following information: (1) accounts receivable—J. Anders $2,500, F. Cone $7,500, T. Dudley $5,000; (2) accounts payable—J. Feeney $10,000, D. Goodman $18,000, and K. Inwood $15,000. The cost of all merchandise sold was 60% of the sales price.

The transactions for January 2011 are as follows.

Jan. 3 Sell merchandise to M. Rensing $5,000, terms 2/10, n/30.
 5 Purchase merchandise from E. Vietti $2,000, terms 2/10, n/30.
 7 Receive a check from T. Dudley $3,500.
 11 Pay freight on merchandise purchased $300.
 12 Pay rent of $1,000 for January.
 13 Receive payment in full from M. Rensing.
 14 Post all entries to the subsidiary ledgers. Issued credit of $300 to J. Anders for returned merchandise.
 15 Send K. Inwood a check for $14,850 in full payment of account, discount $150.
 17 Purchase merchandise from G. Marley $1,600, terms 2/10, n/30.
 18 Pay sales salaries of $2,800 and office salaries $2,000.
 20 Give D. Goodman a 60-day note for $18,000 in full payment of account payable.
 23 Total cash sales amount to $9,100.
 24 Post all entries to the subsidiary ledgers. Sell merchandise on account to F. Cone $7,400, terms 1/10, n/30.
 27 Send E. Vietti a check for $950.
 29 Receive payment on a note of $40,000 from B. Lemke.
 30 Post all entries to the subsidiary ledgers. Return merchandise of $300 to G. Marley for credit.

Instructions
(a) Open general and subsidiary ledger accounts for the following.

101 Cash	301 B. Cortez, Capital
112 Accounts Receivable	401 Sales
115 Notes Receivable	412 Sales Returns and Allowances
120 Merchandise Inventory	414 Sales Discounts
157 Equipment	505 Cost of Goods Sold
158 Accumulated Depreciation—Equipment	726 Sales Salaries Expense
200 Notes Payable	727 Office Salaries Expense
201 Accounts Payable	729 Rent Expense

(b) Record the January transactions in a sales journal, a single-column purchases journal, a cash receipts journal (see Illustration 7-9), a cash payments journal (see Illustration 7-16), and a general journal.

(c) Post the appropriate amounts to the general ledger.

(d) Prepare a trial balance at January 31, 2011.

(e) Determine whether the subsidiary ledgers agree with controlling accounts in the general ledger.

(b) Sales journal $12,400
 Purchases journal $3,600
 Cash receipts journal
 (balancing) $57,600
 Cash payments journal
 (balancing) $22,050
(d) Totals $139,800
(e) Accounts Receivable
 $18,600
 Accounts Payable
 $12,350

PROBLEMS: SET B

Journalize transactions in cash receipts journal; post to control account and subsidiary ledger.

(SO 2, 3, 4)

P7-1B   Kentucky Company's chart of accounts includes the following selected accounts.

101 Cash	401 Sales
112 Accounts Receivable	414 Sales Discounts
120 Merchandise Inventory	505 Cost of Goods Sold
301 Ken Tucky, Capital	

On June 1 the accounts receivable ledger of Kentucky Company showed the following balances: Moose & Son $3,500, Chris Co. $2,800, Cornell Bros. $2,400, and Marx Co. $2,000. The June transactions involving the receipt of cash were as follows.

June 1   The owner, Ken Tucky, invested additional cash in the business $12,000.
      3   Received check in full from Marx Co. less 2% cash discount.
      6   Received check in full from Chris Co. less 2% cash discount.
      7   Made cash sales of merchandise totaling $8,700. The cost of the merchandise sold was $5,000.
      9   Received check in full from Moose & Son less 2% cash discount.
     11   Received cash refund from a supplier for damaged merchandise $450.
     15   Made cash sales of merchandise totaling $6,500. The cost of the merchandise sold was $4,000.
     20   Received check in full from Cornell Bros. $2,400.

Instructions

(a) Balancing totals $38,350

(a) Journalize the transactions above in a six-column cash receipts journal with columns for Cash Dr., Sales Discounts Dr., Accounts Receivable Cr., Sales Cr., Other Accounts Cr., and Cost of Goods Sold Dr./Merchandise Inventory Cr. Foot and crossfoot the journal.
(b) Insert the beginning balances in the Accounts Receivable control and subsidiary accounts, and post the June transactions to these accounts.

(c) Accounts Receivable $0

(c) Prove the agreement of the control account and subsidiary account balances.

Journalize transactions in cash payments journal; post to the general and subsidiary ledgers.

(SO 2, 3, 4)

P7-2B   Starr Company's chart of accounts includes the following selected accounts.

101 Cash	157 Equipment
120 Merchandise Inventory	201 Accounts Payable
130 Prepaid Insurance	306 R. Starr, Drawing

On November 1 the accounts payable ledger of Starr Company showed the following balances: P. McCartney $4,000, J. Lennon $2,100, G. Harrison $800, and J. Lynne $1,300. The November transactions involving the payment of cash were as follows.

Nov. 1   Purchased merchandise, check no. 11, $950.
      3   Purchased store equipment, check no. 12, $1,400.
      5   Paid J. Lynne balance due of $1,300, less 1% discount, check no. 13, $1,287.
     11   Purchased merchandise, check no. 14, $1,700.
     15   Paid G. Harrison balance due of $800, less 3% discount, check no. 15, $776.
     16   R. Starr, the owner, withdrew $400 cash for own use, check no. 16.
     19   Paid J. Lennon in full for invoice no. 1245, $2,100 less 2% discount, check no. 17, $2,058.
     25   Paid premium due on one-year insurance policy, check no. 18, $2,400.
     30   Paid P. McCartney in full for invoice no. 832, $2,900, check no. 19.

Instructions

(a) Balancing totals $13,950

(a) Journalize the transactions above in a four-column cash payments journal with columns for Other Accounts Dr., Accounts Payable Dr., Merchandise Inventory Cr., and Cash Cr. Foot and crossfoot the journal.
(b) Insert the beginning balances in the Accounts Payable control and subsidiary accounts, and post the November transactions to these accounts.

(c) Accounts Payable $1,100

(c) Prove the agreement of the control account and the subsidiary account balances.

Journalize transactions in multi-column purchases journal; post to the general and subsidiary ledgers.

(SO 2, 3, 4)

P7-3B   The chart of accounts of Dickinson Company includes the following selected accounts.

112 Accounts Receivable	401 Sales
120 Merchandise Inventory	412 Sales Returns and Allowances
126 Supplies	505 Cost of Goods Sold
157 Equipment	610 Advertising Expense
201 Accounts Payable	

In May the following selected transactions were completed. All purchases and sales were on account except as indicated. The cost of all merchandise sold was 60% of the sales price.

May 2 Purchased merchandise from Older Company $5,000.
     3 Received freight bill from Fast Freight on Older purchase $250.
     5 Sales were made to May Company $1,300, Coen Bros. $1,800, and Lucy Company $1,000.
     8 Purchased merchandise from Wolfe Company $5,400 and Zig Company $3,000.
    10 Received credit on merchandise returned to Zig Company $350.
    15 Purchased supplies from Michelle's Supplies $600.
    16 Purchased merchandise from Older Company $3,100, and Wolfe Company $4,800.
    17 Returned supplies to Michelle's Supplies, receiving credit $70. (*Hint*: Credit Supplies.)
    18 Received freight bills on May 16 purchases from Fast Freight $325.
    20 Returned merchandise to Older Company receiving credit $200.
    23 Made sales to Coen Bros. $1,600 and to Lucy Company $2,500.
    25 Received bill for advertising from Ole Advertising $620.
    26 Granted allowance to Lucy Company for merchandise damaged in shipment $140.
    28 Purchased equipment from Michelle's Supplies $400.

Instructions

(a) Journalize the transactions above in a purchases journal, a sales journal, and a general journal. The purchases journal should have the following column headings: Date, Account Credited (Debited), Ref., Accounts Payable Cr., Merchandise Inventory Dr., and Other Accounts Dr.
(b) Post to both the general and subsidiary ledger accounts. (Assume that all accounts have zero beginning balances.)
(c) Prove the agreement of the control and subsidiary accounts.

(a) Purchases journal—
     Accounts Payable, Cr.
     $23,495
     Sales column total
     $8,200

(c) Accounts Receivable
     $8,060
     Accounts Payable
     $22,875

P7-4B Selected accounts from the chart of accounts of Valente Company are shown below.

101 Cash	201 Accounts Payable
112 Accounts Receivable	401 Sales
120 Merchandise Inventory	414 Sales Discounts
126 Supplies	505 Cost of Goods Sold
140 Land	610 Advertising Expense
145 Buildings	

Journalize transactions in special journals.

(SO 2, 3, 4)

The cost of all merchandise sold was 65% of the sales price. During October, Valente Company completed the following transactions.

Oct. 2 Purchased merchandise on account from Janet Company $12,000.
      4 Sold merchandise on account to Erik Co. $5,600. Invoice no. 204, terms 2/10, n/30.
      5 Purchased supplies for cash $60.
      7 Made cash sales for the week totaling $6,700.
      9 Paid in full the amount owed Janet Company less a 2% discount.
     10 Purchased merchandise on account from Arduino Corp. $2,600.
     12 Received payment from Erik Co. for invoice no. 204.
     13 Returned $150 worth of damaged goods purchased on account from Arduino Corp. on October 10.
     14 Made cash sales for the week totaling $6,000.
     16 Sold a parcel of land for $20,000 cash, the land's original cost.
     17 Sold merchandise on account to Ed's Warehouse $3,900, invoice no. 205, terms 2/10, n/30.
     18 Purchased merchandise for cash $1,600.
     21 Made cash sales for the week totaling $6,000.
     23 Paid in full the amount owed Arduino Corp. for the goods kept (no discount).
     25 Purchased supplies on account from Paul Martin Co. $190.
     25 Sold merchandise on account to David Corp. $3,800, invoice no. 206, terms 2/10, n/30.
     25 Received payment from Ed's Warehouse for invoice no. 205.
     26 Purchased for cash a small parcel of land and a building on the land to use as a storage facility. The total cost of $26,000 was allocated $16,000 to the land and $10,000 to the building.
     27 Purchased merchandise on account from Mary Co. $6,200.
     28 Made cash sales for the week totaling $5,500.
     30 Purchased merchandise on account from Janet Company $10,000.
     30 Paid advertising bill for the month from the *Gazette*, $290.
     30 Sold merchandise on account to Ed's Warehouse $3,400, invoice no. 207, terms 2/10, n/30.

Valente Company uses the following journals.

1. Sales journal.
2. Single-column purchases journal.
3. Cash receipts journal with columns for Cash Dr., Sales Discounts Dr., Accounts Receivable Cr., Sales Cr., Other Accounts Cr., and Cost of Goods Sold Dr./Merchandise Inventory Cr.
4. Cash payments journal with columns for Other Accounts Dr., Accounts Payable Dr., Merchandise Inventory Cr., and Cash Cr.
5. General journal.

Instructions

Using the selected accounts provided:

(a) Record the October transactions in the appropriate journals.

(b) Foot and crossfoot all special journals.

(c) Show how postings would be made by placing ledger account numbers and check marks as needed in the journals. (Actual posting to ledger accounts is not required.)

(b) Sales journal $16,700
Purchases journal $30,800
Cash receipts journal— Cash, Dr. $53,510
Cash payments journal, Cash, Cr. $42,160

Journalize in purchases and cash payments journals; post; prepare a trial balance; prove control to subsidiary; prepare adjusting entries; prepare an adjusted trial balance.

(SO 2, 3, 4)

P7-5B Presented below are the sales and cash receipts journals for Wicked Co. for its first month of operations.

SALES JOURNAL
S1

Date	Account Debited	Ref.	Accounts Receivable Dr. Sales Cr.	Cost of Goods Sold Dr. Merchandise Inventory Cr.
Feb. 3	C. Lion		4,000	2,400
9	S. Crow		5,000	3,000
12	T. Mann		6,500	3,900
26	W. Oz		5,500	3,300
			21,000	12,600

CASH RECEIPTS JOURNAL
CR1

Date	Account Credited	Ref.	Cash Dr.	Sales Discounts Dr.	Accounts Receivable Cr.	Sales Cr.	Other Accounts Cr.	Cost of Goods Sold Dr. Merchandise Inventory Cr.
Feb. 1	B. Wicked, Capital		23,000				23,000	
2			4,500			4,500		2,700
13	C. Lion		3,960	40	4,000			
18	Merchandise Inventory		120				120	
26	S. Crow		5,000		5,000			
			36,580	40	9,000	4,500	23,120	2,700

In addition, the following transactions have not been journalized for February 2010.

Feb. 2 Purchased merchandise on account from J. Garland for $3,600, terms 2/10, n/30.

7 Purchased merchandise on account from B. Lahr for $23,000, terms 1/10, n/30.

9 Paid cash of $980 for purchase of supplies.

12 Paid $3,528 to J. Garland in payment for $3,600 invoice, less 2% discount.

15 Purchased equipment for $5,500 cash.

16 Purchased merchandise on account from D. Gale $1,900, terms 2/10, n/30.

17 Paid $22,770 to B. Lahr in payment of $23,000 invoice, less 1% discount.

20 B. Wicked withdrew cash of $800 from business for personal use.

21 Purchased merchandise on account from Kansas Company for $6,000, terms 1/10, n/30.

28 Paid $1,900 to D. Gale in payment of $1,900 invoice.

Instructions

(a) Open the following accounts in the general ledger.

101 Cash
112 Accounts Receivable
120 Merchandise Inventory
126 Supplies

157	Equipment	401	Sales
158	Accumulated Depreciation—Equipment	414	Sales Discounts
201	Accounts Payable	505	Cost of Goods Sold
301	B. Wicked, Capital	631	Supplies Expense
306	B. Wicked, Drawing	711	Depreciation Expense

(b) Journalize the transactions that have not been journalized in a one-column purchases journal and the cash payments journal (see Illustration 7-16).

(c) Post to the accounts receivable and accounts payable subsidiary ledgers. Follow the sequence of transactions as shown in the problem.

(d) Post the individual entries and totals to the general ledger.

(e) Prepare a trial balance at February 28, 2010.

(f) Determine that the subsidiary ledgers agree with the control accounts in the general ledger.

(g) The following adjustments at the end of February are necessary.

  (1) A count of supplies indicates that $200 is still on hand.

  (2) Depreciation on equipment for February is $150.

  Prepare the adjusting entries and then post the adjusting entries to the general ledger.

(h) Prepare an adjusted trial balance at February 28, 2010.

*(b) Purchases journal total
$34,500
Cash payments journal—
Cash, Cr. $35,478*

(e) Totals $54,500

*(f) Accounts Receivable
$12,000
Accounts Payable $6,000*

(h) Totals $54,650

PROBLEMS: SET C

Visit the book's companion website at **www.wiley.com/college/weygandt**, and choose the Student Companion site, to access Problem Set C.

COMPREHENSIVE PROBLEM: CHAPTERS 3 TO 7

Packard Company has the following opening account balances in its general and subsidiary ledgers on January 1 and uses the periodic inventory system. All accounts have normal debit and credit balances.

General Ledger

Account Number	Account Title	January 1 Opening Balance
101	Cash	$33,750
112	Accounts Receivable	13,000
115	Notes Receivable	39,000
120	Merchandise Inventory	20,000
125	Office Supplies	1,000
130	Prepaid Insurance	2,000
157	Equipment	6,450
158	Accumulated Depreciation	1,500
201	Accounts Payable	35,000
301	I. Packard, Capital	78,700

Accounts Receivable Subsidiary Ledger

Customer	January 1 Opening Balance
R. Draves	$1,500
B. Hachinski	7,500
S. Ingles	4,000

Accounts Payable Subsidiary Ledger

Creditor	January 1 Opening Balance
S. Kosko	$ 9,000
R. Mikush	15,000
D. Moreno	11,000

Jan. 3 Sell merchandise on account to B. Remy $3,100, invoice no. 510, and J. Fine $1,800, invoice no. 511.

5 Purchase merchandise on account from S. Yost $3,000 and D. Laux $2,700.

7 Receive checks for $4,000 from S. Ingles and $2,000 from B. Hachinski.

8 Pay freight on merchandise purchased $180.

9 Send checks to S. Kosko for $9,000 and D. Moreno for $11,000.

9 Issue credit of $300 to J. Fine for merchandise returned.

10 Summary cash sales total $15,500.

11 Sell merchandise on account to R. Draves for $1,900, invoice no. 512, and to S. Ingles $900, invoice no. 513.

Post all entries to the subsidiary ledgers.

12 Pay rent of $1,000 for January.

13 Receive payment in full from B. Remy and J. Fine.

15 Withdraw $800 cash by I. Packard for personal use.

16 Purchase merchandise on account from D. Moreno for $15,000, from S. Kosko for $13,900, and from S. Yost for $1,500.

17 Pay $400 cash for office supplies.

18 Return $200 of merchandise to S. Kosko and receive credit.

20 Summary cash sales total $17,500.

21 Issue $15,000 note to R. Mikush in payment of balance due.

21 Receive payment in full from S. Ingles.

Post all entries to the subsidiary ledgers.

22 Sell merchandise on account to B. Remy for $3,700, invoice no. 514, and to R. Draves for $800, invoice no. 515.

23 Send checks to D. Moreno and S. Kosko in full payment.

25 Sell merchandise on account to B. Hachinski for $3,500, invoice no. 516, and to J. Fine for $6,100, invoice no. 517.

27 Purchase merchandise on account from D. Moreno for $12,500, from D. Laux for $1,200, and from S. Yost for $2,800.

28 Pay $200 cash for office supplies.

31 Summary cash sales total $22,920.

31 Pay sales salaries of $4,300 and office salaries of $3,600.

Instructions

(a) Record the January transactions in the appropriate journal—sales, purchases, cash receipts, cash payments, and general.

(b) Post the journals to the general and subsidiary ledgers. Add and number new accounts in an orderly fashion as needed.

(c) Trial balance totals $196,820; Adj. T/B totals $196,975

(c) Prepare a trial balance at January 31, 2010, using a worksheet. Complete the worksheet using the following additional information.

(1) Office supplies at January 31 total $700.

(2) Insurance coverage expires on October 31, 2010.

(3) Annual depreciation on the equipment is $1,500.

(4) Interest of $30 has accrued on the note payable.

(5) Merchandise inventory at January 31 is $15,000.

(d) Net income $9,685 Total assets $126,315

(d) Prepare a multiple-step income statement and a statement of owner's equity for January and a classified balance sheet at the end of January.

(e) Prepare and post the adjusting and closing entries.

(f) Post-closing T/B totals $127,940

(f) Prepare a post-closing trial balance, and determine whether the subsidiary ledgers agree with the control accounts in the general ledger.

BROADENING YOUR PERSPECTIVE

FINANCIAL REPORTING AND ANALYSIS

Financial Reporting Problem—Mini Practice Set

BYP7-1 **(You will need the working papers that accompany this textbook in order to work this mini practice set.)**

Bluma Co. uses a perpetual inventory system and both an accounts receivable and an accounts payable subsidiary ledger. Balances related to both the general ledger and the subsidiary ledger for Bluma are indicated in the working papers. Presented below are a series of transactions for

Bluma Co. for the month of January. Credit sales terms are 2/10, n/30. The cost of all merchandise sold was 60% of the sales price.

Jan. 3 Sell merchandise on account to B. Richey $3,100, invoice no. 510, and to J. Forbes $1,800, invoice no. 511.

　　 5 Purchase merchandise from S. Vogel $5,000 and D. Lynch $2,200, terms n/30.

　　 7 Receive checks from S. LaDew $4,000 and B. Garcia $2,000 after discount period has lapsed.

　　 8 Pay freight on merchandise purchased $235.

　　 9 Send checks to S. Hoyt for $9,000 less 2% cash discount, and to D. Omara for $11,000 less 1% cash discount.

　　 9 Issue credit of $300 to J. Forbes for merchandise returned.

　　 10 Summary daily cash sales total $15,500.

　　 11 Sell merchandise on account to R. Dvorak $1,600, invoice no. 512, and to S. LaDew $900, invoice no. 513.

　　 12 Pay rent of $1,000 for January.

　　 13 Receive payment in full from B. Richey and J. Forbes less cash discounts.

　　 15 Withdraw $800 cash by M. Bluma for personal use.

　　 15 Post all entries to the subsidiary ledgers.

　　 16 Purchase merchandise from D. Omara $18,000, terms 1/10, n/30; S. Hoyt $14,200, terms 2/10, n/30; and S. Vogel $1,500, terms n/30.

　　 17 Pay $400 cash for office supplies.

　　 18 Return $200 of merchandise to S. Hoyt and receive credit.

　　 20 Summary daily cash sales total $20,100.

　　 21 Issue $15,000 note, maturing in 90 days, to R. Moses in payment of balance due.

　　 21 Receive payment in full from S. LaDew less cash discount.

　　 22 Sell merchandise on account to B. Richey $2,700, invoice no. 514, and to R. Dvorak $1,300, invoice no. 515.

　　 22 Post all entries to the subsidiary ledgers.

　　 23 Send checks to D. Omara and S. Hoyt in full payment less cash discounts.

　　 25 Sell merchandise on account to B. Garcia $3,500, invoice no. 516, and to J. Forbes $6,100, invoice no. 517.

　　 27 Purchase merchandise from D. Omara $14,500, terms 1/10, n/30; D. Lynch $1,200, terms n/30; and S. Vogel $5,400, terms n/30.

　　 27 Post all entries to the subsidiary ledgers.

　　 28 Pay $200 cash for office supplies.

　　 31 Summary daily cash sales total $21,300.

　　 31 Pay sales salaries $4,300 and office salaries $3,800.

Instructions

(a) Record the January transactions in a sales journal, a single-column purchases journal, a cash receipts journal as shown on page 313, a cash payments journal as shown on page 318, and a two-column general journal.

(b) Post the journals to the general ledger.

(c) Prepare a trial balance at January 31, 2010, in the trial balance columns of the worksheet. Complete the worksheet using the following additional information.

　　(1) Office supplies at January 31 total $900.

　　(2) Insurance coverage expires on October 31, 2010.

　　(3) Annual depreciation on the equipment is $1,500.

　　(4) Interest of $50 has accrued on the note payable.

(d) Prepare a multiple-step income statement and an owner's equity statement for January and a classified balance sheet at the end of January.

(e) Prepare and post adjusting and closing entries.

(f) Prepare a post-closing trial balance, and determine whether the subsidiary ledgers agree with the control accounts in the general ledger.

Exploring the Web

BYP7-2 Microsoft Office Accounting Professional is one of the leading accounting software packages. Information related to this package is found at its website.

Address: http://office.microsoft.com/en-us/accounting/HA102505581033.aspx, or go to **www.wiley.com/college/weygandt**

Instructions

Go to the website shown above and answer the following questions.

(a) What are the top ten reasons to try Microsoft Office Accounting Professional?

(b) Explain the basic features of the payroll add-on service in Microsoft Office Accounting Professional.

CRITICAL THINKING

Decision Making Across the Organization

BYP7-3   Hughey & Payne is a wholesaler of small appliances and parts. Hughey & Payne is operated by two owners, Rich Hughey and Kristen Payne. In addition, the company has one employee, a repair specialist, who is on a fixed salary. Revenues are earned through the sale of appliances to retailers (approximately 75% of total revenues), appliance parts to do-it-yourselfers (10%), and the repair of appliances brought to the store (15%). Appliance sales are made on both a credit and cash basis. Customers are billed on prenumbered sales invoices. Credit terms are always net/30 days. All parts sales and repair work are cash only.

Merchandise is purchased on account from the manufacturers of both the appliances and the parts. Practically all suppliers offer cash discounts for prompt payments, and it is company policy to take all discounts. Most cash payments are made by check. Checks are most frequently issued to suppliers, to trucking companies for freight on merchandise purchases, and to news-papers, radio, and TV stations for advertising. All advertising bills are paid as received. Rich and Kristen each make a monthly drawing in cash for personal living expenses. The salaried re-pairman is paid twice monthly. Hughey & Payne currently has a manual accounting system.

Instructions

With the class divided into groups, answer the following.

(a) Identify the special journals that Hughey & Payne should have in its manual system. List the column headings appropriate for each of the special journals.

(b) What control and subsidiary accounts should be included in Hughey & Payne manual system? Why?

Communication Activity

BYP7-4   Barb Doane, a classmate, has a part-time bookkeeping job. She is concerned about the inefficiencies in journalizing and posting transactions. Jim Houser is the owner of the company where Barb works. In response to numerous complaints from Barb and others, Jim hired two additional bookkeepers a month ago. However, the inefficiencies have continued at an even higher rate. The accounting information system for the company has only a general journal and a general ledger. Jim refuses to install an electronic accounting system.

Instructions

Now that Barb is an expert in manual accounting information systems, she decides to send a letter to Jim Houser explaining (1) why the additional personnel did not help and (2) what changes should be made to improve the efficiency of the accounting department. Write the let-ter that you think Barb should send.

Ethics Case

BYP7-5   Roniger Products Company operates three divisions, each with its own manufactur-ing plant and marketing/sales force. The corporate headquarters and central accounting office are in Roniger, and the plants are in Freeport, Rockport, and Bayport, all within 50 miles of Roniger. Corporate management treats each division as an independent profit center and en-courages competition among them. They each have similar but different product lines. As a competitive incentive, bonuses are awarded each year to the employees of the fastest growing and most profitable division.

Jose Molina is the manager of Roniger's centralized computer accounting operation that enters the sales transactions and maintains the accounts receivable for all three divisions. Jose came up in the accounting ranks from the Bayport division where his wife, several relatives, and many friends still work.

As sales documents are entered into the computer, the originating division is identified by code. Most sales documents (95%) are coded, but some (5%) are not coded or are coded incorrectly. As the manager, Jose has instructed the data-entry personnel to assign the Bayport code to all uncoded and incorrectly coded sales documents. This is done he says, "in order to expedite processing and to keep the computer files current since they are updated daily." All receivables and cash collections for all three divisions are handled by Roniger as one subsidiary accounts receivable ledger.

Instructions
(a) Who are the stakeholders in this situation?
(b) What are the ethical issues in this case?
(c) How might the system be improved to prevent this situation?

"All About You" Activity

BYP7-6 In this chapter you learned about a basic manual accounting information system. Computerized accounting systems range from the very basic and inexpensive to the very elaborate and expensive. Even the most sophisticated systems are based on the fundamental structures and relationships that you learned in this chapter.

Instructions
Go to the book companion site for this text, **www.wiley.com/college/weygandt**, and review the demonstration that is provided for the general ledger software package that is used with this text. Prepare a brief explanation of how the general ledger system works—that is, how it is used, and what information it provides.

Answers to Insight and Accounting Across the Organization Questions

p. 304 Curbing Fraudulent Activity with Software
Q: Why might this software help reduce fraudulent activity by employees?
A: *By pinpointing who used the accounting system and when they used it, the software can hold employees more accountable for their actions. Companies hope that this will reduce efforts by employees to enter false accounting entries, change the dates of transactions, or create unauthorized expenditures. If employees do engage in these activities, there will be significant evidence of their activities.*

p. 307 "I'm John Smith, a.k.a. 13695071642"
Q: Why use numbers to identify names in a computerized system?
A: *Computerized systems process numbers faster than letters. Also, letters sometimes cause problems because you may have two people with the same name. Computerized systems avoid this problem by giving different customers, including those with the same names, different account numbers.*

Answers to Self-Study Questions
1. d **2.** c **3.** a **4.** c **5.** c **6.** c **7.** d **8.** c **9.** a **10.** d **11.** c **12.** d **13.** b **14.** c **15.** c

Fraud, Internal Control, and Cash

STUDY OBJECTIVES

After studying this chapter, you should be able to:

1 Define fraud and internal control.
2 Identify the principles of internal control activities.
3 Explain the applications of internal control principles to cash receipts.
4 Explain the applications of internal control principles to cash disbursements.
5 Describe the operation of a petty cash fund.
6 Indicate the control features of a bank account.
7 Prepare a bank reconciliation.
8 Explain the reporting of cash.

✓ *The Navigator*

✓ The Navigator

Scan **Study Objectives**	▢
Read **Feature Story**	▢
Read **Preview**	▢
Read text and answer **DO IT!**	▢
p. 356 ▢ p. 360 ▢ p. 364 ▢	
p. 371 ▢	
Work **Comprehensive** **DO IT!** p. 374	▢
Review **Summary of Study Objectives**	▢
Answer **Self-Study Questions**	▢
Complete **Assignments**	▢

Feature Story

MINDING THE MONEY IN MOOSE JAW

If you're ever looking for a cappuccino in Moose Jaw, Saskatchewan, stop by Stephanie's Gourmet Coffee and More, located on Main Street. Staff there serve, on average, 650 cups of coffee a day, including both regular and specialty coffees, not to mention soups, Italian sandwiches, and a wide assortment of gourmet cheesecakes.

"We've got high school students who come here, and students from the community college," says owner/manager Stephanie Mintenko, who has run the place since opening it in 1995. "We have customers who are retired,

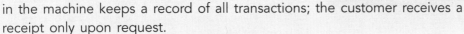

and others who are working people and have only 30 minutes for lunch. We have to be pretty quick."

That means that the cashiers have to be efficient. Like most businesses where purchases are low-cost and high-volume, cash control has to be simple.

"We have an electronic cash register, but it's not the fancy new kind where you just punch in the item," explains Ms. Mintenko. "You have to punch in the prices." The machine does keep track of sales in several categories, however. Cashiers punch a button to indicate whether each item is a beverage, a meal, or a charge for the cafe's Internet connections. An internal tape in the machine keeps a record of all transactions; the customer receives a receipt only upon request.

There is only one cash register. "Up to three of us might operate it on any given shift, including myself," says Ms. Mintenko.

She and her staff do two "cashouts" each day—one with the shift change at 5:00 p.m. and one when the shop closes at 10:00 p.m. At each cashout, they count the cash in the register drawer. That amount, minus the cash change carried forward (the float), should match the shift total on the register tape. If there's a discrepancy, they do another count. Then, if necessary, "we go through the whole tape to find the mistake," she explains. "It usually turns out to be someone who punched in $18 instead of $1.80, or something like that."

Ms. Mintenko sends all the cash tapes and float totals to a bookkeeper, who double-checks everything and provides regular reports. "We try to keep the accounting simple, so we can concentrate on making great coffee and food."

The Navigator

Inside Chapter 8...

As the story about recording cash sales at Stephanie's Gourmet Coffee and More indicates, control of cash is important to ensure that fraud does not occur. Companies also need controls to safeguard other types of assets. For example, Stephanie's undoubtedly has controls to prevent the theft of food and supplies, and controls to prevent the theft of tableware and dishes from its kitchen.

In this chapter, we explain the essential features of an internal control system and how it prevents fraud. We also describe how those controls apply to a specific asset—cash. The applications include some controls with which you may be already familiar, such as the use of a bank.

The content and organization of Chapter 8 are as follows.

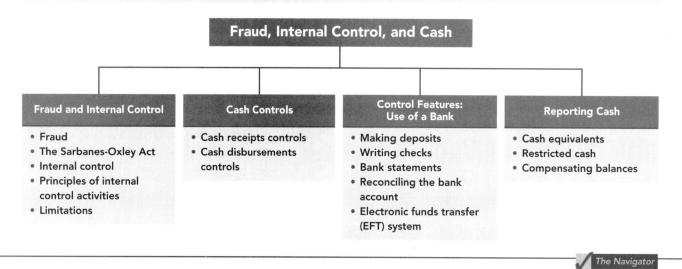

The Navigator

FRAUD AND INTERNAL CONTROL

STUDY OBJECTIVE 1
Define fraud and internal control.

The Feature Story describes many of the internal control procedures used by Stephanie's Gourmet Coffee and More. These procedures are necessary to discourage employees from fraudulent activities.

Fraud

A **fraud** is a dishonest act by an employee that results in personal benefit to the employee at a cost to the employer. Examples of fraud reported in the financial press include:

- A bookkeeper in a small company diverted $750,000 of bill payments to a personal bank account over a three-year period.

- A shipping clerk with 28 years of service shipped $125,000 of merchandise to himself.

- A computer operator embezzled $21 million from Wells Fargo Bank over a two-year period.

- A church treasurer "borrowed" $150,000 of church funds to finance a friend's business dealings.

Why does fraud occur? The three main factors that contribute to fraudulent activity are depicted by the **fraud triangle** in Illustration 8-1.

The most important element of the fraud triangle is **opportunity**. For an employee to commit fraud, the workplace environment must provide opportunities

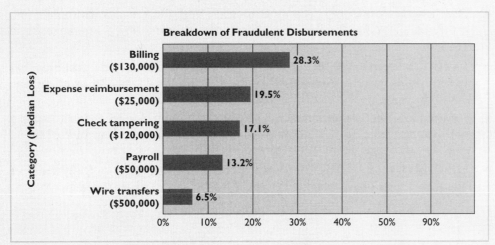

Illustration 8-1
Fraud triangle

that an employee can take advantage of. Opportunities occur when the workplace lacks sufficient controls to deter and detect fraud. For example, inadequate monitoring of employee actions can create opportunities for theft and can embolden employees because they believe they will not be caught.

A second factor that contributes to fraud is **financial pressure**. Employees sometimes commit fraud because of personal financial problems caused by too much debt. Or they might commit fraud because they want to lead a lifestyle that they cannot afford on their current salary.

The third factor that contributes to fraud is **rationalization**. In order to justify their fraud, employees rationalize their dishonest actions. For example, employees sometimes justify fraud because they believe they are underpaid while the employer is making lots of money. Employees feel justified in stealing because they believe they deserve to be paid more.

ETHICS INSIGHT

How Do Employees Steal?

A recent study by the Association of Certified Fraud Examiners found that two-thirds of all employee thefts involved a fraudulent disbursement by an employee. The most common form (28.3% of cases) was fraudulent billing schemes. In these, the employee causes the company to issue a payment to the employee by submitting a bill for nonexistent goods or services, purchases of personal goods by the employee, or inflated invoices. The following graph shows various types of fraudulent disbursements and the median loss from each.

Breakdown of Fraudulent Disbursements

Category (Median Loss)	Percentage
Billing ($130,000)	28.3%
Expense reimbursement ($25,000)	19.5%
Check tampering ($120,000)	17.1%
Payroll ($50,000)	13.2%
Wire transfers ($500,000)	6.5%

Source: 2006 Report to the Nation on Occupational Fraud and Abuse, Association of Certified Fraud Examiners, www.acfe.com/documents/2006_rttn.pdf, p. 14.

 How can companies reduce the likelihood of fraudulent disbursements?

The Sarbanes-Oxley Act

What can be done to prevent or to detect fraud? After numerous corporate scandals came to light in the early 2000s, Congress addressed this issue by passing the **Sarbanes-Oxley Act of 2002 (SOX)**. Under SOX, all publicly traded U.S. corporations are required to maintain an adequate system of internal control. Corporate executives and boards of directors must ensure that these controls are reliable and effective. In addition, independent outside auditors must attest to the adequacy of the internal control system. Companies that fail to comply are subject to fines, and company officers can be imprisoned. SOX also created the Public Company Accounting Oversight Board (PCAOB), to establish auditing standards and regulate auditor activity.

One poll found that 60% of investors believe that SOX helps safeguard their stock investments. Many say they would be unlikely to invest in a company that fails to follow SOX requirements. Although some corporate executives have criticized the time and expense involved in following the SOX requirements, SOX appears to be working well. For example, the chief accounting officer of Eli Lily noted that SOX triggered a comprehensive review of how the company documents controls. This review uncovered redundancies and pointed out controls that needed to be added. In short, it added up to time and money well spent. And the finance chief at General Electric noted, "We have seen value in SOX. It helps build investors' trust and gives them more confidence."[1]

Internal Control

Internal control consists of all the related methods and measures adopted within an organization to safeguard its assets, enhance the reliability of its accounting records, increase efficiency of operations, and ensure compliance with laws and regulations. Internal control systems have five primary components as listed below.[2]

- **A control environment.** It is the responsibility of top management to make it clear that the organization values integrity and that unethical activity will not be tolerated. This component is often referred to as the "tone at the top."

- **Risk assessment.** Companies must identify and analyze the various factors that create risk for the business and must determine how to manage these risks.

- **Control activities.** To reduce the occurrence of fraud, management must design policies and procedures to address the specific risks faced by the company.

- **Information and communication.** The internal control system must capture and communicate all pertinent information both down and up the organization, as well as communicate information to appropriate external parties.

- **Monitoring.** Internal control systems must be monitored periodically for their adequacy. Significant deficiencies need to be reported to top management and/or the board of directors.

---

[1]"Corporate Regulation Must Be Working—There's a Backlash," *Wall Street Journal*, June 16, 2004, p. C1; and Judith Burns, "Is Sarbanes-Oxley Working?" *Wall Street Journal*, June 21, 2004, pp. R8–R9.

[2]The Committee of Sponsoring Organizations of the Treadway Commission, "Internal Control—Integrated Framework," *www.coso.org/publications/executive_summary_integrated_framework.htm* (accessed March 2008).

Principles of Internal Control Activities

Each of the five components of an internal control system is important. Here, we will focus on one component, the control activities. The reason? These activities are the backbone of the company's efforts to address the risks it faces, such as fraud. The specific control activities used by a company will vary, depending on management's assessment of the risks faced. This assessment is heavily influenced by the size and nature of the company.

STUDY OBJECTIVE 2
Identify the principles of internal control activities.

The six principles of control activities are as follows.

- Establishment of responsibility
- Segregation of duties
- Documentation procedures
- Physical controls
- Independent internal verification
- Human resource controls

We explain these principles in the following sections. You should recognize that they apply to most companies and are relevant to both manual and computerized accounting systems.

In the explanations that follow, we have added "Anatomy of a Fraud" stories that describe some recent real-world frauds. At the end of each story, we discuss the missing control activity that, had it been it place, is likely to have prevented or uncovered the fraud.[3]

ESTABLISHMENT OF RESPONSIBILITY

An essential principle of internal control is to assign responsibility to specific employees. **Control is most effective when only one person is responsible for a given task.**

To illustrate, assume that the cash on hand at the end of the day in a Safeway supermarket is $10 short of the cash rung up on the cash register. If only one person has operated the register, the shift manager can quickly determine responsibility for the shortage. If two or more individuals have worked the register, it may be impossible to determine who is responsible for the error. In the Feature Story, the principle of establishing responsibility does not appear to be strictly applied by Stephanie's, since three people operate the cash register on any given shift.

Transfer of cash drawers

Establishing responsibility often requires limiting access only to authorized personnel, and then identifying those personnel. For example, the automated systems used by many companies have mechanisms such as identifying passcodes that keep track of who made a journal entry, who rang up a sale, or who entered an inventory storeroom at a particular time. Use of identifying passcodes enables the company to establish responsibility by identifying the particular employee who carried out the activity.

---

[3]The "Anatomy of a Fraud" stories on pages 350–355 are adapted from *Fraud Casebook: Lessons from the Bad Side of Business*, edited by Joseph T. Wells (Hoboken, NJ: John Wiley & Sons, Inc., 2007). Used by permission. The names of some of the people and organizations in the stories are fictitious, but the facts in the stories are true.

ANATOMY OF A FRAUD

Maureen Frugali was a training supervisor for claims processing at Colossal Healthcare. As a standard part of the claims processing training program, Maureen created fictitious claims for use by trainees. These fictitious claims were then sent to Accounts Payable. After the training claims had been processed, she was to notify the accounts payable department of all fictitious claims, so that they would not be paid. However, she did not inform Accounts Payable about every fictitious claim. She created some fictitious claims for entities that she controlled (that is, she would receive the payment), and she let Accounts Payable pay her.

Total take: $11 million

THE MISSING CONTROL

Establishment of responsibility. The healthcare company did not adequately restrict the responsibility for authoring and approving claims transactions. The training supervisor should not have been authorized to create claims in the company's "live" system.

Source: Adapted from Wells, *Fraud Casebook* (2007), pp. 61–70.

SEGREGATION OF DUTIES

Segregation of duties is indispensable in an internal control system. There are two common applications of this principle:

1. Different individuals should be responsible for related activities.

2. The responsibility for record-keeping for an asset should be separate from the physical custody of that asset.

The rationale for segregation of duties is this: **The work of one employee should, without a duplication of effort, provide a reliable basis for evaluating the work of another employee.** For example, the personnel that design and program computerized systems should not be assigned duties related to day-to-day use of the system. Otherwise, they could design the system to benefit them personally and conceal the fraud through day-to-day use.

Segregation of Related Activities. **Making one individual responsible for related activities increases the potential for errors and irregularities.** For example, companies should assign related *purchasing activities* to different individuals. Related purchasing activities include ordering merchandise, order approval, receiving goods, authorizing payment, and paying for goods or services. Various frauds are possible when one person handles related purchasing activities. For example:

- If a purchasing agent can order goods without obtaining supervisory approval, the likelihood of the purchasing agent receiving kickbacks from suppliers increases.

- If an employee who orders goods also handles receipt of the goods (and invoice) as well as payment authorization, he or she might authorize payment for a fictitious invoice.

These abuses are less likely to occur when companies divide the purchasing tasks.

Similarly, companies should assign related *sales activities* to different individuals. Related selling activities include making a sale, shipping (or delivering) the goods to the customer, billing the customer, and receiving payment. Various frauds are possible when one person handles related sales transactions. For example:

- If a salesperson can make a sale without obtaining supervisory approval, he or she might make sales at unauthorized prices to increase sales commissions.

- A shipping clerk who also has access to accounting records could ship goods to himself.

- A billing clerk who handles billing and receipt could understate the amount billed for sales made to friends and relatives.

These abuses are less likely to occur when companies divide the sales tasks: the salespeople make the sale; the shipping department ships the goods on the basis of the sales order; and the billing department prepares the sales invoice after comparing the sales order with the report of goods shipped.

ANATOMY OF A FRAUD

Lawrence Fairbanks, the assistant vice-chancellor of communications at Aesop University was allowed to make purchases for his department of under $2,500 without external approval. Unfortunately, he also sometimes bought items for himself, such as expensive antiques and other collectibles. How did he do it? He replaced the vendor invoices he received with fake vendor invoices that he created. The fake invoices had descriptions that were more consistent with the communications department's operations. He submitted these fake invoices to the accounting department as the basis for their journal entries and to Accounts Payable as the basis for payment.

Total take: $475,000

THE MISSING CONTROL

Segregation of duties. The university had not properly segregated related purchasing activities. Lawrence was ordering items, receiving the items, and receiving the invoice. By receiving the invoice, he had control over the documents that were used to account for the purchase and thus was able to substitute a fake invoice.

Source: Adapted from Wells, *Fraud Casebook* (2007), pp. 3–15.

Segregation of Record-Keeping from Physical Custody. The accountant should have neither physical custody of the asset nor access to it. Likewise, the custodian of the asset should not maintain or have access to the accounting records. **The custodian of the asset is not likely to convert the asset to personal use when one employee maintains the record of the asset, and a different employee has physical custody of the asset.** The separation of accounting responsibility from the custody of assets is especially important for cash and inventories because these assets are very vulnerable to fraudulent activities.

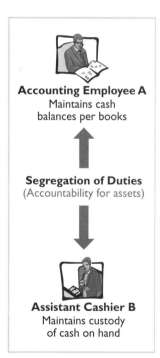

Accounting Employee A
Maintains cash balances per books

Segregation of Duties
(Accountability for assets)

Assistant Cashier B
Maintains custody of cash on hand

ANATOMY OF A FRAUD

Angela Bauer was an accounts payable clerk for Aggasiz Construction Company. She prepared and issued checks to vendors and reconciled bank statements. She perpetrated a fraud in this way: She wrote checks for costs that the company had not actually incurred (e.g., fake taxes). A supervisor then approved and signed the checks. Before issuing the check, though, she would "white-out" the payee line on the check and change it to personal accounts that she controlled. She was able to conceal the theft because she also reconciled the bank account. That is, nobody else ever saw that the checks had been altered.

Total take: $570,000

THE MISSING CONTROL

Segregation of duties. Aggasiz Construction Company did not properly segregate record-keeping from physical custody. Angela had physical custody of the checks, which essentially was control of the cash. She also had recording-keeping responsibility because she prepared the bank reconciliation.

Source: Adapted from Wells, *Fraud Casebook* (2007), pp. 100–107.

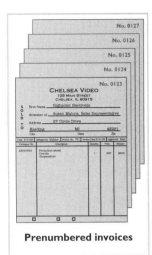

Prenumbered invoices

DOCUMENTATION PROCEDURES

Documents provide evidence that transactions and events have occurred. At Stephanie's Gourmet Coffee and More, the cash register tape is the restaurant's documentation for the sale and the amount of cash received. Similarly, a shipping document indicates that the goods have been shipped, and a sales invoice indicates that the company has billed the customer for the goods. By requiring signatures (or initials) on the documents, the company can identify the individual(s) responsible for the transaction or event. Companies should document transactions when the transaction occurs.

Companies should establish procedures for documents. First, whenever possible, companies should use **prenumbered documents, and all documents should be accounted for**. Prenumbering helps to prevent a transaction from being recorded more than once, or conversely, from not being recorded at all. Second, the control system should require that employees **promptly forward source documents for accounting entries to the accounting department. This control measure helps to ensure timely recording of the transaction** and contributes directly to the accuracy and reliability of the accounting records.

ANATOMY OF A FRAUD

To support their reimbursement requests for travel costs incurred, employees at Mod Fashions Corporation's design center were required to submit receipts. The receipts could include the detailed bill provided for a meal, or the credit card receipt provided when the credit card payment is made, or a copy of the employee's monthly credit card bill that listed the item. A number of the designers who frequently traveled together came up with a fraud scheme: They submitted claims for the same expenses. For example, if they had a meal together that cost $200, one person submitted the detailed meal bill, another submitted the credit card receipt, and a third submitted a monthly credit card bill showing the meal as a line item. Thus, all three received a $200 reimbursement.

Total take: $75,000

THE MISSING CONTROL

Documentation procedures. Mod Fashions should require the original, detailed receipt. It should not accept photocopies, and it should not accept credit card statements. In addition, documentation procedures could be further improved by requiring the use of a corporate credit card (rather than a personal credit card) for all business expenses.

Source: Adapted from Wells, *Fraud Casebook* (2007), pp. 79–90.

PHYSICAL CONTROLS

Use of physical controls is essential. *Physical controls* relate to the safeguarding of assets and enhance the accuracy and reliability of the accounting records. Illustration 8-2 (page 353) shows examples of these controls.

ANATOMY OF A FRAUD

At Centerstone Health, a large insurance company, the mailroom each day received insurance applications from prospective customers. Mailroom employees scanned the applications into electronic documents before the applications were processed. Once the applications are scanned they can be accessed online by authorized employees.

Insurance agents at Centerstone Health earn commissions based upon successful applications. The sales agent's name is listed on the application. However, roughly 15%

Physical Controls

Safes, vaults, and safety
deposit boxes for cash
and business papers

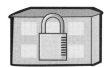

Locked warehouses
and storage cabinets for
inventories and records

Computer facilities
with pass key access
or fingerprint or
eyeball scans

Alarms to
prevent break-ins

Television monitors
and garment sensors
to deter theft

Time clocks for
recording time worked

Illustration 8-2
Physical controls

of the applications are from customers who did not work with a sales agent. Two friends—Alex, an employee in record keeping, and Parviz, a sales agent—thought up a way to perpetrate a fraud. Alex identified scanned applications that did not list a sales agent. After business hours, he entered the mailroom and found the hardcopy applications that did not show a sales agent. He wrote in Parviz's name as the sales agent and then rescanned the application for processing. Parviz received the commission, which the friends then split.

Total take: $240,000

THE MISSING CONTROL

Physical controls. Centerstone Health lacked two basic physical controls that could have prevented this fraud. First, the mailroom should have been locked during nonbusiness hours, and access during business hours should have been tightly controlled. Second, the scanned applications supposedly could be accessed only by authorized employees using their passwords. However, the password for each employee was the same as the employee's user ID. Since employee user-ID numbers were available to all other employees, all employees knew all other employees' passwords. Unauthorized employees could access the scanned applications. Thus, Alex could enter the system pretending to be any other employee.

Source: Adapted from Wells, *Fraud Casebook* (2007), pp. 316–326.

INDEPENDENT INTERNAL VERIFICATION

Most internal control systems provide for **independent internal verification**. This principle involves the review of data prepared by employees. To obtain maximum benefit from independent internal verification:

1. Companies should verify records periodically or on a surprise basis.
2. An employee who is independent of the personnel responsible for the information should make the verification.

3. Discrepancies and exceptions should be reported to a management level that can take appropriate corrective action.

Independent internal verification is especially useful in comparing recorded accountability with existing assets. The reconciliation of the cash register tape with the cash in the register at Stephanie's Gourmet Coffee and More is an example of this internal control principle. Another common example is the reconciliation of a company's cash balance per books with the cash balance per bank and the verification of the perpetual inventory records through a count of physical inventory. Illustration 8-3 shows the relationship between this principle and the segregation of duties principle.

Illustration 8-3
Comparison of segregation of duties principle with independent internal verification principle

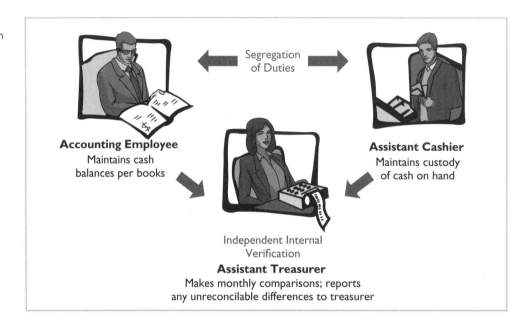

ANATOMY OF A FRAUD

Bobbi Jean Donnelly, the office manager for Mod Fashions Corporations design center, was responsible for preparing the design center budget and reviewing expense reports submitted by design center employees. Her desire to upgrade her wardrobe got the better of her, and she enacted a fraud that involved filing expense-reimbursement requests for her own personal clothing purchases. She was able to conceal the fraud because she was responsible for reviewing all expense reports, including her own. In addition, she sometimes was given ultimate responsibility for signing off on the expense reports when her boss was "too busy." Also, because she controlled the budget, when she submitted her expenses, she coded them to budget items that she knew were running under budget, so that they would not catch anyone's attention.

Total take: $275,000

THE MISSING CONTROL

Independent internal verification. Bobbi Jean's boss should have verified her expense reports. When asked what he thought her expenses for a year were, the boss said about $10,000. At $115,000 per year, her actual expenses were more than ten times what would have been expected. However, because he was "too busy" to verify her expense reports or to review the budget, he never noticed.

Source: Adapted from Wells, *Fraud Casebook* (2007), pp. 79–90.

Large companies often assign independent internal verification to internal auditors. **Internal auditors** are company employees who continuously evaluate the effectiveness of the company's internal control systems. They review the activities of departments and individuals to determine whether prescribed internal controls are being followed. They also recommend improvements when needed. In fact, most fraud is discovered by the company through internal mechanisms such as existing internal controls and internal audits. For example, the alleged fraud at WorldCom, involving billions of dollars, was uncovered by an internal auditor.

HUMAN RESOURCE CONTROLS

Human resource control activities include the following.

1. **Bond employees who handle cash.** Bonding involves obtaining insurance protection against theft by employees. It contributes to the safeguarding of cash in two ways: First, the insurance company carefully screens all individuals before adding them to the policy and may reject risky applicants. Second, bonded employees know that the insurance company will vigorously prosecute all offenders.

2. **Rotate employees' duties and require employees to take vacations.** These measures deter employees from attempting thefts since they will not be able to permanently conceal their improper actions. Many banks, for example, have discovered employee thefts when the employee was on vacation or assigned to a new position.

3. **Conduct thorough background checks.** Many believe that the most important and inexpensive measure any business can take to reduce employee theft and fraud is for the human resources department to conduct thorough background checks. Two tips: (1) Check to see whether job applicants actually graduated from the schools they list. (2) Never use the telephone numbers for previous employers given on the reference sheet; always look them up yourself.

ANATOMY OF A FRAUD

Ellen Lowry was the desk manager and Josephine Rodriquez was the head of housekeeping at the Excelsior Inn, a luxury hotel. The two best friends were so dedicated to their jobs that they never took vacations, and they frequently filled in for other employees. In fact, Ms. Rodriquez, whose job as head of housekeeping did not include cleaning rooms, often cleaned rooms herself, "just to help the staff keep up." These two "dedicated" employees, working as a team, found a way to earn a little more cash. Ellen, the desk manager, provided significant discounts to guests who paid with cash. She kept the cash and did not register the guest in the hotel's computerized system. Instead, she took the room out of circulation "due to routine maintenance." Because the room did not show up as being used, it did not receive a normal housekeeping assignment. Instead, Josephine, the head of housekeeping, cleaned the rooms during the guests' stay.

Total take: $95,000

THE MISSING CONTROL

Human resource controls. Ellen, the desk manager, had been fired by a previous employer after being accused of fraud. If the Excelsior Inn had conducted a thorough background check, it would not have hired her. The hotel fraud was detected when Ellen missed work for a few days due to illness. A system of mandatory vacations and rotating days off would have increased the chances of detecting the fraud before it became so large.

Source: Adapted from Wells, *Fraud Casebook* (2007), pp. 145–155.

ACCOUNTING ACROSS THE ORGANIZATION

SOX Boosts the Role of Human Resources

Under SOX, a company needs to keep track of employees' degrees and certifications to ensure that employees continue to meet the specified requirements of a job. Also, to ensure proper employee supervision and proper separation of duties, companies must develop and monitor an organizational chart. When one corporation went through this exercise it found that out of 17,000 employees, there were 400 people who did not report to anyone, and they had 35 people who reported to each other. In addition, if an employee complains of an unfair firing and mentions financial issues at the company, HR must refer the case to the company audit committee and possibly to its legal counsel.

? Why would unsupervised employees or employees who report to each other represent potential internal control threats?

Limitations of Internal Control

Companies generally design their systems of internal control to provide **reasonable assurance** of proper safeguarding of assets and reliability of the accounting records. The concept of reasonable assurance rests on the premise that the costs of establishing control procedures should not exceed their expected benefit.

To illustrate, consider shoplifting losses in retail stores. Stores could eliminate such losses by having a security guard stop and search customers as they leave the store. But store managers have concluded that the negative effects of such a procedure cannot be justified. Instead, stores have attempted to control shoplifting losses by less costly procedures: They post signs saying, "We reserve the right to inspect all packages" and "All shoplifters will be prosecuted." They use hidden TV cameras and store detectives to monitor customer activity, and they install sensor equipment at exits.

The **human element** is an important factor in every system of internal control. A good system can become ineffective as a result of employee fatigue, carelessness, or indifference. For example, a receiving clerk may not bother to count goods received and may just "fudge" the counts. Occasionally, two or more individuals may work together to get around prescribed controls. Such **collusion** can significantly reduce the effectiveness of a system, eliminating the protection offered by segregation of duties. No system of internal control is perfect.

The size of the business also may impose limitations on internal control. A small company, for example, may find it difficult to segregate duties or to provide for independent internal verification.

> **HELPFUL HINT**
> Controls may vary with the risk level of the activity. For example, management may consider cash to be high risk and maintaining inventories in the stockroom as low risk. Thus management would have stricter controls for cash.

DO IT!

CONTROL ACTIVITIES

Identify which control activity is violated in each of the following situations, and explain how the situation creates an opportunity for a fraud.

1. The person with primary responsibility for reconciling the bank account is also the company's accountant and makes all bank deposits.

2. Wellstone Company's treasurer received an award for distinguished service because he had not taken a vacation in 30 years.

3. In order to save money spent on order slips, and to reduce time spent keeping track of order slips, a local bar/restaurant does not buy prenumbered order slips.

Solution

1. Violates the control activity of segregation of duties. Record-keeping should be separate from physical custody. As a consequence, the employee could embezzle cash and make journal entries to hide the theft.

2. Violates the control activity of human resource controls. Key employees must take vacations. Otherwise, the treasurer, who manages the company's cash, might embezzle cash and use his position to conceal the theft.

3. Violates the control activity of documentation procedures. If pre-numbered documents are not used, then it is virtually impossible to account for the documents. As a consequence, an employee could write up a dinner sale, receive the cash from the customer, and then throw away the order slip and keep the cash.

action plan

✔ Familiarize yourself with each of the control activities summarized on page 349.

✔ Understand the nature of the frauds that each control activity is intended to address.

Related exercise material: **BE8-1**, **BE8-2**, **BE8-3**, **E8-1**, and DO IT! **8-1**.

 The Navigator

CASH CONTROLS

Cash is the one asset that is readily convertible into any other type of asset. It also is easily concealed and transported, and is highly desired. Because of these characteristics, **cash is the asset most susceptible to fraudulent activities**. In addition, because of the large volume of cash transactions, numerous errors may occur in executing and recording them. To safeguard cash and to ensure the accuracy of the accounting records for cash, effective internal control over cash is critical.

Cash Receipts Controls

Illustration 8-4 (page 358) shows how the internal control principles explained earlier apply to cash receipts transactions. As you might expect, companies vary considerably in how they apply these principles. To illustrate internal control over cash receipts, we will examine control activities for a retail store with both over-the-counter and mail receipts.

STUDY OBJECTIVE 3

Explain the applications of internal control principles to cash receipts.

OVER-THE-COUNTER RECEIPTS

In retail businesses, control of over-the-counter receipts centers on cash registers that are visible to customers. A cash sale is rung up on a cash register, with the amount clearly visible to the customer. This activity prevents the cashier from ringing up a lower amount and pocketing the difference. The customer receives an itemized cash register receipt slip and is expected to count the change received. The cash register's tape is locked in the register until a supervisor removes it. This tape accumulates the daily transactions and totals.

At the end of the clerk's shift, the clerk counts the cash and sends the cash and the count to the cashier. The cashier counts the cash, prepares a deposit slip, and deposits the cash at the bank. The cashier also sends a duplicate of the deposit slip to the accounting department to indicate cash received. The supervisor removes the cash register tape and sends it to the accounting department as the basis for a journal entry to record the cash received. Illustration 8-5 (page 359) summarizes this process.

This system for handling cash receipts uses an important internal control principle—segregation of record-keeping from physical custody. The supervisor has access to the cash register tape, but **not** to the cash. The clerk and the cashier have access to the cash, but **not** to the register tape. In addition, the cash register tape provides documentation and enables independent internal verification. Use of these three principles of internal control (segregation of record-keeping from

Cash Receipts Controls

Establishment of Responsibility

Only designated personnel are authorized to handle cash receipts (cashiers)

Physical Controls

Store cash in safes and bank vaults; limit access to storage areas; use cash registers

Segregation of Duties

Different individuals receive cash, record cash receipts, and hold the cash

Independent Internal Verification

Supervisors count cash receipts daily; treasurer compares total receipts to bank deposits daily

Documentation Procedures

Use remittance advice (mail receipts), cash register tapes, and deposit slips

Human Resource Controls

Bond personnel who handle cash; require employees to take vacations; conduct background checks

Illustration 8-4
Application of internal control principles to cash receipts

physical custody, documentation, and independent internal verification) provides an effective system of internal control. Any attempt at fraudulent activity should be detected unless there is collusion among the employees.

In some instances, the amount deposited at the bank will not agree with the cash recorded in the accounting records based on the cash register tape. These differences often result because the clerk hands incorrect change back to the retail customer. In this case, the difference between the actual cash and the amount reported on the cash register tape is reported in a Cash Over and Short account. For example, suppose that the cash register tape indicated sales of $6,956.20 but the amount of cash was only $6,946.10. A cash shortfall of $10.10 exists. To account for this cash shortfall and related cash, the company makes the following entry.

A	=	L	+	OE
+6,946.10				
				−10.10
				+6,956.20

Cash Flows
+6,946.10

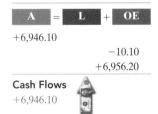

Cash	6,946.10	
Cash Over and Short	10.10	
Sales Revenue		6,956.20
(To record cash shortfall)		

Cash Over and Short is an income statement item. It is reported as miscellaneous expense when there is a cash shortfall, and as miscellaneous revenue when there is

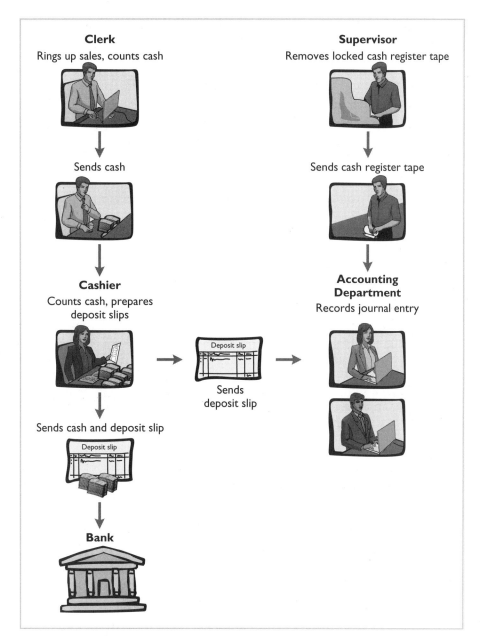

Illustration 8-5
Control of over-the-counter
receipts

an overage. Clearly, the amount should be small. Any material amounts in this account should be investigated.

MAIL RECEIPTS

All mail receipts should be opened in the presence of at least two mail clerks. These receipts are generally in the form of checks. A mail clerk should endorse each check "For Deposit Only." This restrictive endorsement reduces the likelihood that someone could divert the check to personal use. Banks will not give an individual cash when presented with a check that has this type of endorsement.

The mail-receipt clerks prepare, in triplicate, a list of the checks received each day. This list shows the name of the check issuer, the purpose of the payment, and the amount of the check. Each mail clerk signs the list to establish responsibility for the data. The original copy of the list, along with the checks, is then sent to the cashier's department. A copy of the list is sent to the accounting department for recording in the accounting records. The clerks also keep a copy.

This process provides excellent internal control for the company. By employing two clerks, the chance of fraud is reduced; each clerk knows he or she is being observed by the other clerk(s). To engage in fraud, they would have to collude. The customers who submit payments also provide control, because they will contact the company with a complaint if they are not properly credited for payment. Because the cashier has access to cash but not the records, and the accounting department has access to records but not cash, neither can engage in undetected fraud.

DO IT!

CONTROL OVER CASH RECEIPTS

action plan

✔ Differentiate among the internal control principles of (1) establishing responsibility, (2) using physical controls, and (3) independent internal verification.

✔ Design an effective system of internal control over cash receipts.

L. R. Cortez is concerned about the control over cash receipts in his fast-food restaurant, Big Cheese. The restaurant has two cash registers. At no time do more than two employees take customer orders and ring up sales. Work shifts for employees range from 4 to 8 hours. Cortez asks your help in installing a good system of internal control over cash receipts.

Solution

Cortez should assign a cash register to each employee at the start of each work shift, with register totals set at zero. Each employee should be instructed to use only the assigned register and to ring up all sales. Each customer should be given a receipt. At the end of the shift, the employee should do a cash count. A separate employee should compare the cash count with the register tape, to be sure they agree. In addition, Cortez should install an automated system that would enable the company to compare orders rung up on the register to orders processed by the kitchen.

Related exercise material: **BE8-5**, **E8-2**, and DO IT! **8-2**.

 The Navigator

Cash Disbursements Controls

STUDY OBJECTIVE 4
Explain the applications of internal control principles to cash disbursements.

Companies disburse cash for a variety of reasons, such as to pay expenses and liabilities or to purchase assets. **Generally, internal control over cash disbursements is more effective when companies pay by check, rather than by cash.** One exception is **for incidental amounts that are paid out of petty cash.**[4]

Companies generally issue checks only after following specified control procedures. Illustration 8-6 (page 361) shows how principles of internal control apply to cash disbursements.

VOUCHER SYSTEM CONTROLS

Most medium and large companies use vouchers as part of their internal control over cash disbursements. A **voucher system** is a network of approvals by authorized individuals, acting independently, to ensure that all disbursements by check are proper.

The system begins with the authorization to incur a cost or expense. It ends with the issuance of a check for the liability incurred. A **voucher** is an authorization form prepared for each expenditure. Companies require vouchers for all types of cash disbursements except those from petty cash.

---

[4]We explain the operation of a petty cash fund on pages 362–364.

Cash Disbursements Controls

Establishment of Responsibility

Only designated personnel are authorized to sign checks (treasurer) and approve vendors

Physical Controls

Store blank checks in safes, with limited access; print check amounts by machine in indelible ink

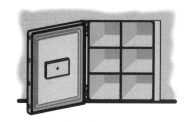

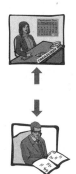

Segregation of Duties

Different individuals approve and make payments; check signers do not record disbursements

Independent Internal Verification

Compare checks to invoices; reconcile bank statement monthly

Documentation Procedures

Use prenumbered checks and account for them in sequence; each check must have an approved invoice; require employees to use corporate credit cards for reimbursable expenses; stamp invoices "paid"

Human Resource Controls

Bond personnel who handle cash; require employees to take vacations; conduct background checks

Illustration 8-6
Application of internal control principles to cash disbursements

The starting point in preparing a voucher is to fill in the appropriate information about the liability on the face of the voucher. The vendor's invoice provides most of the needed information. Then, an employee in accounts payable records the voucher (in a journal called a **voucher register**) and files it according to the date on which it is to be paid. The company issues and sends a check on that date, and stamps the voucher "paid." The paid voucher is sent to the accounting department for recording (in a journal called the **check register**). A voucher system involves two journal entries, one to issue the voucher and a second to pay the voucher.

The use of a voucher system improves internal control over cash disbursements. First, the authorization process inherent in a voucher system establishes responsibility. Each individual has responsibility to review the underlying documentation to ensure that it is correct. In addition, the voucher system keeps track of the documents that back up each transaction. By keeping these documents in one place, a supervisor can independently verify the authenticity of each transaction. Consider, for example, the case of Aesop University presented on page 351. Aesop did not use a voucher system for transactions under $2,500. As a consequence, there was no independent verification of the documents, which enabled the employee to submit fake invoices to hide his unauthorized purchases.

PETTY CASH FUND CONTROLS

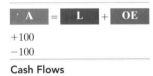

STUDY OBJECTIVE 5

Describe the operation of a petty cash fund.

As you learned earlier in the chapter, better internal control over cash disbursements is possible when companies make payments by check. However, using checks to pay small amounts is both impractical and a nuisance. For instance, a company would not want to write checks to pay for postage due, working lunches, or taxi fares. A common way of handling such payments, while maintaining satisfactory control, is to use a petty cash fund to pay relatively small amounts. The operation of a petty cash fund, often called an **imprest system**, involves three steps: (1) establishing the fund, (2) making payments from the fund, and (3) replenishing the fund.[5]

Establishing The Fund.   In establishing a petty cash fund, a company appoints a petty cash custodian who will be responsible for the fund. Next it determines the size of the fund. Ordinarily, a company expects the amount in the fund to cover anticipated disbursements for a three- to four-week period.

To establish the fund, a company issues a check payable to the petty cash custodian for the stipulated amount. For example, if Laird Company decides to establish a $100 fund on March 1, the journal entry is:

A	=	L	+	OE
+100				
−100				

Cash Flows
no effect

Mar. 1	Petty Cash	100	
	Cash		100
	(To establish a petty cash fund)		

The fund custodian cashes the check and places the proceeds in a locked petty cash box or drawer. Most petty cash funds are established on a fixed-amount basis. The company will make no additional entries to the Petty Cash account unless management changes the stipulated amount of the fund. For example, if Laird Company decides on July 1 to increase the size of the fund to $250, it would debit Petty Cash $150 and credit Cash $150.

Making Payments from the Fund.   The petty cash fund custodian has the authority to make payments from the fund that conform to prescribed management policies. Usually, management limits the size of expenditures that come from petty cash. Likewise, it may not permit use of the fund for certain types of transactions (such as making short-term loans to employees).

Each payment from the fund must be documented on a prenumbered petty cash receipt (or petty cash voucher), as shown in Illustration 8-7 (page 363). Note that the signatures of both the fund custodian and the person receiving payment are required on the receipt. If other supporting documents such as a freight bill or invoice are available, they should be attached to the petty cash receipt.

The fund custodian keeps the receipts in the petty cash box until the fund is replenished. The sum of the petty cash receipts and the money in the fund should equal the established total at all times. Management can (and should) make surprise counts at any time to determine whether the fund is being maintained correctly.

The company does not make an accounting entry to record a payment when it is made from petty cash. Instead, the company recognizes the accounting effects of each payment when it replenishes the fund.

Replenishing the Fund.   When the money in the petty cash fund reaches a minimum level, the company replenishes the fund. The petty cash custodian initiates

---

[5]The term "imprest" means an advance of money for a designated purpose.

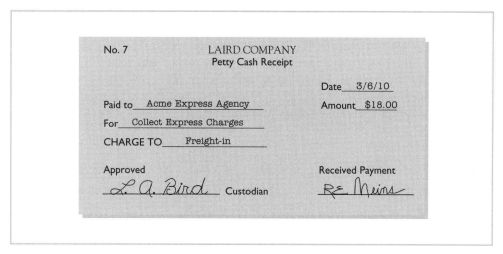

Illustration 8-7
Petty cash receipt

a request for reimbursement. He or she prepares a schedule (or summary) of the payments that have been made and sends the schedule, supported by petty cash receipts and other documentation, to the treasurer's office. Someone in the treasurer's office examines the receipts and supporting documents to verify that they were proper payments from the fund. The treasurer then approves the request and issues a check to restore the fund to its established amount. At the same time, all supporting documentation is stamped "paid" so that it cannot be submitted again for payment.

To illustrate, assume that on March 15 Laird's petty cash custodian requests a check for $87. The fund contains $13 cash and petty cash receipts for postage $44, freight-out $38, and miscellaneous expenses $5. The general journal entry to record the check is:

Mar. 15	Postage Expense	44	
	Freight-out	38	
	Miscellaneous Expense	5	
	Cash		87
	(To replenish petty cash fund)		

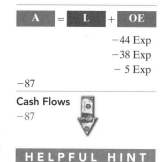

Note that the reimbursement entry does not affect the Petty Cash account. Replenishment changes the composition of the fund by replacing the petty cash receipts with cash. It does not change the balance in the fund.

Occasionally, in replenishing a petty cash fund, the company may need to recognize a cash shortage or overage. This results when the total of the cash plus receipts in the petty cash box does not equal the established amount of the petty cash fund. To illustrate, assume that Laird's petty cash custodian has only $12 in cash in the fund plus the receipts as listed. The request for reimbursement would, therefore, be for $88, and Laird would make the following entry:

HELPFUL HINT
Cash over and short situations result from mathematical errors or from failure to keep accurate records.

Mar. 15	Postage Expense	44	
	Freight-out	38	
	Miscellaneous Expense	5	
	Cash Over and Short	1	
	Cash		88
	(To replenish petty cash fund)		

Conversely, if the custodian has $14 in cash, the reimbursement request would be for $86, and the company would credit Cash Over and Short for $1 (overage). A company reports a debit balance in Cash Over and Short in the income statement as miscellaneous expense. It reports a credit balance in the account as miscellaneous revenue. The company closes Cash Over and Short to Income Summary at the end of the year.

Companies should replenish a petty cash fund at the end of the accounting period, regardless of the cash in the fund. Replenishment at this time is necessary in order to recognize the effects of the petty cash payments on the financial statements.

DO IT!

PETTY CASH FUND

action plan

✔ To establish the fund, set up a separate general ledger account.

✔ Determine how much cash is needed to replenish the fund: subtract the cash remaining from the petty cash fund balance.

✔ Total the petty cash receipts. Determine any cash over or short—the difference between the cash needed to replenish the fund and the total of the petty cash receipts.

✔ Record the expenses incurred according to the petty cash receipts when replenishing the fund.

Bateer Company established a $50 petty cash fund on July 1. On July 30, the fund had $12 cash remaining and petty cash receipts for postage $14, office supplies $10, and delivery expense $15. Prepare journal entries to establish the fund on July 1 and to replenish the fund on July 30.

Solution

July	1	Petty Cash	50	
		Cash		50
		(To establish petty cash fund)		
	30	Postage Expense	14	
		Office Supplies	10	
		Delivery Expense	15	
		Cash Over and Short		1
		Cash ($50 – $12)		38
		(To replenish petty cash)		

Related exercise material: **BE8-9, E8-7, E8-8,** and **DO IT!** 8-3.

 The Navigator

CONTROL FEATURES: USE OF A BANK

STUDY OBJECTIVE 6
Indicate the control features of a bank account.

The use of a bank contributes significantly to good internal control over cash. A company can safeguard its cash by using a bank as a depository and as a clearing house for checks received and written. Use of a bank minimizes the amount of currency that a company must keep on hand. Also, use of a bank facilitates the control of cash because it creates a double record of all bank transactions—one by the company and the other by the bank. The asset account Cash maintained by the company should have the same balance as the bank's liability account for that company. A bank reconciliation compares the bank's balance with the company's balance and explains any differences to make them agree.

Many companies have more than one bank account. For efficiency of operations and better control, national retailers like Wal-Mart and Target may have regional bank accounts. Large companies, with tens of thousands of employees, may have a payroll bank account, as well as one or more general bank accounts. Also, a company may maintain several bank accounts in order to have more than one source for short-term loans when needed.

Making Bank Deposits

An authorized employee, such as the head cashier, should make a company's bank deposits. Each deposit must be documented by a deposit slip (ticket), as shown in Illustration 8-8.

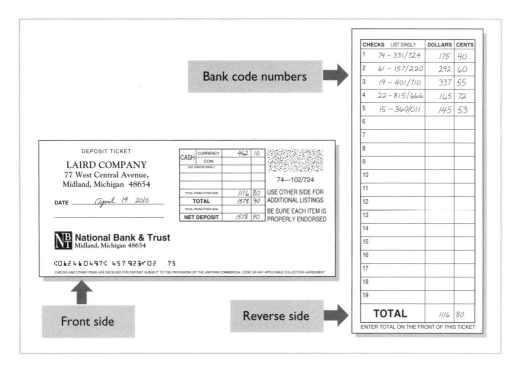

Illustration 8-8
Deposit slip

Deposit slips are prepared in duplicate. The bank retains the original; the depositor keeps the duplicate, machine-stamped by the bank to establish its authenticity.

Writing Checks

Most of us write checks, without thinking very much about them. A **check** is a written order signed by the depositor directing the bank to pay a specified sum of money to a designated recipient. There are three parties to a check: (1) the **maker** (or drawer) who issues the check, (2) the **bank** (or payer) on which the check is drawn, and (3) the **payee** to whom the check is payable. A check is a **negotiable instrument** that one party can transfer to another party by endorsement. Each check should be accompanied by an explanation of its purpose. In many companies, a remittance advice attached to the check, as shown in Illustration 8-9 (page 366) explains the check's purpose.

It is important to know the balance in the checking account at all times. To keep the balance current, the depositor should enter each deposit and check on running-balance memo forms provided by the bank or on the check stubs in the checkbook.

Bank Statements

If you have a personal checking account, you are probably familiar with bank statements. A **bank statement** shows the depositor's bank transactions and

Illustration 8-9
Check with remittance
advice

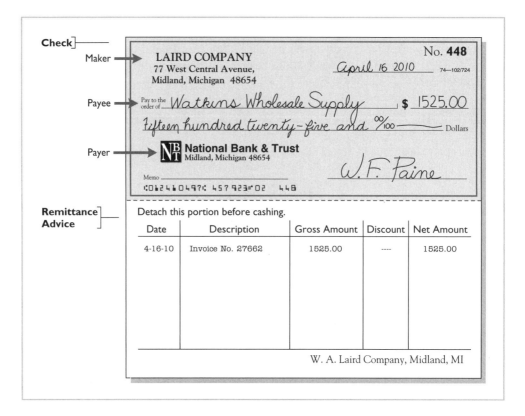

balances.[6] Each month, a depositor receives a statement from the bank. Illustration 8-10 (page 367) presents a typical bank statement. It shows: (1) checks paid and other debits that reduce the balance in the depositor's account, (2) deposits and other credits that increase the balance in the account, and (3) the account balance after each day's transactions.

The bank statement lists in numerical sequence all "paid" checks, along with the date the check was paid and its amount. Upon paying a check, the bank stamps the check "paid"; a paid check is sometimes referred to as a **canceled** check. On the statement the bank also includes memoranda explaining other debits and credits it made to the depositor's account.

DEBIT MEMORANDUM

Some banks charge a monthly fee for their services. Often they charge this fee only when the average monthly balance in a checking account falls below a specified amount. They identify the fee, called a **bank service charge**, on the bank statement by a symbol such as **SC**. The bank also sends with the statement a debit memorandum explaining the charge noted on the statement. Other debit memoranda may also be issued for other bank services such as the cost of printing checks, issuing traveler's checks, and wiring funds to other locations. The symbol **DM** is often used for such charges.

Banks also use a debit memorandum when a deposited check from a customer "bounces" because of insufficient funds. For example, assume that Scott Company, a customer of Laird Company, sends a check for $800 to Laird Company for services provided. Unfortunately, Scott does not have sufficient funds at its bank to pay

---

[6]Our presentation assumes that the depositor makes all adjustments at the end of the month. In practice, a company may also make journal entries during the month as it receives information from the bank regarding its account.

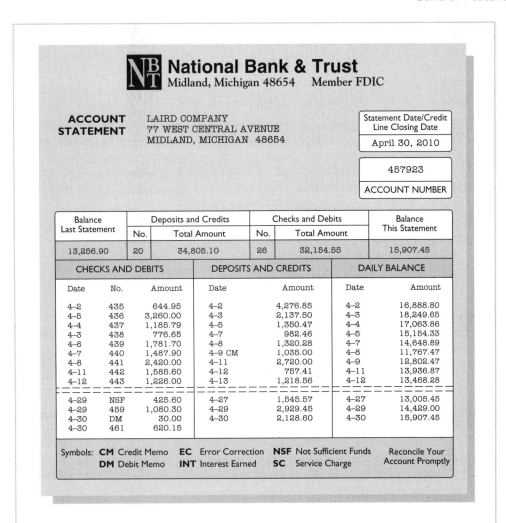

Illustration 8-10
Bank statement

for these services. In such a case, Scott's bank marks the check **NSF** (not sufficient funds) and returns it to Laird's (the depositor's) bank. Laird's bank then debits Laird's account, as shown by the symbol NSF on the bank statement in Illustration 8-10 (above). The bank sends the NSF check and debit memorandum to Laird as notification of the charge. Laird then records an Account Receivable from Scott Company (the writer of the bad check) and reduces cash for the NSF check.

CREDIT MEMORANDUM

Sometimes a depositor asks the bank to collect its notes receivable. In such a case, the bank will credit the depositor's account for the cash proceeds of the note. This is illustrated by the symbol **CM** on the Laird Company bank statement. The bank issues and sends with the statement a credit memorandum to explain the entry. Many banks also offer interest on checking accounts. The interest earned may be indicated on the bank statement by the symbol **CM** or **INT**.

Reconciling the Bank Account

The bank and the depositor maintain independent records of the depositor's checking account. People tend to assume that the respective balances will always agree. In fact, the two balances are seldom the same at any given time. Therefore it is necessary to make the balance per books agree with the

STUDY OBJECTIVE 7
Prepare a bank reconciliation.

balance per bank—a process called **reconciling the bank account**. The lack of agreement between the two balances has two causes:

1. **Time lags** that prevent one of the parties from recording the transaction in the same period as the other party.

2. **Errors** by either party in recording transactions.

Time lags occur frequently. For example, several days may elapse between the time a company mails a check to a payee and the date the bank pays the check. Similarly, when the depositor uses the bank's night depository to make its deposits, there will be a difference of at least one day between the time the depositor records the deposit and the time the bank does so. A time lag also occurs whenever the bank mails a debit or credit memorandum to the depositor.

The incidence of errors depends on the effectiveness of the internal controls of the depositor and the bank. Bank errors are infrequent. However, either party could accidentally record a $450 check as $45 or $540. In addition, the bank might mistakenly charge a check to a wrong account by keying in an incorrect account name or number.

RECONCILIATION PROCEDURE

The bank reconciliation should be prepared by an employee who has no other responsibilities pertaining to cash. If a company fails to follow this internal control principle of independent internal verification, cash embezzlements may go unnoticed. For example, a cashier who prepares the reconciliation can embezzle cash and conceal the embezzlement by misstating the reconciliation. Thus, the bank accounts would reconcile, and the embezzlement would not be detected.

In reconciling the bank account, it is customary to reconcile the balance per books and balance per bank to their adjusted (correct or true) cash balances. The starting point in preparing the reconciliation is to enter the balance per bank statement and balance per books on the reconciliation schedule. The company then makes various adjustments, as shown in Illustration 8-11 (page 369).

The following steps should reveal all the reconciling items that cause the difference between the two balances.

Step 1. Deposits in transit. Compare the individual deposits listed on the bank statement with deposits in transit from the preceding bank reconciliation and with the deposits per company records or duplicate deposit slips. Deposits recorded by the depositor that have not been recorded by the bank are the **deposits in transit**. Add these deposits to the balance per bank.

> **HELPFUL HINT**
> Deposits in transit and outstanding checks are reconciling items because of time lags.

Step 2. Outstanding checks. Compare the paid checks shown on the bank statement with (a) checks outstanding from the previous bank reconciliation, and (b) checks issued by the company as recorded in the cash payments journal (or in the check register in your personal checkbook). Issued checks recorded by the company but that have not yet been paid by the bank are **outstanding checks**. Deduct outstanding checks from the balance per the bank.

Step 3. Errors. Note any errors discovered in the foregoing steps and list them in the appropriate section of the reconciliation schedule. For example, if the company mistakenly recorded as $169 a paid check correctly written for $196, it would deduct the error of $27 from the balance per books. All errors made by the depositor are reconciling items in determining the adjusted cash balance per books. In contrast, all errors made by the bank are reconciling items in determining the adjusted cash balance per the bank.

Step 4. Bank memoranda. Trace bank memoranda to the depositor's records. List in the appropriate section of the reconciliation schedule any unrecorded memoranda. For example, the company would deduct from the balance per books a $5 debit memorandum for bank service charges. Similarly, it would add to the balance per books $32 of interest earned.

Illustration 8-11
Bank reconciliation
adjustments

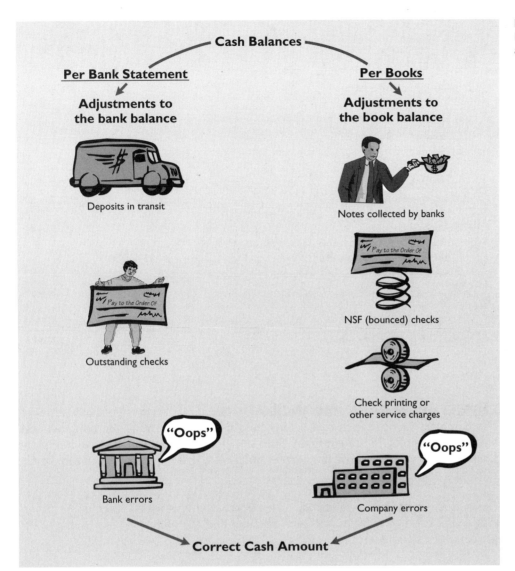

BANK RECONCILIATION ILLUSTRATED

The bank statement for Laird Company, in Illustration 8-10, shows a balance per bank of $15,907.45 on April 30, 2010. On this date the balance of cash per books is $11,589.45. Using the four reconciliation steps, Laird determines the following reconciling items.

Step 1. Deposits in transit: April 30 deposit (received by
   bank on May 1). $2,201.40

Step 2. Outstanding checks: No. 453, $3,000.00; no. 457,
   $1,401.30; no. 460, $1,502.70.   5,904.00

Step 3. Errors: Laird wrote check no. 443 for $1,226.00 and the
   bank correctly paid that amount. However, Laird recorded
   the check as $1,262.00.   36.00

Step 4. Bank memoranda:
   a. Debit—NSF check from J. R. Baron for $425.60   425.60
   b. Debit—Charge for printing company checks $30.00   30.00
   c. Credit—Collection of note receivable for $1,000
      plus interest earned $50, less bank collection fee $15.00   1,035.00

Illustration 8-12 (next page) shows Laird's bank reconciliation.

> **HELPFUL HINT**
>
> Note in the bank statement on page 367 that checks no. 459 and 461 have been paid but check no. 460 is not listed. Thus, this check is outstanding. If a complete bank statement were provided, checks no. 453 and 457 would also not be listed. The amounts for these three checks are obtained from the company's cash payments records.

Illustration 8-12
Bank reconciliation

LAIRD COMPANY Bank Reconciliation April 30, 2010		
Cash balance per bank statement		$15,907.45
Add: Deposits in transit		2,201.40
		18,108.85
Less: Outstanding checks		
No. 453	$3,000.00	
No. 457	1,401.30	
No. 460	1,502.70	5,904.00
Adjusted cash balance per bank		**$12,204.85** ←
Cash balance per books		$11,589.45
Add: Collection of note receivable $1,000, plus interest		
earned $50, less collection fee $15	$1,035.00	
Error in recording check no. 443	36.00	1,071.00
		12,660.45
Less: NSF check	425.60	
Bank service charge	30.00	455.60
Adjusted cash balance per books		**$12,204.85** ←

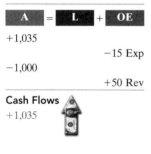

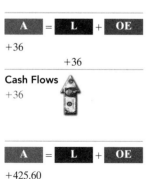

ENTRIES FROM BANK RECONCILIATION

The company records each reconciling item used to determine the **adjusted cash balance per books**. **If the company does not journalize and post these items, the Cash account will not show the correct balance.** Laird Company would make the following entries on April 30.

Collection of Note Receivable. This entry involves four accounts. Assuming that the interest of $50 has not been accrued and the collection fee is charged to Miscellaneous Expense, the entry is:

Apr. 30	Cash	1,035.00	
	Miscellaneous Expense	15.00	
	Notes Receivable		1,000.00
	Interest Revenue		50.00
	(To record collection of note receivable by bank)		

Book Error. The cash disbursements journal shows that check no. 443 was a payment on account to Andrea Company, a supplier. The correcting entry is:

Apr. 30	Cash	36.00	
	Accounts Payable—Andrea Company		36.00
	(To correct error in recording check no. 443)		

NSF Check. As indicated earlier, an NSF check becomes an account receivable to the depositor. The entry is:

Apr. 30	Accounts Receivable—J. R. Baron	425.60	
	Cash		425.60
	(To record NSF check)		

Bank Service Charges. Depositors debit check printing charges (DM) and other bank service charges (SC) to Miscellaneous Expense, because they are usually nominal in amount. The entry is:

Apr. 30	Miscellaneous Expense	30.00	
	Cash		30.00
	(To record charge for printing company checks)		

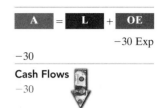

Illustration 8-13
Adjusted balance in cash account

Instead of making four separate entries, Laird could combine them into one compound entry.

After Laird has posted the entries, the Cash account will show the following.

Cash				
Apr. 30 Bal.	11,589.45	Apr. 30	425.60	
30	1,035.00	30	30.00	
30	36.00			
Apr. 30 Bal.	**12,204.85**			

The adjusted cash balance in the ledger should agree with the adjusted cash balance per books in the bank reconciliation in Illustration 8-12.

What entries does the bank make? If the company discovers any bank errors in preparing the reconciliation, it should notify the bank. The bank then can make the necessary corrections in its records. The bank does not make any entries for deposits in transit or outstanding checks. Only when these items reach the bank will the bank record these items.

ELECTRONIC FUNDS TRANSFER (EFT) SYSTEM

It is not surprising that companies and banks have developed approaches to transfer funds among parties without the use of paper (deposit tickets, checks, etc.). Such procedures, called **electronic funds transfers (EFT)**, are disbursement systems that use wire, telephone, or computers to transfer cash balances from one location to another. Use of EFT is quite common. For example, many employees receive no formal payroll checks from their employers. Instead, employers send electronic payroll data to the appropriate banks. Also, individuals now frequently make regular payments such as those for house, car, and utilities by EFT.

EFT transfers normally result in better internal control since no cash or checks are handled by company employees. This does not mean that opportunities for fraud are eliminated. In fact, the same basic principles related to internal control apply to EFT transfers. For example, without proper segregation of duties and authorizations, an employee might be able to redirect electronic payments into a personal bank account and conceal the theft with fraudulent accounting entries.

DO IT!

BANK RECONCILIATION

Sally Kist owns Linen Kist Fabrics. Sally asks you to explain how she should treat the following reconciling items when reconciling the company's bank account: (1) a debit memorandum for an NSF check, (2) a credit memorandum for a note collected by the bank, (3) outstanding checks, and (4) a deposit in transit.

action plan

✔ Understand the purpose of a bank reconciliation.

✔ Identify time lags and explain how they cause reconciling items.

Solution

Sally should treat the reconciling items as follows.

(1) NSF check: Deduct from balance per books.

(2) Collection of note: Add to balance per books.

(3) Outstanding checks: Deduct from balance per bank.

(4) Deposit in transit: Add to balance per bank.

Related exercise material: **BE8-11, BE8-12, BE8-13, BE8-14, E8-9, E8-10, E8-11, E8-12, E8-13,** and **DO IT!** **8-4.**

 The Navigator

REPORTING CASH

STUDY OBJECTIVE 8
Explain the reporting of cash.

Cash consists of coins, currency (paper money), checks, money orders, and money on hand or on deposit in a bank or similar depository. On the balance sheet, companies therefore combine cash on hand, cash in banks, and petty cash and report the total simply as **Cash**. Because it is the most liquid asset owned by a company, cash is listed first in the current assets section of the balance sheet. Some companies use the term "Cash and cash equivalents" in reporting cash, as shown in Illustration 8-14.

Illustration 8-14
Presentation of cash and cash equivalents

EASTMAN KODAK COMPANY
Balance Sheets (partial)

	2006	2005
Current assets (in millions)		
Cash and cash equivalents	$1,469	$1,665

Cash equivalents are short-term, highly liquid investments that can be converted into a specific amount of cash. At the time of purchase, they typically have maturities of three months or less. They include money market funds, bank certificates of deposit, and U.S. Treasury bills and notes.

A company may have cash that is restricted for a special purpose. An example is a payroll bank account for paying salaries and wages. Another would be a plant expansion cash fund for financing new construction. Companies should report **restricted cash** separately on the balance sheet. If a company expects to use the restricted cash **within the next year**, the amount should be reported as a current asset. Otherwise, it should be reported as a noncurrent asset. Since a payroll bank account will be used as early as the next payday, it is reported as a current asset. In contrast, unless the new construction will begin within the next year, cash for plant expansion would be classified as a noncurrent asset (long-term investment).

When making loans to depositors, banks commonly require borrowers to maintain minimum cash balances. These minimum balances, called **compensating balances**, provide the bank with support for the loans. They are a restriction on the use of cash that may affect a company's liquidity. Thus, companies should disclose compensating balances in the notes to the financial statements.

 Be sure to read **ALL ABOUT YOU: Protecting Yourself from Identity Theft** on page 373 for information on how topics in this chapter apply to your personal life.

Protecting Yourself from Identity Theft

As a result of the Sarbanes-Oxley Act, companies have done a lot to improve their internal controls to help protect themselves from both internal and external thieves. What have you done lately to shore up your own personal internal controls? You've heard the stories about hackers cleaning out people's online investment accounts or running up credit card bills that would take you most of your life to pay off. (If you don't have a credit card, they'll open an account for you.) The identity thieves aren't going away. So what can you do to protect yourself? Many of the same common-sense controls discussed in this chapter can be implemented in your personal life.

✹ Some Facts

* Identity thieves determine your identity by going through your mail or trash, stealing your credit cards, redirecting mail through change of address forms, or acquiring personal information you share on unsecured sites. In a recent year, more than 7 million people were victims of identity theft.

* During a single computer-virus outbreak, called the "Hearse," thieves stole 90,000 pieces of personal data.

* The average identity-theft victim spends 600 hours clearing up his or her finances and financial and other records to recover from the crime.

* Victims incur an average of $1,400 in out-of-pocket expenses.

* Consumers have $1.7 trillion worth of assets with online brokerage firms. Many of the largest identity theft losses have been the result of thieves completely cleaning out online brokerage accounts.

* The Federal Trade Commission reports identify theft is the No. 1 fraud complaint among consumers. Phoenix and Las Vegas top the list for identity theft per capita.

✹ About the Numbers

The following chart shows the most common survey responses from victims of identity theft when asked how their information was used by the thieves. (Note that respondents chose more than one type of use.)

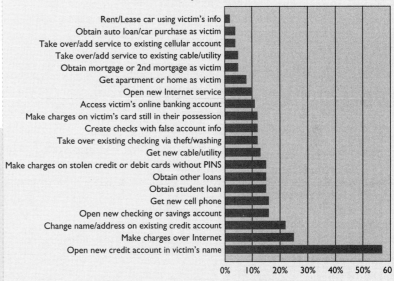

Common Ways That Thieves Use Stolen Identity Information

Source: The Identity Theft Resource Center, *Identity Theft: The Aftermath 2007*, *www.idtheftcenter.org/idaftermath.pdf* (accessed May 2008).

✹ What Do You Think

Do you feel it is safe to store personal financial data (such as Social Security numbers and bank and credit account numbers) on your computer?

YES: I have anti-virus software that will detect and stop any intruder.

NO: Even the best anti-virus software does not detect every kind of intruder.

Sources: Amy Borrus, "Invasion of the Stock Hackers," *Business Week*, November 14, 2005, pp. 38-40; Brian Grow, "Nasty, Brutish, and Sneaky," *Business Week*, April 10, 2006, p. 37; Federal Trade Commission, *www.consumer.gov/idtheft/*.

Comprehensive **DO IT!**

Poorten Company's bank statement for May 2010 shows the following data.

Balance 5/1	$12,650	Balance 5/31	$14,280
Debit memorandum:		Credit memorandum:	
NSF check	$175	Collection of note receivable	$505

The cash balance per books at May 31 is $13,319. Your review of the data reveals the following.

1. The NSF check was from Copple Co., a customer.
2. The note collected by the bank was a $500, 3-month, 12% note. The bank charged a $10 collection fee. No interest has been accrued.
3. Outstanding checks at May 31 total $2,410.
4. Deposits in transit at May 31 total $1,752.
5. A Poorten Company check for $352, dated May 10, cleared the bank on May 25. The company recorded this check, which was a payment on account, for $325.

Instructions

(a) Prepare a bank reconciliation at May 31.
(b) Journalize the entries required by the reconciliation.

action plan

✔ Follow the four steps in the reconciliation procedure (p. 368).

✔ Make sure the adjusted cash balance per bank is equal to the adjusted cash balance per books.

✔ Work carefully to minimize mathematical errors in the reconciliation.

✔ Prepare adjusting entries from reconciling items per books.

✔ Make sure the cash ledger balance after posting the reconciling entries agrees with the adjusted cash balance per books.

Solution to Comprehensive **DO IT!**

(a)

POORTEN COMPANY
Bank Reconciliation
May 31, 2010

Cash balance per bank statement		$14,280
Add: Deposits in transit		1,752
		16,032
Less: Outstanding checks		2,410
Adjusted cash balance per bank		$13,622
Cash balance per books		$13,319
Add: Collection of note receivable $500, plus $15		
interest, less collection fee $10		505
		13,824
Less: NSF check	$175	
Error in recording check	27	202
Adjusted cash balance per books		$13,622

(b)

May 31	Cash	505	
	Miscellaneous Expense	10	
	Notes Receivable		500
	Interest Revenue		15
	(To record collection of note by bank)		
31	Accounts Receivable—Copple Co.	175	
	Cash		175
	(To record NSF check from Copple Co.)		
31	Accounts Payable	27	
	Cash		27
	(To correct error in recording check)		

The Navigator

SUMMARY OF STUDY OBJECTIVES

1 Define fraud and internal control. A fraud is a dishonest act by an employee that results in personal benefit to the employee at a cost to the employer. The fraud triangle refers to the three factors that contribute to fraudulent activity by employees: opportunity, financial pressure, and rationalization. Internal control consists of all the related methods and measures adopted within an organization to safeguard its assets, enhance the reliability of its accounting records, increase efficiency of operations, and ensure compliance with laws and regulations.

2 Identify the principles of internal control. The principles of internal control are: establishment of responsibility; segregation of duties; documentation procedures; physical controls; independent internal verification; and human resource controls such as bonding and requiring employees to take vacations.

3 Explain the applications of internal control principles to cash receipts. Internal controls over cash receipts include: (a) designating specific personnel to handle cash; (b) assigning different individuals to receive cash, record cash, and maintain custody of cash; (c) using remittance advices for mail receipts, cash register tapes for over-the-counter receipts, and deposit slips for bank deposits; (d) using company safes and bank vaults to store cash with access limited to authorized personnel, and using cash registers in executing over-the-counter receipts; (e) making independent daily counts of register receipts and daily comparison of total receipts with total deposits; and (f) bonding personnel that handle cash and requiring them to take vacations.

4 Explain the applications of internal control principles to cash disbursements. Internal controls over cash disbursements include: (a) having specific individuals such as the treasurer authorized to sign checks and approve invoices; (b) assigning different individuals to approve items for payment, pay the items, and record the payment; (c) using prenumbered checks and accounting for all checks, with each check supported by an approved invoice; (d) storing blank checks in a safe or vault with access restricted to authorized personnel, and using a checkwriting machine to imprint amounts on checks; (e) comparing each check with the approved invoice before issuing the check, and making monthly reconciliations of bank and book balances; and (f) bonding personnel who handle cash, requiring employees to take vacations, and conducting background checks.

5 Describe the operation of a petty cash fund. Companies operate a petty cash fund to pay relatively small amounts of cash. They must establish the fund, make payments from the fund, and replenish the fund when the cash in the fund reaches a minimum level.

6 Indicate the control features of a bank account. A bank account contributes to good internal control by providing physical controls for the storage of cash. It minimizes the amount of currency that a company must keep on hand, and it creates a double record of a depositor's bank transactions.

7 Prepare a bank reconciliation. It is customary to reconcile the balance per books and balance per bank to their adjusted balances. The steps in the reconciling process are to determine deposits in transit, outstanding checks, errors by the depositor or the bank, and unrecorded bank memoranda.

8 Explain the reporting of cash. Companies list cash first in the current assets section of the balance sheet. In some cases, they report cash together with cash equivalents. Cash restricted for a special purpose is reported separately as a current asset or as a noncurrent asset, depending on when the cash is expected to be used. ✓ *The Navigator*

GLOSSARY

Bank reconciliation The process of comparing the bank's balance of an account with the company's balance and explaining any differences to make them agree. (p. 364).

Bank service charge A fee charged by a bank for the use of its services. (p. 366).

Bank statement A monthly statement from the bank that shows the depositor's bank transactions and balances. (p. 365).

Bonding Obtaining insurance protection against misappropriation of assets by employees. (p. 355).

Cash Resources that consist of coins, currency, checks, money orders, and money on hand or on deposit in a bank or similar depository. (p. 372).

Cash equivalents Short-term, highly liquid investments that can be converted to a specific amount of cash. (p. 372).

Check A written order signed by a bank depositor, directing the bank to pay a specified sum of money to a designated recipient. (p. 365).

Compensating balances Minimum cash balances required by a bank in support of bank loans. (p. 372).

Deposits in transit Deposits recorded by the depositor but not yet been recorded by the bank. (p. 368).

Electronic funds transfer (EFT) A disbursement system that uses wire, telephone, or computers to transfer funds from one location to another. (p. 371).

Fraud A dishonest act by an employee that results in personal benefit to the employee at a cost to the employer. (p. 346).

Fraud triangle The three factors that contribute to fraudulent activity by employees: opportunity, financial pressure, and rationalization. (p. 346).

Internal auditors Company employees who continuously evaluate the effectiveness of the company's internal control system. (p. 355).

Internal control All of the related methods and activities adopted within an organization to safeguard its assets and enhance the accuracy and reliability of its accounting records. (p. 348).

NSF check A check that is not paid by a bank because of insufficient funds in a customer's bank account. (p. 367).

Outstanding checks Checks issued and recorded by a company but not yet paid by the bank. (p. 368).

Petty cash fund A cash fund used to pay relatively small amounts. (p. 362).

Restricted cash Cash that must be used for a special purpose. (p. 372).

Sarbanes-Oxley Act of 2002 (SOX) Regulations passed by Congress to try to reduce unethical corporate behavior. (p. 348).

Voucher An authorization form prepared for each payment in a voucher system. (p. 360).

Voucher system A network of approvals by authorized individuals acting independently to ensure that all disbursements by check are proper. (p. 360).

SELF-STUDY QUESTIONS

Answers are at the end of the chapter.

(SO 1) **1.** Which of the following is *not* an element of the fraud triangle?
  a. Rationalization.
  b. Financial pressure.
  c. Segregation of duties.
  d. Opportunity.

(SO 1) **2.** An organization uses internal control to enhance the accuracy and reliability of its accounting records and to:
  a. safeguard its assets.
  b. prevent fraud.
  c. produce correct financial statements.
  d. deter employee dishonesty.

(SO 1) **3.** Which of the following was *not* a result of the Sarbanes-Oxley Act?
  a. Companies must file financial statements with the Internal Revenue Service.
  b. All publicly traded companies must maintain adequate internal controls.
  c. The Public Company Accounting Oversight Board was created to establish auditing standards and regulate auditor activity.
  d. Corporate executives and board of directors must ensure that controls are reliable and effective, and they can be fined or imprisoned for failure to do so.

(SO 2) **4.** The principles of internal control do *not* include:
  a. establishment of responsibility.
  b. documentation procedures.
  c. management responsibility.
  d. independent internal verification.

(SO 2) **5.** Physical controls do *not* include:
  a. safes and vaults to store cash.
  b. independent bank reconciliations.
  c. locked warehouses for inventories.
  d. bank safety deposit boxes for important papers.

(SO 3) **6.** Permitting only designated personnel to handle cash receipts is an application of the principle of:
  a. segregation of duties.
  b. establishment of responsibility.
  c. independent check.
  d. human resource controls.

(SO 3) **7.** Which of the following control activities is *not* relevant to when a company uses a computerized (rather than manual) accounting system?
  a. Establishment of responsibility.
  b. Segregation of duties.
  c. Independent internal verification.
  d. All of these control activities are relevant to a computerized system.

(SO 4) **8.** The use of prenumbered checks in disbursing cash is an application of the principle of:
  a. establishment of responsibility.
  b. segregation of duties.
  c. physical controls.
  d. documentation procedures.

(SO 5) **9.** A company writes a check to replenish a $100 petty cash fund when the fund contains receipts of $94 and $3 in cash. In recording the check, the company should:
  a. debit Cash Over and Short for $3.
  b. debit Petty Cash for $94.
  c. credit Cash for $94.
  d. credit Petty Cash for $3.

(SO 6) **10.** The control features of a bank account do *not* include:
  a. having bank auditors verify the correctness of the bank balance per books.
  b. minimizing the amount of cash that must be kept on hand.
  c. providing a double record of all bank transactions.
  d. safeguarding cash by using a bank as a depository.

(SO 7) **11.** In a bank reconciliation, deposits in transit are:
  a. deducted from the book balance.
  b. added to the book balance.
  c. added to the bank balance.
  d. deducted from the bank balance.

(SO 7) **12.** The reconciling item in a bank reconciliation that will result in an adjusting entry by the depositor is:
  a. outstanding checks.
  b. deposit in transit.
  c. a bank error.
  d. bank service charges.

(SO 8) **13.** Which of the following items in a cash drawer at November 30 is *not* cash?
   a. Money orders.
   b. Coins and currency.
   c. A customer check dated December 1.
   d. A customer check dated November 28.

(SO 8) **14.** Which of the following statements correctly describes the reporting of cash?

   a. Cash cannot be combined with cash equivalents.
   b. Restricted cash funds may be combined with Cash.
   c. Cash is listed first in the current assets section.
   d. Restricted cash funds cannot be reported as a current asset.

Go to the book's companion website,
www.wiley.com/college/weygandt,
for Additional Self-Study questions.

 The Navigator

QUESTIONS

1. A local bank reported that it lost $150,000 as the result of an employee fraud. Randal Smith is not clear on what is meant by an "employee fraud." Explain the meaning of fraud to Randal and give an example of frauds that might occur at a bank.

2. Fraud experts often say that there are three primary factors that contribute to employee fraud. Identify the three factors and explain what is meant by each.

3. Identify and describe the five components of a good internal control system.

4. "Internal control is concerned only with enhancing the accuracy of the accounting records." Do you agree? Explain.

5. What principles of internal control apply to most organizations?

6. At the corner grocery store, all sales clerks make change out of one cash register drawer. Is this a violation of internal control? Why?

7. Meg Lucas is reviewing the principle of segregation of duties. What are the two common applications of this principle?

8. How do documentation procedures contribute to good internal control?

9. What internal control objectives are met by physical controls?

10. (a) Explain the control principle of independent internal verification. (b) What practices are important in applying this principle?

11. The management of Sewell Company asks you, as the company accountant, to explain (a) the concept of reasonable assurance in internal control and (b) the importance of the human factor in internal control.

12. McCartney Fertilizer Co. owns the following assets at the balance sheet date.

Cash in bank savings account	$ 8,000
Cash on hand	850
Cash refund due from the IRS	1,000
Checking account balance	12,000
Postdated checks	500

What amount should McCartney report as cash in the balance sheet?

13. What principle(s) of internal control is (are) involved in making daily cash counts of over-the-counter receipts?

14. Jacobs Department Stores has just installed new electronic cash registers in its stores. How do cash registers improve internal control over cash receipts?

15. At Hummel Wholesale Company, two mail clerks open all mail receipts. How does this strengthen internal control?

16. "To have maximum effective internal control over cash disbursements, all payments should be made by check." Is this true? Explain.

17. Joe Griswold Company's internal controls over cash disbursements provide for the treasurer to sign checks imprinted by a checkwriting machine in indelible ink after comparing the check with the approved invoice. Identify the internal control principles that are present in these controls.

18. How do the principles of (a) physical controls and (b) documentation controls apply to cash disbursements?

19. (a) What is a voucher system? (b) What principles of internal control apply to a voucher system?

20. What is the essential feature of an electronic funds transfer (EFT) procedure?

21. (a) Identify the three activities that pertain to a petty cash fund, and indicate an internal control principle that is applicable to each activity. (b) When are journal entries required in the operation of a petty cash fund?

22. "The use of a bank contributes significantly to good internal control over cash." Is this true? Why or why not?

23. Lori Figgs is confused about the lack of agreement between the cash balance per books and the balance per the bank. Explain the causes for the lack of agreement to Lori, and give an example of each cause.

24. What are the four steps involved in finding differences between the balance per books and balance per bank?

25. Kristen Hope asks your help concerning an NSF check. Explain to Kristen (a) what an NSF check is, (b) how it is treated in a bank reconciliation, and (c) whether it will require an adjusting entry.

26. (a) "Cash equivalents are the same as cash." Do you agree? Explain. (b) How should restricted cash funds be reported on the balance sheet?

27. **PEPSICO** At what amount does PepsiCo report cash and cash equivalents in its 2007 consolidated balance sheet?

BRIEF EXERCISES

Identify fraud-triangle concepts.

(SO 1)

BE8-1   Match each situation with the fraud triangle factor—opportunity, financial pressure, or rationalization—that best describes it.

1. An employee's monthly credit card payments are nearly 75% of their monthly earnings.
2. An employee earns minimum wage at a firm that has reported record earnings for each of the last five years.
3. An employee has an expensive gambling habit.
4. An employee has check writing and signing responsibilities for a small company, as well as reconciling the bank account.

Indicate internal control concepts.

(SO 1)

BE8-2   Jim Gaffigan has prepared the following list of statements about internal control.

1. One of the objectives of internal control is to safeguard assets from employee theft, robbery, and unauthorized use.
2. One of the objectives of internal control is to enhance the accuracy and reliability of the accounting records.
3. No laws require U.S. corporations to maintain an adequate system of internal control.

Identify each statement as true or false. If false, indicate how to correct the statement.

Explain the importance of internal control.

(SO 1)

BE8-3   Heather Bailiff is the new owner of Ready Parking. She has heard about internal control but is not clear about its importance for her business. Explain to Heather the four purposes of internal control and give her one application of each purpose for Ready Parking.

Identify internal control principles.

(SO 2)

BE8-4   The internal control procedures in Weiser Company provide that:

1. Employees who have physical custody of assets do not have access to the accounting records.
2. Each month the assets on hand are compared to the accounting records by an internal auditor.
3. A prenumbered shipping document is prepared for each shipment of goods to customers.

Identify the principles of internal control that are being followed.

Identify the internal control principles applicable to cash receipts.

(SO 3)

BE8-5   Knobloch Company has the following internal control procedures over cash receipts. Identify the internal control principle that is applicable to each procedure.

1. All over-the-counter receipts are registered on cash registers.
2. All cashiers are bonded.
3. Daily cash counts are made by cashier department supervisors.
4. The duties of receiving cash, recording cash, and custody of cash are assigned to different individuals.
5. Only cashiers may operate cash registers.

Make journal entries for cash overage and shortfall.

(SO 3)

BE8-6   The cash register tape for Leprechaun Industries reported sales of $6,891.56. Record the journal entry that would be necessary for each of the following situations: (a) Cash to be accounted for exceeds cash on hand by $50.75. (b) Cash on hand exceeds cash to be accounted for by $28.32.

Make journal entry using cash count sheet.

(SO 3)

BE8-7   While examining cash receipts information, the accounting department determined the following information: opening cash balance $150, cash on hand $1,125.74, and cash sales per register tape $990.83. Prepare the required journal entry based upon the cash count sheet.

Identify the internal control principles applicable to cash disbursements.

(SO 4)

BE8-8   Mingenback Company has the following internal control procedures over cash disbursements. Identify the internal control principle that is applicable to each procedure.

1. Company checks are prenumbered.
2. The bank statement is reconciled monthly by an internal auditor.
3. Blank checks are stored in a safe in the treasurer's office.
4. Only the treasurer or assistant treasurer may sign checks.
5. Check signers are not allowed to record cash disbursement transactions.

Prepare entry to replenish a petty cash fund.

(SO 5)

BE8-9   On March 20, Terrell's petty cash fund of $100 is replenished when the fund contains $7 in cash and receipts for postage $52, freight-out $26, and travel expense $10. Prepare the journal entry to record the replenishment of the petty cash fund.

Identify the control features of a bank account.

(SO 6)

BE8-10   Gary Cunningham is uncertain about the control features of a bank account. Explain the control benefits of **(a)** a check and **(b)** a bank statement.

BE8-11 The following reconciling items are applicable to the bank reconciliation for Stormont Company: (1) outstanding checks, (2) bank debit memorandum for service charge, (3) bank credit memorandum for collecting a note for the depositor, (4) deposits in transit. Indicate how each item should be shown on a bank reconciliation.

Indicate location of reconciling items in a bank reconciliation.
(SO 7)

BE8-12 Using the data in BE8-11, indicate **(a)** the items that will result in an adjustment to the depositor's records and **(b)** why the other items do not require adjustment.

Identify reconciling items that require adjusting entries.
(SO 7)

BE8-13 At July 31, Kuhlmann Company has the following bank information: cash balance per bank $7,420, outstanding checks $762, deposits in transit $1,120, and a bank service charge $20. Determine the adjusted cash balance per bank at July 31.

Prepare partial bank reconciliation.
(SO 7)

BE8-14 At August 31, Felipe Company has a cash balance per books of $8,500 and the following additional data from the bank statement: charge for printing Felipe Company checks $35, interest earned on checking account balance $40, and outstanding checks $800. Determine the adjusted cash balance per books at August 31.

Prepare partial bank reconciliation.
(SO 7)

BE8-15 Quirk Company has the following cash balances: Cash in Bank $15,742, Payroll Bank Account $6,000, and Plant Expansion Fund Cash $25,000. Explain how each balance should be reported on the balance sheet.

Explain the statement presentation of cash balances.
(SO 8)

DO IT! REVIEW

DO IT! 8-1 Identify which control activity is violated in each of the following situations, and explain how the situation creates an opportunity for fraud or inappropriate accounting practices.

Identify violations of control activities.
(SO 2)

1. Once a month the sales department sends sales invoices to the accounting department to be recorded.
2. Jay Margan orders merchandise for Rice Lake Company; he also receives merchandise and authorizes payment for merchandise.
3. Several clerks at Dick's Groceries use the same cash register drawer.

DO IT! 8-2 Javier Vasquez is concerned with control over mail receipts at Javy's Sporting Goods. All mail receipts are opened by Nick Swisher. Nick sends the checks to the accounting department, where they are stamped "For Deposit Only." The accounting department records and deposits the mail receipts weekly. Javier asks for your help in installing a good system of internal control over mail receipts.

Design system of internal control over cash receipts.
(SO 3)

DO IT! 8-3 Mengke Company established a $100 petty cash fund on August 1. On August 30, the fund had $9 cash remaining and petty cash receipts for postage $31, office supplies $42, and miscellaneous expense $16. Prepare journal entries to establish the fund on August 1 and replenish the fund on August 30.

Make journal entries for petty cash fund.
(SO 5)

DO IT! 8-4 Linus Hugt owns Linus Blankets. Linus asks you to explain how he should treat the following reconciling items when reconciling the company's bank account.

Explain treatment of items in bank reconciliation.
(SO 7)

1. Outstanding checks
2. A deposit in transit
3. The bank charged to our account a check written by another company
4. A debit memorandum for a bank service charge

EXERCISES

E8-1 Sue Merando is the owner of Merando's Pizza. Merando's is operated strictly on a carry-out basis. Customers pick up their orders at a counter where a clerk exchanges the pizza for cash. While at the counter, the customer can see other employees making the pizzas and the large ovens in which the pizzas are baked.

Identify the principles of internal control.
(SO 2)

Instructions

Identify the six principles of internal control and give an example of each principle that you might observe when picking up your pizza. (*Note*: It may not be possible to observe all the principles.)

Identify internal control weaknesses over cash receipts and suggest improvements.

(SO 2, 3)

E8-2   The following control procedures are used at Gonzales Company for over-the-counter cash receipts.

1. To minimize the risk of robbery, cash in excess of $100 is stored in an unlocked attaché case in the stock room until it is deposited in the bank.
2. All over-the-counter receipts are registered by three clerks who use a cash register with a single cash drawer.
3. The company accountant makes the bank deposit and then records the day's receipts.
4. At the end of each day, the total receipts are counted by the cashier on duty and reconciled to the cash register total.
5. Cashiers are experienced; they are not bonded.

Instructions

(a) For each procedure, explain the weakness in internal control, and identify the control principle that is violated.
(b) For each weakness, suggest a change in procedure that will result in good internal control.

Identify internal control weaknesses over cash disbursements and suggest improvements.

(SO 2, 4)

E8-3   The following control procedures are used in Benton's Boutique Shoppe for cash disbursements.

1. The company accountant prepares the bank reconciliation and reports any discrepancies to the owner.
2. The store manager personally approves all payments before signing and issuing checks.
3. Each week, Benton leaves 100 company checks in an unmarked envelope on a shelf behind the cash register.
4. After payment, bills are filed in a paid invoice folder.
5. The company checks are unnumbered.

Instructions

(a) For each procedure, explain the weakness in internal control, and identify the internal control principle that is violated.
(b) For each weakness, suggest a change in the procedure that will result in good internal control.

Identify internal control weaknesses for cash disbursements and suggest improvements.

(SO 4)

E8-4   At Hutchingson Company, checks are not prenumbered because both the puchasing agent and the treasurer are authorized to issue checks. Each signer has access to unissued checks kept in an unlocked file cabinet. The purchasing agent pays all bills pertaining to goods purchased for resale. Prior to payment, the purchasing agent determines that the goods have been received and verifies the mathematical accuracy of the vendor's invoice. After payment, the invoice is filed by the vendor, and the purchasing agent records the payment in the cash disbursements journal. The treasurer pays all other bills following approval by authorized employees. After payment, the treasurer stamps all bills PAID, files them by payment date, and records the checks in the cash disbursements journal. Hutchingson Company maintains one checking account that is reconciled by the treasurer.

Instructions

(a) List the weaknesses in internal control over cash disbursements.
(b) ━━━► Write a memo to the company treasurer indicating your recommendations for improvement.

Indicate whether procedure is good or weak internal control.

(SO 2, 3, 4)

E8-5   Listed below are five procedures followed by The Beat Company.

1. Several individuals operate the cash register using the same register drawer.
2. A monthly bank reconciliation is prepared by someone who has no other cash responsibilities.
3. Ellen May writes checks and also records cash payment journal entries.
4. One individual orders inventory, while a different individual authorizes payments.
5. Unnumbered sales invoices from credit sales are forwarded to the accounting department every four weeks for recording.

Instructions

Indicate whether each procedure is an example of good internal control or of weak internal control. If it is an example of good internal control, indicate which internal control principle is being followed. If it is an example of weak internal control, indicate which internal control principle is violated. Use the table below.

Procedure	IC Good or Weak?	Related Internal Control Principle
1.		
2.		
3.		
4.		
5.		

E8-6 Listed below are five procedures followed by Collins Company.

Indicate whether procedure is good or weak internal control.

(SO 2, 3, 4)

1. Employees are required to take vacations.
2. Any member of the sales department can approve credit sales.
3. Jethro Bodine ships goods to customers, bills customers, and receives payment from customers.
4. Total cash receipts are compared to bank deposits daily by someone who has no other cash responsibilities.
5. Time clocks are used for recording time worked by employees.

Instructions
Indicate whether each procedure is an example of good internal control or of weak internal control. If it is an example of good internal control, indicate which internal control principle is being followed. If it is an example of weak internal control, indicate which internal control principle is violated. Use the table below.

Procedure	IC Good or Weak?	Related Internal Control Principle
1.		
2.		
3.		
4.		
5.		

E8-7 James Hughes Company established a petty cash fund on May 1, cashing a check for $100. The company reimbursed the fund on June 1 and July 1 with the following results.

Prepare journal entries for a petty cash fund.

(SO 5)

June 1: Cash in fund $2.75. Receipts: delivery expense $31.25; postage expense $39.00; and miscellaneous expense $25.00.

July 1: Cash in fund $3.25. Receipts: delivery expense $21.00; entertainment expense $51.00; and miscellaneous expense $24.75.

On July 10, James Hughes increased the fund from $100 to $150.

Instructions
Prepare journal entries for James Hughes Company for May 1, June 1, July 1, and July 10.

E8-8 Lincolnville Company uses an imprest petty cash system. The fund was established on March 1 with a balance of $100. During March the following petty cash receipts were found in the petty cash box.

Prepare journal entries for a petty cash fund.

(SO 5)

Date	Receipt No.	For	Amount
3/5	1	Stamp Inventory	$39
7	2	Freight-out	21
9	3	Miscellaneous Expense	6
11	4	Travel Expense	24
14	5	Miscellaneous Expense	5

The fund was replenished on March 15 when the fund contained $3 in cash. On March 20, the amount in the fund was increased to $150.

Instructions
Journalize the entries in March that pertain to the operation of the petty cash fund.

Prepare bank reconciliation and adjusting entries.

(SO 7)

E8-9 Anna Pelo is unable to reconcile the bank balance at January 31. Anna's reconciliation is as follows.

Cash balance per bank	$3,560.20
Add: NSF check	690.00
Less: Bank service charge	25.00
Adjusted balance per bank	$4,225.20
Cash balance per books	$3,875.20
Less: Deposits in transit	530.00
Add: Outstanding checks	930.00
Adjusted balance per books	$4,275.20

Instructions
(a) Prepare a correct bank reconciliation.
(b) Journalize the entries required by the reconciliation.

Determine outstanding checks.

(SO 7)

E8-10 On April 30, the bank reconciliation of Galena Company shows three outstanding checks: no. 254, $650, no. 255, $820, and no. 257, $410. The May bank statement and the May cash payments journal show the following.

Bank Statement Checks Paid			Cash Payments Journal Checks Issued		
Date	Check No.	Amount	Date	Check No.	Amount
5/4	254	650	5/2	258	159
5/2	257	410	5/5	259	275
5/17	258	159	5/10	260	890
5/12	259	275	5/15	261	500
5/20	261	500	5/22	262	750
5/29	263	480	5/24	263	480
5/30	262	750	5/29	264	560

Instructions
Using step 2 in the reconciliation procedure, list the outstanding checks at May 31.

Prepare bank reconciliation and adjusting entries.

(SO 7)

E8-11 The following information pertains to Family Video Company.

1. Cash balance per bank, July 31, $7,263.
2. July bank service charge not recorded by the depositor $28.
3. Cash balance per books, July 31, $7,284.
4. Deposits in transit, July 31, $1,500.
5. Bank collected $900 note for Family in July, plus interest $36, less fee $20. The collection has not been recorded by Family, and no interest has been accrued.
6. Outstanding checks, July 31, $591.

Instructions
(a) Prepare a bank reconciliation at July 31.
(b) Journalize the adjusting entries at July 31 on the books of Family Video Company.

Prepare bank reconciliation and adjusting entries.

(SO 7)

E8-12 The information below relates to the Cash account in the ledger of Robertson Company.

Balance September 1—$17,150; Cash deposited—$64,000.
Balance September 30—$17,404; Checks written—$63,746.

The September bank statement shows a balance of $16,422 on September 30 and the following memoranda.

Credits		Debits	
Collection of $1,500 note plus interest $30	$1,530	NSF check: J. E. Hoover	$425
Interest earned on checking account	$45	Safety deposit box rent	$65

At September 30, deposits in transit were $4,450, and outstanding checks totaled $2,383.

Instructions
(a) Prepare the bank reconciliation at September 30.
(b) Prepare the adjusting entries at September 30, assuming (1) the NSF check was from a customer on account, and (2) no interest had been accrued on the note.

E8-13   The cash records of Givens Company show the following four situations.

1. The June 30 bank reconciliation indicated that deposits in transit total $720. During July the general ledger account Cash shows deposits of $15,750, but the bank statement indicates that only $15,600 in deposits were received during the month.
2. The June 30 bank reconciliation also reported outstanding checks of $680. During the month of July, Givens Company books show that $17,200 of checks were issued. The bank statement showed that $16,400 of checks cleared the bank in July.
3. In September, deposits per the bank statement totaled $26,700, deposits per books were $25,400, and deposits in transit at September 30 were $2,100.
4. In September, cash disbursements per books were $23,700, checks clearing the bank were $25,000, and outstanding checks at September 30 were $2,100.

Compute deposits in transit and outstanding checks for two bank reconciliations.

(SO 7)

There were no bank debit or credit memoranda. No errors were made by either the bank or Givens Company.

Instructions
Answer the following questions.

(a) In situation (1), what were the deposits in transit at July 31?
(b) In situation (2), what were the outstanding checks at July 31?
(c) In situation (3), what were the deposits in transit at August 31?
(d) In situation (4), what were the outstanding checks at August 31?

E8-14   Lipkus Company has recorded the following items in its financial records.

Cash in bank	$ 47,000
Cash in plant expansion fund	100,000
Cash on hand	12,000
Highly liquid investments	34,000
Petty cash	500
Receivables from customers	89,000
Stock investments	61,000

Show presentation of cash in financial statements.

(SO 8)

The cash in bank is subject to a compensating balance of $5,000. The highly liquid investments had maturities of 3 months or less when they were purchased. The stock investments will be sold in the next 6 to 12 months. The plant expansion project will begin in 3 years.

Instructions
(a) What amount should Lipkus report as "Cash and cash equivalents" on its balance sheet?
(b) Where should the items not included in part (a) be reported on the balance sheet?
(c) What disclosures should Lipkus make in its financial statements concerning "cash and cash equivalents"?

EXERCISES: SET B

Visit the book's companion website at **www.wiley.com/college/weygandt**, and choose the Student Companion site, to access Exercise Set B.

PROBLEMS: SET A

P8-1A   Luby Office Supply Company recently changed its system of internal control over cash disbursements. The system includes the following features.
    Instead of being unnumbered and manually prepared, all checks must now be prenumbered and written by using the new checkwriting machine purchased by the company. Before a check can be issued, each invoice must have the approval of Sally Morgan, the purchasing agent, and John Countryman, the receiving department supervisor. Checks must be signed by either Ann

Identify internal control principles over cash disbursements.

(SO 2, 4)

Lynn, the treasurer, or Bob Skabo, the assistant treasurer. Before signing a check, the signer is expected to compare the amount of the check with the amount on the invoice.

After signing a check, the signer stamps the invoice PAID and inserts within the stamp, the date, check number, and amount of the check. The "paid" invoice is then sent to the accounting department for recording.

Blank checks are stored in a safe in the treasurer's office. The combination to the safe is known only by the treasurer and assistant treasurer. Each month, the bank statement is reconciled with the bank balance per books by the assistant chief accountant. All employees who handle or account for cash are bonded.

Instructions

Identify the internal control principles and their application to cash disbursements of Luby Office Supply Company.

Journalize and post petty cash fund transactions.

(SO 5)

P8-2A Winningham Company maintains a petty cash fund for small expenditures. The following transactions occurred over a 2-month period.

July 1 Established petty cash fund by writing a check on Cubs Bank for $200.

15 Replenished the petty cash fund by writing a check for $196.00. On this date the fund consisted of $4.00 in cash and the following petty cash receipts: freight-out $94.00, postage expense $42.40, entertainment expense $46.60, and miscellaneous expense $11.20.

31 Replenished the petty cash fund by writing a check for $192.00. At this date, the fund consisted of $8.00 in cash and the following petty cash receipts: freight-out $82.10, charitable contributions expense $45.00, postage expense $25.50, and miscellaneous expense $39.40.

Aug. 15 Replenished the petty cash fund by writing a check for $187.00. On this date, the fund consisted of $13.00 in cash and the following petty cash receipts: freight-out $75.60, entertainment expense $43.00, postage expense $33.00, and miscellaneous expense $37.00.

16 Increased the amount of the petty cash fund to $300 by writing a check for $100.

31 Replenished petty cash fund by writing a check for $284.00. On this date, the fund consisted of $16 in cash and the following petty cash receipts: postage expense $140.00, travel expense $95.60, and freight-out $47.10.

Instructions

(a) July 15, Cash short $1.80

(b) Aug. 31 balance $300

(a) Journalize the petty cash transactions.

(b) Post to the Petty Cash account.

(c) What internal control features exist in a petty cash fund?

Prepare a bank reconciliation and adjusting entries.

(SO 7)

P8-3A On May 31, 2010, James Logan Company had a cash balance per books of $6,781.50. The bank statement from Farmers State Bank on that date showed a balance of $6,404.60. A comparison of the statement with the cash account revealed the following facts.

1. The statement included a debit memo of $40 for the printing of additional company checks.

2. Cash sales of $836.15 on May 12 were deposited in the bank. The cash receipts journal entry and the deposit slip were incorrectly made for $886.15. The bank credited Logan Company for the correct amount.

3. Outstanding checks at May 31 totaled $576.25. Deposits in transit were $1,916.15.

4. On May 18, the company issued check No. 1181 for $685 to Barry Trest, on account. The check, which cleared the bank in May, was incorrectly journalized and posted by Logan Company for $658.

5. A $2,500 note receivable was collected by the bank for Logan Company on May 31 plus $80 interest. The bank charged a collection fee of $20. No interest has been accrued on the note.

6. Included with the cancelled checks was a check issued by Bridgetown Company to Tom Lujak for $800 that was incorrectly charged to Logan Company by the bank.

7. On May 31, the bank statement showed an NSF charge of $680 for a check issued by Sandy Grifton, a customer, to Logan Company on account.

Instructions

(a) Adjusted cash balance per bank $8,544.50

Prepare a bank reconciliation and adjusting entries from detailed data.

(SO 7)

(a) Prepare the bank reconciliation at May 31, 2010.

(b) Prepare the necessary adjusting entries for Logan Company at May 31, 2010.

P8-4A The bank portion of the bank reconciliation for Backhaus Company at November 30, 2010, was as follows.

BACKHAUS COMPANY
Bank Reconciliation
November 30, 2010

Cash balance per bank		$14,367.90
Add: Deposits in transit		2,530.20
		16,898.10
Less: Outstanding checks		

Check Number	Check Amount	
3451	$2,260.40	
3470	720.10	
3471	844.50	
3472	1,426.80	
3474	1,050.00	6,301.80
Adjusted cash balance per bank		$10,596.30

The adjusted cash balance per bank agreed with the cash balance per books at November 30. The December bank statement showed the following checks and deposits.

	Bank Statement				
	Checks			**Deposits**	
Date	**Number**	**Amount**	**Date**	**Amount**	
12-1	3451	$ 2,260.40	12-1	$ 2,530.20	
12-2	3471	844.50	12-4	1,211.60	
12-7	3472	1,426.80	12-8	2,365.10	
12-4	3475	1,640.70	12-16	2,672.70	
12-8	3476	1,300.00	12-21	2,945.00	
12-10	3477	2,130.00	12-26	2,567.30	
12-15	3479	3,080.00	12-29	2,836.00	
12-27	3480	600.00	12-30	1,025.00	
12-30	3482	475.50	Total	$18,152.90	
12-29	3483	1,140.00			
12-31	3485	540.80			
	Total	$15,438.70			

The cash records per books for December showed the following.

	Cash Payments Journal						Cash Receipts Journal	
Date	**Number**	**Amount**	**Date**	**Number**	**Amount**		**Date**	**Amount**
12-1	3475	$1,640.70	12-20	3482	$ 475.50		12-3	$ 1,211.60
12-2	3476	1,300.00	12-22	3483	1,140.00		12-7	2,365.10
12-2	3477	2,130.00	12-23	3484	798.00		12-15	2,672.70
12-4	3478	621.30	12-24	3485	450.80		12-20	2,954.00
12-8	3479	3,080.00	12-30	3486	1,889.50		12-25	2,567.30
12-10	3480	600.00	Total		$14,933.20		12-28	2,836.00
12-17	3481	807.40					12-30	1,025.00
							12-31	1,690.40
							Total	$17,322.10

The bank statement contained two memoranda:

1. A credit of $4,145 for the collection of a $4,000 note for Backhaus Company plus interest of $160 and less a collection fee of $15. Backhaus Company has not accrued any interest on the note.

2. A debit of $572.80 for an NSF check written by D. Chagnon, a customer. At December 31, the check had not been redeposited in the bank.

At December 31 the cash balance per books was $12,485.20, and the cash balance per the bank statement was $20,154.30. The bank did not make any errors, but two errors were made by Backhaus Company.

Instructions

(a) Adjusted balance per books $15,958.40

(a) Using the four steps in the reconciliation procedure, prepare a bank reconciliation at December 31.

(b) Prepare the adjusting entries based on the reconciliation. (*Hint*: The correction of any errors pertaining to recording checks should be made to Accounts Payable. The correction of any errors relating to recording cash receipts should be made to Accounts Receivable.)

Prepare a bank reconciliation and adjusting entries.

(SO 7)

P8-5A Haverman Company maintains a checking account at the Commerce Bank. At July 31, selected data from the ledger balance and the bank statement are shown below.

	Cash in Bank	
	Per Books	**Per Bank**
Balance, July 1	$17,600	$16,800
July receipts	81,400	
July credits		82,470
July disbursements	77,150	
July debits		74,756
Balance, July 31	$21,850	$24,514

Analysis of the bank data reveals that the credits consist of $79,000 of July deposits and a credit memorandum of $3,470 for the collection of a $3,400 note plus interest revenue of $70. The July debits per bank consist of checks cleared $74,700 and a debit memorandum of $56 for printing additional company checks.

You also discover the following errors involving July checks: (1) A check for $230 to a creditor on account that cleared the bank in July was journalized and posted as $320. (2) A salary check to an employee for $255 was recorded by the bank for $155.

The June 30 bank reconciliation contained only two reconciling items: deposits in transit $7,000 and outstanding checks of $6,200.

Instructions

(a) Adjusted balance per books $25,354

(a) Prepare a bank reconciliation at July 31.

(b) Journalize the adjusting entries to be made by Haverman Company at July 31, 2010. Assume that interest on the note has not been accrued.

Identify internal control weaknesses in cash receipts and cash disbursements.

(SO 2, 3, 4)

P8-6A Emporia Middle School wants to raise money for a new sound system for its auditorium. The primary fund-raising event is a dance at which the famous disc jockey Obnoxious Ed will play classic and not-so-classic dance tunes. Tom Wickman, the music and theater instructor, has been given the responsibility for coordinating the fund-raising efforts. This is Tom's first experience with fund-raising. He decides to put the eighth-grade choir in charge of the event; he will be a relatively passive observer.

Tom had 500 unnumbered tickets printed for the dance. He left the tickets in a box on his desk and told the choir students to take as many tickets as they thought they could sell for $5 each. In order to ensure that no extra tickets would be floating around, he told them to dispose of any unsold tickets. When the students received payment for the tickets, they were to bring the cash back to Tom, and he would put it in a locked box in his desk drawer.

Some of the students were responsible for decorating the gymnasium for the dance. Tom gave each of them a key to the money box and told them that if they took money out to purchase materials, they should put a note in the box saying how much they took and what it was used for. After 2 weeks the money box appeared to be getting full, so Tom asked Luke Gilmor to count the money, prepare a deposit slip, and deposit the money in a bank account Tom had opened.

The day of the dance, Tom wrote a check from the account to pay the DJ. Obnoxious Ed, however, said that he accepted only cash and did not give receipts. So Tom took $200 out of the cash box and gave it to Ed. At the dance Tom had Mel Harris working at the entrance to the gymnasium, collecting tickets from students and selling tickets to those who had not prepurchased them. Tom estimated that 400 students attended the dance.

The following day Tom closed out the bank account, which had $250 in it, and gave that amount plus the $180 in the cash box to Principal Foran. Principal Foran seemed surprised that, after generating roughly $2,000 in sales, the dance netted only $430 in cash. Tom did not know how to respond.

Instructions

Identify as many internal control weaknesses as you can in this scenario, and suggest how each could be addressed.

PROBLEMS: SET B

P8-1B   Discount Theater is located in the Mishawaka Mall. A cashier's booth is located near the entrance to the theater. Three cashiers are employed. One works from 1–5 P.M., another from 5–9 P.M. The shifts are rotated among the three cashiers. The cashiers receive cash from customers and operate a machine that ejects serially numbered tickets. The rolls of tickets are inserted and locked into the machine by the theater manager at the beginning of each cashier's shift.

After purchasing a ticket, the customer takes the ticket to an usher stationed at the entrance of the theater lobby some 60 feet from the cashier's booth. The usher tears the ticket in half, admits the customer, and returns the ticket stub to the customer. The other half of the ticket is dropped into a locked box by the usher.

At the end of each cashier's shift, the theater manager removes the ticket rolls from the machine and makes a cash count. The cash count sheet is initialed by the cashier. At the end of the day, the manager deposits the receipts in total in a bank night deposit vault located in the mall. The manager also sends copies of the deposit slip and the initialed cash count sheets to the theater company treasurer for verification and to the company's accounting department. Receipts from the first shift are stored in a safe located in the manager's office.

Identify internal control weaknesses over cash receipts.

(SO 2, 3)

Instructions

(a) Identify the internal control principles and their application to the cash receipts transactions of the Discount Theater.

(b) If the usher and cashier decide to collaborate to misappropriate cash, what actions might they take?

P8-2B   Loganberry Company maintains a petty cash fund for small expenditures. The following transactions occurred over a 2-month period.

Journalize and post petty cash fund transactions.

(SO 5)

July   1   Established petty cash fund by writing a check on Rock Point Bank for $100.
      15   Replenished the petty cash fund by writing a check for $96.90. On this date the fund consisted of $3.10 in cash and the following petty cash receipts: freight-out $51.00, postage expense $20.50, entertainment expense $23.10, and miscellaneous expense $4.10.
      31   Replenished the petty cash fund by writing a check for $95.90. At this date, the fund consisted of $4.10 in cash and the following petty cash receipts: freight-out $43.50, charitable contributions expense $20.00, postage expense $20.10, and miscellaneous expense $12.30.
Aug. 15   Replenished the petty cash fund by writing a check for $98.00. On this date, the fund consisted of $2.00 in cash and the following petty cash receipts: freight-out $40.20, entertainment expense $21.00, postage expense $14.00, and miscellaneous expense $19.80.
      16   Increased the amount of the petty cash fund to $150 by writing a check for $50.
      31   Replenished petty cash fund by writing a check for $137.00. On this date, the fund consisted of $13 in cash and the following petty cash receipts: freight-out $74.00, entertainment expense $43.20, and postage expense $17.70.

Instructions

(a) Journalize the petty cash transactions.

(b) Post to the Petty Cash account.

(c) What internal control features exist in a petty cash fund?

(a) July 15 Cash over $1.80
(b) Aug. 31 balance $150

Prepare a bank reconciliation and adjusting entries.

(SO 7)

P8-3B Wolverine Genetics Company of Flint, Michigan, spreads herbicides and applies liquid fertilizer for local farmers. On May 31, 2010, the company's cash account per its general ledger showed the following balance.

CASH   NO. 101

Date	Explanation	Ref.	Debit	Credit	Balance
May 31	Balance				13,287

The bank statement from Flint State Bank on that date showed the following balance.

FLINT STATE BANK

Checks and Debits	Deposits and Credits	Daily Balance
XXX	XXX	5/31 13,332

A comparison of the details on the bank statement with the details in the cash account revealed the following facts.

1. The statement included a debit memo of $35 for the printing of additional company checks.
2. Cash sales of $1,720 on May 12 were deposited in the bank. The cash receipts journal entry and the deposit slip were incorrectly made for $1,820. The bank credited Wolverine Genetics Company for the correct amount.
3. Outstanding checks at May 31 totaled $1,225, and deposits in transit were $2,100.
4. On May 18, the company issued check no. 1181 for $911 to G. Fischer, on account. The check, which cleared the bank in May, was incorrectly journalized and posted by Wolverine Genetics Company for $119.
5. A $4,000 note receivable was collected by the bank for Wolverine Genetics Company on May 31 plus $80 interest. The bank charged a collection fee of $25. No interest has been accrued on the note.
6. Included with the cancelled checks was a check issued by Carr Company to Henry Ford for $900 that was incorrectly charged to Wolverine Genetics Company by the bank.
7. On May 31, the bank statement showed an NSF charge of $1,308 for a check issued by Bo Sclembech, a customer, to Wolverine Genetics Company on account.

Instructions

(a) Adj. cash bal. $15,107

(a) Prepare the bank reconciliation at May 31, 2010.

(b) Prepare the necessary adjusting entries for Wolverine Genetics Company at May 31, 2010.

Prepare a bank reconciliation and adjusting entries from detailed data.

(SO 7)

P8-4B The bank portion of the bank reconciliation for Chapin Company at October 31, 2010, was as follows.

CHAPIN COMPANY
Bank Reconciliation
October 31, 2010

Cash balance per bank		$6,000
Add: Deposits in transit		842
		6,842
Less: Outstanding checks		

Check Number	Check Amount	
2451	$700	
2470	396	
2471	464	
2472	270	
2474	578	2,408
Adjusted cash balance per bank		$4,434

The adjusted cash balance per bank agreed with the cash balance per books at October 31.
The November bank statement showed the following checks and deposits:

Bank Statement

Checks			Deposits	
Date	Number	Amount	Date	Amount
11-1	2470	$ 396	11-1	$ 842
11-2	2471	464	11-4	666
11-5	2474	578	11-8	545
11-4	2475	903	11-13	1,416
11-8	2476	1,556	11-18	810
11-10	2477	330	11-21	1,624
11-15	2479	980	11-25	1,412
11-18	2480	714	11-28	908
11-27	2481	382	11-30	652
11-30	2483	317	Total	$8,875
11-29	2486	495		
	Total	$7,115		

The cash records per books for November showed the following.

Cash Payments Journal						Cash Receipts Journal	
Date	Number	Amount	Date	Number	Amount	Date	Amount
11-1	2475	$ 903	11-20	2483	$ 317	11-3	$ 666
11-2	2476	1,556	11-22	2484	460	11-7	545
11-2	2477	330	11-23	2485	525	11-12	1,416
11-4	2478	300	11-24	2486	495	11-17	810
11-8	2479	890	11-29	2487	210	11-20	1,642
11-10	2480	714	11-30	2488	635	11-24	1,412
11-15	2481	382	Total		$8,067	11-27	908
11-18	2482	350				11-29	652
						11-30	1,541
						Total	$9,592

The bank statement contained two bank memoranda:

1. A credit of $1,375 for the collection of a $1,300 note for Chapin Company plus interest of $91 and less a collection fee of $16. Chapin Company has not accrued any interest on the note.
2. A debit for the printing of additional company checks $34.

At November 30, the cash balance per books was $5,958, and the cash balance per the bank statement was $9,100. The bank did not make any errors, but two errors were made by Chapin Company.

Instructions

(a) Using the four steps in the reconciliation procedure described on page 368, prepare a bank reconciliation at November 30.

(b) Prepare the adjusting entries based on the reconciliation. (*Hint:* The correction of any errors pertaining to recording checks should be made to Accounts Payable. The correction of any errors relating to recording cash receipts should be made to Accounts Receivable).

P8-5B   Bummer Company's bank statement from Fifth National Bank at August 31, 2010, shows the information on the next page.

(a) Adjusted cash balance per bank $7,191

Prepare a bank reconciliation and adjusting entries.

(SO 7)

Balance, August 1	$11,284	Bank credit memoranda:		
August deposits	47,521	Collection of note		
Checks cleared in August	46,475	receivable plus $105		
Balance, August 31	16,856	interest	$4,505	
		Interest earned	41	
		Bank debit memorandum:		
		Safety deposit box rent	20	

A summary of the Cash account in the ledger for August shows: Balance, August 1, $10,959; receipts $50,050; disbursements $47,794; and balance, August 31, $13,215. Analysis reveals that the only reconciling items on the July 31 bank reconciliation were a deposit in transit for $2,600 and outstanding checks of $2,925. The deposit in transit was the first deposit recorded by the bank in August. In addition, you determine that there were two errors involving company checks drawn in August: (1) A check for $340 to a creditor on account that cleared the bank in August was journalized and posted for $430. (2) A salary check to an employee for $275 was recorded by the bank for $277.

Instructions

(a) Adjusted balance per books $17,831

(a) Prepare a bank reconciliation at August 31.

(b) Journalize the adjusting entries to be made by Bummer Company at August 31. Assume that interest on the note has not been accrued by the company.

Prepare a comprehensive bank reconciliation with theft and internal control deficiencies.

(SO 2, 3, 4, 7)

P8-6B Gazarra Company is a very profitable small business. It has not, however, given much consideration to internal control. For example, in an attempt to keep clerical and office expenses to a minimum, the company has combined the jobs of cashier and bookkeeper. As a result, Johnny Stacatto handles all cash receipts, keeps the accounting records, and prepares the monthly bank reconciliations.

The balance per the bank statement on October 31, 2010, was $15,453. Outstanding checks were: no. 62 for $107.74, no. 183 for $127.50, no. 284 for $215.26, no. 862 for $162.10, no. 863 for $192.78, and no. 864 for $140.49. Included with the statement was a credit memorandum of $340 indicating the collection of a note receivable for Gazarra Company by the bank on October 25. This memorandum has not been recorded by Gazarra Company.

The company's ledger showed one cash account with a balance of $18,608.81. The balance included undeposited cash on hand. Because of the lack of internal controls, Stacatto took for personal use all of the undeposited receipts in excess of $3,226.18. He then prepared the following bank reconciliation in an effort to conceal his theft of cash.

BANK RECONCILIATION

Cash balance per books, October 31		$18,608.81
Add: Outstanding checks		
No. 862	$162.10	
No. 863	192.78	
No. 864	140.49	410.31
		19,019.18
Less: Undeposited receipts		3,226.18
Unadjusted balance per bank, October 31		15,793.00
Less: Bank credit memorandum		340.00
Cash balance per bank statement, October 31		$15,453.00

Instructions

(a) Adjusted balance per books $17,733.31

(a) Prepare a correct bank reconciliation. (*Hint*: Deduct the amount of the theft from the adjusted balance per books.)

(b) Indicate the three ways that Stacatto attempted to conceal the theft and the dollar amount pertaining to each method.

(c) What principles of internal control were violated in this case?

PROBLEMS: SET C

Visit the book's website at **www.wiley.com/college/weygandt**, and choose the Student Companion site, to access Problem Set C.

CONTINUING COOKIE CHRONICLE

(Note: This is a continuation of the Cookie Chronicle from Chapters 1 through 6.)

CCC8   Part 1   Natalie is struggling to keep up with the recording of her accounting transactions. She is spending a lot of time marketing and selling mixers and giving her cookie classes. Her friend John is an accounting student who runs his own accounting service. He has asked Natalie if she would like to have him do her accounting. John and Natalie meet and discuss her business.
Part 2   Natalie decides that she cannot afford to hire John to do her accounting. One way that she can ensure that her cash account does not have any errors and is accurate and up-to-date is to prepare a bank reconciliation at the end of each month. Natalie would like you to help her.

Go to the book's companion website,
www.wiley.com/college/weygandt,
to see the completion of this problem.

BROADENING YOUR PERSPECTIVE

FINANCIAL REPORTING AND ANALYSIS

Financial Reporting Problem: PepsiCo, Inc.

BYP8-1   The financial statements of PepsiCo, Inc., are presented in Appendix A at the end of this textbook.

Instructions
(a) What comments, if any, are made about cash in the report of the independent auditors?
(b) What data about cash and cash equivalents are shown in the consolidated balance sheet?
(c) In its notes to Consolidated Financial Statements, how does PepsiCo define cash equivalents?
(d) In management's letter that assumes "Responsibility for Financial Reporting," what does PepsiCo's management say about internal control? (See page A32 in Appendix A of the back of the book.)

Comparative Analysis Problem: PepsiCo, Inc. vs. The Coca-Cola Company

BYP8-2   PepsiCo's financial statements are presented in Appendix A. Financial statements of The Coca-Cola Company are presented in Appendix B.

Instructions
(a) Based on the information contained in these financial statements, determine each of the following for each company:
  (1) Cash and cash equivalents balance at December 29, 2007, for PepsiCo and at December 30, 2007, for Coca-Cola.
  (2) Increase (decrease) in cash and cash equivalents from 2006 to 2007.
  (3) Cash provided by operating activities during the year ended December 2007 (from statement of cash flows).
(b) What conclusions concerning the management of cash can be drawn from these data?

Exploring the Web

BYP8-3 All organizations should have systems of internal control. Universities are no exception. This site discusses the basics of internal control in a university setting.

Address: **www.bc.edu/offices/audit/controls**, or go to **www.wiley.com/college/weygandt**

Steps: Go to the site shown above.

Instructions
The front page of this site provides links to pages that answer six critical questions. Use these links to answer the following questions.

(a) In a university setting who has responsibility for evaluating the adequacy of the system of internal control?
(b) What do reconciliations ensure in the university setting? Who should review the reconciliation?
(c) What are some examples of physical controls?
(d) What are two ways to accomplish inventory counts?

CRITICAL THINKING

Decision Making Across the Organization

BYP8-4 The board of trustees of a local church is concerned about the internal accounting controls for the offering collections made at weekly services. The trustees ask you to serve on a three-person audit team with the internal auditor of a local college and a CPA who has just joined the church.

At a meeting of the audit team and the board of trustees you learn the following.

1. The church's board of trustees has delegated responsibility for the financial management and audit of the financial records to the finance committee. This group prepares the annual budget and approves major disbursements. It is not involved in collections or record keeping. No audit has been made in recent years because the same trusted employee has kept church records and served as financial secretary for 15 years. The church does not carry any fidelity insurance.
2. The collection at the weekly service is taken by a team of ushers who volunteer to serve one month. The ushers take the collection plates to a basement office at the rear of the church. They hand their plates to the head usher and return to the church service. After all plates have been turned in, the head usher counts the cash received. The head usher then places the cash in the church safe along with a notation of the amount counted. The head usher volunteers to serve for 3 months.
3. The next morning the financial secretary opens the safe and recounts the collection. The secretary withholds $150–$200 in cash, depending on the cash expenditures expected for the week, and deposits the remainder of the collections in the bank. To facilitate the deposit, church members who contribute by check are asked to make their checks payable to "Cash."
4. Each month, the financial secretary reconciles the bank statement and submits a copy of the reconciliation to the board of trustees. The reconciliations have rarely contained any bank errors and have never shown any errors per books.

Instructions
With the class divided into groups, answer the following.

(a) Indicate the weaknesses in internal accounting control over the handling of collections.
(b) List the improvements in internal control procedures that you plan to make at the next meeting of the audit team for (1) the ushers, (2) the head usher, (3) the financial secretary, and (4) the finance committee.
(c) What church policies should be changed to improve internal control?

Communication Activity

BYP8-5 As a new auditor for the CPA firm of Croix, Marais, and Kale, you have been assigned to review the internal controls over mail cash receipts of Manhattan Company. Your review reveals the following: Checks are promptly endorsed "For Deposit Only," but no list of the checks is prepared by the person opening the mail. The mail is opened either by the cashier or by the employee who maintains the accounts receivable records. Mail receipts are deposited in the bank weekly by the cashier.

Instructions

Write a letter to Jerry Mays, owner of the Manhattan Company, explaining the weaknesses in internal control and your recommendations for improving the system.

Ethics Case

BYP8-6 You are the assistant controller in charge of general ledger accounting at Riverside Bottling Company. Your company has a large loan from an insurance company. The loan agreement requires that the company's cash account balance be maintained at $200,000 or more, as reported monthly.

At June 30 the cash balance is $80,000, which you report to Gena Schmitt, the financial vice president. Gena excitedly instructs you to keep the cash receipts book open for one additional day for purposes of the June 30 report to the insurance company. Gena says, "If we don't get that cash balance over $200,000, we'll default on our loan agreement. They could close us down, put us all out of our jobs!" Gena continues, "I talked to Oconto Distributors (one of Riverside's largest customers) this morning. They said they sent us a check for $150,000 yesterday. We should receive it tomorrow. If we include just that one check in our cash balance, we'll be in the clear. It's in the mail!"

Instructions

(a) Who will suffer negative effects if you do not comply with Gena Schmitt's instructions? Who will suffer if you do comply?

(b) What are the ethical considerations in this case?

(c) What alternatives do you have?

"All About You" Activity

BYP8-7 The **All About You** feature in this chapter (page 373) indicates potential security risks that may arise from your personal computer. It is important to keep in mind, however, that there are also many other ways that your identity can be stolen other than from your computer. The federal government provides many resources to help protect you from identity thieves.

Instructions

Go to **http://onguardonline.gov/idtheft.html**, and click on ID Theft Faceoff. Complete the quiz provided there.

Answers to Insight and Accounting Across the Organization Questions

p. 347 How Do Employees Steal?

Q: How can companies reduce the likelihood of fraudulent disbursements?

A: *Some common-sense approaches are to make sure only certain designated individuals can sign checks. In addition, make sure that different personnel approve payments and make payments.*

p. 356 SOX Boosts the Role of Human Resources

Q: Why would unsupervised employees or employees who report to each other represent potential internal control threats?

A. *An unsupervised employee may have a fraudulent job (or may even be a fictitious person—e.g., a person drawing a paycheck without working). Or, if two employees supervise each other, there is no real separation of duties, and they can conspire to defraud the company.*

Authors' Comments on *All About You:* Protecting Yourself from Identity Theft (p. 373)

Most experts discourage storing sensitive financial information on your computer. In recent years there have been countless examples of hackers penetrating sophisticated corporate systems to steal personal data. If hackers can beat sophisticated systems, it is unlikely that you can do better.

The Federal Trade Commission recommends that you frequently update your anti-virus software. Use a firewall program and a secure browser that encrypts all online transactions. If you do store financial information on your computer, make sure that it is password-protected with a password that is an unrecognizable combination of upper- and lower-case letters, numbers, and symbols. Change the password periodically. When you dispose of your old computer, make sure that you use a wiping utility to destroy all information on the hard drive.

Be careful, too, not to focus all of your internal control efforts on your computer. Most identity theft still derives from very non-technical sources—such as your trash can. You should take the following steps to minimize non-computer-related risks: Use passwords on your credit card, bank, and phone accounts. Make sure that all personal information in your home is in a secure place, especially if you have roommates or employ outside help. Don't give out personal information unless you initiated the contact or you are sure you know whom you are dealing with. Deposit outgoing mail in post-office collection boxes (not in your mailbox with the red flag up), and promptly remove all mail from your mailbox. Use a cross-cut shredder to shred all charge receipts, insurance forms, bank statements, etc. that might reveal personal information.

Answers to Self-Study Questions
1. c **2.** a **3.** a **4.** c **5.** b **6.** b **7.** d **8.** d **9.** a **10.** a **11.** c **12.** d **13.** c **14.** c

Chapter 9

Accounting for Receivables

STUDY OBJECTIVES

After studying this chapter, you should be able to:

1 Identify the different types of receivables.

2 Explain how companies recognize accounts receivable.

3 Distinguish between the methods and bases companies use to value accounts receivable.

4 Describe the entries to record the disposition of accounts receivable.

5 Compute the maturity date of and interest on notes receivable.

6 Explain how companies recognize notes receivable.

7 Describe how companies value notes receivable.

8 Describe the entries to record the disposition of notes receivable.

9 Explain the statement presentation and analysis of receivables. ✓ *The Navigator*

✓ *The Navigator*

Scan **Study Objectives**	▪
Read **Feature Story**	▪
Read **Preview**	▪
Read text and answer **DO IT!** p. 406 ▪ p. 409 ▪ p. 413 ▪ p. 415 ▪	
Work **Comprehensive DO IT!** p. 417	▪
Review **Summary of Study Objectives**	▪
Answer **Self-Study Questions**	▪
Complete **Assignments**	▪

Feature Story

A DOSE OF CAREFUL MANAGEMENT KEEPS RECEIVABLES HEALTHY

"Sometimes you have to know when to be very tough, and sometimes you can give them a bit of a break," says Vivi Su. She's not talking about her children, but about the customers of a subsidiary of pharmaceutical company Whitehall-Robins (www.whitehall-robins.com), where she works as supervisor of credit and collections.

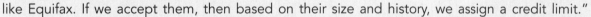

For example, while the company's regular terms are 1/15, n/30 (1% discount if paid within 15 days), a customer might ask for and receive a few days of grace and still get the discount. Or a customer might place orders above its credit limit, in which case, depending on its payment history and the circumstances, Ms. Su might authorize shipment of the goods anyway.

Nearly all of the company's sales come through the credit accounts Ms. Su manages. The process starts with the decision to grant a customer an account in the first place, Ms. Su explains. The sales rep gives the customer a credit application. "My department reviews this application very carefully; a customer needs to supply three good references, and we also run a check with a credit firm like Equifax. If we accept them, then based on their size and history, we assign a credit limit."

Once accounts are established, the company supervises them very carefully. "I get an aging report every single day," says Ms. Su.

"The rule of thumb is that we should always have at least 85% of receivables current—meaning they were billed less than 30 days ago," she continues. "But we try to do even better than that—I like to see 90%." Similarly, her guideline is never to have more than 5% of receivables at over 90 days. But long before that figure is reached, "we jump on it," she says firmly.

At 15 days overdue, Whitehall-Robins phones the client. Often there's a reasonable explanation for the delay—an invoice may have gone astray, or the payables clerk is away. "But if a customer keeps on delaying, and tells us several times that it'll only be a few more days, we know there's a problem," says Ms. Su. After 45 days, "I send a letter. Then a second notice is sent in writing. After the third and final notice, the client has 10 days to pay, and then I hand it over to a collection agency, and it's out of my hands."

Ms. Su knows that management of receivables is crucial to the profitability of Whitehall-Robins. "Receivables are generally the second-largest asset of any company (after its capital assets)," she points out. "So it's no wonder we keep a very close eye on them."

√ *The Navigator*

Inside Chapter 9...

- **When Investors Ignore Warning Signs** (p. 406)
- **How Does a Credit Card Work?** (p. 408)
- *All About You:* **Should You Be Carrying Plastic?** (p. 416)

As indicated in the Feature Story, receivables are a significant asset for many pharmaceutical companies. Because a significant portion of sales in the United States are done on credit, receivables are significant to companies in other industries as well. As a consequence, companies must pay close attention to their receivables and manage them carefully. In this chapter you will learn what journal entries companies make when they sell products, when they collect cash from those sales, and when they write off accounts they cannot collect.

The content and organization of the chapter are as follows.

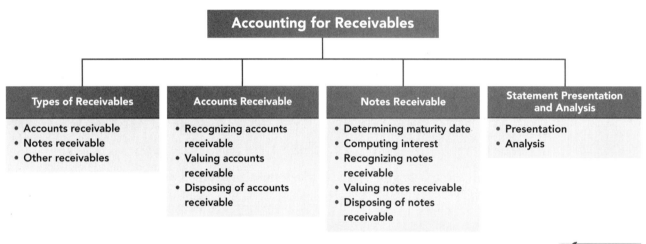

The Navigator

TYPES OF RECEIVABLES

STUDY OBJECTIVE 1

Identify the different types of receivables.

The term **receivables** refers to amounts due from individuals and other companies. Receivables are claims that are expected to be collected in cash. They are frequently classified as (1) accounts receivable, (2) notes receivable, and (3) other receivables.

Accounts receivable are amounts owed by customers on account. They result from the sale of goods and services. Companies generally expect to collect these receivables within 30 to 60 days. Accounts receivable are the most significant type of claim held by a company.

Notes receivable are claims for which formal instruments of credit are issued as proof of the debt. A note receivable normally extends for time periods of 60–90 days or longer and requires the debtor to pay interest. Notes and accounts receivable that result from sales transactions are often called **trade receivables**.

ETHICS NOTE

Companies report receivables from employees separately in the financial statements. The reason: Sometimes those assets are not the result of an "arm's-length" transaction.

Other receivables include nontrade receivables. Examples are interest receivable, loans to company officers, advances to employees, and income taxes refundable. These do not generally result from the operations of the business. Therefore companies generally classify and report them as separate items in the balance sheet.

ACCOUNTS RECEIVABLE

Three accounting issues associated with accounts receivable are:

1. **Recognizing** accounts receivable.
2. **Valuing** accounts receivable.
3. **Disposing of** accounts receivable.

Recognizing Accounts Receivable

Recognizing accounts receivable is relatively straightforward. In Chapter 5 we saw how the sale of merchandise affects accounts receivable. To review, assume that Jordache Co. on July 1, 2010, sells merchandise on account to Polo Company for $1,000 terms 2/10, n/30. On July 5, Polo returns merchandise worth $100 to Jordache Co. On July 11, Jordache receives payment from Polo Company for the balance due. The journal entries to record these transactions on the books of Jordache Co. are as follows.

STUDY OBJECTIVE 2

Explain how companies recognize accounts receivable.

July 1	Accounts Receivable—Polo Company	1,000	
	Sales		1,000
	(To record sales on account)		
July 5	Sales Returns and Allowances	100	
	Accounts Receivable—Polo Company		100
	(To record merchandise returned)		
July 11	Cash ($900−$18)	882	
	Sales Discounts ($900 × .02)	18	
	Accounts Receivable—Polo Company		900
	(To record collection of accounts		
	receivable)		

HELPFUL HINT

These entries are the same as those described in Chapter 5. For simplicity, we have omitted inventory and cost of goods sold from this set of journal entries and from end-of-chapter material.

The opportunity to receive a cash discount usually occurs when a manufacturer sells to a wholesaler or a wholesaler sells to a retailer. The selling company gives a discount in these situations either to encourage prompt payment or for competitive reasons.

Retailers rarely grant cash discounts to customers. In fact, when you use a retailer's credit card (Sears, for example), instead of giving a discount, the retailer charges interest on the balance due if not paid within a specified period (usually 25–30 days).

To illustrate, assume that you use your JCPenney credit card to purchase clothing with a sales price of $300. JC Penney will make the following entry at the date of sale.

ETHICS NOTE

In exchange for lower interest rates, some companies have eliminated the 25-day grace period before finance charges kick in. Be sure you read the fine print in any credit agreement you sign.

Accounts Receivable	300	
Sales		300
(To record sale of merchandise)		

A = L + OE
+300
                    +300 Rev

Cash Flows
no effect

JCPenney will send you a monthly statement of this transaction and any others that have occurred during the month. If you do not pay in full within 30 days, JCPenney adds an interest (financing) charge to the balance due. Although interest rates vary by region and over time, a common rate for retailers is 18% per year (1.5% per month).

The seller recognizes interest revenue when it adds financing charges. Assuming that you owe $300 at the end of the month, and JCPenney charges 1.5% per month on the balance due, the adjusting entry to record interest revenue of $4.50 ($300 × 1.5%) is as follows.

Accounts Receivable	4.50	
Interest Revenue		4.50
(To record interest on amount due)		

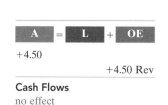

A = L + OE
+4.50
                  +4.50 Rev

Cash Flows
no effect

Interest revenue is often substantial for many retailers.

Valuing Accounts Receivable

STUDY OBJECTIVE 3

Distinquish between the methods and bases companies use to value accounts receivable.

Once companies record receivables in the accounts, the next question is: How should they report receivables in the financial statements? Companies report accounts receivable on the balance sheet as an asset. But determining the **amount** to report is sometimes difficult because some receivables will become uncollectible.

Each customer must satisfy the credit requirements of the seller before the credit sale is approved. Inevitably, though, some accounts receivable become uncollectible. For example, a customer may not be able to pay because of a decline in its sales revenue due to a downturn in the economy. Similarly, individuals may be laid off from their jobs or faced with unexpected hospital bills. Companies record credit losses as debits to **Bad Debts Expense** (or Uncollectible Accounts Expense). Such losses are a normal and necessary risk of doing business on a credit basis.

Two methods are used in accounting for uncollectible accounts: (1) the direct write-off method and (2) the allowance method. The following sections explain these methods.

DIRECT WRITE-OFF METHOD FOR UNCOLLECTIBLE ACCOUNTS

Under the direct write-off method, when a company determines a particular account to be uncollectible, it charges the loss to Bad Debts Expense. Assume, for example, that on December 12 Warden Co. writes off as uncollectible M. E. Doran's $200 balance. The entry is:

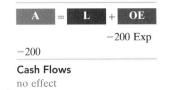

−200

Cash Flows
no effect

Dec. 12	Bad Debts Expense	200	
	Accounts Receivable—M. E. Doran		200
	(To record write-off of M. E. Doran account)		

Under this method, Bad Debts Expense will show only **actual losses** from uncollectibles. The company will report accounts receivable at its gross amount.

Although this method is simple, its use can reduce the usefulness of both the income statement and balance sheet. Consider the following example. Assume that in 2010, Quick Buck Computer Company decided it could increase its revenues by offering computers to college students without requiring any money down and with no credit-approval process. On campuses across the country it distributed one million computers with a selling price of $800 each. This increased Quick Buck's revenues and receivables by $800 million. The promotion was a huge success! The 2010 balance sheet and income statement looked great. Unfortunately, during 2011, nearly 40% of the customers defaulted on their loans. This made the 2011 income statement and balance sheet look terrible. Illustration 9-1 shows the effect of these events on the financial statements if the direct write-off method is used.

Illustration 9-1
Effects of direct write-off method

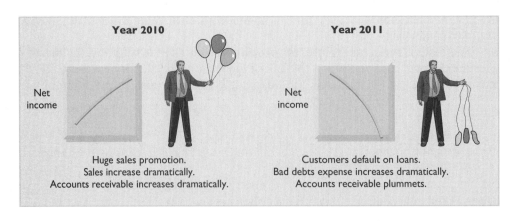

Under the direct write-off method, companies often record bad debts expense in a period different from the period in which they record the revenue. The method does not attempt to match bad debts expense to sales revenues in the income statement. Nor does the direct write-off method show accounts receivable in the balance sheet at the amount the company actually expects to receive. **Consequently, unless bad debts losses are insignificant, the direct write-off method is not acceptable for financial reporting purposes.**

ALLOWANCE METHOD FOR UNCOLLECTIBLE ACCOUNTS

The allowance method of accounting for bad debts involves estimating uncollectible accounts at the end of each period. This provides better matching on the income statement. It also ensures that companies state receivables on the balance sheet at their cash (net) realizable value. Cash (net) realizable value is the net amount the company expects to receive in cash. It excludes amounts that the company estimates it will not collect. Thus, this method reduces receivables in the balance sheet by the amount of estimated uncollectible receivables.

GAAP requires the allowance method for financial reporting purposes when bad debts are material in amount. This method has three essential features:

HELPFUL HINT

In this context, *material* means significant or important to financial statement users.

1. Companies **estimate** uncollectible accounts receivable. They match this estimated expense **against revenues** in the same accounting period in which they record the revenues.

2. Companies debit estimated uncollectibles to Bad Debts Expense and credit them to Allowance for Doubtful Accounts (a contra-asset account) through an adjusting entry at the end of each period.

3. When companies write off a specific account, they debit actual uncollectibles to Allowance for Doubtful Accounts and credit that amount to Accounts Receivable.

Recording Estimated Uncollectibles. To illustrate the allowance method, assume that Hampson Furniture has credit sales of $1,200,000 in 2010. Of this amount, $200,000 remains uncollected at December 31. The credit manager estimates that $12,000 of these sales will be uncollectible. The adjusting entry to record the estimated uncollectibles is:

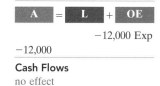

Dec. 31	Bad Debts Expense	12,000	
	Allowance for Doubtful Accounts		12,000
	(To record estimate of uncollectible accounts)		

A = L + OE
−12,000 Exp
−12,000
Cash Flows
no effect

Hampson reports Bad Debts Expense in the income statement as an operating expense (usually as a selling expense). Thus, the estimated uncollectibles are matched with sales in 2010. Hampson records the expense in the same year it made the sales.

Allowance for Doubtful Accounts shows the estimated amount of claims on customers that the company expects will become uncollectible in the future. Companies use a contra account instead of a direct credit to Accounts Receivable because they do not know which customers will not pay. The credit balance in the allowance account will absorb the specific write-offs when they occur. As Illustration 9-2 shows, the company deducts the allowance account from accounts receivable in the current assets section of the balance sheet.

The amount of $188,000 in Illustration 9-2 (page 402) represents the expected **cash realizable value** of the accounts receivable at the statement date. **Companies do not close Allowance for Doubtful Accounts at the end of the fiscal year.**

HELPFUL HINT

Cash realizable value is sometimes referred to as *accounts receivable (net)*.

Illustration 9-2
Presentation of allowance
for doubtful accounts

HAMPSON FURNITURE
Balance Sheet (partial)

Current assets		
Cash		$ 14,800
Accounts receivable	**$200,000**	
Less: Allowance for doubtful accounts	**12,000**	**188,000**
Merchandise inventory		310,000
Prepaid expense		25,000
Total current assets		$537,800

Recording the Write-Off of an Uncollectible Account. As described in the Feature Story, companies use various methods of collecting past-due accounts, such as letters, calls, and legal action. When they have exhausted all means of collecting a past-due account and collection appears impossible, the company should write off the account. In the credit card industry, for example, it is standard practice to write off accounts that are 210 days past due. To prevent premature or unauthorized write-offs, management should formally approve, in writing, each write-off. To maintain good internal control, companies should not give authorization to write off accounts to someone who also has daily responsibilities related to cash or receivables.

To illustrate a receivables write-off, assume that the financial vice-president of Hampson Furniture authorizes a write-off of the $500 balance owed by R. A. Ware on March 1, 2011. The entry to record the write-off is:

+500
−500

Cash Flows
no effect

Mar. 1	Allowance for Doubtful Accounts	500	
	Accounts Receivable—R. A. Ware		500
	(Write-off of R. A. Ware account)		

Bad Debts Expense does not increase when the write-off occurs. **Under the allowance method, companies debit every bad debt write-off to the allowance account rather than to Bad Debts Expense.** A debit to Bad Debts Expense would be incorrect because the company has already recognized the expense when it made the adjusting entry for estimated bad debts. Instead, the entry to record the write-off of an uncollectible account reduces both Accounts Receivable and the Allowance for Doubtful Accounts. After posting, the general ledger accounts will appear as in Illustration 9-3.

Illustration 9-3
General ledger balances
after write-off

Accounts Receivable				Allowance for Doubtful Accounts			
Jan. 1 Bal. 200,000	Mar. 1	500		Mar. 1	500	Jan. 1 Bal. 12,000	
Mar. 1 Bal. 199,500						Mar. 1 Bal. 11,500	

A write-off affects **only balance sheet accounts**—not income statement accounts. The write-off of the account reduces both Accounts Receivable and Allowance for Doubtful Accounts. Cash realizable value in the balance sheet, therefore, remains the same, as Illustration 9-4 shows.

Illustration 9-4
Cash realizable value
comparison

	Before Write-off	After Write-off
Accounts receivable	$200,000	$199,500
Allowance for doubtful accounts	12,000	11,500
Cash realizable value	**$188,000**	**$188,000**

Recovery of an Uncollectible Account.   Occasionally, a company collects from a customer after it has written off the account as uncollectible. The company makes two entries to record the recovery of a bad debt: (1) It reverses the entry made in writing off the account. This reinstates the customer's account. (2) It journalizes the collection in the usual manner.

To illustrate, assume that on July 1, R. A. Ware pays the $500 amount that Hampson had written off on March 1. These are the entries:

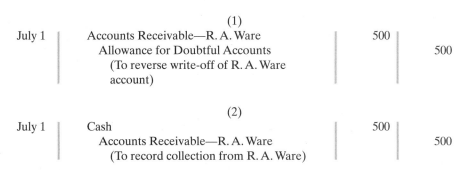

		(1)		
July 1	Accounts Receivable—R. A. Ware		500	
	Allowance for Doubtful Accounts			500
	(To reverse write-off of R. A. Ware			
	account)			

		(2)		
July 1	Cash		500	
	Accounts Receivable—R. A. Ware			500
	(To record collection from R. A. Ware)			

A = L + OE
+500
−500
Cash Flows
no effect

A = L + OE
+500
−500
Cash Flows
+500

Note that the recovery of a bad debt, like the write-off of a bad debt, affects **only balance sheet accounts**. The net effect of the two entries above is a debit to Cash and a credit to Allowance for Doubtful Accounts for $500. Accounts Receivable and the Allowance for Doubtful Accounts both increase in entry (1) for two reasons: First, the company made an error in judgment when it wrote off the account receivable. Second, after R. A. Ware did pay, Accounts Receivable in the general ledger and Ware's account in the subsidiary ledger should show the collection for possible future credit purposes.

Bases Used for Allowance Method.   To simplify the preceding explanation, we assumed we knew the amount of the expected uncollectibles. In "real life," companies must estimate that amount when they use the allowance method. Two bases are used to determine this amount: **(1) percentage of sales**, and **(2) percentage of receivables**. Both bases are generally accepted. The choice is a management decision. It depends on the relative emphasis that management wishes to give to expenses and revenues on the one hand or to cash realizable value of the accounts receivable on the other. The choice is whether to emphasize income statement or balance sheet relationships. Illustration 9-5 compares the two bases.

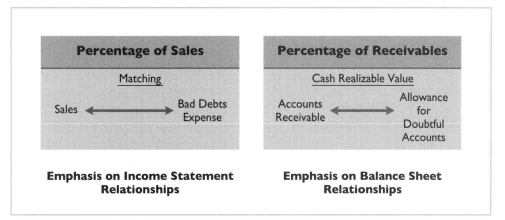

Illustration 9-5
Comparison of bases for estimating uncollectibles

The percentage-of-sales basis results in a better matching of expenses with revenues—an income statement viewpoint. The percentage-of-receivables basis produces the better estimate of cash realizable value—a balance sheet viewpoint. Under both bases, the company must determine its past experience with bad debt losses.

Percentage-of-Sales. In the percentage-of-sales basis, management estimates what percentage of credit sales will be uncollectible. This percentage is based on past experience and anticipated credit policy.

The company applies this percentage to either total credit sales or net credit sales of the current year. To illustrate, assume that Gonzalez Company elects to use the percentage-of-sales basis. It concludes that 1% of net credit sales will become uncollectible. If net credit sales for 2010 are $800,000, the estimated bad debts expense is $8,000 (1% × $800,000). The adjusting entry is:

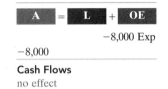

-8,000 Exp

-8,000

Cash Flows
no effect

Dec. 31	Bad Debts Expense	8,000	
	Allowance for Doubtful Accounts		8,000
	(To record estimated bad debts for year)		

After the adjusting entry is posted, assuming the allowance account already has a credit balance of $1,723, the accounts of Gonzalez Company will show the following:

Illustration 9-6
Bad debts accounts after posting

Bad Debts Expense			**Allowance for Doubtful Accounts**	
Dec. 31 Adj.	**8,000**		Jan. 1 Bal.	1,723
			Dec. 31 Adj.	**8,000**
			Dec. 31 Bal.	9,723

This basis of estimating uncollectibles emphasizes the matching of expenses with revenues. As a result, Bad Debts Expense will show a direct percentage relationship to the sales base on which it is computed. **When the company makes the adjusting entry, it disregards the existing balance in Allowance for Doubtful Accounts.** The adjusted balance in this account should be a reasonable approximation of the realizable value of the receivables. If actual write-offs differ significantly from the amount estimated, the company should modify the percentage for future years.

Percentage-of-Receivables. Under the percentage-of-receivables basis, management estimates what percentage of receivables will result in losses from uncollectible accounts. The company prepares an **aging schedule**, in which it classifies customer balances by the length of time they have been unpaid. Because of its emphasis on time, the analysis is often called aging the accounts receivable. In the opening story, Whitehall-Robins prepared an aging report daily.

After the company arranges the accounts by age, it determines the expected bad debt losses. It applies percentages based on past experience to the totals in each category. The longer a receivable is past due, the less likely it is to be collected. Thus, the estimated percentage of uncollectible debts increases as the number of days past due increases. Illustration 9-7 shows an aging schedule for Dart Company. Note that the estimated percentage uncollectible increases from 2 to 40% as the number of days past due increases.

Illustration 9-7
Aging schedule

	A	B	C	D	E	F	G
1					**Number of Days Past Due**		
2			**Not**				
3	**Customer**	**Total**	**Yet Due**	**1–30**	**31–60**	**61–90**	**Over 90**
4	T. E. Adert	$ 600		$ 300		$ 200	$ 100
5	R. C. Bortz	300	$ 300				
6	B. A. Carl	450		200	$ 250		
7	O. L. Diker	700	500			200	
8	T. O. Ebbet	600			300		300
9	Others	36,950	26,200	5,200	2,450	1,600	1,500
10		$39,600	$27,000	$5,700	$3,000	$2,000	$1,900
11	Estimated Percentage Uncollectible		2%	4%	10%	20%	40%
12	Total Estimated Bad Debts	$ 2,228	$ 540	$ 228	$ 300	$ 400	$ 760

HELPFUL HINT

The older categories have higher percentages because the longer an account is past due, the less likely it is to be collected.

Total estimated bad debts for Dart Company ($2,228) represent the amount of existing customer claims the company expects will become uncollectible in the future. This amount represents the **required balance** in Allowance for Doubtful Accounts at the balance sheet date. **The amount of the bad debt adjusting entry is the difference between the required balance and the existing balance in the allowance account.** If the trial balance shows Allowance for Doubtful Accounts with a credit balance of $528, the company will make an adjusting entry for $1,700 ($2,228 − $528), as shown here.

Dec. 31	Bad Debts Expense	1,700	
	Allowance for Doubtful Accounts		1,700
	(To adjust allowance account to total		
	estimated uncollectibles)		

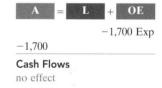

A = L + OE
−1,700 Exp
−1,700
Cash Flows
no effect

After the adjusting entry is posted, the accounts of the Dart Company will show:

Illustration 9-8
Bad debts accounts after posting

Bad Debts Expense		**Allowance for Doubtful Accounts**	
Dec. 31 Adj. **1,700**		Bal.	528
		Dec. 31 Adj. **1,700**	
		Bal.	2,228

Occasionally the allowance account will have a **debit balance** prior to adjustment. This occurs when write-offs during the year have exceeded previous provisions for bad debts. In such a case the company **adds the debit balance to the required balance** when it makes the adjusting entry. Thus, if there had been a $500 debit balance in the allowance account before adjustment, the adjusting entry would have been for $2,728 ($2,228 + $500) to arrive at a credit balance of $2,228. The percentage-of-receivables basis will normally result in the better approximation of cash realizable value.

INVESTOR INSIGHT

When Investors Ignore Warning Signs

Recently Nortel Networks announced that half of its previous year's earnings were "fake." Should investors have seen this coming? Well, there were issues in its annual report that should at least have caused investors to ask questions. The company had cut its allowance for doubtful accounts on all receivables from $1,253 million to $544 million, even though its total balance of receivables remained relatively unchanged.

This reduction in bad debts expense was responsible for a very large part of the company's earnings that year. At the time it was unclear whether Nortel might have set the reserves too high originally and needed to reduce them, or whether it slashed the allowance to artificially boost earnings. But one thing is certain—when a company makes an accounting change of this magnitude, investors need to ask questions.

Source: Jonathan Weil, "Outside Audit: At Nortel, Warning Signs Existed Months Ago," *Wall Street Journal*, May 18, 2004, p. C3.

? When would it be appropriate for a company to lower its allowance for doubtful accounts as a percentage of its receivables?

DO IT!

UNCOLLECTIBLE ACCOUNTS RECEIVABLE

Brule Co. has been in business five years. The ledger at the end of the current year shows:

Accounts Receivable	$30,000 Dr.
Sales	$180,000 Cr.
Allowance for Doubtful Accounts	$2,000 Dr.

Bad debts are estimated to be 10% of receivables. Prepare the entry to adjust the Allowance for Doubtful Accounts.

action plan

✔ Report receivables at their cash (net) realizable value.

✔ Estimate the amount the company does not expect to collect.

✔ Consider the existing balance in the allowance account when using the percentage-of-receivables basis.

Solution

The following entry should be made to bring the balance in the Allowance for Doubtful Accounts up to a balance of $3,000 (0.1 × $30,000):

Bad Debts Expense [(0.1 × $30,000) + $2,000]	5,000	
Allowance for Doubtful Accounts		5,000
(To record estimate of uncollectible accounts)		

Related exercise material: **BE9-3, BE9-4, BE9-5, BE9-6, BE9-7, E9-3, E9-4, E9-5, E9-6,** and **DO IT!** **9-1.**

Disposing of Accounts Receivable

STUDY OBJECTIVE 4

Describe the entries to record the disposition of accounts receivable.

In the normal course of events, companies collect accounts receivable in cash and remove the receivables from the books. However, as credit sales and receivables have grown in significance, the "normal course of events" has changed. Companies now frequently sell their receivables to another company for cash, thereby shortening the cash-to-cash operating cycle.

Companies sell receivables for two major reasons. First, **they may be the only reasonable source of cash**. When money is tight, companies may not be able to borrow money in the usual credit markets. Or, if money is available, the cost of borrowing may be prohibitive.

A second reason for selling receivables is that **billing and collection are often time-consuming and costly**. It is often easier for a retailer to sell the receivables to another party with expertise in billing and collection matters. Credit card companies such as MasterCard, Visa, and Discover specialize in billing and collecting accounts receivable.

SALE OF RECEIVABLES

A common sale of receivables is a sale to a factor. A factor is a finance company or bank that buys receivables from businesses and then collects the payments directly from the customers. Factoring is a multibillion dollar business.

Factoring arrangements vary widely. Typically the factor charges a commission to the company that is selling the receivables. This fee ranges from 1–3% of the amount of receivables purchased. To illustrate, assume that Hendredon Furniture factors $600,000 of receivables to Federal Factors. Federal Factors assesses a service charge of 2% of the amount of receivables sold. The journal entry to record the sale by Hendredon Furniture is as follows.

Cash	588,000	
Service Charge Expense (2% × $600,000)	12,000	
Accounts Receivable		600,000
(To record the sale of accounts receivable)		

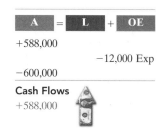

If the company often sells its receivables, it records the service charge expense (such as that incurred by Hendredon) as selling expense. If the company infrequently sells receivables, it may report this amount in the "Other expenses and losses" section of the income statement.

CREDIT CARD SALES

Over one billion credit cards are in use in the United States—more than three credit cards for every man, woman, and child in this country. Visa, MasterCard, and American Express are the national credit cards that most individuals use. Three parties are involved when national credit cards are used in retail sales: (1) the credit card issuer, who is independent of the retailer, (2) the retailer, and (3) the customer. A retailer's acceptance of a national credit card is another form of selling (factoring) the receivable.

Illustration 9-9 (page 408) shows the major advantages of national credit cards to the retailer. In exchange for these advantages, the retailer pays the credit card issuer a fee of 2–6% of the invoice price for its services.

Accounting for Credit Card Sales. The retailer generally considers sales from the use of national credit card sales as *cash sales*. The retailer must pay to the bank that issues the card a fee for processing the transactions. The retailer records the credit card slips in a similar manner as checks deposited from a cash sale.

To illustrate, Anita Ferreri purchases $1,000 of compact discs for her restaurant from Karen Kerr Music Co., using her Visa First Bank Card. First Bank charges a service fee of 3%. The entry to record this transaction by Karen Kerr Music is as follows.

Cash	970	
Service Charge Expense	30	
Sales		1,000
(To record Visa credit card sales)		

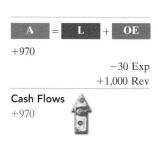

Illustration 9-9
Advantages of credit cards
to the retailer

ACCOUNTING ACROSS THE ORGANIZATION

How Does a Credit Card Work?

Most of you know how to *use* a credit card, but do you know what happens in the transaction and how the transaction is processed? Suppose that you use a Visa card to purchase some new ties at Nordstrom. The salesperson swipes your card, and the swiping machine reads the information on the magnetic strip on the back of the card. The salesperson then types in the amount of the purchase. The machine contacts the Visa computer, which routes the call back to the bank that issued your Visa card. The issuing bank verifies that the account exists, that the card is not stolen, and that you have not exceeded your credit limit. At this point, the slip is printed, which you sign.

Visa acts as the clearing agent for the transaction. It transfers funds from the issuing bank to Nordstrom's bank account. Generally this transfer of funds, from sale to the receipt of funds in the merchant's account, takes two to three days.

In the meantime, Visa puts a pending charge on your account for the amount of the tie purchase; that amount counts immediately against your available credit limit. At the end of the billing period, Visa sends you an invoice (your credit card bill) which shows the various charges you made, and the amounts that Visa expended on your behalf, for the month. You then must "pay the piper" for your stylish new ties.

? Assume that Nordstrom prepares a bank reconciliation at the end of each month. If some credit card sales have not been processed by the bank, how should Nordstrom treat these transactions on its bank reconciliation?

DO IT!

Mehl Wholesalers Co. has been expanding faster than it can raise capital. According to its local banker, the company has reached its debt ceiling. Mehl's suppliers (creditors) are demanding payment within 30 days of the invoice date for goods acquired, but Mehl's customers are slow in paying (60–90 days). As a result, Mehl has a cash flow problem.

Mehl needs $120,000 in cash to safely cover next Friday's payroll. Its balance of outstanding accounts receivables totals $750,000. What might Mehl do to alleviate this cash crunch? Record the entry that Mehl would make when it raises the needed cash.

DISPOSITION OF ACCOUNTS RECEIVABLE

action plan

✔ To speed up the collection of cash, sell receivables to a factor.

✔ Calculate service charge expense as a percentage of the factored receivables.

Solution

Assuming that Mehl Wholesalers factors $125,000 of its accounts receivable at a 1% service charge, it would make the following entry.

Cash	123,750	
Service Charge Expense	1,250	
Accounts Receivable		125,000
(To record sale of receivables to factor)		

Related exercise material: **BE9-8, E9-7, E9-8, E9-9,** and **DO IT!** **9-2.**

 The Navigator

NOTES RECEIVABLE

Companies may also grant credit in exchange for a promissory note. A **promissory note** is a written promise to pay a specified amount of money on demand or at a definite time. Notes receivable give the payee a stronger legal claim to assets than accounts receivable. Promissory notes may be used: (1) when individuals and companies lend or borrow money, (2) when the amount of the transaction and the credit period exceed normal limits, or (3) in settlement of accounts receivable.

In a promissory note, the party making the promise to pay is called the **maker**. The party to whom payment is to be made is called the **payee**. The note may specifically identify the payee by name or may designate the payee simply as the bearer of the note. In the note shown in Illustration 9-10, Calhoun Company is the maker, Wilma Company is the payee. To Wilma Company, the promissory note is a note receivable; to Calhoun Company, it is a note payable.

Illustration 9-10
Promissory note

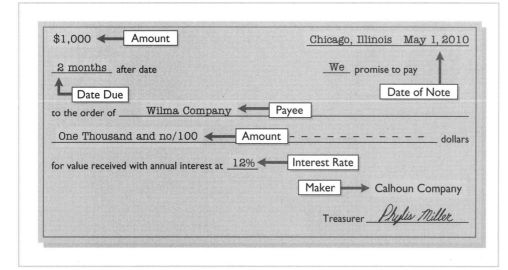

HELPFUL HINT

Who are the two key parties to a note, and what entry does each party make when the note is issued?

Answer:

1. The maker, Calhoun Company, credits Notes Payable.

2. The payee, Wilma Company, debits Notes Receivable.

Like accounts receivable, notes receivable can be readily sold to another party. Promissory notes are negotiable instruments (as are checks), which means that they can be transferred to another party by endorsement.

Companies frequently accept notes receivable from customers who need to extend the payment of an account receivable. They often require such notes from high-risk customers. In some industries (such as the pleasure boat industry), all credit sales are supported by notes. The majority of notes originate from loans.

The basic issues in accounting for notes receivable are the same as those for accounts receivable:

1. **Recognizing** notes receivable.
2. **Valuing** notes receivable.
3. **Disposing of** notes receivable.

On the following pages, we will look at these issues. Before we do, we need to consider two issues that did not apply to accounts receivable: maturity date and computing interest.

Determining the Maturity Date

When the life of a note is expressed in terms of months, you find the date when it matures by counting the months from the date of issue. For example, the maturity date of a three-month note dated May 1 is August 1. A note drawn on the last day of a month matures on the last day of a subsequent month. That is, a July 31 note due in two months matures on September 30.

When the due date is stated in terms of days, you need to count the exact number of days to determine the maturity date. In counting, **omit the date the note is issued but include the due date**. For example, the maturity date of a 60-day note dated July 17 is September 15, computed as follows.

Illustration 9-11
Computation of maturity date

Term of note		60 days
July (31−17)	14	
August	31	45
Maturity date: September		15

Illustration 9-12 shows three ways of stating the maturity date of a promissory note.

Illustration 9-12
Maturity date of different notes

On demand

On a stated date

At the end of a stated period of time

Computing Interest

As indicated in Chapter 3, the basic formula for computing interest on an interest-bearing note is:

Face Value of Note	×	Annual Interest Rate	×	Time in Terms of One Year	=	Interest

Illustration 9-13
Formula for computing interest

The interest rate specified in a note is an **annual** rate of interest. There are many different ways to calculate interest. The time factor in the formula in Illustration 9-13 expresses the fraction of a year that the note is outstanding. When the maturity date is stated in days, the time factor is often the number of days divided by 360. When the due date is stated in months, the time factor is the number of months divided by 12. Illustration 9-14 shows computation of interest for various time periods.

Terms of Note	Interest Computation Face × Rate × Time = Interest
$ 730, 18%, 120 days	$ 730 × 18% × 120/360 = $ 43.80
$1,000, 15%, 6 months	$1,000 × 15% × 6/12 = $ 75.00
$2,000, 12%, 1 year	$2,000 × 12% × 1/1 = $240.00

Illustration 9-14
Computation of interest

The computation above assumed 360 days for the length of the year. Financial instruments actually use 365 days. In order to simplify calculations in our illustrations, we have assumed 360 days. *For homework problems, assume 360 days.*

Recognizing Notes Receivable

To illustrate the basic entry for notes receivable, we will use the $1,000, two-month, 12% promissory note on page 409. Assuming that Calhoun Company wrote the note to settle an open account, Wilma Company makes the following entry for the receipt of the note.

STUDY OBJECTIVE 6
Explain how companies recognize notes receivable.

May 1	Notes Receivable	1,000	
	Accounts Receivable—Calhoun Company		1,000
	(To record acceptance of Calhoun Company note)		

A	=	L	+	OE

+1,000
−1,000

Cash Flows
no effect

The company records the note receivable at its **face value**, the amount shown on the face of the note. No interest revenue is reported when the note is accepted, because the revenue recognition principle does not recognize revenue until earned. Interest is earned (accrued) as time passes.

If a company lends money using a note, the entry is a debit to Notes Receivable and a credit to Cash in the amount of the loan.

Valuing Notes Receivable

Valuing short-term notes receivable is the same as valuing accounts receivable. Like accounts receivable, companies report short-term notes receivable at their **cash (net) realizable value**. The notes receivable

STUDY OBJECTIVE 7
Describe how companies value notes receivable.

allowance account is Allowance for Doubtful Accounts. The estimations involved in determining cash realizable value and in recording bad debts expense and the related allowance are done similarly to accounts receivable.

Disposing of Notes Receivable

STUDY OBJECTIVE 8

Describe the entries to record the disposition of notes receivable.

Notes may be held to their maturity date, at which time the maker must pay the face value plus accrued interest. Sometimes the maker of the note defaults and the payee must make an adjustment to the accounts. At other times the holder of the note speeds up the conversion to cash by selling the note receivable.

HONOR OF NOTES RECEIVABLE

A note is **honored** when its maker pays it in full at its maturity date. For an interest-bearing note, the amount due at maturity is the face value of the note plus interest for the length of time specified on the note.

To illustrate, assume that Betty Co. lends Wayne Higley Inc. $10,000 on June 1, accepting a five-month, 9% interest-bearing note. Interest will be $375 ($10,000 × 9% × 5/12). The maturity value will be $10,375. To obtain payment, Betty Co. (the payee) must present the note either to Wayne Higley Inc. (the maker) or to the maker's designated agent, such as a bank. Assuming that Betty Co. presents the note to Wayne Higley Inc. on the maturity date, Betty Co.'s entry to record the collection is:

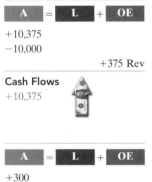

A = L + OE
+10,375
−10,000
            +375 Rev

Cash Flows
+10,375

Nov. 1	Cash	10,375	
	Notes Receivable		10,000
	Interest Revenue		375
	(To record collection of Higley Inc. note)		

If Betty Co. prepares financial statements as of September 30, it must accrue interest. In this case, Betty Co. would make the adjusting entry shown below to record 4 months' interest ($300).

A = L + OE
+300
        +300 Rev

Cash Flows
no effect

Sept. 30	Interest Receivable ($10,000 × 9% × 4/12)	300	
	Interest Revenue		300
	(To accrue 4 months' interest)		

When interest has been accrued, the company must credit Interest Receivable at maturity. In addition, since an additional month has passed, it must record one month of interest revenue. The entry by Betty Co. to record the honoring of the Wayne Higley Inc. note on November 1 is:

A = L + OE
+10,375
−10,000
−300
            +75 Rev

Cash Flows
+10,375

Nov. 1	Cash	10,375	
	Notes Receivable		10,000
	Interest Receivable		300
	Interest Revenue ($10,000 × 9% × 1/12)		75
	(To record collection of note at maturity)		

In this case, Betty Co. credits Interest Receivable because the receivable was established in the adjusting entry of September 30.

DISHONOR OF NOTES RECEIVABLE

A dishonored note is a note that is not paid in full at maturity. A dishonored note receivable is no longer negotiable. However, the payee still has a claim against the maker of the note. Therefore the note holder usually transfers the Notes Receivable account to an Account Receivable.

To illustrate, assume that Wayne Higley Inc. on November 1 indicates that it cannot pay at the present time. The entry to record the dishonor of the note depends on whether Betty Co. expects eventual collection. If it does expect eventual collection, Betty Co. debits the amount due (face value and interest) on the note to Accounts Receivable. It would make the following entry at the time the note is dishonored (assuming no previous accrual of interest).

Nov. 1	Accounts Receivable—Wayne Higley Inc.	10,375	
	Notes Receivable		10,000
	Interest Revenue		375
	(To record the dishonor of Higley Inc. note)		

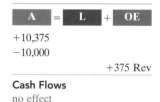

A = L + OE
+10,375
−10,000
                +375 Rev
Cash Flows
no effect

If instead, on November 1, there is no hope of collection, the note holder would write off the face value of the note by debiting the Allowance for Doubtful Accounts. No interest revenue would be recorded because collection will not occur.

SALE OF NOTES RECEIVABLE

The accounting for the sale of notes receivable is recorded similarly to the sale of accounts receivable. The accounting entries for the sale of notes receivable are left for a more advanced course.

DO IT!

Gambit Stores accepts from Leonard Co. a $3,400, 90-day, 12% note dated May 10 in settlement of Leonard's overdue account. (a) What is the maturity date of the note? (b) What is the entry made by Gambit at the maturity date, assuming Leonard pays the note and interest in full at that time?

NOTES RECEIVABLE

action plan

✔ Count the exact number of days to determine the maturity date. Omit the date the note is issued, but include the due date.

✔ Determine whether interest was accrued. The entry here assumes that no interest has been previously accrued on this note.

Solution

(a) The maturity date is August 8, computed as follows.

Term of note:		90 days
May (31−10)	21	
June	30	
July	31	82
Maturity date: August		8

(b) The interest payable at the maturity date is $102, computed as follows.

Face × Rate × Time = Interest
$3,400 × 12% × 90/360 = $102

The entry recorded by Gambit Stores at the maturity date is:

Cash	3,502	
Notes Receivable		3,400
Interest Revenue		102
(To record collection of Leonard note)		

Related exercise material: **BE9-9, BE9-10, BE9-11, E9-10, E9-11, E9-12, E9-13,** and DO IT! **9-3.**

✔ The Navigator

STATEMENT PRESENTATION AND ANALYSIS

Presentation

Companies should identify in the balance sheet or in the notes to the financial statements each of the major types of receivables. Short-term receivables appear in the current assets section of the balance sheet, below short-term investments. Short-term investments appear before receivables, because short-term investments are more liquid (nearer to cash). Companies report both the gross amount of receivables and the allowance for doubtful accounts.

In a multiple-step income statement, companies report bad debts expense and service charge expense as selling expenses in the operating expenses section. Interest revenue appears under "Other revenues and gains" in the nonoperating activities section of the income statement.

Analysis

Investors and corporate managers compute financial ratios to evaluate the liquidity of a company's accounts receivable. They use the **accounts receivable turnover ratio** to assess the liquidity of the receivables. This ratio measures the number of times, on average, the company collects accounts receivable during the period. It is computed by dividing net credit sales (net sales less cash sales) by the average net accounts receivable during the year. Unless seasonal factors are significant, average net accounts receivable outstanding can be computed from the beginning and ending balances of net accounts receivable.

For example, in 2007 Cisco Systems had net sales of $29,462 million for the year. It had a beginning accounts receivable (net) balance of $3,303 million and an ending accounts receivable (net) balance of $3,989 million. Assuming that Cisco's sales were all on credit, its accounts receivable turnover ratio is computed as follows.

Illustration 9-15
Accounts receivable turnover ratio and computation

Net Credit Sales	÷	Average Net Accounts Receivable	=	Accounts Receivable Turnover
$29,462	÷	$\dfrac{\$3,303 + \$3,989}{2}$	=	**8.1 times**

The result indicates an accounts receivable turnover ratio of 8.1 times per year. The higher the turnover ratio the more liquid the company's receivables.

A variant of the accounts receivable turnover ratio that makes the liquidity even more evident is its conversion into an **average collection period** in terms of days. This is done by dividing the turnover ratio into 365 days. For example, Cisco's turnover of 8.1 times is divided into 365 days, as shown in Illustration 9-16, to obtain approximately 45.1 days. This means that it takes Cisco about 45 days to collect its accounts receivable.

Illustration 9-16
Average collection period for receivables formula and computation

Days in Year	÷	Accounts Receivable Turnover	=	Average Collection Period in Days
365 days	÷	8.1 times	=	**45.1 days**

Companies frequently use the average collection period to assess the effectiveness of a company's credit and collection policies. The general rule is that the collection period should not greatly exceed the credit term period (that is, the time allowed for payment).

DO IT!

In 2010, Lebron James Company has net credit sales of $923,795 for the year. It had a beginning accounts receivable (net) balance of $38,275 and an ending accounts receivable (net) balance of $35,988. Compute Lebron James Company's (a) accounts receivable turnover and (b) average collection period in days.

ANALYSIS OF RECEIVABLES

action plan

✔ Review the formula to compute the accounts receivable turnover.

✔ Make sure that both the beginning and ending accounts receivable balances are considered in the computation.

✔ Review the formula to compute the average collection period in days.

Solution

(a)

| Net credit sales | ÷ | Average net accounts receivable | = | Accounts receivable turnover |

| $923,795 | ÷ | $\dfrac{38,275 + 35,988}{2}$ | = | 24.9 times |

(b)

| Days in year | ÷ | Accounts receivable turnover | = | Average collection period in days |

| 365 | ÷ | 24.9 times | = | 14.7 days |

Related exercise material: **BE9-12, E9-14** and **DO IT!** **9-4.**

 The Navigator

 Be sure to read **ALL ABOUT YOU:** *Should You Be Carrying Plastic?* on page 416 for information on how topics in this chapter apply to your personal life.

Should You Be Carrying Plastic?

Smart business people carefully consider their use of credit. They evaluate who they lend to, and how they finance their own operations. They know that getting overextended on credit can destroy their business.

Individuals need to evaluate their personal credit positions using the same thought processes used by business people. Some of you might consider the idea of not having a credit card a ridiculous proposition. But the reality is that the misuse of credit cards brings financial hardship to millions of Americans each year. Credit card companies aggressively market their cards with images of glamour and happiness. But there isn't much glamour in paying an 18% to 21% interest rate, and there is very little happiness to be found in filing for personal bankruptcy.

✺ Some Facts

* About 70% of undergraduates at 4-year colleges carry at least one credit card in their own name. Approximately 22% of college students got their first credit cards in high school.

* The average monthly debt on a college student's charge account, according to one study, is close to $2,000.

* In a recent year, Americans charged more than $1 trillion in purchases with their credit cards. That was more than they spent in cash.

* In the fourth quarter of 2007, the national average of credit card debt per bankcard user rose to $1,694, which was 4.81% higher than in the third quarter.

* Foreclosure filings nationwide soared 57% in January 2008 over the same month in the previous year. Nevada, California, and Florida had the highest foreclosure rates. In a recent month, one of every 167 homes in Nevada was in a stage of foreclosure.

✺ About the Numbers

Presented below is a chart that shows the major causes of personal financial problems. Note the excessive use of credit, which is cited as the number-one cause. This often translates into addiction to credit cards.

Causes of Personal Financial Problems

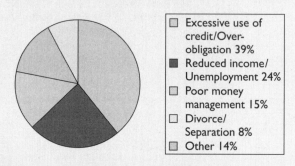

- ☐ Excessive use of credit/Over-obligation 39%
- ■ Reduced income/Unemployment 24%
- ☐ Poor money management 15%
- ☐ Divorce/Separation 8%
- ☐ Other 14%

Source: Debt Solutions of America, *www.becomedebtfree.com* (accessed May 2006).

✺ What Do You Think?

Should you cut up your credit card(s)?

YES: Americans are carrying huge personal debt burdens. Credit cards encourage unnecessary, spontaneous expenditures. The interest rates on credit cards are extremely high, which causes debt problems to escalate exponentially.

NO: Credit cards are a necessity for transactions in today's economy. In fact, many transactions are difficult or impossible to carry out without a credit card. People should learn to use credit cards responsibly.

Sources: Debtsmart, *www.debtsmart.com/pages/debt_stats.html*; Robin Marantz Henig, "Teen Credit Cards Actually Teach Responsibility," *USAToday.com*, July 30, 2001.

The following selected transactions relate to Falcetto Company.

Mar. 1   Sold $20,000 of merchandise to Potter Company, terms 2/10, n/30.
     11   Received payment in full from Potter Company for balance due.
     12   Accepted Juno Company's $20,000, 6-month, 12% note for balance due.
     13   Made Falcetto Company credit card sales for $13,200.
     15   Made Visa credit card sales totaling $6,700. A 3% service fee is charged by Visa.

Apr. 11   Sold accounts receivable of $8,000 to Harcot Factor. Harcot Factor assesses a service charge of 2% of the amount of receivables sold.
     13   Received collections of $8,200 on Falcetto Company credit card sales and added finance charges of 1.5% to the remaining balances.

May 10   Wrote off as uncollectible $16,000 of accounts receivable. Falcetto uses the percentage-of-sales basis to estimate bad debts.

June 30   Credit sales recorded during the first 6 months total $2,000,000. The bad debt percentage is 1% of credit sales. At June 30, the balance in the allowance account is $3,500.

July 16   One of the accounts receivable written off in May was from J. Simon, who pays the amount due, $4,000, in full.

Instructions

Prepare the journal entries for the transactions.

action plan

✔ Generally, record accounts receivable at invoice price.

✔ Recognize that sales returns and allowances and cash discounts reduce the amount received on accounts receivable.

✔ Record a service charge expense on the seller's books when accounts receivable are sold.

✔ Prepare an adjusting entry for bad debts.

✔ Ignore any balance in the allowance account under the percentage-of-sales basis. Recognize the balance in the allowance account under the percentage-of-receivables basis.

✔ Record write-offs of accounts receivable only in balance sheet accounts.

Solution to Comprehensive **DO IT!**

Mar. 1	Accounts Receivable–Potter	20,000	
	Sales		20,000
	(To record sales on account)		
11	Cash	19,600	
	Sales Discounts (2% × $20,000)	400	
	Accounts Receivable—Potter		20,000
	(To record collection of accounts receivable)		
12	Notes Receivable	20,000	
	Accounts Receivable—Juno		20,000
	(To record acceptance of Juno Company note)		
13	Accounts Receivable	13,200	
	Sales		13,200
	(To record company credit card sales)		
15	Cash	6,499	
	Service Charge Expense (3% × $6,700)	201	
	Sales		6,700
	(To record credit card sales)		
Apr. 11	Cash	7,840	
	Service Charge Expense (2% × $8,000)	160	
	Accounts Receivable		8,000
	(To record sale of receivables to factor)		
13	Cash	8,200	
	Accounts Receivable		8,200
	(To record collection of accounts receivable)		

	Accounts Receivable [($13,200 − $8,200) × 1.5%]	75	
	Interest Revenue		75
	(To record interest on amount due)		
May 10	Allowance for Doubtful Accounts	16,000	
	Accounts Receivable		16,000
	(To record write-off of accounts receivable)		
June 30	Bad Debts Expense ($2,000,000 × 1%)	20,000	
	Allowance for Doubtful Accounts		20,000
	(To record estimate of uncollectible accounts)		
July 16	Accounts Receivable—J. Simon	4,000	
	Allowance for Doubtful Accounts		4,000
	(To reverse write-off of accounts receivable)		
	Cash	4,000	
	Accounts Receivable—J. Simon		4,000
	(To record collection of accounts receivable)		

SUMMARY OF STUDY OBJECTIVES

1 Identify the different types of receivables. Receivables are frequently classified as (1) accounts, (2) notes, and (3) other. Accounts receivable are amounts customers owe on account. Notes receivable are claims for which lenders issue formal instruments of credit as proof of the debt. Other receivables include nontrade receivables such as interest receivable, loans to company officers, advances to employees, and income taxes refundable.

2 Explain how companies recognize accounts receivable. Companies record accounts receivable at invoice price. They are reduced by sales returns and allowances. Cash discounts reduce the amount received on accounts receivable. When interest is charged on a past due receivable, the company adds this interest to the accounts receivable balance and recognizes it as interest revenue.

3 Distinguish between the methods and bases companies use to value accounts receivable. There are two methods of accounting for uncollectible accounts: the allowance method and the direct write-off method. Companies may use either the percentage-of-sales or the percentage-of-receivables basis to estimate uncollectible accounts using the allowance method. The percentage-of-sales basis emphasizes the matching principle. The percentage-of-receivables basis emphasizes the cash realizable value of the accounts receivable. An aging schedule is often used with this basis.

4 Describe the entries to record the disposition of accounts receivable. When a company collects an account receivable, it credits Accounts Receivable. When a company sells (factors) an account receivable, a service charge expense reduces the amount received.

5 Compute the maturity date of and interest on notes receivable. For a note stated in months, the maturity date is found by counting the months from the date of issue. For a note stated in days, the number of days is counted, omitting the issue date and counting the due date. The formula for computing interest is: Face value × Interest rate × Time.

6 Explain how companies recognize notes receivable. Companies record notes receivable at face value. In some cases, it is necessary to accrue interest prior to maturity. In this case, companies debit Interest Receivable and credit Interest Revenue.

7 Describe how companies value notes receivable. As with accounts receivable, companies report notes receivable at their cash (net) realizable value. The notes receivable allowance account is the Allowance for Doubtful Accounts. The computation and estimations involved in valuing notes receivable at cash realizable value, and in recording the proper amount of bad debts expense and related allowance are similar to those for accounts receivable.

8 Describe the entries to record the disposition of notes receivable. Notes can be held to maturity. At that time the face value plus accrued interest is due, and the note is removed from the accounts. In many cases, the holder of the note speeds up the conversion by selling the receivable to another party (a factor). In some situations, the maker of the note dishonors the note (defaults), in which case the company transfers the note and accrued interest to an account receivable or writes off the note.

9 Explain the statement presentation and analysis of receivables. Companies should identify in the balance sheet or in the notes to the financial statements each major type of receivable. Short-term receivables are considered current assets. Companies report the gross amount of receivables and the allowance for doubtful accounts. They report bad debts and service charge expenses in the multiple-step income statement as operating (selling) expenses; interest revenue appears under other revenues and gains in the nonoperating activities section of the statement. Managers and investors evaluate accounts receivable for liquidity by computing a turnover ratio and an average collection period.

The Navigator

GLOSSARY

Accounts receivable Amounts owed by customers on account. (p. 398).

Accounts receivable turnover ratio A measure of the liquidity of accounts receivable; computed by dividing net credit sales by average net accounts receivable. (p. 414).

Aging the accounts receivable The analysis of customer balances by the length of time they have been unpaid. (p. 404).

Allowance method A method of accounting for bad debts that involves estimating uncollectible accounts at the end of each period. (p. 401).

Average collection period The average amount of time that a receivable is outstanding; calculated by dividing 365 days by the accounts receivables turnover ratio. (p. 414).

Bad Debts Expense An expense account to record uncollectible receivables. (p. 400).

Cash (net) realizable value The net amount a company expects to receive in cash. (p. 401).

Direct write-off method A method of accounting for bad debts that involves expensing accounts at the time they are determined to be uncollectible. (p. 400).

Dishonored note A note that is not paid in full at maturity. (p. 412).

Factor A finance company or bank that buys receivables from businesses and then collects the payments directly from the customers. (p. 407).

Maker The party in a promissory note who is making the promise to pay. (p. 409).

Notes receivable Claims for which formal instruments of credit are issued as proof of the debt. (p. 398).

Other receivables Various forms of nontrade receivables, such as interest receivable and income taxes refundable. (p. 398).

Payee The party to whom payment of a promissory note is to be made. (p. 409).

Percentage-of-receivables basis Management estimates what percentage of receivables will result in losses from uncollectible accounts. (p. 404).

Percentage-of-sales basis Management estimates what percentage of credit sales will be uncollectible. (p. 404).

Promissory note A written promise to pay a specified amount of money on demand or at a definite time. (p. 409).

Receivables Amounts due from individuals and other companies. (p. 398).

Trade receivables Notes and accounts receivable that result from sales transactions. (p. 398).

SELF-STUDY QUESTIONS

Answers are at the end of the chapter.

(SO 1) **1.** Receivables are frequently classified as:
   a. accounts receivable, company receivables, and other receivables.
   b. accounts receivable, notes receivable, and employee receivables.
   c. accounts receivable and general receivables.
   d. accounts receivable, notes receivable, and other receivables.

(SO 2) **2.** Buehler Company on June 15 sells merchandise on account to Chaz Co. for $1,000, terms 2/10, n/30. On June 20, Chaz Co. returns merchandise worth $300 to Buehler Company. On June 24, payment is received from Chaz Co. for the balance due. What is the amount of cash received?
   a. $700.
   b. $680.
   c. $686.
   d. None of the above.

(SO 3) **3.** Which of the following approaches for bad debts is best described as a balance sheet method?
   a. Percentage-of-receivables basis.
   b. Direct write-off method.
   c. Percentage-of-sales basis.
   d. Both a and b.

(SO 3) **4.** Hughes Company has a credit balance of $5,000 in its Allowance for Doubtful Accounts before any adjustments are made at the end of the year. Based on review and aging of its accounts receivable at the end of the year, Hughes estimates that $60,000 of its receivables are uncollectible. The amount of bad debts expense which should be reported for the year is:
   a. $5,000.
   b. $55,000.
   c. $60,000.
   d. $65,000.

(SO 3) **5.** Use the same information as in question 4, except that Hughes has a debit balance of $5,000 in its Allowance for Doubtful Accounts before any adjustments are made at the end of the year. In this situation, the amount of bad debt expense that should be reported for the year is:

a. $5,000.
b. $55,000.
c. $60,000.
d. $65,000.

(SO 3) **6.** Net sales for the month are $800,000, and bad debts are expected to be 1.5% of net sales. The company uses the percentage-of-sales basis. If the Allowance for Doubtful Accounts has a credit balance of $15,000 before adjustment, what is the balance after adjustment?

a. $15,000.
b. $27,000.
c. $23,000.
d. $31,000.

(SO 3) **7.** In 2010, Roso Carlson Company had net credit sales of $750,000. On January 1, 2010, Allowance for Doubtful Accounts had a credit balance of $18,000. During 2010, $30,000 of uncollectible accounts receivable were written off. Past experience indicates that 3% of net credit sales become uncollectible. What should be the adjusted balance of Allowance for Doubtful Accounts at December 31, 2010?

a. $10,050.
b. $10,500.
c. $22,500.
d. $40,500.

(SO 3) **8.** An analysis and aging of the accounts receivable of Prince Company at December 31 reveals the following data.

Accounts receivable	$800,000
Allowance for doubtful accounts per books before adjustment	50,000
Amounts expected to become uncollectible	65,000

The cash realizable value of the accounts receivable at December 31, after adjustment, is:

a. $685,000.
b. $750,000.
c. $800,000.
d. $735,000.

(SO 6) **9.** One of the following statements about promissory notes is incorrect. The *incorrect* statement is:

a. The party making the promise to pay is called the maker.
b. The party to whom payment is to be made is called the payee.
c. A promissory note is not a negotiable instrument.
d. A promissory note is often required from high-risk customers.

(SO 4) **10.** Which of the following statements about Visa credit card sales is *incorrect*?

a. The credit card issuer makes the credit investigation of the customer.
b. The retailer is not involved in the collection process.

c. Two parties are involved.
d. The retailer receives cash more quickly than it would from individual customers on account.

(SO 4) **11.** Blinka Retailers accepted $50,000 of Citibank Visa credit card charges for merchandise sold on July 1. Citibank charges 4% for its credit card use. The entry to record this transaction by Blinka Retailers will include a credit to Sales of $50,000 and a debit(s) to:

a. Cash	$48,000
and Service Charge Expense	2,000
b. Accounts Receivable	$48,000
and Service Charge Expense	$2,000
c. Cash	$50,000
d. Accounts Receivable	$50,000

(SO 6) **12.** Foti Co. accepts a $1,000, 3-month, 12% promissory note in settlement of an account with Bartelt Co. The entry to record this transaction is as follows.

a. Notes Receivable	1,030	
Accounts Receivable		1,030
b. Notes Receivable	1,000	
Accounts Receivable		1,000
c. Notes Receivable	1,000	
Sales		1,000
d. Notes Receivable	1,020	
Accounts Receivable		1,020

(SO 8) **13.** Ginter Co. holds Kolar Inc.'s $10,000, 120-day, 9% note. The entry made by Ginter Co. when the note is collected, assuming no interest has been previously accrued, is:

a. Cash	10,300	
Notes Receivable		10,300
b. Cash	10,000	
Notes Receivable		10,000
c. Accounts Receivable	10,300	
Notes Receivable		10,000
Interest Revenue		300
d. Cash	10,300	
Notes Receivable		10,000
Interest Revenue		300

(SO 9) **14.** Accounts and notes receivable are reported in the current assets section of the balance sheet at:

a. cash (net) realizable value.
b. net book value.
c. lower-of-cost-or-market value.
d. invoice cost.

(SO 9) **15.** Oliveras Company had net credit sales during the year of $800,000 and cost of goods sold of $500,000. The balance in accounts receivable at the beginning of the year was $100,000, and the end of the year it was $150,000. What were the accounts receivable turnover ratio and the average collection period in days?

a. 4.0 and 91.3 days.
b. 5.3 and 68.9 days.
c. 6.4 and 57 days.
d. 8.0 and 45.6 days.

Go to the book's companion website, **www.wiley.com/college/weygandt**, for additional Self-Study Questions.

 The Navigator

QUESTIONS

1. What is the difference between an account receivable and a note receivable?

2. What are some common types of receivables other than accounts receivable and notes receivable?

3. Texaco Oil Company issues its own credit cards. Assume that Texaco charges you $40 on an unpaid balance. Prepare the journal entry that Texaco makes to record this revenue.

4. What are the essential features of the allowance method of accounting for bad debts?

5. Jerry Gatewood cannot understand why cash realizable value does not decrease when an uncollectible account is written off under the allowance method. Clarify this point for Jerry Gatewood.

6. Distinguish between the two bases that may be used in estimating uncollectible accounts.

7. Eaton Company has a credit balance of $3,500 in Allowance for Doubtful Accounts. The estimated bad debts expense under the percentage-of-sales basis is $4,100. The total estimated uncollectibles under the percentage-of-receivables basis is $5,800. Prepare the adjusting entry under each basis.

8. How are bad debts accounted for under the direct write-off method? What are the disadvantages of this method?

9. DeVito Company accepts both its own credit cards and national credit cards. What are the advantages of accepting both types of cards?

10. An article recently appeared in the *Wall Street Journal* indicating that companies are selling their receivables at a record rate. Why are companies selling their receivables?

11. Pinkston Textiles decides to sell $600,000 of its accounts receivable to First Factors Inc. First Factors assesses a service charge of 3% of the amount of receivables sold. Prepare the journal entry that Pinkston Textiles makes to record this sale.

12. Your roommate is uncertain about the advantages of a promissory note. Compare the advantages of a note receivable with those of an account receivable.

13. How may the maturity date of a promissory note be stated?

14. Indicate the maturity date of each of the following promissory notes:

Date of Note	Terms
(a) March 13	one year after date of note
(b) May 4	3 months after date
(c) June 20	30 days after date
(d) July 1	60 days after date

15. Compute the missing amounts for each of the following notes.

	Principal	Annual Interest Rate	Time	Total Interest
(a)	?	9%	120 days	$ 600
(b)	$30,000	10%	3 years	?
(c)	$60,000	?	5 months	$2,000
(d)	$45,000	8%	?	$1,200

16. In determining interest revenue, some financial institutions use 365 days per year and others use 360 days. Why might a financial institution use 360 days?

17. Cain Company dishonors a note at maturity. What are the options available to the lender?

18. General Motors Corporation has accounts receivable and notes receivable. How should the receivables be reported on the balance sheet?

19. The accounts receivable turnover ratio is 8.14, and average net receivables during the period are $400,000. What is the amount of net credit sales for the period?

20. **PEPSICO** What percentage does PepsiCo's allowance for doubtful accounts represent as a percent of its gross receivables?

BRIEF EXERCISES

BE9-1 Presented below are three receivables transactions. Indicate whether these receivables are reported as accounts receivable, notes receivable, or other receivables on a balance sheet.

(a) Sold merchandise on account for $64,000 to a customer.
(b) Received a promissory note of $57,000 for services performed.
(c) Advanced $10,000 to an employee.

Identify different types of receivables.
(SO 1)

BE9-2 Record the following transactions on the books of Keyser Co.

(a) On July 1, Keyser Co. sold merchandise on account to Maxfield Inc. for $15,200, terms 2/10, n/30.
(b) On July 8, Maxfield Inc. returned merchandise worth $3,800 to Keyser Co.
(c) On July 11, Maxfield Inc. paid for the merchandise.

Record basic accounts receivable transactions.
(SO 2)

BE9-3 During its first year of operations, Henley Company had credit sales of $3,000,000; $600,000 remained uncollected at year-end. The credit manager estimates that $35,000 of these receivables will become uncollectible.

(a) Prepare the journal entry to record the estimated uncollectibles.
(b) Prepare the current assets section of the balance sheet for Henley Company. Assume that in addition to the receivables it has cash of $90,000, merchandise inventory of $130,000, and prepaid expenses of $7,500.

Prepare entry for allowance method and partial balance sheet.
(SO 3, 9)

Prepare entry for write-off; determine cash realizable value.

(SO 3)

BE9-4 At the end of 2010, Delong Co. has accounts receivable of $700,000 and an allowance for doubtful accounts of $54,000. On January 24, 2011, the company learns that its receivable from Ristau Inc. is not collectible, and management authorizes a write-off of $5,400.

(a) Prepare the journal entry to record the write-off.
(b) What is the cash realizable value of the accounts receivable (1) before the write-off and (2) after the write-off?

Prepare entries for collection of bad debts write-off.

(SO 3)

BE9-5 Assume the same information as BE9-4. On March 4, 2011, Delong Co. receives payment of $5,400 in full from Ristau Inc. Prepare the journal entries to record this transaction.

Prepare entry using percentage-of-sales method.

(SO 3)

BE9-6 Nieto Co. elects to use the percentage-of-sales basis in 2010 to record bad debts expense. It estimates that 2% of net credit sales will become uncollectible. Sales are $800,000 for 2010, sales returns and allowances are $45,000, and the allowance for doubtful accounts has a credit balance of $9,000. Prepare the adjusting entry to record bad debts expense in 2010.

Prepare entry using percentage-of-receivables method.

(SO 3)

BE9-7 Linhart Co. uses the percentage-of-receivables basis to record bad debts expense. It estimates that 1% of accounts receivable will become uncollectible. Accounts receivable are $450,000 at the end of the year, and the allowance for doubtful accounts has a credit balance of $1,500.

(a) Prepare the adjusting journal entry to record bad debts expense for the year.
(b) If the allowance for doubtful accounts had a debit balance of $800 instead of a credit balance of $1,500, determine the amount to be reported for bad debts expense.

Prepare entries to dispose of accounts receivable.

(SO 4)

BE9-8 Presented below are two independent transactions.

(a) St. Pierre Restaurant accepted a Visa card in payment of a $150 lunch bill. The bank charges a 4% fee. What entry should St. Pierre make?
(b) Jamar Company sold its accounts receivable of $60,000. What entry should Jamar make, given a service charge of 3% on the amount of receivables sold?

Compute interest and determine maturity dates on notes.

(SO 5)

BE9-9 Compute interest and find the maturity date for the following notes.

	Date of Note	Principal	Interest Rate (%)	Terms
(a)	June 10	$80,000	6%	60 days
(b)	July 14	$50,000	7%	90 days
(c)	April 27	$12,000	8%	75 days

Determine maturity dates and compute interest and rates on notes.

(SO 5)

BE9-10 Presented below are data on three promissory notes. Determine the missing amounts.

	Date of Note	Terms	Maturity Date	Principal	Annual Interest Rate	Total Interest
(a)	April 1	60 days	?	$600,000	9%	?
(b)	July 2	30 days	?	90,000	?	$600
(c)	March 7	6 months	?	120,000	10%	?

Prepare entry for notes receivable exchanged for account receivable.

(SO 6)

BE9-11 On January 10, 2010, Edmunds Co. sold merchandise on account to Jeff Gallup for $13,600, n/30. On February 9, Jeff Gallup gave Edmunds Co. a 10% promissory note in settlement of this account. Prepare the journal entry to record the sale and the settlement of the account receivable.

Compute ratios to analyze receivables.

(SO 9)

BE9-12 The financial statements of Minnesota Mining and Manufacturing Company (3M) report net sales of $20.0 billion. Accounts receivable (net) are $2.7 billion at the beginning of the year and $2.8 billion at the end of the year. Compute 3M's receivables turnover ratio. Compute 3M's average collection period for accounts receivable in days.

DO IT! REVIEW

Prepare entry for uncollectible accounts.

(SO 3)

DO IT! 9-1 Etienne Company has been in business several years. At the end of the current year, the ledger shows:

Accounts Receivable	$ 310,000 Dr.
Sales	2,200,000 Cr.
Allowance for Doubtful Accounts	6,100 Cr.

Bad debts are estimated to be 7% of receivables. Prepare the entry to adjust the Allowance for Doubtful Accounts.

DO IT! 9-2 Ronald Distributors is a growing company whose ability to raise capital has not been growing as quickly as its expanding assets and sales. Ronald's local banker has indicated that the company cannot increase its borrowing for the foreseeable future. Ronald's suppliers are demanding payment for goods acquired within 30 days of the invoice date, but Ronald's customers are slow in paying for their purchases (60–90 days). As a result, Ronald has a cash flow problem.

Prepare entry for factored accounts.

(SO 4)

Ronald needs $160,000 to cover next Friday's payroll. Its balance of outstanding accounts receivable totals $1,000,000. What might Ronald do to alleviate this cash crunch? Record the entry that Ronald would make when it raises the needed cash. (Assume a 2% service charge.)

DO IT! 9-3 Galen Wholesalers accepts from Picard Stores a $6,200, 4-month, 12% note dated May 31 in settlement of Picard's overdue account. (a) What is the maturity date of the note? (b) What is the entry made by Galen at the maturity date, assuming Picard pays the note and interest in full at that time?

Prepare entries for notes receivable.

(SO 5, 8)

DO IT! 9-4 In 2010, Drew Gooden Company has net credit sales of $1,600,000 for the year. It had a beginning accounts receivable (net) balance of $101,000 and an ending accounts receivable (net) balance of $107,000. Compute Drew Gooden Company's (a) accounts receivable turnover and (b) average collection period in days.

Compute ratios for receivables.

(SO 9)

EXERCISES

E9-1 Presented below are selected transactions of Pale Force Company. Pale Force sells in large quantities to other companies and also sells its product in a small retail outlet.

Journalize entries related to accounts receivable.

(SO 2)

March 1 Sold merchandise on account to CC Company for $3,000, terms 2/10, n/30.
     3 CC Company returned merchandise worth $500 to Pale Force.
     9 Pale Force collected the amount due from CC Company from the March 1 sale.
    15 Pale Force sold merchandise for $400 in its retail outlet. The customer used his Pale Force credit card.
    31 Pale Force added 1.5% monthly interest to the customer's credit card balance.

Instructions
Prepare journal entries for the transactions above.

E9-2 Presented below are two independent situations.

Journalize entries for recognizing accounts receivable.

(SO 2)

(a) On January 6, Arneson Co. sells merchandise on account to Cortez Inc. for $9,000, terms 2/10, n/30. On January 16, Cortez Inc. pays the amount due. Prepare the entries on Arneson's books to record the sale and related collection.

(b) On January 10, Mary Dawes uses her Pierson Co. credit card to purchase merchandise from Pierson Co. for $9,000. On February 10, Dawes is billed for the amount due of $9,000. On February 12, Dawes pays $5,000 on the balance due. On March 10, Dawes is billed for the amount due, including interest at 2% per month on the unpaid balance as of February 12. Prepare the entries on Pierson Co.'s books related to the transactions that occurred on January 10, February 12, and March 10.

E9-3 The ledger of Hixson Company at the end of the current year shows Accounts Receivable $120,000, Sales $840,000, and Sales Returns and Allowances $30,000.

Journalize entries to record allowance for doubtful accounts using two different bases.

(SO 3)

Instructions
(a) If Hixson uses the direct write-off method to account for uncollectible accounts, journalize the adjusting entry at December 31, assuming Hixson determines that Fell's $1,400 balance is uncollectible.

(b) If Allowance for Doubtful Accounts has a credit balance of $2,100 in the trial balance, journalize the adjusting entry at December 31, assuming bad debts are expected to be (1) 1% of net sales, and (2) 10% of accounts receivable.

(c) If Allowance for Doubtful Accounts has a debit balance of $200 in the trial balance, journalize the adjusting entry at December 31, assuming bad debts are expected to be (1) 0.75% of net sales and (2) 6% of accounts receivable.

E9-4 Ingles Company has accounts receivable of $93,100 at March 31. An analysis of the accounts shows the information on the next page.

Determine bad debts expense; prepare the adjusting entry for bad debts expense.

(SO 3)

Month of Sale	Balance, March 31
March	$60,000
February	17,600
January	8,500
Prior to January	7,000
	$93,100

Credit terms are 2/10, n/30. At March 31, Allowance for Doubtful Accounts has a credit balance of $1,200 prior to adjustment. The company uses the percentage-of-receivables basis for estimating uncollectible accounts. The company's estimate of bad debts is as follows.

Age of Accounts	Estimated Percentage Uncollectible
1–30 days	2.0%
31–60 days	5.0%
61–90 days	30.0%
Over 90 days	50.0%

Instructions
(a) Determine the total estimated uncollectibles.
(b) Prepare the adjusting entry at March 31 to record bad debts expense.

Journalize write-off and recovery.

(SO 3)

E9-5 At December 31, 2009, Braddock Company had a balance of $15,000 in the Allowance for Doubtful Accounts. During 2010, Braddock wrote off accounts totaling $13,000. One of those accounts ($1,800) was later collected. At December 31, 2010, an aging schedule indicated that the balance in the Allowance for Doubtful Accounts should be $19,000.

Instructions
Prepare journal entries to record the 2010 transactions of Braddock Company.

Journalize percentage of sales basis, write-off, recovery.

(SO 3)

E9-6 On December 31, 2010, Jarnigan Co. estimated that 2% of its net sales of $400,000 will become uncollectible. The company recorded this amount as an addition to Allowance for Doubtful Accounts. On May 11, 2011, Jarnigan Co. determined that Terry Frye's account was uncollectible and wrote off $1,100. On June 12, 2011, Frye paid the amount previously written off.

Instructions
Prepare the journal entries on December 31, 2010, May 11, 2011, and June 12, 2011.

Journalize entries for the sale of accounts receivable.

(SO 4)

E9-7 Presented below are two independent situations.

(a) On March 3, Cornwell Appliances sells $680,000 of its receivables to Marsh Factors Inc. Marsh Factors assesses a finance charge of 3% of the amount of receivables sold. Prepare the entry on Cornwell Appliances' books to record the sale of the receivables.

(b) On May 10, Dale Company sold merchandise for $3,500 and accepted the customer's America Bank MasterCard. America Bank charges a 4% service charge for credit card sales. Prepare the entry on Dale Company's books to record the sale of merchandise.

Journalize entries for credit card sales.

(SO 4)

E9-8 Presented below are two independent situations.

(a) On April 2, Nancy Hansel uses her J. C. Penney Company credit card to purchase merchandise from a J. C. Penney store for $1,500. On May 1, Hansel is billed for the $1,500 amount due. Hansel pays $700 on the balance due on May 3. On June 1, Hansel receives a bill for the amount due, including interest at 1.0% per month on the unpaid balance as of May 3. Prepare the entries on J. C. Penney Co.'s books related to the transactions that occurred on April 2, May 3, and June 1.

(b) On July 4, Kimble's Restaurant accepts a Visa card for a $200 dinner bill. Visa charges a 3% service fee. Prepare the entry on Kimble's books related to this transaction.

Journalize credit card sales, and indicate the statement presentation of financing charges and service charge expense.

(SO 4)

E9-9 Topeka Stores accepts both its own and national credit cards. During the year the following selected summary transactions occurred.

Jan. 15	Made Topeka credit card sales totaling $18,000. (There were no balances prior to January 15.)
20	Made Visa credit card sales (service charge fee 2%) totaling $4,300.
Feb. 10	Collected $10,000 on Topeka credit card sales.
15	Added finance charges of 1% to Topeka credit card balance.

Instructions

(a) Journalize the transactions for Topeka Stores.
(b) Indicate the statement presentation of the financing charges and the credit card service charge expense for Topeka Stores.

E9-10   Orosco Supply Co. has the following transactions related to notes receivable during the last 2 months of 2010.

Journalize entries for notes receivable transactions.

(SO 5, 6)

Nov. 1   Loaned $15,000 cash to Sally Givens on a 1-year, 10% note.
Dec. 11   Sold goods to John Countryman, Inc., receiving a $6,750, 90-day, 8% note.
    16   Received a $4,000, 6-month, 9% note in exchange for Bob Reber's outstanding accounts receivable.
    31   Accrued interest revenue on all notes receivable.

Instructions

(a) Journalize the transactions for Orosco Supply Co.
(b) Record the collection of the Givens note at its maturity in 2011.

E9-11   Record the following transactions for Sandwich Co. in the general journal.

Journalize entries for notes receivable.

(SO 5, 6)

2010

May 1   Received a $7,500, 1-year, 10% note in exchange for Julia Gonzalez's outstanding accounts receivable.
Dec. 31   Accrued interest on the Gonzalez note.
Dec. 31   Closed the interest revenue account.

2011

May 1   Received principal plus interest on the Gonzalez note. (No interest has been accrued in 2011.)

E9-12   Singletary Company had the following select transactions.

Prepare entries for note receivable transactions.

(SO 5, 6, 8)

Apr. 1, 2010   Accepted Wilson Company's 1-year, 12% note in settlement of a $20,000 account receivable.
July 1, 2010   Loaned $25,000 cash to Richard Dent on a 9-month, 10% note.
Dec. 31, 2010   Accrued interest on all notes receivable.
Apr. 1, 2011   Received principal plus interest on the Wilson note.
Apr. 1, 2011   Richard Dent dishonored its note; Singletary expects it will eventually collect.

Instructions

Prepare journal entries to record the transactions. Singletary prepares adjusting entries once a year on December 31.

E9-13   On May 2, Kleinsorge Company lends $7,600 to Everhart, Inc., issuing a 6-month, 9% note. At the maturity date, November 2, Everhart indicates that it cannot pay.

Journalize entries for dishonor of notes receivable.

(SO 5, 8)

Instructions

(a) Prepare the entry to record the issuance of the note.
(b) Prepare the entry to record the dishonor of the note, assuming that Kleinsorge Company expects collection will occur.
(c) Prepare the entry to record the dishonor of the note, assuming that Kleinsorge Company does not expect collection in the future.

E9-14   Bledel Company had accounts receivable of $100,000 on January 1, 2010. The only transactions that affected accounts receivable during 2010 were net credit sales of $1,000,000, cash collections of $900,000, and accounts written off of $30,000.

Compute receivables turnover and average collection period.

(SO 9)

Instructions

(a) Compute the ending balance of accounts receivable.
(b) Compute the accounts receivable turnover ratio for 2010.
(c) Compute the average collection period in days.

EXERCISES: SET B

Visit the book's companion website at **www.wiley.com/college/weygandt**, and choose the Student Companion site, to access Exercise Set B.

PROBLEMS: SET A

Prepare journal entries related to bad debts expense.

(SO 2, 3, 9)

P9-1A At December 31, 2009, Leis Co. reported the following information on its balance sheet.

Accounts receivable	$960,000
Less: Allowance for doubtful accounts	80,000

During 2010, the company had the following transactions related to receivables.

1.	Sales on account	$3,200,000
2.	Sales returns and allowances	50,000
3.	Collections of accounts receivable	2,810,000
4.	Write-offs of accounts receivable deemed uncollectible	90,000
5.	Recovery of bad debts previously written off as uncollectible	24,000

Instructions

(a) Prepare the journal entries to record each of these five transactions. Assume that no cash discounts were taken on the collections of accounts receivable.

(b) Accounts receivable $1,210,000 ADA $14,000

(b) Enter the January 1, 2010, balances in Accounts Receivable and Allowance for Doubtful Accounts, post the entries to the two accounts (use T accounts), and determine the balances.

(c) Bad debts expense $101,000

(c) Prepare the journal entry to record bad debts expense for 2010, assuming that an aging of accounts receivable indicates that expected bad debts are $115,000.

(d) Compute the accounts receivable turnover ratio for 2010.

Compute bad debts amounts.

(SO 3)

P9-2A Information related to Hermesch Company for 2010 is summarized below.

Total credit sales	$2,200,000
Accounts receivable at December 31	825,000
Bad debts written off	33,000

Instructions

(a) What amount of bad debts expense will Hermesch Company report if it uses the direct write-off method of accounting for bad debts?

(b) Assume that Hermesch Company estimates its bad debts expense to be 2% of credit sales. What amount of bad debts expense will Hermesch record if it has an Allowance for Doubtful Accounts credit balance of $4,000?

(c) Assume that Hermesch Company estimates its bad debts expense based on 6% of accounts receivable. What amount of bad debts expense will Hermesch record if it has an Allowance for Doubtful Accounts credit balance of $3,000?

(d) Assume the same facts as in (c), except that there is a $3,000 debit balance in Allowance for Doubtful Accounts. What amount of bad debts expense will Hermesch record?

(e) What is the weakness of the direct write-off method of reporting bad debts expense?

Journalize entries to record transactions related to bad debts.

(SO 2, 3)

P9-3A Presented below is an aging schedule for Zillmann Company.

☒ Worksheet.xls							▢▣☒
▣ **File** **Edit** **View** **Insert** **Format** **Tools** **Data** **Window** **Help**							
	A	B	C	D	E	F	G
1					**Number of Days Past Due**		
2			Not				
3	Customer	Total	Yet Due	1–30	31–60	61–90	Over 90
4	Arndt	$ 22,000		$10,000	$12,000		
5	Blair	40,000	$ 40,000				
6	Chase	57,000	16,000	6,000		$35,000	
7	Drea	34,000					$34,000
8	Others	132,000	96,000	16,000	14,000		6,000
9		$285,000	$152,000	$32,000	$26,000	$35,000	$40,000
10	Estimated Percentage Uncollectible		3%	6%	13%	25%	60%
11	Total Estimated Bad Debts	$ 42,610	$ 4,560	$ 1,920	$ 3,380	$ 8,750	$24,000
12							

At December 31, 2010, the unadjusted balance in Allowance for Doubtful Accounts is a credit of $12,000.

Instructions

(a) Journalize and post the adjusting entry for bad debts at December 31, 2010.

(b) Journalize and post to the allowance account the following events and transactions in the year 2011.

    (1) On March 31, a $1,000 customer balance originating in 2010 is judged uncollectible.

    (2) On May 31, a check for $1,000 is received from the customer whose account was written off as uncollectible on March 31.

(c) Journalize the adjusting entry for bad debts on December 31, 2011, assuming that the unadjusted balance in Allowance for Doubtful Accounts is a debit of $800 and the aging schedule indicates that total estimated bad debts will be $28,600.

(a) Bad debts expense $30,610

(c) Bad debts expense $29,400

P9-4A Wall Inc. uses the allowance method to estimate uncollectible accounts receivable. The company produced the following aging of the accounts receivable at year end.

Journalize transactions related to bad debts.

(SO 2, 3)

⊠ Worksheet.xls							□回区
🖹 File Edit View Insert Format Tools Data Window Help							
	A	**B**	**C**	**D**	**E**	**F**	**G**
1			\multicolumn{5}{c}{**Number of Days Outstanding**}	
2							
3		**Total**	**0–30**	**31–60**	**61–90**	**91–120**	**Over 120**
4	Accounts receivable	375,000	220,000	90,000	40,000	10,000	$15,000
5	% uncollectible		1%	4%	5%	8%	10%
6	Estimated bad debts						
7							

Instructions

(a) Calculate the total estimated bad debts based on the above information.

(b) Prepare the year-end adjusting journal entry to record the bad debts using the aged uncollectible accounts receivable determined in (a). Assume the current balance in Allowance for Doubtful Accounts is a $8,000 debit.

(c) Of the above accounts, $5,000 is determined to be specifically uncollectible. Prepare the journal entry to write off the uncollectible account.

(d) The company collects $5,000 subsequently on a specific account that had previously been determined to be uncollectible in (c). Prepare the journal entry(ies) necessary to restore the account and record the cash collection.

(e) Comment on how your answers to (a)–(d) would change if Wall Inc. used 3% of *total* accounts receivable, rather than aging the accounts receivable. What are the advantages to the company of aging the accounts receivable rather than applying a percentage to total accounts receivable?

(a) Tot. est. bad debts $11,510

P9-5A At December 31, 2010, the trial balance of Worcester Company contained the following amounts before adjustment.

Journalize entries to record transactions related to bad debts.

(SO 3)

	Debits	**Credits**
Accounts Receivable	$385,000	
Allowance for Doubtful Accounts		$ 2,000
Sales		950,000

Instructions

(a) Based on the information given, which method of accounting for bad debts is Worcester Company using—the direct write-off method or the allowance method? How can you tell?

(b) Prepare the adjusting entry at December 31, 2010, for bad debts expense under each of the following independent assumptions.

    (1) An aging schedule indicates that $11,750 of accounts receivable will be uncollectible.

    (2) The company estimates that 1% of sales will be uncollectible.

(c) Repeat part (b) assuming that instead of a credit balance there is an $2,000 debit balance in Allowance for Doubtful Accounts.

(d) During the next month, January 2011, a $3,000 account receivable is written off as uncollectible. Prepare the journal entry to record the write-off.

(e) Repeat part (d) assuming that Worcester uses the direct write-off method instead of the allowance method in accounting for uncollectible accounts receivable.

(f)   What type of account is Allowance for Doubtful Accounts? How does it affect how accounts receivable is reported on the balance sheet at the end of the accounting period?

(b) (2) $9,500

Prepare entries for various notes receivable transactions.

(SO 2, 4, 5, 8, 9)

P9-6A Mendosa Company closes its books monthly. On September 30, selected ledger account balances are:

Notes Receivable	$33,000
Interest Receivable	170

Notes Receivable include the following.

Date	Maker	Face	Term	Interest
Aug. 16	Chang Inc.	$ 8,000	60 days	8%
Aug. 25	Hughey Co.	9,000	60 days	10%
Sept. 30	Skinner Corp.	16,000	6 months	9%

Interest is computed using a 360-day year. During October, the following transactions were completed.

Oct. 7 Made sales of $6,900 on Mendosa credit cards.
12 Made sales of $900 on MasterCard credit cards. The credit card service charge is 3%.
15 Added $460 to Mendosa customer balance for finance charges on unpaid balances.
15 Received payment in full from Chang Inc. on the amount due.
24 Received notice that the Hughey note has been dishonored. (Assume that Hughey is expected to pay in the future.)

Instructions
(a) Journalize the October transactions and the October 31 adjusting entry for accrued interest receivable.

(b) Accounts receivable $16,510

(c) Total receivables $32,630

(b) Enter the balances at October 1 in the receivable accounts. Post the entries to all of the receivable accounts.
(c) Show the balance sheet presentation of the receivable accounts at October 31.

Prepare entries for various receivable transactions.

(SO 2, 4, 5, 6, 7, 8)

P9-7A On January 1, 2010, Kloppenberg Company had Accounts Receivable $139,000, Notes Receivable $25,000, and Allowance for Doubtful Accounts $13,200. The note receivable is from Sara Rogers Company. It is a 4-month, 12% note dated December 31, 2009. Kloppenberg Company prepares financial statements annually. During the year the following selected transactions occurred.

Jan. 5 Sold $20,000 of merchandise to Dedonder Company, terms n/15.
20 Accepted Dedonder Company's $20,000, 3-month, 9% note for balance due.
Feb. 18 Sold $8,000 of merchandise to Ludwig Company and accepted Ludwig's $8,000, 6-month, 9% note for the amount due.
Apr. 20 Collected Dedonder Company note in full.
30 Received payment in full from Sara Rogers Company on the amount due.
May 25 Accepted Jenks Inc.'s $4,000, 3-month, 7% note in settlement of a past-due balance on account.
Aug. 18 Received payment in full from Ludwig Company on note due.
25 The Jenks Inc. note was dishonored. Jenks Inc. is not bankrupt; future payment is anticipated.
Sept. 1 Sold $12,000 of merchandise to Lena Torme Company and accepted a $12,000, 6-month, 10% note for the amount due.

Instructions
Journalize the transactions.

PROBLEMS: SET B

Prepare journal entries related to bad debts expense.

(SO 2, 3, 9)

P9-1B At December 31, 2009, Dill Imports reported the following information on its balance sheet.

Accounts receivable	$250,000
Less: Allowance for doubtful accounts	15,000

During 2010, the company had the following transactions related to receivables.

1. Sales on account	$2,400,000
2. Sales returns and allowances	45,000
3. Collections of accounts receivable	2,250,000
4. Write-offs of accounts receivable deemed uncollectible	12,000
5. Recovery of bad debts previously written off as uncollectible	3,000

Instructions

(a) Prepare the journal entries to record each of these five transactions. Assume that no cash discounts were taken on the collections of accounts receivable.

(b) Enter the January 1, 2010, balances in Accounts Receivable and Allowance for Doubtful Accounts. Post the entries to the two accounts (use T accounts), and determine the balances.

(c) Prepare the journal entry to record bad debts expense for 2010, assuming that an aging of accounts receivable indicates that estimated bad debts are $22,000.

(d) Compute the accounts receivable turnover ratio for the year 2010.

(b) Accounts receivable
 $343,000
 ADA $6,000

(c) Bad debts expense
 $16,000

P9-2B   Information related to Bee Company for 2010 is summarized below.

Compute bad debts amounts.
(SO 3)

Total credit sales	$1,100,000
Accounts receivable at December 31	369,000
Bad debts written off	22,150

Instructions

(a) What amount of bad debts expense will Bee Company report if it uses the direct write-off method of accounting for bad debts?

(b) Assume that Bee Company decides to estimate its bad debts expense to be 2% of credit sales. What amount of bad debts expense will Bee record if Allowance for Doubtful Accounts has a credit balance of $3,000?

(c) Assume that Bee Company decides to estimate its bad debts expense based on 6% of accounts receivable. What amount of bad debts expense will Bee Company record if Allowance for Doubtful Accounts has a credit balance of $4,000?

(d) Assume the same facts as in (c), except that there is a $2,000 debit balance in Allowance for Doubtful Accounts. What amount of bad debts expense will Bee record?

(e) ⬛▬▬▷ What is the weakness of the direct write-off method of reporting bad debts expense?

P9-3B   Presented below is an aging schedule for Jafar Company.

Journalize entries to record transactions related to bad debts.
(SO 2, 3)

⊠ Worksheet.xls

🖹 File   Edit   View   Insert   Format   Tools   Data   Window   Help

	A	B	C	D	E	F	G
1					**Number of Days Past Due**		
2			**Not**				
3	**Customer**	**Total**	**Yet Due**	**1–30**	**31–60**	**61–90**	**Over 90**
4	Akers	$ 30,000		$ 13,500	$16,500		
5	Baietto	45,000	$ 45,000				
6	Comer	75,000	22,500	7,500		$45,000	
7	DeJong	57,000					$57,000
8	Others	189,000	138,000	22,500	19,500		9,000
9		$396,000	$205,500	$43,500	$36,000	$45,000	$66,000
10	Estimated Percentage Uncollectible		2%	6%	10%	25%	50%
11	Total Estimated Bad Debts	$ 54,570	$ 4,110	$ 2,610	$ 3,600	$ 11,250	$33,000
12							

At December 31, 2010, the unadjusted balance in Allowance for Doubtful Accounts is a credit of $16,000.

Instructions

(a) Journalize and post the adjusting entry for bad debts at December 31, 2010.

(b) Journalize and post to the allowance account the following events and transactions in the year 2011.

   (1) March 1, a $1,900 customer balance originating in 2010 is judged uncollectible.

   (2) May 1, a check for $1,900 is received from the customer whose account was written off as uncollectible on March 1.

(c) Journalize the adjusting entry for bad debts on December 31, 2011. Assume that the unadjusted balance in Allowance for Doubtful Accounts is a debit of $2,000, and the aging schedule indicates that total estimated bad debts will be $42,300.

(a) Bad debts expense
 $38,570

(c) Bad debts expense
 $44,300

Journalize transactions related to bad debts.

(SO 2, 3)

P9-4B The following represents selected information taken from a company's aging schedule to estimate uncollectible accounts receivable at year end.

		Number of Days Outstanding				
	Total	0–30	31–60	61–90	91–120	Over 120
Accounts receivable	$375,000	$220,000	$90,000	$40,000	$10,000	$15,000
% uncollectible		1%	4%	5%	8%	10%
Estimated bad debts						

Worksheet.xls — File Edit View Insert Format Tools Data Window Help

Instructions

(a) Tot. est. bad debts $10,100

(a) Calculate the total estimated bad debts based on the above information.

(b) Prepare the year-end adjusting journal entry to record the bad debts using the allowance method and the aged uncollectible accounts receivable determined in (a). Assume the current balance in the Allowance for Doubtful Accounts account is a $3,000 credit.

(c) Of the above accounts, $1,600 is determined to be specifically uncollectible. Prepare the journal entry to write off the uncollectible accounts.

(d) The company subsequently collects $700 on a specific account that had previously been determined to be uncollectible in (c). Prepare the journal entry(ies) necessary to restore the account and record the cash collection.

(e) Explain how establishing an allowance account satisfies the matching principle.

Journalize entries to record transactions related to bad debts.

(SO 3)

P9-5B At December 31, 2010, the trial balance of Liquid Snake Company contained the following amounts before adjustment.

	Debits	Credits
Accounts Receivable	$250,000	
Allowance for Doubtful Accounts		$ 1,100
Sales		600,000

Instructions

(a) (2) $12,000

(a) Prepare the adjusting entry at December 31, 2010, to record bad debts expense under each of the following independent assumptions.
  (1) An aging schedule indicates that $12,500 of accounts receivable will be uncollectible.
  (2) The company estimates that 2% of sales will be uncollectible.

(b) Repeat part (a) assuming that instead of a credit balance, there is a $1,100 debit balance in Allowance for Doubtful Accounts.

(c) During the next month, January 2011, a $3,200 account receivable is written off as uncollectible. Prepare the journal entry to record the write-off.

(d) Repeat part (c) assuming that Liquid Snake Company uses the direct write-off method instead of the allowance method in accounting for uncollectible accounts receivable.

(e) What are the advantages of using the allowance method in accounting for uncollectible accounts as compared to the direct write-off method?

Prepare entries for various notes receivable transactions.

(SO 2, 4, 5, 8, 9)

GLS

P9-6B Marty Co. closes its books monthly. On June 30, selected ledger account balances are:

Notes Receivable	$57,000
Interest Receivable	420

Notes Receivable include the following.

Date	Maker	Face	Term	Interest
May 16	Rice Inc.	$12,000	60 days	10%
May 25	Smelter Co.	30,000	60 days	9%
June 30	Kupp Corp.	15,000	6 months	12%

During July, the following transactions were completed.

July 5 Made sales of $7,200 on Marty Co. credit cards.

14 Made sales of $1,000 on Visa credit cards. The credit card service charge is 3%.

14 Added $510 to Marty Co. credit card customer balances for finance charges on unpaid balances.

15 Received payment in full from Rice Inc. on the amount due.

25 Received notice that the Smelter Co. note has been dishonored. (Assume that Smelter Co. is expected to pay in the future.)

Instructions

(a) Journalize the July transactions and the July 31 adjusting entry for accrued interest receivable. (Interest is computed using 360 days.)

(b) Enter the balances at July 1 in the receivable accounts. Post the entries to all of the receivable accounts.

(c) Show the balance sheet presentation of the receivable accounts at July 31.

(b) Accounts receivable $38,160

(c) Total receivables $53,310

P9-7B   On January 1, 2010, Furball Company had Accounts Receivable $98,000 and Allowance for Doubtful Accounts $8,100. Furball Company prepares financial statements annually. During the year the following selected transactions occurred.

Prepare entries for various receivable transactions.

(SO 2, 4, 5, 6, 7, 8)

Jan. 5 Sold $10,800 of merchandise to Kandle Company, terms n/30.

Feb. 2 Accepted a $10,800, 4-month, 10% promissory note from Kandle Company for the balance due.

12 Sold $13,500 of merchandise to Lowe Company and accepted Lowe's $13,500, 2-month, 10% note for the balance due.

26 Sold $7,000 of merchandise to Barrel Co., terms n/10.

Apr. 5 Accepted a $7,000, 3-month, 8% note from Barrel Co. for the balance due.

12 Collected Lowe Company note in full.

June 2 Collected Kandle Company note in full.

July 5 Barrel Co. dishonors its note of April 5. It is expected that Barrel will eventually pay the amount owed.

15 Sold $12,000 of merchandise to Bushel Co. and accepted Bushel's $12,000, 3-month, 12% note for the amount due.

Oct. 15 Bushel Co.'s note was dishonored. Bushel Co. is bankrupt, and there is no hope of future settlement.

Instructions

Journalize the transactions.

PROBLEMS: SET C

Visit the book's companion website at **www.wiley.com/college/weygandt**, and choose the Student Companion site, to access Problem Set C.

CONTINUING COOKIE CHRONICLE

(*Note:* This is a continuation of the Cookie Chronicle from Chapters 1 through 8.)

CCC9   One of Natalie's friends, Curtis Lesperance, runs a coffee shop where he sells specialty coffees and prepares and sells muffins and cookies. He is eager to buy one of Natalie's fine European mixers, which would enable him to make larger batches of muffins and cookies. However, Curtis cannot afford to pay for the mixer for at least 30 days. He asks Natalie if she would be willing to sell him the mixer on credit. Natalie comes to you for advice.

Go to the book's companion website, **www.wiley.com/college/weygandt,** *to see the completion of this problem.*

BROADENING YOUR PERSPECTIVE

FINANCIAL REPORTING AND ANALYSIS

Financial Reporting Problem: SEK Company

BYP9-1 SEK Company sells office equipment and supplies to many organizations in the city and surrounding area on contract terms of 2/10, n/30. In the past, over 75% of the credit customers have taken advantage of the discount by paying within 10 days of the invoice date.

The number of customers taking the full 30 days to pay has increased within the last year. Current indications are that less than 60% of the customers are now taking the discount. Bad debts as a percentage of gross credit sales have risen from the 2.5% provided in past years to about 4.5% in the current year.

The company's Finance Committee has requested more information on the collections of accounts receivable. The controller responded to this request with the report reproduced below.

SEK COMPANY
Accounts Receivable Collections
May 31, 2010

The fact that some credit accounts will prove uncollectible is normal. Annual bad debts write-offs have been 2.5% of gross credit sales over the past 5 years. During the last fiscal year, this percentage increased to slightly less than 4.5%. The current Accounts Receivable balance is $1,400,000. The condition of this balance in terms of age and probability of collection is as follows.

Proportion of Total	Age Categories	Probability of Collection
62%	not yet due	98%
20%	less than 30 days past due	96%
9%	30 to 60 days past due	94%
5%	61 to 120 days past due	91%
2½%	121 to 180 days past due	75%
1½%	over 180 days past due	30%

The Allowance for Doubtful Accounts had a credit balance of $29,500 on June 1, 2009. SEK has provided for a monthly bad debts expense accrual during the current fiscal year based on the assumption that 4.5% of gross credit sales will be uncollectible. Total gross credit sales for the 2009–10 fiscal year amounted to $2,900,000. Write-offs of bad accounts during the year totaled $102,000.

Instructions

(a) Prepare an accounts receivable aging schedule for SEK Company using the age categories identified in the controller's report to the Finance Committee showing the following.
  (1) The amount of accounts receivable outstanding for each age category and in total.
  (2) The estimated amount that is uncollectible for each category and in total.
(b) Compute the amount of the year-end adjustment necessary to bring Allowance for Doubtful Accounts to the balance indicated by the age analysis. Then prepare the necessary journal entry to adjust the accounting records.
(c) In a recessionary environment with tight credit and high interest rates:
  (1) Identify steps SEK Company might consider to improve the accounts receivable situation.
  (2) Then evaluate each step identified in terms of the risks and costs involved.

Comparative Analysis Problem: PepsiCo, Inc. vs. The Coca-Cola Company

BYP9-2 PepsiCo, Inc.'s financial statements are presented in Appendix A. Financial statements of The Coca-Cola Company are presented in Appendix B.

Instructions

(a) Based on the information in these financial statements, compute the following 2007 ratios for each company. (Assume all sales are credit sales and that PepsiCo's receivables on its balance sheet are all trade receivables.)

(1) Accounts receivable turnover ratio.

(2) Average collection period for receivables.

(b) What conclusions about managing accounts receivable can you draw from these data?

Exploring the Web

BYP9-3 **Purpose:** To learn more about factoring services.

Address: **www.invoicebankers.com**, or go to **www.wiley.com/college/weygandt**

Steps: Go to the website and answer the following questions.

(a) What are some of the benefits of factoring?

(b) What is the range of the percentages of the typical discount rate?

(c) If a company factors its receivables, what percentage of the value of the receivables can it expect to receive from the factor in the form of cash, and how quickly will it receive the cash?

CRITICAL THINKING

Decision Making Across the Organization

BYP9-4   Molly and Joe Mayne own Campus Fashions. From its inception Campus Fashions has sold merchandise on either a cash or credit basis, but no credit cards have been accepted. During the past several months, the Maynes have begun to question their sales policies. First, they have lost some sales because of refusing to accept credit cards. Second, representatives of two metropolitan banks have been persuasive in almost convincing them to accept their national credit cards. One bank, City National Bank, has stated that its credit card fee is 4%.

The Maynes decide that they should determine the cost of carrying their own credit sales. From the accounting records of the past 3 years they accumulate the following data.

	2010	2009	2008
Net credit sales	$500,000	$600,000	$400,000
Collection agency fees for slow-paying customers	2,450	2,500	2,400
Salary of part-time accounts receivable clerk	4,100	4,100	4,100

Credit and collection expenses as a percentage of net credit sales are: uncollectible accounts 1.6%, billing and mailing costs 0.5%, and credit investigation fee on new customers 0.15%.

Molly and Joe also determine that the average accounts receivable balance outstanding during the year is 5% of net credit sales. The Maynes estimate that they could earn an average of 8% annually on cash invested in other business opportunities.

Instructions

With the class divided into groups, answer the following.

(a) Prepare a table showing, for each year, total credit and collection expenses in dollars and as a percentage of net credit sales.

(b) Determine the net credit and collection expense in dollars and as a percentage of sales after considering the revenue not earned from other investment opportunities.

(c) Discuss both the financial and nonfinancial factors that are relevant to the decision.

Communication Activity

BYP9-5   Rene Mai, a friend of yours, overheard a discussion at work about changes her employer wants to make in accounting for uncollectible accounts. Rene knows little about accounting, and she asks you to help make sense of what she heard. Specifically, she asks you to explain the differences between the percentage-of-sales, percentage-of-receivables, and the direct write-off methods for uncollectible accounts.

Instructions
In a letter of one page (or less), explain to Rene the three methods of accounting for uncollectibles. Be sure to discuss differences among these methods.

Ethics Case

BYP9-6   The controller of Ruiz Co. believes that the yearly allowance for doubtful accounts for Ruiz Co. should be 2% of net credit sales. The president of Ruiz Co., nervous that the stockholders might expect the company to sustain its 10% growth rate, suggests that the controller increase the allowance for doubtful accounts to 4%. The president thinks that the lower net income, which reflects a 6% growth rate, will be a more sustainable rate for Ruiz Co.

Instructions
(a) Who are the stakeholders in this case?
(b) Does the president's request pose an ethical dilemma for the controller?
(c) Should the controller be concerned with Ruiz Co.'s growth rate? Explain your answer.

"All About You" Activity

BYP9-7   As the **All About You** feature in this chapter (page 416) indicates, credit card usage in the United States is substantial. Many startup companies use credit cards as a way to help meet short-term financial needs. The most common forms of debt for startups are use of credit cards and loans from relatives.

Suppose that you start up Brothers Sandwich Shop. You invested your savings of $20,000 and borrowed $70,000 from your relatives. Although sales in the first few months are good, you see that you may not have sufficient cash to pay expenses and maintain your inventory at acceptable levels, at least in the short term. You decide you may need to use one or more credit cards to fund the possible cash shortfall.

Instructions
(a) Go to the Web and find two sources that provide insight into how to compare credit card terms.
(b) Develop a list, in descending order of importance, as to what features are most important to you in selecting a credit card for your business.
(c) Examine the features of your present credit card. (If you do not have a credit card, select a likely one online for this exercise.) Given your analysis above, what are the three major disadvantages of your present credit card?

Answers to Insight and Accounting Across the Organization Questions

p. 406 When Investors Ignore Warning Signs
Q: When would it be appropriate for a company to lower its allowance for doubtful accounts as a percentage of its receivables?
A: *It could do so if the company's collection experience had improved, or was expected to improve, and therefore the company expected lower defaults as a percentage of receivables.*

p. 408 How Does a Credit Card Work?
Q: Assume that Nordstrom prepares a bank reconciliation at the end of each month. If some credit card sales have not been processed by the bank, how should Nordstrom treat these transactions on its bank reconciliation?
A: *Nordstrom would treat the credit card receipts as deposits in transit. It has already recorded the receipts as cash. Its bank will increase Nordstrom's cash account when it receives the receipts.*

Authors' Comments on *All About You*: Should You Be Carrying Plastic? (p. 416)

We aren't going to tell you to cut up your credit card(s). Well, we aren't going to tell *all* of you to do so. Credit cards, when used properly, can serve a very useful purpose. They provide great convenience, are widely accepted, and can be a source of security in an emergency. But too many

Americans use credit cards inappropriately. When businesses purchase short-term items such as inventory and supplies, they use short-term credit, which they expect to pay back very quickly. The same should be true of your credit card. When you make purchases of everyday items, you should completely pay off those items within a month or two. If you don't, you are living beyond your means, and you will soon dig yourself a deep financial pit.

Longer-term items should not be purchased with credit cards, since the interest rate is too high. If you currently have a large balance on your credit card(s), we encourage you to cut up your card(s) until you have paid off your balance(s).

Answers to Self-Study Questions

1. d   **2.** c   **3.** a   **4.** b   **5.** d   **6.** b   **7.** b   **8.** d   **9.** c   **10.** c   **11.** a   **12.** b   **13.** d   **14.** a   **15.** c

Chapter 10

Plant Assets, Natural Resources, and Intangible Assets

STUDY OBJECTIVES

After studying this chapter, you should be able to:

1 Describe how the cost principle applies to plant assets.
2 Explain the concept of depreciation.
3 Compute periodic depreciation using different methods.
4 Describe the procedure for revising periodic depreciation.
5 Distinguish between revenue and capital expenditures, and explain the entries for each.
6 Explain how to account for the disposal of a plant asset.
7 Compute periodic depletion of natural resources.
8 Explain the basic issues related to accounting for intangible assets.
9 Indicate how plant assets, natural resources, and intangible assets are reported.

✓ *The Navigator*

✓ *The Navigator*

Scan **Study Objectives**

Read **Feature Story**

Read **Preview**

Read text and answer **DO IT!** p. 442
p. 449   p. 452   p. 457

Work **Comprehensive** **DO IT!** p. 461
p. 462

Review **Summary of Study Objectives**

Answer **Self-Study Questions**

Complete **Assignments**

Feature Story

HOW MUCH FOR A RIDE TO THE BEACH?

It's spring break. Your plane has landed, you've finally found your bags, and you're dying to hit the beach—but first you need a "vehicular unit" to get you there. As you turn away from baggage claim you see a long row of rental agency booths. Many are names you are familiar with—Hertz, Avis, and Budget. But a booth at the far end catches your eye—Rent-A-Wreck (*www.rent-a-wreck.com*). Now there's a company making a clear statement!

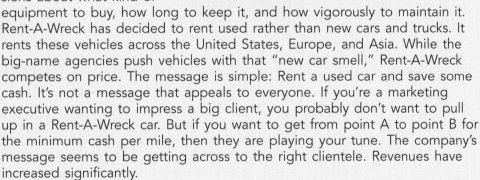

Any company that relies on equipment to generate revenues must make decisions about what kind of equipment to buy, how long to keep it, and how vigorously to maintain it. Rent-A-Wreck has decided to rent used rather than new cars and trucks. It rents these vehicles across the United States, Europe, and Asia. While the big-name agencies push vehicles with that "new car smell," Rent-A-Wreck competes on price. The message is simple: Rent a used car and save some cash. It's not a message that appeals to everyone. If you're a marketing executive wanting to impress a big client, you probably don't want to pull up in a Rent-A-Wreck car. But if you want to get from point A to point B for the minimum cash per mile, then they are playing your tune. The company's message seems to be getting across to the right clientele. Revenues have increased significantly.

When you rent a car from Rent-A-Wreck, you are renting from an independent business person who has paid a "franchise fee" for the right to use the Rent-A-Wreck name. In order to gain a franchise, he or she must meet financial and other criteria, and must agree to run the rental agency according to rules prescribed by Rent-A-Wreck. Some of these rules require that each franchise maintain its cars in a reasonable fashion. This ensures that, though you won't be cruising down Daytona Beach's Atlantic Avenue in a Mercedes convertible, you can be reasonably assured that you won't be calling a towtruck.

Inside Chapter 10...

The accounting for long-term assets has important implications for a company's reported results. In this chapter, we explain the application of the cost principle of accounting to property, plant, and equipment, such as Rent-A-Wreck vehicles, as well as to natural resources and intangible assets such as the "Rent-A-Wreck" trademark. We also describe the methods that companies may use to allocate an asset's cost over its useful life. In addition, we discuss the accounting for expenditures incurred during the useful life of assets, such as the cost of replacing tires and brake pads on rental cars.

The content and organization of Chapter 10 are as follows.

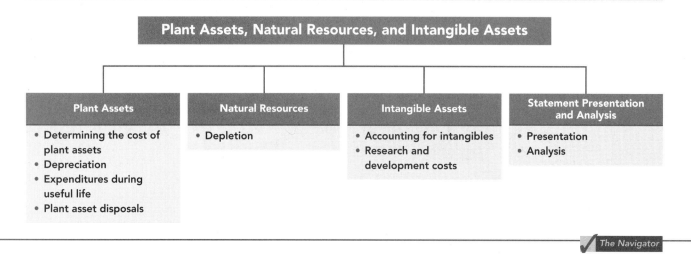

Plant Assets, Natural Resources, and Intangible Assets

Plant Assets	Natural Resources	Intangible Assets	Statement Presentation and Analysis
• Determining the cost of plant assets • Depreciation • Expenditures during useful life • Plant asset disposals	• Depletion	• Accounting for intangibles • Research and development costs	• Presentation • Analysis

✔ *The Navigator*

SECTION 1 Plant Assets

Plant assets are resources that have three characteristics: they have a physical substance (a definite size and shape), are used in the operations of a business, and are not intended for sale to customers. They are also called **property, plant, and equipment; plant and equipment;** and **fixed assets**. These assets are expected to provide services to the company for a number of years. Except for land, plant assets decline in service potential over their useful lives.

Because plant assets play a key role in ongoing operations, companies keep plant assets in good operating condition. They also replace worn-out or outdated plant assets, and expand productive resources as needed. Many companies have substantial investments in plant assets. Illustration 10-1 shows the

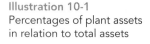

Illustration 10-1
Percentages of plant assets in relation to total assets

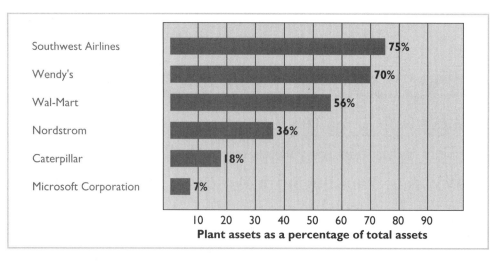

Southwest Airlines 75%
Wendy's 70%
Wal-Mart 56%
Nordstrom 36%
Caterpillar 18%
Microsoft Corporation 7%

10 20 30 40 50 60 70 80 90
Plant assets as a percentage of total assets

percentages of plant assets in relation to total assets of companies in a number of industries.

DETERMINING THE COST OF PLANT ASSETS

The cost principle requires that companies record plant assets at cost. Thus Rent-A-Wreck records its vehicles at cost. **Cost consists of all expenditures necessary to acquire the asset and make it ready for its intended use**. For example, the cost of factory machinery includes the purchase price, freight costs paid by the purchaser, and installation costs. Once cost is established, the company uses that amount as the basis of accounting for the plant asset over its useful life.

In the following sections, we explain the application of the cost principle to each of the major classes of plant assets.

Land

Companies acquire **land** for use as a site upon which to build a manufacturing plant or office. The cost of land includes (1) the cash purchase price, (2) closing costs such as title and attorney's fees, (3) real estate brokers' commissions, and (4) accrued property taxes and other liens assumed by the purchaser. For example, if the cash price is $50,000 and the purchaser agrees to pay accrued taxes of $5,000, the cost of the land is $55,000.

Companies record as debits (increases) to the Land account all necessary costs incurred to make land **ready for its intended use**. When a company acquires vacant land, these costs include expenditures for clearing, draining, filling, and grading. Sometimes the land has a building on it that must be removed before construction of a new building. In this case, the company debits to the Land account all demolition and removal costs, less any proceeds from salvaged materials.

To illustrate, assume that Hayes Manufacturing Company acquires real estate at a cash cost of $100,000. The property contains an old warehouse that is razed at a net cost of $6,000 ($7,500 in costs less $1,500 proceeds from salvaged materials). Additional expenditures are the attorney's fee, $1,000, and the real estate broker's commission, $8,000. The cost of the land is $115,000, computed as follows.

Land	
Cash price of property	$100,000
Net removal cost of warehouse	6,000
Attorney's fee	1,000
Real estate broker's commission	8,000
Cost of land	**$115,000**

Illustration 10-2
Computation of cost of land

When Hayes records the acquisition, it debits Land for $115,000 and credits Cash for $115,000.

Land Improvements

Land improvements are structural additions made to land. Examples are driveways, parking lots, fences, landscaping, and underground sprinklers. The cost of land improvements includes all expenditures necessary to make the improvements ready for their intended use. For example, the cost of a new parking lot for Home Depot includes the amount paid for paving, fencing, and lighting. Thus Home Depot debits to Land Improvements the total of all of these costs.

Land improvements have limited useful lives, and their maintenance and replacement are the responsibility of the company. Because of their limited useful life, companies expense (depreciate) the cost of land improvements over their useful lives.

Buildings

Buildings are facilities used in operations, such as stores, offices, factories, warehouses, and airplane hangars. Companies debit to the Buildings account all necessary expenditures related to the purchase or construction of a building. When a building is **purchased**, such costs include the purchase price, closing costs (attorney's fees, title insurance, etc.) and real estate broker's commission. Costs to make the building ready for its intended use include expenditures for remodeling and replacing or repairing the roof, floors, electrical wiring, and plumbing. When a new building is **constructed**, cost consists of the contract price plus payments for architects' fees, building permits, and excavation costs.

In addition, companies charge certain interest costs to the Buildings account: Interest costs incurred to finance the project are included in the cost of the building when a significant period of time is required to get the building ready for use. In these circumstances, interest costs are considered as necessary as materials and labor. However, the inclusion of interest costs in the cost of a constructed building is **limited to the construction period**. When construction has been completed, the company records subsequent interest payments on funds borrowed to finance the construction as debits (increases) to Interest Expense.

Equipment

Equipment includes assets used in operations, such as store check-out counters, office furniture, factory machinery, delivery trucks, and airplanes. The cost of equipment, such as Rent-A-Wreck vehicles, consists of the **cash purchase price, sales taxes, freight charges, and insurance during transit paid by the purchaser**. It also includes expenditures required in assembling, installing, and testing the unit. However, Rent-A-Wreck does not include motor vehicle licenses and accident insurance on company vehicles in the cost of equipment. These costs represent annual recurring expenditures and do not benefit future periods. Thus, they are treated as expenses as they are incurred.

To illustrate, assume Merten Company purchases factory machinery at a cash price of $50,000. Related expenditures are for sales taxes $3,000, insurance during shipping $500, and installation and testing $1,000. The cost of the factory machinery is $54,500, computed as follows.

Illustration 10-3
Computation of cost of factory machinery

Factory Machinery	
Cash price	$50,000
Sales taxes	3,000
Insurance during shipping	500
Installation and testing	1,000
Cost of factory machinery	**$54,500**

Merten makes the following summary entry to record the purchase and related expenditures:

Factory Machinery	54,500	
Cash		54,500
(To record purchase of factory machine)		

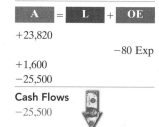

A = L + OE
+54,500
−54,500

Cash Flows
−54,500

For another example, assume that Lenard Company purchases a delivery truck at a cash price of $22,000. Related expenditures consist of sales taxes $1,320, painting and lettering $500, motor vehicle license $80, and a three-year accident insurance policy $1,600. The cost of the delivery truck is $23,820, computed as follows.

Delivery Truck

Cash price	$22,000
Sales taxes	1,320
Painting and lettering	500
Cost of delivery truck	**$23,820**

Illustration 10-4
Computation of cost of delivery truck

Lenard treats the cost of the motor vehicle license as an expense, and the cost of the insurance policy as a prepaid asset. Thus, Lenard makes the following entry to record the purchase of the truck and related expenditures:

Delivery Truck	23,820	
License Expense	80	
Prepaid Insurance	1,600	
Cash		25,500
(To record purchase of delivery truck and related expenditures)		

A = L + OE
+23,820
−80 Exp
+1,600
−25,500

Cash Flows
−25,500

ACCOUNTING ACROSS THE ORGANIZATION

Many U.S. Firms Use Leases

Leasing is big business for U.S. companies. For example, business investment in equipment in a recent year totaled $709 billion. Leasing accounted for about 31% of all business investment ($218 billion).

Who does the most leasing? Interestingly major banks, such as Continental Bank, J.P. Morgan Leasing, and US Bancorp Equipment Finance, are the major lessors. Also, many companies have established separate leasing companies, such as Boeing Capital Corporation, Dell Financial Services, and John Deere Capital Corporation. And, as an excellent example of the magnitude of leasing, leased planes account for nearly 40% of the U.S. fleet of commercial airlines. In addition, leasing is becoming increasingly common in the hotel industry. Marriott, Hilton, and InterContinental are increasingly choosing to lease hotels that are owned by someone else.

 Why might airline managers choose to lease rather than purchase their planes?

DO IT!

COST OF PLANT ASSETS

Assume that Drummond Heating and Cooling Co. purchases a delivery truck for $15,000 cash, plus sales taxes of $900 and delivery costs of $500. The buyer also pays $200 for painting and lettering, $600 for an annual insurance policy, and $80 for a motor vehicle license. Explain how each of these costs would be accounted for.

action plan

✔ Identify expenditures made in order to get delivery equipment ready for its intended use.

✔ Treat operating costs as expenses.

Solution

The first four payments ($15,000, $900, $500, and $200) are expenditures necessary to make the truck ready for its intended use. Thus, the cost of the truck is $16,600. The payments for insurance and the license are operating costs and therefore are expensed.

Related exercise material: **BE10-1, BE10-2, E10-1, E10-2, E10-3, and DO IT! 10-1.**

 The Navigator

DEPRECIATION

STUDY OBJECTIVE 2

Explain the concept of depreciation.

As explained in Chapter 3, depreciation **is the process of allocating to expense the cost of a plant asset over its useful (service) life in a rational and systematic manner**. Cost allocation enables companies to properly match expenses with revenues in accordance with the matching principle (see Illustration 10-5).

Illustration 10-5
Depreciation as a cost allocation concept

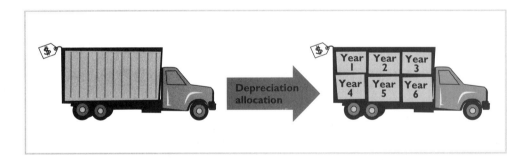

It is important to understand that **depreciation is a process of cost allocation. It is not a process of asset valuation**. No attempt is made to measure the change in an asset's market value during ownership. So, the **book value** (cost less accumulated depreciation) of a plant asset may be quite different from its market value.

Depreciation applies to three classes of plant assets: land improvements, buildings, and equipment. Each asset in these classes is considered to be a **depreciable asset**. Why? Because the usefulness to the company and revenue-producing ability of each asset will decline over the asset's useful life. Depreciation **does not apply to land** because its usefulness and revenue-producing ability generally remain intact over time. In fact, in many cases, the usefulness of land is greater over time because of the scarcity of good land sites. Thus, **land is not a depreciable asset**.

⚖ ETHICS NOTE

When a business is acquired, proper allocation of the purchase price to various asset classes is important, since different depreciation treatment can materially affect income. For example, buildings are depreciated, but land is not.

During a depreciable asset's useful life its revenue-producing ability declines because of **wear and tear**. A delivery truck that has been driven 100,000 miles will be less useful to a company than one driven only 800 miles.

Revenue-producing ability may also decline because of obsolescence. **Obsolescence** is the process of becoming out of date before the asset physically wears out. For example, major airlines moved from Chicago's Midway Airport to Chicago-O'Hare International Airport because Midway's runways were too short for jumbo jets. Similarly, many companies replace their computers long before they originally planned to do so because improvements in new computing technology make the old computers obsolete.

Recognizing depreciation on an asset does not result in an accumulation of cash for replacement of the asset. The balance in Accumulated Depreciation represents the total amount of the asset's cost that the company has charged to expense. It is not a cash fund.

Note that the concept of depreciation is consistent with the going-concern assumption. The **going-concern assumption** states that the company will continue in operation for the foreseeable future. If a company does not use a going-concern assumption, then plant assets should be stated at their market value. In that case, depreciation of these assets is not needed.

Factors in Computing Depreciation

Three factors affect the computation of depreciation:

1. **Cost.** Earlier, we explained the issues affecting the cost of a depreciable asset. Recall that companies record plant assets at cost, in accordance with the cost principle.

2. **Useful life.** Useful life is an estimate of the expected *productive life*, also called *service life*, of the asset. Useful life may be expressed in terms of time, units of activity (such as machine hours), or units of output. Useful life is an estimate. In making the estimate, management considers such factors as the intended use of the asset, its expected repair and maintenance, and its vulnerability to obsolescence. Past experience with similar assets is often helpful in deciding on expected useful life. We might reasonably expect Rent-A-Wreck and Avis to use different estimated useful lives for their vehicles.

3. **Salvage value.** Salvage value is an estimate of the asset's value at the end of its useful life. This value may be based on the asset's worth as scrap or on its expected trade-in value. Like useful life, salvage value is an estimate. In making the estimate, management considers how it plans to dispose of the asset and its experience with similar assets.

ALTERNATIVE TERMINOLOGY

Another term sometimes used for salvage value is *residual value*.

Illustration 10-6 summarizes the three factors used in computing depreciation.

Illustration 10-6
Three factors in computing depreciation

HELPFUL HINT

Depreciation expense is reported on the income statement. Accumulated depreciation is reported on the balance sheet as a deduction from plant assets.

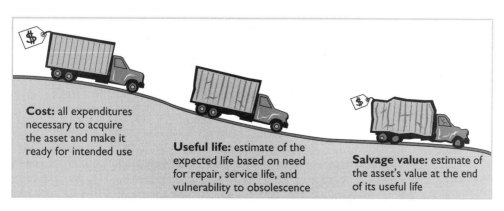

Cost: all expenditures necessary to acquire the asset and make it ready for intended use

Useful life: estimate of the expected life based on need for repair, service life, and vulnerability to obsolescence

Salvage value: estimate of the asset's value at the end of its useful life

Depreciation Methods

STUDY OBJECTIVE 3

Compute periodic depreciation using different methods.

Depreciation is generally computed using one of the following methods:

1. Straight-line
2. Units-of-activity
3. Declining-balance

Each method is acceptable under generally accepted accounting principles. Management selects the method(s) it believes to be appropriate. The objective is to select the method that best measures an asset's contribution to revenue over its useful life. Once a company chooses a method, it should apply it consistently over the useful life of the asset. Consistency enhances the comparability of financial statements. Depreciation affects the balance sheet through accumulated depreciation and the income statement through depreciation expense.

We will compare the three depreciation methods using the following data for a small delivery truck purchased by Barb's Florists on January 1, 2010.

Illustration 10-7
Delivery truck data

Cost	$13,000
Expected salvage value	$ 1,000
Estimated useful life in years	5
Estimated useful life in miles	100,000

Illustration 10-8 (in the margin) shows the use of the primary depreciation methods in 600 of the largest companies in the United States.

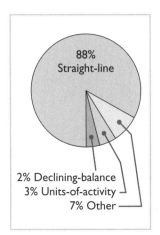

Illustration 10-8
Use of depreciation methods in 600 large U.S. companies

STRAIGHT-LINE

Under the **straight-line method**, companies expense the same amount of depreciation for each year of the asset's useful life. It is measured solely by the passage of time.

In order to compute depreciation expense under the straight-line method, companies need to determine depreciable cost. **Depreciable cost** is the cost of the asset less its salvage value. It represents the total amount subject to depreciation. Under the straight-line method, to determine annual depreciation expense, we divide depreciable cost by the asset's useful life. Illustration 10-9 shows the computation of the first year's depreciation expense for Barb's Florists.

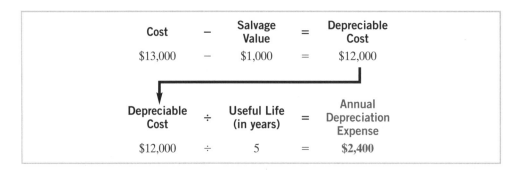

Illustration 10-9
Formula for straight-line method

Alternatively, we also can compute an annual **rate** of depreciation. In this case, the rate is 20% (100% ÷ 5 years). When a company uses an annual straight-line rate, it applies the percentage rate to the depreciable cost of the asset. Illustration 10-10 shows a **depreciation schedule** using an annual rate.

Illustration 10-10
Straight-line depreciation
schedule

	Computation		Annual Depreciation Expense	End of Year	
Year	Depreciable Cost	× Depreciation Rate =	Annual Depreciation Expense	Accumulated Depreciation	Book Value
2010	$12,000	20%	$2,400	$ 2,400	$10,600*
2011	12,000	20	2,400	4,800	8,200
2012	12,000	20	2,400	7,200	5,800
2013	12,000	20	2,400	9,600	3,400
2014	12,000	20	2,400	12,000	1,000

BARB'S FLORISTS

*Book Value = Cost − Accumulated depreciation = ($13,000 − $2,400).

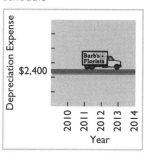

Note that the depreciation expense of $2,400 is the same each year. The book value (computed as cost minus accumulated depreciation) at the end of the useful life is equal to the expected $1,000 salvage value.

What happens to these computations for an asset purchased **during** the year, rather than on January 1? In that case, it is necessary to **prorate the annual depreciation** on a time basis. If Barb's Florists had purchased the delivery truck on April 1, 2010, the company would own the truck for nine months of the first year (April–December). Thus, depreciation for 2010 would be $1,800 ($12,000 × 20% × 9/12 of a year).

The straight-line method predominates in practice. Such large companies as Campbell Soup, Marriott, and General Mills use the straight-line method. It is simple to apply, and it matches expenses with revenues when the use of the asset is reasonably uniform throughout the service life. For simplicity, Rent-A-Wreck is probably using the straight-line method of depreciation for its vehicles.

UNITS-OF-ACTIVITY

Under the **units-of-activity method**, useful life is expressed in terms of the total units of production or use expected from the asset, rather than as a time period. The units-of-activity method is ideally suited to factory machinery. Manufacturing companies can measure production in units of output or in machine hours. This method can also be used for such assets as delivery equipment (miles driven) and airplanes (hours in use). The units-of-activity method is generally not suitable for buildings or furniture, because depreciation for these assets is more a function of time than of use.

To use this method, companies estimate the total units of activity for the entire useful life, and then divide these units into depreciable cost. The resulting number represents the depreciation cost per unit. The depreciation cost per unit is then applied to the units of activity during the year to determine the annual depreciation expense.

To illustrate, assume that Barb's Florists drives its delivery truck 15,000 miles in the first year. Illustration 10-11 shows the units-of-activity formula and the computation of the first year's depreciation expense.

Illustration 10-11
Formula for units-of-activity method

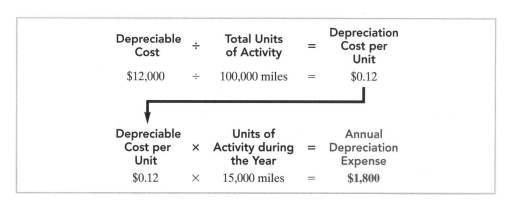

The units-of-activity depreciation schedule, using assumed mileage, is as follows.

Illustration 10-12
Units-of-activity depreciation
schedule

| | Computation | | | Annual | End of Year | |
| | Units of | | Depreciation | Depreciation | Accumulated | Book |
Year	Activity	×	Cost/Unit	= Expense	Depreciation	Value
2010	15,000		$0.12	**$1,800**	$ 1,800	$11,200*
2011	30,000		0.12	**3,600**	5,400	7,600
2012	20,000		0.12	**2,400**	7,800	5,200
2013	25,000		0.12	**3,000**	10,800	2,200
2014	10,000		0.12	**1,200**	12,000	**1,000**

BARB'S FLORISTS

*($13,000 − $1,800).

This method is easy to apply for assets purchased mid-year. In such a case, the company computes the depreciation using the productivity of the asset for the partial year.

The units-of-activity method is not nearly as popular as the straight-line method (see Illustration 10-8, page 444), primarily because it is often difficult for companies to reasonably estimate total activity. However, some very large companies, such as Chevron and Boise Cascade (a forestry company), do use this method. When the productivity of an asset varies significantly from one period to another, the units-of-activity method results in the best matching of expenses with revenues.

DECLINING-BALANCE

The **declining-balance method** produces a decreasing annual depreciation expense over the asset's useful life. The method is so named because the periodic depreciation is based on a **declining book value** (cost less accumulated depreciation) of the asset. With this method, companies compute annual depreciation expense by multiplying the book value at the beginning of the year by the declining-balance depreciation rate. **The depreciation rate remains constant from year to year, but the book value to which the rate is applied declines each year.**

At the beginning of the first year, book value is the cost of the asset. This is so because the balance in accumulated depreciation at the beginning of the asset's useful life is zero. In subsequent years, book value is the difference between cost and accumulated depreciation to date. Unlike the other depreciation methods, the declining-balance method does not use depreciable cost. That is, **it ignores salvage value in determining the amount to which the declining-balance rate is applied**. Salvage value, however, does limit the total depreciation that can be taken. Depreciation stops when the asset's book value equals expected salvage value.

A common declining-balance rate is double the straight-line rate. The method is often called the **double-declining-balance method**. If Barb's Florists uses the double-declining-balance method, it uses a depreciation rate of 40% (2 × the straight-line rate of 20%). Illustration 10-13 shows the declining-balance formula and the computation of the first year's depreciation on the delivery truck.

Illustration 10-13
Formula for declining-
balance method

Book Value at Beginning of Year	×	Declining-Balance Rate	=	Annual Depreciation Expense
$13,000	×	40%	=	**$5,200**

The depreciation schedule under this method is as follows.

BARB'S FLORISTS

	Computation				End of Year	
Year	Book Value Beginning of Year	× Depreciation Rate	=	Annual Depreciation Expense	Accumulated Depreciation	Book Value
2010	$13,000	40%		**$5,200**	$ 5,200	$7,800
2011	7,800	40		**3,120**	8,320	4,680
2012	4,680	40		**1,872**	10,192	2,808
2013	2,808	40		**1,123**	11,315	1,685
2014	1,685	40		685*	12,000	**1,000**

*Computation of $674 ($1,685 × 40%) is adjusted to $685 in order for book value to equal salvage value.

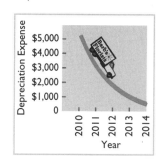

Illustration 10-14
Double-declining-balance depreciation schedule

The delivery equipment is 69% depreciated ($8,320 ÷ $12,000) at the end of the second year. Under the straight-line method, the truck would be depreciated 40% ($4,800 ÷ $12,000) at that time. Because the declining-balance method produces higher depreciation expense in the early years than in the later years, it is considered an **accelerated-depreciation method**. The declining-balance method is compatible with the matching principle. It matches the higher depreciation expense in early years with the higher benefits received in these years. It also recognizes lower depreciation expense in later years, when the asset's contribution to revenue is less. Some assets lose usefulness rapidly because of obsolescence. In these cases, the declining-balance method provides the most appropriate depreciation amount.

> **HELPFUL HINT**
>
> The method recommended for an asset that is expected to be significantly more productive in the first half of its useful life is the declining-balance method.

When a company purchases an asset during the year, it must prorate the first year's declining-balance depreciation on a time basis. For example, if Barb's Florists had purchased the truck on April 1, 2010, depreciation for 2010 would become $3,900 ($13,000 × 40% × 9/12). The book value at the beginning of 2011 is then $9,100 ($13,000 − $3,900), and the 2011 depreciation is $3,640 ($9,100 × 40%). Subsequent computations would follow from those amounts.

COMPARISON OF METHODS

Illustration 10-15 compares annual and total depreciation expense under each of the three methods for Barb's Florists.

Year	Straight-Line	Units-of-Activity	Declining-Balance
2010	$ 2,400	$ 1,800	$ 5,200
2011	2,400	3,600	3,120
2012	2,400	2,400	1,872
2013	2,400	3,000	1,123
2014	2,400	1,200	685
	$12,000	$12,000	$12,000

Illustration 10-15
Comparison of depreciation methods

Annual depreciation varies considerably among the methods, but **total depreciation is the same for the five-year period** under all three methods. Each method is acceptable in accounting, because each recognizes in a rational and systematic manner the decline in service potential of the asset. Illustration 10-16 (page 448) graphs the depreciation expense pattern under each method.

Illustration 10-16
Patterns of depreciation

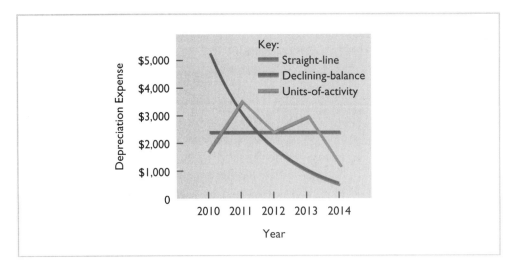

Depreciation and Income Taxes

The Internal Revenue Service (IRS) allows corporate taxpayers to deduct depreciation expense when they compute taxable income. However, the IRS does not require the taxpayer to use the same depreciation method on the tax return that is used in preparing financial statements.

Many corporations use straight-line in their financial statements to maximize net income. At the same time, they use a special accelerated-depreciation method on their tax returns to minimize their income taxes. Taxpayers must use on their tax returns either the straight-line method or a special accelerated-depreciation method called the **Modified Accelerated Cost Recovery System** (MACRS).

Revising Periodic Depreciation

STUDY OBJECTIVE 4

Describe the procedure for revising periodic depreciation.

Depreciation is one example of the use of estimation in the accounting process. Management should periodically review annual depreciation expense. If wear and tear or obsolescence indicate that annual depreciation estimates are inadequate or excessive, the company should change the amount of depreciation expense.

When a change in an estimate is required, the company makes the change in **current and future years**. **It does not change depreciation in prior periods.** The rationale is that continual restatement of prior periods would adversely affect confidence in financial statements.

HELPFUL HINT

Use a step-by-step approach: (1) determine new depreciable cost; (2) divide by remaining useful life.

To determine the new annual depreciation expense, the company first computes the asset's depreciable cost at the time of the revision. It then allocates the revised depreciable cost to the remaining useful life.

To illustrate, assume that Barb's Florists decides on January 1, 2013, to extend the useful life of the truck one year because of its excellent condition. The company has used the straight-line method to depreciate the asset to date, and book value is $5,800 ($13,000 − $7,200). The new annual depreciation is $1,600, computed as follows.

Illustration 10-17
Revised depreciation computation

Book value, 1/1/13	$5,800	
Less: Salvage value	1,000	
Depreciable cost	$4,800	
Remaining useful life	3 years	(2013–2015)
Revised annual depreciation ($4,800 ÷ 3)	**$1,600**	

Barb's Florists makes no entry for the change in estimate. On December 31, 2013, during the preparation of adjusting entries, it records depreciation expense of $1,600. Companies must describe in the financial statements significant changes in estimates.

DO IT!

On January 1, 2010, Iron Mountain Ski Corporation purchased a new snow-grooming machine for $50,000. The machine is estimated to have a 10-year life with a $2,000 salvage value. What journal entry would Iron Mountain Ski Corporation make at December 31, 2010, if it uses the straight-line method of depreciation?

STRAIGHT-LINE DEPRECIATION

action plan

✔ Calculate depreciable cost (Cost − Salvage value).

✔ Divide the depreciable cost by the estimated useful life.

Solution

$$\text{Depreciation expense} = \frac{\text{Cost} - \text{Salvage value}}{\text{Useful life}} = \frac{\$50,000 - \$2,000}{10} = \$4,800$$

The entry to record the first year's depreciation would be:

Dec. 31	Depreciation Expense	4,800	
	Accumulated Depreciation		4,800
	(To record annual depreciation on snow-grooming machine)		

Related exercise material: **BE10-3, BE10-4, BE10-5, BE10-6, BE10-7, E10-5, E10-6, E10-7, E10-8,** and **DO IT!** **10-2.**

 The Navigator

EXPENDITURES DURING USEFUL LIFE

During the useful life of a plant asset, a company may incur costs for ordinary repairs, additions, or improvements. **Ordinary repairs** are expenditures to **maintain** the operating efficiency and productive life of the unit. They usually are fairly small amounts that occur frequently. Examples are motor tune-ups and oil changes, the painting of buildings, and the replacing of worn-out gears on machinery. Companies record such repairs as debits to Repair (or Maintenance) Expense as they are incurred. Because they are immediately charged as an expense against revenues, these costs are often referred to as **revenue expenditures**.

Additions and improvements are costs incurred to **increase** the operating efficiency, productive capacity, or useful life of a plant asset. They are usually material in amount and occur infrequently. Additions and improvements increase the company's investment in productive facilities. Companies generally debit these amounts to the plant asset affected. They are often referred to as **capital expenditures**. Most major U.S. corporations disclose annual capital expenditures.

Companies must use good judgment in deciding between a revenue expenditure and capital expenditure. For example, assume that Rodriguez Co. purchases a number of wastepaper baskets. Although the proper accounting would appear to be to capitalize and then depreciate these wastepaper baskets over their useful life, it would be more usual for Rodriguez to expense them immediately. This practice is justified on the basis of **materiality**. Materiality refers to the impact of an item's size on a company's financial

STUDY OBJECTIVE 5

Distinguish between revenue and capital expenditures, and explain the entries for each.

ETHICS NOTE

WorldCom perpetrated the largest accounting fraud in history by treating $7 billion of "line costs" as capital expenditures. *Line costs* are rental payments to access other companies' networks. Like any other rental payment, they should have been expensed as incurred. Instead, capitalization delayed expense recognition to future periods and thus boosted current-period profits.

operations. The **materiality principle** states that if an item would not make a difference in decision making, the company does not have to follow GAAP in reporting that item.

PLANT ASSET DISPOSALS

STUDY OBJECTIVE 6

Explain how to account for the disposal of a plant asset.

Companies dispose of plant assets in three ways—retirement, sale, or exchange—as Illustration 10-18 shows. Whatever the method, at the time of disposal the company must determine the book value of the plant asset. As noted earlier, book value is the difference between the cost of a plant asset and the accumulated depreciation to date.

Retirement
Equipment is scrapped or discarded.

Sale
Equipment is sold to another party.

Exchange
Existing equipment is traded for new equipment.

Illustration 10-18
Methods of plant asset disposal

At the time of disposal, the company records depreciation for the fraction of the year to the date of disposal. The book value is then eliminated by (1) debiting (decreasing) Accumulated Depreciation for the total depreciation to date, and (2) crediting (decreasing) the asset account for the cost of the asset. In this chapter we examine the accounting for the retirement and sale of plant assets. In the appendix to the chapter we discuss and illustrate the accounting for exchanges of plant assets.

Retirement of Plant Assets

To illustrate the retirement of plant assets, assume that Hobart Enterprises retires its computer printers, which cost $32,000. The accumulated depreciation on these printers is $32,000. The equipment, therefore, is fully depreciated (zero book value). The entry to record this retirement is as follows.

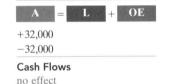

+32,000
−32,000

Cash Flows
no effect

Accumulated Depreciation—Printing Equipment	32,000	
Printing Equipment		32,000
(To record retirement of fully depreciated equipment)		

HELPFUL HINT

When a company disposes of a plant asset, the company must remove from the accounts all amounts related to the asset. This includes the original cost in the asset account and the total depreciation to date in the accumulated depreciation account.

What happens if a fully depreciated plant asset is still useful to the company? In this case, the asset and its accumulated depreciation continue to be reported on the balance sheet, without further depreciation adjustment, until the company retires the asset. Reporting the asset and related accumulated depreciation on the balance sheet informs the financial statement reader that the asset is still in use. Once fully depreciated, no additional depreciation should be taken, even if an asset is still being used. In no situation can the accumulated depreciation on a plant asset exceed its cost.

If a company retires a plant asset before it is fully depreciated, and no cash is received for scrap or salvage value, a loss on disposal occurs. For example, assume that Sunset Company discards delivery equipment that cost $18,000 and has accumulated depreciation of $14,000. The entry is as follows.

Accumulated Depreciation—Delivery Equipment	14,000		
Loss on Disposal	4,000		
Delivery Equipment		18,000	
(To record retirement of delivery equipment at a loss)			

A	=	L	+	OE
+14,000				
				−4,000 Exp
−18,000				

Cash Flows
no effect

Companies report a loss on disposal in the "Other expenses and losses" section of the income statement.

Sale of Plant Assets

In a disposal by sale, the company compares the book value of the asset with the proceeds received from the sale. If the proceeds of the sale **exceed** the book value of the plant asset, **a gain on disposal occurs**. If the proceeds of the sale **are less than** the book value of the plant asset sold, **a loss on disposal occurs**.

Only by coincidence will the book value and the fair market value of the asset be the same when the asset is sold. Gains and losses on sales of plant assets are therefore quite common. For example, Delta Airlines reported a $94,343,000 gain on the sale of five Boeing B727-200 aircraft and five Lockheed L-1011-1 aircraft.

GAIN ON DISPOSAL

To illustrate a gain, assume that on July 1, 2010, Wright Company sells office furniture for $16,000 cash. The office furniture originally cost $60,000. As of January 1, 2010, it had accumulated depreciation of $41,000. Depreciation for the first six months of 2010 is $8,000. Wright records depreciation expense and updates accumulated depreciation to July 1 with the following entry.

July 1	Depreciation Expense	8,000		
	Accumulated Depreciation—Office Furniture		8,000	
	(To record depreciation expense for the first			
	6 months of 2010)			

A	=	L	+	OE
				−8,000 Exp
−8,000				

Cash Flows
no effect

After the accumulated depreciation balance is updated, the company computes the gain or loss. Illustration 10-19 shows this computation for Wright Company, which has a gain on disposal of $5,000.

Cost of office furniture	$60,000
Less: Accumulated depreciation ($41,000 + $8,000)	49,000
Book value at date of disposal	11,000
Proceeds from sale	16,000
Gain on disposal	**$ 5,000**

Illustration 10-19
Computation of gain on disposal

Wright records the sale and the gain on disposal as follows.

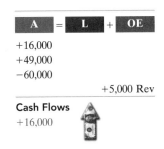

A	=	L	+	OE
+16,000				
+49,000				
−60,000				
				+5,000 Rev

Cash Flows
+16,000

July 1	Cash	16,000	
	Accumulated Depreciation—Office Furniture	49,000	
	Office Furniture		60,000
	Gain on Disposal		5,000
	(To record sale of office furniture at a gain)		

Companies report a gain on disposal in the "Other revenues and gains" section of the income statement.

LOSS ON DISPOSAL

Assume that instead of selling the office furniture for $16,000, Wright sells it for $9,000. In this case, Wright computes a loss of $2,000 as follows.

Illustration 10-20
Computation of loss on disposal

Cost of office furniture	$60,000
Less: Accumulated depreciation	49,000
Book value at date of disposal	11,000
Proceeds from sale	9,000
Loss on disposal	**$ 2,000**

Wright records the sale and the loss on disposal as follows.

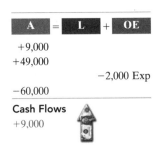

A	=	L	+	OE
+9,000				
+49,000				
				−2,000 Exp
−60,000				

Cash Flows
+9,000

July 1	Cash	9,000	
	Accumulated Depreciation—Office Furniture	49,000	
	Loss on Disposal	2,000	
	Office Furniture		60,000
	(To record sale of office furniture at a loss)		

Companies report a loss on disposal in the "Other expenses and losses" section of the income statement.

DO IT!

PLANT ASSET DISPOSAL

Overland Trucking has an old truck that cost $30,000, and it has accumulated depreciation of $16,000 on this truck. Overland has decided to sell the truck. (a) What entry would Overland Trucking make to record the sale of the truck for $17,000 cash? (b) What entry would Overland trucking make to record the sale of the truck for $10,000 cash?

action plan

✔ At the time of disposal, determine the book value of the asset.

✔ Compare the asset's book value with the proceeds received to determine whether a gain or loss has occurred.

Solution

(a) Sale of truck for cash at a gain:

	Cash	17,000	
	Accumulated Depreciation—Truck	16,000	
	Truck		30,000
	Gain on Disposal [$17,000 − ($30,000 − $16,000)]		3,000
	(To record sale of truck at a gain)		

(b) Sale of truck for cash at a loss:

Cash	10,000	
Loss on Disposal [$10,000 − ($30,000 − $16,000)]	4,000	
Accumulated Depreciation—Truck	16,000	
Truck		30,000
(To record sale of truck at a loss)		

Related exercise material: **BE10-9, BE10-10, E10-9, E10-10,** and **DO IT!** **10-3.**

SECTION 2 Natural Resources

Natural resources consist of standing timber and underground deposits of oil, gas, and minerals. These long-lived productive assets have two distinguishing characteristics: (1) They are physically extracted in operations (such as mining, cutting, or pumping). (2) They are replaceable only by an act of nature.

The acquisition cost of a natural resource is the price needed to acquire the resource **and** prepare it for its intended use. For an already-discovered resource, such as an existing coal mine, cost is the price paid for the property.

The allocation of the cost of natural resources to expense in a rational and systematic manner over the resource's useful life is called **depletion**. (That is, *depletion* is to natural resources as *depreciation* is to plant assets.) **Companies generally use the units-of-activity method** (learned earlier in the chapter) **to compute depletion.** The reason is that **depletion generally is a function of the units extracted during the year**.

Under the units-of-activity method, companies divide the total cost of the natural resource minus salvage value by the number of units estimated to be in the resource. The result is a **depletion cost per unit of product.** They then multiply the depletion cost per unit by the number of units extracted and sold. The result is the **annual depletion expense.** Illustration 10-21 shows the formula to compute depletion expense.

> **HELPFUL HINT**
>
> On a balance sheet, natural resources may be described more specifically as *timberlands*, *mineral deposits*, *oil reserves*, and so on.

> **STUDY OBJECTIVE 7**
>
> Compute periodic depletion of natural resources.

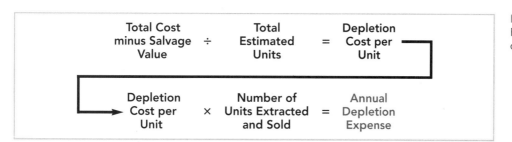

Illustration 10-21
Formula to compute depletion expense

To illustrate, assume that Lane Coal Company invests $5 million in a mine estimated to have 10 million tons of coal and no salvage value. In the first year, Lane extracts and sells 800,000 tons of coal. Using the formulas above, Lane computes the depletion expense as follows:

$$\$5,000,000 \div 10,000,000 = \$0.50 \text{ depletion cost per ton}$$

$$\$0.50 \times 800,000 = \$400,000 \text{ annual depletion expense}$$

> **ETHICS NOTE**
>
> Investors were stunned at news that Royal Dutch/Shell Group had significantly overstated its reported oil reserves—and perhaps had done so intentionally.

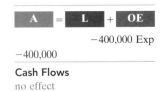

Cash Flows
no effect

Lane records depletion expense for the first year of operation as follows.

Dec. 31	Depletion Expense	400,000	
	Accumulated Depletion		400,000
	(To record depletion expense on coal deposits)		

The company reports the account Depletion Expense as a part of the cost of producing the product. Accumulated Depletion is a contra-asset account, similar to accumulated depreciation. It is deducted from the cost of the natural resource in the balance sheet, as Illustration 10-22 shows.

Illustration 10-22
Statement presentation of accumulated depletion

LANE COAL COMPANY
Balance Sheet (partial)

Coal mine	$5,000,000	
Less: Accumulated depletion	400,000	$4,600,000

Many companies do not use an Accumulated Depletion account. In such cases, the company credits the amount of depletion directly to the natural resources account.

Sometimes, a company will extract natural resources in one accounting period but not sell them until a later period. In this case, the company does not expense the depletion until it sells the resource. It reports the amount not sold as inventory in the current assets section.

SECTION 3 Intangible Assets

Intangible assets are rights, privileges, and competitive advantages that result from the ownership of long-lived assets that do not possess physical substance. Evidence of intangibles may exist in the form of contracts or licenses. Intangibles may arise from the following sources:

1. Government grants, such as patents, copyrights, and trademarks.
2. Acquisition of another business, in which the purchase price includes a payment for the company's favorable attributes (called *goodwill*).
3. Private monopolistic arrangements arising from contractual agreements, such as franchises and leases.

Some widely known intangibles are Microsoft's patents, McDonald's franchises, Apple's trade name iPod, J.K. Rowlings' copyrights on the Harry Potter books, and the trademark Rent-A-Wreck in the Feature Story.

ACCOUNTING FOR INTANGIBLE ASSETS

STUDY OBJECTIVE 8

Explain the basic issues related to accounting for intangible assets.

Companies record intangible assets at cost. Intangibles are categorized as having either a limited life or an indefinite life. If an intangible has a **limited life**, the company allocates its cost over the asset's useful life using a process similar to depreciation. The process of allocating the cost of intangibles is referred to as **amortization**. The cost of intangible assets with **indefinite lives should not be amortized**.

To record amortization of an intangible asset, a company increases (debits) Amortization Expense, and decreases (credits) the specific intangible asset. (Unlike depreciation, no contra account, such as Accumulated Amortization, is usually used.)

Intangible assets are typically amortized on a straight-line basis. For example, the legal life of a patent is 20 years. Companies **amortize the cost of a patent over its 20-year life or its useful life, whichever is shorter**. To illustrate the computation of patent amortization, assume that National Labs purchases a patent at a cost of $60,000. If National estimates the useful life of the patent to be eight years, the annual amortization expense is $7,500 ($60,000 ÷ 8). National records the annual amortization as follows.

Dec. 31	Amortization Expense—Patent	7,500	
	Patent		7,500
	(To record patent amortization)		

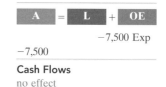

A = L + OE
−7,500 Exp
−7,500

Cash Flows
no effect

Companies classify Amortization Expense—Patents as an operating expense in the income statement.

There is a difference between intangible assets and plant assets in determining cost. For plant assets, cost includes both the purchase price of the asset and the costs incurred in designing and constructing the asset. In contrast, cost for an intangible asset includes **only the purchase price**. Companies expense any costs incurred in developing an intangible asset.

Patents

A **patent** is an exclusive right issued by the U.S. Patent Office that enables the recipient to manufacture, sell, or otherwise control an invention for a period of 20 years from the date of the grant. A patent is nonrenewable. But companies can extend the legal life of a patent by obtaining new patents for improvements or other changes in the basic design. **The initial cost of a patent is the cash or cash equivalent price paid to acquire the patent.**

The saying, "A patent is only as good as the money you're prepared to spend defending it" is very true. Many patents are subject to litigation. Any legal costs an owner incurs in successfully defending a patent in an infringement suit are considered necessary to establish the patent's validity. **The owner adds those costs to the Patent account and amortizes them over the remaining life of the patent.**

The patent holder amortizes the cost of a patent over its 20-year legal life or its useful life, whichever is shorter. Companies consider obsolescence and inadequacy in determining useful life. These factors may cause a patent to become economically ineffective before the end of its legal life.

Copyrights

The federal government grants **copyrights** which give the owner the exclusive right to reproduce and sell an artistic or published work. Copyrights extend for the life of the creator plus 70 years. The cost of a copyright is the **cost of acquiring and defending it**. The cost may be only the $10 fee paid to the U.S. Copyright Office. Or it may amount to much more if an infringement suit is involved.

The useful life of a copyright generally is significantly shorter than its legal life. Therefore, copyrights usually are amortized over a relatively short period of time.

Trademarks and Trade Names

A **trademark** or **trade name** is a word, phrase, jingle, or symbol that identifies a particular enterprise or product. Trade names like Wheaties, Game Boy, Frappuccino, Kleenex, Windows, Coca-Cola, and Jeep create immediate product identification.

They also generally enhance the sale of the product. The creator or original user may obtain exclusive legal right to the trademark or trade name by registering it with the U.S. Patent Office. Such registration provides 20 years of protection. The registration may be renewed indefinitely as long as the trademark or trade name is in use.

If a company purchases the trademark or trade name, its cost is the purchase price. If a company develops and maintains the trademark or trade name, any costs related to these activities are expensed as incurred. Because trademarks and trade names have indefinite lives, they are not amortized.

Franchises and Licenses

When you fill up your tank at the corner Shell station, eat lunch at Taco Bell, or rent a car from Rent-A-Wreck, you are dealing with franchises. A **franchise** is a contractual arrangement between a franchisor and a franchisee. The franchisor grants the franchisee the right to sell certain products, provide specific services, or use certain trademarks or trade names, usually within a designated geographical area.

Another type of franchise is that entered into between a governmental body (commonly municipalities) and a company. This franchise permits the company to use public property in performing its services. Examples are the use of city streets for a bus line or taxi service, use of public land for telephone and electric lines, and the use of airwaves for radio or TV broadcasting. Such operating rights are referred to as **licenses**. **When a company can identify costs with the purchase of a franchise or license, it should recognize an intangible asset.** Companies should amortize the cost of a limited-life franchise (or license) over its useful life. If the life is indefinite, the cost is not amortized. Annual payments made under a franchise agreement are recorded as **operating expenses** in the period in which they are incurred.

ACCOUNTING ACROSS THE ORGANIZATION

ESPN Wins Monday Night Football Franchise

What is a well-known franchise worth? Recently ESPN outbid its rivals for the right to broadcast Monday Night Football. At a price of $1.1 billion per year—nearly twice what rival ABC paid in previous years—it isn't clear who won and who lost.

When bidding for a unique franchise like Monday Night Football, management must consider many factors to determine a price. As part of the deal, ESPN also got wireless rights and Spanish-language telecasts. By its estimation, ESPN will generate a profit of $200 million per year from Monday Night Football. ABC was losing $150 million per year.

Another factor in the decision was ESPN management's concern that if ESPN didn't win the bid, a buyer would emerge that would use Monday Night Football as a launching pad for a new sports network. ESPN doesn't want any more competitors than it already has. It is hard to put a price tag on the value of keeping the competition to a minimum.

Source: Ronald Grover and Tom Lowry, "A Ball ESPN Couldn't Afford to Drop," *BusinessWeek*, May 2, 2005, p. 42.

 How should ESPN account for the $1.1 billion per year franchise fee?

Goodwill

Usually, the largest intangible asset that appears on a company's balance sheet is goodwill. **Goodwill** represents the value of all favorable attributes that relate to a company. These include exceptional management, desirable location, good customer relations, skilled employees, high-quality products, and harmonious relations with labor unions. Goodwill is unique: Unlike assets such as investments and plant assets, which can be sold *individually* in the marketplace, goodwill can be identified only with the business as a whole.

If goodwill can be identified only with the business as a whole, how can its amount be determined? One could try to put a dollar value on the factors listed above (exceptional management, desirable location, and so on). But the results would be very subjective, and such subjective valuations would not contribute to the reliability of financial statements. **Therefore, companies record goodwill only when an entire business is purchased. In that case, goodwill is the excess of cost over the fair market value of the net assets (assets less liabilities) acquired.**

In recording the purchase of a business, the company debits (increases) the net assets at their fair market values, credits (decreases) cash for the purchase price, and debits goodwill for the difference. **Goodwill is not amortized** (because it is considered to have an indefinite life). Companies report goodwill in the balance sheet under intangible assets.

RESEARCH AND DEVELOPMENT COSTS

Research and development costs are expenditures that may lead to patents, copyrights, new processes, and new products. Many companies spend considerable sums of money on research and development (R&D). For example, in a recent year IBM spent over $6.15 billion on R&D.

Research and development costs present accounting problems. For one thing, it is sometimes difficult to assign the costs to specific projects. Also, there are uncertainties in identifying the extent and timing of future benefits. As a result, companies usually record R&D costs **as an expense when incurred**, whether the research and development is successful or not.

To illustrate, assume that Laser Scanner Company spent $3 million on R&D. This expenditure resulted in two highly successful patents, obtained with $20,000 in lawyers' fees. The company would add the lawyers' fees to the patent account. The R&D costs, however, cannot be included in the cost of the patent. Instead, the company would record the R&D costs as an expense when incurred.

Many disagree with this accounting approach. They argue that expensing R&D costs leads to understated assets and net income. Others, however, argue that capitalizing these costs will lead to highly speculative assets on the balance sheet. It is difficult to determine who is right. The controversy illustrates how difficult it can be to establish proper guidelines for financial reporting.

> **HELPFUL HINT**
> Research and development (R&D) costs are not intangible assets. But because they may lead to patents and copyrights, we discuss them in this section.

DO IT!

Match the statement with the term most directly associated with it.

CLASSIFICATION CONCEPTS

Copyright	Depletion
Intangible asset	Franchise
Research and development costs	

1. _____ The allocation of the cost of a natural resource to expense in a rational and systematic manner.

2. _____ Rights, privileges, and competitive advantages that result from the ownership of long-lived assets that do not possess physical substance.

3. _____ An exclusive right granted by the federal government to reproduce and sell an artistic or published work.

action plan

✔ Know that the accounting for intangibles often depends on whether the item has a finite or indefinite life.

✔ Recognize the many similarities and differences between the accounting for natural resources, plant assets, and intangible assets.

4. _____ A right to sell certain products or services or to use certain trademarks or trade names within a designated geographic area.

5. _____ Costs incurred by a company that often lead to patents or new products. These costs must be expensed as incurred.

Solution

1. Depletion
2. Intangible assets
3. Copyright
4. Franchise
5. Research and development

Related exercise material: **BE10-11, BE10-12, E10-11, E10-12, E10-13,** and **DO IT!** **10-4.**

 The Navigator

STATEMENT PRESENTATION AND ANALYSIS

Presentation

STUDY OBJECTIVE 9

Indicate how plant assets, natural resources, and intangible assets are reported.

Usually companies combine plant assets and natural resources under "Property, plant, and equipment" in the balance sheet. They show intangibles separately. Companies disclose either in the balance sheet or the notes the balances of the major classes of assets, such as land, buildings, and equipment, and accumulated depreciation by major classes or in total. In addition, they should describe the depreciation and amortization methods that were used, as well as disclose the amount of depreciation and amortization expense for the period.

Illustration 10-23 shows the financial statement presentation of property, plant, and equipment and intangibles by The Procter & Gamble Company (P&G) in its 2007 balance sheet. The notes to P&G's financial statements present greater details about the accounting for its long-term tangible and intangible assets.

Illustration 10-23
P&G's presentation of property, plant, and equipment, and intangible assets

P&G

THE PROCTER & GAMBLE COMPANY
Balance Sheet (partial)
(in millions)

	June 30	
	2007	**2006**
Property, plant, and equipment		
Buildings	$ 6,380	$ 5,871
Machinery and equipment	27,492	25,140
Land	849	870
	34,721	31,881
Accumulated depreciation	(15,181)	(13,111)
Net property, plant, and equipment	19,540	18,770
Goodwill and other intangible assets		
Goodwill	56,552	55,306
Trademarks and other intangible assets, net	33,626	33,721
Net goodwill and other intangible assets	$90,178	$89,027

Illustration 10-24 shows another comprehensive presentation of property, plant, and equipment, from the balance sheet of Owens-Illinois. The notes to the financial statements of Owens-Illinois identify the major classes of property, plant, and equipment. They also indicate that depreciation and amortization are by the straight-line method, and depletion is by the units-of-activity method.

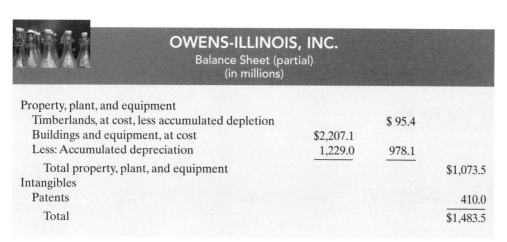

OWENS-ILLINOIS, INC. Balance Sheet (partial) (in millions)			
Property, plant, and equipment			
Timberlands, at cost, less accumulated depletion		$ 95.4	
Buildings and equipment, at cost	$2,207.1		
Less: Accumulated depreciation	1,229.0	978.1	
Total property, plant, and equipment			$1,073.5
Intangibles			
Patents			410.0
Total			$1,483.5

Illustration 10-24
Owens-Illinois' presentation of property, plant, and equipment, and intangible assets

Analysis

Using ratios, we can analyze how efficiently a company uses its assets to generate sales. The **asset turnover ratio** analyzes the productivity of a company's assets. It tells us how many dollars of sales a company generates for each dollar invested in assets. This ratio is computed by dividing net sales by average total assets for the period. The formula in Illustration 10-25 shows the computation of the asset turnover ratio for The Procter & Gamble Company. P&G's net sales for 2007 were $76,476 million. Its total ending assets were $138,014 million, and beginning assets were $135,695 million.

Net Sales	÷	Average Total Assets	=	Asset Turnover Ratio
$76,476	÷	$\dfrac{\$138,014 + \$135,695}{2}$	=	.56 times

Illustration 10-25
Asset turnover formula and computation

Thus, each dollar invested in assets produced $0.56 in sales for P&G. If a company is using its assets efficiently, each dollar of assets will create a high amount of sales. This ratio varies greatly among different industries—from those that are asset intensive (utilities) to those that are not (services).

Be sure to read **ALL ABOUT YOU: *Buying a Wreck of Your Own*** on page 460 for information on how topics in this chapter apply to your personal life.

Buying a Wreck of Your Own

The opening story to this chapter discusses car rental company Rent-A-Wreck. Recall that Rent-A-Wreck determined it can maximize its profitability by buying and renting used, rather than new, cars. What about *you*? Could you maximize your economic well-being by buying a used car rather than a new one?

❂ Some Facts

* In a recent year, nearly 17 million new cars were sold in the U.S., compared to sales of 44 million used cars.

* The cost of an average new car has risen in recent years, to about $22,000. The price of the average used car has actually been falling, and is now about $8,100.

* Financial institutions typically require a down payment of at least 10% of the value of a vehicle on a vehicle loan. Thus, the average new car will require a much higher down payment. However, interest rates on used-car loans are higher than on new-car loans.

* A new car typically loses at least 30% of its value during the first two years, and about 40 to 50% after three years. Some brands maintain their value better than others.

* The price of new cars has increased faster than average annual incomes in recent years.

* To keep monthly car payments down, car companies will now provide financing for up to six years. (It used to be two or three years.) With such a long loan, you might end up "upside down on the loan"—that is, you might actually owe more money than the car is worth if you decide to sell the car before the end of the loan.

❂ About the Numbers

There are many costs to consider in deciding whether to buy a new or used car. These costs include the down payment, monthly loan payments, insurance, maintenance and repair costs, and state (department of motor vehicle) fees. The graph below compares the total costs over five years for the typical new versus used car.

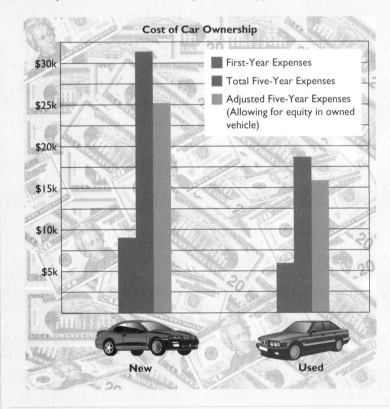

Cost of Car Ownership

Legend:
- First-Year Expenses
- Total Five-Year Expenses
- Adjusted Five-Year Expenses (Allowing for equity in owned vehicle)

New / Used

Source for graph: Phillip Reed, "Compare the Costs: Buying vs. Leasing vs. Buying a Used Car," *www.edmunds.com/advice/buying/articles/47079/article.html* (accessed May 2006).

❂ What Do You Think?

Should you buy a new car?

YES: I have enough stress in my life. I don't want to worry about my car breaking down—and if it does break down, I want it to be covered by a warranty. Besides, I have an image to maintain—I don't want to be seen in anything less than the latest styling and the latest technology.

NO: I'm a college student, and I need to keep my costs down. Also, used cars are a lot more dependable than they used to be. In addition, my self-image is strong enough that I don't need a fancy new car to feel good about myself (despite what the car advertisements say).

Source: Michelle Krebs, "Should You Buy New or Used?" *www.cars.com/go/advice*, May 3, 2005.

Comprehensive **DO IT!** *1*

DuPage Company purchases a factory machine at a cost of $18,000 on January 1, 2010. DuPage expects the machine to have a salvage value of $2,000 at the end of its 4-year useful life.

During its useful life, the machine is expected to be used 160,000 hours. Actual annual hourly use was: 2010, 40,000; 2011, 60,000; 2012, 35,000; and 2013, 25,000.

Instructions

Prepare depreciation schedules for the following methods: (a) straight-line, (b) units-of-activity, and (c) declining-balance using double the straight-line rate.

action plan

✔ Under the straight-line method, apply the depreciation rate to depreciable cost.

✔ Under the units-of-activity method, compute the depreciation cost per unit by dividing depreciable cost by total units of activity.

✔ Under the declining-balance method, apply the depreciation rate to **book value** at the beginning of the year.

Solution to Comprehensive DO IT! *1*

(a)

Straight-Line Method

| | Computation | | | Annual | End of Year | |
| | Depreciable | | Depreciation | Depreciation | Accumulated | Book |
Year	Cost*	×	Rate	= Expense	Depreciation	Value
2010	$16,000		25%	$4,000	$ 4,000	$14,000**
2011	16,000		25%	4,000	8,000	10,000
2012	16,000		25%	4,000	12,000	6,000
2013	16,000		25%	4,000	16,000	2,000

*$18,000 − $2,000.
**$18,000 − $4,000.

(b)

Units-of-Activity Method

| | Computation | | | Annual | End of Year | |
| | Units of | | Depreciation | Depreciation | Accumulated | Book |
Year	Activity	×	Cost/Unit	= Expense	Depreciation	Value
2010	40,000		$0.10*	$4,000	$ 4,000	$14,000
2011	60,000		0.10	6,000	10,000	8,000
2012	35,000		0.10	3,500	13,500	4,500
2013	25,000		0.10	2,500	16,000	2,000

*($18,000 − $2,000) ÷ 160,000.

(c)

Declining-Balance Method

| | Computation | | | Annual | End of Year | |
| | Book Value Beginning of | | Depreciation | Depreciation | Accumulated | Book |
Year	Year	×	Rate*	= Expense	Depreciation	Value
2010	$18,000		50%	$9,000	$ 9,000	$9,000
2011	9,000		50%	4,500	13,500	4,500
2012	4,500		50%	2,250	15,750	2,250
2013	2,250		50%	250**	16,000	2,000

*¼ × 2.
**Adjusted to $250 because ending book value should not be less than expected salvage value.

Comprehensive **DO IT!** *2*

On January 1, 2010, Skyline Limousine Co. purchased a limo at an acquisition cost of $28,000. The vehicle has been depreciated by the straight-line method using a 4-year service life and a $4,000 salvage value. The company's fiscal year ends on December 31.

Instructions

Prepare the journal entry or entries to record the disposal of the limousine assuming that it was:

(a) Retired and scrapped with no salvage value on January 1, 2014.

(b) Sold for $5,000 on July 1, 2013.

action plan

✔ At the time of disposal, determine the book value of the asset.

✔ Recognize any gain or loss from disposal of the asset.

✔ Remove the book value of the asset from the records by debiting Accumulated Depreciation for the total depreciation to date of disposal and crediting the asset account for the cost of the asset.

Solution to Comprehensive DO IT! 2

(a)	1/1/14	Accumulated Depreciation—Limousine	24,000	
		Loss on Disposal	4,000	
		Limousine		28,000
		(To record retirement of limousine)		
(b)	7/1/13	Depreciation Expense	3,000	
		Accumulated Depreciation—Limousine		3,000
		(To record depreciation to date of disposal)		
		Cash	5,000	
		Accumulated Depreciation—Limousine	21,000	
		Loss on Disposal	2,000	
		Limousine		28,000
		(To record sale of limousine)		

The Navigator

SUMMARY OF STUDY OBJECTIVES

1 Describe how the cost principle applies to plant assets. The cost of plant assets includes all expenditures necessary to acquire the asset and make it ready for its intended use. Cost is measured by the cash or cash equivalent price paid.

2 Explain the concept of depreciation. Depreciation is the allocation of the cost of a plant asset to expense over its useful (service) life in a rational and systematic manner. Depreciation is not a process of valuation, nor is it a process that results in an accumulation of cash.

3 Compute periodic depreciation using different methods. Three depreciation methods are:

Method	Effect on Annual Depreciation	Formula
Straight-line	Constant amount	Depreciable cost ÷ Useful life (in years)
Units-of-activity	Varying amount	Depreciation cost per unit × Units of activity during the year
Declining-balance	Decreasing amount	Book value at beginning of year × Declining-balance rate

4 Describe the procedure for revising periodic depreciation. Companies make revisions of periodic depreciation in present and future periods, not retroactively. They determine the new annual depreciation by dividing the depreciable cost at the time of the revision by the remaining useful life.

5 Distinguish between revenue and capital expenditures, and explain the entries for each. Companies incur revenue expenditures to maintain the operating efficiency and productive life of an asset. They debit these expenditures to Repair Expense as incurred. Capital expenditures increase the operating efficiency, productive capacity, or expected useful life of the asset. Companies generally debit these expenditures to the plant asset affected.

6 Explain how to account for the disposal of a plant asset. The accounting for disposal of a plant asset through retirement or sale is as follows:

(a) Eliminate the book value of the plant asset at the date of disposal.

(b) Record cash proceeds, if any.

(c) Account for the difference between the book value and the cash proceeds as a gain or loss on disposal.

7 **Compute periodic depletion of natural resources.** Companies compute depletion cost per unit by dividing the total cost of the natural resource minus salvage value by the number of units estimated to be in the resource. They then multiply the depletion cost per unit by the number of units extracted and sold.

8 **Explain the basic issues related to accounting for intangible assets.** The process of allocating the cost of an intangible asset is referred to as amortization. The cost of intangible assets with indefinite lives are not amortized. Companies normally use the straight-line method for amortizing intangible assets.

9 **Indicate how plant assets, natural resources, and intangible assets are reported.** Companies usually combine plant assets and natural resources under property, plant, and equipment; they show intangibles separately under intangible assets. Either within the balance sheet or in the notes, companies should disclose the balances of the major classes of assets, such as land, buildings, and equipment, and accumulated depreciation by major classes or in total. They also should describe the depreciation and amortization methods used, and should disclose the amount of depreciation and amortization expense for the period. The asset turnover ratio measures the productivity of a company's assets in generating sales.

GLOSSARY

Accelerated-depreciation method Depreciation method that produces higher depreciation expense in the early years than in the later years. (p. 447).

Additions and improvements Costs incurred to increase the operating efficiency, productive capacity, or useful life of a plant asset. (p. 449).

Amortization The allocation of the cost of an intangible asset to expense over its useful life in a systematic and rational manner. (p. 454).

Asset turnover ratio A measure of how efficiently a company uses its assets to generate sales; calculated as net sales divided by average total assets. (p. 459).

Capital expenditures Expenditures that increase the company's investment in productive facilities. (p. 449).

Copyright Exclusive grant from the federal government that allows the owner to reproduce and sell an artistic or published work. (p. 455).

Declining-balance method Depreciation method that applies a constant rate to the declining book value of the asset and produces a decreasing annual depreciation expense over the useful life of the asset. (p. 446).

Depletion The allocation of the cost of a natural resource to expense in a rational and systematic manner over the resource's useful life. (p. 453).

Depreciation The process of allocating to expense the cost of a plant asset over its useful (service) life in a rational and systematic manner. (p. 442).

Depreciable cost The cost of a plant asset less its salvage value. (p. 444).

Franchise (license) A contractual arrangement under which the franchisor grants the franchisee the right to sell certain products, provide specific services, or use certain trademarks or trade names, usually within a designated geographical area. (p. 456).

Going-concern assumption States that the company will continue in operation for the foreseeable future. (p. 443).

Goodwill The value of all favorable attributes that relate to a business enterprise. (p. 456).

Intangible assets Rights, privileges, and competitive advantages that result from the ownership of long-lived assets that do not possess physical substance. (p. 454).

Licenses Operating rights to use public property, granted to a business enterprise by a governmental agency. (p. 456).

Materiality principle If an item would not make a difference in decision making, a company does not have to follow GAAP in reporting it. (p. 450).

Natural resources Assets that consist of standing timber and underground deposits of oil, gas, or minerals. (p. 453).

Ordinary repairs Expenditures to maintain the operating efficiency and productive life of the unit. (p. 449).

Patent An exclusive right issued by the U.S. Patent Office that enables the recipient to manufacture, sell, or otherwise control an invention for a period of 20 years from the date of the grant. (p. 455).

Plant assets Tangible resources that are used in the operations of the business and are not intended for sale to customers. (p. 438).

Research and development (R&D) costs Expenditures that may lead to patents, copyrights, new processes, or new products. (p. 457).

Revenue expenditures Expenditures that are immediately charged against revenues as an expense. (p. 449).

Salvage value An estimate of an asset's value at the end of its useful life. (p. 443).

Straight-line method Depreciation method in which periodic depreciation is the same for each year of the asset's useful life. (p. 444).

Trademark (trade name) A word, phrase, jingle, or symbol that identifies a particular enterprise or product. (p. 455).

Units-of-activity method Depreciation method in which useful life is expressed in terms of the total units of production or use expected from an asset. (p. 445).

Useful life An estimate of the expected productive life, also called service life, of an asset. (p. 443).

APPENDIX Exchange of Plant Assets

Ordinarily, companies record a gain or loss on the exchange of plant assets. The rationale for recognizing a gain or loss is that most exchanges have **commercial substance**. An exchange has commercial substance if the future cash flows change as a result of the exchange.

To illustrate, Ramos Co. exchanges some of its equipment for land held by Brodhead Inc. It is likely that the timing and amount of the cash flows arising from the land will differ significantly from the cash flows arising from the equipment. As a result, both Ramos and Brodhead are in different economic positions. Therefore **the exchange has commercial substance**, and the companies recognize a gain or loss in the exchange. Because most exchanges have commercial substance (even when similar assets are exchanged), we illustrate only this type of situation, for both a loss and a gain.

Loss Treatment

To illustrate an exchange that results in a loss, assume that Roland Company exchanged a set of used trucks plus cash for a new semi-truck. The used trucks have a combined book value of $42,000 (cost $64,000 less $22,000 accumulated depreciation). Roland's purchasing agent, experienced in the second-hand market, indicates that the used trucks have a fair market value of $26,000. In addition to the trucks, Roland must pay $17,000 for the semi-truck. Roland computes the cost of the semi-truck as follows

Illustration 10A-1
Cost of semi-truck

Fair value of used trucks	$26,000
Cash paid	17,000
Cost of semi-truck	$43,000

Roland incurs a loss on disposal of $16,000 on this exchange. The reason is that the book value of the used trucks is greater than the fair market value of these trucks. The computation is as follows.

Illustration 10A-2
Computation of loss on disposal

Book value of used trucks ($64,000−$22,000)	$42,000
Fair market value of used trucks	26,000
Loss on disposal	**$16,000**

In recording an exchange at a loss, three steps are required: (1) Eliminate the book value of the asset given up, (2) record the cost of the asset acquired, and (3) recognize the loss on disposal. Roland Company thus records the exchange on the loss as follows.

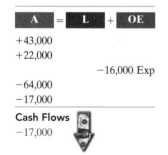

A = L + OE
+43,000
+22,000
−16,000 Exp
−64,000
−17,000
Cash Flows
−17,000

Semi-truck	43,000	
Accumulated Depreciation—Used Trucks	22,000	
Loss on Disposal	16,000	
Used Trucks		64,000
Cash		17,000
(To record exchange of used trucks for semi-truck.)		

Gain Treatment

To illustrate a gain situation, assume that Mark Express Delivery decides to exchange its old delivery equipment plus cash of $3,000 for new delivery equipment. The book value of the old delivery equipment is $12,000 (cost $40,000 less accumulated depreciation $28,000). The fair market value of the old delivery equipment is $19,000.

The cost of the new asset is the fair market value of the old asset exchanged plus any cash paid (or other consideration given up). The cost of the new delivery equipment is $22,000 computed as follows.

Fair market value of old delivery equipment	$19,000
Cash paid	3,000
Cost of new delivery equipment	**$22,000**

Illustration 10A-3
Cost of new delivery equipment

A gain results when the fair market value of the old delivery equipment is greater than its book value. For Mark Express there is a gain of $7,000 on disposal, computed as follows.

Fair market value of old delivery equipment	$19,000
Book value of old delivery equipment ($40,000−$28,000)	12,000
Gain on disposal	**$ 7,000**

Illustration 10A-4
Computation of gain on disposal

Mark Express Delivery records the exchange as follows.

Delivery Equipment (new)	22,000	
Accumulated Depreciation—Delivery Equipment (old)	28,000	
Delivery Equipment (old)		40,000
Gain on Disposal		7,000
Cash		3,000
(To record exchange of old delivery equipment for new delivery equipment)		

A = L + OE

+22,000
+28,000
−40,000
                +7,000 Rev
−3,000

Cash Flows
−3,000

In recording an exchange at a gain, the following three steps are involved: (1) Eliminate the book value of the asset given up, (2) record the cost of the asset acquired, and (3) recognize the gain on disposal. Accounting for exchanges of plant assets becomes more complex if the transaction does not have commercial substance. This issue is discussed in more advanced accounting classes.

SUMMARY OF STUDY OBJECTIVE FOR APPENDIX

10   Explain how to account for the exchange of plant assets. Ordinarily companies record a gain or loss on the exchange of plant assets. The rationale for recognizing a gain or loss is that most exchanges have commercial substance. An exchange has commercial substance if the future cash flows change as a result of the exchange.

Note: All **asterisked** Questions, Exercises, and Problems relate to material in the appendix to the chapter.

SELF-STUDY QUESTIONS

Answers are at the end of the chapter.

(SO 1) **1.** Erin Danielle Company purchased equipment and incurred the following costs.

Cash price	$24,000
Sales taxes	1,200
Insurance during transit	200
Installation and testing	400
Total costs	$25,800

What amount should be recorded as the cost of the equipment?
  a. $24,000.
  b. $25,200.
  c. $25,400.
  d. $25,800.

2. Depreciation is a process of: (SO 2)
  a. valuation.
  b. cost allocation.

c. cash accumulation.

d. appraisal.

(SO 3) **3.** Micah Bartlett Company purchased equipment on January 1, 2009, at a total invoice cost of $400,000. The equipment has an estimated salvage value of $10,000 and an estimated useful life of 5 years. The amount of accumulated depreciation at December 31, 2010, if the straight-line method of depreciation is used, is:

a. $80,000.

b. $160,000.

c. $78,000.

d. $156,000.

(SO 3) **4.** Ann Torbert purchased a truck for $11,000 on January 1, 2009. The truck will have an estimated salvage value of $1,000 at the end of 5 years. Using the units-of-activity method, the balance in accumulated depreciation at December 31, 2010, can be computed by the following formula:

a. ($11,000 ÷ Total estimated activity) × Units of activity for 2010.

b. ($10,000 ÷ Total estimated activity) × Units of activity for 2010.

c. ($11,000 ÷ Total estimated activity) × Units of activity for 2009 and 2010.

d. ($10,000 ÷ Total estimated activity) × Units of activity for 2009 and 2010.

(SO 3) **5.** Jefferson Company purchased a piece of equipment on January 1, 2010. The equipment cost $60,000 and had an estimated life of 8 years and a salvage value of $8,000. What was the depreciation expense for the asset for 2011 under the double-declining-balance method?

a. $6,500.

b. $11,250.

c. $15,000.

d. $6,562.

(SO 4) **6.** When there is a change in estimated depreciation:

a. previous depreciation should be corrected.

b. current and future years' depreciation should be revised.

c. only future years' depreciation should be revised.

d. None of the above.

(SO 4) **7.** Able Towing Company purchased a tow truck for $60,000 on January 1, 2010. It was originally depreciated on a straight-line basis over 10 years with an assumed salvage value of $12,000. On December 31, 2012, before adjusting entries had been made, the company decided to change the remaining estimated life to 4 years (including 2012) and the salvage value to $2,000. What was the depreciation expense for 2012?

a. $6,000.

b. $4,800.

c. $15,000.

d. $12,100.

(SO 5) **8.** Additions to plant assets are:

a. revenue expenditures.

b. debited to a Repair Expense account.

c. debited to a Purchases account.

d. capital expenditures.

(SO 6) **9.** Bennie Razor Company has decided to sell one of its old manufacturing machines on June 30, 2010. The machine was purchased for $80,000 on January 1, 2006, and was depreciated on a straight-line basis for 10 years assuming no salvage value. If the machine was sold for $26,000, what was the amount of the gain or loss recorded at the time of the sale?

a. $18,000.

b. $54,000.

c. $22,000.

d. $46,000.

(SO 7) **10.** Maggie Sharrer Company expects to extract 20 million tons of coal from a mine that cost $12 million. If no salvage value is expected, and 2 million tons are mined and sold in the first year, the entry to record depletion will include a:

a. debit to Accumulated Depletion of $2,000,000.

b. credit to Depletion Expense of $1,200,000.

c. debit to Depletion Expense of $1,200,000.

d. credit to Accumulated Depletion of $2,000,000.

(SO 8) **11.** Which of the following statements is *false*?

a. If an intangible asset has a finite life, it should be amortized.

b. The amortization period of an intangible asset can exceed 20 years.

c. Goodwill is recorded only when a business is purchased.

d. Research and development costs are expensed when incurred, except when the research and development expenditures result in a successful patent.

(SO 8) **12.** Martha Beyerlein Company incurred $150,000 of research and development costs in its laboratory to develop a patent granted on January 2, 2010. On July 31, 2010, Beyerlein paid $35,000 for legal fees in a successful defense of the patent. The total amount debited to Patents through July 31, 2010, should be:

a. $150,000.

b. $35,000.

c. $185,000.

d. $170,000.

(SO 9) **13.** Indicate which of the following statements is *true*.

a. Since intangible assets lack physical substance, they need be disclosed only in the notes to the financial statements.

b. Goodwill should be reported as a contra-account in the owner's equity section.

c. Totals of major classes of assets can be shown in the balance sheet, with asset details disclosed in the notes to the financial statements.

d. Intangible assets are typically combined with plant assets and natural resources and shown in the property, plant, and equipment section.

(SO 9) **14.** Lake Coffee Company reported net sales of $180,000, net income of $54,000, beginning total assets of $200,000, and ending total assets of $300,000. What was the company's asset turnover ratio?

a. 0.90

b. 0.20

c. 0.72

d. 1.39

(SO 10) *15. Schopenhauer Company exchanged an old machine, with a book value of $39,000 and a fair market value of $35,000, and paid $10,000 cash for a similar new machine. The transaction has commercial substance. At what amount should the machine acquired in the exchange be recorded on Schopenhauer's books?

  a. $45,000.
  b. $46,000.
  c. $49,000.
  d. $50,000.

*16. In exchanges of assets in which the exchange has commer- (SO 10) cial substance:

  a. neither gains nor losses are recognized immediately.
  b. gains, but not losses, are recognized immediately.
  c. losses, but not gains, are recognized immediately.
  d. both gains and losses are recognized immediately.

Go to the book's companion website, **www.wiley.com/college/weygandt**, for Additional Self-Study questions.

QUESTIONS

1. Tim Hoover is uncertain about the applicability of the cost principle to plant assets. Explain the principle to Tim.

2. What are some examples of land improvements?

3. Dain Company acquires the land and building owned by Corrs Company. What types of costs may be incurred to make the asset ready for its intended use if Dain Company wants to use (a) only the land, and (b) both the land and the building?

4. In a recent newspaper release, the president of Keene Company asserted that something has to be done about depreciation. The president said, "Depreciation does not come close to accumulating the cash needed to replace the asset at the end of its useful life." What is your response to the president?

5. Robert is studying for the next accounting examination. He asks your help on two questions: (a) What is salvage value? (b) Is salvage value used in determining periodic depreciation under each depreciation method? Answer Robert's questions.

6. Contrast the straight-line method and the units-of-activity method as to (a) useful life, and (b) the pattern of periodic depreciation over useful life.

7. Contrast the effects of the three depreciation methods on annual depreciation expense.

8. In the fourth year of an asset's 5-year useful life, the company decides that the asset will have a 6-year service life. How should the revision of depreciation be recorded? Why?

9. Distinguish between revenue expenditures and capital expenditures during useful life.

10. How is a gain or loss on the sale of a plant asset computed?

11. Mendez Corporation owns a machine that is fully depreciated but is still being used. How should Mendez account for this asset and report it in the financial statements?

12. What are natural resources, and what are their distinguishing characteristics?

13. Explain what depletion is and how it is computed.

14. What are the similarities and differences between the terms depreciation, depletion, and amortization?

15. Pendergrass Company hires an accounting intern who says that intangible assets should always be amortized over their legal lives. Is the intern correct? Explain.

16. Goodwill has been defined as the value of all favorable attributes that relate to a business enterprise. What types of attributes could result in goodwill?

17. Kenny Sain, a business major, is working on a case problem for one of his classes. In the case problem, the company needs to raise cash to market a new product it developed. Joe Morris, an engineering major, takes one look at the company's balance sheet and says, "This company has an awful lot of goodwill. Why don't you recommend that they sell some of it to raise cash?" How should Kenny respond to Joe?

18. Under what conditions is goodwill recorded?

19. Often research and development costs provide companies with benefits that last a number of years. (For example, these costs can lead to the development of a patent that will increase the company's income for many years.) However, generally accepted accounting principles require that such costs be recorded as an expense when incurred. Why?

20. McDonald's Corporation reports total average assets of $28.9 billion and net sales of $20.5 billion. What is the company's asset turnover ratio?

21. Resco Corporation and Yapan Corporation operate in the same industry. Resco uses the straight-line method to account for depreciation; Yapan uses an accelerated method. Explain what complications might arise in trying to compare the results of these two companies.

22. Lopez Corporation uses straight-line depreciation for financial reporting purposes but an accelerated method for tax purposes. Is it acceptable to use different methods for the two purposes? What is Lopez's motivation for doing this?

23. You are comparing two companies in the same industry. You have determined that May Corp. depreciates its plant assets over a 40-year life, whereas Won Corp. depreciates its plant assets over a 20-year life. Discuss the implications this has for comparing the results of the two companies.

24. Wade Company is doing significant work to revitalize its warehouses. It is not sure whether it should capitalize these costs or expense them. What are the implications for current-year net income and future net income of expensing versus capitalizing these costs?

25. **PEPSICO** What classifications and amounts are shown in PepsiCo's Note 4 to explain its total property, plant, and equipment (net) of $11,228 million?

26. When assets are exchanged in a transaction involving commercial substance, how is the gain or loss on disposal computed?

*27. Tatum Refrigeration Company trades in an old machine on a new model when the fair market value of the old machine is greater than its book value. The transaction has commercial substance. Should Tatum recognize a gain on disposal? If the fair market value of the old machine is less than its book value, should Tatum recognize a loss on disposal?

BRIEF EXERCISES

Determine the cost of land.
(SO 1)

BE10-1 The following expenditures were incurred by Obermeyer Company in purchasing land: cash price $70,000, accrued taxes $3,000, attorneys' fees $2,500, real estate broker's commission $2,000, and clearing and grading $3,500. What is the cost of the land?

Determine the cost of a truck.
(SO 1)

BE10-2 Neeley Company incurs the following expenditures in purchasing a truck: cash price $30,000, accident insurance $2,000, sales taxes $1,500, motor vehicle license $100, and painting and lettering $400. What is the cost of the truck?

Compute straight-line depreciation.
(SO 3)

BE10-3 Conlin Company acquires a delivery truck at a cost of $42,000. The truck is expected to have a salvage value of $6,000 at the end of its 4-year useful life. Compute annual depreciation for the first and second years using the straight-line method.

Compute depreciation and evaluate treatment.
(SO 3)

BE10-4 Ecklund Company purchased land and a building on January 1, 2010. Management's best estimate of the value of the land was $100,000 and of the building $200,000. But management told the accounting department to record the land at $220,000 and the building at $80,000. The building is being depreciated on a straight-line basis over 20 years with no salvage value. Why do you suppose management requested this accounting treatment? Is it ethical?

Compute declining-balance depreciation.
(SO 3)

BE10-5 Depreciation information for Conlin Company is given in BE10-3. Assuming the declining-balance depreciation rate is double the straight-line rate, compute annual depreciation for the first and second years under the declining-balance method.

Compute depreciation using the units-of-activity method.
(SO 3)

BE10-6 Speedy Taxi Service uses the units-of-activity method in computing depreciation on its taxicabs. Each cab is expected to be driven 150,000 miles. Taxi no. 10 cost $33,500 and is expected to have a salvage value of $500. Taxi no. 10 is driven 30,000 miles in year 1 and 20,000 miles in year 2. Compute the depreciation for each year.

Compute revised depreciation.
(SO 4)

BE10-7 On January 1, 2010, the Ramirez Company ledger shows Equipment $29,000 and Accumulated Depreciation $9,000. The depreciation resulted from using the straight-line method with a useful life of 10 years and salvage value of $2,000. On this date, the company concludes that the equipment has a remaining useful life of only 4 years with the same salvage value. Compute the revised annual depreciation.

Prepare entries for delivery truck costs.
(SO 5)

BE10-8 Firefly Company had the following two transactions related to its delivery truck.

1. Paid $45 for an oil change.
2. Paid $400 to install special shelving units, which increase the operating efficiency of the truck.

Prepare Firefly's journal entries to record these two transactions.

Prepare entries for disposal by retirement.
(SO 6)

BE10-9 Prepare journal entries to record the following.

(a) Gomez Company retires its delivery equipment, which cost $41,000. Accumulated depreciation is also $41,000 on this delivery equipment. No salvage value is received.
(b) Assume the same information as (a), except that accumulated depreciation is $39,000, instead of $41,000, on the delivery equipment.

Prepare entries for disposal by sale.
(SO 6)

BE10-10 Chan Company sells office equipment on September 30, 2010, for $20,000 cash. The office equipment originally cost $72,000 and as of January 1, 2010, had accumulated depreciation of $42,000. Depreciation for the first 9 months of 2010 is $5,250. Prepare the journal entries to (a) update depreciation to September 30, 2010, and (b) record the sale of the equipment.

Prepare depletion expense entry and balance sheet presentation for natural resources.
(SO 7)

BE10-11 Olpe Mining Co. purchased for $7 million a mine that is estimated to have 35 million tons of ore and no salvage value. In the first year, 6 million tons of ore are extracted and sold.

(a) Prepare the journal entry to record depletion expense for the first year.
(b) Show how this mine is reported on the balance sheet at the end of the first year.

BE10-12 Galena Company purchases a patent for $120,000 on January 2, 2010. Its estimated useful life is 10 years.

(a) Prepare the journal entry to record patent expense for the first year.
(b) Show how this patent is reported on the balance sheet at the end of the first year.

Prepare patent expense entry and balance sheet presentation for intangibles.
(SO 8)

BE10-13 Information related to plant assets, natural resources, and intangibles at the end of 2010 for Spain Company is as follows: buildings $1,100,000; accumulated depreciation—buildings $650,000; goodwill $410,000; coal mine $500,000; accumulated depletion—coal mine $108,000. Prepare a partial balance sheet of Spain Company for these items.

Classify long-lived assets on balance sheet.
(SO 9)

BE10-14 In its 2007 annual report Target reported beginning total assets of $37.3 billion; ending total assets of $44.6 billion; property and equipment (net) of $24.1 billion; and net sales of $61.5 billion. Compute Target's asset turnover ratio.

Analyze long-lived assets.
(SO 9)

*BE10-15 Rivera Company exchanges old delivery equipment for new delivery equipment. The book value of the old delivery equipment is $31,000 (cost $61,000 less accumulated depreciation $30,000). Its fair market value is $19,000, and cash of $5,000 is paid. Prepare the entry to record the exchange, assuming the transaction has commercial substance.

Prepare entry for disposal by exchange.
(SO 10)

*BE10-16 Assume the same information as BE10-15, except that the fair market value of the old delivery equipment is $38,000. Prepare the entry to record the exchange.

Prepare entry for disposal by exchange.
(SO 10)

DO IT! REVIEW

DO IT! 10-1 African Lakes Company purchased a delivery truck. The total cash payment was $27,900, including the following items.

Negotiated purchase price	$24,000
Installation of special shelving	1,100
Painting and lettering	900
Motor vehicle license	100
Annual insurance policy	500
Sales tax	1,300
Total paid	$27,900

Explain how each of these costs would be accounted for.

Explain accounting for cost of plant assets.
(SO 1)

DO IT! 10-2 On January 1, 2010, Pine Grove Country Club purchased a new riding mower for $15,000. The mower is expected to have an 8-year life with a $1,000 salvage value. What journal entry would Pine Grove make at December 31, 2010, if it uses straight-line depreciation?

Calculate depreciation expense and make journal entry.
(SO 2)

DO IT! 10-3 Ritenour Manufacturing has an old factory machine that cost $50,000. The machine has accumulated depreciation of $28,000 and a fair value of $26,000. Ritenour has decided to sell the machine.

(a) What entry would Ritenour make to record the sale of the truck for $26,000 cash?
(b) What entry would Ritenour make to record the sale of the truck for $15,000 cash?

Make journal entries to record plant asset disposal.
(SO 6)

DO IT! 10-4 Match the statement with the term most directly associated with it.

Goodwill	Amortization
Intangible assets	Franchise
Research and development costs	

Match intangibles classifications concepts.
(SO 7, 8)

1. _____ Rights, privileges, and competitive advantages that result from the ownership of long-lived assets that do not possess physical substance.
2. _____ The allocation of the cost of an intangible asset to expense in a rational and systematic manner.
3. _____ A right to sell certain products or services, or use certain trademarks or trade names within a designated geographic area.
4. _____ Costs incurred by a company that often lead to patents or new products. These costs must be expensed as incurred.
5. _____ The excess of the cost of a company over the fair market value of the net assets required.

EXERCISES

Determine cost of plant acquisitions.

(SO 1)

E10-1   The following expenditures relating to plant assets were made by Spaulding Company during the first 2 months of 2010.

1. Paid $5,000 of accrued taxes at time plant site was acquired.
2. Paid $200 insurance to cover possible accident loss on new factory machinery while the machinery was in transit.
3. Paid $850 sales taxes on new delivery truck.
4. Paid $17,500 for parking lots and driveways on new plant site.
5. Paid $250 to have company name and advertising slogan painted on new delivery truck.
6. Paid $8,000 for installation of new factory machinery.
7. Paid $900 for one-year accident insurance policy on new delivery truck.
8. Paid $75 motor vehicle license fee on the new truck.

Instructions
(a) ⬛━━━▶ Explain the application of the cost principle in determining the acquisition cost of plant assets.
(b) List the numbers of the foregoing transactions, and opposite each indicate the account title to which each expenditure should be debited.

Determine property, plant, and equipment costs.

(SO 1)

E10-2   Trudy Company incurred the following costs.

1. Sales tax on factory machinery purchased	$5,000
2. Painting of and lettering on truck immediately upon purchase	700
3. Installation and testing of factory machinery	2,000
4. Real estate broker's commission on land purchased	3,500
5. Insurance premium paid for first year's insurance on new truck	880
6. Cost of landscaping on property purchased	7,200
7. Cost of paving parking lot for new building constructed	17,900
8. Cost of clearing, draining, and filling land	13,300
9. Architect's fees on self-constructed building	10,000

Instructions
Indicate to which account Trudy would debit each of the costs.

Determine acquisition costs of land.

(SO 1)

E10-3   On March 1, 2010, Penner Company acquired real estate on which it planned to construct a small office building. The company paid $80,000 in cash. An old warehouse on the property was razed at a cost of $8,600; the salvaged materials were sold for $1,700. Additional expenditures before construction began included $1,100 attorney's fee for work concerning the land purchase, $5,000 real estate broker's fee, $7,800 architect's fee, and $14,000 to put in driveways and a parking lot.

Instructions
(a) Determine the amount to be reported as the cost of the land.
(b) For each cost not used in part (a), indicate the account to be debited.

Understand depreciation concepts.

(SO 2)

E10-4   Chris Rock has prepared the following list of statements about depreciation.

1. Depreciation is a process of asset valuation, not cost allocation.
2. Depreciation provides for the proper matching of expenses with revenues.
3. The book value of a plant asset should approximate its market value.
4. Depreciation applies to three classes of plant assets: land, buildings, and equipment.
5. Depreciation does not apply to a building because its usefulness and revenue-producing ability generally remain intact over time.
6. The revenue-producing ability of a depreciable asset will decline due to wear and tear and to obsolescence.
7. Recognizing depreciation on an asset results in an accumulation of cash for replacement of the asset.
8. The balance in accumulated depreciation represents the total cost that has been charged to expense.
9. Depreciation expense and accumulated depreciation are reported on the income statement.
10. Four factors affect the computation of depreciation: cost, useful life, salvage value, and residual value.

Instructions
Identify each statement as true or false. If false, indicate how to correct the statement.

E10-5   Younger Bus Lines uses the units-of-activity method in depreciating its buses. One bus was purchased on January 1, 2010, at a cost of $168,000. Over its 4-year useful life, the bus is expected to be driven 100,000 miles. Salvage value is expected to be $8,000.

Compute depreciation under units-of-activity method.
(SO 3)

Instructions
(a) Compute the depreciation cost per unit.
(b) Prepare a depreciation schedule assuming actual mileage was: 2010, 26,000; 2011, 32,000; 2012, 25,000; and 2013, 17,000.

E10-6   Kelm Company purchased a new machine on October 1, 2010, at a cost of $120,000. The company estimated that the machine will have a salvage value of $12,000. The machine is expected to be used for 10,000 working hours during its 5-year life.

Determine depreciation for partial periods.
(SO 3)

Instructions
Compute the depreciation expense under the following methods for the year indicated.

(a) Straight-line for 2010.
(b) Units-of-activity for 2010, assuming machine usage was 1,700 hours.
(c) Declining-balance using double the straight-line rate for 2010 and 2011.

E10-7   Brainiac Company purchased a delivery truck for $30,000 on January 1, 2010. The truck has an expected salvage value of $2,000, and is expected to be driven 100,000 miles over its estimated useful life of 8 years. Actual miles driven were 15,000 in 2010 and 12,000 in 2011.

Compute depreciation using different methods.
(SO 3)

Instructions
(a) Compute depreciation expense for 2010 and 2011 using (1) the straight-line method, (2) the units-of-activity method, and (3) the double-declining balance method.
(b) Assume that Brainiac uses the straight-line method.
   (1) Prepare the journal entry to record 2010 depreciation.
   (2) Show how the truck would be reported in the December 31, 2010, balance sheet.

E10-8   Jerry Grant, the new controller of Blackburn Company, has reviewed the expected useful lives and salvage values of selected depreciable assets at the beginning of 2010. His findings are as follows.

Compute revised annual depreciation.
(SO 4)

Type of Asset	Date Acquired	Cost	Accumulated Depreciation 1/1/10	Useful Life in Years		Salvage Value	
				Old	Proposed	Old	Proposed
Building	1/1/04	$800,000	$114,000	40	50	$40,000	$37,000
Warehouse	1/1/05	100,000	25,000	25	20	5,000	3,600

All assets are depreciated by the straight-line method. Blackburn Company uses a calendar year in preparing annual financial statements. After discussion, management has agreed to accept Jerry's proposed changes.

Instructions
(a) Compute the revised annual depreciation on each asset in 2010. (Show computations.)
(b) Prepare the entry (or entries) to record depreciation on the building in 2010.

E10-9   Presented below are selected transactions at Ingles Company for 2010.

Jan.   1   Retired a piece of machinery that was purchased on January 1, 2000. The machine cost $62,000 on that date. It had a useful life of 10 years with no salvage value.

Journalize entries for disposal of plant assets.
(SO 6)

June 30   Sold a computer that was purchased on January 1, 2007. The computer cost $40,000. It had a useful life of 5 years with no salvage value. The computer was sold for $14,000.

Dec. 31   Discarded a delivery truck that was purchased on January 1, 2006. The truck cost $39,000. It was depreciated based on a 6-year useful life with a $3,000 salvage value.

Instructions
Journalize all entries required on the above dates, including entries to update depreciation, where applicable, on assets disposed of. Ingles Company uses straight-line depreciation. (Assume depreciation is up to date as of December 31, 2009.)

Journalize entries for disposal of equipment.

(SO 6)

E10-10   Beka Company owns equipment that cost $50,000 when purchased on January 1, 2007. It has been depreciated using the straight-line method based on estimated salvage value of $5,000 and an estimated useful life of 5 years.

Instructions

Prepare Beka Company's journal entries to record the sale of the equipment in these four independent situations.

(a) Sold for $28,000 on January 1, 2010.
(b) Sold for $28,000 on May 1, 2010.
(c) Sold for $11,000 on January 1, 2010.
(d) Sold for $11,000 on October 1, 2010.

Journalize entries for natural resources depletion.

(SO 7)

E10-11   On July 1, 2010, Hurtig Inc. invested $720,000 in a mine estimated to have 800,000 tons of ore of uniform grade. During the last 6 months of 2010, 100,000 tons of ore were mined and sold.

Instructions

(a) Prepare the journal entry to record depletion expense.
(b) Assume that the 100,000 tons of ore were mined, but only 80,000 units were sold. How are the costs applicable to the 20,000 unsold units reported?

Prepare adjusting entries for amortization.

(SO 8)

E10-12   The following are selected 2010 transactions of Franco Corporation.

Jan. 1   Purchased a small company and recorded goodwill of $150,000. Its useful life is indefinite.
May 1   Purchased for $90,000 a patent with an estimated useful life of 5 years and a legal life of 20 years.

Instructions

Prepare necessary adjusting entries at December 31 to record amortization required by the events above.

Prepare entries to set up appropriate accounts for different intangibles; amortize intangible assets.

(SO 8)

E10-13   Herzogg Company, organized in 2010, has the following transactions related to intangible assets.

1/2/10	Purchased patent (7-year life)	$560,000
4/1/10	Goodwill purchased (indefinite life)	360,000
7/1/10	10-year franchise; expiration date 7/1/2018	440,000
9/1/10	Research and development costs	185,000

Instructions

Prepare the necessary entries to record these intangibles. All costs incurred were for cash. Make the adjusting entries as of December 31, 2010, recording any necessary amortization and reflecting all balances accurately as of that date.

Calculate asset turnover ratio.

(SO 9)

E10-14   During 2010 Nasra Corporation reported net sales of $4,900,000 and net income of $1,500,000. Its balance sheet reported average total assets of $1,400,000.

Instructions

Calculate the asset turnover ratio.

Journalize entries for exchanges.

(SO 10)

*E10-15   Presented below are two independent transactions. Both transactions have commercial substance.

1. Sidney Co. exchanged old trucks (cost $64,000 less $22,000 accumulated depreciation) plus cash of $17,000 for new trucks. The old trucks had a fair market value of $36,000.
2. Lupa Inc. trades its used machine (cost $12,000 less $4,000 accumulated depreciation) for a new machine. In addition to exchanging the old machine (which had a fair market value of $9,000), Lupa also paid cash of $3,000.

Instructions

(a) Prepare the entry to record the exchange of assets by Sidney Co.
(b) Prepare the entry to record the exchange of assets by Lupa Inc.

Journalize entries for the exchange of plant assets.

(SO 10)

*E10-16   Coran's Delivery Company and Enright's Express Delivery exchanged delivery trucks on January 1, 2010. Coran's truck cost $22,000. It has accumulated depreciation of $15,000 and a fair market value of $4,000. Enright's truck cost $10,000. It has accumulated depreciation of $8,000 and a fair market value of $4,000. The transaction has commercial substance.

Instructions

(a) Journalize the exchange for Coran's Delivery Company.
(b) Journalize the exchange for Enright's Express Delivery.

EXERCISES: SET B

Visit the book's companion website at **www.wiley.com/college/weygandt**, and choose the Student Companion site, to access Exercise Set B.

PROBLEMS: SET A

P10-1A Diaz Company was organized on January 1. During the first year of operations, the following plant asset expenditures and receipts were recorded in random order.

Determine acquisition costs of land and building.

(SO 1)

Debits

1. Cost of filling and grading the land	$ 4,000
2. Full payment to building contractor	700,000
3. Real estate taxes on land paid for the current year	5,000
4. Cost of real estate purchased as a plant site (land $100,000 and building $45,000)	145,000
5. Excavation costs for new building	35,000
6. Architect's fees on building plans	10,000
7. Accrued real estate taxes paid at time of purchase of real estate	2,000
8. Cost of parking lots and driveways	14,000
9. Cost of demolishing building to make land suitable for construction of new building	15,000
	$930,000

Credits

10. Proceeds from salvage of demolished building	$ 3,500

Instructions

Analyze the foregoing transactions using the following column headings. Insert the number of each transaction in the Item space, and insert the amounts in the appropriate columns. For amounts entered in the Other Accounts column, also indicate the account titles.

Totals
Land $162,500
Building $745,000

Item	Land	Building	Other Accounts

P10-2A In recent years, Juresic Transportation purchased three used buses. Because of frequent turnover in the accounting department, a different accountant selected the depreciation method for each bus, and various methods were selected. Information concerning the buses is summarized below.

Compute depreciation under different methods.

(SO 3)

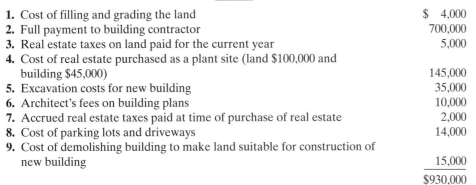

Bus	Acquired	Cost	Salvage Value	Useful Life in Years	Depreciation Method
1	1/1/08	$ 96,000	$ 6,000	5	Straight-line
2	1/1/08	120,000	10,000	4	Declining-balance
3	1/1/09	80,000	8,000	5	Units-of-activity

For the declining-balance method, the company uses the double-declining rate. For the units-of-activity method, total miles are expected to be 120,000. Actual miles of use in the first 3 years were: 2009, 24,000; 2010, 34,000; and 2011, 30,000.

Instructions

(a) Compute the amount of accumulated depreciation on each bus at December 31, 2010.

(b) If bus no. 2 was purchased on April 1 instead of January 1, what is the depreciation expense for this bus in (1) 2008 and (2) 2009?

(a) Bus 2, 2009, $90,000

P10-3A On January 1, 2010, Pele Company purchased the following two machines for use in its production process.

Compute depreciation under different methods.

(SO 3)

Machine A: The cash price of this machine was $38,000. Related expenditures included: sales tax $1,700, shipping costs $150, insurance during shipping $80, installation and testing costs $70, and $100 of oil and lubricants to be used with the machinery during its first year of operations. Pele estimates that the useful life of the machine is 5 years with a $5,000 salvage value remaining at the end of that time period. Assume that the straight-line method of depreciation is used.

Machine B: The recorded cost of this machine was $160,000. Pele estimates that the useful life of the machine is 4 years with a $10,000 salvage value remaining at the end of that time period.

Instructions

(a) Prepare the following for Machine A.

(1) The journal entry to record its purchase on January 1, 2010.

(2) The journal entry to record annual depreciation at December 31, 2010.

(b) Calculate the amount of depreciation expense that Pele should record for machine B each year of its useful life under the following assumptions.

(1) Pele uses the straight-line method of depreciation.

(2) Pele uses the declining-balance method. The rate used is twice the straight-line rate.

(3) Pele uses the units-of-activity method and estimates that the useful life of the machine is 125,000 units. Actual usage is as follows: 2010, 45,000 units; 2011, 35,000 units; 2012, 25,000 units; 2013, 20,000 units.

(c) Which method used to calculate depreciation on machine B reports the highest amount of depreciation expense in year 1 (2010)? The highest amount in year 4 (2013)? The highest total amount over the 4-year period?

Calculate revisions to depreciation expense.

(SO 3, 4)

P10-4A At the beginning of 2008, Lehman Company acquired equipment costing $90,000. It was estimated that this equipment would have a useful life of 6 years and a residual value of $9,000 at that time. The straight-line method of depreciation was considered the most appropriate to use with this type of equipment. Depreciation is to be recorded at the end of each year.

During 2010 (the third year of the equipment's life), the company's engineers reconsidered their expectations, and estimated that the equipment's useful life would probably be 7 years (in total) instead of 6 years. The estimated residual value was not changed at that time. However, during 2013 the estimated residual value was reduced to $5,000.

Instructions

Indicate how much depreciation expense should be recorded each year for this equipment, by completing the following table.

Year	Depreciation Expense	Accumulated Depreciation
2008		
2009		
2010		
2011		
2012		
2013		
2014		

2014 depreciation expense, $12,800

Journalize a series of equipment transactions related to purchase, sale, retirement, and depreciation.

(SO 3, 6, 9)

P10-5A At December 31, 2010, Jimenez Company reported the following as plant assets.

Land		$ 4,000,000
Buildings	$28,500,000	
Less: Accumulated depreciation—buildings	12,100,000	16,400,000
Equipment	48,000,000	
Less: Accumulated depreciation—equipment	5,000,000	43,000,000
Total plant assets		$63,400,000

During 2011, the following selected cash transactions occurred.

April 1 Purchased land for $2,130,000.

May 1 Sold equipment that cost $780,000 when purchased on January 1, 2007. The equipment was sold for $450,000.

June 1 Sold land purchased on June 1, 2001 for $1,500,000. The land cost $400,000.

July 1 Purchased equipment for $2,000,000.

Dec. 31 Retired equipment that cost $500,000 when purchased on December 31, 2001. No salvage value was received.

Instructions

(a) Journalize the above transactions. The company uses straight-line depreciation for buildings and equipment. The buildings are estimated to have a 50-year life and no salvage value. The equipment is estimated to have a 10-year useful life and no salvage value. Update depreciation on assets disposed of at the time of sale or retirement.

(b) Record adjusting entries for depreciation for 2011.

(c) Prepare the plant assets section of Jimenez's balance sheet at December 31, 2011.

(b) Depreciation Expense—
building $570,000;
equipment $4,772,000
(c) Total plant assets
$61,270,000

P10-6A   Puckett Co. has office furniture that cost $75,000 and that has been depreciated $50,000. Record the disposal under the following assumptions.

Record disposals.

(SO 6)

(a) It was scrapped as having no value.

(b) It was sold for $21,000.

(c) It was sold for $31,000.

P10-7A   The intangible assets section of Redeker Company at December 31, 2010, is presented below.

Prepare entries to record transactions related to acquisition and amortization of intangibles; prepare the intangible assets section.

(SO 8, 9)

Patent ($70,000 cost less $7,000 amortization)	$63,000
Franchise ($48,000 cost less $19,200 amortization)	28,800
Total	$91,800

The patent was acquired in January 2010 and has a useful life of 10 years. The franchise was acquired in January 2007 and also has a useful life of 10 years. The following cash transactions may have affected intangible assets during 2011.

Jan. 2   Paid $45,000 legal costs to successfully defend the patent against infringement by another company.

Jan.–June   Developed a new product, incurring $140,000 in research and development costs. A patent was granted for the product on July 1. Its useful life is equal to its legal life.

Sept. 1   Paid $50,000 to an extremely large defensive lineman to appear in commercials advertising the company's products. The commercials will air in September and October.

Oct. 1   Acquired a franchise for $100,000. The franchise has a useful life of 50 years.

(b) Amortization Expense—
Patents $12,000
Amortization Expense—
Franchise $5,300
(c) Total intangible assets
$219,500

Instructions

(a) Prepare journal entries to record the transactions above.

(b) Prepare journal entries to record the 2011 amortization expense.

(c) Prepare the intangible assets section of the balance sheet at December 31, 2011.

P10-8A   Due to rapid turnover in the accounting department, a number of transactions involving intangible assets were improperly recorded by the Thorne Company in 2010.

Prepare entries to correct errors made in recording and amortizing intangible assets.

(SO 8)

1. Thorne developed a new manufacturing process, incurring research and development costs of $136,000. The company also purchased a patent for $60,000. In early January, Thorne capitalized $196,000 as the cost of the patents. Patent amortization expense of $9,800 was recorded based on a 20-year useful life.

2. On July 1, 2010, Thorne purchased a small company and as a result acquired goodwill of $92,000. Thorne recorded a half-year's amortization in 2010, based on a 50-year life ($920 amortization). The goodwill has an indefinite life.

Instructions

Prepare all journal entries necessary to correct any errors made during 2010. Assume the books have not yet been closed for 2010.

1. R&D Exp. $136,000

P10-9A   Lebo Company and Ritter Corporation, two corporations of roughly the same size, are both involved in the manufacture of in-line skates. Each company depreciates its plant assets using the straight-line approach. An investigation of their financial statements reveals the following information.

Calculate and comment on asset turnover ratio.

(SO 9)

	Lebo Co.	Ritter Corp.
Net income	$ 800,000	$1,000,000
Sales	1,200,000	1,080,000
Average total assets	2,500,000	2,000,000
Average plant assets	1,800,000	1,000,000

Instructions

(a) For each company, calculate the asset turnover ratio.

(b) ━━━━━ Based on your calculations in part (a), comment on the relative effectiveness of the two companies in using their assets to generate sales and produce net income.

PROBLEMS: SET B

Determine acquisition costs of land and building.

(SO 1)

P10-1B Dewey Company was organized on January 1. During the first year of operations, the following plant asset expenditures and receipts were recorded in random order.

Debits

1. Accrued real estate taxes paid at time of purchase of real estate	$ 5,000
2. Real estate taxes on land paid for the current year	7,500
3. Full payment to building contractor	500,000
4. Excavation costs for new building	19,000
5. Cost of real estate purchased as a plant site (land $75,000 and building $25,000)	100,000
6. Cost of parking lots and driveways	18,000
7. Architect's fees on building plans	9,000
8. Installation cost of fences around property	6,000
9. Cost of demolishing building to make land suitable for construction of new building	17,000
	$681,500

Credit

10. Proceeds from salvage of demolished building	$ 3,500

Instructions

Analyze the foregoing tranactions using the following column headings. Insert the number of each transaction in the Item space, and insert the amounts in the appropriate columns. For amounts entered in the Other Accounts column, also indicate the account title.

Totals

Land $118,500
Building $528,000

Item	Land	Building	Other Accounts

Compute depreciation under different methods.

(SO 3)

P10-2B In recent years, Pablo Company purchased three machines. Because of heavy turnover in the accounting department, a different accountant was in charge of selecting the depreciation method for each machine, and each selected a different method. Information concerning the machines is summarized below.

Machine	Acquired	Cost	Salvage Value	Useful Life in Years	Depreciation Method
1	1/1/07	$105,000	$ 5,000	10	Straight-line
2	1/1/08	150,000	10,000	8	Declining-balance
3	11/1/10	100,000	15,000	6	Units-of-activity

For the declining-balance method, the company uses the double-declining rate. For the units-of-activity method, total machine hours are expected to be 25,000. Actual hours of use in the first 3 years were: 2010, 2,000; 2011, 4,500; and 2012, 5,500.

Instructions

(a) Machine 2, 2009, $28,125

(a) Compute the amount of accumulated depreciation on each machine at December 31, 2010.

(b) If machine 2 had been purchased on May 1 instead of January 1, what would be the depreciation expense for this machine in (1) 2008 and (2) 2009?

Compute depreciation under different methods.

(SO 3)

P10-3B On January 1, 2010, Arlo Company purchased the following two machines for use in its production process.

Machine A: The cash price of this machine was $55,000. Related expenditures included: sales tax $2,750, shipping costs $100, insurance during shipping $75, installation and testing costs $75, and $90 of oil and lubricants to be used with the machinery during its first year of operation. Arlo estimates that the useful life of the machine is 4 years with a $5,000 salvage value remaining at the end of that time period.

Machine B: The recorded cost of this machine was $100,000. Arlo estimates that the useful life of the machine is 4 years with a $10,000 salvage value remaining at the end of that time period.

Instructions

(a) Prepare the following for Machine A.

   (1) The journal entry to record its purchase on January 1, 2010.

   (2) The journal entry to record annual depreciation at December 31, 2010, assuming the straight-line method of depreciation is used.

(b) Calculate the amount of depreciation expense that Arlo should record for machine B each year of its useful life under the following assumption.

   (1) Arlo uses the straight-line method of depreciation.

   (2) Arlo uses the declining-balance method. The rate used is twice the straight-line rate.

   (3) Arlo uses the units-of-activity method and estimates the useful life of the machine is 25,000 units. Actual usage is as follows: 2010, 5,500 units; 2011, 7,000 units; 2012, 8,000 units; 2013, 4,500 units.

(c) Which method used to calculate depreciation on machine B reports the lowest amount of depreciation expense in year 1 (2010)? The lowest amount in year 4 (2013)? The lowest total amount over the 4-year period?

(a) (2) $13,250

P10-4B   At the beginning of 2008, Anfernee Company acquired equipment costing $200,000. It was estimated that this equipment would have a useful life of 6 years and a residual value of $20,000 at that time. The straight-line method of depreciation was considered the most appropriate to use with this type of equipment. Depreciation is to be recorded at the end of each year.

   During 2010 (the third year of the equipment's life), the company's engineers reconsidered their expectations, and estimated that the equipment's useful life would probably be 7 years (in total) instead of 6 years. The estimated residual value was not changed at that time. However, during 2013 the estimated residual value was reduced to $5,000.

Calculate revisions to depreciation expense.

(SO 3, 4)

Instructions

Indicate how much depreciation expense should be recorded for this equipment each year by completing the following table.

Year	Depreciation Expense	Accumulated Depreciation
2008		
2009		
2010		
2011		
2012		
2013		
2014		

2014 depreciation expense, $31,500

P10-5B   At December 31, 2010, Starkey Company reported the following as plant assets.

Land		$ 2,000,000
Buildings	$20,000,000	
Less: Accumulated depreciation—buildings	8,000,000	12,000,000
Equipment	30,000,000	
Less: Accumulated depreciation—equipment	4,000,000	26,000,000
Total plant assets		$40,000,000

Journalize a series of equipment transactions related to purchase, sale, retirement, and depreciation.

(SO 3, 6, 9)

During 2011, the following selected cash transactions occurred.

April 1   Purchased land for $1,200,000.

May 1   Sold equipment that cost $420,000 when purchased on January 1, 2007. The equipment was sold for $240,000.

June 1   Sold land purchased on June 1, 2001, for $1,000,000. The land cost $340,000.

July 1   Purchased equipment for $1,100,000.

Dec. 31   Retired equipment that cost $300,000 when purchased on December 31, 2001. No salvage value was received.

Instructions

(a) Journalize the above transactions. Starkey uses straight-line depreciation for buildings and equipment. The buildings are estimated to have a 50-year useful life and no salvage value.

The equipment is estimated to have a 10-year useful life and no salvage value. Update depreciation on assets disposed of at the time of sale or retirement.

(b) Record adjusting entries for depreciation for 2011.

(c) Prepare the plant assets section of Starkey's balance sheet at December 31, 2011.

P10-6B Bobby's has delivery equipment that cost $40,000 and that has been depreciated $26,000. Record the disposal under the following assumptions.

(a) It was scrapped as having no value.

(b) It was sold for $29,000.

(c) It was sold for $10,000.

P10-7B The intangible assets section of Time Company at December 31, 2010, is presented below.

Patent ($100,000 cost less $10,000 amortization)	$ 90,000
Copyright ($60,000 cost less $24,000 amortization)	36,000
Total	$126,600

The patent was acquired in January 2010 and has a useful life of 10 years. The copyright was acquired in January 2007 and also has a useful life of 10 years. The following cash transactions may have affected intangible assets during 2011.

Jan. 2 Paid $45,000 legal costs to successfully defend the patent against infringement by another company.

Jan.–June Developed a new product, incurring $230,000 in research and development costs. A patent was granted for the product on July 1. Its useful life is equal to its legal life.

Sept. 1 Paid $125,000 to an Xgames star to appear in commercials advertising the company's products. The commercials will air in September and October.

Oct. 1 Acquired a copyright for $200,000. The copyright has a useful life of 50 years.

Instructions

(a) Prepare journal entries to record the transactions above.

(b) Prepare journal entries to record the 2011 amortization expense for intangible assets.

(c) Prepare the intangible assets section of the balance sheet at December 31, 2011.

(d) Prepare the note to the financials on Time's intangibles as of December 31, 2011.

P10-8B Due to rapid turnover in the accounting department, a number of transactions involving intangible assets were improperly recorded by Wasp Company in 2010.

1. Wasp developed a new manufacturing process, incurring research and development costs of $110,000. The company also purchased a patent for $50,000. In early January, Wasp capitalized $160,000 as the cost of the patents. Patent amortization expense of $8,000 was recorded based on a 20-year useful life.

2. On July 1, 2010, Wasp purchased a small company and as a result acquired goodwill of $200,000. Wasp recorded a half-year's amortization in 2010, based on a 50-year life ($2,000 amortization). The goodwill has an indefinite life.

Instructions

Prepare all journal entries necessary to correct any errors made during 2010. Assume the books have not yet been closed for 2010.

P10-9B McLead Corporation and Gene Corporation, two corporations of roughly the same size, are both involved in the manufacture of canoes and sea kayaks. Each company depreciates its plant assets using the straight-line approach. An investigation of their financial statements reveals the following information.

	McLead Corp.	Gene Corp.
Net income	$ 300,000	$ 325,000
Sales	1,100,000	990,000
Average total assets	1,000,000	1,050,000
Average plant assets	750,000	770,000

Instructions

(a) For each company, calculate the asset turnover ratio.

(b) Based on your calculations in part (a), comment on the relative effectiveness of the two companies in using their assets to generate sales and produce net income.

PROBLEMS: SET C

Visit the book's companion website at **www.wiley.com/college/weygandt**, and choose the Student Companion site, to access Problem Set C.

COMPREHENSIVE PROBLEM: CHAPTERS 3 TO 10

Winterschid Company's trial balance at December 31, 2010, is presented below. All 2010 transactions have been recorded except for the items described below and on page 480.

	Debit	Credit
Cash	$ 28,000	
Accounts Receivable	36,800	
Notes Receivable	10,000	
Interest Receivable	–0–	
Merchandise Inventory	36,200	
Prepaid Insurance	3,600	
Land	20,000	
Building	150,000	
Equipment	60,000	
Patent	9,000	
Allowance for Doubtful Accounts		$ 500
Accumulated Depreciation—Building		50,000
Accumulated Depreciation—Equipment		24,000
Accounts Payable		27,300
Salaries Payable		–0–
Unearned Rent		6,000
Notes Payable (short-term)		11,000
Interest Payable		–0–
Notes Payable (long-term)		35,000
Winterschid, Capital		113,600
Winterschid, Drawing	12,000	
Sales		900,000
Interest Revenue		–0–
Rent Revenue		–0–
Gain on Disposal		–0–
Bad Debts Expense	–0–	
Cost of Goods Sold	630,000	
Depreciation Expense—Buildings	–0–	
Depreciation Expense—Equipment	–0–	
Insurance Expense	–0–	
Interest Expense	–0–	
Other Operating Expenses	61,800	
Amortization Expense—Patents	–0–	
Salaries Expense	110,000	
Total	$1,167,400	$1,167,400

Unrecorded transactions

1. On May 1, 2010, Winterschid purchased equipment for $13,200 plus sales taxes of $600 (all paid in cash).
2. On July 1, 2010, Winterschid sold for $3,500 equipment which originally cost $5,000. Accumulated depreciation on this equipment at January 1, 2010, was $1,800; 2010 depreciation prior to the sale of the equipment was $450.
3. On December 31, 2010, Winterschid sold for $9,000 on account inventory that cost $6,300.
4. Winterschid estimates that uncollectible accounts receivable at year-end is $4,000.
5. The note receivable is a one-year, 8% note dated April 1, 2010. No interest has been recorded.
6. The balance in prepaid insurance represents payment of a $3,600 6-month premium on September 1, 2010.

7. The building is being depreciated using the straight-line method over 30 years. The salvage value is $30,000.
8. The equipment owned prior to this year is being depreciated using the straight-line method over 5 years. The salvage value is 10% of cost.
9. The equipment purchased on May 1, 2010, is being depreciated using the straight-line method over 5 years, with a salvage value of $1,800.
10. The patent was acquired on January 1, 2010, and has a useful life of 10 years from that date.
11. Unpaid salaries at December 31, 2010, total $2,200.
12. The unearned rent of $6,000 was received on December 1, 2010, for 3 months rent.
13. Both the short-term and long-term notes payable are dated January 1, 2010, and carry a 9% interest rate. All interest is payable in the next 12 months.

Instructions

(a) Prepare journal entries for the transactions listed above.

(b) Totals $1,201,290

(b) Prepare an updated December 31, 2010, trial balance.

(c) Prepare a 2010 income statement and an owner's equity statement.

(d) Total assets $260,400

(d) Prepare a December 31, 2010, classified balance sheet.

CONTINUING COOKIE CHRONICLE

(Note: This is a continuation of the Cookie Chronicle from Chapters 1 through 9.)

CCC10 Natalie is also thinking of buying a van that will be used only for business. Natalie is concerned about the impact of the van's cost on her income statement and balance sheet. She has come to you for advice on calculating the van's depreciation.

Go to the book's companion website,
www.wiley.com/college/weygandt,
to see the completion of this problem.

BROADENING YOUR PERSPECTIVE

FINANCIAL REPORTING AND ANALYSIS

Financial Reporting Problem: PepsiCo, Inc.

BYP10-1 The financial statements and the Notes to Consolidated Financial Statements of PepsiCo, Inc. are presented in Appendix A.

Instructions

Refer to PepsiCo's financial statements and answer the following questions.

(a) What was the total cost and book value of property, plant, and equipment at December 29, 2007?

(b) What method or methods of depreciation are used by the company for financial reporting purposes?

(c) What was the amount of depreciation and amortization expense for each of the three years 2005–2007?

(d) Using the statement of cash flows, what is the amount of capital spending in 2007 and 2006?

(e) Where does the company disclose its intangible assets, and what types of intangibles did it have at December 29, 2007?

Comparative Analysis Problem: PepsiCo, Inc. vs. The Coca-Cola Company

BYP10-2 PepsiCo's financial statements are presented in Appendix A. Financial statements of The Coca-Cola Company are presented in Appendix B.

 PEPSICO

Instructions
(a) Compute the asset turnover ratio for each company for 2007.
(b) What conclusions concerning the efficiency of assets can be drawn from these data?

Exploring the Web

BYP10-3 A company's annual report identifies the amount of its plant assets and the depreciation method used.

Address: www.reportgallery.com, or go to **www.wiley.com/college/weygandt**

Steps
1. From Report Gallery Homepage, choose **Search by Alphabet**, and pick a letter.
2. Select a particular company.
3. Choose the most recent **Annual Report**.
4. Follow instructions below.

Instructions
(a) What is the name of the company?
(b) At fiscal year-end, what is the net amount of its plant assets?
(c) What is the accumulated depreciation?
(d) Which method of depreciation does the company use?

CRITICAL THINKING

Decision Making Across the Organization

BYP10-4 Reimer Company and Lingo Company are two proprietorships that are similar in many respects. One difference is that Reimer Company uses the straight-line method and Lingo Company uses the declining-balance method at double the straight-line rate. On January 2, 2008, both companies acquired the following depreciable assets.

Asset	Cost	Salvage Value	Useful Life
Building	$320,000	$20,000	40 years
Equipment	110,000	10,000	10 years

Including the appropriate depreciation charges, annual net income for the companies in the years 2008, 2009, and 2010 and total income for the 3 years were as follows.

	2008	2009	2010	Total
Reimer Company	$84,000	$88,400	$90,000	$262,400
Lingo Company	68,000	76,000	85,000	229,000

At December 31, 2010, the balance sheets of the two companies are similar except that Lingo Company has more cash than Reimer Company.
 Sally Vogts is interested in buying one of the companies. She comes to you for advice.

Instructions
With the class divided into groups, answer the following.

(a) Determine the annual and total depreciation recorded by each company during the 3 years.
(b) Assuming that Lingo Company also uses the straight-line method of depreciation instead of the declining-balance method as in (a), prepare comparative income data for the 3 years.
(c) Which company should Sally Vogts buy? Why?

Communication Activity

BYP10-5 The following was published with the financial statements to American Exploration Company.

AMERICAN EXPLORATION COMPANY
Notes to the Financial Statements

Property, Plant, and Equipment—The Company accounts for its oil and gas exploration and production activities using the successful efforts method of accounting. Under this method, acquisition costs for proved and unproved properties are capitalized when incurred.... The costs of drilling exploratory wells are capitalized pending determination of whether each well has discovered proved reserves. If proved reserves are not discovered, such drilling costs are charged to expense.... Depletion of the cost of producing oil and gas properties is computed on the units-of-activity method.

Instructions

Write a brief memo to your instructor discussing American Exploration Company's note regarding property, plant, and equipment. Your memo should address what is meant by the "successful efforts method" and "units-of-activity method."

Ethics Case

BYP10-6 Buster Container Company is suffering declining sales of its principal product, non-biodegradeable plastic cartons. The president, Dennis Harwood, instructs his controller, Shelly McGlone, to lengthen asset lives to reduce depreciation expense. A processing line of automated plastic extruding equipment, purchased for $3.1 million in January 2010, was originally estimated to have a useful life of 8 years and a salvage value of $300,000. Depreciation has been recorded for 2 years on that basis. Dennis wants the estimated life changed to 12 years total, and the straight-line method continued. Shelly is hesitant to make the change, believing it is unethical to increase net income in this manner. Dennis says, "Hey, the life is only an estimate, and I've heard that our competition uses a 12-year life on their production equipment."

Instructions

(a) Who are the stakeholders in this situation?

(b) Is the change in asset life unethical, or is it simply a good business practice by an astute president?

(c) What is the effect of Dennis Harwood's proposed change on income before taxes in the year of change?

 ## "All About You" Activity

BYP10-7 Both the "All About You" story and the Feature Story at the beginning of the chapter discussed the company Rent-A-Wreck. Note that the tradename Rent-A-Wreck is a very important asset to the company, as it creates immediate product identification. As indicated in the chapter, companies invest substantial sums to ensure that their product is well-known to the consumer. Test your knowledge of who owns some famous brands and their impact on the financial statements.

Instructions

(a) Provide an answer to the five multiple-choice questions below.

    (1) Which company owns both Taco Bell and Pizza Hut?

        (a) McDonald's.   **(c)** Yum Brands.

        (b) CKE.   **(d)** Wendy's.

    (2) Dairy Queen belongs to:

        (a) Breyer.   **(c)** GE.

        (b) Berkshire Hathaway.   **(d)** The Coca-Cola Company.

(3) Phillip Morris, the cigarette maker, is owned by:
- (a) Altria.
- (b) GE.
- (c) Boeing.
- (d) ExxonMobil.

(4) AOL, a major Internet provider, belongs to:
- (a) Microsoft.
- (b) Cisco.
- (c) NBC.
- (d) Time Warner.

(5) ESPN, the sports broadcasting network, is owned by:
- (a) Procter & Gamble.
- (b) Altria.
- (c) Walt Disney.
- (d) The Coca-Cola Company.

(b) How do you think the value of these brands is reported on the appropriate company's balance sheet?

Answers to Insight and Accounting Across the Organization Questions

p. 441 Many U.S. Firms Use Leases

Q: Why might airline managers choose to lease rather than purchase their planes?

A: *The reasons for leasing include favorable tax treatment, better financing options, increased flexibility, reduced risk of obsolescence, and low airline income.*

p. 456 ESPN Wins Monday Night Football Franchise

Q: How should ESPN account for the $1.1 billion per year franchise fee?

A: *Since this is an annual franchise fee, ESPN should expense it each year, rather than capitalizing and amortizing it.*

Authors' Comments on *All About You: Buying a Wreck of Your Own* (p. 460)

As the data in the box suggest, this decision can have significant implications for your personal budget. For many college students, vehicle costs are among their biggest expenses—and vehicle expenses often offer the greatest opportunities for savings. But for many people their vehicle choice is not just about how to get around. Some view their car as an expression of their personality. That said, many people simply don't realize just how much this particular expression of their personality is actually costing them.

You should approach this decision using the skills you have acquired in your business studies. Evaluate your transportation needs, collect information about all of your alternatives, and understand exactly what the real costs are of each. For example, everyone knows that the original purchase price of a new car is higher than a used car, but few people stop to consider the fact that insurance costs and annual motor vehicle costs on a new vehicle are also much higher.

We cannot tell you whether a new or used car is right for you, but we do hope that we have convinced you to carefully consider all aspects of the financial implications of your decision the next time you shop for new wheels. In later chapters we will provide you with additional tools to help you evaluate this decision.

Answers to Self-Study Questions

1. d **2.** b **3.** d **4.** d **5.** b **6.** b **7.** d **8.** d **9.** a **10.** c **11.** d **12.** b **13.** c **14.** c ***15.** a ***16.** d

Chapter 11

Current Liabilities and Payroll Accounting

STUDY OBJECTIVES

After studying this chapter, you should be able to:

1 Explain a current liability, and identify the major types of current liabilities.

2 Describe the accounting for notes payable.

3 Explain the accounting for other current liabilities.

4 Explain the financial statement presentation and analysis of current liabilities.

5 Describe the accounting and disclosure requirements for contingent liabilities.

6 Compute and record the payroll for a pay period.

7 Describe and record employer payroll taxes.

8 Discuss the objectives of internal control for payroll.

✓ *The Navigator*

✓ *The Navigator*

Scan **Study Objectives**

Read **Feature Story**

Read **Preview**

Read text and answer **DO IT!**
p. 489   p. 494   p. 501   p. 505

Work **Comprehensive DO IT!** p. 507

Review **Summary of Study Objectives**

Answer **Self-Study Questions**

Complete **Assignments**

Feature Story

FINANCING HIS DREAMS

What would you do if you had a great idea for a new product, but couldn't come up with the cash to get the business off the ground? Small businesses often cannot attract investors. Nor can they obtain traditional debt financing through bank loans or bond issuances. Instead, they often resort to unusual, and costly, forms of nontraditional financing.

Such was the case for Wilbert Murdock. Murdock grew up in a New York housing project, and always had great ambitions. This ambitious spirit led him

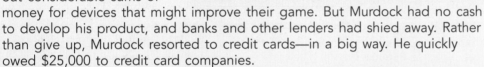

into some business ventures that failed: a medical diagnostic tool, a device to eliminate carpal-tunnel syndrome, custom-designed sneakers, and a device to keep people from falling asleep while driving.

Another idea was computerized golf clubs that analyze a golfer's swing and provide immediate feedback. Murdock saw great potential in the idea: Many golfers are willing to shell out considerable sums of money for devices that might improve their game. But Murdock had no cash to develop his product, and banks and other lenders had shied away. Rather than give up, Murdock resorted to credit cards—in a big way. He quickly owed $25,000 to credit card companies.

While funding a business with credit cards might sound unusual, it isn't. A recent study found that one-third of businesses with fewer than 20 employees financed at least part of their operations with credit cards. As Murdock explained, credit cards are an appealing way to finance a start-up because "credit-card companies don't care how the money is spent." However, they do care how they are paid. And so Murdock faced high interest charges and a barrage of credit card collection letters.

Murdock's debt forced him to sacrifice nearly everything in order to keep his business afloat. His car stopped running, he barely had enough money to buy food, and he lived and worked out of a dimly lit apartment in his mother's basement. Through it all he tried to maintain a positive spirit, joking that, if he becomes successful, he might some day get to appear in an American Express commercial.

Source: Rodney Ho, "Banking on Plastic: To Finance a Dream, Many Entrepreneurs Binge on Credit Cards," *Wall Street Journal*, March 9, 1998, p. A1.

✓ The Navigator

Inside Chapter 11...

Inventor-entrepreneur Wilbert Murdock, as you can tell from the Feature Story, had to use multiple credit cards to finance his business ventures. Murdock's credit card debts would be classified as *current liabilities* because they are due every month. Yet by making minimal payments and paying high interest each month, Murdock used this credit source long-term. Some credit card balances remain outstanding for years as they accumulate interest.

Earlier, we defined liabilities as creditors' claims on total assets and as existing debts and obligations. These claims, debts, and obligations must be settled or paid at some time **in the future** by the transfer of assets or services. The future date on which they are due or payable (maturity date) is a significant feature of liabilities. This "future date" feature gives rise to two basic classifications of liabilities: (1) current liabilities and (2) long-term liabilities. We will explain current liabilities, along with payroll accounting, in this chapter. We will explain long-term liabilities in Chapter 15.

The content and organization of Chapter 11 are as follows.

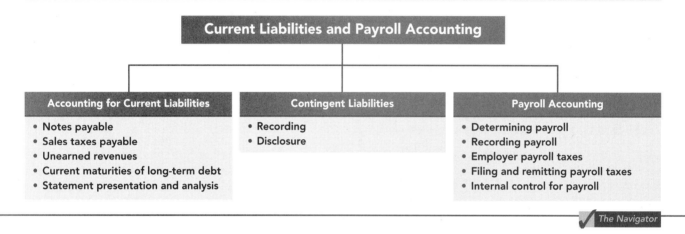

Current Liabilities and Payroll Accounting

Accounting for Current Liabilities	Contingent Liabilities	Payroll Accounting
• Notes payable	• Recording	• Determining payroll
• Sales taxes payable	• Disclosure	• Recording payroll
• Unearned revenues		• Employer payroll taxes
• Current maturities of long-term debt		• Filing and remitting payroll taxes
• Statement presentation and analysis		• Internal control for payroll

✓ *The Navigator*

ACCOUNTING FOR CURRENT LIABILITIES

STUDY OBJECTIVE 1

Explain a current liability, and identify the major types of current liabilities.

As explained in Chapter 4, a **current liability** is a debt with two key features: (1) The company reasonably expects to pay the debt from existing current assets or through the creation of other current liabilities. (2) The company will pay the debt within one year or the operating cycle, whichever is longer. Debts that do not meet **both criteria** are classified as long-term liabilities. Most companies pay current liabilities within one year out of current assets, rather than by creating other liabilities.

Companies must carefully monitor the relationship of current liabilities to current assets. This relationship is critical in evaluating a company's short-term debt-paying ability. A company that has more current liabilities than current assets may not be able to meet its current obligations when they become due.

Current liabilities include notes payable, accounts payable, and unearned revenues. They also include accrued liabilities such as taxes, salaries and wages, and interest payable. In previous chapters we explained the entries for accounts payable and adjusting entries for some current liabilities. In the following sections, we discuss other types of current liabilities.

STUDY OBJECTIVE 2

Describe the accounting for notes payable.

Notes Payable

Companies record obligations in the form of written promissory notes, called **notes payable**. Notes payable are often used instead of accounts payable because they give the lender formal proof of the obligation in case legal remedies are needed to collect the debt. Notes payable usually require the borrower to pay interest. Companies frequently issue them to meet short-term financing needs.

Notes are issued for varying periods. **Those due for payment within one year of the balance sheet date are usually classified as current liabilities.**

To illustrate the accounting for notes payable, assume that First National Bank agrees to lend $100,000 on March 1, 2010, if Cole Williams Co. signs a $100,000, 12%, four-month note. With an interest-bearing promissory note, the amount of assets received upon issuance of the note generally equals the note's face value. Cole Williams Co. therefore will receive $100,000 cash and will make the following journal entry.

Mar. 1	Cash	100,000	
	Notes Payable		100,000
	(To record issuance of 12%, 4-month note to First National Bank)		

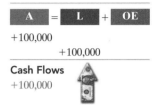

A = L + OE
+100,000
     +100,000

Cash Flows
+100,000

Interest accrues over the life of the note, and the company must periodically record that accrual. If Cole Williams Co. prepares financial statements on June 30, it makes an adjusting entry at June 30 to recognize interest expense and interest payable of $4,000 ($100,000 × 12% × 4/12). Illustration 11-1 shows the formula for computing interest, and its application to Cole Williams Co.'s note.

Face Value of Note	×	Annual Interest Rate	×	Time in Terms of One Year	=	Interest
$100,000	×	12%	×	4/12	=	**$4,000**

Illustration 11-1
Formula for computing interest

Cole Williams makes an adjusting entry as follows:

June 30	Interest Expense	4,000	
	Interest Payable		4,000
	(To accrue interest for 4 months on First National Bank note)		

A = L + OE
           −4,000 Exp
    +4,000

Cash Flows
no effect

In the June 30 financial statements, the current liabilities section of the balance sheet will show notes payable $100,000 and interest payable $4,000. In addition, the company will report interest expense of $4,000 under "Other expenses and losses" in the income statement. If Cole Williams Co. prepared financial statements monthly, the adjusting entry at the end of each month would have been $1,000 ($100,000 × 12% × 1/12).

At maturity (July 1, 2010), Cole Williams Co. must pay the face value of the note ($100,000) plus $4,000 interest ($100,000 × 12% × 4/12). It records payment of the note and accrued interest as shown below.

July 1	Notes Payable	100,000	
	Interest Payable	4,000	
	Cash		104,000
	(To record payment of First National Bank interest-bearing note and accrued interest at maturity)		

A = L + OE
        −100,000
        −4,000
−104,000

Cash Flows
−104,000

Sales Taxes Payable

As a consumer, you know that many of the products you purchase at retail stores are subject to sales taxes. Many states also are now collecting sales taxes on purchases made on the Internet. Sales taxes are expressed as a stated percentage of the sales price. The retailer collects the tax from the

STUDY OBJECTIVE 3
Explain the accounting for other current liabilities.

customer when the sale occurs. Periodically (usually monthly), the retailer remits the collections to the state's department of revenue.

Under most state sales tax laws, the selling company must ring up separately on the cash register the amount of the sale and the amount of the sales tax collected. (Gasoline sales are a major exception.) The company then uses the cash register readings to credit Sales and Sales Taxes Payable. For example, if the March 25 cash register reading for Cooley Grocery shows sales of $10,000 and sales taxes of $600 (sales tax rate of 6%), the journal entry is:

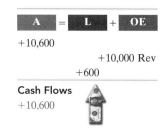

+10,600

+10,000 Rev
+600

Cash Flows
+10,600

Mar. 25	Cash	10,600	
	Sales		10,000
	Sales Taxes Payable		600
	(To record daily sales and sales taxes)		

When the company remits the taxes to the taxing agency, it debits Sales Taxes Payable and credits Cash. The company does not report sales taxes as an expense. It simply forwards to the government the amount paid by the customers. Thus, Cooley Grocery serves only as a **collection agent** for the taxing authority.

Sometimes companies do not ring up sales taxes separately on the cash register. To determine the amount of sales in such cases, divide total receipts by 100% plus the sales tax percentage. To illustrate, assume that in the above example Cooley Grocery rings up total receipts of $10,600. The receipts from the sales are equal to the sales price (100%) plus the tax percentage (6% of sales), or 1.06 times the sales total. We can compute the sales amount as follows.

$$\$10,600 \div 1.06 = \$10,000$$

HELPFUL HINT

Alternatively, Cooley could find the tax by multiplying sales by the sales tax rate ($10,000 × .06).

Thus, Cooley Grocery could find the sales tax amount it must remit to the state ($600) by subtracting sales from total receipts ($10,600 − $10,000).

Unearned Revenues

A magazine publisher, such as Sports Illustrated, receives customers' checks when they order magazines. An airline company, such as American Airlines, receives cash when it sells tickets for future flights. Through these transactions, both companies have incurred **unearned revenues**—revenues that are received before the company delivers goods or provides services. How do companies account for unearned revenues?

1. When a company receives the advance payment, it debits Cash, and credits a current liability account identifying the source of the unearned revenue.

2. When the company earns the revenue, it debits the Unearned Revenue account, and credits an earned revenue account.

To illustrate, assume that Superior University sells 10,000 season football tickets at $50 each for its five-game home schedule. The university makes the following entry for the sale of season tickets:

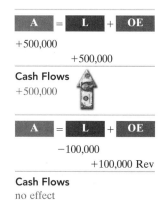

+500,000

+500,000

Cash Flows
+500,000

Aug. 6	Cash	500,000	
	Unearned Football Ticket Revenue		500,000
	(To record sale of 10,000 season tickets)		

As the school completes each of the five home games, it earns one-fifth of the revenue. The following entry records the revenue earned.

−100,000

+100,000 Rev

Cash Flows
no effect

Sept. 7	Unearned Football Ticket Revenue	100,000	
	Football Ticket Revenue		100,000
	(To record football ticket revenue earned)		

Organizations report any balance in an unearned revenue account (in Unearned Football Ticket Revenue, for example) as a current liability in the balance sheet.

As they earn the revenue, a transfer from unearned revenue to earned revenue occurs. Unearned revenue is material for some companies. In the airline industry, for example, tickets sold for future flights represent almost 30% of total current liabilities. At United Air Lines, unearned ticket revenue is its second largest current liability, recently amounting to over $1.6 billion.

Illustration 11-2 shows specific unearned and earned revenue accounts used in selected types of businesses.

Type of Business	Account Title	
	Unearned Revenue	**Earned Revenue**
Airline	Unearned Passenger Ticket Revenue	Passenger Revenue
Magazine publisher	Unearned Subscription Revenue	Subscription Revenue
Hotel	Unearned Rental Revenue	Rental Revenue
Insurance company	Unearned Premium Revenue	Premium Revenue

Illustration 11-2
Unearned and earned revenue accounts

Current Maturities of Long-Term Debt

Companies often have a portion of long-term debt that comes due in the current year. That amount is considered a current liability. For example, assume that Wendy Construction issues a five-year interest-bearing $25,000 note on January 1, 2010. Each January 1, starting January 1, 2011, $5,000 of the note is due to be paid. When Wendy Construction prepares financial statements on December 31, 2010, it should report $5,000 as a current liability. It would report the remaining $20,000 on the note as a long-term liability. Current maturities of long-term debt are often termed **long-term debt due within one year**.

It is not necessary to prepare an adjusting entry to recognize the current maturity of long-term debt. The company will recognize the proper statement classification of each balance sheet account when it prepares the balance sheet.

DO IT!

You and several classmates are studying for the next accounting examination. They ask you to answer the following questions.

CURRENT LIABILITIES

1. If cash is borrowed on a $50,000, 6-month, 12% note on September 1, how much interest expense would be incurred by December 31?
2. How is the sales tax amount determined when the cash register total includes sales taxes?
3. If $15,000 is collected in advance on November 1 for 3-months' rent, what amount of rent revenue is earned by December 31?

action plan

✔ Use the interest formula: Face value of note × Annual interest rate × Time in terms of one year.

✔ Divide total receipts by 100% plus the tax rate to determine sales; then subtract sales from the total receipts.

✔ Determine what fraction of the total unearned rent was earned this year.

Solution

1. $50,000 × 12% × 4/12 = $2,000
2. First, divide the total cash register receipts by 100% plus the sales tax percentage to find the sales amount. Second, subtract the sales amount from the total cash register receipts to determine the sales taxes.
3. $15,000 × 2/3 = $10,000

Related exercise material: **BE11-2, BE11-3, BE11-4, E11-1, E11-2, E11-3, E11-4, and DO IT! 11-1.**

The Navigator ✔

Statement Presentation and Analysis

PRESENTATION

As indicated in Chapter 4, current liabilities are the first category under liabilities on the balance sheet. Each of the principal types of current liabilities is listed separately. In addition, companies disclose the terms of notes payable and other key information about the individual items in the notes to the financial statements.

Companies seldom list current liabilities in the order of liquidity. The reason is that varying maturity dates may exist for specific obligations such as notes payable. A more common method of presenting current liabilities is to list them by **order of magnitude**, with the largest ones first. Or, as a matter of custom, many companies show notes payable first, and then accounts payable, regardless of amount. Then the remaining current liabilities are listed by magnitude. (*Use this approach in your homework.*) The following adapted excerpt from the balance sheet of Caterpillar Inc. illustrates its order of presentation.

Illustration 11-3
Balance sheet presentation of current liabilities

CATERPILLAR®

CATERPILLAR INC.
Balance Sheet
December 31, 2007
(in millions)

Assets

Current assets	$25,477
Property, plant and equipment (net)	9,997
Other long-term assets	20,658
Total assets	$56,132

Liabilities and Stockholders' Equity

Current liabilities	
Short-term borrowings (notes payable)	$ 5,468
Accounts payable	4,723
Accrued expenses	3,178
Accrued wages, salaries, and employee benefits	1,126
Customer advances	1,442
Dividends payable	225
Other current liabilities	951
Long-term debt due within one year	5,132
Total current liabilities	22,245
Noncurrent liabilities	25,004
Total liabilities	47,249
Stockholders' equity	8,883
Total liabilities and stockholders' equity	$56,132

ANALYSIS

Use of current and noncurrent classifications makes it possible to analyze a company's liquidity. **Liquidity** refers to the ability to pay maturing obligations and meet unexpected needs for cash. The relationship of current assets to current liabilities is critical in analyzing liquidity. We can express this relationship as a dollar amount (working capital) and as a ratio (the current ratio).

The excess of current assets over current liabilities is **working capital**. Illustration 11-4 shows the formula for the computation of Caterpillar's working capital (dollar amounts in millions).

$$\underset{\text{Assets}}{\text{Current}} - \underset{\text{Liabilities}}{\text{Current}} = \underset{\text{Capital}}{\text{Working}}$$

$$\$25,477 - \$22,245 = \$3,232$$

Illustration 11-4
Working capital formula and computation

As an absolute dollar amount, working capital offers limited informational value. For example, $1 million of working capital may be far more than needed for a small company but be inadequate for a large corporation. Also, $1 million of working capital may be adequate for a company at one time but inadequate at another time.

The **current ratio** permits us to compare the liquidity of different-sized companies and of a single company at different times. The current ratio is calculated as current assets divided by current liabilities. The formula for this ratio is illustrated below, along with its computation using Caterpillar's current asset and current liability data (dollar amounts in millions).

$$\underset{\text{Assets}}{\text{Current}} \div \underset{\text{Liabilities}}{\text{Current}} = \underset{\text{Ratio}}{\text{Current}}$$

$$\$25,477 \div \$22,245 = 1.15:1$$

Illustration 11-5
Current ratio formula and computation

Historically, companies and analysts considered a current ratio of 2:1 to be the standard for a good credit rating. In recent years, however, many healthy companies have maintained ratios well below 2:1 by improving management of their current assets and liabilities. Caterpillar's ratio of 1.15:1 is adequate but certainly below the standard of 2:1.

CONTINGENT LIABILITIES

With notes payable, interest payable, accounts payable, and sales taxes payable, we know that an obligation to make a payment exists. But suppose that your company is involved in a dispute with the Internal Revenue Service (IRS) over the amount of its income tax liability. Should you report the disputed amount as a liability on the balance sheet? Or suppose your company is involved in a lawsuit which, if you lose, might result in bankruptcy. How should you report this major contingency? The answers to these questions are difficult, because these liabilities are dependent—contingent—upon some future event. In other words, a **contingent liability** is a potential liability that may become an actual liability in the future.

STUDY OBJECTIVE 5

Describe the accounting and disclosure requirements for contingent liabilities.

How should companies report contingent liabilities? They use the following guidelines:

1. If the contingency is **probable** (if it is *likely* to occur) **and** the amount can be **reasonably estimated**, the liability should be recorded in the accounts.

2. If the contingency is only **reasonably possible** (if it *could* happen), then it needs to be disclosed only in the notes that accompany the financial statements.

3. If the contingency is **remote** (if it is *unlikely* to occur), it need not be recorded or disclosed.

ACCOUNTING ACROSS THE ORGANIZATION

Contingencies: How Big Are They?

Contingent liabilities abound in the real world. Consider the following: Manville Corp. filed for bankruptcy when it was hit by billions of dollars in asbestos product-liability claims. Companies having multiple toxic waste sites are faced with cleanup costs that average $10 to $30 million and can reach as high as $500 million depending on the type of waste. For life and health insurance companies and their stockholders, the cost of diseases such as diabetes, Alzheimer's, and AIDS is like an iceberg: Everyone wonders how big such costs really are and what damage they might do in the future. And frequent-flyer programs are so popular that airlines at one time owed participants more than 3 million round-trip domestic tickets. That's enough to fly at least 5.4 billion miles—free for the passengers, but at what future cost to the airlines?

 Why do you think most companies disclose, but do not record, contingent liabilities?

Recording a Contingent Liability

Product warranties are an example of a contingent liability that companies should record in the accounts. Warranty contracts result in future costs that companies may incur in replacing defective units or repairing malfunctioning units. Generally, a manufacturer, such as Black & Decker, knows that it will incur some warranty costs. From prior experience with the product, the company usually can reasonably estimate the anticipated cost of servicing (honoring) the warranty.

The accounting for warranty costs is based on the matching principle. **The estimated cost of honoring product warranty contracts should be recognized as an expense in the period in which the sale occurs.** To illustrate, assume that in 2010 Denson Manufacturing Company sells 10,000 washers and dryers at an average price of $600 each. The selling price includes a one-year warranty on parts. Denson expects that 500 units (5%) will be defective and that warranty repair costs will average $80 per unit. In 2010, the company honors warranty contracts on 300 units, at a total cost of $24,000.

At December 31, it is necessary to accrue the estimated warranty costs on the 2010 sales. Denson computes the estimated warranty liability as follows.

Illustration 11-6
Computation of estimated product warranty liability

Number of units sold	10,000
Estimated rate of defective units	× 5%
Total estimated defective units	500
Average warranty repair cost	× $80
Estimated product warranty liability	**$40,000**

The company makes the following adjusting entry.

A	=	L	+	OE
				−40,000 Exp
		+40,000		

Cash Flows
no effect

Dec. 31	Warranty Expense	40,000	
	Estimated Warranty Liability		40,000
	(To accrue estimated warranty costs)		

Denson records those repair costs incurred in 2010 to honor warranty contracts on 2010 sales as shown below.

Jan. 1–	Estimated Warranty Liability	24,000	
Dec. 31	Repair Parts		24,000
	(To record honoring of 300 warranty contracts on 2010 sales)		

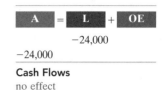

A	=	L	+	OE
		−24,000		
−24,000				

Cash Flows
no effect

The company reports warranty expense of $40,000 under selling expenses in the income statement. It classifies estimated warranty liability of $16,000 ($40,000 − $24,000) as a current liability on the balance sheet.

In the following year, Denson should debit to Estimated Warranty Liability all expenses incurred in honoring warranty contracts on 2010 sales. To illustrate, assume that the company replaces 20 defective units in January 2011, at an average cost of $80 in parts and labor. The summary entry for the month of January 2011 is:

Jan. 31	Estimated Warranty Liability	1,600	
	Repair Parts		1,600
	(To record honoring of 20 warranty contracts on 2010 sales)		

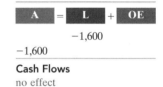

A	=	L	+	OE
		−1,600		
−1,600				

Cash Flows
no effect

Disclosure of Contingent Liabilities

When it is probable that a company will incur a contingent liability but it cannot reasonably estimate the amount, or when the contingent liability is only reasonably possible, only disclosure of the contingency is required. Examples of contingencies that may require disclosure are pending or threatened lawsuits and assessment of additional income taxes pending an IRS audit of the tax return.

The disclosure should identify the nature of the item and, if known, the amount of the contingency and the expected outcome of the future event. Disclosure is usually accomplished through a note to the financial statements, as illustrated by the following.

YAHOO! INC.
Notes to the Financial Statements

Contingencies. From time to time, third parties assert patent infringement claims against the company. Currently the company is engaged in several lawsuits regarding patent issues and has been notified of a number of other potential patent disputes. In addition, from time to time the company is subject to other legal proceedings and claims in the ordinary course of business, including claims for infringement of trademarks, copyrights and other intellectual property rights.... The Company does not believe, based on current knowledge, that any of the foregoing legal proceedings or claims are likely to have a material adverse effect on the financial position, results of operations or cash flows.

Illustration 11-7
Disclosure of contingent liability

The required disclosure for contingencies is a good example of the use of the full-disclosure principle. The **full-disclosure principle** requires that companies disclose all circumstances and events that would make a difference to financial statement users. Some important financial information, such as contingencies, is not easily reported in the financial statements. Reporting information on contingencies in the notes to the financial statements will help investors be aware of events that can affect the financial health of a company.

DO IT!

CURRENT LIABILITIES

Lepid Company has the following account balances at December 31, 2010.

Notes payable ($80,000 due after 12/31/11)	$200,000
Unearned revenue	75,000
Other long-term debt ($30,000 due in 2011)	150,000
Salaries payable	22,000
Other accrued expenses	15,000
Accounts payable	100,000

In addition, Lepid is involved in a lawsuit. Legal counsel feels it is probable Lepid will pay damages of $38,000 in 2011.

(a) Prepare the current liability section of Lepid's December 31, 2010, balance sheet.

(b) Lepid's current assets are $504,000. Compute Lepid's working capital and current ratio.

action plan

✔ Determine which liabilities will be paid within one year or the operating cycle and include those as current liabilities.

✔ If the contingent liability is probable and reasonably estimable, include it as a current liability.

✔ Use the formula for working capital: Current assets − Current liabilities.

✔ Use the formula for the current ratio: Current assets ÷ Current liabilities.

Solution

(a) Current liabilities

Notes payable due in 2011	$120,000
Accounts payable	100,000
Unearned revenue	75,000
Lawsuit liability	38,000
Salaries payable	22,000
Other accrued expenses	15,000
Long-term debt due within one year	30,000
Total current liabilities	$400,000

(b) Working capital = Current assets − Current liabilities = $504,000 − $400,000 = $104,000

Current ratio: Current assets ÷ Current liabilities = $504,000 ÷ $400,000 = 1.26:1

Related exercise material: **BE11-6, E11-5, E11-6, E11-7, E11-8, and DO IT! 11-2.**

 The Navigator

PAYROLL ACCOUNTING

Payroll and related fringe benefits often make up a large percentage of current liabilities. Employee compensation is often the most significant expense that a company incurs. For example, Costco recently reported total employees of 103,000 and labor and fringe benefits costs which approximated 70% of the company's total cost of operations.

Payroll accounting involves more than paying employees' wages. Companies are required by law to maintain payroll records for each employee, to file and pay payroll taxes, and to comply with state and federal tax laws related to employee compensation.

The term "payroll" pertains to both salaries and wages. Managerial, administrative, and sales personnel are generally paid **salaries**. Salaries are often expressed in terms of a specified amount per month or per year rather than an hourly rate. Store clerks, factory employees, and manual laborers are normally paid **wages**. Wages are based on a rate per hour or on a piecework basis (such as per unit of product). Frequently, people use the terms "salaries" and "wages" interchangeably.

The term "payroll" does not apply to payments made for services of professionals such as certified public accountants, attorneys, and architects. Such professionals are independent contractors rather than salaried employees. Payments to them are called **fees**. This distinction is important because government regulations relating to the payment and reporting of payroll taxes apply only to employees.

Determining the Payroll

Determining the payroll involves computing three amounts: (1) gross earnings, (2) payroll deductions, and (3) net pay.

GROSS EARNINGS

Gross earnings is the total compensation earned by an employee. It consists of wages or salaries, plus any bonuses and commissions.

Companies determine total **wages** for an employee by multiplying the hours worked by the hourly rate of pay. In addition to the hourly pay rate, most companies are required by law to pay hourly workers a minimum of 1½ times the regular hourly rate for overtime work in excess of eight hours per day or 40 hours per week. In addition, many employers pay overtime rates for work done at night, on weekends, and on holidays.

For example, assume that Michael Jordan, an employee of Academy Company, worked 44 hours for the weekly pay period ending January 14. His regular wage is $12 per hour. For any hours in excess of 40, the company pays at one-and-a-half times the regular rate. Academy computes Jordan's gross earnings (total wages) as follows.

Type of Pay	Hours	×	Rate	=	Gross Earnings
Regular	40	×	$12	=	$480
Overtime	4	×	18	=	72
Total wages					**$552**

Illustration 11-8
Computation of total wages

This computation assumes that Jordan receives 1½ times his regular hourly rate ($12 × 1.5) for his overtime hours. Union contracts often require that overtime rates be as much as twice the regular rates.

An employee's **salary** is generally based on a monthly or yearly rate. The company then prorates these rates to its payroll periods (e.g., biweekly or monthly). Most executive and administrative positions are salaried. Federal law does not require overtime pay for employees in such positions.

Many companies have bonus agreements for employees. One survey found that over 94% of the largest U.S. manufacturing companies offer annual bonuses to key executives. Bonus arrangements may be based on such factors as increased sales or net income. Companies may pay bonuses in cash and/or by granting employees the opportunity to acquire shares of company stock at favorable prices (called stock option plans).

ETHICS NOTE
Bonuses often reward outstanding individual performance, but successful corporations also need considerable teamwork. A challenge is to motivate individuals while preventing an unethical employee from taking another's idea for his or her own advantage.

PAYROLL DEDUCTIONS

As anyone who has received a paycheck knows, gross earnings are usually very different from the amount actually received. The difference is due to payroll deductions.

Payroll deductions may be mandatory or voluntary. Mandatory deductions are required by law and consist of FICA taxes and income taxes. Voluntary deductions are at the option of the employee. Illustration 11-9 (page 496) summarizes common types of payroll deductions. Such deductions do not result in payroll tax expense to the employer. The employer is merely a collection agent, and subsequently transfers the deducted amounts to the government and designated recipients.

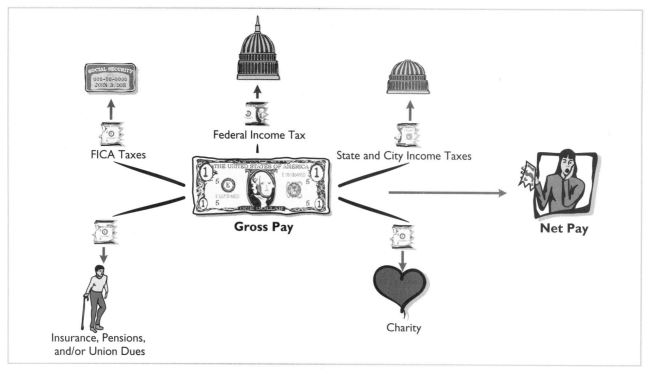

Illustration 11-9
Payroll deductions

FICA Taxes. In 1937 Congress enacted the Federal Insurance Contribution Act (FICA). **FICA taxes are designed to provide workers with supplemental retirement, employment disability, and medical benefits.** In 1965, Congress extended benefits to include Medicare for individuals over 65 years of age. The benefits are financed by a tax levied on employees' earnings. FICA taxes are commonly referred to as **Social Security taxes**.

Congress sets the tax rate and the tax base for FICA taxes. When FICA taxes were first imposed, the rate was 1% on the first $3,000 of gross earnings, or a maximum of $30 per year. The rate and base have changed dramatically since that time! In 2008, the rate was 7.65% (6.2% Social Security plus 1.45% Medicare) on the first $102,000 of gross earnings for each employee.[1] For purpose of illustration in this chapter, we will assume a rate of 8% on the first $100,000 of gross earnings, or a maximum of $8,000. Using the 8% rate, the FICA withholding for Jordan for the weekly pay period ending January 14 is $44.16 ($552 × 8%).

Income Taxes. Under the U.S. pay-as-you-go system of federal income taxes, employers are required to withhold income taxes from employees each pay period. Three variables determine the amount to be withheld: (1) the employee's gross earnings; (2) the number of allowances claimed by the employee; and (3) the length of the pay period. The number of allowances claimed typically includes the employee, his or her spouse, and other dependents.

Withholding tables furnished by the Internal Revenue Service indicate the amount of income tax to be withheld. Withholding amounts are based on gross wages and the number of allowances claimed. Separate tables are provided for weekly, biweekly, semimonthly, and monthly pay periods. Illustration 11-10 shows

---

[1]The Medicare provision also includes a tax of 1.45% on gross earnings in excess of $102,000. In the interest of simplification, we ignore this 1.45% charge in our end-of-chapter assignment material. We assume zero FICA withholdings on gross earnings above $100,000.

Illustration 11-10
Withholding tax table

MARRIED Persons — **WEEKLY** Payroll Period

(For Wages Paid in 2008)

If the wages are —		And the number of withholding allowances claimed is —										
At least	But less than	0	1	2	3	4	5	6	7	8	9	10
		The amount of income tax to be withheld is —										
490	500	56	48	40	32	24	17	9	1	0	0	0
500	510	57	49	42	34	26	18	10	3	0	0	0
510	520	59	51	43	35	27	20	12	4	0	0	0
520	530	60	52	45	37	29	21	13	6	0	0	0
530	540	62	54	46	38	30	23	15	7	0	0	0
540	550	63	55	48	40	32	24	16	9	1	0	0
550	560	65	57	49	41	33	26	18	10	2	0	0
560	570	66	58	51	43	35	27	19	12	4	0	0
570	580	68	60	52	44	36	29	21	13	5	0	0
580	590	69	61	54	46	38	30	22	15	7	0	0
590	600	71	63	55	47	39	32	24	16	8	1	0
600	610	72	64	57	49	41	33	25	18	10	2	0
610	620	74	66	58	50	42	35	27	19	11	4	0
620	630	75	67	60	52	44	36	28	21	13	5	0
630	640	77	69	61	53	45	38	30	22	14	7	0
640	650	78	70	63	55	47	39	31	24	16	8	0
650	660	80	72	64	56	48	41	33	25	17	10	2
660	670	81	73	66	58	50	42	34	27	19	11	3
670	680	83	75	67	59	51	44	36	28	20	13	5
680	690	84	76	69	61	53	45	37	30	22	14	6

the withholding tax table for Michael Jordan (assuming he earns $552 per week and claims two allowances). For a weekly salary of $552 with two allowances, the income tax to be withheld is $49.

In addition, most states (and some cities) require **employers** to withhold income taxes from employees' earnings. As a rule, the amounts withheld are a percentage (specified in the state revenue code) of the amount withheld for the federal income tax. Or they may be a specified percentage of the employee's earnings. For the sake of simplicity, we have assumed that Jordan's wages are subject to state income taxes of 2%, or $11.04 (2% × $552) per week.

There is no limit on the amount of gross earnings subject to income tax withholdings. In fact, under our progressive system of taxation, the higher the earnings, the higher the percentage of income withheld for taxes.

Other Deductions. Employees may voluntarily authorize withholdings for charitable, retirement, and other purposes. All voluntary deductions from gross earnings should be authorized in writing by the employee. The authorization(s) may be made individually or as part of a group plan. Deductions for charitable organizations, such as the United Way, or for financial arrangements, such as U.S. savings bonds and repayment of loans from company credit unions, are made individually. Deductions for union dues, health and life insurance, and pension plans are often made on a group basis. We will assume that Jordan has weekly voluntary deductions of $10 for the United Way and $5 for union dues.

NET PAY

Academy determines net pay by subtracting payroll deductions from gross earnings. Illustration 11-11 (page 498) shows the computation of Jordan's net pay for the pay period.

ALTERNATIVE TERMINOLOGY

Net pay is also called *take-home pay.*

Illustration 11-11
Computation of net pay

Gross earnings		$552.00
Payroll deductions:		
FICA taxes	$44.16	
Federal income taxes	49.00	
State income taxes	11.04	
United Way	10.00	
Union dues	5.00	119.20
Net pay		**$432.80**

Assuming that Michael Jordan's wages for each week during the year are $552, total wages for the year are $28,704 (52 × $552). Thus, all of Jordan's wages are subject to FICA tax during the year. In comparison, let's assume that Jordan's department head earns $2,000 per week, or $104,000 for the year. Since only the first $100,000 is subject to FICA taxes, the maximum FICA withholdings on the department head's earnings would be $8,000 ($100,000 × 8%).

ACCOUNTING ACROSS THE ORGANIZATION

Taxes Are the Largest Slice of the Pie

In 2008, Americans worked 74 days to afford their federal taxes and 39 more days to afford state and local taxes, according to the Tax Foundation. Each year this foundation calculates the mathematical average of tax collections in the United States, using a formula that divides the year's total tax collections (federal, state, and local taxes) by all income earned (the "national income"). The resulting national "tax burden" varies each year, and the tax burden also varies by state.

National taxation in 2008 was a bigger burden than average expenditures on housing and household operation (60 days), health and medical care (50 days), food (35 days), transportation (29 days), recreation (21 days), or clothing and accessories (13 days).

Source: www.taxfoundation.org/taxfreedomday/ (accessed June 2008). For a map of tax burden by states, see Figure 6 at that site.

? If the information on 2008 taxation depicted your spending patterns, on what date (starting on January 1) will you have earned enough to pay all of your taxes? This date is often referred to as Tax Freedom Day.

Recording the Payroll

Recording the payroll involves maintaining payroll department records, recognizing payroll expenses and liabilities, and recording payment of the payroll.

MAINTAINING PAYROLL DEPARTMENT RECORDS

To comply with state and federal laws, an employer must keep a cumulative record of each employee's gross earnings, deductions, and net pay during the year. The record that provides this information is the **employee earnings record**. Illustration 11-12 (next page) shows Michael Jordan's employee earnings record.

Companies keep a separate earnings record for each employee, and update these records after each pay period. The employer uses the cumulative payroll data on the earnings record to: (1) determine when an employee has earned the maximum earnings subject to FICA taxes, (2) file state and federal payroll tax returns (as explained

Academy Company.xls

File　Edit　View　Insert　Format　Tools　Data　Window　Help

ACADEMY COMPANY
Employee Earnings Record
For the Year 2010

Name	Michael Jordan	Address	2345 Mifflin Ave.
Social Security Number	329-36-9547		Hampton, Michigan 48292
Date of Birth	December 24, 1964	Telephone	555-238-9051
Date Employed	September 1, 2005	Date Employment Ended	
Sex	Male	Exemptions	2
Single _____	Married　x		

2010		Gross Earnings				Deductions						Payment	
Period Ending	Total Hours	Regular	Overtime	Total	Cumulative	FICA	Fed. Inc. Tax	State Inc. Tax	United Way	Union Dues	Total	Net Amount	Check No.
1/7	42	480.00	36.00	516.00	516.00	41.28	43.00	10.32	10.00	5.00	109.60	406.40	974
1/14	44	480.00	72.00	552.00	1,068.00	44.16	49.00	11.04	10.00	5.00	119.20	432.80	1028
1/21	43	480.00	54.00	534.00	1,602.00	42.72	46.00	10.68	10.00	5.00	114.40	419.60	1077
1/28	42	480.00	36.00	516.00	2,118.00	41.28	43.00	10.32	10.00	5.00	109.60	406.40	1133
Jan. Total		1,920.00	198.00	2,118.00		169.44	181.00	42.36	40.00	20.00	452.80	1,665.20	

Illustration 11-12
Employee earnings record

later), and (3) provide each employee with a statement of gross earnings and tax withholdings for the year. Illustration 11-16 on page 504 shows this statement.

In addition to employee earnings records, many companies find it useful to prepare a **payroll register**. This record accumulates the gross earnings, deductions, and net pay by employee for each pay period. Illustration 11-13 presents Academy Company's payroll register. It provides the documentation for preparing a paycheck

Illustration 11-13
Payroll register

Academy Company.xls

File　Edit　View　Insert　Format　Tools　Data　Window　Help

ACADEMY COMPANY
Payroll Register
For the Week Ending January 14, 2010

		Earnings			Deductions						Paid		Accounts Debited	
Employee	Total Hours	Regular	Over-time	Gross	FICA	Federal Income Tax	State Income Tax	United Way	Union Dues	Total	Net Pay	Check No.	Office Salaries Expense	Wages Expense
Office Salaries														
Arnold, Patricia	40	580.00		580.00	46.40	61.00	11.60	15.00		134.00	446.00	998	580.00	
Canton, Matthew	40	590.00		590.00	47.20	63.00	11.80	20.00		142.00	448.00	999	590.00	
Mueller, William	40	530.00		530.00	42.40	54.00	10.60	11.00		118.00	412.00	1000	530.00	
Subtotal		5,200.00		5,200.00	416.00	1,090.00	104.00	120.00		1,730.00	3,470.00		5,200.00	
Wages														
Bennett, Robin	42	480.00	36.00	516.00	41.28	43.00	10.32	18.00	5.00	117.60	398.40	1025		516.00
Jordan, Michael	44	480.00	72.00	552.00	44.16	49.00	11.04	10.00	5.00	119.20	432.80	1028		552.00
Milroy, Lee	43	480.00	54.00	534.00	42.72	46.00	10.68	10.00	5.00	114.40	419.60	1029		534.00
Subtotal		11,000.00	1,010.00	12,010.00	960.80	2,400.00	240.20	301.50	115.00	4,017.50	7,992.50			12,010.00
Total		16,200.00	1,010.00	17,210.00	1,376.80	3,490.00	344.20	421.50	115.00	5,747.50	11,462.50		5,200.00	12,010.00

for each employee. For example, it shows the data for Michael Jordan in the wages section. In this example, Academy Company's total weekly payroll is $17,210, as shown in the gross earnings column (column E, row 24).

Note that this record is a listing of each employee's payroll data for the pay period. In some companies, a payroll register is a journal or book of original entry. Postings are made from it directly to ledger accounts. In other companies, the payroll register is a memorandum record that provides the data for a general journal entry and subsequent posting to the ledger accounts. At Academy Company, the latter procedure is followed.

RECOGNIZING PAYROLL EXPENSES AND LIABILITIES

From the payroll register in Illustration 11-13, Academy Company makes a journal entry to record the payroll. For the week ending January 14 the entry is:

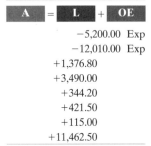

A = L + OE		
−5,200.00 Exp		
−12,010.00 Exp		
+1,376.80		
+3,490.00		
+344.20		
+421.50		
+115.00		
+11,462.50		

Cash Flows
no effect

Jan. 14	Office Salaries Expense	5,200.00	
	Wages Expense	12,010.00	
	FICA Taxes Payable		1,376.80
	Federal Income Taxes Payable		3,490.00
	State Income Taxes Payable		344.20
	United Way Payable		421.50
	Union Dues Payable		115.00
	Salaries and Wages Payable		11,462.50
	(To record payroll for the week ending January 14)		

The company credits specific liability accounts for the mandatory and voluntary deductions made during the pay period. In the example, Academy debits Office Salaries Expense for the gross earnings of salaried office workers, and it debits Wages Expense for the gross earnings of employees who are paid at an hourly rate. Other companies may debit other accounts such as Store Salaries or Sales Salaries. The amount credited to Salaries and Wages Payable is the sum of the individual checks the employees will receive.

RECORDING PAYMENT OF THE PAYROLL

A company makes payments by check (or electronic funds transfer) either from its regular bank account or a payroll bank account. Each paycheck is usually accompanied by a detachable **statement of earnings** document. This shows the employee's gross earnings, payroll deductions, and net pay, both for the period and for the year-to-date. Academy Company uses its regular bank account for payroll checks. Illustration 11-14 (next page) shows the paycheck and statement of earnings for Michael Jordan.

Following payment of the payroll, the company enters the check numbers in the payroll register. Academy Company records payment of the payroll as follows.

A = L + OE		
−11,462.50		
−11,462.50		

Cash Flows
−11,462.50

Jan. 14	Salaries and Wages Payable	11,462.50	
	Cash		11,462.50
	(To record payment of payroll)		

Many medium- and large-size companies use a payroll processing center that provides payroll record-keeping services. Companies send the center payroll information about employee pay rates and hours worked. The center maintains the payroll records and prepares the payroll checks. In most cases, it costs less to process the payroll through the center than if the company did so internally.

Illustration 11-14
Paycheck and statement of earnings

AC	ACADEMY COMPANY 19 Center St. Hampton, MI 48291		No. 1028

January 14, 2010 $\frac{62-1113}{610}$

Pay to the
order of _Michael Jordan_ $ _432.80_

Four Hundred Thirty-two and $\frac{80}{100}$ _____ Dollars

City Bank & Trust
P.O. Box 3000
Hampton, MI 48291

For _Payroll_   _Randall E. Barnes_

⑆00324477⑆ ⑆1028

DETACH AND RETAIN THIS PORTION FOR YOUR RECORDS

NAME				SOC. SEC. NO.	EMPL. NUMBER	NO. EXEMP	PAY PERIOD ENDING
Michael Jordan				329-36-9547		2	1/14/10

REG. HRS.	O.T. HRS.	OTH. HRS. (1)	OTH. HRS. (2)	REG. EARNINGS	O.T. EARNINGS	OTH. EARNINGS (1)	OTH. EARNINGS (2)	GROSS
40	4			480.00	72.00			$552.00

FED. W/H TAX	FICA	STATE TAX	LOCAL TAX	OTHER DEDUCTIONS				NET PAY
				(1)	(2)	(3)	(4)	
49.00	44.16	11.04		10.00	5.00			432.80

YEAR TO DATE								
FED. W/H TAX	FICA	STATE TAX	LOCAL TAX	OTHER DEDUCTIONS				NET PAY
				(1)	(2)	(3)	(4)	
92.00	85.44	21.36		20.00	10.00			$839.20

HELPFUL HINT

Do any of the income tax liabilities result in payroll tax expense for the employer?

Answer: No. The employer is acting only as a collection agent for the government.

DO IT!

In January, gross earnings in Ramirez Company were $40,000. All earnings are subject to 8% FICA taxes. Federal income tax withheld was $9,000, and state income tax withheld was $1,000. (a) Calculate net pay for January, and (b) record the payroll.

PAYROLL

action plan

✔ Determine net pay by subtracting payroll deductions from gross earnings.

✔ Record gross earnings as Salaries and Wages Expense, record payroll deductions as liabilities, and record net pay as Salaries and Wages Payable.

Solution

(a) Net pay: $40,000 − (8% × $40,000) − $9,000 − $1,000 = $26,800

(b) | Salaries and Wages Expense | 40,000 | |
| --- | --- | --- |
| FICA Taxes Payable | | 3,200 |
| Federal Income Taxes Payable | | 9,000 |
| State Income Taxes Payable | | 1,000 |
| Salaries and Wages Payable | | 26,800 |
| (To record payroll) | | |

Related exercise material: **BE11-8, BE11-7, E11-10, E11-11, E11-12, E11-13,** and **DO IT! 11-3.**

 ✔ The Navigator

Employer Payroll Taxes

Payroll tax expense for businesses results from three taxes that governmental agencies levy **on employers**. These taxes are: (1) FICA, (2) federal unemployment tax, and (3) state unemployment tax. These taxes plus

STUDY OBJECTIVE 7

Describe and record employer payroll taxes.

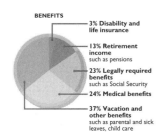

such items as paid vacations and pensions (discussed in the appendix to this chapter) are collectively referred to as **fringe benefits**. As indicated earlier, the cost of fringe benefits in many companies is substantial. The pie chart in the margin shows the pieces of the benefits "pie."

FICA TAXES

Each employee must pay FICA taxes. In addition, employers must match each employee's FICA contribution. The matching contribution results in **payroll tax expense** to the employer. The employer's tax is subject to the same rate and maximum earnings as the employee's. The company uses the same account, FICA Taxes Payable, to record both the employee's and the employer's FICA contributions. For the January 14 payroll, Academy Company's FICA tax contribution is $1,376.80 ($17,210.00 × 8%).

FEDERAL UNEMPLOYMENT TAXES

The Federal Unemployment Tax Act (FUTA) is another feature of the federal Social Security program. Federal unemployment taxes provide benefits for a limited period of time to employees who lose their jobs through no fault of their own. The FUTA tax rate is 6.2% of taxable wages. The taxable wage base is the first $7,000 of wages paid to each employee in a calendar year. Employers who pay the state unemployment tax on a timely basis will receive an offset credit of up to 5.4%. Therefore, the net federal tax rate is generally 0.8% (6.2%–5.4%). This rate would equate to a maximum of $56 of federal tax per employee per year (0.8% × $7,000). State tax rates are based on state law.

The **employer** bears the entire federal unemployment tax. There is no deduction or withholding from employees. Companies use the account Federal Unemployment Taxes Payable to recognize this liability. The federal unemployment tax for Academy Company for the January 14 payroll is $137.68 ($17,210.00 × 0.8%).

HELPFUL HINT

Both the employer and employee pay FICA taxes. Federal unemployment taxes and (in most states) the state unemployment taxes are borne entirely by the employer.

STATE UNEMPLOYMENT TAXES

All states have unemployment compensation programs under state unemployment tax acts (SUTA). Like federal unemployment taxes, state unemployment taxes provide benefits to employees who lose their jobs. These taxes are levied on employers.[2] The basic rate is usually 5.4% on the first $7,000 of wages paid to an employee during the year. The state adjusts the basic rate according to the employer's experience rating: Companies with a history of stable employment may pay less than 5.4%. Companies with a history of unstable employment may pay more than the basic rate. Regardless of the rate paid, the company's credit on the federal unemployment tax is still 5.4%.

Companies use the account State Unemployment Taxes Payable for this liability. The state unemployment tax for Academy Company for the January 14 payroll is $929.34 ($17,210.00 × 5.4%). Illustration 11-15 (next page) summarizes the types of employer payroll taxes.

RECORDING EMPLOYER PAYROLL TAXES

Companies usually record employer payroll taxes at the same time they record the payroll. The entire amount of gross pay ($17,210.00) shown in the payroll register in Illustration 11-13 is subject to each of the three taxes mentioned above. Accordingly,

---

[2]In a few states, the employee is also required to make a contribution. *In this textbook, including the homework, we will assume that the tax is only on the employer.*

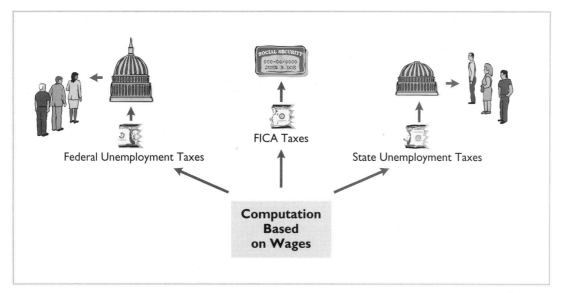

Illustration 11-15
Employer payroll taxes

Academy records the payroll tax expense associated with the January 14 payroll with the following entry.

					A = L + OE
Jan. 14	Payroll Tax Expense	2,443.82			−2,443.82 Exp
	FICA Taxes Payable		1,376.80		+1,376.80
	Federal Unemployment Taxes Payable		137.68		+137.68
	State Unemployment Taxes Payable		929.34		+929.34
	(To record employer's payroll taxes on				**Cash Flows**
	January 14 payroll)				no effect

Note that Academy uses separate liability accounts instead of a single credit to Payroll Taxes Payable. Why? Because these liabilities are payable to different taxing authorities at different dates. Companies classify the liability accounts in the balance sheet as current liabilities since they will be paid within the next year. They classify Payroll Tax Expense on the income statement as an operating expense.

Filing and Remitting Payroll Taxes

Preparation of payroll tax returns is the responsibility of the payroll department. The treasurer's department makes the tax payment. Much of the information for the returns is obtained from employee earnings records.

For purposes of reporting and remitting to the IRS, the company combines the FICA taxes and federal income taxes that it withheld. **Companies must report the taxes quarterly**, no later than one month following the close of each quarter. The remitting requirements depend on the amount of taxes withheld and the length of the pay period. Companies remit funds through deposits in either a Federal Reserve bank or an authorized commercial bank.

Companies generally file and remit federal unemployment taxes **annually** on or before January 31 of the subsequent year. Earlier payments are required when the tax exceeds a specified amount. Companies usually must file and pay state unemployment taxes by the **end of the month following each quarter**. When payroll taxes are paid, companies debit payroll liability accounts, and credit Cash.

Employers also must provide each employee with a Wage and Tax Statement (Form W-2) by January 31 following the end of a calendar year. This statement shows gross earnings, FICA taxes withheld, and income taxes withheld for the year. The required W-2 form for Michael Jordan, using assumed annual data, is shown in Illustration 11-16. The employer must send a copy of each employee's Wage and Tax Statement (Form W-2) to the Social Security Administration. This agency subsequently furnishes the Internal Revenue Service with the income data required.

Illustration 11-16
W-2 form

22222	Void ☐	**a** Employee's social security number 329-36-9547	For Official Use Only ▶ OMB No. 1545-0008	
b Employer identification number (EIN) 36-2167852			**1** Wages, tips, other compensation 26,300.00	**2** Federal income tax withheld 2,248.00
c Employer's name, address, and ZIP code Academy Company 19 Center St. Hampton, MI 48291			**3** Social security wages 26,300.00	**4** Social security tax withheld 2,104.00
			5 Medicare wages and tips 26,300.00	**6** Medicare tax withheld
			7 Social security tips	**8** Allocated tips
d Control number			**9** Advance EIC payment	**10** Dependent care benefits
e Employee's first name and initial Last name Suff. Michael Jordan 2345 Mifflin Ave. Hampton, MI 48292			**11** Nonqualified plans	**12a** See instructions for box 12
			13 Statutory employee ☐ Retirement plan ☐ Third-party sick pay ☐	**12b**
			14 Other	**12c**
				12d
f Employee's address and ZIP code				

15 State Employer's state ID number MI 423-1466-3	**16** State wages, tips, etc. 26,300.00	**17** State income tax 526.00	**18** Local wages, tips, etc.	**19** Local income tax	**20** Locality name

Form **W-2** Wage and Tax Statement   **2007**   Department of the Treasury—Internal Revenue Service

Copy A For Social Security Administration — Send this entire page with Form W-3 to the Social Security Administration; photocopies are **not** acceptable.

For Privacy Act and Paperwork Reduction Act Notice, see back of Copy D.

Cat. No. 10134D

Internal Control for Payroll

Chapter 8 introduced internal control. As applied to payrolls, the objectives of internal control are (1) to safeguard company assets against unauthorized payments of payrolls, and (2) to ensure the accuracy and reliability of the accounting records pertaining to payrolls.

Irregularities often result if internal control is lax. Frauds involving payroll include overstating hours, using unauthorized pay rates, adding fictitious employees to the payroll, continuing terminated employees on the payroll, and distributing duplicate payroll checks. Moreover, inaccurate records will result in incorrect paychecks, financial statements, and payroll tax returns.

Payroll activities involve four functions: hiring employees, timekeeping, preparing the payroll, and paying the payroll. For effective internal control, companies should assign these four functions to different departments or individuals. Illustration 11-17 (next page) highlights these functions and illustrates their internal control features.

Payroll Function

Hiring Employees

Internal control feature: Human Resources department documents and authorizes employment.

Fraud prevented: Fictitious employees are not added to payroll.

Timekeeping

Internal control feature: Supervisors monitor hours worked through time cards and time reports.

Fraud prevented: Employee works appropriate hours.

Payroll Function

Preparing the Payroll

Internal control feature: Two (or more) employees verify payroll amounts; supervisor approves.

Fraud prevented: Payroll calculations are accurate and relevant.

Paying the Payroll

Internal control feature: Treasurer signs and distributes prenumbered checks.

Fraud prevented: Checks are not lost from theft; endorsed check provides proof of payment.

Illustration 11-17
Internal control for payroll

DO IT!

In January, the payroll supervisor determines that gross earnings for Halo Company are $70,000. All earnings are subject to 8% FICA taxes, 5.4% state unemployment taxes, and 0.8% federal unemployment taxes. Halo asks you to record the employer's payroll taxes.

EMPLOYER'S PAYROLL TAXES

action plan

✔ Compute the employer's payroll taxes on the period's gross earnings.
✔ Identify the expense account(s) to be debited.
✔ Identify the liability account(s) to be credited.

Solution

The entry to record the employer's payroll taxes is:

Payroll Tax Expense	9,940	
FICA Taxes Payable ($70,000 × 8%)		5,600
Federal Unemployment Taxes Payable ($70,000 × 0.8%)		560
State Unemployment Taxes Payable ($70,000 × 5.4%)		3,780
(To record employer's payroll taxes on January payroll)		

Related exercise material: **BE11-9, BE11-10, E11-12, E11-14,** and **DO IT!** **11-4.**

 The Navigator

 Be sure to read **ALL ABOUT YOU: *Your Boss Wants to Know If You Jogged Today*** on page 506 for information on how topics in this chapter apply to your personal life.

Your Boss Wants to Know If You Jogged Today

As you saw in this chapter, compensation packages often include fringe benefits in addition to basic salary. Health insurance is one benefit that many employers offer. In recent years, as the cost of health insurance has sky-rocketed, many employers either have shifted some of the cost of health insurance onto employees, or have discontinued health insurance coverage altogether.

✷ Some Facts

* Health-care spending in the U.S. was $1.9 trillion in 2004, and is projected to be $2.9 trillion by 2009. It is four times the amount spent on national defense and represents 16% of U.S. gross domestic product.

* About 45 million Americans are without any form of health insurance. Many of these people are employed, but their jobs don't provide a health-care benefit.

* For employers, the average cost of health-care benefits per employee is about $6,700 per year.

* The rate of increase of employer health-care costs has slowed somewhat as employers raised the employee share of premiums and raised deductibles (the amount of a bill that the employee pays before insurance coverage begins).

* More than 30% of small employers have a deductible of $1,000 for employee health insurance.

✷ About the Numbers

As the graph below shows, private health insurance, such as that provided by employers, pays for less than half of health-care costs in the U.S. If employers continue to cut their health-care benefits, more of the burden will shift to the government or to individuals as out-of-pocket costs.

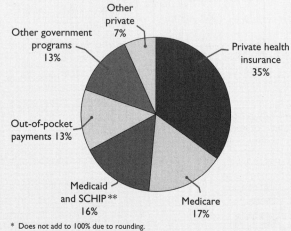

The Nation's Health-Care Dollar: Where it Comes From*

- Other private 7%
- Other government programs 13%
- Private health insurance 35%
- Out-of-pocket payments 13%
- Medicaid and SCHIP ** 16%
- Medicare 17%

* Does not add to 100% due to rounding.
** State Children's Health Insurance Program.

Source: Data for 2004, from Centers for Medicare and Medicaid Services, Office of the Actuary, National Health Statistics Group.

✷ What Do You Think?

Suppose you own a business. About a quarter of your employees smoke, and an even higher percentage are overweight. You decide to implement a mandatory health program that requires employees to quit smoking and to exercise regularly, with regular monitoring. If employees do not participate in the program, they will have to pay their own insurance premiums. Is this fair?

YES: It is the responsibility of management to try to maximize a company's profit. Employees with unhealthy habits drive up the cost of health insurance because they require more frequent and more costly medical attention.

NO: What people do on their own time is their own business. This represents an invasion of privacy, and is a form of discrimination.

Source: Dee Gill, "Get Healthy . . . Or Else," *Inc.* Magazine, April 2006; "Health Insurance Cost," The National Coalition on Health Care, *www.nchc.org/facts/cost.shtml* (accessed May 2006).

Indiana Jones Company had the following selected transactions.

Feb. 1 Signs a $50,000, 6-month, 9%-interest-bearing note payable to CitiBank and receives $50,000 in cash.

10 Cash register sales total $43,200, which includes an 8% sales tax.

28 The payroll for the month consists of Sales Salaries $32,000 and Office Salaries $18,000. All wages are subject to 8% FICA taxes. A total of $8,900 federal income taxes are withheld. The salaries are paid on March 1.

28 The company develops the following adjustment data.
1. Interest expense of $375 has been incurred on the note.
2. Employer payroll taxes include 8% FICA taxes, a 5.4% state unemployment tax, and a 0.8% federal unemployment tax.
3. Some sales were made under warranty. Of the units sold under warranty, 350 are expected to become defective. Repair costs are estimated to be $40 per unit.

Instructions

(a) Journalize the February transactions.

(b) Journalize the adjusting entries at February 28.

action plan

✔ To determine sales, divide the cash register total by 100% plus the sales tax percentage.

✔ Base payroll taxes on gross earnings.

✔ Expense warranty costs in the period in which the sale occurs.

Solution to Comprehensive DO IT!

(a) Feb. 1	Cash	50,000	
	Notes Payable		50,000
	(Issued 6-month, 9%-interest-bearing note to CitiBank)		
10	Cash	43,200	
	Sales ($43,200 ÷ 1.08)		40,000
	Sales Taxes Payable ($40,000 × 8%)		3,200
	(To record sales and sales taxes payable)		
28	Sales Salaries Expense	32,000	
	Office Salaries Expense	18,000	
	FICA Taxes Payable (8% × $50,000)		4,000
	Federal Income Taxes Payable		8,900
	Salaries Payable		37,100
	(To record February salaries)		
(b) Feb. 28	Interest Expense	375	
	Interest Payable		375
	(To record accrued interest for February)		
28	Payroll Tax Expense	7,100	
	FICA Taxes Payable		4,000
	Federal Unemployment Taxes Payable		400
	(0.8% × $50,000)		
	State Unemployment Taxes Payable		2,700
	(5.4% × $50,000)		
	(To record employer's payroll taxes on February payroll)		
28	Warranty Expense (350 × $40)	14,000	
	Estimated Warranty Liability		14,000
	(To record estimated product warranty liability)		

✔ The Navigator

SUMMARY OF STUDY OBJECTIVES

1 **Explain a current liability, and identify the major types of current liabilities.** A current liability is a debt that a company can reasonably expect to pay (1) from existing current assets or through the creation of other current liabilities, and (2) within one year or the operating cycle, whichever is longer. The major types of current liabilities are notes payable, accounts payable, sales taxes payable, unearned revenues, and accrued liabilities such as taxes, salaries and wages, and interest payable.

2 **Describe the accounting for notes payable.** When a promissory note is interest-bearing, the amount of assets received upon the issuance of the note is generally equal to the face value of the note. Interest expense accrues over the life of the note. At maturity, the amount paid equals the face value of the note plus accrued interest.

3 **Explain the accounting for other current liabilities.** Companies record sales taxes payable at the time the related sales occur. The company serves as a collection agent for the taxing authority. Sales taxes are not an expense to the company. Companies initially record unearned revenues in an Unearned Revenue account. As the company earns the revenue, a transfer from unearned revenue to earned revenue occurs. Companies report the current maturities of long-term debt as a current liability in the balance sheet.

4 **Explain the financial statement presentation and analysis of current liabilities.** Companies should report the nature and amount of each current liability in the balance sheet or in schedules in the notes accompanying the statements. The liquidity of a company may be analyzed by computing working capital and the current ratio.

5 **Describe the accounting and disclosure requirements for contingent liabilities.** If the contingency is *probable* (likely to occur) and the amount is reasonably estimable, the company should record the liability in the accounts. If the contingency is only *reasonably possible* (it could happen), then it should be disclosed only in the notes to the financial statements. If the possibility that the contingency will happen is *remote* (unlikely to occur), it need not be recorded or disclosed.

6 **Compute and record the payroll for a pay period.** The computation of the payroll involves gross earnings, payroll deductions, and net pay. In recording the payroll, companies debit salaries (or wages) expense for gross earnings, credit individual tax and other liability accounts for payroll deductions, and credit salaries (wages) payable for net pay. When the payroll is paid, companies debit Salaries and Wages Payable, and credit Cash.

7 **Describe and record employer payroll taxes.** Employer payroll taxes consist of FICA, federal unemployment taxes, and state unemployment taxes. The taxes are usually accrued at the time the company records the payroll, by debiting Payroll Tax Expense and crediting separate liability accounts for each type of tax.

8 **Discuss the objectives of internal control for payroll.** The objectives of internal control for payroll are (1) to safeguard company assets against unauthorized payments of payrolls, and (2) to ensure the accuracy of the accounting records pertaining to payrolls.

GLOSSARY

Bonus Compensation to management and other personnel, based on factors such as increased sales or the amount of net income. (p. 495).

Contingent liability A potential liability that may become an actual liability in the future. (p. 491).

Current ratio A measure of a company's liquidity; computed as current assets divided by current liabilities. (p. 491).

Employee earnings record A cumulative record of each employee's gross earnings, deductions, and net pay during the year. (p. 498).

Federal unemployment taxes Taxes imposed on the employer by the federal government that provide benefits for a limited time period to employees who lose their jobs through no fault of their own. (p. 502).

Fees Payments made for the services of professionals. (p. 494).

FICA taxes Taxes designed to provide workers with supplemental retirement, employment disability, and medical benefits. (p. 496).

Full-disclosure principle Requires that companies disclose all circumstances and events that would make a difference to financial statement users. (p. 493).

Gross earnings Total compensation earned by an employee. (p. 495).

Net pay Gross earnings less payroll deductions. (p. 497).

Notes payable Obligations in the form of written promissory notes. (p. 486).

Payroll deductions Deductions from gross earnings to determine the amount of a paycheck. (p. 495).

Payroll register A payroll record that accumulates the gross earnings, deductions, and net pay by employee for each pay period. (p. 499).

Salaries   Employee pay based on a specified amount rather than an hourly rate. (p. 494).

Statement of earnings   A document attached to a paycheck that indicates the employee's gross earnings, payroll deductions, and net pay. (p. 500).

State unemployment taxes   Taxes imposed on the employer by states that provide benefits to employees who lose their jobs. (p. 502).

Wage and Tax Statement (Form W-2)   A form showing gross earnings, FICA taxes withheld, and income taxes withheld, prepared annually by an employer for each employee. (p. 504).

Wages   Amounts paid to employees based on a rate per hour or on a piece-work basis. (p. 494).

Working capital   A measure of a company's liquidity; computed as current assets minus current liabilities. (p. 491).

APPENDIX **Additional Fringe Benefits**

In addition to the three payroll-tax fringe benefits, employers incur other substantial fringe benefit costs. Two of the most important are paid absences and post-retirement benefits.

STUDY OBJECTIVE 9
Identify additional fringe benefits associated with employee compensation.

Paid Absences

Employees often are given rights to receive compensation for absences when they meet certain conditions of employment. The compensation may be for paid vacations, sick pay benefits, and paid holidays. When the payment for such absences is **probable** and the amount can be **reasonably estimated**, the company should accrue a liability for paid future absences. When the amount cannot be reasonably estimated, the company should instead disclose the potential liability. Ordinarily, vacation pay is the only paid absence that is accrued. The other types of paid absences are only disclosed.[3]

To illustrate, assume that Academy Company employees are entitled to one day's vacation for each month worked. If 30 employees earn an average of $110 per day in a given month, the accrual for vacation benefits in one month is $3,300. Academy records the liability at the end of the month by the following adjusting entry.

Jan. 31	Vacation Benefits Expense	3,300	
	Vacation Benefits Payable		3,300
	(To accrue vacation benefits expense)		

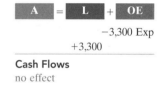

A	=	L	+	OE
				−3,300 Exp
		+3,300		

Cash Flows
no effect

This accrual is required by the matching principle. Academy would report Vacation Benefits Expense as an operating expense in the income statement, and Vacation Benefits Payable as a current liability in the balance sheet.

Later, when Academy pays vacation benefits, it debits Vacation Benefits Payable and credits Cash. For example, if employees take 10 days of vacation in July, the entry is:

July 31	Vacation Benefits Payable	1,100	
	Cash		1,100
	(To record payment of vacation benefits)		

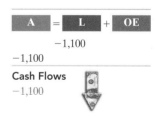

A	=	L	+	OE
		−1,100		
−1,100				

Cash Flows
−1,100

The magnitude of unpaid absences has gained employers' attention. Consider the case of an assistant superintendent of schools who worked for 20 years and rarely took a vacation or sick day. A month or so before she retired, the school district discovered that she was due nearly $30,000 in accrued benefits. Yet the school district had never accrued the liability.

---

[3]The typical U.S. company provides an average of 12 days of paid vacations for its employees, at an average cost of 5% of gross earnings.

Post-Retirement Benefits

Post-retirement benefits are benefits that employers provide to retired employees for (1) pensions and (2) health care and life insurance. Companies account for both types of post-retirement benefits on the accrual basis. The cost of post-retirement benefits is getting steep. For example, General Motors' pension and health-care costs for retirees in a recent year totaled $6.2 billion, or approximately $1,784 per vehicle produced.

The average American has debt of approximately $10,000 (not counting the mortgage on their home) and has little in the way of savings. What will happen at retirement for these people? The picture is not pretty—people are living longer, the future of Social Security is unclear, and companies are cutting back on post-retirement benefits. This situation may lead to one of the great social and moral dilemmas this country faces in the next 40 years. The more you know about post-retirement benefits, the better you will understand the issues involved in this dilemma.

PENSIONS

A **pension plan** is an agreement whereby employers provide benefits (payments) to employees after they retire. The most popular type of pension plan used is the 401(k) plan. A 401(k) plan works as follows: As an employee, you can contribute up to a certain percentage of your pay into a 401(k) plan, and your employer will match a percentage of your contribution. These contributions are then generally invested in stocks and bonds through mutual funds. These funds will grow without being taxed and can be withdrawn beginning at age 59-1/2. If you must access the funds earlier, you may be able to do so, but a penalty usually occurs along with a payment of tax on the proceeds. Any time you have the opportunity to be involved in a 401(k) plan, you should avail yourself of this benefit!

The accounting for a 401(k) plan by the company is straightforward. When the company makes a contribution on behalf of the employee, it debits Pension Expense and credits Cash for the amount contributed. For example, Mark Hatfield, an employee of Veri Company, contributes $11,000 to his 401(k) plan. Veri Company matches this contribution, and records the expense with the following entry.

Pension Expense	11,000	
Cash		11,000
(To record contribution to 401(k) plan.)		

If the pension expense is not funded during the year, the company credits Pension Liability.

A 401(k) plan is often referred to as a **defined-contribution plan**. In a defined-contribution plan, the plan defines the contribution that an employer will make but not the benefit that the employee will receive at retirement.

The other type of pension plan is a **defined-benefit plan**. In a defined-benefit plan, the employer agrees to pay a defined amount to retirees, based on employees meeting certain eligibility standards. The amount of the benefit is usually based on years of service and average salary over a period of years. Employers are at risk with defined-benefit plans because they must contribute enough to meet the cost of benefits that the plan defines. Many large companies have defined-benefit plans. The accounting for these plans is complex. Many companies are starting to utilize 401(k) plans more extensively instead.

POST-RETIREMENT HEALTH-CARE AND LIFE INSURANCE BENEFITS

Providing medical and related health-care benefits for retirees was at one time an inexpensive and highly effective way of generating employee goodwill. This practice has now turned into one of corporate America's most worrisome financial problems. Runaway medical costs, early retirement, and increased longevity are sending the liability for retiree health plans through the roof.

Companies estimate and expense post-retirement costs during the working years of the employee because the company benefits from the employee's services during this period. However, the company rarely sets up funds to meet the cost of the future benefits. It follows a pay-as-you-go basis for these costs. The major reason is that the company does not receive a tax deduction until it actually pays the medical bill.

SUMMARY OF STUDY OBJECTIVE FOR APPENDIX

9 Identify additional fringe benefits associated with employee compensation. Additional fringe benefits associated with wages are paid absences (paid vacations, sick pay benefits, and paid holidays), and post-retirement benefits (pensions and health care and life insurance).

GLOSSARY FOR APPENDIX

Pension plan   An agreement whereby an employer provides benefits to employees after they retire. (p. 510).

Post-retirement benefits   Payments by employers to retired employees for health care, life insurance, and pensions. (p. 510).

*__Note:__ All **asterisked** Questions, Exercises, and Problems relate to material in the appendix to the chapter.

SELF-STUDY QUESTIONS

Answers are at the end of the chapter.

(SO 1)   **1.** The time period for classifying a liability as current is one year or the operating cycle, whichever is:
  a. longer.
  b. shorter.
  c. probable.
  d. possible.

(SO 1)   **2.** To be classified as a current liability, a debt must be expected to be paid:
  a. out of existing current assets.
  b. by creating other current liabilities.
  c. within 2 years.
  d. both (a) and (b).

(SO 2)   **3.** Maggie Sharrer Company borrows $88,500 on September 1, 2010, from Sandwich State Bank by signing an $88,500, 12%, one-year note. What is the accrued interest at December 31, 2010?
  a. $2,655.
  b. $3,540.
  c. $4,425.
  d. $10,620.

(SO 2)   **4.** RS Company borrowed $70,000 on December 1 on a 6-month, 12% note. At December 31:
  a. neither the note payable nor the interest payable is a current liability.
  b. the note payable is a current liability, but the interest payable is not.
  c. the interest payable is a current liability but the note payable is not.
  d. both the note payable and the interest payable are current liabilities.

5. Becky Sherrick Company has total proceeds from sales (SO 3) of $4,515. If the proceeds include sales taxes of 5%, the amount to be credited to Sales is:
  a. $4,000.
  b. $4,300.
  c. $4,289.25.
  d. No correct answer given.

6. Sensible Insurance Company collected a premium of (SO 3) $18,000 for a 1-year insurance policy on April 1. What amount should Sensible report as a current liability for Unearned Insurance Premiums at December 31?
  a. $0.
  b. $4,500.
  c. $13,500.
  d. $18,000.

7. Working capital is calculated as: (SO 4)
  a. current assets minus current liabilities.
  b. total assets minus total liabilities.
  c. long-term liabilities minus current liabilities.
  d. both (b) and (c).

8. The current ratio is computed as: (SO 4)
  a. total assets divided by total liabilities.
  b. total assets divided by current liabilities.

c. current assets divided by total liabilities.

d. current assets divided by current liabilities.

(SO 5)   **9.** A contingent liability should be recorded in the accounts when:

a. it is probable the contingency will happen, but the amount cannot be reasonably estimated.

b. it is reasonably possible the contingency will happen, and the amount can be reasonably estimated.

c. it is probable the contingency will happen, and the amount can be reasonably estimated.

d. it is reasonably possible the contingency will happen, but the amount cannot be reasonably estimated.

(SO 5)   **10.** At December 31, Hanes Company prepares an adjusting entry for a product warranty contract. Which of the following accounts is/are included in the entry?

a. Miscellaneous Expense.

b. Estimated Warranty Liability.

c. Repair Parts/Wages Payable.

d. Both (a) and (b).

(SO 6)   **11.** Andy Manion earns $14 per hour for a 40-hour week and $21 per hour for any overtime work. If Manion works 45 hours in a week, gross earnings are:

a. $560.   **c.** $650.

b. $630.   **d.** $665.

(SO 6)   **12.** When recording payroll:

a. gross earnings are recorded as salaries and wages payable.

b. net pay is recorded as salaries and wages expense.

c. payroll deductions are recorded as liabilities.

d. More than one of the above.

(SO 7)   **13.** Employer payroll taxes do *not* include:

a. federal unemployment taxes.

b. state unemployment taxes.

c. federal income taxes.

d. FICA taxes.

(SO 7)   **14.** FICA Taxes Payable was credited for $7,500 in the entry when Antonio Company recorded payroll. When Antonio Company records employer's payroll taxes, FICA Taxes Payable should be credited for:

a. $0.

b. $7,500.

c. $15,000.

d. some other amount.

(SO 8)   **15.** The department that should pay the payroll is the:

a. timekeeping department.

b. human resources department.

c. payroll department.

d. treasurer's department.

(SO 9)   ***16.** Which of the following is *not* an additional fringe benefit?

a. Post-retirement pensions.

b. Paid absences.

c. Paid vacations.

d. Salaries.

Go to the book's companion website, **www.wiley.com/college/weygandt**, for additional Self-Study Questions.

QUESTIONS

1. Jill Loomis believes a current liability is a debt that can be expected to be paid in one year. Is Jill correct? Explain.

2. Frederickson Company obtains $40,000 in cash by signing a 9%, 6-month, $40,000 note payable to First Bank on July 1. Frederickson's fiscal year ends on September 30. What information should be reported for the note payable in the annual financial statements?

3. (a) Your roommate says, "Sales taxes are reported as an expense in the income statement." Do you agree? Explain.

(b) Planet Hollywood has cash proceeds from sales of $7,400. This amount includes $400 of sales taxes. Give the entry to record the proceeds.

4. Baylor University sold 10,000 season football tickets at $80 each for its five-game home schedule. What entries should be made (a) when the tickets were sold, and (b) after each game?

5. What is liquidity? What are two measures of liquidity?

6. What is a contingent liability? Give an example of a contingent liability that is usually recorded in the accounts.

7. Under what circumstances is a contingent liability disclosed only in the notes to the financial statements?

Under what circumstances is a contingent liability not recorded in the accounts nor disclosed in the notes to the financial statements?

8. What is the difference between gross pay and net pay? Which amount should a company record as wages or salaries expense?

9. Which payroll tax is levied on both employers and employees?

10. Are the federal and state income taxes withheld from employee paychecks a payroll tax expense for the employer? Explain your answer.

11. What do the following acronyms stand for: FICA, FUTA, and SUTA?

12. What information is shown in a W-2 statement?

13. Distinguish between the two types of payroll deductions and give examples of each.

14. What are the primary uses of the employee earnings record?

15. (a) Identify the three types of employer payroll taxes.

(b) How are tax liability accounts and payroll tax expense accounts classified in the financial statements?

16. You are a newly hired accountant with Batista Company. On your first day, the controller asks you to identify the main internal control objectives related to payroll accounting. How would you respond?

17. What are the four functions associated with payroll activities?

*18. Identify two additional types of fringe benefits associated with employees' compensation.

*19. Often during job interviews, the candidate asks the potential employer about the firm's paid absences policy. What are paid absences? How are they accounted for?

*20. What are two types of post-retirement benefits?

*21. Explain how a 401(k) plan works.

*22. What is the difference between a defined-contribution pension plan and a defined-benefit pension plan?

BRIEF EXERCISES

BE11-1 Buffaloe Company has the following obligations at December 31: (a) a note payable for $100,000 due in 2 years, (b) a 10-year mortgage payable of $300,000 payable in ten $30,000 annual payments, (c) interest payable of $15,000 on the mortgage, and (d) accounts payable of $60,000. For each obligation, indicate whether it should be classified as a current liability. (Assume an operating cycle of less than one year.)

Identify whether obligations are current liabilities.
(SO 1)

BE11-2 Hanna Company borrows $80,000 on July 1 from the bank by signing a $80,000, 10%, one-year note payable.

(a) Prepare the journal entry to record the proceeds of the note.
(b) Prepare the journal entry to record accrued interest at December 31, assuming adjusting entries are made only at the end of the year.

Prepare entries for an interest-bearing note payable.
(SO 2)

BE11-3 Leister Auto Supply does not segregate sales and sales taxes at the time of sale. The register total for March 16 is $15,540. All sales are subject to a 5% sales tax. Compute sales taxes payable, and make the entry to record sales taxes payable and sales.

Compute and record sales taxes payable.
(SO 3)

BE11-4 Emporia State University sells 4,000 season basketball tickets at $180 each for its 12-game home schedule. Give the entry to record (a) the sale of the season tickets and (b) the revenue earned by playing the first home game.

Prepare entries for unearned revenues.
(SO 3)

BE11-5 Yahoo! Inc.'s 2006 financial statements contain the following selected data (in thousands).

Analyze liquidity.
(SO 4)

| Current assets | $3,449,533 | Current liabilities | $1,204,052 |
| Total assets | 10,831,834 | Total liabilities | 2,265,419 |

Compute **(a)** working capital and **(b)** current ratio.

BE11-6 On December 1, Diaz Company introduces a new product that includes a one-year warranty on parts. In December, 1,000 units are sold. Management believes that 5% of the units will be defective and that the average warranty costs will be $80 per unit. Prepare the adjusting entry at December 31 to accrue the estimated warranty cost.

Prepare adjusting entry for warranty costs.
(SO 5)

BE11-7 Cindy Neuer's regular hourly wage rate is $16, and she receives an hourly rate of $24 for work in excess of 40 hours. During a January pay period, Cindy works 47 hours. Cindy's federal income tax withholding is $95, and she has no voluntary deductions. Compute Cindy Neuer's gross earnings and net pay for the pay period.

Compute gross earnings and net pay.
(SO 6)

BE11-8 Data for Cindy Neuer are presented in BE11-7. Prepare the journal entries to record **(a)** Cindy's pay for the period and **(b)** the payment of Cindy's wages. Use January 15 for the end of the pay period and the payment date.

Record a payroll and the payment of wages.
(SO 6)

BE11-9 In January, gross earnings in Vega Company totaled $70,000. All earnings are subject to 8% FICA taxes, 5.4% state unemployment taxes, and 0.8% federal unemployment taxes. Prepare the entry to record January payroll tax expense.

Record employer payroll taxes.
(SO 7)

BE11-10 Rodriquez Company has the following payroll procedures.

(a) Supervisor approves overtime work.
(b) The human resources department prepares hiring authorization forms for new hires.
(c) A second payroll department employee verifies payroll calculations.
(d) The treasurer's department pays employees.

Identify the payroll function to which each procedure pertains.

Identify payroll functions.
(SO 8)

Record estimated vacation benefits.

(SO 9)

*BE11-11   At Tagaci Company employees are entitled to one day's vacation for each month worked. In January, 80 employees worked the full month. Record the vacation pay liability for January assuming the average daily pay for each employee is $120.

DO IT! REVIEW

Answer questions about current liabilities.

(SO 2, 3)

DO IT! 11-1   You and several classmates are studying for the next accounting examination. They ask you to answer the following questions:

1. If cash is borrowed on a $70,000, 9-month, 12% note on August 1, how much interest expense would be incurred by December 31?
2. The cash register total including sales taxes is $42,000, and the sales tax rate is 5%. What is the sales taxes payable?
3. If $42,000 is collected in advance on November 1 for 6-month magazine subscriptions, what amount of subscription revenue is earned by December 31?

Prepare current liabilities section and compute liquidity measures.

(SO 4, 5)

DO IT! 11-2   Moth Company has the following account balances at December 31, 2010.

Notes payable ($60,000 due after 12/31/11)	$100,000
Unearned revenue	70,000
Other long-term debt ($90,000 due in 2011)	250,000
Salaries payable	32,000
Utilities payable	13,000
Accounts payable	50,000

In addition, Moth is involved in a lawsuit. Legal counsel feels it is probable Moth will pay damages of $85,000 in 2011.

(a) Prepare the current liability section of Moth's 12/31/10 balance sheet.
(b) Moth's current assets are $570,000. Compute Moth's working capital and current ratio.

Calculate net pay and record payroll.

(SO 6)

DO IT! 11-3   In January, gross earnings in Alexi Company were $60,000. All earnings are subject to 8% FICA taxes. Federal income tax withheld was $14,000, and state income tax withheld was $1,600. (a) Calculate net pay for January, and (b) record the payroll.

Record employer's payroll taxes.

(SO 7)

DO IT! 11-4   In January, the payroll supervisor determines that gross earnings for Bond Company are $110,000. All earnings are subject to 8% FICA taxes, 5.4% state unemployment taxes, and 0.8% federal unemployment taxes. Bond asks you to record the employer's payroll taxes.

EXERCISES

Prepare entries for interest-bearing notes.

(SO 2)

E11-1   Rob Judson Company had the following transactions involving notes payable.

July 1, 2010	Borrows $50,000 from Third National Bank by signing a 9-month, 12% note.
Nov. 1, 2010	Borrows $60,000 from DeKalb State Bank by signing a 3-month, 10% note.
Dec. 31, 2010	Prepares adjusting entries.
Feb. 1, 20011	Pays principal and interest to DeKalb State Bank.
Apr. 1, 20011	Pays principal and interest to Third National Bank.

Instructions
Prepare journal entries for each of the transactions.

Prepare entries for interest-bearing notes.

(SO 2)

E11-2   On June 1, Melendez Company borrows $90,000 from First Bank on a 6-month, $90,000, 12% note.

Instructions
(a) Prepare the entry on June 1.
(b) Prepare the adjusting entry on June 30.
(c) Prepare the entry at maturity (December 1), assuming monthly adjusting entries have been made through November 30.
(d) What was the total financing cost (interest expense)?

E11-3   In providing accounting services to small businesses, you encounter the following situations pertaining to cash sales.

1. Warkentinne Company rings up sales and sales taxes separately on its cash register. On April 10, the register totals are sales $30,000 and sales taxes $1,500.
2. Rivera Company does not segregate sales and sales taxes. Its register total for April 15 is $23,540, which includes a 7% sales tax.

Journalize sales and related taxes.

(SO 3)

Instructions
Prepare the entry to record the sales transactions and related taxes for each client.

E11-4   Guyer Company publishes a monthly sports magazine, *Fishing Preview*. Subscriptions to the magazine cost $20 per year. During November 2010, Guyer sells 12,000 subscriptions beginning with the December issue. Guyer prepares financial statements quarterly and recognizes subscription revenue earned at the end of the quarter. The company uses the accounts Unearned Subscriptions and Subscription Revenue.

Journalize unearned subscription revenue.

(SO 3)

Instructions
(a) Prepare the entry in November for the receipt of the subscriptions.
(b) Prepare the adjusting entry at December 31, 2010, to record subscription revenue earned in December 2010.
(c) Prepare the adjusting entry at March 31, 2011, to record subscription revenue earned in the first quarter of 2011.

E11-5   Hiatt Company sells automatic can openers under a 75-day warranty for defective merchandise. Based on past experience, Hiatt estimates that 3% of the units sold will become defective during the warranty period. Management estimates that the average cost of replacing or repairing a defective unit is $20. The units sold and units defective that occurred during the last 2 months of 2010 are as follows.

Record estimated liability and expense for warranties.

(SO 5)

Month	Units Sold	Units Defective Prior to December 31
November	30,000	600
December	32,000	400

Instructions
(a) Determine the estimated warranty liability at December 31 for the units sold in November and December.
(b) Prepare the journal entries to record the estimated liability for warranties and the costs incurred in honoring 1,000 warranty claims. (Assume actual costs of $20,000.)
(c) Give the entry to record the honoring of 500 warranty contracts in January at an average cost of $20.

E11-6   Brad Hoey Co. is involved in a lawsuit as a result of an accident that took place September 5, 2010. The lawsuit was filed on November 1, 2010, and claims damages of $1,000,000.

Record and disclose contingent liabilities.

(SO 5)

Instructions
(a) At December 31, 2010, Brad Hoey's attorneys feel it is remote that Brad Hoey will lose the lawsuit. How should the company account for the effects of the lawsuit?
(b) Assume instead that at December 31, 2010, Brad Hoey's attorneys feel it is probable that Brad Hoey will lose the lawsuit, and be required to pay $1,000,000. How should the company account for this lawsuit?
(c) Assume instead that at December 31, 2010, Brad Hoey's attorneys feel it is reasonably possible that Brad Hoey could lose the lawsuit, and be required to pay $1,000,000. How should the company account for this lawsuit?

E11-7   Jewett Online Company has the following liability accounts after posting adjusting entries: Accounts Payable $63,000, Unearned Ticket Revenue $24,000, Estimated Warranty Liability $18,000, Interest Payable $8,000, Mortgage Payable $120,000, Notes Payable $80,000, and Sales Taxes Payable $10,000. Assume the company's operating cycle is less than 1 year, ticket revenue will be earned within 1 year, warranty costs are expected to be incurred within 1 year, and the notes mature in 3 years.

Prepare the current liability section of the balance sheet.

(SO 1, 2, 3, 4, 5)

Instructions

(a) Prepare the current liabilities section of the balance sheet, assuming $30,000 of the mortgage is payable next year.

(b) Comment on Jewett Online Company's liquidity, assuming total current assets are $300,000.

Calculate liquidity ratios.
(SO 4)

E11-8 Kroger Co.'s 2007 financial statements contained the following data (in millions).

Current assets	$ 6,755	Accounts receivable	$ 773
Total assets	21,215	Interest expense	488
Current liabilities	7,581	Income tax expense	633
Total liabilities	16,292	Net income	1,115
Cash	189		

Instructions

Compute these values:

(a) Working capital.   **(b)** Current ratio.

Calculate current ratio and working capital before and after paying accounts payable.
(SO 4)

E11-9 The following financial data were reported by 3M Company for 2006 and 2007 (dollars in millions).

3M COMPANY
Balance Sheets (partial)

	2007	2006
Current assets		
Cash and cash equivalents	$1,896	$1,447
Accounts receivable, net	3,362	3,102
Inventories	2,852	2,601
Other current assets	1,728	1,796
Total current assets	$9,838	$8,946
Current liabilities	$5,362	$7,323

Instructions

(a) Calculate the current ratio and working capital for 3M for 2006 and 2007.

(b) Suppose that at the end of 2007 3M management used $200 million cash to pay off $200 million of accounts payable. How would its current ratio and working capital have changed?

Compute net pay and record pay for one employee.
(SO 6)

E11-10 Joyce Kieffer's regular hourly wage rate is $15, and she receives a wage of 1½ times the regular hourly rate for work in excess of 40 hours. During a March weekly pay period Joyce worked 42 hours. Her gross earnings prior to the current week were $6,000. Joyce is married and claims three withholding allowances. Her only voluntary deduction is for group hospitalization insurance at $25 per week.

Instructions

(a) Compute the following amounts for Joyce's wages for the current week.
   (1) Gross earnings.
   (2) FICA taxes. (Assume an 8% rate on maximum of $90,000.)
   (3) Federal income taxes withheld. (Use the withholding table in the text, page 497.)
   (4) State income taxes withheld. (Assume a 2.0% rate.)
   (5) Net pay.

(b) Record Joyce's pay, assuming she is an office computer operator.

Compute maximum FICA deductions.
(SO 6)

E11-11 Employee earnings records for Medenciy Company reveal the following gross earnings for four employees through the pay period of December 15.

C. Ogle	$93,500	D. Delgado	$96,100
L. Jeter	$97,600	T. Spivey	$104,000

For the pay period ending December 31, each employee's gross earnings is $4,000. The FICA tax rate is 8% on gross earnings of $100,000.

Instructions
Compute the FICA withholdings that should be made for each employee for the December 31
pay period. (Show computations.)

E11-12 Alvamar Company has the following data for the weekly payroll ending January 31.

*Prepare payroll register and
record payroll and payroll tax
expense.*

(SO 6, 7)

| | Hours | | | | | | Hourly | Federal Income Tax | Health |
Employee	M	T	W	T	F	S	Rate	Withholding	Insurance
M. Hashmi	8	8	9	8	10	3	$12	$34	$10
E. Benson	8	8	8	8	8	2	13	37	25
K. Kern	9	10	8	8	9	0	15	58	25

Employees are paid 1½ times the regular hourly rate for all hours worked in excess of 40 hours per
week. FICA taxes are 8% on the first $100,000 of gross earnings. Alvamar Company is subject to 5.4%
state unemployment taxes and 0.8% federal unemployment taxes on the first $7,000 of gross earnings.

Instructions
(a) Prepare the payroll register for the weekly payroll.
(b) Prepare the journal entries to record the payroll and Alvamar's payroll tax expense.

E11-13 Selected data from a February payroll register for Gerfield Company are presented
below. Some amounts are intentionally omitted.

*Compute missing payroll
amounts and record payroll.*

(SO 6)

Gross earnings:		State income taxes	$(3)
Regular	$8,900	Union dues	100
Overtime	(1)	Total deductions	(4)
Total	(2)	Net pay	$7,660
Deductions:		Accounts debited:	
FICA taxes	$ 800	Warehouse wages	(5)
Federal income taxes	1,140	Store wages	$4,000

FICA taxes are 8%. State income taxes are 3% of gross earnings.

Instructions
(a) Fill in the missing amounts.
(b) Journalize the February payroll and the payment of the payroll.

E11-14 According to a payroll register summary of Ruiz Company, the amount of employees'
gross pay in December was $850,000, of which $90,000 was not subject to FICA tax and $750,000
was not subject to state and federal unemployment taxes.

*Determine employer's payroll
taxes; record payroll tax
expense.*

(SO 7)

Instructions
(a) Determine the employer's payroll tax expense for the month, using the following rates:
FICA 8%, state unemployment 5.4%, federal unemployment 0.8%.
(b) Prepare the journal entry to record December payroll tax expense.

*E11-15 Cerner Company has two fringe benefit plans for its employees:

*Prepare adjusting entries for
fringe benefits.*

(SO 9)

1. It grants employees 2 days' vacation for each month worked. Ten employees worked the entire month of March at an average daily wage of $120 per employee.
2. In its pension plan the company recognizes 10% of gross earnings as a pension expense.
   Gross earnings in March were $40,000. No contribution has been made to the pension fund.

Instructions
Prepare the adjusting entries at March 31.

*E11-16 Serenity Corporation has 20 employees who each earn $120 a day. The following
information is available.

*Prepare journal entries for
fringe benefits.*

(SO 9)

1. At December 31, Serenity recorded vacation benefits. Each employee earned 5 vacation
   days during the year.
2. At December 31, Serenity recorded pension expense of $100,000, and made a contribution
   of $70,000 to the pension plan.
3. In January, 18 employees used one vacation day each.

Instructions
Prepare Serenity's journal entries to record these transactions.

EXERCISES: SET B

Visit the book's companion website at **www.wiley.com/college/weygandt**, and choose the Student Companion site, to access Exercise Set B.

PROBLEMS: SET A

Prepare current liability entries, adjusting entries, and current liabilities section.

(SO 1, 2, 3, 4, 5)

P11-1A   On January 1, 2010, the ledger of Mane Company contains the following liability accounts.

Accounts Payable	$52,000
Sales Taxes Payable	7,700
Unearned Service Revenue	16,000

During January the following selected transactions occurred.

Jan. 5   Sold merchandise for cash totaling $22,680, which includes 8% sales taxes.
   12   Provided services for customers who had made advance payments of $10,000. (Credit Service Revenue.)
   14   Paid state revenue department for sales taxes collected in December 2009 ($7,700).
   20   Sold 800 units of a new product on credit at $50 per unit, plus 8% sales tax. This new product is subject to a 1-year warranty.
   21   Borrowed $18,000 from UCLA Bank on a 3-month, 8%, $18,000 note.
   25   Sold merchandise for cash totaling $12,420, which includes 8% sales taxes.

Instructions
(a) Journalize the January transactions.
(b) Journalize the adjusting entries at January 31 for (1) the outstanding notes payable, and (2) estimated warranty liability, assuming warranty costs are expected to equal 7% of sales of the new product. (*Hint:* Use one-third of a month for the UCLA Bank note.)

(c) Current liability total $84,640

(c) Prepare the current liabilities section of the balance sheet at January 31, 2010. Assume no change in accounts payable.

Journalize and post note transactions; show balance sheet presentation.

(SO 2)

P11-2A   The following are selected transactions of Winsky Company. Winsky prepares financial statements quarterly.

Jan.   2   Purchased merchandise on account from Yokum Company, $30,000, terms 2/10, n/30.
Feb.   1   Issued a 9%, 2-month, $30,000 note to Yokum in payment of account.
Mar. 31   Accrued interest for 2 months on Yokum note.
Apr.   1   Paid face value and interest on Yokum note.
July   1   Purchased equipment from Korsak Equipment paying $11,000 in cash and signing a 10%, 3-month, $40,000 note.
Sept. 30   Accrued interest for 3 months on Korsak note.
Oct.   1   Paid face value and interest on Korsak note.
Dec.   1   Borrowed $15,000 from the Otago Bank by issuing a 3-month, 8% note with a face value of $15,000.
Dec. 31   Recognized interest expense for 1 month on Otago Bank note.

Instructions
(a) Prepare journal entries for the listed transactions and events.
(b) Post to the accounts Notes Payable, Interest Payable, and Interest Expense.
(c) Show the balance sheet presentation of notes and interest payable at December 31.

(d) $1,550

(d) What is total interest expense for the year?

Prepare payroll register and payroll entries.

(SO 6, 7)

P11-3A   Del Hardware has four employees who are paid on an hourly basis plus time-and-a half for all hours worked in excess of 40 a week. Payroll data for the week ended March 15, 2010, are presentd below.

Employee	Hours Worked	Hourly Rate	Federal Income Tax Withholdings	United Fund
Joe Devena	40	$15.00	$?	$5.00
Mary Keener	42	15.00	?	5.00
Andy Dye	44	13.00	60	8.00
Kim Shen	46	13.00	61	5.00

Devena and Keener are married. They claim 0 and 4 withholding allowances, respectively. The following tax rates are applicable: FICA 8%, state income taxes 3%, state unemployment taxes

5.4%, and federal unemployment 0.8%. The first three employees are sales clerks (store wages expense). The fourth employee performs administrative duties (office wages expense).

Instructions

(a) Prepare a payroll register for the weekly payroll. (Use the wage-bracket withholding table in the text for federal income tax withholdings.)

(b) Journalize the payroll on March 15, 2010, and the accrual of employer payroll taxes.

(c) Journalize the payment of the payroll on March 16, 2010.

(d) Journalize the deposit in a Federal Reserve bank on March 31, 2010, of the FICA and federal income taxes payable to the government.

(a) Net pay $1,944.20; Store wages expense $1,843

(b) Payroll tax expense $352.16

(d) Cash paid $636.80

P11-4A The following payroll liability accounts are included in the ledger of Armitage Company on January 1, 2010.

Journalize payroll transactions and adjusting entries.

(SO 6, 7, 9)

Peachtree

FICA Taxes Payable	$760.00
Federal Income Taxes Payable	1,204.60
State Income Taxes Payable	108.95
Federal Unemployment Taxes Payable	288.95
State Unemployment Taxes Payable	1,954.40
Union Dues Payable	870.00
U.S. Savings Bonds Payable	360.00

In January, the following transactions occurred.

Jan. 10   Sent check for $870.00 to union treasurer for union dues.

12   Deposited check for $1,964.60 in Federal Reserve bank for FICA taxes and federal income taxes withheld.

15   Purchased U.S. Savings Bonds for employees by writing check for $360.00.

17   Paid state income taxes withheld from employees.

20   Paid federal and state unemployment taxes.

31   Completed monthly payroll register, which shows office salaries $26,600, store wages $28,400, FICA taxes withheld $4,400, federal income taxes payable $2,158, state income taxes payable $454, union dues payable $400, United Fund contributions payable $1,888, and net pay $45,700.

31   Prepared payroll checks for the net pay and distributed checks to employees.

At January 31, the company also makes the following accrued adjustments pertaining to employee compensation.

1. Employer payroll taxes: FICA taxes 8%, federal unemployment taxes 0.8%, and state unemployment taxes 5.4%.

***2.** Vacation pay: 6% of gross earnings.

Instructions

(a) Journalize the January transactions.

(b) Journalize the adjustments pertaining to employee compensation at January 31.

(b) Payroll tax expense $7,810; Vacation benefits expense $3,300

P11-5A For the year ended December 31, 2010, Blasing Electrical Repair Company reports the following summary payroll data.

Prepare entries for payroll and payroll taxes; prepare W-2 data.

(SO 6, 7)

Gross earnings:	
Administrative salaries	$200,000
Electricians' wages	370,000
Total	$570,000
Deductions:	
FICA taxes	$ 38,800
Federal income taxes withheld	174,400
State income taxes withheld (3%)	17,100
United Fund contributions payable	27,500
Hospital insurance premiums	17,200
Total	$275,000

Blasing Company's payroll taxes are: FICA 8%, state unemployment 2.5% (due to a stable employment record), and 0.8% federal unemployment. Gross earnings subject to FICA taxes total $485,000, and gross earnings subject to unemployment taxes total $135,000.

(a) Wages Payable $295,000
(b) Payroll tax expense
     $43,255

Instructions

(a) Prepare a summary journal entry at December 31 for the full year's payroll.

(b) Journalize the adjusting entry at December 31 to record the employer's payroll taxes.

(c) The W-2 Wage and Tax Statement requires the following dollar data.

Wages, Tips, Other Compensation	Federal Income Tax Withheld	State Income Tax Withheld	FICA Wages	FICA Tax Withheld

Complete the required data for the following employees.

Employee	Gross Earnings	Federal Income Tax Withheld
Jane Eckman	$59,000	$28,500
Sharon Bishop	26,000	10,200

PROBLEMS: SET B

Prepare current liability entries, adjusting entries, and current liabilities section.

(SO 1, 2, 3, 4, 5)

P11-1B   On January 1, 2010, the ledger of Software Company contains the following liability accounts.

Accounts Payable	$30,000
Sales Taxes Payable	5,000
Unearned Service Revenue	12,000

During January the following selected transactions occurred.

Jan. 1   Borrowed $20,000 in cash from Platteville Bank on a 4-month, 6%, $20,000 note.
      5   Sold merchandise for cash totaling $9,752, which includes 6% sales taxes.
     12   Provided services for customers who had made advance payments of $8,000. (Credit Service Revenue.)
     14   Paid state treasurer's department for sales taxes collected in December 2009, $5,000.
     20   Sold 900 units of a new product on credit at $44 per unit, plus 6% sales tax. This new product is subject to a 1-year warranty.
     25   Sold merchandise for cash totaling $16,536, which includes 6% sales taxes.

Instructions

(a) Journalize the January transactions.

(b) Journalize the adjusting entries at January 31 for (1) the outstanding notes payable, and (2) estimated warranty liability, assuming warranty costs are expected to equal 5% of sales of the new product.

(c) Current liability total
     $59,944

(c) Prepare the current liabilities section of the balance sheet at January 31, 2010. Assume no change in accounts payable.

Journalize and post note transactions and show balance sheet presentation.

(SO 2)

P11-2B   The following are selected transactions of Donn Company. Donn prepares financial statements *quarterly*.

Jan.   2   Purchased merchandise on account from Stein Company, $20,000, terms 2/10, n/30.
Feb.   1   Issued a 12%, 2-month, $20,000 note to Stein in payment of account.
Mar. 31   Accrued interest for 2 months on Stein note.
Apr.   1   Paid face value and interest on Stein note.
July   1   Purchased equipment from Morelli Equipment paying $12,000 in cash and signing a 10%, 3-month, $25,000 note.
Sept. 30   Accrued interest for 3 months on Morelli note.
Oct.   1   Paid face value and interest on Morelli note.
Dec.   1   Borrowed $15,000 from the Federated Bank by issuing a 3-month, 12% note with a face value of $15,000.
Dec. 31   Recognized interest expense for 1 month on Federated Bank note.

Instructions

(a) Prepare journal entries for the above transactions and events.

(b) Post to the accounts, Notes Payable, Interest Payable, and Interest Expense.

(d) $1,175

(c) Show the balance sheet presentation of notes and interest payable at December 31.

(d) What is total interest expense for the year?

Prepare payroll register and payroll entries.

(SO 6, 7)

P11-3B   John's Drug Store has four employees who are paid on an hourly basis plus time-and-a-half for all hours worked in excess of 40 a week. Payroll data for the week ended February 15, 2010, are shown at the top of the page 521.

Employees	Hours Worked	Hourly Rate	Federal Income Tax Withholdings	United Fund
J. Uddin	39	$12.00	$ 34	$–0–
B. Conway	42	11.00	20	10.00
S. Becker	44	10.00	51	5.00
L. Blum	46	10.00	36	5.00

Uddin and Conway are married. They claim 2 and 4 withholding allowances, respectively. The following tax rates are applicable: FICA 8%, state income taxes 3%, state unemployment taxes 5.4%, and federal unemployment 0.8%. The first three employees are sales clerks (store wages expense). The fourth employee performs administrative duties (office wages expense).

Instructions
(a) Prepare a payroll register for the weekly payroll.
(b) Journalize the payroll on February 15, 2010, and the accrual of employer payroll taxes.
(c) Journalize the payment of the payroll on February 16, 2010.
(d) Journalize the deposit in a Federal Reserve bank on February 28, 2010, of the FICA and federal income taxes payable to the government.

(a) Net pay $1,521.99; Store wages expense $1,401.00

(b) Payroll tax expense $268.52

(d) Cash paid $443.56

P11-4B The following payroll liability accounts are included in the ledger of Pettibone Company on January 1, 2010.

FICA Taxes Payable	$ 540
Federal Income Taxes Payable	1,100
State Income Taxes Payable	210
Federal Unemployment Taxes Payable	54
State Unemployment Taxes Payable	365
Union Dues Payable	200
U.S. Savings Bonds Payable	300

Journalize payroll transactions and adjusting entries.

(SO 6, 7, 9)

In January, the following transactions occurred.

Jan. 10 Sent check for $200 to union treasurer for union dues.
   12 Deposited check for $1,640 in Federal Reserve bank for FICA taxes and federal income taxes withheld.
   15 Purchased U.S. Savings Bonds for employees by writing check for $300.
   17 Paid state income taxes withheld from employees.
   20 Paid federal and state unemployment taxes.
   31 Completed monthly payroll register, which shows office salaries $17,400, store wages $22,500, FICA taxes withheld $3,192, federal income taxes payable $2,540, state income taxes payable $500, union dues payable $300, United Way contributions payable $1,300, and net pay $32,068.
   31 Prepared payroll checks for the net pay and distributed checks to employees.

At January 31, the company also makes the following accruals pertaining to employee compensation.

1. Employer payroll taxes: FICA taxes 8%, state unemployment taxes 5.4%, and federal unemployment taxes 0.8%.
*2. Vacation pay: 5% of gross earnings.

Instructions
(a) Journalize the January transactions.
(b) Journalize the adjustments pertaining to employee compensation at January 31.

(b) Payroll tax expense $5,665.80; Vacation benefits expense $1,995

P11-5B For the year ended December 31, 2010, L. Ullman Company reports the following summary payroll data.

Prepare entries for payroll and payroll taxes; prepare W-2 data.

(SO 6, 7)

Gross earnings:		Deductions:	
Administrative salaries	$150,000	FICA taxes	$ 29,600
Electricians' wages	240,000	Federal income taxes withheld	78,000
Total	$390,000	State income taxes withheld (3%)	11,700
		United Fund contributions payable	17,000
		Hospital insurance premiums	12,000
		Total	$148,300

L. Ullman Company's payroll taxes are: FICA 8%, state unemployment 2.5% (due to a stable employment record), and 0.8% federal unemployment. Gross earnings subject to FICA taxes total $370,000, and gross earnings subject to unemployment taxes total $90,000.

Instructions

(a) Wages Payable $241,700

(b) Payroll tax expense $32,570

(a) Prepare a summary journal entry at December 31 for the full year's payroll.

(b) Journalize the adjusting entry at December 31 to record the employer's payroll taxes.

(c) The W-2 Wage and Tax Statement requires the dollar data shown below.

Wages, Tips, Other Compensation	Federal Income Tax Withheld	State Income Tax Withheld	FICA Wages	FICA Tax Withheld

Complete the required data for the following employees.

Employee	Gross Earnings	Federal Income Tax Withheld
R. Lowski	$50,000	$18,300
K. Monez	24,000	4,800

PROBLEMS: SET C

Visit the book's companion website at **www.wiley.com/college/weygandt**, and choose the Student Companion site, to access Problem Set C.

CONTINUING COOKIE CHRONICLE

(*Note:* This is a continuation of the Cookie Chronicle from Chapters 1 through 10.)

CCC11 Recall that Cookie Creations sells fine European mixers that it purchases from Kzinski Supply Co. Kzinski warrants the mixers to be free of defects in material and workmanship for a period of one year from the date of original purchase. If the mixer has such a defect, Kzinski will repair or replace the mixer free of charge for parts and labor.

Go to the book's companion website,
www.wiley.com/college/weygandt,
to see the completion of this problem.

BROADENING YOUR PERSPECTIVE

FINANCIAL REPORTING AND ANALYSIS

Financial Reporting Problem: PepsiCo, Inc.

BYP11-1 The financial statements of PepsiCo, Inc. and the Notes to Consolidated Financial Statements appear in Appendix A.

Instructions

Refer to PepsiCo's financial statements and answer the following questions about current and contingent liabilities and payroll costs.

(a) What were PepsiCo's total current liabilities at December 29, 2007? What was the increase/decrease in PepsiCo's total current liabilities from the prior year?

(b) In PepsiCo's Note 2 ("Our Significant Accounting Policies"), the company explains the nature of its contingencies. Under what conditions does PepsiCo recognize (record and report) liabilities for contingencies?

(c) What were the components of total current liabilities on December 29, 2007?

Comparative Analysis Problem: PepsiCo, Inc. vs. The Coca-Cola Company

BYP11-2 PepsiCo, Inc.'s financial statements are presented in Appendix A. Financial statements of The Coca-Cola Company are presented in Appendix B.

Instructions

(a) At December 29, 2007, what was PepsiCo's largest current liability account? What were its total current liabilities? At December 31, 2007, what was Coca-Cola's largest current liability account? What were its total current liabilities?

(b) Based on information contained in those financial statements, compute the following 2007 values for each company.

(1) Working capital.

(2) Current ratio.

(c) What conclusions concerning the relative liquidity of these companies can be drawn from these data?

Exploring the Web

BYP11-3 The Internal Revenue Service provides considerable information over the Internet. The following site answers payroll tax questions faced by employers.

Address: www.irs.ustreas.gov/formspubs/index.html, or go to **www.wiley.com/college/weygandt**

Steps

1. Go to the site shown above.

2. Choose **View Online, Tax Publications**.

3. Choose **Publication 15, Circular E, Employer's Tax Guide**.

Instructions

Answer each of the following questions.

(a) How does the government define "employees"?

(b) What are the special rules for Social Security and Medicare regarding children who are employed by their parents?

(c) How can an employee obtain a Social Security card if he or she doesn't have one?

(d) Must employees report to their employer tips received from customers? If so, how?

(e) Where should the employer deposit Social Security taxes withheld or contributed?

CRITICAL THINKING

Decision Making Across the Organization

BYP11-4 Kensingtown Processing Company provides word-processing services for business clients and students in a university community. The work for business clients is fairly steady throughout the year. The work for students peaks significantly in December and May as a result of term papers, research project reports, and dissertations.

Two years ago, the company attempted to meet the peak demand by hiring part-time help. This led to numerous errors and much customer dissatisfaction. A year ago, the company hired four experienced employees on a permanent basis in place of part-time help. This proved to be much better in terms of productivity and customer satisfaction. But, it has caused an increase in annual payroll costs and a significant decline in annual net income.

Recently, Valarie Flynn, a sales representative of Metcalfe Services Inc., has made a proposal to the company. Under her plan, Metcalfe will provide up to four experienced workers at a daily rate of $75 per person for an 8-hour workday. Metcalfe workers are not available on an hourly basis. Kensingtown would have to pay only the daily rate for the workers used.

The owner of Kensingtown Processing, Donna Bell, asks you, as the company's accountant, to prepare a report on the expenses that are pertinent to the decision. If the Metcalfe plan is adopted, Donna will terminate the employment of two permanent employees and will keep two permanent employees. At the moment, each employee earns an annual income of $21,000. Kensingtown pays

8% FICA taxes, 0.8% federal unemployment taxes, and 5.4% state unemployment taxes. The unemployment taxes apply to only the first $7,000 of gross earnings. In addition, Kensingtown pays $40 per month for each employee for medical and dental insurance. Donna indicates that if the Metcalfe Services plan is accepted, her needs for temporary workers will be as follows.

Months	Number of Employees	Working Days per Month
January–March	2	20
April–May	3	25
June–October	2	18
November–December	3	23

Instructions

With the class divided into groups, answer the following.

(a) Prepare a report showing the comparative payroll expense of continuing to employ permanent workers compared to adopting the Metcalfe Services Inc. plan.

(b) What other factors should Donna consider before finalizing her decision?

Communication Activity

BYP11-5 Jack Quaney, president of the Ramsberg Company, has recently hired a number of additional employees. He recognizes that additional payroll taxes will be due as a result of this hiring, and that the company will serve as the collection agent for other taxes.

Instructions

In a memorandum to Jack Quaney, explain each of the taxes, and identify the taxes that result in payroll tax expense to Ramsberg Company.

Ethics Case

BYP11-6 Daniel Longan owns and manages Daniel's Restaurant, a 24-hour restaurant near the city's medical complex. Daniel employs 9 full-time employees and 16 part-time employees. He pays all of the full-time employees by check, the amounts of which are determined by Daniel's public accountant, Gina Watt. Daniel pays all of his part-time employees in currency. He computes their wages and withdraws the cash directly from his cash register.

Gina has repeatedly urged Daniel to pay all employees by check. But as Daniel has told his competitor and friend, Steve Hill, who owns the Greasy Diner, "My part-time employees prefer the currency over a check. Also, I don't withhold or pay any taxes or workmen's compensation insurance on those cash wages because they go totally unrecorded and unnoticed."

Instructions

(a) Who are the stakeholders in this situation?

(b) What are the legal and ethical considerations regarding Daniel's handling of his payroll?

(c) Gina Watt is aware of Daniel's payment of the part-time payroll in currency. What are her ethical responsibilities in this case?

(d) What internal control principle is violated in this payroll process?

 ## "All About You" Activity

BYP11-7 As indicated in the **All About You** on page 506, medical costs are substantial and rising. But will they be the most substantial expense over your lifetime? Not likely. Will it be housing or food? Again, not likely. The answer is in the *Accounting Across the Organization* box on page 498: taxes. On average, Americans work 74 days to afford their federal taxes. Companies, too, have large tax burdens. They look very hard at tax issues in deciding where to build their plants and where to locate their administrative headquarters.

Instructions

(a) Determine what your state income taxes are if your taxable income is $60,000 and you file as a single taxpayer in the state in which you live.

(b) Assume that you own a home worth $200,000 in your community and the tax rate is 2.1%. Compute the property taxes you would pay.

(c) Assume that the total gasoline bill for your automobile is $1,200 a year (300 gallons at $4 per gallon). What are the amounts of state and federal taxes that you pay on the $1,200?

(d) Assume that your purchases for the year total $9,000. Of this amount, $5,000 was for food and prescription drugs. What is the amount of sales tax you would pay on these purchases? (Many states do not levy a sales tax on food or prescription drugs. Does yours?)

(e) Determine what your Social Security taxes are if your income is $60,000.

(f) Determine what your federal income taxes are if your taxable income is $60,000 and you file as a single taxpayer.

(g) Determine your *total* taxes paid based on the above calculations, and determine the percentage of income that you would pay in taxes based on the following formula: Total taxes paid ÷ Total income.

Answers to Insight and Accounting Across the Organization Questions

p. 492 Contingencies: How Big Are They?

Q: Why do you think most companies disclose, but do not record, contingent liabilities?

A: *A contingent liability may be probable, but often its amount is difficult to determine. If it cannot be determined, the company is not required to accrue it as a liability.*

p. 498 Taxes Are the Largest Slice of the Pie

Q: If the information on 2008 taxation depicted your spending patterns, on what date (starting on January 1) will you have earned enough to pay all of your taxes?

A: *As indicated in the story, it takes 113 (74 + 39) days to pay your taxes. Thus, April 23 is Tax Freedom Day. For the past 26 years Tax Freedom Day has occurred in April, except for the year 2000 when it occurred in May.*

Authors' Comments on *All About You:* Your Boss Wants to Know If You Jogged Today (p. 506)

A company's insurance premiums would be substantially lower if its employees did not smoke and if they were in better shape. Some argue that employees with unhealthy habits increase the share of insurance premiums that all employees have to pay. Also, unhealthy employees miss more days of work and thus burden healthy employees. On the other hand, some argue that this approach discriminates in favor of "healthy" people. Also, it is not illegal to smoke or to be overweight. Should an employer really be able to dictate against non-illegal behavior that employees do on their own time? The cost of health care is a huge problem in the U.S., with no easy answers.

Answers to Self-Study Questions

1. a   **2.** d   **3.** b   **4.** d   **5.** b   **6.** b   **7.** a   **8.** d   **9.** c   **10.** b   **11.** d   **12.** c   **13.** c
14. b   **15.** d   *****16.** d

Chapter 12

Accounting for Partnerships

STUDY OBJECTIVES

After studying this chapter, you should be able to:

1 Identify the characteristics of the partnership form of business organization.
2 Explain the accounting entries for the formation of a partnership.
3 Identify the bases for dividing net income or net loss.
4 Describe the form and content of partnership financial statements.
5 Explain the effects of the entries to record the liquidation of a partnership.

 The Navigator

✓ The Navigator

Scan **Study Objectives**	▨
Read **Feature Story**	▨
Read **Preview**	▨
Read text and answer **DO IT!** p. 532 ▨ p. 538 ▨ p. 541 ▨ p. 544 ▨	
Work **Comprehensive DO IT!** p. 545	▨
Review **Summary of Study Objectives**	▨
Answer **Self-Study Questions**	▨
Complete **Assignments**	▨

Feature Story

FROM TRIALS TO THE TOP TEN

In 1990 Cliff Chenfield and Craig Balsam gave up the razors, ties, and six-figure salaries they had become accustomed to as New York lawyers. Instead, they set up a partnership, Razor & Tie Music (www.razorandtie.com), in Cliff's living room. Ten years later, it became the only record company in the country that had achieved success in selling music both on television and in stores. Razor & Tie's entertaining and effective TV commercials have yielded unprecedented sales for multi-artist music compilations. At the same time, its hot retail label has been behind some of the most recent original, progressive releases from artists such as Kelly Sweet, All That Remains, EndeverafteR, Angelique Kidjo, Ryan Shaw, Dave Barnes, Twisted Sister, Dar Williams, Danko Jones, and Yerba Buena.

Razor & Tie may be best known for its wildly popular *Kidz Bop* CD series, the top-selling children's audio product in the United States. Advertised on

Nickelodeon, the Cartoon Network, and elsewhere, *Kidz Bop* titles have sold over 7 million copies. Seven of the 11 releases in the series have "gone Gold."

Razor & Tie got its start with its first TV release, *Those Fabulous '70s* (100,000 copies sold), followed by *Disco Fever* (over 300,000 sold).

After restoring the respectability of the oft-maligned music of the 1970s, the partners forged into the musical '80s with the same zeal that elicited success with their first releases. In 1993, Razor & Tie released *Totally '80s*, a collection of Top-10 singles from the 1980s that has sold over 450,000 units. Featuring the tag line, "The greatest hits from the decade when communism died and music videos were born," *Totally '80s* was the best-selling direct-response album in the country in 1993.

In 1995, Razor & Tie broke into the contemporary music world with *Living in the '90s*, the most successful record in the history of the company. Featuring a number of songs that were still hits on the radio at the time the package initially aired, *Living in the '90s* was a blockbuster. It received Gold certification in less than nine months and rewrote the rules on direct-response albums. For the first time, contemporary music was available through an album offered only through direct-response spots. Razor & Tie pursued that same strategy with its 2002 introduction of the *Kidz Bop* titles.

How has Razor & Tie carved out its sizable piece of the market? Through the complementary talents of the two partners. Their imagination and savvy, along with exciting new releases planned for the coming years, ensure Razor & Tie continued growth.

✓ The Navigator

Inside Chapter 12...

It is not surprising that when Cliff Chenfield and Craig Balsam began Razor & Tie, they decided to use the partnership form of organization. Both saw the need for hands-on control of their product and its promotion. In this chapter, we will discuss reasons why businesses select the partnership form of organization. We also will explain the major issues in accounting for partnerships.

The content and organization of Chapter 12 are as follows.

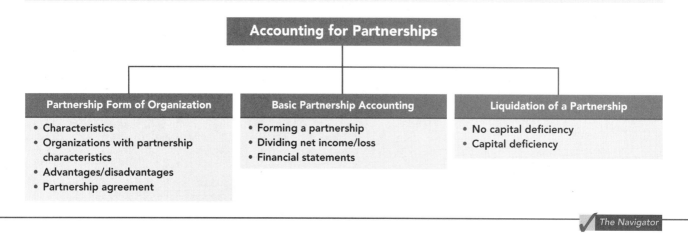

Accounting for Partnerships

Partnership Form of Organization	Basic Partnership Accounting	Liquidation of a Partnership
• Characteristics • Organizations with partnership characteristics • Advantages/disadvantages • Partnership agreement	• Forming a partnership • Dividing net income/loss • Financial statements	• No capital deficiency • Capital deficiency

✓ *The Navigator*

PARTNERSHIP FORM OF ORGANIZATION

A **partnership** is an association of two or more persons to carry on as co-owners of a business for profit. Partnerships are sometimes used in small retail, service, or manufacturing companies. Also accountants, lawyers, and doctors find it desirable to form partnerships with other professionals in the field.

Characteristics of Partnerships

Partnerships are fairly easy to form. People form partnerships simply by a verbal agreement, or more formally, by written agreement. We explain the principal characteristics of partnerships in the following sections.

Association of Individuals

ASSOCIATION OF INDIVIDUALS

A partnership is a legal entity. A partnership can own property (land, buildings, equipment), and can sue or be sued. **A partnership also is an accounting entity.** Thus, the personal assets, liabilities, and transactions of the partners are excluded from the accounting records of the partnership, just as they are in a proprietorship.

The net income of a partnership is not taxed as a separate entity. But, a partnership must file an information tax return showing partnership net income and each partner's share of that net income. Each partner's share is taxable at **personal tax rates**, regardless of the amount of net income each withdraws from the business during the year.

Mutual Agency

MUTUAL AGENCY

Mutual agency means that each partner acts on behalf of the partnership when engaging in partnership business. The act of any partner is binding on all other partners. This is true even when partners act beyond the scope of their authority, so long as the act appears to be appropriate for the partnership. For example, a partner of a grocery store who purchases a delivery truck creates a binding contract in the name of the partnership, even if the partnership agreement denies this authority. On the other hand, if a partner in a law firm purchased a snowmobile for the partnership, such an act would not be binding on the partnership. The purchase is clearly outside the scope of partnership business.

LIMITED LIFE

Corporations have unlimited life. Partnerships do not. A partnership may be ended voluntarily at any time through the acceptance of a new partner or the withdrawal of a partner. It may be ended involuntarily by the death or incapacity of a partner. **Partnership dissolution** occurs whenever a partner withdraws or a new partner is admitted. Dissolution does not necessarily mean that the business ends. If the continuing partners agree, operations can continue without interruption by forming a new partnership.

Limited Life

UNLIMITED LIABILITY

Each partner is **personally and individually liable** for all partnership liabilities. Creditors' claims attach first to partnership assets. If these are insufficient, the claims then attach to the personal resources of any partner, irrespective of that partner's equity in the partnership. Because each partner is responsible for all the debts of the partnership, each partner is said to have **unlimited liability**.

CO-OWNERSHIP OF PROPERTY

Partners jointly own partnership assets. If the partnership is dissolved, each partner has a claim on total assets equal to the balance in his or her respective capital account. This claim does not attach to **specific assets** that an individual partner contributed to the firm. Similarly, if a partner invests a building in the partnership valued at $100,000 and the building is later sold at a gain of $20,000, the partners all share in the gain.

Unlimited Liability

Partnership net income (or net loss) is also co-owned. **If the partnership contract does not specify to the contrary, all net income or net loss is shared equally by the partners.** As you will see later, though, partners may agree to unequal sharing of net income or net loss.

Co-ownership of Property

Organizations with Partnership Characteristics

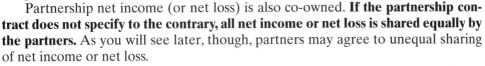

If you are starting a business with a friend and each of you has little capital and your business is not risky, you probably want to use a partnership. As indicated above, the partnership is easy to establish and its cost is minimal. These types of partnerships are often called **regular partnerships**. However if your business is risky—say, roof repair or providing some type of professional service—you will want to limit your liability and not use a regular partnership. As a result, special forms of business organizations with partnership characteristics are now often used to provide protection from unlimited liability for people who wish to work together in some activity.

The special partnership forms are: limited partnerships, limited liability partnerships, and limited liability companies. These special forms use the same accounting procedures as those described for a regular partnership. In addition, for taxation purposes, all the profits and losses pass through these organizations (similar to the regular partnership) to the owners, who report their share of partnership net income or losses on their personal tax returns.

LIMITED PARTNERSHIPS

In a limited partnership, one or more partners have **unlimited liability** and one or more partners have **limited liability** for the debts of the firm. Those with unlimited

INTERNATIONAL NOTE

Much of the funding for successful new U.S. businesses comes from "venture capital" firms, which are organized as limited partnerships. To develop its own venture capital industry, China believes that it needs the limited liability form. Therefore, China has taken steps to model its partnership laws to allow for limited partnerships like those in the U.S.

HELPFUL HINT

In an LLP, *all* partners have limited liability. There are no general partners.

liability are **general partners**. Those with limited liability are **limited partners**. Limited partners are responsible for the debts of the partnership up to the limit of their investment in the firm.

The words "Limited Partnership," or "Ltd.," or "LP" identify this type of organization. For the privilege of limited liability, the limited partner usually accepts less compensation than a general partner and exercises less influence in the affairs of the firm. If the limited partners get involved in management, they risk their liability protection.

LIMITED LIABILITY PARTNERSHIP

Most states allow professionals such as lawyers, doctors, and accountants to form a **limited liability partnership** or "LLP." The LLP is designed to protect innocent partners from malpractice or negligence claims resulting from the acts of another partner. LLPs generally carry large insurance policies as protection against malpractice suits. These professional partnerships vary in size from a medical partnership of three to five doctors, to 150 to 200 partners in a large law firm, to more than 2,000 partners in an international accounting firm.

LIMITED LIABILITY COMPANIES

A hybrid form of business organization with certain features like a corporation and others like a limited partnership is the **limited liability company**, or "LLC." An LLC usually has a limited life. The owners, called **members**, have limited liability like owners of a corporation. Whereas limited partners do not actively participate in the management of a limited partnership (LP), the members of a limited liability company (LLC) can assume an active management role. For income tax purposes, the IRS usually classifies an LLC as a partnership.

ACCOUNTING ACROSS THE ORGANIZATION

Limited Liability Companies Gain in Popularity

The proprietorship form of business organization is still the most popular, followed by the corporate form. But whenever a group of individuals wants to form a partnership, the limited liability company is usually the popular choice.

One other form of business organization is a *subchapter S corporation*. A subchapter S corporation has many of the characteristics of a partnership—especially, taxation as a partnership—but it is losing its popularity. The reason: It involves more paperwork and expense than a limited liability company, which in most cases offers similar advantages.

? Why do you think that the use of the limited liability company is gaining in popularity?

Illustration 12-1 (next page) summarizes different forms of organizations that have partnership characteristics.

Advantages and Disadvantages of Partnerships

Why do people choose partnerships? One major advantage of a partnership is to combine the skills and resources of two or more individuals. In addition, partnerships are easily formed and are relatively free from government regulations and restrictions. A partnership does not have to contend with the "red tape" that a

	Major Advantages	Major Disadvantages
**Regular Partnership** General Partners	Simple and inexpensive to create and operate.	Owners (partners) personally liable for business debts.
**Limited Partnership** General Limited Partners Partners	Limited partners have limited personal liability for business debts as long as they do not participate in management. General partners can raise cash without involving outside investors in management of business.	General partners personally liable for business debts. More expensive to create than regular partnership. Suitable mainly for companies that invest in real estate.
**Limited Liability Partnership**	Mostly of interest to partners in old-line professions such as law, medicine, and accounting. Owners (partners) are not personally liable for the malpractice of other partners.	Unlike a limited liability company, owners (partners) remain personally liable for many types of obligations owed to business creditors, lenders, and landlords. Often limited to a short list of professions.
**Limited Liability Company**	Owners have limited personal liability for business debts even if they participate in management.	More expensive to create than regular partnership.

Illustration 12-1
Different forms of organizations with partnership characteristics

Source: *www.nolo.com* (accessed June 2006).

corporation must face. Also, partners generally can make decisions quickly on substantive business matters without having to consult a board of directors.

On the other hand, partnerships also have some major disadvantages. **Unlimited liability** is particularly troublesome. Many individuals fear they may lose not only their initial investment but also their personal assets, if those assets are needed to pay partnership creditors.

Illustration 12-2 summarizes the advantages and disadvantages of the regular partnership form of business organization. As indicated in the previous section,

Advantages	Disadvantages
Combining skills and resources of two or more individuals	Mutual agency
Ease of formation	Limited life
Freedom from governmental regulations and restrictions	Unlimited liability
Ease of decision making	

Illustration 12-2
Advantages and disadvantages of a partnership

different types of partnership forms have evolved to reduce some of the disadvantages.

DO IT!

PARTNERSHIP ORGANIZATION

Indicate whether each of the following statements is true or false.

_____ 1. Partnerships have unlimited life. Corporations do not.

_____ 2. Partners jointly own partnership assets. A partner's claim on partnership assets does not attach to specific assets.

_____ 3. In a limited partnership, the general partners have unlimited liability.

_____ 4. The members of a limited liability company have limited liability, like shareholders of a corporation, and they are taxed like corporate shareholders.

_____ 5. Because of mutual agency, the act of any partner is binding on all other partners.

action plan

✔ When forming a business, carefully consider what type of organization would best suit the needs of the business.

✔ Keep in mind the new, "hybrid" organizational forms that have many of the best characteristics of partnerships and corporations.

Solution

1. False. Corporations have unlimited life. Partnerships do not.
2. True.
3. True.
4. False. The members of a limited liability company are taxed like partners in a partnership.
5. True.

Related exercise material: **E12-1** and **DO IT!** 12-1.

 The Navigator

The Partnership Agreement

ETHICS NOTE

A well-developed partnership agreement reduces ethical conflict among partners. It specifies in clear and concise language the process by which the partners will resolve ethical and legal problems. This issue is especially significant when the partnership experiences financial distress.

Ideally, the agreement of two or more individuals to form a partnership should be expressed in a written contract, called the **partnership agreement** or **articles of co-partnership**. The partnership agreement contains such basic information as the name and principal location of the firm, the purpose of the business, and date of inception. In addition, it should specify relationships among the partners, such as:

1. Names and capital contributions of partners.
2. Rights and duties of partners.
3. Basis for sharing net income or net loss.
4. Provision for withdrawals of assets.
5. Procedures for submitting disputes to arbitration.
6. Procedures for the withdrawal or addition of a partner.
7. Rights and duties of surviving partners in the event of a partner's death.

We cannot overemphasize the importance of a written contract. The agreement should attempt to anticipate all possible situations, contingencies, and disagreements. The help of a lawyer is highly desirable in preparing the agreement.

ACCOUNTING ACROSS THE ORGANIZATION

How to Part Ways Nicely

What should you do when you and your business partner do not agree on things, to the point where you are no longer on speaking terms? Given how heated business situations can get, this is not an unusual occurrence. Unfortunately, in many instances the partners do everything they can to undermine the other partner, eventually destroying the business. In some instances people even steal from the partnership because they either feel that they "deserve it" or they assume that the other partners are stealing from them.

It would be much better to follow the example of Jennifer Appel and her partner. They found that after opening a successful bakery and writing a cookbook, they couldn't agree on how the business should be run. The other partner bought out Ms. Appel's share of the business, and Ms. Appel went on to start her own style of bakery, which she ultimately franchised.

Source: Paulette Thomas, "As Partnership Sours, Parting Is Sweet," *Wall Street Journal,* July 6, 2004, p. A20.

 How can partnership conflicts be minimized and more easily resolved?

BASIC PARTNERSHIP ACCOUNTING

We now turn to the basic accounting for partnerships. The major accounting issues relate to forming the partnership, dividing income or loss, and preparing financial statements.

Forming a Partnership

Each partner's initial investment in a partnership is entered in the partnership records. The partnership should record these investments at the **fair market value of the assets at the date of their transfer to the partnership.** All partners must agree to the values assigned.

To illustrate, assume that A. Rolfe and T. Shea combine their proprietorships to start a partnership named U.S. Software. The firm will specialize in developing financial modeling software packages. Rolfe and Shea have the following assets prior to the formation of the partnership.

> **STUDY OBJECTIVE 2**
>
> Explain the accounting entries for the formation of a partnership.

	Book Value		Market Value	
	A. Rolfe	**T. Shea**	**A. Rolfe**	**T. Shea**
Cash	$ 8,000	$ 9,000	$ 8,000	$ 9,000
Office equipment	5,000		4,000	
Accumulated depreciation	(2,000)			
Accounts receivable		4,000		4,000
Allowance for doubtful accounts		(700)		(1,000)
	$11,000	$12,300	$12,000	$12,000

Illustration 12-3
Book and market values of assets invested

*Items under **owners' equity** (OE) in the accounting equation analyses (in margins) are not labeled in this partnership chapter. Nearly all affect partners' **capital** accounts.*

The partnership records the investments as follows.

Investment of A. Rolfe

Cash	8,000	
Office Equipment	4,000	
A. Rolfe, Capital		12,000
(To record investment of Rolfe)		

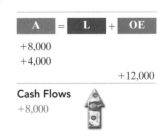

A	=	L	+	OE
+8,000				
+4,000				
				+12,000

Cash Flows
+8,000

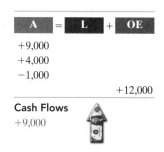

Investment of T. Shea

Cash	9,000	
Accounts Receivable	4,000	
Allowance for Doubtful Accounts		1,000
T. Shea, Capital		12,000
(To record investment of Shea)		

Note that the partnership records neither the original cost of the office equipment ($5,000) nor its book value ($5,000 − $2,000). It records the equipment at its fair market value, $4,000. The partnership does not carry forward any accumulated depreciation from the books of previous entities (in this case, the two proprietorships).

In contrast, the gross claims on customers ($4,000) are carried forward to the partnership. The partnership adjusts the allowance for doubtful accounts to $1,000, to arrive at a cash (net) realizable value of $3,000. A partnership may start with an allowance for doubtful accounts because it will continue to collect existing accounts receivable, some of which are expected to be uncollectible. In addition, this procedure maintains the control and subsidiary relationship between Accounts Receivable and the accounts receivable subsidiary ledger.

After formation of the partnership, the accounting for transactions is similar to any other type of business organization. For example, the partners record all transactions with outside parties, such as the purchase or sale of merchandise inventory and the payment or receipt of cash, the same as would a sole proprietor.

The steps in the accounting cycle described in Chapter 4 for a proprietorship also apply to a partnership. For example, the partnership prepares a trial balance and journalizes and posts adjusting entries. A worksheet may be used. There are minor differences in journalizing and posting closing entries and in preparing financial statements, as we explain in the following sections. The differences occur because there is more than one owner.

Dividing Net Income or Net Loss

Partners equally share partnership net income or net loss unless the partnership contract indicates otherwise. The same basis of division usually applies to both net income and net loss. It is customary to refer to this basis as the **income ratio**, the **income and loss ratio**, or the **profit and loss (P&L) ratio**. Because of its wide acceptance, we will use the term income ratio to identify the basis for dividing net income and net loss. The partnership recognizes a partner's share of net income or net loss in the accounts through closing entries.

CLOSING ENTRIES

As in the case of a proprietorship, a partnership must make four entries in preparing closing entries. The entries are:

1. Debit each revenue account for its balance, and credit Income Summary for total revenues.

2. Debit Income Summary for total expenses, and credit each expense account for its balance.

3. Debit Income Summary for its balance, and credit each partner's capital account for his or her share of net income. Or, credit Income Summary, and debit each partner's capital account for his or her share of net loss.

4. Debit each partner's capital account for the balance in that partner's drawing account, and credit each partner's drawing account for the same amount.

The first two entries are the same as in a proprietorship. The last two entries are different because (1) there are two or more owners' capital and drawing accounts, and (2) it is necessary to divide net income (or net loss) among the partners.

To illustrate the last two closing entries, assume that AB Company has net income of $32,000 for 2010. The partners, L. Arbor and D. Barnett, share net income and net loss equally. Drawings for the year were Arbor $8,000 and Barnett $6,000. The last two closing entries are:

Dec. 31	Income Summary	32,000	
	L. Arbor, Capital ($32,000 × 50%)		16,000
	D. Barnett, Capital ($32,000 × 50%)		16,000
	(To transfer net income to partners' capital accounts)		
Dec. 31	L. Arbor, Capital	8,000	
	D. Barnett, Capital	6,000	
	L. Arbor, Drawing		8,000
	D. Barnett, Drawing		6,000
	(To close drawing accounts to capital accounts)		

A = L + OE
−32,000
+16,000
+16,000
Cash Flows no effect

A = L + OE
−8,000
−6,000
+8,000
+6,000
Cash Flows no effect

Assume that the beginning capital balance is $47,000 for Arbor and $36,000 for Barnett. After posting the closing entries, the capital and drawing accounts will appear as shown in Illustration 12-4.

Illustration 12-4
Partners' capital and drawing accounts after closing

L. Arbor, Capital			
12/31 Clos.	8,000	1/1 Bal.	47,000
		12/31 Clos.	16,000
		12/31 Bal.	55,000

D. Barnett, Capital			
12/31 Clos.	6,000	1/1 Bal.	36,000
		12/31 Clos.	16,000
		12/31 Bal.	46,000

L. Arbor, Drawing			
12/31 Bal.	8,000	12/31 Clos.	8,000

D. Barnett, Drawing			
12/31 Bal.	6,000	12/31 Clos.	6,000

As in a proprietorship, the partners' capital accounts are permanent accounts; their drawing accounts are temporary accounts. Normally, the capital accounts will have credit balances, and the drawing accounts will have debit balances. Drawing accounts are debited when partners withdraw cash or other assets from the partnership for personal use.

INCOME RATIOS

As noted earlier, the partnership agreement should specify the basis for sharing net income or net loss. The following are typical income ratios.

STUDY OBJECTIVE 3
Identify the bases for dividing net income or net loss.

1. A fixed ratio, expressed as a proportion (6:4), a percentage (70% and 30%), or a fraction (2/3 and 1/3).
2. A ratio based either on capital balances at the beginning of the year or on average capital balances during the year.
3. Salaries to partners and the remainder on a fixed ratio.
4. Interest on partners' capital balances and the remainder on a fixed ratio.
5. Salaries to partners, interest on partners' capital, and the remainder on a fixed ratio.

The objective is to settle on a basis that will equitably reflect the partners' capital investment and service to the partnership.

A **fixed ratio** is easy to apply, and it may be an equitable basis in some circumstances. Assume, for example, that Hughes and Lane are partners. Each contributes the same amount of capital, but Hughes expects to work full-time in the partnership and Lane expects to work only half-time. Accordingly, the partners agree to a fixed ratio of 2/3 to Hughes and 1/3 to Lane.

A **ratio based on capital balances** may be appropriate when the funds invested in the partnership are considered the critical factor. Capital ratios may also be equitable when the partners hire a manager to run the business and do not plan to take an active role in daily operations.

The three remaining ratios (items 3, 4, and 5) give specific recognition to differences among partners. These ratios provide salary allowances for time worked and interest allowances for capital invested. Then, the partnership allocates any remaining net income or net loss on a fixed ratio.

Salaries to partners and interest on partners' capital are not expenses of the partnership. Therefore, these items do not enter into the matching of expenses with revenues and the determination of net income or net loss. For a partnership, as for other entities, salaries expense pertains to the cost of services performed by employees. Likewise, interest expense relates to the cost of borrowing from creditors. But partners, as owners, are not considered either **employees** or **creditors**. When the partnership agreement permits the partners to make monthly withdrawals of cash based on their "salary," the partnership debits these withdrawals to the partner's drawing account.

SALARIES, INTEREST, AND REMAINDER ON A FIXED RATIO

Under income ratio (5) in the list above, the partnership must apply salaries and interest **before** it allocates the remainder on the specified fixed ratio. **This is true even if the provisions exceed net income. It is also true even if the partnership has suffered a net loss for the year.** The partnership's income statement should show, below net income, detailed information concerning the division of net income or net loss.

To illustrate, assume that King and Lee are co-partners in the Kingslee Company. The partnership agreement provides for: (1) salary allowances of $8,400 to King and $6,000 to Lee, (2) interest allowances of 10% on capital balances at the beginning of the year, and (3) the remainder equally. Capital balances on January 1 were King $28,000, and Lee $24,000. In 2010, partnership net income is $22,000. The division of net income is as follows.

Illustration 12-5
Income statement with division of net income

KINGSLEE COMPANY
Income Statement (partial)
For the Year Ended December 31, 2010

	Sales	$200,000		
	Net income	$ 22,000		

Division of Net Income

	Sara King	Ray Lee	Total
Salary allowance	$ 8,400	$6,000	$14,400
Interest allowance on partners' capital			
Sara King ($28,000 × 10%)	2,800		
Ray Lee ($24,000 × 10%)		2,400	
Total interest allowance			5,200
Total salaries and interest	11,200	8,400	19,600
Remaining income, $2,400			
($22,000 − $19,600)			
Sara King ($2,400 × 50%)	1,200		
Ray Lee ($2,400 × 50%)		1,200	
Total remainder			2,400
Total division of net income	$12,400	$9,600	$22,000

Kingslee records the division of net income as follows.

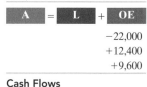

Dec. 31	Income Summary	22,000	
	Sara King, Capital		12,400
	Ray Lee, Capital		9,600
	(To close net income to partners' capital)		

A = L + OE
−22,000
+12,400
+9,600

Cash Flows
no effect

Now let's look at a situation in which the salary and interest allowances *exceed* net income. Assume that Kingslee Company's net income is only $18,000. In this case, the salary and interest allowances will create a deficiency of $1,600 ($19,600 − $18,000). The computations of the allowances are the same as those in the preceding example. Beginning with total salaries and interest, we complete the division of net income as shown in Illustration 12-6.

	Sara King	Ray Lee	Total
Total salaries and interest	$11,200	$8,400	$19,600
Remaining deficiency ($1,600)			
($18,000 − $19,600)			
Sara King ($1,600 × 50%)	(800)		
Ray Lee ($1,600 × 50%)		(800)	
Total remainder			(1,600)
Total division	**$10,400**	**$7,600**	**$18,000**

Illustration 12-6
Division of net income—
income deficiency

Partnership Financial Statements

The financial statements of a partnership are similar to those of a proprietorship. The differences are due to the number of owners involved. The income statement for a partnership is identical to the income statement for a proprietorship except for the division of net income, as shown earlier.

The owners' equity statement for a partnership is called the **partners' capital statement**. It explains the changes in each partner's capital account and in total partnership capital during the year. Illustration 12-7 shows the partners' capital statement for Kingslee Company. It is based on the division of $22,000 of net income in Illustration 12-5. The statement includes assumed data for the additional investment and drawings. The partnership prepares the partners' capital statement from the income statement and the partners' capital and drawing accounts.

STUDY OBJECTIVE 4
Describe the form and content of partnership financial statements.

KINGSLEE COMPANY
Partners' Capital Statement
For the Year Ended December 31, 2010

	Sara King	Ray Lee	Total
Capital, January 1	$28,000	$24,000	$52,000
Add: Additional investment	2,000		2,000
Net income	12,400	9,600	22,000
	42,400	33,600	76,000
Less: Drawings	7,000	5,000	12,000
Capital, December 31	**$35,400**	**$28,600**	**$64,000**

Illustration 12-7
Partners' capital statement

HELPFUL HINT

As in a proprietorship, partners' capital may change due to (1) additional investment, (2) drawings, and (3) net income or net loss.

The balance sheet for a partnership is the same as for a proprietorship except for the owner's equity section. For a partnership, the balance sheet shows the capital balances of each partner. The owners' equity section for Kingslee Company would show the following.

Illustration 12-8
Owners' equity section of a partnership balance sheet

KINGSLEE COMPANY
Balance Sheet (partial)
December 31, 2010

Total liabilities (assumed amount)		$115,000
Owners' equity		
Sara King, Capital	$35,400	
Ray Lee, Capital	28,600	
Total owners' equity		64,000
Total liabilities and owners' equity		$179,000

DO IT!

DIVISION OF NET INCOME

action plan

✔ Compute net income exclusive of any salaries to partners and interest on partners' capital.

✔ Deduct salaries to partners from net income.

✔ Apply the partners' income ratios to the remaining net income.

✔ Prepare the closing entry distributing net income or net loss among the partners' capital accounts.

LeeMay Company reports net income of $57,000. The partnership agreement provides for salaries of $15,000 to L. Lee and $12,000 to R. May. They will share the remainder on a 60:40 basis (60% to Lee). L. Lee asks your help to divide the net income between the partners and to prepare the closing entry.

Solution

The division of net income is as follows.

	L. Lee	R. May	Total
Salary allowance	$15,000	$12,000	$27,000
Remaining income $30,000 ($57,000 − $27,000)			
L. Lee (60% × $30,000)	18,000		
R. May (40% × $30,000)		12,000	
Total remaining income			30,000
Total division of net income	$33,000	$24,000	$57,000

The closing entry for net income therefore is:

Income Summary	57,000	
L. Lee, Capital		33,000
R. May, Capital		24,000
(To close net income to partners'		
capital accounts)		

Related exercise material: **BE12-3, BE12-4, BE12-5, E12-4, E12-5,** and **DO IT!** **12-2.**

The Navigator

LIQUIDATION OF A PARTNERSHIP

STUDY OBJECTIVE 5

Explain the effects of the entries to record the liquidation of a partnership.

Liquidation of a business involves selling the assets of the firm, paying liabilities, and distributing any remaining assets. Liquidation may result from the sale of the business by mutual agreement of the partners, from the death of a partner, or from bankruptcy. **Partnership liquidation** ends both the legal and economic life of the entity.

From an accounting standpoint, the partnership should complete the accounting cycle for the final operating period prior to liquidation. This includes preparing adjusting entries and financial statements. It also involves preparing closing entries and a post-closing trial balance. Thus, only balance sheet accounts should be open as the liquidation process begins.

In liquidation, the sale of noncash assets for cash is called **realization**. Any difference between book value and the cash proceeds is called the **gain or loss on realization**. To liquidate a partnership, it is necessary to:

1. Sell noncash assets for cash and recognize a gain or loss on realization.
2. Allocate gain/loss on realization to the partners based on their income ratios.
3. Pay partnership liabilities in cash.
4. Distribute remaining cash to partners on the basis of their **capital balances**.

Each of the steps must be performed in sequence. The partnership must pay creditors **before** partners receive any cash distributions. Also, an accounting entry must record each step.

When a partnership is liquidated, all partners may have credit balances in their capital accounts. This situation is called no capital deficiency. Or, one or more partners may have a debit balance in the capital account. This situation is termed a capital deficiency. To illustrate each of these conditions, assume that Ace Company is liquidated when its ledger shows the following assets, liabilities, and owners' equity accounts.

> **ETHICS NOTE**
> The process of selling noncash assets and then distributing the cash reduces the likelihood of partner disputes. If, instead, the partnership distributes noncash assets to partners to liquidate the firm, the partners would need to agree on the value of the noncash assets, which can be very difficult to determine.

Assets		Liabilities and Owners' Equity	
Cash	$ 5,000	Notes payable	$15,000
Accounts receivable	15,000	Accounts payable	16,000
Inventory	18,000	R. Arnet, Capital	15,000
Equipment	35,000	P. Carey, Capital	17,800
Accum. depr.—equipment	(8,000)	W. Eaton, Capital	1,200
	$65,000		$65,000

Illustration 12-9
Account balances prior to liquidation

No Capital Deficiency

The partners of Ace Company agree to liquidate the partnership on the following terms: (1) The partnership will sell its noncash assets to Jackson Enterprises for $75,000 cash. (2) The partnership will pay its partnership liabilities. The income ratios of the partners are 3 : 2 : 1, respectively. The steps in the liquidation process are as follows.

1. Ace sells the noncash assets (accounts receivable, inventory, and equipment) for $75,000. The book value of these assets is $60,000 ($15,000 + $18,000 + $35,000 − $8,000). Thus Ace realizes a gain of $15,000 on the sale. The entry is:

(1)

Cash	75,000	
Accumulated Depreciation–Equipment	8,000	
Accounts Receivable		15,000
Inventory		18,000
Equipment		35,000
Gain on Realization		15,000
(To record realization of noncash assets)		

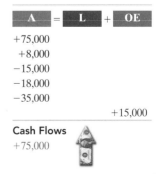

A	=	L	+	OE
+75,000				
+8,000				
−15,000				
−18,000				
−35,000				
				+15,000

Cash Flows
+75,000

2. Ace allocates the $15,000 gain on realization to the partners based on their income ratios, which are 3:2:1. The entry is:

A	=	L	+	OE
				−15,000
				+7,500
				+5,000
				+2,500

Cash Flows
no effect

(2)

Gain on Realization	15,000	
R. Arnet, Capital ($15,000 × 3/6)		7,500
P. Carey, Capital ($15,000 × 2/6)		5,000
W. Eaton, Capital ($15,000 × 1/6)		2,500
(To allocate gain to partners' capital accounts)		

3. Partnership liabilities consist of Notes Payable $15,000 and Accounts Payable $16,000. Ace pays creditors in full by a cash payment of $31,000. The entry is:

A	=	L	+	OE
		−15,000		
		−16,000		
−31,000				

Cash Flows
−31,000

(3)

Notes Payable	15,000	
Accounts Payable	16,000	
Cash		31,000
(To record payment of partnership liabilities)		

4. Ace distributes the remaining cash to the partners on the basis of **their capital balances**. After posting the entries in the first three steps, all partnership accounts, including Gain on Realization, will have zero balances except for four accounts: Cash $49,000; R. Arnet, Capital $22,500; P. Carey, Capital $22,800; and W. Eaton, Capital $3,700, as shown below.

Cash		R. Arnet, Capital		P. Carey, Capital		W. Eaton, Capital	
Bal. 5,000 | (3) 31,000		| Bal. 15,000		| Bal. 17,800		| Bal. 1,200	
(1) 75,000 |		| (2) 7,500		| (2) 5,000		| (2) 2,500	
Bal. 49,000 |		| Bal. 22,500		| Bal. 22,800		| Bal. 3,700	

Illustration 12-10
Ledger balances before
distribution of cash

Ace records the distribution of cash as follows.

A	=	L	+	OE
				−22,500
				−22,800
				−3,700
−49,000				

Cash Flows
−49,000

(4)

R. Arnet, Capital	22,500	
P. Carey, Capital	22,800	
W. Eaton, Capital	3,700	
Cash		49,000
(To record distribution of cash to partners)		

After posting this entry, all partnership accounts will have zero balances.

A word of caution: **Partnerships should not distribute remaining cash to partners on the basis of their income-sharing ratios.** On this basis, Arnet would receive three-sixths, or $24,500, which would produce an erroneous debit balance of $2,000. The income ratio is the proper basis for allocating net income or loss. **It is not a proper basis for making the final distribution of cash to the partners.**

ALTERNATIVE TERMINOLOGY

The schedule of cash payments is sometimes called a *safe cash payments schedule.*

SCHEDULE OF CASH PAYMENTS

The **schedule of cash payments** shows the distribution of cash to the partners in a partnership liquidation. A cash payments schedule is sometimes prepared to determine the distribution of cash to the partners in the liquidation of a partnership.

The schedule of cash payments is organized around the basic accounting equation. Illustration 12-11 shows the schedule for Ace Company. The numbers in parentheses refer to the four required steps in the liquidation of a partnership. They also identify the accounting entries that Ace must make. The cash payments schedule is especially useful when the liquidation process extends over a period of time.

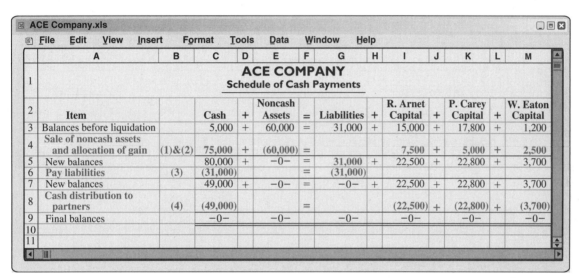

ACE Company.xls

File Edit View Insert Format Tools Data Window Help

ACE COMPANY
Schedule of Cash Payments

Item		Cash	+	Noncash Assets	=	Liabilities	+	R. Arnet Capital	+	P. Carey Capital	+	W. Eaton Capital
Balances before liquidation		5,000	+	60,000	=	31,000	+	15,000	+	17,800	+	1,200
Sale of noncash assets and allocation of gain	(1)&(2)	75,000	+	(60,000)	=			7,500	+	5,000	+	2,500
New balances		80,000	+	–0–	=	31,000	+	22,500	+	22,800	+	3,700
Pay liabilities	(3)	(31,000)			=	(31,000)						
New balances		49,000	+	–0–	=	–0–	+	22,500	+	22,800	+	3,700
Cash distribution to partners	(4)	(49,000)			=			(22,500)	+	(22,800)	+	(3,700)
Final balances		–0–		–0–		–0–		–0–		–0–		–0–

Illustration 12-11
Schedule of cash payments, no capital deficiency

DO IT!

The partners of Grafton Company have decided to liquidate their business. Noncash assets were sold for $115,000. The income ratios of the partners Kale D., Croix D., and Marais K. are 2:3:3, respectively. Complete the following schedule of cash payments for Grafton Company.

GRAFTON Company.xls

File Edit View Insert Format Tools Data Window Help

Item	Cash	+	Noncash Assets	=	Liabilities	+	Kale D., Capital	+	Croix D., Capital	+	Marais K., Capital
Balances before liquidation	10,000		85,000		40,000		15,000		35,000		5,000
Sale of noncash assets and allocation of gain											
New balances											
Pay liabilities											
New balances											
Cash distribution to partners											
Final balances											

PARTNERSHIP LIQUIDATION

action plan

✔ First, sell the noncash assets and determine the gain.

✔ Allocate the gain to the partners based on their income ratios.

✔ Use cash to pay off liabilities.

✔ Distribute remaining cash on the basis of their capital balances.

Solution

GRAFTON Company.xls

File   Edit   View   Insert   Format   Tools   Data   Window   Help

	A	B	C	D	E	F	G	H	I	J	K	L
1	Item	Cash	+	Noncash Assets	=	Liabilities	+	Kale D., Capital	+	Croix D., Capital	+	Marais K., Capital
2	Balances before liquidation	10,000		85,000		40,000		15,000		35,000		5,000
3	Sale of noncash assets and allocation of gain	115,000		(85,000)				7,500[a]		11,250[b]		11,250[b]
4	New balances	125,000		–0–		40,000		22,500		46,250		16,250
5	Pay liabilities	(40,000)				(40,000)						
6	New balances	85,000		–0–		–0–		22,500		46,250		16,250
7	Cash distribution to partners	85,000						(22,500)		(46,250)		(16,250)
8	Final balances	–0–		–0–		–0–		–0–		–0–		–0–

[a]30,000 × 2/8
[b]30,000 × 3/8

Related exercise material: **BE12-6, E12-8, E12-9, E12-10,** and **DO IT!** **12-3.**

Capital Deficiency

A capital deficiency may result from recurring net losses, excessive drawings, or losses from realization suffered during liquidation. To illustrate, assume that Ace Company is on the brink of bankruptcy. The partners decide to liquidate by having a "going-out-of-business" sale. They sell merchandise at substantial discounts, and sell the equipment at auction. Cash proceeds from these sales and collections from customers total only $42,000. Thus, the loss from liquidation is $18,000 ($60,000 − $42,000). The steps in the liquidation process are as follows.

1. The entry for the realization of noncash assets is:

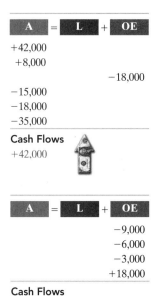

(1)

Cash	42,000	
Accumulated Depreciation—Equipment	8,000	
Loss on Realization	18,000	
Accounts Receivable		15,000
Inventory		18,000
Equipment		35,000
(To record realization of noncash assets)		

2. Ace allocates the loss on realization to the partners on the basis of their income ratios. The entry is:

(2)

R. Arnet, Capital ($18,000 × 3/6)	9,000	
P. Carey, Capital ($18,000 × 2/6)	6,000	
W. Eaton, Capital ($18,000 × 1/6)	3,000	
Loss on Realization		18,000
(To allocate loss on realization to partners)		

3. Ace pays the partnership liabilities. This entry is the same as the previous one.

(3)

Notes Payable	15,000	
Accounts Payable	16,000	
Cash		31,000
(To record payment of partnership liabilities)		

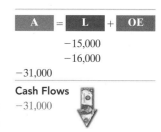

A = L + OE

−15,000
−16,000
−31,000

Cash Flows
−31,000

4. After posting the three entries, two accounts will have debit balances—Cash $16,000, and W. Eaton, Capital $1,800. Two accounts will have credit balances—R. Arnet, Capital $6,000, and P. Carey, Capital $11,800. All four accounts are shown below.

Cash				R. Arnet, Capital				P. Carey, Capital				W. Eaton, Capital			
Bal.	5,000	(3)	31,000	(2)	9,000	Bal.	15,000	(2)	6,000	Bal.	17,800	(2)	3,000	Bal.	1,200
(1)	42,000														
Bal.	16,000					Bal.	6,000			Bal.	11,800	Bal.	1,800		

Illustration 12-12
Ledger balances before distribution of cash

Eaton has a capital deficiency of $1,800, and so owes the partnership $1,800. Arnet and Carey have a legally enforceable claim for that amount against Eaton's personal assets. Note that the distribution of cash is still made on the basis of capital balances. But the amount will vary depending on how Eaton settles the deficiency. Two alternatives are presented in the following sections.

PAYMENT OF DEFICIENCY

If the partner with the capital deficiency pays the amount owed the partnership, the deficiency is eliminated. To illustrate, assume that Eaton pays $1,800 to the partnership. The entry is:

(a)

Cash	1,800	
W. Eaton, Capital		1,800
(To record payment of capital deficiency by Eaton)		

A = L + OE

+1,800
+1,800

Cash Flows
+1,800

After posting this entry, account balances are as follows.

Cash				R. Arnet, Capital				P. Carey, Capital				W. Eaton, Capital			
Bal.	5,000	(3)	31,000	(2)	9,000	Bal.	15,000	(2)	6,000	Bal.	17,800	(2)	3,000	Bal.	1,200
(1)	42,000													(a)	1,800
(a)	1,800					Bal.	6,000			Bal.	11,800				
Bal.	17,800											Bal.	–0–		

Illustration 12-13
Ledger balances after paying capital deficiency

The cash balance of $17,800 is now equal to the credit balances in the capital accounts (Arnet $6,000 + Carey $11,800). Ace now distributes cash on the basis of these balances. The entry is:

R. Arnet, Capital	6,000	
P. Carey, Capital	11,800	
Cash		17,800
(To record distribution of cash to the partners)		

A = L + OE

−6,000
−11,800
−17,800

Cash Flows
−17,800

After posting this entry, all accounts will have zero balances.

NONPAYMENT OF DEFICIENCY

If a partner with a capital deficiency is unable to pay the amount owed to the partnership, the partners with credit balances must absorb the loss. The partnership allocates the loss on the basis of the income ratios that exist between the partners with credit balances.

The income ratios of Arnet and Carey are $3:2$, or 3/5 and 2/5, respectively. Thus, Ace would make the following entry to remove Eaton's capital deficiency.

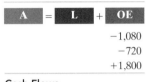

Cash Flows
no effect

(a)

R. Arnet, Capital ($1,800 × 3/5)	1,080	
P. Carey, Capital ($1,800 × 2/5)	720	
W. Eaton, Capital		1,800
(To record write-off of capital deficiency)		

After posting this entry, the cash and capital accounts will have the following balances.

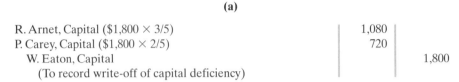

Cash				R. Arnet, Capital				P. Carey, Capital				W. Eaton, Capital			
Bal.	5,000	(3)	31,000	(2)	9,000	Bal.	15,000	(2)	6,000	Bal.	17,800	(2)	3,000	Bal.	1,200
(1)	42,000			(a)	1,080			(a)	720						(a)	1,800
Bal.	16,000					Bal.	4,920			Bal.	11,080			Bal.	–0–

Illustration 12-14
Ledger balances after nonpayment of capital deficiency

Cash Flows
–16,000

The cash balance ($16,000) now equals the sum of the credit balances in the capital accounts (Arnet $4,920 + Carey $11,080). Ace records the distribution of cash as:

R. Arnet, Capital	4,920	
P. Carey, Capital	11,080	
Cash		16,000
(To record distribution of cash to the partners)		

After posting this entry, all accounts will have zero balances.

DO IT!

PARTNERSHIP LIQUIDATION

action plan

✔ Allocate any unpaid capital deficiency to the partners with credit balances, based on their income ratios.

✔ After distribution of the deficiency, distribute cash to the remaining partners, based on their capital balances.

Kessington Company wishes to liquidate the firm by distributing the company's cash to the three partners. Prior to the distribution of cash, the company's balances are: Cash $45,000; Rollings, Capital (Cr.) $28,000; Havens, Capital (Dr.) $12,000; and Ostergard, Capital (Cr.) $29,000. The income ratios of the three partners are 4:4:2, respectively. Prepare the entry to record the absorption of Havens' capital deficiency by the other partners and the distribution of cash to the partners with credit balances.

Solution

Rollings, Capital ($12,000 × 4/6)	8,000	
Ostergard, Capital ($12,000 × 2/6)	4,000	
Havens, Capital		12,000
(To record write-off of capital deficiency)		
Rollings, Capital ($28,000 − $8,000)	20,000	
Ostergard, Capital ($29,000 − $4,000)	25,000	
Cash		45,000
(To record distribution of cash to partners)		

Related exercise material: **E12-10** and **DO IT!** **12-4**.

Comprehensive **DO IT!**

On January 1, 2010, the capital balances in Hollingsworth Company are Lois Holly $26,000, and Jim Worth $24,000. In 2010 the partnership reports net income of $30,000. The income ratio provides for salary allowances of $12,000 for Holly and $10,000 to Worth and the remainder equally. Neither partner had any drawings in 2010.

Instructions

(a) Prepare a schedule showing the distribution of net income in 2010.
(b) Journalize the division of 2010 net income to the partners.

action plan

✔ Compute the net income of the partnership.

✔ Allocate the partners' salaries.

✔ Divide the remaining net income among the partners, applying the income/loss ratio.

✔ Journalize the division of net income in a closing entry.

Solution to Comprehensive **DO IT!**

(a)   Net income   30,000

Division of Net Income

	Lois Holly	Jim Worth	Total
Salary allowance	$12,000	$10,000	$22,000
Remaining income $8,000 ($30,000 − $22,000)			
Lois Holly ($8,000 × 50%)	4,000		
Jim Worth ($8,000 × 50%)		4,000	
Total remainder			8,000
Total division of net income	$16,000	$14,000	$30,000

(b) 12/31/10 | Income Summary | | 30,000 | |
	Lois Holly, Capital			16,000
	Jim Worth, Capital			14,000
	(To close net income to partners' capital)			

The Navigator

SUMMARY OF STUDY OBJECTIVES

1 **Identify the characteristics of the partnership form of business organization.** The principal characteristics of a partnership are: (a) association of individuals, (b) mutual agency, (c) limited life, (d) unlimited liability, and (e) co-ownership of property.

2 **Explain the accounting entries for the formation of a partnership.** When formed, a partnership records each partner's initial investment at the fair market value of the assets at the date of their transfer to the partnership.

3 **Identify the bases for dividing net income or net loss.** Partnerships divide net income or net loss on the basis of the income ratio, which may be (a) a fixed ratio, (b) a ratio based on beginning or average capital balances, (c) salaries to partners and the remainder on a fixed ratio, (d) interest on partners' capital and the remainder on a fixed ratio, and (e) salaries to partners, interest on partners' capital, and the remainder on a fixed ratio.

4 **Describe the form and content of partnership financial statements.** The financial statements of a partnership are similar to those of a proprietorship. The principal differences are: (a) The partnership shows the division of net income on the income statement. (b) The owners' equity statement is called a partners' capital statement. (c) The partnership reports each partner's capital on the balance sheet.

5 **Explain the effects of the entries to record the liquidation of a partnership.** When a partnership is liquidated, it is necessary to record the (a) sale of noncash assets, (b) allocation of the gain or loss on realization, (c) payment of partnership liabilities, and (d) distribution of cash to the partners on the basis of their capital balances.

The Navigator

GLOSSARY

Capital deficiency A debit balance in a partner's capital account after allocation of gain or loss. (p. 539).

General partner A partner who has unlimited liability for the debts of the firm. (p. 530).

Income ratio The basis for dividing net income and net loss in a partnership. (p. 534).

Limited liability company A form of business organization, usually classified as a partnership for tax purposes and usually with limited life, in which partners, who are called *members*, have limited liability. (p. 530).

Limited liability partnership A partnership of professionals in which partners are given limited liability and the public is protected from malpractice by insurance carried by the partnership. (p. 530).

Limited partner A partner whose liability for the debts of the firm is limited to that partner's investment in the firm. (p. 532).

Limited partnership A partnership in which one or more general partners have unlimited liability and one or more partners have limited liability for the obligations of the firm. (p. 529).

No capital deficiency All partners have credit balances after allocation of gain or loss. (p. 539).

Partners' capital statement The owners' equity statement for a partnership which shows the changes in each partner's capital account and in total partnership capital during the year. (p. 537).

Partnership An association of two or more persons to carry on as co-owners of a business for profit. (p. 528).

Partnership agreement A written contract expressing the voluntary agreement of two or more individuals in a partnership. (p. 532).

Partnership dissolution A change in partners due to withdrawal or admission, which does not necessarily terminate the business. (p. 529).

Partnership liquidation An event that ends both the legal and economic life of a partnership. (p. 538).

Schedule of cash payments A schedule showing the distribution of cash to the partners in a partnership liquidation. (p. 540).

APPENDIX **Admission and Withdrawal of Partners**

The chapter explained how the basic accounting for a partnership works. We now look at how to account for a common occurrence in partnerships—the addition or withdrawal of a partner.

Admission of a Partner

The admission of a new partner results in the **legal dissolution** of the existing partnership and the beginning of a new one. From an economic standpoint, however, the admission of a new partner (or partners) may be of minor significance in the continuity of the business. For example, in large public accounting or law firms, partners are admitted annually without any change in operating policies. **To recognize the economic effects, it is necessary only to open a capital account for each new partner.** In the entries illustrated in this appendix, we assume that the accounting records of the predecessor firm will continue to be used by the new partnership.

A new partner may be admitted either by (1) purchasing the interest of one or more existing partners or (2) investing assets in the partnership. The former affects only the capital accounts of the partners who are parties to the transaction. The latter increases both net assets and total capital of the partnership.

PURCHASE OF A PARTNER'S INTEREST

The **admission** of a partner **by purchase of an interest** is a personal transaction between one or more existing partners and the new partner. Each party acts as an individual separate from the partnership entity. The individuals involved negotiate the price paid. It may be equal to or different from the capital equity acquired. The purchase price passes directly from the new partner to the partners who are giving up part or all of their ownership claims.

Any money or other consideration exchanged is the personal property of the participants and **not** the property of the partnership. Upon purchase of an interest, the new partner acquires each selling partner's capital interest and income ratio.

Accounting for the purchase of an interest is straightforward. The partnership records record only the changes in partners' capital. **Partners' capital accounts are debited for any ownership claims sold.** At the same time, the new partner's capital account is credited for the capital equity purchased. Total assets, total liabilities, and total capital remain unchanged, as do all individual asset and liability accounts.

To illustrate, assume that L. Carson agrees to pay $10,000 each to C. Ames and D. Barker for 33⅓% (one-third) of their interest in the Ames–Barker partnership. At the time of the admission of Carson, each partner has a $30,000 capital balance. Both partners, therefore, give up $10,000 of their capital equity. The entry to record the admission of Carson is:

C. Ames, Capital	10,000	
D. Barker, Capital	10,000	
L. Carson, Capital		20,000
(To record admission of Carson by purchase)		

The effect of this transaction on net assets and partners' capital is shown below.

Illustration 12A-1
Ledger balances after purchase of a partner's interest

Net Assets	C. Ames, Capital		D. Barker, Capital		L. Carson, Capital
60,000	10,000	30,000	10,000	30,000	20,000
		Bal. 20,000		Bal. 20,000	

Note that net assets remain unchanged at $60,000, and each partner has a $20,000 capital balance. Ames and Barker continue as partners in the firm, but the capital interest of each has changed. The cash paid by Carson goes directly to the individual partners and not to the partnership.

Regardless of the amount paid by Carson for the one-third interest, the entry is exactly the same. If Carson pays $12,000 each to Ames and Barker for one-third of the partnership, the partnership still makes the entry shown above.

INVESTMENT OF ASSETS IN A PARTNERSHIP

The admission of a partner by an investment of assets is a transaction between the new partner and the partnership. Often referred to simply as admission by investment, the transaction **increases both the net assets and total capital of the partnership**.

Assume, for example, that instead of purchasing an interest, Carson invests $30,000 in cash in the Ames–Barker partnership for a 33⅓% capital interest. In such a case, the entry is:

Cash	30,000	
L. Carson, Capital		30,000
(To record admission of Carson by investment)		

The effects of this transaction on the partnership accounts would be:

Net Assets		C. Ames, Capital	D. Barker, Capital	L. Carson, Capital
60,000		30,000	30,000	30,000
30,000				
Bal. 90,000				

Illustration 12A-2
Ledger balances after
investment of assets

Note that both net assets and total capital have increased by $30,000.

Remember that Carson's one-third capital interest might not result in a one-third income ratio. The new partnership agreement should specify Carson's income ratio, and it may or may not be equal to the one-third capital interest.

The comparison of the net assets and capital balances in Illustration 12A-3 shows the different effects of the purchase of an interest and admission by investment.

Illustration 12A-3
Comparison of purchase of
an interest and admission
by investment

Purchase of an Interest		Admission by Investment	
Net assets	**$60,000**	**Net assets**	**$90,000**
Capital		Capital	
C. Ames	$20,000	C. Ames	$30,000
D. Barker	20,000	D. Barker	30,000
L. Carson	20,000	L. Carson	30,000
Total capital	**$60,000**	**Total capital**	**$90,000**

When a new partner purchases an interest, the total net assets and total capital of the partnership *do not change*. When a partner is admitted by investment, both the total net assets and the total capital *change*.

In the case of admission by investment, further complications occur when the new partner's investment differs from the capital equity acquired. When those amounts are not the same, the difference is considered a **bonus** either to (1) the existing (old) partners or (2) the new partner.

Bonus to Old Partners. For both personal and business reasons, the existing partners may be unwilling to admit a new partner without receiving a bonus. In an established firm, existing partners may insist on a bonus as compensation for the work they have put into the company over the years. Two accounting factors underlie the business reason: First, total partners' capital equals the **book value** of the recorded net assets of the partnership. When the new partner is admitted, the fair market values of assets such as land and buildings may be higher than their book values. The bonus will help make up the difference between fair market value and book value. Second, when the partnership has been profitable, goodwill may exist. But, the partnership balance sheet does not report goodwill. The new partner is usually willing to pay the bonus to become a partner.

A bonus to old partners results when the new partner's investment in the firm is greater than the capital credit on the date of admittance. The bonus results in **an increase in the capital balances of the old partners. The partnership allocates the bonus to them on the basis of their income ratios before the admission of the new partner.** To illustrate, assume that the Bart–Cohen partnership, owned by Sam Bart and Tom Cohen, has total capital of $120,000. Lea Eden acquires a 25% ownership (capital) interest in the partnership by making a cash investment of $80,000. The procedure for determining Eden's capital credit and the bonus to the old partners is as follows.

1. **Determine the total capital of the new partnership:** Add the new partner's investment to the total capital of the old partnership. In this case the total capital of the new firm is $200,000, computed as follows.

Total capital of existing partnership	$120,000
Investment by new partner, Eden	80,000
Total capital of new partnership	$200,000

2. **Determine the new partner's capital credit:** Multiply the total capital of the new partnership by the new partner's ownership interest. Eden's capital credit is $50,000 ($200,000 × 25%).

3. **Determine the amount of bonus:** Subtract the new partner's capital credit from the new partner's investment. The bonus in this case is $30,000 ($80,000 − $50,000).

4. **Allocate the bonus to the old partners on the basis of their income ratios:** Assuming the ratios are Bart 60%, and Cohen 40%, the allocation is: Bart $18,000 ($30,000 × 60%) and Cohen $12,000 ($30,000 × 40%).

The entry to record the admission of Eden is:

Cash	80,000	
Sam Bart, Capital		18,000
Tom Cohen, Capital		12,000
Lea Eden, Capital		50,000
(To record admission of Eden and bonus to old partners)		

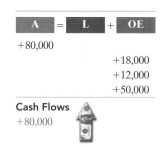

```
 A  =  L  +  OE
+80,000
              +18,000
              +12,000
              +50,000
Cash Flows
+80,000
```

Bonus to New Partner.   A bonus to a new partner results when the new partner's investment in the firm is less than his or her capital credit. This may occur when the new partner possesses special attributes that the partnership wants. For example, the new partner may be able to supply cash that the firm needs for expansion or to meet maturing debts. Or the new partner may be a recognized expert in a relevant field. Thus, an engineering firm may be willing to give a renowned engineer a bonus to join the firm. The partners of a restaurant may offer a bonus to a sports celebrity in order to add the athlete's name to the partnership. A bonus to a new partner may also result when recorded book values on the partnership books are higher than their market values.

A bonus to a new partner results in a **decrease in the capital balances of the old partners**. **The amount of the decrease for each partner is based on the income ratios before the admission of the new partner.** To illustrate, assume that Lea Eden invests $20,000 in cash for a 25% ownership interest in the Bart–Cohen partnership. The computations for Eden's capital credit and the bonus are as follows, using the four procedures described in the preceding section.

1. Total capital of Bart–Cohen partnership		$120,000
Investment by new partner, Eden		20,000
Total capital of new partnership		$140,000
2. **Eden's capital credit** (25% × $140,000)		$ 35,000
3. **Bonus to Eden** ($35,000 − $20,000)		$ 15,000
4. Allocation of bonus to old partners:		
Bart ($15,000 × 60%)	$9,000	
Cohen ($15,000 × 40%)	6,000	$ 15,000

Illustration 12A-4
Computation of capital credit and bonus to new partner

A	=	L	+	OE
+20,000				
				−9,000
				−6,000
				+35,000

Cash Flows
+20,000

The partnership records the admission of Eden as follows:

Cash	20,000	
Sam Bart, Capital	9,000	
Tom Cohen, Capital	6,000	
Lea Eden, Capital		35,000
(To record Eden's admission and bonus)		

Withdrawal of a Partner

STUDY OBJECTIVE 7

Describe the effects of the entries when a partner withdraws from the firm.

Now let's look at the opposite situation—the withdrawal of a partner. A partner may withdraw from a partnership **voluntarily**, by selling his or her equity in the firm. Or, he or she may withdraw **involuntarily**, by reaching mandatory retirement age or by dying. The withdrawal of a partner, like the admission of a partner, legally dissolves the partnership. The legal effects may be recognized by dissolving the firm. However, it is customary to record only the economic effects of the partner's withdrawal, while the firm continues to operate and reorganizes itself legally.

As indicated earlier, the partnership agreement should specify the terms of withdrawal. The withdrawal of a partner may be accomplished by (1) payment from partners' personal assets or (2) payment from partnership assets. The former affects only the partners' capital accounts. The latter decreases total net assets and total capital of the partnership.

PAYMENT FROM PARTNERS' PERSONAL ASSETS

Withdrawal by payment from partners' personal assets is a personal transaction between the partners. **It is the direct opposite of admitting a new partner who purchases a partner's interest.** The remaining partners pay the retiring partner directly from their personal assets. **Partnership assets are not involved in any way, and total capital does not change.** The effect on the partnership is limited to changes in the partners' capital balances.

To illustrate, assume that partners Morz, Nead, and Odom have capital balances of $25,000, $15,000, and $10,000, respectively. Morz and Nead agree to buy out Odom's interest. Each of them agrees to pay Odom $8,000 in exchange for one-half of Odom's total interest of $10,000. The entry to record the withdrawal is:

A	=	L	+	OE
				−10,000
				+5,000
				+5,000

Cash Flows
no effect

J. Odom, Capital	10,000	
A. Morz, Capital		5,000
M. Nead, Capital		5,000
(To record purchase of Odom's interest)		

The effect of this entry on the partnership accounts is shown below.

Net Assets		A. Morz, Capital		M. Nead, Capital		J. Odom, Capital	
50,000			25,000		15,000	10,000	10,000
			5,000		5,000		
			Bal. 30,000		Bal. 20,000	Bal.	−0−

Illustration 12A-5
Ledger balances after payment from partners' personal assets

Note that net assets and total capital remain the same at $50,000.

What about the $16,000 paid to Odom? You've probably noted that it is not recorded. The entry debited Odom's capital only for $10,000, not for the $16,000 that she received. Similarly, both Morz and Nead credit their capital accounts for only $5,000, not for the $8,000 they each paid.

After Odom's withdrawal, Morz and Nead will share net income or net loss equally unless they indicate another income ratio in the partnership agreement.

PAYMENT FROM PARTNERSHIP ASSETS

Withdrawal by payment from partnership assets is a transaction that involves the partnership. **Both partnership net assets and total capital decrease as a result.** Using partnership assets to pay for a withdrawing partner's interest is the **reverse** of admitting a partner through the investment of assets in the partnership.

Many partnership agreements provide that the amount paid should be based on the fair market value of the assets at the time of the partner's withdrawal. When this basis is required, some maintain that any differences between recorded asset balances and their fair market values should be (1) recorded by an adjusting entry, and (2) allocated to all partners on the basis of their income ratios. This position has serious flaws. Recording the revaluations violates the cost principle, which requires that assets be stated at original cost. It also violates the going-concern assumption, which assumes the entity will continue indefinitely. The terms of the partnership contract should not dictate the accounting for this event.

In accounting for a withdrawal by payment from partnership assets, the partnership should not record asset revaluations. Instead, it should consider any difference between the amount paid and the withdrawing partner's capital balance as **a bonus** to the retiring partner or to the remaining partners.

Bonus to Retiring Partner.   A partnership may pay a bonus to a retiring partner when:

1. The fair market value of partnership assets is more than their book value,

2. There is unrecorded goodwill resulting from the partnership's superior earnings record, or

3. The remaining partners are eager to remove the partner from the firm.

The partnership deducts the bonus from the remaining partners' capital balances on the basis of their income ratios at the time of the withdrawal.

To illustrate, assume that the following capital balances exist in the RST partnership: Roman $50,000, Sand $30,000, and Terk $20,000. The partners share income in the ratio of 3 : 2 : 1, respectively. Terk retires from the partnership and receives a cash payment of $25,000 from the firm. The procedure for determining the bonus to the retiring partner and the allocation of the bonus to the remaining partners is as follows.

1. **Determine the amount of the bonus:** Subtract the retiring partner's capital balance from the cash paid by the partnership. The bonus in this case is $5,000 ($25,000 − $20,000).

2. **Allocate the bonus to the remaining partners on the basis of their income ratios:** The ratios of Roman and Sand are 3 : 2. Thus, the allocation of the $5,000 bonus is: Roman $3,000 ($5,000 × 3/5) and Sand $2,000 ($5,000 × 2/5).

The partnership records the withdrawal of Terk as follows.

B. Terk, Capital	20,000	
F. Roman, Capital	3,000	
D. Sand, Capital	2,000	
Cash		25,000
(To record withdrawal of and bonus to Terk)		

The remaining partners, Roman and Sand, will recover the bonus given to Terk as the partnership sells or uses the undervalued assets.

HELPFUL HINT

Compare this entry to the one on page 552.

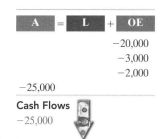

A = L + OE

−20,000
−3,000
−2,000
−25,000

Cash Flows
−25,000

Bonus to Remaining Partners. The retiring partner may give a bonus to the remaining partners when:

1. Recorded assets are overvalued,
2. The partnership has a poor earnings record, or
3. The partner is eager to leave the partnership.

In such cases, the cash paid to the retiring partner will be less than the retiring partner's capital balance. **The partnership allocates (credits) the bonus to the capital accounts of the remaining partners on the basis of their income ratios.**

To illustrate, assume instead that the partnership pays Terk only $16,000 for her $20,000 equity when she withdraws from the partnership. In that case:

1. The bonus to remaining partners is $4,000 ($20,000 − $16,000).
2. The allocation of the $4,000 bonus is: Roman $2,400 ($4,000 × 3/5) and Sand $1,600 ($4,000 × 2/5).

Under these circumstances, the entry to record the withdrawal is:

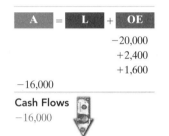

HELPFUL HINT

Compare this entry to the one on page 551.

A = L + OE		
−20,000		
+2,400		
+1,600		
−16,000		

Cash Flows
−16,000

B. Terk, Capital	20,000	
F. Roman, Capital		2,400
D. Sand, Capital		1,600
Cash		16,000
(To record withdrawal of Terk and bonus to remaining partners)		

Note that if Sand had withdrawn from the partnership, Roman and Terk would divide any bonus on the basis of their income ratio, which is 3 : 1 or 75% and 25%.

DEATH OF A PARTNER

The death of a partner dissolves the partnership. But partnership agreements usually contain a provision for the surviving partners to continue operations. When a partner dies, it usually is necessary to determine the partner's equity at the date of death. This is done by (1) determining the net income or loss for the year to date, (2) closing the books, and (3) preparing financial statements. The partnership agreement may also require an independent audit and a revaluation of assets.

The surviving partners may agree to purchase the deceased partner's equity from their personal assets. Or they may use partnership assets to settle with the deceased partner's estate. In both instances, the entries to record the withdrawal of the partner are similar to those presented earlier.

To facilitate payment from partnership assets, some partnerships obtain life insurance policies on each partner, with the partnership named as the beneficiary. The partnership then uses the proceeds from the insurance policy on the deceased partner to settle with the estate.

SUMMARY OF STUDY OBJECTIVES FOR APPENDIX

6 **Explain the effects of the entries when a new partner is admitted.** The entry to record the admittance of a new partner by purchase of a partner's interest affects only partners' capital accounts. The entries to record the admittance by investment of assets in the partnership (a) increase both net assets and total capital and (b) may result in recognition of a bonus to either the old partners or the new partner.

7 **Describe the effects of the entries when a partner withdraws from the firm.** The entry to record a withdrawal from the firm when the partners pay from their personal assets affects only partners' capital accounts. The entry to record a withdrawal when payment is made from partnership assets (a) decreases net assets and total capital and (b) may result in recognizing a bonus either to the retiring partner or the remaining partners.

GLOSSARY FOR APPENDIX

Admission by investment Admission of a partner by investing assets in the partnership, causing both partnership net assets and total capital to increase. (p. 547).

Admission by purchase of an interest Admission of a partner in a personal transaction between one or more existing partners and the new partner; does not change total partnership assets or total capital. (p. 546).

Withdrawal by payment from partners' personal assets Withdrawal of a partner in a personal transaction between partners; does not change total partnership assets or total capital. (p. 550).

Withdrawal by payment from partnership assets Withdrawal of a partner in a transaction involving the partnership, causing both partnership net assets and total capital to decrease. (p. 551).

*Note: All **asterisked** Questions, Exercises, and Problems relate to material in the appendix to the chapter.

SELF-STUDY QUESTIONS

Answers are at the end of the chapter.

(SO 1) **1.** Which of the following is *not* a characteristic of a partnership?
   a. Taxable entity
   b. Co-ownership of property
   c. Mutual agency
   d. Limited life

(SO 1) **2.** A partnership agreement should include each of the following except:
   a. names and capital contributions of partners.
   b. rights and duties of partners as well as basis for sharing net income or loss.
   c. basis for splitting partnership income taxes.
   d. provision for withdrawal of assets.

(SO 1) **3.** The advantages of a partnership do *not* include:
   a. ease of formation.
   b. unlimited liability.
   c. freedom from government regulation.
   d. ease of decision making.

(SO 2) **4.** Upon formation of a partnership, each partner's initial investment of assets should be recorded at their:
   a. book values.
   b. cost.
   c. market values.
   d. appraised values.

(SO 2) **5.** Ben and Sam Jenkins formed a partnership. Ben contributed $8,000 cash and a used truck that originally cost $35,000 and had accumulated depreciation of $15,000. The truck's market value was $16,000. Sam, a builder, contributed a new storage garage. His cost of construction was $40,000. The garage has a market value of $55,000. What is the combined total capital that would be recorded on the partnership books for the two partners?
   a. $79,000.
   b. $60,000.
   c. $75,000.
   d. $90,000.

(SO 3) **6.** The NBC Company reports net income of $60,000. If partners N, B, and C have an income ratio of 50%, 30%, and 20%, respectively, C's share of the net income is:
   a. $30,000.
   b. $12,000.

   c. $18,000.
   d. No correct answer is given.

(SO 3) **7.** Using the data in (4) above, what is B's share of net income if the percentages are applicable after each partner receives a $10,000 salary allowance?
   a. $12,000
   b. $20,000
   c. $19,000
   d. $21,000

(SO 3) **8.** To close a partner's drawing account, an entry must be made that:
   a. debits that partner's drawing account and credits Income Summary.
   b. debits that partner's drawing account and credits that partner's capital account.
   c. credits that partner's drawing account and debits that partner's capital account.
   d. credits that partner's drawing account and debits the firm's dividend account.

(SO 4) **9.** Which of the following statements about partnership financial statements is true?
   a. Details of the distribution of net income are shown in the owners' equity statement.
   b. The distribution of net income is shown on the balance sheet.
   c. Only the total of all partner capital balances is shown in the balance sheet.
   d. The owners' equity statement is called the partners' capital statement.

(SO 5) **10.** In the liquidation of a partnership it is necessary to (1) distribute cash to the partners, (2) sell noncash assets, (3) allocate any gain or loss on realization to the partners, and (4) pay liabilities. These steps should be performed in the following order:
   a. (2), (3), (4), (1).
   b. (2), (3), (1), (4).
   c. (3), (2), (1), (4).
   d. (3), (2), (4), (1).

Use the following account balance information for Creekville Partnership to answer questions 11 and 12. Income ratios are 2:4:4 for Harriet, Mike, and Elly, respectively.

Assets		Liabilities and Owners' Equity	
Cash	$ 9,000	Accounts payable	$ 21,000
Accounts		Harriet, Capital	23,000
receivable	22,000	Mike, Capital	8,000
Inventory	73,000	Elly, Capital	52,000
	$104,000		$104,000

(SO 5) **11.** Assume that, as part of liquidation proceedings, Creekville sells its noncash assets for $85,000. The amount of cash that would ultimately be distributed to Elly would be:
   a. $52,000.
   b. $48,000.
   c. $34,000.
   d. $86,000.

(SO 5) **12.** Assume that, as part of liquidation proceedings, Creekville sells its noncash assets for $60,000. As a result, one of the partners has a capital deficiency which that partner decides not to repay. The amount of cash that would ultimately be distributed to Elly would be:
   a. $52,000.
   b. $38,000.
   c. $24,000.
   d. $34,000.

(SO 6) ***13.** Louisa Santiago purchases 50% of Leo Lemon's capital interest in the K & L partnership for $22,000. If the capital balance of Kate Kildare and Leo Lemon are $40,000 and $30,000, respectively, Santiago's capital balance following the purchase is:

   a. $22,000.
   b. $35,000.
   c. $20,000.
   d. $15,000.

*14. Capital balances in the MEM partnership are Mary, Capital (SO 6) $60,000, Ellen, Capital $50,000, and Mills, Capital $40,000, and income ratios are 5 : 3 : 2, respectively. The MEMO partnership is formed by admitting Oleg to the firm with a cash investment of $60,000 for a 25% capital interest. The bonus to be credited to Mills, Capital in admitting Oleg is:
   a. $10,000.
   b. $7,500.
   c. $3,750.
   d. $1,500.

*15. Capital balances in the MURF partnership are Molly, (SO 7) Capital $50,000, Ursula, Capital $40,000, Ray, Capital $30,000, and Fred, Capital $20,000, and income ratios are 4 : 3 : 2 : 1, respectively. Fred withdraws from the firm following payment of $29,000 in cash from the partnership. Ursula's capital balance after recording the withdrawal of Fred is:
   a. $36,000.
   b. $37,000.
   c. $38,000.
   d. $40,000.

Go to the book's companion website, **www.wiley.com/college/weygandt**, for Additional Self-Study questions.

 The Navigator

QUESTIONS

1. The characteristics of a partnership include the following: (a) association of individuals, (b) limited life, and (c) co-ownership of property. Explain each of these terms.

2. Jerry Kerwin is confused about the partnership characteristics of (a) mutual agency and (b) unlimited liability. Explain these two characteristics for Jerry.

3. Brent Houghton and Dick Kreibach are considering a business venture. They ask you to explain the advantages and disadvantages of the partnership form of organization.

4. Why might a company choose to use a limited partnership?

5. Sampson and Stevens form a partnership. Sampson contributes land with a book value of $50,000 and a fair market value of $65,000. Sampson also contributes equipment with a book value of $52,000 and a fair market value of $57,000. The partnership assumes a $20,000 mortgage on the land. What should be the balance in Sampson's capital account upon formation of the partnership?

6. W. Mantle, N. Cash, and W. DiMaggio have a partnership called Outlaws. A dispute has arisen among the partners. Mantle has invested twice as much in assets as the other two partners, and he believes net income and net losses should be shared in accordance with the capital ratios. The partnership agreement does not specify the division of profits and losses. How will net income and net loss be divided?

7. Blue and Grey are discussing how income and losses should be divided in a partnership they plan to form. What factors should be considered in determining the division of net income or net loss?

8. M. Carson and R. Leno have partnership capital balances of $40,000 and $80,000, respectively. The partnership agreement indicates that net income or net loss should be shared equally. If net income for the partnership is $36,000, how should the net income be divided?

9. S. McMurray and F. Kohl share net income and net loss equally. (a) Which account(s) is (are) debited and credited to record the division of net income between the partners? (b) If S. McMurray withdraws $30,000 in cash for personal use in lieu of salary, which account is debited and which is credited?

10. Partners T. Evans and R. Meloy are provided salary allowances of $30,000 and $25,000, respectively. They divide the remainder of the partnership income in a ratio of 3 : 2. If partnership net income is $45,000, how much is allocated to Evans and Meloy?

11. Are the financial statements of a partnership similar to those of a proprietorship? Discuss.

12. How does the liquidation of a partnership differ from the dissolution of a partnership?

13. Bobby Donal and Bill Spader are discussing the liquidation of a partnership. Bobby maintains that all cash should be distributed to partners on the basis of their income ratios. Is he correct? Explain.

14. In continuing their discussion from Question 13, Bill says that even in the case of a capital deficiency, all cash should still be distributed on the basis of capital balances. Is Bill correct? Explain.

15. Lowery, Keegan, and Feeney have income ratios of 5 : 3 : 2 and capital balances of $34,000, $31,000, and $28,000, respectively. Noncash assets are sold at a gain. After creditors are paid, $109,000 of cash is available for distribution to the partners. How much cash should be paid to Keegan?

16. Before the final distribution of cash, account balances are: Cash $23,000; S. Penn, Capital $19,000 (Cr.); L. Pattison, Capital $12,000 (Cr.); and M. Jeter, Capital $8,000 (Dr.). Jeter is unable to pay any of the capital deficiency. If the income-sharing ratios are 5 : 3 : 2, respectively, how much cash should be paid to L. Pattison?

*17. Linda Ratzlaff decides to purchase from an existing partner for $50,000 a one-third interest in a partnership. What effect does this transaction have on partnership net assets?

*18. Steve Renn decides to invest $25,000 in a partnership for a one-sixth capital interest. How much do the partnership's net assets increase? Does Renn also acquire a one-sixth income ratio through this investment?

*19. Kate Robidou purchases for $72,000 Grant's interest in the Sharon-Grant partnership. Assuming that Grant has a $66,000 capital balance in the partnership, what journal entry is made by the partnership to record this transaction?

*20. Tracy Harper has a $39,000 capital balance in a partnership. She sells her interest to Kim Remington for $45,000 cash. What entry is made by the partnership for this transaction?

*21. Debbie Perry retires from the partnership of Garland, Newlin, and Perry. She receives $85,000 of partnership assets in settlement of her capital balance of $77,000. Assuming that the income-sharing ratios are 5 : 3 : 2, respectively, how much of Perry's bonus is debited to Newlin's capital account?

*22. Your roommate argues that partnership assets should be revalued in situations like those in question 21. Why is this generally not done?

*23. How is a deceased partner's equity determined?

24. Why is PepsiCo not a partnership?

BRIEF EXERCISES

BE12-1   Jennifer DeVine and Stanley Farrin decide to organize the ALL-Star partnership. DeVine invests $15,000 cash, and Farrin contributes $10,000 cash and equipment having a book value of $3,500. Prepare the entry to record Farrin's investment in the partnership, assuming the equipment has a fair market value of $5,000.

Journalize entries in forming a partnership.
(SO 2)

BE12-2   Beck and Cey decide to merge their proprietorships into a partnership called Fresh Start Company. The balance sheet of Cey Co. shows:

Accounts receivable	$16,000	
Less: Allowance for doubtful accounts	1,200	$14,800
Equipment	20,000	
Less: Accumulated depreciation	7,000	13,000

The partners agree that the net realizable value of the receivables is $13,500 and that the fair market value of the equipment is $11,000. Indicate how the four accounts should appear in the opening balance sheet of the partnership.

Prepare portion of opening balance sheet for partnership.
(SO 2)

BE12-3   Held Bond Co. reports net income of $70,000. The income ratios are Held 60% and Bond 40%. Indicate the division of net income to each partner, and prepare the entry to distribute the net income.

Journalize the division of net income using fixed income ratios.
(SO 3)

BE12-4   ESU Co. reports net income of $55,000. Partner salary allowances are Espino $15,000, Sears $5,000, and Utech $5,000. Indicate the division of net income to each partner, assuming the income ratio is 50 : 30 : 20, respectively.

Compute division of net income with a salary allowance and fixed ratios.
(SO 3)

BE12-5   Joe & Sam Co. reports net income of $28,000. Interest allowances are Joe $7,000 and Sam $5,000; salary allowances are Joe $15,000 and Sam $10,000; the remainder is shared equally. Show the distribution of income on the income statement.

Show division of net income when allowances exceed net income.
(SO 3)

BE12-6   After liquidating noncash assets and paying creditors, account balances in the Heartley Co. are Cash $19,000, A Capital (Cr.) $8,000, L Capital (Cr.) $7,000, and F Capital (Cr.) $4,000. The partners share income equally. Journalize the final distribution of cash to the partners.

Journalize final cash distribution in liquidation.
(SO 5)

*BE12-7   Alpha Co. capital balances are: Ace $30,000, Bly $25,000, and Cox $20,000. The partners share income equally. Day is admitted to the firm by purchasing one-half of Cox's interest for $13,000. Journalize the admission of Day to the partnership.

Journalize admission by purchase of an interest.
(SO 6)

Journalize admission by invest-ment.

(SO 6)

*BE12-8   In Decker Co., capital balances are Menke $40,000 and Hibbett $50,000. The partners share income equally. Kosko is admitted to the firm with a 45% interest by an investment of cash of $52,000. Journalize the admission of Kosko.

Journalize withdrawal paid by personal assets.

(SO 7)

*BE12-9   Capital balances in Midway Co. are Messer $40,000, Isch $30,000, and Denny $18,000. Messer and Isch each agree to pay Denny $12,000 from their personal assets. Messer and Isch each receive 50% of Denny's equity. The partners share income equally. Journalize the with-drawal of Denny.

Journalize withdrawal paid by partnership assets.

(SO 7)

*BE12-10   Data pertaining to Midway Co. are presented in BE12-9. Instead of payment from personal assets, assume that Denny receives $24,000 from partnership assets in withdrawing from the firm. Journalize the withdrawal of Denny.

DO IT! REVIEW

Analyze statements about part-nership organization.

(SO 1)

DO IT! 12-1   Indicate whether each of the following statements is true or false.

_____ **1.** Each partner is personally and individually liable for all partnership liabilities.
_____ **2.** If a partnership dissolves, each partner has a claim to the specific assets he/she contributed to the firm.
_____ **3.** In a limited partnership, all partners have limited liability.
_____ **4.** A major advantage of regular partnership is that it is simple and inexpensive to create and operate.
_____ **5.** Members of a limited liability company can take an active management role.

Divide net income and prepare closing entry.

(SO 3)

DO IT! 12-2   Villa America Company reported net income of $85,000. The partnership agree-ment provides for salaries of $25,000 to S. Wiborg and $18,000 to G. Murphy. They divide the re-mainder 40% to Wiborg and 60% to Murphy. S. Wiborg asks your help to divide the net income between the partners and to prepare the closing entry.

Complete schedule of partner-ship liquidation payments.

(SO 5)

DO IT! 12-3   The partners of Clash Company have decided to liquidate their business. Noncash assets were sold for $125,000. The income ratios of the partners M. Jones, J. Strummer, and P. Simonon are 3:2:3, respectively. Complete the following schedule of cash payments for Clash Company

	CLASH Company.xls											
	File Edit View Insert Format Tools Data Window Help											
	A	**B**	**C**	**D**	**E**	**F**	**G**	**H**	**I**	**J**	**K**	**L**
1	Item	Cash	+	Noncash Assets	=	Liabilities	+	M. Jones, Capital	+	J. Strummer, Capital	+	P. Simonon, Capital
2	Balances before liquidation	15,000		90,000		40,000		20,000		32,000		13,000
3	Sale of noncash assets and allocation of gain											
4	New balances											
5	Pay liabilities											
6	New balances											
7	Cash distribution to partners											
8	Final balances											

Prepare entries to record absorption of capital deficiency and distribution of cash.

(SO 5)

DO IT! 12-4   Granger Company wishes to liquidate the firm by distributing the company's cash to the three partners. Prior to the distribution of cash, the company's balances are: Cash $66,000; Niles, Capital (Cr.) $47,000; Dowagiac, Capital (Dr.) $21,000; and Vandalia, Capital (Cr.) $40,000. The income ratios of the three partners are 3:3:4, respectively. Prepare the entry to record the absorption of Dowagiac's capital deficiency by the other partners and the distribution of cash to the partners with credit balances.

EXERCISES

E12-1 Shani Davis has prepared the following list of statements about partnerships.

1. A partnership is an association of three or more persons to carry on as co-owners of a business for profit.
2. The legal requirements for forming a partnership can be quite burdensome.
3. A partnership is not an entity for financial reporting purposes.
4. The net income of a partnership is taxed as a separate entity.
5. The act of any partner is binding on all other partners, even when partners perform business acts beyond the scope of their authority.
6. Each partner is personally and individually liable for all partnership liabilities.
7. When a partnership is dissolved, the assets legally revert to the original contributor.
8. In a limited partnership, one or more partners have unlimited liability and one or more partners have limited liability for the debts of the firm.
9. Mutual agency is a major advantage of the partnership form of business.

Identify characteristics of partnership.
(SO 1)

Instructions
Identify each statement as true or false. If false, indicate how to correct the statement.

E12-2 K. Meissner, S. Cohen, and E. Hughes are forming a partnership. Meissner is transferring $50,000 of personal cash to the partnership. Cohen owns land worth $15,000 and a small building worth $80,000, which she transfers to the partnership. Hughes transfers to the partnership cash of $9,000, accounts receivable of $32,000 and equipment worth $19,000. The partnership expects to collect $29,000 of the accounts receivable.

Journalize entry for formation of a partnership.
(SO 2)

Instructions
(a) Prepare the journal entries to record each of the partners' investments.
(b) What amount would be reported as total owners' equity immediately after the investments?

E12-3 Jack Herington has owned and operated a proprietorship for several years. On January 1, he decides to terminate this business and become a partner in the firm of Herington and Kaspar. Herington's investment in the partnership consists of $12,000 in cash, and the following assets of the proprietorship: accounts receivable $14,000 less allowance for doubtful accounts of $2,000, and equipment $20,000 less accumulated depreciation of $4,000. It is agreed that the allowance for doubtful accounts should be $3,000 for the partnership. The fair market value of the equipment is $13,500.

Journalize entry for formation of a partnership.
(SO 2)

Instructions
Journalize Herington's admission to the firm of Kaspar and Herington.

E12-4 F. Calvert and G. Powers have capital balances on January 1 of $50,000 and $40,000, respectively. The partnership income-sharing agreement provides for (1) annual salaries of $20,000 for Calvert and $12,000 for Powers, (2) interest at 10% on beginning capital balances, and (3) remaining income or loss to be shared 60% by Calvert and 40% by Powers.

Prepare schedule showing distribution of net income and closing entry.
(SO 3)

Instructions
(a) Prepare a schedule showing the distribution of net income, assuming net income is (1) $50,000 and (2) $36,000.
(b) Journalize the allocation of net income in each of the situations above.

E12-5 O. Guillen (beginning capital, $60,000) and K. Williams (beginning capital $90,000) are partners. During 2010, the partnership earned net income of $70,000, and Guillen made drawings of $18,000 while Williams made drawings of $24,000.

Prepare journal entries to record allocation of net income.
(SO 3)

Instructions
(a) Assume the partnership income-sharing agreement calls for income to be divided 45% to Guillen and 55% to Williams. Prepare the journal entry to record the allocation of net income.

(b) Assume the partnership income-sharing agreement calls for income to be divided with a salary of $30,000 to Guillen and $25,000 to Williams, with the remainder divided 45% to Guillen and 55% to Williams. Prepare the journal entry to record the allocation of net income.

(c) Assume the partnership income-sharing agreement calls for income to be divided with a salary of $40,000 to Guillen and $35,000 to Williams, interest of 10% on beginning capital, and the remainder divided 50%–50%. Prepare the journal entry to record the allocation of net income.

(d) Compute the partners' ending capital balances under the assumption in part (c).

Prepare partners' capital statement and partial balance sheet.

(SO 4)

E12-6   For Starrite Co., beginning capital balances on January 1, 2010, are Gary Stark $20,000 and Jim Nyland $18,000. During the year, drawings were Stark $8,000 and Nyland $5,000. Net income was $30,000, and the partners share income equally.

Instructions

(a) Prepare the partners' capital statement for the year.

(b) Prepare the owners' equity section of the balance sheet at December 31, 2010.

Prepare a classified balance sheet of a partnership.

(SO 4)

E12-7   Moe, Larry, and Curly are forming The Stooges Partnership. Moe is transferring $30,000 of personal cash and equipment worth $25,000 to the partnership. Larry owns land worth $18,000 and a small building worth $75,000, which he transfers to the partnership. There is a long-term mortgage of $20,000 on the land and building, which the partnership assumes. Curly transfers cash of $7,000, accounts receivable of $36,000, supplies worth $3,000, and equipment worth $22,000 to the partnership. The partnership expects to collect $32,000 of the accounts receivable.

Instructions

Prepare a classified balance sheet for the partnership after the partners' investments on December 31, 2010.

Prepare cash payments schedule.

(SO 5)

E12-8   The Best Company at December 31 has cash $20,000, noncash assets $100,000, liabilities $55,000, and the following capital balances: Rodriguez $45,000 and Escobedo $20,000. The firm is liquidated, and $110,000 in cash is received for the noncash assets. Rodriguez and Escobedo income ratios are 60% and 40%, respectively.

Instructions

Prepare a schedule of cash payments.

Journalize transactions in a liquidation.

(SO 5)

E12-9   Data for The Best Company are presented in E12-8.

Instructions

Prepare the entries to record:

(a) The sale of noncash assets.

(b) The allocation of the gain or loss on realization to the partners.

(c) Payment of creditors.

(d) Distribution of cash to the partners.

Journalize transactions with a capital deficiency.

(SO 5)

E12-10   Prior to the distribution of cash to the partners, the accounts in the NJF Company are: Cash $28,000, Newell Capital (Cr.) $17,000, Jennings Capital (Cr.) $15,000, and Farley Capital (Dr.) $4,000. The income ratios are 5 : 3 : 2, respectively.

Instructions

(a) Prepare the entry to record (1) Farley's payment of $4,000 in cash to the partnership and (2) the distribution of cash to the partners with credit balances.

(b) Prepare the entry to record (1) the absorption of Farley's capital deficiency by the other partners and (2) the distribution of cash to the partners with credit balances.

Journalize admission of a new partner by purchase of an interest.

(SO 6)

*E12-11   J. Lynn, M. Oller, and F. Tate share income on a 5 : 3 : 2 basis. They have capital balances of $30,000, $26,000, and $18,000, respectively, when Doc Duran is admitted to the partnership.

Instructions

Prepare the journal entry to record the admission of Doc Duran under each of the following assumptions.

(a) Purchase of 50% of Lynn's equity for $19,000.
(b) Purchase of 50% of Oller's equity for $12,000.
(c) Purchase of 33⅓% of Tate's equity for $9,000.

---

*E12-12   G. Olde and R. Young share income on a 6 : 4 basis. They have capital balances of $100,000 and $70,000, respectively, when K. Twener is admitted to the partnership.

Journalize admission of a new partner by investment.

(SO 6)

Instructions

Prepare the journal entry to record the admission of K. Twener under each of the following assumptions.

(a) Investment of $90,000 cash for a 30% ownership interest with bonuses to the existing partners.
(b) Investment of $50,000 cash for a 30% ownership interest with a bonus to the new partner.

---

*E12-13   B. Cates, V. Elder, and S. Nguyen have capital balances of $50,000, $40,000, and $32,000, respectively. Their income ratios are 5 : 3 : 2. Nguyen withdraws from the partnership under each of the following independent conditions.

Journalize withdrawal of a partner with payment from partners' personal assets.

(SO 7)

1. Cates and Elder agree to purchase Nguyen's equity by paying $17,000 each from their personal assets. Each purchaser receives 50% of Nguyen's equity.
2. Elder agrees to purchase all of Nguyen's equity by paying $22,000 cash from her personal assets.
3. Cates agrees to purchase all of Nguyen's equity by paying $26,000 cash from her personal assets.

Instructions

Journalize the withdrawal of Nguyen under each of the assumptions above.

---

*E12-14   H. Barrajas, T. Dingler, and R. Fisk have capital balances of $95,000, $75,000, and $60,000, respectively. They share income or loss on a 5 : 3 : 2 basis. Fisk withdraws from the partnership under each of the following conditions.

Journalize withdrawal of a partner with payment from partnership assets.

(SO 7)

1. Fisk is paid $68,000 in cash from partnership assets, and a bonus is granted to the retiring partner.
2. Fisk is paid $56,000 in cash from partnership assets, and bonuses are granted to the remaining partners.

Instructions

Journalize the withdrawal of Fisk under each of the assumptions above.

---

*E12-15   Carson, Letterman, and O'Brien are partners who share profits and losses 50%, 30%, and 20%, respectively. Their capital balances are $100,000, $60,000, and $40,000, respectively.

Journalize entry for admission and withdrawal of partners.

(SO 6, 7)

Instructions

(a) Assume Stewart joins the partnership by investing $80,000 for a 25% interest with bonuses to the existing partners. Prepare the journal entry to record his investment.
(b) Assume instead that Carson leaves the partnership. Carson is paid $120,000 with a bonus to the retiring partner. Prepare the journal entry to record Carson's withdrawal.

EXERCISES: SET B

Visit the book's companion website at **www.wiley.com/college/weygandt**, and choose the Student Companion site, to access Exercise Set B.

PROBLEMS: SET A

Prepare entries for formation of a partnership and a balance sheet.

(SO 2, 4)

P12-1A The post-closing trial balances of two proprietorships on January 1, 2010, are presented below.

	Patrick Company		Samuelson Company	
	Dr.	**Cr.**	**Dr.**	**Cr.**
Cash	$ 14,000		$12,000	
Accounts receivable	17,500		26,000	
Allowance for doubtful accounts		$ 3,000		$ 4,400
Merchandise inventory	26,500		18,400	
Equipment	45,000		29,000	
Accumulated depreciation—equipment		24,000		11,000
Notes payable		18,000		15,000
Accounts payable		22,000		31,000
Patrick, Capital		36,000		
Samuelson, Capital				24,000
	$103,000	$103,000	$85,400	$85,400

Patrick and Samuelson decide to form a partnership, Pasa Company, with the following agreed upon valuations for noncash assets.

	Patrick Company	Samuelson Company
Accounts receivable	$17,500	$26,000
Allowance for doubtful accounts	4,500	4,000
Merchandise inventory	28,000	20,000
Equipment	23,000	16,000

All cash will be transferred to the partnership, and the partnership will assume all the liabilities of the two proprietorships. Further, it is agreed that Patrick will invest an additional $5,000 in cash, and Samuelson will invest an additional $19,000 in cash.

Instructions

(a) Patrick, Capital $38,000
Samuelson, Capital
$24,000

(c) Total assets $172,000

(a) Prepare separate journal entries to record the transfer of each proprietorship's assets and liabilities to the partnership.
(b) Journalize the additional cash investment by each partner.
(c) Prepare a classified balance sheet for the partnership on January 1, 2010.

Journalize divisions of net income and prepare a partners' capital statement.

(SO 3, 4)

P12-2A At the end of its first year of operations on December 31, 2010, CNU Company's accounts show the following.

Partner	Drawings	Capital
Reese Caplin	$23,000	$48,000
Phyllis Newell	14,000	30,000
Betty Uhrich	10,000	25,000

The capital balance represents each partner's initial capital investment. Therefore, net income or net loss for 2010 has not been closed to the partners' capital accounts.

Instructions

(a) (1) Caplin $18,000
(2) Caplin $19,000
(3) Caplin $15,700

(a) Journalize the entry to record the division of net income for the year 2010 under each of the following independent assumptions.
   (1) Net income is $30,000. Income is shared 6 : 3 : 1.
   (2) Net income is $37,000. Caplin and Newell are given salary allowances of $15,000 and $10,000, respectively. The remainder is shared equally.
   (3) Net income is $19,000. Each partner is allowed interest of 10% on beginning capital balances. Caplin is given a $12,000 salary allowance. The remainder is shared equally.
(b) Prepare a schedule showing the division of net income under assumption (3) above.

(c) Caplin $40,700

(c) Prepare a partners' capital statement for the year under assumption (3) above.

P12-3A   The partners in New Yorker Company decide to liquidate the firm when the balance sheet shows the following.

Prepare entries with a capital deficiency in liquidation of a partnership.

(SO 5)

NEW YORKER COMPANY
Balance Sheet
May 31, 2010

Assets		Liabilities and Owners' Equity	
Cash	$ 27,500	Notes payable	$ 13,500
Accounts receivable	25,000	Accounts payable	27,000
Allowance for doubtful accounts	(1,000)	Wages payable	4,000
Merchandise inventory	34,500	M. Mantle, Capital	33,000
Equipment	21,000	W. Mays, Capital	21,000
Accumulated depreciation—equipment	(5,500)	D. Snider, Capital	3,000
Total	$101,500	Total	$101,500

The partners share income and loss 5 : 3 : 2. During the process of liquidation, the following transactions were completed in the following sequence.
1. A total of $55,000 was received from converting noncash assets into cash.
2. Gain or loss on realization was allocated to partners.
3. Liabilities were paid in full.
4. D. Snider paid his capital deficiency.
5. Cash was paid to the partners with credit balances.

Instructions
(a) Prepare the entries to record the transactions.
(b) Post to the cash and capital accounts.
(c) Assume that Snider is unable to pay the capital deficiency.
  (1) Prepare the entry to allocate Snider's debit balance to Mantle and Mays.
  (2) Prepare the entry to record the final distribution of cash.

(a) Loss on realization
$19,000
Cash paid: to Mantle
$23,500; to Mays
$15,300

*P12-4A   At April 30, partners' capital balances in SKG Company are: S. Seger $52,000, J. Kensington $54,000, and T. Gomez $18,000. The income sharing ratios are 5:4:1, respectively. On May 1, the SKGA Company is formed by admitting D. Atchley to the firm as a partner.

Journalize admission of a partner under different assumptions.

(SO 6)

Instructions
(a) Journalize the admission of Atchley under each of the following independent assumptions.
  (1) Atchley purchases 50% of Gomez's ownership interest by paying Gomez $16,000 in cash.
  (2) Atchley purchases 33⅓% of Kensington's ownership interest by paying Kensington $15,000 in cash.
  (3) Atchley invests $66,000 for a 30% ownership interest, and bonuses are given to the old partners.
  (4) Atchley invests $46,000 for a 30% ownership interest, which includes a bonus to the new partner.
(b) Kensington's capital balance is $32,000 after admitting Atchley to the partnership by investment. If Kensington's ownership interest is 20% of total partnership capital, what were (1) Atchley's cash investment and (2) the bonus to the new partner?

(a) (1) Atchley $9,000
(2) Atchley $18,000
(3) Atchley $57,000
(4) Atchley $51,000

*P12-5A   On December 31, the capital balances and income ratios in FAD Company are as follows.

Journalize withdrawal of a partner under different assumptions.

(SO 7)

Partner	Capital Balance	Income Ratio
J. Fagan	$60,000	50%
P. Ames	40,000	30%
K. Durham	26,000	20%

Instructions
(a) Journalize the withdrawal of Durham under each of the following assumptions.
  (1) Each of the continuing partners agrees to pay $18,000 in cash from personal funds to purchase Durham's ownership equity. Each receives 50% of Durham's equity.
  (2) Ames agrees to purchase Durham's ownership interest for $25,000 cash.

(a) (1) Ames, Capital $13,000
(2) Ames, Capital $26,000
(3) Bonus $8,000
(4) Bonus $4,000

(3) Durham is paid $34,000 from partnership assets, which includes a bonus to the retiring partner.

(4) Durham is paid $22,000 from partnership assets, and bonuses to the remaining partners are recognized.

(b) If Ames's capital balance after Durham's withdrawal is $42,400 what were (1) the total bonus to the remaining partners and (2) the cash paid by the partnership to Durham?

PROBLEMS: SET B

Prepare entries for formation of a partnership and a balance sheet.

(SO 2, 4)

P12-1B The post-closing trial balances of two proprietorships on January 1, 2010, are presented below.

	John Company		Calvin Company	
	Dr.	**Cr.**	**Dr.**	**Cr.**
Cash	$ 10,000		$ 8,000	
Accounts receivable	18,000		30,000	
Allowance for doubtful accounts		$ 2,000		$ 3,000
Merchandise inventory	35,000		20,000	
Equipment	60,000		35,000	
Accumulated depreciation—equipment		28,000		15,000
Notes payable		20,000		
Accounts payable		30,000		40,000
John, Capital		43,000		
Calvin, Capital				35,000
	$123,000	$123,000	$93,000	$93,000

John and Calvin decide to form a partnership, John-Calvin Company, with the following agreed upon valuations for noncash assets.

	John Company	Calvin Company
Accounts receivable	$18,000	$30,000
Allowance for doubtful accounts	2,500	4,000
Merchandise inventory	38,000	25,000
Equipment	40,000	22,000

All cash will be transferred to the partnership, and the partnership will assume all the liabilities of the two proprietorships. Further, it is agreed that John will invest an additional $3,500 in cash, and Calvin will invest an additional $16,000 in cash.

Instructions

(a) John, Capital $53,500
Calvin, Capital $41,000

(a) Prepare separate journal entries to record the transfer of each proprietorship's assets and liabilities to the partnership.

(b) Journalize the additional cash investment by each partner.

(c) Total assets $204,000

(c) Prepare a classified balance sheet for the partnership on January 1, 2010.

Journalize divisions of net income and prepare a partners' capital statement.

(SO 3, 4)

P12-2B At the end of its first year of operations on December 31, 2010, KAT Company's accounts show the following.

Partner	Drawings	Capital
H. Krik	$15,000	$40,000
N. Andres	10,000	25,000
S. Thabo	5,000	15,000

The capital balance represents each partner's initial capital investment. Therefore, net income or net loss for 2010 has not been closed to the partners' capital accounts.

Instructions

(a) Journalize the entry to record the division of net income for 2010 under each of the independent assumptions shown on the next page.

(1) Net income is $50,000. Income is shared 5:3:2.
(2) Net income is $40,000. Kirk and Andres are given salary allowances of $15,000 and $10,000, respectively. The remainder is shared equally.
(3) Net income is $37,000. Each partner is allowed interest of 10% on beginning capital balances. Kirk is given an $20,000 salary allowance. The remainder is shared equally.
(b) Prepare a schedule showing the division of net income under assumption (3) above.
(c) Prepare a partners' capital statement for the year under assumption (3) above.

(a) (1) Kirk $25,000
    (2) Kirk $20,000
    (3) Kirk $27,000

(c) Kirk $52,000

P12-3B   The partners in Apache Company decide to liquidate the firm when the balance sheet shows the following.

Prepare entries and schedule of cash payments in liquidation of a partnership

(SO 5)

APACHE COMPANY
Balance Sheet
April 30, 2010

Assets		Liabilities and Owners' Equity	
Cash	$30,000	Notes payable	$20,000
Accounts receivable	25,000	Accounts payable	30,000
Allowance for doubtful accounts	(2,000)	Wages payable	2,500
Merchandise inventory	35,000	Scottie, Capital	28,000
Equipment	20,000	Spock, Capital	13,650
Accumulated depreciation—equipment	(8,000)	Kirk, Capital	5,850
Total	$100,000	Total	$100,000

The partners share income and loss 5:3:2. During the process of liquidation, the transactions below were completed in the following sequence.

1. A total of $57,000 was received from converting noncash assets into cash.
2. Gain or loss on relization was allocated to partners.
3. Liabilities were paid in full.
4. Cash was paid to the partners with credit balances.

Instructions
(a) Prepare a schedule of cash payments.
(b) Prepare the entries to record the transactions.
(c) Post to the cash and capital accounts.

(a) Loss on realization $13,000
    Cash paid: to Scottie
    $21,500; to Kirk $3,250

*P12-4B   At April 30, partners' capital balances in BAB Company are: Barney $30,000. Andy $16,000, and Bea $15,000. The income-sharing ratios are 5:3:2, respectively. On May 1, the BABE Company is formed by admitting Ellen to the firm as a partner.

Journalize admission of a partner under different assumptions.

(SO 6)

Instructions
(a) Journalize the admission of Ellen under each of the following independent assumptions.
   (1) Ellen purchases 50% of Bea's ownership interest by paying Bea $6,000 in cash.
   (2) Ellen purchases 50% of Andy's ownership interest by paying Andy $10,000 in cash.
   (3) Ellen invests $29,000 cash in the partnership for a 40% ownership interest that includes a bonus to the new partner.
   (4) Ellen invests $24,000 in the partnership for a 20% ownership interest, and bonuses are given to the old partners.
(b) Andy's capital balance is $24,000 after admitting Ellen to the partnership by investment. If Andy's ownership interest is 24% of total partnership capital, what were (1) Ellen's cash investment and (2) the total bonus to the old partners?

(a) (1) Ellen, Capital $7,500
    (2) Ellen $8,000
    (3) Ellen $36,000
    (4) Ellen $17,000

*P12-5B   On December 31, the capital balances and income ratios in Canasta Company are as follows.

Journalize withdrawal of a partner under different assumptions.

(SO 7)

Partner	Capital Balance	Income Ratio
A. Heart	$100,000	60%
L. Club	51,000	30
B. Spade	25,000	10

(a) (1) Club, Capital $12,500
    (2) Club, Capital $25,000
    (3) Bonus $9,000
    (4) Bonus $6,000

Instructions

(a) Journalize the withdrawal of Spade under each of the following independent assumptions.

  (1) Each of the remaining partners agrees to pay $15,000 in cash from personal funds to purchase Spade's ownership equity. Each receives 50% of Spade's equity.

  (2) Club agrees to purchase Spade's ownership interest for $22,000 in cash.

  (3) From partnership assets, Spade is paid $34,000, which includes a bonus to the retiring partner.

  (4) Spade is paid $19,000 from partnership assets. Bonuses to the remaining partners are recognized.

(b) If Club's capital balance after Spade's withdrawal is $55,000, what were (1) the total bonus to the remaining partners and (2) the cash paid by the partnership to Spade?

PROBLEMS: SET C

Visit the book's companion website at **www.wiley.com/college/weygandt**, and choose the Student Companion site, to access Problem Set C.

CONTINUING COOKIE CHRONICLE

(*Note:* This is a continuation of the Cookie Chronicle from Chapters 1 through 11.)

CCC12 Natalie's high school friend, Katy Peterson, has been operating a bakery for approximately 18 months. Because Natalie has been so successful operating Cookie Creations, Katy would like to have Natalie become her partner. Katy believes that together they will create a thriving cookie-making business. Natalie is quite happy with her current business set-up. Up until now, she had not considered joining forces with anyone. However, Natalie thinks that it may be a good idea to establish a partnership with Katy, and decides to look into it.

Go to the book's companion website, **www.wiley.com/college/weygandt**, *to see the completion of this problem.*

BROADENING YOUR PERSPECTIVE

FINANCIAL REPORTING AND ANALYSIS

Exploring the Web

BYP12-1 This exercise is an introduction to the Big Four accounting firms, all of which are partnerships.

Addresses

Deloitte & Touche	**www.deloitte.com/**
Ernst & Young	**www.ey.com/**
KPMG	**www.us.kpmg.com/**
PricewaterhouseCoopers	**www.pw.com/**

or go to **www.wiley.com/college/weygandt**

Steps

1. Select a firm that is of interest to you.

2. Go to the firm's homepage.

Instructions
(a) Name two services provided by the firm.
(b) What is the firm's total annual revenue?
(c) How many clients does it service?
(d) How many people are employed by the firm?
(e) How many partners are there in the firm?

CRITICAL THINKING

Decision Making Across the Organization

BYP12-2 Richard Powers and Jane Keckley, two professionals in the finance area, have worked for Eberhart Leasing for a number of years. Eberhart Leasing is a company that leases high-tech medical equipment to hospitals. Richard and Jane have decided that, with their financial expertise, they might start their own company to provide consulting services to individuals interested in leasing equipment. One form of organization they are considering is a partnership.

 If they start a partnership, each individual plans to contribute $50,000 in cash. In addition, Richard has a used IBM computer that originally cost $3,700, which he intends to invest in the partnership. The computer has a present market value of $1,500.

 Although both Richard and Jane are financial wizards, they do not know a great deal about how a partnership operates. As a result, they have come to you for advice.

Instructions
With the class divided into groups, answer the following.

(a) What are the major disadvantages of starting a partnership?
(b) What type of document is needed for a partnership, and what should this document contain?
(c) Both Richard and Jane plan to work full-time in the new partnership. They believe that net income or net loss should be shared equally. However, they are wondering how they can provide compensation to Richard Powers for his additional investment of the computer. What would you tell them?
(d) Richard is not sure how the computer equipment should be reported on his tax return. What would you tell him?
(e) As indicated above, Richard and Jane have worked together for a number of years. Richard's skills complement Jane's and vice versa. If one of them dies, it will be very difficult for the other to maintain the business, not to mention the difficulty of paying the deceased partner's estate for his or her partnership interest. What would you advise them to do?

Communication Activity

BYP12-3 You are an expert in the field of forming partnerships. Daniel Ortman and Sue Stafford want to establish a partnership to start "Pasta Shop," and they are going to meet with you to discuss their plans. Prior to the meeting you will send them a memo discussing the issues they need to consider before their visit.

Instructions
Write a memo in good form to be sent to Ortman and Stafford.

Ethics Case

BYP12-4 Elizabeth and Laurie operate a beauty salon as partners who share profits and losses equally. The success of their business has exceeded their expectations; the salon is operating quite profitably. Laurie is anxious to maximize profits and schedules appointments from 8 a.m. to 6 p.m. daily, even sacrificing some lunch hours to accommodate regular customers. Elizabeth schedules her appointments from 9 a.m. to 5 p.m. and takes long lunch hours. Elizabeth regularly makes significantly larger withdrawals of cash than Laurie does, but, she says, "Laurie, you needn't worry, I never make a withdrawal without you knowing about it, so it is properly recorded in my drawing account and charged against my capital at the end of the year." Elizabeth's withdrawals to date are double Laurie's.

Instructions

(a) Who are the stakeholders in this situation?

(b) Identify the problems with Elizabeth's actions and discuss the ethical considerations of her actions.

(c) How might the partnership agreement be revised to accommodate the differences in Elizabeth's and Laurie's work and withdrawal habits?

 ## "All About You" Activity

BYP12-5   As the text in this chapter indicates, the partnership form of organization has advantages and disadvantages. The chapter noted that different types of partnerships have been developed to minimize some of these disadvantages. Alternatively, an individual or company can choose the proprietorship or corporate form of organization.

Instructions

Go to two local businesses that are different, such as a restaurant, a retailer, a construction company, a professional office (dentist, doctor, etc.), and find the answers to the following questions.

(a) What form of organization do you use in your business?

(b) What do you believe are the two major advantages of this form of organization for your business?

(c) What do you believe are the two major disadvantages of this form of organization for your business?

(d) Do you believe that eventually you may choose another form of organization?

(e) Did you have someone help you form this organization (attorney, accountant, relative, etc.)?

 ## Answers to Insight and Accounting Across the Organization Questions

p. 530 Limited Liability Companies Gain in Popularity

Q: Why do you think that the use of the limited liability company is gaining in popularity?

A: *The LLC is gaining in popularity because owners in such companies have limited liability for business debts even if they participate in management. As a result, the LLC form has a distinct advantage over regular partnerships. In addition, the other limited type partnerships discussed in Illustration 12-1 are restrictive as to their use. As a result, it is not surprising that limited liability companies are now often used as the form of organization when individuals want to set up a partnership.*

p. 533 How to Part Ways Nicely

Q: How can partnership conflicts be minimized and more easily resolved?

A: *First, it is important to develop a business plan that all parties agree to. Second, it is vital to have a well-thought-out partnership agreement. Third, it can be useful to set up a board of mutually agreed upon and respected advisors to consult when making critical decisions.*

Answers to Self-Study Questions

1. a   **2.** c   **3.** b   **4.** c   **5.** a   **6.** b   **7.** c   **8.** c   **9.** d   **10.** a   **11.** b   **12.** d   *****13.** d   *****14.** d   *****15.** b

SPECIMEN FINANCIAL STATEMENTS:
PepsiCo, Inc.

THE ANNUAL REPORT

Once each year a corporation communicates to its stockholders and other interested parties by issuing a complete set of audited financial statements. The **annual report**, as this communication is called, summarizes the financial results of the company's operations for the year and its plans for the future. Many annual reports are attractive, multicolored, glossy public relations pieces, containing pictures of corporate officers and directors as well as photos and descriptions of new products and new buildings. Yet the basic function of every annual report is to report financial information, almost all of which is a product of the corporation's accounting system.

The content and organization of corporate annual reports have become fairly standardized. Excluding the public relations part of the report (pictures, products, etc.), the following are the traditional financial portions of the annual report:

- Financial Highlights
- Letter to the Stockholders
- Management's Discussion and Analysis
- Financial Statements
- Notes to the Financial Statements
- Management's Report on Internal Control
- Management Certification of Financial Statements
- Auditor's Report
- Supplementary Financial Information

In this appendix we illustrate current financial reporting with a comprehensive set of corporate financial statements that are prepared in accordance with generally accepted accounting principles and audited by an international independent certified public accounting firm. We are grateful for permission to use the actual financial statements and other accompanying financial information from the annual report of a large, publicly held company, PepsiCo, Inc.

FINANCIAL HIGHLIGHTS

Companies usually present the financial highlights section inside the front cover of the annual report or on its first two pages. This section generally reports the total or per share amounts for five to ten financial items for the current year and one or more previous years. Financial items from the income statement and the balance sheet that typically are presented are sales, income from continuing operations, net income, net income per share, net cash provided by operating activities, dividends per common share, and the amount of capital expenditures. The financial highlights section from PepsiCo's Annual Report is shown on page A-2.

The financial information herein is reprinted with permission from the PepsiCo, Inc. 2007 Annual Report. The complete financial statements are available through a link at the book's companion website.

Financial Highlights

PepsiCo, Inc. and Subsidiaries
($ in millions except per share amounts; all per share amounts assume dilution)

	2007	2006	Chg(a)
Summary of Operations			
Total net revenue	$39,474	$35,137	12%
Division operating profit(b)	$8,025	$7,307	10%
Total operating profit(c)	$7,272	$6,569	11%
Net income(d)	$5,599	$5,065	11%
Earnings per share(d)	$3.38	$3.00	13%
Other Data			
Management operating cash flow(e)	$4,551	$4,065	12%
Net cash provided by operating activities	$6,934	$6,084	14%
Capital spending	$2,430	$2,068	17%
Common share repurchases	$4,300	$3,000	43%
Dividends paid	$2,204	$1,854	19%
Long-term debt	$4,203	$2,550	65%

(a) Percentage changes are based on unrounded amounts.
(b) Excludes corporate unallocated expenses and restructuring and impairment charges. See page 86 for a reconciliation to the most directly comparable financial measure in accordance with GAAP.
(c) Excludes restructuring and impairment charges. See page 86 for a reconciliation to the most directly comparable financial measure in accordance with GAAP.
(d) Excludes restructuring and impairment charges and certain tax items. See page 86 for a reconciliation to the most directly comparable financial measure in accordance with GAAP.
(e) Includes the impact of net capital spending. Also, see "Our Liquidity and Capital Resources" in Management's Discussion and Analysis.

PepsiCo Estimated Worldwide Retail Sales: $98 Billion*

*Includes estimated retail sales of all PepsiCo products, including those sold by our partners and franchised bottlers.

Largest PepsiCo Brands

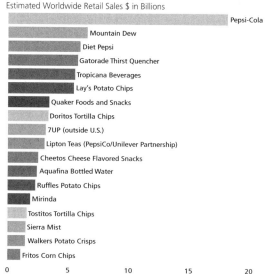

Estimated Worldwide Retail Sales $ in Billions

PepsiCo has 18 mega-brands that generate $1 billion or more each in annual retail sales.

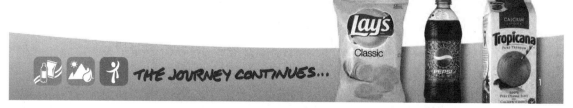

LETTER TO THE STOCKHOLDERS

Nearly every annual report contains a letter to the stockholders from the chairman of the board or the president, or both. This letter typically discusses the company's accomplishments during the past year and highlights significant events such as mergers and acquisitions, new products, operating achievements, business philosophy, changes in officers or directors, financing commitments, expansion plans, and future prospects. The letter to the stockholders is signed by Indra Nooyi, Chairman of the Board and Chief Executive Officer, of PepsiCo.

Only a short summary of the letter is provided below. The full letter can be accessed at the book's companion website at **www.wiley.com/college/weygandt.**

Delivering Performance with Purpose in 2007

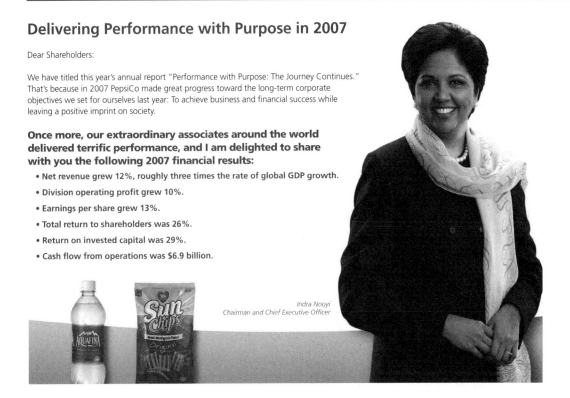

Dear Shareholders:

We have titled this year's annual report "Performance with Purpose: The Journey Continues." That's because in 2007 PepsiCo made great progress toward the long-term corporate objectives we set for ourselves last year: To achieve business and financial success while leaving a positive imprint on society.

Once more, our extraordinary associates around the world delivered terrific performance, and I am delighted to share with you the following 2007 financial results:

- Net revenue grew 12%, roughly three times the rate of global GDP growth.
- Division operating profit grew 10%.
- Earnings per share grew 13%.
- Total return to shareholders was 26%.
- Return on invested capital was 29%.
- Cash flow from operations was $6.9 billion.

Indra Nooyi
Chairman and Chief Executive Officer

MANAGEMENT'S DISCUSSION AND ANALYSIS

The **management's discussion and analysis (MD&A)** section covers three financial aspects of a company: its results of operations, its ability to pay near-term obligations, and its ability to fund operations and expansion. Management must highlight favorable or unfavorable trends and identity significant events and uncertainties that affect these three factors. This discussion obviously involves a number of subjective estimates and opinions. In its MD&A section, PepsiCo breaks its discussion into four major headings: Our Business, Our Critical Accounting Policies, Our Financial Results, and Our Liquidity and Capital Resources. You can access the full MD&A section at **www.wiley.com/college/weygandt.**

FINANCIAL STATEMENTS AND ACCOMPANYING NOTES

The standard set of financial statements consists of: (1) a comparative income statement for three years, (2) a comparative statement of cash flows for three years, (3) a comparative balance sheet for two years, (4) a statement of stockholders' equity for three years, and (5) a set of accompanying notes that are considered an integral part of the financial statements. The auditor's report, unless stated otherwise, covers the financial statements and the accompanying notes. PepsiCo's financial statements and accompanying notes plus supplementary data and analyses follow.

Consolidated Statement of Income

PepsiCo, Inc. and Subsidiaries

Fiscal years ended December 29, 2007, December 30, 2006 and December 31, 2005

(in millions except per share amounts)	2007	2006	2005
Net Revenue	$39,474	$35,137	$32,562
Cost of sales	18,038	15,762	14,176
Selling, general and administrative expenses	14,208	12,711	12,252
Amortization of intangible assets	58	162	150
Operating Profit	7,170	6,502	5,984
Bottling equity income	560	553	495
Interest expense	(224)	(239)	(256)
Interest income	125	173	159
Income before Income Taxes	7,631	6,989	6,382
Provision for Income Taxes	1,973	1,347	2,304
Net Income	$ 5,658	$ 5,642	$ 4,078
Net Income per Common Share			
Basic	$3.48	$3.42	$2.43
Diluted	$3.41	$3.34	$2.39

See accompanying notes to consolidated financial statements.

Net Revenue

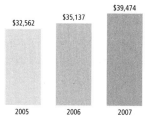

Operating Profit

Net Income

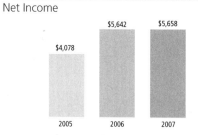

Net Income per Common Share

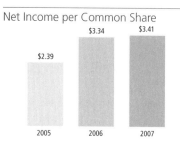

Consolidated Statement of Cash Flows

PepsiCo, Inc. and Subsidiaries
Fiscal years ended December 29, 2007, December 30, 2006 and December 31, 2005

(in millions)	2007	2006	2005
Operating Activities			
Net income	$ 5,658	$ 5,642	$ 4,078
Depreciation and amortization	1,426	1,406	1,308
Stock-based compensation expense	260	270	311
Excess tax benefits from share-based payment arrangements	(208)	(134)	–
Cash payments for merger-related costs and restructuring charges	–	–	(22)
Pension and retiree medical plan contributions	(310)	(131)	(877)
Pension and retiree medical plan expenses	535	544	464
Bottling equity income, net of dividends	(441)	(442)	(414)
Deferred income taxes and other tax charges and credits	118	(510)	440
Change in accounts and notes receivable	(405)	(330)	(272)
Change in inventories	(204)	(186)	(132)
Change in prepaid expenses and other current assets	(16)	(37)	(56)
Change in accounts payable and other current liabilities	500	223	188
Change in income taxes payable	128	(295)	609
Other, net	(107)	64	227
Net Cash Provided by Operating Activities	6,934	6,084	5,852
Investing Activities			
Capital spending	(2,430)	(2,068)	(1,736)
Sales of property, plant and equipment	47	49	88
Proceeds from (Investment in) finance assets	27	(25)	–
Acquisitions and investments in noncontrolled affiliates	(1,320)	(522)	(1,095)
Cash proceeds from sale of PBG stock	315	318	214
Divestitures	–	37	3
Short-term investments, by original maturity			
More than three months — purchases	(83)	(29)	(83)
More than three months — maturities	113	25	84
Three months or less, net	(413)	2,021	(992)
Net Cash Used for Investing Activities	(3,744)	(194)	(3,517)
Financing Activities			
Proceeds from issuances of long-term debt	2,168	51	25
Payments of long-term debt	(579)	(157)	(177)
Short-term borrowings, by original maturity			
More than three months — proceeds	83	185	332
More than three months — payments	(133)	(358)	(85)
Three months or less, net	(345)	(2,168)	1,601
Cash dividends paid	(2,204)	(1,854)	(1,642)
Share repurchases — common	(4,300)	(3,000)	(3,012)
Share repurchases — preferred	(12)	(10)	(19)
Proceeds from exercises of stock options	1,108	1,194	1,099
Excess tax benefits from share-based payment arrangements	208	134	–
Net Cash Used for Financing Activities	(4,006)	(5,983)	(1,878)
Effect of exchange rate changes on cash and cash equivalents	75	28	(21)
Net (Decrease)/Increase in Cash and Cash Equivalents	(741)	(65)	436
Cash and Cash Equivalents, Beginning of Year	1,651	1,716	1,280
Cash and Cash Equivalents, End of Year	$ 910	$ 1,651	$ 1,716

See accompanying notes to consolidated financial statements.

 **PEPSICO**

Consolidated Balance Sheet

PepsiCo, Inc. and Subsidiaries
December 29, 2007 and December 30, 2006

(in millions except per share amounts)	2007	2006
ASSETS		
Current Assets		
Cash and cash equivalents	$ 910	$ 1,651
Short-term investments	1,571	1,171
Accounts and notes receivable, net	4,389	3,725
Inventories	2,290	1,926
Prepaid expenses and other current assets	991	657
Total Current Assets	10,151	9,130
Property, Plant and Equipment, net	11,228	9,687
Amortizable Intangible Assets, net	796	637
Goodwill	5,169	4,594
Other nonamortizable intangible assets	1,248	1,212
Nonamortizable Intangible Assets	6,417	5,806
Investments in Noncontrolled Affiliates	4,354	3,690
Other Assets	1,682	980
Total Assets	$34,628	$29,930
LIABILITIES AND SHAREHOLDERS' EQUITY		
Current Liabilities		
Short-term obligations	$ –	$ 274
Accounts payable and other current liabilities	7,602	6,496
Income taxes payable	151	90
Total Current Liabilities	7,753	6,860
Long-Term Debt Obligations	4,203	2,550
Other Liabilities	4,792	4,624
Deferred Income Taxes	646	528
Total Liabilities	17,394	14,562
Commitments and Contingencies		
Preferred Stock, no par value	41	41
Repurchased Preferred Stock	(132)	(120)
Common Shareholders' Equity		
Common stock, par value 1 2/3¢ per share (authorized 3,600 shares, issued 1,782 shares)	30	30
Capital in excess of par value	450	584
Retained earnings	28,184	24,837
Accumulated other comprehensive loss	(952)	(2,246)
	27,712	23,205
Less: repurchased common stock, at cost (177 and 144 shares, respectively)	(10,387)	(7,758)
Total Common Shareholders' Equity	17,325	15,447
Total Liabilities and Shareholders' Equity	$34,628	$29,930

See accompanying notes to consolidated financial statements.

Consolidated Statement of Common Shareholders' Equity

PepsiCo, Inc. and Subsidiaries
Fiscal years ended December 29, 2007, December 30, 2006 and December 31, 2005

(in millions)	2007 Shares	2007 Amount	2006 Shares	2006 Amount	2005 Shares	2005 Amount
Common Stock	1,782	$ 30	1,782	$ 30	1,782	$ 30
Capital in Excess of Par Value						
Balance, beginning of year		584		614		618
Stock-based compensation expense		260		270		311
Stock option exercises/RSUs converted(a)		(347)		(300)		(315)
Withholding tax on RSUs converted		(47)		–		–
Balance, end of year		450		584		614
Retained Earnings						
Balance, beginning of year		24,837		21,116		18,730
Adoption of FIN 48		7		–		–
Adjusted balance, beginning of year		24,844		–		–
Net income		5,658		5,642		4,078
Cash dividends declared — common		(2,306)		(1,912)		(1,684)
Cash dividends declared — preferred		(2)		(1)		(3)
Cash dividends declared — RSUs		(10)		(8)		(5)
Balance, end of year		28,184		24,837		21,116
Accumulated Other Comprehensive Loss						
Balance, beginning of year		(2,246)		(1,053)		(886)
Currency translation adjustment		719		465		(251)
Cash flow hedges, net of tax:						
Net derivative (losses)/gains		(60)		(18)		54
Reclassification of losses/(gains) to net income		21		(5)		(8)
Adoption of SFAS 158		–		(1,782)		–
Pension and retiree medical, net of tax:						
Net pension and retiree medical gains		464		–		–
Reclassification of net losses to net income		135		–		–
Minimum pension liability adjustment, net of tax		–		138		16
Unrealized gain on securities, net of tax		9		9		24
Other		6		–		(2)
Balance, end of year		(952)		(2,246)		(1,053)
Repurchased Common Stock						
Balance, beginning of year	(144)	(7,758)	(126)	(6,387)	(103)	(4,920)
Share repurchases	(64)	(4,300)	(49)	(3,000)	(54)	(2,995)
Stock option exercises	28	1,582	31	1,619	31	1,523
Other, primarily RSUs converted	3	89	–	10	–	5
Balance, end of year	(177)	(10,387)	(144)	(7,758)	(126)	(6,387)
Total Common Shareholders' Equity		$17,325		$15,447		$14,320

	2007	2006	2005
Comprehensive Income			
Net income	$5,658	$5,642	$4,078
Currency translation adjustment	719	465	(251)
Cash flow hedges, net of tax	(39)	(23)	46
Minimum pension liability adjustment, net of tax	–	5	16
Pension and retiree medical, net of tax:			
Net prior service cost	(105)	–	–
Net gains	704	–	–
Unrealized gain on securities, net of tax	9	9	24
Other	6	–	(2)
Total Comprehensive Income	$6,952	$6,098	$3,911

(a) Includes total tax benefits of $216 million in 2007, $130 million in 2006 and $125 million in 2005.
See accompanying notes to consolidated financial statements.

Notes to Consolidated Financial Statements

Note 1 — Basis of Presentation and Our Divisions

Basis of Presentation

Our financial statements include the consolidated accounts of PepsiCo, Inc. and the affiliates that we control. In addition, we include our share of the results of certain other affiliates based on our economic ownership interest. We do not control these other affiliates, as our ownership in these other affiliates is generally less than 50%. Our share of the net income of our anchor bottlers is reported in our income statement as bottling equity income. Bottling equity income also includes any changes in our ownership interests of these affiliates. Bottling equity income includes $174 million, $186 million and $126 million of pre-tax gains on our sales of PBG stock in 2007, 2006 and 2005, respectively. See Note 8 for additional information on our significant noncontrolled bottling affiliates. Intercompany balances and transactions are eliminated. In 2005, we had an additional week of results (53rd week). Our fiscal year ends on the last Saturday of each December, resulting in an additional week of results every five or six years.

Beginning in the first quarter of 2007, income for certain non-consolidated international bottling interests was reclassified from bottling equity income and corporate unallocated results to PI's division operating results, to be consistent with PepsiCo's internal management accountability. Prior period amounts have been adjusted to reflect this reclassification.

Raw materials, direct labor and plant overhead, as well as purchasing and receiving costs, costs directly related to production planning, inspection costs and raw material handling facilities, are included in cost of sales. The costs of moving, storing and delivering finished product are included in selling, general and administrative expenses.

The preparation of our consolidated financial statements in conformity with generally accepted accounting principles requires us to make estimates and assumptions that affect reported amounts of assets, liabilities, revenues, expenses and disclosure of contingent assets and liabilities. Estimates are used

in determining, among other items, sales incentives accruals, tax reserves, stock-based compensation, pension and retiree medical accruals, useful lives for intangible assets, and future cash flows associated with impairment testing for perpetual brands, goodwill and other long-lived assets. Actual results could differ from these estimates.

See "Our Divisions" below and for additional unaudited information on items affecting the comparability of our consolidated results, see "Items Affecting Comparability" in Management's Discussion and Analysis.

Tabular dollars are in millions, except per share amounts. All per share amounts reflect common per share amounts, assume dilution unless noted, and are based on unrounded amounts. Certain reclassifications were made to prior years' amounts to conform to the 2007 presentation.

Our Divisions

We manufacture or use contract manufacturers, market and sell a variety of salty, sweet and grain-based snacks, carbonated and non-carbonated beverages, and foods through our North American and international business divisions. Our North American divisions include the U.S. and Canada. Division results are based on how our Chief Executive Officer assesses the performance of and allocates resources to our divisions. For additional unaudited information on our divisions, see "Our Operations" in Management's Discussion and Analysis. The accounting policies for the divisions are the same as those described in Note 2, except for the following certain allocation methodologies:

- stock-based compensation expense,
- pension and retiree medical expense, and
- derivatives.

Stock-Based Compensation Expense

Our divisions are held accountable for stock-based compensation expense and, therefore, this expense is allocated to our divisions as an incremental employee compensation cost. The allocation of stock-based compensation expense in 2007 was approximately 29% to FLNA, 17% to PBNA, 34% to PI, 4% to QFNA and 16% to corporate unallocated expenses. We had similar allocations of stock-based compensation expense to our divisions in 2006 and 2005. The expense allocated to our divisions excludes any impact of changes in our Black-Scholes assumptions during the year which reflect market conditions over which division management has no control. Therefore, any variances between allocated expense and our actual expense are recognized in corporate unallocated expenses.

Pension and Retiree Medical Expense

Pension and retiree medical service costs measured at a fixed discount rate, as well as amortization of gains and losses due to demographics, including salary experience, are reflected in division results for North American employees. Division results also include interest costs, measured at a fixed discount rate, for retiree medical plans. Interest costs for the pension plans, pension asset returns and the impact of pension funding, and gains and losses other than those due to demographics, are all reflected in corporate unallocated expenses. In addition, corporate unallocated expenses include the difference between the service costs measured at a fixed discount rate (included in division results as noted above) and the total service costs determined using the Plans' discount rates as disclosed in Note 7.

Derivatives

Beginning in the fourth quarter of 2005, we began centrally managing commodity derivatives on behalf of our divisions. Certain of the commodity derivatives, primarily those related to the purchase of energy for use by our divisions, do not qualify for hedge accounting treatment. These derivatives hedge underlying commodity price risk and were not entered into for speculative purposes. Such derivatives are marked to market with the resulting gains and losses recognized in corporate unallocated expenses. These gains and losses are subsequently reflected in division results when the divisions take delivery of the underlying commodity. Therefore, division results reflect the contract purchase price of the energy or other commodities.

In the second quarter of 2007, we expanded our commodity hedging program to include derivative contracts used to mitigate our exposure to price changes associated with our purchases of fruit. Similar to our energy contracts, these contracts do not qualify for hedge accounting treatment and are marked to market with the resulting gains and losses recognized in corporate unallocated expenses. These gains and losses are then subsequently reflected in divisional results.

New Organizational Structure

In the fourth quarter of 2007, we announced a strategic realignment of our organizational structure. For additional unaudited information on our new organizational structure, see "Our Operations" in Management's Discussion and Analysis. In the first quarter of 2008, our historical segment reporting will be restated to reflect the new structure. The segment amounts and discussions reflected in this annual report reflect the management reporting that existed through fiscal year-end 2007.

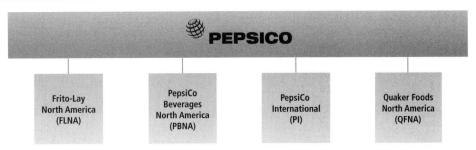

	Net Revenue			Operating Profit		
	2007	2006	2005	2007	2006	2005
FLNA	$11,586	$10,844	$10,322	$2,845	$2,615	$2,529
PBNA	10,230	9,565	9,146	2,188	2,055	2,037
PI	15,798	12,959	11,376	2,322	2,016	1,661
QFNA	1,860	1,769	1,718	568	554	537
Total division	39,474	35,137	32,562	7,923	7,240	6,764
Corporate	–	–	–	(753)	(738)	(780)
	$39,474	$35,137	$32,562	$7,170	$6,502	$5,984

Net Revenue

Division Operating Profit

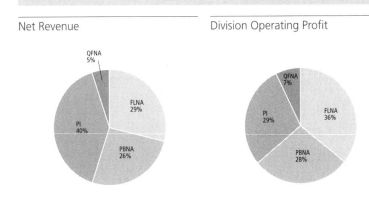

Corporate

Corporate includes costs of our corporate headquarters, centrally managed initiatives, such as our ongoing business transformation initiative in North America, unallocated insurance and benefit programs, foreign exchange transaction gains and losses, and certain commodity derivative gains and losses, as well as profit-in-inventory elimination adjustments for our noncontrolled bottling affiliates and certain other items.

Other Division Information

	Total Assets			Capital Spending		
	2007	2006	2005	2007	2006	2005
FLNA	$ 6,270	$ 5,969	$ 5,948	$ 624	$ 499	$ 512
PBNA	7,130	6,567	6,316	430	492	320
PI	14,747	11,571	10,229	1,108	835	667
QFNA	1,002	1,003	989	41	31	31
Total division	29,149	25,110	23,482	2,203	1,857	1,530
Corporate(a)	2,124	1,739	5,331	227	211	206
Investments in bottling affiliates	3,355	3,081	2,914	–	–	–
	$34,628	$29,930	$31,727	$2,430	$2,068	$1,736

(a) Corporate assets consist principally of cash and cash equivalents, short-term investments, and property, plant and equipment.

Total Assets   Capital Spending   Net Revenue   Long-Lived Assets

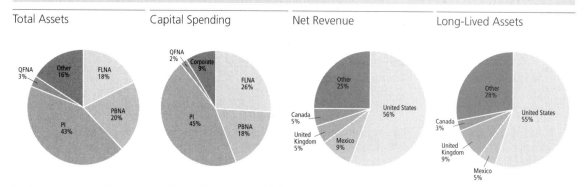

	Amortization of Intangible Assets			Depreciation and Other Amortization		
	2007	2006	2005	2007	2006	2005
FLNA	$ 9	$ 9	$ 3	$ 437	$ 432	$ 419
PBNA	11	77	76	302	282	264
PI	38	76	71	564	478	420
QFNA	–	–	–	34	33	34
Total division	58	162	150	1,337	1,225	1,137
Corporate	–	–	–	31	19	21
	$58	$162	$150	$1,368	$1,244	$1,158

	Net Revenue(a)			Long-Lived Assets(b)		
	2007	2006	2005	2007	2006	2005
U.S.	$21,978	$20,788	$19,937	$12,498	$11,515	$10,723
Mexico	3,498	3,228	3,095	1,067	996	902
United Kingdom	1,987	1,839	1,821	2,090	1,995	1,715
Canada	1,961	1,702	1,509	699	589	582
All other countries	10,050	7,580	6,200	6,441	4,725	3,948
	$39,474	$35,137	$32,562	$22,795	$19,820	$17,870

(a) Represents net revenue from businesses operating in these countries.
(b) Long-lived assets represent property, plant and equipment, nonamortizable intangible assets, amortizable intangible assets, and investments in noncontrolled affiliates. These assets are reported in the country where they are primarily used.

Note 2 — Our Significant Accounting Policies

Revenue Recognition

We recognize revenue upon shipment or delivery to our customers based on written sales terms that do not allow for a right of return. However, our policy for DSD and chilled products is to remove and replace damaged and out-of-date products from store shelves to ensure that our consumers receive the product quality and freshness that they expect. Similarly, our policy for warehouse-distributed products is to replace damaged and out-of-date products. Based on our historical experience with this practice, we have reserved for anticipated damaged and out-of-date products. For additional unaudited information on our revenue recognition and related policies, including our policy on bad debts, see "Our Critical Accounting Policies" in Management's Discussion and Analysis. We are exposed to concentration of credit risk by our customers, Wal-Mart and PBG. In 2007, Wal-Mart (including Sam's) represented approximately 12% of our total net revenue, including concentrate sales to our bottlers which are used in finished goods sold by them to Wal-Mart; and PBG represented approximately 9%. We have not experienced credit issues with these customers.

Sales Incentives and Other Marketplace Spending

We offer sales incentives and discounts through various programs to our customers and consumers. Sales incentives and discounts are accounted for as a reduction of revenue and totaled $11.3 billion in 2007, $10.1 billion in 2006 and $8.9 billion in 2005. While most of these incentive arrangements have terms of no more than one year, certain arrangements, such as fountain pouring rights, extend beyond one year. Costs incurred to obtain these arrangements are recognized over the shorter of the economic or contractual life, as a reduction of revenue, and the remaining balances of $287 million at December 29, 2007 and $297 million at December 30, 2006 are included in current assets and other assets on our balance sheet. For additional unaudited information on our sales incentives, see "Our Critical Accounting Policies" in Management's Discussion and Analysis.

Other marketplace spending, which includes the costs of advertising and other marketing activities, totaled $2.9 billion in 2007, $2.7 billion in 2006 and $2.8 billion in 2005 and is reported as selling, general and administrative expenses. Included in these amounts were advertising expenses of $1.9 billion in 2007, $1.7 billion in 2006 and $1.8 billion in 2005. Deferred advertising costs are not expensed until the year first used and consist of:

* media and personal service prepayments,
* promotional materials in inventory, and
* production costs of future media advertising.

Deferred advertising costs of $160 million and $171 million at year-end 2007 and 2006, respectively, are classified as prepaid expenses on our balance sheet.

Distribution Costs

Distribution costs, including the costs of shipping and handling activities, are reported as selling, general and administrative expenses. Shipping and handling expenses were $5.1 billion in 2007, $4.6 billion in 2006 and $4.1 billion in 2005.

Cash Equivalents

Cash equivalents are investments with original maturities of three months or less which we do not intend to rollover beyond three months.

Software Costs

We capitalize certain computer software and software development costs incurred in connection with developing or obtaining computer software for internal use when both the preliminary project stage is completed and it is probable that the software will be used as intended. Capitalized software costs include only (i) external direct costs of materials and services utilized in developing or obtaining computer software, (ii) compensation and related benefits for employees who are directly associated with the software project and (iii) interest costs incurred while developing internal-use computer software. Capitalized software costs are included in property, plant and equipment on our balance sheet and amortized on a straight-line basis when placed into service over the estimated useful lives of the software, which approximate five to seven years. Net capitalized software and development costs were $652 million at December 29, 2007 and $537 million at December 30, 2006.

Commitments and Contingencies

We are subject to various claims and contingencies related to lawsuits, taxes and environmental matters, as well as commitments under contractual and other commercial obligations. We recognize liabilities for contingencies and commitments when a loss is probable and estimable. For additional information on our commitments, see Note 9.

Research and Development

We engage in a variety of research and development activities. These activities principally involve the development of new products, improvement in the quality of existing products, improvement and modernization of production processes, and the development and implementation of new technologies to enhance the quality and value of both current and proposed product lines. Consumer research is excluded from research and development costs and included in other marketing costs. Research and development costs were $364 million in 2007, $282 million in 2006 and $280 million in 2005 and are reported as selling, general and administrative expenses.

Other Significant Accounting Policies

Our other significant accounting policies are disclosed as follows:

- Property, Plant and Equipment and Intangible Assets — Note 4, and for additional unaudited information on brands and goodwill, see "Our Critical Accounting Policies" in Management's Discussion and Analysis.
- Income Taxes — Note 5, and for additional unaudited information, see "Our Critical Accounting Policies" in Management's Discussion and Analysis.
- Pension, Retiree Medical and Savings Plans — Note 7, and for additional unaudited information, see "Our Critical Accounting Policies" in Management's Discussion and Analysis.
- Risk Management — Note 10, and for additional unaudited information, see "Our Business Risks" in Management's Discussion and Analysis.

Recent Accounting Pronouncements

In September 2006, the SEC issued SAB 108 to address diversity in practice in quantifying financial statement misstatements. SAB 108 requires that we quantify misstatements based on their impact on each of our financial statements and related disclosures. On December 30, 2006, we adopted SAB 108. Our adoption of SAB 108 did not impact our financial statements.

In September 2006, the FASB issued SFAS 157 which defines fair value, establishes a framework for measuring fair value, and expands disclosures about fair value measurements. The provisions of SFAS 157 are effective as of the beginning of our 2008 fiscal year. However, the FASB has deferred the effective date of SFAS 157, until the beginning of our 2009 fiscal year, as it relates to fair value measurement requirements for nonfinancial assets and liabilities that are not remeasured at fair value on a recurring basis. We are currently evaluating the impact of adopting SFAS 157 on our financial statements. We do not expect our adoption to have a material impact on our financial statements.

In February 2007, the FASB issued SFAS 159 which permits entities to choose to measure many financial instruments and certain other items at fair value. The provisions of SFAS 159 are effective as of the beginning of our 2008 fiscal year. Our adoption of SFAS 159 will not impact our financial statements.

In December 2007, the FASB issued SFAS 141R and SFAS 160 to improve, simplify, and converge internationally the accounting for business combinations and the reporting of noncontrolling interests in consolidated financial statements. The provisions of SFAS 141R and SFAS 160 are effective as of the beginning of our 2009 fiscal year. We are currently evaluating the impact of adopting SFAS 141R and SFAS 160 on our financial statements.

Note 3 — Restructuring and Impairment Charges

2007 Restructuring and Impairment Charge

In 2007, we incurred a charge of $102 million ($70 million after-tax or $0.04 per share) in conjunction with restructuring actions primarily to close certain plants and rationalize other production lines across FLNA, PBNA and PI. The charge was comprised of $57 million of asset impairments, $33 million of severance and other employee-related costs and $12 million of other costs and was recorded in selling, general and administrative expenses in our income statement. Employee-related costs primarily reflect the termination costs for approximately 1,100 employees. Substantially all cash payments related to this charge are expected to be paid by the end of 2008.

A summary of the restructuring and impairment charge by division is as follows:

	Asset Impairments	Severance and Other Employee Costs	Other Costs	Total
FLNA	$19	$ –	$ 9	$ 28
PBNA	–	11	–	11
PI	38	22	3	63
	$57	$33	$12	$102

2006 Restructuring and Impairment Charge

In 2006, we incurred a charge of $67 million ($43 million after-tax or $0.03 per share) in conjunction with consolidating the manufacturing network at FLNA by closing two plants in the U.S., and rationalizing other assets, to increase manufacturing productivity and supply chain efficiencies. The charge was comprised of $43 million of asset impairments, $14 million of severance and other employee-related costs and $10 million of other costs. Employee-related costs primarily reflect the termination costs for approximately 380 employees. All cash payments related to this charge were paid by the end of 2007.

2005 Restructuring Charge
In 2005, we incurred a charge of $83 million ($55 million after-tax or $0.03 per share) in conjunction with actions taken to reduce costs in our operations, principally through headcount reductions. Of this charge, $34 million related to FLNA, $21 million to PBNA, $16 million to PI and $12 million to Corporate. Most of this charge related to the termination of approximately 700 employees. As of December 30, 2006, all terminations had occurred, and as of December 29, 2007, no accrual remains.

Note 4 — Property, Plant and Equipment and Intangible Assets

	Average Useful Life	2007	2006	2005
Property, plant and equipment, net				
Land and improvements	10 – 34 yrs.	$ 864	$ 756	
Buildings and improvements	20 – 44	4,577	4,095	
Machinery and equipment, including fleet and software	5 – 14	14,471	12,768	
Construction in progress		1,984	1,439	
		21,896	19,058	
Accumulated depreciation		(10,668)	(9,371)	
		$ 11,228	$ 9,687	
Depreciation expense		$1,304	$1,182	$1,103
Amortizable intangible assets, net				
Brands	5 – 40	$ 1,476	$1,288	
Other identifiable intangibles	3 – 15	344	290	
		1,820	1,578	
Accumulated amortization		(1,024)	(941)	
		$ 796	$ 637	
Amortization expense		$58	$162	$150

Property, plant and equipment is recorded at historical cost. Depreciation and amortization are recognized on a straight-line basis over an asset's estimated useful life. Land is not depreciated and construction in progress is not depreciated until ready for service. Amortization of intangible assets for each of the next five years, based on average 2007 foreign exchange rates, is expected to be $62 million in 2008, $60 million in 2009, $60 million in 2010, $59 million in 2011 and $59 million in 2012.

Depreciable and amortizable assets are only evaluated for impairment upon a significant change in the operating or macroeconomic environment. In these circumstances, if an evaluation of the undiscounted cash flows indicates impairment, the asset is written down to its estimated fair value, which is based on discounted future cash flows. Useful lives are periodically evaluated to determine whether events or circumstances have occurred which indicate the need for revision. For additional unaudited information on our amortizable brand policies, see "Our Critical Accounting Policies" in Management's Discussion and Analysis.

Nonamortizable Intangible Assets
Perpetual brands and goodwill are assessed for impairment at least annually. If the carrying amount of a perpetual brand exceeds its fair value, as determined by its discounted cash flows, an impairment loss is recognized in an amount equal to that excess. No impairment charges resulted from the required impairment evaluations. The change in the book value of nonamortizable intangible assets is as follows:

	Balance, Beginning 2006	Acquisitions	Translation and Other	Balance, End of 2006	Acquisitions	Translation and Other	Balance, End of 2007
FLNA							
Goodwill	$ 145	$139	$ –	$ 284	$ –	$ 27	$ 311
PBNA							
Goodwill	2,164	39	–	2,203	146	20	2,369
Brands	59	–	–	59	–	–	59
	2,223	39	–	2,262	146	20	2,428
PI							
Goodwill	1,604	183	145	1,932	236	146	2,314
Brands	1,026	–	127	1,153	–	36	1,189
	2,630	183	272	3,085	236	182	3,503
QFNA							
Goodwill	175	–	–	175	–	–	175
Corporate							
Pension intangible	1	–	(1)	–	–	–	–
Total goodwill	4,088	361	145	4,594	382	193	5,169
Total brands	1,085	–	127	1,212	–	36	1,248
Total pension intangible	1	–	(1)	–	–	–	–
	$5,174	$361	$271	$5,806	$382	$229	$6,417

Note 5 — Income Taxes

	2007	2006	2005
Income before income taxes			
U.S.	$4,085	$3,844	$3,175
Foreign	3,546	3,145	3,207
	$7,631	$6,989	$6,382
Provision for income taxes			
Current: U.S. Federal	$1,422	$ 776	$1,638
Foreign	489	569	426
State	104	56	118
	2,015	1,401	2,182
Deferred: U.S. Federal	22	(31)	137
Foreign	(66)	(16)	(26)
State	2	(7)	11
	(42)	(54)	122
	$1,973	$1,347	$2,304
Tax rate reconciliation			
U.S. Federal statutory tax rate	35.0%	35.0%	35.0%
State income tax, net of U.S. Federal tax benefit	0.9	0.5	1.4
Lower taxes on foreign results	(6.5)	(6.5)	(6.5)
Tax settlements	(1.7)	(8.6)	–
Taxes on AJCA repatriation	–	–	7.0
Other, net	(1.8)	(1.1)	(0.8)
Annual tax rate	25.9%	19.3%	36.1%
Deferred tax liabilities			
Investments in noncontrolled affiliates	$1,163	$1,103	
Property, plant and equipment	828	784	
Intangible assets other than nondeductible goodwill	280	169	
Pension benefits	148	–	
Other	136	248	
Gross deferred tax liabilities	2,555	2,304	
Deferred tax assets			
Net carryforwards	722	667	
Stock-based compensation	425	443	
Retiree medical benefits	528	541	
Other employee-related benefits	447	342	
Pension benefits	–	38	
Deductible state tax and interest benefits	189	–	
Other	618	592	
Gross deferred tax assets	2,929	2,623	
Valuation allowances	(695)	(624)	
Deferred tax assets, net	2,234	1,999	
Net deferred tax liabilities	$ 321	$ 305	
Deferred taxes included within:			
Assets:			
Prepaid expenses and other current assets	$325	$223	
Liabilities:			
Deferred income taxes	$646	$528	
Analysis of valuation allowances			
Balance, beginning of year	$624	$532	$564
Provision/(benefit)	39	71	(28)
Other additions/(deductions)	32	21	(4)
Balance, end of year	$695	$624	$532

For additional unaudited information on our income tax policies, including our reserves for income taxes, see "Our Critical Accounting Policies" in Management's Discussion and Analysis.

In 2007, we recognized $129 million of non-cash tax benefits related to the favorable resolution of certain foreign tax matters. In 2006, we recognized non-cash tax benefits of $602 million, substantially all of which related to the IRS's examination of our consolidated income tax returns for the years 1998 through 2002. In 2005, we repatriated approximately $7.5 billion in earnings previously considered indefinitely reinvested outside the U.S. and recorded income tax expense of $460 million related to the AJCA. The AJCA created a one-time incentive for U.S. corporations to repatriate undistributed international earnings by providing an 85% dividends received deduction.

Reserves

A number of years may elapse before a particular matter, for which we have established a reserve, is audited and finally resolved. The number of years with open tax audits varies depending on the tax jurisdiction. Our major taxing jurisdictions and the related open tax audits are as follows:

- the U.S. — in 2006, the IRS issued a Revenue Agent's Report (RAR) related to the years 1998 through 2002. We are in agreement with their conclusion, except for one matter which we continue to dispute. We made the appropriate cash payment during 2006

to settle the agreed-upon issues, and we do not anticipate the resolution of the open matter will significantly impact our financial statements. In 2007, the IRS initiated their audit of our U.S. tax returns for the years 2003 through 2005;
- Mexico — in 2006, we completed and agreed with the conclusions of an audit of our tax returns for the years 2001 through 2005;
- the United Kingdom — audits have been completed for all taxable years prior to 2004; and
- Canada — audits have been completed for all taxable years through 2004. We are disputing some of the adjustments for the years 1999 through 2004. We do not anticipate the resolution of the 1999 through 2004 tax years will significantly impact our financial statements. The Canadian tax return for 2005 is currently under audit and no adjustments are expected to significantly impact our financial statements.

While it is often difficult to predict the final outcome or the timing of resolution of any particular tax matter, we believe that our reserves reflect the probable outcome of known tax contingencies. We adjust these reserves, as well as the related interest, in light of changing facts and circumstances. Settlement of any particular issue would usually require the use of cash. Favorable resolution would be recognized as a reduction to our annual tax rate in the year of resolution.

For further unaudited information on the impact of the resolution of open tax issues, see "Other Consolidated Results."

In 2006, the FASB issued FIN 48, which clarifies the accounting for uncertainty in tax positions. FIN 48 requires that we recognize in our financial statements the impact of a tax position, if that position is more likely than not of being sustained on audit, based on the technical merits of the position. We adopted the provisions of FIN 48 as of the beginning of our 2007 fiscal year. As a result of our adoption of FIN 48, we recognized a $7 million decrease to reserves for income taxes, with a corresponding increase to opening retained earnings.

As of December 29, 2007, the total gross amount of reserves for income taxes, reported in other liabilities, was $1.5 billion. Of that amount, $1.4 billion, if recognized, would affect our effective tax rate. Any prospective adjustments to our reserves for income taxes will be recorded as an increase or decrease to our provision for income taxes and would impact our effective tax rate. In addition, we accrue interest related to reserves for income taxes in our provision for income taxes and any associated penalties are recorded in selling, general and administrative expenses. The gross amount of interest accrued, reported in other liabilities, was $338 million as of December 29, 2007, of which $34 million was recognized in 2007.

A rollforward of our reserves in 2007 for all federal, state and foreign tax jurisdictions, is as follows:

Balance, beginning of year	$1,435
FIN 48 adoption adjustment to retained earnings	(7)
Reclassification of deductible state tax and interest benefits to other balance sheet accounts	(144)
Adjusted balance, beginning of year	1,284
Additions for tax positions related to the current year	264
Additions for tax positions from prior years	151
Reductions for tax positions from prior years	(73)
Settlement payments	(174)
Statute of limitations expiration	(7)
Currency translation adjustment	16
Balance, end of year	$1,461

Carryforwards and Allowances

Operating loss carryforwards totaling $7.1 billion at year-end 2007 are being carried forward in a number of foreign and state jurisdictions where we are permitted to use tax operating losses from prior periods to reduce future taxable income. These operating losses will expire as follows: $0.5 billion in 2008, $5.6 billion between 2009 and 2027 and $1.0 billion may be carried forward indefinitely. We establish valuation allowances for our deferred tax assets if, based on the available evidence, it is more likely than not that some portion or all of the deferred tax assets will not be realized.

Undistributed International Earnings

At December 29, 2007, we had approximately $14.7 billion of undistributed international earnings. We intend to continue to reinvest earnings outside the U.S. for the foreseeable future and, therefore, have not recognized any U.S. tax expense on these earnings.

Mexico Tax Legislation

In October 2007, Mexico enacted new tax legislation effective January 1, 2008. The deferred tax impact was not material and is reflected in our effective tax rate in 2007.

Note 6 — Stock-Based Compensation

Our stock-based compensation program is a broad-based program designed to attract and retain employees while also aligning employees' interests with the interests of our shareholders. A majority of our employees participate in our stock-based compensation program, which includes our broad-based SharePower program established in 1989 to grant an annual award of stock options to all eligible employees, based on job level or classification and, in the case of international employees, tenure as well. In addition, members of our Board of Directors participate in our stock-based compensation program in connection with their service on our Board. Beginning in 2007, members of our Board of Directors no longer receive stock-based compensation grants. Stock options and restricted stock units (RSU) are granted to employees under the shareholder-approved 2007 Long-Term Incentive Plan (LTIP), our only active stock-based plan. Stock-based compensation expense was $260 million in 2007, $270 million in 2006 and $311 million in 2005. Related income tax benefits recognized in earnings were $77 million in 2007, $80 million in 2006 and $87 million in 2005. Stock-based compensation cost capitalized in connection with our ongoing business transformation initiative was $3 million in 2007, $3 million in 2006 and $4 million in 2005. At year-end 2007, 67 million shares were available for future stock-based compensation grants.

Method of Accounting and Our Assumptions

We account for our employee stock options, which include grants under our executive program and broad-based SharePower program, under the fair value method of accounting using a Black-Scholes valuation model to measure stock option expense at the date of grant. All stock option grants have an exercise price equal to the fair market value of our common stock on the date of grant and generally have a 10-year term. The fair value of stock option grants is amortized to expense over the vesting period, generally three years. Executives who are awarded long-term incentives based on their performance are offered the choice of stock options or RSUs. Executives who elect RSUs receive one RSU for every four stock options that would have otherwise been granted. Senior officers do not have a choice and are granted 50% stock options and 50% RSUs. RSU expense is based on the fair value of PepsiCo stock on the date of grant and is amortized over the vesting period, generally three years. Each RSU is settled in a share of our stock after the vesting period. Vesting of RSU awards for senior officers is contingent upon the achievement of pre-established performance targets. There have been no reductions to the exercise price of previously issued awards, and any repricing of awards would require approval of our shareholders.

On January 1, 2006, we adopted SFAS 123R under the modified prospective method. Since we had previously accounted for our stock-based compensation plans under the fair value provisions of SFAS 123, our adoption did not significantly impact our financial position or our results of operations. Under SFAS 123R, actual tax benefits recognized in excess of tax benefits previously established upon grant are reported as a financing cash inflow. Prior to adoption, such excess tax benefits were reported as an operating cash inflow.

Our weighted-average Black-Scholes fair value assumptions are as follows:

	2007	2006	2005
Expected life	6 yrs.	6 yrs.	6 yrs.
Risk free interest rate	4.8%	4.5%	3.8%
Expected volatility	15%	18%	23%
Expected dividend yield	1.9%	1.9%	1.8%

The expected life is the period over which our employee groups are expected to hold their options. It is based on our historical experience with similar grants. The risk free interest rate is based on the expected U.S. Treasury rate over the expected life. Volatility reflects movements in our stock price over the most recent historical period equivalent to the expected life. Dividend yield is estimated over the expected life based on our stated dividend policy and forecasts of net income, share repurchases and stock price.

A summary of our stock-based compensation activity for the year ended December 29, 2007 is presented below:

Our Stock Option Activity	Options[a]	Average Price[b]	Average Life (years)[c]	Aggregate Intrinsic Value[d]
Outstanding at December 30, 2006	127,749	$44.24		
Granted	11,671	65.12		
Exercised	(28,116)	39.34		
Forfeited/expired	(2,496)	56.04		
Outstanding at December 29, 2007	108,808	$47.47	5.26	$3,216,316
Exercisable at December 29, 2007	75,365	$42.65	3.97	$2,590,994

(a) Options are in thousands and include options previously granted under Quaker plans. No additional options or shares may be granted under the Quaker plans.
(b) Weighted-average exercise price.
(c) Weighted-average contractual life remaining.
(d) In thousands.

Our RSU Activity	RSUs[a]	Average Intrinsic Value[b]	Average Life (years)[c]	Aggregate Intrinsic Value[d]
Outstanding at December 30, 2006	7,885	$53.38		
Granted	2,342	65.21		
Converted	(2,361)	47.83		
Forfeited/expired	(496)	$57.73		
Outstanding at December 29, 2007	7,370	$58.63	1.28	$567,706

(a) RSUs are in thousands.
(b) Weighted-average intrinsic value at grant date.
(c) Weighted-average contractual life remaining.
(d) In thousands.

Other Stock-Based Compensation Data	2007	2006	2005
Stock Options			
Weighted-average fair value of options granted	$13.56	$12.81	$13.45
Total intrinsic value of options exercised[a]	$826,913	$686,242	$632,603
RSUs			
Total number of RSUs granted[a]	2,342	2,992	3,097
Weighted-average intrinsic value of RSUs granted	$65.21	$58.22	$53.83
Total intrinsic value of RSUs converted[a]	$125,514	$10,934	$4,974

(a) In thousands.

At December 29, 2007, there was $287 million of total unrecognized compensation cost related to nonvested share-based compensation grants. This unrecognized compensation is expected to be recognized over a weighted-average period of 1.5 years.

Note 7 — Pension, Retiree Medical and Savings Plans

Our pension plans cover full-time employees in the U.S. and certain international employees. Benefits are determined based on either years of service or a combination of years of service and earnings. U.S. and Canada retirees are also eligible for medical and life insurance benefits (retiree medical) if they meet age and service requirements. Generally, our share of retiree medical costs is capped at specified dollar amounts, which vary based upon years of service, with retirees contributing the remainder of the costs.

Other gains and losses resulting from actual experience differing from our assumptions and from changes in our assumptions are also determined at each measurement date. If this net accumulated gain or loss exceeds 10% of the greater of plan assets or liabilities, a portion of the net gain or loss is included

in expense for the following year. The cost or benefit of plan changes that increase or decrease benefits for prior employee service (prior service cost/(credit)) is included in earnings on a straight-line basis over the average remaining service period of active plan participants, which is approximately 11 years for pension expense and approximately 13 years for retiree medical expense.

On December 30, 2006, we adopted SFAS 158. In connection with our adoption, we recognized the funded status of our Plans on our balance sheet as of December 30, 2006 with subsequent changes in the funded status recognized in comprehensive income in the years in which they occur. In accordance with SFAS 158, amounts prior to the year of adoption have not been adjusted. SFAS 158 also requires that, no later than 2008, our

assumptions used to measure our annual pension and retiree medical expense be determined as of the balance sheet date, and all plan assets and liabilities be reported as of that date. Accordingly, as of the beginning of our 2008 fiscal year, we will change the measurement date for our annual pension and retiree medical expense and all plan assets and liabilities from September 30 to our year-end balance sheet date. As a result of this change in measurement date, we will record an after-tax $7 million reduction to 2008 opening shareholders' equity which will be reflected in our 2008 first quarter Form 10-Q.

Selected financial information for our pension and retiree medical plans is as follows:

	Pension				Retiree Medical	
	2007	2006	2007	2006	2007	2006
	U.S.		International			
Change in projected benefit liability						
Liability at beginning of year	$5,947	$5,771	$1,511	$1,263	$1,370	$1,312
Service cost	244	245	59	52	48	46
Interest cost	338	319	81	68	77	72
Plan amendments	147	11	4	8	–	–
Participant contributions	–	–	14	12	–	–
Experience (gain)/loss	(309)	(163)	(155)	20	(80)	(34)
Benefit payments	(319)	(233)	(46)	(38)	(77)	(75)
Settlement/curtailment loss	–	(7)	–	(6)	–	–
Special termination benefits	–	4	–	–	–	1
Foreign currency adjustment	–	–	96	126	9	–
Other	–	–	31	6	7	48
Liability at end of year	$6,048	$5,947	$1,595	$1,511	$1,354	$1,370
Change in fair value of plan assets						
Fair value at beginning of year	$5,378	$5,086	$1,330	$1,099	$ –	$ –
Actual return on plan assets	654	513	122	112	–	–
Employer contributions/funding	69	19	58	30	77	75
Participant contributions	–	–	14	12	–	–
Benefit payments	(319)	(233)	(46)	(38)	(77)	(75)
Settlement/curtailment loss	–	(7)	–	–	–	–
Foreign currency adjustment	–	–	91	116	–	–
Other	–	–	26	(1)	–	–
Fair value at end of year	$5,782	$5,378	$1,595	$1,330	$ –	$ –
Reconciliation of funded status						
Funded status	$(266)	$(569)	$ –	$(181)	$(1,354)	$(1,370)
Adjustment for fourth quarter contributions	15	6	107	13	19	16
Adjustment for fourth quarter special termination benefits	(5)	–	–	–	–	–
Net amount recognized	$(256)	$(563)	$107	$(168)	$(1,335)	$(1,354)
Amounts recognized						
Other assets	$ 440	$ 185	$187	$ 6	$ –	$ –
Other current liabilities	(24)	(19)	(3)	(2)	(88)	(84)
Other liabilities	(672)	(729)	(77)	(172)	(1,247)	(1,270)
Net amount recognized	$(256)	$(563)	$107	$(168)	$(1,335)	$(1,354)
Amounts included in accumulated other comprehensive loss (pre-tax)						
Net loss	$1,136	$1,836	$287	$475	$276	$ 364
Prior service cost/(credit)	156	13	28	24	(88)	(101)
Total	$1,292	$1,849	$315	$499	$188	$ 263
Components of the (decrease)/increase in net loss						
Change in discount rate	$(292)	$(123)	$(224)	$ 2	$(50)	$(30)
Employee-related assumption changes	–	(45)	61	6	(9)	–
Liability-related experience different from assumptions	(17)	5	7	6	(21)	(4)
Actual asset return different from expected return	(255)	(122)	(25)	(30)	–	–
Amortization of losses	(136)	(164)	(30)	(29)	(18)	(21)
Other, including foreign currency adjustments and 2003 Medicare Act	–	(3)	23	46	10	17
Total	$(700)	$(452)	$(188)	$ 1	$(88)	$(38)
Liability at end of year for service to date	$5,026	$4,998	$1,324	$1,239		

Components of benefit expense are as follows:

	Pension						Retiree Medical		
	2007	2006	2005	2007	2006	2005	2007	2006	2005
	U.S.			International					
Components of benefit expense									
Service cost	$ 244	$ 245	$ 213	$ 59	$ 52	$ 32	$ 48	$ 46	$ 40
Interest cost	338	319	296	81	68	55	77	72	78
Expected return on plan assets	(399)	(391)	(344)	(97)	(81)	(69)	–	–	–
Amortization of prior service cost/(credit)	5	3	3	3	2	1	(13)	(13)	(11)
Amortization of net loss	136	164	106	30	29	15	18	21	26
	324	340	274	76	70	34	130	126	133
Settlement/curtailment loss	–	3	–	–	–	–	–	–	–
Special termination benefits	5	4	21	–	–	–	–	1	2
Total	$ 329	$ 347	$ 295	$ 76	$ 70	$ 34	$130	$127	$135

The estimated amounts to be amortized from accumulated other comprehensive loss into benefit expense in 2008 for our pension and retiree medical plans are as follows:

	Pension		Retiree Medical
	U.S.	International	
Net loss	$56	$20	$ 7
Prior service cost/(credit)	20	3	(12)
Total	$76	$23	$ (5)

The following table provides the weighted-average assumptions used to determine projected benefit liability and benefit expense for our pension and retiree medical plans:

	Pension						Retiree Medical		
	2007	2006	2005	2007	2006	2005	2007	2006	2005
	U.S.			International					
Weighted-average assumptions									
Liability discount rate	6.2%	5.8%	5.7%	5.8%	5.2%	5.1%	6.1%	5.8%	5.7%
Expense discount rate	5.8%	5.7%	6.1%	5.2%	5.1%	6.1%	5.8%	5.7%	6.1%
Expected return on plan assets	7.8%	7.8%	7.8%	7.3%	7.3%	8.0%			
Rate of salary increases	4.7%	4.5%	4.4%	3.9%	3.9%	4.1%			

The following table provides selected information about plans with liability for service to date and total benefit liability in excess of plan assets:

	Pension				Retiree Medical	
	2007	2006	2007	2006	2007	2006
	U.S.		International			
Selected information for plans with liability for service to date in excess of plan assets						
Liability for service to date	$(364)	$(387)	$(72)	$(286)		
Fair value of plan assets	$–	$1	$13	$237		
Selected information for plans with benefit liability in excess of plan assets						
Benefit liability	$(707)	$(754)	$(384)	$(1,387)	$(1,354)	$(1,370)
Fair value of plan assets	$–	$1	$278	$1,200		

Of the total projected pension benefit liability at year-end 2007, $658 million relates to plans that we do not fund because the funding of such plans does not receive favorable tax treatment.

Future Benefit Payments and Funding
Our estimated future benefit payments are as follows:

	2008	2009	2010	2011	2012	2013-17
Pension	$290	$315	$350	$385	$425	$2,755
Retiree medical[a]	$95	$100	$105	$110	$115	$640

(a) Expected future benefit payments for our retiree medical plans do not reflect any estimated subsidies expected to be received under the 2003 Medicare Act. Subsidies are expected to be approximately $10 million for each of the years from 2008 through 2012 and approximately $70 million in total for 2013 through 2017.

These future benefits to beneficiaries include payments from both funded and unfunded pension plans.

In 2008, we expect to make pension contributions of up to $150 million, with up to $75 million expected to be discretionary. Our cash payments for retiree medical are estimated to be approximately $85 million in 2008.

Pension Assets
Our pension plan investment strategy is reviewed annually and is established based upon plan liabilities, an evaluation of market conditions, tolerance for risk, and cash requirements for benefit payments. Our investment objective is to ensure that funds are available to meet the plans' benefit obligations when they are due. Our overall investment strategy is to prudently invest plan assets in high-quality and diversified equity and debt securities to achieve our long-term return expectation. As part of our investment strategy, we employ certain equity strategies which, in addition to investing in U.S. and international common and preferred stock, include investing in certain equity- and debt-based securities used collectively to generate returns in excess of certain equity-based indices. Debt-based securities represent approximately a third of our equity strategy portfolio as of year-end 2007 and 2006. Our investment policy also permits the use of derivative instruments to enhance the overall return of the portfolio. Our expected long-term rate of return on U.S. plan assets is 7.8%, reflecting estimated long-term rates of return of 9.3% from our equity strategies, and 5.8% from our fixed income strategies. Our target investment allocation is 60% for equity strategies and 40% for fixed income strategies. Our actual pension plan asset allocations, consistent with our investment approach and with how we view and manage our overall investment portfolio, for the plan years 2007 and 2006, are as follows:

	Actual Allocation	
Asset Category	**2007**	2006
Equity strategies	**61%**	61%
Fixed income strategies	**38%**	39%
Other, primarily cash	**1%**	–
Total	**100%**	100%

The expected return on pension plan assets is based on our historical experience, our pension plan investment strategy and our expectations for long-term rates of return. We use a market-related valuation method for recognizing investment gains or losses. For this purpose, investment gains or losses are the difference between the expected and actual return based on the market-related value of assets. This market-related valuation method recognizes investment gains or losses over a five-year period from the year in which they occur, which has the effect of reducing year-to-year volatility. Pension expense in future periods will be impacted as gains or losses are recognized in the market-related value of assets over the five-year period.

Pension assets include 5.5 million shares of PepsiCo common stock with a market value of $401 million in 2007, and 5.5 million shares with a market value of $358 million in 2006. Our investment policy limits the investment in PepsiCo stock at the time of investment to 10% of the fair value of plan assets.

As of December 29, 2007, approximately 3%, or approximately $165 million, of securities in the investment portfolio of our U.S. pension plans are subprime mortgage holdings. We do not believe that the ultimate realization of such investments will result in a material impact to future pension expense, future contributions or the funded status of our plans.

Retiree Medical Cost Trend Rates
An average increase of 8.5% in the cost of covered retiree medical benefits is assumed for 2008. This average increase is then projected to decline gradually to 5% in 2014 and thereafter. These assumed health care cost trend rates have an impact on the retiree medical plan expense and liability. However, the cap on our share of retiree medical costs limits the impact. A 1-percentage-point change in the assumed health care trend rate would have the following effects:

	1% Increase	1% Decrease
2007 service and interest cost components	$5	$(4)
2007 benefit liability	$55	$(48)

Savings Plan

Our U.S. employees are eligible to participate in 401(k) savings plans, which are voluntary defined contribution plans. The plans are designed to help employees accumulate additional savings for retirement. We make matching contributions on a portion of eligible pay based on years of service. In 2007 and 2006, our matching contributions were $62 million and $56 million, respectively.

For additional unaudited information on our pension and retiree medical plans and related accounting policies and assumptions, see "Our Critical Accounting Policies" in Management's Discussion and Analysis.

Note 8 — Noncontrolled Bottling Affiliates

Our most significant noncontrolled bottling affiliates are PBG and PAS. Sales to PBG reflect approximately 9% of our total net revenue in 2007 and approximately 10% in 2006 and 2005.

The Pepsi Bottling Group

In addition to approximately 35% and 38% of PBG's outstanding common stock that we own at year-end 2007 and 2006, respectively, we own 100% of PBG's class B common stock and approximately 7% of the equity of Bottling Group, LLC, PBG's principal operating subsidiary. Bottling equity income includes $174 million, $186 million and $126 million of pre-tax gains on our sales of PBG stock in 2007, 2006 and 2005, respectively.

PBG's summarized financial information is as follows:

	2007	2006	2005
Current assets	$ 3,086	$ 2,749	
Noncurrent assets	10,029	9,178	
Total assets	$13,115	$11,927	
Current liabilities	$ 2,215	$2,051	
Noncurrent liabilities	7,312	7,252	
Minority interest	973	540	
Total liabilities	$10,500	$9,843	
Our investment	$2,022	$1,842	
Net revenue	$13,591	$12,730	$11,885
Gross profit	$6,221	$5,830	$5,540
Operating profit	$1,071	$1,017	$1,023
Net income	$532	$522	$466

Our investment in PBG, which includes the related goodwill, was $507 million and $500 million higher than our ownership interest in their net assets at year-end 2007 and 2006, respectively. Based upon the quoted closing price of PBG shares at year-end 2007 and 2006, the calculated market value of our shares in PBG exceeded our investment balance, excluding our investment in Bottling Group, LLC, by approximately $1.7 billion and $1.4 billion, respectively.

Additionally, in 2007, we formed a joint venture with PBG, comprising our concentrate and PBG's bottling businesses in Russia. PBG holds a 60% majority interest in the joint venture and consolidates the entity. We account for our interest of 40% under the equity method of accounting.

PepsiAmericas

At year-end 2007 and 2006, we owned approximately 44% of PAS, and their summarized financial information is as follows:

	2007	2006	2005
Current assets	$ 922	$ 675	
Noncurrent assets	4,386	3,532	
Total assets	$5,308	$4,207	
Current liabilities	$ 903	$ 694	
Noncurrent liabilities	2,274	1,909	
Minority interest	273	—	
Total liabilities	$3,450	$2,603	
Our investment	$1,118	$1,028	
Net revenue	$4,480	$3,972	$3,726
Gross profit	$1,823	$1,608	$1,562
Operating profit	$436	$356	$393
Net income	$212	$158	$195

Our investment in PAS, which includes the related goodwill, was $303 million and $316 million higher than our ownership interest in their net assets at year-end 2007 and 2006, respectively. Based upon the quoted closing price of PAS shares at year-end 2007 and 2006, the calculated market value of our shares in PAS exceeded our investment by $855 million and $173 million, respectively.

Additionally, in 2007, we completed the joint purchase of Sandora, LLC with PAS.

PAS holds a 60% majority interest in the joint venture and consolidates the entity. We account for our interest of 40% under the equity method of accounting.

Related Party Transactions

Our significant related party transactions include our noncontrolled bottling affiliates. We sell concentrate to these affiliates, which they use in the production of CSDs and non-carbonated beverages. We also sell certain finished goods to these

affiliates, and we receive royalties for the use of our trademarks for certain products. Sales of concentrate and finished goods are reported net of bottler funding. For further unaudited information on these bottlers, see "Our Customers" in Management's Discussion and Analysis. These transactions with our bottling affiliates are reflected in our consolidated financial statements as follows:

	2007	2006	2005
Net revenue	$4,874	$4,837	$4,633
Selling, general and administrative expenses	$91	$87	$143
Accounts and notes receivable	$163	$175	
Accounts payable and other current liabilities	$106	$62	

Such amounts are settled on terms consistent with other trade receivables and payables. See Note 9 regarding our guarantee of certain PBG debt.

In addition, we coordinate, on an aggregate basis, the contract negotiations

of sweeteners and other raw material requirements for certain of our bottlers. Once we have negotiated the contracts, the bottlers order and take delivery directly from the supplier and pay the suppliers directly. Consequently, these

transactions are not reflected in our consolidated financial statements. As the contracting party, we could be liable to these suppliers in the event of any nonpayment by our bottlers, but we consider this exposure to be remote.

Note 9 — Debt Obligations and Commitments

	2007	2006
Short-term debt obligations		
Current maturities of long-term debt	$ 526	$ 605
Commercial paper (4.3% and 5.3%)	361	792
Other borrowings (7.2% and 7.3%)	489	377
Amounts reclassified to long-term debt	(1,376)	(1,500)
	$ –	$ 274
Long-term debt obligations		
Short-term borrowings, reclassified	$1,376	$1,500
Notes due 2008-2026 (5.3% and 6.0%)	2,673	1,148
Zero coupon notes, $375 million due 2008-2012 (13.3%)	285	299
Other, due 2008-2016 (6.1% and 6.1%)	395	208
	4,729	3,155
Less: current maturities of long-term debt obligations	(526)	(605)
	$4,203	$2,550

The interest rates in the above table reflect weighted-average rates at year-end.

In the second quarter of 2007, we issued $1 billion of senior unsecured notes maturing in 2012. We used a portion of the proceeds from the issuance of the notes to repay existing short-term debt of $500 million, bearing interest at 3.2% per year and maturing on May 15, 2007, with the balance of the proceeds used primarily for general corporate purposes. Additionally, in the second quarter of 2007, we extended the maturity of our $1.5 billion unsecured revolving credit agreement by one year to 2012, and, in the third quarter of 2007, we increased the amount of this agreement from $1.5 billion to $2 billion. Funds borrowed under this agreement may be used for general corporate purposes, including supporting our outstanding commercial paper issuances. This line of credit remains unused as of December 29, 2007.

In the third quarter of 2007, we updated our U.S. $2.5 billion euro medium term note program following the expiration of the existing program. Under the program, we may issue unsecured notes under mutually agreed upon terms with the purchasers of the notes. Proceeds from any issuance of notes may be used for general corporate purposes, except as otherwise specified in the related prospectus. As of December 29, 2007, we have no outstanding notes under the program.

In the fourth quarter of 2007, we issued $1 billion of senior unsecured notes maturing in 2013. We used the proceeds from the issuance of the notes for general corporate purposes, including the repayment of outstanding short-term indebtedness.

As of December 29, 2007, we have reclassified $1.4 billion of short-term debt to long-term based on our intent and ability to refinance on a long-term basis.

In addition, as of December 29, 2007, $806 million of our debt related to borrowings from various lines of credit is maintained for our international divisions. These lines of credit are subject to normal banking terms and conditions and are fully committed to the extent of our borrowings.

Interest Rate Swaps

In connection with the issuance of the $1 billion notes in the second quarter of 2007, we entered into an interest rate swap to effectively convert the interest rate from a fixed rate of 5.15% to a variable rate based on LIBOR. We previously entered into an interest rate swap in 2004 to effectively convert the interest rate of a specific debt issuance from a fixed rate to a variable rate. This interest rate swap matured in May 2007. The terms of the swaps match the terms of the debt they modify. The notional amounts of the interest rate swaps outstanding at December 29, 2007 and December 30, 2006 were $1 billion and $500 million, respectively.

At December 29, 2007, approximately 56% of total debt, after the impact of the related interest rate swap, was exposed to variable interest rates, compared to 63% at December 30, 2006. In addition to variable rate long-term debt, all debt with maturities of less than one year is categorized as variable for purposes of this measure.

Cross Currency Interest Rate Swaps

In 2004, we entered into a cross currency interest rate swap to hedge the currency exposure on U.S. dollar denominated debt of $50 million held by a foreign affiliate. The terms of this swap match the terms of the debt it modifies. The swap matures in 2008. The unrealized loss related to this swap was approximately $8 million at December 29, 2007, resulting in a U.S. dollar liability of $58 million. The unrealized gain related to this swap was less than $1 million at December 30, 2006, resulting in a U.S. dollar liability of $50 million.

We also entered into cross currency interest rate swaps to hedge the currency exposure on U.S. dollar denominated intercompany debt of $45 million at December 29, 2007 and $95 million at December 30, 2006. The terms of the swaps match the terms of the debt they modify. The net unrealized losses related to these swaps was less than $1 million at December 29, 2007 and December 30, 2006. The outstanding swap matures in 2008.

Long-Term Contractual Commitments[a]

Payments Due by Period	Total	2008	2009-2010	2011-2012	2013 and beyond
Long-term debt obligations[b]	$ 2,827	$ –	$ 171	$1,340	$1,316
Interest on debt obligations[c]	938	184	300	285	169
Operating leases	1,105	260	340	191	314
Purchasing commitments	3,767	1,182	1,713	509	363
Marketing commitments	1,251	329	551	278	93
Other commitments	248	44	127	75	2
	$10,136	$1,999	$3,202	$2,678	$2,257

(a) Reflects non-cancelable commitments as of December 29, 2007 based on year-end foreign exchange rates and excludes any reserves for income taxes under FIN 48 as we are unable to reasonably predict the ultimate amount or timing of settlement of our reserves for income taxes.
(b) Excludes short-term borrowings reclassified as long-term debt of $1,376 million and includes $273 million of accrued interest related to our zero coupon notes.
(c) Interest payments on floating-rate debt are estimated using interest rates effective as of December 29, 2007.

Most long-term contractual commitments, except for our long-term debt obligations, are not recorded on our balance sheet. Non-cancelable operating leases primarily represent building leases. Non-cancelable purchasing commitments are primarily for oranges and orange juice, packaging materials and cooking oil. Non-cancelable marketing commitments are primarily for sports marketing. Bottler funding is not reflected in our long-term contractual commitments as it is negotiated on an annual basis. See Note 7 regarding our pension and retiree medical obligations and discussion below regarding our commitments to noncontrolled bottling affiliates and former restaurant operations.

Off-Balance-Sheet Arrangements
It is not our business practice to enter into off-balance-sheet arrangements, other than in the normal course of business. However, certain guarantees were necessary to facilitate the separation of our bottling and restaurant operations from us. In connection with these transactions, we have guaranteed $2.3 billion of Bottling Group, LLC's long-term debt through 2012 and $18 million of YUM! Brands, Inc.'s (YUM) outstanding obligations, primarily property leases, through 2020. The terms of our Bottling Group, LLC debt guarantee are intended to preserve the structure of PBG's separation from

us and our payment obligation would be triggered if Bottling Group, LLC failed to perform under these debt obligations or the structure significantly changed. Our guarantees of certain obligations ensured YUM's continued use of certain properties. These guarantees would require our cash payment if YUM failed to perform under these lease obligations. See Note 8 regarding contracts related to certain of our bottlers.

See "Our Liquidity and Capital Resources" in Management's Discussion and Analysis for further unaudited information on our borrowings.

Note 10 — Risk Management

We are exposed to market risks arising from adverse changes in:
- commodity prices, affecting the cost of our raw materials and energy,
- foreign exchange risks, and
- interest rates.

In the normal course of business, we manage these risks through a variety of strategies, including the use of derivatives. Certain derivatives are designated as either cash flow or fair value hedges and qualify for hedge accounting treatment, while others do not qualify and are marked to market through earnings. See "Our Business Risks" in Management's Discussion and Analysis for further unaudited information on our business risks.

For cash flow hedges, changes in fair value are deferred in accumulated other comprehensive loss within shareholders' equity until the underlying hedged

item is recognized in net income. For fair value hedges, changes in fair value are recognized immediately in earnings, consistent with the underlying hedged item. Hedging transactions are limited to an underlying exposure. As a result, any change in the value of our derivative instruments would be substantially offset by an opposite change in the value of the underlying hedged items. Hedging ineffectiveness and a net earnings impact occur when the change in the value of the hedge does not offset the change in the value of the underlying hedged item. If the derivative instrument is terminated, we continue to defer the related gain or loss and include it as a component of the cost of the underlying hedged item. Upon determination that the underlying hedged item will not be part of an actual transaction, we recognize the related gain or loss in net income in that period.

We also use derivatives that do not qualify for hedge accounting treatment. We account for such derivatives at market value with the resulting gains and losses reflected in our income statement. We do not use derivative instruments for trading or speculative purposes, and we limit our exposure to individual counterparties to manage credit risk.

Commodity Prices
We are subject to commodity price risk because our ability to recover increased costs through higher pricing may be limited in the competitive environment in which we operate. This risk is managed through the use of fixed-price purchase orders, pricing agreements, geographic diversity and derivatives. We use derivatives, with terms of no more than two years, to economically hedge

price fluctuations related to a portion of our anticipated commodity purchases, primarily for natural gas, diesel fuel and fruit. For those derivatives that qualify for hedge accounting, any ineffectiveness is recorded immediately. However, such commodity cash flow hedges have not had any significant ineffectiveness for all periods presented. We classify both the earnings and cash flow impact from these derivatives consistent with the underlying hedged item. During the next 12 months, we expect to reclassify net gains of $1 million related to cash flow hedges from accumulated other comprehensive loss into net income. Derivatives used to hedge commodity price risks that do not qualify for hedge accounting are marked to market each period and reflected in our income statement.

Foreign Exchange

Our operations outside of the U.S. generate 44% of our net revenue, with Mexico, the United Kingdom and Canada comprising 19% of our net revenue. As a result, we are exposed to foreign currency risks. On occasion, we enter into hedges, primarily forward contracts with terms of no more than two years, to reduce the effect of foreign exchange rates. Ineffectiveness of these hedges has not been material.

Interest Rates

We centrally manage our debt and investment portfolios considering investment opportunities and risks, tax consequences and overall financing strategies. We may use interest rate and cross currency interest rate swaps to manage our overall interest expense and foreign exchange

risk. These instruments effectively change the interest rate and currency of specific debt issuances. These swaps are entered into concurrently with the issuance of the debt that they are intended to modify. The notional amount, interest payment and maturity date of the swaps match the principal, interest payment and maturity date of the related debt. These swaps are entered into only with strong creditworthy counterparties and are settled on a net basis.

Fair Value

All derivative instruments are recognized on our balance sheet at fair value. The fair value of our derivative instruments is generally based on quoted market prices. Book and fair values of our derivative and financial instruments are as follows:

	2007		2006	
	Book Value	Fair Value	Book Value	Fair Value
Assets				
Cash and cash equivalents[a]	$910	$910	$1,651	$1,651
Short-term investments[b]	$1,571	$1,571	$1,171	$1,171
Forward exchange contracts[c]	$32	$32	$8	$8
Commodity contracts[d]	$10	$10	$2	$2
Prepaid forward contracts[e]	$74	$74	$73	$73
Interest rate swaps[f]	$36	$36	$–	$–
Cross currency interest rate swaps[f]	$–	$–	$1	$1
Liabilities				
Forward exchange contracts[c]	$61	$61	$24	$24
Commodity contracts[d]	$7	$7	$29	$29
Debt obligations	$4,203	$4,352	$2,824	$2,955
Interest rate swaps[g]	$–	$–	$4	$4
Cross currency interest rate swaps[g]	$8	$8	$–	$–

The above items are included on our balance sheet under the captions noted or as indicated below. In addition, derivatives qualify for hedge accounting unless otherwise noted below.

(a) Book value approximates fair value due to the short maturity.

(b) Principally short-term time deposits and includes $189 million at December 29, 2007 and $145 million at December 30, 2006 of mutual fund investments used to manage a portion of market risk arising from our deferred compensation liability.

(c) The 2007 asset includes $20 million related to derivatives that do not qualify for hedge accounting and the 2007 liability includes $5 million related to derivatives that do not qualify for hedge accounting. The 2006 liability includes $10 million related to derivatives that do not qualify for hedge accounting. Assets are reported within current assets and other assets, and liabilities are reported within current liabilities and other liabilities.

(d) The 2007 asset includes $10 million related to derivatives that do not qualify for hedge accounting and the 2007 liability includes $7 million related to derivatives that do not qualify for hedge accounting. The 2006 liability includes $28 million related to derivatives that do not qualify for hedge accounting. Assets are reported within current assets and other assets, and liabilities are reported within current liabilities and other liabilities.

(e) Included in current assets and other assets.

(f) Asset included within other assets.

(g) Reported in other liabilities.

This table excludes guarantees, including our guarantee of $2.3 billion of Bottling Group, LLC's long-term debt. The guarantee had a fair value of $35 million at December 29, 2007 and December 30, 2006 based on our estimate of the cost to us of transferring the liability to an independent financial institution. See Note 9 for additional information on our guarantees.

Note 11 — Net Income per Common Share

Basic net income per common share is net income available to common shareholders divided by the weighted average of common shares outstanding during the period. Diluted net income per common share is calculated using the weighted average of common shares outstanding adjusted to include the effect that

would occur if in-the-money employee stock options were exercised and RSUs and preferred shares were converted into common shares. Options to purchase 2.7 million shares in 2007, 0.1 million shares in 2006 and 3.0 million shares in 2005 were not included in the calculation of diluted earnings per common share

because these options were out-of-the-money. Out-of-the-money options had average exercise prices of $65.18 in 2007, $65.24 in 2006 and $53.77 in 2005.

The computations of basic and diluted net income per common share are as follows:

	2007		2006		2005	
	Income	Shares[a]	Income	Shares[a]	Income	Shares[a]
Net income	$5,658		$5,642		$4,078	
Preferred shares:						
Dividends	(2)		(2)		(2)	
Redemption premium	(10)		(9)		(16)	
Net income available for common shareholders	$5,646	1,621	$5,631	1,649	$4,060	1,669
Basic net income per common share	$3.48		$3.42		$2.43	
Net income available for common shareholders	$5,646	1,621	$5,631	1,649	$4,060	1,669
Dilutive securities:						
Stock options and RSUs	–	35	–	36	–	35
ESOP convertible preferred stock	12	2	11	2	18	2
Diluted	$5,658	1,658	$5,642	1,687	$4,078	1,706
Diluted net income per common share	$3.41		$3.34		$2.39	

(a) Weighted-average common shares outstanding.

Note 12 — Preferred Stock

As of December 29, 2007 and December 30, 2006, there were 3 million shares of convertible preferred stock authorized. The preferred stock was issued only for an ESOP established by Quaker and these shares are redeemable for common stock by the ESOP participants. The preferred stock accrues dividends at an annual rate

of $5.46 per share. At year-end 2007 and 2006, there were 803,953 preferred shares issued and 287,553 and 320,853 shares outstanding, respectively. The outstanding preferred shares had a fair value of $108 million as of December 29, 2007 and $100 million as of December 30, 2006. Each share is

convertible at the option of the holder into 4.9625 shares of common stock. The preferred shares may be called by us upon written notice at $78 per share plus accrued and unpaid dividends. Quaker made the final award to its ESOP plan in June 2001.

	2007		2006		2005	
	Shares	Amount	Shares	Amount	Shares	Amount
Preferred stock	0.8	$41	0.8	$41	0.8	$41
Repurchased preferred stock						
Balance, beginning of year	0.5	$120	0.5	$110	0.4	$ 90
Redemptions	–	12	–	10	0.1	19
Balance, end of year	0.5	$132	0.5	$120	0.5	$110[a]

(a) Does not sum due to rounding.

Note 13 — Accumulated Other Comprehensive Loss

Comprehensive income is a measure of income which includes both net income and other comprehensive income or loss. Other comprehensive income or loss results from items deferred from recognition into our income statement. Accumulated other comprehensive loss is separately presented on our balance sheet as part of common shareholders' equity. Other comprehensive income/(loss) was $1,294 million in 2007, $456 million in 2006 and $(167) million in 2005. The accumulated balances for each component of other comprehensive loss were as follows:

	2007	2006	2005
Currency translation adjustment	$ 213	$ (506)	$ (971)
Cash flow hedges, net of tax[a]	(35)	4	27
Unamortized pension and retiree medical, net of tax[b]	(1,183)	(1,782)	–
Minimum pension liability adjustment[c]	–	–	(138)
Unrealized gain on securities, net of tax	49	40	31
Other	4	(2)	(2)
Accumulated other comprehensive loss	$ (952)	$(2,246)	$(1,053)

(a) Includes $3 million after-tax gain in 2007 and 2006 and no impact in 2005 for our share of our equity investees' accumulated derivative activity.
(b) Net of taxes of $645 million in 2007 and $919 million in 2006.
(c) Net of taxes of $72 million in 2005. Also includes $120 million for our share of our equity investees' minimum pension liability adjustments, net of tax.

Note 14 — Supplemental Financial Information

	2007	2006	2005
Accounts receivable			
Trade receivables	$3,670	$3,147	
Other receivables	788	642	
	4,458	3,789	
Allowance, beginning of year	64	75	$ 97
Net amounts charged/(credited) to expense	5	10	(1)
Deductions[a]	(7)	(27)	(22)
Other[b]	7	6	1
Allowance, end of year	69	64	$ 75
Net receivables	$4,389	$3,725	
Inventories[c]			
Raw materials	$1,056	$ 860	
Work-in-process	157	140	
Finished goods	1,077	926	
	$2,290	$1,926	

(a) Includes accounts written off.
(b) Includes currency translation effects and other adjustments.
(c) Inventories are valued at the lower of cost or market. Cost is determined using the average, first-in, first-out (FIFO) or last-in, first-out (LIFO) methods. Approximately 14% in 2007 and 19% in 2006 of the inventory cost was computed using the LIFO method. The differences between LIFO and FIFO methods of valuing these inventories were not material.

	2007	2006
Other assets		
Noncurrent notes and accounts receivable	$ 121	$149
Deferred marketplace spending	205	232
Unallocated purchase price for recent acquisitions	451	196
Pension plans	635	197
Other	270	206
	$1,682	$980
Accounts payable and other current liabilities		
Accounts payable	$2,562	$2,102
Accrued marketplace spending	1,607	1,444
Accrued compensation and benefits	1,287	1,143
Dividends payable	602	492
Other current liabilities	1,544	1,315
	$7,602	$6,496

	2007	2006	2005
Other supplemental information			
Rent expense	$303	$291	$228
Interest paid	$251	$215	$213
Income taxes paid, net of refunds	$1,731	$2,155	$1,258
Acquisitions[a]			
Fair value of assets acquired	$ 1,611	$ 678	$ 1,089
Cash paid and debt issued	(1,320)	(522)	(1,096)
SVE minority interest eliminated	–	–	216
Liabilities assumed	$ 291	$ 156	$ 209

(a) In 2005, these amounts include the impact of our acquisition of General Mills, Inc.'s 40.5% ownership interest in SVE for $750 million. The excess of our purchase price over the fair value of net assets acquired was $250 million and reported in goodwill. We also reacquired rights to distribute global brands for $263 million which is included in other nonamortizable intangible assets.

ADDITIONAL INFORMATION

In addition to the financial statements and accompanying notes, companies are required to provide a report on internal control over financial reporting and to have an auditor's report on the financial statements. In addition, PepsiCo has provided a report indicating that financial reporting is management's responsibility. Finally, PepsiCo also provides selected financial data it believes is useful. The two required reports are further explained below.

Management's Report on Internal Control over Financial Reporting

The Sarbanes-Oxley Act of 2002 requires managers of publicly traded companies to establish and maintain systems of internal control over the company's financial reporting processes. In addition, management must express its responsibility for financial reporting, and it must provide certifications regarding the accuracy of the financial statements.

Auditor's Report

All publicly held corporations, as well as many other enterprises and organizations engage the services of independent certified public accountants for the purpose of obtaining an objective, expert report on their financial statements. Based on a comprehensive examination of the company's accounting system, accounting records, and the financial statements, the outside CPA issues the auditor's report.

The standard auditor's report identifies who and what was audited and indicates the responsibilities of management and the auditor relative to the financial statements. It states that the audit was conducted in accordance with generally accepted auditing standards and discusses the nature and limitations of the audit. It then expresses an informed opinion as to (1) the fairness of the financial statements and (2) their conformity with generally accepted accounting principles. It also expresses an opinion regarding the effectiveness of the company's internal controls. All of this additional information for PepsiCo is provided on the following pages.

Management's Responsibility for Financial Reporting

To Our Shareholders:

At PepsiCo, our actions — the actions of all our associates — are governed by our Worldwide Code of Conduct. This code is clearly aligned with our stated values — a commitment to sustained growth, through empowered people, operating with responsibility and building trust. Both the code and our core values enable us to operate with integrity — both within the letter and the spirit of the law. Our code of conduct is reinforced consistently at all levels and in all countries. We have maintained strong governance policies and practices for many years.

The management of PepsiCo is responsible for the objectivity and integrity of our consolidated financial statements. The Audit Committee of the Board of Directors has engaged independent registered public accounting firm, KPMG LLP, to audit our consolidated financial statements and they have expressed an unqualified opinion.

We are committed to providing timely, accurate and understandable information to investors. Our commitment encompasses the following:

Maintaining strong controls over financial reporting. Our system of internal control is based on the control criteria framework of the Committee of Sponsoring Organizations of the Treadway Commission published in their report titled *Internal Control — Integrated Framework*. The system is designed to provide reasonable assurance that transactions are executed as authorized and accurately recorded; that assets are safeguarded; and that accounting records are sufficiently reliable to permit the preparation of financial statements that conform in all material respects with accounting principles generally accepted in the U.S. We maintain disclosure controls and procedures designed to ensure that information required to be disclosed in reports under the Securities Exchange Act of 1934 is recorded, processed, summarized and reported within the specified time periods. We monitor these internal controls through self-assessments and an ongoing program of internal audits. Our internal controls are reinforced through our Worldwide Code of Conduct, which sets forth our commitment to conduct business with integrity, and within both the letter and the spirit of the law.

Exerting rigorous oversight of the business. We continuously review our business results and strategies. This encompasses financial discipline in our strategic and daily business decisions. Our Executive Committee is actively involved — from understanding strategies and alternatives to reviewing key initiatives and financial performance. The intent is to ensure we remain objective in our assessments, constructively challenge our approach to potential business opportunities and issues, and monitor results and controls.

Engaging strong and effective Corporate Governance from our Board of Directors. We have an active, capable and diligent Board that meets the required standards for independence, and we welcome the Board's oversight as a representative of our shareholders. Our Audit Committee is comprised of independent directors with the financial literacy, knowledge and experience to provide appropriate oversight. We review our critical accounting policies, financial reporting and internal control matters with them and encourage their direct communication with KPMG LLP, with our General Auditor, and with our General Counsel. We also have a senior compliance officer to lead and coordinate our compliance policies and practices.

Providing investors with financial results that are complete, transparent and understandable. The consolidated financial statements and financial information included in this report are the responsibility of management. This includes preparing the financial statements in accordance with accounting principles generally accepted in the U.S., which require estimates based on management's best judgment.

PepsiCo has a strong history of doing what's right. We realize that great companies are built on trust, strong ethical standards and principles. Our financial results are delivered from that culture of accountability, and we take responsibility for the quality and accuracy of our financial reporting.

Management's Report on Internal Control over Financial Reporting

To Our Shareholders:

Our management is responsible for establishing and maintaining adequate internal control over financial reporting, as such term is defined in Rule 13a-15(f) of the Exchange Act. Under the supervision and with the participation of our management, including our Chief Executive Officer and Chief Financial Officer, we conducted an evaluation of the effectiveness of our internal control over financial reporting based upon the framework in *Internal Control — Integrated Framework* issued by the Committee of Sponsoring Organizations of the Treadway Commission. Based on that evaluation, our management concluded that our internal control over financial reporting is effective as of December 29, 2007.

KPMG LLP, an independent registered public accounting firm, has audited the consolidated financial statements included in this Annual Report and, as part of their audit, has issued their report, included herein, on the effectiveness of our internal control over financial reporting.

During our fourth fiscal quarter of 2007, we continued migrating certain of our financial processing systems to SAP software. This software implementation is part of our ongoing global business transformation initiative, and we plan to continue implementing such software throughout other parts of our businesses over the course of the next few years. In connection with the SAP implementation and resulting business process changes, we continue to enhance the design and documentation of our internal control processes to ensure suitable controls over our financial reporting.

Except as described above, there were no changes in our internal control over financial reporting that have materially affected, or are reasonably likely to materially affect, our internal control over financial reporting during our fourth fiscal quarter of 2007.

Peter A. Bridgman
Senior Vice President and Controller

Richard Goodman
Chief Financial Officer

Indra K. Nooyi
Chairman of the Board of Directors and
Chief Executive Officer

Report of Independent Registered Public Accounting Firm

The Board of Directors and Shareholders
PepsiCo, Inc.:
We have audited the accompanying Consolidated Balance Sheet of PepsiCo, Inc. and Subsidiaries ("PepsiCo, Inc." or the "Company") as of December 29, 2007 and December 30, 2006, and the related Consolidated Statements of Income, Cash Flows and Common Shareholders' Equity for each of the years in the three-year period ended December 29, 2007. We also have audited PepsiCo, Inc.'s internal control over financial reporting as of December 29, 2007, based on criteria established in Internal Control — Integrated Framework issued by the Committee of Sponsoring Organizations of the Treadway Commission ("COSO"). PepsiCo, Inc.'s management is responsible for these consolidated financial statements, for maintaining effective internal control over financial reporting, and for its assessment of the effectiveness of internal control over financial reporting, included in Management's Report on Internal Control over Financial Reporting. Our responsibility is to express an opinion on these consolidated financial statements and an opinion on the Company's internal control over financial reporting based on our audits.

We conducted our audits in accordance with the standards of the Public Company Accounting Oversight Board (United States). Those standards require that we plan and perform the audits to obtain reasonable assurance about whether the financial statements are free of material misstatement and whether effective internal control over financial reporting was maintained in all material respects. Our audits of the consolidated financial statements included examining, on a test basis, evidence supporting the amounts and disclosures in the financial statements, assessing the accounting principles used and significant estimates made by management, and evaluating the overall financial statement presentation. Our audit of internal control over financial reporting included obtaining an understanding of internal control over financial reporting, assessing the risk that a material weakness exists, and testing and evaluating the design and operating effectiveness of internal control based on the assessed risk. Our audits also included performing such other procedures as we considered necessary in the circumstances. We believe that our audits provide a reasonable basis for our opinions.

A company's internal control over financial reporting is a process designed to provide reasonable assurance regarding the reliability of financial reporting and the preparation of financial statements for external purposes in accordance with generally accepted accounting principles. A company's internal control over financial reporting includes those policies and procedures that (1) pertain to the maintenance of records that, in reasonable detail, accurately and fairly reflect the transactions and dispositions of the assets of the company; (2) provide reasonable assurance that transactions are recorded as necessary to permit preparation of financial statements in accordance with generally accepted accounting principles, and that receipts and expenditures of the company are being made only in accordance with authorizations of management and directors of the company; and (3) provide reasonable assurance regarding prevention or timely detection of unauthorized acquisition, use, or disposition of the company's assets that could have a material effect on the financial statements.

Because of its inherent limitations, internal control over financial reporting may not prevent or detect misstatements. Also, projections of any evaluation of effectiveness to future periods are subject to the risk that controls may become inadequate because of changes in conditions, or that the degree of compliance with the policies or procedures may deteriorate.

In our opinion, the consolidated financial statements referred to above present fairly, in all material respects, the financial position of PepsiCo, Inc. as of December 29, 2007 and December 30, 2006, and the results of its operations and its cash flows for each of the years in the three-year period ended December 29, 2007, in conformity with accounting principles generally accepted in the United States of America. Also in our opinion, PepsiCo, Inc. maintained, in all material respects, effective internal control over financial reporting as of December 29, 2007, based on criteria established in Internal Control — Integrated Framework issued by COSO.

KPMG LLP

New York, New York
February 15, 2008

Selected Financial Data (in millions except per share amounts, unaudited)

Quarterly	First Quarter	Second Quarter	Third Quarter	Fourth Quarter
Net revenue				
2007	$7,350	$9,607	$10,171	$12,346
2006	$6,719	$8,714	$9,134	$10,570
Gross profit				
2007	$4,065	$5,265	$5,544	$6,562
2006	$3,757	$4,852	$5,026	$5,740
Restructuring and impairment charges[a]				
2007	–	–	–	$102
2006	–	–	–	$67
Tax benefits[b]				
2007	–	–	$(115)	$(14)
2006	–	–	–	$(602)
Net income				
2007	$1,096	$1,557	$1,743	$1,262
2006	$947	$1,375	$1,494	$1,826
Net income per common share — basic				
2007	$0.67	$0.96	$1.08	$0.78
2006	$0.57	$0.83	$0.90	$1.11
Net income per common share — diluted				
2007	$0.65	$0.94	$1.06	$0.77
2006	$0.56	$0.81	$0.89	$1.09
Cash dividends declared per common share				
2007	$0.30	$0.375	$0.375	$0.375
2006	$0.26	$0.30	$0.30	$0.30
2007 stock price per share[c]				
High	$65.54	$69.64	$70.25	$79.00
Low	$61.89	$62.57	$64.25	$68.02
Close	$64.09	$66.68	$67.98	$77.03
2006 stock price per share[c]				
High	$60.55	$61.19	$65.99	$65.99
Low	$56.00	$56.51	$58.65	$61.15
Close	$59.34	$59.70	$64.73	$62.55

2006 results reflect our change in reporting calendars of certain operating units within PI.

(a) The restructuring and impairment charge in 2007 was $102 million ($70 million or $0.04 per share after-tax). The restructuring and impairment charge in 2006 was $67 million ($43 million or $0.03 per share after-tax). See Note 3.

(b) In 2007, represents non-cash tax benefits related to the favorable resolution of certain foreign tax matters. In 2006, represents non-cash tax benefits primarily related to the IRS's examination of our consolidated income tax returns for the years 1998 through 2002. See Note 5.

(c) Represents the composite high and low sales price and quarterly closing prices for one share of PepsiCo common stock.

Five-Year Summary	2007	2006	2005
Net revenue	$39,474	$35,137	$32,562
Net income	$5,658	$5,642	$4,078
Income per common share — basic	$3.48	$3.42	$2.43
Income per common share — diluted	$3.41	$3.34	$2.39
Cash dividends declared per common share	$1.425	$1.16	$1.01
Total assets	$34,628	$29,930	$31,727
Long-term debt	$4,203	$2,550	$2,313
Return on invested capital[a]	28.9%	30.4%	22.7%

Five-Year Summary (cont.)	2004	2003
Net revenue	$29,261	$26,971
Income from continuing operations	$4,174	$3,568
Net income	$4,212	$3,568
Income per common share — basic, continuing operations	$2.45	$2.07
Income per common share — diluted, continuing operations	$2.41	$2.05
Cash dividends declared per common share	$0.85	$0.63
Total assets	$27,987	$25,327
Long-term debt	$2,397	$1,702
Return on invested capital[a]	27.4%	27.5%

(a) Return on invested capital is defined as adjusted net income divided by the sum of average shareholders' equity and average total debt. Adjusted net income is defined as net income plus net interest expense after-tax. Net interest expense after-tax was $63 million in 2007, $72 million in 2006, $62 million in 2005, $60 million in 2004 and $72 million in 2003.

• Includes restructuring and impairment charges of:

	2007	2006	2005	2004	2003
Pre-tax	$102	$67	$83	$150	$147
After-tax	$70	$43	$55	$96	$100
Per share	$0.04	$0.03	$0.03	$0.06	$0.06

• Includes Quaker merger-related costs of:

	2003
Pre-tax	$59
After-tax	$42
Per share	$0.02

• In 2007, we recognized $129 million ($0.08 per share) of non-cash tax benefits related to the favorable resolution of certain foreign tax matters. In 2006, we recognized non-cash tax benefits of $602 million ($0.36 per share) primarily in connection with the IRS's examination of our consolidated income tax returns for the years 1998 through 2002. In 2005, we recorded income tax expense of $460 million ($0.27 per share) related to our repatriation of earnings in connection with the AJCA. In 2004, we reached agreement with the IRS for an open issue related to our discontinued restaurant operations which resulted in a tax benefit of $38 million ($0.02 per share).

• On December 30, 2006, we adopted SFAS 158 which reduced total assets by $2,016 million, total common shareholders' equity by $1,643 million and total liabilities by $373 million.

• The 2005 fiscal year consisted of 53 weeks compared to 52 weeks in our normal fiscal year. The 53rd week increased 2005 net revenue by an estimated $418 million and net income by an estimated $57 million ($0.03 per share).

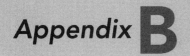

SPECIMEN FINANCIAL STATEMENTS:
The Coca-Cola Company

THE COCA-COLA COMPANY AND SUBSIDIARIES
CONSOLIDATED STATEMENTS OF INCOME

Year Ended December 31,	2007	2006	2005
(In millions except per share data)			
NET OPERATING REVENUES	**$ 28,857**	$ 24,088	$ 23,104
Cost of goods sold	**10,406**	8,164	8,195
GROSS PROFIT	**18,451**	15,924	14,909
Selling, general and administrative expenses	**10,945**	9,431	8,739
Other operating charges	**254**	185	85
OPERATING INCOME	**7,252**	6,308	6,085
Interest income	**236**	193	235
Interest expense	**456**	220	240
Equity income—net	**668**	102	680
Other income (loss)—net	**173**	195	(93)
Gains on issuances of stock by equity method investees	**—**	—	23
INCOME BEFORE INCOME TAXES	**7,873**	6,578	6,690
Income taxes	**1,892**	1,498	1,818
NET INCOME	**$ 5,981**	$ 5,080	$ 4,872
BASIC NET INCOME PER SHARE	**$ 2.59**	$ 2.16	$ 2.04
DILUTED NET INCOME PER SHARE	**$ 2.57**	$ 2.16	$ 2.04
AVERAGE SHARES OUTSTANDING	**2,313**	2,348	2,392
Effect of dilutive securities	**18**	2	1
AVERAGE SHARES OUTSTANDING ASSUMING DILUTION	**2,331**	2,350	2,393

Refer to Notes to Consolidated Financial Statements.

The financial information herein is reprinted with permission from The Coca-Cola Company 2007
Annual Report. The accompanying Notes are an integral part of the consolidated financial statements. The complete financial statements are available through a link at the book's companion
website.

THE COCA-COLA COMPANY AND SUBSIDIARIES
CONSOLIDATED BALANCE SHEETS

December 31,	2007	2006
(In millions except par value)		
ASSETS		
CURRENT ASSETS		
Cash and cash equivalents	$ 4,093	$ 2,440
Marketable securities	215	150
Trade accounts receivable, less allowances of $56 and $63, respectively	3,317	2,587
Inventories	2,220	1,641
Prepaid expenses and other assets	2,260	1,623
TOTAL CURRENT ASSETS	12,105	8,441
INVESTMENTS		
Equity method investments:		
Coca-Cola Enterprises Inc.	1,637	1,312
Coca-Cola Hellenic Bottling Company S.A.	1,549	1,251
Coca-Cola FEMSA, S.A.B. de C.V.	996	835
Coca-Cola Amatil Limited	806	817
Other, principally bottling companies and joint ventures	2,301	2,095
Cost method investments, principally bottling companies	488	473
TOTAL INVESTMENTS	7,777	6,783
OTHER ASSETS	2,675	2,701
PROPERTY, PLANT AND EQUIPMENT—net	8,493	6,903
TRADEMARKS WITH INDEFINITE LIVES	5,153	2,045
GOODWILL	4,256	1,403
OTHER INTANGIBLE ASSETS	2,810	1,687
TOTAL ASSETS	$ 43,269	$ 29,963
LIABILITIES AND SHAREOWNERS' EQUITY		
CURRENT LIABILITIES		
Accounts payable and accrued expenses	$ 6,915	$ 5,055
Loans and notes payable	5,919	3,235
Current maturities of long-term debt	133	33
Accrued income taxes	258	567
TOTAL CURRENT LIABILITIES	13,225	8,890
LONG-TERM DEBT	3,277	1,314
OTHER LIABILITIES	3,133	2,231
DEFERRED INCOME TAXES	1,890	608
SHAREOWNERS' EQUITY		
Common stock, $0.25 par value; Authorized—5,600 shares;		
Issued—3,519 and 3,511 shares, respectively	880	878
Capital surplus	7,378	5,983
Reinvested earnings	36,235	33,468
Accumulated other comprehensive income (loss)	626	(1,291)
Treasury stock, at cost—1,201 and 1,193 shares, respectively	(23,375)	(22,118)
TOTAL SHAREOWNERS' EQUITY	21,744	16,920
TOTAL LIABILITIES AND SHAREOWNERS' EQUITY	$ 43,269	$ 29,963

Refer to Notes to Consolidated Financial Statements.

THE COCA-COLA COMPANY AND SUBSIDIARIES

CONSOLIDATED STATEMENTS OF CASH FLOWS

Year Ended December 31, (In millions)	2007	2006	2005
OPERATING ACTIVITIES			
Net income	$ **5,981**	$ 5,080	$ 4,872
Depreciation and amortization	**1,163**	938	932
Stock-based compensation expense	**313**	324	324
Deferred income taxes	**109**	(35)	(88)
Equity income or loss, net of dividends	**(452)**	124	(446)
Foreign currency adjustments	**9**	52	47
Gains on issuances of stock by equity investees	**—**	—	(23)
Gains on sales of assets, including bottling interests	**(244)**	(303)	(9)
Other operating charges	**166**	159	85
Other items	**99**	233	299
Net change in operating assets and liabilities	**6**	(615)	430
Net cash provided by operating activities	**7,150**	5,957	6,423
INVESTING ACTIVITIES			
Acquisitions and investments, principally beverage and bottling companies	**(5,653)**	(901)	(637)
Purchases of other investments	**(99)**	(82)	(53)
Proceeds from disposals of other investments	**448**	640	33
Purchases of property, plant and equipment	**(1,648)**	(1,407)	(899)
Proceeds from disposals of property, plant and equipment	**239**	112	88
Other investing activities	**(6)**	(62)	(28)
Net cash used in investing activities	**(6,719)**	(1,700)	(1,496)
FINANCING ACTIVITIES			
Issuances of debt	**9,979**	617	178
Payments of debt	**(5,638)**	(2,021)	(2,460)
Issuances of stock	**1,619**	148	230
Purchases of stock for treasury	**(1,838)**	(2,416)	(2,055)
Dividends	**(3,149)**	(2,911)	(2,678)
Net cash provided by (used in) financing activities	**973**	(6,583)	(6,785)
EFFECT OF EXCHANGE RATE CHANGES ON CASH AND CASH EQUIVALENTS	**249**	65	(148)
CASH AND CASH EQUIVALENTS			
Net increase (decrease) during the year	**1,653**	(2,261)	(2,006)
Balance at beginning of year	**2,440**	4,701	6,707
Balance at end of year	$ **4,093**	$ 2,440	$ 4,701

Refer to Notes to Consolidated Financial Statements.

THE COCA-COLA COMPANY AND SUBSIDIARIES
CONSOLIDATED STATEMENTS OF SHAREOWNERS' EQUITY

Year Ended December 31,	2007	2006	2005
(In millions except per share data)			
NUMBER OF COMMON SHARES OUTSTANDING			
Balance at beginning of year	**2,318**	2,369	2,409
Stock issued to employees exercising stock options	**8**	4	7
Purchases of stock for treasury[1]	**(35)**	(55)	(47)
Treasury stock issued to employees exercising stock options	**23**	—	—
Treasury stock issued to former shareholders of glacéau	**4**	—	—
Balance at end of year	**2,318**	2,318	2,369
COMMON STOCK			
Balance at beginning of year	$ **878**	$ 877	$ 875
Stock issued to employees exercising stock options	**2**	1	2
Balance at end of year	**880**	878	877
CAPITAL SURPLUS			
Balance at beginning of year	**5,983**	5,492	4,928
Stock issued to employees exercising stock options	**1,001**	164	229
Tax (charge) benefit from employees' stock option and restricted stock plans	**(28)**	3	11
Stock-based compensation	**309**	324	324
Stock purchased by former shareholders of glacéau	**113**	—	—
Balance at end of year	**7,378**	5,983	5,492
REINVESTED EARNINGS			
Balance at beginning of year	**33,468**	31,299	29,105
Adjustment for the cumulative effect on prior years of the adoption of Interpretation No. 48	**(65)**	—	—
Net income	**5,981**	5,080	4,872
Dividends (per share—$1.36, $1.24 and $1.12 in 2007, 2006 and 2005, respectively)	**(3,149)**	(2,911)	(2,678)
Balance at end of year	**36,235**	33,468	31,299
ACCUMULATED OTHER COMPREHENSIVE INCOME (LOSS)			
Balance at beginning of year	**(1,291)**	(1,669)	(1,348)
Net foreign currency translation adjustment	**1,575**	603	(396)
Net gain (loss) on derivatives	**(64)**	(26)	57
Net change in unrealized gain on available-for-sale securities	**14**	43	13
Net change in pension liability	**392**	—	—
Net change in pension liability, prior to adoption of SFAS No. 158	**—**	46	5
Net other comprehensive income adjustments	**1,917**	666	(321)
Adjustment to initially apply SFAS No. 158	**—**	(288)	—
Balance at end of year	**626**	(1,291)	(1,669)
TREASURY STOCK			
Balance at beginning of year	**(22,118)**	(19,644)	(17,625)
Stock issued to employees exercising stock options	**428**	—	—
Stock purchased by former shareholders of glacéau	**66**	—	—
Purchases of treasury stock	**(1,751)**	(2,474)	(2,019)
Balance at end of year	**(23,375)**	(22,118)	(19,644)
TOTAL SHAREOWNERS' EQUITY	$ **21,744**	$ 16,920	$ 16,355
COMPREHENSIVE INCOME			
Net income	$ **5,981**	$ 5,080	$ 4,872
Net other comprehensive income adjustments	**1,917**	666	(321)
TOTAL COMPREHENSIVE INCOME	$ **7,898**	$ 5,746	$ 4,551

[1] Common stock purchased from employees exercising stock options numbered approximately zero shares, zero shares and 0.5 million shares for the years ended December 31, 2007, 2006 and 2005, respectively.

Refer to Notes to Consolidated Financial Statements.

Appendix C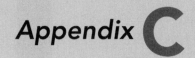

Time Value of Money

STUDY OBJECTIVES

After studying this appendix, you should be able to:

1 Distinguish between simple and compound interest.
2 Identify the variables fundamental to solving present value problems.
3 Solve for present value of a single amount.
4 Solve for present value of an annuity.
5 Compute the present value of notes and bonds.

Would you rather receive $1,000 today or a year from now? You should prefer to receive the $1,000 today because you can invest the $1,000 and earn interest on it. As a result, you will have more than $1,000 a year from now. What this example illustrates is the concept of the **time value of money**. Everyone prefers to receive money today rather than in the future because of the interest factor.

NATURE OF INTEREST

Interest is payment for the use of another person's money. It is the difference between the amount borrowed or invested (called the **principal**) and the amount repaid or collected. The amount of interest to be paid or collected is usually stated as a **rate** over a specific period of time. The rate of interest is generally stated as an **annual rate**.

The amount of interest involved in any financing transaction is based on three elements:

1. **Principal (p):** The original amount borrowed or invested.
2. **Interest Rate (i):** An annual percentage of the principal.
3. **Time (n):** The number of years that the principal is borrowed or invested.

Simple Interest

Simple interest is computed on the principal amount only. It is the return on the principal for one period. Simple interest is usually expressed as shown in Illustration C-1 on the next page.

> **STUDY OBJECTIVE 1**
> Distinguish between simple and compound interest.

Illustration C-1
Interest computation

Interest	=	Principal _p_	×	Rate _i_	×	Time _n_

For example, if you borrowed $5,000 for 2 years at a simple interest rate of 12% annually, you would pay $1,200 in total interest computed as follows:

$$\text{Interest} = p \times i \times n$$
$$= \$5{,}000 \times .12 \times 2$$
$$= \$1{,}200$$

Compound Interest

Compound interest is computed on principal **and** on any interest earned that has not been paid or withdrawn. It is the return on the principal for two or more time periods. Compounding computes interest not only on the principal but also on the interest earned to date on that principal, assuming the interest is left on deposit.

To illustrate the difference between simple and compound interest, assume that you deposit $1,000 in Bank Two, where it will earn *simple interest* of 9% per year, and you deposit another $1,000 in Citizens Bank, where it will earn compound interest of 9% per year *compounded annually*. Also assume that in both cases you will not withdraw any interest until three years from the date of deposit. Illustration C-2 shows the computation of interest you will receive and the accumulated year-end balances.

Illustration C-2
Simple versus compound interest

Bank Two				Citizens Bank		
Simple Interest Calculation	Simple Interest	Accumulated Year-end Balance		Compound Interest Calculation	Compound Interest	Accumulated Year-end Balance
Year 1 $1,000.00 × 9%	$ 90.00	$1,090.00		Year 1 $1,000.00 × 9%	$ 90.00	$1,090.00
Year 2 $1,000.00 × 9%	90.00	$1,180.00		Year 2 $1,090.00 × 9%	98.10	$1,188.10
Year 3 $1,000.00 × 9%	90.00	$1,270.00		Year 3 $1,188.10 × 9%	106.93	$1,295.03
	$ 270.00		$25.03 Difference		$ 295.03	

Note in Illustration C-2 that simple interest uses the initial principal of $1,000 to compute the interest in all three years. Compound interest uses the accumulated balance (principal plus interest to date) at each year-end to compute interest in the succeeding year—which explains why your compound interest account is larger.

Obviously, if you had a choice between investing your money at simple interest or at compound interest, you would choose compound interest, all other things—especially risk—being equal. In the example, compounding provides $25.03 of additional interest income. For practical purposes, compounding assumes that unpaid interest earned becomes a part of the principal, and the accumulated balance at the end of each year becomes the new principal on which interest is earned during the next year.

Illustration C-2 indicates that you should invest your money at the bank that compounds interest annually. Most business situations use compound interest. Simple interest is generally applicable only to short-term situations of one year or less.

PRESENT VALUE VARIABLES

The **present value** is the value now of a given amount to be paid or received in the future, assuming compound interest. The present value is based on three variables: (1) the dollar amount to be received (future amount), (2) the length of time until the amount is received (number of periods), and (3) the interest rate (the discount rate). The process of determining the present value is referred to as **discounting the future amount**.

STUDY OBJECTIVE 2
Identify the variables fundamental to solving present value problems.

In this textbook, we use present value computations in measuring several items. For example, Chapter 15 computed the present value of the principal and interest payments to determine the market price of a bond. In addition, determining the amount to be reported for notes payable and lease liabilities involves present value computations.

PRESENT VALUE OF A SINGLE AMOUNT

To illustrate present value, assume that you want to invest a sum of money that will yield $1,000 at the end of one year. What amount would you need to invest today to have $1,000 one year from now? Illustration C-3 shows the formula for calculating present value.

STUDY OBJECTIVE 3
Solve for present value of a single amount.

$$\text{Present Value} = \text{Future Value} \div (1 + i)^n$$

Illustration C-3
Formula for present value

Thus, if you want a 10% rate of return, you would compute the present value of $1,000 for one year as follows:

$$PV = FV \div (1 + i)^n$$
$$= \$1,000 \div (1 + .10)^1$$
$$= \$1,000 \div 1.10$$
$$= \$909.09$$

We know the future amount ($1,000), the discount rate (10%), and the number of periods (1). These variables are depicted in the time diagram in Illustration C-4.

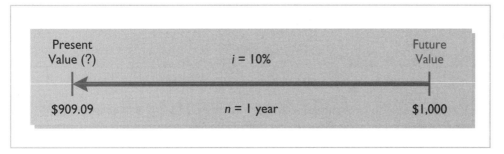

Illustration C-4
Finding present value if discounted for one period

Present Value (?)	$i = 10\%$	Future Value
$909.09	$n = 1$ year	$1,000

If you receive the single amount of $1,000 **in two years**, discounted at 10% [$PV = \$1,000 \div (1 + .10)^2$], the present value of your $1,000 is $826.45 [($1,000 ÷ 1.21), depicted as shown in Illustration C-5 on the next page.

Illustration C-5
Finding present value if
discounted for two periods

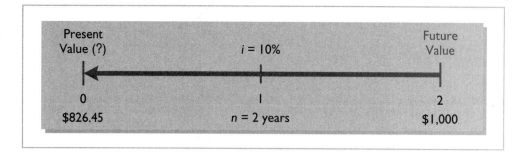

You also could find the present value of your amount through tables that show the present value of 1 for *n* periods. In Table 1, below, *n* (represented in the table's rows) is the number of discounting periods involved. The percentages (represented in the table's columns) are the periodic interest rates or discount rates. The 5-digit decimal numbers in the intersections of the rows and columns are called the **present value of 1 factors**.

When using Table 1 to determine present value, you multiply the future value by the present value factor specified at the intersection of the number of periods and the discount rate.

TABLE 1
Present Value of 1

(*n*) Periods	4%	5%	6%	8%	9%	10%	11%	12%	15%
1	.96154	.95238	.94340	.92593	.91743	.90909	.90090	.89286	.86957
2	.92456	.90703	.89000	.85734	.84168	.82645	.81162	.79719	.75614
3	.88900	.86384	.83962	.79383	.77218	.75132	.73119	.71178	.65752
4	.85480	.82270	.79209	.73503	.70843	.68301	.65873	.63552	.57175
5	.82193	.78353	.74726	.68058	.64993	.62092	.59345	.56743	.49718
6	.79031	.74622	.70496	.63017	.59627	.56447	.53464	.50663	.43233
7	.75992	.71068	.66506	.58349	.54703	.51316	.48166	.45235	.37594
8	.73069	.67684	.62741	.54027	.50187	.46651	.43393	.40388	.32690
9	.70259	.64461	.59190	.50025	.46043	.42410	.39092	.36061	.28426
10	.67556	.61391	.55839	.46319	.42241	.38554	.35218	.32197	.24719
11	.64958	.58468	.52679	.42888	.38753	.35049	.31728	.28748	.21494
12	.62460	.55684	.49697	.39711	.35554	.31863	.28584	.25668	.18691
13	.60057	.53032	.46884	.36770	.32618	.28966	.25751	.22917	.16253
14	.57748	.50507	.44230	.34046	.29925	.26333	.23199	.20462	.14133
15	.55526	.48102	.41727	.31524	.27454	.23939	.20900	.18270	.12289
16	.53391	.45811	.39365	.29189	.25187	.21763	.18829	.16312	.10687
17	.51337	.43630	.37136	.27027	.23107	.19785	.16963	.14564	.09293
18	.49363	.41552	.35034	.25025	.21199	.17986	.15282	.13004	.08081
19	.47464	.39573	.33051	.23171	.19449	.16351	.13768	.11611	.07027
20	.45639	.37689	.31180	.21455	.17843	.14864	.12403	.10367	.06110

For example, the present value factor for one period at a discount rate of 10% is .90909, which equals the $909.09 ($1,000 × .90909) computed in Illustration C-4. For two periods at a discount rate of 10%, the present value factor is .82645, which equals the $826.45 ($1,000 × .82645) computed previously.

Note that a higher discount rate produces a smaller present value. For example, using a 15% discount rate, the present value of $1,000 due one year from now is $869.57, versus $909.09 at 10%. Also note that the further removed from the present the future value is, the smaller the present value. For example, using the same discount rate of 10%, the present value of $1,000 due in **five years** is $620.92, versus the present value of $1,000 due in **one year**, which is $909.09.

The following two demonstration problems (Illustrations C-6, C-7) illustrate how to use Table 1.

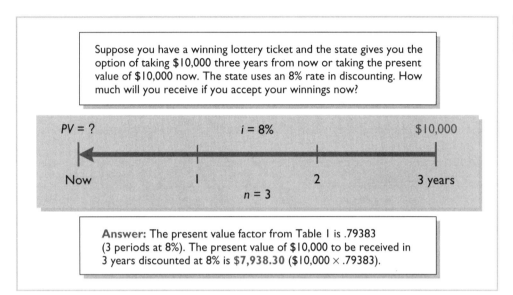

Illustration C-6
Demonstration problem—
Using Table 1 for *PV* of 1

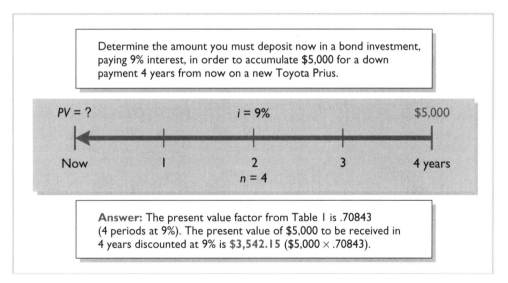

Illustration C-7
Demonstration problem—
Using Table 1 for *PV* of 1

PRESENT VALUE OF AN ANNUITY

The preceding discussion involved the discounting of only a single future amount. Businesses and individuals frequently engage in transactions in which a *series* of equal dollar amounts are to be received or paid periodically. Examples of a series of periodic receipts or payments are loan agreements, installment sales, mortgage notes, lease (rental) contracts, and pension obligations. As discussed in Chapter 15, these periodic receipts or payments are **annuities**.

STUDY OBJECTIVE 4

Solve for present value of an annuity.

The **present value of an annuity** is the value now of a series of future receipts or payments, discounted assuming compound interest. In computing the present value of an annuity, you need to know: (1) the discount rate, (2) the number of discount periods, and (3) the amount of the periodic receipts or payments.

To illustrate how to compute the present value of an annuity, assume that you will receive $1,000 cash annually for three years at a time when the discount rate is 10%. Illustration C-8 depicts this situation, and Illustration C-9 shows the computation of its present value.

Illustration C-8
Time diagram for a three-year annuity

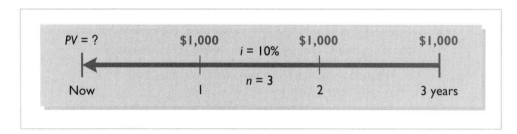

Illustration C-9
Present value of a series of future amounts computation

Future Amount	×	Present Value of 1 Factor at 10%	=	Present Value
$1,000 (one year away)		.90909		$ 909.09
1,000 (two years away)		.82645		826.45
1,000 (three years away)		.75132		751.32
		2.48686		$2,486.86

This method of calculation is required when the periodic cash flows are not uniform in each period. However, when the future receipts are the same in each period, there are two other ways to compute present value. First, you can multiply the annual cash flow by the sum of the three present value factors. In the previous example, $1,000 × 2.48686 equals $2,486.86. The second method is to use annuity tables. As illustrated in Table 2 below, these tables show the present value of 1 to be received periodically for a given number of periods.

TABLE 2
Present Value of an Annuity of 1

(n) Periods	4%	5%	6%	8%	9%	10%	11%	12%	15%
1	.96154	.95238	.94340	.92593	.91743	.90909	.90090	.89286	.86957
2	1.88609	1.85941	1.83339	1.78326	1.75911	1.73554	1.71252	1.69005	1.62571
3	2.77509	2.72325	2.67301	2.57710	2.53130	2.48685	2.44371	2.40183	2.28323
4	3.62990	3.54595	3.46511	3.31213	3.23972	3.16986	3.10245	3.03735	2.85498
5	4.45182	4.32948	4.21236	3.99271	3.88965	3.79079	3.69590	3.60478	3.35216
6	5.24214	5.07569	4.91732	4.62288	4.48592	4.35526	4.23054	4.11141	3.78448
7	6.00205	5.78637	5.58238	5.20637	5.03295	4.86842	4.71220	4.56376	4.16042
8	6.73274	6.46321	6.20979	5.74664	5.53482	5.33493	5.14612	4.96764	4.48732
9	7.43533	7.10782	6.80169	6.24689	5.99525	5.75902	5.53705	5.32825	4.77158
10	8.11090	7.72173	7.36009	6.71008	6.41766	6.14457	5.88923	5.65022	5.01877
11	8.76048	8.30641	7.88687	7.13896	6.80519	6.49506	6.20652	5.93770	5.23371
12	9.38507	8.86325	8.38384	7.53608	7.16073	6.81369	6.49236	6.19437	5.42062
13	9.98565	9.39357	8.85268	7.90378	7.48690	7.10336	6.74987	6.42355	5.58315
14	10.56312	9.89864	9.29498	8.24424	7.78615	7.36669	6.98187	6.62817	5.72448
15	11.11839	10.37966	9.71225	8.55948	8.06069	7.60608	7.19087	6.81086	5.84737
16	11.65230	10.83777	10.10590	8.85137	8.31256	7.82371	7.37916	6.97399	5.95424
17	12.16567	11.27407	10.47726	9.12164	8.54363	8.02155	7.54879	7.11963	6.04716
18	12.65930	11.68959	10.82760	9.37189	8.75563	8.20141	7.70162	7.24967	6.12797
19	13.13394	12.08532	11.15812	9.60360	8.95012	8.36492	7.83929	7.36578	6.19823
20	13.59033	12.46221	11.46992	9.81815	9.12855	8.51356	7.96333	7.46944	6.25933

Table 2 shows that the present value of an annuity of 1 factor for three periods at 10% is 2.48685.[1] (This present value factor is the total of the three individual present value factors, as shown in Illustration C-9.) Applying this amount to the annual cash flow of $1,000 produces a present value of $2,486.85.

The following demonstration problem (Illustration C-10) illustrates how to use Table 2.

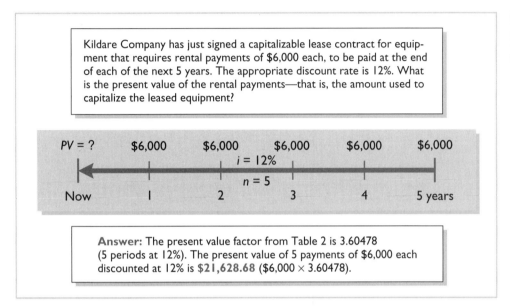

Illustration C-10
Demonstration problem—
Using Table 2 for *PV* of an annuity of 1

Kildare Company has just signed a capitalizable lease contract for equipment that requires rental payments of $6,000 each, to be paid at the end of each of the next 5 years. The appropriate discount rate is 12%. What is the present value of the rental payments—that is, the amount used to capitalize the leased equipment?

PV = ? $6,000 $6,000 $6,000 $6,000 $6,000
                          i = 12%
                          n = 5
Now   1   2   3   4   5 years

Answer: The present value factor from Table 2 is 3.60478 (5 periods at 12%). The present value of 5 payments of $6,000 each discounted at 12% is **$21,628.68** ($6,000 × 3.60478).

TIME PERIODS AND DISCOUNTING

In the preceding calculations, the discounting was done on an *annual* basis using an *annual* interest rate. Discounting may also be done over shorter periods of time such as monthly, quarterly, or semiannually.

When the time frame is less than one year, you need to convert the annual interest rate to the applicable time frame. Assume, for example, that the investor in Illustration C-8 received $500 **semiannually** for three years instead of $1,000 annually. In this case, the number of periods becomes six (3 × 2), the discount rate is 5% (10% ÷ 2), the present value factor from Table 2 is 5.07569, and the present value of the future cash flows is $2,537.85 (5.07569 × $500). This amount is slightly higher than the $2,486.86 computed in Illustration C-9 because interest is paid twice during the same year; therefore interest is earned on the first half year's interest.

COMPUTING THE PRESENT VALUE OF A LONG-TERM NOTE OR BOND

The present value (or market price) of a long-term note or bond is a function of three variables: (1) the payment amounts, (2) the length of time until the amounts are paid, and (3) the discount rate. Our illustration uses a five-year bond issue.

STUDY OBJECTIVE 5

Compute the present value of notes and bonds.

---

[1]The difference of .00001 between 2.48686 and 2.48685 is due to rounding.

The first variable—dollars to be paid—is made up of two elements: (1) a series of interest payments (an annuity), and (2) the principal amount (a single sum). To compute the present value of the bond, we must discount both the interest payments and the principal amount—two different computations. The time diagrams for a bond due in five years are shown in Illustration C-11.

Illustration C-11
Present value of a bond time diagram

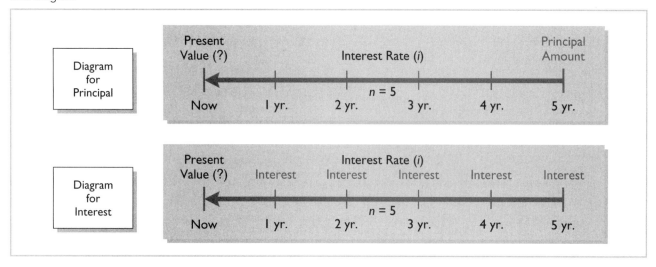

When the investor's market interest rate is equal to the bond's contractual interest rate, the present value of the bonds will *equal* the face value of the bonds. To illustrate, assume a bond issue of 10%, five-year bonds with a face value of $100,000 with interest payable **semiannually** on January 1 and July 1. If the discount rate is the same as the contractual rate, the bonds will sell at face value. In this case, the investor will receive the following: (1) $100,000 at maturity, and (2) a series of ten $5,000 interest payments [($100,000 × 10%) ÷ 2] over the term of the bonds. The length of time is expressed in terms of interest periods—in this case—10, and the discount rate per interest period, 5%. The following time diagram (Illustration C-12) depicts the variables involved in this discounting situation.

Illustration C-12
Time diagram for present value of a 10%, five-year bond paying interest semiannually

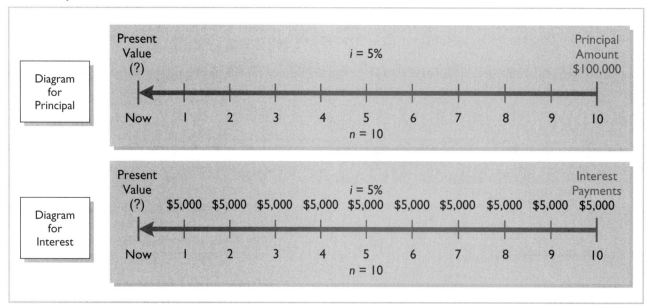

Illustration C-13 shows the computation of the present value of these bonds.

10% Contractual Rate—10% Discount Rate	
Present value of principal to be received at maturity	
$100,000 × *PV* of 1 due in 10 periods at 5%	
$100,000 × .61391 (Table 1)	$ 61,391
Present value of interest to be received periodically	
over the term of the bonds	
$5,000 × *PV* of 1 due periodically for 10 periods at 5%	
$5,000 × 7.72173 (Table 2)	38,609*
Present value of bonds	**$100,000**

*Rounded

Illustration C-13
Present value of principal and interest—face value

Now assume that the investor's required rate of return is 12%, not 10%. The future amounts are again $100,000 and $5,000, respectively, but now a discount rate of 6% (12% ÷ 2) must be used. The present value of the bonds is $92,639, as computed in Illustration C-14.

10% Contractual Rate—12% Discount Rate	
Present value of principal to be received at maturity	
$100,000 × .55839 (Table 1)	$55,839
Present value of interest to be received periodically	
over the term of the bonds	
$5,000 × 7.36009 (Table 2)	36,800
Present value of bonds	**$92,639**

Illustration C-14
Present value of principal and interest—discount

Conversely, if the discount rate is 8% and the contractual rate is 10%, the present value of the bonds is $108,111, computed as shown in Illustration C-15.

10% Contractual Rate—8% Discount Rate	
Present value of principal to be received at maturity	
$100,000 × .67556 (Table 1)	$ 67,556
Present value of interest to be received periodically	
over the term of the bonds	
$5,000 × 8.11090 (Table 2)	40,555
Present value of bonds	**$108,111**

Illustration C-15
Present value of principal and interest—premium

The above discussion relies on present value tables in solving present value problems. Many people use spreadsheets such as Excel or Financial calculators (some even on websites) to compute present values, without the use of tables. Many calculators, especially "financial calculators," have present value (*PV*) functions that allow you to calculate present values by merely inputting the proper amount, discount rate, and periods, and pressing the PV key. Appendix D illustrates how to use a financial calculator in various business situations.

SUMMARY OF STUDY OBJECTIVES

1 **Distinguish between simple and compound interest.** Simple interest is computed on the principal only, while compound interest is computed on the principal and any interest earned that has not been withdrawn.

2 **Identify the variables fundamental to solving present value problems.** The following three variables are fundamental to solving present value problems: (1) the future amount, (2) the number of periods, and (3) the interest rate (the discount rate).

3 **Solve for present value of a single amount.** Prepare a time diagram of the problem. Identify the future amount, the number of discounting periods, and the discount (interest) rate. Using the present value of a single amount table, multiply the future amount by the present value factor specified at the intersection of the number of periods and the discount rate.

4 **Solve for present value of an annuity.** Prepare a time diagram of the problem. Identify the future annuity pay-

ments, the number of discounting periods, and the discount (interest) rate. Using the present value of an annuity of 1 table, multiply the amount of the annuity payments by the present value factor specified at the intersection of the number of periods and the interest rate.

5 **Compute the present value of notes and bonds.** To determine the present value of the principal amount: Multiply the principal amount (a single future amount) by the present value factor (from the present value of 1 table) intersecting at the number of periods (number of interest payments) and the discount rate.

To determine the present value of the series of interest payments: Multiply the amount of the interest payment by the present value factor (from the present value of an annuity of 1 table) intersecting at the number of periods (number of interest payments) and the discount rate. Add the present value of the principal amount to the present value of the interest payments to arrive at the present value of the note or bond.

GLOSSARY

Annuity A series of equal dollar amounts to be paid or received periodically. (p. C5).

Compound interest The interest computed on the principal and any interest earned that has not been paid or withdrawn. (p. C2)

Discounting the future amount(s) The process of determining present value. (p. C3).

Interest Payment for the use of another's money. (p. C1).

Present value The value now of a given amount to be paid or received in the future assuming compound interest. (p. C3).

Present value of an annuity The value now of a series of future receipts or payments, discounted assuming compound interest. (p. C5).

Principal The amount borrowed or invested. (p. C1).

Simple interest The interest computed on the principal only. (p. C1).

BRIEF EXERCISES

Use tables to solve exercises.

Use present value tables.

BEC-1 For each of the following cases, indicate (a) to what interest rate columns, and (b) to what number of periods you would refer in looking up the discount rate.

1. In Table 1 (present value of 1):

	Annual Rate	Number of Years Involved	Compounding Per Year
(a)	12%	6	Annually
(b)	10%	15	Annually
(c)	8%	12	Semiannually

2. In Table 2 (present value of an annuity of 1):

	Annual Rate	Number of Years Involved	Number of Payments Involved	Frequency of Payments
(a)	8%	20	20	Annually
(b)	10%	5	5	Annually
(c)	12%	4	8	Semiannually

Determine present values. **BEC-2** **(a)** What is the present value of $30,000 due 8 periods from now, discounted at 8%? **(b)** What is the present value of $30,000 to be received at the end of each of 6 periods, discounted at 9%?

BEC-3   Ramirez Company is considering an investment that will return a lump sum of $600,000 5 years from now. What amount should Ramirez Company pay for this investment in order to earn a 10% return?

Compute the present value of a single-sum investment.

BEC-4   LaRussa Company earns 9% on an investment that will return $700,000 8 years from now. What is the amount LaRussa should invest now in order to earn this rate of return?

Compute the present value of a single-sum investment.

BEC-5   Polley Company sold a 5-year, zero-interest-bearing $36,000 note receivable to Valley Inc. Valley wishes to earn 10% over the remaining 4 years of the note. How much cash will Polley receive upon sale of the note?

Compute the present value of a single-sum zero-interest-bearing note.

BEC-6   Marichal Company issues a 3-year, zero-interest-bearing $60,000 note. The interest rate used to discount the zero-interest-bearing note is 8%. What are the cash proceeds that Marichal Company should receive?

Compute the present value of a single-sum zero-interest-bearing note.

BEC-7   Colaw Company is considering investing in an annuity contract that will return $40,000 annually at the end of each year for 15 years. What amount should Colaw Company pay for this investment if it earns a 6% return?

Compute the present value of an annuity investment.

BEC-8   Sauder Enterprises earns 11% on an investment that pays back $100,000 at the end of each of the next 4 years. What is the amount Sauder Enterprises invested to earn the 11% rate of return?

Compute the present value of an annuity investment.

BEC-9   Chicago Railroad Co. is about to issue $200,000 of 10-year bonds paying a 10% interest rate, with interest payable semiannually. The discount rate for such securities is 8%. How much can Chicago expect to receive for the sale of these bonds?

Compute the present value of bonds.

BEC-10   Assume the same information as in BEC-9 except that the discount rate is 10% instead of 8%. In this case, how much can Chicago expect to receive from the sale of these bonds?

Compute the present value of bonds.

BEC-11   Berghaus Company receives a $75,000, 6-year note bearing interest of 8% (paid annually) from a customer at a time when the discount rate is 9%. What is the present value of the note received by Berghaus Company?

Compute the present value of a note.

BEC-12   Troutman Enterprises issued 8%, 8-year, $1,000,000 par value bonds that pay interest semiannually on October 1 and April 1. The bonds are dated April 1, 2010, and are issued on that date. The discount rate of interest for such bonds on April 1, 2010, is 10%. What cash proceeds did Troutman receive from issuance of the bonds?

Compute the present value of bonds.

BEC-13   Ricky Cleland owns a garage and is contemplating purchasing a tire retreading machine for $16,280. After estimating costs and revenues, Ricky projects a net cash flow from the retreading machine of $2,800 annually for 8 years. Ricky hopes to earn a return of 11% on such investments. What is the present value of the retreading operation? Should Ricky Cleland purchase the retreading machine?

Compute the value of a machine for purposes of making a purchase decision.

BEC-14   Martinez Company issues a 10%, 6-year mortgage note on January 1, 2010, to obtain financing for new equipment. Land is used as collateral for the note. The terms provide for semi-annual installment payments of $78,978. What were the cash proceeds received from the issuance of the note?

Compute the present value of a note.

BEC-15   Durler Company is considering purchasing equipment. The equipment will produce the following cash flows: Year 1, $30,000; Year 2, $40,000; Year 3, $60,000. Durler requires a minimum rate of return of 12%. What is the maximum price Durler should pay for this equipment?

Compute the maximum price to pay for a machine.

BEC-16   If Carla Garcia invests $2,745 now, she will receive $10,000 at the end of 15 years. What annual rate of interest will Carla earn on her investment? (*Hint:* Use Table 1.)

Compute the interest rate on a single sum.

BEC-17   Sara Altom has been offered the opportunity of investing $51,316 now. The investment will earn 10% per year and at the end of that time will return Sara $100,000. How many years must Sara wait to receive $100,000? (*Hint:* Use Table 1.)

Compute the number of periods of a single sum.

BEC-18   Stacy Dains purchased an investment for $11,469.92. From this investment, she will receive $1,000 annually for the next 20 years, starting one year from now. What rate of interest will Stacy's investment be earning for her? (*Hint:* Use Table 2.)

Compute the interest rate on an annuity.

BEC-19   Diana Rossi invests $8,559.48 now for a series of $1,000 annual returns, beginning one year from now. Diana will earn a return of 8% on the initial investment. How many annual payments of $1,000 will Diana receive? (*Hint:* Use Table 2.)

Compute the number of periods of an annuity.

Compute the amount to be invested.

BEC-20 Minitori Company needs $10,000 on January 1, 2013. It is starting a fund on January 1, 2010.

Instructions

Compute the amount that must be invested in the fund on January 1, 2010, to produce a $10,000 balance on January 1, 2013 if.

(a) The fund earns 8% per year compounded annually.
(b) The fund earns 8% per year compounded semiannually.
(c) The fund earns 12% per year compounded annually.
(d) The fund earns 12% per year compounded semiannually.

Compute the amount to be invested.

BEC-21 Venuchi Company needs $10,000 on January 1, 2015. It is starting a fund to produce that amount.

Instructions

Compute the amount that must be invested in the fund to produce a $10,000 balance on January 1, 2015, if:

(a) The initial investment is made January 1, 2010, and the fund earns 6% per year.
(b) The initial investment is made January 1, 2012, and the fund earns 6% per year.
(c) The initial investment is made January 1, 2010, and the fund earns 10% per year.
(d) The initial investment is made January 1, 2012, and the fund earns 10% per year.

Select the better payment option.

BEC-22 Letterman Corporation is buying new equipment. It can pay $39,500 today (option 1), or $10,000 today and 5 yearly payments of $8,000 each, starting in one year (option 2).

Instructions

Which option should Letterman select? (Assume a discount rate of 10%.)

Compute the cost of an investment, amount received, and rate of return.

BEC-23 Carmen Corporation is considering several investments.

Instructions

(a) One investment returns $10,000 per year for 5 years and provides a return of 10%. What is the cost of this investment?
(b) Another investment costs $50,000 and returns a certain amount per year for 10 years, providing an 8% return. What amount is received each year?
(c) A third investment costs $70,000 and returns $11,971 each year for 15 years. What is the rate of return on this investment?

Select the best payment option.

BEC-24 You are the beneficiary of a trust fund. The fund gives you the option of receiving $5,000 per year for 10 years, $9,000 per year for 5 years, or $30,000 today.

Instructions

If the desired rate of return is 8%, which option should you select?

Compute the semiannual car payment.

BEC-25 You are purchasing a car for $24,000, and you obtain financing as follows: $2,400 down payment, 12% interest, semiannual payments over 5 years.

Instructions

Compute the payment you will make every 6 months

Compute the present value of bonds.

BEC-26 Contreras Corporation is considering purchasing bonds of Jose Company as an investment. The bonds have a face value of $40,000 with a 10% interest rate. The bonds mature in 4 years and pay interest semiannually.

Instructions

(a) What is the most Contreras should pay for the bonds if it desires a 12% return?
(b) What is the most Contreras should pay for the bonds if it desires an 8% return?

Compute the present value of bonds.

BEC-27 Garcia Corporation is considering purchasing bonds of Fred Company as an investment. The bonds have a face value of $90,000 with a 9% interest rate. The bonds mature in 6 years and pay interest semiannually.

Instructions

(a) What is the most Garcia should pay for the bonds if it desires a 10% return?
(b) What is the most Garcia should pay for the bonds if it desires an 8% return?

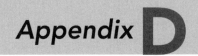

Using Financial Calculators

Business professionals, once they have mastered the underlying concepts in Appendix C, often use a financial (business) calculator to solve time value of money problems. In many cases, they must use calculators if interest rates or time periods do not correspond with the information provided in the compound interest tables.

To use financial calculators, you enter the time value of money variables into the calculator. Illustration D-1 shows the five most common keys used to solve time value of money problems.[1]

Illustration D-1
Financial calculator keys

where

N = number of periods

I = interest rate per period (some calculators use I/YR or i)

PV = present value (occurs at the beginning of the first period)

PMT = payment (all payments are equal, and none are skipped)

FV = future value (occurs at the end of the last period)

In solving time value of money problems in this appendix, you will generally be given three of four variables and will have to solve for the remaining variable. The fifth key (the key not used) is given a value of zero to ensure that this variable is not used in the computation.

PRESENT VALUE OF A SINGLE SUM

To illustrate how to solve a present value problem using a financial calculator, assume that you want to know the present value of $84,253 to be received in five years, discounted at 11% compounded annually. Illustration D-2 pictures this problem.

---

[1]On many calculators, these keys are actual buttons on the face of the calculator; on others they appear on the display after the user accesses a present value menu.

Illustration D-2
Calculator solution for
present value of a single sum

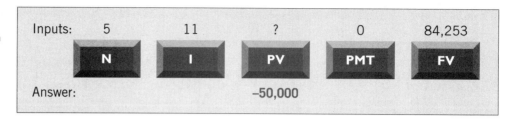

The diagram shows you the information (inputs) to enter into the calculator: N = 5, I = 11, PMT = 0, and FV = 84,253. You then press PV for the answer: −$50,000. As indicated, the PMT key was given a value of zero because a series of payments did not occur in this problem.

Plus and Minus

The use of plus and minus signs in time value of money problems with a financial calculator can be confusing. Most financial calculators are programmed so that the positive and negative cash flows in any problem offset each other. In the present value problem above, we identified the $84,253 future value initial investment as a positive (inflow); the answer −$50,000 was shown as a negative amount, reflecting a cash outflow. If the 84,253 were entered as a negative, then the final answer would have been reported as a positive 50,000.

Hopefully, the sign convention will not cause confusion. If you understand what is required in a problem, you should be able to interpret a positive or negative amount in determining the solution to a problem.

Compounding Periods

In the problem above, we assumed that compounding occurs once a year. Some financial calculators have a default setting, which assumes that compounding occurs 12 times a year. You must determine what default period has been programmed into your calculator and change it as necessary to arrive at the proper compounding period.

Rounding

Most financial calculators store and calculate using 12 decimal places. As a result, because compound interest tables generally have factors only up to 5 decimal places, a slight difference in the final answer can result. In most time value of money problems, the final answer will not include more than two decimal points.

PRESENT VALUE OF AN ANNUITY

To illustrate how to solve a present value of an annuity problem using a financial calculator, assume that you are asked to determine the present value of rental receipts of $6,000 each to be received at the end of each of the next five years, when discounted at 12%, as pictured in Illustration D-3.

Illustration D-3
Calculator solution for
present value of an annuity

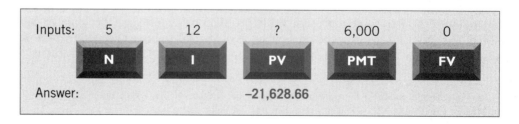

In this case, you enter N = 5, I = 12, PMT = 6,000, FV = 0, and then press PV to arrive at the answer of $21, 628.66.

USEFUL APPLICATIONS OF THE FINANCIAL CALCULATOR

With a financial calculator you can solve for any interest rate or for any number of periods in a time value of money problem. Here are some examples of these applications.

Auto Loan

Assume you are financing a car with a three-year loan. The loan has a 9.5% nominal annual interest rate, compounded monthly. The price of the car is $6,000, and you want to determine the monthly payments, assuming that the payments start one month after the purchase. This problem is pictured in Illustration D-4.

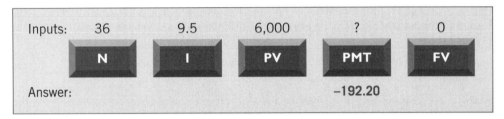

Illustration D-4
Calculator solution for auto loan payments

To solve this problem, you enter N = 36 (12 × 3), I = 9.5, PV = 6,000, FV = 0, and then press PMT. You will find that the monthly payments will be $192.20. Note that the payment key is usually programmed for 12 payments per year. Thus, you must change the default (compounding period) if the payments are other than monthly.

Mortgage Loan Amount

Let's say you are evaluating financing options for a loan on a house. You decide that the maximum mortgage payment you can afford is $700 per month. The annual interest rate is 8.4%. If you get a mortgage that requires you to make monthly payments over a 15-year period, what is the maximum purchase price you can afford? Illustration D-5 depicts this problem.

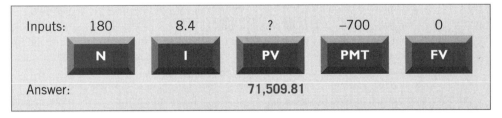

Illustration D-5
Calculator solution for mortgage amount

You enter N = 180 (12 × 15 years), I = 8.4, PMT = −700, FV = 0, and press PV. You find a present value of $71,509.81—the maximum house price you can afford, given that you want to keep your mortgage payments at $700. Note that by changing any of the variables, you can quickly conduct "what-if" analyses for different situations.

SUMMARY OF LEARNING OBJECTIVE

1 Use a financial calculator to solve time value of money problems. Financial calculators can be used to solve the same and additional problems as those solved with time value of money tables. One enters into the financial calculator the amounts for all but one of the unknown elements of a time value of money problem (periods, interest rate, payments, future or present value). Particularly useful situations involve interest rates and compounding periods not presented in the tables.

BRIEF EXERCISES

Determine interest rate.

BED-1 Reba McEntire wishes to invest $19,000 on July 1, 2010, and have it accumulate to $49,000 by July 1, 2020.

Instructions
Use a financial calculator to determine at what exact annual rate of interest Reba must invest the $19,000.

Determine interest rate.

BED-2 On July 17, 2010, Tim McGraw borrowed $42,000 from his grandfather to open a clothing store. Starting July 17, 2011, Tim has to make 10 equal annual payments of $6,500 each to repay the loan.

Instructions
Use a financial calculator to determine what interest rate Tim is paying.

Determine interest rate.

BED-3 As the purchaser of a new house, Patty Loveless has signed a mortgage note to pay the Memphis National Bank and Trust Co. $14,000 every 6 months for 20 years, at the end of which time she will own the house. At the date the mortgage is signed the purchase price was $198,000, and Loveless made a down payment of $20,000. The first payment will be made 6 months after the date the mortgage is signed.

Instructions
Using a financial calculator, compute the exact rate of interest earned on the mortgage by the bank.

Various time value of money situations.

BED-4 Using a financial calculator, solve for the unknowns in each of the following situations.

(a) On June 1, 2010, Shelley Long purchases lakefront property from her neighbor, Joey Brenner, and agrees to pay the purchase price in seven payments of $16,000 each, the first payment to be payable June 1, 2011. (Assume that interest compounded at an annual rate of 7.35% is implicit in the payments.) What is the purchase price of the property?

(b) On January 1, 2010, Cooke Corporation purchased 200 of the $1,000 face value, 8% coupon, 10-year bonds of Howe Inc. The bonds mature on January 1, 2020, and pay interest annually beginning January 1, 2011. Cooke purchased the bonds to yield 10.65%. How much did Cooke pay for the bonds?

Various time value of money situations.

BED-5 Using a financial calculator, provide a solution to each of the following situations.

(a) Bill Schroeder owes a debt of $35,000 from the purchase of his new sport utility vehicle. The debt bears annual interest of 9.1% compounded monthly. Bill wishes to pay the debt and interest in equal monthly payments over 8 years, beginning one month hence. What equal monthly payments will pay off the debt and interest?

(b) On January 1, 2010, Sammy Sosa offers to buy Mark Grace's used snowmobile for $8,000, payable in five equal annual installments, which are to include 8.25% interest on the unpaid balance and a portion of the principal. If the first payment is to be made on December 31, 2010, how much will each payment be?

Appendix E

Standards of Ethical Conduct for Management Accountants

Management accountants have an obligation to the organizations they serve, their profession, the public, and themselves to maintain the highest standards of ethical conduct. In recognition of this obligation, the **Institute of Management Accountants (IMA)** has published and promoted the following standards of ethical conduct for management accountants.[1]

IMA STATEMENT OF ETHICAL PROFESSIONAL PRACTICE

Members of IMA shall behave ethically. A commitment to ethical professional practice includes: overarching principles that express our values, and standards that guide our conduct.

Principles

IMA's overarching ethical principles include: Honesty, Fairness, Objectivity, and Responsibility. Members shall act in accordance with these principles and shall encourage others within their organizations to adhere to them.

Standards

A member's failure to comply with the following standards may result in disciplinary action.

I. COMPETENCE

Each member has a responsibility to:

1. Maintain an appropriate level of professional expertise by continually developing knowledge and skills.
2. Perform professional duties in accordance with relevant laws, regulations, and technical standards.
3. Provide decision support information and recommendations that are accurate, clear, concise, and timely.
4. Recognize and communicate professional limitations or other constraints that would preclude responsible judgment or successful performance of an activity.

---

[1]Reprinted by permission of the Institute of Management Accountants, *www.imanet.org/pdf/981.pdf*.

II. CONFIDENTIALITY

Each member has a responsibility to:

1. Keep information confidential except when disclosure is authorized or legally required.
2. Inform all relevant parties regarding appropriate use of confidential information. Monitor subordinates' activities to ensure compliance.
3. Refrain from using confidential information for unethical or illegal advantage.

III. INTEGRITY

Each member has a responsibility to:

1. Mitigate actual conflicts of interest. Regularly communicate with business associates to avoid apparent conflicts of interest. Advise all parties of any potential conflicts.
2. Refrain from engaging in any conduct that would prejudice carrying out duties ethically.
3. Abstain from engaging in or supporting any activity that might discredit the profession.

IV. CREDIBILITY

Each member has a responsibility to:

1. Communicate information fairly and objectively.
2. Disclose all relevant information that could reasonably be expected to influence an intended user's understanding of the reports, analyses, or recommendations.
3. Disclose delays or deficiencies in information, timeliness, processing, or internal controls in conformance with organization policy and/or applicable law.

Resolution of Ethical Conflict

In applying the Standards of Ethical Professional Practice, you may encounter problems identifying unethical behavior or resolving an ethical conflict. When faced with ethical issues, you should follow your organization's established policies on the resolution of such conflict. If these policies do not resolve the ethical conflict, you should consider the following courses of action:

1. Discuss the issue with your immediate supervisor except when it appears that the supervisor is involved. In that case, present the issue to the next level. If you cannot achieve a satisfactory resolution, submit the issue to the next management level. If your immediate superior is the chief executive officer or equivalent, the acceptable reviewing authority may be a group such as the audit committee, executive committee, board of directors, board of trustees, or owners. Contact with levels above the immediate superior should be initiated only with your superior's knowledge, assuming he or she is not involved. Communication of such problems to authorities or individuals not employed or engaged by the organization is not considered appropriate, unless you believe there is a clear violation of the law.
2. Clarify relevant ethical issues by initiating a confidential discussion with an IMA Ethics Counselor or other impartial advisor to obtain a better understanding of possible courses of action.
3. Consult your own attorney as to legal obligations and rights concerning the ethical conflict.

Chapter 1 Page 3 Jeff Greenberg/PhotoEdit Page 11 Brent Holland/iStockphoto Page 23 iStockphoto

Chapter 2 Page 49 NBAE/Getty Images Page 58 Mike Stewart/Corbis Sygma Page 70 PhotoDisc, Inc./Getty Images

Chapter 3 Page 94 Witte Thomas E/Gamma Presse, Inc. Page 98 Kevin Winter/Getty Images, Inc Page 106 iStockphoto

Chapter 4 Page 145 Brian Bahr/Getty Images, Inc Page 157 Alex Slobodkin/iStockphoto Page 162 Christian Lagereek/iStockphoto Page 164 Lowell Sannes/iStockphoto Page 165 Denis Vorob'yev/iStockphoto Page 166 Nikki Ward/iStockphoto Page 167 Vladislav Gurfinkel/iStockphoto Page 168 iStockphoto

Chapter 5 Page 199 Stone/Getty Images, Inc Page 203 Marco Coda/iStockphoto Page 210 iStockphoto

Chapter 6 Page 249 Pathaithai Chungyam/iStockphoto Page 251 Bjorn Kindler/iStockphoto Page 262 PhotoDisc, Inc./Getty Images Page 262 Scott Olson/Getty Images

Chapter 7 Page 301 Henry Chaplin/iStockphoto Page 304 Sean Locke/iStockphoto Page 307 Andrejs Zavadskis/ iStockphoto

Chapter 8 Page 345 Valerie Loiseleux/iStockphoto Page 356 Terence John/Retna

Chapter 9 Page 397 Charles Orrico/SUPERSTOCK Page 406 Joe Polillio/Getty Images, Inc Page 408 Michael Braun/iStockphoto

Chapter 10 Page 437 David Trood/Getty Images, Inc Page 441 iStockphoto Page 456 Andy Lions/Photonica/Getty Images, Inc Page 459 Linda Steward/iStockphoto

Chapter 11 Page 485 Cary Westfall/iStockphoto Page 492 Steve Diblee/iStockphoto Page 498 Catherine dee Auvil/iStockphoto

Chapter 12 Page 527 Charles Taylor/iStockphoto Page 530 Malcolm Romain/iStockphoto Page 533 PhotoDisc/Getty Images, Inc.

COMPANY INDEX

Contra accounts:
for assets, 103–104
for revenue, 209, 210
Control, internal, *see* Internal control
Control accounts, 305–306
Control environment, 348
Co-ownership of property, 529
Copyrights, 455
Corporations, 10
owner's equity accounts in, 168
subchapter S, 530
Correcting entries, 160–162, 370
Cost(s):
in computation of depreciation, 443
of copyrights, 455
depreciable, 444
freight, 205, 223
line, 449
of patents, 455
for plant assets, 439–442
research and development, 457–458
warranty, 492
Cost flows, in merchandising companies, 201–203
Cost flow assumptions/methods:
average-cost, 258–259
effects of, 260–261
first-in, first-out, 255–257
in inventory costing, 255–263
last-in, first-out, 257–258
in perpetual inventory systems, 271–274
Costing, inventory, 254–263
consistency principle in, 262
cost flow assumptions, 255–262
lower-of-cost-or-market, 262–263
specific identification method, 254–255
Cost of goods sold, 200–202, 221–222
Cost principle (historical cost principle), 9, 439
CPAs (certified public accountants), 29
Credits, 51–54, 68
Credit agreements, 399
Credit balance, 51
Credit cards, 407–408, 416, 485
Crediting accounts, 51
Credit losses, 400
Credit memorandum (CM), 367
Creditors, 12
Creditors' subsidiary ledger, 305
Credit purchases, 15–17, 315–316
Credit terms, 206
Cross-footing a journal, 314
Current assets, 164
Current liabilities, 486–491
on classified balance sheet, 166–167
current maturities of long-term debt, 489
notes payable, 486–487
order of listing, 490
sales taxes payable, 487–488
statement presentation and analysis, 490–491
unearned revenues, 488–489
Current ratio, 491
Current replacement cost, 263
Customers, as external users, 7
Customers' subsidiary ledger, 305

D
Days in inventory, 267
Debits, 51–54, 68
Debit balance, 51
Debiting accounts, 51
Debit memorandum (DM), 366, 367
Decisions, social impact of, 160
Declining-balance depreciation, 446–448
Deferrals, 99–100
adjusting entries for, 100–107, 119–122
alternative treatment of, 119–122
basic relationships for, 122
Defined-benefit plans, 510
Defined-contribution plans, 510
Depletion (natural resources), 453
Depreciable cost, 444
Depreciation:
accumulated, 165
adjusting entries for, 102–104
computing, 443
declining-balance method, 446–448
and income taxes, 443
of plant assets, 442–449
recognizing, 443
revising estimates of, 448–449
straight-line method, 444–445, 447–448
units-of-activity method, 445–448
Depreciation schedule, 444–445
Direct write-off method, 400–401
Disbursements, 347, 360–364
Disbursements journal, 317–319
Disclosure, of contingent liabilities, 493
Discounts:
cash, 399
purchase, 206–207
sales, 210
Discounting, time value of money and, C7
Discount period, 206–207
Dishonored notes, 412–413
Disposal:
of accounts receivable, 406–408
of notes receivable, 412–413
of plant assets, 450–453
Divestments, owner's drawings as, 19
DM, *see* Debit memorandum
Documentation procedures, 352
Dollar signs, use of, 70
Donnelly, Bobbi Jean, 354
Dot-coms, 94
Double-declining-balance method, 446–447
Double-entry system, 51–54
Drawings (by owners), 13, 19, 52–53
Dual posting, 320
Duties:
rotating, 355
segregation of, 350–351

E
Earnings statement, 22. *See also* Income statement
Economic entity assumption, 9–10
Edmondson, David, 72, 92
Electronic funds transfers (EFTs), 371
Electronic spreadsheets, 146. *See also* Worksheets
Employee compensation, *see* Payroll accounting
Employee earnings record, 498–499
Employee theft, 268
Employer payroll taxes, 501–503
The End of Work (Jeremy Rifkin), 198
Enterprise resource planning (ERP) systems, 304
Equipment, cost of, 440–441
ERP (enterprise resource planning) systems, 304
Errors, 49
in bank accounts, 368
correcting entries for, 160–162
inventory, 263–265
irregularities vs., 69
in trial balances, 70
Estimating:
depreciation, 448–449
inventories, 274–277
uncollectible accounts, 401–405
Ethics issues:
appearance of liquidity, 166
arm's-length transactions, 398
backdating sales, 108
computer-system tampering, 304
credit agreements, 399
and economic entity assumption, 9
employee theft, 347
errors in statements, 161
financial aid applications, 25
in financial reporting, 7–8, 209
fraudulent disbursements, 347
fraudulent documents, 55
inventory fraud, 264
inventory overstatement, 253
motivating employees, 495
partnership agreements, 532
partnership liquidations, 539
in personal financial reporting, 25
petty cash funds, 364
purchase price allocation, 442
in recording transactions, 70
salad oil company fraud, 252
social impact of decisions, 160
software for fraud control, 304
specific identification method, 255
standards of conduct for management accountants, E1–E2
Europe, accounting in, 51
European Union, 9
Exchange of plant assets, 464–465
Expenses:
accrued, 100, 108–111
in double-entry system, 53–54
owner's equity decrease from, 13
payroll, 500
prepaid, 100–104, 119–121, 755
recognizing, 97–98
on single-step income statement, 217
transaction analysis for, 17
Expense reports, fraudulent, 354
External transactions, 14
External users, 6–7

F
Face value, of notes, 411
Factors, 407
FAFSA (Free Application for Federal Student Aid), 25
Fairbanks, Lawrence, 351
FASB, *see* Financial Accounting Standards Board
FBI (Federal Bureau of Investigation), 30
Federal Insurance Contribution Act (FICA), 496
Federal Trade Commission, 7
Federal unemployment taxes, 501, 502
Federal Unemployment Tax Act (FUTA), 502
Fees, 494
FICA (Federal Insurance Contribution Act), 496
FICA taxes, 495–496, 501, 502
FIFO, *see* First-in, first-out
Financial Accounting Standards Board (FASB), 8, 9
Financial calculators, D1–D3
Financial literacy, 3
Financials (Oracle), 304
Financial statements, 5, 20–27. *See also* *individual statements*
from adjusted trial balance, 115–117
balance sheet, 20–23
current liabilities on, 490–491
depreciation on, 103–104
effect of cost flow methods on, 260–261
income statement, 20–22
intangible assets on, 458–459
inventories on, 265–267
for merchandising companies, 214–219
natural resources on, 458
owner's equity statement, 20–22
partners' capital statement, 537
for partnerships, 537–538
plant assets on, 458–459
receivables on, 414–415
statement of cash flows, 20, 21, 23–24
time periods for, 96
from worksheets, 150, 151
Finished goods inventory, 250

Chapter Content

ACCOUNTING EQUATION (Chapter 2)

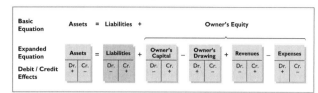

ADJUSTING ENTRIES (Chapter 3)

	Type	Adjusting Entry	
Deferrals	1. Prepaid expenses 2. Unearned revenues	Dr. Expenses Dr. Liabilities	Cr. Assets Cr. Revenues
Accruals	1. Accrued revenues 2. Accrued expenses	Dr. Assets Dr. Expenses	Cr. Revenues Cr. Liabilities

Note: Each adjusting entry will affect one or more income statement accounts and one or more balance sheet accounts.

Interest Computation

Interest = Face value of note × Annual interest rate × Time in terms of one year

CLOSING ENTRIES (Chapter 4)

Purpose: (1) Update the Owner's Capital account in the ledger by transferring net income (loss) and Owner's Drawing to Owner's Capital. (2) Prepare the temporary accounts (revenue, expense, Owner's Drawing) for the next period's postings by reducing their balances to zero.

Process

1. Debit each revenue account for its balance (assuming normal balances), and credit Income Summary for total revenues.
2. Debit Income Summary for total expenses, and credit each expense account for its balance (assuming normal balances).

   STOP AND CHECK: Does the balance in your Income Summary Account equal the net income (loss) reported in the income statement?

3. Debit (credit) Income Summary, and credit (debit) Owner's Capital for the amount of net income (loss).
4. Debit Owner's Capital for the balance in the Owner's Drawing account and credit Owner's Drawing for the same amount.

   STOP AND CHECK: Does the balance in your Owner's Capital account equal the ending balance reported in the balance sheet and the owner's equity statement? Are all of your temporary account balances zero?

ACCOUNTING CYCLE (Chapter 4)

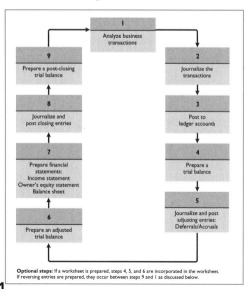

Optional steps: If a worksheet is prepared, steps 4, 5, and 6 are incorporated in the worksheet. If reversing entries are prepared, they occur between steps 9 and 1 as discussed below.

INVENTORY (Chapters 5 and 6)

Ownership

Freight Terms	Ownership of goods on public carrier resides with:	Who pays freight costs:
FOB shipping point	Buyer	Buyer
FOB destination	Seller	Seller

Perpetual vs. Periodic Journal Entries

Event	Perpetual	Periodic*
Purchase of goods	Inventory Cash (A/P)	Purchases Cash (A/P)
Freight (shipping point)	Inventory Cash	Freight-In Cash
Return of goods	Cash (or A/P) Inventory	Cash (or A/P) Purchase Returns and Allowances
Sale of goods	Cash (or A/R) Sales Cost of Goods Sold Inventory	Cash (or A/R) Sales No entry
End of period	No entry	Closing or adjusting entry required

Cost Flow Methods

- Specific identification
- First-in, first-out (FIFO)
- Weighted average
- Last-in, first-out (LIFO)

FRAUD, INTERNAL CONTROL, AND CASH (Chapter 8)

The Fraud Triangle

Opportunity

Finanical pressure — Rationalization

Principles of Internal Control Activities

- Establishment of responsibility
- Segregation of duties
- Documentation procedures
- Physical controls
- Independent internal verification
- Human resource controls

Bank Reconciliation

Bank	Books
Balance per bank statement Add: Deposit in transit Deduct: Outstanding checks Adjusted cash balance	Balance per books Add: Unrecorded credit memoranda from bank statement Deduct: Unrecorded debit memoranda from bank statement Adjusted cash balance

Note: 1. Errors should be offset (added or deducted) on the side that made the error.
      2. Adjusting journal entries should only be made on the books.

STOP AND CHECK: Does the adjusted cash balance in the Cash account equal the reconciled balance?

RECEIVABLES (Chapter 9)

Methods to Account for Uncollectible Accounts

Direct write-off method	Record bad debts expense when the company determines a particular account to be uncollectible.
Allowance methods: Percentage-of-sales	At the end of each period estimate the amount of credit sales uncollectible. Debit Bad Debts Expense and credit Allowance for Doubtful Accounts for this amount. As specific accounts become uncollectible, debit Allowance for Doubtful Accounts and credit Accounts Receivable.
Percentage-of-receivables	At the end of each period estimate the amount of uncollectible receivables. Debit Bad Debts Expense and credit Allowance for Doubtful Accounts in an amount that results in a balance in the allowance account equal to the estimate of uncollectibles. As specific accounts become uncollectible, debit Allowance for Doubtful Accounts and credit Accounts Receivable.

Chapter Content

PLANT ASSETS (Chapter 10)

Presentation

Tangible Assets	Intangible Assets
Property, plant, and equipment	Intangible assets (Patents, copyrights, trademarks, franchises, goodwill)
Natural resources	

Computation of Annual Depreciation Expense

Straight-line	$\dfrac{\text{Cost} - \text{Salvage value}}{\text{Useful life (in years)}}$
Units-of-activity	$\dfrac{\text{Depreciable cost}}{\text{Useful life (in units)}} \times \text{Units of activity during year}$
Declining-balance	Book value at beginning of year $\times$ Declining balance rate* *Declining-balance rate $= 1 \div$ Useful life (in years)

Note: If depreciation is calculated for partial periods, the straight-line and declining-balance methods must be adjusted for the relevant proportion of the year. Multiply the annual depreciation expense by the number of months expired in the year divided by 12 months.

SHAREHOLDERS' EQUITY (Chapter 13)

Comparison of Equity Accounts

Proprietorship	Partnership	Corporation
Owner's equity Name, Capital	Partner's equity Name, Capital Name, Capital	Stockholders' equity Common stock Retained earnings

No-Par Value vs. Par Value Stock Journal Entries

No-Par Value	Par Value

Cash
     Common Stock
	Cash
	     Common Stock (par value)
	     Paid-in Capital in Excess of Par Value

DIVIDENDS (Chapter 14)

Comparison of Dividend Effects

	Cash	Common Stock	Retained Earnings
Cash dividend	↓	No effect	↓
Stock dividend	No effect	↑	↓
Stock split	No effect	No effect	No effect

BONDS (Chapter 15)

Premium	Market interest rate < Contractual interest rate
Face Value	Market interest rate = Contractual interest rate
Discount	Market interest rate > Contractual interest rate

INVESTMENTS (Chapter 16)

Comparison of Long-Term Bond Investment and Liability Journal Entries

Event	Investor	Investee

Purchase / issue of bonds	Debt Investments
	     Cash
		Cash
		     Bonds Payable

Interest receipt / payment	Cash
	     Interest Revenue
		Interest Expense
		     Cash

Comparison of Cost and Equity Methods of Accounting for Long-Term Stock Investments

Event	Cost	Equity

Acquisition	Stock Investments
	     Cash
		Stock Investments
		     Cash

Investee reports earnings	No entry	Stock Investments Investment Revenue

Investee pays dividends	Cash
	     Dividend Revenue
		Cash
		     Stock Investments

Trading and Available-for-Sale Securities

Trading	Report at fair value with changes reported in net income.
Available-for-sale	Report at fair value with changes reported in the stockholders' equity section.

STATEMENT OF CASH FLOWS (Chapter 17)

Cash flows from operating activities (**indirect method**)

Net income		
Add:	Losses on disposals of assets	$ X
	Amortization and depreciation	X
	Decreases in current assets	X
	Increases in current liabilities	X
Deduct:	Gains on disposals of assets	(X)
	Increases in current assets	(X)
	Decreases in current liabilities	(X)
Net cash provided (used) by operating activities		$ X

Cash flows from operating activities (**direct method**)

Cash receipts
    (Examples: from sales of goods and services to customers, from receipts of interest and dividends on loans and investments) $ X
Cash payments
    (Examples: to suppliers, for operating expenses, for interest, for taxes)   (X)
Cash provided (used) by operating activities $ X

PRESENTATION OF NON-TYPICAL ITEMS (Chapter 18)

Prior period adjustments (Chapter 14)	Statement of retained earnings (adjustment of beginning retained earnings)
Discontinued operations	Income statement (presented separately after "Income from continuing operations")
Extraordinary items	Income statement (presented separately after "Income before extraordinary items")
Changes in accounting principle	In most instances, use the new method in current period and restate previous years results using new method. For changes in depreciation and amortization methods, use the new method in the current period, but do not restate previous periods.

MANAGERIAL ACCOUNTING (Chapter 19)

Characteristics of Managerial Accounting

Primary Users	Internal users
Reports	Internal reports issued as needed
Purpose	Special purpose for a particular user
Content	Pertains to subunits, may be detailed, use of relevant data
Verification	No independent audits

Types of Manufacturing Costs

Direct materials	Raw materials directly associated with finished product
Direct labor	Work of employees directly associated with turning raw materials into finished product
Manufacturing overhead	Costs indirectly associated with manufacture of finished product

JOB ORDER AND PROCESS COSTING (Chapters 20 and 21)

Types of Accounting Systems

Job order	Costs are assigned to each unit or each batch of goods
Process cost	Costs are applied to similar products that are mass-produced in a continuous fashion

Job Order and Process Cost Flow

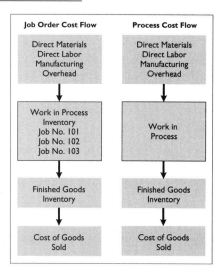

COST-VOLUME-PROFIT (Chapter 22)

Types of Costs

Variable costs	Vary in total directly and proportionately with changes in activity level
Fixed costs	Remain the same in total regardless of change in activity level
Mixed costs	Contain both a fixed and a variable element

CVP Income Statement Format

	Total	Per Unit
Sales	$xx	$xx
Variable costs	xx	xx
Contribution margin	xx	$xx
Fixed costs	xx	
Net income	$xx	

Contribution Margin per Unit

$$\text{Contribution margin per unit} = \text{Unit selling price} - \text{Unit variable costs}$$

Breakeven Point

$$\text{Breakeven point in units} = \text{Fixed costs} \div \text{Contribution margin per unit}$$

Target Net Income

$$\text{Required sales in units} = (\text{Fixed costs} + \text{Target net income}) \div \frac{\text{Contribution}}{\text{margin per unit}}$$

BUDGETS (Chapter 23)

Components of the Master Budget

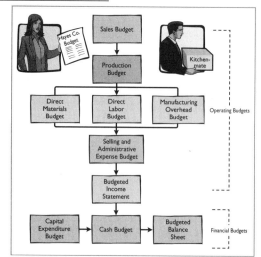

Chapter Content

RESPONSIBILITY ACCOUNTING (Chapter 24)

Types of Responsibility Centers

Cost	Profit	Investment
Expenses only	Expenses and Revenues	Expenses and Revenues and ROI

Return on Investment

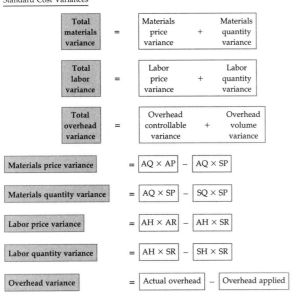

STANDARD COSTS (Chapter 25)

Standard Cost Variances

$$\text{Total materials variance} = \text{Materials price variance} + \text{Materials quantity variance}$$

$$\text{Total labor variance} = \text{Labor price variance} + \text{Labor quantity variance}$$

$$\text{Total overhead variance} = \text{Overhead controllable variance} + \text{Overhead volume variance}$$

$$\text{Materials price variance} = (AQ \times AP) - (AQ \times SP)$$

$$\text{Materials quantity variance} = (AQ \times SP) - (SQ \times SP)$$

$$\text{Labor price variance} = (AH \times AR) - (AH \times SR)$$

$$\text{Labor quantity variance} = (AH \times SR) - (SH \times SR)$$

$$\text{Overhead variance} = \text{Actual overhead} - \text{Overhead applied}$$

INCREMENTAL ANALYSIS AND CAPITAL BUDGETING (Chapter 26)

Incremental Analysis

1. Identify the relevant costs associated with each alternative. Relevant costs are those costs and revenues that differ across alternatives. Choose the alternative that maximizes net income.
2. Opportunity costs are those benefits that are given up when one alternative is chosen instead of another one. Opportunity costs are relevant costs.
3. Sunk costs have already been incurred and will not be changed or avoided by any future decision. Sunk costs are not relevant costs.

Annual Rate of Return

$$\text{Annual rate of return} = \frac{\text{Expected annual net income}}{\text{Average investment}}$$

Cash Payback

$$\text{Cash payback period} = \frac{\text{Cost of capital investment}}{\text{Net annual cash flow}}$$

Discounted Cash Flow Approaches

Net Present Value	Internal Rate of Return
Compute net present value (a dollar amount). If net present value is zero or positive, accept the proposal. If net present value is negative, reject the proposal.	Compute internal rate of return (a percentage). If internal rate of return is equal to or greater than the minimum required rate of return, accept the proposal. If internal rate of return is less than the minimum rate, reject the proposal.

RAPID REVIEW
Financial Statements

Order of Preparation

Statement Type	Date
1. Income statement	For the period ended
2. Retained earnings statement	For the period ended
3. Balance sheet	As of the end of the period
4. Statement of cash flows	For the period ended

Income Statement (perpetual inventory system)

Name of Company Income Statement For the Period Ended		
Sales revenues		
Sales	$ X	
Less: Sales returns and allowances	X	
Sales discounts	X	
Net sales		$ X
Cost of goods sold		X
Gross profit		X
Operating expenses		
(Examples: store salaries, advertising, delivery, rent,		
depreciation, utilities, insurance)		X
Income from operations		X
Other revenues and gains		
(Examples: interest, gains)	X	
Other expenses and losses		
(Examples: interest, losses)	X	X
Income before income taxes		X
Income tax expense		X
Net income		$ X

Income Statement (periodic inventory system)

Name of Company Income Statement For the Period Ended			
Sales revenues			
Sales		$ X	
Less: Sales returns and allowances		X	
Sales discounts		X	
Net sales			$ X
Cost of goods sold			
Beginning inventory		X	
Purchases	$ X		
Less: Purchase returns and allowances	X		
Net purchases	X		
Add: Freight in	X		
Cost of goods purchased		X	
Cost of goods available for sale		X	
Less: Ending inventory		X	
Cost of goods sold			X
Gross profit			X
Operating expenses			
(Examples: store salaries, advertising, delivery, rent,			
depreciation, utilities, insurance)			X
Income from operations			X
Other revenues and gains			
(Examples: interest, gains)		X	
Other expenses and losses			
(Examples: interest, losses)		X	X
Income before income taxes			X
Income tax expense			X
Net income			$ X

Retained Earnings Statement

Name of Company Retained Earnings Statement For the Period Ended	
Retained earnings, beginning of period	$ X
Add: Net income (or deduct net loss)	X
	X
Deduct: Dividends	X
Retained earnings, end of period	$ X

STOP AND CHECK: Net income (loss) presented on the retained earnings statement must equal the net income (loss) presented on the income statement.

Balance Sheet

Name of Company Balance Sheet As of the End of the Period			
Assets			
Current assets			
(Examples: cash, short-term investments, accounts			
receivable, merchandise inventory, prepaids)			$ X
Long-term investments			
(Examples: investments in bonds, investments in stocks)			X
Property, plant, and equipment			
Land		$ X	
Buildings and equipment	$ X		
Less: Accumulated depreciation	X	X	X
Intangible assets			X
Total assets			$ X
Liabilities and Stockholders' Equity			
Liabilities			
Current liabilities			
(Examples: notes payable, accounts payable, accruals,			
unearned revenues, current portion of notes payable)			$ X
Long-term liabilities			
(Examples: notes payable, bonds payable)			X
Total liabilities			X
Stockholders' equity			
Common stock			X
Retained earnings			X
Total liabilities and stockholders' equity			$ X

STOP AND CHECK: Total assets on the balance sheet must equal total liabilities and stockholders' equity; and, ending retained earnings on the balance sheet must equal ending retained earnings on the retained earnings statement.

Statement of Cash Flows

Name of Company Statement of Cash Flows For the Period Ended	
Cash flows from operating activities	
Note: May be prepared using the direct or indirect method	
Cash provided (used) by operating activities	$ X
Cash flows from investing activities	
(Examples: purchase / sale of long-term assets)	
Cash provided (used) by investing activities	X
Cash flows from financing activities	
(Examples: issue / repayment of long-term liabilities,	
issue of stock, payment of dividends)	
Net cash provided (used) by financing activities	X
Net increase (decrease) in cash	X
Cash, beginning of the period	X
Cash, end of the period	$ X

STOP AND CHECK: Cash, end of the period, on the statement of cash flows must equal cash presented on the balance sheet.

Using the Information in the Financial Statements

Ratio	Formula	Purpose or Use
Liquidity Ratios		
1. Current ratio	$\dfrac{\text{Current assets}}{\text{Current liabilities}}$	Measures short-term debt-paying ability.
2. Acid-test (quick) ratio	$\dfrac{\text{Cash + Short-term investments + Receivables (net)}}{\text{Current liabilities}}$	Measures immediate short-term liquidity.
3. Receivables turnover	$\dfrac{\text{Net credit sales}}{\text{Average net receivables}}$	Measures liquidity of receivables.
4. Inventory turnover	$\dfrac{\text{Cost of goods sold}}{\text{Average inventory}}$	Measures liquidity of inventory.
Profitability Ratios		
5. Profit margin	$\dfrac{\text{Net income}}{\text{Net sales}}$	Measures net income generated by each dollar of sales.
6. Asset turnover	$\dfrac{\text{Net sales}}{\text{Average assets}}$	Measures how efficiently assets are used to generate sales.
7. Return on assets	$\dfrac{\text{Net income}}{\text{Average assets}}$	Measures overall profitability of assets.
8. Return on common stockholders' equity	$\dfrac{\text{Net income − Preferred dividends}}{\text{Average common stockholders' equity}}$	Measures profitability of owners' investment.
9. Earnings per share (EPS)	$\dfrac{\text{Net income − Preferred dividends}}{\text{Weighted average common shares outstanding}}$	Measures net income earned on each share of common stock.
10. Price-earnings (P-E) ratio	$\dfrac{\text{Market price per share of stock}}{\text{Earnings per share}}$	Measures ratio of the market price per share to earnings per share.
11. Payout ratio	$\dfrac{\text{Cash dividends}}{\text{Net income}}$	Measures percentage of earnings distributed in the form of cash dividends.
Solvency Ratios		
12. Debt to total assets ratio	$\dfrac{\text{Total debt}}{\text{Total assets}}$	Measures percentage of total assets provided by creditors.
13. Times interest earned	$\dfrac{\text{Income before income taxes and interest expense}}{\text{Interest expense}}$	Measures ability to meet interest payments as they come due.
14. Free cash flow	Cash provided by operating activities − Capital expenditures − Cash dividends	Measures the amount of cash generated during the current year that is available for the payment of additional dividends or for expansion.

WileyPLUS combines robust course management tools with the complete online text and all of the interactive teaching and learning resources you and your students need in one easy to use system.

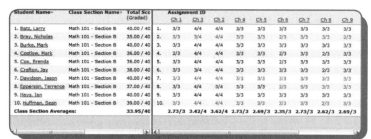

⊕ *Algorithmically generated, end-of-chapter exercises and problems allow a number of students to take the same assignment with differing variables.*

⊕ *Assessment and Homework Management tools help instructors monitor students' progress individually—or by class.*

"I received an A in accounting because WileyPLUS *helped me understand the material by practicing."*
— *Student Crista Dixon, University of Nevada, Reno*

www.wileyplus.com

Wiley is committed to making your entire *WileyPLUS* experience productive & enjoyable by providing the help, resources, and personal support you & your students need, when you need it. It's all here: www.wileyplus.com –

TECHNICAL SUPPORT:

- A fully searchable knowledge base of FAQs and help documentation, available 24/7
- Live chat with a trained member of our support staff during business hours
- A form to fill out and submit online to ask any question and get a quick response
- **Instructor-only** phone line during business hours: 1.877.586.0192

FACULTY-LED TRAINING THROUGH THE WILEY FACULTY NETWORK:
Register online: www.wherefacultyconnect.com

Connect with your colleagues in a complimentary virtual seminar, with a personal mentor in your field, or at a live workshop to share best practices for teaching with technology.

1ST DAY OF CLASS...AND BEYOND!
Resources You & Your Students Need to Get Started & Use *WileyPLUS* from the first day forward.

- 2-Minute Tutorials on how to set up & maintain your *WileyPLUS* course
- User guides, links to technical support & training options
- *WileyPLUS for Dummies*: Instructors' quick reference guide to using *WileyPLUS*
- Student tutorials & instruction on how to register, buy, and use *WileyPLUS*

YOUR *WileyPLUS* ACCOUNT MANAGER:

Your personal *WileyPLUS* connection for any assistance you need!

QuickStart

SET UP YOUR *WileyPLUS* COURSE IN MINUTES!

Selected *WileyPLUS* courses with QuickStart contain pre-loaded assignments & presentations created by subject matter experts who are also experienced *WileyPLUS* users.

Interested? See and try WileyPLUS *in action!*
Details and Demo: *www.wileyplus.com*

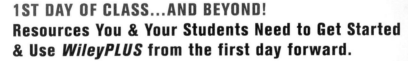